THE MOVEMENT

THE MOVEMENT

Anti-Persecution Gazette

AND

REGISTER OF PROGRESS

A WEEKLY JOURNAL

OF

REPUBLICAN POLITICS, ANTI-THEOLOGY
AND UTILITARIAN MORALS

EDITED BY

G. JACOB HOLYOAKE

Volume I, Number 1, [December 16, 1843] - Volume II, Number 68, April 2, 1845 & *The Circular*, Numbers 1 - 4, [May 1] - August 1, 1845

[1843 - 1845]

AUGUSTUS M. KELLEY · PUBLISHERS
NEW YORK 1970

First Published 1843-1845

(London: *Printed & Published by* G. Jacob Holyoake, *40 Holywell Street, Strand*, 1843-1845)

Reprinted 1970 by
AUGUSTUS M. KELLEY · PUBLISHERS
REPRINTS OF ECONOMIC CLASSICS
New York New York 10001

. . . .

I S B N 0 678 00679 2
L C N 79 120546

. . . .

PRINTED IN THE UNITED STATES OF AMERICA
by SENTRY PRESS, NEW YORK, N. Y. 10019

THE MOVEMENT,

Anti=Persecution Gazette,

AND

REGISTER OF PROGRESS:

A WEEKLY JOURNAL

OF

REPUBLICAN POLITICS, ANTI-THEOLOGY, & UTILITARIAN MORALS.

EDITED BY G. JACOB HOLYOAKE,
ASSISTED BY M. Q. RYALL.

"Maximise Morals, Minimise Religion."--Bentham.

VOL. I.

London:

PRINTED AND PUBLISHED BY G. JACOB HOLYOAKE,
40, HOLYWELL STREET, STRAND,
AND SOLD BY ALL BOOKSELLERS AND NEWSVENDERS IN TOWN AND COUNTRY.

PREFACE.

The *Movement*, like a great nation, has four histories—political, moral, pecuniary, and intellectual—but it does not, like a nation, require Rapin or Niebuhr to write them.

It will be fresh in the recollection of our subscribers how the local authorities, and the Attorney Generals of England and Scotland sought to suppress the *Oracle of Reason*. They were determined it should not be published, but its conductors thought differently. It is true the editors went into prison—but then their work came out—and for once (the cases are solitary) right baffled might. At the commencement of the *Movement* (it being pledged to tread in the *Oracle's* steps) it was said that prosecutions of a more effective character would be renewed. But as the simple idea of perfect duty excludes that of fear, we issued our weekly number with the same nonchalance that we took our breakfasts. It seemed so natural to express honest opinions, that in what way it could be wrong we could not conceive, and integrity appeared so useful that we would not. Thus we have no merit to claim, and no apologies to make—we have not written from bravado, but from simplicity, and we have known no policy but that of not knowing expediency. This is the political and moral history of the *Movement*. Its pecuniary history is recorded in the enthusiasm and support of Atheists in England, Scotland, and Ireland—its intellectual history must be written by the reader. To the searcher after truth only a clue (in this case our Index) can be given—no bias, no recommendation. *He* is an auditor of the accounts we have kept between truth and error, and should have no advice from the Secretaries as to the balance he is to declare in their favour.

G. JACOB HOLYOAKE,
M. QUESTELL RYALL.

INDEX.

A delicate experiment	7
ANTI-PERSECUTION UNION, the,	5, 14, 27, 72, 109, 126, 305, 316, 323, 327, 391, 431
A work of supererogation	23
A messenger from God	24
A religious genius	24
ANTI-PERSECUTION UNION Subscriptions,	8, 16, 24, 40, 48, 56, 64, 72, 80, 88, 96, 104, 112, 120, 128, 136, 152, 160, 168, 184, 200, 208, 216, 224, 232, 240, 248, 256, 264, 272, 280, 292, 304, 316, 328, 340, 352, 360, 376, 392, 400, 407, 408, 416, 424, 432, 440, 448, 456, 464
Arrival extraordinary	39
A clerical truism	40
Another inquiry after Moses	48
An unexpected chance	48
Alliance and ignorance	48
Anti-slavery decision	56
Atheistical soiree	56
A hunt after the Devil	65
Advice to a friend	71
Addresses,	80, 128, 211, 300
A lesson to Atheists	89
Anti-supernaturalism	92
Algernon Sydney	96
Atheism, character of	97, 290
Atheism, practical ends of	98, 176
An athiest in court	119
An abstract of Rules of L.A.S	125
Alliance of ignorance and servitude	126
A duellist's apology for murder	128
A new office for the clergy	128
A tardy conscience	128
A generous barber	128
A specimen prayer	135
Answer of the prison directors, etc.	150
An Irish Editor, etc.	153
Abernethy's demonstration	169
A bone for theologians	208
An improvement in verdicts	224
Atheistical relics, etc.	224, 270, 440
Address to Madame d'Arusmont	227
A new phenomenon	232
A veteran publicist	240
Amendment of the law	249
A Manchester matice in a new light	254
Anniversary of the storming the Bastile	255
A victim to religion	256
Analogical speculations	260
Applications to parliament	278
A new estimate, etc.	281
Address to R. Owen	287
Another melancholy instance	306
A bigot in grain	306
A physician	340
Abner Kneeland	350, 116
Another specimen of religious swindling	355
A correspondent's wish	363
A christian's estimate, etc.	376
Admirable defence, etc.	393
A spicy bit of progress	406
A new book wanted	416
A phœnix	421
Anti-clerical artillery	426
A card of character	447
Alphabet of materialism	449
Belly and the back, the	3
Bronterre O'Brien	16, 23, 40, 416
Balance Sheet of the Anti-persecution Union	32, 127, 175, 291, 408
Bentham	96
Belgium, its laws and liberties	99
Blasphemy laws and Protestan practice	155
Byron and Shelley	181
Baptism	399
Beneficial influence of infidelity	399
Biography of Francis Wright	423
Branch A 1	111, 432, 448, 463
Bible god	277
Bishop of Down	362
"Border Watch" on infidelity	396
Blasphemous bible	128
CORRESPONDENTS, notice to,	8, 16, 24, 32, 48, 56, 64, 72, 80, 88, 96, 104, 112, 120, 128, 136, 144, 152, 160, 168, 176, 192, 200, 216, 224, 232, 240, 248, 256, 264, 72, 280, 292, 304, 316, 328, 340, 352, 360, 368, 376, 392, 400, 418, 432, 440, 456, 464
Correspondence	314, 455, 461
Christianity, benefits of to woman	24
Character making and Character hunting	26
Contemporary sayings and doings	31
Continental communism	31, 369
Civilisation in Scotland	33
Controversy, religious	38
Celestio-inferno-super-humano-mundanities	58

Call to the unconverted 37	Erasmus 104
Conspiracy protected 120	Equality 104
Christian conversion, etc. 96, 149, 198, 237, 242, 250, 315, 335, 361	Examination of Butler's Analogy ... 157
	Extension of the franchise 223
Christianity's liberallity 159	Emma Martins's serials ... 239, 314
Churchman abroad 159	Effects of religion on nations ... 303
Common sense 168	Etzler's Visions 207
Christianity a barrier to political liberty 174	F. Gilder 72
Conservatism and reform 222	Freedom of expression ... 104, 217
Christianity bewitched 248	Filial ingratitude 111
Conventialism 304	Fashionable religion 119
Christian portraiture of christians ... 332	Foreign progress 184
Chemical design 338	Factitious griefs 239
Controversies 366	Fancy envelope 315
Church consecration fees 367	Fatal sentence, etc. 224
Continental progress 375	Franchise, the 240
Coming round 378	Friends of free discussion, to the .. 136
Censorship 386	Gatherings 16
Christianity weighed, etc. 399	— abroad 77
Character of Gen. Assembly, Scotland 431	Gratifying decision 56
Challenge to Mr Holyoake ... 439, 456	Gratuitous instruction 30
Concluding letter from Mr. Gillespie ... 444	Government control of education 31
Chameleon, the 232	Glasgow 56, 39
Chinese and their religion ... 214, 222	God idea, the 48
Confederacy of Priests and Lawyers 215	— metaphysical origin of ... 185
Canker of religion 141	God and nature 168
Cant of authority 447	God's instruments 186
Doctrines of the Concordists, 21, 67, 110, 182, 302, 317	Godwin 207
	Guidance of the feelings 248
Discussion, curious 29, 45, 93	German students 351
Dr. Graham's lecture 77	— Atheism 439
Decline of faith 95	Galashiels 359, 391, 431
Dr. Strauss 95	Geology and the Bible ... 394, 451
Discovery of truth 104	God belief and God believers 437, 453
Death of F. Holyoake 136	God's word and God's works 442
Dr. Kalley and religious liberty in Portugal 159	Gillespian controversy 13, 90, 101, 105, 114, 140, 193, 293, 307, 319, 326, 364, 405, 440.
Dr. Macnab on morals 179	
Diderot 224	Government of Harmony 254
Dr. Fossati's address 262	Galashiels operative 403
Discussions 316, 328, 340, 352, 360, 368, 376	God of nature 178, 235, 245
Derby 351	Herbert Marsh, the Rev. 129
Devil cheated 368	Hint to persecutors 232
Deity 424	Honest confessions 253
Democracy 456	Hint to the heaven-bound 262
Derby Mercury, to the 277	How is man's character formed ? ... 350
Democratic Banquet 367	Hawick 351
Design argument 389	Home Mission Humbug ... 432, 444
Duty of the next Congress 146	Home missions 422, 444, 456, 463
Decision of Sir Peter Laurie .. 207	Height of credulity 176
Democratic friends of all nations .. 397	Hull Magistrates 418, 463
Education 8	Introduction 1
Ebenezer Elliot 12	Influence of faith 8
Editorialities 17	Infidelity in Ireland 9
Errata 24, 88, 120, 160, 340, 36∞432, 448, 464	Impracticabilities 25
	Interesting intelligence 40
English repudiations 36	Is Socialism a religious system ? ... 50
Emigration ... 59, 78, 120, 203, 240, 399	Importance of petitions 142
Edinburgh 80, 95, 184, 391	Insanity 173
Discussions 206, 272	Important public discussion 187
Electro-physiology 94	Irreligion in the American Congress 255

Instruction, rational and scholastic 257, 265, 298
Instructions of the chief of the Capuchins ... 267, 278, 289
Ipswich 351
Is the bible true? 365
Improvement class ... 368, 376, 400
Infidel tract society ... 286, 406, 429
Investigators 349
Jews and Gentiles ... 118, 128, 189, 201
Jesuits and Jesus 441
Kalley correspondence 5, 25, 40, 48, 83, 85, 161, 164, 280, 329, 341, 456. 415.
Keenan's Dr. Lectures 63, 70, 79, 102, 440
Kotzebue 96
Kohl on Bibles 367
Letters from friends 12
Liberty of the press in Paris ... 31
Letters on History, De Lamartine's 46, 75, 100, 103.
Leicester... ... 72, 95, 313
Letter of J. P. Greaves ... 76, 158
Letters from Mr. Paterson 13, 83, 172, 325, 365, 427.
Library of Reason ... 136, 351
L'abbe Maurette 160
Legal oppression 176
— contingencies 424
Library talk 188
Legends 279
Lectures 316, 328, 340, 352, 360, 368, 376, 432, 440, 443, 456, 464
Lectures to the Socialists of England 349, 363
Letter from Father Pinello, etc. ... 351
Love one another 359
Letter from Mr. Lloyd Jones ... 438
Latin 440
Late fraternal meeting ... 391
Late Acting Governor 440, 446
"Last of the Martyrs" ... 407
Morality of Infidels 25
Miners' struggle 277
Morality of the bible ... 421
Madeira people ... 447
Meeting at Stockport ... 133
Mr. Finlay, imprisonment of, ... 7
Mrs. Martin 8, 111, 174, 315, 336, 390, 447
Mr. Paterson ... 10, 27, 64, 124, 259
Mr. Sergeant Talfourd ... 20
Moses and the Apostles in danger of arrest ... 23
Medical recipes for moral invalids ... 23
Morals, points of 26
Mr. George White, the liberation of ... 31
Moses, another enquiry after ... 48
Milton's Satan 48
Mr. Southwell ... 55, 456, 464
Mutual exchanges 55
Methodism 56
Man thinking 69

Mr. H. Wood 72
M. A. L. 80
Mr. Sanderson 80
Mr. Ellis 111
Murray on the bible 136
Mr. J. M'Neil 158
Mr. Knox's case 158
Magisterial courtesy to an Atheist ... 160
Mahometan, versus Christian theology 176
Miss Frances Wright 197
Morality superior to religion ... 199
Mr. T. R. Perry's petition ... 205, 212
Modesty of Christianity ... 215
Mr. Macaulay 224
Mr. Robert Owen ... 279, 304, 407
Making the best of it ... 288, 447
Mr. Campbell and the Concordists 325, 414
Milan 371, 385
Men of business 373
Mirabeau's Erotica Biblion ... 395
Mr. Johnson's case ... 398, 404, 448
Mr. Robinson 416
Mr. L. Beckwith 424
Mrs. Morrison 439
Mr. Lloyd Jones's denial ... 447
Notices 24, 32, 63, 80, 104, 136, 152, 168, 192, 200, 208, 216, 224, 240, 248, 256, 263, 272, 280, 292, 304, 316, 340, 352, 360, 368, 392, 408, 424.
Natural Theology and Sentimental Theists ... 34, 43, 52, 74
National Hall 48, 464
Names instead of things ... 104
News for Atheists 152
Nicholas of Russia 208
Notable things 228
Notes from the North ... 258
Napoleon Buonaparte 371
New definition of god 422
New Socialist Executive ... 285, 301
"National Reformer" ... 407, 422
Northern star in London ... 448
One hundred pounds reward ... 23
Other movements ... 40
O'Connell and Jesus Christ, etc. 113, 289
On the Insanity of mankind ... 123
Oppression 144
Obening of Investigation Hall ... 400
Obituaries 408
Oath taking 422
Our friends abroad 425
Ominous admissions 40
Owen R. D., election of ... 339
Principles of Naturalism ... 2, 11, 19
Prison discipline 8
Pope, Alexander 20
Progress of Christianity ... 23
Precise intelligence 32
Precept, the first 39
Pantheism in France 40
Principle 45

Phonography	... 55	Religionism	... 273
Paine	56, 208	"Rational Day and Sunday Scholar's Magazine"	.. 150
Practical Grammar, criticisms upon	... 337		
Praying jenny company	107, 120	Rev. Mr. Lee of Campsie	... 352
Pemberton, Charles	... 62	Right of public meetings	... 273
Prospectus for a philosophical Institute	64	Rosherville Gardens, the	... 227
Practical bearings of the God contest	91	Rev. Sidney Smith	... 12
P. Lecount, R.N.	... 111	Religion versus scepticism	... 313
Persecution	128, 390, 424	Report of the farewell breakfast	287, 339
Petitioning	130, 261, 315	Remarks, etc.	... 345
Presentation of the Sheffield petition	136	Rustic ruminations	... 359
Pleasing exertions	... 143	Reverence for the reverends	... 392
Prosecutions for blasphemy	... 143	Raising religious wind	... 430
Public meetings	144, 431, 433	Religious light defined	... 432
Protean goddities	... 145	Recent discussion	.. 407
Practical direction on petitions	... 171	Ruling classes	.. 111
Pro bono publico	... 174	Right of admission to Public Lectures	439
Pauper rank	... 174	Rev. Mr. Phillips	.. 440
Posts and providence	... 176	Scheme of universal progression	4, 10, 28, 49.
Policy	... 176		
Plato	... 184	Signs of liberality in the christian zodiac	... 15
Peel, Providence and Co.	... 192		
Proselytism at Madeira	... 210	Speak out	... 18
Progress	234, 241, 267, 288, 315, 347, 424	Summary	... 22
Popular outbreaks in Germany	... 243	Specialities	... 39
Post-office revelations	... 224	Socialism	41, 56, 356, 448
Publication of opinion	... 262	School books	.. 69
Providential interposition	... 262	Scotland	.. 70
Political virtue	... 292	Scottish Union	96, 120
Power of circumstances	... 301	Shelly	.. 104
Priestcraft	... 303	Social reform association	.. 109
Plain preaching	... 316	Special intolerance	.. 135
Prescription	... 30	Slow advances of reason	.. 167
Parsons, pumps and policemen	... 349	Supplementary observations, etc.	.. 170
Public discussion, etc.	... 400	Science and religion	.. 196
Paterson testimonial	289, 407, 429	Songs	216, 223, 440
Propagandism and Paterson	... 414	Sentence of Maria Joaquina for blasphemy	.. 225
Preston	128, 424		
Plebeian	... 429	Sensible ideas of god notions	.. 236
Papers on Harmony Hall	... 432	Society of propagandists	.. 261
Popular concerts	... 468	Social and political parallel	.. 263
Query for the Movement	.. 61	Still to be achieved	.. 314
Questions for Christians to answer	... 370	Strong Owenism	.. 315
Questions of Zapata	.. 68	Sex of the Holy Ghost	... 49
Repeal argument, a "Standard"	... 22	Statistics of demoralization	... 68
Result of oligarchical rule	... 31	Statue of Byron	... 229
Rights of man	... 31	Social Reformers of Hampshire	... 233
Religious controversy	38, 362	Sceptic's death	... 263
Republicanism	... 39	Sir James Graham	... 268
Religion, origin and practice of,	40, 56, 176, 314	Socialists in England	.. 392
		Sweet uses of religion	.. 69
Registration	... 56	Scotch Trials	.. 144
Roalfe, Miss	15, 56, 64, 87, 103, 136	Socialist Parliament	.. 209
Review	76, 166	Supremacy of man considered	.. 212
Religious intelligence, &c.	80, 95	The mountain sermon	... 42
Reason v. religion	... 96	The "Beacon"	... 56
Received	144, 263	Theory of parties	... 57
Rum, gunpowder, and missionaries	... 183	The Movement	30, 48, 63, 279, 339, 358, 392, 463,
Reply to C. Southwell, etc.	193, 274, 283		
Reasoning with the religious	... 206	The Oracle	63, 439, 456
Reply to Madame d'Arusmont	... 242	Tyranny and toleration	... 66

Thought in bondage 263	Value of Mahometans 200
Theosophers 270	Viewing matters in the right light .. 208
Thoroughfare law 351	Votes of the House of Commons 184, 272, 280, 340
The trial 39	
The devil at court 231	Visit to Harmony 401, 409, 417, 428, 440, 456.
Trade mysteries 248	
The recanting witch-killer 66	Wesleyan educational movement .. 31
The man Jesus Christ 154	Woman's co-operation indispensable .. 49
The Chartists 8, 73	W. B. C. Norwich 56
Theory of Regular Gradation .. 413	W. M., Glasgow 56
Theory of heat and vital principle .. 69	W. Anderson, Glasgow 56
The *a posteriori* argument 76	W. McNeil 64
The deluge 79	W. de Britaine 164
The last judgment 79	Whitechapel case 144
Truth independent of majorities .. 112	White quakers 424
The sublime 119	Woman's co-operation 144
The *a priori* God 121	Works of William Gillespie 228
Theology and politics 826	Working class capacity for governing 231
Temple of Juggernaut 151	Whitechapel 95, 279
The "Northampton Herald" .. 184	Words and deeds 297
Thoughts on reading 202	Witchcraft 314
Unitarians 151	Weitling .. 328, 352, 353, 367, 392
Union, its supporters and retarders .. 116	What I admire, etc.  345
Unity form of government 63	Worcester 351
Useful information 363	Woodbridge 376
Voluntary, the 55, 98	W. J. Fox 431, 448, 456
Von Rotteck's history of the world .. 149	Worth preserving 432
Vegetable diet defended 158	Zeal 405

THE MOVEMENT;
And Anti-Persecution Gazette.

"Maximize morals, minimize religion."—BENTHAM.

No. 1.)   EDITED BY G. JACOB HOLYOAKE.   (PRICE 1½d.
ASSISTED BY M. Q. RYALL.

INTRODUCTION.

A periodical, like a well ordered poem, should resemble human life—its exordium should be simple, and should promise little. This accords with our tastes: we have no talents for mere profession, and we make none.

In these days, when publications teem from the press, the editor of every new one has to tax his ingenuity to find out its distinctive features; but distinctive features come to us. We stand alone, in principle and practice. Competition, which so disturbs the equilibrium of others, affects not us. It is not *fashionable* yet to plagiarise our sentiments, nor *prudent* to imitate our manner. The fates have given the "Movement," ample space to *move* in.

After a severe struggle with law and religion, materialism has been rescued from the philosopher's closet, and its elements presented to the world. But this has been done in vain, unless the better rules of life, deducible from it, are pressed on the attention, and commended to the practice of the world.

At present, all intentions are tinctured, and all endeavors warped, by supernaturalism. The young are trained, and the old are induced, to consider humanity as beside their true interest, and this world of only secondary importance. The question is no less than one of human conduct wrongly directed, and involves the national bowing down at the shrine of error. This fatal mistake demands vigorous and effectual correction. Reason and humanity alike cry aloud for the annihilation of the pernicious delusion.

Religion, like the Pensylvanian debt, we deem to be "a broad, blazing, refulgent, meridian fraud,"—a libel on human nature —the sink of virtue, and the grave of independence. It has confounded moral distinctions, obscured political rights, and trampled on the tenderest affections. Never was pronounced a precept of higher import, never was taught a duty of greater magnitude than —" Maximize morals, minimize religion."

While we write, Thomas Paterson is dragging out an unjust, severe, and degrading imprisonment in the Perth Penitentiary. A living man—generous and brave, of kind impulses and noble bearing, built up in a stone sepulchre for fifteen months because he had dared openly to denounce a blighting and malignant faith. The cant about christianity's mild and benign influence is an outrage on our best feelings. Piety and infamy are weird sisters. If any tell us that we mistake the spirit of true religion, our answer is, the *Penitentiary of Perth*.

Shall we be reminded that the christians who set on foot the prosecution, and Lord Chief Justice Clerk, who added insult to the vengeance of his sentence, are the "creatures of circumstances." Be it so. Are the circumstances, therefore, less infamous, or christianity less hateful? Admitting the admonition of such philosophy, that faith is doubly detestable which has not only victimized Paterson, but debased his prosecutors, disgraced his jury, and made his judge at once inhuman and unjust. The rising indignation at Paterson's oppressors we transfer, with concentrated intensity, to the system which built them up.

With this system we proclaim unceasing war. Nor shall we do so in vain. We have full confidence in human endeavors.

> If we do but watch the hour,
> There *never yet* was human power
> That *could evade*, if unforgiv'n,
> The patient search and vigil long
> Of them who treasure up a wrong.

In the name of friendship and freedom— in the name of Paterson, and every other victim of similar injustice, *that* "hour" we *will* watch.

The same determination we hope to bring to other great questions we agitate. Our exertions may be in vain;—still we shall make them. They who will not attempt fruitless things are unfitted for moral reformers. He who must first be assured of success before making exertions, will never achieve great good.

Those whose chief merit consists in making their actions square with existing customs, and are content to seek freedom in the hollow paths of life, will see "no use" in the course we propose to pursue. But for such we do not, we *cannot* write. We have *felt* the fashionable iniquity against which we protest, and cannot shut our eyes to the wrong that lies in our way, and "strike the harp in praise of our own vehement content."

What we conscientiously think wrong, we shall honestly and earnestly oppose; and hope to have the suffrages of all good men with us.

THE PRINCIPLES OF NATURALISM.

It does not appear, from any true history or experience of the mind's progress, that any man, by formal deductions of his discursive power, ever reasoned himself into the belief of a God.—"Encyclopædia Britannica," page 305, article, Moral Philosophy.

Naturalism signifies a system of reasoning and belief founded on known phenomena. Philosophers style it Materialism, and religious people call it Atheism.

Viewed in relation to religion, the most prominent feature of naturalism is the rejection of the belief in a deity. The province of this article is to state, in a plain manner, a few of the reasons on which that rejection is founded.

All men do not view the question of the existence of deity with the profundity of Spinoza, or the meditative acumen of Strauss. The majority of mankind regard chiefly its bold and broad features. This may be less erudite, but it is more practical. No question is properly examined until its bolder traits are described; nor fully understood until mankind at large have been enabled to view them. It will, therefore, be useful to the present question in its most obvious bearings, and for this purpose the presumptive evidence against the belief in deity and religion in general must first be offered to the reader's notice. These presumptive evidences may thus be set forth:—

1.—We may doubt the general soundness of the belief in deity, because the most ignorant have ever been the primest believers and stoutest defenders of the dogma.
2.—We may question the beneficial effects of such belief, since it has been most encouraged by the most criminal governments.
3.—We may suspect that believers themselves were never reasonably assured of its truth, since they have ever found it easier to annihilate than answer those who have urged objections to their opinions.
4.—We may challenge its moral influence; for the most atrocious monsters have always been its most zealous supporters, and its professors the most enduring foes of liberty, virtue, improvement and truth.

These considerations are not offered as decisive on the question. They have no other pretensions in the writer's estimation than that of forming an easy introduction to the more argumentative part of the subject. In popular parlance, naturalism is a question between Atheists and Theists. We shall therefore use these designations, not for the mere sake of employing terms which in some ears sound objectionably, but because such terms are better understood. It has been deemed honest in all ages to use words in their popular acceptation. To put a private construction on public terms can only serve to conceal our meaning, which we do not want—or to confuse our readers, which we much desire to avoid. Our purpose is to inform, not to mystify, and where we cannot teach, we have no ambition to puzzle.

In stating the question between the Atheists and the Theists, it will be required that I define the Theists; but I must be excused doing this, seeing that they have never satisfactorily defined themselves. Therefore I shall begin by defining the Atheists.

The Atheist is one who believes nothing of any designer, mind, intelligence, cause, power, spirit, principle, or person, distinct from the material universe.

The principles of the Atheist are fair and simple, and may be thus stated:—

The Atheist believes in the eternity of matter. This is the first of the great principles on which he rests. He believes that something must have existed from all eternity, for in the words of Paley—"Most assuredly, there never was a time in which nothing existed, because that condition must have continued. The universal *blank* must have remained; nothing could rise up out of it; nothing could ever have existed since; nothing could exist now." But as matter exists now—matter—or in other words, the material universe, is that something which has existed from all eternity. The opinion that matter is eternal is founded on the self-evident truism, *Ex nihilo nihil fit*,—"From nothing, nothing can be made," —or nothing come. But that which came from nothing could have had no beginning, therefore matter had no beginning; and what had no beginning is uncaused, therefore the universe is uncaused and, consequently, self-existent.

The Atheist believes in the infinity of matter. Matter is universal. Imagination cannot bound it. The child instinctively enquires what is there at the end of the world? Infancy pictures something there; and when the telescope has pierced beyond the remotest star, the astronomer still finds new worlds to contemplate. The sailor who said he had travelled until he could not thrust a sixpence between his nose and the moon, only expressed the general truth, that matter is present everywhere.

These are the ancient principles of Atheism, and hence the Atheist concludes that, since the universe is eternal, it could not have had a Creator; and since it is self existent, a sustaining deity is not wanted; and, as matter is infinite, the existence of anything independent of matter is impossible.

(*To be continued.*)

THE BELLY AND THE BACK.

"*The greatness of the little, and the littleness of the great.*—*Robespierre.*"

"The back and the belly!" "Isn't it ungenteel," observes Miss Jenkins. "Quite vulgar," adds her aunt Stubbs. "Positively low," chimes in Sir Augustus Frederick Montague—Of course. Mr. and Mrs. Jenkins pay £200. per annum for the three Miss Jenkinses, who are all parlor boarders, and from teazing a sampler to torturing a pianoforte, and murdering the French, they severally run through the "regular gradations" of a genteel young ladies' orthodox boarding school. What have the Jenkinses to do with backs and bellies? As for Mrs. Stubbs—Widow Stubbs, she is far too stout, starched and, since her dear departed common councilman and tallow-chandler's lamented (?) death, far too comfortable to trouble herself about backs and bellies—at all events, the backs and bellies of other people. Sir Augustus Frederick Montague, having on his side the "accident of birth," and an estate to make his name "respectable," could not descend to anything low. Backs and bellies and poor people and paupers are voted troublesome subjects and insufferably low, and interdicted accordingly. With all this array of "respectability" before my eyes—all sneers, gibes, or deprecation to the contrary, notwithstanding—I will, without the help of God, or blessing of Providence, but with the strongest facts, the best reasoning, and the most earnest appeals it is in my power to set forth, I will endeavour to plead the cause of the belly and the back, which is the foundation of all that goes to the improvement of suffering humanity.

There is the cant of political and the cant of social reform, as well as the usually recognised cants that infest this canting age. Be it the province of the "Movement" to fall as little as may be into this muddy track—to evince that earnestness and simplicity which sincere convictions will prompt—and to convey as much of accurate information as our opportunities will permit. Never sacrificing truth to originality—never too conceited to seek knowledge from others, nor too inflated to acknowledge the obligation, it may be that our repository of ardent endeavour and uncompromising truthfulness shall be instrumental in rescuing some noble efforts from the cant stigma of vulgarity.— Vulgar things may be ennobled, and the tinsel of conventional grandeur be stripped from the puppets and idols which serfs set up to worship. For this reason have I chosen to front one of my first papers with its title, humble, but homely and pregnant of meaning. In this, also, have I chosen a motto which I first heard Mr. Bronterre O'Brien give as a toast at a Chartist convivial meeting. Right glad was I, on a more recent occasion, to hear the "political schoolmaster" scornfully deride the high-sounding and empty phrases with which the pseudo-philanthropists endeavour to amuse the starving. Well did he say that the only argument they need is a loaf. The only way to their brains is through their stomachs.—And so it ought to be. The first useful knowledge is to teach them to get food, or force others to yield it. In the absence of loaves and coats, to give, to shew the way to get them is the next best thing. If the starving cannot be reached by a three-half-penny periodical, the next in gradation can —the hard-striving, toil-worn operative; the frugal, industrious middle man. These are the men to address. When enlightened, they soon convert the other "classes," or illuminate the dupes of their own. Robert Owen might have talked till he was hoarse, written till he was blind, and worked till he dropped, among the comfortable, rich, and titled classes. He changed his course, addressed himself to the active and industrious many. The intelligent among them, perceiving how vitally his recommendations touched their interests, took the enquiry in hand. Thus was formed one of the most remarkable instances of the formation of public opinion which modern times can instance. With the Chartists the same thing has happened. Chartism and Socialism, two of the most important practicable developments of the theories of political and social reform—two of the most energetic organizations on behalf of the belly and the back, sprung from the active, industrious, ill-paid, suffering artisans, operated on by appeals from men made potent and influential by the occasion which called them forth. A few plain and resolute men, with whatever defects of knowledge or conduct some might be charged, plentifully scattered the few truths, or half truths, they knew, the germination of which has produced, and is producing, a crop which must largely add to the improvement of the physical condition of the many.

Political and Social Science will teach us first to feed the hungry, clothe the naked, and shelter the houseless—and keep them so. And most and best of all—teach them how to keep themselves so. It would else be no science, but sentimental quackery, as stagnating as monopoly, as love-destroying as competition, as revolting as "coarser food" and Malthusian economy, and as pernicious as religion. Quackery, hero-worship, and priestianity have impudently stalked forth, or stealthily crept in, among our plans and organizations for extensive reform. It must be part of the business of MOVEMENT men to denounce the one, and drag to light the other. This course, while demonstrating the soundness of doctrines which will live and thrive after the most severe and searching examination will come home not only to the "business and bosoms," but to the bellies and backs of all men.

M. Q. R.

SCHEME OF UNIVERSAL PROGRESSION.

"Man never is, but always to be, blest," would almost appear, to be more than the splenetic effusion of a poet, if we refer to the condition of man in almost every state of civilization, and to the numberless failures of schemes of improvement. There are those who expect it will ever be thus. The religious world pronounce man to be radically bad—tending to evil continually. Despairing of a solution to the difficulties which appear to surround his destiny, both as an individual and a species, they act with this as they do with natural facts that are strange to them, invent one difficulty to remove another. The miseries in this ball of earth not being referred by them to man's ignorance and errors, they invent a world to come, in which the balance sheet is to be drawn up, and our accounts totted up of happiness and misery, virtue and vice, in order that a fair total may be made out. Thus deficits are to be made good, and surpluses to be deducted, by the great unseen, unknown, and incomprehensible Auditor General of accounts. "Sooner shall the rich man pass through the eye of a needle," says the biblical Cocker, than he shall taste of the nice things in store for them who please the almighty arithmetician," and " blessed are the poor," for they shall have all the best places hereafter.— This may be a highly satisfactory way to the religionists or anti-naturals to help themselves out of difficulties which they had before pitched themselves into. For those who don't take things on trust; who not only assert but practise the "right of private judgment;" who not only advise others, but themselves prove all things"—for such, both duties and places celestial and infernal, and all appertaining to them, set them on no better track to account for social inequalities than they were on before.

Another set of opinions, if not equally absurd, are, at least, equally unsatisfactory. They are, however entitled to respect, as professing the guidance of reason. Such are the views of those who consider mankind as unimprovable material, or incapable of eventually and permanently acting or being acted upon for good. If we revert to the progress made in various directions and at different times, a ready answer is forthcoming—they have fallen back into their original condition or something equally as bad. And again, that the advance or improvement so called, is fictitious. While they have advanced in one direction, there have been counterbalancing disadvantages in another; or what have appeared to be advantages were mere diversions which tickled the fancy of the imaginative and formed speculation and business for the leisurely. Such reasoners add that there have been always, are now, and will ever continue to be, rich and poor; the rich trying to make the poor more poor, and the poor man striving to possess themselves of the accumulations of the rich. That industry and idleness, talents and dulness, always continuing, will always cause one set of men to prey on their fellows. That the former qualities, like the precious metals, being the scarcer, the preyers will continue to be least, and the preyed on the most numerous. From the former will continue to be supplied the governing, and from the latter the governed classes. That which we call, say they, political and social meliorations, are but changes of names, not things. For instance, though not openly robbed, our houses broken into, or ourselves knocked down in the street by titled footpads, we are pinched and defrauded by monied footpads, who obtain their ends as effectually by bits of paper as their ancestors used by bits of steel. The difference, say they, is between robbing and swindling. Human progression is a fond fiction. Man is but following the ordinary rules of nature in devouring his weaker fellow-creatures. Mention greater cheapness in articles of commerce, they refer you to stinted means of obtaining the necessaries of life. Speak of the less frequent occurrence of personal violence, and you are met by a reference to the increased frequency of fraud. If less bloodthirstiness be viewed in criminal punishments, more refined barbarity is instanced. If the diffusion of letters is brought forward, you are met by an alleged falling off in the independent exercise of vigorous judgment and powerful memory. If allusions be made to political and social agitation as evidence of our superior progress in unitedness and energetic action, we are brought back to the long continued and determined opposition to class privileges and domination evinced in the celebrated agrarian contest waged in the palmy days of Rome. The decline and fall of nations are cited as illustrations of the non improvability of the species man. As nations have advanced, declined, and fallen, we are told, so will they continue to do. These advances we are informed in the first place are more fictitious than real. Next, if real, they are invariably succeeded by lapses and degeneration. Mankind, in fact, cannot be permanently meliorated in his condition, or if so, only here and there, in patches.

This theory, however—cold, unsatisfactory and discouraging as it is, merits attention. It is offered by cool, deliberate, reflective men—by those who appeal to history, facts, and judgment, instead of legends, fictions, and imagination. For these reasons they are entitled, I repeat, to respectful attention. Appealing to the same or similar facts, following "the right rule of reason" with perfect sincerity, and drawing the inferences with no less regard to truth, it may be anticipated that the conclusions arrived at in this investigation may not be less unworthy of presentation to thinking men. Much of what is affirmed by the class of philosophers who have been quoted, may be granted, without, as I consider, necessarily leading to the same conclusions. And many of these affirmations, by a more precise and searching examination, may, in my opinion, be with great propriety called into question. Space will not permit the development of these views. I expect to be able to conclude this subject in the next.

M. Q. R.

THE ANTI-PERSECUTION UNION.

The Union have completed their arrangements to address their friends and the public through the pages of the "Movement." They commence by presenting their correspondence with Dr. Kalley, of Madeira.

THE KALLEY CORRESPONDENCE.

40, Holywell-street, Strand, London.
Sep. 12, 1843.

Dear Doctor.—The Anti-Persecution Union of London have heard of your unjust imprisonment with great regret. The distance between you and them makes no diminution in their sympathy. They condole with the victims of religious oppression in every clime.

It is enough for the Union to know that you are imprisoned for expressing theological opinions, to establish your claim to their protection. According to the Scotch newspaper, the *Witness*, your alleged offence is against the mother of god. Mother or father, it makes no difference to the Anti-Persecution Union; they contend for every man's right to express his opinions on these parties, unchecked by any power but the power of opinion.

It may console you to know that the union will not censure you for having gone "too far," or condemn you for having been too rash. They chill you not with the cant of pseudo-liberalism about your shocking people's prejudices, or violating their feelings. They hold your feelings, and your prejudices to be as sacred as those of your oppressors! Nor will the Union treat you as your own brethen in this country, and Scotland, are now treating persons in your condition. The union will not stigmatise you as a wretch, brand you as a miscreant and hold you up to public execration—put you without the pale of human sympathies, and call upon the authorities to put you without the pale of legal protection.

On the contrary the Union offer you their hearty support, and beg to know, if possible, per return of post, in what manner they can best serve you.

They enclose you two addresses put forth by the Union, which will serve *to guide your decision*—and they are happy to add the Scottish Anti-persecution Union have already put forth an appeal to the public on your behalf.

Signed on behalf of the London Anti-Persecution Union,

G. JACOB HOLYOAKE, Secretary.

Dr. Kalley's Reply.

Jail of Funchal, Madeira,
9th Nov., 1843.

Dear Sir.—I received your letter, of the 13th of Sept., when confined to bed with fever, or I should have answered it sooner.

I beg you will return my sincere thanks to the London Anti-Persecution Union for the expression of sympathy, and offer of assistance, contained in it.

When suffering from injustice at the hands of enemies, it is refreshing to know that others sympathize with us; and in this world, where sorrow and suffering so much abound, our kind Creator has graciously connected some of our purest and richest enjoyments on earth with the succour of the oppressed and afflicted, even though they may have injured us and deserved punishment.

It seems no great stretch of credence to believe —nay, it seems to be a natural inference, that He who formed our nature so as to enjoy such delightful emotions from doing good to our fellow-creatures, is Himself merciful, and delights in succouring the afflicted, even though they may have deserved heavy chastisement for having neglected his counsels, and trampled upon his laws.

But if He be merciful, what becomes of his justice? A God unjust is inconceivable: and perfect justice rewards *every individual act strictly in accordance with its desert.* There seems no room for the exercise of *that* in the Creator, which is a source of such delight in the Creature.

Unassisted reason cannot reconcile justice, with mercy, towards the guilty. But there is in man a natural pleasure in seeing difficulties overcome which appeared insurmountable, and this is particularly the case when the difficulties seem to stand in the way of our own well-being. Consequently it is natural to feel intense interest and pleasure in the demonstration of the manner in which the Creator can be, and is, a Just God and a Saviour.

I believe that the true reason of my imprisonment is because I have endeavoured to show that the great Creator of all cannot sell his favor or barter his mercy; but that, in the scheme of christianity, He appears most glorious in conferring a free salvation on guilty creatures through a crucified Redeemer; and because I have urged the duty of entertaining towards him feelings corresponding to His character as a *Just* and *Merciful* God.

No doubt many who profess to worship the Creator as possessed of these two glorious attributes, have persecuted, and, by persecution, have thought they did Him service. To me persecution seems altogether inconsistent with the gospel and character of Jesus. Instead of having recourse to injuries, the true christian, confident in the excellence of his cause, will employ only the weapons provided for him by his master; such as universal philanthropy, and reasonable evidence. And if, through the imperfection of our nature He be ever tempted to desire that fire from heaven should destroy those who despise such a God, and will not receive Christ, the words of this heavenly teacher afford a reasonable reproof:—"Ye know not what manner of spirit ye are of; for the son of man is not come to destroy men's lives, but to save."

I long despised the writings of the prophets and apostles: I regarded all professors of christianity as fools or knaves, and thought it a noble thing to shake off the trammels of what I called superstition; and when I first visited Madeira twelve years ago, if any one had told me I should be a prisoner here for explaining the Holy Scriptures, I should have said that that was utterly impossible. I was determined that I should not be deceived, and I am not deceived. Though biassed by such views and feelings, I could not, on the most calm and careful examination of evidence, resist the conviction that christianity is truth. I know that it is most precious truth, worth suffering for, even unto death.

Perhaps some of the members of your Union may think this letter irrelevant and intrusive.—Those of them whose views on these important subjects harmonize with what is stated will not, I am sure, be offended with me; on the other hand, I think I cannot better requite the kind sympathy of those who hold different sentiments than by laying before them truths which have been the source of so much pleasure to myself.

Desiring that He who formed and continually supports us may give us all wisdom to do his will here, and fit us for the enjoyment of his friendship for ever, I am

Most respectfully yours,
ROBERT R. KALLEY, M. D.

G. JACOB HOLYOAKE, ESQ.,
Secretary to the London Anti-Persecution Union.

The Answer of the Union.

40, Holywell-street, Strand,
London, Dec. 1843.

My Dear Kalley.—The London Anti-Persecution Union have received your letter accepting their proffered assistance, with much gratification. Your disagreement with many of them in opinion, by no means diminished the interest with which they perused its contents.

The unaffected candour of your communication very much commends you to their esteem. Great dignity is reflected on your character by the earnest tone in which your sentiments are stated, and by the fortitude with which you appear to support your unjust imprisonment. Such conduct must greatly advance, in Madeira, the cause you have at heart, and we greatly rejoice that no enemy can deprive you of this consolation.

One passage in your letter struck me as remarkable, it being *exactly* the contrary of my own experience; and as you have given it as illustrative of your present sentiments, you may not deem it irrelevant if I write it out as illustrative of my own—

"I long despised the writings of unbelievers and Atheists: I regarded all professors of infidelity as fools or knaves, and thought it a noble thing to shake off the trammels of what I called unbelief; and when I first began to think for myself, some twelve years ago, if any one had told me that I should have been a prisoner in Gloucester, for explaining the pernicious influence of the holy Scriptures, I should have said that that was utterly impossible. I was determined that I should not be deceived, and I am not deceived. Though biassed by such views and feelings, I could not, on the most calm and careful examination of evidence, resist the conviction that Atheism is true. I know that it is most precious truth—worth suffering for, even unto death."

You will understand me to speak here individually, and not officially—to be giving my own experience, and not that of the Union.

If not already aware, I can inform you that a public meeting was held in the Waterloo Rooms, Edinburgh, on Sept. 11, on your behalf; the Lord Provost in the chair, and Dr. Candlish a principal speaker. On that occasion Mr. Southwell, Mr. Jeffery, and Mr. Paterson were in attendance to express their sympathy for your situation; but they were brutally dragged from the meeting to prison, at the instigation of the Lord Provost and your friends. Subsequently, Mr. Jeffery was held to bail, and Mr. Paterson imprisoned for the *offence*, because their opinion of religion did not conform to the Edinburgh orthodox standard! Since this, Mr. Paterson has been sentenced to fifteen months imprisonment—felon treatment for the same offence in kind, though different in degree as that for which you are suffering. Upon reading this narrative, we know that you will blush for your brethren. But the Anti-Persecution Union extend their protection to Mr. Paterson, and they extend it to you, and rejoice in the opportunity in returning good for evil.

We are delighted to inform you that the Earl of Aberdeen, the Secretary of Foreign Affairs, has ordered an enquiry into your case, and we hope soon to be able to welcome you again to liberty.

I am directed, by the Union, to remit you five pounds; and, were not their funds just now exhausted by recent cases in this country, they would have the pleasure of remitting you a much larger sum.

I have taken the precaution of registering this letter to ensure its safe delivery, and shall be pleased to hear from you at your earliest convenience.

You would greatly oblige us by saying, in your next, if your imprisonment is solitary—whether you are treated as a felon—deprived of the visits of friends—of the company of books, and used with harshness and brutality, as are the victims in Scotland. We desire to contrast Madeira with Edinborough zeal for God. The statistics of blasphemy are the prime revelations of religious iniquity.

I am, dear sir,
On behalf of the London Anti-Persecution Union, most respectfully yours,
G. JACOB HOLYOAK, Secretary.

To Robert R. Kalley, M.D., Prisoner for Blasphemy, Funchal Gaol, Madeira.

THE IMPRISONMENT OF MR. FINLAY, OF EDINBURGH.

As you have already been informed, Finlay was last week indicted to appear before the Sheriff's Court on the old charge, which, in his case, we thought was entirely dropped. I can give no other reason for the revival of this prosecution than the vexation of the authorities at finding the sale of blasphemy going on as briskly as ever. Finlay's case will excite more sympathy than either of the preceding ones. The trial took place yesterday. Finlay read his defence which lasted upwards of an hour. It was truly excellent. The age of the prisoner, his earnest manner, his correct language and noble sentiments commanded the respect of all persons present. The Sheriff complimented him upon the manner in which he had conducted the defence, but sentenced him to *sixty* days imprisonment, *felon* treatment, in the jail of Edinburgh.

His family is thus left without the means of subsistence, making another call upon our funds if we had any. We hope that the London Union will be able to send us some assistance.

H. JEFFERY.

I believe there is not to be another number of the "ORACLE," and therefore I have not written to Chilton, Finlay's case I suppose will be noticed in the "MOVEMENT."

A DELICATE EXPERIMENT.

A recent number of a well-known journal contained a report of progress, which stated, that in order to the "full discussion" of a certain knotty subject, that lectures on it should be read; and "that the result has proved satisfactory. The statements were listend to with the utmost attention, evincing *an advanced state of the public mind.*" On reading this we much admired the delicate experiment by which this result had been arrived at; for to us it evinced a "very advanced state of" observing ingenuity. The public mind, in London, according to the last census, may be set down at one million and a half, and the portion of which met on the occasion in question was probably one hundred. Therefore the opinion of the "advanced state of the public mind" was arrived at from the inspection of the fifteenth thousandth part of it. We knew that the physician, by placing his finger on one artery, could judge of the state of the circulation through all, but was not aware the circulation of "new views" through the veins of the public could be so easily and "satisfactorily" ascertained. We purpose sending the first numbers of the "MOVEMENT" to this institution, to have their merits discussed; and, should the "result prove satisfactory," we shall have the gratification of knowing that the "advanced state of the public mind" has declared in our favour.

INFLUENCE OF FAITH.

Let us hear no more of the wickedness of following reason. It is the brightest gem of our being, the choicest gift of nature; it is the doer of all that is grand; and its triumphs are unattended with sorrow, and unstained with blood; whilst on the other hand, the triumphs of faith have been at the expence of the best interests of the human race. It has bent the knee and prostrated the minds of sages like Galilee; it has made one portion of mankind reckless in tyranny and another portion rank hypocrites, to escape the inflictions of such tyranny. Its progress has been over broken hearts, and shattered intellects, and accompanied with the tears, the sighs, the groans, and the blood of millions of its victims.—*Lloyd Jones—Freaks of faith.*

POPE IMPROVED.

For modes of faith let graceless zealots fight, His can't be wrong whose life is in the right.

So sung Pope—but seeing that faith vitiates reasoning, is always in collision with the moral virtues, and continually leads its votaries wrong, Pope's couplet ought to stand thus:—

For modes of faith let graceless zealots fight, He has *no faith* whose life is in the right.

FAMILY CONNECTIONS.

SIN, the pestiferous offspring of IGNORANCE, flourishes not less when associated with her younger sister DEVOTION.—*Emma Martin.*

THE SOCIALISTS.—A proposal from the Central Board is now being submitted to the Society of "Rationalists" to raise, by joint stock shares, the sum of £25,000 for carrying on operations at their estate in Hampshire, to complete the arrangements for preliminary community.

THE CHARTISTS of Southwark and Lambeth have bestirred themselves for the purpose of securing a place for meeting. They have opened a spacious room; the first meeting was attended by O'Connor, O'Brien and Parry—Toasts given—" The Charter " —" The People, " The legitimate source of wealth"—and " Civil & Religious Liberty."

MRS. MARTIN continues her Lectures, which are announced in weekly addresses, obtainable at the Social Institutions.

PRISON DICIPLINE.—Two inmates of the Pentonville Prison, subject to the experiment of the disciplinarian process, have been removed in a state of insanity to Bethlem Hospital.

EDUCATION.—A Meeting to promote this object, by the opening of a Day School, took place during the week at the Social Hall, Whitechapel. Mr. Saul in the chair.

SUBSCRIPTIONS
For the Anti-Persecution Union.

	£ s d
A Friend, Canterbury	0 5 0
Mrs. Baker, London,	0 1 6
(Per Mr. S. Miller.)	
A few Friends	0 17 6
A few Factory Lads, at a Night School, North Moor, Oldham	0 2 6
(Per Mr. Morrish, Bristol.)	
Collector, 17	0 6 0
Ditto 27	0 14 0
Ditto 29	0 1 0
Ditto 30	0 2 0
Mr. Park, Collector 23	0 11 0
Mr. Dobell	0 2 6
Mr. Savage, junior	0 1 0
Mr. McCullough, Collector 20	0 1 8
A few Friends, Lisson Grove	0 2 6
Mr. Johnson, Collector 15	0 5 2
Mr. G. Brace Morgan, Worcester	0 10 0
A few Friends, Maidstone	0 14 0
(Per Mr. Alexander Dickson.)	

G. J. HOLYOAKE, Secretary.

NOTICE TO CORRESPONDENTS.

It is usual to commence a first number by giving numerous answers to Correspondents, but we defer this until next week, for the plain reason that we have not any yet.

Printed and Published by G. J. HOLYOAKE, 40, Holywell-street, Strand, London.

THE MOVEMENT
And Anti=Persecution Gazette.

"Maximize morals, minimize religion."—BENTHAM.

No. 2.   EDITED BY G. JACOB HOLYOAKE, ASSISTED BY M. Q. RYALL.   PRICE 1½d.

INFIDELITY IN IRELAND.

The *Belfast Vindicator*, a few days ago, had an article entitled "Infidel Publications—New English Invasion." It was founded on "A call to the police," made by the *Belfast Chronicle*. My readers will find the whole article reprinted in the past number of the *New Moral World*. It appears that copies of a paper, headed "Beauties of the Bible," had by some unknown hands been largely distributed in the town. Not an infidel word is said to appear on the paper—it was the pure (?) Bible and nothing but the Bible. Yet the editor of the *Chronicle*" calls on the police authorities to find out the fabricators of the vile document." The editor of the *Vindicator* follows up in pious order, saying, "in truth the police would be most profitably employed in such business." The editor then proceeds to stigmatise infidels as "fellows," and before he concludes tells us that "In Ireland, there is an orthodoxy of morals in which all religious sects agree."

Christianity has marked impudence for her own. Who are the men that this *Christian* calls "fellows?" When in England have Socialism and St. Simonianism been preached, and the consequences been frightful? Where are the ruined sons and daughters, and the bereaved parents who have to curse the day they first heard of Socialism? Their names would be a fortune to Brindley or Barker—verily, one must go from home to learn news. This *Catholic* christian also sneers at the condition of England under an episcopalian church, and thinks it by no means marvellous that social and infidel preachers can obtain *willing* audiences—but, he continues, "Thank heaven, the socialists have no field for their *work of iniquity* in Ireland. In England, where Socialism and St. Simonianism are openly preached to willing audiences, the consequences are frightful. Many honest parents have to curse such creeds for the loss of their sons and ruin of their daughters."

Is there indeed! Why the catholic declares it to be grossly immoral to permit the indiscriminate reading of the Bible—a book which the catholic Shiel declared to be the records of a carnal people, and parts of which a virtuous woman would rather *die* than utter—yet the protestant declares it to be perfectly moral, and essentially christian, for both laity and clergy to read, mark, learn and *inwardly digest* that book.

The protestant declares celibacy to be unnatural, and, of course, immoral, and that the practice of it leads to the grossest immoralities—yet the catholic clergy are forbidden to marry, and their general chastity is much questioned.

The protestant declares the most important institution of the catholic church, the Confessional, to be immoral, and the source of innumerable immoralities—and doubtless the questions put to females are very indecent—yet the catholic believes the practice of confession unquestionably moral, and conducive to the welfare and happiness of the community.

Lastly, the catholic believes the agitation for repeal to be both moral and legal—whilst the protestant decries it as immoral and illegal, and is prepared to oppose it by the bayonet and the bludgeon, the use of which is declared by the catholic as immoral and tyrannical.

Where then is the "Orthodoxy of morals in which *all* religious Irish sects agree?"

In the same paper, and in the same column as the extract I have quoted, there is an energetic appeal to the Irish to give no occasion or excuse to the government to use force for the suppression of repeal, and the editor thus speaks of the police, whose aid he invokes for the extermination of infidelity.

" The courage which would induce a man to resent by violence *the vulgar bigotry of a low scoundrel* who is more familiar with his bludgeon than either bible or prayer-book, is a merely animal instinct, which all men, with rare exceptions, possess, but which all men do not know how to exercise aright."

To be subject to "*the vulgar bigotry* of a LOW SCOUNDREL," is doubtless very objectionable in the case of a repealer—but the exercise of vulgar bigotry and low scoundrelism in the case of an atheist, is exceedingly proper, highly commendable, and just! Would anything but "vulgar bigotry" advocate the suppression of opinion by means of the strong arms and heavy bludgeons of the police?"

In law, the receiver is considered worse than the thief, for it is asserted that if there were no receivers there would be no thieves—and in justice, the advocate for the suppression of opinion by force should be considered fully as culpable, if not more so, as the adopter of the suggestion. There is "vulgar bigotry" in the press, as well as in the police—men who are far "more familiar" with slander than with argument, with appeals to the magistrate and the minions of the law, than with common sense, for the refutation of principles and opinions which they would find a difficulty in otherwise overturning.

The repealer advocates the repeal of the union now existing between England and Ireland—the atheist the repeal of the union now and from time immemorial existing between ignorance and humanity. The repealer declares that England has bound Ireland in fetters, and robs her inhabitants of wealth and happiness—the atheist says that the god-idea has bound men hand and foot and leaves them an easy prey to priests and tyrants, who plunder and murder them for their own aggrandisement and amusement. The repealer is of opinion that the repeal of the legislative union between England and Ireland would restore Ireland to tranquillity and happiness—and the atheist is of opinion that the repeal of the god-idea would make all men infinitely more happy and prosperous than they have yet been. Both the repealer and the atheist employ the same means to obtain their object—lectures, public meetings, and the press—yet the repealer *recommends* the use of physical force and the strong arm of the law for the suppression of atheism, whilst he denounces as villanous the use of any such force for the suppression of repeal. What miserable inconsistency is here —what a deplorable prostitution of mind is visible in such conduct. The editor of the *Vindicator* may rest assured that physical force will be as innoxious against infidelity, as he declares it would be against repeal.

W. CHILTON.

Mr. PATERSON.

One principal object of the *Movement's* existence is to draw public attention to the condition and claims of the conscientious victims of our indefinable, judge-invented, witchcraft, blasphemy laws. In another part of this number will be found two letters from the Perth Penitentiary. Mr Paterson's destination was not known to his London friends immediately after his sentence. It was considered advisable to learn from authentic sources, his exact position before letters were addressed to him. Now it is known that correspondence will afford him pleasure and alleviation. In writing, his friends will guard against expressions that may be made a pretext for withholding their letters. Upon receiving Mr. Paterson's first communication, the Anti-Persecution Union instantly sent him a remittance of stamps and money, as he mentions in his second letter. One part of that communication we had already anticipated. Before his second letter arrived I had written remarks for the *Movement* to this effect,---let no one be deterred from writing because Mr. Paterson may not be allowed to answer. The pleasure of reading will be as great a relief to him as if he could reply, and he will the more highly esteem the kindness he is not expected to requite. Even if he is not permitted to read letters, still let them be written to him—the odium of keeping them from him, will be increased by every letter sent. This I speak from experience. Our friends will do well to keep a registry of all their communications, the date when posted, the enclosures and the place of posting, that such particulars may be handed to Mr. Paterson on his liberation as will enable him to ascertain if any letters are detained, or to institute a proper inquiry if they should be affirmed not to have reached the gaol. The treatment of Mr. Paterson, Mr. Finlay, and others in Scotland, in its solitary confinement and cruel discipline, literally equals the brutality of the old inquisition. It is catholic torture under a protestant christian name. In the name of humanity let public meetings be held, and petitions, memorials and protestations against these proceedings be sent to the Queen, the Parliament, and Sir James Graham.

G. J. H.

SCHEME OF UNIVERSAL PROGRESSION.

II.

The question of "progression" has not been usually treated, as far as it has come under my observation, in a way calculated to bring the enquiry to a satisfactory conclusion. For the most part indeed the subject has not taken the form of enquiry. It has been usually disposed of with a dash of the pen or a flippant remark in which "depravity of human nature" on the one hand, or "faith in humanity" and "aspirations after the good and true and beautiful," on the other hand, have taken the place of sober discussion. Most religionists belong to the *depraved* school, and sucking philosophers to the *aspiration* party. To gain my adhesion to the doctrine of depravity, the *apple* story must be cleared up. It has never yet been demonstrated to my satisfaction that for the mistakes of my great grandfather's earliest ancestor on the paternal side, I must earn my bread by the sweat of my brow and my helpmeet must bring forth her kind in anguish. The only chance the depravity doctrine has to keep it from falling is to lean on the crutch of Revelation. But what has revelation to lean upon? Oh, I had forgotten—faith—faith! it may do very well for intellectual cripples, but for people who can walk alone, it is found to be much better let alone. I think I have given ample space to the depraved part of the subject, let others show their depravity, and glory in it, as beggars do their sores. I do not aspire to the honor of association with human depravity, therefore beg to disown all fellowship with depraved humans. Now to grapple with the frigid philosopher who, contemptuously or misanthropically viewing our species, considers that they may be most aptly denominated an incorrigible set of grovelling Yahoos. Thus is the argument urgently set forth by the caustic author of *the Yahoo*.

"The present 'all-accomplished' Yahoo breed
May boast their 'spread of intellect' indeed.
The 'best of education's' now the word,
From tripe and dogs' meat vendors, to my lord.
But does this lacker change the Yahoo's nature?
Is he not still the same vile silly creature?
The spread of intellect, so much his boast,
Is but leaf-gold spread on a rotten post.
Polished he may be, varnish'd high enough,
But still 'tis ornament on paltry stuff."

This is throwing cold water on our "aspirations" with a vengeance. However well administered and applicable the castigation, let us have another look before we write ourselves down incorrigible. Is it really true that we have not lastingly mended in any direction? Have we always been sliding forward one step and slipping back another? Does history convey accurate impressions on the condition of the people? Does history indeed tell us anything at all about the condition of the people? Had history any people at all, properly so called? Had science progressed in the ratio in which it now advances? Had it reached the point to which it has now arrived in various branches? Had it obtained so secure a foundation or advanced so far in all directions? Was positive knowledge diffused among so large a proportion of the population? Were the masses better fed, clothed and lodged? Is religious error more prevalent than formerly? Is conduct on the whole less calculated to promote the general happiness?—Are the numerous classes better or worse capacitated to manage their own business—that is, surveillance over the acts of the legislative and executive bodies who control the nation's affairs? Are there a greater or less number on the whole who take part in the choice of their governors? Are they nearer or farther off the point of self government? Are there not increased facilities for rapidly communicating every new idea and fact to the uttermost confines of the globe? I beg of you, readers of the *Movement*, to answer these questions for yourselves—It is the best possible discipline to anticipate a writer—In the present instance you must do so if you pursue the subject, for Mr. Holyoake has just intimated that the columns will be crowded by a press of interesting and stirring matter which personally concerns every friend of freedom. Such subjects justly claim pre-eminence. I must therefore break off for the present.

M. Q. R.

THE PRINCIPLES OF NATURALISM.
II.

Man must persist in the belief that the incomprehensible is comprehensible—otherwise he would inquire into nothing.—*Goethe*.

Every body who reasons must do it from some acknowledged axioms, on which arguments can be built and to which an opponent can be referred. The atheist takes for granted his own existence, as also that of the material universe. This is the common ground which all are at liberty to appropriate. The rest is to be attained by a fair enquiry into the nature of things.

The atheist professes to be guided solely by human reason, and to deem nothing certain that is not founded on facts, and nothing probable, that is not in accordance with experience.

The atheist takes into his investigation the great metaphysical principle that all our ideas have material prototypes.

A great noise is sometimes made about the nature of the proof that the atheist ought to expect from the theist. Though before these questions were generally discussed, the theist would pretend that he had demonstrable proof. But investigation has taught him modesty. The proofs of deity's existence the atheist requires, depend on the theist's degree of positiveness. If the theist declares positively, that there is a deity the atheist is free to demand positive proof. If the theist believes it as probable only, the atheist would only expect probability. If the theist thought it an uncertain subject, the atheist would reason on his conjectures. The expectations of the atheist are measured by the proceedings of the theist.

These enquiries concerning religion and the gods will be very much simplified, as mathematical enquiries are, by a careful attention to the meaning of terms. If occasion arises to use the terms of theism, deity seems a preferable term to god—because it is more vague and indefinite, and is consequently more expressive, of the idea attached to it. IT is a better term than *he* or *she* because it signifies an ignorance of the gender of deity. The use of terms which imply ignorance on this question is much to be commended, because they better accord with our actual want of information about it. The atheist does not talk of nature's *laws*, because such a phrase gives the idea of a *law-giver* besides being incorrect in other respects. The atheist understanding nothing of law-givers, consistently avoids the use of terms which sanction such erroneous notions. Nature's modes of operation seems a better phrase than nature's laws. *Creation* is a term unsuited to the views of the atheist. Creation signifies something made out of nothing—a performance not easily understood. Perhaps we might talk of the creations of *forms*, but not of the creation of *matter*. The term *world* must not be confounded with the *universe*. The universe is a collective name for all the material things evident to our senses, but the *world* generally implies no more than the planet on which we live. An atheist does not say that the world has existed for ever, but that the *matter* of which it is composed has existed for ever. The atheist and theist should patiently learn the precise sense in which each uses his respective terms. As these papers are unstudied effusions and written rather for plainness than effect, I may, in my desire to unmystify this subtle subject, fall into some inaccuracies. But should I be found to advance anything unreasonable I will promise to give it up to the first religionist who points it out, as he can from long habit deal much better with things unreasonable than I can.

THE REV. SIDNEY SMITH.
To the Editor of the Movement.

Sir.—All the world has been filled with admiration of Sidney Smith's letter on 'American Repudiation," but I have thought one passage in it of very questionable tendency. I am duly aware of the presumption of breaking a lance with such an accomplished wit, but still I think that a man's strong sense of right should never be dazzled by the brilliancy of any talent, nor should an honest conviction be smothered in deference to superior power.

This splendid canon tells us that "the Pensylvanian people having once tasted of the dangerous luxury of dishonesty can never be brought back to the homely rule of right." But is it not a false and dangerous thing to represent dishonesty as a luxury? Is it a luxury for the Pensylvanians to have been dishonest—to have been lashed by Sidney Smith, and to have earned an infamous reputation which a century of rectitude will hardly wipe away?

Then is it proper to talk of the "homely rule of right?" A just action though every hour performed is never low and never mean. Right doing is a perennial flower, and ever fresh and pure as the morning dew.

I. T.

EBENEZER ELLIOTT.

Sir.—A few days ago I stepped into the chapel of an eminent divine to hear a sermon on "miracles," when, to my great surprise, I heard *Ebenezer Elliott* quoted in support of a very crude theory, and I determined to write the *Movement* on the subject —for if such glorious cant-hating men as Elliott are becoming pulpit authorities, we are indeed *moving* on. The line adduced in the sermon occurs in one of the poet's earliest poems.—It is thus :

" O, what a miracle is nature !"

Now, Sir, a miracle is generally considered as something *contrary* to nature, and all nature contrary to itself is surely the strangest contrary ever known. I put it to you, Mr. Editor, whether it would not be more reasonable to consider the line in question as a poetical raphsody than a scriptural or any other verity.
M.

[To be sure it would.—*Editor.*]

LETTERS FROM FRIENDS.

Agreeably to a request expressed in the "*Oracle of Reason*" last week, Mrs. Baker forwards her name and address to the Editor of the forthcoming periodical, as one most anxious for the extensive circulation of the "*Movement*," and for the propagation of Atheistical principles generally, being firmly convinced that the dissemination of those principles alone can emancipate the human race from its present degraded state of ignorance and superstition.

Lambeth.

Let us have the *Movement* by all means. From the character of the proceedings in Scotland it is time some of us were on the *move*.

H. Bradley, Bagnigge Wells-road.

I hope to see the *Movement* like the *Oracle*—bold in the expression of opinion. We must be uncompromising and daring. My means are limited, but I will promote the sale of the *Movement* among my friends —take two copies myself, and send you a weekly subscription to aid in covering the losses incurred.

M. A. Liddle, Poplar.

Every success to the *Movement*. My endeavor will be to get it on the parson's carpet as well as on the poor man's floor.

W. B. Inverton, near Bath.

The *New Moral World* was once bold and uncompromising, and gave us all high hope that our deliverance from priestly domination was near—but the task Herculean seems reserved for other hands. The *Movement* will have a more extensive circulation than its predecessor the *Oracle*. Our friends are much pleased with the prospectus, and I shall hail the *Movement* as the centre of a new organization round which all friends interested in the free expression of thought will rally. I will send you an annual subscription of ten shillings, and shall be proud to become a collector to the *Anti-Persecution Union*.

J. Hindle, Ashton-under-line.

Was sorry to hear of the imprisonment of Paterson. Memorialise Sir James Graham. Don't forget Mr. Gillespie. As for myself I shall not only take in the *Movement*, but if you find it does not pay, I will give you a donation either more or less according to the inadequacy of its payment.

H. Uttley, Burnley.

The above are extracted from a number of a similarly cordial character from Bristol, Leeds, Sheffield, Edinburgh. etc. etc.— Ed. of *M*.

TO MR. W. GILLISPIE.

Sir.—On the part of the "Philalethean Society" of Edinburgh, your "a priori argument for a first great cause," was transmitted to the conductors of the *Oracle of Reason* for their reply. That work is now in the hands of Mr. Southwell, who will probably send, shortly, to the pages of the "Movement" his opinion of your production.

To fill up the vacancy that will exist, until the labor the Blasphemy cases in Edinburgh have imposed on Mr. Southwell' shall permit him to reply—the "Society of Atheists" of London beg to send you Mr. Holyoake's a posteriori argument against the existence of a God, as displayed in his work entitled "Paley refuted in his own words."

You are doubtless aware that the a posteriori argument for God's existence is deemed of far more potency by the whole theological world than the a priori one. It is of more plausible theory and of more popular acceptation. As the Philaletheans of Edinburgh have "challenged" an answer to your a priori production, the London Society of Atheists challenge a reply to Mr. Holyoake's a posteriori work. The reciprocation of replies may prove mutually advantageous.

I am your obedient servant,
J. Mc. Cullough,
Secretary.
12, Chandos St., Strand, London,
Dec. 20, 1843.

A VOICE FROM PERTH PENITENTIARY.

Nov. 25th, 1843.—Prison, Perth.

My dear Holyoake.—I avail myself of the Governor's permission to inform you of my removal to Perth, and likewise that letters can reach me if sent properly. Although I am endeavoring to make the "best of a bad bargain," yet I cannot help feeling a little chagrined at not receiving a *single note* from *one* of the many butterflies that fluttered about me in the sunshine. Has the shade sent them into their original nothingness? It may be, and it very likely is, that I have brought down the ire of friends as well as authority. But it concerns me most, to know, that I acted in accordance with my judgment, and fools'-bolts will be shot whichever way one acts. Let my friends, Budge, Jeffrey, Southwell and others round you, know my feelings on this matter.

A petition should be presented to Sir J. Graham on the subject of "Felon Treatment," with the remarks of the Lord Justice Clerk on that matter at the conclusion of my defence. I certainly was not justly treated at my trial. The "wickedness" of the indicted passages could not *constitutionally* be proven, seeing I was not allowed to show their truth, as you no doubt are aware, and his lordship forgot to point out a single statute that prevented me from selling a book. Nor should the fact be omitted, that while punishment for overt acts are yearly being ameliorated, those for expression of opinion are increasing in severity.

Hope Miss Roalfe is doing well in the shop—should much like to hear from W. J. B.—Is he still in Hamburgh? I will notice all letters every three months, or earlier if possible. Have no postage stamps.

Love to Dr. Kalley and all friends.

Yours truly,
Thomas Paterson.

SECOND LETTER.

My dear H.—Yours of 1st and 5th received. The governor has permitted me *once more* to write that I may explain that the money remitted me is of no service—as nothing can be purchased here. You must please preserve, until the end of my imprisonment, whatever may be subscribed for me.

No *printed* enclosures reach me; but the "Treatise on Practical Grammar" which you inform me you are preparing for the Press, I have requested to be permitted to receive, and it is promised that I shall if it contains nothing objectionable. Thank the Union for the £1 and five shillings' worth of stamps.

Please to explain that I cannot reply oftener than every three months and that my friends must write me for what pleasure I receive—not for what I can give.

Will you write A. Trevelyan, Esq. *from me*, that he may apply to Mr. Hill, the Prison Inspector for Scotland, for permission to send me "Chambers' Information," bound. Also for the use of writing paper for me. They will afford my thoughts employment. Be good enough to explain why I write only to you. It is necessary that I send to some one quarter whence all my friends will hear of me. The trouble I give you, I know you will forgive. I do not feel at liberty to say more about my imprisonment than that the Pentonville New Model Prison is the nearest I can think of.

Yours truly,
T. PATERSON.

ADDRESS OF THE ANTI-PERSECUTION UNION.

The friends of freedom of expression must be greatly gratified by the articles which have recently appeared in the papers, entirely condemning any interference with the utterance of thought. Since the commencement of the Scotch agitation, newspapers circulating in remote and important districts have contended with boldness for full liberty of speech. The principles of free discussion have been more extensively and earnestly elucidated than at any former period. This is the more valuable as the Scotch cases have exhibited the most determined and uncompromising opposition to religion. The writers who have nobly thrown their shield of protection round these victims, are men who understand, appreciate and are prepared to claim the full measure of liberty for their fellow-men.

It is necessary, as this address will probably be read by new friends, to repeat that the great object of the Anti-Persecution Union, is to secure a free discussion of theological opinions. They have nothing to do with the sentiments of any party—christian or atheist; Dr. Kalley or Thomas Paterson are alike to them. They defend the claim of both to speak their thoughts in their own words, and their own way. The Union holds that neither magistrate nor judge should be allowed to dictate to any man what he shall think on theology, nor how he shall express himself. The tyranny of one man saying to another "you shall think *my* thoughts," is only equalled by the insolence of saying "you ought to adopt *my* manner." Whatever may be found objectionable in the utterance of opinion can best be controlled and regulated by opinion.

The fate of Mr. Paterson is well known. Mr. Finlay, a noble old man, the father-in-law of Mr. Robinson, has been taken from his home in Edinburgh and sentenced to Sixty days imprisonment—which he bravely preferred to the ignominy of paying a fine of £10. for the offence! of having sold an ordinary infidel book. In thus suffering himself, at his time of life, to be thrown into a felon's cell, rather than abandon a high principle, he has set a proud example, and must command more than the sympathy the Union claims for him, the support of all honorable men. His wife and family are left destitute, for Finlay is not rich. If christianity demands the sacrifice of his grey hairs, let humanity preserve his wife and children from privations.

The storm of blasphemy still rages—the vindictiveness in the case of Finlay, and the brutality displayed in the cases of others, has generated a tempest of opposition. Mr. Mc.Neil, of Campsie, stands over for trial, and Miss Roalfe—the young lady whose spirited manifesto was lately published, has been apprehended, and only liberated on bail to the amount of £60. Neither age nor sex, the sensibility of woman, nor the venerableness of age is spared ; and we are reminded again of the horrors of the inquisition and the fearful nature of religion.

On Sunday evening, Mrs. Martin, who is the foremost among women in the defence of the uncompromising lovers of liberty, made an eloquent appeal to her audience in the City-road, and received nearly £3. for the funds of the Union. This excellent instance of what has been already done, is the best example of what should be done. Miss Roalfe's case should receive the serious attention of her sex. Women ought to command the direct support and assistance of women. They will never attain their fair measure of liberty unless they defend one another with spirit and resolution from brutality and injustice. They should permit neither the political nor the religious tyrant to trample them down. Let ladies become at once collectors for the Anti-Persecution Union.

The recent remittance to Dr. Kalley of Madeira has contributed to diminish the Anti-Persecution funds. The Union anxious to prove that they did not merely talk of equal liberality to christian and atheist, embraced the first opportunity of proving it. If christians will not help infidels when they are the victims of injustice—they perhaps will assist one of themselves in that situation, and therefore earnest appeals should be made to them for contributions for so "catholic" an association.

G. Jacob Holyoake, Sec.

THE APPREHENSION AND TREATMENT OF MISS ROALFE.

The following from Miss Roalfe to the Secretary of the London Anti-Persecution Union will be read with interest and concern by the friends of liberty.

Edinbro', Dec. 14, 1843.

My dear sir.—a combination of circumstances prevented me from fulfilling my promise of writing to you yesterday. In the first place I found my home, as you may well suppose, in a wretched state of disorder on my return from prison. It took the greater part of yesterday to restore it to anything like a degree of comfort. Next I had the shop filled with persons who called to see me, some prompted by regard, and others by curiosity, and last though not least, the house was surrounded by a riotous mob, whose hissings and hootings at times almost stunned me. Never did I witness such a scene as took place the night of my liberation; the moment it was ascertained that I was at home, a crowd began to assemble, and in about half an hour some hundreds of persons had collected, and before ten o-clock they baffled all description. If you can imagine an *Indian war-whoop* then you may form some idea of the yells of these disciples of the meek and lowly Jesus.— Several of the committee of the Anti-P. U. were at my house, some of whom attempted to put up the shutters; but part were seized by the mob, and others were struck, one young man in particular was struck by a medical student on the head with his stick, which cut it open. At last with the assistance of a number of the police, we succeeded in dispersing the mob. I fear, however, that I shall experience considerable annoyance for some time to come, as I am blessed with a neighbour who is a Methodist local preacher, and who is the principal actor in the scene.

I am not aware at what Court I shall be tried, but I *fear* at the Sheriff's; I say I *fear*, because although I should, no doubt, have a shorter term of *imprisonment* if tried at that court, yet, as I intend to defend *myself*, it would more benefit the cause to which I am devoted, to be tried at the High Court of Justiciary.

At my seizure I did not lose a great deal of stock. I had taken the precaution to remove the principal part, having received intimation that the " Fiscal " intended to honor me with a visit. I sold last week two books to a person who I was informed was a sheriff's officer; another was waiting outside the shop. The books I sold him were the " Trinity of Trinities" and the " Bible an improper book." As the man went out of the shop I heard some of the persons outside the shop say—" *She's nick'd*," which seems to be the Lord's way of settling business in these parts.

The examination was a private one, and the books with which I am charged to have vended, are those before-named, and copies of the *Oracle of Reason,* 91, 94, and 100; also " God *versus* Paterson," " Godology," and one " Home thrust."

When committed to prison I was put into a wretched stone cell, and after waiting in vain for my dismissal I was told by the turnkey that the lights were about to be extinguished and that I had better go to bed, as there was very little chance that I should leave that night. But on preparing for rest guess my surprise and disgust, on discovering my bed covered with *vermin !* I instantly made an alarm and insisted on being removed into another cell, which was accordingly done. I stated that I should make a complaint, but as the turnkey was particularly civil I said no more about it. Since my return home however I have had considerable difficulty in freeing myself from the impurities of that place.

Mr. Finlay, jun., has just brought me a letter from his father who has written for his tools; he is therefore allowed to work at his own trade. He is quite well in health, and desires to be remembered to all friends.

M. ROALFE.

SIGNS OF LIBERALITY IN THE CHRISTIAN ZODIAC.

The progress of infidelity is almost as marked as the spread of catholicism. If you need any proof of it, you may find such proof in the efforts which are at present made toward the public preaching of infidelity. Until lately it confined itself to the use of the machinery of the press. Now it lifts up its voice in the pulpit and the lecture room, and has provided for itself a regular organization which bears an analogy to that of christian churches. I need not tell you that I look upon this movement as an erroneous and a dangerous one. I believe christianity to be a revelation from God. But I cannot refrain from doing justice even to the unbelief which prevails around us.— *Rev. J. Gordon, Protestantism.*

We hate persecution in every shape whether directed, as in Edinburgh, against infidel and blasphemous publications, or as throughout Scotland, against the members of the free church.

In a prison of the Island of Madeira lies Dr Kalley, incarcerated by the authorities for blasphemy; in Edinburgh gaol Paterson and his friend are immured for the same crime. If it be the part of the civil magistrate to act as the physical force champion of the Almighty, which of the above authorities in the above cases are in the right? —*Nonconformist.*

In Edinburgh they have been prosecuting one Paterson, a man who acquired some notoriety in London, a short time ago, for vending blasphemous publications. He has been sentenced to fifteen months imprisonment and will come forth at the close of it, a martyr, and doubtless, sell blasphemy with greater vigor, and at a higher price, than ever. Not by such means shall we silence the blasphemer, nay, we thus give him a hundred tongues instead of one. Moreover, we thus violate the principles of religious freedom. This Paterson *may* have a conscience and deep convictions of his own, with which high courts of justiciary have no right to meddle. The law may give them the power, but cannot give them the right.—*Essex and Herts Mercury.*

Blasphemy, as far as we can understand the term simply, means that a man is of another religion than that established in the country in which he lives. You are a blasphemer, says the lawgiver in Madeira, because you refuse to worship the Virgin Mary. Had we a Jewish establishment of religion, the harmless seller of sausages, for aught we know, might share the fate of Paterson, and Kalley. This is quite right, if government has the right to prescribe what shall be the creed and worship of its subjects. We cannot see how, with any face at all, the presbyterians of Edinburgh can exclaim against the conduct of the government of Madeira, whilst their own conduct is equally illiberal. To us they seem marvellously inconsistent— they, at least, should have, if not the sense, the decency to be dumb.—*Philanthropist.*

In the present number of the Philanthropist we have an excellent article on religious persecution, in which the writer takes precisely the same view as we did, on the occasion of the imprisonment of Holyoake for blasphemy. He shows that the persecution of Dr Hoby in Denmark, of Dr Kalley in Madeira, and of Paterson in Edinburgh, are all *equally* indefensible.— *Cheltenham Free Press.*

Mr. Bronterre O'Brien.—The friends of this able advocate of the poor man's claims, intend honoring him with a *Soiree* and Ball at the Rotunda Theatre on the first Tuesday in January next. We shall give further particulars in our next number. Every friend of political and social liberty should endeavor to be present at this *Soiree.*

GATHERINGS.

The Anti-Persecution Union contemplates issuing elegant cards and cases for the use of their collectors.—Mrs. Martin continues to publish weekly addresses to the Metropolitan congregations. One of the recent addresses contained some quaint strictures on the murder of Jesus Christ.—Mr. Buchanan has just concluded a three nights' discussion with a Mr. Leigh on the Existence of the Devil.—Mr. Holyoake, on Sunday evening, a course of three lectures at the Rotunda on Practical Socialism. The first lecture answered the question in the negative—" Is socialism a religious system." The second considered " Home Colonization as a poor man's speculation," and the third will be on " Socialism as it ought to be."—An old gentleman has cordially promised his support for the *Movement,* who has been cheerfully "living without God in the world" for half a century. — De Lamartine has lately written some splendid letters on history and literature, which have appeared in the *Independent Review*—the organ of the French communists.—The *New Moral World* has devoted a column this week to the interests of the Anti-Persecution Union.

NOTICE TO CORRESPONDENTS.

Now we are able to appear in this department.

C.R. sends us some jokes and we were charged extra postage for his letter. Was he parsimonious in the use of his stamps, or was it owing to the *heavy* nature of his enclosures?

G. N. signs himself a "*Constant* Reader." We feel complimented. Has he done nothing but read our first number since it was issued? We cannot conceive how he can as yet be a *Constant* reader in any other sense.

J. S. sends us some very tame poetry, but we beg thus early to say to him and others, that we do not want what Ben Jonson denominated

" ———Verses as smooth and soft as cream,
In which there is neither depth nor stream."

E. H.'s Opera of the " Gods" declined. Common Sense, Anti-Priestcraft, and W., Oldham, received.

SUBSCRIPTIONS

For the Anti-Persecution Union.

W. B., Inverton	£0 1 0
Mr. Palmer, an old subscriber	0 2 6
Mr. Ascott, first weekly subscription	0 1 0
Pr. Mrs. Martin, at the Hall of Science, City Road, on Dec. 17.	
A Foe to oppression	0 10 0
A Recent Convert	0 10 0
M.P. a lady	0 3 0
Given at Doors	1 15 8½

G. J. Holyoake, secretary.

Printed and Published by G. J. Holyoake,
40, Holywell-street, Strand, London.
Saturday, Dec. 23, 1843.

THE MOVEMENT
And Anti-Persecution Gazette.

"Maximize morals, minimize religion."—BENTHAM.

No. 3.   EDITED BY G. JACOB HOLYOAKE. ASSISTED BY M. Q. RYALL.   PRICE 1½d.

EDITORIALITIES.

We have to deal with personalities, or more properly, if we may coin a word, with editorialities.—BRISTOL MERCURY.

A few friends have expressed their opinion that the price of the *Movement* will be thought dear at its size. Each, however, says that *he* does not care, but fears that *others* will. It is a consolation to discover that friends find no fault. We might say much in extenuation; we might, by comparisons with other works of a similar kind, draw an inference in favour of the *Movement's* price; we might show that no work, except the *Oracle*, was ever cheaper; we might talk of risks and expenses not incurred by other journalists—but we care not to make these defences. We think the public wrong in their rage for literary quantity, and are not disposed to pander to it. They who must write much will often be forced to write without due deliberation, and thereby tax people for hasty, unwise advice. To the industrious a great book *is* a great evil. Shelves are loaded, time wasted, and patience exhausted. It is better to say much in few than in many words. Spartan sententiousness is best adapted to periodicals; it comprises brevity, economy, vigour, and spirit. So far the plan of the *Movement* accords with our wishes; but what we wish and what we are coerced to, are the same thing. The *Movement* must be three half-pence, or the Anti-Persecution Union, and Atheist, can have no organ. If all who *wish* us well would do well for us, the case would be wonderfully different. As it is, we can only calculate upon the few who ever stand steadily by their principles, and do something more than merely *hope* that we shall succeed. To cover expenses, with the moderate sale we expect, the price must be what we have fixed; and, finding that this must be the case, we do, as in the affairs of common life—make no higgling with fate. If nobody will buy the *Movement* at its present price, why there is an end of it. But we think better of the world than this, and hope, while persecution exists, to be enabled to retain this favourable opinion.

Some have supposed that there will exist an antagonism between the *Movement* and the *New Moral World*. Nothing of the kind. Both papers labour to attain the same great objects—liberty and happiness; but the *Movement* takes a different field of exertion. I think the *New Moral World* should have embraced the *Movement*, and wish that it would. *We* add theology to political economy. The errors of the priests are not less dangerous than the mistakes of capitalists. Socialism will be criticised in the *Movement*, but not in the spirit of antagonism. The present policy of Socialists I think not sound—the interpretation of Socialism not correct—the measures neither so vigorous nor practical as they might be; but they *may be* right. I arrogate no infallibility; I only venture to explain differences. I question not the Central Board's integrity—assume no dishonesty; I only impugn their judgment, and desire, if, indeed, I am able, to improve, not condemn.

We are fully persuaded with the author of the "*Clockmaker*," that "decency is a manly virtue ;" and on no occasion will the *Movement* exhibit a wilful forgetfulness of this truth. But, be it remembered, that our notions of decency and indecency will not be measured by false conventionalism, by prudery and fashion, but, as far as our power lies, from the *nature* of *things*. Hence many, who are delighted with the surface phraseology of the day, will start at some of our expressions; but let them examine our subjects, and pause before they require us to sacrifice plain, useful statements that we may tickle the ears of the genteel. We shall ridicule folly, whether sacred or profane; and laugh or frown people into what we think right in the pleasantest way possible. But as M. Q. R. has expressed it in another place, we shall be discriminate; not join in the vulgar laugh at well-intended efforts, although they may not be characterised by the wisdom we could wish. There is positive vice and criminal folly enough in the world on which to exercise wit, sarcasm, and ridicule.   G. J. H.

SPEAK OUT!

It is of paramount importance for infidels, so called, to make a bold stand, gain a firmer position, display their strength and numbers, and, by individual as well as collective efforts, to resist all impertinent interference with their thoughts, words, and actions.—Resolution and singleness of purpose are essential among both the heterodox and the orthodox. We must be prepared to make sacrifices, and practice truth and candour, instead of subterfuge and prevarication.

Do we, or do we not desire to be understood to think as we do think? Is it a light matter to conform to or to dissent from prevailing opinions on subjects so deeply affecting our habits and institutions as religion? Is it of no moment that our claims to exemption from religious imposts, and the hundreds of legal interferences, should not only be pressed upon public attention, but overlooked, nay more, remain absolutely unknown or concealed? Let any who has conscientiously and deliberately arrived at the conclusion that the religion of the land, in all its varieties, is erroneous, ask himself a few practical questions in connection with the new relations that thus arise between himself and his fellow countrymen. Did he deem it his duty, as a member of a religious denomination, to acquaint himself with its tenets, observe its precepts, conform to its rules of worship, aid in the sustaining of its external machinery or organization? How can he absolve himself from similar duties in a contrary direction, after his fuller examination and final rejection of what he before considered pure and vital truth? The more deeply his former opinions influenced him, the more comprehensive their scope, the more effective their operation in building up the thoughts and actuating the conduct of others, the more readily they united with, or introduced a basis for, institutional arrangements, by so much the more imperatively necessary did it become for him to avow his new convictions, and not only avow but proclaim them.

There is another, and, if possible, still more important view to take of this subject. Others continue to be affected and acted upon by the sentiments or system now discarded, in whose interests and welfare we are personally or indirectly concerned. Childhood is dangerously susceptible to the influence of stirring narrative, entertaining romance, or wondrous relations, and unable to discriminate between truth and fiction, detect motives, and separate the tinsel of glory from the pure ore of virtue, It is necessarily misled by whatever dogma is insidiously introduced among the legends, fables, and marvels which form the staple of all old and sacred history; it thus becomes Christian, Mahometan, Pagan, according to its locality—God-worshipper in every locality. And who are most fearfully answerable for the instilling of these pernicious frauds and delusions? who suffer the youthful intellect to be taken prisoner, confined, bound, warped, and moulded according to the frightful distortions which religious dogmas, in all climes and periods, have produced to frighten, degrade, and enslave the community? Who—to reduce the accusation to the least possible extent that may be warranted by facts—permit their own children to be subjected to the absurd and and immoral schemes of trickery, absurdity, and monstrosity, which go under the generic term of religion? Those, of course, who having themselves seen through priestly artifice, and become emancipated from congregational dupery, are in the true position to expose and withstand those frauds and errors which had exercised so blighting an influence on themselves. For my part, I know of no business, no connections of kindred, profession, or society, no personal interests or obstacles, that can outweigh the tremendous charge which devolves on the parent, the guardian, or protector, and which imposes the irresistible necessity of shielding the youth under the sphere of his influence from the narrowing effects of religious systems. The timid and irresolute may say,—I cannot myself instruct, I cannot afford a tutor; a school for development of the faculties, instruction in realities, the rejection of speculative theories and unnatural dogmas, and the pursuance of moral training, is not within my reach. Granted. The so called National Schools are hot-beds of superstition; the dissenting seminaries and sabbath-schools are the same; the British and Foreign Schools, which make the bible a text-book, and undertake much more than they can accomplish, though they accomplish much less than they ought, are not exempt these charges, The Rational Schools are scarcely more than in embryo, in many instances possessed of very inadequate means and appliances, and too expensive for persons in humble circumstances with large families. All this is true. But before these difficulties are deemed insuperable, let us ask the atheist, or infidel, or rationalist, or anti-supernaturalist, or by whatever other term he would choose to be designated, has he adopted a plain, straightforward, manly course in regard to his dissent? Let us ascertain if he has avowed his opinions when called upon; if he has gone a step further and announced them. Let us know if he has advanced a little further still, and manfully defending his sentiments, set forth in unequivocal terms the superiority, sublimity, and truth which he must suppose to be characteristic of the reformed opinions. Has he, still venturing a step onward, taken measures to make others participators in the fact-based convictions, improved sentiments, and more humanizing influences which his fortunate emancipation from religious thraldom have produced in himself. Above all, has he made any efforts, in conjunction with others, or stimulated any to commence instructing the rising generation in the ennobling study of nature, instead of the contemptible guesses about Gods. Has he strengthened any of the efforts of the Socialist Branches in the establishment of new religious academies, or has he opposed them when endeavouring, Janus like, to show two faces, each simpering and smiling, one to the infidel world and one to the religious world? Has he done or attempted to do these things? Or has he, with bated breath, and down-cast look, and deprecatory mien, when taxed by a reverend divine with soul-destroying error and most damnable heresy, has he hummed and hawed, and part confessed, and part denied, and part excused himself, and falteringly essayed to disguise the features, alter the proportions, or disown the connection subsisting between him and his new love, reason, after his most just repudiation of the hag superstition. Has he, Jew-Abraham like, denied his wife, subjecting her to adulterous intercourse," lest for his wife's sake they should slay him," or Jew-Peter like, denied his master lest he should share in the disgrace and fall of his acknowledged Leader? If he be so weak and deplorable a truckler, if he cannot make a sacrifice, aye, a sacrifice of magnitude, for the sustaining and propagating of his principles and the protection of the community, especially the younger portions, from the debasing effects of church influence and chapel influence, and "christian instruction;" if he do nothing towards resisting interference with the "rights of conscience," substantially and not nominally, whether attacked by parish, parliament, or people—then is he fitter for a victim of the Juggernaut car of Christianity, than to roam as a freeman over the enlightened realms of reason, and working out for the rising generation a perpetual citizenship in this only true republic.

M. Q. R.

THE PRINCIPLES OF NATURALISM.

III.

To what end, said Candid, was the world formed? To turn our brains, said Martin.—VOLTAIRE'S CANDID; OR ALL FOR THE BEST.

The curious concerning the definition of the universe, will find Ocellus Lueanus very intelligible and instructive on this subject. This remark has reference to what was said about the universe, in the last Paper, on Naturalism. For all effects, the atheist, in common with other persons, allows causes, but does not allow that the universe is an *effect*, but the *cause* of all effects which we witness. *Good Sense*, a terse, philosophical, and argumentative work, first reprinted in this country by Carlile, is, perhaps, the best work which the student can consult on this question of cause and effect, as connected with naturalism. Chance is a term which has, when used by materialists, a meaning the opposite of that ascribed to it by divines. With the materialist, it expresses merely the known effect of an unknown cause; while the theologian uses it to signify something proceeding from no cause at all. It would be well if materialists would disuse the word and employ some new one. The opposite meanings attached to it lead to frequent misunderstandings.

The chief cause that operates to prevent the theist from seeing the reasonableness of naturalism, is his poor opinion of matter. He lives in the world—sees infinite marvellous things which nature hourly produces; and yet he gives such powers no credit for their productions. Of nature he knows little and believes little. His custom is to look beyond nature for causes which lie before him in daily life. Plotinus used to say that "nature was a thing which did only do, but did not know;" but Plotinus, like many of his followers, forgot to inform us how he came to know that: if nature made him its especial confident, he might have apprised us of the fact. Those who know most of nature believe most in its powers. Science is against Plotinus.

The theist has his wonders and marvels; the materialist finds all things equally wonderful. Why things are as they are, is, doubtless, an ingenious question to ask; but it is one to which neither philosophy nor folly has yet given a satisfactory answer. It would be as wonderful why they should not be, and puzzle the curious just as much, in this case, as in the other. The theist refers to God; the atheist confesses his ignorance; he dogmatises not where he understands nothing, and is without facts on which to base his theory. On the other hand, the theist is confident in the proportion of his ignorance, and will present his imaginings where he should present his facts. Atheism is modesty; theism presumption. The atheist looks carefully to his experience and his facts, and founds his earnest opinions only on them. But,

Where men of judgment creep and feel their way,
The positive pronounce without dismay.

It would be well if a classification were made of all the mysteries of metaphysics. All our abstract terms should be analyzed, and the material nature of them explained. Properly speaking, we have no abstract terms. Love, truth, virtue, are plain matter of fact, material things, when divested of the fogs in which spiritual metaphysics has enveloped them. In the same manner all the technical terms, entering into theological discussions, should be carefully examined, and their intelligible nature settled. By eternity, is simply meant all the time that has preceded, and that we expect will succeed our existence. Yet it is classed among the bewildering notions of men. The clergyman approached the definite, who said, eternity "is for ever and ever, and five or six everlastings o-top of that. After millions and trillions of years has rolled away in eternity, it will be a hundred thousand years to breakfast time."

The idea called deity, means either a person or a principle. With those who deal in a personality, as Paley did, it is a pleasant thing to argue—one can understand them. They may be wrong, but they are intelligible. But the men with a principle are metaphysical, theological jesuits; they slip about like greased lightning. If they mean by a principle what other people mean by the term—a rule, then a principle-deity is practical atheism. No man would think of worshipping a deistical principle, any sooner than he would an electrical principle. A principle is no more an object of homage than smoke or clover. Again, a principle is nothing distinct from matter; and this idea of such distinctness is the inseparable idea of all deities. The atheist never forgets this; and when mind, intelligence, or power, is cited as a deity, he makes this sole reply—none of these is distinct from matter. They are all plain properties of matter; of spirit he can say nothing, because he can understand nothing. Spirit is the sole perqusite of saints.

We are told a grave and remarkable truth in the Encyclopædia Britanica, probably by Sir James Mackintosh, in the assurance that no man ever reasoned himself into the belief of the existence of deity. As we reason ourselves, without difficulty, into the belief of all reasonable opinions, we can only fail to reason ourselves into the belief of deity's existence, because it is not a reasonable thing. When Pythagoras said he could not speak of deity without a solecism, he expressed what the sagacity of Goethe has more strikingly reiterated, "They who enquire into deity must persist in believing the incomprehensible comprehensible;" in other words, must persist in contradicting themselves. Surely this should admonish us that human powers should be employed only about human subjects. We should not, like Candid, continue to ask unanswerable questions, but should content ourselves with saying, each with Protagoras, "of the gods I know nothing." G. J. H.

CORRESPONDENCE.

To the Editor of the Movement.

ALEXANDER POPE.

Sir,—In your first number you give a couplet from Pope, also an emendation of it. Perhaps you would admit an admirer of that poet—for Pope is a favourite of mine—to make a suggestion in his favour. You know it is archly supposed that Milton knew very well what he was about when he wrote *Paradise Lost*, and made Satan the hero of his poem. Now, may we not credit Pope with similar shrewdness? I will only quote one line from his famous *Universal Prayer*:—

Thou first great cause LEAST understood.

Is there no inuendo here? What, pray to that which of all things we *least* understand? *Cui boni?* To what purpose? We know that Bolingbroke was the personal friend of Pope. With such an aquaintance no doubt that Pope saw as far into the theological millstone as most people. M.

MR. SERJEANT TALFOURD.

Sir,—As I have read all the works on natural theology that have fallen in my way for a long time past, you would, peradventure, deem me qualified to trouble you with the following remark.

Looking over the other day the case of "Gregory v. Brunswick." I was struck with this remark by Serjeant Talfourd:—
"*The character of Hamlet was most human, and being the most human was most like the divine.*" I know we have no right to

expect lawyers to be theologians, but we have a right to guess what they mean; and as Mr. Serjeant Talfourd differs from ordinary lawyers in many things, being known as an elegant critic and clever writer, I guess that he means what he says. If, then, that which is most human is most like the divine, the divine itself must be human; and when we are perfectly divine we shall be perfectly human. Whether this is pantheism, or atheism, I cannot tell; but it makes deity into a great material man. Can the learned Serjeant be a believer in the absurdities of natural theology?   I. T

DOCTRINES OF THE CONCORDISTS

"We agree to differ."

In accordance with an intimation in the prospectus, an exposition by an acknowledged authority is now presented of a phase of opinion offering remarkable contrast to those which it is the principal object of the Movement to propogate and familiarize. Comment is dispensed with till a further development shall sufficiently acquaint the reader with these views to enable him to form a judgment on their meaning and value. The turn of thought, style, and language, so dissimilar to the usage of the writers, and the experience of the readers of this journal, will, at least, afford features of interest. To say more now, would be prejudging the question.

To those wholly ignorant, or but partially informed of these doctrines and their expounders, it will be well to state that guiding maxims for conduct, for associative arrangments, and for educative efforts, emanate from the theory; and that zealous and active men are devoting themselves to carrying out the practice. Alcott and Graham, of America, Wright, Lane, Oldham, and the late Mr. Greaves, who edited Pestalozzi's letters, have chiefly contributed, by personal experiment or otherwise, to advance these views. The *Graham Journal*, of America, I believe also Emerson's *Dial*, the *Healthian*, and other tracts by the concordists of Ham Common; the occasional tracts of Mr. Wright, a teacher of great zeal and amiability, and the present Concordium experiment are all, more or less, exemplifications of the spirit which governs these men, call them mystics, theologists, philosophers, or what we will.

I doubt not that freethinkers, in the true sense of the word, will concur in reprobating the tendency to vulgar ridicule, with which it is the fashion to assail those who travel widely from the beaten path. Ridicule is permissible, and not only so, but just and appropriate, when applied to its legitimate purposes. Impudent pretensions, hypocrisy, and tyranny, are properly the buts for ridicule the most caustic, or exposure the most severe. A self-devoted intentness and earnestness of purpose, assiduous exertions to work out a great and noble object, should command our respect and win our esteem, however we may be disposed to question the accuracy of the principles, or the efficiency of the practice.

Such has appeared to be the course of the Concordists, or "Sacred Socialists," as they have been termed, and their co-thinkers across the Atlantic. Unless we find these appearances deceptive, they are entitled to a friendly and encouraging regard, rather than to a scornful and derisive repulse. A severity of examination may be applied to their views; but having no sufficient grounds to impugn their motives, or doubt their sincerity, it is just to meet them in the pages of a truth-seeking work in a congenial spirit.

With these introductory observations, I beg to usher Mr. Oldham as expositor of the Concordists into the arena of the *Movement*.   M. Q. R.

EXPOSITION.

I.

We affirm, first, as an indispensable axiom, that prior to all motion there must be a primary mover which is never moved; before all manifestation there *is* that which can never be manifested; antecedent to all creation, the Creator *is*, and is ever creating, itself being the only *uncreated*. Of this we can affirm nothing; we are obliged to admit it, although it be ineffable, and can only proceed to speak of its appearances, its outbirths, its masks, clothings, or operations. These manifestations, be they what they may, whether physical, psychical, or spiritual, are always of a triune character. This triad manner of exhibition of primary laws and principles in all things, has been generally admitted by writers, especially theologians, in all ages, under various terms. Christians have uniformly in England designated it by the words Father, Son, and Spirit, which terms we admit as expressive of the triune idea as any others; but to avoid the unmeaning manner in which they are too generally passed over, and the personal idea which is attached to them, we prefer usually the words love, wisdom, power.

These words, with us, express the idea of the triune primary being Law; the highest essential universe manifestation, which enters into, and is the immutable basis of existence; from this law all essences, and all existences, have their origin. Hence emanate all loves, affinities, attractions, and inclinations, or dispositions; all intellect, intellections, reason, intelligence, understanding, and knowledge; all motion, operations, and vitalized existencies, in whatsoever spheres they may appear. All existence, whether visible or invisible to soul or sense, having their origin from hence; all actions, things, words, thoughts, perceptions, conceptions, affections, and beings, may be classified under, and belong to this threefold category, because this universal law is the substratum of all that exists, without which nothing can be, live, perceive, feel, or love. It is the essence in all existence; it is that in which all things inhere, that which is the good in all good feelings, thoughts, actions, and things; the truth, wisdom, or light in all true, wise, and intelligent or enlightened natures; the power, strength, and efficiency in all powerful, strong, durable things, and beings; it pervades and permeates all things, and is their very radix; it is the real in all realities; the essential *I* in all ideas and idealities; and the vital actor in all acts and actualities. From this universal, loving, intelligent, vital love, all universal principles proceed, and which are the exponents or representatives of it to man. The real Man is created the image of this being Law. It is the basis of his existence, his origin. It is the love in his will and affections, the light in his reason and understanding, the life in his actions and energies. Man, as at present existing, however, is degraded, degenerate; he is not born in an harmonious relationship in all his faculties with this universe love; his essences and instincts are deranged, confounded, and out of order. His will, if in harmonic relation with love, would be wholly enlovened; his intellect, if in perfect harmony with wisdom, would be throughout an enlightened reflection of truth, and his energies, if uniformly pervaded by life, would be powerful and unfailing in all their operations.

W. OLDHAM.

A STANDARD REPEAL ARGUMENT.—In the *Standard's* leading article of Dec. 19 occur the following observations :—" The *state of Ireland!* the phrase might be stereotyped for daily use, any time within the last half century—*that is, ever since Ireland became an object of close observation in this country* [our own Italics]. The *state of Ireland* is bad. But why ? Because the social state of Ireland is just the state of of all Europe, England and Holland only excepted, down to a period within the memory of men now living, the state of Ireland is that which must be the state of every country where the comparatively rich are separated, by a very wide chasm, from the very poor. Where such wide separation exists, poverty *will be infamous*; they who have anything will struggle to retain and augment his possessions, to avoid the danger of falling into infamy : one of their most obvious means will be to extort, from all beneath them, as much as can be obtained by any means, cruel or otherwise." After a quotation from an Italian writer, illustrating his view, the editor proceeds,—" The state of Romagna, however, as described above, was the average state of all Europe, England and Holland only excepted, until the middle of the last century. Ireland formed no exception; and, therefore, *the state of Ireland* was not the hacknied topic that it has become. Some of the European nations have approached to the condition of England, through the fiery process of war and revolution ; and Ireland, happily, by her connection with those countries [we suppose England and Holland are meant] spared these calamities, is now to be reformed by a gentler but not less certain process, complete incorporation with the country that has served as a model for all others that have really advanced towards good government and a happy social state."

Inference.—Ireland is the only country in Europe remaining in the state of semi-barbarism which prevailed a century ago. Ireland is the only country in Europe under the immediate and contiguous sway of England ; ergo, Ireland's connection with England is the cause of her semi-barbarism.

SUMMARY.

Another letter from De Lamartine on " Church State and Instructions," has appeared in some of the French Papers.— The Anti-Persecution Union have passed votes of acknowledgemnt to the Editors of the *Northern Star* and *New Moral World*, for the services they have recently rendered to the cause of theological liberty.—Cosmopolite, of Edinburgh, has issued an address to the Christians of that city on the current prosecutions for blasphemy ; he asserts that there are numerous individuals willing to tread in the footsteps of the martyrs of truth.—M. Finlay is working at his trade in gaol, and continues in good health and spirits.—Very lately, a bill was exhibited in the shop windows at the West end of London, offering five shillings reward for the restoration of a supplement to an atheistical work which had been lost. —The office of secretary is vacant at the John Street Institution, Mr. Wilson, the gentleman who held that situation, being removed to the Central Board.—Mr. Jeffery, of Edinburgh, has the happiness of marrying this week. It is not generally known that atheists fall in love like other people.—Mrs. Martin has suffered from illness during the week, but we are happy to state that she is recovering.—The report, going the round of the papers, that some persons have been poisoned by a Socialist relative, has been promptly and satisfactorily contradicted in the *New Moral World*.

MOSES AND THE APOSTLES IN DANGER OF ARREST.—The *Belfast Chronicle* commenting on the paper entitled "Beauties of the Bible," referred to in the article "Infidelity in Ireland," "most earnestly calls on the police authorities to use every means in their power to discover the *fabricators* of this vile document." Now, we have reason to believe that this said "vile document" was verbatim from the writings of Moses, Ezekiel, and the apostles. These were the "fabricators" of the sentences, and are, of course, the parties aimed at by the *Belfast Chronicle* and the police. The people of Belfast may expect to read on their walls, one of these fine mornings, the following bill:—

£100 REWARD.

WHEREAS, it has been represented to the "police authorities," by the *Belfast Chronicle*, that a certain evil-disposed Jew named Moses, a prophet called Ezekiel, and sundry apostles, *alias* evangelists, *alias* Matthew, Luke, Paul, and John, were the original "fabricators" of a certain "vile document," purporting to be "Beauties of the Bible," a book they are supposed to have written. This is to give notice, that the above reward will be paid, on the discovery and conviction of the aforesaid offenders, who are supposed to have absconded. A free pardon will be granted to any accomplice who will impeach his fellows.

By order of the " Police Authorities" of Belfast.

GOD SAVE THE QUEEN,—of course.

PROGRESS OF CHRISTIANITY.—Within the last two years Bristol and Gloucester gaols have declared in favour of the "truth as it is in Jesus." Tothil Fields has been a believer in the same doctrines for a whole month. The Tolbooth of Edinburgh, Stirling gaol, and the Perth Penitentiary, have lately come over to the same side ; and, in foreign parts, Funchal prison is acknowledged to be in Christianity's favour. Verily, "the knowledge of the Lord is covering the earth as the waters cover the sea."

MEDICAL RECIPES FOR MORAL INVALIDS.

To CURE AFFECTIONS OF THE HEART.— Take neutral policy in large quantities ; don't see any use in the discussion of an unfashionable topic ; live under a unity form of government ; and if any one goes farther than you, persuade yourself that they "provoke authority." All troublesome pulsations of sympathy will soon cease.

To CORRECT ONE-SIDEDNESS.—Read a *liberal* notice of a theological discussion. It will infallibly enable you to " see faults on both sides."

A WORK OF SUPEREROGATION.—The Rev. Walter Scott, theological tutor of Airdale College, has just published an expensive work on " The Existence of Evil Spirits." Any laboured demonstration of such beings is surely uncalled for. Their exsistence is a truism. We meet with *evil spirits* every day ; and among the ranks of the rev. gentleman's own brethren in the faith we could select a whole troop. At a prosecution for blasphemy they may be found in swarms.

" BRONTERRE O'BRIEN.—The *Soiree* and *Ball*, in honour of this gentleman, are fixed for Tuesday, Jan. 2, and will be held in the large theatre of the Rotunda, Blackfriar's Road. Need we urge a numerous attendance of politicians on this occasion ? Surely the friends of politial improvement require no stimulus to be present for the gratifying purpose of expressing their appreciation of Mr. O'Brien's exertions on behalf of the dignity and rights of industry. Tickets to be had at Mr. Hetherington's, and numerous other places.

THE BENEFITS OF CHRISTIANITY TO WOMEN.—This has ever been a prominent boast with Christians, and called forth thousands of the most pathetic homilies and deeply sentimental poems. But we were never able to discover the *practical evidence* of its truth. On the contrary, facts are directly against it. Christanity benefit women ! Yes—as vultures benefit lambs—attacking and devouring them.

The poorer class of women, always the largest and most meritorious class, are obliged, in all Christian countries, to become mere drudges to obtain even a decent subsistence; and when it is earned, they must give a portion of it to some lazy drone of a priest, or else submit to hear themselves styled as worthless. This is the condition of women in this country—Christian as it is. In Christian England, women are used as beasts of burden! as proved by the "Commissioners' Report of the employment of women and children in coal mines." Glorious benefits of Christianity !—*Boston Investigator.*

A MESSENGER FROM GOD.

Elder Knapp is to visit Salem this summer. He announces the fact in the following terms : " I expect, by divine permission, sometime next August, to commence a battle in Massachusetts, in Salem. I think it is time the devil was routed there. He has got a strong hold in that city, but by prayer and faith we can drive him from the field."—The Elder is powerful, to be sure ; but not quite enough so to fulfil his expectation. We must say, however, that he is fully competent to "RAISE *the devil*," and so the people of Salem will find to their cost.—*Boston Investigator.*

A RELIGIOUS GENIUS.—A man in white habiliments, with snowy head and beard, by name of Silas Samson, is going about among the Millerites, preaching a new doctrine. He believes that the resurrection is already past, and that we are now in heaven!—*American Paper.*

The papers call this a " Gross Delusion," but I consider it a gross delusion to say so. This man *is* a first-rate religious genius. His equal has never arisen. He is the formost man among all new religion inventors. Adopt his creed, and the mystery of godliness is plain. Death and the White Horse has gone prancing by. We have cheated Charon; we have passed the river Jordan; we *are* all saved; we are all saved! we are now in Paradise, and a pretty place it is! It is to be hoped that Silas will soon send a few missionaries here. Our true religions must be all a mistake. Lamson for ever!

NOTICE.

Many persons have written to enquire how they can obtain the *Movement* in Oldham, Dover, and other places. If they did not see an advertisement in the *Penny Satirist* of last week, explaining this, we copy for them the following notice from it.

NOTICE.—Order the *Movement* of your bookseller or newsman. If neglect occurs, write to the Editor, 40, Holywell-street, Strand, London, who will order it to be sent to any part of town or country, on the receipt of two penny postage stamps in a pre-paid letter.

Errata in No. 1—omitted last week. In paragraph marked 1, on page 2, for "primest" read *firmest* ; and in the last line of the third paragraph of the letter to Dr. Kalley, for " in" read *of.*

NOTICE TO CORRESPONDENTS.

ESPERANZA is thanked for his remarks. Would he occasionally favour us in the same way, and with a little more explicitness.

J. MELLON, Oldham ; and G. SMITH, Salford, will find their communications, respecting price, considered in the first article in this Number.

W. ROBINSON, Atheist, Manchester.—His suggestion cannot be acted on with a periodical, Only works already completed can be printed as he proposes.

G. HAMMOND, R. DOYLE, Discussion at Branch A. 1. received.

SUBSCRIPTIONS
For the Anti-Persecution Union.

SCOTTISH UNION.

From Friends in Arbroath	. .	0 10 0
From Friends in Dundee	. .	0 3 0
From the London Union	. .	3 0 0

H. JEFFERY, Secretary.

ENGLISH UNION.

Mr. Dobell, for Mr. Paterson	. .	0 1 6
From Christians at the Rotunda	. .	0 5 7
(Per Mr. G. Smith, Salford Collector.)		
Mr. Capper	. .	0 5 0
Mr. Haward	. .	0 5 0
Tr. J. Hadfield	. .	0 1 0
Mr. J. Stonier	. .	0 1 0
Mr. H. Walker	. .	0 1 0
Mr. J. Rawson	. .	0 1 0
Mr. T. Mash	. .	0 2 6
Mr. J. Higginbotham	. .	0 1 0
Mr. J. Denton	. .	0 1 0
Mr. S. J.	. .	0 1 0
Mr. J. Mason	. .	0 1 0
Several Friends	. .	0 8 7

G. J. HOLYOAKE, Secretary.

Printed and Published by G. J. HOLYOAKE, 40, Holywell-street, Strand, London. Saturday, Dec. 30, 1843.

THE MOVEMENT
And Anti-Persecution Gazette.
"Maximize morals, minimize religion."—BENTHAM.

No. 4.   EDITED BY G. JACOB HOLYOAKE, ASSISTED BY M. Q. RYALL.   PRICE 1½d.

DR. KALLEY'S LETTER.

In Dr. Kalley's singular letter, published in our first number, a passage is found which deserves remark. The reader is asked "if Deity be merciful, what becomes of his justice? Unassisted reason cannot reconcile justice with mercy towards the guilty." This is true, and is a candid acknowledgment of the contradiction existing between the commonly received notions of the attributes of that supposed being. Men believe according to the evidence presented to them; and if a deity be the author of all things, it is the author of man's peculiar constitution, and of all the evidence which forms his opinions. Therefore, if we do not believe in deity's existence, through the want of proper and sufficient evidence, there can be no guilt imputed to us, and we need no mercy. Justice will remember our natural condition and acquit us. Again, men's actions are caused by the influences which operate in their formation, and on their organization; and if deity be the great cause of all things, it caused *these* things; it caused our conduct, whether good or bad. A just deity, supposing again, for the sake of argument, one to exist, would recollect this order of existence and action, and would allow, if accountability there be, that it was accountable to us, rather than we to it. Mercy would be an insult in this case, where men stand in the dignity and equality of justice. So men of "unassisted reason" must conclude. We belong to this class of persons. We have nothing but common reason to guide us. We are not, like the Doctor, able to see invisible things. No grace, or holy spirit, or help from above, has given us a second sight. It is gratifying to find that the views of mercy and justice, explained above, are reasonable views, and nothing more. That they are not crude or sophistical, but the plain teachings, of ordinary common sense. How the Doctor came by anything superior to reason, it would, indeed, be delightful to know. How he came into the possession of more than the ordinary share of sense allotted to mortals, is an interesting speculation; and I venture to assert, that he would benefit mankind more, by enlightening them on this point, than by preaching protestantism to the already bewildered catholics of Madeira.

The fate of the Doctor's letter in Scotland, is as remarkable as its contents. It was sent by the Secretary of the Scottish Anti-Persecution Union to the editors of the christian papers, in which Dr. Kalley has been lauded, and sympathy for him expressed. But, with one exception, that of the *Scotsman*, no editor published it. Why was this? The assistance offered to Dr. Kalley, by the Union, was unconditional, and in no degree compromised his sentiments. Is it regarded as a crime in the Doctor to have, in his distress, accepted of infidel sympathy and assistance? Is it wrong in a christian, under any circumstances, to have the fellowship of good feeling, with those who differ from him, in opinion? Is religion ever to be a barrier between man and his fellow man, forbidding the acceptance of kind acts, and the expression of generous sympathy? So it seems. The Doctor is slighted because he has held communication with infidels, who were drawn to him by a desire to assist, and not by any care to proselytise him. We shall be sorry if the well intentioned offers of the Anti-Persecution Union shall in any way injure the Doctor among his own friends; and we hope that the light this transaction throws on the nature of religion, will discover to all men its hollow pretensions, and unhappy, antisocial, misanthropic tendency.

G. J. H.

THE MORALITY OF INFIDELS.—I think all the heretics I have known have been virtuous men. They have the virtue of fortitude, or they would not venture to own their heresy; and they cannot afford to be deficient in any of the other virtues, as that would give advantage to their enemies, and they have not, like *orthodox* sinners, such a number of friends to excuse or justify them.—*Franklin*.

IMPRACTICABILITIES.—"To reclaim a fanatic by persuasion and to convince a heratic by stripes."

POINTS OF MORALS.
CHARACTER-MAKING AND CHARACTER-HUNTING.

The man who is continually running after his character, seldom has a character worth the chase.
FRANCIS PLACE.

Character may be considered as the sum of our value as members of society, and the estimation in which we are held. There may exist an utter disproportion, or absolute agreement between a man's intrinsic value, and the estimation in which he is held by others. The discrepancy between the value which people commonly set on themselves, and the estimate of others is so obvious, as to have become proverbial. An illustration of this is furnished in the familiar phrase of "I should like to buy him at my price, and sell him at his own." "Know thyself," the reputed wise saying of one of the seven sages of Greece, is anything but a mere gingle of words, or turn of expression, fine to the ear, but void to the sense. The precept, if precept can, contains a world of meaning. To know thyself is the first step to all that is good, excellent, and noble. It is essential to the discipline of self-control, and self-regulation, without which nothing important can be achieved while we occupy a place in a society needing reformation.

We may make a fair start by asking ourselves three questions. Is the attainment of character desirable? What sort of character do we deem it most useful to attain? How shall we set about attaining and retaining it? The first query may be thus answered:—The difference between a man with a character, and a characterless man, is two-fold, inasmuch as self-respect, and general esteem, on the one hand, or self-abandonment and general contempt on the other, form the two absolutely dissimilar results. A great amount of pleasurable, or unpleasurable feeling, must result from either of these two conditions, or the individual must be in a most unpromising state of moral stagnation.

But here a most important distinction presents itself. Having determined that the acquisition of character is desirable, whom shall we choose as judges? Where shall we seek a standard? The only conclusive answer is afforded by referring to the degree of intelligence to which we have arrived, or the integrity and capacity of those among whom we mix.

It is susceptible of easy proof, that in whatever society or community we are thrown, the value of the opinion of others must, ultimately or primarily, be dependent on our own. If we defer ever so much to the judgment of others, we must, at one stage or other of the process, refer to ourselves, for no other purpose than to test or determine the degree of dependence to be placed on external decisions. How much more, then, do we establish the existence of a standard of our own in those cases in which we refer to ourselves, to determine whether our actions should be approved or disapproved. The enquiry confines itself only to this limit—not what standard shall we set up—but shall we set up a standard of character at all. The apprehension of conceit and presumption is got rid of by recollecting that we must at last judge of the judgers, decide upon the deciders. The process then is greatly simplified by being our own judges and deciders. The rigor or impartiality with which we sit in judgment on ourselves, will depend on the advancement we have made in general intelligence, self-knowledge, and the ascertainment of the relations subsisting between ourselves and the external world. Whenever we have ability, courage, and impartiality enough to look to, and be governed rather by our own approbation than that of others, we shall have advanced far on the road to that greatest and most difficult of all reformations, self-reformation.

The qualification of family, the patronage of connection, the support of a coterie, the adhesion of a party may be pleasant, profitable, and flattering; but the self-approval, based on a calm and comprehensive review of our actions, thoughts, and impulses, yields to none of these for the production of solid and permanent satisfaction. Purity of intentions, integrity of action, thus obtain their proper sovereignty over fashion and conventionalism.

It is this immeasurably superior influence that sustains men in pursuing a consistent and uniform course, regardless alike of the sneers of ridicule, the venom of calumny, or the thunders of denunciation. It is this which stimulates the true lover of his species to pursue an undeviating course in winning liberty for his fellow men, regardless of the sneer of the cold-hearted of his own party, or the fine and the dungeon of his oppressors. This firmness of purpose in the pursuit of what is deemed good, has been promoted and stimulated in the Carliles, the Owens, the Patersons, and others of a like stamp, by the sustaining conviction of right. These are not the men to "run after character;" the last consideration with such as devote themselves to the interests of humanity, is not what others will think of them, but what ought they to think of themselves.

M. Q. R.

THE CASE OF PATERSON.

The following extract from a letter of one of our most valued friends, received from the continent a few days since, is deserving a place in the *Movement*, and I send it to you for insertion. Perhaps you can state if anything has been done as recommended. W. C.

"The punishment of Paterson is horrible: but a very good lawyer assured me that he could not receive the treatment of a felon for the offence he was found guilty of; that the prisons of England and Scotland are both under the regulation of the Secretary of State, and, therefore, he should be addressed without delay.—What impudence for the judge to say, according to the *Times*, that in any part of the United Kingdom, Paterson, if again found guilty, would meet with still severer punishment. He has nothing on earth to do with England, or the decision of any judge in it. I suppose he was dreaming of a new invasion of England, by the covenanters, in the time of Charles. There was one consolatory feature, that the jury took three quarters of an hour to consider, and only decided by a majority; therefore if there were some dissentients, and if he had been before a jury in England, where all must agree, he would consequently have been acquitted. The Anti-Persecution Union should bestir themselves to try and get him redress. I wish Paterson could have answered that infernal speech of the judge; or at any rate, that it may be answered by the facts, contrary to anticipation, which will prove to him that he has not so speedily extirpated blasphemy by persecution. What difference is there between the offences of O'Connell and Paterson? O'Connell is charged with uttering and publishing, conspiring thereby against government, and leading to overt acts; and Paterson simply of the first, without any intentions of the second. I should like to know whether, if found guilty, they will treat O'Connell as a felon, and give him a prison suit to wear. Were there not some Chartists tried and found guilty in Scotland, how were they used? If there is a *personal* punishment apart from imprisonment, such as wearing a peculiar dress, shaving the head, or what not, for the expression of opinion, there is not only an inquisition, but *torture* still existing in Scotland, when it does no longer in Spain."

Memorandum.—The collecting of particulars, relative to Paterson's trial, not obtainable through the public press, would serve the victims of religious oppression.

ADDRESS OF THE ANTI-PERSECUTION UNION

TO ITS COLLECTORS AND FRIENDS.

The Committee this week present their report of receipts and expenditure for the quarter ending December 26, and congratulate their collectors and friends on its favourable and encouraging appearance. Though, compared with the objects of the Union, and the powers and duty of the public, it is meagre enough, yet, when contrasted with the past quarter's report, it bears gratifying signs of improvement.

The balance in hand, the Committee feel it their duty to say, should be kept in hand; and they hope that the contributions of the next quarter will not only meet all current demands on the Union, but will greatly augment that balance which must be kept for the persons in prison, and who are not permitted to receive what has been subscribed for them. On the liberation of these victims of a sanguinary religious law, they should be placed in better circumstances than before. Those who are sacrificed because of their struggles for liberty deserve a higher reward than that which money can furnish; but whatever advantages that can give them should truly be theirs.

The subscriptions which the Committee have received, possess a value in their eyes beyond that which commercially attaches to them, because it has been given freely and ungrudgingly. The independence of thought and expression, which the Committee labour to promote, has pervaded all they have done. Their official letters to the Branches of the Rational Society, and other public bodies, contained, in every case, this sentence:—"We make no appeal to the *cold.*" But if any friends of honest heterodoxy are disposed to assist our objects, we shall be proud of their help; and if not, we are content to struggle alone. It has been the glory of the Union that the victims, whom they have had the honour to defend, have been women and men of integrity and spirit, who have preferred a jail to stooping to injustice; but who have never asked the help of the parsimonious, or accepted the hollow sympathy of the Laodiceans of liberty. The Union has never *begged*—no fraction has been accepted as a *charity.* What has been given has been given by the generous and the free.

The Committee are gratified with the confidence with which they have been honoured by subscribers. This, while they hold office, they will always merit. They believe that in no case has a farthing been entrusted to them, or any of their collectors, which has not been promptly acknowledged, and correctly accounted for. To guarrantee fidelity, in this respect, the Secretary desires, that if any complaints do, or should exist, that they may be made at once to the auditors, who were appointed at a public meeting, and who are men of known integrity.

The names and addresses of the Auditors are, Mr. Allen Davenport, No. 2, Waterloo Terrace, Waterloo Town; and Mr. Joshua Hopkins, No. 6, Wood-street, North, King's-square, Goswell-road, London.   G. JACOB HOLYOAKE, Secretary.

SCHEME OF UNIVERSAL PROGRESSION.
II.

"It may be asked, whether there be a universal civilization of the human species, a destiny for humanity; and whether there has been transmitted, from age to age, 'something which cannot be lost, which must increase, form a store, and thus be passed on to the end of time?"—GUIZOT.

In pursuing further the subject of Universal Progression, it will be well to touch upon a very common and injurious error in such investigations generally, and especially with such a one as the present. When a thought arises which leads us into a new channel, one which has not been ordinarily followed by those with whom we mix, we are apt to become enamoured of it, and to allow a weight and importance to which it is not entitled. Thus it is with many reasoners on the state and prospects of our species. The prominent manner in which some political and social evils have have been forced on their attention has led to a violent revulsion of feeling as to the possibility of effecting a permanently beneficial change. Finding so much that is actually bad in the condition of the majority, they have not stopped to inquire whether or not such condition, or a worse, was the fate of a still larger majority at a bygone period. It is forgotten that we learn and see things of present time in their stern realities. The sentiments, habits, and actions of our ancestors are viewed through the mellowed hues of history, decked in the gorgeous trappings of romance, and adorned by the captivating graces and splendid imagery of poetry. A luxurious mansion, the model of taste, elegance, and sumptuousness; a chivalrous baron, lady fair, and stalwart yeomanry, dwindle, when viewed without the gloss of exaggeration, into very contemptible places and persons, with tastes, habits, and enjoyments of the most brutally low description. "Distance lends enchantment to the view." These magnificient abodes of the romancist or historian—being generally convertible terms in reference to by-gone times—have turned out, by closer inspection, to be nasty, dark, dingy, ill-constructed, ill-ventilated places; the earthen floor strewn with straw, kept filthy by an accumulation from the refuse of the table; the garb of both male and female such in kind, quality, and condition, as would cause it to be rejected by one of the meanest artizans of the present day; the food bad and often scanty, and from the badness of its preparation, and the scarcity of good vegetables and wholesome grain, continually subjecting the consumers, especially the humbler portion of the community, to virulent, eruptive, and other serious disorders. The valiant knights have turned out murderous marauders, the "ladies fair," coarse, vulgar, and ignorant kitchen wenches, and the stalwart yeomanry miserable starvlings. Our Saxon ancestors, with their manliness, vigour, and democracy, were eaten up by Danes, Romans, and Normans, each preying and preyed on in turn. Our "Saxon institutions," lauded as they have been, by constitutional writers, have recognized the transference of man, wife, and children, with the soil, as beasts of burthen. Yet were they improvements on the previous more barbaric and despotic systems, just as some fundamental alterations made in modern times have bettered those which preceded. Why, our glorious ancestors have been set up as models in shape, make, and stature, as well as wisdom and virtue. The remains of their barbarous and brutal enactments continually being struck off the statute-books, or sunk into desuetude, attest the value of the one department of progress. The specimens of their armour preserved in the tower, and minor curiosity shops, exhibit the other. Actual measurement has determined that an average-sized adult of the present day can hardly squeeze himself into the generality of these coats of mail.

Another test of the condition of a people, and worth a hundred theories and conjectures—the comparative increase of population in a given period—strengthens these considerations.

But, perhaps, no stronger evidence, no more satisfactory series of facts, directly bearing on the subject, can be adduced than the tables of the comparative duration of life for as long a series of years as can be attained with any degree of accuracy. The statistics of the duration of human life show a most decided and positive increase of the present over previous generations. Tables furnishing these calculations may be referred to in the pages of *Chamber's Edinburgh Journal*, which, being a readily accessible source of information, may be consulted to verify the statement. Thus, by inquiring more, and diving deeper into these matters, we may obtain data which will put us into a fair train of investigation. Crude speculation and illogical inferences will give way to the surer, safer, and more satisfactory results established by the inductive process.

An impartial examination, then, of the condition of our ancestors in manners, morals, habits, political liberty, health, strength, and long life—important elements or evidences of progress—will turn the current of our thoughts into another channel, bring us to juster conclusions, and enlarge and liberalize our conceptions of humanity. M. Q. R.

CURIOUS DISCUSSION,
At Branch, A 1.

On Sunday morning, November 12, the President called the attention of the members to a very important resolution which had been submitted to the branch on the Sunday previous, by Mr. Hanhart. Mr. Hanhart rose to open the proceedings—said he had been on a visit to Harmony Hall, and while there, he had paid considerable attention to the management of the school, and after having conversed with the schoolmaster and managers, he found some difficulty was felt for want of something to produce that moral effect, and due subordination on the part of the children, which exist in religious schools. He had given the subject much reflection and study, and would submit to their serious attention the following resolution:—"That the words 'God' and 'religion,' as used by Mr. Owen in the 'Outline' and the Sixth Social Tract, shall continue to be used in the schools of the Rational Society. He believed it was necessary to fill up a vacancy which existed in the school; he believed there was a feeling in the human mind, but especially in children, which looked up to some great power in the phenomena and operations of Nature. It was necessary to give this feeling and that power some precise terms, and he thought his resolution would suit that purpose.

Mr. Hardy seconded the resolution.

Mr. Wilson had observed that there was a strong feeling of veneration, or admiration, in children; and he thought that, by directing their young minds to facts, as developed in the works of Nature, their feelings and manners would be very much softened and refined.

Mr. Clark, President, could see no objection to the resolution; something *tangible* was wanted, and those who generally discuss the question never come to anything tangible or decisive. We were aware that there must be A CAUSE of all existence from the very fact of existence; but belief in a God does not constitute a religion; real religion was nothing more than a system of morals.

Mr. Rowley thought that to teach the use of words to children, which could not be defined or explained, would only tend to confuse and embarrass them. If the children were taught the principles of the society, it would be sufficient, without using words which were surrounded with mystery, and which nobody could explain anything at all about.

Mr. M'Cullough said he had been brought up in religious society, and had some experimental knowledge of the general acceptation and practical use, which the words "*God*" and "*religion*" had in the religious world. The Social Institutions, throughout the country, were the schools in which he had lost his superstitious impressions about "God" and "religion;" and it was with peculiar feelings, therefore, that he rose to oppose such a resolution in in a social institution, He would meet the question with a direct negative by moving the following amendment:—"That the words NATURE and MORALITY be substituted for the words 'God' and 'religion.'" As regards the word "God," Mr. Hanhart had based his motion on the presumption that that paragraph in the "Outline" was correct, viz.,—"That all facts yet known to man, indicate that there is an external or internal cause of all existences, by the fact of their existence, &c." He (Mr. M'C.) based his amendment on the thorough conviction that it was incorrect; "all existences" proved nothing but "the *fact* of their existence;" the words "*cause*" and "*effect*" only applied to Nature in her "*internal*" operations; but, when carried to the "*aggregate of Nature*," they ceased to have any meaning. He believed that when the Socialist spoke of God, he meant Nature. We should use words which expressed our real meanings. Would the term "Nature" not convey all we intended by the term "God?" Did not the field of "Nature" embrace all that they could teach in their schools? He considered the term "Nature" preferable to "God," from the fact that, with the meaning of the former, all men would agree; but, with the latter all would disagree. As to the term "Religion," Mr. Clark has said that "belief in a God did not constitute a religion;" he (Mr. M'C.) would take the term in its universal acceptation, and he found it inseparably connected with priests, ceremonial worship, and blind faith in senseless creeds. What was the Socialists' definition of "religion?" "The unceasing practice of promoting the happiness of every man, woman, and child, to the greatest extent in our power." Would the religious world agree with them in calling *this* "religion?" But all men would admit that it was "*morality*;" and he considered this beautiful description of pure morality to be disgraced by its connection with the term "religion." The words "nature" and "morality," then, were terms which expressed all they could intend to convey in their tuition of the rising youth; their real meanings would be acceded to by all men; and they were, therefore, preferable to the words in the resolution, which could only tend to lead astray.

Mr. Blunt seconded the amendment. As a matter of expediency, he could have tolerated the use of the terms "*God*" and "*religion*" in the old world; but when he saw an attempt to introduce them into our community schools, he would certainly oppose it. The definition of "religion," in the "Outline," was pure morality, and reminded him of the description of morality by Miss Frances Wright, and it was disparaging to morality to term it "religion,"

Mr. Hartly adjourned the meeting to the following Sunday morning.

THE CIRCULATION AND SUPPORT OF THE MOVEMENT.

To the Editor of the Movement.

Sir,—There are three venders of liberal publications in this town; I order a *Movement* of each, and leave them a day or two in the respective shops that other persons may have an opportunity of seeing the paper and purchasing if they please. If the two numbers that I do not want are purchased, I lose nothing; if no one buys them I have two copies to give away, in which case I can be charitable at a small expense. This is no time to be idle; it is absolutely necessary that every one, who takes to himself the name of Socialist, or Atheist, should be as active at least as the sons of delusion. H. ROCHE, Derby.

Sir,—The *Movement* ought to be twice its size, without any increase of price. The various religious parties subscribe most liberally for the support of their own particular dogmas. The money which even the poor subscribe is immense. Cannot something be subscribed for philosophy and freedom? Is there no zeal among any portion of the people except for their own degradation? Devise some plan, Mr. Editor, and I will eagerly act upon it. Suppose that one hundred readers of the *Movement* would guarrantee, within a fortnight, to subscribe two shillings and sixpence, and endeavour to get a friend that would do the same. Speak out, Sir, upon this point, and let us see what can be done. E. H. S.

[NOTE.—We cannot speak out, if public application for money is meant. We will support the *Movement* with determination, so long as nothing humiliating or mean is required for that purpose. The preface to the second volume of the *Oracle* gave the history of the struggles and the sacrifices made for the cause of Atheism and free expression. That history is before our friends, and to them, I think, we need no other appeal. If any are disposed to send us assistance it will be accepted; and we offer this explanation relative to the manner of its employment and our intentions. The expences of publishing the *Movement* are fixed at the lowest possible sum; and all money sent for the support of the *Movement*, that exceed the deficiencies of that sum, will be either employed in enlarging the paper, or be paid into the funds of the Anti-Persecution Union. If E. H. S. acts on his advice, and others imitate him, their remittances will be employed as I have stated. Accurate accounts are kept of all we receive and all we expend, which any donor, who desires it, may see on calling at the office, or authorizing a friend to do so, on her or his behalf. Ed. of M.]

GRATUITOUS INSTRUCTION.

Mr. G. Hammond of the Whitechapel Branch, has written to express his willingness—if a suitable room is found him—to give gratuitous and efficient instruction in Gurney's System of Short-Hand to such members and friends of the Anti-Persecution Union as may be desirous of that accomplishment. The time required to perfect pupils will be two hours per week for three months. Mr. Hammond thinks that other persons might be found to offer gratuitous tuition to the same parties in other branches of art or science. The proposal is a laudable one, and we recommend all persons who wish to participate in its benefits, or are able to promote the scheme, to write to us, or communicate at once to Mr. Hammond.

CONTEMPORARY SAYINGS AND DOINGS.

LIBERTY OF THE PRESS IN PARIS.—An important decision has recently been given in an alleged libel case, in which freedom of scientific comment was mixed up with imputations on character. The court drew a wide line of distinction, by which full immunity was guarranteed in the discussion of merely scientific subjects. The literary and scientific men of France have taken a lively interest in the case, and addresses from all quarters have poured into the capital, expressive of an earnest desire for non-interference on the part of the law with freedom of expression.

CONTINENTAL COMMUNISM.—An elaborate article appeared in the *Times* newspaper, of Friday week, on the strength and condition of communist associations in France, Germany, Switzerland, &c., and the struggles between them and the authorities.

WESLEYAN EDUCATIONAL MOVEMENT.—I would have been much better pleased if the Wesleyans had united with all who were desirous of promoting education among the people, *instead of making their movement sectarian.*—*Charles Hindley, M.P.*

GOVERNMENT CONTROL OF EDUCATION.—In a work recently published, under the title of *France; her Government Institutions Considered and Exposed*; an immense amount of fatally pernicious influence is stated to be exercised by the French Government. Of 20,000 teachers appointed by Government, none dare give an independent electoral vote at the peril of his place. The number of functionaries under the centralized system of France is so great, and their officials are so completely under the control of the ministry, that an overwhelming preponderance is ensured among the electoral body.

"THE PEOPLE," a journal expressly and exclusively devoted to the interests of the operative classes and trades' unions, has started contemporaneously with our own publication. It will be a pleasing evidence of progress if this journal succeeds in establishing itself. There is still room for plenty of "people's" advocates. What an important day in a "calendar of progress," will be the 16th December!

RESULT OF OLIGARCHICAL RULE.—A debt, exceeding in amount the weight of all the precious metals on the earth, and to pay the bare interest of which, the industry of the living and the unborn are mortgaged to the last generation—a colonial empire rendered an annual loss by tariffs—ten millions of people living on the dietary of cattle—another million and a half immured in workhouses—and six millions of adults deprived of all the rights of citizenship.—*Sentinel.*

The report that appeared in the *Times* a few days ago, of the libellous application of Mr. Crawford to the magistrates of Union Hall Police Office, concerning the South London Hall of Science, has been corrected by a subsequent report in the *Times,* of the explanation of Mr. Crawford's unjust conduct, made by Mr. Benson Lear, the secretary of the Rotunda, to Mr. Traill, the magistrate at the Union Hall.

THE LIBERATION OF MR. GEORGE WHITE.

Mr. White suffered with unflinching firmness a severe imprisonment in Wakefield, a few years ago, for the expression of his political opinions; and on Monday next he will be liberated from an imprisonment of eight months in the Queen's Bench for the same offence. Mr. White possesses a calibre not easily subdued by severities. He is one of those few and invaluable men on whom reliance could be placed in the last struggle for liberty. In Birmingham he is sincerely respected by the most unbending party that radical town possesses, a party characterised by the safe but unfashionable qualities of bluntness and integrity. Mr. White deserves well of working men, who will only discharge a duty by being present in large numbers at the following celebrations of his return to liberty, which we have gratification in announcing.

Monday, Jan. 8th.—A dinner, concert, and ball, at the Political Institute, Turnagain-lane.—*Tuesday,* 9th.—A public meeting at the Hall of Science, 81, Whitechapel. — *Wednesday,* 10th. — A public meeting at the Chartist Hall, Blackfriarsroad; and a public dinner at the Bricklayers' Arms, Homer-street, Paddington.

Birmingham.—An operative meeting at Duddeston-row, on Mr. White's arrival from London by the train at one o'clock on Monday, 15th of January; and a grand tea party and ball in the evening, in the Mechanics' Institution. Tea on the table at five o'clock. Feargus O'Connor, Esq., will attend.

Rights of Man.—To say that private men have nothing to do with government, is to say that private men have nothing to do with their own happiness or misery; that people ought not to concern themselves whether they be naked or clothed, fed or starved, deceived or instructed, protected or destroyed.—*Gordon. Cato's Letters.*

BALANCE SHEET OF THE ANTI-PERSECUTION UNION,
For the Quarter ending December 26, 1843.

RECEIPTS.					EXPENDITURE.			
September 26, Balance in hand	£0	7	6		Oct. 3, Mr. J. Mc Neil, Stirling	£0	10	0
Oracle No. 96	2	3	4		Dec. 17, Public Meeting, Rotunda Bills, posting, Hire of hall, etc.	1	1	0
Do., — 97	0	5	1		Dec. 19, New covers for Paterson's Trial	0	10	0
Do., — 98	2	18	10		— 16, Mr. Paterson, Edinburgh	1	0	0
Do., — 99	0	11	3		— 25, Do. Do.	1	0	0
Do., — 100	4	7	6		Nov. 1, Do. Do.	1	0	0
Do., — 101	6	10	9½		— 6, Do. Do.	1	0	0
Do., — 102	4	15	8½		Dec. 1, Do. Perth Penitentiary	0	5	0
Do., — 103	2	7	5		— 5, Do. Do.	1	0	0
Movement, No. 1	4	17	4		Nov. 7, To George Hinton, Esq., solicitor, Bristol, in settlement of bill Queen v. Southwell	2	0	0
Do., — 2	3	3	2½		Nov. 7, To expense of Public Meeting, Hall of Science, Manchester, 1000 Union Addresses, etc.	0	17	0
Do., — 3	1	16	2		Nov. 12, Assistant Secretary	1	10	0
					— 12, Dr. Kalley, Madeira	5	0	0
					— 12, Letters to and from Madeira	0	5	5
					— 13, To Scottish Union	1	0	0
Audited by us and found correct,					— 18, Do. Do.	2	0	0
JOSHUA HOPKINS,					To general correspondence papers for press and circulation, printing, etc.	3	3	7½
ALLEN DAVENPORT.					To balance in Treasurer's hand	11	2	1
	£34	4	1½			£34	4	1½

DR. KALLEY.—As the public mind has of late been much and painfully interested in the present unmerited position of Dr. Kalley, of Madeira, the following extract from a letter, dated the 23rd and 29th ult., from that island, will be read with satisfaction :—" You ask me about Dr. Kalley. He is still in gaol. Some say he will soon be set free, others are doubtful. The people here—I mean those who put him in—would be right glad to see him out again. They seem to be aware that they have got into a sad scrape. He claims remuneration, and a large sum too, for what he has lost, and for false imprisonment. In the mean time, his labours are going on; he has as much as he can do in prison. People are not forbidden to speak with him, and many hundred tracts are distributed. In fact, I think the cause has been greatly promoted by the late events. People have been led to think, and to ask the reason of all this. In the mean time, he enjoys excellent health, and the society of his wife; and Mrs. and Miss Crawford (his mother and sister-in-law) are almost constantly with him. All the strangers call upon him; the other day, when I went to see him, I found the Duchess of Manchester with him."—PATRIOT.

PRECISE INTELLIGENCE.—An Extraordinay Supplement of the "Staats Courant" says—" At half-past twelve o'clock Colonel Spengler arrived from Berlin with the melancholy intelligence that the ALMIGHTY had been pleased to take unto Himself His Majesty King William Frederick, Count of Nassau, on the 12th instant, at half-past eight o'clock in the morning."

Could the editor of the "Courant" tell us WHERE the Count was taken to, and WHEN he arrived at the place of his destination. He who has obtained such an accurate particular of the celestial movement in one instance can, no doubt, do it in others.—ED. OF M.

NOTICE.—A few complete copies of Vol. II. of the " Oracle of Reason," price 5s. 6d., boards, can be had on application at Mr. Hetherington's, 40, Holywell Street, Strand.

REPLIES.—W. M., Glasgow. Send "Oracle" etc., orders to M. Ryall.---W. Cooke and W. Anderson's orders received

TO CORRESPONDENTS.

ANTI-PRIESTCRAFT.—CANTERBURY is informed that the 5s. in stamps, which he says, in his letter of Dec. 4, 1843, he "sent to Chilton," has never been received by Mr. Chilton. Will ANTI-PRIESTCRAFT inquire at the Post Office concerning that letter?

R. DOYLE.—His communication is written with lead; if he will honour it with INK, it shall receive attention. Above all things controversy should be plain, otherwise we may dispute about misunderstandings instead of the infinity of matter.

T. BIDWELL.—Received. His 6d. was duly handed in, but the Union can only acknowledge, separately, sums of one shilling and upwards. It would be too expensive separately to acknowledge all the small sums which are subscribed. Such small sums are sent in by the collector of them under the head "several friends" so much. T. B.'s 6d. has been memorandomed, as we expected another, and when received the one shilling will be acknowledged. His former 6d. he will find in ORACLE 103, as coming from "J. B. Hoxton." That was the printer's error. It should have been T. B. Hoxton. It was explained to the satisfaction of Mr. Hetherington, who paid it in.

H. ROCHE, Derby.—Please express an acknowledgement for the pretty advertisement of the "Movement."

J. M.—Superstition—declined.

Received, "Belfast Chronicle."

To our Scottish Correspondents.—How is it that we have received no accounts of the meetings in Dundee in favour of free discussion?

Received by C. S., G. J. H., and T. P. of "W. W." 1 10 0
———— Mr. Mc Neil, H. J., and Miss R. of "W. J." 0 15 0

Printed and Published by G. J. HOLYOAKE,
40, Holywell-street, Strand, London.
Saturday, Jan. 6, 1844.

THE MOVEMENT
And Anti=Persecution Gazette.
"Maximize morals, minimize religion."—BENTHAM.

No. 5.   EDITED BY G. JACOB HOLYOAKE, ASSISTED BY M. Q. RYALL.   PRICE 1½d.

CIVILIZATION IN SCOTLAND.

Civilization is the refining influence of literature and science diffused over the manners and institutions of men. It softens the harshness of ignorance and the rancour of parties, wherever reason can prevail. Its friend is knowledge, but, like the other benefactors of humanity, its foe is religion.

The assemblies, courts and streets of Scotland, have, lately, afforded melancholy evidence of this truth. Acts of injustice, insult and barbarism, from the contemplation of which, decency and feeling shrink, have been perpetrated by a people renowned for their fervent piety and deep christian spirit. Yes; and perpetrated, be it proclaimed far and wide, solely in consequence of their piety and their christianity.

In any meeting in the three kingdoms, called by infidels, for the consideration of the cases of the victims of persecution, any person—the saintly persecutor himself—would be willingly and fairly heard. The liberty which infidels claim for their friends, they would concede to others; but, at the Waterloo Rooms, Edinburgh, with the spirit of christianity incarnated in no less a person than the Lord Provost, Mr. Paterson and his friends narrowly escaped with their lives, because, holding opposite opinions on religious points, they sought to speak at that christian meeting. The impartiality an atheist would be ashamed to forget, a christian never knows. That same meeting persecuted Paterson for his opinions; while, with characteristic inconsistency, they were protesting against persecution—while Dr. Kalley was writing from his gaol in Madeira, that no "christian has recourse to injuries, and that he relies on universal philanthropy and reasonable evidence." Is it that christianity observes the sense of consistency which influences other men? or is that, like the hyena, it sets up the sounds of humanity only to decoy the credulous traveller to his destruction?

Next, we find christianity on the bench, in the person of Judge Hope. Not only did this judge inflict on Paterson a dreadful sentence, but mocked at his victim as he held him in his power. Told him he "had prayed to Almighty God to vouchsafe him comfort and peace, and sentenced him to fifteen months' imprisonment—that he had prayed to the Redeemer to show mercy to Paterson, to whom *he* would show neither humanity nor justice. Judge Hope said that " the court had no reason to believe that much, if any, impression had been made by the efforts of Paterson and Robinson," which was confessing this christian prosecution was uncalled for and vindictive; that it was not required by public utility, but by—christian revenge. Yet this judge and Paterson's prosecutors would be among the loudest insisters in favour of christianity's benign and civilizing influence. Verily, we may apply to Judge Hope, and his fellow christians, the language of Sidney Smith:— They soar above all men in what they say, and sink below all the world in what they do. They float on the heaven of declamation about the glory and truth of christianity, and fall down to feed on the offal and garbage of persecution.

A short time ago Miss Roalfe was liberated on bail, having been apprehended for the publication of her opinions. To any one a gaol is an appalling place—a den of systematic cruelty—a professed manufactory of misery—a place where the fortunate part of society torture and kill the unfortunate—a place where joy and affection are never permitted to come. A woman, whatever may be her courage, may well feel distress at being made the inmate of such a place. Yet, on Miss Roalfe's return to her home—left wretched and desolate by the visit of Christ—she was surrounded by a savage and fiendish mob of christians. I was going to say *brutal* mob, but *brutes* would have betrayed some instinctive sensibility of a woman's feelings and the conduct due to her. Cannibals would have displayed regard on such an occasion, but not this pious Edinburgh mob. Not satisfied that their vindictiveness would be amply gratified on the bench, they yelled on, and medical students and methodist preachers, mingled in the inhuman and disgraceful scene. The spirit of christianity, when beheld in the refined inuindoes of the prosecuting counsel, in the affected concern of the judge, or in the pretended regard for the public welfare by the press, is modified by public opinion and general intelligence. In these garb it is not less fatal to liberty, but less offensive to the eye. But in the mob, genuine bible christianity exhibits itself. Fresh from the pulpit, the sacramental-table, and the prayer-meeting, unsophisticated and unrefined, in all its savagery, violence, yells and threats—*there it is*. To other than pious people one might reason of delicacy and humanity with a chance of success; but to these, expostulation and reproof would be vain and idle; they are neither men nor women, but christians, and they have nothing human about them but their flesh and bones. That these men are sound christians there is no doubt, and that they are a disgrace to civilization is no less certain; they kneel daily at the throne of grace, and go about the world a living infamy—they may "die in the arms of Jesus," but they would disgrace the purlieus of Billingsgate.

To use a phrase of Pemberton's, one might as well attempt to draw two mountains together with a diachylon plaister, as to convince some persons of the demoralizing tendency of piety. Facts and evidence make no more impression on them than hail on the helmet of Achilles. They appear to rejoice in a *convenient* obtuseness—their insensibility is supernatural. The Lord Provost may imprison infidels at an anti-persecution meeting; Judge Hope may rival the inquisitors in cool malignity; an Edinburgh mob may violate decency and humanity—each and all under the influence, in the name, and for the special glory of christianity; and yet some sapient saint will tell us that these men are professors, and not possessors—that it is not christianity, but the *want* of it. As well might we be told by some thick and thin patron of night, that though night obscures the face of nature, conceals her hues, deprives vegetation of light and warmth; throws her mantle over thieves and assassins, yet it is not night, bless your soul! that does all these things, but the *want of night*. As reasonable is all this, as is the assertion that it is not christianity, which does *what christianity does*, but the want of it.

The charm and perfection of the social compact, is when individuals arrive at that state of civilization in which they mutually concede to each other that freedom of action, and independence of opinion and expression, which is enjoyed without the pale of society. When the refinements of knowledge and sense of justice lead to this result, all the benefits of the savage are united to the higher advantages of the social state. But religion is ever the greatest barrier to this order of things. The tyranny which society collectively arrogates, and coarsely acts out, the religious man ingloriously usurps and exhibits in his own person, in all its grossness, for the triumph of his miserable faith, and for trampling on the infidel consciences of other men. In the streets, at public meetings, and on the bench, clothed in law and ermine, we have traced exhibitions of this rude vulgarity. It is no assumption made by party spirit, but a fact in the history of progress, that religion, of all things, is that which clings to prejudice and injustice the longest, and adopts improvements the latest. May we live to wipe the foul blot of religion from the fair face of humanity. May civilization extend her conquests over piety, that the belief in gods, like the belief in witches, may no longer disgrace our courts of justice, and dishonour our common nature.

G. J. H.

SENTIMENTAL THEISTS, AND NATURAL THEOLOGY.

Written for the Investigator, by CHARLES SOUTHWELL.

"The Argument of Design equal to Nothing; or Nieuentytt and Paley versus David Hume and Saint Paul. By Fidia (late Victorious) Analysis."—
London: Smith, Elder, & Co., 65, Cornhill; and W. Blackwood & Sons, Edinburgh.—One Shilling.
"Paley Refuted in his own Words." By George Jacob Holyoake.—
London: Hetherington.—Price Sixpence; boards, one Shilling.
"Natural Theology Exposed." The arguments of Paley, Brougham, and the Bridgewater Treatises on this subject, examined. By George Ensor.—
London: Hetherington; and Watson.—One Penny.

I.

There is a manifest disposition, on the part of leading theologians, to set aside reason as an unfit guide in matters of religion. Since christianity appeared in its Jewish dress, its priests have, with unbroken uniformity, preached the insufficiency of reason; but never with more zeal than at the present day. Rarely, indeed, are they *now* heard admonishing their flocks to seek "a *reason* for the faith within them?" No; the preaching greatly in vogue, at this opinional crisis, is the very opposite of Saint Peter's, instead of waxing eloquent in praise of *reason*, instead of glorifying it as the "most precious gift of God to man;" they denounce it as the bane of morals, and religion's mortal foe. In truth, reason is just now the terror of Europe's clergy; their *accuser*, and go we into conventicle or church, from clerical lips, we hear little or no reasoning, not directed against the practice of relying *upon* reason. The amazing spread of Atheism in England and Germany, during the last two years, has seriously alarmed the clergy: that alarm is natural, it is quite natural; they who have everything to lose and nothing to gain by a change of direction in the current of thought, should do all they can to keep it in old channels. The clergy of Europe *feel*, to use their favorite word, that the march of infidelity must be stopped, or christianity will hardly outlive the present century. The Puseyite movement is an attempt, a feeble, but, still a *cunning* attempt, to arrest the tide of reason. Like many other cunning people, those "unprotestantizers of England's church," are damaging the cause they manœuvered to serve. Sworn enemies of reason, they have, without, perhaps, knowing it, proved themselves the christian faith's most formidable enemies. They are the men, who, more than any other class of religionists, have at once given strength to Atheism; and an impetus to that anti-rational *feeling* which is now agitating Europe. All churchmen are not Puseyites, but an immense majority of our church are, more or less, infected with the Puseyite spirit. The Oxford heresy has already effected a partial, and promises to effect a complete revolution; not only as regards this or that christian church, but in men's opinion of christianity itself. The abettors of that heresy are as unscrupulous a band of sacerdotal conspirators, as ever plotted to corrupt the reason, that they might enslave the bodies of men. They would feign, to borrow the expressive phrase of Milton, "stiffen us into uniformity by the starch of tradition." Popery, in all but name, is the object for which they struggle: for *that* they stigmatize a disposition to investigate religious questions as "irreverent:" for *that* they laud the spirit of persecution as a spirit springing from an intense and earnest love of christian truth; for *that* they avow their determination to "unprotestantize" the very church, whose bread they eat, and whose doctrines they are sworn to defend; for *that* they rave, like bedlamites, about the curse of reason, and efficacy of *their* faith; the impiety, the soul damning sin, of proving and judging *their* true religion before we believe and maintain it. Yes, for *that* they have the audacity to say, and the measureless impudence to print *their* balderdash as the wisdom of inspiration, that none may doubt, save at "the peril of their souls."

A writer, in *Blackwood*,[*] who is, probably, in league with this modest club of godly unprotestantizers, bids us remember that, in more cases than academic dignitaries may be willing to admit, the heart (where a man has one) is the only safe, the only legitimate ruler of the head, and that a mere metaphysician, and solitary speculator, however properly trimmed—

"One whose smooth-rubbed soul can cling,
Nor form nor feeling, great or small;
A reasoning self sufficing thing,
An intellectual all in all,

may write very famous books, profound even to unintelligibility; but never can be a philosopher." Now, I may not be an excellent judge of the heart's intellectual functions; not, indeed, being aware that hearts performed such functions: and as to the hearts being "the only legitimate ruler of the head;" I must say the terms are pretty, but thus strung together "profound even to unintelligibility;" and certainly am of opinion that their clever writer "never can be a philosopher." As, however, he is a sworn enemy to "an intellectual all in all," I presume he would kindly take under his wing any intellectual *half-in-half*. This model philosopher, would divide his convictions between brain and heart, sometimes thinking, sometimes feeling his way to truth; not "a reasoning self-sufficing thing," nor one whose soul has been "rubbed into smoothness," such being mere metaphysicians and solitary speculators, however "properly trimmed;" but individuals who arrive at one set of convictions by the road of experience and observation; by another set without travelling for them at all, being convinced of their truth by intuition — such model philosophers are, of course, "reasoners to the end of their tether." Not an inch farther do they reason; but if you cannot take things by the head, seize them by the tail, say the Arabs; and if you cannot know any more through the brains, lay hold and rely on the heart, say these model philosophers. Wonderful organ this heart; and as wonderful are the model philosophers, who by it are guided through

[*] See "Blackwood's Magazine," No. cccxxv, Art. Frederick Schlegel.

all the mazes of the dark past, and darker future; who, in so many instances, find it "the only legitimate ruler of the head," and who, by its almost magical aid, believe; 'they know not why, and care not wherefore." Sterne, in the redolence of good nature, loved *critics* to be *pleased*, they knew not why, nor cared not wherefore, and the writer in *Blackwood*, (a sly fox,) is very anxious that those who criticize religion, should act "upon the same good natured principle." He does not, however, augur a speedy termination to his amiable anxiety; for he complains that "the modern world has fallen altogether into a practical Atheism by the idolatry of mere reason; whereas all true greatness comes not down from the head, but up from the heart of man." There is, then, if this complaint be well founded, a vast amount of practical Atheism in modern society. But what is practical Atheism? the writer in *Blackwood* has not distinctly informed us. Those words "*practical Atheism*" will bear a whole legion of interpretations. Some individuals would not object to say, as Mongey did, "I have the *honor* to be an Atheist." Others may easily be found who would as soon be called, and thought robbers, or even murderers, as Atheists. Evidently these two classes of individuals very differently understand the words "practical Atheism." The exact meaning affixed to them, by the contributor of *Blackwood*, I don't know, but guess him to mean something bordering on the terrible conduct pursued, or acts performed, that none would perform or pursue, save "intellectual all-in-alls;" in whom faith in the incredible is stone dead: those "idolaters of mere reason," who are misguided enough to be guided by "the light of nature and the evidence of their senses;" who are irrational enough to declare with Locke, that hoping to think soundly through other mens brains, is no more than expecting to see clearly through other mens eyes; who, moreover, commit the unpardonable offence of rejecting the doctrines taught by christian priests, as "profound even to unintelligibility."

ENGLISH REPUDIATIONS.

The newspapers, American and English, have indulged in much recrimination, as to the non-payment of debts, and appropriation of property, occurring in the history of the two nations. The Americans did not seem to know some facts, and the English prints have taken care not to acknowledge them. The Americans quote our conduct to the Jews; for many years they supplied the necessities of the nation, till, having no more to satisfy the public rapacity, they were put to death, and forbidden the country. The next great and general confiscation of property, occurred at the Reformation, when the church was divided between the king and the nobles. But, under Edward III., occurred the refusal to pay a foreign debt, when several of the principal mercantile houses at Florence failed, in consequence of the non-payment of sums lent to the English king. Henry VIII. twice borrowed money from his subjects, and was exonerated by parliament from paying. But the great fact of national bankruptcy, established under Charles II., and legalized by William III., and Queen Anne, may be said still to attach to us. I copy the following account of the whole transaction from p. 685, vol. ii. of the *Pictorial History of England*. "At the revolution, (1688,) with the exception of about 580,000*l*. of arrears due to the army, and 60,000*l*. to the late king's servants, to meet both of which charges, there was money sufficient in the exchequer, and in the hands of the receiver of taxes, the only debt due by the state, was the sum of 1,328,526*l*. which had been seized by Charles II. on shutting up the exchequer in 1672. Interest had been originally paid upon this sum, at the rate of 5 per cent., but had been discontinued in the last year of Charles's reign; from which date, to the discredit of the government of William, as well as of that of James II. no provision was made for the just claims of the persons from whom this money had been taken, till the year 1700, (the last of William's reign,) when the hereditary excise was charged with interest upon the whole, from the year 1705, (Queen Anne's reign) at the rate of 3 per cent. and the principal was made redeemable on the payment of half its amount, or 664,263*l*. The unfortunate bankers and merchants, therefore, to whom this money properly belonged, after it had been borrowed from them, in the first instance, without their consent, and then detained from them without any interest being paid upon it for above twenty years, during which space it would, at the then customary rate of interest, have accumulated three times its original amount, were now further mulcted or robbed of one half of the sum which had hitherto been admitted to be legally due to them. In fact, the entire amount to which they were plundered by this arrangement, considerably exceeded three millions sterling. King Charles's shutting of the exchequer has been deservedly reprobated ; but the injustice and hardship of that measure, which consisted simply in forcing a loan from the subject, for which, however, the ordinary rate of interest was paid, were not to be compared to this winding up and conclusion of the affair by the government of King William. The 664,263*l.* thus ultimately awarded in satisfaction of equitable claims to six times the amount, was called the bankers' debt, and *still remains undischarged*, although long ago incorporated with other public debts, in that vast pile, of which it may in a manner be regarded as the foundation stone." Hume assigns as a reason for the parliament of Henry the VIIIth not paying the king's debts, that they did not wish to encourage a system of national indebtedness, and therefore hoped to prevent people lending money which would not be returned to them. Hume was against national debts, and frequently in his writings, and that in common with all other great political and financial writers, prognosticates their end in England. The above facts may not exonerate the Pennsylvanians, but they ought to check our affectation of exemplary integrity. W. J. B.

CALL TO THE UNCONVERTED.

A man who is the mainstay of anything at all, should have calves that do not shrink from inspection, and sinews somewhat stouter than a weaver's.
TIMES.

" You had better mind your own business than trouble yourself about matters that don't concern you." " Pray," quoth the person addressed, " what do you call my own business; and what, matters that don't concern me?" I mean what you get your living by, which, I think, would be much better minded if you would give up going to those chartist and socialist meetings. " I'm sure they can't do you or your family, or anybody else, any good; and you'll get your discharge, some day or other, for it. Just tell me whether it will put a coat on your back, or a dinner on your table?" I will, most readily—for as I think that the foundation of reform is the supplying one's wants, without a prospect of this sort, I would agree with you, that to join the socialists, and chartists, and free traders, is time thrown away. I will grant you, to begin with, that every one for himself, and God for us all, is the way with people in general. " How does this apply to those that govern?" Why, as they are few and rich, and we are many and poor, and the many and the poor don't send them to manage the business of the country, they will take good care to keep all they have, and to get all they can. As their interest is not our interest, and everyone will look to his own before anybody elses, we are still left in the lurch. " And how can you alter it?" How has everything been altered that has been changed for the better? Could not the word of one man, without law and without jury, put us in prison and keep us on the same spot of ground all our lives along with the cattle, sell us with the cattle, or take us away, and if we had got anything for our own use, take it away without either law or appeal. " Well, such as you had nothing to do with altering things of this sort." Aye, there's the rub, it is just because we have had nothing to do with these things, that much better alterations have not taken place, and that so many are able and willing to work and can't so much as get a living. "Well, but you that have such hard work to get a living, had better leave such things to people that have more time and are better off." People that have more time, and are better off, have their own interests to look to, which do not happen to be ours, and never will be till we are as well off as themselves; and that we never shall be, till we have as much to do with government as they have. " But the Socialists have nothing to do with the government, they want to get land for themselves, and don't trouble themselves about what the government is doing, or intends to do." That is either a mistake of yours, or an error of theirs, in my opinion. However, whichever way that may be, the Socialists have very good plans for altering things for the better, by clubbing together. It is because we have been kept so much apart, and been made jealous or afraid of one another, or been persuaded that we can do no good for ourselves, and that we must have employers who will always keep the profits and give us the work to do; it is because of all this, that we are apt to fancy, as you do, that we can do nothing for our own advantage, but keep to our work like beasts of burden, and let things around us go on as they will.

Political and social reform must make the people, the producing people, " the mainstay of the country," or they are nothing worth;—they must, as a consequence, " have calves that do not shrink from inspection," or we had better, as one of the interlocutors recommends, mind our own business, and not concern ourselves with what does not belong to our calling or profession;—our population should have " sinews somewhat stouter than a weaver's," through the instrumentality of social and political changes, or all efforts in these directions would amount to something worse than useless. Social and political reforms are hand-maidens—the utmost political alterations, however great, could not, consistently with a nation's freedom, do more than allow the people to obtain, or protect them in obtaining, a better living, and ensure for them ample security in carrying out social reform. The utmost social reform, however advanced, and however admirably calculated to effect the purposes of better living, the obtainment of higher morals, education, and knowledge than heretofore, would still fail, and, Roman like, fall to pieces through external assailants, had it not the security of government protection, or government non-interference.

Science, the arts, education, each is—all are found—indispensable; but first let us have the substratum. No work, organ, agitation, or proceeding, can have the interests of humanity at heart that does not first consider the means of obtaining for all, competency and leisure—this is a test for all associative efforts of magnitude. Anti-supernaturalism, free discussion, however remote they may appear in their bearings on these questions, nevertheless, affect the matter deeply. If the altar, backed up by the priest and church, be abolished, men's pockets, as well as their thoughts, will be their own. Well clothed, and well fed slaves are as much my abhorrence as that of any man breathing; but ill clothed, and ill fed freemen, seem to be very like irreconcilable or incompatible, things; and if compatible, or reconcilable, it is high time that their impropriety and undesirableness should be forcibly indicated, and that the most advanced of the vehicles for thought, should busy themselves in pointing out the connection of reforms, or movement, in all directions, with that of the supplying of the animal wants.

M. Q. R.

RELIGIOUS CONTROVERSY.

The following address to the Catholic, Church of England, and Dissenting Congregations of the Metropolis, from the pen of Mrs. Martin, will be acceptable to our friends in the country who cannot obtain intelligence of what is doing here. It is the fourth weekly address, and was issued in the last week in December. Many thousand copies have been circulated of the several addresses. Mrs. Martin's style is pointed and effective; she archly calculates that they to whom she speaks will not read much; and she takes care that if they read at all, they shall do it to some purpose. Here is the address mentioned—the others are of an equally excellent character.

To the Christians of the Metropolis.

Friends,—Now your Christmas Festivities are ended, you will have time again to think upon subjects of more permanent interest; and I, and Jesus, may venture to ask a share in your cogitations; and I hope we shall turn your thoughts into fruitful channels.

Do you know who Jesus was before he was born? Paul says he was "GOD over all. Blessed for evermore," and who ventures to doubt it? The same authority tells us, that by his birth "he was made a little lower than the angels," which of course you all believe. Would it not be "straining at a gnat," indeed, to ask, how the "God over ALL" could be made *lower* than some of his own creatures?

Is your faith orthodox on the question of his paternity? This is an important point.

Who was the father of Jesus? Luke vaguely tells us, that he "was SUPPOSED (*to be*) the son of Joseph," but that he "should be CALLED the son of GOD." If HE was GOD, and there is but *one* GOD, two *indisputable* points, it means that he was his OWN father. Happy would it be for many a mother, could *she* and *others* believe that her child had been its own father!

Have you rightly weighed the important purpose for which he was *sent?* SENT! Then who sent him? Necessarily some *one* greater than himself! If there is any greater than himself, he could not be GOD; and if not God, what was he?

If you should think it more likely that he was Joseph's son, than his *own*, your curiosity will perhaps be excited, like mine, to know *who* was Joseph? Matthew says, "he was the son of Jacob," but Luke affirms that he was "the son of Heli." Of BOTH, gentle reader? or neither? Could you settle it by Act of Parliament?

It would be interesting to know where the little Jesus was nursed. Matthew informs us, that Joseph and Mary took him into Egypt, and was there until the death of Herod: but Luke assures us that "when they had performed all things according to the law, they returned into Galilee, to their own city, Nazareth." *Which* of the Evangelists, since they were *both* inspired, has written falsely? or, who has corrupted the text? and, where was God when they did so?

You are doubtless aware, that the Devil presumed to *tempt* God with various offers of things which were already his own; that Jesus was "driven of the spirit," that is, one part of the Godhead, drove another part of it into the wilderness, *immediately* after his baptism, on purpose to be so tempted by the aforesaid Devil ; and that the said God fasted for forty days, and thereupon was " an hungered." So Mark, *no doubt*, TRULY writes. But, now then, does John prove that on the third day after his baptism he was at a feast in Cana of Galilee ? *Gentle reader*, which must I give up ? The miracle, or the temptation ?

" How happy could I be with either,
Were t'other dear charmer away !"

Where is the Christian Instruction Society ? It will leave me bewildered in the *labyrinth* of the " mystery of Godliness," until I inadvertently write *Blasphemy*.

I have asked them, and the *learned (?)* clergy, for rational answers to knotty questions ; they *wont* answer them, because they are asked by a *woman*, yet they obtained Christ from the same source. I wonder they did not object to *him* on that account.

Believe me, friends, 'tis not that they *will not*, it would be their glory to do so : I shall tell you *in confidence* they *cannot*. No. If your priests *had* answers, they would *bring* them ; but their weaker-than-woman's arms, have not nerve enough to cleanse the Augean stable of Christendom of the filth with which Devotion has filled it. Suffer the Hercules THOUGHT to *fulfil* that salutary task, and you will then know me to be

The friend of the whole human race,
and of the undisguised truth,
EMMA MARTIN.

THE FIRST PRECEPT.

The Anti Persecution-Union have just issued the annexed Precept for the extension of its usefulness in Leicester. They will be happy to receive applications for others, from friends in the principal Towns.

(Copy.) PRECEPT No. I.

Anti Persecution Union Office,
40, Holywell Street, Strand, London.
January 1, 1843.

To Mr. William Henry Holyoak.

" The London Anti Persecution Union to establish the Free Discussion of Theological Opinions, and to protect the Victims of Intolerance and Bigotry," having been applied to by William Henry Holyoak for authority to establish the operations of the Union in Leicester, and having reasons to confide in the honour and integrity of the said W. H. Holyoak, the aforesaid Union do hereby authorize him to promote the formation of a Committee, to be called " The Leicester Committee of the London Anti Persecution Union." This Committee, Secretary, Treasurer, and Auditors of Accounts, are to be appointed by a public meeting in that town. The names and addresses of the Secretary of the Committee and Auditors of Accounts, to be forwarded to the London Union. All monies collected in the name, and for the Anti Persecution Union, are to be forwarded to that Union at convenient times. This Committee will be, to all intents and purposes, the acknowledged Committee of the London Anti Persecution Union, so long as these conditions are complied with, and no longer.

By order and on behalf of the
Anti Persecution Union,
GEORGE JACOB HOLYOAKE.

SPECIALITIES.

THE TRIAL.—Miss Roalfe has not yet been apprised of the time of her trial.

GLASGOW.—The public meeting held in the Social Institution in favour of freedom of expression, was very numerously attended. The Rev. John Taylor, who was expected, did not attend. The meeting was addressed by Mr. Peddie, of Edinburgh, Mr. Southwell, and others. Miss Roalfe explained her intentions and sentiments; urged the necessity of perseverance to obtain the abrogation of the laws affecting conscientious opinion and expression. She was received with enthusiasm, and heard with attention. No report of the resolutions and speeches have reached us yet.

ARRIVAL EXTRAORDINARY.—Mr. Baker, of the united order of blasphemers, London, has arrived in Edinburgh to take the superintendence of the Atheistical Depôt in Nicholson-street, in the absence of Miss Roalfe.

REPUBLICANISM.—Every man would be a republican if he did not expect to carry off, sooner or later, from under another system, what never could belong to him rightfully, and what cannot (he thinks) accrue to him from this.—*Landor*.

THE POOR in resenting an injury, are ungrateful—in submitting in silence, are base and cowardly.—*The Savage*.

ORIGIN AND PRACTICE OF RELIGION.

"The origin and practice of religion is described in 'the guarantee of liberty and harmony,' in the following parable :—

'The main road through life is rugged, thorny, dusty, and exposed to all the inclemencies and extremities of temperature. This is the path trodden by the great multitude; upon it you see a countless throng of starved, mournful, haggard, crippled beings, creeping along, with the sweat on their brows, and casting an anxious look to the termination of their sufferings.

Delightful avenues lead along both sides of this miserable main road; they are shaded by the most beautiful fruit trees; refreshing fountains spring up at short distances, and pleasant seats are established to rest the limbs of the high and mighty, the nobles, the public functionaries, the rich merchants, and other privileged, favoured individuals, who alone maintain the prerogative to walk in these charming alleys.

'These privileged classes, discovering that they were far too small in number to keep the multitude on the road of misery if it chose to leave it, and that even the best organised police and army might one day become insufficient to control the mass, or would see through the game, discover where the real strength and their real interest lay, and side with the people, invented what they called religion, or the hope of a future world, with reward and punishment. They designated a certain number of their own as priests, who preached to the people, that for all their present privation they would meet more than adequate reward in the future world, while the rich would then atone for all their present enjoyment.

'The priests soon succeeded in impressing the multitude with this so-called heavenly truth. They called themselves pastors of the flock, and as the shepherd manages his herd by forcing the leading sheep a certain way, so did they lead the multitude by directing the foremost. They taught some to regard as sinful the wish to quit the road of misery and share the abundance of the privileged; and the rest believed also ;—the poor man dying of hunger, who to save himself extended his hand towards one of the succulent fruits so abundant in the privileged walks, was stigmatized as a criminal even by his starving brethren.

'Thus has the mass of the population been led on the road of misery and privation by the mummeries of religion, which is led by it still, and there are but few that see through the diabolical game that is played with them, and fewer still that have the courage to resent it, and make it known. 'But the hour is coming.'"—The TIMES of Dec. 29, 1843; article, the "Communists in Germany."

INTERESTING INTELLIGENCE.

THE SOIREE IN HONOUR OF MR. O'BRIEN.—This was held on Tuesday at the Rotunda. Mr. Morling, of Brighton, was called to the chair. He stated the great respect in which Mr. O'B. was held in Brighton, and that he had himself come expressly to London to pay his respects to him. Mr. Neesom gave "the Sovereignty of the People," another gentleman gave "the Press ;" Mr. Morling, "the health and prosperity of Mr. Bronterre O'Brien. Mr. O'B. replied in a short and interesting speech. An agreeable discussion followed, concerning the extent to which democratic principles had spread. We observed Mr. Watson, Mr. Moore, Mr. R. Carlile, jun., among the company. J. H. Parry, Esq., would have taken the chair but for pressing engagements which detained him away.

OTHER MOVEMENTS.—"We have assisted at the birth of two 'movements,' both of which, we fondly believe, will tell favourably upon our country's welfare—the one political, the other ecclesiastical ; the first already strong, the other having only just opened its young eyes to the light of day—complete suffrage, and the separation of church and state."—NONCONFORMIST.

A CLERICAL TRUISM.—"We controverted, and ever will controvert, the non-establishment principle but the voluntary contributions of our people we have never been ashamed to ask, and have at all times thankfully received.---MANIFESTO OF SCOTCH FREE CHURCH.

OMINOUS ADMISSIONS.—The efficiency of the non-establishment principle has not been proved as yet by the Free Church of Scotland. At the present time our funds come so wofully short of the demands upon them, that we are glad to receive the aid of our Christian Friends in England and Ireland, aye, and in America, to enable us to prosecute the glorious end of making the free church commensurate with the boundaries of our beloved country.—Ibid.

THE SEX OF THE HOLY GHOST.—Mrs. Martin lately delivered a lecture in the John Street Institution on "The Holy Ghost, HER nature, offices, and laws."

DR. KALLEY.—We have learned, from authority in which we place great confidence, that a letter has been received from Dr. Kalley, stating that orders had been given which ought to have secured his liberation, and that, from his liberation not having taken place, he believed that he was in the hands of the Inquisition.—WITNESS.

PANTHEISM IN FRANCE.—The dispute between the university and the clergy of France, is now the passion of the day, and constantly furnishes new topics to the Parisian press. The dispute is by no means a new event, as months ago the Dean of the University of Paris uttered these memorable words : —"If the university believe in Pantheism, nothing shall prevent his teaching it." Besides the French believers in Pantheism, it has numerous adherents in the United States, in Germany, &c. Emmerson, in Boston, the late Professor Hegel, of Berlin, are amongst the foremost. The name is of Greek origin (Pan-theos,) and means the belief in the universality of Deity.

SUBSCRIPTIONS
for the Anti Persecution Union.
At the Rotunda, on Dec. 24, 1843.
(Per Mr. H.)

		£	s	d
S. B.	-	0	2	6
Messrs. Side, Ascott, Friend and Punting		0	4	0
Several Friends	-	0	2	1
Mr. Farn, Liverpool, for the Scottish Union		0	4	0
J. Whiddon	-	0	1	0
A Friend, per Mr. G. A. Fleming	-	1	0	0

(Per Mr. Cook, Bradford.)

		£	s	d
By Collection	-	0	6	6
A Friend	-	0	2	6
Mr. Morling, Brighton	-	0	1	0

(Per Mr. Morrish, Bristol.)

		£	s	d
Collector, No. 17	-	0	10	0
Ditto 19	-	0	3	0
Ditto 27	-	0	7	0
W. J. B., Esq. for Miss Roalfe	-	5	0	0
Mr. Friend	-	0	1	0

G. J. HOLYOAKE, Secretary.

J. WILLS, Sheffield.—Sends verses which appear to be a new version of one of Dr. Watts's hymns. He does not say if it is sung in the schools. I have no room but for the first lines :—

When'ere I take my walks abroad
How many rich I see;
What shall I think of thee, O Lord,
For thy neglect of me?

Printed and Published by G. J. HOLYOAKE,
40, Holywell-street, Strand, London.
Saturday, Jan. 13, 1844.

THE MOVEMENT
And Anti=Persecution Gazette.

"Maximize morals, minimize religion."—BENTHAM.

No. 6.   EDITED BY G. JACOB HOLYOAKE, ASSISTED BY M. Q. RYALL.   PRICE 1½d.

SOCIALISM.

"When Unitarianism was unknown Nonconformity was a crime. Till Infidelity began to assume a popular form Unitarianism was a crime.—The 'odium theologicum' is always transferred to the new-comers."—WESTMINSTER REVIEW.

If this is no new, it is a very pretty old truth. Let whatever may be said to the contrary, upon the principle here laid down, Atheism has benefitted Socialism, even as the world goes, for it has made it respectable. The *New Moral World* was once an infidel paper, but when Atheism arose, it became religious. Those who fear going "too far," sometimes think that Atheism has damaged Socialism in the eyes of the religious world. Nothing of the sort. Socialism could not, by itself, have attained in a century the reputation for orthodoxy which the budding of Atheism, in two short years, has given it. Those who believe that the prosperity of the Rational Society depends on its freedom from irreligion, have more to thank Atheists for than they have to thank themselves.

It is a pleasant thing to write on Socialism. There is no fear of offending any one. "Silence will not retard, and opposition will only accelerate its progress." Its friends are apathetic and say nothing about it; still it goes on, and should any one write in opposition to it, he directly helps it forward. Socialists are happy people! nothing disquiets, nothing offends them. Let a man do what he will, he is sure to serve them.

The reader will conclude, and rightly, from this, that I am not a believer in the dogma that silence will not retard, and opposition will accelerate, truth. In some cases, and with a certain class of men, the maxim is true; but, as the world goes, it is deceptive and false. The Bishop of Exeter taught me that truth, in the hands of *prudent* men, could be endangered. If I thought that persecution accelerated truth, I would not be Secretary another day to the Anti-persecution Union. It is because I have seen truth stabbed with saintly daggers that I hate persecution, and do not much admire persecutors.

I am about to offer a few papers on Socialists and Socialism, because one of the objects of the *Movement* is commending its opinions to thinking parties, and as Socialists stand highest in our esteem, they seem first to claim our attention.

I have long been a member of the Society, and, for many reasons, I prefer it to all others. It has less religion than any other public body; it permits greater liberty of opinion among its members; and its objects are more comprehensive and radical than those of chartism or complete suffrage. Still, it is not a faultless system, nor are its members past improvement; and many points never debated in the *New Moral World* are worthy of earnest attention.

That good will result I doubt not. I have unwavering confidence in the smallest effort for the betterance of things. Socialism possesses vast powers for good, then why should it be all dormancy? It has let slip the strong affection which bound men to it, not because it was erroneous, but because it has been unwise. The interest which was felt *in* it is still felt *for* it; but it has removed itself from its earliest friends; it has drawn around itself a conventional circle, over which the poor man cannot step. What did not Socialism promise when its voice first gladdened the ear of competition-cursed man? Armed with some intelligence and much truth, what is it not able to accomplish? Yet what is its position?

Day after day, day after day,
It sticks—nor breath, nor motion:
As idle as a painted ship
Upon a painted ocean.

By what right, or for what purpose, did we formerly move the nation—alarm the legislature—mix in meetings, distribute tracts? To show the world that we were wanton disturbers? Socialists have gone too far to retreat with honour. If they do retreat, like the wolf-boy of Æsop, when they next profess to be in earnest, nobody will believe them.

I use the term Socialists in preference to *Rationalists*, because I am not willing to assume for myself any pre-eminence of sense. That we may mean by the appellation, only that we aim at rationality, does not remove the objection. It is doing what frankness never does—putting private significations upon public words. Individual definitions cannot weigh against those of society. The ablest pen-advocate Socialism ever had, W. Hawkes Smith, says, "For my own part, I prefer the appellative Socialism. It expresses indifferently well that the parties ranging themselves as its advocates, desire to conduct their affairs, in some way or other, on the combinative principle for mutual advantage. It excludes necessity, real or imagined, of attachment 'through thick and thin' to the views and opinions of any single individual, however well-qualified, generally, he may be to direct. It avoids, also, the seeming vanity of assuming that within its pale, and there alone, is reason to be found. It is more completely descriptive than the term co-operation, because this last may seem merely to involve the wise use, for mutual benefit, of the physical energies of the band; while Socialism necessarily includes the gradually perfected use of all the powers and faculties, producing, in the end, a state of society in which the intellectual and the moral shall also be fully brought into action, each by each, for the good of all, himself included; and plenty, leisure, knowledge, loving-kindness, and happiness prevail, being produced on principles which inviolably connect these conditions. Co-operation may serve a provident society, a joint-stock manufacturing or farming concern, as proposed by Mr. Babbage, a saving's bank, a mutual insurance company. Socialism refuses to be confined within the range of any individual object. Its name is 'Legion, for it is many.' It is the universal workman, the schoolmaster, the preacher, the economical director, and house-steward —it is production and distribution—it is education, natural philosophy, logic, and ethics; health, wealth, and contentment." Hawkes Smith wrote with the comprehensiveness of the philosopher, and warmth of the enthusiast, nor dreamed that his favourite science would officially dwindle into a joint-stock company of "prime minds," who would confine Socialism, in a "business-like manner," to a speculation of capitalists.

In a very few papers I shall examine the natural limitations of parties, treat of the "*Dis*advantages of Union,"—of the *advan*tages we all know—enquire whether "Socialism is a religious system," analyse "Home Colonization," and ask for whom it is intended? and notice a few other matters of moment. In doing all this I only ask the Socialist, with whom I have long laboured, and sincerely regard, to remember the saying of Montaigne, that "the plain-dealing remonstrances of a friend differ as widely from the rancour of an enemy as the friendly probe of a physician from the dagger of an assassin." I do not seek controversy, nor desire it. I have no "Quixotic ambition," but if any person disputes my facts and conclusions, and desires to reply in the *Movement*, the same space I shall occupy shall be at his or her service. G. J. H.

THE MOUNTAIN SERMON.
CHARITY.

Sincerity is a virtue, and whatever may be the motives of men, it is better that their actions, good or bad, were done openly, and judged by the tribunal of the public. The business of mankind is with man, and it is unwise to make human actions, relative, not to earth, but to heaven, and imaginary consequences hereafter. The best source of the affections is to be found in themselves, and the result of reason, which sees its own happiness in the happiness of the greatest number. The almsgiving of the sermon on the mount, has no one worldly object in view, but promises a greater reward, in the estimation of believers, than any it can receive on earth. True charity only looks to the justice of the donation, and cares little whether it be known or not, except as the publicity of a good act may induce others to do the same. Generosity contemplates no other reward, than the good which was the object of the donation; but, if I part with my money from a preconceived idea that I get a reward in heaven, or here on earth as a return from heaven, that was the object, and not the good of mankind. Thousands give, and are inclined to give, from sympathy and love of their fellow creatures; they are not desirous of display, and are so far from expecting a reward here or hereafter, that they, probably, have quickly forgotten the occasion of their good offices. On the other hand, the pious must be always looking to the great account book, which they are told is to be opened at the last day, or are expecting already an interest on the investment made in the treasury of the father, "who will reward openly." When the object of charity is heaven, and not man, almsgiving will look more to the salvation of the soul, than the benefit of the man. Money will go only to the faithful, or the conversion of infidels. Man, as man, is entirely overlooked in these sentiments of Jesus, as human nature is everywhere, in his mouth, made a sacrifice to heaven.

The respect due to charity is a better guide to men, than the secret or open almsgiving which only seeks glory in heaven. According to Jesus, a man is to be stupidly indifferent as to the object concerned in his charity; it is not to be done for men, but for God, and, therefore, "his left hand is not to know what his right hand doth." This has been a capital maxim for priesthood, in all times; make us the deposit of your secret pecuniary interest with heaven, say they, and remain in entire ignorance of your and our doings with man, so long as you have the saving knowledge of your reward in heaven. When the woman emptied a precious box of ointment over him, he was particularly pleased with this extravagant act of almsgiving in a woman, who did not obtain what she had got by the best means, but who obtained the pardon of her sins, by this charity, in the proper quarter. It is forbidden, in the old Jew book, to receive the price of prostitution; but as Jesus had no objection, it has been a rule, with the church, to make this a source of emolument. Brothels a long time formed part of the ecclesiastical revenues.

SENTIMENTAL THEISTS, AND NATURAL THEOLOGY.

II.

"As no man can rise to the perception of higher principles than those of which he is himself conscious, when weak men throw their 'divinity' into action, they necessarily impart to their idea something of their own weakness and infirmity. The mass of religious people end in worshipping a fancied monster. They may continue to call this idol of their fabrication, this reflection of their own vices, 'most wise,' and 'most merciful,' but they attribute to their fearful phantom their own hateful passions and narrow views. It may be laid down as a general rule, that there are no bounds to the credulity of mankind. When reason is once cried down and distrusted, men become the dupes of their own delusions."—THE BOOK OF REASON.

In the past chapter were enumerated, according to theologians, the crimes of atheists, and all who commit them, are without doubt perpetrators of practical atheism. To correct the modern world's tendency to such alarming practice, the contributor to *Blackwood* before-mentioned would put an end to investigation as far as the mysterious truths of Christianity are concerned; or better still, because more liberal, extinguish practical atheism by reasonings not to be resisted, that reason is a dangerous and faith a safe guide to those who seek religious truth.

I can attach no other meaning to his words, which are, indeed (excepting, of course, those "profound to unintelligibility,") so very fine as to make all who read them deeply regret that fine words neither butter parsnips—a fact of which the sagacious Lord Duberly assures us—nor make falsehood less false or less mischievous. How pretty is the phrase, "true greatness comes not down from the head, but up from the heart of man," yet it contains an ugly sense. The sense is that when, in the course of our speculations about God and worlds, about which none know any thing, but respecting which priests affect to know a great deal, we read or hear what the head cannot understand, the *heart* is forthwith, by some process no human head can pretend to an acquaintance with, to accomplish. These "model philosophers" would have us use our heads, so long as they avail us in the pious work of agreeing with *them;* but when *their* speculations are not *our* speculations, when *their* divine truth appears to *us* rank lies, then we are to give our brains the bag, and call up from the heart the *quantum suff.* of "believing spirit." Those who do not this are " wretched infidels," " miserable blasphemers," wretches so wretched, and miserables so miserable, that eminent divines have, in the plenitude of that "greatness which cometh up from christian hearts," recommended their brethren to put such "atrocious miscreants" "beyond the pale of civilization," or, better still, blow them into eternity from the mouths of cannon. Alas, poor atheists! where are they to look for succour when even those very philosophers and divines who were themselves charged with atheism, hated them so fervently. The first of these recommendations was given by John Locke, whose works are among the best specimens of "practical atheism" extant. The other is ascribed to Joseph Addison, who ranks among the most charitable of christians, the most pleasing of essayists, and the most shallow of philosophers. This horror of atheists is no wise as touching, nor his expressed desire that they should be "blown from cannon carefully pointed towards Tartary," a *very* remarkable circumstance, for his piety was unquestionable, and his faith in Christianity thorough and unwavering. But that Locke, who sneered so witheringly at the appealers to *faith* when, and only when, reason was against them; who was, by the *sentimentalists* of his day *stigmatized*(?) as an atheist for exploding the "innate idea" fallacy—that he should have joined the crew of reason vilifiers; that he should have raised his voice to put atheists "beyond the pale of civilization", is indeed astounding. The writer in *Blackwood* applies the term "base" to Helvetius, and "impious" to all other reasoners of the non-sentimental school; but that can surprise no one, for the contributors to that magazine are either parsons or their allies, whose *interest* and *business* it is to blackguard Rationalists, and run down practical atheism. When informed that Lord Brougham said, before a committee of the House of Lords, that he believed men who blaspheme (that is, question or deny the truth of his Lordship's religion) are not rational beings, not men to be reasoned with, I was by no means amazed; for Lord Brougham, in consideration no doubt of the service he has rendered humanity, is by common sense *patented* to scribble trash, talk nonsense, and play off fantastic tricks before high heaven, which, if angels *could* weep, would assuredly make them do so. In 1830 the Rev. Robert Taylor claimed his Lordship as *one of us*, and perhaps he still is one of us; but if he is, I devoutly hope he wont say so; for were he to avow himself, or be generally known as a practical atheist, the cause of atheism would be seriously damaged, such being my estimate of his Lordship's *moral*, or rather immoral influence. Anything he might say, either in or out of Parliament, against blasphemers, would neither surprise nor annoy me. But John Locke was a profound thinker and excellent man, decidedly one of the best as he was the wisest of professing christians; his writings I admire, and for his memory entertain feelings almost reverential; it therefore pains as well as astonishes me that he should have stooped to vulgar prejudice, and strengthened the enemies of reason by denouncing its best friends as unworthy to be admitted within the "pale of civilized society." If, like the writer in *Blackwood*, he had thought all wickedness comes from reason, and every virtue under heaven from some vague something no one knows what, called feeling or sentiment, intolerant expressions, such as the one complained of, might have been expected to flow from his pen; but every one who has looked into his works is aware that no writer ever more strenuously or successfully insisted upon the necessity of exercising reason upon religious as well as other topics. The present crusade against Rationalists is headed by men who differ with Locke in *toto*, as to the absolute sufficiency of reason. Decidedly the most able opponents of the hourly strengthening anti-theistic movement, are those who have given up as worse than useless the writings of Clarke and Paley—men who broadly tell us that no proof can be furnished of God's existence, and that the *a priori* demonstration of Clarke, and *a posteriori* reasonings of Paley, are utterly worthless *except to the atheist*. There is now before me No. 2 of "Lay Sermons on the Theory of Christianity, by a Company of Brethren," which professes in its title-page to show "The Argument of Design equal to Nothing, or Nieuentytt and Paley versus David Hume and Saint Paul." "The Lay Brother" who wrote this remarkable "sermon" announces himself as Fidian, (late Victorious) Analysis. An odd name that, and one meaning methinks, as the sermon surely does, much more than meets the eye. Let us see what this mysterious Mr. Analysis says by way of apology for tumbling down the whole system of Natural Theology:—

"The first writer of note who states the argument of design as a formal proof, was the Dutch mathematician Nieuentytt, in whose religious philosophy is to be found the original of that classical analogy of a watch which was afterwards expounded by Howe, and then illustrated and enforced with so much perspicacity and elegance by Dr. Paley. The last was the first to urge it with such effect as to secure it a standing in the world. His Natural Theology is read by every body, and is a text-book at the Universities. It has gone through many editions, even a cheap one for the people, and is a standard work. It has been lately presented anew under the united auspices of Lord Brougham and Sir Charles Bell. Lastly, the late Earl of Bridgewater has bequeathed the world eight well-paid treatises, all emulous of demonstrating Him 'who is past finding out.' I would not run counter to such high authorities if I were not convinced that the cause of Christianity has suffered from these attempts to afford it external aid. Their direct tendency is to rob the religion of faith of its essential character; and this of 'design' encourages those who reject our most holy faith in the implied conclusion, that either God must be to be found in Nature by research, or not exist all. Hence come insincere atheism, idolatrous scientific theism, and worthless half-belief in God. These are my motives and defence."

George Jacob Holyoake, towards the conclusion of his "Paley Refuted in his own Words," admonishes us that "the preceding enquiry is conducted solely on the principle of human reason; that no other standard is appealed to; that men have no safer guide, no nobler faculty than reason: that he who abandons reason, in any pursuit, degrades himself as a man, becomes the dupe of every religious knave, and the prey of every political opponent; that instead of dispelling his fears by manly enquiry, he converts them into tyrants, and himself into their trembling, crawling slaves; and adds, " I fully agree with the Bishop of Salisbury, that unless religion is shown to harmonize with the light of nature and reason, that all the arguments in the world cannot conclude in its favour"—all of which is tangibility itself. No man can miscomprehend it, or woman either. Reason, and reason alone, is the authority acknowledged; and, unquestionably, Mr. Holyoake's essay demonstrates that Paley's completest refutation is to be found in Paley's own words. The sermon of Fidian Analysis is wide as the poles from the Refutation of George Jacob Holyoake, yet do they both tell with crushing effect upon natural theology. Analysis calls the reasoning of our Paleys and Butlers " unnatural demonstrations" of God's existence; so does Holyoake; but strangely different are their conclusions, from that, perhaps, the only speculative *fact* common to both.—*God is*, exclaims Analysis; and presently almost reconciles one to his dogmatism, by the candid avowal that *He* can " be apprehended only by Faith." Nor does he leave his reader sceptical as to whether Nature be not the God which *is;* for though he talks about God being " in one sense alone; the one reality," which is a mystical kind of talk, enough to make the least suspicious suspect him of " a pantheising deification of nature;" the context perfectly establishes his orthodoxy, as regards belief in a *regular* God, *not* nature, neither matter, nor spirit, nor both—such is the God of Analysis. Stranger still, he rejects absolutely "the false light of scientific theism," as " only idolatry of a better kind than fire-worship and the like," which seems tantamount to "practical atheism;" but Analysis is no more Atheist than Pantheist, for he distinctly declares his belief in the being of God at which he arrived "by the way of faith." Nay, he promises in this very Sermon to furnish, some time or other, " an analytical exhibition of the true way of believing in the ineffable and incomprehensible Being in question.

PRINCIPLE.

Sir,—Observing that your correspondent, I. T., has drawn attention to a serious oversight in the Rev. Sidney Smith's letter on "American Repudiation," I also am encouraged to venture a remark. It will be, Sir, on the principle laid down by I. T. that wrong ought to be exposed, because it is wrong, regardless from whom it may proceed, or by what versatility of invention supported.

The *Times* says that "no animal alive, neither man nor monkey, squeaks so amusingly when it is hurt, as does the Rev. Sidney Smith"—and it might have been added, nor speaks so eloquently. Perhaps your readers will remember, that towards the conclusion of the " plundered canon's" letter this passage occurs:—" It is not for Gin Sling alone and Sherry Cobler that man is to live, but for those great principles against which no argument can be listened to—principles which give to every power a double power above their functions and their offices, which are the books, the arts, the academies that teach, lift up and nourish the world." My objection arises in this way, Mr. Editor: Most men have their fears of somebody, and I have mine of the bigots. Now some sound christians—Mr. Editor, keep a look out on "sound" christians—appropriate this passage, and say the belief in God, depravity, and the bible, are " great principles," and on the authority of the Rev. Sidney Smith, such, as against them "*no argument can be listened to.*" My opinion is, that with all great principles we may safely take great liberties. The greater they are the less likely are we to injure them by enquiry and discussion. As a body who finds fault, should amend, if possible, I beg to suggest, that if Sidney—it seems degrading to style HIM the *Rev.* Smith—had said, " those great principles against which no arguments can be successfully urged," he would have said enough for his purpose, and not have awakened my nervous fear of the saints.

Yours, M.

CURIOUS DISCUSSION,

At Branch, A 1.

II.

Mr. Clark, president, rose and said:—In the absence of anyone else he would do his best to state to the meeting what the question was. It appeared that the subjects of theology and religion had been left in a very undecided state by the society: it appeared, also, that when Mr. Hanhart visited the school at Harmony, he found something tangible and definite was wanted on this subject; and as Mr. H. had some belief in the existence of a God, he wished to have it taught.

Mr. Hanhart.—No! no! no! that was not what he meant.

When he visited the school at Harmony Hall, he found *something* like a devotion or a contemplation wanted to direct the minds of the children to. He believed there was some directing power in nature—that children might be taught to contemplate that power in the phenomena of nature under the name of God, with good results. Mr. Owen, in the "Outline," had called this power, God, and that was the reason why he moved the resolution.

A Voice.—You should define what God is.

Mr. Clark.—We believe in no Gods, whatever, consequently we cannot define what it is.

Mr. Hardy said, when he looked at the effect produced in religious schools, he certainly did believe that religion was necessary among children. He had observed in religious families and schools, that prayers had a good moral effect on the minds of children, and, therefore, he believed that some devotion or religion was actually necessary.

Mr. Mc Cullough.—His arguments in support of his amendment were not yet answered; his attention had been directed to the sixth social tract, by Mr. Hanhart, as fully expressing his (Mr. H.) opinion on the great power "which moves the atom and controls the aggregate of nature;" but he had yet to learn that the aggregate of nature was controlled by a power similar to that by which the atom was directed. The atom was directed by a power *external* to itself; but the aggregate of nature having no power *external* to itself, cannot, in its integral capacity, be under the control of any such Power. The sixteenth social tract told him " that an eternal and *uncaused* existence had ever filled the universe;" he could fully subscribe to this proposition, but how did the "*uncaused existence*" of the sixth social tract comport with the "*external cause* of all existences" spoken of in the "Outline?" Did not the "*all existences*" of the latter necessarily include the "*uncaused existence*" of the former? or, rather, were they not two distinct doctrines wholly at variance with each other? Mr. Hanhart was of opinion that some " devotion" or " contemplation " was wanted in the schools, in order to produce due subordination on the part of children; and it is believed that children were intuitively devotional; but he (Mr. Mc C.) did not think so; he believed that devotional feelings were the result of education. If religious feeling appeared at any time to be innate in children, it might be viewed as a physiological result from their being born under religious institutions; but, supposing that children possessed strong veneration, there was a sufficient field for its development, without directing it to unknown powers, respecting which nothing could be taught. Children could be instructed to venerate their teachers and parents, and to admire good conduct.

He had spent ten or twelve years under the influence of " prayers" and religious devotion; and he denied that they had produced good effects. He knew, from his experience in the religious world, that religion alienated the affections of youth from their parents, and enabled them to commit every species of crime, under the religious plea " we must obey God rather than man." The arguments he had urged for the use of the words "nature" and "morality," in preference to "god" and "religion," had not yet been answered, or attempted to be answered, and until they were answered, he would call on the gentlemen opposite to withdraw their resolution.

DE LAMARTINE'S LETTER ON HISTORY.

A friend has favoured us with a free translation of this letter, which is presented to readers of the *Movement*, from a conviction that the views it contains are instructive. In the translation nothing is pretended to, except the solidity of the ideas—elegance of diction, and accuracy of idiom—if any are lost, must be set down as having been disregarded for plain sense. It is intended to make the *Movement*, as far as possible, original, whether good or bad. But Lamartine's letter is not deemed a departure from this rule, as his letter, though it has appeared in the *Independent Review*—that being a French Communist organ—may not be accessible to the majority of our readers. There is no objection to reprints, if in books professing to be reprints; but, in the present custom of publishing the same thing in nearly every paper, it often happens that a man has the same article in a dozen books. By disregarding this practice, one may give the *Movement* a little freshness, if not value.

Ed. of M.

" Saint Point, 6th August, 1843.

"Hitherto the people have been much flattered, showing that they are not yet sufficiently estimated; for one flatters only what one wishes to seduce. Why have they been flattered? Because the people have been made a *means* of, instead of an *end*.

One said to one another, the force is there; we want it for overthrowing governments, whom we dislike, or for absorbing nationalities for which we vie; let us call the people to us; intoxicate them with themselves; tell them that right is in numbers, and that their will is justice; that God is with great armies; that glory is the amnesty of history; that all means are good for securing the victory to popular causes; and that crimes even are extinguished by the grandeur and security of the results: they will believe us; follow us; lend us their material forces, and when, by the help of their arms, blood, and even of their crimes, we shall have displaced tyranny and upset Europe; we shall disband the people, and tell them, in our turn, be silent; work and obey! This is the way in which they have been hitherto addressed. Thus have the views of courts been carried into the streets, and given the people such a taste for flattery, such a want for complacencies, and caresses, that after the example of some sovereignties of the empire below, they would not be spoken to but on the knees. This, however, is not the way; they ought to be spoken to upright, on a level, face to face. They are neither more or less than the other elements of the nation. The number is nothing. Take one after another of the individuals who compose a mass, what do you find? The same ignorance, the same errors, the same passions, and often the same vices, as elsewhere. Is there any cause for falling down on ones knees? No. Multiply as much as you like all these ignorances, vices, passions, and miseries by millions of men, who will not have changed their nature, you will ever have but a multitude. Let us, therefore, overlook number, and let us respect truth alone.

It is truth only which you ought to have in view in writing history for the use of the people; and do not believe that you will be less read, less heard, and less popular for that. The people have depraved tastes, adulation and lying; but they have also natural tastes—truth and courage. They respect those who dare them; those who fear them, they despise. There are wild beasts who devour but those who flee them, or who fall before them. The people are as the lion, whom one ought not to approach sideways, but directly in front, eye fixed on eye, the hand grasping his mane, with that firm familiarity and confidence, which prove that you devote yourself, but that you respect yourself, and which says to the multitudes—count yourselves as much as you like; I—I feel myself.

"This said, which point of view will you select for writing your popular history? There are three principal ones in which you may place yourself. The point of glory, of patriotism, of civilization, or of the morality of the actions, you will have to relate. If you write in the point of view of glory, you will vastly please a warlike nation, who have been dazzled long before they were enlightened, and whom this dazzling has so often blinded to the real value of the men and things that glittered in their horizon. If you place yourself in the exclusive point of view of their patriotism, you will rouse the passions of a people, who have, for their sublime egotism, the very excuse of their salvation and greatness; and who, feeling themselves so great and strong, could believe, sometimes, that they were alone, and that Europe recognized herself in them. But neither the one nor the other of these points of view will give you the real truth; that is to say, general truth; they will give you the French truth only; now, the French truth is but true at Paris; step beyond the frontiers and it becomes a lie. It is not to this truth, limited by the boundaries of a nation, that you will devote instruction and reduce the intelligence of a people? What remains, then, for you to choose? The universal and permanent point of view; that is to say, the point of view of the morality of the individual and national actions, which you will have to describe. All the others are in a false and conventional light; this one only stands in a complete and divine light; this one alone can guide the uncertainty of human judgments through the maze of prejudices, opinions, passions, personal and national egotism, and can tell the people—this is good; this is bad; this is great.

(*To be continued.*)

WOMAN'S CO-OPERATION INDISPENSABLE. —Those who allow the influence which female graces have in contributing to polish the manners of men, would do well to reflect how great an influence female morals must also have on their conduct. How much then is it to be regretted that women should ever sit down contented to polish, when they are able to reform—to entertain where they might instruct.—*Blair.*

Oppression, under the color of justice, is always more formidable from the arts which are used to disguise its malignity.

ANOTHER ENQUIRY AFTER MOSES.—At a meeting of the Belfast Protestant Operative Association a few days ago, Mr. Withers is reported in the "Belfast Chronicle" to have said:—" Since he came into that hall he was informed, that the corners of the streets of Belfast were placarded with a notice of a publication called—' The Beauties of the Bible,' a publication so iniquitous, so vile, so awful, that he almost wondered that the WRITERS of it ' had not ere this experienced the full vengeance of God's wrath.' "—Moses and the Evangelist may say, save us from our friends.

AN UNEXPECTED CHANCE.—A recent number of the " Times " contained this advertisement :—Wanted, a decidedly serious young man as clerk. The particular section of Christ's church, to which he may belong, is immaterial, if his views of divine truth are scriptural.—We recommend some of our readers to apply without delay. Applications to be made to W. and Y., Mr. Suter's, Cheapside.

EMBELLISHMENTS OF THE MOVEMENT.—The paper just referred to, informs us, in the same advertisement, that—Three youths are wanted who write good hands. Those will be preferred who bear marks of TRUE religion.—If W. and Y. will favour us with a sketch of those much disputed marks, as soon as he discovers them, we will promise an engraving of them in an early number. We did not think there was such a short and easy method of deciding the controversy concerning genuine religion.

MILTON'S SATAN.—Nothing can exceed the energy and magnificence of the character of Satan, as expressed in " Paradise Lost." It is a mistake to suppose that he could ever have been intended for the popular personification of evil. Implacable hate, patient cunning, and a sleepless refinement of device to inflict the extremest anguish on an enemy, these things are evil ; and although venial in a slave, are not to be forgiven in a tyrant ; and although redeemed by much that ennobles his defeat in one subdued, are marked by all that dishonours his conquest in the victor. Milton's Devil, as a moral being, is as far superior to his God, as one who perseveres in some purpose which he has conceived to be excellent, in spite of adversity and torture, is to one who in the cold security of undoubted triumph, inflicts the most horrible revenge upon his enemy, not from any mistaken notion of inducing him to repent of a perseverance in enmity, but with the alleged design of exasperating him to deserve new torments."—Shelley's Defence of Poetry."

THE GOD IDEA.—Greenlanders cannot conceive of invisible things.

Otaheitian families have each a guardian spirit, and some gods in general, but abhor the idea of future punishment. They admit the immortality of the soul, and degrees of future eminence and happiness. The priests have great power.

Carolinas.—The people believe in certain celestial spirits; but there are no objects of worship except a kind of crocodile.

Pelew Islands.—There is no appearance of religion of any kind, but an idea that the soul survives the body.

New Zealanders bury their dead, and believe that on the third day resurrected, the heart is separated from the body, and carried to the clouds by a spirit. They have no place of worship, but the priests address the gods for prosperity.

Van Dieman's Land.—The natives have neither rites nor ceremonies, religious or otherwise ; but are, in every respect, exactly as nature left them.

New Hollanders are utter strangers to religion, and have no idea of a future state.

DR. KALLEY.—It was stated that the Doctor was out on bail, but the account required corroboration. It is more than probable that he is now at liberty. A long account, from himself, appeared in the " Patriot," 11th January.

Common sense cannot enable men to judge where the experience of common life cannot be applied.—DRUMMOND.

ALLIANCE OF IGNORANCE.—As the blindness of mankind has caused their slavery, in return, their state of slavery is made a pretence for continuing them in a state of blindness.

NATIONAL HALL.—First monthly "conversazione" on Thursday, pleasant and profitable. Want of room and time prevents report.

On Tuesday, January 23, the first of a series of practical lectures on Emigration, will be delivered at the Rotunda, Blackfriars Road, by a gentleman just returned from the Western States of America.

Received by Mrs. Martin, and M. Q. R.
—of W. J. - - - - - 0 10 0

SUBSCRIPTIONS
for the Anti Persecution Union.

N. Marston - - - -	0 1 0
T. Bidwell, Hoxton - -	0 1 0
B. J., Bristol, for addresses -	0 1 0

G. J. Holyoake, Secretary.

TO CORRESPONDENTS.

W. TALBERT, Birmingham, will find that the plan he proposes may be carried out by proper parties applying to the A. P. Union for a " precept" similar to that published in the last " Movement," as being issued to Leicester.

Received — W. TALBERT, Birmingham ; R. WHITEMAN, Harbro'; EX EMIGRANT, and R. REDBURN.

T. BIDWELL.—His communication is handed to Mr. Ryall.

J. MELLOR, Oldham.—We are obliged by his exertions to circulate the " Movement."

ANTI-PERSECUTIONIST.—Read the excellent article on "Religious Persecutions," re-published in the "New Moral World" on Dec. 30, 1843, from the "Westminster Review."

AN INFIDEL LOOKER-ON.—Would he and other of our friends, who wish us to see this or that article, send us—if convenient, the paper itself—whether new or old, even if published at the next door to us. Some how or other, though we greatly desire it, we cannot see everything. The first we heard of the excellent article in the Catholic newspaper, the "Tablet," on the " Kalley correspondence" published in No. 1 of the "Movement," was in a letter from a correspondent at Brussels.

SUPPLY OF THE MOVEMENT.

The difficulties and obstacles occurring in the supply of the "Movement," have induced me to make the following arrangements.

Regular Subscribers living within Two Miles of the Publishing Office, in Holywell Street, are supplied with the weekly numbers of the "Movement," carriage free.

Monthly Parts are delivered Four Miles from the Office.

A single Number is sent by post, on receipt of a pre-paid letter, containing two penny stamps.

M. RYALL.

NOW READY.—The First Monthly part of the "Movement," stitched in a neat stiff Wrapper, price 7d.

Printed and Published by G. J. HOLYOAKE,
40, Holywell-street, Strand, London.
Saturday, Jan. 20, 1844.

THE MOVEMENT

And Anti-Persecution Gazette.

"Maximize morals, minimize religion."—BENTHAM.

No. 7.   EDITED BY G. JACOB HOLYOAKE, ASSISTED BY M. Q. RYALL.   PRICE 1½d.

SCHEME OF UNIVERSAL PROGRESSION.

IV-

"The time appears to have arrived, when a transition from that state in which mankind have undergone the ordeal of thorns and difficulties necessary to form a guiding experience in the approaching and more happy state, is to take place. Great and extraordinary interests have been awakened, stupendous powers for producing happiness and extirpating misery have been called into action; brands have been snatched from the bright fire of reason, which are already showing, and will soon universally show, the proper direction of their powers. PROGRESSION is the word, innovations strange and mighty in their essence, and powerful in their operation, fronted with a growing intelligence, are succeeding the semi-barbarous conditions of all nations, and science is now imparting her giant energies to facilitate the change."---PROSPECTS AND PLEASURES OF RATIONALITY.

Having already sketched the theologically orthodox notions on the subject of human capabilities, and not only quoted, but argued for, the "frigid philosophers," it will hardly be deemed out of place to let the "aspiration school" be heard in turn. The anonymous writer, from whom the above remarks are extracted, is both aspirant and expectant of great and mighty changes. Were his enthusiasm not sobered by reflection and guided by judgment, it might be deemed visionary rather than rational. The qualifying observations which follow indicate a tempered and reasonable expectation, rather than a blind and self-delusive zeal. "This change is, and must be, so great in its nature, and so universally prevailing in its influence, that I would wish to be freed from the implication of supposing the world possible to be regenerated in a day. This is impossible—that change will extend over many years, and seize on the human race at many points." Obviously a disciple of the revered philanthropist, he is yet far from being led away by excess of enthusiasm to conceive that the recognition of new principles, however true, and the re-organization of old society, however fundamental, can be effected on a sudden; or that the stupendous work of remedying ages of misguidance can be performed in the off-hand style of a feat of legerdemain. Not only must the work, if the work be possible, be one of slow and gradual change, but must, after the ordinary course of events, be accomplished through much endurance, peril, and suffering, to those who pass through the transition states, whether as guides or followers. The changes *must* seize on the human race at many points. Those who consider man's destinies bound up with the adoption of one particular notion, and that notion of a sectional character, betray either the ignorance or the impudence of the quack doctor, who warrants a cure for all the ills the flesh is heir to, by the administration of a single bolus. Had mankind progressed in every department but one, "the short and easy method" would be to supply that one deficiency. But our errors neither are nor can be in one direction only. Human knowledge is not capable of the distinct, defined, and abrupt divisions or partitions, which you can apply to a weight or a measure. It would be impossible to represent the extent and limitation of knowledge by the terms one hundred, and then assert that ninety-nine divisions, neither more nor less, had been mastered. There is so gradual, so intimate and imperceptible a blending of all sorts of knowledge, it has been found impossible to assign to its various branches completely arbitrary limits. This is one of the most potent arguments that can be urged in favour of the general diffusion of knowledge; or, perhaps better, the diffusion of general knowledge. The Social system is by so much better, more comprehensive and effectual than all previous systems, as it embraces a greater number of reforms, seizes on the human race at a greater number of points. This will be more largely and fully insisted on after some further elucidation of the general views of the progressionists, and a thorough sifting of the objections already advanced on behalf of their opponents. A class of pertinent and cogent objections, represented by a few queries, are admirably met by the following observation:—"Mankind and society in general, in accordance with the most palpable laws of nature, have passed from one stage to another and experienced a continued improvement." Absolute slavery, vassalage or feudalism, and competetive labour, are several instances of this passage from one stage to another. Co-operative labour and communism have yet to be introduced with other concomitant advantages. This however, is not the illustration above alluded to—it occurs in the following sentence :— "*Apparent interruptions* of the immense chain are, of themselves, only so many necessary consequences of advancement; they are but the *backward ripple* on the vast ocean of necessity, as its mighty waters roll on in their eternal progress." I would rather have left out eternal progress, which are mere expletives, like the words god, divine, &c., when a sentence requires rounding off—not having the pleasure of an acquaintance with the author, I know not if he would think I had unwarrantably clipped the pinions of his oratory, and injured its fair proportions. The thought at any rate is worthy of the greatest care, culture, and diffusion. If we seem to have remained stationary in departments of progress—if we can note an apparent or actual retrogression, it will put us upon asking, is the whole ocean of knowledge to recede entirely from us, leaving a dry and desert waste? or do we see but the "backward ripple," which on its return will assist, with newly-acquired and increased energy, to roll forward the tide of plenty and happiness. M. Q. R.

IS SOCIALISM A RELIGIOUS SYSTEM?

Socialism, in its aspirations and objects, is what the *Times* has designated it—the natural offspring of the age. It is an attempt to annihilate wrong on a grand scale; it comes to relieve the heart-sickening strife of competition in its grossness; it is the embodiment of the popular hope of happiness, and constitutes, in its finer forms, the poetical dream of bliss.

But this same Socialism is a strange anomaly. Born of philosophy, kicked about by parliament, and diluted into religion by its alarmed advocates, it has become the wonder and contempt of men. Socialism, in its advent so glorious, and in its promises so thrilling, is now only felt as a cold neutrality, and known as an egotistical, plausibly-supported, branch-extended, popular mistake.

Did one in ten who took out the sixty or seventy charters of the Social Branches think that he was joining a religious society? Does one single philosopher, who ever contemplated Socialism's facts, believe Socialism to be connected with religion? Mr. Owen denounced *all* religions; the missionaries attacked them; and until Exeter's bishop arose, every man was in earnest to rid philosophy and the world of the incubus of piety. But now all this was a mistake. The Central Board's agents gravely inform the public and themselves—for *they* were formerly without the knowledge—that Socialism has nothing to do with religion; community is its sole business, notwithstanding Mr. Owen's former declaration, and the testimony of every man's experience, that "if religion is carried into community, a paradise will be no longer found there."

Mr. Troup, of the Montrose Review, was right in declaring Socialism atheistical, and this is one of the few things in which Mr. Brindley was correct. But as, in these days, people prefer judging for themselves, here are the facts.

Mr. Owen, in his "Instructions to the Missionaries," as President of Congress, in 1839, says distinctly, "Should you be challenged to discuss the dogmas of the Christians, state that you have not time for such discussions, which tend to increase the general insanity of the world upon these mystical and endless imaginations of the human brain." With the full conviction that religion only increased *insanity*, that it was a mystical, endless imagination," could Mr. Owen intend Socialists to be religious, and the lecturers to go forth with a "rational" INSANITY, an unending "imagination" of their own?

Not only, according to "our venerable Founder," are we religionless, but we are officially so. The eighth Congress Report, page 183, informs us that, on the motion of Messrs. Fleming and Newall, it was unanimously agreed that we cease to call ourselves RELIGIONISTS. One official organ has always been the "New *Moral*," and not the *Religious* "World;" and Congress agreed to return to primitive simplicity and purity, and abandon even the name of "RELIGIONISTS."* If Socialism is religious, this decision was dishonest; we ought to retain every name which explains our principles.

In a "Glossary of Terms proposed to be used by Socialists," by a committee of Branch A 1, and published in "The New Moral World," April 1, 1839, religion is defined as "speculative opinions concerning the IMAGINARY being called God."—a very satisfactory exposition of the the "true religion" of Branch A 1. The same Glossary tells us that "Morality is the HIGHEST

* The present "Official Declaration of Socialist Principles" does not mention religion.

of all human obligations;" and, consequently, as there cannot be two HIGHESTS, religion, if it be an obligation at all, is a LOWER obligation. Here we have morality right atheistically exalted above religion. The Socialist, in taking the name of Christian, displays his sagacity; for, if he did not take the appellation, nobody would give it, or guess that it belonged to him.

In law 18 of the old "Constitution" of the Socialists, in several Congresses confirmed, religion is defined as the practice of CHARITY; but as charity is a vice of fashion, a conventional and degrading substitute for justice, such religion is without recommendation in the Atheist's eye; and as charity, of itself, is without God, it is unacceptable in the Christian's.

The sixth Social Tract, an official expositor of our divinity, commences thus:— "We have been requested to state what will be the religion of the New Moral World. We reply, It will be the unceasing practice of promoting the happiness of all, and this religion every child in the New Moral World will be taught." Write the passage thus: "We have been requested to state what will be the BUSINESS of the New Moral World. We reply, It will be the unceasing practice of promoting the happiness of all, and this every child will be taught." Could Aristotle, the prince of logicians, discover a particle of difference in the meaning of these two? If this sixth Tract statement of religion is religion, what is morality? We might as well call a Chartist a Tory, or a Methodist a Unitarian, as call the New Moral World people religionists.

In the present Constitution of Socialists—the orthodox production of last Congress, the foundation of Socialism is set forth as facts. Its "objects," with one exception, that of charity, are moral. Its "principles" are metaphysical, and its "means" human. A religious lynx could not find a kindred principle in the whole system. Dr. Barrow, one of the authors of the "Christian Institutes" received in our universities, declares that the "belief in God's existence is the foundation of ALL religion —the principal article in all the creeds of all the world." But who can find, or gather God, from facts—from Socialism? Not merely Mr. Owen, the Congresses, Branch A 1, or the Social Tracts, but Socialism's own principles, declare it to be a godless system. It is without bible, revelation, or faith. It knows nothing of immortality, future rewards and punishments, and teaches that men are the creatures of naturally and humanly devised circumstances, uninfluenced by a deity, and unaccountable to one.

It will not do to say chemistry or geometry embraces none of these points, and by parity of reasoning should be called atheistical. These sciences relate to the properties of earth and air, and of lines and angles. But Socialism proposes to educate, employ, govern, and conduct, the human family by facts and reason, without religion. Now, if religion be true, it is momentous, and ought to occupy our first attention. It is no LOWER, but a HIGHEST obligation. My former appreciation of religion teaches me so; nor would I, did my former faith remain, have any connection with any system, promise or realise what it might, if it did not rest upon religion.

The Rev. C. Birch, of Cheltenham, is reported in "The New Moral World" of March 17, 1842, to have said, "Not till the verdict against Christianity has been pronounced can Socialism put forth its claims." Considering how seldom rev. gentlemen tell us any clear truth, the Rev. C. Birch merits canonization for this saying. It is true—no religious man can be a Socialist.

Let the foregoing facts be impartially weighed, and how idle, how beside truth is the declaration, that discussions on religion are no part of Socialism. Socialists profess to surround men with wise and beneficial circumstances, or they profess nothing. Nearly all the world says religion is a great circumstance, and it is a pernicious and fearful circumstance. But Mr. Owen says he will reject it as tending to "insanity," as an endless imagination. What! without discussion? Will this man of reason give no reason for his rejection of "christian dogmas?" And if he does reason, must he not discuss? He who cannot give sound reasons against religion should embrace religion; and he who would cavalierly denounce the faith of his fellow men, and refuse to justify his scepticism by argument, deserves not attention, be he Robert Owen, or G. J. H.

I deliberately write without any desire to impugn any man's professions, that no Socialist is religious in the common acceptation of the term; and that it is only by what, to me, seems jesuitically attaching religious terms to common every-day *feelings*, after Mr. Lloyd Jones's and "The New Moral World" fashion, that Socialism can be dressed out in the wretched nomenclature of orthodoxy. Socialism is a communitarian modification of atheism, and, when it is taught with a just plainness, it will be as much respected as it was formerly feared. I do not care that Socialists should proclaim themselves Atheists, but that they should not go out of their way to prove themselves Christians. I would have "The New Moral World" as bold and consistent as "The Zoist."

Let me guard the reader against a common but incorrect supposition that I think because Socialists once opposed religion they should do it now. No one would more readily admit than I myself that the practice or profession of yesterday should be abandoned to-day if proved to be incorrect. But I contend that neither from the Founder, the expositors, nor the principles of Socialism does any good reason appear to justify the changes I have hinted at. If in the warmth of writing I have let slip any word giving the impression that I impute this change to dishonourable calculation, I reiterate that I question not the intentions of what has been done, but the soundness of what has been said.

G. J. H.

SENTIMENTAL THEISTS, AND NATURAL THEOLOGY.

III.

Fidian Analysis ends his strange sermon with a short formal statement of the "way of faith," for believing in the ineffable and incomprehensible being whom we left at the end of Chap II. His, that is, Fidian's ability to do this—if it can be done—I am not even sceptical about. He has begun the work (I give his own words) by "sifting the far-famed argument of design," and a splendid beginning it is—note it well, truth-loving reader:—

"That conception of divinity to which it is too common, in these days of superannuated rationalism in religion, to think that the cumulative evidence of design enables the mind to ascend, is a scientific guess, or proposition assumed, in order to render the mechanism of the world intelligible. Those who hold by it, or suppose they do, seek refuge from what would else appear an inextricable complexity of wonderful harmonies, and unintelligible adaptations in the play of multitudinous nature, in the supposition of an intelligent First Cause, a Designer like themselves in kind, but infinitely above them in degree of faculty, an Almighty Man. The exposition and inculcation of this argument is not confined to the Theists; on the contrary, the best authors are to be found among such as have devoted themselves to the honourable task of bringing science to the aid of revelation. The more is the pity; for, apart from a previous or simultaneous act of faith, the so called argument proves either nothing, or so infinitely less than the infinitude that is sought after, as to be, in comparison of truth, equal to nothing. Pity, at least, for the present interests of religion; for we cannot but believe that even this has tended, and tends, towards the consummation of that great good we all hope for, and love to think about. I wish to convince you that the illustrious argument of Paley and the Bridgewater Treatises is inconclusive; that it is now fraught with danger to the success of that gospel of faith which its promulgators profess their anxious readiness to defend; and, lastly, that though thus impotent and insidious in itself, yet after the reception of Jehovah by our common human faith, it gloriously illustrates his goodness, wisdom, and power............ A bubble rises from the bottom of a solitary pool, basking in the sun among the hills, clothed about with a slender film of rainbow hue, the bonny bell floats like a thing of light over the mantling ripple of its little sea, till the tiny craft is broken on the tiny bed of a water-lily, and away fly its crew of dancing atoms, hither, thither, and every whither!

A timid breath at first, a transient touch,
How soon it swells from little into much!

What a wondrous combination of means and ends! how remote the instrumentality employed from the effects produced, and how worthy of a God! Suppose, then, a million instances like this; recall to mind the curious cases you have read in Paley and the Bridgewaters; find many more in the records of science—for every page is full of them; search out the undiscovered multitudes of similar examples in the open book of nature, which is a written strain of the loftiest music from beginning to end; and you have the data which the natural theologians endeavour to generalize. The survey of these crowding facts, like that of every other class of observations, suggests the inexhaustible inquiry of research, How are they to be understood? What is their meaning? Where is the theory? The method of inquisition is the same here as elsewhere. Is there any similar class of facts of which we *know* the explanation? Yes, there is one. In the works of human art, in the mechanism of a watch, the construction of asteam-engine, in every product of art, there are adaptations of one result to another, completely resembling those which are found in the world which art attempts to imitate and control. In truth, all art consists in the institution of such mutual relations and such productions of effects by fitly-chosen means. Now, the explanation of this set of facts is ready beforehand. Art is the product of a designing mind, and the designer is man. Accordingly, the substance of the Paleyan argument is this: The facts of adaptation discovered in nature are radically like the facts of adaptation discovered in art, and the inference is, that they resemble them in origin as well as resulting character. Nature is the product of a designing mind, and the designer is God. This is the argument of design, and it is essentially cumulative in its power; for the greater the number, and more striking the kind of evidences of design that can be gathered around it, the stronger does it appear to become. I have some strictures to make upon it, with the sincere hope of convincing you that without a *previous or simultaneous act of faith*, or *intuitive belief*, conscious or unconscious, it is wholly inadequate to the purpose for which it was constructed.

" The fact is this :—If there be any genuine analogy between man, the designer of the works of art, and the inferred designer of the works of nature, it must be complete and extensible in the inference to all the essential characteristics of the known designer—man. How then does man design? By reducing discovered truth to his own uses, and making combinations of natural forms and qualities : he knows the expansive force of steam, as well as the law of latent heat, and makes a steam engine ; he creates nothing. So that the Deity, inferred from evidence of design, does, for all that the argument of analogy makes out, discover truth, apply it to his own uses, and make combinations of forms and qualities. He knows the repulsive force of matter, as well as the law of gravitation, and makes a solar system. He creates nothing.

"This is Hume's analysis, though otherwise expressed, and very differently intentioned ; and its force is irresistible. Hume was the best analyst, as a mere analyst, that Britain has produced. A sincere and not uncharitable man, he detested the plausible, and never rested till he stripped it bare, and hooted it out of his presence. If he had believed in God by faith, I had only need have repeated his voice; as it is, you see how searching and indisputable his analysis is, so far as it extends.

" All that the boasted argument *a posteriori*, as it is called, for the existence of a God ever tends to establish, is the existence of designers, not that that is the Supreme, whom science, 'falsely so called,' is thus ambitious of demonstrating, like any other theorem. I find a watch on a solitary moor, examine its parts and relationships, and infer a designer; but I go further. I know that watchmakers construct similar combinations of mechanical power, and infer a watchmaker. Again, I am born into a world full of peerless contrivances and stupendous mechanism; I discover that it is only a little part of the system of the glorious sun, and that, in its turn, of the vast looming firmament in which it burns as a bright point, which again is only one complicated particle in an indefinite universe of firmaments on firmaments growing ever on and on athwart the boundless abyss of immensity, throughout the year of eternity, and finding power and goodness every where, only goodness and power, I may infer a designer, if that will satisfy my heart; but I cannot take another step; *I never beheld or heard of a universe-maker, and I dare not infer a God*. I might, indeed, surmise that this designer may, in reality, be that Jehovah who is represented in the Bible of the Hebrews, even in the Koran of Mahomet, and, above all, in the gospel of Christ, as the Creator and Preserver of all things, Himself being the only absolute underived Being; but that is all, and it is not a discovery; it is not proof ; it is only one conjecture based upon another.

Once more ; grant the natural theologian leave to pass from the conception of a mere maker to that of a true creator. The creative attribute is not human indeed, but is it therefore divine? Brutes are incapable of reason, it is man's prerogative; but man is not therefore divine in relation to the irrational creation. So that for all that design can prove, in combination even with the granted conceptions of creative powers, there may be more creators than one. But allowing that the inferred designer really spoke the world into existence, and He alone, still that creative designer may not be God after all, for divinity, if proved at all, must be proved to be almighty in power, inexhaustible in wisdom, and boundless in love: but the universe cannot be proved to be anywise infinite in the literal sense of infinitude ; it is only indefinitely vast, its magnitude compared with true immensity, being a trifle for all our telescopes can disclose, and the attributes of its inferred creator may be less than infinite in kind and degree. Whatever is less than infinitude is infinitely less; and whatever is infinitely less than anything, is nothing. *Then is* NOT *God ?*"

This is the whole argument *against* design, as I find it in this Long Sermon. For one of a company of christian brethren it is a rare production. So skilfully has he explained by his " analytical procedure" how the being of God is not to be known, so satisfactorily has he established that Paley's "Illustrious" argument is inadequate to the purposes for which it was constructed; that I look forward with impatient anxiety for the two promised discourses "containing an analytical exhibition" of the true way of comprehending the "Incomprehensible One." I long for as clear an "exhibition" of what God *is* as he has vouchsafed of what He is *not*. *This is not God*; are the startling words with which he dismisses the idol whose worship sprung from the "lifeless faith of scientific theism." *This is God*, are words that will doubtless in "Lay Sermons" to come, stare us full in the face ; and though my faith in the power of human heads or human hearts to find out Him, confessedly "past finding out," is utterly dead; yet I unhesitatingly pledge myself to "apprehend God as the Incomprehensible One, *when* "Analysis" shall have "exhibited" as clearly what He *is*, as he already has what He is *not*. The pledge to do this has been given in the Sermon now under consideration ; and may it be speedily redeemed. Yes, Fidian (late victorious) Analysis, if an honest gentleman of his word, will by and by teach us how to know God otherwise than by discovery; and then, oh delicious moment! "the world and all the world" will be known without being discovered; "the sublimest commentary and illustration of his transcending attributes." The method of coming at this most sublime of all knowledge, the "Sermon" also informs us, is the method of the Book of Job and the Psalms of David, in both of which the Divine Majesty is tacitly understood as being, of course, the Jehovah, or one independent reality; and his attributes are only illuminated by the contemplation of his handiwork; all of which is to me "profound even to unintelligibility." This is unfortunate, and certainly arises from one of two causes : the bluntness of my perceptions, or the stupid sublimity of the paragraph,—I, as in duty bound, decide in my own favour; and not without reason, or I have lost the use of mine; for to understand a writer who pronounces and *proves* the design argument worthless, who plainly states God is to be known *otherwise* than by discovery, who follows up that statement by a string of jargons about "world and all the worlds offering the sublimest commentary and illustration of his transcending attributes," &c.; and who then, by way of apex to the column of nonsense, refers us to the Book of Job and David's Psalms for a "method" of understanding "Divine Majesty;"—I say to get at the meaning of such a writer, is what readers may fail to do without being charged as *unreasonable*. Any one more patient than Job, and shrewder than Aristotle, might, perhaps, so far profit by this marvellous "method" as to proceed with some chance of success on a voyage of discovery after the undiscoverable God. But with all its faults, which are neither few nor unimportant, I admire this "Lay Sermon" exceedingly; the pains obviously taken by the author to bewilder and dazzle by out of the way phrases and rhetorical tricks, is a capital fault ; no less than Miss Carolina Wilhelmina Skeggs, "I likes fine writings and fine peoples;" but as the ridiculous is the sublimer next door neighbour, so is the very fine within a hair's breadth of the foolish. This "Lay Sermon" abounds in passages of great force and beauty, worthy of Milton himself ; not a few, however, are foolishly fine, while others are so studiedly obscure as to be either uninterpretable or only to be interpreted in a sense their author would shrink from admitting to be the true one : take, for example, this passage—" Ah ! they have toyed too lightly with the Creative Attribute who have thought to climb up to its awful sanctuary, where it dwelleth evermore in the omnific word of Godhead, by piling stone upon stone in endless erection of a faithless science of final causation and a great first cause. Why Jehovah is not the infinite source, not the first cause, but the cause of the first cause, of all things ; *and even that in an altogether metaphorical mode.*" Now, let any man consider this entire passage ; let him note well the part of it I have printed in italics; and then ask himself whether those words mean anything unless they mean *Atheism*. I do not accuse their author of indirectly teaching disbelief in the being of God under cover of a direct attack on what he calls scientific theism; and would scorn to *insinuate* a charge, which, if just, ought to be honestly made; but the passage here quoted is as atheistical in appearance as any to be found in the works of Stewart or D'Holbach. It is evident that if Jehovah, the only God, "Analysis" believes to be, is not the first cause of all things; but the first cause of the first cause; and even *that* in a mode altogether metaphorical, *He* cannot *actually* exist at all; for a cause first or last, altogether metaphorical in *mode*, must be altogether metaphorical in fact, not to mention the inherent and monstrous absurdity inseparable from the conception of sources of infinite sources, and first causes of first causes. The truth is, and the most momentous of truths too, that there is no limit to the absurdities into which philosophers run when bent on believing in God with the heart, if they *can't* with the head. What "the practical back door" was to Kant, feeling, or faith, or sentiment, or light within, (for many names are given to this infallible delusion), is to those who, like our "Analysis," deny that the being of God can be evidenced by reasoning, while insisting upon living faith in such being, as *the* wisdom, compared with which all other wisdom is as foolishness; then attempt to escape through this sentimental "back door." I hesitate not to pronounce a virtual abandonment of theism, unscientific as well as scientific, a Jesuitical giving up of God; a wretched, paltry, quibbling subterfuge that every rationalist should, to borrow the words of " Analysis" himself. " hoot out of his presence."

" THE VOLUNTARY :

UNDER THE DIRECTION OF THE EVANGELICAL VOLUNTARY CHURCH ASSOCIATION."

The editor of this paper, in an article on " the case of Dr. Kalley," in his last number, insinuated that the Doctor has been imposed on by the title of the " Anti Persecution Union ;" but when it is remembered that the Union only corresponded with Dr. Kalley for the purpose of offering him assistance, and that they have remitted to him 5*l*., it will be seen that the extent of their criminality—if proven—is that they have imposed on the Doctor 5*l*., an imposition which most persons would forgive. The public will perceive, from the following letter to the editor of the *Voluntary*, that the Union will neither " deceive" the Doctor for evil nor good, and that they have spoken to him with careful and premeditated explicitness.

To the Editor of the Voluntary.

Sir,—In your article on " The Case of Dr. Kalley," in your January number, you state that " the officer of the Anti Persecution Union has entered into a correspondence with Dr. Kalley, and that the Doctor, deceived by its plausible name, has freely responded to the official expression of its sympathy." As this implies that I have misled Dr. Kalley by the neutral name of the Anti-Persecution Union, I take the liberty of enclosing you a copy of the letter which I addressed to the Doctor, and also the two addresses which were enclosed in the letter. Upon perusing them I think you will acquit me of any intention of imposing on Dr. Kalley, or of leaving it even possible that the Doctor could be " deceived by the official expression of the sympathy " of the Anti Persecution Union; indeed the Doctor's reply, which I also forward you, proves that he did very well understand us.

We shall be sorry if our correspondence with the Doctor shall, in any way, diminish the interest which his religious friends may feel in his welfare, but it is due to ourselves to distinctly assert that we have acted with perfect frankness towards him; and it is but justice to him to own that his acceptance of our assistance has not, in our opinion, identified him in the remotest degree with our individual sentiments. We offered Dr. Kalley our assistance, not our opinions; we corresponded with him as a victim of persecution, not as a Christian. The Anti-Persecution Union knows no distinction of sects or parties.

We have remitted the Doctor £5., and when his acknowledgment is received a copy of it shall be forwarded to your office.

Respectfully soliciting the insertion of this explanation,

I am, yours, &c.

G. JACOB HOLYOAKE,

Sec. to the Anti Persecution Union.

40, Holywell Street, Strand.

16*th January*, 1844.

MR. SOUTHWELL'S RELEASE FUND.—The committee for procuring Mr. Southwell's release from Bristol gaol were discharged from their lengthened and laborious duties on Wednesday the 10th instant. A full dividend of 1*l*. was paid to each shareholder who applied for it. Some shares not being claimed, a surplus remained, which Mr. Redburn moved be given to the Anti-Persecution Union; but it was ultimately decided that it be paid over to the John Street Institution.

PHONOGRAPHY.—Mr. J. Merrin is conducting a Phonographic class at the Tower Street Mutual Instruction Society's room, 16, Great Tower Street. The subscription to the institution is 1*s*. per quarter ; to the phonographic class, 6*d*. per quarter. The class meets on Wednesday evenings at half past eight.

MUTUAL EXCHANGE.—A society is, we hear, in the course of formation on the Surrey side of the water, having for its object the raising a capital of 1,000*l*., in small shares, in order to establish a bazaar for the mutual exchange of goods for provisions and other necessaries on equitable terms, chiefly for the purpose of enabling small tradesmen to find a fair market for their goods.—*Sentinel*.

FRAGMENTS OF PROGRESS.

PAINE.—A public supper to commemorate the birth of Paine will take place at the "Rock, Lisson Grove, Marylebone, on January 29th. Mr. Benbow, who assisted at the exhumation of Paine's bones, is to take the chair.

REGISTRATION.—Memoranda for votes have gone the round of the newspaper press. They should be carefully acted upon by all reformers.

RELIGION.— A young man named Gibson became so excited at the Wesleyan class meeting in London Passage, White Cross Street, on Wednesday evening, Dec. 27, that he fell down in extreme terror, fainted away, and has since remained in a dangerous state.

METHODISM.—It was stated, at the new year's eve meeting, in Great Queen Street Chapel, London, that notwithstanding an increase of numbers among the Wesleyan body, during the last two years, from want of funds their operations have been greatly crippled, and some of their promising stations, in various parts of the country, abandoned.

"THE BEACON."—Another bit of heterodoxy has appeared, styling itself "A Summary of the best Arguments in Morals and Religion." Such an undertaking, well-conducted, would be invaluable to free-thinkers. The shortness of the time precludes a fair examination, and it would be premature to pronounce on the merit of a first or second number.

ANTI-SLAVERY DECISION.—The Royal Court of Paris has decided that slaves from any part of the world recover their liberty the moment they set foot on the French soil.

CHRISTIAN APOLOGIES FOR CRIME.—"Suddenly tempted by the devil." The phrase is a most convenient one, every way calculated to bring balm to uneasy consciences, and reconcile a scoundrel to the commission of any deed, no matter how atrocious. Should a man, for instance, feel disposed to walk off with his neighbour's wife, to forge his name to a blank bill, to set his house on fire, or commit a burglary on another's goods and chattels—what more easy for him than to stifle the stern upbraidings of remorse by the accommodating reflection that he is "tempted by the devil."—SUN.

GRATIFYING DECISION AT BRANCH A 1.—On Sunday evening last, at the conclusion of the lecture, Mr. Robert Clarke, the energetic and talented President of the Branch, announced that they had that morning come to a resolution expressive of their approval of the objects of the "Anti-Persecution Union," their confidence in the manner in which it was conducted, and determination to support it. He then, in a very cordial spirit, recommended both the Union and its organ, the "Movement," to the attention of the audience.

ATHEISTICAL SOIREE.—We are informed that a Soiree of this character is in contemplation in one of the northern towns, at which nobody but NO-GOD PEOPLE will be privileged to take a part. Further particulars will appear as arrangements are matured.

SOCIALISM.—Mr. Southwell has just held a two-night discussion with a Mr. Pinkerton, who charged Mr. Owen's marriage doctrines as "absurd, beastly, and immoral." Mr. Southwell conducted the defence of Mr. Owen's views to admiration, and demolished Mr. Pinkerton's positions to the satisfaction of the audience, and to more than Mr. P.'s satisfaction: admitting that the twelve lectures were not wisely worded, Mr. S. contended that they were excellently meant.

MISS ROALFE.

Before this number is in the hands of our readers, Miss Roalfe will be an inmate of a dungeon, classed with thieves and treated as one, for the CRIME of having published infidel books. She received notice to prepare for trial in the Sheriff's Court on Tuesday last. That we can foretel the result with infallible prescience is a proof of the undying virulence which is mixed up with that precious compound—true christianity. If our law officers should charge a person with blasphemy for having boiled a tea kettle on a Sunday, there is not a sound christian jury in the three kingdoms that would not find a verdict of guilty. We hate the Hindoo religion for its burning of widows; we hate mythologic, savage and catholic rites for their bloody and cruel orgies, and shall we not hate christianity for its immolation of men and women in gaols for the conservation of its absurd and dangerous tenets. Victim after victim is immured, and now Miss Roalfe is added to the number. Will it only be registered as an ordinary transaction? Will it pass by as a tale told? No; it will remain for ever in the memories of those who love integrity of expression; and while the regard for freedom and truth exists, christianity will be detested.

GLASGOW.—A public meeting has been held in this town on behalf of Dr. Kalley. It was called on a requisition to the Lord Provost and held in the Gælic church. Baillie Anderson was in the chair. Dr. Heugh, Mr. A. Mitchell, Dr. Bates, Mr. Jno. Wright, Dr. Wills, Dr. Watson, and Mr. Thompson, of Nile Street, were the speakers on the foreign sympathy side. Mr. Southwell, Mr. Adams, a chartist preacher, and an Irishman, whose name we cannot learn, spoke in favour of a home sympathy for those suffering for conscience sake in Scotland. Mr. Adams declared his intention was to move a resolution that should bring out the "insincerity" of the gentlemen on the platform; and two policemen stepped up to him, seemingly for the purpose of removing him; but they did not do it. Mr. Southwell drew a parallel between Dr. Kalley and the Edinburgh victims; he was often interrupted by the disapprobation of the meeting; but by the intervention of the chairman—who behaved with more justice than the Lord Provost of Edinburgh—Mr. Southwell was heard to the end.

TO CORRESPONDENTS.

W. B. C., NORWICH.—Received. His communication was mislaid by those to whose care it was entrusted, and only found when W. B. C.'s inquiry arrived. "The Recanting Witch-Killer" accepted.

Received.—T. A., Worcester; N., PRESTON, Glasgow; M. A. LIDDLE.

W. M., Glasgow.—The back Oracles now ready for him.

W. ANDERSON, Glasgow.—Nos. 2 and 3 of "Oracle" not yet able to get. The other publications he can have as proposed.

The notice of the Glasgow meeting was compiled from the "Watchman." No account has been forwarded by any of our friends to the "Movement" office. This is mentioned that we may be acquitted of neglecting matters of such direct interest. We cannot go to Glasgow to take notes, and our friends must not blame us for their omissions.

ANTI-PERSECUTION UNION,

Subscriptions received.

Mr. Johnson, Coll. 15	-	-	-	-	-	0	9	0
Master William Palmer	-	-	-	-	-	0	2	6
Stephen Balkwill	-	-	-	-	-	0	2	6
Isaac Messeder	-	-	-	-	-	0	1	0
Mr. Atkinson	-	-	-	-	-	0	1	0
William Smith	-	-	-	-	-	0	1	0
R. Whiteman, Harbro'	-	-	-	-	-	0	2	6

G. J. Holyoake, Secretary.

Printed and Published by G. J. HOLYOAKE,
40, Holywell-street, Strand, London.
Saturday, Jan. 27, 1844.

THE MOVEMENT
And Anti-Persecution Gazette.

"Maximize morals, minimize religion."—BENTHAM.

No. 8.   EDITED BY G. JACOB HOLYOAKE, ASSISTED BY M. Q. RYALL.   PRICE 1½d.

THE THEORY OF PARTIES.

All agree that knowledge is power, and that division is weakness. "Divide and conquer," "sow disunion," are considered the maxims of knavish rulers; yet I have seen knowledge break up Radicals into Chartists and Socialists, and again into Complete Suffragists. "The Beacon," an American paper, edited by the secretary of the U. S. Philosophical Society, of which R. D. Owen is a director, says that "Robert Owen tells them, the Reformers, that their evils are to be cured by the "Cooperative system," and that the want of it has produced the present state; without, however, denying the influence of bad governments, or the necessity of reform. He goes with the Chartists in principles, but withholds the physical influence of his followers, and consequently weakens the moral influence of the body. Mr. Owen, a reformer himself, he divides the reformers of England." Mr. Owen and his friends, with their new knowledge of social polity, did more than the government to break up Trades' Unions which had cost the labour of years, the liberties of many, and the hard earnings of millions of poor men. Every increase of knowledge has split up the friends of liberty. How is it—who solves the paradox—that this power has generated weakness? Either many parties are not evils, or knowledge is not power.

Nothing is more common than for the Socialist and Suffragist of only yesterday's growth, to exclaim against the rise of new parties, while they are yet sweating with the toil of adding to the world's perplexity their own parties. Some inconsistency is here, which perhaps a brief exposition of the doctrine of parties would explain.

In the world of political economy a division of labour is found to favour production. If every lady had to make her own pins before using them, and to sail to the Indies for sugar and to China for leaves, before sitting down to tea, how many of these conveniences and luxuries would be foregone! But pin-making is rapidly performed by the division of labour; and by sailors being set apart for the purposes of importation, tea and sugar are brought to every fire-side. The same principle holds good in the worlds of intellect and action. Newton by devoting himself to mathematics, Euler to algebra, Voltaire to theology, and Paine to politics, threw the concentrated light of their understandings on these subjects, and advanced them more in their lives than the mass of mankind would, by their piece-meal and partial attention, in centuries. In the same manner, philosophical institutions, political societies, and discussion classes, do more than individuals can for promoting science, liberty, and truth. David Hume assures us that "Parties from *principles*, especially abstract speculative principles, are known only to modern times, and are, perhaps, the most extraordinary and unaccountable *phenomena* which ever yet appeared in human affairs." But if the views just represented are correct, they are no longer "unaccountable." They have risen with the progress of knowledge to meet the wants of the world. All important affairs are now conducted by unions, and all unions are parties. It is true that some people affect to be of no party, and paradoxically form a party to cry down all parties. Neutrality is criminality. If wrong is redressed, no one blesses the neutral man; and when evil triumphs, curses fall on him, for he has allowed oppression and he shares the crime. Party is in itself good, and the only question is its proper direction.

Whenever a distinct, useful object is to be obtained, it is justifiable to form a party to obtain it, no matter what the predicted consequences may be. Progression is tardy, because so few are brave enough to trust to first acts to rectify themselves. It was proper to supersede Attwood's half and half 10*l.* Radicals by sterling universal-suffrage Chartists. A distinct object is seen in Chartism; but "Complete Suffragists" are *non sequiturs*. Because they adopt a more conventional way of seeking Chartism, it forms no justification for splitting up Reformers, by setting up a new party. Suffragists may be very well-meaning people, but if persons are to form new parties for every fresh *manner* of agitation, we shall have parties for wearing our hats in this particular way, or strapping our boots in that. But if Suffragists consider their objects broadly distinct from Chartists, in that distinction they have their justification. Socialism is distinct from Chartism, because Chartism asks for rights —Socialism for happiness. Chartism considers the means, Socialism the end. If this difference forms not a broad and useful distinction Socialism is an incumbrance, and ought to fall back into Chartism. A new party, unless established for the attainment of a new and great object, is a nuisance.

A party, if true wisdom actuates its members, will never be narrowed so as to exclude, but widened so as to embrace, all possible objects, that men may not be driven to division. The universal party, if ever it appears, must include all aims. Hence, I contended in the last number, that the Socialists forgot their universal professions when, from the political and moral, they excluded theological discussion. There ought not to have been "Oracles of Reason," "Anti-Persecution Unions," or "Movements." Socialism was wide enough to embrace them all. But these papers and party have been forced into separate existence by an unwise policy, and the authors have blamed us more than once for the consequences of their own folly. Atheism, and the Anti-Persecution Union, will work in union if they are permitted; but if not, they will work. Truth and liberty must know no repose while man is erring and wretched. G. J. H.

CELESTIO-INFERNO-SUPER-HUMANO-MUNDANITIES.

The Angels, quoth the immortal bard of ours,
Who sang in strains mellifluous and grand,
Of God, the Devil, Hell, and Human Souls,
Discoursed of doctrines deep and subtleties
Much, to our mortal senses, too abstruse.
Puffed up with vain conceit, inquisitive,
Grasping at shadows, with the substance near,
Man, silly man, intent on things divine,
Has peered and pried, guessed, wondered evermore,
At his own fancies and imaginings,
Forgetful ever that such lofty themes—
Which to the beings of his dreaming hours,
The phantom tenants of the ethereal space—
Might well employ their superhuman thoughts—
Bewildered quite our earth-born brains,
Unless perchance angelic natures we
Had first attained, united, or subjoined
Unto our grosser corporeity. OLD EPIC.

Sir Walter Scott had an artful way of placing under a quaint verse of his own manufacture, the words "Old Play." Why should not a similar license be allowed to me? Had I added my own "M. Q. R." would the very best judges of Milton imagine directly——but modesty forbids me to proceed—I would not rob the illustrious dead of their honors.

Should not man speculate? He does and will, whether he should or not. If he will do so it saves us from the trouble of determining whether or not he ought. Truly, but there may be wrong ways of speculating—such as speculations taken for, and insisted on, as realities, and forced on others, at the peril of losing life, liberty, property, and reputation. Among all speculations, however substantial or shadowy, none serve to perplex and demoralize so largely as those which appertain to the celestial, the infernal, and the superhuman in general. "God" and the "Devil," "Hell" and the "Soul," have strangely deranged the humanities. By them and for them priests have juggled, soldiers have fought, lawyers chicaned, kings have been enthroned, nobles have oppressed, landlords and money lords have griped and ground, philosophers have bewildered themselves, and the people have——paid.

Soul! God!! Devil!!! Hell!!!!—what complicated perplexities, what sublimated immaterialities, what monstrous phantasies, and what abhorrent enormities have not these speculations called forth when taught and accepted as realities? Should we then dismiss these subjects with contempt or disgust? Not while they are sincerely and conscientiously entertained by the few or the many. Who shall presume to decide in what particular instances, under what peculiarities, or apparent absurdities of belief, sincerity and conscientiousness abide? None. Then none can condemn, however they may differ, or disapprove, or oppose. When guesses, speculations, doctrines, and principles, grow into acts of interference, lead their adherents into abuse and calumny of non-believers or opponents, exposure becomes just. When personal interference is the result, resistance is a duty. When active oppression is practised, self-preservation may warrant a defensive or aggressive course in return, the right measure of which would be appropriately determined by our comparative strength and judgment.

On matters pertaining to the Celestio-inferno-superhumano-mundanities, some of the latest considerations are offered in some tracts by Owen Howell, published by Cousins—the titles run as follows :—" The Immortality of the Soul: twelve reasons for believing the doctrine. The Almighty God: twelve reasons for believing in his existence. The Devil: twelve reasons for disbelieving his existence. An eternal Hell: twelve reasons for not believing in the doctrine."

Perhaps some of the "Movement" readers would like to handle them, or send some suggestions by way of getting their hand in. I shall wait a little, and return to the subject. M. Q. R.

EMIGRATION.
To the Editor of the "Movement."

Sir,—Believing the conductors of the "Movement" will not be particular as to what or where they move, and that it will be of no consequence whether they speak of Harmony establishment in Hants, or community establishments in the "Far West," I send you a copy of a letter which I have received from Mr. G. White, one of Mr. Hunt's party. I know many are very anxious to hear from them; and to all true Socialists I am sure the information will be gratifying. Mr. G. White was well known to most Socialists in London by his zealous labours as the Secretary of the Social Tract Society, to which he devoted much valuable time for several years; I had the pleasure of working with him, and hope again some day to have the pleasure of doing so in the "Far West." The letter inclosed will act, I have no doubt, as a wholesome antidote to the "weak inventions of the enemy" which appeared a week or two ago in the shape of a letter from Mr. Lloyd Jones, the object of which letter, in my opinion, and in the opinions of many others, was to frighten those who had thought of bettering their condition in a distant country. It is not the first time that gentleman has felt uncomfortable upon that subject, as *some of those far away could testify.* He is permitted to say what he thinks proper in the pages of the "New Moral World," and no one is allowed to call in question his dicta.

Some parties, I perceive, by the "N. M. W." this week, are in that predicament—valuable letters are refused from old friends and co-operators abroad. Does the Editor fear the information will be injurious to the "Harmony establishment;" and are we to understand that that establishment is to be kept up by all others being kept down? I thought Mr. Owen had propounded views which were to benefit the whole human race; and that the Rational Society was founded to extend those views, and to act as a lever to move the whole world to adopt its principles, and that the "N. M. W." was to be the organ whereby the principles of the said Society were to be extended to the great family of man without distinction of *class, sect, country,* or *colour*; but I find in the "N. M. World's" answers to two correspondents, who have claimed the privilege of replying to Mr. Jones's "attack," "that the columns of the said paper are to be devoted to the advocacy of Moral and Social changes *at home.*"

Permit me, sir, to introduce to your readers Mr. White's letter, and to say that any one desiring information upon the subject of co-operative emigration, may obtain it by applying by letter (prepaid) to John Campbell Smith (*late of the Central B..ard*), No. 91, Tavistock Row, Covent Garden; or to Mr. William Thorp, 23, John Street, Tottenham Court Road.

R. REDBURN.

Magnanago, Milwankie County, Wisconsin Territory, United States, N.A.
November 14, 1843.

My Dear F. M. B. S.—I received your very kind co-operative letter of September 20, on the 9th of November, which removed the great anxiety which I had so long felt through your delay in answering; therefore I trust you will be more punctual for the future. You must excuse me writing to each separately, as the postage of letters, both in receiving and sending, cost me 27 cents, or about one-third, nearly, the price of a quarter of an acre of first-rate land. I regret much that you were unable to see me on the morning the St. James sailed, as I am sure we all felt the disappointment; but I hope ere long we shall meet again, under more favourable circumstances, in the land of liberty and plenty, never more to part. I will endeavour to provide such a home, that I shall have little difficulty in prevailing on you to accept. Am glad to hear that W—— has got such a respectable appointment; but I am afraid that, in England, his talents will not meet with that patronage they deserve. In America, where skill and industry are much better rewarded, even in our small schools, an assistant gets about 26*l.* a-year for six hours' attendance per day. This sum will purchase more than one hundred acres of land, capable of soon being made as good as any in England. Look at this—compare it with the beggarly stipend of an assistant in England; besides, there is a great desire for education here, and I dare say you will be surprised to hear that we have in every township which is six miles square, a section of one square mile for the support of a school; the school-houses are also used for meetings, discussions, or anything undecided upon by the inhabitants. I was at one of their debates last Friday, which afforded me great pleasure, as I observed general good feeling exhibited. It will give you some idea of emigration to this territory, when I state the fact, that at one of its ports (Milwankie), there are frequently landed from two to three thousand emigrants; and from this place, including the above port, there were not more than 20 houses eight years ago; now Milwankie alone contains between four and five thousand inhabitants. Much has been said about the want of society in the back woods of America, but I can assure you that I have met with more real kindness and intelligence amongst our neighbours, than ever I observed in a mixed number in England. Many of the landholders are men of education, far above the farmers and tradesmen of the old country; and I feel well assured that either Mr. C—— or W—— might obtain an excellent living in, or near, some of the large cities or towns, and, in a few years, make themselves independent; for men of talent are highly respected here, and would be certain of support. I will now, agreeably to your request, proceed to give you some account of our estate :—It consists of near 300 acres of excellent land, called the Burr back openings, which are very similar in appearance to the parks of the English aristocracy, being studded with clumps of oak-trees. This description of land is considered the best in the States, as it is quickly cleared. The soil is a rich black mould, which can be easily tilled, after the first ploughing. It is 30 miles from Milwankie, eight from ——, and five from the town of Magnanago. We bought it of the government for one and a quarter dollar per acre, or 5s. 2½d. English money. Part of it had been pre-empted (which is allowing a person to take a piece of land under certain restrictions, and paying for it at the end of twelve months), by a person from whom we purchased the piece, comprising a log-house 18 feet by 13, a good stable, and about three acres fenced and cultivated. These improvements cost us about 39l. Some other land we afterwards purchased, adjoining Spring Lake, which abounds with splendid trout, prickeral, &c. The scenery here is most delightful. There is also a running stream which will probably, ultimately, be of great service for driving machinery. Our house, which is 27 feet by 18, is now nearly completed, as also a seven-stall cow-shed; we have also built a root-house, which will be most useful for preserving our vegetables from the frost. The voyage across the Atlantic was to me like a trip of pleasure, with the exception of the fogs on the banks of Newfoundland, which gave me a very severe cold for a week. However, after we had passed the banks, the weather cleared up, and made the rest of the voyage to N. Y. very pleasant. Here we staid about thirty hours, and then proceeded up the Hudson, through the most delightful scenery I ever beheld, (with the exception of the Niagara Falls, which I will presently notice) to Troy, where we staid about a day, where we engaged for our exclusive use a fine canal-boat to take us to Buffalo, a distance of 360 miles. In our route we visited Rochester Falls, (but unfortunately the water was scarce), Ronce, Syracuse, Jordan; Byron, Newark, Port Gibson, Palmyra, Pittsburgh, celebrated for its salt-works, Brockport, Albion, Lockport; the whole of these towns are situated on the banks of the Erie canal, in the State of N. Y.; many of these places have sprung up in the course of a few years, and are now of great importance. Lockport has five locks, built in a very superior manner of granite, rising nearly 100 feet, and have a very imposing appearance when the boats are passing through. After a very pleasant trip of six days, we arrived at Buffalo, which is considered the depôt of the western world. Here we staid near a week, which gave us an opportunity of visiting the Niagara Falls: we started about eight o'clock in the morning, per steam boat, for the wonder of the world; and, from the description, I was led to believe it was something grand; but, although my imagination was somewhat excited, I did not expect to have seen a sight that would have created such intense feelings of pleasure as I felt; but I will give you a more minute description in my next. The following are the prices of a few articles we have purchased :—two horses, waggon, and harness, 38l.; two cows, calf (one of which is of superior description), 5l.; a fine bullock, which we have killed, cost rather less than 1d. per lb.; mutton, 2½d.; pork, 2½d.; best flour, 7s. per 100 lbs.; butter, 7½d.; eggs, 6d. per dozen; sugar, 4½d.; tea, 2s. 6d. to 3s.; coffee, 6d.; candles, 6d. to 9d.; soap, 4½d.; potatoes, 1s. 4d. per bushel; turnips, 4d.; whiskey, 1s. 3d. per gallon; brandy, 3s.; nails, 3d. per lb.; 1-inch oak board, 1l. 12s. per 1000 feet; pine, 2l. per 1000; boots, 12s. per pair; wheat, 1s. 9d. per bushel; oats, 1s. 3d.; clothing, with the exception of woollen cloths and flannels, is about the same price as in England. We have a saw-mill about 3 miles distant; another, 8; and two great mills within 9 miles. The mail passes within a mile of the house, and it is expected a road will be shortly made to pass direct through our grounds, which will much enhance their value. Several of our friends have settled near us, and are doing very well; in fact, it is almost impossible to do otherwise, for the means of production are so great. I hope father and the whole of you will think seriously of coming out here, as he would be able to live like a prince on his capital. I will give you one instance of a purchase made by an acquaintance of mine, since I have been here:—he bought a farm of 80 acres fenced, 10 acres under cultivation with growing crops, a good house and stable, for rather less than 60*l.*; he has since been offered 20*l.* for the crops on eight acres. Now there are plenty of opportunities like this, not that there are any objections to the situation, but because the Yankies are a roving race, and will generally sell if they can get a few dollars by so doing. There are several men in this neighbourhood who came here with scarcely a farthing, but who have now large farms well stocked. I am sorry that I have not been able to hear from Redburn and other friends; give my kind respects to them; let them see this letter, or copy it for them.

I remain,
your affectionate son and brother,
GEORGE WHITE.

P. S.—When you write, direct as above, and send a long letter.

QUERY FOR THE "MOVEMENT."

Mr. Editor—What do you think of a thorough out and out Atheist who can spend 1*s.* per week in Tobacco, yet cannot afford 1*s.* per year to assist those who are imprisoned for teaching Atheism? Is he not a man of *Smoke?*

Anti-tobacconist—*Harbro'*.
Editor—Yes.

TRIAL OF MISS ROALFE.

Can Christianity exercise hate?

We, the prophets of the "Movement," last week predicted the conviction of Miss Roalfe by the "elect" in Edinburgh; and true as the needle to the pole is the christian to persecution: we this week record the confirmation. Mr. Jeffrey writes, "Miss Roalfe has been sentenced to sixty days' imprisonment in the jail of Edinburgh, of course to be treated as a common felon. The usual forms were gone through in the Sheriff's Court. The lengthy indictment was read, and witnesses were called to prove the sale of the works libelled. Miss R. cross-examined the witnesses with considerable skill, elicited from them that they had been sent to purchase the books for the purposes of prosecution, and that, though some of them had read the works, they did not find their morals in the least degree corrupted by the perusal. After all the witnesses had been called, counsel for the prosecution spoke for a short time in the customary legal style, content to earn his fee with the smallest possible trouble to himself. Miss R. was then asked if she wished to say anything in her own defence. In a brief extempore speech, which was listened to with much attention and respect, she pointed out the folly and injustice of these prosecutions. She denied having sold the publications indicted with a wicked and felonious intent, for she had vended them, not with an intention to demoralize, but to improve and elevate the public mind. Her object was to disseminate truth, and no terrors of authority should prevent her from acting in accordance with the dictates of her conscience. She concluded by saying that *when liberated from prison, she would again pursue the course for which she was about to suffer.* The Sheriff said he was a mere instrument for administering the law; what the law was, in this matter, had been decided by a superior court, and he had no alternative but to pass sentence upon the prisoner.

The court was crowded to excess, and when Miss R. was led away by the officers to the jail, the assembled multitude, unable to restrain their feelings, gave her three hearty expressions of applause. Infidels were delighted, and christians forgot their rancour.

Miss R. is a heroine, an example to her sex, age, and to the other sex also. For her sake, for the sake of other martyrs, for the sake of freedom and truth, will not those who call themselves liberals now bestir themselves, and show by their *deeds* that they are really friends of liberty?"

Miss Roalfe elicited from the witnesses that they were sent to her shop by the Procurator Fiscal. Only *one* out of the four witnesses had read the works which they swore were blasphemous. When Miss Roalfe asked the one who had read the books what impression they made on him, he replied "none whatever." Miss Roalfe then asked him if he was any the less moral in consequence of having read them, at which he seemed, as the Dutch say, "flabbergasted;" the question set the court in a titter, and when the man replied "*no*," the place rang with laughter. The books prosecuted were 91 of the "Oracle," the "Home Thrust at the Atrocious Trinity," "Godology," and "The Bible an Improper Book for Youth."

The authorities endeavoured to keep the trial secret—"some men love darkness"— but an address from Mr. Baker, who is now keeping open Miss Roalfe's shop, and supplying blasphemy to the customers, brought a crowded court. Strong disapprobation was expressed on the Sheriff passing sentence, and he threatened, if it was repeated, to clear the court.

This is the brief detail of the events of the trial; of the consequences I have said little. As there are some feelings too strong for utterance, so there is indignation too great for expression. Denunciation seems cold in this case. Nothing will satisfy but *acts*. In the words of Mr. Jeffrey, the friends of liberty must show themselves "by their deeds."

G. J. H.

CHARLES PEMBERTON.

A volume has lately been published by C. Fox, entitled "The Remains of Charles Reece Pemberton, edited by John Fowler, Secretary to the Sheffield Mechanics' Institution." A plate is prefixed to the volume, a portrait of Pemberton, which is perhaps the most pleasing, intelligent, and generous face ever engraved. Portraits are generally gorgon, stony, leaden heads, made to be looked at, but this is Pemberton himself looking at you. Our great men on paper, in most cases, appear as if they were trying to look great—as if they knew the world was inspecting them; but Pemberton is unassuming, is vivacity, intelligence, and sensibility.

As the reader passes through this charming volume, he will thank the editor who has given it to the world. Every page is full of the strangest romance and purest morality. Montaigne said in his famous essays "reader, this is a book altogether without guile;" and this highest praise belongs, with greater truth than any book published to the "Autobiography of Pel Verjuice." Strangely, and unbelievably as it will sound, Pel Verjuice has neither guile nor cant. This book should be in every library that the poor man visits throughout the land. No young man should deem his course of reading complete, unless it embraces Pemberton's autobiography, letters, and dramas. He is ignorant of rare loveliness who has not tasted Pemberton's variety, freshness, and truth. How genius is built up by its own self-relyings—how glorious is integrity—what rich fields of beauty the truthful man finds in the world, and how much of joy he spreads around him, constitute the teachings of this book.

People will tell us of the public mind not being prepared; that *all* is cold, sordid, selfish. That good may not be performed—that men may not be honest—the world will not appreciate bold good. That the world will not reward on the scale it should, is true; but that the highest virtue will not find appreciators is false. Men forget that the world would be better if it was oftener invited to admire excellence; that it would be more faithful if truth was oftener shown to it. Weak good men keep back their good, and wonder the world does not faster improve. Let the world see truth as much as it sees falsehood; let the right example be as often before it as the wrong is now; let the number of good men equal the knaves; and the natural goodness of human nature is my proof that the world will soon better by the example. Pemberton stood out among men a hater of cant—a foe of hypocrisy. He spurned deceit as openly as other men cling to custom or hug "respectability;" and Pemberton WAS appreciated. Any one of his friends felt more real love for him than the whole world feels for half its lauded heroes.

One might descant through a whole "Movement" without weariness on the pleasing views the "Remains" presents, and the useful principles it elucidates. But short, necessarily short, as this notice must be, it shall not pass unadorned with something of Pemberton. Here is an extract—no, not an "extract"—that is a dry, cold, formal, pedantic, phrase—here is a gush of feeling:—

"ENGLAND.

"O verdant, flowery, and lovely England! I look upon the soft, and bright, and gladdening decorations which nature has spread over thee with lavish hand. I cast my memory's eye over all else on which I have gazed, over all on which my foot has trodden; and to thy demi-paradise turn again with an increased ardour of affection, from the comparison—and while I exclaim, "Oh beautiful, most beautiful!" I feel as I could cling to each tree, and shrub, and flower, with a lover's fondness, as my bosom swells with admiration, joy, and rapture. But when I look among thy people, all the glorious exultation dries up from my heart, and bitterness succeeds the draught which heaven mingled. I see one-third of thy twelve millions have no other use for sense or reason than to study new indulgences, and find fresh sources of life's enjoyment; all the others are toiling to administer those enjoyments, and supplying those sources,—struggling to endure existence, or battling with misery while life endures."

How much pain have cost us the evils that have never happened!

DR. KEENAN'S LECTURES
AT THE POLYTECHNIC INSTITUTION.

Physiology and medicine will one day acknowledge themselves indebted to Dr. Keenan. This gentleman is delivering a course of six lectures on the "True Functions of the Lungs." The first was listened to on Jan. 27, by a numerous audience, with great interest. It was full of startling and original views. The light of facts was thrown over the dreams of theory. It is high praise, but his lecture much resembled one of Emerson's orations, so replete was it with novelty's charm and truth's effect. The Doctor commenced by remarking that men with large chests were distinguished for their vivacity, proceeding from the large quantities of oxygen consumed. He said that the quality of a sensation depended on the climate, and quantity of feeling on the chest's capacity. All motion had a common origin, which was the combination of oxygen with an oxydizable base. In proof of which he had galvanic and electric machines set in motion, and identified his theory with the cause of their action. He referred the origin of life to the same principle, considered man to be an electro-motive machine, and explained that the true use of food and air was not, as Liebig and his followers supposed, to produce *heat*, but to generate the electro-moving power. It was this power, and not the mind or will, as considered by the old metaphysicians, which caused motion in man. We all knew that the will would not move a paralytic limb, and that a man might lie down and die within sight of his own door, with all the *will* in the world to reach it; but if he had not the electro-power requisite he could not. Air evidently served a more general requirement than the supply of heat. If it aided in the formation of heat only, then warm animals would not require it equally with cold ones; but it was afforded to hot and cold alike for the purpose of motion. The racing horse breathed most when most hot, not to gain heat surely, of which he had too much, but to gain power which he was exhausting. By an effective display of facts Dr. K. supported his opinion that food was only in part employed in nourishing the body, and part in supplying the lungs. He contended that hydro-carburets, such as butter, wine, and the like, were requisite and useful in producing power. Temperance people, who reasoned chemically in favour of their views, were misled, as he had been, by the crude and erroneous theories of the continental physiologists. It was no disparagement to call wine a stimulant, such term, if it implied anything, implied an accession of power, to which no objection could be made. It was in man as in steam-engines, we wanted but matter to make, and power to move; but physiologists had done little to account for motion. A lengthened report, which our space will not permit, would be necessary to enumerate circumstantially all the novel views Dr. K. advanced. The admission to a single lecture is 3s., and those of our readers who can make it convenient to attend will be amply repaid. The Doctor illustrates his views by the fine galvanic and and electric apparatus around him.

UNITY FORM OF GOVERNMENT.—I have been on a visit to a wise man, a *very* wise man, who has followed from his youth up the whim, and all very wise men have whims, of restoring the neglected school of Pythagoras to its pristine greatness. Accordingly he has selected and brought up some dozen submissive persons to his full satisfaction, for not one of them dare know his right hand from his left but on his master's authority, doubly backed by that of the great founder. They have, in short, no tongue of their own, no will of their own, and no thought of their own. You cannot conceive a more perfect community; one more virtuously insipid, more scientifically absurd, or more wisely ignorant. The whole place is an abode of the blessed—a house with twelve bodies in it, and *one* brain to serve them all. Once more, it was a perfect household—with the men, all peace, method, virtue, learning, and absurdity—with the women, all silence, order, ignorance, and modesty.

FRANCES WRIGHT.

NOTICES.

THE MOVEMENT.—Orders for supplying subscribers, at their own residences, to be addressed to M. Ryall.

Agent for Birmingham, Mr. Nicholls, 61, Broad Street.

Part II., price 7d., now ready.

THE ORACLE.—A few copies of the second volume may be had.

The back numbers of the "Oracle," with few exceptions, can now be supplied. Write to M. Ryall.

Bronterre O'Brien lectures on Sunday afternoon, between the hours of two and five, at the Rotunda.

M. Ryall has opened a Philosophical Lending Library. The particulars are described in the second Part of the "Movement."

THE MOVEMENT.

PROSPECTUS FOR A PHILOSOPHICAL INSTITUTE.

THE ROTUNDA is about to change its occupancy, or be left vacant: so important an arena for philosophical investigation ought not to be lost to the cause of philanthropy and reason.

The late want of success which will compel BRANCH LIII. of the RATIONALISTS to relinquish those Premises, seems to have arisen from the want of a RESIDENT DIRECTORY, which, with energy, intelligence, and unanimity, should at all times be able to preserve consistency and order, so much needed to attract attention and obtain public support.

Under these circumstances a few friends of freedom and progression have ascertained that Mrs. Martin would have no objection to engage in this undertaking, if enabled to do so. As that Lady is well known as the uncompromising opponent of superstition in all its chameleon forms, and although not the advocate exclusively of any party, is yet the candid approver and able Teacher of that which she finds excellent in all, she seems precisely fitted for the management of the Rotunda, eminently calculated to adorn it by her talents, give it efficiency by her energy, and conduct it with that nice propriety which would merit for it great public support.

In the event of Mrs. Martin becoming the proprietor of this establishment, she will devote it, as far as possible, to the dissemination of useful knowledge—the unchecked avowal of mental conviction; in fine, to the establishment of the Reign of Reason, by the promotion of knowledge, virtue, and freedom.

ARRANGEMENTS WILL BE MADE FOR

1. Lectures, by talented persons of all parties, on Scientific and Philosophical Questions; on Political, Religious, and Social Reform.
[MRS. MARTIN WILL USUALLY LECTURE ON SUNDAYS.]
2. A Weekly Discussion on subjects of popular interest, especially Theology.
3. Sunday Soirees, for Conversation and Intellectual Recreation, commencing at 4 P. M.
4. A Philosophical Library, and a Reading Room, supplied with books as well as periodicals. The books will also be circulated among the Subscribers.
5. Rational Education Classes and Schools.
6. Select Recreative Assemblies, a Dancing Class, etc.

MEANS.

A considerable sum has already been expended on the Premises, which yet require many improvements and repairs. A comparatively moderate sum (£250) is necessary, to enable a new occupant to have the advantage of what is already spent. It is proposed to raise this sum by £5 and £1 subscriptions.

FIVE POUND SUBSCRIBERS

Will be entitled to a Transferable and Saleable Ticket of Admission to all the Sunday Meetings, the Weekly Discussion, and to the Library and Reading Room, until their money is repaid; a quarter's notice of the withdrawal of which will be required, and be sufficient for its recall.

ONE POUND SUBSCRIBERS

Will be entitled to a Transferable Ticket, admitting two to the same advantages as those enumerated during one year from the date of opening.

Persons willing to assist in this undertaking will please to signify their intentions, addressed to the Secretary below. They are respectfully informed that their subscriptions, to be of service, must be immediate, as Mrs. Martin must be in possession of the sum required in a few days, or it will be too late for its purpose.

If ultimately sufficient money should not be received, what may have been then subscribed will be promptly returned.

G. JACOB HOLYOAKE, HON. SEC.

A Meeting of Mrs. Martin's Friends will be held on TUESDAY, February 6th, at the Rotunda, to receive the results of this notice, and take the immediate steps necessary.

ANTI-PERSECUTION UNION,
Subscriptions received.

M. A. Liddle, Coll. 36.	-	-	-	0 1 6
J. Wood, Harbro,	-	-	-	0 2 6
W. Cooke, Bradford	-	-	-	0 1 0
J. Drummond, Preston	-	-	-	0 1 6

G. J. Holyoake, Secretary.

TO CORRESPONDENTS.

H. WOOD, New Town, Edinburgh.—We have written to this person for his address. If he will be good enough to send it, we shall be happy to furnish the explanation he asks.

PATERSON'S TRIAL.—Any friend will greatly serve us by forwarding any of the newspaper reports of Mr. Paterson's last trial in Scotland.

H. COCKS, Bristol.—Sends us an article on the "Jew Book Humbug." He earnestly desires to impress on his Bristol friends the necessity of forming a Branch of the Anti-persecution Union in that city as an antidote to the bigotted outpourings of Mr. Roper and the malevolence of Mr. Wood. We can safely assure him that our friends already there will be glad of his co-operation in carrying out his laudable desires.

D. R.— Mr. H. W. Holyoak, of Leicester, is not a relative of the Editor of the "Movement," though of the same age, and devoted to the same cause.

W. M'NEIL.—Will this gentleman send us his address?

R. W.—Says that he cannot see the truth of the remark on the 1st. page of the "Movement" "respecting those unwilling to engage in a fruitless agitation." He says, "if an agitation appears fruitless what motives have we to enter into it?" We answer, perhaps R. W. is right, and that no one would exert himself if he was sure that no good result would ensue. But no man who does a good act is warranted in thinking it will be useless. A well-meant effort, like "a thing of beauty, is a joy for ever." Still, we cannot always see the end of our course. People have said, What good will the Anti-Persecution Union do? You cannot put down the priests, and the task has SEEMED hopeless. Still we pressed on. The fruitlessness of our labour deterred us not. We did literally, with our eyes open, make "fruitless attempts," and rich rewards have often crowned our persistency. Reformers are sure to find those who will represent their every attempt as hopeless, and unless they are able to work in the teeth of despair, they are unequal to their high work.

Printed and Published by G. J. HOLYOAKE,
40, Holywell-street, Strand, London.
Saturday, Feb. 3, 1844.

THE MOVEMENT
And Anti-Persecution Gazette.

"Maximize morals, minimize religion."—BENTHAM.

No. 9.   EDITED BY G. JACOB HOLYOAKE, ASSISTED BY M. Q. RYALL.   PRICE 1½d.

A HUNT AFTER THE DEVIL.

A few hundred Bible Contradictions, and a few other Odd Matters. By John P. Y., M.D.

A work with this quaint title was a short time ago issued from the press in three volumes, and it is greatly to be regretted that it has not generally been brought under the notice of reviewers. It is a book of rare excellence, caustic wit, and acute argument. Such a brilliant demolition of the bible probably never appeared in any age or nation. It combines the strong sense of "The Age of Reason" with deeper research than the "Diegesis." Every page is a battering ram in full play against the walls of inspiration. Natural eloquence and classic lore, crowds of arguments and accurate reference, are combined and displayed with mathematical precision and unequalled brevity. Egyptian sage and Catholic priest, Chinese philosopher and Methodist parson, Indian seers and Hebrew rabbies, Greeks, Romans, and English, all ages, languages, arts, sciences, the earth's bowels and the milky way, are all overrun in Dr. P. Y.'s learned, earnest, nimble, and indefatigable "Hunt after the Devil."

The "Bible Contradictions," and the brilliant array of arguments against the bible's inspiration, are chiefly of a novel and original character. But were they not so, they have a merit from the brevity and perspicuity of their arrangement which would win for them general acceptation. I can appreciate the original thinker, and watch his rise with the intensest interest; but if we were all Waldo Emersons and Thomas Carlyles, the eye of practice would be blinded by universal brilliancy, and the world would come to a stand still. These men throw their light over future ages, and the full glory of their light will be seen in the happiness of coming generations. So of the sages of by-gone times—their light is falling on us, and those men who popularize their works, and so exhibit their thinkings that all the world understand them, may be likened to glasses which concentrate the sun's rays, and reflect them with new power on surrounding objects. Your philosophers throw their broad beams on the world, and your practical men reflect them on the business of life. The philosopher may be more eminent, but the practical man is not less useful; both are necessary, and neither must scorn the other. Without the practical man the philosopher would live in vain, and without the philosopher the practical man would grope in the dark.

I make these remarks because nothing is more common, when a good argument is again diffused, than to hear some reader of Celsus or Origen object to it because it was once advanced by those ancients. It may be so, but was it advanced to this generation? Did the priest-ridden working man of this day hear it? Has he time to explore the caves of ancient learning, and bring to light the hidden gems? Then is it not high service rendered, to bring these lights from under the bushel, and set them on the hill—to make the writing on the wall so bold and legible that the poor man, who must run to live, may be enabled to read as he runs? The man who concentrates the rays of knowledge, and flashes them on mankind, performs a high and useful duty. These are the real men of progression. *They* stimulate action—they conduct the world. This is the province of the orator, and it was by overlooking this view that Hazlitt erred in his delineation, and Bulwer undervalued the office of the orator. It is no objection to great speeches that they are not readable; they are not intended for it. Your book-writer is to be read; the orator to be heard. Hazlitt and Bulwer criticise the orator as unwisely as he who should apply a mathematical formula to decide a question in morals, or a point in history. If a great speech makes a great impression, no matter that it cannot be read, it has done its work and fulfilled its mission. Its errand was practical—it was to set the multitude to work. Homer's Iliad and Bacon's Organon are, doubtless, greater works than

Demosthenes' speeches; but both were fitted to their spheres if judged aright. Bacon wrote for posterity; Demosthenes spoke for his generation. The province of Bacon was to set men to think; that of Demosthenes to make men act. The orator takes men as they are; the philosopher as they should be. Doubtless men like Elliot and Emerson may talk their high thinkings to public assemblies, but they would still be poets and philosophers, not orators. They would instruct, not move. The fine speech of Shiel in defence of J. O'Connell is a readable production, but those parts which most delight the world would move the jury least. In tone, gesture, will, and sympathy, lie the orator's chief power, but these cannot be conveyed on paper. The object of this apparent digression is to satisfy the reader that there are two classes of men, thinkers and popularizers, men who spread knowledge as well as those who increase it; and that those who spread with care and talent are among the benefactors of mankind. This I remark, that the learned critic may not underrate the important work of Dr. P. Y. if here and there, in his thousands of facts and criticisms, some ten should be discovered peculiar to another age and hand.

Dr. P. Y. is a firm believer in the god fiction; but while he believes in that, he seems determined to believe in nothing else without reasonable evidence. The Doctor commences by saying "I have always been puzzled whenever I have attempted to find out what was the end of us human beings. Here we are, generation after generation; we rise, grow up, perchance get old, and fall—for what purpose? If we exclude the few who add to the stores of human knowledge, I see none, except that we exist to humbug, to be humbugged, and to pay our taxes. These seem the main duties of morality. Nevertheless, under all our distress, there is one consolation, that a bull terrier dog is, if anything, rather worse than a human being." For the present I shall content myself with transcribing one specimen of the " Contradictions," and return, on future occasions, to the consideration of the contents of these vivacious volumes. We are told in the Chronicles, quotes Dr. P., that "thirty and two years old was he when he began to reign, and he reigned in Jerusalem eight years, and the inhabitants of Jerusalem made Ahaziah, his *youngest* son, king in his stead. Forty and two years old was Ahaziah when he began to reign"—just two years older than his father ! G. J. H.

Tyranny itself is to me a less odious word than toleration.—LANDOR.

THE RECANTING WITCH-KILLER.

" Thou shalt not suffer a witch to live."
" There shall not be found amongst you an enchanter, or a witch, or a charmer, or a consulter with familiar spirits, or a wizard, or a necromancer." GOD JEHOVAH.

In a recent number of Chamber's Journal there appears an article of which the following is an abridgment:—

GOVERNOR SEWALL.

[From the Gift, an American Annual.]

"How unlike that of Cotton Mather (a witch-finder and persecutor in New England) was the conduct of Judge Sewall, of Salem, who had presided on the bench during the trials for sorcery that disgraced the year 1692, and who had pronounced sentence of death on the victims. When the frightful excitement of fanaticism and superstition had passed away, and reason and humanity had resumed their empire, he was one of the first to regret the part he had taken in it through his official situation. Sixteen years afterwards, one Sunday at the close of public worship, Judge Sewall left his seat, and advanced towards the pulpit, where he handed up to the minister a paper, which he requested him to read aloud to the congregation, desiring them all to remain and hear it. This paper was an acknowledgment of sincere recantation and deep repentance for having, in his capacity of judge, sentenced to death so many innocent people. He stated that he now believed himself to have acted, at that time, under a delusion, that remorse had soon come upon him, and that he had ever since done all in his power to benefit the families of those who had suffered by his sentence, and to make all possible atonement for his misguided severity. And he now humbly, and in the presence of the assembled church, expressed his sorrow and compunction, and tremblingly implored the forgiveness of God. While this memorial was read to the congregation (amongst which were many relatives of the victims of the year 1692), Judge Sewall stood at the foot of the pulpit in an attitude of the deepest sorrow and contrition, with his head bowed down, his eyes cast on the ground, and his hands crossed humbly on his breast. That such a man must have believed himself right in doing the wrong for which he afterwards so conscientiously endeavoured to atone, can admit of no doubt."

Here's a precious farce! Governor Sewall, in the strict obedience of his God's commands *(vide ut supra)* assists, as set forth by the reflecting contributor to " The

Gift," in bringing "nineteen unoffending persons to an ignominious and unmerited death;" but, becoming afterwards subject to certain "compunctious visitings of nature," he repents of his zeal in the service of his sanguinary God, and doubting, perhaps, in spite of his "Bible," if there ever were a veritable witch in existence, actually begs said God's pardon for implicitly obeying his supreme behests!

I would crave of all reasonable men an answer to this question: Would witch-finding and witch-killing have ever taken place if God-finding (and God-killing) had not pre-occurred?

Deists are continually enquiring, What harm is there in the belief in a God! Beside a thousand other instances of the pernicious influence of Goddism, here is one; for, since there is just as much reason for the existence of witches as for the existence of Gods, the frightful evil of witch-finding excitements (or something equivalent) will naturally arise amongst fanatical and ignorant deists of all sects. Be it remembered, these things have always originated with "*Bible Christians*."

"Thou shalt not suffer a witch to live."

Would there, I ask, have been a belief in witches, even amongst ever-credulous christians, but for their God's recognition of such beings in his laws delivered by Moses, and the inspired record of the witch of Endor? We learn from the latter that this witch of Endor exhibited her power to Saul by raising Samuel from the dead to give a reason for God's shabby conduct, which "heaven's high majesty" refused to give, viz., that Saul was to be sent to the right about because he did not "obey the voice of the Lord, and execute his fierce wrath on Amalek."

No, Saul was too *reasonable* and *humane;* David was the boy!

To the influence of "the Bible," then, the "precious Bible," must be traced all such cases as that of Judge Sewall, who believed himself right in doing the wrong for which he afterwards endeavoured to atone; aye! and even cases wherein there has been no recantation, for mark you, reader, it is when "REASON and HUMANITY resume their empire," not religion and Godly piety, that the rage for witch-destroying discontinues.

How near to the truth do men sometimes approach without arriving at it! Doubtless, though both the original writer, and the Edinburgh transcribers of the article we have been reviewing, would be as much shocked at and prejudiced against the bare truth itself as would have been the fanatic Judge Sewall if told, in the midst of his witch-killing career, that he was grossly criminal in endeavouring to act in accordance with God Jehovah's recognition of the existence of witches, and in obedience of his commands for their extermination.

"Thou shalt not suffer a witch to live."

Well, well, witches are now no more where reason and humanity have progressed and maintained their sway; and "The Movement" will not cease, I hope, before the same may be said of the God idea. W. B. C.

THE DOCTRINES OF THE CONCORDISTS.

II.

In our last article under this head we spoke of the primary-being-source, and man's relation to the same. We said the real man is created the image of the universe law. By the real man we mean the universal man—genus, of which men are the species. This universal humanity nature is the pure three-fold representative of the triune spirit. Men, or the individual species, are the impure or imperfect representations of the same. The former of these, as yet, exists not in the actual sphere. It is real and ideal, not yet actualized. We can, therefore, only treat of the actual or individual man, who, whether viewed in the mass, or singly, is constitutionally at variance with the primary law. A divergency has somewhere taken place. We can conceive of a being of kindly feeling, of clear intellect, and of certain and successful action, but to find this perfect man existing in the actual world we cannot. We do not undertake to determine how this defection occurred, but so it is. Wherever this constitutional defect originated, it is practically perpetuated by false generation. Here it is that evil, misery, and degradation is ensured to us. Here alone can evil be successfully attacked; all human elevation must commence with pure generation. To ascertain the true universe-generative-law and its requirements, and to yield a perfect obedience to the same, should be man's chief study, as it would ensure his highest good. Whilst man remains in a dislocated position with the primary laws, and continue to generate in this false position, it is in vain to expect much else than painful uneasiness in his whole character. When man's antecedent relations are correct, his consequent associations will be happy; but so long as he remains in disjunctive association with the spirit, so long must his transactions with men be defective, and productive of vexation and misery. No modification of man's external circumstances can permanently alleviate his internal disquiet.

Man is unhappy from what he *is*, not from what he does. He cannot be improved by altering his doings any more than by punishing him for them; a better constitution is needed, which will ensure better conduct, better associative arrangements and better institutions. His untruthful conduct with his fellows arises from his defective relation with truth. His unloving conduct with men has its origin in a constitution out of harmony with love, and his unsuccessful conduct from his partial affinity with power. In fact, upon man's constitutional relationship with the antecedent spirit depends all his consequent conduct.

Man occupies a middle position between the infinite and the finite, which may be termed the indefinite. His attention should be awakened to his antecedent relations as immensely more important than his consequent ones. Upon the former his happiness depends, both as a recipient and a transmitter of good. As a man is natured or faculited, so he associates; no higher than he is natured can he associate. It is in vain to call upon him to exercise faculties that are not yet developed in him. The imperfect man essays to effect a perfect work, and finds to his disappointment he is constantly foiled. He needs to be directed to the creative source for higher faculties and instincts, in which to receive and enjoy the highest good, and exhibit it to others.

In our next we propose to speak of man's relation to the outward or consequent world. W. OLDHAM.

THE STATISTICS OF DEMORALIZATION.

(FOR 1843.)

A friend has favoured us with the following list of receipts of various religious societies and speculations during the past year. Those who ask "What's the good of discussing about religion, and spreading atheism?" we point to that list. That money ought to have been employed in placing the industrious poor in communities, or some places where labour would meet its reward. Had the money been merely wasted the evil would be light; but worse than being useless, it has been expended for bad purposes. Its office has been to make men religious, and it is your religious men who are the prime curse of the earth. They prop up any oppression if it come but in the name of God; they oppose knowledge; they imprisoned Mrs. Adams in Cheltenham, and now they have imprisoned Miss Roalfe in Edinburgh. The list appears to be the voluntary, and not to include the enormous mass of forced monies. Let us register this lamentable folly of our species, and hope for better things.

Baptist Missionary	£51,631
Baptist Home Missionary	5,270
Baptist Irish	2,314
Baptist Colonial Missionary	238
Bible Translation (Baptist)	3,488
British and Foreign Bible*	92,476
British and Foreign Sailor's	2,205
British Reformation*	1,196
Christian Knowledge*	78,940
Christian Instruction	1,152
Church Missionary	115,100
Church of Scotland Missionary	6,909
—— Jewish Mission	4,474
—— Colonial	4,268
Church Pastoral Aid	17,562
Colonial Church	3,149
Colonial Missionary	2,970
District Visiting	405
Home Missionary	7,788
Irish	3,877
Irish Evangelical, about	3,403
Jews, for propagating Christianity among them	25,066
—— Operative Converts' Instit.	1,037
London City Mission	6,741
London Missionary	78,450
Lord's Day Observance	930
Moravian Missionary	5,324
National School, annual subscription about	12,000
Naval and Military Bible*	3,251
Propagation of the Gospel	71,091
Prayer Book and Homily	2,590
Protestant Association	1,528
Religious Tract	52,605
Sailor's Home	2,225
Sunday School Union*	10,301
Trinitarian Bible*	2,337
Wesleyan Missionary	98,253

* The total of the receipts of the Societies thus marked includes sales of publications.

THE QUESTIONS OF ZAPATA.
—*Hetherington, London.*

Dominico Zapata was a professor of theology in the university of Salamanca in 1629, and he presented to the junta of doctors this string of brilliant Questions. It is difficult to believe they were not written by Voltaire, so sparkling and satirical are they. The Questions of Zapata form the richest little book that has issued from the press for years, and Mr. Hetherington must have been in a waggish mood when he determined to publish it. After the learned and dry argument with which the bible is often assailed and defended, one turns with delight to the racy Zapata. His queries fall like an anodyne of wit on the weary spirit. Let those who think persecution does no harm calculate on the consequences of this book not being widely circulated since 1629. Had it been read since that time by every person who has read the bible, Christendom would have been thoroughly infidel. The translator of Zapata, who, by the by, is a lady, has imbibed the spirit of her original, and thus quaintly concludes the book: "Zapata having had no answer to his questions, set about preaching. He disengaged truth from falsehood; he taught and practised virtue. He was mild, benevolent, modest, and was BURNT at Valladolid, in the year of our Lord 1631."

THEORY OF HEAT AND VITAL PRINCIPLE.—*By Arthur Trevelyan.*

Mr. Trevelyan holds the opinion that all heat is the same, and proceeds from one source, the sun. Solar, electric, flame heat, he regards as but different names for one principle, and agrees with Professor Leslie that light is but diffused heat. The "Theory of Vital Principle" is this, that "the primary principle of life is *heat*, which is the cause of all excitability and sensibility." This is the substance of these interesting theories, which have been rejected by the "Chemical Gazette" on the ground of being "entirely opposed to those generally received," and by the "Electrical Magazine" because they "involve a complete revolution in established views, and would require extensive investigation to confirm them." The "Chemical Gazette" does itself little honour by professing itself a conservator of received notions rather than a searcher after truth; and the "Electrical Magazine" should have made known new theories involving a revolution in established views, that those who could afford "extensive investigation" might make it. Mr. Trevelyan's theory of vital principle deserves attention because it promises a solution to the causes of human phenomena which not only simplifies our metaphysical and theological speculations, but may have an important influence on medicine. If an opportunity presents itself I will contrast Mr. Trevelyan's theories with Dr. Keenan's views of the same phenomena.

SCHOOL BOOKS.

Mr. John Ellis has published, in addition to his first book for children entitled "Lessons on Words and Objects," a *second* book for the same young parties, on words and objects, containing a tabular view of the comparative heights and lengths of the mountains and rivers of the world. Also two smaller books, one entitled "Songs for Children," the other the "Pictorial Reading and Spelling Book." The wood cuts in this last book are not from the graver of Linton or Kenny Meddows. The pig reminds me of that famous fellow mentioned by Daniel as disconcerting the whole Jewish nation when stuck on the gates of Jerusalem. Still the pictures will answer their end, that of pleasing their juvenile inspectors. The table prefixed to the "Second Book on Words and Objects" is neat and instructive, and the whole arrangement of the matter pleasing. These are the best books of the kind extant, and I hope Mr. Ellis will complete the series he promises on Natural Phenomena and the Nature of Man. Cobbett was the first to present a useful school-book tolerably free from goddism. The Chambers' books are infected; Mr. Ellis's are not entirely free, but they contain little more than the ghost of God, which is a great recommendation.

MAN THINKING.—This is an Oration of R. Waldo Emerson, published in this country by Mudie. It is one of those fine productions which induced Carlyle to make the author known on this side the earth. The Oration is not so much "Man Thinking" as Emerson thinking. It is full of fine thoughts, is eminently calculated to awaken the germs of talent any where, but well adapted to fulfil its special mission, that of raising the AMERICAN SCHOLAR to the high position required by the glory of America and her republican institutions. America must become both studious and modest, or its modern brightness will fade away, and its institutions become a reproach.

THE SWEET USES OF RELIGION.

[FROM COBBETT'S REGISTER.]

When the borough men select schoolmasters and furnish books, what volumes of tracts we shall have! In what sweet notes will be sung to us the endless blessings of passive obedience, non-resistance, ragged backs frozen joints, parching lips, and hungry bellies! How seriously it will be told us by a smooth-tongued hack, that as God has ordained, that the noisy and lazy, and gormandizing cuckoo shall suck the eggs of the hedge sparrow, lay its own eggs in the nest, and make the poor hedge sparrow hatch and feed the young; that we are to let our children starve to death, while we contentedly labor for pensioned masters and pensioned misses, the progeny of boroughmongers!

Come little children list to me,
  While I describe your duty,
And kindly lead your eyes to see
  Of lowliness the beauty.

Tis true your bony backs are bare,
  Your lips too dry for spittle;
Your eyes as dead as whiting's are,
  Your bellies growl for vict'al.

But, dearest children, O, believe!
  Believe not treacherous senses!
'Tis they your infant hearts deceive
  And lead into offences.

When frost assails your joints by day,
  And ice by night torments ye,
'Tis to remind you *oft to pray,*
  And of *your sin repent* ye.

At parching lips when you repine,
  And when your belly hungers,
You covet what by *right divine*
  Belongs to boroughmongers.

Let dungeons, gags, and hangman's noose,
  Make you content and humble,
Your heavenly crown you'll surely lose
  If here on earth you grumble.
                      COBBETT.

SCOTLAND.—Mr. Paterson writes, at the end of his first three months, and desires to acknowledge the receipt of letters respectively from Mr. Chilton, Talbert, and A. Campbell. Other friends who have written have seen his acknowledgment. A letter from W. J. B. has been detained by reason of some plain comments on christian justice. Mr. P. says "Get Hornblower, Dent, Davis, Merriman, and other friends, to copy me pieces on logic, morals, and philosophy. Such I may be allowed to receive if *written,* and not from their nature objectionable. I could say much on prison discipline, if allowed to do so. I still live at Perth—shall be glad of letters—they are the only lights that gild my cell. I have read those I have about 6000 times over."

Mr. Finlay writes to say that he is well and cheerful, and that he is still Thomas Finlay the INFIDEL. This was written on January 19; on Monday last he was liberated, and a Ball and Soiree were held in honour thereof. Miss Roalfe's conduct has occasioned universal admiration, out and out bigots of course excepted.

Mr. Baker writes "Infidelity in Edinburgh has become somewhat respectable. We were the 'new-comers' upon whom was transferred the '*Odium Theologicum.*' Envious of our growing respectability here, the saints wish to 'rob us of that which cannot enrich themselves, but which will make us poor indeed'—the good name we bear.

"Would you could have seen the sapients on the bench look at each other when Miss Roalfe asked the witness, the only witness that had read any of the prosecuted books, 'what effect was produced upon his mind?' The persecutor's own witness declaring 'he did not consider himself the less moral in consequence of having read the books.'

"With evidence of this kind, how, I ask, could the 'children of grace' dare to prosecute any more, upon the same pretence that poor Finlay and Paterson are incarcerated in a cold cell, solitary confinement, subjected to all the treatment of common felons, the pretence of protecting public morals! Monstrous! is it the 19th century or the 9th in which we live?

"Since the trial of Miss Roalfe, some friends(?), I make no doubt, pious christians, have been in the habit of paying me a visit, for what purpose, think you? 'Aye, there's the rub.' It was not for 'God v. Paterson,' 'Trinity of Trinities,' 'Godology,' 'The Bible an Improper Book for Youth,' 'A Home Thrust at the Atrocious Trinity,' nor 'God's Gifts.' No, I say not for any of these books; but for *Fanny Hill, The Exquisite, Aristotle,* &c.,

"Now, can you see what 'God's People' would be at? I usually tell such parties that 'we don't sell indecent books, but have no doubt that they can be got at some *Religious Tract Warehouse,* or, perhaps, the Bible will suit them."

I am having copied, "Man Thinking," and posting it as fast as it is ready to Paterson. This may suggest to our friends in what way they may contribute to his amusement.   G. J. H.

DR. KEENAN'S SECOND LECTURE.

The novel and highly interesting views on the subject of man, in connection with physiology, pathology, chemistry, &c., were developed and maintained with a force of reasoning and a copiousness of illustration which charmed and instructed a most intelligent audience.

The use, operations, and effects of food,

its two-fold nature, as distinguished according to the most recent researches of physiologists and chemists, into respiratory and nutritive, and the beautiful correspondence of its action, in the animal machine, with that of the zinc plate in the galvanic machine, formed the principal topics of the evening's discourse.

The rationale of situation, air, climate, foods, was explained. Thus localities confined between hills, in which a stagnation of air was the consequence, were seen to produce the most direful diseases. Cretinism, one of the forms of disease most prominently conspicuous to visitors of the hills of Switzerland, was asserted to be more or less prevalent, in various forms and modifications, under similar circumstances in our own country. Oxydization should go on, and for this a continual motion of the air must prevail. The conditions necessary for the healthy, vigorous action of the animal, or of the electro-motive machine to generate greater power, vivacity, and flow of spirits, were increased oxydization of the blood, for which oxydizable food taken in by the mouth, and oxygenised air by the nostrils, were essential. These operations were facilitated as already described by width and expansiveness of chest, which gave greater command over their hearers to the orator, the lawyer, the divine, the actor. Liebig's theory of the generation of heat was then considered and combatted, motion being substituted by the lecturer for the heat theory of the great chemist. What Liebig denominated the disintegration of the tissues, or the gradual destruction and re-production of the animal fibre, was pronounced by the doctor as a tissue of gross errors. Were we renewed about every seven years, according to commonly received notions, we should be re-juvenised, instead of acquiring old brittle bones and rigid muscles, and marks would not continue from childhood, to old age.

The doctor ran through a few striking phenomena connected with some leading species or remarkable individuals belonging to the animal kingdom, expatiated on the protection afforded to the electro-motive machinery by the respective coverings of skin, hair, feathers,—of the peculiarities of the gymnotus, or electrical eel, &c., with a profusion of interesting facts bearing pointedly on the views he was propounding. The nature and properties of oxygenised and non-oxygenised food were discoursed on, as butter, wine, &c., on the one hand, and albumen of egg, red fibre of meat, blood, on the other. Dr. Keenan insisted on the importance in every stage of the process of discussing fundamentals, and aptly illustrated the instance of the great divergence of the summit of a wall or building arising from a very slight deviation at its base.

He very modestly repudiated all intention of being understood to settle the truth, but in helping to narrow the track others would at any rate be enabled, with the greater ease and satisfaction, to arrive at true results, or approach nearer. He differed from Liebig, he begged it to be understood, in no cavilling or captious spirit, and admirably drew a line of distinction between a due regard for, and deference to, men of such distinguished ability, and that fatal servility which had so long thrown impediments in the paths of science.

The Doctor is next to take into consideration the effects of intoxicating liquors as to benefits or disadvantages, the production of strength and weakness, adaptation of the constitution to climate and profession, false calculations of teachers and parents.

The tenth, seventeenth, and twenty-fourth of February, and second of March, are the appointed days. The lectures are delivered in the theatre of the Polytechnic Institution, at eight in the evening.

ADVICE TO A FRIEND.—Lord Clarendon commends that sentiment of Seneca in which that ancient reproaches mankind for the common complaint, that men in place and authority are never at liberty, never at leisure to be spoken to Yet, says Seneca, with all their business, they do sometimes give audiences, while men generally are never vacant, never at liberty to speak to themselves. The idea here conveyed opens a fountain of profound and useful thought. This self-study is *the* source of individual improvement. You will find nothing more profitable than to often employ yourself with yourself. It is one of the great consolations that though you cannot speak to others you cannot be prevented speaking to yourself. Then do this. Begin with the first moment of consciousness, and trace up all subsequent sensations. Recal all old thoughts, events, acts. Enquire what your experience has been—become familiar with it. Go over it and over it, until every principal event can be called up at pleasure. Ask what they have taught you. Deduce maxims of worldly wisdom from your own connections with the world. Trace the rise of your knowledge—classify it, sum it up. Find out the guides of your conduct, the principles which regulate your reasonings, the axioms of your life The best of men are those who have best understood themselves. Gibbon, Pemberton, Emerson, owe their freshness and beauty to this. No man knows others who does not know himself. The world is never so well seen as through the spectacles of our own experience.

LEICESTER.—The branch of the Rational Society in this town have issued an address to the public, containing these spirited sentiments.

They find that the System they are promulgating is misrepresented (either through ignorance or design) by preachers of religion; that *they* are its most determined opponents; that *they* place the two Systems in antagonism before the public mind —until at last the conclusion has been forced upon them, that before the truths of that system can make great way among the minds of the people, the errors of religion must be removed.

Hitherto they have refrained from making any direct attack upon religious error, from a disposition not unnecessarily to wound the feelings of any individual; but believing that the *principles* of religion are demonstrably false; they think the time is come when they should be brought to the test of reason and of public examination.

Some say religion is too sacred and holy a thing to be brought into the arena of public debate. We reply—we *cannot* regard *that* holy or sacred which appears to our minds *false*. We say to the public teachers of this religion, that as we hold *them* to be sincere believers in the *truth* and beneficial influence of the religion they from week to week expound, they are morally bound to come forward and defend that truth and beneficial influence against *those* who as *sincerely* believe that this religion is false, and of necessity leads to erroneous practice.

THE ANTI-PERSECUTION UNION.—To ensure the assistance of the friends of real freedom, the Union need only state the fact that four persons are at this moment suffering in the dungeon's gloom, merely for publishing what they conceive to be the truth on theological matters. The Union would ask the Christian observer of these proceedings—Does persecution form part and parcel of Christianity? If it does not, then should the Christian assist the Union in endeavouring to establish the right of free discussion, for the truth can never suffer from free enquiry. We surely cannot investigate too closely that which we are told concerns our eternal welfare.

To the lukewarm, who affirm that the Law of Blasphemy will not affect them or their children, as they have assured to them a religious education, the Union would suggest that experience teaches that we cannot ensure our opinions for an hour; and as we cannot foresee what circumstances our children may be placed in, it becomes our duty to endeavour to procure for them the right to express their opinions upon all subjects. Until this is the case we shall never arrive at that state of freedom necessary for the true happiness of the human family. To obtain this is the object of the Anti-Persecution Union: need more be said to enlist the aid of honest men. W. H. B.

THE "BOY CLARKE."—Wants a place —who knows of one?

TO CORRESPONDENTS.

F. GILDER.—We have handed his letter the Secretary of the Atheistical Society. If his suggestions are adopted, he will see some recommendation on the subject.

Mr. H. WOOD.—We have written to him at "Edinburgh, New Town," the address he gives, but have received no answer. No tidings of him can be learned, in Edinburgh, by our friends. Unless he reveals himself, we shall not publish his letter.

MR. THORNLEY, Huddersfield.—Will receive a parcel through Mr. Cleave.

Received. — "The Regenerator," and "Lines on Thomas Paine, by J. Watkins."

ADDRESSES.

Mr. Paterson, Gaol, Perth.
Miss Roalfe, Gaol, Edinburgh.

ANTI-PERSECUTION UNION,

Subscriptions received.

Per Mr. Holyoak, Leicester.
Mr. Plant - - - - -	0	1	0
Mr. Gimson - - - - -	0	1	0
Mrs. and Mr. Chamberlin - -	0	2	0
Mr. Cook - - - - -	0	1	0
Mr. Hall - - - - -	0	1	0
Per Friends	0	7	6
Mr. Coltman, a very ancient friend of the persecuted, Leicester -	0	3	6
From a dozen Christians averse to persecution, collected by W. B. C.	0	6	0
W. B. C. - - - - -	0	2	0
A. or Z. - - - - -	1	0	0
A Friend, per Mrs. Martin - -	0	2	6
Mr. Goosey - - - - -	0	1	0

G. J. Holyoake, Secretary.

Printed and Published by G. J. HOLYOAKE, 40, Holywell-street, Strand, London.
Saturday, Feb. 10, 1844.

THE MOVEMENT
And Anti=Persecution Gazette.

"Maximize morals, minimize religion."—BENTHAM.

No. 10.   EDITED BY G. JACOB HOLYOAKE, ASSISTED BY M. Q. RYALL.   PRICE 1½d

THE CHARTISTS AND THEIR CENSORS.

A LETTER *from Mr. Lovett to Messrs. Donaldson and Mason.* A LETTER *from J. H. Parry to F. O'Connor.* AN ANSWER *to J. H. Parry by George White.* A LETTER *to J. H. Parry by F. O'Connor.* AN IMPEACHMENT *of F. O'Connor by John Watkins.* THE REJECTED LETTERS *of W. Hill.* A LETTER *from F. O'Connor to the Rev. W. Hill, and* A SCABBARD *for F. O'Connor's Sword.*

THESE are a series of pamphlets which have lately inundated the Chartist world. Upon their several merits and faults it would be difficult to pronounce an impartial opinion. It would seem that Chartists had turned for a time from the examination of their principles to the criticism of themselves—and the complete Suffragists from the extension of their views to the destruction of O'Connor. It really appears of less importance to build up republicanism, than to pull down the proprietor of the *Northern Star.* How far persons ought to be considered as affecting principles, is a question in policy and morals, little understood, and far from being settled. He would do no mean service to Reformers who should put this point in a clear and conclusive light. When the great National Petition was presented in the Commons, Mr. Roebuck paved the way to its rejection, by informing the house that it was drawn up by disreputable parties. If this was the case —though I do not believe a word of it—out of the three-and-a-half millions said to have signed it, certainly three millions did not know, nor did they care who drew it up. They signed it because they approved its contents, and those only were the legitimate grounds of discussion, and not Mr. Roebuck's estimation of Mr. Feargus O'Connor. The *American Beacon,* quoted from in a recent number, says that Mr. Robert Owen is considered to be the "tool of the aristocracy." But no sound Socialist cares one jot whether this is so or not. What Mr. Owen *is,* does not affect the truth of what Mr. Owen *says.* Socialism is excellent in itself, and if it is not, Mr. Owen being an archangel, won't make it any better. If socialism comes from the aristocracy it is certainly one of the best things they ever helped the nation to, either by accident or design. So of Chartism, its merits and demerits are quite independent of Mr. Lovett, or Feargus O'Connor, of the *Nonconformist* or the *Northern Star.* It is the prime mistake of parties to divide about men rather than measures. Bad men sometimes say the best of things, and good men often give pernicious advice. The question of character belongs rather to the closet than to the forum, it is doubtless one of vast importance, but it oftener divides than enlightens "King Mob." With Mr. O'Connor I have had little intercourse, but judging of him from these pamphlets he does *not* appear to the great disadvantage that his numerous and highly incensed enemies set forth. Of the "tools" of Mr. O'Connor, as they are contemptuously termed, I do know something, and what it is I am proud to state, at this time, when storms of odious epithets are showering on them. Mr. George White is a plain blunt man, but he is honest. At the hands of the government he has suffered severely and borne it as bravely as any one. The *Sheffield Iris,* edited by a gentleman whom all who know him lastingly esteem, led me, many years ago, to regard Mr. Julian Harney, as a traitor in the pay of the government. But I believe the editor of the *Iris* to have been misled. Filled with these ungenerous suspicions, I first saw Mr. Harney at those Birmingham riots, which led to Mr. Lovett's and Collins's imprisonments. Mr. Harney lived opposite my door, and, unkind to him, I watched him with a jealous eye. Subsequently, I invited him to my house in Sheffield, and what I saw and heard in his unguarded moments fixed him in my esteem and confidence. And Mr. Paterson, whom no cold hearted man ever yet beguiled, highly esteemed him. The way of a working man is hard—if he sinks under his fetters he is called slave and coward—if he breaks them off, the law grasps at him with bloody fangs—if he eludes the clutch, his brethren stigmatize him *tool* and *spy.* A poor man is struck down by his enemies, because he struggles for liberty, and is spurned by his friends because he does it in some unconventional way—as though a man, maddened with oppression, could always put on holiday smiles, and exhibit the blandness he cannot feel. Let us hope for humanity's sake, that this wrong is done unwillingly. Those who know the working classes best, and have mixed with them most, who have lived on their hearths, enjoyed their confidence, shared their suffering and struggles will believe them worthy of the noblest cause, and the leaders, rising from their ranks, incapable of becoming, knowingly, the tools of any man.

G. J. H.

SENTIMENTAL THEISTS AND NATURAL THEOLOGY.

IV.

I HAVE said that that paltry jesuitry by which anything is pretended and nothing is honestly meant, every Rationalist should "hoot out of his presence:" Holyoake in his "Paley" has done this, and herein lies not the least of his merits—"Detesting the plausible, and never resting till he has stripped it bare;" he will have nothing to do with sentiment where sentiment has nothing to do with him or his philosophy. Everything he writes is not only intelligible but consistent. His readers don't find an appeal to reason in one page, and an appeal to sentiment in another; here an injunction to draw down wisdom from the head—there to pump it up from the heart. No, he appeals to the principle of human reason, solely, as a fallible standard to be sure, but still a standard men's senses can judge of—still a standard infinitely nearer perfection than any other, and still a standard to the test of which sentimentarians themselves, struggle as they may, must bring their systems. Mr. Holyoake says with much point (p. 34.) that "Paley himself pays homage to reason, for he commences his enquiry appealing to it. But that which guided his first steps, should have guided his last." Undoubtedly it should. No such thing however. Mr. Holyoake's pamphlet demonstrates that Paley's guide at the beginning of his argument was dispensed with at the end of it. Paley's attachment to reason, is precisely the sort of attachment manifested by almost all theists, lay or clerical, scientific or unscientific, who have come within the circle of my experience. With few exceptions I have found them favourable to reason when reason was favourable to them; the majority of them are constantly so far liberal, and no farther. An amusing illustration of this peculiar liberality fell under my notice while in Bristol. When a bookseller there, a foreigner came into my shop upon a certain occasion, and after examining the library, talked very fluently for nearly a couple of hours; I listened with pleasure as well as attention, (for his command of words and the extensiveness of his general information, perfectly astonished me), contenting myself by interjecting a phrase now and then; most admirably did he reason against bad political and religious systems; urging with much vehemence of gesture, the absolute necessity of enlightening humanity; of emancipating nations by freeing them from the pernicious influence of priestcraft, which blessed results he assured me, could never be *un fait accompli*, until superstitious nations should be made so far reasonable as to embrace Deism. And why not Atheism, I interposed? Oh, he exclaimed, at the same time raising his hands, and nearly burying his head between his shoulders: Atheism is *terribille mar haaarte, mar haaarte*, tells me there is *von* God. Ah, rejoined I, perhaps so, but it is your *head*, not your *heart*, at which I aim. But no, his "believing spirit," so far as related to God, I found "immovable," though on all other topics he followed "the light of nature and reason." The horror depicted in his countenance when the word Atheism was mentioned, the abruptness with which he broke off the conversation and hurried out of the shop, convinced me that he had no objection to reason if I had stopped at Whiggery in politics and Deism in religion. Atheism he abhorred, because he felt it was abominable; his heart told him so. Deism he loved, because he knew it was reasonable, his head assured him so. Verily he is a rationalist worthy to be associated with our Paleys and Broughams, and Blackwood writers. By scouting the unprincipled principle of these blind leaders of a blind world, Mr. Holyoke has done that world more service than it is yet prepared rightly to estimate. The time has come when the friends of human melioration and progress should "speak out" in reprobation of those least consistent of inconsistent enemies, who play "fast and loose" with reason, extolling it as a "divine faculty," when some selfish end is to be achieved by its use, and denouncing it as devilish, when more is to be gained by its abuse. Thus, to borrow the expressive words of an atheistical philosopher, John Stewart" the disciple of reason is bewildered and lost, and man is hoodwinked, like the miller's horse, to make him move in the same beaten track.

Let us be consistent, "Consistency," says Mr. Holyoake, "is the rarest of intellectual powers, as it is the rarest of moral virtues." It is so. Now to vamp up reason in one page, and cry it down in the next, is gross inconsistency. Undoubtedly there are mysteries reason cannot furnish an explanation of.

The fact is frankly admitted by its advocates. Atheists are consistent advocates of reason; they do not use it to-day and abuse it to-morrow; Mr. Holyoake in the introduction to his pamphlet states that "The existence of Deity is a question upon which research has been employed to no purpose, and learning has been expended in vain. Ingenuity has not been able to show more than that nothing can be known. The penetration of the man of science, and the zeal of the devotee have been alike baffled, and the honest saint has agreed with the sceptic, that incomprehensible is God's name. In all ages the sober have sat down with the conviction of Simonides, that study has brought with it no satisfaction, and that the more they have thought, the less they have understood. Under these circumstances it would be wise, as Locke expresses it, to sit down in quiet ignorance of this subject, which has been found beyond the reach of our capacities."

This is the language of good sense; the opinion it bodies forth is forcing its way through all the ramifications of societarian prejudices with wonderful rapidity. There does not exist any power adequate to stop, or even impede its progress. Sentimental theists, and all other reasoners "thus far and no farther," have placed themselves in a position analogous to that of the idiot, who drew back the bolts of the flood-gate, and was borne away by the torrent. Yes, the bolts of reason's flood-gate have been drawn back by the priests themselves; our Paleys, our Clarkes, and our Fenelons. These are the rash priests, who, by their vain attempts to reason us into belief in the being of a God, have done more than any other writers to let in upon the world a deluge of Atheism which is carrying dismay into the hearts of priests, for they feel that in its destructive course every vestige of religion will be swept away. Never was Christianity in a condition more rickety, or the Christian's God in a condition more perilous. Natural theology is attacked on all sides, and fast sinking into the grave of contempt. Yet, if natural theology perish, Christianity must perish with it. Lord Brougham admits, that without the prop of natural theology, the truths of revelation would have no other bases than vague tradition.

DE LAMARTINE'S LETTERS ON HISTORY.

II.

If you would form the judgment of the masses, and withdraw them from the immoral theory of success, do something which has not been done before: give *history a conscience*. This is the work of the time; this is the work worthy of the people, and the enterprise worthy of yourself. By an historical plan of this kind you may not so immediately gratify the excitable feelings of the masses, but you will a thousand times better serve their cause, interests, and reason. For instance, here is one of the greatest events of the century; one of those days that decide the fate of a revolution—a nation and an empire—the 18th Brumaire. You will, no doubt, have to relate it; how will you consider it in the point of view of glory? It is dazzling, it glitters like an unsheathed sword in the sun, it whirlwinds like the dust of a passing squadron, filling the ears with noise, and the eyes with brightness. A man from afar off issued from the camp, preceded by his name, supported by his renown, accustomed to discipline. Tired of the slowness, the resistance, and importunate noise of a discussing government; and impatient of the sluggish and collective work of the liberty to be founded, he avails himself of a moment of discouragement of the public spirit, mounts at the head of some grenadiers, cuts to pieces with his sword the whole of this republican machine, and says to the empire "you can but talk, I am for action." He succeeds; the revolution falls into his own hands—he transforms it to his fancy, not knowing how to make a nation of it—he makes an army, whom he throws upon the world—infatuates with victories, and causes to place the crown on his head. Is it not glorious! Trumpet it forth—blazon it all before the masses. They will be dazzled —will you have instructed them?

Would you consider the same event in the point of view of national patriotism? The people see themselves everywhere in the image of their *victorious* army; French patriotism expands to the extent of the Continent; it says "Europe is myself;" The fact so presented, you would thus fanaticise the masses as an event which has deprived them of all the fruits of the revolution before they were ripe, and of all moral conquests of the eighteenth century. Will you have elevated them?

Finally, would you regard this event in the point of view of the morality of the action, and of true civilization? All is changed; here is a man, whom the free government of his country have entrusted with an army for defending it against factions, and, who turns it into a military faction against this government. Here is a revolution—terrible, anarchical, bloody; which, by the sole power of the public spirit, and by the free play of civil re-actions, had gone through the most deplorable crises; washed its hands, ashamed of the blood odiously shed; blushed at the proscriptions; began to find its centre of gravity between demagogism and despotism, and the unorganized movements of which tended every day to moderation, and to a regularity and permanency of liberty. This man appears; he arrests the revolutionary movement at the very moment when it had disenthralled itself: sets up a re-action against a liberty that commenced already to re-act by itself, and, arming himself with the instruments of the revolution itself, he crushes the rising liberty with the fragments she has overthrown for her breaking forth. He re-builds an old regimen with things and names of yesterday; he forces the press to retrograde to the censorship; the rostrum to silence, equality to a noblesse of Plebeians; liberty to the prisons of state; philosophy and independance of worship to a concordat, to a state religion—instrument of power, to a coronation, to the oppression and captivity of a pontiff. He stifles all over Europe the love and pacific dissemination of such ideas, in order to employ only the odious arms of violence and conquest. What is the end of this drama, with one sole actor, instead of the great national and European drama, which the revolution, when regular and left to its own impulse, could have shown during these last thirty years? You see it—but one name more in history, and Europe is twice in Paris; the limits of France more confined by the distrustful unquietness of the suspicious West; and England realising without a rival, the universal monarchy of the seas; in France herself, reason, liberty, and the masses infinitely retarded by this episode of glory, and having, perhaps, to pass more than a century in regaining the ground lost in one single day. This is the 18th Brumaire in its three views. Need I tell you mine?

(To be continued.)

THE A POSTERIORI ARGUMENT AND ATTRIBUTES OF DEITY.

THE *a posteriori* argument, though founded on a mere *petitio principii*, exercises a powerful influence, by moulding and directing men in consentaneity with the will and interest of the priestarchy. It may, therefore, be useful to present its fallacy in every distinct point of view:

Whether there is or is not perfect adaptation—whether adaptation proves anything more than suitability of circumstances—or whether suitable circumstances must necessarily be preceded by intelligence, I will not now dispute, but will allow that design is manifested in the object we behold.

Origen Bachelor has been good enough to tell us that "less than infinite wisdom could not construct the veriest insect." He also asks "What finite being could sustain himself on nothing, and roll one twinkling star, or sweep a flaming comet through the mighty void. This is the illogical rant of theology —to be sure it is sublime, but then it is only sublime nonsense. Animals are finite in extent and operation, therefore, if wisdom, goodness, and power be displayed in their organizations, they can only be so to a limited extent. *Infinite properties can only be displayed through infinite manifestations.* But man, being finite, can never become cognizant of infinite manifestations, and he is only justified in admitting infinity when its denial involves an absurdity or impossibility.

It may probably be objected that there is an infinite manifestation of design, because the universe is infinite in extent. But we do not know that things are in a similar condition everywhere. Because this part of the universe exhibits marks of design, it is not reasonable to conclude that this condition is universal, and similar marks exists everywhere. No reasons are known why things should or should not be different in other parts of the universe. We cannot judge of that of which we are ignorant. We can only comprehend a finite portion of the universe, and perceive a limited number of facts, which, on theological premises, merely prove a limited amount of wisdom, goodness, and power. The Theists then, even admitting the ground of their reasoning to be correct, have no authority whatever for affirming the existence of a deity infinitely wise, good, and powerful.

RICHARD DOYLE.

REVIEW.

LETTERS *of J. P. Greaves to Alexander Campbel.* Concordium Press.

THIS is an interesting exposition of the cogitation of that eccentric and benevolent mystic James Pierrepont Greaves. But with all its strangeness, that which is said by the friend of Pestalozzi, for such was Mr. Greaves, deserves attention. The letters are addressed to a gentleman who combines the mystic, the good-natured, and the intelligible in the prettiest proportions imaginable. The "Life," prefixed to the letters, is well written and full of interest. I do not intend this remark to apply to that passage which tells us that "On the morning of the 11th of March, 1842, the love-prepared soul was withdrawn from its earthly mansion to the more *extensive sphere of celestial activity.*" Here Mr. Greaves's life retires beyond all criticism, where neither senses nor interest can follow, and only Mr. Campbell can see into the deep secret. Nine axioms are prefixed to the "Letters," but only the third can be understood by ordinary mortals, and that one is an old favourite from Euclid, meaning that things which are equal to the same thing are equal to one another.

The strange terms which Greaves employs very much impairs the usefulness of his letters. I quarrel not with his style, but with those dim and spiritualized conceptions which gave it birth. He seems perpetually to hold converse with dusky sprites, flitting to and fro in the twilight of imagination, belonging neither to nature nor strong fancy. Mr. Greaves resembled a fossil remain of a past age. He was more the child of mythology than of the order of Rationalists. The ancients would have made him the teacher of the Sybils, and Shakspere would have wedded him to Hecate. Still, I have so much faith that there is good in him, that I will get my friend Campbell to initiate me that I may find it out.

DR. GRAHAM'S LECTURE on *Chastity*, republished at the Concordium Press.

It is a delightful thing to praise, but it cannot always be done honestly. In Dr. Graham's book there is but the *object* of it that is worthy of commendation. If the great subject of a book merits approval, it is undoubtedly much in its favour, but good objects should always be accompanied by great graces. The "Lecture on Chastity" is grave, which it need not be. It is a book of one or two eminently useful ideas with their natural charms, obscured by heavy long-drawn sentences, and buried under heaps of verboseness. The lecture should have been re-written. It would have been invested with grace and vivacity, condensed to half its present size, and made far more useful and instructive. This should have been done, as its subject is one of first importance, and is supported by facts which deserve careful attention.

With all its drawbacks, Dr. Graham's lecture contains valuable information, and should be in the hands of all young persons. Chastity is a difficult subject to treat. The world finds ready fault with its great vices, but will scarcely permit any one to give the proper information for their correction. The doctor's subject requires to be touched with a bold and delicate hand. Nothing is of more importance, in societarian questions, than the preservation of delicacy of thought and conduct. Few men are qualified to treat the choice refinements of life and love so as to remedy the errors of ignorance, without offending delicacy of sentiment. The physiology of "chastity," Dr. Graham treats with propriety, and he advances the most satisfactory reasons for temperance in love of any author with whom I am acquainted.

FOURIERISM.—A series of papers under the head of "Phalansterian Tracts" are being issued from the Phalanx Office. No. 1 is on *National Emigration*, No. 2 on *High Rents and Low Wages*. They promise to be a popular and useful exposition of the views of this intelligent order of reformers.

GATHERINGS ABROAD.

EDUCATION and the press are declared free in Belgium; there are universities and primary schools supported by government, but not equal to the wants of the population. The University at Brussells is called the free, because open to all classes: at Louvain there is a university confined to Catholicism. The professors of philosophy, morals and history inculcate indirectly Pantheism, and speak against religion to the horror of the Catholic party. Education being free, the Catholics have established seminaries, which teach at a lower price than any other schools, and, consequently, to their own profit or the increase of religion. The same complaint is made in France—the reason is obvious, if the clergy is paid in each country, they have that to depend upon besides education; and, therefore, can make it comparatively gratuitous on their part. Throughout Europe, at least France, Belgium, and England, there is a great struggle between parties to get education into their hands, on the issue of the competition depends in a great measure the destinies of mankind. The anti-movement party, the ecclesiastical and aristocratical, are fully aware that education given by themselves, is the best way to make the human mind subservient to their persuasions and interests. Besides public money they have more than others private funds at their disposal, and have the vantage ground over their antagonists. There are 35,000 priests in France; in Belgium there have never been so many since the time of the Austrians, when Joseph II. fell, in the endeavour to crush them. In England there are 10,000 of the established church, they can employ superstition in their favor, the authority of the upper classes is given them over the low, and the unwilling dare not resist, but are obliged to go along with the current of society and public opinion, which has, at present, all the elements of power.

The press being entirely free in Belgium gives the most umbrage to the clergy. Association appears to be unfettered, and they have entered into one, only to allow certain newspapers and books to be read by the Catholic party. Nearly all the principal journals of Belgium, to the number of half-a-dozen, are mentioned by name as forbidden to be read. The literature of Belgium being entirely French, it is to be supposed the reading would be of a very free character, but the Catholics, with the Archibishop of Malines at the head of their society for good books, would put France *hors de cambat* in their index expurgatorius. The priests cannot yet boast of a Times newspaper in their favor, and the present ministry in Belgium is not considered the Catholic *par excellence*. The Queen is considered a fanatic, and gives all her influence and exertions in favor of the clergy; the King does not lead but follows the most powerful party. The poor are supported chiefly by voluntary contributions, and the clergy in their quality of alms-givers get all the influence which the distributions of money gives. There was a democratic petition presented to the houses, said to have had a million of signatures, demanding employment, and the suffrage, but on some informality the petition was not received, and the number were said to have been exaggerated. There is a large sort of poor-house at Brussels where beggars are sent, on the same principle as the union workhouses in England, women and children in one department, the men in another. There are said to be a population of 100,000 in Brussels, and 33,000 in the last three years' account were said to have received charity, but it was hinted that not really more than 23,000 poor had actually been on the books; the money for 10,000 having found its way into other pockets. Belgium on the whole having a greater population than England, has large tracts of waste land, to the cultivation of which at the present moment, the Chambers have turned their attention, but have not yet made their arrangements. The value of land is said to rise in Belgium—famous for its good agriculture, and for small farms, particularly in the province of Flanders.

W. J. B.

PERSECUTION OF THE JEWS IN LITHUANIA.

WARSAW, JAN. 22.—You will with difficulty credit the extent to which the persecution of the Jews of this country by order of the Government of His Majesty the Emperor Nicholas is extending. I shall, however, be brief in my reference to it.

An Imperial ukase has been received in Lithuania directing the authorities of towns and other localities inhabited by Jews to transport those unhappy persons, amounting to 36,000 families, to a distance of 12 leagues from their several actual places of residence. This cruel ukase was further to receive its execution before the 18th inst., so that, at a moderate estimate, 150,000 persons of both sexes, and of all ages and conditions, are at this moment, in the midst of all the rigours of a Lithuanian winter, expelled their houses, and forced to seek a resting-place in strange countries, and not merely among strangers, but among people predisposed to view them as outcasts, and objects for extortion, persecution, and violence.

Sacrificing a great principle in order to protect a suffering race, Europe interfered between the Greeks and their butchers. Here is a case for intervention not less urgent. Will the Christian Powers of Europe remain silent and inactive in the presence of such horrors?—*Times*, Feb. 8.

THE DELUGE.

A fine conception of this subject may be seen in a window in Chancery-lane. It is an engraving of a painting said to have been executed by Girodèt, purchased by Napoleon for £10,000, and by him placed in the Louvre at Paris. Girodèt also received the coronet and £2000, being the prize offered for the best historical painting. The lithographic, of which I speak, is extremely scarce and beautiful. Girodèt has not crowded a multitude of awful objects together, but has drawn one scene, which alone strikes the observer with a full and overwhelming sense of the desolation and agony of a drowning world. One solitary rock that seems to enter the bursting cataracts in the skies, is all of earth that is beheld, and that is nearly covered, while all around is one dreary waste of haze and water. Up this rock a man has climbed with his aged father on his back, who seems blind with age, and clips with feeble hands his son's neck. With one hand his son is dragging up his wife who hangs apparently lifeless with a fine child on her bosom, and an elder child nearly enveloped in water is supporting himself by clinging to her hair. With these to support with one hand, and the weight of his father on his shoulders, the son grasps the single bough of an old tree, which is bending and giving way every moment There they hang with the clouds bursting above, the tree bending, and the ocean of waters rising higher and higher. In the fearful agony of this scene, the spectator wonders how a God of mercy and love could look on that spectacle unmoved. A demon would have rushed to their deliverance. This picture is a most eloquent argument against the monstrous fiction of the deluge; it is given as the reason that men were depraved and lost to virtue. Such noble devotion as this son exhibits in periling his own life to save his wife and children and his aged father, cannot be surpassed in the history of humanity. It is the noblest part of filial affection. One feels, on seeing the poor old man joining his feeble hands to hold on his son, and as the wife saving, even when senseless, her child from death, that the son and husband deserve all the heavens that ever were conceived. The plate is proposed to be published in this country by subscription of 10s. for one impression, and £1 for India proofs. I could not desire more than that a copy might be hung up in every chapel in the kingdom.

G. J. H.

EMIGRATION.

THE Albion Phalanx Emigration Association meet every Monday evening at eight o'clock, at the Devon and Exeter coffee-house, Tottenham-court-road, and every Wednesday evening at Sutterby's coffee-house, opposite the Rotunda, Blackfriars-road. The Democratic Co-operative Society for emigrating to the Western States of North America, meet at Hudson's coffee-house, Upper Wellington-street, Covent-garden. Secretary, Mr. C. Sully, 11, Roll's-buildings, Fetterlane.

Interesting lectures on EMIGRATION are being delivered every Wednesday evening at the Turnagain-lane Institution, by a gentleman who lately emigrated to the Western States.

THE LAST JUDGMENT.

THE following elegant description of the last judgment was once delivered to a Coventry audience in a lecture on Socialism by a gentleman from Manchester, who is now an accredited ex-pounder of " the principles." It is a curious reminiscence of original Socialistic true Christianity. The lecturer commenced thus:—

" I am going to preach you a sermon : my text is, ' Inasmuch as ye did it not unto the least of these my brethren, ye did it not unto me.' Well, let us suppose that we are present at the day of judgment ;—well there sits God Almighty on a great three-legged stool —I beg pardon, I mean a throne—no matter, there he sits; the religious world march up to take heaven by storm, when the judge calls out, ' Hillo! where do you come from ? what have you been doing in the other world?' ' O Lord,' answer they, ' we are the believers; we went to places of worship; we had to do with Bible and Religious Tract Societies ; we were the religionists of the world.' ' O don't bother me with your stuff; tell me what you have been doing for your fellow men.' ' O Lord,' reply the religious, ' we had not time to do anything for them.' ' Stand on one side,' says the judge. Presently he sees in the distance a lot of trembling gloomy characters, and calls out to them, ' Well, what have you been doing in the other world.' ' Lord, we did not believe; we did not worship.' Oh don't bother me with that stuff; what have you been doing for your fellow men ?' The second lot answer that they had been doing all they could in that respect ; whereupon the judge laid hold of their heels and chucked them up into heaven ; but turning to the first lot, he lifts up his foot and says, ' Go to hell with you ! you are bothering me as you did in the other world.' "

DR. KEENAN'S THIRD LECTURE.

THE lecture room of the Polytechnic Institution was attended on Saturday evening by a more numerous audience than before, and Mr. Keenan's address kept alive the attention of his hearers with unabated interest to the end. The operations of the animal machine, more especially those of the stomach and lungs, were considered in relation to the influence upon the system, of one class of food in particular. Food having hitherto been considered only as nutritive, or for supplying the waste, and wear and tear of the body, all foods that were supposed unfitted for assimilation, or, in other words, that were not absorbed by, and become part of, the blood, have been supposed useless or pernicious. This error arose from ignorance of the true functions of the lungs and the action of the blood. The human machine had been viewed in a different light, from other machines, which precisely resembled it. A supply in both cases was needed, not only for the sustainment of the apparatus, but the motive force, which caused it to work. How beautiful and perfect the resemblance, was seen by comparing the human body with the galvanic battery, and the hydroelective machine, both of which are combined in each individual. The nerves of the one corresponded with the wires of the other, in each a fluid passed rapidly through small tubes, being the blood traversing the veins of the one machine, and the steam rushing through the iron pipes of the other. Our researches once directed in this track, this simple and beautiful analogy once obtained, we had the key to hitherto unsolvable mysteries. Knowing that the blood, previously considered as altogether for nourishment or re-production, was also the origin of the motive force, we are enabled to approximate to more correct views theologically and practically. Thus, alcoholic drinks have been, without qualification, reprehended on account of their non-affinities or non-similitude with the blood, being found to contain no phosphate of lime for the formation of the bones, and other requisites for the building up of the animal machine; ascertained to be non-digestible, and therefore non-nutritive—they have been by some theorists utterly condemned as unfit for supplying the system. We are taught on the contrary by rightly considering the subject that, wines, spirits, and other stimulants, however injurious to those with certain functional derangements, as for instance diseased liver, may under other circumstances act beneficially. In the one set of cases nutrition is imperfectly performed, while the motive forces require no extra propulsion, in the other the nutritive functions act energetically, while motion is imperfectly generated. These are but further developments of the important fundamental doctrine of the double functions of food, the nutritive and the respiratory.

Small chested persons—those who are located in a stagnant and humid atmosphere, may advantageously have recourse to the more oxygenised food. A glass of wine or spirituous liquor, will, in such cases, prove beneficial; the every-day experience of men shown in their national customs have frequently anticipated the discoveries of philosophers; the Dutch and French are examples of this. Poets have equally hit upon the truth—men of science thus frequently do not precede to discover, but follow to explain. The subject, however novel and interesting, must be closed for want of space, the bare enumeration of topics would trespass too far on the limits of this half sheet; a full notice would not be contained in an entire number.

EDINBURGH.—That precious journal the *Edinburgh Evening Post*, edited apparently like our *Morning Post*, by some inimitable Jenkins, has given an article on Miss Roalfe's trial. The charming scribe, in a long tissue of ferocious abuse, calls reason a *vile* goddess—infidelity the spawn of vice; and, after exhausting his vocabulary of these elegancies, argues that infidelity should be suppressed by the law, on the ground of its vulgarity and indecency.

RELIGIOUS INTELLIGENCE.—The Rev. Mr. Sperry, who has been for some years in the receipt of a handsome salary for preaching against Catholicism in Pennsylvania, has been detected at Pottsville, in that state, in the sanctified error of "vending obscene books."

NOTICES.

Mr. Southwell, on the 16th of last month, handed to Miss Roalfe £2 17s. 10d. being the balance (expences being paid) of collection at the Social Hall, Glasgow.

A friend has three complete volumes, in boards, of the NEW MORAL WORLD, of the years 1838-9 and 40, to be sold for 9s. Some person making-up sets may desire these. They can be had at the office.

Mr. George Smith, of 5, Greengate, Salford, is still the authorised collector of the Anti-Persecution Union. Do our friends in Manchester understand what this gentleman was appointed for?

ADDRESSES.

Miss Matilda Roalfe, prisoner for blasphemy, Gaol, Edinburgh.
Mr. Thomas Paterson, prisoner for blasphemy, Goal, Perth.
The Secretary of the Anti-Persecution Union, G. Jacob Holyoake, 5, Paul's-alley, Paternoster-row.

ANSWERS TO CORRESPONDENTS.

J. N., Canterbury.—Have not received the 5s.

M. A. L.—Everybody supposes that everybody else writes to our friends in Gaol, and, consequently, few persons do write. It would be happy for those incarcerated, if everyone would suppose that no one else has written.

MR. SANDERSON.—No one has refuted "Paley Refuted."

J. W.—The lines spoken at the Marylebone Supper have arrived too late for insertion.

SUBSCRIPTIONS FOR ANTI-PERSECUTION UNION.

A few friends, Stratford, per Mr. G. Dixon	0 10	6
Pr. Mr. H. Morrish, Bristol:—		
Coll. 17	0 8	6
19	0 1	0
27	0 6	0
30	0 1	0
J. Smith, Stepney, Fourth Subscription	0 1	0
Pr. Mr. Dent	0 1	8
A few friends at Audsley, near Barnsley, per Mr. Lingard .	0 4	0
Mr. Hilton, London, per G. Smith, Salford	0 1	0
Henry Walker	0 1	0
G. Smith	0 1	0
Three friends	0 1	1

G. J. H. *Sec.*

Printed and Published by G. J. HOLYOAKE, 40, Holywell-street, Strand, Saturday, Feb. 17, 1844.

THE MOVEMENT
And Anti=Persecution Gazette.

"Maximize morals, minimize religion."—BENTHAM.

No. 11.   EDITED BY G. JACOB HOLYOAKE, ASSISTED BY M. Q. RYALL.   PRICE 1½d

SENTIMENTAL THEISTS AND NATURAL THEOLOGY.
v.

By demolishing natural theology, we destroy all confidence in revelation, for no sane man can believe a heap of vague traditions to be the pure word of God. It is because Atheists agree with Lord Brougham, that if natural theology is false, what Jews and Christians call revelation must be false too, that they have taken so much pains to explode the *à posteriori* fallacy. As to Dr. Clarke's famous *à priori* ditto. not a single defender of it can now be found even in the orthodox ranks. Mr. Holyoake quotes Dr. Reid, Dugald Stewart, and Lord Brougham, who are unanimous in condemnation of Dr. Samuel Clarke's performance. Dr. Reid confessed himself unable to determine whether Clarke's speculations about Deity were "as solid as they are sublime," or "the wanderings of the imagination in a region beyond the limits of human understanding." Dugald Stewart refers to this "candid acknowledgment of Dr. Reid's, and then acknowledges himself not ashamed to confess doubts and difficulties" upon the same subject. Lord Brougham declares his belief that "very few men have ever formed a distinct apprehension of the nature of Dr. Clarke's celebrated argument, and that hardly any person has ever been at all satisfied with it." So much for the *à priori* demonstration of God-existence. It died after a "fitful fever" of short duration, was decently interred, to the great regret of many who thought so "sublime" a demonstration deserved immortality. Reid, Stewart, and Brougham were the men who lent most efficient aid to the interesting work of consigning it to that building which "lasts till doomsday." Dr. Clarke's argument being dead and buried, in order to get rid of the God-idea altogether, Atheists have nothing more to do than expose the sophistries of Paley.—But what do I write? Why they *have* done this, Mr. Holyoake has *completely* defeated Paley in his own words. If any one doubt my veracity, let him read the pamphlet, and he will doubt no longer. It may be had for sixpence, which is one reason why I give no more quotations; another is, that to do it justice, I should quote it entire.

George Ensor's "Natural Theology Exposed," is a smartly written pamphlet, which may be had for a penny, and carefully read in half an hour. No person who is doubtful as to the solidity of the *à priori* argument, as stated by Paley, Brougham, and the Bridgewater Treatise writers, should be without a copy of this "Exposition." Its author handles those gentlemen respectfully, but roughly. After quoting Lord Brougham's important admission that natural theology is a science, the truths of which are discovered by induction like the truths of natural or moral philosophy, he observes, "The subject is therefore necessarily relieved from the limits of faith or belief, as contradistinguished from reason, and of course detached from all peculiarities connected with particular religions." To admit faith in this discussion would evidently be to mistake the object and the means of the debate, and offend against Bacon's repeated warning "to give faith nothing that is not faith's."

Ensor has not, nor did Bacon tell, what amount or sort of intellectual property faith can legitimately lay claim to, or we rationally offer. This *advice* of Bacon's is analogous to the *reply* we are told Jesus Christ gave to certain Jews who said, "Master, is it lawful to pay tribute to Cæsar or not?" Both are much admired, without being very well understood. Christ's reply was an enigmatical evasion, for the Jews could not have been ignorant that they should give unto Cæsar the things which were Cæsar's; but then what were Cæsar's things, Christ should, but he did not, inform them. In like manner Bacon advised us to give faith nothing that is not faith's—advice no one can question the wisdom of, but he did not tell us what we owed to faith. In a letter to the Archbishop of Canterbury, which appeared in No. 9 of the *Investigator*, I endeavoured to show his Grace that reason must be convinced of faith's efficacy, before faith itself can come into play, and that it is not only wise to set up reason as the standard measure of all things, but that in point of fact it is the only standard measure and exponent of all things which can be set up. To that letter I refer not only those who think there is a "moral guide superior to reason, but the rather numerous section of investigators, who imagine we can have faith independently of our reasoning faculty. I do not conclude that Ensor made this vulgar mistake, but as he quotes approvingly Bacon's "Warnings," it may be that the fallacy involved therein did not strike him. Whatever his opinions upon this nice point, his writings prove him an able and consistent reasoner. Nothing can be better than his descriptions of the Bridgewater Treatises. Of that written by Dr. Roget, he says, "The Doctor, according to his account, had admitted only such facts as afford manifest evidences of design." Yet in speaking of thorny prickles, &c. on different plants, he dogmatises that they are intended particularly to prevent them from the molestation of animals, and he instances a nettle. Why should a nettle be so preserved, instead of thousands of other plants? But is the nettle unmolested? No, for he says that fifty different species of insects feed upon it. Verily we may, with the old Roman in Shakspere remark "We call a nettle but a nettle, and the faults of fools folly." This is, however, but the beginning and basis of the extravagance, for he subjoins, " The sting of the nettle is of this class, and its structure bears a striking analogy to that of the poisonous fangs of serpents." Why is the rattle snake, which by the bye, bears to be thawed and frozen alternately, without ceasing to live—protected by so potent a defence; or rather, why is he armed against all animals that may inadvertently approach his retreat, and thus derive from his fangs and poison, the title of *crotalus horridus* (the horrid crotalus.)

"The arguers and interpreters of final causes are not less at variance with facts than with circumstances. Professor Buckland declares that the stays of the plesiosaurus were intended to protect the frailty of the form of this extinct race, because without this peculiar instrument, it would be destitute of defence—that it was made weak by nature to be artificially strengthened by nature. Again, these writers are enraptured with the provident arrangement which enables the gazelle, antelope, deer, &c., by their swiftness and watchfulness to escape their natural enemies, and then they express equal admiration that their natural enemies have their feet covered with hair to deaden the sound of their approaching feet, and further that they are particularly formed for surprise, by bounding on their prey." Dr. Roget adds, " Lions and tigers who feed on gazelles, and the like, have jaws and teeth formed for mastication and the destruction of life." Thus it is clear these final causes counteract each other—one set of animals are qualified by nature to eat the other, and these are aided by nature not to be eaten by them, though they supply their means of living. * * * * The final causers also say that nature always acts by the simplest means. Why the *crotalus horridus* just mentioned has two hundred vertebræ—the common earth worm has more than half that number of holes in its back for vital purposes. Lyonnet counted in one species of caterpillar, four thousand muscular bands, and Roget speaks of the eye of the codfish in the following words:—'This little spherical body, scarcely larger than a pea, is composed of five millions of fibres, which lock into one another by means of more than sixty-two thousand five hundred millions of teeth.' I am not so monstrously absurd as to object to nature in the arrangement of the world and of its inhabitants, but I object to the self-sufficiency of the animal man, that atom on the fidgets, assuming that his capacity embraces the principles, progress, and destination of all beings animate and inanimate."

The self sufficiency so sharply reproved by Ensor, stands methinks in the same relation to natural theology as Lord Brougham instructs us that natural theology does to revelation. By destroying that self-sufficiency, we shall without doubt remove one main obstruction to the march of pure reason. Those imbeciles, so well named by Ensor, "atoms on the fidgets," who are possessed with the notion that they are equal to the task of explaining " highest universals," are strong in numbers and influence, though contemptible in point of intellect. The parties here pointed at are of course Theists, for Atheists deny that any human capacity can embrace "the principles, progress, and destination of all beings, animate and inanimate." They are charged with displaying "the pride of reason," but in truth, it is Theists who are proud of their reason; so proud indeed as to imagine that through its instrumentality the *unknowable* may be clearly comprehended. Miss Frances Wright, a decidedly atheistical writer, reprobates as childish and idle, all attempts to explain nature. She warns those who persist in the fruitless attempt, that with every truth they may discover will be mixed a thousand errors; and for one matter of fact they will charge their brain with a thousand fancies. But this result, so painful to the rationalist, is rejoiced at by the priest who sees in fanciful speculation and ridiculous error, the bulwarks of his authority. That bulwark, thanks to the diffusers of *really* useful knowledge, is becoming daily weaker and weaker. Natural theology is fast falling into contempt, and with it every vestige of faith in revelation. As to Sentimental The-

ism, it is so much like Atheism, that I strongly recommend its professors to admit with Cicero, that there is nothing more perfect than the universe, which is wise, and on this account, GOD.
CHARLES SOUTHWELL.

LETTER FROM MR. PATERSON.
(*Abstract.*)
Highland Home, Feb. 3, 1844.
DEAR H———,
Thanks are too common place. Both yours received, and they have risen my blood, which was below *freezing* point. Miss R. sent me *Chambers' Information*, and *Hill's Text Book*. The Chaplain put his veto on the latter, and *Chambers' Information* lies at the lodge, and cannot be admitted without an order from the PRISON BOARD, which sits at Edinburgh. In reply to your queries, I have to say that *all the rules of the prison apply to me*. I go to bed at 9 p.m., rise at 6 a.m.—work and sleep in the same cell. I can't explain now the quantity of work—some days I have one hour to spare, some days two. The prison library, like other prison libraries, I suppose—No books can be had on Saturday or Sunday, except the Bible. No going out of my cell to chapel. The cell is so constructed that I can hear without moving. My confinement is strictly solitary; I never speak to any one but the governor, and once a week to the chaplain. About twenty minutes walking in the air daily, Sundays excepted. Surgeon humane—the governor kind, or I should not have written three times instead of once. Once a quarter is the rule. My health is impaired—I take medicine as regularly as my food, or life would be miserable. No visitors are admitted without an order from the board at Edinburgh. In short *there* must be your field of exertion. You say you are "all anxious to alleviate my condition," and I believe you. Get for me *Chambers' Information*, writing paper, and liberty to purchase food when I am inclined to study, and consequently fall short in my work. You cannot think what I suffer for want of paper to write on. The chaplain manages that department, and he refused me a sheet to put down a few little matters of a private nature, which I wished not to forget. Get me liberty to write oftener, when I promise you the "Leviathan letters" which you say I ought to write. I shall be delighted with phonography, and overjoyed at a letter from your correspondent. Mr. Hammond, you say, has promised his attentions to the collectors of the A. P. U.; could he transfer a little of his generosity to one of the *collected*. Glad of the copy sent of Emerson's "Man Thinking." Chilton and Southwell are both dead—may my last end be like theirs. I wish some young enthusiast would send me weekly lessons in French. Mr. B. and I were planning a trip to Paris about the time that the Lord Advocate was planning to send me to the north pole.

One word in conclusion, I shall endeavour to practise some of your philosophy. If you can do anything for me, well and good—if not, say so. I only tell you what I want, because you court my wishes. If you labour under the notion that I repent having placed myself in this position, you are wrong, for I am prepared to suffer death, for what I think right and just. Yours,
T. PATERSON.

[*Note*.—With regard to the above letter, our friends will be pleased to hear that the Anti-Persecution Union have been for some time incessantly occupied in consulting legal authorities, and preparing drafts of applications to proper parties on Mr. Paterson's behalf, and hope soon to be able to report progress.]
G. J. H.

SECOND LETTER FROM DR. KALLEY.
Jail of Funchal, Madeira,
MY DEAR SIR,   Dec. 28, 1843.
I received yesterday your favor of the 5th current, inclosing a Bank of England five pound note, No. 58,496; and am sorry that in my letter of the 9th ult., while I sincerely thanked your committee for their sympathy and kind offer of assistance, I did not expressly decline pecuniary aid. I did not anticipate that they would have inferred from my letter that I wished that kind of assistance, and regret that you have had the trouble of sending it. As I am not in want of money I take the liberty of returning the sum which you so promptly transmitted to me, and feel as much obliged to you as if I had retained it.

Before receiving your first favor of the 13th Sept., I had already heard of the disturbance in the meeting at Edinburgh, and could not help regretting that the Anti-Persecution Union there, had not rather called a separate meeting of a political nature, in which they might have unanimously expressed their sentiments, without clashing with those of the christians. This would not have exposed them to the painful results to which you refer, and it would have advanced more efficiently the cause of religious liberty, for the influence upon our government must have been much more powerful from two unanimous meetings, than from one so discordant and disagreeable to both parties.

In reply to your inquiries, I mention that I am allowed the use of my books, and in accordance with the law of this country, (that prisoners be allowed apartments proportioned to their rank) I have the most comfortable rooms in the prison.

When the sister of one of the Portuguese ministers of state was dangerously ill, about five weeks ago, I was permitted to go and see her professionally, and since that time, when an influential person has had a certificate from another physician stating that his life was in danger, the judge has given leave for me to visit him for half an hour, not for my benefit, but, as he declares, for the sake of humanity, and I am always accompanied by a guard. This jail has no court in which the prisoners may take exercise, so that these visits, to the apparently dying, are the only occasions on which, during five months, I have been out of this house.

There was a paper affixed to the outer door of the jail by order of the administrador do Conselho, forbidding all Portuguese subjects to hear me speak about religion; another, signed by the judge, was fixed to the door of my rooms, warning all the aforesaid subjects against hearing me read the Bible, or speak about religious matters, under pain of prosecution, while a warrant officer was sent to me by the said judge, with a written order, forbidding my singing of the Bible, as they denominate my praising God.

My speaking to the other prisoners was held to be an "almost intolerable insult to the laws and authorities of the Province" for which, and for having given some food to those who had only one meal per day, I was forbidden to see them for a time.

The jailer has orders to watch me narrowly, by spying through the key hole, listening at the door, and by every secret means in his power, and to report all to the public prosecutor and judge.

My nearest neighbours, on the same floor with me, are two individuals imprisoned on a charge of murder. We are all three treated in exactly the same manner, with the exception of the aforesaid professional walks, the interdicts, and espionage.

No member of my family, or English friend, is prohibited from visiting me during the day, but only three Portuguese friends are allowed to be present at a time.

One of the city common sewers runs along the wall of that part of the prison where I am confined; it is not covered, and during the summer when there is no rain to clear it, and the sun beats on its abominable contents, it emits the most horribly offensive stench that I ever smelt, so that however intense the heat, no circulation of air can be endured.

I am imprisoned without any sentence of a competent authority, and denied bail in direct opposition to the laws of the country, on the plea that my crimes are punishable with death. These are declared to be blasphemy, and abetting heresy and apostacy.

You will be sorry to hear that the instigators and principal supporters of this persecution are avowed infidels and atheists. One of the most violent of them declared to a friend of mine (who is himself a deist) "that he does not believe any such nonsense as that there is a God;" and I am not aware of there being one bigot, or one believer in christianity among them. Christianity is opposed to the spirit of persecution; it commands universal benevolence, not in word only, but in deed and in truth—not to friends only, but to enemies. It commands all to render good for evil, and if any one do not sincerely strive to follow this rule, his conduct is inconsistent with christianity. Many regard such inconsistent conduct of professing christians as a disproof of christianity; but as their conduct does not afford a reason for condemning the command to do good for evil, so neither can it be a reason for condemning the many other most wise, benevolent, and noble maxims which are embodied in the christian system. If we be warranted to condemn a creed because of the conduct of some of its professors, then the conduct of my persecutors must warrant the condemnation of those views which you have espoused so warmly, but which I sincerely hope you will not long retain.

I will suppose you possessed of all the knowledge requisite for examining and weighing the various proofs of the existence of a God; and that you have employed that knowledge in searching all earth—all the phenomena of mineral, vegetable, and animal kingdoms; and further, that you have been able to show, by unanswerable argument, that earth does not display any proof of the being of a God; and supposing all this, I maintain that, even in that case you could not have a rational certainty in atheism, for there might be a God, though earth should exhibit no trace of his being or operations. In order to be rationally certain that there is no God, it would be necessary for you not only to examine all earth, but all space; for if any one portion of the universe remained unsearched you could not have a reasonable certainty that there does not exist there such proofs as must convince even you that there is a God. There God might be. It is evident then, that creatures, such as we are, never can, by any possibility, attain to a rational certainty in atheism. The atheist doubts the existence of God—he finds much that appears to him to strengthen his doubts —but he has no rational certainty in atheism, and a state of doubt and uncertainty on any subject that affects our most important interests is painful. As long, indeed, as a man can persuade himself that his interests are not affected he may be content with uncertainty. But who that understands the words will dare to say that his interests are not affected by the existence or non-existence of Deity. Should it prove true that there is such a God as the christian believes in, would it not affect your interests?

When a man feels himself irresistibly hurried on to death, and knows that he can live only a few hours, uncertainty as to whether or not there is an Almighty Being, who hates evil, and will punish it, becomes agony. The possibility of an hereafter of retribution, (and you cannot rationally deny its possibility), brings horror; and often those who most daringly deny the existence of God, heaven, and hell, while in health, are overwhelmed with anguish and despair at last. A veil may cover such things from the world, but it is hard to hide them from the physician. One of the character mentioned, and whom I well knew, cried out, when nearing death, "tell me, tell me, what is truth;" and I have witnessed scenes which most painfully proved, that in the hour of greatest need, atheism deserts its advocates, and leaves them unsupported and miserable.

Since you deny the existence of a God, I suppose that you may maintain that the vast system of the universe—the movement of its greatest orbs—and the changes in its most minute particles, are all governed by general laws. Who then, is the law-giver? who devised the laws? who enforces them? who has done so during the long succession of ages? "Nature," you may, perhaps, reply —they are laws of nature—nature does it all. —be it so. Then nature must be wise, for there are, in every department, proofs of consummate wisdom designing certain ends. Nature must be kind, for in every part of our frames, and all around, there exist the clearest proofs of benevolence. Nature must be possessed of a power so great as to be to us inconceivable; else, how could it raise the waves, keep the sea in constant motion, and sweep the planets in their courses, with that amazing rapidity with which they perform them?

Perhaps you will answer me, as an atheist once did in the beginning of a mortal disease, " I see no wisdom, I see no goodness, I see no power." My answer to him was " of course you do not—you cannot. Wisdom and power, and goodness, are not visible things. I may know how to perform a difficult surgical operation; you cannot see my knowledge, though you may be convinced of its existence by seeing the operation performed correctly. I may have a strong desire of benefiting you, but you cannot see my goodness; you may have such proofs of it as to convince you of its existence; but the thing itself cannot be perceived by any of your senses; and so with power and all moral and intellectual faculties."

We have as clear evidence of the existence of wisdom, power, and goodness in the arrangement and government of the universe, as you can have of their existence in any person by the works which you see him perform. If you grant that nature possesses such properties, and that there is visible proof of their existence in its amazing system and operation, then, I say, that this existing wise benevolent power which you call nature, I call God. It gave me life—gives me health—forms and supports the smallest insect, and overrules all. It changes bread into blood, and blood into flesh within my body every day, and performs thousands of other changes equally amazing, none of which could I perform by any wisdom of which I am possessed. It is free to act where it chooses, as is plain from the fact that it does not sustain the life and health of all indiscriminately. My affection and gratitude are due for its kindness to me, and these are the essence of the worship which I render to God. But I do not owe affection and gratitude for natural gifts only. Christianity unfolds many infinitely stronger motives for our love to our Creator, demonstrating that God is love, and full of mercy, that he had pity on his rebellious creature, when man had cast off the fear and the love of God, and wished to disbelieve his existence. It assures us that God is a just God, and merciful; that He is waiting to be gracious to us, and desires nothing from us but our salvation from every evil, both from sin and from suffering: is this unreasonable? Is it inconsistent with the greatness and excellence of that wise and ruling benevolent power which you call nature? Desiring that that God on whom you are constantly dependent for every good, but whose being you deny and ungratefully wish to forget, may mercifully lead you to know and love the truth ere it be too late, I remain, most sincerely, your well-wisher.

·Robert R. Kalley.

REPLY OF THE ANTI-PERSECUTION UNION.

London, 5, Paul's-alley, Paternoster-row, *Feb.* 16, 1844.

Dear Dr.—I acknowledge yours of Dec. 28, returning the £5 remitted in my last. After the comments of the christian journals we expected you would feel compelled to return it, although your own liberality might incline you not to treat us with disrespect. Your friends have regarded it ill that we should feel sympathy for you, until we have feared that our endeavours to serve you would operate to your disadvantage. To counteract this as far as lay in our power, we have overlooked the severity of the *Tablet*, and publicly disclaimed what the *Voluntary* ungenerously insinuated. Nor should we publish this correspondence but that your letter seems well calculated to set you right with your religious friends. It is intended to reprove the Scottish Union, to identify atheists with your persecutors, and contains elaborate arguments in favor of theism, all of which we rejoice in making known, both for your satisfaction, and that the truth may appear.

Undoubtedly "two unanimous meetings would have been more effective than one discordant" assembly. But Mr. Southwell, Mr. Jeffery, and others, must have prejudged your friends in a manner that you yourself would condemn, had they assumed that intolerance rather than reason would prevail. Could they forsee that it wonld be "clashing with christians" to solicit an extension of their sympathy from Funchal to Calton Jail. Though the Lord Provost might find it convenient to distinguish between the blasphemers at home and abroad, yet, at a public meeting it would have been more decent to have heard Messrs. Jeffery and Paterson, than to imprison them. It is with pleasure I write that at a meeting of your friends in Glasgow, this more courteous conduct was to a great extent pursued.

We shall print with willingness the painful narrative of your condition. Though less fearful than that of persons indicted for blasphemy in Scotland, it is not less to be deprecated and earnestly protested against, as a dangerous and unjust infringement of the liberty of expression.

You are right: I *am* " sorry to hear that Atheists are among your persecutors," and if you will favour me with their names and addresses, I will certainly find out by what ratiocination *they* connect such execrable conduct with their principles. That they should imitate Christians in this unenviable particular, and differ from them in every thing else, is strange. They cannot persecute for their own glory, and they have not, like believers, the glory of God to do it for. Besides, Atheists must rejoice in your efforts to spread Protestantism among Catholics, since the dissent from one religion paves the way for dissent from all. In your former letter you said, " I believe that the true reason of my imprisonment is because I have endeavoured to show that the great Creator of all cannot sell his favour or barter his mercy." But how Atheists, who do not believe in a Creator, can care whether it is said that it barters favour or not, I am at a loss to determine. Apart from these difficulties, it strikes us as strange that " *avowed* Atheists " should enjoy immunity " to instigate " and power " to support " public proceedings in a country where Christianity is the state and popular religion, and a Presbyterian preacher is ranked as a blasphemer.

You imply that I would object to Atheism being condemned on account of the conduct of its professors. Nothing of the sort. If Atheists do not repudiate persecution, and do all in their power to put it down, whether it proceeds from Christians or from any of themselves, they will justly be held to approve it. If, like Christians, they permit it to be done in their name, defend it from their books, and only protest against it when directed against themselves, the infamy ought ever to lie at their door.

I now arrive at that part of your letter where you cease to write to me as the representative of a party, and address me as an individual. I will also meet you on the same ground, and speak with the candour of one who has nothing to conceal, and with the humility of a young man willing to be instructed. I do this as you do not put me without the pale of courtesy because I am an Atheist, but seek to convince me by reason, to which all men are bound to listen. Though I am not won by your arguments, nor cannot concur in your views, I sincerely appreciate your kind intentions.

If Christianity is true, I grant it will " affect my interest." That " there *may be* a God" I admit, and when I *know* it, or see reasonable evidence to believe it, my conduct will be, as it ever has been—moulded according to my views of my duty. At present nothing under my notice, either in the shape of nature, or argument, is satisfactory on the subject. I therefore confine my study to morality, which I can better understand, and conform my practice to the extent of my knowledge. If I knew more of my duty I would hasten to do more. Acting and feeling thus, I expect the approval of Deity, should there prove to be one, since I have acted up to all that the ability that it has given, enables me. In this respect you resemble me. You do not *know*, you only *suppose* you are right. Your Catholic brethren who have higher pretensions than yourself to the possession of true religion, consider you a blasphemer of God, and in the end it may prove so. What then is *your* prospect? Will you not rely on your *intention*, plead that you acted to the best of your knowledge? Such a plea would be allowed by a just man.

and "who shall say that man is more just than God?" If a God is not just, it matters little what you or I believe or do. When I assume that there " may be a God," so I reason and so I rely.

In prosperity I have believed these things, and in adversity I have tried them, on the bed of sickness and the gloom of the prison I have weighed them, and my conscience has confirmed my convictions. Persons who are thoughtless and vain, who take up opinions without examination, and echo them because they are novel, may ask in death, for the first time, "tell me what is truth," but men accustomed to commune with themselves and follow the dictates of reason, are not thus deserted by confidence. However persons may die under your care Atheists here as frequently die at peace with the world and themselves as other men. Personally, I shrink from the presumption of expecting future life. Because I enjoy existence now, I cannot consider any Deity under obligation to continue it hereafter. Pleased with this strange world in which I unexpectedly find myself, however I may wish, I see no right claim, and no decency in expecting another. Immortality will not more delight than surprise me.

You ask me " who is the lawgiver of nature?" I know not. If I did, how could I be an Atheist? I do not understand the term as applied to nature. Certain operations pass before my eyes; they astonish, they delight, they charm me, but there is the beginning and the end of my knowledge, so far as final causes are concerned. Apart from faith and creeds do you know more?

I will not be disingenuous, as the Atheist, you mention, was, and pretend I cannot see wisdom and goodness *because they are " invisible things."* I will not deny that there are adaptabilities, advantages, and enjoyments afforded by nature, but if these are assumed as evidences of " wisdom and goodness, and power," which would imply that I thought them things *intended* or *designed*, then must we also assume that the inadaptabilities, disadvantages and miseries seen in nature, are evidences of folly, malice, or impotence. That I think nature imperfect in some respects you will tell me is owing to my limited faculties. True. But—

Say first of God above and man below,
What can I reason but from what I know.

When I have infinite knowledge, I shall draw infinite conclusions, but till that is the case, you must permit me to follow the plain and humble course of judging according to the evidence I see.

If the life, animation, and materiality, which I see around me be Deity—if what I call Nature you call God—the difference between us is not great, unless you employ a term which mankind will regard as disingenuous on your lips. If, as you say, " nature gives men life and health, forms and supports the smallest insect, and *overrules all*," how can we be " rebellious creatures," since we never move but as Nature directs?

I could desire that when you " wish me well," you would not charge me with insincerity and ingratitude. Perhaps you are not aware of it, but you stab me as you appear to pour on me your benedictions. You say I *" ungratefully wish to forget* God." How can I wish to forget what I do not know? You insinuate that I have a secret assurance of what I publicly deny;—then why have you pretended to reason to convince me of what you believe I am already convinced? If you have written these words deliberately, you must think me a hypocrite, and you idly desire that " God may mercifully lead me to know" what you believe I already know. If I have received a benefit from Deity, and am ungrateful to my benefactor, what a wretch you make me! The man who has done me a kind act or spoken to me a kind word, humble though he might be, was never yet forgotten or disregarded; and though he may since have become my enemy, I always remembered his kindness. Could my knowledge embrace a Deity—could I trace its benefits and adore its will,—I should, if a noble character, honour, serve, and adore it—for ever.

With unqualified wishes for your liberty and happiness, I am, yours respectfully,
G. JACOB HOLYOAKE,
Sec. Anti-Persecution Union.

MISS ROALFE AND HER PERSECUTORS, OR ERROR, VERSUS TRUTH.

MR. EDITOR—From the *facts* I have to state, it will be evident to all parties that Miss Roalfe really acted the part of a heroine on her trial, that she took her stand in the strictest sense of the word upon principle, and upon principle alone. She never attempted to meddle with the case legally, but boldly and unhesitatingly denied the justice of such prosecutions whether legal or not. She did this in the very teeth of the Procurator Fiscal himself; knowing full well that it would subject her to all the horrors of prison discipline, with communications from friends cut off on every side, and to the most rigid solitary confinement. Can we say too much, or too highly estimate her conduct, when, had she been disposed, to take advantage of legal quibbles, she might have escaped the law most effectually; for the sheriff told her that if she said that she was ignorant of the contents of the books when she sold them, why then it would be a very different thing, in fact the case would fall to the ground. Besides, in the quotations made from those books prosecuted, there are some of the most palpable blunders possible to be made, not simply one or two, for in no less than a dozen different places the books are falsely quoted by the over-zealous supporters of God's Holy Word; and had Miss Roalfe thought proper to avail herself of these things, she might have escaped their clutches. She knew of all those legal flaws before the day of trial. I subjoin a few of the misquotations:—

1st. Page 73, "God v. Paterson." In quoting Mr. Southwell's article, the "Jew Book," it stands in page 7 of the indictment as follows:—"It is a book which contains passages so outrageously disgusting and scandalously indecent, that were it called the word of God, no modest woman would suffer it to be read in her house." While it stands in God v. Paterson, "that were it not called &c," so that the entire sense is altered, and persons prosecuted for selling a book which never contained the words indicted.

2nd. In page 14, the Indictment in quoting page 76 of "God v. Paterson," instead of leaving out a word, they have thought proper to put one in, which is not to be found in the book, last line but one the words holy, holy, are quoted, while only one "holy" is there.

3rd. The article "God checkmated by the Devil," must certainly have had a very extraordinary effect upon the copyer, more than the reading of it did upon M'Levie the witness; for there are seven misquotations altogether.

Page 15 Indictment, 78 "God v. Paterson," in line 7, the word "that" is in the Indictment and not in the copy.

Page 17 Indictment, the word "not" is inserted instead of the word "did."

Same page, the word "shortly" is made to precede the words "he promised," instead of "in better plight."

Page 18 Indictment, 78 "God v. Paterson," line 7, second paragraph of "God checkmated by the devil," the word "all" is left out.

Page 19 Indictment, line 10, second paragraph, the word "them" is left out. Three lines lower down the word "will" is put instead of the word "shall."

Page 24 Indictment, 79 "God v. Paterson," last line but one of the second paragraph, the word "and" is left out.

In 91, *Oracle*, the word "up" is left out, page 29 Indictment. Same page, *Oracle*, pape 30 Indictment, when speaking of the Jews, Egyptians, and their jewels, the word "of" is inserted when it has no business there; and in "Godology," third paragraph, the word "before" is left out in the Indictment.

I make no further remarks, but that we cannot fail to think that Miss Roalfe knowing all this, and not taking the advantage of it, set a worthy example, for when contending against a bad law, should we take advantage of it, it would seem that we thought it of some value.

I will send you a copy of "God v. Paterson," and "Godology," marked, so that you can see the difference. W. BAKER.

P. S. I have sent a parcel to you containing a sample of bread, cheese, pea-soup, Scotch kale or porridge, and treacle water, with an account of how much of each is given to the prisoners at a meal in Calton Gaol, the bread and cheese is that which Mr. Finlay had for his dinner on Sunday, the day before he was liberated. I propose that they should be taken care of, to form, with a copy of all the prosecuted books, papers, and indictments, summons, and other relics of Infidel martyrdom, an *Infidel Museum*. A copy of all Infidel works might be deposited with you, so as to form a library for reference, such as is not to be found in any place in the United Kingdom. W. B.

[NOTE.—M. Ryall, W. J. Baker, and several of us have long had in contemplation the establishment of an extensive and unique *Museum*, in which not only infidel relics, but the gods of all nations, as far as practicable, shall be assembled and arranged in mythological order. More of this anon.—ED. M.

The Report of Dr. Keenan's lecture is unavoidably postponed.

ERRATA IN NO. 10.—In page 73, col. 2, line 37, for "unkind" read unknown. In page 79, col. 2, line 56, for "theologically" read theoretically. In page 80, col. 1, line 22, for "oxygenized" read oxydizable.

ANSWERS TO CORRESPONDENTS.

Received from J. M. C. "The Philalethean Society." "Belgium, its Constitution and Laws, by W. J. B." Remittance to M. Q. R. from W. Cooke for "Oracles."

J. M.—"The Hunt after the Devil" is in three vols. £1 7s.: published by Hetherington, London.

SUBSCRIPTIONS FOR THE ANTI-PERSECUTION UNION.
Returned from Dr. R. Kalley,
  Madeira £5 0 0
B. Armfield, Doncaster . . 0 1 0
W. B. B. 0 10 0
Per Mrs. Martin—Collection at
  Institution, City Road . . 1 6 8
                      G. J. H., *Sec.*

Printed and Published by G. J. HOLYOAKE,
40, Holywell-street, Strand,
Saturday, Feb. 24, 1844.

THE MOVEMENT

And Anti=Persecution Gazette.

"Maximize morals, minimize religion."—BENTHAM.

No. 12.   EDITED BY G. JACOB HOLYOAKE, ASSISTED BY M. Q. RYALL.   PRICE 1½d.

A LESSON TO ATHEISTS.

WE may assert that atheism leaves us free to combine a course of conduct, and a line of practice, distinct from all others in their nature, and superior to all others in importance. To make this appear has been one of the great objects of the *Movement*, and to make it generally felt is now of more consequence than ever.

Scepticism and infidelity, as commonly understood, are only higher stages of religion. They have less of error and more of liberality than religion itself, but they have none of that vitality, calibre, or distinctness of purpose, which alone can constitute a *cause*, or gather up into a focus the strong sympathies of men. Atheism has exhibited this phase, it must continue energetically, or give up its best pretensions; atheists have put on decision and determination — they must unswervingly hold this bold and distinctive character, or relinquish the proud position of men of progress, and sink into mere commonplace infidels.

The great success of theologians in creating a public opinion against infidels, has been owing to their taunts, that infidels wanted courage. Infidels, said they, are bold while they are safe, but in danger they sink into littleness and often into meanness. Leslie threw about his scorn, and Robert Hall his withering sneers, and the common-place christian, who could imitate these champions of abuse in nothing else, could imitate them in this; and down to the days of Brindley and Exeter's Bishop, vituperation and jibes have been the principal stock in trade of christian disputants. Carlile and his brave confederates threw huge confusion over this line of policy, and raised infidelity to the honour of being feared. Atheism, in its modern dawn, from the pen and from the prison of Mr. Southwell, has been of the character of dare-devilism. It has been charged with all sorts of violence, but few have charged it with cowardice. The long and continually increasing list of victims, both of men and women, has at least established atheism's capacity for persistency. So far, if it has not commanded admiration, it has at least commanded respect. Those who would not allow that we were right, have at length conceded that we are in earnest.

But this reputation, though desirable in itself, and absolutely indispensable for any great public effort, is only sufficient to satisfy, and not to stimulate. The stimulus must come from the clear perception of the benefits which atheistical views can confer, and in profound and undying conviction of their importance. This conviction and importance, the *Movement* was designed to create, and must labour unceasingly to complete.

It is even with Socialists as it is with the Christian. If one conceals sentiments, in order not to offend Christian prejudices, instead of acknowledging the forbearance, the Christian calls out hypocrite and coward, and if one insists but mildly on atheism's tendency and importance, in order to avoid collision with the careful and worldly-wise socialist, he sneers at the "inutility" of one's proceedings, the " waste of energy" we exhibit—says our " contest," in which labour is given, liberty is risked, and every fervent aspiration enlisted, is one of "words, words, words," holds up those who think with us to public derision, and endeavours to cover us with contempt.

What I allude to is this, In the *New Moral World* of Saturday, Feb. 10th, 1844, No. 33, and page 264, appeared two letters, under the head of " Religious Controversy." The first letter is from " T. A.," its purport is to induce the Socialists to abandon the absurdity of professing in their outline a *Rational Religion*, and the argument is shrewdly put. The second letter is from Mr. Jackson of Leeds, and justly impugns the flagrant inconsistency of Socialists in calling themselves Christians, when neither their sentiments nor practice agrees with christianity. These were charges which professed lovers of reason should have met with reason—not with derision. But what was the editor's answer? this; " What excites the indignation of both correspondents? Words, words, words!! Would our readers like to see our columns usually occupied by such matter? We hope the parties who enjoy such verbal warfare, will find out a more *suitable organ* in future."

This would be inexcusable in those " voilent and abusive Atheists" who conduct *Oracles* and *Movements*, but with what grace comes it from those "prime minds" and smooth conventionalists, who lecture us continually on our "inexperience," in not treating Christian opponents with a due regard to their feelings! These letters are from old and earnest fellow-workers in the same cause with Mr. Fleming; our "abuse" is of men who attack with bigot fury, the life, liberty, and property of the atheist.

There is no mistaking the meaning of the passage I have quoted. The editor assumes T. A. and W. Jackson to be of the atheistical school, and intends his remarks to be taken as an answer to all troublesome disputants on theology. These are his first words: "Some parties are disposed to complain because the *New Moral World* does not devote some of its space to religious disputation, or rather ANTI-theological essays. For this course many good reasons have been and can be given; but, as the best way of illustrating its utility, we insert the two last communications on the subject of religion." Nothing can be clearer, he treats his correspondents as anti-theological, i.e., atheistical objectors, and as such I shall consider them. Of Mr. Jackson I know little, but his letter, intrinsically, deserves regard. "T. A." is Mr. Timothy Allen, the secretary of the Worcester branch, who has been for years a faithful, laborious, and intelligent officer of socialism; and certainly his communication, if it did not command approval, at least merited, at the hands of the editor of the N. M. W., decency of reception. Mr. Allen never approved of atheism, but he is one of those whom I have often esteemed worthy of an attempt to convince of its value. The editor, in dismissing these letters, expressed a wish that "fanaticism" may soon be banished the world, insinuating thereby, that these writers are actuated by a fanatical spirit, but our readers will be of opinion that "fanaticism's" partial spirit has not yet forsaken the pages of the Rational Gazette.

With the *New Moral World* I have no personal quarrel, and want none, and do not intend these remarks to be taken cynically, they are purely defensive, they make no attack, they repel one. The establishment of communities have all my sympathies. I do not think the project is pursued with a decision and boldness worthy of the great objects professed, but here ends my complaint. The notice I now comment on is not one calculated to excite anger, but to awaken far different emotions. It teaches a lesson to atheists which no enemy could inculcate. That the reputedly calculating, and better-to-be-safe, editor of the *New Moral World* should feel that he could venture to treat atheistical objectors so cavalierly is a severe censure on the supineness of atheists, who have not taken more care to make the value of their principles and objects more extensively felt. T. A. and W. Jackson are desired to find some "more suitable organ for the contest of words," that is, they must send them to the *Movement*. This is plain enough for the wilfully blind to see. It is published to the readers of the *New Moral World* in both hemispheres, that the atheists of England and conductors of the *Movement*, are engaged in a mere "contest of words," and that they possess an organ for the patronage and publication of fanatical contributions.

However wise, and it is wise, rarely to appropriate inuendoes, it is sometimes safer to pass by open charges, than not to adopt some insinuations. Inuendoes are sometimes as clear as indictments. The *New Moral World's* insinuation that atheists are men of wordy disputes is a reproach on atheists generally.

It will now be our duty to contrast atheism with mere communism, atheism's practical bearings must receive full attention, its principles must be weighed in the balance of utility with those of religion and pseudo-rationalism; less quarter must be shown to parties or policy, atheism's merits, if it has any, must be seen, let it come in contact with what it may, and a verdict must be pronounced. One can endure to be hated, and even enjoy it, but never to be despised.

I blame not the *New Moral World*. If the editor sees clearly that he may safely so speak of atheistical efforts, atheists deserve it—the fault is theirs, and the contempt is due; and if this contumely is merited any more, may it descend in copious showers. G. J. H.

THE PHILALETHEAN SOCIETY.

Edinburgh, Feb. 6, 1844.

SIR,—I beg to acknowledge receipt of a copy of No. 2 of the *Movement*, containing a letter, addressed by you to Mr. W. Gillespie, in which you state that his "Argument à priori for the being and attributes of God," which the Philalethean Society long ago challenged any Atheist to answer, is now in the hands of Mr. Southwell; and in which letter you also state that the London Society of Atheists now challenge a reply to Mr. Holyoake's work, entitled "Paley Refuted in his own Words."

Since Mr. Gillespie received your letter, accompanied by a copy of Mr. Holyoake's work, I have had some correspondence with him. And, in answer to your letter, I now beg to make the following observations:—

In the *first place* it is no answer to the challenge given by the Philalethean Society to answer the *à priori* argument, for you to invite them or Mr. Gillespie to reply to Mr. Holyoake's answer to the *à posteriori* argument. If the existence of God can be proved in the *first* way, it is altogether immaterial whether in can be proved in the *second* way or not; for if it can be proved in *one* way that is sufficient to destroy the atheistical theory. It is impossible, therefore, to look upon your challenge to Mr. Gillespie as being in any way relevant to the challenge of the Philalethean Society, or to regard it as being to any extent an answer to that society's challenge to you.

In the *second place* you do not challenge the Philalethean Society, but Mr. Gillespie. If the London Atheists choose to challenge the Philalethean Society, I do not think that challenge would be declined. I may, however, mention that that society is much inclined to look upon your challenge as being an excuse for delay, and as indicating a desire on the part of the London Atheists to evade answering Mr. Gillespie's work, by involving the Philalethean Society in a discussion as to the validity of the *à posteriori* instead of the *à priori* argument; and, therefore, the Philalethean Society will make it a condition of any acceptance of any challenge which you may give, that an answer to Mr. Gillespie's work shall be at least commenced in the pages of the *Movement* before they commence a reply to Mr. Hollyoake's work. This is quite reasonable, seeing that it is about a year since the Philalethean Society's challenge was accepted, and the long promised answer seems just as far advanced as it was the day the challenge was accepted.

I am, sir, your obedient servant,
C. CLARK,
V. P. Philalethean Society,
To Mr. M'CULLOUGH,
12, Chandos-street, Strand, London.

[I will thank you to send me two copies of the number of the *Movement*, in which this letter may be inserted.]

ANSWER OF THE ATHEISTICAL SOCIETY.

2, Chandos-street, Strand, London,
Feb. 16, 1844.

Sir,—Certainly the work we transmitted to Mr. Gillespie, is no answer to the one long ago sent to the conductors of the *Oracle of Reason*. It was not so intended.

If it is necesary "to challenge"—if one may continue to employ, on a peaceable matter, such a belligerent term—the Philalethean Society in preference to Mr. Gillespie, we respectfully do so, and I am instructed to transmit you a copy of "Paley Refuted in his own Words" for your reply.

The condition you name, that the reply to Mr. Gillespie's work, shall commence before you begin to reply to Mr. Holyoake's, is reasonable. Mr. Gillespie's work was not received by us, or it should have been attended to before. I am, yours obediently,
J. M'CULLOUGH,
Secretary to the Atheistical Society.
To Mr. C. CLARK,
V. P. Philalethean Society, Edinburgh.

[*Note.*—Of this correspondence I desire to state that Mr. Ryall in the *Oracle* took the blame on himself for the delay that had occurred in replying to Mr. Gillespie's work, though he explained why he had neglected it. I think that the Philalethean Society might, with perfect justice, have been much more severe towards us for permitting so much time to elapse. Expecting that those of my friends who were cognizant of the Philalethean challenge, would be anxious to answer it, I did not put myself forward. Should the Philalethians publish that we cannot refute Mr. G.'s book, I should not complain. Except from hearsay, I knew nothing of Mr. G.'s performance until lately, when I borrowed a copy of the argument from Mr. Chilton. A reply shall appear in the next *Movement*, or following number. Mr. Southwell's answer will have the preference, should it arrive in time.
ED. M.]

PRACTICAL BEARINGS OF THE GOD-CONTEST.

A FEW words on the subject of God-notions and their influences may be considered as timely and appropriate. Numerous questions have been asked by lookers-on, objections raised by opponents, and various views offered by friends on these topics. Why raise an opposition on a merely speculative point, one not belonging to the sphere of action, is a frequent question. It was put but recently by a supporter of liberal action, theologically and politically. If speculations were unproductive of results, good or bad, they would be innocent at least, and not legitimate objects of opposition. If, on the contrary, the most baneful practical results occurred, exposure became necessary. It might, for instance, be very harmless to believe in the man-in-the-moon; it might, to go a step further, be no detriment to believe he knew what was going forward on his neighbouring planet, the earth. The supposition even that he built our world, or further, that he presided over our destinies and determined them, might not yet be extensively objectionable. But if, to these speculations concerning the existence of the man-in-the-moon, others were added which purported to reveal his certain commands relative to the inhabitants of our planet, then it becomes quite time to enquire into the certainty of his existence, or the authenticity of his commands. When, besides, these speculations not only lead to revelations of authority, pronounced by self-styled favorites, or their partizans or followers, ages after their supposed existence; when these laws and commandments are found to enter into every thought, word, and action, to grant certain privileges to a favoured class, to doom the rest to unremitting toil, slavery, and intellectual prostration, for the sake of this minority — then does the man-in-the-moon speculation become not only a matter of objection, but a cause of wide-spread misery, which should not be suffered to continue an hour after it is practicable to uproot it. If so, the only consideration is, not is it to be done, but how is it most effectually to be done. By restraining the moon-struck devotees, whether dupes or cheats, from promulgating their speculations? No; for this would be following the very course we should reprobate in them. By showing their fallacies, or the uncertainty of their statements as bases of action. In all this it would by no means follow that the opponents of the moonites could prove there is no man in the moon, or should even dogmatically assert that there is no such individual. It would be quite sufficient for utterly destroying the moon notion, as a basis of morals, politics, or social action to show the uncertainty or improbability of the man in the moon doctrine. So stand the God notion, its influences, and the Atheists. A guess or speculation is laid down as a reality, supposed to be proved by tradition, records, or observation; it influences thought, controuls words, and directs conduct; the thoughts, words, and conduct under such influences, are found, while supposed pleasing to the fancied author of certain commandments, to be directly opposed to the interests of humanity. Some, instead of beating round the little abuses of those set apart as interpreters of those speculations, set about uprooting the entire foundation of the great structure of ignorance, fraud, or hypocrisy. The Atheist consistently comes forward, leaving the sect and doctrinal, and church, and priest squabbles to be settled among the belligerents, and cuts the ground from under the whole. He is the true, the only great emancipator.

To come to examples, what was it that invaded the homes, plundered the property, seized, bound, and confined the persons of Southwell, Adams, Holyoake, Paterson, Finlay, M'Neile, Matilda Roalfe! what was it but a speculation or notion. The offence was none against life, limb, or property, but against the man in the moon; call him Budh, Brama, Jupiter, Jehovah, Jesus, or Ghost. Whether moon-rakers, wonder-workers, soothsayers, inspirationists, revelationists, and all sorts of mystery-men, with their Godish and devilish malignity, cheat or are cheated, is not so much our concern, as whether they act upon their godly notions, and teach others, particularly our children, their own sublimated folly and wickedness.

If ever and anon victimised, we have not worked for nought. The *Oracle* did not hurl its missives two years for nothing. Paterson's establishments in London and Edinburgh were not carried on without effect. The *Movement* does not address its thousand subscribers, and several thousand readers without demonstrable good. Atheistical agitation, it may be confidently anticipated, will not be without its achievements. The operations of the *Union* have already been attended with most gratifying success. The Atheists, notwithstanding their victimization, have much to look upon with gratulation, and are warranted in looking forward to still more extensive and lasting practical results.   M. Q. R.

ANTI-SUPERNATURALISM.

To the Editor of the Movement.

Sir,—The *Inquirer* of last Saturday contains a long article upon the doings and opinions of certain parties calling themselves Anti-Supernaturalists. These individuals believe the Deity has never at any time resorted to supernatural agency, either for the manisfestation of his will, or the accomplishment of his purposes; they are for the most part, Ministers of the Unitarian churches, and members of Unitarian congregations. Thus much may be gathered from the article in the *Inquirer*.

It is natural to suppose that parties holding these opinions have little reverence for the scriptures in their professed capacity as a revelation from God, and I should think can retain little of what we have been accustomed to understand by the term christianity. If a man rejects the notion of miraculous agency in matters of religion, in what light can he contemplate the supernatural stories recorded in the Old and New Testament? He must consider them grossly exaggerated, or utterly fabulous, and their writers either the dupes of their own credulity, or the designing narrators of that which they knew to be false. He may be a Mono-Theist, he may still continue to personify and worship a First Cause; but these are the only characteristics which distinguish him from the Infidel.

The Anti-Supernaturalists have made an advance in the right direction; an advance which the opponents of superstition will contemplate with peculiar satisfaction, emanating as it does from a society whose members are remarkable for their learning and ability, and for the liberal spirit in which their religious investigations and controversies, have been prosecuted. Unitarianism has been truly styled the stepping-stone to infidelity; its advocates are the most philosophical of christian sects, and encourage freedom of enquiry to a greater extent than any other religious society; and whenever liberty of thought and expression are countenanced and encouraged, falsehood will be rejected, and truth evolved.

Yours in the advocacy of freedom,
Manchester, Feb. 9, 1844. J. N.

ADJOURNED DISCUSSIONS AT BRANCH A.1.

Sunday, November 26th. 1843.

Mr. REDBURN rose to support the amendment. He had thought that the beau ideal of education was to be carried out at Harmony, that "truth without mystery, mixture of error or fear of man," was to prevail instead of disputations on what god and religion were wanted. They found out, it seems, a gap which wanted filling up, and they must cram a god and religion in to fill it up. Then came the question, What sort of god? which was answered by one of our "moral philosophers," saying, each have a god of his own, in accordance with the authorised right of private judgment. Why they would introduce another heathen mythology. Where would be the charity so much vaunted when once the baneful and immoral doctrines of god and religion came to fill up the pretended gap; he was told of Christian Socialism, why the idea was absurd, it would puzzle a conjurer to understand what the head teacher at Harmony had been talking about. If the conductors of schools would acquaint themselves with the nature of the brain, physiologically and phrenologically, they would have no occasion to find gaps to fill with the pestilent words and horrid ideas of god and religion. He concluded with recommending that the words "god and religion" should be struck out for "nature and morality."

A speaker, whose name was not announced, was surprised to hear such remarks. Why did not Socialists abide by the outline—the laws of which were our religion. Did not think the term plain and explicit. The Atheists who raised it as a watchword were most uncharitable; their persecuting spirit was seen in the French revolution; he hoped they would have no power here, and that their disputes and divisions would be put an end to.

Mr. Dunn was of opinion that the gentleman who spoke last had only risen to abuse the Atheists, not to speak to the motion; it was one thing to abuse, vilify, and asperse the Atheists, but it was a very different thing to answer them and their arguments. Individuals seemed to be afraid of discussion, for his own part he had no such fears. Discussion only tended to expose the truth, and to shed fresh light, lustre, and beauty upon the principles of our society. When he studied the philosophy of the Social System, he could deduce nothing else but the doctrines of materialism, therefore he could see no utility in substituting the words "God and Religion," where "Nature and Morality" was meant, and for that reason he would support the amendment.

Mr. Hardy had heard nothing sufficient to alter his opinion: admitted there was much superstitious nonsense about religion, but thought there was something in it beneficial to the mind. Reason is applicable to children; prayer induces the child to curb its faculties and keep within bounds. We don't know what God is, but it is a better term than that of nature, which teaches animals to prey on one another. Matter is not external, there are indications in nature of superintendence and design which was as difficult to exclude as works of human invention—

The speaker was here called to order, as diverging into the "Existence of God, and Design" questions. After some interruptions he proceeded in the same strain.

The discussion was re-opened by Mr. M'Cullough, after being declined by the adjourner. Mr. M'Cullough need not deal with the observations of Mr. Hardy, which were not the question; should it be entertained, he should be happy to take part in it. Mr. Hanhart's argument for the use of the word God in the Socialist school, that it had been universally in use fell to the ground, as rational practice was not determined by old customs, but utility.

Mr. Clark thought the word "religion" not baneful in the sense in which Mr. Owen had used it, being merely the feeling in man which produced morality. The facts of nature proved a cause, he reasoned from one fact to another until he arrived at a first cause, that cause he called "God;" he believed that god to be universal; he could see nothing in nature to substitute for that god, nor could the human mind reason for a moment without reference to the word "God."

Mr. Campbell Smith thought, that if they applied the moral part of religion to the mind, it would have no injurious tendency, but it was the custom of the religious world to touch the imagination rather than develop the reasoning powers. Religion should be stated as it is generally understood, and not as they themselves understand it: he preferred the word "Morality," because its meaning could not lead astray. He could see no harm in the use of the word "God," when explained according to the views of the Society, but the term "Nature" would answer much better, as it suited every purpose of their own, and could not lead the mind astray. He disapproved of deciding the present debate by the vote, as that could not settle the question, and might offend the minority. "Prayers," he believed, had not always an unalloyed good effect on the mind.

Mr. Sturges. The subject of debate was not a question of ideas, but a clothing of ideas with certain meanings. The motion and amendment contained four important words, "God," "Religion," "Nature," and Morality;" none of them were applicable. Education is a development of the mental powers, a drawing out of the faculties, and not a putting into the mind any ideas from without.

Mr. M'Cullough differed very much from Mr Clark, respecting Mr. Owen's remarks on religion. He did not think that Mr. Owen had expressed his opinion in the "best possible manner," and he was much surprised to hear that Mr. Southwell had said so. He thought that Mr. Owen had penned his opinions on religious matters in a very loose and inconclusive manner: he would again urge his opinion, that no "facts" in nature proved a "first cause." That every effect in nature had a cause, was true, but the words cause and effect, order and disorder, being but relative terms, they were in nowise applicable to nature as a whole. Mr. Clark had put the effect before the cause, when he said "religion was the feeling that produced morality." Morality consisted in making our fellow-beings happy, and then followed that feeling of universal love referred to by Mr. Clark; this feeling existed in the breast of the Socialist more exquisitely than it possibly could do in religionists. "Coming to the vote" had been objected to as not being calculated to "settle the question." Had the question been the existence of Deity voting would have been absurd, but the present motion was a recommendation to the Harmony school on the use of certain words, and in this sense he thought the opinion of the branch ought to be put to the vote.

Mr. Rowley thought that Mr. Clark's "God" was as much the last cause as the first cause; they should not teach children words which had no meaning; such a system would only confuse and mystify the youthful mind, the child when educated aright would not feel any "gap" whatever, and he much objected to "religion," because it had produced evil.

Mr. Swan: The "gap" was in the teacher, and not in the child. A teacher should express his ignorance at once, if he did not understand the enquiries of children: this would be better than answering the child by words which neither of them could ever understand.

ELECTRO PHYSIOLOGY.

The most interesting and animated lectures of the course have been delivered by Dr. Keenan since the last report. The leading idea, the consequences of which he considers of such vast importance and calculated to lead to such great results, that the electro-motive action and machinery are alike the characteristic of the galvanic or electrical apparatus and the human organization, was traced and expanded throughout a multitudinous array of physiological, chemical, and mechanical facts. The hitherto unrecognized function of food for *moving;* the proper action and application of medicaments, the effects of climate on temper, health and craniological development were severally treated. Medical science, said the doctor, might be made, by a knowledge of these fundamental principles, as precise in its deductions as the mathematics. Food and air might be chosen in precise accordance with the peculiarity of the animal machine. Food easy of digestion, in other words, most easy of combination with air, and air most fitted for combination with food, might be obtained by very simple observation. Combustion consists of the combination of air with the fuel in the same manner as with the food, two-thirds of which should combine with the air. Our own firesides would instruct us in these particulars. Where and when the fire burns brightest, the spirits and strength proportionably increase. The aching of rheumatic limbs, the shooting of corns, and such other bodily ailments are ruled by the same laws, and subject to the same influences as those which regulate our household fires—in the one case a plentiful supply of air, in the other deficient oxydisement takes place. Low, marshy, moist soil and stagnant air produce a differently organized race from elevated dry situations, visited by exhilarating breezes. The Flemings and the French illustrate this point. The brute, as well as human animals, share these influences. The gross, heavy, prize sheep, and dull phlegmatic stolid people which some soils and climates produce are sufficient examples.

The necessity is here shown of proportioning the motive to the sustentative food. If the superfluous food which is so enormously used is not expended in producing energy, where does it go? It is laid up in fat, precisely as in the Lincolnshire prize sheep, and with the same amount of grossness and impurity.

The old notions of the schools and colleges are passed from mouth to mouth without challenge, and the scientific themselves are tardy in repudiating them. We hear a man with the authority of an archbishop pronouncing that our bodies are continually changing, and are entirely renewed once in seven years, thus as it were in a spirit of inspiration announcing a continuous set of resurrections; this of course in brute animals exactly as in man.

The theory of the animal continually wasting away and consuming, showing what Liebig has called the "disintegration of the tissues," or continually tearing away of the fibre, should never surely have outlived recent admirable physiological discoveries.

The mechanical and mercantile genius of England, the sentimental and emotionary temperaments of the Irish, and the calculating and ratiocinative bias of the Scotch, were illustrated by their respective Commerce and Railways, Roman Catholicism and Presbyterianism.

Very full notes have been taken of the course, but want of space and press of matter prevent any but a mere fragmentary notice.

DECLINE OF FAITH.—E. H. writes, " I have lately been much engaged, directly and indirectly, in investigating the opinions held by the workmen employed in the trades and manufactories of London and other large places, and I find that two-thirds of the inmates of our shops and warehouses hold either deistical or atheistical opinions, and a portion of the other third no great admirers of the priestcraft." E. H. expresses a regret, in which we join, that these parties are not aroused to a sense of their duty, to the necessity of asserting their opinions, and defending their brethren from persecution. He thinks the Atheistical Society's attention should be called to this question.

DR. STRAUSS.—This famous rationalist has lately married a celebrated singer of Berlin.

EDINBURGH.—A friend in Glasgow wrote two letters to Miss Roalfe, one without her address, the second one had his address, and immediately both were returned, with a note to the effect that it was useless to write, for she was *not allowed to receive or answer letters.* I have written every week, at least twice, but no answer. I applied at the gates, and was told prisoners were allowed to receive and answer letters. I wrote to the governor on the subject, and he answered "that my letters were given to the matron, to be given to the prisoner *when it was judged proper.*" I wrote to Sir James Graham on the subject, and sent a copy of the governor's letter; he has sent me an answer, that my letter has been referred to the General Prison Board of Scotland.
W. B.

LEICESTER.—At a public meeting held on Sunday, February 4th, in the Social Institution, Mr. W. Cook in the chair, it was resolved, that a committee of the Anti-Persecution Union should be formed in that town. Mr. W. H. Holyoak was appointed secretary; Mr. W. Cook, treasurer; and Messrs. J. Chamberlin and G. Read, auditors. It was further resolved, that 3d. per quarter, paid in advance, be the smallest amount of subscription from members.

SOCIAL INSTITUTION, WHITECHAPEL.—Discusion on Saturday evening—Was the existence of Christ, a reality or an allegory.

RELIGIOUS SUBLIMITY.—Some body in Boston has sent us a pamphlet of 12 pages entitled, "Revival Hymns; principally selected by the Rev. R. H. Neale: set to some of the most familiar and useful Revival Tunes. Arranged by H. W. Day." It is decently printed, and the tunes may be good, but we have no taste that way and cannot judge. But many of the hymns—shade of Tom Shaw, what shall we say of them?—are the most simple, weak, puerile and sickening trash, that was ever rhymed on paper. From "Satan's kingdom is tumbling down," we select the following:

" Saint Paul and Silas bound in jail,
Would pray and sing in spite of hell—
They made the prison loudly ring,
Although opposed by hell's dark king.
       Shout! shout!"

Again—

" Young David's weapon seemed but dull,
Yet broke Goliah's brazen skull."

Bro. Cummings of the Christian Mirror, thus speaks of this couplet: " Pity another skull could not have been broken, before this product saw the light." We suspect the fellow's skull was already broken.

From " Come hear me tell"—

" Then I began to weep and cry
And looked this way and that to fly,
It grieved me so that I must die;
I strove salvation for to buy."

This reminds us of the poem addressed to the Maine militia, by a Down East poet—and we advise Mr. Neale to insert it in the next edition of his hymns:

" Come out, ye Continentalers,
  We're going for to go,
To fight the red-coat army
  We're plaguey cute you know."

How perfect the rhyme in the following, to say nothing of its harmony:—

" Stand fast in faith, fight for your king,
And soon the victory you shall win,
When Satan comes to tempt your minds,
Then meet him with these blessed lines."

We should think such lines would frighten the old rascal—for he has something of a taste for good poetry.—*American Paper.*

SCOTTISH UNION.—A public meeting on behalf of freedom of expression, was held in St. Cecilia's Hall, Edinburgh. Speeches were delivered by Messrs. Affleck, (chairman). Peddie, Jeffrey, Southwell, Tankard, and others.

CHRISTIAN CONVERSION EXTRAORDINARY.—The Bishop of Calcutta recently exposed himself and his system of proselytism most egregiously. He had, at Calcutta, an immensely rich Rajah, whom he had converted, as he thought. A public assembly was held at Calcutta, the governor-general, the whole staff, with the military and naval officers, were present, and all the civil officers were assembled. The bishop examined the Hindoo on the christian faith. The man answered, mechanically, in the affimative to all the bishop had said. But at last the bishop went too far, and asked him whether his answers were really those of conscientious conviction. A dead pause was in the assembly; immense expectations were raised. The bishop said, as literally as we remember, "on your conscience, which do you consider the best religion?" The Hindoo, with the usual solemnity of his race, replied in the following words, and not in very good English:—"I have considered this question very considerably, and I have given it a great deal of consideration, and I consider that the Christian religion is the best for the Christians, and the Hindoo religion is the best for Hindoos." The whole meeting burst out in a roar of laughter, and even the governor-general could not keep his countenance. It is under such disgusting circumstances of imposition that the bishops and migratory clergymen will fleece our poor, and rob them of the sums which are necessary for their sustenance and comfort.—*Dispatch.*

REASON *v.* RELIGION.—We are frequently asked, what we "intend to give the people if we take religion from them?" If by religion is meant those contradictory and incomprehensible systems, which no one has been able to reconcile; those dogmas which, without examination, are everywhere received as truths; we reply, that, in place of these absurdities, we recommend the cultivation of REASON. While Religion tells its votaries that their only safety is in a blind submission to their spiritual guides, Reason teaches man that his happiness consists in reciprocating benefits to his fellow men. While an inexorable priesthood are vainly denouncing eternal perdition on all who question the truth of their mandates, Nature lays open her volume, in which the most attractive inducements to virtue are presented to the sight, and the vicious insensibly impelled to pay her homage. This is our substitute for what is called Religion. This alone is sufficient to guarantee human happiness. The errors of education, the vortex of discordant systems, in which mankind are ingulphed, popular opinion, and family connections—all of these combine to retain them in bondage, and perpetuate their misery. It is our object to break the charm; to promote inquiry and investigation, by stimulating our fellow citizens, freely and fearlessly to exercise their intellectual faculties. In no other way can morality be fixed on a permanent basis; by no other means can felicity be assured to mortals.

Only by making the ruling few uneasy, can the oppressed many obtain a particle of relief.—BENTHAM.

A happy people will never rebel.—KOTZEBUE.

A weight of chains, number of stripes, hardness of labour, and other effects of a master's cruelty, may make one servitude more miserable than another; but he is a slave, who serves the best and gentlest man in the world, as well as he who serves the worst—and he does serve him if he must obey his commands, and depend upon his will.—ALGERNON SYDNEY.

A noble heart will disdain to subsist like a drone upon honey gathered by other's labour, like vermin, to filch its food out of the public granary, or, like a shark, to prey upon the lesser fry: but will rather outdo his private obligations to other men's care and toil, by considerable service and beneficence to the public.—BARONNE.

ANSWERS TO CORRESPONDENTS.

G. SMITH. —The application on Mrs. Martin's account was successful. That lady has some time been in possession of the means requisite for taking the Rotunda, and if terms can be come to with the landlord, she will shortly enter on the premises.

Received—W. Oldham.—" Belfast Vindicator." C. J. Savage.—Phil. Blasphemy relics from Edinburgh.

SUBSCRIPTIONS FOR THE ANTI-PERSECUTION UNION.

Per G. Smith, Salford.

Mr. Kalley	. . .	£0 1 0
,, J. Partington	. .	0 1 0
,, H. Moss	. .	0 1 0
J. Allen, London	. .	0 1 0
J. B. and L.	. .	0 1 0
Mr. Teed and Mr. Marsden	.	0 1 0
J. Dyoson, per Mr. Watson	-	0 2 0

G. J. H., *Sec.*

Printed and Published by G. J. HOLYOAKE, 40, Holywell-street, Strand, Saturday, March 2, 1844.

THE MOVEMENT

And Anti=Persecution Gazette.

"Maximize morals, minimize religion."—BENTHAM.

No. 13.   EDITED BY G. JACOB HOLYOAKE,   PRICE 1½d.
            ASSISTED BY M. Q. RYALL.

CHARACTER OF ATHEISM.

By our general tone, temper, and matter, we have sufficiently shown how wide and intense an interest we take in the world's doings. We have evinced how close, in our opinion, is the alliance between Atheism in theory and morality in practice. The less we think of other worlds, the more we think of this—the less we hope of the future, the greater is our anxiety to rationalise, to improve, and increase the happiness of the present. Were our pages more extensive, no fact of progress should go unregistered, no effort of improvement should pass by uncheered, and no enemy, in principle, of liberty and joy should escape unlashed. When Atheists, as a body, are more sensible of their interests and duty, they will put the means of doing this into our or some one else's power. With greater means, we should carry out with pleasure and satisfaction these cherished objects. Meanwhile, our friends must make allowances for any occasional omissions of matter or topics which to them may seem desirable, and even to be called for.

The article, on which I commented last week, entitled "Religious Controversy," is a common instance of the misappropriation of that term. Atheistical controversy was the controversy intended. Between these terms a practical distinction obtains. Religious controversy relates to the *improvement* of religion—atheistical controversy to the *destruction* of it. Nor was it hardly consistent in the writer of that article to condemn in such unmeasured terms even religious controversy—which sometimes has its uses, when a subsequent No. of the *New Moral World* contains an article on "Analogy and Theology;" in which is discussed the question of the consistency of Christian ideas with Analogy.

Discussions on religion have at least produced the good predicted by L'Estrange—they have at last brought religion itself into contempt. They were the *distinctions* of religion, which Sheil denounced as "fatal, disastrous, and detestable;" and even Socialistic true Christianity might not improperly be included in the same category. We would go farther than Mr. Sheil, and denounce religion itself as being the cause of these fatal and pernicious distinctions.

The *New Moral World* asks—"Ought not the spirit out of which such monstrous evils as fanaticism arise, to be checked and discouraged by all who sincerely desire to benefit their fellow-men?" But how can this spirit be checked except by Atheism? Will not the upas tree always flourish while the root is left sound? Who can "discourage" evil so effectually as they who labour to destroy the cause?

To merely deplore the flourishing of fanaticism and leave its root and source untouched—to labour vainly for the improvement of that which requires extermination, much more resembles "a contest of words, words, words," than open, uncompromising, atheistical controversy.

Religion, that keeps men ignorant, makes them superstitious and bigoted, in process of time throws off its infamous and degrading coils—or rather knowledge and reason pulls them off, and then the man begins to appear—something of the goodness of human nature looks out—liberty begins to be appreciated—reason is listened to, and the trembling precincts of faith are left for the bolder speculations of improvement. The religious men who undergo this favourable change are sceptics and infidels. Such persons have thrown off the dominion of the bible, the slavish regard of priests, and the grosser corruptions of faith; but they still retain the fundamental error of religion and the effeminacy of piety.

Besides these natural and enduring defects of feeling, judgment, and opinion, they stand before the world inconsistent and absurd. However sound the Deist may consider his views, they are at the mercy of such men as Leslie and Faber, who pursue them with relentless severity. The Socialists have to drag through the mire of religious contempt their atheistical principles. Nor has their profession of religion saved them from the haughty insolence of the Bishop of Exeter, or the low abuse of the Schoolmaster of March. Atheism in the felon's dock borne down by the arm of the law—by magisterial tyranny and christian rage, never yet suffered such contempt. It has been hated but not despised.

In argument, Deism and Socialistic Christianity fare no better: they can only be supported by evasion and subterfuge, by plentiful interlardings of reserved meanings, and new interpretations of commonly received words. By the employment of plain, sound reasoning, these views have hitherto failed of support. It is no mean presumptive evidence in favour of Atheism, that it needs only a fair field—that it despises subterfuge—that it needs no mystery, but can always promote its plain purposes by plain means.   G. J. H.

PRACTICAL ENDS OF ATHEISM.

A leading characteristic of our Journal cannot fail to have impressed the least attentive reader. The pettinesses of sectarian controversy, strictures of individual character in the religious world, church imposition and dominancy, and the various hacknied topics on which the "liberal" press so largely dilate, have been made to give place to the discussion of fundamentals. Priests, churches, and sects, necessarily arising out of the notion of the supernatural, the principal phase of which is the god-idea, must be abolished when the god-foundation is uprooted. When fallacies are detected and exposed in fundamentals, all the multitudinous deductions of error thence arising, are swept away. It is, in fact, uprooting the tree instead of meddling with the branches. It is the true radical method in theology. As was expressed in the pages of the *Oracle*—" We war not with the church but with the altar; not with the form of worship, but with worship itself; not with the attributes but the existence of deity." Thus leaving to the small railers, and abusers of all sorts, to amuse their circles of readers, by pelting with harmless and ineffectual missiles the grosser religious delinquents; we have directed heavy blows at the vital parts of religion. Finding easy, credulous people easily tickled and deceived by such nice phrases as "abuses of religion," when, in reality, religion is none other than one monstrous abuse, we have deemed it a principal business to keep to the prolific source of this widely ramified evil. However "negative" our course, it is productive of the most extensively positive results. As god's blessing or god's curse, god's commands, likings, dislikings or favouritisms are unceremoniously dragged into every word and deed of the business of life, the business of life must be materially and positively influenced by turning out this god-influence. If we find god in all sorts of rules, laws and regulations affecting us individually and collectively, —when we find that a queen cannot open her mouth, nor the legislature pass an act, nor a parish beadle bawl out a notice without more or less of god interference, surely the attacking of the god notion is a very practical course. Instead of putting god upon half-pay, for which half-measure, my colleague was censured by both godists and anti-godists,—we atheists would allow it no pay at all. We certainly do not talk of diminishing the supplies, reforming church abuses, pruning down the enormous revenues of the priesthood—episcopalian and dissenting,—down with their god, and down they must come!

But widely extensive and practically operative as all atheistical advocacy is calculated to be, it has been by no means to this alone that we have confined our efforts. Our pages, to the utmost extent of our limited space, have been the depositaries of every fact and argument and sentiment that was found to bear upon the happiness of the community.
M. Q. R.

THE "VOLUNTARY," AND THE ANTI-PERSECUTION UNION.

It is due to the editor of the *Voluntary* to have earlier acknowledged that he did the Anti-Persecution Union the justice to admit that we did furnish Dr. Kalley with most ample means of knowing our sentiments. He also publishes the letter which was addressed to him in the Union's defence; and which appeared in *Movement*, No. 7. According to my promise in that letter, I forwarded a few days ago to the editor of the *Voluntary*, Dr. Kalley's second letter. At the same time I expressed a hope that he would do the Union the justice to correct the erroneous opinion he had formed concerning us. On the same day I addressed, for reasons which will be seen, the following letter to the Editor, and from a sense of fairness, it becomes us to publish it.

To the Editor of the Voluntary.

Sir,—I left, this morning, a letter for you, at your publisher's, in which I expressed a hope that you would "feel yourself justified in correcting the impressions you had published concerning the Anti-Persecution Union's correspondence with Dr. Kalley." I have since procured your February number, and find that you have very handsomely done this. I therefore respectfully apologise for the unnecessary remark in my letter of this morning. Had I been aware that you had published my first letter to you, I should not have used the remark which occurs in my reply to Dr. Kalley's "second" letter. This error I will hasten to publicly correct. In publishing, in the *Voluntary*, the explanation of the Anti-Persecution Union, you have done us a justice which we did not expect, and to which we are unaccustomed, but it is an act which we shall always be happy to acknowledge.

I am, Sir, yours respectfully,
G. JACOB HOLYOAKE,
Sec. to the A. P. U.

It will be remembered that in my first letter to the *Voluntary*, I enclosed to the editor my whole correspondence with Dr. Kalley up to that period—and in addition to publishing the explanation of the Union, the editor presents to his readers, our first letter to Dr. Kalley, and the Doctor's reply. In the first letter to the Doctor, these words occur—" According to the Scotch newspaper, the *Witness*, your alleged offence is against the mother of god. Mother or father, it makes no difference to the Anti-Persecution Union—they contend for every man's right to express his opinions on these parties, unchecked by any power, but the power of opinion." This must be new doctrine to the readers of the *Voluntary*, and members of the " Evangelical Voluntary Church Association." The editor says, that " the Union is composed, in part, if not wholly, of avowed infidels, and having under its protection, persons of the most infamous character and pursuits," but we pass by this, in consideration of his general fairness towards us. He further adds, that "the notice that Dr. Kalley has obtained from us, conveys a severe rebuke to his fellow Christians in England!" I wonder how many "rebukes" it will take to make them better. Incorrigible dogs! G. J. H.

BELGIUM, ITS LAWS & LIBERTIES.
For the Movement.

Perhaps a short account of the Belgian Constitution may be interesting to your readers, as it is the most liberal in Europe, and said to be the model for the new Greek Constitution. The chamber of representatives is composed of deputies elected by citizens, paying a certain sum in taxes, according to the constitution. The sum required to make an elector cannot exceed one hundred florins in direct taxation, nor be below twenty florins. A person must have passed his twenty-fifth year to be eligible as a member—no property qualification is required. The members are elected for four years. The half, renewable every two years. In case of dissolution, the chamber is entirely renewed. Members are paid two-hundred florins monthly, during the session. Those who inhabit the town where the session is held, are not paid. In place of a hereditary house of lords, they have a senate, elected by those who elect the members of the chamber of representatives. The number of senators is equal to half of that of the representatives. The senators are elected for eight years, the half renewable every four years. The members of the senate just as the representatives, are entirely renewed in case of dissolution. A member of the senate must be at least forty years old, and must pay at least one thousand florins in direct taxation. Senators do not receive any pay for their services. The King can declare war, make treaties of peace, alliance and commerce. He can confer titles of nobility, without attaching any privilege to them. The following are some of the other portions of their political code. Under the title of Belgians and their rights, the national Congress on the 7th of February, 1831, decreed amongst other articles: that except in the case of a flagrant offence, no one can be arrested, except in virtue of an ordinance, with the cause assigned, by the judge, which must be signified at the moment of arrest, or at latest in twenty-four hours.—Your readers will recollect that Mr. Holyoake was arrested without a warrant. By our statute of William III. an Englishman convicted of blasphemy, is deprived of all civil rights—Civil death is abolished; it cannot be re-established, says the thirteenth article, under the head of rights. The fourteenth article says, the liberty of worship, that of its public exercise, as well as the liberty of manifesting his opinions on every matter, are guaranteed, saving the repression of crimes committed on the occasion of using those liberties. The fifteenth article, says, no one can be obliged in any manner to concur in the acts and ceremonies of worship, nor observe its days of repose. The sixteenth, says, the state has no right to interfere either in the nomination or installation of the ministers of any worship, nor to prevent their corresponding with their superiors, and publishing their acts; having in this latter case the ordinary responsibility in matters of the press and publication. The civil marriage must always precede the nuptial benediction, unless there shall be exceptions established by law. Seventeenth: Instruction is free, every preventive measure is forbidden. The repression of offences is only regulated by the law. Public instruction given at the expence of the state is equally regulated by the law. Eighteenth: The press is free; the censure can never be re-established; no caution can be exacted from the writers, editors, or printers. When the author is known, and lives in Belgium, the editor, printer, or distributor cannot be pursued. Nineteenth: The Belgians have the right to assemble peaceably and without arms, in conforming themselves to the laws which regulate the exercise of this right, without however having to submit it to any previous authority. This disposition does not apply to assemblies in the open air, which remain entirely subject to laws of police. Twentieth: The Belgians have the right of association; this right cannot be made subject to any preventative measure. Twenty-first: Every one has the right of addressing to the public authorities, petitions signed by one or several persons. Article Eight: Decree on the jury, says, Offences of the press, and those political, shall be proceeded against in prosecution, and in court, as in matters criminal. However, contrary to article 133 of the code of criminal prosecution, the court may discharge the defendant from the prosecution, if the majority of judges pronounce in his favour. If the accused is brought before the court of assizes, he ought to appear in person, and he will have a distinct place from others accused for crime. Previous imprisonment can never take place for simple offences, political, or of the press. In a decree upon the press, July 20, 1831, Article first, says, All those will be reputed, accomplices in every crime or offence committed, who, either by discourses pronounced in a public place before a re-union of individuals, or by placards fixed up, or by writings, printed or not, sold or distributed, shall have provoked directly to commit them. Second: Whoever wickedly and publicly shall have attacked the obligatory force of the laws, or provoked direct disobedience of them, will be punished with imprisonment, from six months to three years. By Art. sixth: truth is made the justification of libel. Article Ninth: The defendant of an offence committed in publication, and only incurring the pain of imprisonment, if residing in Belgium, shall not be imprisoned before condemnation. By Art. Tenth: Prosecutions of the press are only to be made by the persons calumniated. Calumny of the king and royal family, and all public functionaries, may be prosecuted officially. The jury will occupy themselves first with the enquiry, whether the defendant is the author of the publication. The printer takes the place of the writer, should he not be discovered. By Art. Thirteenth: Every person mentioned in a journal, whether by name, or indirectly, will have the right of forcing the insertion of an answer, provided that it does not exceed a thousand letters in writing, or double the space occupied by the article which shall have provoked it. The answer must be inserted, at latest, the next day after the answer shall have been deposited at the bureau, or the editor looses twenty florins each day of delay.

In the bulletin officiel, Oct. 16, 1830, is the following, on the liberty of the press, of speech and of teaching. The provisional government, considering that the domain of intelligence is essentially free, considering that it is incumbent to cause to disappear for ever the trammels by which power has hitherto chained the press in its expression, its march, and its developments, makes the following decree: Article first, It is free for every citizen, or citizens, associated for a religious or philosophical object, whatever it may be, to profess their opinions as they understand them, and to spread them by *all the possible means of persuasion and conviction*. All laws or regulations which cramp the free manifestation of opinions and the propogation of doctrines, by the way of speech, press, or instruction, are abolished. Of the liberty of association, the same bulletin officiel, as before, published the following: The provisional government considering that the trammels put upon the liberty of association, are infractions upon the rights of individual and political liberty, order, Article first,—It is allowed to citizens to associate as they understand it, for objects political, religious, philosophical, literary, industrial, and commercial. W. J. B.

DE LAMARTINE'S LETTERS ON HISTORY.
III.

You can put to the same test every episode of the French revolution; you will always discover these three aspects—the purely individual aspect, glory; the exclusively national, patriotism; and the moral aspect, civilization. Considering these various points of view in a strictly logical manner, you will always find that glory, and even patriotism, severed from national morality, are barren as respects the nation, and the real progress of the human race; in short, that there is no glory without honesty; no patriotism without humanity; no success without justice.

How admirable is such a history; how beneficial for the people; what a pledge for their future power is given into their hands with such a book! To teach the people by the facts, by the plots, by the hidden sense of those great historical dramas, of which men see only the scenery and the actors, without discerning the plan—to teach them to know, to judge, to moderate themselves, to enable them to distinguish those that serve them from those that mislead them, those that dazzle them from those that enlighten them—to enable them to point out each man, each great event of their own history, to weigh them, not by the false weight of the passions of the day, of prejudices, of hatred, of national vanities, of confined patriotism, but by the just and real weight of universal conscience of the human race, and of the utility of the action for civilization—to convince them that history is not a series of mere chances, a confused mixture of men and things, but a progressing march through centuries, where each nationality has a post, a part assigned to it; where each social class itself has its relative importance in the eyes of God; to teach the people to respect themselves, to take part in the progressive accomplishment of the great providential designs—in a word, to create for them a moral sense, and instruct them to exercise this moral sense on their governments, on their great men and on themselves—this is to give the people much more than the empire, much more than the power, much more than the government; this is to give them a conscience, judgment, the sovereignty of themselves; this is to place them above all governments. *The day when they are really worthy of reigning they will reign.* It matters then very little under what name and in what form governments are after all, but the mould into which the statue of the people is cast, and where it takes the form comformable to its more or less perfect nature. Of what use changing twenty times the mould if you do not change the clay—it will always be clay. It is the people who are to be modified; governments will modify themselves to the people's image, for, like people, like government. When a people complain of theirs, it is because they are not worth having another.

But your attempt to popularise history has awaked a thought which has slept these ten years in my soul, a thought which by turns I have presented for realisation to the great parties and governments of my country, and which they dropped with indifference to the ground, because it was not a weapon of war for fighting, but an instrument of melioration and peace for fashioning the nation. The thought is this, I said to myself;—our liberty of the press, our government of discussion and publicity, our industrial movement, especially our primary instruction instituted in our forty thousand parishes lavishly spread elementary instruction throughout the inferior regions of the population. All this gives the faculty, the habit, and creates a want of reading among the masses of the people! but after having created in them this want, what is given them for its gratification? What is written for them? Nothing. The education of us, sons of the rich, privileged by leisure, goes on without interruption through our youth, and even our life. After the elementary teaching which we imbibe in the laps of our mothers, colleges receive us, from which we pass to the great courses of the universities; we hear the illustrious masters, whom the state pays for us in the chief towns; sciences, philosophy, human letters, politics—all is poured forth in full cups, and if it is not enough, inexhaustable libraries are opened to us; numberless reviews and journals, for which our fortune permits us to subscribe, work for us the whole day or the whole night, in order to nourish our intelligence every morning with the bloom of all human knowledge.

With such a diet perish alone what *cannot* live, the incapable or the indifferent. Life is a study till death. For the children of the people, of all this, there is absolutely nothing. They, too, however, have their portion of leisure. The holidays, or days of rest. There is not one trade in which some portion of the day or of the year may not be devoted to study. How many unoccupied hours have your five hundred thousand soldiers in their garrisons, your sixty thousand sailors on the decks of their vessels, when the sea is calm, and the wind favourable; how many have your numberless workmen, who repose or fatigue themselves with idleness generally forty-eight hours a week? how many have the women, the old men, the children at home, the shepherds in the fields? And where is the intellectual nourishment of these masses? Where is this moral and daily bread of the people? Nowhere. A catechism, or songs; this is their diet. Some gloomy crimes related in atrocious verses, represented in hideous features, and hung up in their cottage or their attic—this is their library, their art, their museum.

Among the more enlightened may be seen some journals exclusively political, which slip from time to time into the workshop or the inn of the village, and bring them the counter-blow of our parliamentary debates, names of men to be hated, and some popularities to tear to pieces, exactly as one throws rags to the dogs to be torn off; this is their civil education. What sort of people do you expect from all this?

Well, I thought to fulfil this vow in the moral and intellectual life of the masses, not only by books which one takes up, reads once, and lays aside for ever; but by the sole book which never ends, which re-commences every day; which one reads in spite of one's self, so to speak—and, by an insatiable instinct of curiosity and novelty, which is one of the natural appetites of man, namely by the daily book, by popular journalism! for journalism is not a caprice, it is the succession itself of time, noticed hour by hour on the dial of the human mind.

(*To be concluded in our next number.*)

MR. GILLESPIE'S ARGUMENT.

Glasgow, March 2nd, 1844.

DEAR GEORGE.—I take shame to myself for not commencing long ere this my promised reply to Gillespie's "monster" argument for the being and attributes of God, with which certain persons who rejoice in the name "Philalethean," seem so strangely enamoured, more especially as they have expressed themselves through their V. P., Mr. C. Clark, "much inclined to look upon your challenge to Mr. Gillespie as being an excuse for delay and as indicating a desire on the part of the London Atheists, to evade answering Mr. Gillespie's work. By way, however, of lame apology for myself, I wish two important particulars to be taken cognizance of; one, that like yourself, I knew nothing except from hearsay of Mr. Gillespie's performance until lately, (about a month since,) when with some difficulty I obtained a copy; the other is, that since I came here my health has been strangely affected. These matters would not have been referred to, save and except only for the satisfaction of London Atheists, who have been almost charged with evasion, because I neglected to do what I pledged myself to do, and shall commence to do early in the coming week, so that our suspicious challengers of the Philalethean Society, will not much longer be unattended to. For a note appended to Mr. M'Cullough's answer to Mr. Clark, you say that should the Philaletheans publish us as a set of incapables, you should not complain—nor should I, but if the members of that society are wise, they will wait yet a little while, as it would be rather awkward if they published us incapable of refuting Mr. Gillespie's book just as our refutation of his book appeared. I therefore strongly recommend them to bridle their impatience for a fortnight longer.

I am well pleased to find the circulation of the *Movement* so great, though it should be far greater, and here I may take occasion to observe, that in the report of "Adjourned Discussion at Branch A1," given in the current number, our able friend Mr. M'Cullough said he was "much surprised to hear that Mr. Southwell had said certain things about Mr. Owen;" and well he might, if he heard any one declare that I had said Mr. Owen "expressed his opinion (respecting god, religion, &c.,) in the best possible manner," for I never thought so, and certainly never said so, except perhaps when fast asleep. In lieu of thinking that Mr. Owen has written about religion in the best possible manner, I am of opinion that he has written more inconsistently, and no less absurdly about it than the *Times'* editor, or the followers of Johanna Southcott. I have, as you know, invariably refused to defend Mr. Owen's words, though ever ready to stand up for the excellence of his intentions, and (religion always excepted) the truth of his meanings. Of course you are at liberty to publish so much or little of this letter as you think proper.   C. SOUTHWELL.

THE DEATHS OF MESSRS. SOUTHWELL AND CHILTON.

IN No. 11 Mr. Paterson, in one of his dry jokes, says "Chilton and Southwell are both dead—may my last end be like theirs." Upon this a valuable friend writes in anxious simplicity—

My dear sir,—I have been astonished by reading in Paterson's letter in the *Movement* of yesterday, that Chilton and Southwell were both dead. Surely this is some error. It is not long since that I was in correspondence with Chilton, upon the most friendly terms. It cannot be. Else, why have not regular notices appeared, if such events as they took place? I am quite bewildered; pray enlighten me, if possible, per return of post.

It is a shame to spoil this joke by explanation. If half the world were dead, Paterson shut up in his stone cell, in Perth, could not find it out. Messrs. Southwell and Chilton have been as much surprised as our correspondent, to find that they were "dead." "They are not dead, but sleeping." Not having written to Paterson with their accustomed regularity, they had become *non est inventus* to him—and as they are at large in the world, in the enjoyment of liberty and love, Paterson archly hopes that *his* last end may be like theirs."   G. J. H.

DR. KEENAN'S CONCLUDING LECTURE.

THE Doctor further explained his views of the functions of the lungs, brain and spine, the influence upon health and the digestion, of partial brain-work and the importance of exact knowledge on these subjects for the guidance of parents and instructors. The weaning of children was introduced as illustrative—a comparison was instituted between the injurious action of the improper and indigestible food generally permitted to the infant at this period, and the prejudicial operation of too laborious an employment of one part of the brain, at the expense of the other portion, and the spine. The result in each case was the withdrawal of the required energy from the back of the brain and spine, and consequent debility of the whole system. The forcing of children to exercise the thinking powers at the expense of the emotional was reprobated as highly injudicious.

We were scarcely more than mere animals at the earlier stages of existence, and the vital and emotional powers only were properly called into action. If a child shows an indisposition to acquire knowledge, it is both absurd and cruel to force it, or rather attempt to force it. When a desire to learn is felt, learning becomes easy, pleasurable, and a healthful exercise of the faculties; if the desire is unfelt, learning becomes painful drudgery; we have no business to compel unwilling studies. The province of the judicious parent or teacher is to actuate the child by a motive. If we wish to direct the attention to arithmetic, geometry, grammar let us extract these sciences and arts from his tops, marbles, and every-day topics Rules before practice are reversing the order of progress. Let him count his marbles, measure the objects around him, such as interest him, weigh, and compute the comparative weights of his companions, let him correct his speech by present familiar examples; from these courses deduce, or let him deduce rules.

Excellently did the Doctor by the force of cogent reasoning, based on observation of facts, physiologically and practically, draw the same conclusions as Rousseau has, with such a combination of eloquence and simplicity advocated in his *Emilius*.

The Doctor supplies a continual fount of interesting facts and accurate conclusions, admirably subservient to the advocacy of advanced views in social, economical, political, moral, and philosophical reform.

This last lecture of the course was received with as marked attention and manifestations of pleasure as any of his previous addresses. Addresses indeed they may be more properly called, and perhaps on account of this peculiarity there is about them the charm of novelty, not only in matter, but in manner. We ordinarily hear in philosophical lectures, a carefully concocted and elaborate dissertation, each part of which has been methodically pre-arranged. Regularity and order are by this mode certainly secured; but the freshness, vivacity, and point, pervading the Doctor's discourses are, by the old routine, unattainable. There is a familiarity, too, about these, as it were, impromptu efforts, peculiarly suitable to unscientific people. It is to be desired that the Doctor may step out from the scientific and somewhat exclusive circle of the "Polytechnic," and visit the humbler regions of the vulgar. His style and manner, thoroughly versed though he appears to be, in all the scientific departments of his subject, would excellently suit the apprehensions of a mixed audience. This is said with reference rather to his copious, beautiful, and useful illustrations, than to the main object he has in view, the electro-physiological expositions. The former must always please and instruct,—the latter have to be submitted to the test of discussion by competent investigators.

One word with the Doctor on his god-almightyisms;—a free comment on these points, cannot now subject us to the charge of atheistical bigotry. Comment was withheld on this head, while respectful attention was paid to his facts and philosophy.

On the conclusion of these lectures, some remarks on these divine excrescences may be neither mistimed nor misplaced. In bidding the worthy lecturer farewell, we will take leave to refer him to a fact—a little fact—but one that speaks volumes. Will he please to recall the occasion of his remark in refutation of Liebig's doctrine, of the disintegration of the tissues in which he designated the notion of our " shaking ourselves to pieces, in order to be continually renovated, as a libel on the wisdom of a great and adorable creator." It was a very nice, pretty, and well rounded wind up of a section of his argument; and albeit quite as well turned and constructed as previous little points which had elicited general applause, this particular peroration fell still-born, stale, flat, and unprofitable on the assembled ear! The god-almighty clap-trap, that will shake the walls of Exeter Hall by the responsive applause of the saints and apish vulgarians who mob round them, is mere senseless noise— *vox et preterea nihil*, among an intelligent, investigative audience.

It is high time for scientific men to discard the religious rhodomontade of the theologers. Every man to his trade. We attend scientific lectures and read scientific treatises, not for spiritual, but material information. We need not know and do not care whether a public instructor believes in one "great and adorable creator," or five hundred—in a good and evil personified principle, *i. e.*, a god and a devil—or a triplicate personification, *i.e.*, god, christ, and ghost. We don't want to be cozened out of our time or money by the substitution of divinity for philosophy. Divinity shops abound, and from the supply exceeding the demand, their merchandise is to be had as cheap as dirt—it is, in fact, quite "a drug in the market,"—Then away with it to the pulpit. Let not the platform of science be discredited by godly cant. These animadversions, it is but just to say, are far more applicable to the generality of lecturers than to the gentleman who has given rise to them; but, to quote an applicable Jewish saying, " where much is given much should be required;" so of the Doctor,—with his activity of brain in the direction of analysis and ratiocination, added to a capacity and willingness to impart his information, the cant of god-almightyism is specially offensive to the intelligent, and insidious to the uninformed.

MISS ROALFE.—We give the following important and interesting news on the authority of a correspondent. The Glasgow branch of the Rational Society intend presenting Miss Roalfe with the sum of £10, being the amount of the fine the authorities required her to pay as an alternative of imprisonment. The presentation is to take place at a soirée to be held in the Hall on the occasion of her liberation.

NOTICE.—If any friends can send us Nos. 2 and 3 and 38 of the *Oracle* any reasonable expence will be paid, and they will much oblige many anxious contributors who are waiting to complete volumes.

Just Published, price 6d., " Christianity proved Idolatry ; or a short and easy method with the Christians :" by Charles Southwell.

In the Press, and will shortly be published, neatly bound in cloth lettered, price 1s. 6d., " PRACTICAL GRAMMAR ; or Composition Divested of Difficulties," with select examples from the writings of elegant authors ; containing all that is necessary for ordinary purposes and no more, and intended for the use of those who have little time to study: by G. J. Holyoake. " No department of knowledge is like grammar: a person may conceal his ignorance of any other art; but every time he speaks, he publishes his ignorance of this. There can be no greater imputation on the intelligence of any man than that he should talk from the cradle to the tomb and never talk well."—G. J. H. London : Watson, 5, Paul's-alley, Paternoster-row.

Riches are attended with luxury, and luxury ends in despotism.—*Erasmus.*

EQUALITY.—A state of cultivated equality is that state which, in speculation and theory, appears most consonant to the nature of man, and most conducive to the extensive diffusion of felicity.—*Godwin.*

NAMES INSTEAD OF THINGS.— It is a mockery of our fellow creatures' wrongs to call them equal in rights, when, by bitter compulsion of their wants, we make them inferior to us in all that can soften the heart, or dignify the understanding.—*Coleridge.*

The state of society in which we live is a mixture of feudal savageness and imperfect civilisation.—SHELLEY.

Never do an act of which you doubt the justice.

Have care of an ox before you, of an ass behind you, and of a priest on either side of you.—*W. de Britaine.*

FREEDOM OF EXPRESSION.—The spirit of society on this subject, may be looked upon as the thermometer of civilization.—*Bailey.*

DISCOVERY OF TRUTH.—Men doubt before they understand, and in the propagation of knowledge, it happens that fathers doubt before sons argue ; thus two, and sometimes three, generations are required to attain rational resolutions.—*Ensor.*

ANSWERS TO CORRESPONDENTS.

PHIL.—Will he favour us with one or two of his papers ?

J. THORNTON. — The *Investigator* closed at No. 28, but a little page, index, and preface, appeared. Would Mr. T. favour us with the pamphlet he quotes from ?

"A CONVERT FROM METHODISM, BY THE ORACLE OF REASON," in a letter of some drollery, assures us that he does not intend purchasing any more gospel truth until he gets a receipt from the Lord for the money already laid out in that commodity. —We wish he may get it.

C. HARRISON, Northampton, says that, " a few friends to liberty are about to establish a Sunday School, to teach morality without priestcraft," and they desire to be informed what books to procure. There are no books that *precisely* meet the wants of a children's school. Much has yet to be done before this department will be perfect in the eye of the moralist and unsectarian educator. Mr. Ellis's books and Chamber's 1st, 2nd, and 3rd Reading Books, are the plainest, but they are intended rather for Infant than general schools. Chamber's Introduction to the Sciences, and Peter Parley's Tales, published by Tegg and Son, will be found very useful.

J. C. S. objects to the article on "The Chartists and their Censors," and sends several facts for publication, on individual character, which have been published again and again. In stating what I knew, my only object was to adduce a little on the other side that something like fair play might obtain. To continue the personal discussion which I deprecated would be inconsistent. J. C. S. concludes by saying that he thinks " the working classes should not place implicit confidence in any leader, but use their own discretion." With this I agree, and the sole purpose of my article was to enforce it.

SUBSCRIPTIONS TO THE ANTI-PERSECUTION UNION.

W. Arnott, Pocklington . .	£0 5	0
J. N., Canterbury . .	0 5	0
Subscriptions collected by Mr. Alexander Campbell :—		
An Enemy to Persecution .	0 10	0
A Friend to Humanity and Justice	0 10	0
A Concordist . .	0 2	6
A Paterialist . . .	0 2	6
A sacred Socialist . .	0 2	6
One who wishes to be a love-spirit agent for the emancipation of humanity from the evils of degeneration.	0 2	6
Per Mr. H. Morrish, Bristol :—		
Coll. 17	0 7	6
Ditto 19	0 2	0
Ditto 27	0 5	6

G. J. H., *Sec.*

Printed and Published by G. J. HOLYOAKE, 40, Holywell-street, Strand, Saturday, March 9, 1844.

THE MOVEMENT
And Anti=Persecution Gazette.

"Maximize morals, minimize religion."—BENTHAM.

| No. 14. | EDITED BY G. JACOB HOLYOAKE, ASSISTED BY M. Q. RYALL. | PRICE 1½d. |

FALLACY OF "THE ARGUMENT A PRIORI," FOR THE BEING AND ATTRIBUTES OF GOD, AS THAT ARGUMENT IS STATED BY WILLIAM GILLESPIE.

THIS "grand" argument just amounts to a grand absurdity! that is, if conclusions logically flowing from absurd assumptions, are themselves absurd, which I take to be undeniable.

The very clever person, who writes himself " Antitheos," has published a " Refutation of the argument à priori for the being and attributes of god;" showing the irrelevancy of that argument, as well as the fallacious reasoning of Dr. Samuel Clarke and others, *especially* of Mr. Gillespie in support of it. But it seems to me, the author of that " Refutation" has not exactly overturned the " Argument à priori for the being and attributes of god," as laid down by Gillespie; nay, his " Refutation," ably written though it certainly is, has in nowise damaged, but rather lent an appearance of strength to that argument, because containing a very foolish admission, which Gillespie has turned to excellent account, in his " Examination of Antitheos's ' Refutation of the argument à priori, for the being and attributes of god:' " Take an example:—

Gillespie asserts the *existence* of infinity of extension; and it will be seen by and bye, that the mighty argument we London Atheists are so confidently " challenged" to attack, is not worth the paper on which it is so pompously laid out, unless that unproved, unprovable, and most idle *assertion*, turns out, under Gillespie's wonder-working hand, an Atheist confounding *truth*. I shall be excused, therefore, without doubt, by readers in general, and Gillespie's admirers in particular, for taking some pains to prove that there is no such *thing* as infinity of extension, and *consequently* that Gillespie, in assuming as the basis of his " Argument that there *is*," has assumed unwarrantably; and Antitheos in admitting the assumption, did foolishly.

That there may be " no mistake," I shall here quote a little.

" Infinity of extension is necessarily existing."

This is the starting, the very first proposition in Gillespie's book, and here are the reasons he seems to consider sufficient to satisfy even Atheists—

" For even when the mind endeavours to remove from it the idea of infinity of extension, it cannot, after all its efforts, avoid leaving still there, the idea of such infinity. Let there be ever so much endeavour to displace this idea, that is, conceive infinity of extention non-existent, every one, by a review or reflex examination of his own thoughts, will find it is utterly beyond his power to do so.

" Now, since even when we would remove infinity of extension out of our mind, we prove it must exist, by necessarily leaving the thought behind, or by substituting (so to speak) infinity of extension, for infinity of extension taken away. From this it is manifest, infinity of extension is necessarily existing; for everything, the existence of which we *cannot but* believe, which we *always suppose*, even though we *would not*, is necessarily existing.

" To deny that infinity of extension exists is, therefore, an utter contradiction. Just as much a contradiction as this, 1 is equal to 1; *therefore*, 1 is not equal to 1, but to 2; 2 not being identical with 1. As thus, infinity of extension is ever present to the mind, though we desire to banish it; *therefore* it can be removed from the mind. This is just an application of the greatest of all contradictions—a thing can be and not be, at the same time."

The reader has now before him Proposition I. of that "grand" argument London Atheists have been defied to grapple with, together with some *reasons* for its acceptance, deemed by its author so solid, and so perfectly irresistible, that he who shall in spite of them, venture " to deny that infinity of extension exists," must prepare to find himself classed among utterers of "utter contradictions." Nevertheless, I do deny that infinity of extension exists; and will prove, " in proper time and place," that matter is the only existence; yea, I will *demonstrate* that infinity of extension no more *exists*, necessarily or unnecessarily, than does infinity of time or infinity of motion. We *demonstrate*, says this "grand" argument's author, that a thing is not, only by proving that it cannot be,* and *therefore* the Philalethian Society will strike their divine colours, and notwithstanding past blusters, publish a candid admission of their error, if I contrive to *demonstrate* that infinity of extension is not by proving that it cannot be.

But loving to do everything decently and in order, before proceeding to prove that the "grand" argument's fundamental proposition is a fundamental fallacy, I will adduce the promised evidence that Antitheos has unwarily admitted, to the great joy, and perhaps surprise of Gillespie, that this very fundamental blunder is incontestable truth.

At page 43 of his "Refutation," I find these words:—

The first proposition—"Infinity of extension is necessarily existing"—it would be absurd in the extreme to deny. No more can we imagine any limit prescribable to extension, than we can imagine the outside of a house to be in the inside of it.

"Thus," observes Gillespie,† "Antitheos admits, to the fullest extent, the truth of proposition I. *To me, this is a most important admission,* for if that proposition is granted, (and who can rationally deny it?) I undertake to make out all the rest by *necessary consequence.*"

Now, I marvel not that Gillespie should *make much* of the "most important admission," but I do marvel greatly, that so shrewd a thinker as Antitheos should have furnished him with it; for of all admissions that could be made to such an antagonist, it is at once the most silly and important; every atom of the "grand" argument must survive or perish with it. The author of that argument may well be excused for *chuckling*, when he found the rotten proposition, every other proposition in his book rests upon suddenly converted by the mistake of a talented opponent into a safe and sound *point d'appui*, but patience good reader, for

"Let Hercules himself do what he may,
Cats will mew, and dogs will have their day."

As with dogs, so with arguments of the *spurious* kind, which "have their day," and then drop unwept, unhonoured, and unseen into that bottomless grave where all sorts of exploded error hides its *despised* head. But I must back to the point.

Infinity of extension is necessarily existing, according to the "Argument," and as my desire is to give this *decisive* proposition all the advantage it can derive from the authority of great names, I gladly take this opportunity of mentioning that Locke declared it "near as hard to conceive any existence, or to have an idea of any real being, with a perfect negation of all manner of expansion, as it is to have the idea of any real existence, with a perfect negation of all manner of duration."

Dr. Samuel Clarke, another "great name," observes that "extension does not belong to *thought,* because thought is not a being. But there is *need* of extension to the existence of every being, to a being which has or has not thought, or any other quality whatsoever."

Here are two first-rate authorities, of whom it must be confessed Gillespie has sufficient reason to boast, as giving respectability (in appearance) to the "infinity of extension" dogma. Many other authorities, almost equally respectable, might be adduced on the *same* side, but what availeth it though *all* authority were on that side, if *truth* is on the other.

Gillespie in the "Introduction" to his "Argument," says "if reason can with certainty pronounce anything, it may pronounce this *decision,* that extension and existence are so necessary to each other, that there can be no existence without extension. Talk of a substance which has no extension, you present us with words of amusement.

"If there be a subject on which *authority* should be of weight, such a subject, 'tis plain, is the debate, whether we must conceive that to deny extension, is to deny existence. And, 'tis well, that in behalf of the position, that existence cannot be without extension; there are two as great authorities in speculations of this nature, as can anywhere be found."

These words are in the "Introduction," followed by those quotations from Locke and Clarke given above. They are "most important," and (without offence, be it said,) furnish as pretty a specimen of the *self-damnatory* mode of reasoning, as any of the very many pretty specimens I have had the "great good fortune" to cast my eye upon, though a tolerably industrious reader. But pretty though it may be, dissected it must be, for the special benefit of the Philalethean Society, who I hope will reward me for my pains, by turning "proper Atheists," and publicly announce the fact as a "necessary consequence" of my skilful *cutting up.* This is no joke though jocularly said, and in seriousness most sober I promise to *demonstrate* in the next *Movement* that there is no such *thing*, and *consequently* no such *existence* as extension, and that Gillespie is *quite right* when he asserts there can be no existence without extension, though *quite wrong* when he calls extension an existence, for as already remarked, and as shall be clearly shown, extension no more exists than time or motion. CHARLES SOUTHWELL.

[*Notes.*—* An Examination (p. 88) of Antitheos's " Refutation of the argument *à priori* for the being and attributes of a god."

† Examination of Antitheos's refutation, page 39.

THE PRAYING JENNY COMPANY.
(*The latest invention.*)

DR. P. Y. in the learned work we reviewed in No. 9, says, " We think we have done wonders by making the giant steam do what he does, but the followers of the Grand Llama have beaten us hollow; they have got PRAYING JENNIES. They believe that as often as the substance on which a prayer is written is turned over, it is the same as if they said the prayer, which they are mostly unable to do, as Calmucs do not often learn to read. Their praying jenny the *Kerada*, is like a barrel churn; the prayers of all the family are put inside two cylinders, and some one gives them a turn round, which answers for all the rest. A bottle jack would save this trouble; or if they like to erect a public one by subscription, with a water wheel, the whole village population need never go to church unless there is a drought. The prayers are all in the Tangotian, or sacred language."

This paragraph meeting the eye, or rather eyes, of a number of *calculating* christians, it suggested to them the possibility of founding an entirely new sect, which should be enabled to compete with any other "house in the trade." They propose that the steam engines throughout the country, which at every glut of the foreign markets, have to stand still, be immediately, on such an occurrence, set to work turning cylinders duly filled with prayers. These cylinders being first made by the out-of-work mechanics who perambulate the country in the fruitless search for employment.

Unbeneficed clergymen and supernumerary saints are to prepare the prayers. Never before was such a happy junction of political economy and piety. Steam engines, mechanics, and saints, may now ply heaven with scientific regularity, not a soul need go to the devil in all the three kingdoms, and this can be accomplished without interfering with the business of the nation in the slightest degree. When this plan is in full operation, or rather when the cylinders are full of prayers, and making them constant, endless, infinite, and innumerable revolutions, all churches and chapels, from Saint Paul's downward, may be used for scientific instruction, and the study of morals and man. It has been predicted that Duprez will make an immense hit at Drury Lane this season, but this new prayer churning may be expected to throw all ordinary hits into the shade. The advanced spirit of the times seems to have advanced on purpose to meet this production of Calmuc ingenuity, and the wants of the age will be discovered by future historians to have been simply the want of this generalization of Keradas.

The greatest possible ingenuity has been expended by the founders of this new sect in endeavouring to hit on a suitable soubriquet whereby to designate themselves. It was proposed that they should call themselves " Christian Turners," but as it appeared that this title would perhaps identify their project with the common end of Christian Schemes —that of "turning a penny," it was abandoned. The *Latest* day saints was thought of as a rivaller to "*Latter* day saints," but ultimately it was decided that their cognomen ought to indicate the new union of science with salvation, and that therefore they should be known as the *Cylindrical Saints*. Also, as it appeared that they would be nothing unless they were everything, it was further agreed that they should be known as the *Universal Rotatory Prayer Association*.

We have been frequently told by modern sages that "the world can't go on without a god," whether there is one or not to go on with, and, that "we must have a religion of some sort." Ever anxious to oblige every body, we have at last yielded to these sagacious solicitations, and present to the notice and approval of these gentry the following

PROSPECTUS
OF THE
CYLINDRICAL SAINTS
AND
UNIVERSAL ROTATORY PRAYER ASSOCIATION.

CAPITAL—EIGHTEENPENCE.
PATRONS—THE UTILITARIANS.
MANAGERS, *Pro. Tem.*—THE POOR-LAW COMMISSIONERS.

Principle. The principal principle of this Association is "Cheap Salvation," cheaper than Hetherington's, which is sold at three pence!!!

Capital. It will be asked what is the capital for? As this Society assumes with the Llamaites, that prayers *turned* are as good as prayers *said*, it will be necessary, in this country, to prove this dogma from scripture, and the whole of the capital is offered as a prize for the best essay on this subject. From the well known ease with which any thing can be proved from the Bible, it appeared that eighteenpence would amply cover all the trouble. The *Independents* not being bound to any thing in particular, have already sent in a specimen, and one is expected from the Puseyites next week.

A deputation has been appointed to wait on the *Anti-League*, to solicit their assistance in carrying out the objects of this society. The manufacturers naturally join the Corn Law League when their mills are standing idle; and as this association offers tenders to Cobden and Bright for the use of all superfluous steam engines for prayer-churning, the threatened revolution by the Corn Law League may be expected to give place to the *revolution* of cylinders, to the great joy of the Anti-League, and the prosperity of this association.

The heads of the houses at Oxford are to be addressed on the objects of this society, as it is likely to be a facile engine in the dissemination of Puseyism; since prayers to the mother of god can be just as easily churned, as those addressed to the rest of the family.

A sub-committee of ladies from the Tract Society have been appointed, under the title of "The Keradäan Sisters." Their province is, to visit the houses of the poor, to induce them to attach a domestic kerada to their bottle jack, that those who have not a joint of meat to turn, may turn a can of prayers. No plan equal to this has been devised for teaching the poor contentment, and *turning* the carnal man into the spiritual.

The limits of a prospectus warn us to be brief, and we can only add that *Sir Andrew Agnew* has consented to bring the objects of this association before Parliament early ·in the sessions.

J. *Silk* Buckinhám is to deliver a lecture at the British Institute, at the conclusion of his present course on Palestine,—subject, "The Calmuc Kerada, an illustration of scripture prophecy."

The Poor-Law Commissioners are merely *pro. tem.* directors, for the sake of saving the gruel of the unemployed, until Sir R. Peel has found time to consider the "Condition of England question." Her Majesty's government are likely to give their attention to this subject about the year 1986.

When Franklin saw his father say grace over a rump steak, he, in the true spirit of a utilitarian, asked why he did not say grace over the whole cow, and so save all future trouble. How Franklin would have rejoiced could he have foreseen the rise of the *Cylindrical Saints!* Talk of going to heaven by act of parliament, the old fashioned way of our ancestors—we go to heaven by steam! Shades of Savary and Watt, who can compass the uses of thy inventions?

At a meeting of the directors on Saturday night, unanimous thanks were voted to Dr. P. Y., for bringing, in his great work, this invention before the country, and he was appointed engineer to the association, and constructor of cylinders in general.

End of the Prospectus.

DE LAMARTINE'S LETTERS ON HISTORY.

(*Concluded.*)

To engage as co-operators in the enterprize without regard to opinion or party, by the very sentiment of the good to be effected, and by adequate and honourable remuneration for their work, all men who, in France or in Europe, march at the head of thought, of philosophy, of science, of literature, of arts, and even of trades; to request of each a certain number of articles on each of the departments of the particular knowledge in which he excels, from this our moral philosophy; from that, history—the other science—another, poetry—another, politics; but general politics only, and in their unanimous principles, without any animate and actual polemic against men and governments; to induce them to bring all these high thoughts within the reach of the least abstract mind, in clear, precise, substantial terms; to translate themselves, to coin themselves, so to speak, from the learned into the vulgar language; to associate with this elementary, successive and varied instruction, the narration of the principal national and European facts, the complete chronicle of the day in the whole universe; to cause the brightness of day to penetrate into the domiciles of the people, and to let these masses of men share in their proportion, and without cost, the activity of the religious, philosophic, scientific, literary, and political life, as they partake in physical life of cheaper, but not less nourishing food—this is the thought; I have no time to develop it here, but suffice it to say, that for realising it, not more than a million of francs would be required. Yes, it would be sufficient that a million of well-intentioned citizens subscribe to this subsidy for the masses one franc a year only, one of those small pieces of money that slip between the fingers without being retained, or which the thoughtless a thousand times in the year throw away for the least fancy of the day, to realize this thought. Thus would civilization descend like a cloud on the inferior regions, and pour forth its fertilizing rain and dew. What a moral revolution would not this effect within ten years on the intelligence, on the ideas, on the customs of the mass; this daily and universal infiltration of light into their darkness—of thought into their drowsiness.

They are in the shade—put them in the sun; all would ferment, all would germinate, all would fructify. I do not fear to affirm that in a few years your political people would be changed. But, you will tell me, why do you not execute it? Because I have not the million myself alone; because there is not, at the present time in France, the idea which weighs against a dollar. Let the good citizens find the million; I will undertake to find the men.

Those men would in fact be the real moral power of the nation, the administrators of public thought, the permanent committee of modern civilization. Is this no temptation for noble and ambitious devotedness? Yes, there are, in this day, everywhere two kinds of governments, the one who administer, and the other who reign. Those who reign are those who think. They are above the former; but this government of public thought, like the other, wants unity of action and of organs. The popular journal thus conceived, would be the code of this government of thought; association would be their budget and army; the first writers of the century would be their ministers. Let us reflect on it. There is in this time something grander than to be minister of the houses, or of the crown; it is to be minister of opinion.

A. DE LAMARTINE.

ADDRESS OF THE ANTI-PERSECUTION UNION TO ITS COLLECTORS AND FRIENDS.

THE committee of the Anti-Persecution Union have pleasure in announcing that they now have ready to issue Subscription Cards, in convenient cases. The cards are so contrived that the subscription given can be properly registered in a moment—entirely superseding the old and inconvenient subscription books.

All Collectors, therefore, are desired to return, to the Secretary, their books made up to the day of sending, that the new cards and cases may be forwarded to them.

Any person, in town or country, willing to become a collector, may obtain a collector's card, on application to the secretary, by giving a reference, if the party applying is unknown to the Union.

The Union would remind their collectors and friends, that the trial of Mr. Paterson, is the property of the Union, and that those who promote its sale, will not only diffuse the principles of the Union, but increase its funds.

The trial is that of Mr. Paterson for Placard Blasphemy in London. A large edition of it was generously presented to the Union by W. J. B., and its price has been reduced to 6d. that its circulation may be extended. It contains ninety-two pages of the size of the *Movement*, of the most extraordinary matter ever published, and when it is remembered that the magistrates insolently said, that no reports of Mr. Paterson's trial should appear by the press, it becomes every man's duty to disappoint such tyrannical malice, by largely promoting its diffusion.

To imprison a man for the avowal of his opinions, and deny him the privilege of being heard in his own defence, is a double injustice that every man is called upon to promptly and vigorously resist.

It is only by bringing public opinion to bear on persecutors, that we can hope to annihilate the infamous race. In courts of law, the Wetherells, Jardines, and judges, would behave as brutally as they do bigotedly, was it not for the consciousness that their deeds will be published to the world. It is for this reason that the committee are preparing the *Scotch Trials* for the press. The Anti-Persecution Union cannot cancel the verdicts of christian juries, and godly judges, but they can damn them on the pages of history to everlasting fame. They cannot shorten the imprisonment of the victims, and can perhaps do but little to diminish the torture they are subjected to, but they can win for them the respect of all just men, and the gratitude of posterity.

Hitherto the Union has had an indefinite constitution. Every person subscribing to its funds has been considered a member, but it has now been determined to issue *Members cards* at 6d. each, by which persons taking them, will become *registered Member* of the Union. Consciousness of this, it is hoped, will perpetually stimulate to active exertion, in promoting its objects. *Members cards* will be renewed quarterly—the subscription will be at the rate of a half-penny per week. The subscription cards, before spoken of, are for registering the larger donations of members, or contributions of indifferent persons.

Collectors can obtain *Members cards* to issue in their localities, on application to the Secretary.

I am desired to state, as a general notice, that any respectable person, of known integrity, may obtain, on application to the Secretary, authority to call a public meeting in the town in which he resides, in the name of the Anti-Persecution Union, to appoint a committee to collect subscriptions, and aid in carrying out the objects of the Union generally. G. JACOB HOLYOAKE, Sec.

SOCIAL REFORM ASSOCIATION.
Re-organization of Society.

A MEETING on this important subject will be held every Sunday, when will be debated a plan for a new state of society, in which poverty, vice, and misery, will be displaced by plenty, virtue, and happiness. Meetings held at the Social Hall, corner of Broadway and Grand Sts. Public Discussions in the afternoons at 3, discourses delivered by the members in the evenings at 7. Admission free.

The celebrated and talented Madam F. W. Darusmont, (better known as Frances Wright,) is expected in the city in a few days, and will be invited to address the meeting on the next, or following Sunday.—J. R. SMITH, President.—*From the Regenerator, an excellent American journal.*

THE DOCTRINES OF THE CONCORDISTS.
III.

HAVING briefly noticed in our last article, man's origin and antecedent relations, we have now to speak of the affinity he bears to the objects of nature, and the devices of his fellows on the stage of human life, to which he is introduced here to act his part with the numerous actors in this sphere of wonder and confusion. Man is a generated compound mode of the divine will, in harmonious or disjunctive relation with the infinite spirit, a good or bad representative of divinity. He is somewhat like a mirror in which the spirit reflects itself, the correct or incorrect likeness depends upon the quality of the mirror, and the nature of the beholder. One looks into him and beholds nothing but deformity, not one trace of the universal beauty is discernible; another looks into this living glass and discovers some fine lineaments of the divine image, and declares of it accordingly, each gives his own partial view more or less faithfully; every one differs from the other according as he is organised and developed. This occasions the vast variety and contrariety of human life. Man's relations to society are more or less strong, as he is more or less intensively related to spirit. He who is intensively natured in unity with the creator will attach but little importance to the relations in human society. Benevolence and integrity will mark all his conduct on earth, but his individual attachments will be held lightly, and but little regarded, being constantly actuated by the universal, he feels but little in common with the *merely* individual being. The essences composing the particular constitution and the different modes of compounding them determine the degree and kind of effect which the surrounding circumstances will have upon it. No external circumstances can alter the essential or inner organism, they can modify the accidental character, but never can touch his essential character.

The future man lies in his distinctive essence encradled in the germal embryo. Rank and fortune have no part in this deep definement of identity; true, indeed, caste and station and other contingencies affect his position in this false world of appearances, but *essentially* he is what he is by birth. Generation or re-generation casts the essential die; education and association give the colouring polish. Education does much to modify the external character, to refine and soften the manners and give the sectarian tinge to the outer man; it may give him the Christian, the Mahometan, or any other external appearance, but never makes a good or a bad man, with respect to essence, or to good itself, or the universal laws. Each being comes into the world with essences, faculties, inclinations and propensities, *peculiarly* compounded, so that whatever may be his developing conditions he differs from all other individuals. The inward character is as much fixed at birth, as the oak's specific character is fixed in the acorn. No change of circumstances can ever evolve from the acorn the elm tree. *A tree* indeed may grow from the oak or elm seed, but the specific nature of the tree will be just according to the germal essences enfolded in the seed. Conditions might very much affect its height, its size, or its health and whole external aspect, but they can never touch its vital specific order in the vegetable kingdom, unless by introducing another nature by a new birth or graft. Very much is effected in the vegetable and animal world by the training process, great superiority and beauty is by this means obtained in gardens and in different species of animals, also with mankind this training becomes so popular that man himself is by some declared to be the creature of circumstance, though no creature ever received its vital germs, its peculiar characteristics from any hand but the creating-spirit. All vital, truthful, loveful, operations are of this origin. Man's relation to the creation commences at birth; the first is to its mother, she is the child's first teacher. Here commences his education and conditionating care; every act towards the child is important; every feeling, look, or action, should be in harmony with the universal laws, and subserve the inner end which is working in the child.

Whatever may be the station of society into which the child is introduced, it must be carefully tended with a constant regard to its inner nature, and its antecedent affinity to spirit. No obstructions shold be offered to the unfoldings of vitality, intelligence, and affection within it. The parent's affectionate attention should ever be vigilantly active in watching and supplying the demands made by the inner law, in distinction from the little selfish petulance or desires of the inferior nature which may occasionally appear. The parents should scrupulously obey the universal laws in the child, and see that the child at no time infringes the same. The most assiduous and affectionate attention and skill should be paid to supply the best conditions for the child's development as a universal being.

The great business of the parents and other educators should be to assist the pupils to feel in their own being the one grand causer, and to connect every feeling, perception, and act with it until the spirit and soul are brought into vital co-operation at all times. This affected, the being is secured in benevolence, intelligence and energy, through a life of happiness and usefulness.

The being having reached what is called the age of manhood, in whatsoever circumstances he may find himself placed, it is his duty to submit at all times to the highest good and clearest truth he finds made known to him, taking all his instruction from the universal laws, whether these instructions militate or not against the laws established by men. He is not called upon directly to antagonise with the customs of men any further than a faithful submission and obedience to the universal will demands of him. In all his most active life a perfect passivity to universal laws is his highest duty and happiness.

Some of the *particular* relations in human society may form the subject of our next paper. W. OLDHAM.

FILIAL INGRATITUDE. — The Leicester Branch have determined on abandoning the *Paternal* form of government.

P. LECOUNT, R. N.—This gentleman has addressed a letter to the editor of the *Midland Observer*, detailing the cure of all kinds of *pain*, by a method he has discovered, and which, in 400 trials, has failed only once. The high scientific character of this gentleman, is a sufficient guarantee that there is no deception played off. He states that it is not mesmerism nor electricity, nor galvanism nor magnetism, and few persons are better able than the discoverer of this new art, to detect the presence of these elements. This announcement demands the attention of the scientific. All experiments are made gratuitously, and an offer is made to perform them publicly.

BLASPHEMY LAWS.—"Among modern laws, the French code pénal contains no provisions for the punishment of persons reviling God or christianity, except where such conduct amounts to a violation of the right of religious freedom, or an interruption of the exercise of public worship. The additions made to the code pénal in 1825, under the head of 'Sacrilege,' have but imperfectly supplied this deficiency. The Prussian law punishes "gross blasphemies of God publicly uttered, and giving general offence," with imprisonment from two to six months: and revilings of any religious communities allowed by the state, and disturbances during divine service are visited with a somewhat *higher* degree of punishment. The Austrian code declares that, "whosoever shall blaspheme God, in speeches, writings, or actions or shall interrupt any religions allowed by' the state or shall by the indecent abuse of vessels used for divine service, or otherwise by actions, speeches or writings, publicly manifest contempt for religion, "shall be punished according to the degree of scandal occasioned, and the degree of malice in the offender, with heavy imprisonment, for any period between one year and ten years." The Bavarian code makes no direct mention of blasphemy as an offence, but contains provisions for punishing a disturbance of public worship, attended by personal violence, with imprisonment for any period between one and six years, and a disturbance by opprobrious words without personal violence, with imprisonment for any period from one month to six months. We may here observe that in none of these laws, nor in the laws of any country with which we are acquainted, excepting the laws of England, and those states of America which have adopted the common law, is it declared to be a crime simply to deny the truth of the doctrines of natural or revealed religion; offences of this class being invariably made to consist in the use of indecent, railing, or scurrilous language on such subjects.

Now Ready—Part III of the *Movement*, in a stiff wrapper, price 7d.

MRS. MARTIN has just commenced, at the City-road Hall, a series of Sunday Evening "Sermons for the People. No. I;—The Throne and the Loom."

THE BRANCH A 1 committee, to aid the Anti-Persecution Union by collecting funds, have been indefatigable in their exertions. Some of the results will be found under the head of "Subscriptions." They have tendered their valuable co-operation for the important Public Meeting shortly to be held to petition parliament on behalf of Paterson.

MR. ELLIS, on Sunday week, delivered an able and animated lecture on the "Impolicy of Prosecutions for Blasphemy," at Branch A 1. At the conclusion a collection was made on behalf of the Anti-Persecution Union.

THE RULING CLASSES.—The blindness of one part of mankind, co-operating with the phrenzy and villany of the other, has been the real builder of this respectable fabric of political society.—*Burke.*

New and Interesting Work—"*The Scotch Trials,*" *under the Superintendence of the Anti-Persecution Union.*

On SATURDAY, MARCH 23rd, the day of Miss Roalfe's liberation, will be published, price 2d., 16 pages, size of the *Movement*, No. 1, of

THE TRIAL OF THOMAS PATERSON,
FOR BLASPHEMY.
Before the High Court of Justiciary, Edinburgh; with the whole of his Bold and Effective
DEFENCE.
ALSO, THE TRIALS OF
THOMAS FINLAY AND MISS MATILDA ROALFE,
(For Blasphemy), in the Sheriff's Court.
With Notes, and a Special Dissertation on Blasphemy Prosecutions in general. By the Secretary of the Anti-Persecution Union.

Mr. Paterson at the conclusion of his intrepid address, was sentenced to *fifteen months solitary confinement.* The best eulogium of this defence is the fact that the Lord Chief Justice found it necessary to go out of his way to deprecate it, and declare the Court's satisfaction that it was not likely to have great effect in influencing the public mind in favour of the sentiments which it contained. What his lordship really thought is shown by his sentence. What the Anti-Persecution Union think is proved by their publishing it, and they are also curious to ascertain if his judgeship is as much of a wizard as a bigot.

Wednesday the Eighth day of November, 1843, will long be remembered in Scotland, as on that day an individual had the moral hardihood to avow, and *justify,* on the floor of its High Court of Justiciary, his disbelief in a God—that individual was Thomas Paterson.—*Oracle of Reason.*

Mr. Finlay's defence was truly excellent. The age of the prisoner, his earnest manner, his correct language, and noble sentiments, commanded the respect of all present.—*Movement.*

The court was crowded to excess, and when Miss Roalfe was led away by the officers of the jail, the assembled multitude, unable to restrain their feelings, gave her three hearty expressions of applause. Infidels were delighted, and Christians forgot their rancour.—*Ibid.*

Miss Roalfe conducted her own defence. She admitted the sale of the works libelled, knowing perfectly that they contained a denial of the truth of the Christian religion, and were calculated to bring it into contempt; but denied that she sold them wickedly and feloniously. Indeed, so little did she consider her conduct criminal, that *soon as she should be at liberty, she intended to resume the same practice.*—*Scotch Paper.*

TRUTH, INDEPENDENT OF MAJORITIES.—As ten millions of circles can never make a square, so the united voices of myriads cannot lend the smallest foundation to falsehood.—*Goldsmith.*

TO CORRESPONDENTS.
RECEIVED.—J. C. F., A. T., H. Cooke, but too late.
J. R. H. BAIRSTOW.— His interesting letter shall receive early attention.

SUBSCRIPTIONS TO THE ANTI-PERSECUTION UNION.
The Branch A 1 Committee, for collecting funds in aid of the A. P. Union, per Mr. W. M. Waterson £6 12 2
A Friend, per Mr. Palmer . 0 1 0
G. J. H., *Sec.*

Printed and Published by G. J. HOLYOAKE, 40, Holywell-street, Strand, Saturday, March 16, 1844.

THE MOVEMENT
And Anti=Persecution Gazette.

"Maximize morals, minimize religion."—BENTHAM.

No. 14.   EDITED BY G. JACOB HOLYOAKE, ASSISTED BY M. Q. RYALL.   PRICE 1½d.

O'CONNELL AND JESUS CHRIST.

THE practical uses of Atheism were never better exemplified than in Ireland, at this moment. Religion in its most virulent, and in its best forms, can always be made subservient to the causes of oppression and delusion. When reason and justice begin to make way in the world, then religion never failingly comes in to stop their progress. Patriots may labour, and Philanthropists may toil for the emancipation of man, but let them beware if religion has taken root around them. Their plans and exertions are doomed, sooner or later, to be frustrated. They may hope to work with religion, but vain is the hope. They may think to take advantage of it as the instrument of their benevolent ameliorations, but they mistake its insidious nature. It is a trap that will ultimately take them. It is a viper that will surely sting all those who patronise it. The Repealers of Ireland have exerted themselves for the deliverance of their country, their arguments and the justice of their cause have confounded their opponents, and now these opponents have resorted to their most potent and fatal weapon—they have lustily raised the cry of "blasphemers." The repealers have talked largely of religion, thinking to better promote their designs thereby.—Mr. O'Connell has been commented for his deep policy in flattering religious prejudices, for his denunciation of Socialists and other irreligious parties, but now all this is being repaid with compound interest. The religious prejudices he has fostered, are being turned against him. Every pulsation of piety he has promoted, adds stings to the cry of "blasphemer" raised against repealers.

It appears that the *Nation* newspaper has taken it into its Catholic head, to style Jesus Christ a "convicted *criminal*," the propriety of which designation few unprejudiced people will doubt. It then proceeds to draw a parallel between this Gallilean "conspirator" and O'Connell, under the head of "convicted criminals." The *Nation* thus proceeds:—

"He was astonished that members of that house should *dare* to cheer a convicted conspirator.'—*Mr. Ferrand's Speech.*

"History has some examples of convicted conspirators who were not altogether disreputable characters!—conspirators whose memory all good men revere, and whose conviction is the very thing that has advanced their principles and made their names immortal.

"Jesus of Nazareth was a convicted conspirator. 'We found this fellow,' said his accusers, 'perverting the nation and forbidding to give tribute to Cæsar.' 'He stirreth up the people, teaching through all Jewry, beginning from Galilee unto this place.' Nay, that conspirator held *monster meetings*, 5,000 and 7,000 at a time, until the Scribes and Elders of the people exclaimed—'Perceive ye how ye prevail nothing; behold the world is gone after him.' And he sought to *bring the ordinary tribunals of the country into disrespect*, and to induce the people to adopt other modes of settling their disputes—'Agree with thine adversary whilst thou art in the way, lest he hale thee to the judge, and the judge deliver thee to the magistrate.' Such were the counts in that indictment, and, before a court of Scribes and Pharisees, his chance of acquittal was slender. In that day, too, there were factions men who exasperated the people against their true benefactor, and so perverted their sense of justice, that when the Governor offered to release Jesus, the cry was—'Away with this man, and release unto us Barabbas'—(say Oastler)—'now Barabbas was a robber.'

"And the Son of God was crucified between two thieves, and those that passed by, amongst whom was some progenitor of Busfield Ferrand, reviled him, wagging their heads. His degradation and abasement were, in the eyes of those Ferrands complete. He was a *convicted conspirator*. Their only wonder was, that the Arimathean thought it not beneath him to bury the convict in his own tomb. And now, behold! that criminal is the Saviour of the world, and those base Jews, and their children's children, have become an hissing and an abomination to the ends of the earth."

The *Belfast News-letter*, calls this "a monstrous piece of impiety"—"a recklessly infidel article," and "most daring profanity." The *Londonderry Sentinel* rises higher, and designates it as "most atrocious blasphemy," "a daring insult to the great founder of the

Christian religion, and bearing an affinity to the unpardonable sin against the holy ghost!" The *Evening Mail* brings up the rear of this pious bombast and hypocrisy.—"The mischievous genius of Voltaire never conceived, nor the diabolical pen of Paine ever executed a more dreadful and awfully blasphemous article than that of the *Nation*." At the risk of incurring the high displeasure of all these worthy editors, I affirm that no sober infidel, certainly no atheist, would give a fraction for the comparison, or would wish to be coupled in such a parallel. According to the Evangelists, Jesus Christ went vagabondising up and down the country, and if he was now to appear and play the same tricks in Ireland, he would meet with no better fate than he is fabled to have done at the hands of the Jews. These very papers, just cited, would treat him as they do Joshua Jacobs. But the *Londonderry Sentinel* lets out the secret of its admiration of Christ. "Christ," says the sapient editor, "was the son of God—O'Connell the son of a Kerry bogtrotter.--O'Connell has defied the civil powers as far as he was able, but *Christ taught an unhesitating and active obedience to civil rulers.—render unto Cæsar the things which are Cæsar's, was his precept.*" Yes, and for this reason we should feel little flattered by a comparison with such a precept given. Here is the key-stone to priestly laudation of Christ. Oppression is secure under his influence. The consistent Christian is bound to render whatever the reigning Cæsar may choose to call his dues. This is a weapon more potent on a Christian populace than reason and justice. Repealers have fostered this enemy, and they may expect to feel its power. Religion is a two-edged sword, and those who play with it should not complain when they are cut by it—other than Repeal Societies may profit by the lesson.   G. J. H.

FALLACY OF "AN ARGUMENT, A PRIORI," ON THE BEING & ATTRIBUTE OF GOD, AS THAT ARGUMENT IS STATED BY WILLIAM GILLESPIE.

THAT Infinity of Extension necessary exists, is the first and fundamental proposition of our author—that there is no such a thing as extension, I have engaged, and shall now attempt to demonstrate.

What our author understands by extension, it is by no means easy to understand, but, as he announces it infinite, and talks very knowingly about the indivisibility of its parts, I guess him to understand by extension a something, seeing that nothing cant have a material *parts*, or properly be called *boundless;* though, something, our author's extension certainly is not, as at page 45 and elsewhere, he "demonstrates" most cleverly that "the material universe cannot be the substratum of infinity of extension."

Our author is not only sure that infinity of extension necessarily exists, but also that none can help having an idea thereof, for, says he even when the mind endeavours to remove from it the idea of infinity of extension, it cannot after all its efforts, avoid having still there the idea of such infinity.

If this were so, why then indeed: *but* the truth is (and that it is the truth, any one may convince himself by five minutes wholesome reflection,) that the only thing, *i.e.* real existence of, which it is possible to think at all, is matter; and I tell our author that it is not infinity of extension, but, infinity of matter we *cannot but* believe, which we *always suppose*, even though we *would not*. I tell him too, that the entire language of his "argument," though carefully framed to hide, does very plainly exhibit, its sophistry.

We are told in the course of that argument, that the parts of infinity of extension, are necessarily indivisible from each other, really or mentally. At page 41. Book I., we are gravely instructed that the parts of infinity of extension being necessarily immovable among themselves, it is a *necessary consequence* that that, the parts of which are *movable* among themselves, is not infinity of extension.

A sentence (thought Shakspeare's clown,) *is but a cheveril glove to a good wit—how easily it may be turned the wrong side outward.* So I think too, of such sentences as the two odd ones just quoted ; and without being at all disposed to write myself down "good wit," I do consider myself wit enough to turn our author's sentences the "wrong side outward."

The parts of infinity of extension are necessarily indivisible from each other, really or mentally.

This is sentence the first, and richly deserves first to be turned wrong side outward.

It is perfectly obvious, that nought save matter can be conceived to have parts, properly so called ; Matter being the only existence, properly so called, and without denying that our author has an idea of extension, I assert the non-existence of extension in the same way, that without denying he has a distinct idea of duration, I distinctly assert the non-exisience of duration.

It is usual and very convenient to talk about the parts of time and duration, but except our author and some few others, through much learning made mad metaphysicians, none can be found mistified enough to assert the reality, that is to say the *existence* of time.

Whatever exists, exists in *some* form, *somewhere*; we are sure too, it has *some* weight, *some* density, in short, *some* of all those properties or attributes which cannot, *even in thought*, be separated from realities.

According to our author, (page 51.) infinity of duration and the being of infinity of duration are *identical, not different;* which is quite true, and right for once he undoubtedly is, but, a million identical nothings wont amount to a single non-identical something. Let it be granted that infinity of duration, and the being of infinity of duration are *identical* not *different*, we stand far off as ever from the *monstrous absurdity*, that "infinity of duration is necessarily existing."

Our author says, (page 49), the truth of this proposition (infinity of duration is necessarily existing), is evident, from the same sort of consideration as shows there is necessarily infinity of extension; but, unluckily for "the truth of this proposition," the sort of consideration alluded to is not the right sort. But I must be grave, and seriously ask my Philalethean "challengers" whether the one being of infinity of duration; the one being of infinity of expansion; the one being of infinity of extension; the one simple and unique being of infinity of expansion and duration; the one intelligent all-knowing, all-powerful, necessarily indivisible, necessary immovable, necessarily free, and necessarily (it should be added) *impossible* being, our author has thought fit to make a god of, is not the most comical of deities. I ask them to consider that though infinite extension, infinite expansion, and infinite duration, may *on paper* look like a very pretty trinity in unity; the three in one have neither length, breadth, or thickness as body hath—they are not real—they exist nowhere. They can neither be bottled off by the pint like wine, or cut and eaten by the pound like cheese—no; and, wherefore, no? They are *ideal* not *real* things.

Our author ought to know that *extension*, oftener called *space*, is a word philosophers have agreed shall represent a certain class of ideas, generated in us by *the order of things existing.* Our author ought to know that *duration*, oftener called *time*, is a word philosophers have agreed shall represent a certain class of ideas generated in us by *the order of things successive.*

But though our author knows so little of this kind of knowledge, he knows vastly more than it is possible to know about sundry other kinds of knowledge, as for example:—he knows the parts of infinity of extension are necessarily indivisible from each other *in spite* of the fact, that, infinity of extension has no parts; he knows, *certainly*, (see page 56), that some parts of the material universe are divisible from each other *in spite* of the fact that save in the sense of partial consideration only (to borrow a sentence himself to freely uses) the parts of matter are necessarily indivisible; he knows (marvellous man) that the parts of infinity of expansion (which exists in precisely the *same* manner that infinity of extension does) are immovable among themselves, and is quite certain that some parts of the material universe are movable among themselves *in spite* of the fact that infinite expansion is infinite nothing, of course therefore, without parts, and *in spite* of the fact that (except in the sense of partial consideration only) the parts of the material universe are NOT *movable among themselves.*

I am aware that our author has declared (page 76 of An Examination of Anti-Theos' Refutation) he has something very different from the parts of matter in view, when he speaks of parts in the sense of partial consideration only, but I am fully as well aware that there are no other parts (properly so called) than the parts of matter; fully as well aware too that matter is the *only* infinite, and therefore, our author instead of saying anything so absurd as that "the parts of infinity of extension are necessarily indivisible from each other, really or mentally, *should* have said that the parts of infinity of matter (save in the sense of partial consideration only) are necessary indivisible from each other, really or mentally. This conclusion is inevitable—it is " the conclusion to which the rulers of philosophy entitle us to come," and our author is "challenged" to prove it fallacious, and having failed, as assuredly he will fail, to accomplish the impossible task, I hope he will be invited, and that he will cheerfully accept the invitation to become *one of us.*

But I must not, while indulging in anticipation so pleasing, forget that before concluding, another sentence must "be turned the wrong side outward." Here it is *as it is.* The parts of infinity of extension being necessarily unmovable among themselves; it is a *necessary consequence* that that, the parts of which are movable among themselves, is not infinity of extension. Here it is *as it should be.* The parts of infinity of matter being necessarily immovable among themselves (except in the sense of partial consideration only), it is a *necessary consequence* that that, the parts of which (in the sense explained), are movable among themselves, *is* infinity of matter.

Our author's sentence thus turned wrong side outward relatively to *his* argument, and right side outward relatively to *my* argument, is an exceedingly valuable, though rather a clumsy looking one—indeed, our author's entire work might easily be converted into one of the very best Atheistical books extant, and so soon as convenient I propose to *atheise* the whole argument, by the cheap process of substituting about a score of *proper* words for an equal number of *improper* ones. Thus in the new edition:

Infinity of *matter* is necessarily existing, will stand, *Proposition I.* Infinity of matter is necessarily indivisable, will stand, *Proposition II.* Infinity of matter is necessarily immovable, will stand, *Proposition III.* There is necessarily a being of infinity of matter, will stand, *Proposition IV.*

The being of infinity of matter is necessarily of unity of simplicity, will stand, *Proposition V.*

Here are five of our author's propositions stated atheistically, *i. e. as they ought to be stated*, by the simple substitution in every case of *matter* for *extension*, and in like manner all his other propositions may be altered to the full stretch of "grossest" atheism; aye, and they shall be too, in due time.

Thus, it seems, that after all the fuss made about it, our author's "grand" argument is a grand mistake. It rests upon the most ridiculous of metaphysical fallacies. All existence, properly so called, necessarily exists. This our author well understands, but then he don't appear to understand that matter is the only *existence*, properly so called, and therefore the only *necessarily existing being*.

If extension is ideal (and who in his senses can doubt it?) our author's whole argument must be false, as already shown.

If extension is real, it is matter, and our author stands proved a dishonest Atheist, or an Atheist so stupid as not to know he is one—atheism claiming for *matter* precisely what he claims for *extension*.

If extension is not matter, it is nothing, for *matter* and *something* being convertible terms, to somethingise extension is to materialise it—*a demonstration* that the *infinite extension* of our author is just an *infinite nothing*, the *parts* of which are without doubt "necessarily indivisible from each other, really or mentally."

Our author says "there can be no existence without extension," but he omits to add, "nor extension without existence." "Talk," says he, "of substance which has no extension, you present us with words of amusement." Talk, say I, of extension, which has no substance, you present us with words without meaning.

It is no more possible to have an idea of extension, where there is nothing extended, than to have an idea of motion where there is nothing moved. And certainly it would be no more ridiculous to declare motion an infinite, and necessarily indivisible being, than to assert, as does our author, that extension is an infinite, and necessarily an existing being.

When he succeeds in proving motion an infinite being, he may possibly succeed in proving extension an infinite being, duration an infinite being, expansion an infinite being, and all three infinite beings, but *one* infinite being. After getting thus far with his "argument," he may venture a step further, and demonstrate upon principles strictly mathematical, that the "one infinite being is simple, unique, necessarily intelligent, necessarily all-knowing, necessarily all-powerful, and necessarily all-free."

But having, I conceive, redeemed my pledge, that is to say, *demonstrated* the non-existence of extension, and *consequent* fallacy of our author's *fundamental* proposition, I very willingly take leave of his "grand argument," though, of course, in the confident expectation that my "challengers" *will with all convenient speed either answer what is here written, or acknowledge it unanswerable.*

CHARLES SOUTHWELL.
Edinburgh, March 15, 1844.

THE UNION,
ITS SUPPORTERS AND RETARDERS.

IT is thought by some, that those brave friends who have borne the brunt of the battle of free discussion, are entitled to sympathy and support. It is deemed a matter intimately affecting all who like to think for themselves, and who would that others had the same liberty; by such is it deemed a matter of important concernment, that individuals have gone forth proclaiming their opinions, or giving currency to those of others, without stopping to enquire if they have found favour in the sight of authority. There are those who think that freedom of expression is worth having, is worth striving for, nay, even risking life, liberty, and wealth to obtain. Such as these think that it is incumbent on all who have an identity of opinion and sentiment with these pioneers of freedom, to sympathise with them, to cheer them onward, to countenance and assist them —when clutched by the fangs of the law, to aid in extricating them—if fined, to bear the cost—if imprisoned, to soothe, alleviate, and soften the moments of suffering or privation, by all the means which stronger ties of respect, admiration, and even affection will inspire. These are the thoughts which some cherish—the sentiments by which they are actuated—the deeds which they admire. There are those who, besides their admiration of the noble self-sacrifices, besides an approval of efforts to aid them on the part of others, do *themselves* lend a helping hand. There may be others also, and doubtless are, more who are ready to crown such high thoughts, noble sentiments, profound admiration, as well as distant support, with deeds of their own. From among such, is the UNION against persecution, and for the defence of its victims, supported.

There are also those, it must be acknowledged, who look with lack-lustre eye at the description of difficulties encountered in the defence of free opinions—who hear, emotionless, the recital of sufferings undergone for maintaining truth, who are too dull to connect such sufferings and endurance with their own liberties, or too spiritless to acknowledge and avow the championship of their rights by others.

Mortified and ashamed at what he deems the discreditable supineness of the free-thinkers, a correspondent from Salford, Mr. George Smith, asks the reason of the "disgraceful apathy on the part of the professing friends of free discussion, in the late trials and convictions for blasphemy (?) in Scotland, and why they quietly suffer a single fellow-creature, male or female, to be immured within the walls of a loathsome and filthy dungeon, at the instigation of a few ignorant bigots, for daring to exercise those first and chief characteristics of humanity, 'Reason and Speech,' and especially when such indignity and suffering are heaped upon a woman." He adds, "the cold indifference generally speaking, manifested by the enlightened and liberal public, at the injustice and torture inflicted upon Paterson and others for having given publicity to their opinions astonished me,— but I am thoroughly astounded, shall I say disgusted, at the apathetic chillness shown towards Miss Roalfe, who is wasting in prison, under the tender mercies of the loving Christians of Scotland, and yet they raise not their voice nor put forth an effort to snatch her from the deadly clutch of so relentless a monster." Our friend of Salford thinks that tyrannies like these should "raise the ire of every right minded man, and nerve him to her defence, if not to her rescue." His indignation at the monstrous oppression on the one side, and craven endurance on the other, together with the fervent emotion into which he is carried, prompt him to ejaculate, "Oh! for a few bold spirits of the chivalrous age of knighthood, when none was thought worthy who would not cheerfully risk his life in defence of injured woman!" Our Salford friend is not alone in thinking that the valourous deeds of old have no parallel in these our degenerate days—that the mantle of ancient chivalry has not descended on our recreant knights. I will not stop to enquire how far the spirit of trade, or aggrandisement, of intense competitive life differs from the spirit of adventure and magnanimity, distinguishing the periods of monopoly. Nor is this the moment to discuss how far the crisis of competition which seems to threaten, and the transition state between it and co-operative life, are calculated to beget or retard a similar spirit. Whether it is to be considered that the intense gain-striving of a commercial era, tend to sharpen the selfish and blunt the social feelings; certain it is, that the work of succour and support to our noble and devoted friends who have voluntarily exposed themselves to the heat of persecution, has been too scantily performed to satisfy our hearty friends. That which has been most effectually accomplished, is known to be the doing of of a small minority of kindred spirits. Thrice honoured are the few! Out of their miserable pittances, still more stinted and precarious from their rejection of popular delusions, and consequent bribes, have they contributed to uphold the pioneers of liberty.

What shall we say of those who, having had the advantages of emancipation from the vile thraldom of their god-ridden fellow-men, do yet hug the chains of a debasing and mercenary worship, a worship of the god Mammon! To account for the adverse, the indifferent, the reluctant, the lukewarm, or the heartless in the Christian world, we look to the creed. In faith, worship, and stooping to authority, we can find the root of all such retardation or obstruction to the enlighted liberators of the human intellect. The coveted approximation to despotic deity induces consequent alienation from all that concerns human progress. Those devoted to the spiritualities are sadly negligent of the humanities. But to what shall we trace sham-liberalism or illiberalism in the ranks of infidelity?—Humiliating as the acknowledgement is, we have seen among us those who credit and debit, and measure and weigh, and tot up; who haggle and chaffer and screw—the very impersonification of day-book and ledger, and who, had they a soul, would have it locked up in one of Chubb's trebly-bolted safes—who have till and cashbox as legibly depicted in the lines of their countenance as if tattood there—and who, if appealed to for their persecuted brethren, declare that "they have nothing to give— they really can't afford it!" The poor Mammonites would fear lest a dole for our Union might make them members of another Union. —There are they who toil, and drudge, and slave, and sweat, and sew; who ticket, and post, and puff, and strain their faculties to their utmost tension to obtain and secure custom; these are your business men and nothing else, "they are too much engaged, too busy, really they can't attend to it."—There are they who value a standing and position in life, as if it was the rightful substitute of independence, liberty, self-respect and all the manly virtues; who have bowed, sneaked cringed and fawned into place, office or emolument, unmindful of all but low, narrow despicable expediency. Such time-servers, if addressed on behalf of the persecuted, think "they should not have thrust themselves forward," "they have brought it on themselves," "they should have respected the prejudices of society.—There are the Egoists, as the French style them, fellows wrapped up in self, who cannot see in any body or anything, aught of interest but what ministers to the gratification of their appetites, or tends to personal enjoyment; such intensity of selfishness, like other characteristics of the retardists and obstructives, or other useless or pernicious units who make up the aggregate of society, may coexist with any and every class of opinion more or less, or with no opinion at all. It may be discovered in all ranks and grades from the clown to the prince, it may be even seen lurking in the reform ranks; and this lets us into the secret, that the reform and public spirit is the profession—selfishness the pervading and ascendant quality with such as these.

We must never forget that the infidel world has been for the most part born, nursed and schooled in godism and its accursedly debasing influences; we cannot hope to have entirely escaped the contagion.

Shall we then calculate on the proportion of the useless, or pernicious, or the half and half people, who may be encountered in our ranks? assuredly not. Such support as we can give or obtain by the pen, the tongue, the purse, or the person should be continued with or without, or dispite of all foreign aid.

Mr. Smith's recommendation and statement are among the desirable courses of action, he says " I would recommend that simultaneous public meetings be held in *all the branches*, and a correct state of public opinion on these disgraceful prosecutions presented to the legislature forthwith. Manchester is about calling a meeting on the subject from which will be presented a petition to parliament for their immediate release. When our society was young it could then put forth its infant strength with giant effect and with equal ease crush the malignity of a *magistrate*, a *peer* or a *father in god*; but now that it has increased in muscle and sinew by age it minds not to use its power in defence of its bravest and most honest friends."

The conduct pursued by the Edinburgh infidels with regard to Miss Roalfe, since the date of our correspondent's letter is precisely of the right stamp. It shows a just appreciation of the *manful* and energetic conduct of that young lady. They have determined that she shall be benefited to the extent that her persecutors intended she should be injured, in presenting her with the amount of the £10 fine she so devotedly refused to pay, as the alternative of escaping imprisonment. Such is also the honourable conduct of the fellow-workmen of our atheistical brother *Knox*, whose upright bearing in the court of law is recorded in the present number.

The Union's present quarter's subscriptions too, which yield a return averaging about £200 yearly income, would by many be estimated as a favourable indication of the spirit of the freethinkers, taking into calculation their numbers and means.

These are the sunny, glowing, cheering points of the picture. There is still then, much encouragment for the timid and irresolute. Those who have well deliberated, carefully reflected, conscientiously determined, will continue their well appointed course by the force of their own self-sustaining energy.

There remains then for the ardent friend of truth, for the champion of liberty, for the true liberator, the same course hitherto pursued by our most gallant and devoted band, a steady pursuance of the plan marked out, whether it be in the most unobserved track, or on the platform of public observation. Above all, it is the most excellent, the most exalted sphere of action, to mark out and pursue a career though unknown, unheeded, or unsupported, to act his part though the world hang back. The applauses of a party, the approbation of the mighty, the support of a society must not enter into his calculation, if they come, they come unlooked for. Let not such wait for leaguing or confederacy, but Onward! as if the fate of the cause depended on his individual exertions.

M. Q. R.

THE JEWS.

One would suppose that nothing could still the fierceness of Christian disputants. Yes, I know a charm that will work that wonder; throw into the midst of them a Jew, and all their fangs will be fixed in him;—the unfortunate, the despised, the insulted, the persecuted Jew, who has been now nineteen centuries under the hand of affliction, robbed, tortured, and murdered in almost every country under heaven, and deprived of his civil rights throughout almost all the world. Alas! with what heartfelt pleasure is it that I stop for one short minute to pour oil into his wounds.

In Protestant Germany they are only allowed to live in certain numbers in certain towns; in Protestant Sweden not at all. In other parts they can only be married in certain numbers every year, and cannot be apprenticed to any trade. A Jew seems to live only to be persecuted. It is such a thoroughly cowardly thing, too, striking a man when he is down; and for what! For doing that which ought to command our respect and esteem— for adhering through fire, or through water, through plunder, and bloodshed, and death, to the religion which his fathers have followed for more than 3000 years. He is ever the same; his existence is almost a miracle—yet there he stands with his phylacteries as he was before the Tabernacle. With his amiable and deeply religious prayer book, most of it as old as the days of Ezra, and his one God, he looks like some emblem of eternity in the midst of time. To be esteemed and respected a Jew only requires to be known, and I may say the same of his literature; but what do we know of him? If he is well dressed, we think of money bags, and bonds, and securities, and usury; if he is ill dressed, we remember black lead pencils, oranges, and old clothes. This is the end of our knowledge. I, who in all parts of the earth have shared with him my hospitality and partaken of his—I, to whom the face of a Jew always appears the face of a friend—can conscientiously assert, that in all the exalted feelings of the human race I never found the Jew below his fellow mortals. I once owed my life to a Jew. I believe there are very few to be discovered who have not more than an average warmth of heart. In their religious duties they would shame many Christians, and of their patience and resignation under their manifold sufferings, mental and bodily, all can speak. Truly it needs much resignation, for even the immortal Shakspeare has, among others, lifted his hand against the Jew, I hope unknowingly. In his *Merchant of Venice* he has dramatised a fact; but, tell it not in Gath, it was the Christian who demanded so bitterly his pound of flesh, and that pound of flesh was to be cut from the body of a helpless Jew.— Dr. P. Y. "*Hunt after the Devil.*"

AN ATHEIST IN COURT.
To the Editor of the Movement.

Sir,— Last week, Thomas Knox, a public Atheist, was summoned to appear as a witness on behalf of a policeman who had been assaulted. When the book was tendered to him, he desired to be affirmed, and one of the magistrates, a Unitarian, enquired why he objected to be sworn, Mr. Knox answered because he did not believe in future rewards and punishments. "But," says the magistrate, "do you not believe in a God?" when Knox answered in a firm tone "No," which caused a sensation in the court, with the ejaculation of "poor fellow, he does not believe in a god." He was immediately ordered down, and on applying for remuneration for loss of time (from nine till one o'clock), he was informed "that his evidence was of no use—that he should have told them he was an Atheist, and then they would not have put his name on the list, and there was nothing for him." So much for the case, now for the remarks, especially by the Infidels thereon. The majority I have talked with condemn Thomas Knox's proceeding, nineteen twentieths would have taken the oath, and those that would have refused would have done it in a more philosophical or gentlemanly way. Thus it is always with the quick sighted, when anything is done, they can show how much better it might have been done, although these gifted individuals are frequently backward in experimenting. Mr. Knox stood on principle, and he does not now regret that he did so. A few of his fellow Infidels (working men), have made up to him the value of the half-day's work which was wasted by the court. Leaving it to time to sanction the course he has adopted.

Yours respectfully,
A. Q. Campbell.
Leicester, March 10th, 1844.

[We insert this case, having no reason to doubt its correctness, but our correspondent would have obliged us by more explicitness, stating the particular police office, day of the month when the transaction took place, and the name of the magistrate. We hope the day is not far distant when a legislatorial use will be made of these facts. Assuming the correctness of our correspondent's version of the case, we have no hesitation in saying that Mr. Knox's conduct has our warmest approval. The working men who made up his loss behaved in a generous and praiseworthy manner. We value their warm sympathy higher than the "quick-sightedness" of Mr. Knox's cold critics.

THE SUBLIME.
In the Unitarian Hymn Book, which has for its motto, "I will sing with the spirit and with the understanding also," the following lines occur for the exercise of the understanding!

"On Cherub and on Cherubim,
Full royally he rode;
And on the wings of mighty wind,
Came flying all abroad."

What would be said if infidels appreciated and sung such sublimity as this. It would be triumphantly quoted on every occasion, to degrade infidel intellect.

Should these gentlemen set themselves up with a Pictorial Hymn Book, we may expect an engraving of a Cherubim riding the Almighty on his shoulders, as one school-boy rides another.

FASHIONABLE RELIGION.
The first Daughter of the Duke of Wirtemberg, was the first wife of the present Emperor of Austria. She embraced the Catholic faith, and died very young, two days before the Emperor Joseph the Second, at Vienna. The present Empress Dowager, late wife to Paul,

became a proselyte to the Greek religion, on her arrival at Petersburg. The son of the Duke of Wirtemberg, who succeeded him in the Dukedom, was a Protestant, *it being his interest to profess that religion for the security of his inheritance*. Prince Ferdinand, who was in the Austrian service, and a long time Governor of Vienna, was a Catholic, *as he could not otherwise have enjoyed that office*. Prince Louis, who held a Commission under the Prussian monarch, followed the religion of the country where he served—and the other princes, who were in the employment of Sweden, and other countries, found no difficulty in conforming themselves to the religion of the sovereigns under whom they served. None of them having any established forms of worship, they naturally embraced that which conduced most to their aggrandisement, emolument, or dignity.—*Secret Memoirs of the Royal Family of France during the French Revolution*, Vol. I. page 277. Published by Treuttel, Wurtz, and Richter, Soho Square, 1826.

THE CYLINDRICAL SAINTS.

EVER anxious to promote the cause of *true* religion now it has appeared, we again bestow a notice on the *Cylindrical Saints*. We have offered this body the use of our mahogany box for the receipt of their communications, and announce on their behalf that they will be happy to receive specimens of prayers. Several persons of " experience " are expected to try their hands; and, next week we shall probably present a few samples.

CONSPIRACY PROTECTED.—The *Northern Star* of Saturday week says, that in a poem by Hoffman, the German poet, who was lately expelled the Prussian dominions, and his works prohibited, the following word appears;—" Steurverweigerungsverfassungsmassigberechfig," meaning a man exempt by the constitution from the payment of taxes. We would sugggest to Mr. O'Connell that the Repealers be forthwith known as " Steurverweigerungsverfassungsmassigberechfiggians." He will be an acute attorney-general who will be able to penetrate conspiracy beneath a title like this. A Clontarf meeting of *Steurverweigerungsverfassungsmassigberechfiggians* would be taken for a meeting of the old builders of Babel. The indictment of these parties would be a curiosity.

THE SCOTCH UNION.—We are desired to state that the excellent (intended) defence of Mr. Thomas Finlay, which was prepared when he was first brought to trial, and which the Union published at 6d., is now to be had at 3d. The committee have determined on this reduction, that the interesting facts and reasoning therein contained may be widely circulated. Anti-Persecutionists will feel it their duty to aid this important object.

EMIGRATION.—On Sunday evening, 17th of March, Mr. Hunt's, Mr. Sully's, and Mr. Smith's party of Social emigrants met at the Parthenium, St. Martin's-lane.—Mr. Sully reported the refusal by the *New Moral World* of his reply to Mr. L. Jones's letter in that journal, condemning emigration. A committee was appointed to induce the next " congress " to constitute the *New Moral World* an organ of foreign as well as home colonization. The next meeting takes place on Sunday evening, 12th of May.

ERRATA.—We are desired, for the satisfaction of subscribers to the A. P. U., to state that in No. 3, " Mr. T. Mash 2s. 6d. should be Thomas Wesh." In No. 12, " Mr. Kalley 'ls., should be Mr. Katley." And that in No. 13 the first subscription should be " A few Friends," Pocklington." Collectors will oblige the printer by writing proper names in the plainest manner.

TO CORRESPONDENTS.

Received.—" The Regenerator." The circular of the Wesleyan Chapel, Canterbury. J. Emery.

W. B. C.—His erratum would be no improvement. It is not needed.

J. A. thinks that if we had read the Gillespie controversy, we should not esteem it worth the trouble we take with it. He has a friend who can prove the " existence of an intelligent first cause from facts acknowledged by all, if afforded an opportunity." We beg to assure J. A. that his friend shall have that opportunity in the *Movement*, and we shall anxiously expect such promising papers.

W. ROSE is thanked for his kind promises. The " Uses and Beauties of Euclid " will appear in due time.

SUBSCRIPTIONS TO THE ANTI-PERSECUTION UNION.

W. C. L.	£0 10	6
John Cook, Infidel Repository, Ipswich . . .	0 1	0
J. M'E. and Mr. Shute . .	0 1	0
E. Johnson, Col. 15 . .	0 6	0
J. Emery, W. W. Williams .	0 1	0
Per Mr. George Smith, Salford, Thomas Walsh . . .	0 1	0
M. J. Hall, late of Stockport .	0 1	0
Mr. Park, London, per Mr. Stewart	0 10	0

G. J. H., *Sec.*

Printed and Published by G. J. HOLYOAKE, 40, Holywell-street, Strand, Saturday, March 23, 1844.

THE MOVEMENT
And Anti=Persecution Gazette.

"Maximize morals, minimize religion."—BENTHAM.

No. 16.   EDITED BY G. JACOB HOLYOAKE, ASSISTED BY M. Q. RYALL.   PRICE 1½d

THE A PRIORI GOD.

THE Argument of Mr. Gillespie, transmitted to the conductors of the *Oracle*, is, I suppose the one submitted to the public. Of the refutation as set forth by Mr. Southwell, it would not be becoming to speak, that is now the Philaletheans' province. But Mr. Gillespie's Argument, apart from its logical relevancy, is open to criticism and comment.

The Argument is displayed as an *à priori* argument, for the being and attributes of a first great cause. But a "great cause" or a little cause, no cause so obscure as Mr. Gillespie's ever yet peered in the twilight of theology.

Mr. Gillespie's god is the driest god in the world. The way of the Lord was never so arid before.

As this argument is recommended to us by the Philalethean Society of Edinburgh, and as these gentlemen profess to silence Atheism by argument, instead of by law, as they essay "to peaceably repress infidelity," whether the Philalethean mountain should labour with mystery or with mice, its every delivery deserves our attention.

Whatever could induce this redoubtable body to desire a refutation of this argument, Aristotle could scarcely determine. Conversation can do the dumb no good, and this argument is so choked with the pedantry of the schools, that *speaking* is out of the question! It is buried beneath the weight of *Prologomenas, Scholimus, a, b,* and *c, Propositions, divisions, corrollaries,* and *sub-propositions.* To all practical and popular purposes it is dead. It is a modern mummy in metaphysical wrappers. Its meaning is hermetically sealed in learning jargon. Job and Mr. Gillespie must have been twins. Let he who doubts that god is past finding out read Mr. Gillespie's demonstrations of his existence, and he will be sceptical of the fact no more.

A certain *Presbyterian Review* has declared this production to be "an approach to a *perfectly colourless* and diaphanous simplicity." Had the critic pronounced that the performance could be easily *seen through,* he would have himself have more nearly "approached" the truth. Great truths are solid, and the grandeur of argument is always found to consist in plain effective statements.

When Euclid and Tacquet descant on a mathematical theorem, they favour their reader with axioms, definitions, and postulates—they place before him points, lines, and angles, surfaces and solids, and with these substantial auxiliaries to meaning, one hangs with delightful rapture over their lucid arguments. But Mr. Gillespie disdains to perform so kind an office for his reader, but leaves him to grope through the infinities of subtle extension as he best can. If the object aimed at was placed on a hill, the reader could see if it was reachable by reason, but Mr. Gillespie conceals it in a quagmire or a pitfall, as though he intended that when the bewildered traveller has lost his way, he shall at least be entrapped if he cannot be convinced.

If by "infinity of extension," the abstraction with which Mr. Gillespie sets out, the reader suspected that it was put for what the pulpits proclaim as "God over all, blessed for ever more," he would narrowly inspect such an artful premise. What Christian ever dreamed in his most frantic moments that his "crucified Saviour," is "infinity of extension!" and the holy spirit that guides him is an "immoveable being!!" yet these are the literal results which Mr. Gillespie by Aristotlean ratiocination brings out of his fundamental proposition. I do not here declare that Mr. Gillespie has not succeeded, but if he has, his performance is a wonderful work, not more calculated to surprise us, than to astonish his own brethren.

G. J. H.

SUBSTANCE OF A LECTURE,
Delivered in Liverpool on behalf of Mr. Paterson,
By J. C. FARN.

I AM of opinion that the right of free discussion should be possessed by every member of society, and that to deprive any individual of it, is a violation of the rights of man, and, consequently, an act of injustice; any infringement of the liberty of the press, is a blow struck at the well-being of society; and therefore, cannot be sanctioned on the ground of public utility. I have long held, as an incontrovertable doctrine, the natural equality of man; and, therefore it is, I affirm that any infringement of the right of free discussion, is an act of injustice. The principles of human nature and human society, which I advocate, forbid me to countenance, in any way, persecutions in matters of opinion. The right of free discussion is the only distinction between a free man and a slave. We know well that entire uniformity of opinion is impossible; and therefore, we should agree amicably to differ with each other on matters of opinion. As we are all liable to err, why should any claim infallibility? Such pretentions are as absurd as they are unjust. If none are infallible, how can any body of men claim the censorship of the press? Yet the British priesthood claim it in the present day; imitating, in their desire to tyranise, the conduct of the priesthood in all climes and in all stages of the world. I claim for every member of society the liberty of opinion, and the right to express, without fear, the dictates of his conscience on all subjects. Had it not been for some liberty of discussion, we should have still been the feudal barons' slaves, compelled to fight his battles without having any interest in the contest. Had all free inquiry been crushed by the iron hand of the persecutors, the dark cloud of Paganism would have overshadowed this country to the present hour. Had inquiry been neglected, savage could not have been changed to civilised life. And shall we tamely resign into the hands of intolerant priesthood, that principle which has done so much for the world, and is destined to do still more. Forbid it reason! forbid it common sense! No! The hand of the persecutor must be checked in the nineteenth century, if it never has been before. There must be no wavering policy where such great interests are at stake, as the liberty of the press. It is not the cause of sect or party, it is neither more nor less than the cause of universal liberty.

Once destroy liberty of conscience, and we may bid farewell to the progress of society, human improvement, and the triumph of truth. Once allow unchallenged tyranny, in matters of opinion and to despotism there will be no end. Then, indeed, would intolerance triumph over the dignity of human nature, and trample with impunity on the claims of reason, justice, and truth. Rather than I would submit to such a degrading bondage, I would abandon human society and retire henceforth to the solitude of the forest. Is there no more noble contest for the priesthood to engage in, than that of attempting to paralyse the noblest faculties of our nature. No better cause than that of injustice to engage their atttention. Must their dominion be perpetuated by the destruction of human liberty? The priesthood have always been the friends of the oppressor, and the enemies of the oppressed. They have not attempted to remove the evils of the world; but, on the contrary, they have added to their number and force. " If we do not destroy the press," said Cardinal Wolsey, " the press will destroy us!" It is this fear that has generated the present prosecution. It is the legitimate offspring of a Stae Church

If history teaches us one thing more than another, it is this—" Beware of the Priests " or you will feel, and that bitterly too, the consequence of neglect. Yes! in the nineteenth century, men are imprisoned because they loved liberty, and sought the improvement of society. It is the duty of all classes, sects, and parties to struggle for civil and religious liberty; for where the *one is not*, the other cannot be. As the Church and State have united for evil, the people must unite for good. We must deprive the serpent of its sting and nip the poisonous herb in the bud. It is the duty of a Government to protect the expression of opinion, and not to coerce it by the strong arm of the law; to do so is a violation of the social compact, and pernicious to the well-being of society, in its most extensive sense. If society does not protect its members, it is of no value whatever. Persecution is not defenceable on the ground of public utility, as it never makes sincere converts; it may irritate, but it never can convince. It may deluge the world with blood, but it cannot make all think alike; for this is impossible with that variety of natural constitution which is the characteristic of our common nature. And yet our political governors are determined to enslave our bodies, and an intolerant Church our minds. Thanks, however to the increase of human intelligence; such dominion, if we do our duty, will soon draw to a close; it will sink into oblivion, " and like the baseless fabric of a vision leave not a wreck behind." And then such proceedings will be considered as the offspring of an ignorant and a barbarous age. Then shall we possess that liberty of thought and action to which we are justly entitled, and enjoy that happiness of which we are all in search of, though hitherto we have searched in vain. A State Church has always been a persecuting one, in our country and in every other. As the Church of Rome in this country is, politically speaking, dead, I shall not disturb its ashes; peace be to its memory, although it did not allow peace to the world in the days of its power. The first founder of the Protestant Church was a determined persecutor. In her reign an act was passed, entitled, " The Act of Uniformity," which prohibited any one from following a clergyman who was not of the established religion, under pain of forfeiting all they possessed for the first offence, a year's imprisonment for the second, and imprisonment for life for the third; while it imposed a fine of a shilling on those who did not attend the church on Sundays. The Protestant priesthood did not oppose the enactment of these laws, and therefore they are fairly chargeable with them, as they who allow oppression share the crime. I beg of you to bear this in mind, or any charge against them may appear unreasonable and unjust. These laws were not allowed to remain a dead letter. The Quakers were ruinously fined for not attending the established church. In Bristol alone, in one year, they paid in fines, or what is the same thing, the Church plundered for the payment to the amount of £16,440. The Church is now plundering the Society of Friends to the amount of £14,000 per annum. I have no doubt the priests would like to levy fines for non-attendance at church in 1844. It would materially increase their salaries, and enable them to preach to the people contentment in their situation still more than they do now, as they would have more interest in doing so, though they have sufficient of that already.

In the reign of William the Third an act was passed, relating to apostacy from the Christian religion; it is even now on the statute book, though it has been for a long time a dead letter. But, to prevent a revival of its monstrous influence, we ought to seek its repeal.

"By the 9th and 10th of William the Third, chap. 32, it is provided, that if any person educated in, or having made profession of, the Christian religion, shall, by writing, printing, teaching, or advised speaking, deny the Christian religion to be true, or the Holy Scriptures to be of Divine authority, he shall, upon the first offence, be rendered incapable to hold any office or place of trust: and for the second be incapable of bringing any action, be executor, legatee, or purchaser of lands, and suffer three years' imprisonment. Such disabilities may for once be avoided by a public recantation within four months after statute of apostacy.

In a speech at Sheffield, Mr. Ward, the Member of Parliament of that town, spoke as follows, about twelve months ago—" I have mentioned persecution. You are told that the Catholic is a persecuting church; but look back at the history of the last three hundred years. Recollect the parable of the mote and the beam. Recollect the last, the blackest, and the most enduring instance of persecution on record. Recollect the Penal laws which were passed by a Protestant legislature. Did you eve read these laws? It is scarcely fifty years since the worst part of them was repealed. Look at them, and remember that they were made by Protestants against their Catholic neighbours. Look at the premiums that were offered for the treachery of children against parents; at the prohibition of the possession of property by Catholics; at the denunciation of the priests, and the price set on their heads; at the prohibition of the education of Catholic children at home, while it was made misprison of treason to send them abroad for education; and yet they are now denounced for their ignorance. Recollect the 'Nameless Statute,' as it is justly called to this day. I once mentioned it in the House of Commons and Sir Robert Peel took a note of it, and attempted to gainsay me, but he found that I was right, and that this atrocity had really been sanctioned by both branches of the legislature of Protestant Ireland. After trying all other penalties, both Houses of Parliament passed a law, inflicting on every Catholic priest who should be found in the discharge of his duty, a qualification for the guardianship of the Grand Seignior's seraglio. This act was passed by an Irish Protestant legislature. Let the Protestants blush for it, and never again name the persecutions of Protestants by Catholics, while this 'nameless statute' is on record."

I call upon reformers of all grades to join in the present struggle for civil and religious liberty, lest there should be a recurrence of those evils from which we have partially escaped. I have come forward on the present occasion, not because my own opinions, or those of the society to which I belong, have been attacked, but to perform my duty as a member of general society, and as an advocate of the rights of man. (Cheers.)

ON THE INSANITY OF MANKIND.

Insanity is inseparable from cerebral imperfection, therefore the fate of all the human race.

SANITY can never on any occasion deviate from REASON; and, as no one is at all times. Rational, therefore, all mankind are either INSANE or EXTRA-INSANE.

Sanity is the attribute of perfection alone; and all the human race being (at present) imperfect (*i.e.* having brains, the different organs of which are unequally balanced), Insanity *must* be the result. Those individuals who aver that they can draw the line of demarcation between the Sane (so called) and the Insane, must, in the first place, prove that they themselves are perfectly Sane; and who is to judge?

In Vol. XVII. page 60, of the Phrenological Journal, we find the following agreement to the foregoing:—There is no individual in whom a harmonious balance of the mental powers is to be found, and consequently, if we speak with rigorous exactness, "*no human mind is in its right state.*"

Those who commit irrational acts,—*i. e.*, acts injurious to themselves or others,—cannot be sane, and therefore not responsible for their actions—should not be punished as criminals, but treated as lunatics; *as well might we punish men born and brought up in this island for not possessing the lauguage, manners, and customs, of the Chinese.—How can we expect men to practise that which they have never learnt?*

Can we by wishing "make one hair white or black?" or can we "add one cubit to our stature?"—can we *will* ourselves geometers, astronomers, poets, painters, or mechanics, without possessing talents suited to attaining such knowledge? or can we *will* the alteration of our views, moral, political, or religious, without conviction? No; then, how can we be *free agents?* for in the former it is natural talent which gives us the *inclination,* and *forces* us (involuntarily) to attain such knowledge; in the latter, it is *conviction* which *compels* us (involuntarily) to alter our opinions, unless a pretended change is made (as too often is the case) from selfish motives; thus, also is free agency an attribute of Perfection alone.

Our thoughts, words, and deeds arise *involuntarily* from cerebration (*i. e.* the action of the brain) and the circumstances we are placed in at the time those organs of the brain are excited, which produce such manifestations; thus, none but the *ignorant* or *Extra-insane* (fancying themselves free agents) *blame* or *praise* their fellow-men for their actions and opinions.

Education makes a most material difference in the conduct of many persons through life; in fact, unless the individuals have good reasoning faculties, and possess moral courage, they but seldom (externally) after the opinions engrafted on their cerebral organs in childhood, however adverse such opinions may be to all logical deductions.

Although education has a great effect in forming the cerebration, still, when the individual is capable of reflection, opinions often, in after life, become much modified, provided there is honesty enough to own it.

In Vol. XVII. page 89, of the Phrenological Journal, among the reviews occurs the following passage:—"*To us,*" says the writer, "*it appears that the criminal's knowledge of his act being against law, so far from increasing his guilt,* (if there be any) *establishes its diminution. It proves a greater amount of mental alienation, for it implies a mind not under the regulation of the ordinary rules of prudence and common sense. By it the homicide exhibits himself as uncontrolled by the strongest principle in the reasoning-man's nature—self-preservation. To send such men as these to the scaffold is not to serve, but to insult, justice.*"

Nothing exhibits the *Insanity* of the human race in a greater degree than the following individuals being esteemed *sane*: viz., *duellists, assassins, men hired to destroy the lives of those who never injured them, as soldiers and hangmen, and other murderers; gamblers and thieves; liars and other deceivers; drinkers of alcholic liquors, whether in excess or not, and users of other narcotics, except as medicines; non-restrainers of their anger; haters of their fellow-men; revengers of injuries; persecutors for opinions, &c. &c., and all those who commit acts injurious to themselves or others.* Can a man be *sane* who, at any time, commits acts at variance with reason? and is it rational for a man to injure himself.

To the *ignorant* the following may appear absurd; but it is nevertheless a fact, that persons can, by examination of the *map* of the brain, as laid down on the *exterior surface* of the head, *minutely* describe the talents, opinions, morals, and animal feelings of the individuals: thus even religious *feeling* cannot escape them, it being *quite easy* (by means of the brain map) to *decide* whether or not the individual is *sincere* in his profession of religion, and the *amount* of his belief.

ARTHUR TREVELYAN.

CASE OF MR. PATERSON.

MR. PATERSON desires me to acknowledge several letters which he has received from friends. I have done so privately, with the exception of Mr. Knox and Mr. Campbell's letters of Leicester. Mr. C.'s first, contained too much news, and the last too strong language.

From this it will be concluded that Mr. Paterson has been permitted to write again: *Chambers' Information,* writing paper, and a dictionary, have been allowed him. Mr. Paterson sends his "respects to Miss M. Roalfe, and says, that, was it not for the weather, and one or two other trifling obstacles, he would be present at her liberation. He hopes that I shall have a curacy vacant at the expiration of his own sentence, as he shall relish it more than ever." The Anti Persecution Union have addressed the following

APPLICATION ON BEHALF OF MR. PATERSON.
(*Copy.*)

To the General Prison Board of Scotland:
My Lords and Gentlemen.—I am instructed by the Anti-Persecution Union of London, to apply to you on behalf of Thomas Paterson, a prisoner in Perth Gaol. Mr. Paterson was sentenced in the High Court of Justiciary, Edinburgh, on November 8, 1843, to fifteen month's imprisonment for the aledged offence of blasphemy.

Immediately after his sentence he was removed to Perth Gaol, and has since been treated, in every respect, as a felon—has been kept in solitary confinement—not permitted by the rules of the gaol, to write oftener than once in three months—not allowed to see visitors—and is compelled to labour to the exclusion of time for study, for moral and intellectual improvement—is forced to live on the prison diet without reference to his former habits, and is degraded by being compelled to wear the prison dress.

Your applicants do not contend that the conduct of Mr. Paterson which led to his incarceration was not very objectionable in the eyes of his Christian fellow-countrymen, but it cannot be denied that his conduct resulted from conscientious conviction, and the degree of his punishment seems to your applicants, and also to many enlightened christians in the country, greatly to exceed anything that his offence called for, and his treatment has excited very general pain and disapprobation, as the resolutions of many public meetings, both in England and Scotland, testify. Indeed, so much difference of opinion prevails as to the wisdom and justice of subjecting persons to imprisonment for such offences as Mr. Paterson's, that Parliament will shortly be solicited, to advise Her Majesty to order his liberation.

But while Mr. Paterson remains imprisoned, your applicants earnestly hope that your board will see reason to ameliorate his sufferings, as far as the discretionary power in your hands will permit.

Your applicants have reason to fear that the effects of solitary confinement may end in insanity, of which many unhappy cases have recently occurred to prisoners at Pentonville, who have been under the discipline to which Mr. Paterson is subjected. Whatever may be the bitterness with which Mr. Paterson may be regarded, your applicants are unwilling to believe that his prosecutors intend to deprive him of his reason. The bare supposition is too horrible to be entertained, and to melancholy for contemplation. Your applicants, therefore, entreat your Lordships to remove him at once from solitary confinement, permit him to see visitors at stated and not unfrequent periods, and to write weekly to his friends, which will contribute greatly to preserve the proper tone of his feelings.

Since enlightened legislature has inseparably connected the improvement of the prisoner with the punishment of his alleged offence, your applicants trust that your Lordships will not deem it unreasonable in them, to request that Mr. Paterson be relieved from compulsory labour, or left sufficient time for reading and study, a privilege which, considering his former reflecting habits, will not contribute less to his improvement than to his health.

Your applicants desire that Mr. Paterson be permitted, with the sanction of the surgeon, to provide himself with a more agreeable dietary than that which the prison affords.

Permission given to Mr. Paterson to wear his own dress, though trifling in some eyes, is important in your applicants'. By being clad in the degrading livery of felony, Mr. Paterson's feelings must be continually lacerated, or his self-respect destroyed. This is a punishment from which a felon would be exempt, because it is a degradation which a felon would not feel. Your applicants trust that your Lordships will not deem it necessary to punish the conscientious publication of opinions with more severity than the committal of deliberate crime.

Your applicants have learned with pleasure, that a few books and writing paper have been allowed Mr. Paterson, and they hope they may regard these things as an earnest of future lenity.

The anxiety your applicants feel for Mr. Paterson's welfare, will, they trust, excuse them for intruding this application on your Lordships' attention.

I have the honour to be,
My Lords and Gentlemen,
Yours very respectfully,
G. JACOB HOLYOAKE.
Secretary to the Anti-Persecution Union.
Office of the A. P. U.
5, Paul's-alley, Paternoster-row,
London, 22d March 1843.

AN ABSTRACT OF THE RULES, &c.
OF THE
LONDON ATHEISTICAL SOCIETY.

ITS objects are—to establish the right of free discussion on all religious subjects—and to obtain from the legislature a repeal of all Acts of Parliament interfering with the right of conscience.

Its means will be by a Union of all parties favourable to our views—delivery of lectures—distribution of tracts—and the collection of a fund to support those members who may be prosecuted.

The Society will be conducted by a committee of five, assisted by a secretary and treasurer, who will present a report of their proceedings each half year. The accounts will be audited by two persons elected for that purpose.

The Society will meet monthly to discuss any subject that may be agreed upon. The public will be admitted free. Donations will be received to aid in carrying out the objects.
T. P.

The Atheist of London have at length accomplished a much desired object, the establishment of a society, for the consideration of their peculiar opinions. This is a long wished for consummation, and must merit the approval of all who justly appreciate the value of civil liberty, and moral progress. The formation of this society, exhibits another instance of the short sighted and suicidal policy of our would-be conscience masters in high quarters. The malignity and unjust hate heretofore bestowed on the atheist by the thoughtless multitude, have been, under the fostering hand of persecution converted into sympathy, active support and admiration for the victims of religious intolerance, and hence, as a natural consequence, the formation of a Union for mutual protection and defence. The London Atheistical Society desire the adherence of every atheist in the kingdom. Every atheist should for fraternity's sake become a member of this society. To give force and potency to our efforts, association is necessary. To afford encouragement to each other support should be counted on, and every event in which an atheist takes a prominent part, chronicled. By these means shall we become powerful, and by scrupulous attention to active duties, a useful section of reformers. The open avowal of atheism is a responsibility none but a vrituous man will dare, and which none but honest men will venture upon. Such men we have, and such we look to have, and such only do we care to have. Atheism must cease to be the scapegoat for the consequences of religious villany, it must have a practical embodiment in every act of its professors. Truth should be its shield, candour and consistency its supporters, and the welfare of man its motto. Every member must possess fortitude to maintain for it this character in the various positions he may occupy in society.

Any communication addressed to the secretary, Mr. T. Powell, at the office of the *Movement*, will be immediately attended to, and any information relating to the society furnished. C. DENT.

EXTENSION OF THE ANTI-PERSECUTION UNION.

Church Gate, Leicester, March 6, 1844.
DEAR HOLYOAKE,—I have often thought while reading your *Movement* that the scope of the Anti-Persecution Union was by no means wide enough. It seems too exclusively confined to persecution directed against theological heresy alone, while by far the greater part of government or local prosecutions, have been, and are now, directed against political heresy.

I have ever appreciated the gratuitous and effective assistance you have personally given us, when struggling either for the release of our victims, or the mitigation of their treatment—at Bristol and still more recently at Leicester, on behalf of Cooper.

The more immediate object of my present communication is to ask whether a more general union might not be raised, whose object should comprise in common, the relief and release of all prisoners incarcerated for opinions' sake, and whether, such a union might not in your opinion be far more effective in the collcetion of funds, in the getting up of petitions, and in obtaining the release of those who are thus unjustly prosecuted for, whether theological or political heresy.
Yours truly,
J. R. H. BAIRSTOW.

The subject of Mr. Bairstow's letter is one of the deepest interest to the Anti-Persecution Union. It formerly professed to defend the expression of *all* opinions, "political" of course included. The objects were limited to theological, because the committee disliked parading a universal profession, which their limited means and organization did not enable to carry out. But now their position is better understood and better established, they would be happy to extend their exertions into the political sphere, if a practicable plan of doing so could be devised. Mr. Ruffey Ridley who is a valuable member of the Anti-Persecution Committee, has promised to give this subject attention. Any suggestions Mr. Bairstow may find leisure to give, will be sure to meet with patient consideration. The free expression of political opinions is of vast importance, and if the Anti-Persecution Union received a nationa character, no doubt that great good would result from its operations in every department of public discussion. Let our friends meditate on the practicability of this,
G. J. H.

THEOLOGY AND POLITICS.—In a coffee-house in Red Cross-street, within a couple of doors from Barbican, may be seen in large, bold, unmistakable characters, the following:
—POLITICAL and THEOLOGICAL DISCUSSIONS every Monday and Thursday evenings, at half-past 8. The value of the PROTESTANT REFORMATION was announced as the particular subject in the course of debate. No shrinkers these in Barbican to all appearances. "Better to be safe" and "conformity to the prejudices of society," do not appear to be recognized as guiding phrases among them. But why do they not let us know what they are about, instead of waiting till the chapter of accidents should lead one of the *Movement's* conductors into that district?

ALLIANCE OF IGNORANCE AND SERVITUDE.—As the blindness of mankind has caused their slavery, in return, their state of slavery is made a pretence for continuing them in a state of blindness.—*Burke.*

BALANCE SHEET OF THE SCOTTISH ANTI-PERSECUTION UNION.

RECEIPTS.

	£	s.	d.
Nov. 10, 1843, Collection in Clyde-street Hall, at Reorganization of Union	0	4	8
,, Ditto Waterloo Rooms, public meeting	2	5	7¾
,, Sale of Addresses	0	6	11
Donations, Cosmopolite	1	0	0
Collections, J. Wood	0	5	0
Do. W. Anderson	0	5	0
Do. R. Peddie	0	5	0
Do. R. Hamilton	0	5	0
Do. George Brown	0	5	0
Do. John Brown	0	5	0
Do. R. Martin	0	4	0
Do. R. Cranston	5	19	6
Dec. London Union, 3 Remittances			
From No. 3, 10s.; No. 4, 6s. 6d.; No. 8, 9s.; No. 5, 5s.; No. 7, 1s. 3d.½; No. 11, 3s. 3d. No. 16, 8s.; No. 20, 1s.; Collecting Books, making	2	3	0
Collected by Miss Roalfe	0	3	2
Do. Mr. Baker in Robinson's Shop	0	3	0
Member's Tickets	0	16	0
Mr. Burns	0	5	0
From three Friends	0	2	3¼
,, Dundee ditto	0	3	0
,, Arbroath ditto	0	10	0
Feb. 1844. Falkirk	0	14	0
,, 21, Collection, Public Meeting, St. Cecilia Hall	1	2	0
	17	17	2¼

A true Copy abridged from the Cash Book.
J. W. *Treasurer, A. P. U.*
March 11, 1844.

EXPENDITURE.

	£	s.	d.
Petty cash to Secretary for books, postage, &c.	0	7	6
Assistant to do. as per minutes, Nov. 22.	0	5	0
Nov. 21, 1843. Rent of Waterloo Room, public meeting	5	10	0
Committee Room, 6 nights	0	6	0
Dec. 25. Mr. Peddie and Miss Roalfe's expenses to Glasgow	0	8	0
Mr. Southwell from Glasgow to Edinburgh, twice	1	7	10
Feb. 21, 1144. Rent of St. Cecilia Hall, public meeting	2	10	0
Paid for Miss Roalfe's Bail Bond and Fees	0	3	6
Do. Mrs. Finlay, 7s. week during Mr. Finlay's Incarceration	2	16	0
Do. Mr. Hunter for a board	0	4	0
Do. Bill Sticker	0	9	6
Do. Mr. Glass, printer, to acct.	1	0	0
Do. Mr. Elder, printer, in full for bills	2	12	0
Do. for 3 paid letters to members	0	0	3
Do. Policeman at Waterloo Room, Voluntary	0	2	0
Expenditure	18	1	7
Receipts	17	17	2¼
Balance due to Treasurer	0	4	4¾

A true copy abridged from the Account Book.
March 11, 1844. J. W., *Treasurer A. P. U.*

Having examined the above accounts, we hereby certify they are correct. } W. BAKER, } W. LOGAN, } *Auditors.*

Edinburgh, *March 16th,* 1844. HENRY JEFFREY, *Sec.*

A DUELLIST'S APOLOGY FOR MURDER.—Lieut. Monro, in his letter in the *Morning Chronicle*, begins by saying that "Providence, for some wise purpose," permitted him to shoot his brother-in-law, Colonel Fawcett. From which it follows that, since that duel has called forth general, just, and unqualified disapprobation, the "wise purposes of providence" are acquiring a doubtful reputation.

THE BLASPHEMOUS BIBLE.—A poet has written some verses which appeared in *The Times* of March 18, entitled "THE CRY," in which he introduced the well-known scripture text which says that the "poor shall not cease out of the land," and which has been so long the rich man's excuse for not removing poverty from our starving population. The poet speaks of it in these lines—

Mock God with some *blasphemous* text,
  Pointing out with a scriptural hand
How in this world, if not in the next,
  "The poor" must still cumber the land.

We should be visited with six months' for saying this. "That in a captain is but a choleric word, which in a corporal is rank blasphemy."

THE PRESTON MAGISTRATES.—A short time ago, the Solons of Preston closed the Social Hall in that town, upon which the Central Board sent Mr. Lloyd Jones down to deliver Lectures in *defiance* of the magistrates. Mr. Jones did as he was bidden, was not interfered with, and the hall in Preston is now kept open. We are glad that the Central Board sent Mr. Jones down, and we are doubly glad that Mr. Jones went, and we are doubly glad at the success which attended the bold step, for it is of importance that Social Halls should be kept open as well as Atheistical book shops. We are glad also that "*running into the lion's mouth*," supposed to be the exclusive business of Mr. Paterson, is becoming fashionable.

LIBERATION OF MISS ROALFE.—Mr. Southwell writes, "Miss Roalfe was liberated this morning (March 23.) She looks better than my anticipative faculty had pictured her. She is in excellent spirits, and by no meanns sorry for the past, or fearful of the future."

A TARDY CONSCIENCE.—Mr. Wood of Walworth informs us that a Mr. Aday of the same district has supplied him with *thirteen* numbers of the *Movement*, but when about to hand him the *fourteenth* it appeared to him to be an unchristian act, and his conscience stung him.

A GENEROUS BARBER.—A friend in Leicester has commenced *shaving* for the benefit of the victims of intolerance. The proceeds of his labours are added to the funds of the Anti-Persecution Union. This is certainly one of the drollest ways in which industry and ingenuity ever sought to support the cause of liberty. Such a man would make the fortune of a Methodist Missionary. Was he one of their converts he would be extolled as an astonishing instance of the gospel's power.

PERSECUTION IN FRANCE.—A man named Michel, the author of a book entitled "Caducite des Religions pretendues Revelées," was tried by the Court of Assize, on Friday, and convicted of "outrage against religion and public, and religious morality," and sentenced to six month's imprisonment, and a fine of 2,000f. The seized copies of the book were ordered to be destroyed.—*Lloyd's London Newspaper.*

On Tuesday Evening next, the Atheistical Society will hold its First Public Meeting at the Parthenium, St. Martin's-lane, at half-past Eight o'Clock, to admit Members and to discuss the following question—"The Moral Obligations of Atheism."

ADDRESS.— J. M'Cullough, 24, Cecil-court, St. Martin's-lane.

TO CORRESPONDENTS.

RECEIVED.—"Christian Mysteries." W. Rose's enclosures. A No. 38, "Vegetable Diet, Defended by Dr. Alcott." "Letters of J. P. Greaves, parts 2 and 3."

J. HINDLE.—His opinions are always valued by us. The phrase "incorrigible dogs" was written in laughing irony—not in earnest. If taken seriously it is objectionable. The enlargement of the *Movement* cannot at present take place. The "incorporation" he speaks of, is not practicable.

"A SINCERE WELL-WISHER."—His letter is very interesting, coming from one who has read little on metaphysical subjects.

Received by C. S. from "W. W."	0 10	0
,, by Miss R., H. J., and J. Mc N. from "W. J."	0 15	0

SUBSCRIPTIONS TO THE ANTI-PERSECUTION UNION.

A Friend	£0 10	0
Per Mr. John Hindle, Ashton-under-Lyne	0 14	10
W. J. B. for Miss Roalfe on her liberation	1 0	0
Mr. Liddle, Col. 36	0 1	0
Mr. Messeder and friends	0 1	0

G. J. H., Sec.

Printed and Published by G. J. HOLYOAKE, 40, Holywell-street, Strand, Saturday, March 30, 1844.

THE MOVEMENT
And Anti=Persecution Gazette.

"Maximize morals, minimize religion."—BENTHAM.

No. 17.   EDITED BY G. JACOB HOLYOAKE, ASSISTED BY M. Q. RYALL.   PRICE 1½d

THE REV. HERBERT MARSH.

THIS bright luminary of the Established Church has been, we are glad to find, very generally condemned by his brethren. The *Northampton Herald*, in particular, goes so far as to condemn its neighbour, the *Northampton Mercury*, for publishing the prosecution of Nathalie Miard, by Marsh. "No right-minded mother," exclaims the *Herald*, "No virtuous wife, no chaste daughter, ought to be made acquainted with the impurities of the French brothels," the haunts of the Rev. Herbert Marsh.

The editor of the *Herald* is a clergyman, and as one he must be aware that the bible is as full of impurities as revolting to decency as those with which the Rev. Herbert Marsh has been connected. If then, the editor of the *Northampton Herald* is as consistent as he professes to be indignant, he will give our friend "Cosmopolite" the benefit of his approval, and help to circulate Cosmopolite's useful tract, "The Bible an Improper Book for Youth." While delinquent and obscene clergymen are cried down, consistency requires that delinquent and obscene books should not be cried up. The clerical editor of the *Northampton Herald* should not, in his pulpit, recommend to "right minded mothers, virtuous wives, and chaste daughters," a book of Jewish brothel history, as vile as the Rev. Mr. Marsh's history. This clergyman editor cannot, from sheer disgust, publish in his own paper the report of Marsh's amours, how then can he suffer his parishioners to read those of Lot, Judah, David, Solomon, and the Holy Ghost? Surely "right minded mothers, virtuous wives, and chaste daughters," can have no sympathy with the Virgin Mary?

We do not consider the conduct of this disgusting delinquent minister, Marsh, as resulting from his christian principles, and yet we charge persecution on christianity. This difference is voluntarily mentioned for the sake of drawing attention to the reason of it. Christians generally, of all sects, and all the newspaper organs of piety, from the *Times* downward, have condemned and denounced Mr. Marsh's conduct, and even the bishops have been, to some extent, in earnest in their endeavours to prevent the repetition of his practices. We allow this to be a sufficient indication that they do not find in their religious principles that which encourages disgusting licentiousness. They evidently feel the incongruity between what Mr. Marsh has been guilty of, and what they believe to be orthodoxly proper. But is it so with persecution? Do christians of all sects denounce the persecutors? What religious newspapers condemned the conduct of Maitland the preacher, who was witness against Mr. Holyoake in Cheltenham. What bishops censured the Rev. Mr. Close, whose paper dictated Mr. Holyoake's apprehension? Have christians held up to public reprobation the Rev. Mr. Lee, of Campsie, who so recently caused the imprisonment of Mr. M'Neile? Has the *Times* newspaper execrated the Procurator Fiscal, of Edinburgh, who incarcerated poor old Finlay and Miss Roalfe? What church dignitaries have reprimanded the Lord Justice Hope and Lord Moncreiff, who sentenced Mr. Paterson to fifteen months solitary confinement? What steps have been taken by Christians to prevent the recurrence of this conduct? Who has discovered any incongruity between these barbarous and savage practices, and the belief of religious tenets? On the contrary, these persecutors have been held to promote the "glory of god and the cause of true religion." Therefore it is that we discover in christianity something not only congenial to persecution, but that which nourishes, supports, and defends it. Let the loathsome persecutor meet the execrations properly showered on the head of the loathsome libertine. The man who stops free discussion is a greater enemy to mankind than he who violates the decencies of society. He who seeks to stifle truth is a greater criminal than the parson who squanders his tithes with courtezans, and he is far more depraved who fills dungeons with conscientious martyrs for liberty, than he who fills brothels by his indiscretion. In our opinion, the Maitlands, Closes, Lees, Fiscals, Hopes, and Moncreifts, are actuated by more pernicious principles than the Marshs. Marsh sets a bad example—they perform bad actions. He strikes at decency—they at liberty. He injures himself—they others. Wherefore should he be condemned and they honoured? We condemn him in the name of decency, and execrate them in the name of truth. G. J. H.

PETITIONING.

In the 83rd number of the *Oracle* are published some reflections on the etiquette of petitioning, which I wish to recall to the recollection of the readers of the *Movement*, especially as the friends of the Anti-Persecution-Union have now to exert themselves in this department. Petitions, and also the resolutions of public meetings respecting our imprisoned friends, require to be expressed with studied propriety, that a correct public opinion may be speedily formed. Before offering the suggestions I intended, I will introduce a petition forwarded by Mr. Paterson to the care of Joseph Hume, M. P., to be laid before the House of Commons, or the Home Secretary, as may be found most judicious.

" *To the Honourable the Commons, &c.*
" *The Petition of Thomas Paterson, prisoner, Perth Gaol.*

" Respectfully sheweth—That your petitioner was sentenced in the High Court of Justiciary, Edinburgh, on the 5th of November, 1843, to fifteen months imprisonment, for the alleged offence of blasphemy. That he was immediately brought to Perth Prison, and has been subsequently treated in every respect as a felon. He is deprived of his own clothing, and subjected to solitary confinement in one small cell night and day—compelled to labour, and allowed only the prison diet. That the rules under which he is placed, only permit him to write one letter in three months, and that he is not allowed to see visitors. Your petitioner finds his health to be impaired by the close confinement, want of proper exercise, and the nature of his unvaried and unrelished food.

" The offence alleged against your petitioner is that of " Selling and publishing works intended to libel the scriptures," but in reality, these works were of a controversial and matter of fact description—very necessary to throw light on a much disputed subject; and from the fact of their relation to a disputed topic, did your petitioner consider he was benefitting the public by affording all the information he could on the question. Eminent divines have said, " that to the objections of Infidels do they owe many of the evidences of their faith, which, but for these objectors, would have remained unknown and unnoticed." If, therefore, divinity be true, as your House doubtless believes, your petitioner claims to be considered an auxiliary of the church, and as rather deserving of thanks than a gaol.

' Your petitioner considers the persecution from which he is suffering, a disgrace to the intelligence of the age—for his imprisonment is an assumption that truth cannot stand without the law's support. Besides, the injustice is committed of punishing conscientious conviction. Sincerity may pertain to those in the right as well as those in the wrong, since opinions result from organization, education, and association. The only well ascertained effect of penal inflictions for opinions is that they make hypocrites or martyrs—and laws which do so must be injurious to society. Your petitioner knows not any instance in which persecution converted the individual punished. Your petitioner is very far from being converted, or even convinced he acted wrongly, and he considers a religion requiring the law's protection undeserving of attention. The cruelty with which your petitioner is punished demonstrates religious immorality as well as inutility. Your petitioner considers that even if opinions, were dangerous, or led to dishonest acts, the punishment of these actions is the only legitimate object of legislative control, and a sufficient safeguard to the public weal.

" Your petitioner also thinks that persecution for opinion's sake betrays a deficiency of sober reflection—an ignorance of history and of the faculties of mankind—a want of knowledge of the world, which ought to meet with the censure of your House. Your petitioner has found the enlightened treat opinion as a thing of time and place. They see that what is right in Asia is considered very wrong in Africa, and that "blasphemy" in Madeira is first-rate gospel in Scotland—that it is merely a matter of geography. Less of this ludicrous diversity would exist if opinions were generally permitted to be brought to the test of free discussion. Your petitioner regrets that the sentiments of Lord Brougham on this subject have had so little weight with his countrymen. Had the Christians of Scotland the knowledge and liberality as his Lordship, your petitioner would now be in the enjoyment of his liberty.

" Your petitioner further considers he was unjustly treated on his trial, as the Lord Justice Clerk was evidently an interested party in your petitioner's prosecution, by mixing up his strong prejudices in his various remarks to your petitioner and the jury, and thus converting the judgment seat into an inquisitorial office. Your petitioner was quite prepared to show that the charges in the indictment of " libelling the scriptures," were not true, unless truth is libellous. But your petitioner was not allowed to do this, "because," said his lordship, "the law does not allow you to prove that the bible contains such and such passages." These charges therefore the law ought not to have brought against me. From ignorance of the law, and understanding from his lordship that part of the charge should be withdrawn, your petitioner desisted from that part of his defence, but at the conclusion, his lordship prejudiced your petitioner to the jury in his summing up, by still insisting that he *had* "libelled the scriptures;" and to that circumstance, and the violent religious prejudices of the jury, your petitioner attributes their verdict againt him.

"Your petitioner is not sensible of having committed any crime. He has acted conscientiously and to the best of his judgment. He consider the publication of all opinions valuable, and the correct way of checking dangerous ones is by soundly educating the people. In accordance with this view your petitioner disseminated cheap, and he believed useful literature amongst them; and however erroneous others may consider his opinions, he acted from conviction alone. By Lord Campbell's New Libel Bill, it is allowed that "Truth and good intentions may be received in extenuation of any libel." The truth of his views your petitioner is ready to prove, and his good intentions are manifested in the circumstances under which his views were published. If further proof is required, a reference to Mr. Jardine of Bow-street will be satisfactory.

"You petitioner is willing at any time to defend the general sentiments contained in any or all the works he published or sold, as he believes they are calculated to instruct, elevate, and refine his fellow countymen.

"For these reasons, your petitioner hopes you will pray Her Majesty to abrogate all laws infringing the right of "private judgment," and at once order the release of your petitioner; or at least ameliorate his punishment, by removing him from solitary confinement—giving him leave to purchase other food—relieving him from compulsory labour—permitting him to see friends, write weekly, and have moral and scientific books from his own library.

"And your petitioner as in duty bound will feel obliged.   THOMAS PATERSON.

"Dated, Perth Prison, March 15, 1844."

This petition, which is a proper and manly one from Mr. Paterson, would not be proper from his friends, except under peculiar circumstances. If they should send such a petition with the view of ameliorating Mr. Paterson's condition, they would undoubtedly take an unlikely course to effect their object. If their intention was to set forth their strong anti-religious convictions, such petition as the preceding would answer the purpose well.

Mr. Paterson has an undoubted right to take which course he pleases. He prefers in his petition, evidently to set forth his unchanged convictions and voluntarily perils any amelioration of his condition, for the sake of exhibiting to those in authority his untamed resolution to stand by the conduct he conscientiously pursued. This is brave in him, and is to be admired. It is for his friends to solicit the relaxation of the iron severity with which he and others are treated.

In drawing up petitions to Parliament, one object only should be in view. No mixture of purposes should appear. Many political petitions sent for the recent victims of legislatorial misrule were very faulty in this respect. It was no uncommon thing to find a petition specially intended to procure privileges for some one incarcerated, containing several clauses in favour of the "Six Points," thus confounding two very distinct things together, and compelling the discussion of the Charter, when prison discipline was professedly the question. A petition against blasphemy laws, a memorial in favour of freedom of discussion, or on behalf of some victim, should each relate respectively to the one subject upon which it professes to treat, and be brief, plain, and argumentative.

A public meeting has been lately held in Sheffield, Mr. S. Ironside in the chair. Resolutions were ably spoken to by Messrs. J. Watts, Hanson, Nelson, Bradley, Rotheram, and Stevenson. A petition was adopted, which I subjoin. It has been forwarded by Mr. Ironside to Lord Warncliffe, for presentation in the House of Lords, and to Henry George Ward, M. P., for presentation in the Commons.

"*The Petition of a Public Meeting holden in the Hall of Science, Sheffield, on the 19th day of March,* 1844."

"Humbly sheweth—That, in the opinion of your petitioners, the best mode of combatting error is to find its source, and to oppose it with evidence of the truth; that for this purpose the free expression of opinion upon all subjects by all parties is advisable; that as belief or opinion depends upon evidence and the mental capacity for its reception, erroneous opinion is a misfortune—the punishment of which is immoral and unjust.

"Your petitioners would call the particular attention of you right Honourable House to the cases of Messrs. Robinson and Paterson, of Edinburgh, now suffering the treatment of common felons, for exercising their legal calling, and publishing opinions by them believed true. Your petitioners would suggest that such punishment can only set a premium on gross hypocrisy, and can never serve the cause of truth. Your petitioners would more especially call for your interference in the case of Miss Roalfe, of Edinburgh, confined for 60 days for vending blasphemy. The only definition of blasphemy with which your petitioners are acquainted, is " bringing God, Religion, or the Bible into contempt ; " your petitioners have been taught that English law requires direct proof of crime before punishment can be inflicted, whereas in the case of Miss Roalfe, the only witness, who had read the prosecuted works, admitted in evidence, "that his religious opinions were not thereby changed, and his morals had not thereby suffered. This witness seems to your petitioners to have clearly proved the innocence instead of the guilt of the prosecuted, and yet she suffers confinement as a felon.

"Your petitioners, therefore, hope your right Honourable House will see it wise to order the release of all the above persons, and to abolish for ever punishments for opinions.

"And your petitioners, &c."

That part of the petition which relates to the Scotch victims is excellent. The first part is not couched with such just propriety. Both the English and the Scotch judges, who have most weight at the bar and in the country, have declared that penalties are not directed against opinion. Men, say they, may entertain any sentiments provided they are not expressed publicly. Indeed, the recent struggles for freedom of speech have reduced the question to a still narrower compass. The most eminent judges of the land have declared that any subject may be discussed, speculative or practical, provided that the opinions advanced be expressed in a "temperate argumentative manner, without levity or ridicule." They profess not to enquire whether opinion is true or false, but to be anxious only for the preservation of decency, and the feelings of the public. The point to be gained then is the *free unrestricted expression* of conscientious theological opinion. It is unnecessary, if not beside the question in dispute, to argue that " erroneous opinion is a misfortune." The truth or error of the opinions advanced, the fortune or misfortune of the holders are not now to be defended —but the unrestricted expression of conscientious opinion without the visitation of legal penalties. In many cases true opinion cannot be known until it has been fully discussed. It must be shown—if it can be shown—that the legal definitions of the decency and propriety of discussion are partial, unwise or unjust—or that it would be better to permit the feelings of the community to be outraged than to punish the conscientious convictions of any man. If it can be proved that men are stirred up to determined support of persecuted opinion, and that in the particular instance in question that the evil is increased by the severity which is intended to suppress it, the argument will be valid against the policy of such prosecutions. As soon as final communication are received for the General Prison Board of Scotland, and the Secretary of State, a memorial of the following kind will be proposed to public meetings in London :—

The Memorial to the Commons House of Great Britain and Ireland, adopted by a public meeting holden in ———

Sheweth—That Mr. Thomas Paterson was sentenced in the High Court of Justiciary, Edinburgh, on Nov. 9, 1843, to 15 months imprisonment, for the publication of Atheistical sentiments ; and, in the opinion of your memorialists, such sentence was an unwise exercise of the powers of the law, for the public utility cannot, in this age, be promoted by visiting with legal penalties the conscientious convictions of any man. Your memorialists. therefore, pray your House to take such steps as will lead to the immediate release of the aforsaid Thomas Paterson, and to the repeal of all laws affecting the unrestricted publication of theological opinions.

II. That the said Thomas Paterson is subjected to all the horrors of solitary confinement, from which your memorialists fear that insanity will result. That he is only permitted to write to his friends once in three months. That he is not permitted to see visitors, nor allowed leisure time for study and improvement—in the event, therefore, of your House not seeing sufficient reason to adopt measures for his liberation, your memorialists earnesty pray that you will advise that he said Thomas Paterson be removed at once from solitary confinement, have the privilege of seeing friends, and be permitted to purchase food when he is inclined to spend a por'ion of that time in study which must now be occupied with work before food is supplied him.

This memorial is a memorial, because a petition is humiliating. It is addressed merely to the " Commons," because it will not be fulsome. It asks the liberation of Mr. Paterson, consistently with its request of the repeal of all blasphemy laws. It is frank about Mr. Paterson's offence, and specifies it as atheism, and not mere blasphemy. It brings the mildest accusation against the law, that of being unwise, and requires Mr. Paterson's liberation, and the law's repeal on the highest grounds—those of public utility and private integrity. In the event of the

House not seeing sufficient reason, which it is sure not, to advise Mr. Paterson's liberation, the memorial provides for the betterment of his treatment. G. J. H.

THE STOCKPORT MEETING.
(*To the Editor of the Movement.*)

MY DEAR SIR,—It affords me much satisfaction to acquaint you that last week a public meeting was held in this town, to consider the cases of Miss Roalfe and Messrs. Paterson and Robinson. The audience, though not quite so numerous as I expected, was a very spirited one—for Stockport remarkably so. It was truly gratifying to find, that in a place where that grand curse of the age—our present factory system—reigns supreme, and in its most hideous features, all popular energy and enthusiasm were not paralysed,—that there still could be found in the hearts of the people a few drops of that love of justice and fair play to all parties, which is always ready to soothe the persecuted and inspire them onward in their noble endeavours to resist those who have the brutality to prosecute men for not swallowing, in all humility, the orthodox bolus of the day. I laid before the meeting the particulars of the prosecutions, more especially that of Miss Roalfe, which drew forth a torrent of indignation that must even have made a *christian* blush. Speeches were also delivered by Messrs, Allinson, Watts, James Cooper and Joseph Smith; at the close of whose address a subscription was entered into to defray the expenses of the meeting, and support the "Anti Persecution Union." The subscription is still open, and, when it amounts to something worth sending, will be forwarded to the proper quarter.

It is certainly, sir, high time that these holy pranks we put a stop to, which can only be done by rallying round those who are their victims. Do the political and religious despots of the age really imagine that they will frighten men from enjoying the noblest rights appertaining to humanity, by victimising those who dare to exercise it? Vain mortals! Let them glance at the past, let them read the history of such attempts, and learn a lesson of shame and humiliation. Did the banishment of the enlightened Anaxagoras, the first sceptic of any note, extinguish the blaze of truth which burst from his master-mind? No! It only imparted to it additional splendour and glory. Did the death of the virtuous philanthropist of Athens suppress the views he developed? No! Though the poisonous hemlock destroyed the man—the flesh and blood—it harmed not his opinions, *they* were impervious to its deadly sting, *they* still were left to spread their light through the length and breadth of the fairest state immortalized in the pantheon of history. Did the incarceration of the venerable philosopher of Florence obliterate his discoveries? No! Though the priestly chain shackled the man, his *opinions* were fetterless, indestructible, indelable, immortal. Even when his hoary locks were bent at the shrine of superstition, he could not but exclaim, as if in mockery of their priestly arrogance and brutality, "It is so, it is so!" No, sir, persecution has never chained *mind*, fettered *intellect*, imprisoned *thought*. For ages has it defied all the unhallowed powers of kingcraft and priestcraft to subdue it. Their sceptres cannot crush it, their mitres cannot awe it, their scaffolds cannot strangle it, their faggots cannot burn it, their dungeons cannot enclose it, their guns, bayonets, bludgeons, curses and indictments cannot annihilate it! They calm the whirlwind in its terrific fury—they may still the earthquake in its disasterous convulsions—they may arrest the lightning in its awful flashes—they may stem the ocean in its foaming torrents, but *opinion* they cannot touch. It is omnipotent, it bursts all bounds, and wings its way to the minds and hearts of mankind. As Campbell has nobly sung—

"Tyrants! in vain ye trace the wizard ring,
In vain ye limit minds unwearied spring."

I say, then, to those who would wish to crush the liberties, and above all, the *mental* liberty of the people, to be cautious, to think before they strike. France, Switzerland, the United States, the Texas stand up as land-marks to warn them of their danger. The spirits of their murdered sons cry out, Beware!

It is not inherent in the nature of things, that injustice and intolerance should always hold their brutal sway: they must eventually sink beneath the mighty tide of mind and civilization. Let us, then, hasten that glorious day, when every man, aye, and every *woman*, too, dare *speak* what they think, *write* what they think, *publish* what they think, without dread of the kingly bauble, or the priestly rod. Till this *desiderata* be realized, little permanent improvement may be anticipated in other ways. They will, as they hitherto have done, nip in the bud all that is beautiful and good, noble and great—blast the fairest efforts of the best of men—cripple and paralyze their usefulness—disappoint and deaden their enthusiasm. To the struggle, then; it is a mighty one, a glorious one, a struggle which requires and deserves all the energy which a warm and devoted spirit can command. Our efforts must be crowned with success sooner or later. The day *must* come when we shall behold, as Moore exclaims,

"Earth's shrines and thrones before our banner fall,
When the glad slave shall at these feet lay down

His broken chain, the tyrant lord his crown,
The priest his book, the conqueror his wreath."
ROBT. COOPER.

BIBLE APOLIGIES FOR PERSECUTION.

Extracted from a petition to the House of Commons by Mr. Southwell when in Bristol Goal.

I. There was a law to restrain the expression or publication of certain religious opinions held by Unitarians, and others, during the reign of William the Third; also, that in the reign of George the Third, when those so termed blasphemers, grew rich, numerous, and powerful, the statute of William was swept away, but, at no period of our history has there been a law of parliament against blasphemers, nor has parliament ever yet attempted to deal with the subject, which plainly shews, either that parliament thought it too contemptible to be worth the notice of the legislature, or too fugitive in its character to be laid hold of.

All those punished before the reign of William, for the too free expression of heterodox opinions, were punished under the authority of common law; judge made law, as Bentham styles it, which common, or judge made law, abolished by the statute of William, was revived upon the repeal of that statute, in the reign of George the Third, and men, in this so called free country, are tried for an offence, against which there is absolutely no law, and are thrust into a dungeon, for a longer or shorter period, according to the temper, whim, or caprice of a judge. Those charged with blasphemy, have, it is true, in common with felons or murderers, the advantage of trial by jury, but, in consequence of the state of the law, or rather in the absence of all law touching blasphemy, together with the excessive ignorance of juries in general, they are but ill qualified to decide rationally upon the subject.

It is usual with those who are incompetent to treat the question of persecution for opinions sake upon its own merits, and its influence upon the destinies of mankind, to fly to scripture for what they are pleased to consider divine sanction, to deal cruelly with heretics and infidels. If any line of conduct deserve the term wicked, it in this, and those who pursue it, are generally weak-minded, but dangerous men, who seek, in biblical texts, oaam lsier tt strengthen the hands of tyranny, and an apology for its crimes. The Bible furnishes weapons for all classes and orders of disputants, and will serve him best, who is most dexterous in the use of them. We live in a christian country in which the bible is generally received as the revealed will of a god; but he must indeed be a shallow christian, who cannot see through so gross an artifice, as appealing for authority to inflict vengence upon our fellow creatures to a volume that furnishes arguments for every class of reasoners. It is usual to refer to the mosaic law, in justification of imprisoning, or even killing any man, whom some dozen men may think fit to call a blasphemer. By the jewish law, it was decreed, that all blasphemers should *"die the death,"* but christians are not tied to the mosaic law; and philosophers only value laws as they tend to protect our rights and liberties. To talk, as some men do, when it suits their purpose, about abiding by the mosaic law, is preposterous in the extreme. for that law, though probably well suited to the ideas and capacities of jewish people, would sit with an ill grace upon the far more civilized society of the present day. But if the mosaic law is to be followed out, at all events, the spirit of it adopted as regards blasphemy, what reason can there be why it should not in all other respects. By the jewish laws, the husband could cast off his wife, nothing more being necessary, than simply handing her a writing of devorcement, for no other reason, than the unhappy wife "no longer found favour in his eyes"; and this license, for it can hardly be called liberty, was allowed the Jews, "on account of the hardness of their hearts," but, surely, no man in his senses, would say that such a law should serve as a model for us, or that modern ideas of justice and utility are to be squared with the notfons of a hard-hearted race who lived four thousand years since.

All christians admit that though the law came by Moses, that grace and truth came by Jesus Christ, who, if he did not introduce a new religion, gave, at least, a new dispensation, and taught opinions as repugnant to old jewish law, as his conduct was repugnant to jewish practice. He taught that loving ones neighbour was fulfilling of the law. An eye for an eye, and a tooth for a tooth, gave place to the new commandment. A new commandment, said Jesus, I give unto you, that ye love one another, as I have loved you, that is, if we have the truth on the matter. So that there is no greater difference between darkness and light, than the difference between the law of Moses and the law of Christ. The law of Moses was the law of violence and revenge, and the law of Christ, is said to be that of love and gentleness.

If isolated scripture texts are to be adduced in justification of religious persecution, why should not the infidel avail himself of the texts which favour his own views of the question. By such a course there will no difficulty in proving or disproving any thing; even the devil, it has been observed, can quote scripture for his purpose. Your Petitioner could easily show by such dishonest courses, that Luther, Calvin, Knox, and others, (whose names was revered by Protestants) were blasphemers, and merited condign punishment; that the patriot Hampden was a violator of god's law, and a most pernicious traitor, and that the glorious revolution in 1688, as it is styled, was a most scandalous resistance to divine ordinances. Saint Paul taught that there was no power but of god; and that whosoever, therefore, resisteth the power, resisteth the divine ordinance of god, and that they that resist shall receive to themselves damnation,

These passages are quoted, in order to serve as a warning against the practice so common, which is as ridiculous ss abominable, of making ancient opinions an apology for modern wickedness.

A SPECIMEN PRAYER.

OUR space will not at present permit the Committee of the "Universal Rotary Prayer Association" to present the sample prayers they contemplate. Some very affecting productions are received from a gentleman whose god is "feeling." Something not a little extraordinary has been executed by one who has discovered that the great question of specutive philosophy is but "words, words, words." We have only room for the following from an old correspondent.

To the Hero of Theology.

It is with prayers as with enterprises, the difficulty is to begin—but since "words alter *nothing*," I will at once say, O, god, if there be a god, for god's sake say so. If a mortal may address he knows not what, I would mention that men have been anxious to know thee for 6,000 years, and, for all we know to the contrary, a great while longer. Need it be added, that we should be greatly served by god telling us what it is, or by doing the next best thing, telling us that it won't tell us. Evidence of religion we must have—but of the kind of evidence we are not particularly nice, provided it is satisfactory. If a beggar may do with thee as our state beggars do with us, be choosers, we should choose the evidence of miracles. Feeding a few thousand with manna, as of old, will be particularly acceptable both to the hungry and the poor-law commissioners, who are not much addicted to feeding the hungry with anything. Making five loaves feed 5,000 again would highly gratify, if not convert our heterodox poor, for it is well known that loaves do not go half far enough in our day. "Christ and a crust" used to be thought poor fare, but a vast many people are obliged to put up with Christ alone. It is unnecessary to say more to one who, if report speaks truly, knows all, both of the sceptic's darkness and the poor man's wants. AN OLD HAND.

Ordered to be Churned Immediately.

SPECIAL INTOLERANCE!!

To the Editor of the Movement

SIR,—The Lord has declared war against us. On Friday week, the street-keeper took away the announcement board which contained the question for discussion on Saturday evening—viz., "Was the existence of Christ a reality or an allegory?" At our meeting on Sunday morning, it was agreed that another board containing the same words should be hung up where the other was taken from (at the entrance of the institution.) It was so, and the board hung two days, and we heard nothing from the saints; however, "on the third they rose again," and whilst the boy was in the act of hanging it up, he was seized and taken before the magistrate at Lambeth-street. The President, Secretary, Mr. Edwards, and I, attended at the magistrate's office; when we got in we found nearly the whole of the parish authorities there ready for us, an individual who sat alongside of the magistrate, stated the case, and the magistrate, the Hon. G. C. Norton, fined the boy £2, or a month's imprisonment, without hearing any one in defence. Mr. Edwards attempted to speak, but was ordered out of court. Our Secretary made an attempt, but was silenced immediately. Our President was ordered to stand forward, as the honourable magistrate said he must be a curiosity. Not wishing the boy to suffer, we paid the fine, but do not intend to let the matter drop. R. DRAPER.

This is an important case, and demands immediate and active attention. So serious an infringement of the liberty of publication, must not be allowed to pass unredressed. I am informed by an eye witness in court, that the clerk was pleased in the plenitude of his theologico-legal wisdom to apply seven epithets to the announcement board, beginning with blasphemous, and rising to a unique climax of orthodox description.

It is distinctly stated that the decision come to, was not on the ground of a nuisance committed by placing the board on improper premises, but on the ground of the blasphemous nature of the notice. If so, this decision is of questionable wisdom in two important particulars. First, the notice comes within the limits of that discussion recently allowed by the most eminent judges of the land. Secondly, the court was not legally competent to adjudicate in a case of blasphemy. Bad as the law is, it provides a jury to decide that point; and the Hon. G. C. Norton should have dismissed the boy, and ordered an action to be commenced by indictment. Mr. Draper paid the £2, and liberated the lad, or he would have been committed. Somebody, not a lad, must do this act again, and try the question if the decision was of the nature reported. Application has been made to the Central Board for their assistance. The legal advice of Mr. Ashurst, of Mr. Thomas, or some other able lawyer must be taken as to the proper steps to be pursued. More of this next week.

[ED. of M.

PRESENTATION OF THE SHEFFIELD PETITION.

Curzon Street, Mar. 26, 1844.

SIR,—I beg to acknowledge the receipt of your letter of the 23rd inst. and of the Petition to which it refers, which I presented to the House of Lords last night.

I am, sir,
Your very humble servant,
WHARNCLIFFE.

Mr. Isaac Ironside.

To THE FRIENDS OF FREE DISCUSSION. —Mr. Thomas Finlay desires to acknowledge in the *Movement*, that since he was apprehended on the 3rd of June last, on the charge of blasphemy he has received the following sums from parties who wished to support and aid him, in what they were pleased to consider his sufferings and exertions in the cause of human emancipation.

From a valued friend, who allotted
5s. weekly to Mrs. Finlay during
his imprisonment . . £7 0 0
From the Scottish Anti-Persecution Union, to Mrs. Finlay,
weekly, 7s. 2 16 0
From the London A. P. U. . 3 0 0
From Friends in London . 3 0 0
Per Richard Carlile, jun., Son of
Carlile the First . . . 1 0 0

MURRAY ON THE BIBLE.—Mr. Murray assures us that "*Who* is applied to persons, and *which* to animals and *inanimate* things." Now, as Moses tells the Israelites of the lord their god *which* brought them out of the land of Egypt, it follows, as a matter of course, that the great hero of the Old Testament was either an *animal* or a *block*. Oh, Mr. Murray!

LIBRARY OF REASON.—The purchasers of this work are assured by the proprietors of the *Oracle*, its originators, that the delay in the publication is not caused by neglect on their part; an individual whose co-operation they obtained, and who is part proprietor, being the sole cause. Either the present proprietors, or other individuals, will shortly re-commence the publication.

MISS ROALFE'S SOIREE.—The soiree and ball in honour of Miss Roalfe, was held on Monday, March 25, in the Calton Convening Room, Mr. Charles Southwell, M.C., Mr. Robert Affleck, chairmen. On Miss Roalfe entering the room, three rounds of enthusiastic cheering greeted her. There was a good band, good accomodation, good attendance, and good everything, not excepting good profits. The greatest satisfaction was felt, and the affair was considered to exceed anything of the kind that had taken place among our Edinburgh friends.

DIED, March 7th, 1844, aged 25, Mr. Fredric Holyoake (eldest brother of G. Jacob Holyoake), in the house of his brother-in-law, Mr. Edward Nicholls, Broad-street, Birmingham. His friends in Wolverton will be pleased to hear that his exertions to introduce Social and liberal principles in that place, was a source of satisfaction to him, and added to the equanimity with which he passed from life. A wife survives him, for whose welfare his last and kindest wishes were expressed. He was an Odd Fellow, and was borne to his grave by his brotherhood, and interred in the Birmingham Cemetery. The service used was read by his valued friend, W. B. Smith.

TO CORRESPONDENTS.

R. N.—Paper received—obliged.

J. MOTHERWELL shall receive a No. 28 of *Oracle* as soon as one can be obtained.

T. E.—Part 4, for *April*, of the *Movement* was ready for delivery on "Magazine day."

W. BROOM will oblige us by sending a friend to read his letter. It is written in characters which were obsolete before the invasion of Julius Cæsar.

ERRATUM.—In *Movement* 13, page 102, col. 2, par. 2, for "*if* such events, as they took place?" read, *of* such events, as they took place?

NOTICE.—The *Members'* Tickets just issued will extend over the next quarter.

In the next number will be published an answer to the question "What ought the Social Congress to do?

SUBSCRIPTIONS TO THE ANTI-PERSECUTION UNION.

Mr. W. Watts and a few Friends £0 10 0

In last week's list, for "Mr. Messeder and Friends, 1s.," read 1s. 6d.

The Meeting of the Committee of the Union will be held in Hudson's coffee-house, on Monday evening, April 8th, at half-past 8 o'clock.

All persons having any demands on the Anti-Persecution Union, will please send in their bills immediately. Collectors having money in hand will oblige by forwarding it, as the Quarterly Balance Sheet is about to be made up.

G. J. H., *Sec.*

Printed and Published by G. J. HOLYOAKE,
40, Holywell-street, Strand,
Saturday, April 6, 1844.

THE MOVEMENT
And Anti=Persecution Gazette.

"Maximize morals, minimize religion."—BENTHAM.

No. 18.   EDITED BY G. JACOB HOLYOAKE, ASSISTED BY M. Q. RYALL.   PRICE 1½d

WHAT OUGHT CONGRESS TO DO?

IT is not necessary to repeat the interest I have never ceased to feel in the efficacy of home colonization. At this period the annual discussion is proceeding throughout the Social branches on the question "What ought Congress to do," and since no one will be free to blame an erroneous decision who has not endeavoured to advise a wise one, I will present a few thoughts on this subject. In No. 6 of the *Movement* I promised to treat certain questions, of which a few yet remain to be considered. These I will endeavour to include in this article, as a press of atheistical discussions will probably occupy all spare space or some time hence.

Four principal things have contributed to damp socialistic ardour—a vague notion of the parties for whom home colonization is intended—the inconsistent reprehension of atheistical discussion—the doctrine of the manners of the working classes—and the influence of the paternal form of government.

FOR WHOM IS HOME COLONIZATION INTENDED.—Let those who have imbibed the flattering notions of human equality which the Platoes and Mores have pictured, and those dreams of human perfection which the Shelleys have embodied in song, and who would learn how widely different is fact from fiction, and how remote is the dawn of humanity's brighter day from the realities of 1844—let such read the "Developement" of the plans and principles of communities by Robert Owen. In this book the profound and masterly views of society, which eminently distinguish Mr. Owen, are set forth in diagrams and figures, and though the result is strikingly calculated to damp enthusiasm, it can hardly fail to awaken that cool determination whereby progression only can be achieved, and the condition of humanity permanently improved.

The slow advance of the Tytherly experiment has been owing to the miscalculation of the working classes as to the part they are to take in its perfection. This evil can be corrected only by greater frankness than is now practised towards them. Mr. Owen, in his "Instructions to the Missionaries," in 1839, speaks to the purpose on this point—his words are " the middle class is the *only* efficient *directing* class in society—the working class never did *direct* any permanent successful operations." In his Egytian Hall Lectures in 1841, he declares that " the working classes are too inexperienced even to know their real position, and that they will pass from one error to another, until, like Peter the Great, they will be *beaten* into a knowledge of the powers against which they have to contend, and of the means effectually to overcome them." Certainly a charming fate. Mr. Owen's estimate of the conditions of the working classes is, that they are powerless, penniless and prostrate at the feet of the capitalist, at the door of the poor house, or the mouth of the grave. Since falsehood has its degress of comparison, I suppose we must set this down as an *atrocious* truth. But if it be truth most useful is it, that it be told.

In the "Developement" it is set down that the expence of each home colony will be £700,000, and that the number of active adult persons in each will be 1548. The question is, when will the working classes be able to erect one of these communities? Why, if 1548 persons paid 1s. per week, they would be 173 years in establishing one!

This is the fair and sunny side of the picture. In these home colonies there are to be three classes—one of hired labourers, and one of candidates—the third is the members' class, the class in which every Socialist naturally expects that he will be. This class comprises only 360 persons. In our present branches there are not 360 persons able to pay 1s. per week, but if there were, they would be 747 years in erecting one of these communities!! The present members of the Universal Community Society of the Rational Religionists will be jolly old fellows when they enter into it. I guess they will have the requisite "experience" by that time. What an abundant answer does this afford to those silly people who prate about Socialism breaking up the foundations of society, and putting dangerous power into the hands of the working classes. Socialism, as advocated by Mr. Owen, is the most inoxous thing that ever agitated a nation, or alarmed a bishop.

I only aduce these facts, for the purpose I suppose that Mr. Owen has adduced them that of convincing Socialists, by the rhetoric of facts, that they *alone* are incapable of carrying out their founder's views. Two years ago when I endeavoured to make the Sheffield Socialists wise on these points, they looked at me with astonishment, and rewarded me with malevolence. During the utterance of these statements at the Rotunda, a short time since, many very sober and estimable members of the branch exhibited as much trepidation as though I was burning title deeds of Queenwood.

Could I stoop to apologize to these parties for speaking well intended truths, my defence would be *it is so written in the book*. And I might expose their ignorance of their founder's writings. But I prefer to say, if these things are true, it is better that we know them. For working men to conceal from themselves their true condition, is to imitate the weakness of the ostrich, that thrusts his head into the bush, and fancies he is free from danger.

Mr. Owen has always contended that there must be a union of the middle and working classes, and nothing can be clearer, after the exposition I have given, that *his* views only can be carried out by such means. It is then the business of congress to tell us plainly, if they intend following out Mr. Owen's plans, how this union is to be effected, and what working men must do to promote it.

The Tytherly experiment has been aptly compared to the coffin of Mahomet, suspended between two rocks, the canaille and the aristocracy. Its present position is dubious —a position in which no practical experiment ought ever to be found. It is too fine for the poor man's ambition, and too mean for the rich man's wants. With Mr. Owen as director, the confidence of working capitalists cannot be obtained. The intentions of Mr. Owen all admire, but his business abilities no one can trust. He knows no difference between the poor man's pocket, and the rich man's bank—but expends the contents of both alike. Congress must determine the character of this important experiment. They talk largely of business-like habits, they must talk business-like sense. Let them gather up again the sympathies of the poor, and exhibit the link which binds the redemption of poverty with the triumphs of their glorious philosophy.

Of Atheistical Discussions.—I neither deny the right nor the propriety of any body of men declaring that the conduct which they formerly pursued is wrong, but I deny that this declaration can be consistently made, while the same principles are professed, from which the former conduct flowed. In the article "Is Socialism a Religious System?" I proved that Socialism is essentially atheistic in principle, and that its premises necessarily include atheistic discussion. These facts have not been disputed, and until they are proved erroneous, it follows that heterodox controversy legitimately belongs to modern rationalism, and can never be openly or tacitly condemned without inconsistency. In reply to this position, it is commonly said that community is the sole object for which Socialists are banded together. Granted. But what kind of communities? Are they to be composed of well-fed and sleek men, who, like yard-dogs, will show the mark of the collar, or of men happy, intelligent, and free? If no mixture of error is to be there, all questions must be freely canvassed. It will not do to say, "Can't we pursue home-colonization, and leave the discussion of theology to others?" This is an evasion of the argument I know that the world cannot go on without a division of labour. I know, with the *Edinburgh Review*, that "if the piano-forte maker is compelled to add the business of a baker to his own, that we shall have much worse music and much worse bread." I know that society will be thrown into confusion, if it is to be made the duty of every association which is formed for one good object, to promote every other good object. But I deny that community is *one* simple object. It is world-making on a small scale. It embraces theogical disquisitions and political speculation, as much as political economy. If the science of circumstances is, as it is said to be, *universal*, if the phrase is not unmeaning jargon, it embraces *all* circumstances. If, indeed, the Central Board or Congress—there is little difference in the meaning of these terms now —choose to confine "community" to buying land, creating wealth, and driving bargains, I question not their right—but let them, at the same time, be candid and confess their decision, and not, parrot-like, repeat professions which will have become dead letters. Let them concede the principles they formerly held, and set before us their new ones; it will save them from the charge of inconsistency, and us from disappointed expectations. I grant that political economy is the great feature of community plans, that it is of more importance than Atheism. Freedom from religious dogmas will leave a man more free to act for the good of his fellows, and more anxious to promote their improvement, but how the physical elevation of man is to be effected it belongs to the science of society to tell. But while I allow that this science is the principal object, Atheism is a subordinate that cannot be overlooked without departure from professed principles. exhibiting either weakness or ignorance. It is narrow, mean, sordid and selfish, to reduce man to a mere wealth-making animal. He has other thoughts than those connected with buildings and banks —the greatness of human nature is not found in the wants but the relations of life, and these relations theology or atheism can alone determine.

OF THE MANNER OF THE WORKING CLASSES.—Socialism has, during the last few years, been made to consist more in manner than principle. What the members have thought or felt, has been considered of far less importance than how they acted. Here has lain a grave error. It has been truly said that the principle, that "Nothing can be too insignificant for the attention of the wisest, which is not too insignificant to give pleasure or pain to the meanest, it is the characteristic of the Baconian philosophy." And this would be the glorious principle of social philosophy, if its philosophy was candidly expounded. I agree that *manner* is all-important, but differ from Socialists' accredited agents as to the way in which the essential manner is to be produced. All the attempts hitherto made to teach manners have proved failures. We have had the exterior of benevolence without the reality—we have had the cant of prime minds from very inferior men—we have had exhibited a contempt for all parties without commanding the confidence of any. "O," say the St. Johns who lean upon Mr. Owen's bosom, "we don't mean that the working classes should behave in this or that manner, but that they should exhibit a kindness of bearing." Very fine gentlemen! but in all soberness, in all earnestness, what do you mean by a kind bearing? Do you mean what we have already had—the affectation of philanthropy with the coldness of contempt? It has been the fashion to restrain the show of opposition, from the fear of wounding the feelings of others, but, at the same time, by silence, a look, a sneer, or a laugh, ye have blighted the feelings you pretended to regard more effectually than a curse or a blow would have done. If this is kindness of bearing, perish such kindness, and that false and hollow philosophy which gave it birth!

The *Oracle of Reason* established a new principle for the creation of manner, one indeed plainly deducible from the philosophy of circumstances, but one which Mr. Owen had never pointed out, nor his disciples understood. It was—that as conception is the ruler of style, so feeling is the governor of manners. That we must proceed to alter a man's style as we would his faith, by giving him a new understanding of things. To generate a kind bearing towards the middle classes, we must show that there is a foundation for the poor man's confidence. We ought to be told what concessions must be made, what servility must be practised. We must have explained what will be the assumptions of the middle class, and how they intend to lord it over inexperienced industry. No real union will ever exist without the frankest understanding. No bargain will ever be come to, until we know the terms. By the phrase, "the bearing the working classes," much more is implied than is revealed. The men who have advised this bearing have never yet, either through false prudence, or want of courage, told what they intend. Behind the "paternal form of government" they have concealed the intended dominion of wealth, by the phrase "business habits" they have veiled over middle class supremacy, and by "unity" has been meant passive obedience and non-resistance.

This conduct has resulted less from any intention to deceive than from weakness. It has resulted from the *paternal* feeling—from the pernicious belief that it was necessary to treat the industrious like children. The result is that distrust has been nurtured, when a wiser and franker treatment would have generated confidence and regard.

THE PATERNAL FORM OF GOVERNMENT. —The paternal government is the government of Tories, of tyranny, and of retrogression. "We shall believe in the paternal doctrine," says Mr. Macauley in answer to Mr. Gladstone, when you can show us some government which loves its subjects as a father loves a child, and which is as superior in intelligence to its subjects, as a father is to a child. "Will the presidents of this government "select our nurses, decide on our education, overlook our pastimes, fix the hours of our recreations, prescribe what ballads shall be sung, what tunes shall be played, what books shall be read, and what physic shall be swallowed? Why should they not choose our wives, limit our expenses, and stint us to a certain number of dishes of meat, glasses of wine, and cups of tea." These things fall within the legitimate duties of the paternal office if consistently acted up to. Such has been my experience of the paternal government, that I would not willingly make a president of the very best god that ever was invented. I think I speak not in ignorance of the nature of government. I know that in the savage and social state, man is equally under a despotism. Nature is as despotic as laws, but the difference in the influence is vast. A tyrant is not more tyrannical than a majority, but the chances of justice with a majority are a thousand to one over those with an individual. Government is but a degree of despotism, but in the degree lies the difference between slavery and freedom. I have lived under all forms of government, and have felt none so degrading as the paternal. The mockery of freedom, and the reality of supercilious controul are its chief characteristics. If democracy is too changing and uncertain for the conduct of communities, cancel old agreements, eschew openly popular controul, put them under individual and interested management, let them become joint-stock companies or savings' banks, or what you will; but delude not the mass with the shadow of influence and government when the substance has departed. It may be necessary that the poor man be excluded from the management even of his own money, but it cannot be necessary that he be excluded and deceived too. Let the true relation be candidly explained.

Briefly, Congress ought to give Tytherly experiment a decisive, intelligible, and practical character. If anything can be relied upon, proceeding from a person who has written so many contradictory things on religion as Mr. Owen, the following words in his last book of the *New Moral World* are unequivocal as to the propriety of atheistical discussion. "There must be now a mighty effort made to throw off religion—this incubus on the happiness of all in every country. Men, for the permanent well-being of their race must meet this monster evil—openly encounter it, follow it to its strongest holds and last retreat, and destroy it root and branch for ever." If this is not idle bombast, it means that atheism should be earnestly diffused—for in no other way can religion's "root and branch be cut off." The prejudices of inexperience must be met with candour. Since the good sense of the majority of branches have reduced the paternal government to nearly a dead letter, it was unnecessary to bestow a word upon it, but that if popular support is to be sought, congress must lay its ban on this prime paralyser of enthusaism.

I had parted from this subject when Mr. Geo. Bird gave it as his opinion that the congress must not fail to change the society's name. He speaks solely with reference to the health of the members who having been annually indulged with a new soubriquet might suffer from the want of one this year. He thinks that the awkardness which would attach to any other society in changing its name does not attach to us—we have become used to it, and the world expects it from us. We shall astonish posterity not more with what we do, than with what we call ourselves. But I see great difficulty in giving up our present name—the self complacency of passing ourselves off as Rationalists, a name as high in the morality, as god in theology, and one standing for the world's highest conception of virtue—is too gratifying to petty vanity to be given up. To give up the name of Rationalist is to allow that other people and parties may have wisdom, as well as ourselves—a most irrational supposition! Then the Chartist might be considered right, and the Atheist practical—this would never do! It must still be the Socialist's glorious prerogative to sneer at politics and petition Parliament, to cry up religion and declare them all to be founded in error, and to rejoice in the name of *Rationalists?* G. J. H.

THE GILLESPIAN CONTROVERSY.

To the Editor of the Movement.

Torbanehill, near Bathgate, N. B. 30th March, 1844.

SIR,—Mr. Southwell has at length published strictures on my "Argument, *à priori*," &c. The controversy was transferred from the *Oracle of Reason* to the *Movement*, and it was understood that "if I thought it necessary to reply to any part of the answer to my argument, the reply should also be inserted in the *Oracle*," (see *Oracle*, No. 98, p. 362.) I suppose that any reply which I may make to Mr. Southwell's strictures, will be admitted into the *Movement*. Fair play is all I ask. Be so good as to let me hear from you on the subject. I am, sir,

Your obedient servant,
WILLIAM GILLESPIE.

Irrespective of anything promised in the *Oracle*, Mr. Gillespie may claim at our hands the insertion of his Reply. He has a right to the same space which Mr. Southwell occupied with his "Strictures." Whatever Mr. Gillespie may send, if it does not very much exceed in quantity Mr. Southwell's remarks, will be promptly and cheerfully inserted.—ED. M.

THE CANKER OF RELIGION.

THE following letter, headed "Sir Robert Peel and Factory Labor," and addressed to the editor of the *Times*, affords a notable example of morality of the theological cast. It was afterwards quoted in the *Post*, and doubtless has run the usual newspaper routine by this time.

"Sir,—Perhaps the following reminiscence may not be *mal-à-propos* at the present moment.

"In the year 1820 the 'Bill for the Regulation of Factories' passed, and a great boon it was to the operatives; it was called 'Peel's Bill,' being worked through Parliament by the late Sir R. Peel. The whole, however, was the work of a philanthropic individual, the late Mr. N. Gould, of Manchester, who spent many years and many thousands [it is said above £20,000.] in accomplishing, to a small extent, an object so dear to him.

"To facilitate his operations, he engaged a house in Dover-street. I was one evening assisting him in his laborious occupation, when the present Premier walked in; he burst out with, 'Well, Gould, how do you get on?' 'Why, Robert lad, we do get on, but we meet with opposition where we did not expect it.' 'I told you you would find it hard work; however, I wish you success sincerely.' 'Ay, Robert, there's no doubt of our success man! our cause is just, it's righteous, it's holy, it must succeed.' 'Well, Gould, what can I do for you, though I fear you will not carry all your objects?' 'Well, Robert, we must take what we can get; but we'll fight hard in so good a cause.' 'Well, Gould, good night.' As Mr. Peel passed me he put his hand on the table, evidently leaving something on it. "Ay, Robert,' said Mr. Gould, 'thou art a good fellow," giving him at the same time a shake of the hand, and a slap on the shoulder, as he wished him 'Good night.'

"Mr. Gould turned round and took up the paper, smiling, 'What is it?' said I. 'Ay, lad, it's a £50 note—Peel's a good fellow; but he little thinks what a drop in a bucket this is. Never mind, lad, we'll take it; it's well meant,'—and he put it in his pocket.

"The sequel is curious; about half an hour afterwards the notorious Robert Owen walked in, proffering his services in the most urgent manner upon Mr. Gould, to be employed in any way, either the most laborious or the most trivial; but on all this Mr. Gould put a negative, telling Owen he had enough to do of his own, he would not trouble him, his philanthropy had other objects, &c., and he was fairly bowed out. At this refusal of assistance so zealously offered, I expressed my extreme surprise, upon which Mr. Gould walked up to me, put a hand on each shoulder, and said 'Lad! dost know Owen?' 'No,' said I, 'beyond his Lanark hills, and his puffing his own philanthropy and his falsehoods.' 'Why, lad, I know him well—Owen is an Atheist."

"Your very old and constant reader,
March 26. VERAX."

Take this thoroughly disgraceful case in connection with the recent conduct of the House of Commons on Lord Ashley's proposed factory measure, and the comments of the press on the proceedings. Can anything convey a more wretched picture of the hollowness or hypocrisy of the so-called people's friends, together with a miserably fanaticized state of public opinion, to either encourage or permit such conduct—baseness!

Allowing the abridgement-of-labor proposal, all the merit its supporters claim for it, suppose a public man having agreed to urge forward the measure, being asked by a manufacturing constituency, why he had rejected the support of Mr. So-and-so, a tried friend to his own work-people—who had in his own factory done that best of all possible things —himself set the example of shortening the time of labor, drawn up and presented memorials to the legislature on the subject, first, or nearly first, directed public attention to it, in short, brought his example, wealth, influence and untiring energy to bear on the object he held so important to the poor. Let it be supposed that an oppressed, over-worked and under-paid population of a manufacturing district were to demand why the co-operation of such a man—and such a man was Robert Owen—was rejected—and let the answer be —" Why, lads, I know him well—Owen is an Atheist."—What would be the indignant cry of a suffering people? What, at least, would it be if not maddened by fanaticism, " Drivelling dotard! what is it to you or us, what you call him, or whether he *guesses* differently from you, in things we none of us know; if he judges and acts rightly and humanely in things we all of us feel."

Truly we ought to redouble our labors— aye, increase them tenfold—a hundred fold —*Movements*, and a hundred publications should form a strong and vigorously increasing nucleus of opinion in every town in the empire. Every Atheist is urgently called on to make it a part of his business to promote the *de-fanaticising* operations of every plain-spoken journal or society.

BUTLER'S ANALOGY.

MR. GRINFIELD concluded his lectures on the "Analogy" of Bishop Butler, on Monday evening, to an audience "fit though few;" for although the lecture room was not filled, he was listend to with profound attention. It should not be forgotten that the learned prelate, besides the services which he has rendered to truth by his great work, has nearer claims upon our regard by his having been Bishop of Bristol, and by his having confided his bones, as it were, to our keeping. The sense of this honour was manifested, in 1834, by an elegant mural monument being erected in the Cathedral to his memory. The just and beautiful inscription from the pen of a celebrated native of our city, Dr. Southey, was quoted by Mr. Grinfield, and may not inaptly be introduced here:—" Others had established the historic and prophetic grounds of the Christian religion, and that sure testimony to its truth which is found in its perfect adaptation to the heart of man: it was reserved for him to develope its analogy to the condition and course of nature; and, laying his strong foundations in the depths of that great argument, there to construct another and an irretragable proof: thus rendering philosophy subservient to faith, and finding in outward and visible things the type and pledge of those within the veil." Lest any should suppose that Dr. Butler's usefulness, as a defender of religion, is confined to the educated classes, Mr. Grinfield, in the course of his lectures, adduced anecdotes which had been communicated to him by his friends, one of which we quote, as showing that the reasoning of his "Analogy" may be understood and appreciated by the intelligent of all classes.

"When my brother (writes the lady who furnished the lecturer with these particulars) was first ordained to his curacy in Leicestershire, he found a regularly organised body of Deists in that and the two adjoining parishes, who met together one evening in the week, to read the works of Paine and other infidel publications. Finding the church almost deserted, he went round his parish to expostulate with his parishioners. In reply to his inquiries as to the cause of their non-attendance, the answer very generally made was expressive of their disbelief of the bible; but, when they were pressed on the subject, he in general found much ignorance as to their own principles; and one and all referred him to 'Master Loombes, a stocking maker, 'who would be able to answer every question.' He found Master Loombes a shrewd, intelligent man, about 60 years of age, who brought forward the usual objections, and had much to say for himself; but it was clear that he had never before conversed with any one who was able to answer him, and appeared staggered at some of the replies which were made; but, at the same time, was much more candid and open to conviction than could be expected. After a long conversation, he was asked whether he would read a book on the subject, with the deep thought and serious consideration which if deserved. Loombes acquiesced in the request, and my brother gave him 'Butler's Analogy,' which, after a few weeks, he returned, with these words, 'The arguments, sir, are unanswerable; I am quite convinced;' and then expressed his intention of coming to church (where he had not been for 40 years). The following Sunday Loombes came, with the whole body of Deists, who quite filled the gallery, and from that time the infidel club was completely broken up, both in that and the adjoining parishes; and the sensation produced by the conversion of these apostles of infidelity was so great that the church became quite thronged." These circumstances occured about 1807. Upon this the lecturer remarked, that although Butler wrote principally for academies, and though his work is used in Oxford and Cambridge examinations, it is striking to find that the clearness and the force of his appeals to *present* realities, in favour of things *unseen*, has found its way to the minds of stocking manufacturers. It was a fine proof, also, of the intellectual capacity, seconded by conscience, of the labouring portion of our countrymen.—*Bristol Mercury*, *March* 23, 1844.

[Will our Bristol correspondent who favored us with this report, be kind enough to send us an abstract of Mr. Grinfield's lectures. Butler's Analogy demands an able analysis. We have heard many people laud it, but never met with one who understood it. We know a barrister who carried it round the Oxford circuit with him for several years in the vain hope of being able to find out what Butler was at, and though he wanted neither will nor power, as many of his published works to which we could refer would testify, yet Butler's darkness was too much for him. We suspect 'Master Loombes' was gifted with a second sight. Will some Mr. Greenfield or Leicestershire Curate try Butler's converting power upon us? The bishop was a deep thinker, and obscurity is a fault not peculiar to him alone. In soberness, we should he obliged if some able Butlerian would pour out the force of the bishop's philosophy in the *Movement's* pages.]

IMPORTANCE OF PETITIONS.

I was glad to hear from Mr. Finlay that Mr. Hume is to present a petition to Parliament from Edinburgh, "On the freedom of opinion and abrogation of all laws interfering therewith." This is the true way of forwarding our cause and making it known to the public. This should be followed up by every place where a petition could be got up. I know from experience the effect that can be produced by acting in this manner, for I continued year after year to get up petitions against tithes and church cess, until at length the tithe prector was dismissed, the tithe system modified, tithes reduced, and church cess wholly and solely abolished!!!

Your duty as editor in this case should be to notice in the *Movement* every petition that is presented, and even to publish in full every petition, or at least its prayer; this would tend to enlighten all who read your publication, and stimulate them to follow the example set them. Mr. Smith mentions that Manchester is about calling a meeting to petition, and I find from the 7th Report of the Select Committee of the House of Commons, on public petitions, of the 4th and 5th of March, that Carlisle has already moved in this business, as the following extract will shew:—"Blasphemy—For alteration of law.—March 5th.—Petition of the Members of the Working Men's Mental Improvement Society of Carlisle. Signed in behalf of the society, J. B. HANSON, *Chairman.* Presented by Thomas Duncombe, Esq., M. P."

The petitioners pray the House to abrogate all laws interfering with freedom of opinion, and all enactments or regulations relative to blasphemy.

Now, sir, I ask you how many have heard of this petition being presented? Very few indeed!! This would not have been so if it had been mentioned by you, with an observation that no notice was taken of its presentation by the newspapers. Every petition I got up I had published in the papers, and when presented I took the opportunity of mentioning by whom presented, so that the public could not but be acquainted with the fact. I wrote the petitions myself on a sheet of vellum paper, and called on each individual tithe payer to obtain his signature, and always forwarded it to a different member for presentation. Thus, without any expense, I attained my object, and if you only follow my example, you also must succeed; you will at least open the eyes of the public to a subject that few ever think of—"freedom of thinking and expressing their opinion," whatever it may be, without being fined or imprisoned.

FROM A CORRESPONDENT.

PLEASING EXERTIONS.

Ipswich Infidel Repository.
Upper Orwell Street,
March 10th, 1844.

MY Dear Sir,—I have sent you 1s. for the Union, which I shall continue, if possible, once a-month during the summer. I am willing to become a regular collector, and will do my utmost to get contributors. There is not a very great field to work in at present in this part of the *Christian* world, but I think I see signs of improvement. Though only a journeyman shoemaker, I am not exactly beneath notice. I have been visited by several of the earth's curse, (parsons and their tools). They first tried persuasion, but that brought them into *discussion.* They then tried bombast, that answered equally as well, for I made short work with them by ordering them out of my shop. They have tried their hand again in another way, (at least so I suspect,) for a young *gentleman*, a stranger, came and asked me if I could get him Fanny Hill, but I told him I dealt in infidelity, not in obscenity; but most likely, if he wanted such things as those, he could get them at some of the respectable booksellers who promote Christianity, (an idea that I gleaned from the *Movement,*) which answered beautifully, and I have since enjoyed quite a holiday.

I take two numbers of the *Movement*; one I send to some parson or leading man, the other I lend to those likely to read them. Hoping soon to see Free Discussion universally acknowledged and *acted* upon, I remain your fellow, though humble, labourer,

JOHN COOK.

[We do not insert this letter because the writer has gleaned an idea from the *Movement*, nor because he takes two numbers weekly, but because it is one of many instances which have come to our notice, of Atheists in humble circumstances labouring unnoticed and unrewarded, save by the honourable consciousness of doing good, to diffuse a spirit of enquiry around them.—ED. of M.]

PROSECUTION FOR BLASPHEMY.

THE Priests are again making desperate efforts to recover that horrible supremacy wrested from them by the Great Revolution. We announced in our last the condemnation and sentence of M. Michel for "blasphemy," the following additional and interesting particulars are supplied by the correspondent of the *Dispatch*.—The Court Assize for the Department of the Seine has just condemned M. Toussaint Michel to six months' imprisonment and a fine of 2,000 francs, (£80,) for having written and published a work entitled " Conducité des Religions Pretendues Revelées," (" The Decline of Religions Pretending to be revealed"). The barrister who defended M. Michel entered into a long disquisition to prove the truth of the author's propositions, and quoted passages from the Bible and Koran for the purpose of showing that these works are repugnant to common sense and common decency. The judges and jury listed with great attention to this speech, which occupied several hours in delivery, and did not once attempt to interrupt the mode of reasoning adopted by the learned counsel. This religious prosecution is, I believe, the first undertaken since the revolution of 1830 ; and was probably allowed in order to propitiate the clergy, whose virulence against the university daily gains ground. Whether it be wise or just to prosecute or punish a man for his religious opinions need not be argued in the nineteenth century; but this I may mention, that such a process must be pre-eminenily absurd in a country where the works of Voltaire, Bayle, Volney, and the thousand and one anti-religious writings are far more common than bibles and prayer books. It is considered no disgrace for those works to be seen upon drawing-room tables in France ; and no library, public or private, would be deemed complete without them. Some years ago, there died in the south of France, at a very advanced age, a priest of the name of Jean Messlier; and upon his will being opened, it was discovered that he had written a book against the Christian religion, which he desired might be immediately published. This book concludes with an apology for having, for so many years, preached a creed in which its author did not believe, and expresses a hope "that God would forgive him for having aided in the propagation of a system at variance with the eternal omnipotence, omniscience, and mercy." This work was published; and there is not a man in France who can read that has not read it. No means are adopted to suppress the sale of this and similar books, but they are actually to be found in the Royal library and that of the University—libraries of public resort for literary men, like that of the British Museum in England. To prosecute, then, a man for his religious opinions, in the face of facts like these, is a most monstrous proceeding, and one (amongst innumerable others) indicative of a desire on the part of the King to return to the old tyrannies which, it was hoped, the revolution of 1830 had abolished for ever.—*Northern Star.*

[Could some one favour us with Michel's address?—ED. of M.

THE SCOTCH TRIALS, OR THE REGISTER OF RELIGIOUS INIQUITY.— This work has now progressed to the 4th number, and should be in the possession of every friend of free discussion in Great Britain. The 4th number contains the Trial and Defence of Mr. Finlay. We venture to predict that Mr. Finlay's defence will both astonish and delight the reader. No previous defence has been so appropriate to the defendant and so apposite to the case, so plain, earnest, and convincing. The 5th, and last, number will contain Miss Roalfe's interesting case, with her own account of the disgraceful and harsh treatment she received while imprisoned.

PUBLIC MEETINGS.— An excellent and expressive placard, of which the following is a copy, has lately been posted on the walls of Leicester:—"'God's People' and their doings. The committee of the Leicester Branch of the London Anti-Persecution Union respectfully call the attention of Atheists, Infidels, and the public generally, to the workings of the blasphemy law, as recently exhibited in the prosecutions in Scotland. The doings to which they refer are, the imprisonment of Thomas Paterson, Henry Robinson, Thomas Finlay, and Matilda Roalfe, for the priest-made and Christianity-sanctioned offence of blasphemy, the terms of their imprisonment varying from sixty days to fifteen months. The case of Thomas Paterson demands especial attention. He is confined in Perth Penitentiary, and subjected to a felon's treatment; his confinement is solitary, and his health so impaired as to be under the necessity of taking medicine as regularly as food, and is at this moment suffering privations as painful to be borne as they are disgraceful to his Christian persecutors. The committee therefore announce that a public meeting will be held in the Social Institution, upper end of the Market-place, Leicester, on Monday evening, to memorialize the Prison Board at Edinburgh on behalf of Thomas Paterson, and to adopt a Petition to Parliament for the abrogation of the Blasphemy Law.

"Friends to freedom! attend and assist the Leicester Branch of the London Anti-Persecution Union to establish the Free Discussion of Theological Opinions, and to protect the victims of intolerance and bigotry."

WHITECHAPEL CASE.—The Central Board are investigating this transaction. Positive results will be soon made known.

WOMAN'S CO-OPERATION INDISPENSIBLE. —Those who allow the influence which female graces have in contributing to polish the manners of men, would do well to reflect how great an influence female morals must also have on their conduct. How much then, is it to be regretted that women should ever sit down contented to polish, when they are able to reform—to entertain when they might instruct.—*Blair.*

OPPRESSION under the colour of justice is always more formidable from the arts which are used to disguise its malignity.

TO CORRESPONDENTS.

G. HAMMOND. By the very authority he quotes it is acknowledged that the custom of considering *cherubim* as a singular has now become the law. The distinction for which G. H. contends would be ascribed to pedantry. The word as used by us, is more in accordance with the genius of our language, and more consonant with the rules we should always follow. It is as unwise to be the slave of Hebrew grammars as the slave of Hebrew gods. In admitting a word into our language, it becomes us to act, as we do, when we admit a stranger into our country, expect him to conform to our laws.

W. OLDHAM.—Received.

RECEIVED

For G. J. H., from "W.W."	. 0 10	0
For T. Paterson, from "W.W."	. 0 10	0
For T. Paterson, from "W. J."	. 0 2	0
For Mrs. Martin, from "W. J."	. 0 5	0

Printed and Published by G. J. HOLYOAKE,
40, Holywell-street, Strand,
Saturday, April 13, 1844.

THE MOVEMENT
And Anti=Persecution Gazette.

"Maximize morals, minimize religion."—BENTHAM.

No. 19.　　　EDITED BY G. JACOB HOLYOAKE,　　　PRICE 1½d.
　　　　　　　ASSISTED BY M. Q. RYALL.

PROTEAN GODDITIES.

EVERYBODY knows—at least every body who has read Ovid, Lemprière, Tooke's Pantheon, or some such classicality, what a queer fellow Proteus was—how, when anybody tried to catch him in one shape, he suddenly, when hard pressed, jumped into another; if close pursued as a bear, he would roar before you as a lion; if overcome in this shape he would elude you as a mouse; if discovered in this form he would crackle up as a bonfire, or nearly quenched in this similitude, he would spurt and sparkle before your eyes as a stream or fountain, or ape the vegetation of an oak or a cabbage. From a brute to a human animal, or vice versa, was to him but an easy transition—had he known the newly discovered Yahoo tribe he could have been both at once. These Protean transformations, extreme and multitudinous as they are fabled to be, are yet paralleled, if not surpassed, by our modern mystery-men. The turns, changes, wheelings, twistings, distortions, manœuvres, sorts, patterns, varieties, and metamorphoses of our one-god men would set up a whole heathen mythology. Speak we of a primitive and pre-Adamite god, figuring away before we base-born worms were manufactured out of dust or bones, our auditor professes no acquaintanceship with such a deity. We refer him to—"In the beginning God created the heavens and the earth," and he cuts us off by cutting off the authority. Another bows to the authority, but hocus-pocuses the words—with him, beginning is not beginning—created is not created—heavens is not heavens. Thus he makes his errata to suit his reading. For "in the beginning," read *in times past;* for "created," read *formed;* for "heavens and earth," read *planetary system.* He thus cooks up his god to suit his palate. Two or three little upstart difficulties that can't be overcome must be smothered. He tells you it cannot be conceived that our little contemptible speck should have been made in the beginning, and the heavens, or sun, moon, stars and planets, for its express accommodation, or that of the crawling atoms upon it. It is too much of a burlesque that a god-almighty should be said to create what he cannot but see, *never was not*—this appears too barefaced a contradiction to pass current. Thus he promotes his god from a special favourer of us earth-worms, to a world-controller-general, and sinks him from a creator to a manufacturer in one fell swoop. Leaving Adam and Eve, and the rib and the apple, the fig leaf, the serpent, and all that, to the "vulgar herd," you try to fix your god-almighty man to the portrait of their patron-god by the Egyptio-Chaldaic-Babylonish-gipsy-pedlar-Jews, whose queer disjointed jumbles from "Moses, the king of the conjurers to Peter and Paul, the last of the gang," set so many god-struck brains a-wool gathering. What says my Protean god-almighty man to this? he protests against the narrow conceptions of those who would paint *his* god in such colours. His god is "no respecter of persons, no favourer of families, tribes, or nations; his bountiful care extends over all his people, and his people are all mankind." Oh, Moses, the meek, who smashed the mile-stones, and brained the Egyptian, hear this!—Oh all ye big and little saints, snugly ensconced in Abraham's bosom, won't you jump out of your hiding places at such profanity? Verily, oh, god-almighty man, if you believe not Moses and the prophets, (and they had peeps at, and talks with Yahouah, and ought to know,) neither will you believe though one rose from the dead. This very goddist who has cast off the old prophet, takes up the new; he that makes but small work of Abraham, Isaac, and Jacob, and has no great opinion of David and Solomon, the intermediate characters and their god-notions, is "hail fellow, well met," with the Nazarene and his apostles, and their daft of a god. All the menaces, denunciations, and thunderings which plentifully season the gospel divinity-dish are to him the spiritual condiments for every-day meals—the god-notions that belong to all their faith, authority, and damnation dogmas, are familiar to, and influential with him, though he thinks the "old law" and old god-notions of the old Jews are quite superseded by the new law and new god-notions of the converted Jews.

A bible goddist will have a new testament god, but drest up according to a receipt of his own—with him god's elections, upbraidings, threatenings, punishings, damnings, with all such other manifestations as displease his distorted vision are cast aside, and his god is decked out with attributes of his own invention, in which the milk of all the more honourable traits of character, which win our admiration in our fellow-men, are sought to be added to this phantasm. Here we have another god-believer professing to fashion his notions according to new testament spirit and phraseology, yet picking and choosing a lot here and there, to his fancy, garbling some, adding and rejecting others. How are we to take these god-people? I have painted but the bible sort, or rather *a few* of the bible sort as yet. Many more biblists and non-biblists, each with gods of their own class or sect, remain undescribed. Are not these already sufficient to show their Protean nature? Truly Proteus must be the type of the genus. M. Q. R.

THE DUTY OF THE NEXT CONGRESS DEDUCED FROM THE HISTORY OF SOCIALISM, BY A MISSIONARY OF SEVEN YEARS' STANDING.

To the Editor of the Movement.

SIR,—I perceive by the *New Moral World* that the most influential London Branch of the Rational Society has taken into its consideration, What ought the next Congress to do? As one of the avowed objects of your journal is the promotion of Communism, I make no scruple in sending you a few remarks on the above question. In doing so, I shall he somewhat antagonistic, not however from choice but from necessity—not from a desire to find fault, but with a view of rendering the experience of the past useful for the future.

The best way of deciding what the next Congress should do, in my opinion, is to consider the history of Socialism from first to last, to consider what measures have retarded, and what measures have promoted the success of the cause. Mr. Owen, I believe, first appeared as a writer, in the year 1812, as the author of a series of beautiful essays on the formation of character. In them are to be found none of those sweeping denunciations of religion for which a few years later the writer became so remarkable. Even religionists must admire the moderation of his tone. He seems to have acted on the principle laid down in the third essay, viz., "While erroneous customs prevail in any country it would evince an ignorance of human nature to offend against them unless the community are convinced of their error," for in these Essays he merely proposes a slight modification of the Church established by law, so slight indeed that a superficial observer might suppose that he was one of the real "friends of the church." Three years later, when he brought the Factory Question before the public for the first time, the same caution characterised all his sayings and doings for the benefit of the world. He did not think it prudent at that juncture to declare that the *triune* cause of moral evil was private property, religion and marriage, as he has since so frequently done. All at once, in the year 1818, he forgot all his former caution, and 'came out' in a manner that astounded those who had watched his proceedings with some little interest, and in a manner that lost him all the popularity and support his *caution* had gained. He probably thought that the time for temporising was past, and that the whole truth might be told. Mr. Owen has frequently declared that he does not regret the step he took in 1818, and yet it is difficult to account for his *truckling* policy of late years upon any other principle than that of regret; for if the blow of 1818 was well thought of, and well done, it should have been followed by additional ones from that time to the present. How Mr. Owen could suppose that he had done all that was required, when he declared the erroneous foundation of all religions, and yet knew that the doctrine of *necessity* was by no means new to the religionists of the world, can only be accounted for by the fact that he has always been in the *habit* of disregarding the objections that have been brought against his view of men and things. He seems to consider a *wave of the hand* quite sufficient to refute, and uttering the word *inexperience* quite sufficient to overthrow the best opponent and the best argument upon the opposite side. But, Mr. Editor, if the experience of one of the *inexperienced* is worth anything, it teaches this—that general denunciations may stagger, but cannot convince an opponent that he is in the wrong. General denunciations are all very well in their place, but they are not omnipotent. To give them their proper weight they must be followed up by *detailed* refutation, and to that mode Mr. Owen it not attached, but absolutely condemns, and yet I affirm that the good that has been done is owing more to the latter than the former method. Of this I am fully convinced after mixing with the warfare, as vigorously as possible, during the last seven years.

In the year 1826 we find Mr. Owen in America still denouncing the religions of the world, if possible more strenuously than before. Declaring that if all the sacred writings were gathered into one immense heap and consumed, that it would be the most glorious fire that ever was kindled for the interest of the human race. All this time, that is from 1812 to 1826, his principal efforts were directed against the religions of the world, his politics being in some measure kept in the back ground, as though they could not properly be considered, until the theological rubbish was thoroughly removed out of the way.

In 1830 Mr. Owen delivered a course of lectures which are more remarkable for what they did *not*, rather than what they *did* say on the subject of religion. The style is somewhat between that of 1812 and that of 1818. Mr. Owen, in my opinion, gave the first check to the progress of his principles in 1834 by the delivery of his, too well known, ten lectures on the marriages of the world. I have no hesitation in saying that by far the greater part of the prejudice that exists upon the subject of Socialism is owing to these lectures—they are so carelessly worded and so loosely written, that people easily misconceive their meaning, and opponents pervert their aim. The principles propounded in these lectures are substantially correct, but the phraseology is remarkably defective, often leading the mind astray instead of leading it into the right path. This deficient perspicuity is no doubt owing to the fact that the reports of the lectures were merely reprints of progress from the first volume of the *New Moral World*, in a separate form, avowedly to cure the prejudice then said to exist, while the fact was, that before they were published in this separate form, no prejudice of importance existed, because the lectures were comparatively speaking unknown.

In 1833 Mr. Owen proposed some regulations for marriage and divorce, far better calculated to form a sound public opinion upon this delicate subject than anything he had published before, or has published since. Yet so recklessly were these ten lectures given to the world, that these regulations found no place in the report. *Before* this period, Owen was condemned for advocating divorce, *after* this he was denounced as one who wished to destroy the regulated intercourse of the sexes, as one who recommended promiscuous intercourse and desired to degrade man to a level and even below the level of the brute.

I am the more particular in dwelling upon this point, because it has hitherto been sadly overlooked. It has been, and still is, the dragchain upon the progress of Socialism, and, in fact, *has done all the harm that is usually attributed to the anti-religious lectures that have been given, and the theological discussions that have taken place*. Had these lectures never appeared in their present form prejudice from other causes would still have existed, but not by any means equal to that which exists at the present time.

In 1835 Mr. Owen organised a society for the diffusion of the principles of the rational system; and so necessary did he consider, at that time, a theological warfare, that rejecting one of the principal orthodox doctrines was made a *fundamental principle of the society*. I allude to the bad-by-nature doctrine, upon which, as all know, depends the doctrine of the atonement, and other truly Christian absurdities. This was, in f ct, a declaration of war against the Christian world, and as such ought to have been continued, or given up with an acknowledgement that the founder was in the wrong.

In 1837 Mr. Owen went farther than ever he did before. In his discussion with Mr. Roebuck is to be found some of the " most atrocious" blasphemy ever uttered by mortal man; not merely blasphemy against the bible as a book, but against the bible-god—declaring that a more ignorant, inconsistent, cruel being never entered into the diseased imagination of men. And his final address to the Congress of 1837 is still more remarkable, as showing that Mr. Owen then thought that general denunciations were not sufficient, but that detailed argument was required; for, in a series of proposition, he, with logical accuracy, shows up what he calls ' this foolery' in fine style. Even the *New Moral World* seemed smitten with the anti-theological mania, for in that year letters against the bible, of a serial character, were admitted, and by inference approved. From this time to the Congress of 1839, theological discussions were the order of the day, so much so, that the people supposed that the only object of the Socialist was the overthrow of religion. Discussions on religion were frequently taking place in most parts of the country; their success was duly reported, and their triumph welcomed. The editor of the *New Moral World* sharing in the glory and sharing in the fight.

At length, about the middle of the year 1839, Mr. Owen seemed all at once to discover that he or his disciples were going too far, and in a letter of advice to the Social missionaries, tells them to decline discussions on the mysteries of the Chistians, Jews, &c., &c., &c., but without giving any substantial reasons for the change. This was the more inconsistent, as Mr. Owen himself, had by his writings, led them into these controversies he now so much condemned, and from which they could not escape without being justly branded as cowards and misrepresenters for their retreat. Even the letters that conveyed this advice contained many disputed propositions, and, in fact, involved them in these controversies more than ever. The letters were but little noticed at the time, but when, in 1840, the Bishop of Exeter made his attack in the House of Lords, attention was called to the subject by the Birmingham Central Board; a circular was sent to the various branches and lecturers of the society, warning the branches of the danger that attended these theological controversies, and the odium they created, and warning the missionaries, that if they persisted in engaging in them, that they must instantly cease to be the missionaries of the society; and for a time this threat partially had the desired effect upon some of the parties thus addressed.

But this was not the only misfortune that befel the society in this eventful year, for, at the Congress of 1840, Mr. Owen produced the first draft of that scheme of home colonization, which was afterwards declared by the Central Board to the Congress of 1842 as their desire to carry out, and that the buildings at Harmony were the introductory part of that plan. I may here state, for the sake of those who have not read the developement," that this plan differs from all its predecessors in one particular, for it no longer provides that the great *political* principle of the society should be practically carried out, viz., equality of education and condition.

Previous to this Congress of 1842, many errors had been committed both in the theoretical and practical management of the society's affairs. The subscriptions had fallen off, both for agitating and for community purposes, Galpin, as the organ of the Central Board, affirming, as one of the reasons for the decline, the fondness for theological discussion, whilst it was notorious to all but this "closet theorist" and others like him, that the most prosperous branches in the society were those that retained the original plan of agitation, those who made their meeting places schools for the people in the widest sense of the term.

For some time previous to this congress of 1842, the confidence of the working classes had been on the decline, both in England and Scotland, and has not as yet, and I fear will not for some time, be restored. It was prophesied, however, that if the changes proposed by the Galpin board were carried into effect by the Congress, that the funds would be found to carry out the "Developement" plan of community—a plan more remarkable for its extensive proposals, than for its suitability to the means of the society by which it was to be carried into practice—more remarkable for its theoretical splendour than for its feasibility during the present age. Whilst the thousands came in from the few individuals composing the Home Colonization Society in 1842, all seemed, in the opinion of the Central Board, to go on well. The men who had been so instrumental in bringing before the public the principles of the society, were allowed one after another to retire into private life, or to depend upon the success of their individual exertions to forward the cause, so much so that the great principle of associative labour was forgotten in the agitation, and had been during the preceding twelve months. The consequence was that the society dwindled into a mere shadow of what it was.

During the first two years of the organized Rationalists, they made but little progress, because they adopted no forcible method of bringing their operations to bear upon the public mind. At the end of that period, but four branches had been formed. The Congress of 1837 were aware of this slow progress, and appointed two men to preach the principles of the society, and two others not formally appointed, set out on very successful lecturing tours. During the year this agitation soon aroused public attention; the demand for information and for books rapidly increased, and six missionaries were appointed at the next Congress, that of 1838, and two more shortly after. This gave a most important impulse to the movement. Friends were discovered and made in most of the manufacturing districts. Adherents were delighted, and enemies appalled at the success of the cause. But what was the charm that caused this shaking among the dry bones —the talents of the men—no! the novelty of the thing—no! it was the *truth of their principles*, boldly and fearlessly expressed, in all their bearings upon the condition of mankind. Their lectures embraced freedom in politics, freedom in commerce, and freedom of religion, freedom of thought and speech, and freedom from the degradation of labour, by social industrial independence. Then honesty was considered the best policy, but temperance (*i. e.* abstinence) was not considered the best physic. A change then came over the spirit of the dream, and during the last two years the society has done little or nothing to accomplish the great object it originally had in view. It may be urged by the inexperienced that religion is still denounced in the same way as at first, though more moderate in degree, and that the same energy is not now required as formerly. To which it may be replied that it is quite time to talk about vantage ground when we really possess it, but in the meantime, let us remember that superstition is ever active for evil, and always a barrier of good. Even the *New Moral World*, at one time the most interesting periodical of the day, is both in letter and in spirit, behind many of the publications of this day. It requires the stimulus of an enlarged policy to make it what it ought to become, for it ought to be the denouncer of all that is wrong, and the supporter of all that is right. It ought to cure—not pander to prejudice, and should, in the liberality of its management, be an example for the world of letters to imitate and admire.

If I have written to any purpose, I have shown that the alteration in the policy of the society has done a great deal of harm to the cause, and the remedy, in that case of course, is to return to the original principles and policy of the society, making such alterations in pecuniary matters as are required by the circumstances of the times, for I regret to say that experience has taught us no wisdom except in the latter respect. I think we have gained some valuable knowledge in pecuniary matters, and therefore I wish it to be retained and used, but let us not endeavour to gain the pounds, shillings, and pence, at the cost of continued mental servitude.

I am well aware that many may urge that the vigorous agitation I recommend to be resumed, cannot take place because of the state of the funds, but in answer to that I beg to say that a well ordered agitation would produce the funds requisite for the purpose, providing we have no idlers in the ranks. Let each man strive to make the income *great*, and the expenditure *small*, and the thing is done. Above all things, let us have no more hirelings in the camp, let us have men of principle, men who really feel a pleasure in the progress of the cause in which they are engaged. Instead of talking so much about the detailed practical operations of the estate the Rationalists possess, let them furnish all the cash required in the shortest possible period, but at the same time watch its expenditure with a jealous eye, taking care that all disbursements be upon the principle of accommodating the largest number of members in the shortest period of time; and when it is once proved that the capitalists can obtain a better security and greater interest by investing in home colonies than in any competing transactions, then shall we gain a pecuniary triumph, and our only business will then be to give to capital its due, and to take care that it has no more.

Last, but not least, let no man abandon the Rational Society in despair, let him try to make it as efficient as it is capable of being made. It should form no part of the philosophy of progressive reformers to abandon the most forward movement, because it is not all they desire, for that is not the way to reform the world, but it is the way to *deform* it, and that in the most effectual manner.

Trusting, Mr. Editor, that your labours will not be in vain,   I am, yours,
A Lecturer of Seven Years Standing.

Christian Mysteries—*Richard Carlile, Paternoster-row.*—This is an excellent reprint of a "Dialogue between a Christian Missionary and a Chinese Mandarin," from the pen of that prince of infidel wits, Voltaire. The "getting up" of this tract is in admirable keeping with its character, and the reputation of its publisher's name. It purposes to be printed "For the Promotion of Christian Knowledge, by Richard Carlile, of 2, Lovell's-court, Paternoster-row, opposite the Religious Tract Society." The bible references in the tract, are given, as they always should be, in marginal notes, and nothing interrupts the stream of satire, argument, ridicule and wit, which sets in on the first page and rushes on to the last. A copy of the "Christian Mysteries" should be put into the hands of every saint in the kingdom. The pious of our day, worship the Bible as Catholics did the virgin — this Dialogue is the antidote to such transparent folly. We trust that Mr. Carlile will often treat the world to these choice morsels, by which men will be so agreeably reminded of his father's memory and of his own usefulness.

Von Rotteck's History of the World.—A few sets of this fine work, of which so many thousand copies have been sold on the continent, have been brought to this country by Mr. Stollmeyer. The work is in four volumes, bound in leather and lettered, at £1, only. Copies can be had on application at the *Movement* office. We only mention this that so excellent a work may be more widely circulated. It ought to be a recommendation that Mr. Stollmeyer's copies were printed in America, bound by democrats, in leather which grew on the hides of republican cows. But higher praise than this remains—the *Times* lauded the learned character of the work, but declared its philosophy too high, save for the comprehension of the few—which interpreted means, that it is too liberal for the many. A general history, like Rotteck's, differs from a universal history. A history of the stones, windows, walls, and parts of a house, is its universal history, but its general history describes it as a whole, its fittings, proportions, magnificence, and uses. Rotteck does not, as his critics have said, take his reader on to a high mountain and show him all the kingdoms of the world at once, for this is impossible. He does what is better, takes him to the margin of Time's broad stream, and placing him at that spot where chronology commences, points out to him the villages, cities, nations and dynasties of the world as they float slowly down—the exploits of the heroic Trojan, the learned Egyptian, the graceful Greek, the superstitious Jew, the bold Roman, the rough Scandinavian—the Crusader in his infatuation, the Lutheran in his coarseness, and the Methodist in his fanaticism. Barbarism, deformity, and civilization's progress are painted with a master-hand, and written with a poet's fire. The book's philosophy we have not space to analyse and can only wish it English readers.

THE RATIONAL DAY AND SUNDAY SCHOLARS' MAGAZINE. — *Cleave, Heywood, and Hobson.*

This is a little monthly publication, price 1¼d., intended for children, and is vastly superior to the pious trash which issues from Sunday schools and religious book depositories. Each number contains light instructive tales on science, morals, and natural objects, with greater freedom from cant than we were prepared to expect. If a writer of a dissertation on poetry should introduce directions for mending saucepans, everybody would exclaim against the vile junction of the tinker and the bard, yet the same thing is done every day in school books with the approbation of the *discerning* public. Epics and kettles are not wider asunder than religion and morals, and yet they are perpetually jumbled in every book we meet. The *Rational Magazine* is a great improvement in this respect. The training of youth is so important, and correct phraseology and thought, of so much consequence in first impressions, that the editor, if he be worthy of his office, will excuse two remarks, which may prove useful suggestions to him. On page 92, Mamma is made to say "Why is an object called animate?" and William answers without much elegance, propriety, or philosophy, "Because it has *got* life." I will not enquire where the "object" *got* life from, for that neither Mamma, William, nor the editor of the *Rational Magazine* is prepared to answer, but put it to the writer whether the shorter answer "Because it has life," would not be an improvement in simplicity, as laid down in philology and in truth so far as we know it. On page 76, children are properly told that the reward of duty is "pleasure, respect, and quiet." This is good sense and proper teaching; but on page 48, it is said that,

" That if little insects are kind to each other,
All children most certainly ought."

But if children are to be kind because insects are kind, why may not children quarrel because dogs snarl? This insidious principle of imitation lies deep at the root of theological morals, and ought to have no place in a *Rational* magazine. Infants *can* learn better reasons for kindness. Page 78 presents a fine sentiment of Socrates—"Respect yourself, but honour your parents," but page 79 contains a questionable precept from Chambers—"Children are *bound* to obey their parents." Editor of the *Rational Magazine*, how came you to think that Chambers could improve Socrates? If manly children are to be reared-slavish, submission must not be taught by teachers, nor exacted by parents. The independence of the child is the cradle of the man's freedom. I know not the editor of this magazine, but I will not esteem him so low as to class him with those idle people who think any reason or precept good enough for a child. The editor gives evidence that he appreciates his task of instructor, let him appreciate infant intellect, and never forget that the child is man and woman's minature.

The editor of this magazine professes to be a "schoolmaster," but if this is true, he has double pursuits, or he has a double object, that of writing for big and little children at the same time, which is not the way to achieve success. A true schoolmaster lives the life and thinks the thoughts of his children. But this "schoolmaster" uses fine terms which the genuine teacher would feel at once to be unsuitable to children-capacity. A little more of the spirit and child-nature of Pestalozzi in its conductor, and the *Magazine* will become valuable.

ANSWER OF THE PRISON DIRECTORS OF SCOTLAND, TO THE APPLICATION OF THE ANTI-PERSECUTION UNION.

Chambers of the General Board of Directors of Prisons,
Edinburgh, 27th March, 1844.

SIR,—I am directed by the General Board of Directors of Prisons in Scotland, to acknowledge the receipt of your letter of 22nd inst., with its enclosure; and to acquaint you in reply, that the regulations of the General Prison at Perth, in which Thomas Paterson is at present confined, are established by Act of Parliament, (2nd and 3rd Vict. c. 42), and by orders in furtherance of that Act, and under the authority of the Secretary of State, which are obligatory on the Board.

I am, sir,
Your obedient servant,
LUD. COLQUHOUN.

Mr. G. Jacob Holyoake,
5, Paul's Alley,
Paternoster Row, London.

FREE PUBLICATION OF OPINION.—I have at all times opposed persecution for opinion sake, and would never interfere with anything a man might write or sell in the way of opinion. Every man should be allowed to publish, and to sell what he pleases. Without that, there *is not liberty of the press*, and without the power of communicating opinion, we cannot say that we live in a country that enjoys freedom of opinion—unless, indeed, it is liberty to abuse and vilify any other religion than that supported by law. That is denominated freedom of opinion by some—not by me."—*Extract from Letters of Joseph Hume, Esq., M.P. on the Scotch Cases.*

TEMPLE OF JUGGERNAUT.

A DESPATCH has been sent out from the Court of Directors of the East India Company to the Governor-General of India, relative to the temple of Juggernaut, and the superintendence of the native religious institutions. They transmit with it copies of a publication respecting the present state of the temple, in which are statements to the effect, that patronage and support, notwithstanding the abolition of the pilgrim-tax, are still afforded to Juggernaut, in the annual payment of 60,000 rupees for the maintenance of the temple, the fees of the pilgrim hunters, the embellishments of the idol, and the pomp of the festivals. They further request to be informed as to whether the trade of the Purkarees, or pilgrim-hunters, is continued, and the authority of the police employed to impress the labouring classes to drag the idol's car at the great festivals. Also, whether the trade of the Purkarees is sanctioned by the Government—whether the superstition at Juggernaut " is now flourishing beyond all experience," and whether the loss of life among the pilgrims is as high as 50,000 yearly? The despatch intimates that it is the express desire of the Court that the authority of the police may be employed on all occasions in preventing the people from dragging the idol's car.—*Globe.*

More Christian impudence and one-sidedness! On what possible pretence can the Juggernaut mob be interfered with in the dragging of their idol's car, any more than the Christian mob, who fling up their greasy caps and fill the air with their blatant bellowings when suffered to approach the car of our puppet royalty, and whose slavish admiration of the idol of the day, often prompts them to unyoke his car, and thrust their own persons into the harness of the other brutes who drew him. If our own Christian Juggernauts are not drawn about, it is only because churches and chapels are not upon wheels.

THE UNITARIANS.

UNITARIANISM has for some time been in rather a languishing state in Glasgow, as must be the case with every system which attempts a truce between reason and superstition, and which, while it checks the zeal of fanaticism, prevents the developement of full-grown reason's strength. Socialism, too, has done much in this locality to thin the numbers of the Unitarian body. Lately, however, they have been aroused from their slumber, by the appearance of a division in their own ranks — a split which is likely to render these semi-orthodox people still weaker. It was whispered in the congregation, that the Rev. J. Taylor, their minister, was sceptical overmuch, that his faith was not sufficiently strong as to the curing of blind men with spittle; lame men taking up their beds and walking, without so much as an application of "Holloway's Ointment," the playing of the devil with the pigs, and other sublime evidences of the messiahship of Jesus. These whispers swelled into an audible voice, upon which he was "requested to embody and print for circulation through the congregation, his religious opinions and views." This the reverend gentleman did with boldness, and to his honour be it named, at a sacrifice of his salary of £250 per annum. He contended that all that is necessary for union in worship is, a belief in a Supreme Being of perfect attributes, who requires the practice of morality from his creatures; that other articles of belief are of quite minor consideration, or are only incumbrances which should be lopped off. "*A rational man,*" says he, "*does not blindly submit to the authority of Jesus, is not a disciple of his in a sense different from that in which he may be said to be a disciple of Newton, or Plato, or Socrates.*" Mr. Taylor declares himself to be an "*anti-supernatural Christian,*" an advocate of "*unadulterated Theism,*" and a disbeliever of "*reputed miracles recorded in the Christian scriptures including the bodily resurrection of Christ.*" This was rather too strong meat for the weak stomachs of many of the reverend gentlemen's hearers. Their brains were dizzy with this new doctrine. The orthodox Unitarians, who prided themselves upon having " some religion," who plumed themselves upon the "respectability" of their body, who scowled upon the "vulgar infidelity" of the Socialists, and who would not lift a little finger to rescue Paterson from the hellish dungeon of an insanity-producing, silent-system torture house; these same despisers of all who went " too far," became greatly alarmed and sorely troubled. Mr. Taylor was called to account.—Three or four stormy meetings of the congregation were held; and finally Mr. Taylor was deposed from his ministry by a very small majority. Fallacious as we deem his deistical views, it is but just to admire the honesty of the man, and refer to his conduct as worthy of imitation.

These events are pleasing signs of the times. They indicate the decay of supernaturalism, and the approach of a brighter day, when

reason being paramount, virtue and happiness will attend in her train. H. J.
Glasgow, 22*th March* 1844.

NEWS FOR ATHEISTS.—At a meeting of the London City Mission, held last night in Kensington, it was stated by a Mr. Owen that of the entire population of London, amounting to two millions one hundred thousand, there are only eighty thousand recognised Christians, consequently, there are upwards of two millions of persons without religion in London, or twenty unbelievers to one Christian. Does not this open a wide field for the spread of Atheism? and, with a knowledge of those facts before us, are we not bound as men devoted to one cause—the spread of truth, and the downfall of error—to use every means in our power to unite and spread our principles far and wide, when so large a field is open to us for our operations? It was farther stated that the London City Mission Society have in hand upwards of seven thousand pounds. The Atheistical Society would turn that sum to good account. It was farther stated by one of the missionaries that in the course of his labours he visited a place where there were sixteen shoe makers at work, who were, to a man, avowed Atheists; after a great deal of labour on his part he was enabled to convert but two of them. I have mentioned these facts because I thought they would not only be interesting, but would show the necessity for an atheistical society in London, as well as show that we have not so much to dread from the number of Christians as might at first be supposed. R. PAYNE, Kensington.

JUST PUBLISHED.—" Why am I an Infidel: Why are you a Christian?" By Charles Southwell.—" *Truth is a higher word than Christianity.*"

NOTICE.—The subscribers to the fund for placing Mrs. Martin in possession of the Rotunda, and securing to the people the advantages of a "Philosophical Institute," are respectfully informed that it cannot be obtained for any such object.

As the disappointment has not arisen from the want of funds if any eligible premises should be found, the owner of which does not trouble himself about whether his tenant believes in a God or no,* such an institution as that proposed will be established before the winter season. In the mean time all the subscriptions received will be returned, on application at the Hall of Science, City-road, on Sunday evening, April 28th, after the Lecture; or will be sent to the subscribers on their forwarding their present addresses to the secretary.

Those subscribers whose money was offered by letter, and not sent for, are respectfully thanked for their proffered assistance, which is not unappreciated though for the present declined.
G. J. HOLYOAKE, *Hon. Sec.*

* The only reason yet assigned for the landlord's refusal of the Rotunda to Mrs. Martin, is, that she does not believe in a God (vide *Morning Herald*). Branch 53 spent several hundred pounds upon his premises—he has taken forcible possession of them, without allowing a shilling for the repairs and fixtures, and is now applying for arrears of rent, after refusing Mrs. Martin as tenant, who would have enabled the tenants to pay that rent by her purchase of the said fixtures. *His* belief in a *God* has not taught him justice—how should it? Would that this was the first instance in which a *belief in a God* and gross *injustice to man* had been associated!

TO CORRESPONDENTS.

D. PALMER.—Received the "Midnight Cry," the organ of the Millerites. Do the American Saints never go to bed? They appear to be up all night, and to have a "Cry" for every hour. The Recording Angel can never have any peace in those parts.

B. ARMFIELD.—If you can find a trusty, active friend, leave the card with him, otherwise bring it.

J. W. C.—Has obliged us for his communication. It is left at Mr. Hetherington's for him.

TO-MORROW Mr. Buchanan lectures at the Literary and Scientific Institution, Laurence-street, Birmingham. On Sunday, April 21, Mr. Richardson, of Coventry, commences a course of Lectures on *English History*, in the same Hall.

SUBSCRIPTIONS TO THE ANTI-PERSECUTION UNION.
From the Leicester Branch of the Anti-Persecution Union:—First quarterly account.

9 Members at 6d. per quarter	£0	4 6
20 Do. at 3d. ,,	. 0	5 0
1 Do. at 4d. ,,	. 0	0 4
The A. P. U. Barber .	. 0	3 3
J. Drummond, London .	. 0	1 0
Per Mr. Johnson, card 5 .	. 0	3 6
Per Mr. Morrish, Bristol:—		
Card 11 . . .	. 0	6 0
,, 13 . . .	. 0	2 0
,, 14 . . .	. 0	6 9
,, 12 . . .	. 0	2 7

G. J. H., *Sec.*

Printed and Published by G. J. HOLYOAKE, 40, Holywell-street, Strand, Saturday, April 20, 1844.

THE MOVEMENT

And Anti=Persecution Gazette.

"Maximize morals, minimize religion."—BENTHAM.

No. 20.   EDITED BY G. JACOB HOLYOAKE, ASSISTED BY M. Q. RYALL.   PRICE 1½d.

AN IRISH EDITOR, A LONDON MAGISTRATE, AND A YORKSHIRE PARSON.

A PRETTILY diversified medley this! but, heterogeneous as the compound may seem, no sooner shall we apply the touch-stone of religion, than the ignoble similarity of its ingredients will appear. As kings agree concerning one text of scripture only, viz., that all the world should be taxed—in like manner Christians, of all creeds and latitudes, agree to tax humanity by their injustice, and perplex it with their folly.

A marvellously monotonous parody has lately appeared in the *Dublin Evening Mail*, on the third chapter of Daniel. These are two of the best verses—

"Then, in the reign of Peel, the Anythingarian an herald cried aloud—To you it is commanded, O people,

"That ye fall down and worship the golden image that Stanley, the Whig, has set up. And whoso falleth not down and worshippeth, if he be of the religion of the true God, and so declared to be by the laws of the land, shall be cut off from all favour of the said King Peel, the Anythingarian."

Upon reading this idle performance, the editor of the *Belfast News Letter* exclaims "irreverent parody!" "profane squib!"—and thus sagely discourseth—

"We can laugh at wit, admire even the ingenuity of a pun, and can relish the "broad grins" of caricature; but, while we despise the Pharisaic hypocrisy of cant in all its forms, we can hold no terms with the writer who sits down to turn into effective ridicule the mysteries of the records of revelation. Exercise your genius if you will, but leave sacred things untouched—we would not scruple to parody the productions of the highest names in English or other literature, and something of this nature may have been done by us in a sportive mood; but the realities of Christianity have upon society a bearing too decided to be thus trifled with."

If we have one opinion on the question more strong than another, it is, that if the "realities of Christianity" can be used to advance the cause of general liberty, they are susceptible of a more useful application than we were prepared to expect. When the editor of the *Mail* was obliged to have recourse to the man of the "fiery furnace," and the "lion's den" to illustrate his arguments, he must have been "sorely straitened" for something to say. But if Daniel the prophet can be of any service to the cause of repeal, "it is commanded unto you, O, Editor of the *Belfast News Letter*, that you do not interfere to prevent the only good that the said Daniel is ever likely to render mankind."

But, editor of the *News-Letter*, by what right do you parody "the highest productions of literature," if other persons are not to parody productions of prophets and saints? Be it known unto you O Editor! that many persons have a reverence, as great, for the "highest productions of literature," as thou hast for the productions of Daniel—and if you "can hold no terms with the writer who ridicules the records of revelation," in reciprocal dealing, that writer can hold no terms with the editor of the *Belfast News-Letter*, who ridicules the more useful records of literature. If this editor parodies that "highest literature" which the infidel admires, while he hold "no terms" with the infidel who parodies revelation—he acts with injustice and sets an example, which, if generally followed, would convert the calm discussion of truth and liberty, into a ferocious contention. To ridicule folly, whether sacred or profane, is the common privilege of all men, and cannot be disturbed without turning literature into a bear garden, and controversy into a savage battle.

Next to the one-sided distinction of this Irish editor, who by the way does not scruple to employ ridicule himself, but only objects to others employing the same weapon against himself—next to this impartial saint, stands the Hon. Mr. Norton of Melbourne notoriety, who imprisoned the boy belonging to the Whitechapel Branch, for hanging out the notice of a discussion on the question—" Is the existence of Christ an allegory or a reality." Men are literally baited by priests to believe in the Lord Jesus Christ—the sceptic is anathematized, inconceivable interests are declared to hang on this great dogma—for it our faith is demanded and our money taken

—we have every right which interest and intellect can give us to inquire into its truth yet if we ask, is it a reality or an allegory? —what are the grounds on which the priestmen disturb our peace and possess themselves of our property? the Hon. Mr. Norton decides that it is *blasphemous, licentious, obscene, seditious and disgraceful.* These men having been bereft, by religion, of any sense of decency or justice, seem to fancy all other people blind to their arrogance, or incapable of feeling or resenting their insolence.

A few evenings ago, the Rev. B. Parsons of York, appeared at the Tottenham Court Road Chapel, and preached a Charity Sermon. Mr. Parsons is a man of considerable ability—able in the conception of his theme, but uncouth and feeble in its execution, and apparently weak enough to believe what he says. In one part of his sermon, he apostrophized unbelievers, and challenged them to stand up and avow certain sentiments which he repeated in a tone not be mistaken—many were present, in the chapel, who would willingly have made the avowal, but they would have been answered with a night's lodging in the station-house. Such is the meanness to which religion descends—to challenge when no one can answer, and to claim a victory which the jailer has won. It is said that the higher the monkey climbs the more he shows his offensive parts, so when religion climbs to the heights of eloquence, the more it exposes its dastard nature and detestable spirit.

G. J. H.

THE NAME JESUS CHRIST,
AND SOME "POINTS OF VIEW" IN WHICH TO CONSIDER IT.

To those who have been accustomed to receive with implicit credence the nursery tales of gods, devils, and hobgoblins, most in vogue, the casting a doubt upon the existence of a popular divinity is sure to be met, if not with indignation, at least with astonishment, or perhaps derision. The professed unbeliever, who has habituated himself to the contemplation of the grossest absurdities among religious creedists and to place them to the account of ignorance or infatuation, is prepared for denials or attempts at disproof of the most widely spread and cherished dogmas however respectabilized by the antiquity of ages, or surrounded by the halo of sanctity. Among the sceptical world may by cited two more classes or sections. There are those who have trodden in a beaten track of infidelity, and who are almost as timidly sensitive to alarm at the slightest deviation as the most unexceptionably orthodox. From the mere doubter or disbeliever of the godhead of Jesus to the *pivotal* atheist, will be found weak or irresolute people who fear to take one step more, and who look with a sort of alarm or distrust on those who have advanced a stage beyond themselves. The others remaining to be noticed are those who, influenced by a wholesome scepticism, and instigated by an untiring regard for truth, on whichever side it may be found—whether accordant or differing with preconceived opinions—hesitate not to direct their investigations into a fresh channel, and fairly and legitimately shape their conclusions to the reasoning processes which new and extended evidence enables them to command. From these remarks it may be concluded that the one class of thinkers—the last named—are alone qualified, or at least pre-eminently qualified—"other things being equal,"—to come to just conclusions respecting questions which continue to enlist the prejudices besetting not only the religious, but the majority of the irreligious portions of society. Reflections of this character, a searching self-scrutiny, are admirable preparatives for a free, bold and candid investigation. Thus braced for the work we can enter with a just, instead of an overweening and misplaced confidence, on the consideration of a subject deeply and vitally affecting ourselves or our contemporaries.

The existence or non-existence as a superhuman or a human being of Jesus Christ—the Christ of the evangelical writings—may be deemed, and with great apparent propriety, as too insignificant a matter to merit such preliminaries, or such painstaking research. We, of the *Movement*, having gone to the root of religious enquiry by dealing with the subject of *god-existence* in its essence, can consistently pass by questions of mode in such existence, and degree in supernatural agencies in general. It may be, nevertheless, gratifying to those who have not progressed further than midway between the opinions of the Theist and the Atheist to have presented to them a statement, slightly, instead of so distantly, in advance of their own. This may furnish a standing reason for any deviations from ordinary routine. Another reason for a notice of the Christ-controversy is, that the Atheist, whether or not he might deem it advisable to enter into discussion on the subject, should at all events be prepared for meeting it. He might not, or need not, or perhaps cannot have made himself master of the principal historical data, but he may acquaint himself, by a comparatively small sacrifice of time or attention, with a sufficient number of facts, statements, or reasonings to help him to a probable conclusion. He may not be enabled to satisfy himself of the positive existence or non existence, as a historical personage, of the reputed founder of the Christian religions, but he may determine, and bring others to the same conclusions, that sufficient evidence is capable of being adduced from historical and antiquarian, as well as scientific researches, to throw doubt upon his reputed birth, life, death, and achievements.

With religion, to cause doubt is to destroy. It is well to disprove, but this is always difficult and next door to impossible. It is sufficient to show that the religionist *cannot prove his* dogmas or statements—his system thence necessarily falls to the ground. Whether Dupuis with others has succeeded in proving the astronomical origin of all religions, we can look with sufficient interest and satisfaction at what he has done, if he has only succeeded in shaking their foundations, and depriving them of the authenticity to which they laid claim. Some further considerations strengthen this view of the subject. The amazing research and erudition necessary for the examination of these critical points of ancient history, legend and fable, entirely preclude the ordinary student from a thorough sifting of the subject. He who must rely on others, is continually dependent on their honesty, liable to be swerved by their prejudices, and to have his judgment guided or misdirected by their capacity. History, unless profound antiquarians and linguists, we must take on the credit of others, reasoning on opinions we may more or less exercise for ourselves. The great utility then, of such admirable works as Dupuis' and Volney's, Higgins's Anacalypsis, with others of the like cast, is to direct students into the right channel for more extended researches, and for the accumulation of fresh material for further elucidations. The chief advantages of the spirited and popular compilations from works of like magnitude and value, as the "Existence of Christ Disproved, by a German Jew," and "Christianity Proved Idolatry, by Charles Southwell," are their gathering together of a number of curious historical or legendary recitals, or scientific observations but little known, or entirely unknown to the general reader, causing a spirit of enquiry, and above all, *throwing doubt* upon the assumed "external or historical evidences of the truth of the Christian religion." The points of view, as Delamartine would say, in which men have been in the habit of considering the Christ of the New Testament, have been as varied as chameleon hues. From a radical reformer, partaking of the good and bad qualities of his fellow creatures, to a man specially missioned by god—thence to a sinless man—a miracle-working man and prophet—a god-man—a part of a tri-partite deity—an ancient solar deity—thence to a mere fictional being or figment of the imagination, he has been represented. Advocates are not now wanting for the maintenance of each of these views. The last of these points of view are those in which they come before us in the recent pamphlet by Mr. Southwell. A rapid survey is taken of the principal theological systems, a comparison is sedulously instituted between the sayings and doings of our Bible Christ and those of the various bygone christs, messiahs, redeemers, saviours, &c., who have figured in the principal mythologies.

The double position is maintained, that our Christ is but a copy, and a very base copy, of their Christs, being but "a fabulous character," and that the Jesus Christ so called, of the Holy Evangelists, did not even exist as a preacher and sufferer under Pontius Pilate. The tract is concluded by the assertion of the "pagan origin of the New Testament maxims—that Christ never existed, and that christianity is neither more nor less than a new version of old fables."

Freethinkers, or any thinkers at all, who may not have directed their attention into this channel, will find in *Christianity Proved Idolatry*, much that will instruct, amuse, or startle. Materials for thinking abound in its few, cheap, and diminutive pages, and a strong stimulus is given to pursue investigations of so curious and interesting a character. Those even who may possess a copy of "The Existence of Christ Disproved," will find this "a short and easy method" to refresh their memories, and afford them a condensed summary of the contents of the more rare, bulky, and expensive work. M. Q. R.

BLASPHEMY LAWS AND PROTESTANT PRACTICE.

(*From Mr. Southwell's Petition when in Bristol Gaol.*)

II.

There is no law against blasphemy, not a single scrap of legislation anywhere exists. Parliament never yet enacted a law against blasphemy, for the very sufficient reason, that blasphemy cannot be defined, and to make a law against an undefinable crime would be preposterous. Your petitioner asked the judge, upon the trial, to define blasphemy, but he was referred to the jury, and thus the judge shifted the burthen of reply from his own shoulders to the shoulders of those who were even less able to bear it. If a man destroy his neighbour, or steal a horse, there is not the slightest difficulty in defining his offence, but no one ever did, or ever will, define blasphemy; so that on all trials for that imaginary offence, the whole question turns upon the opinions of twelve men, who are often as little capable of determining truly, as twelve blocks of wood; and the punishment of the victim is entirely contingent upon the capricious dictum of the judge. Blasphemy, like heresy, admits of no clear definition; and generally means any opinions in any country which are considered dangerous to the interests of the established religion, or fatal to the interest of the priests. The first Protestants in England and Germany, and the Huguenots of France were called heretics and blasphemers, nor have the Protestants failed in their turn to attach opprobrious epithets to all who have dared to separate from her communion. The Catholics burnt Cranmer and Ridley for their abominable heresies; but neither Cranmer nor Ridley was brought to the stake without having first brought others there. John Calvin was so hated, that the more orthodox used to call their dogs Calvin, as a mark of their contempt for that reformer. Calvin fled from persecution; but when Servetus fled to HIM for refuge, thinking that kindred suffering would not deny its sympathy, he was brought to the stake by his *friend*. The absurdity as well as wickedness of coercing conscience, or casting men into dungeons for the expression of their honest convictions is clearly shewn by all history. Not to mention the cruelties practised by Henry the Eighth upon the Lutherans; the atrocities of Mary; or the hardly less atrocious persecutions of Elizabeth; your petitioner will just remind your Honourable House of the startling fact, that Fox, an author of great credit, computes that in the Netherlands alone from the time that the edict of Charles the Fifth was promulgated against the reformers, there had been fifty thousand persons hanged, beheaded, buried alive, or burnt, on account of religion; and that in France the number had also been considerable; yet in both countries, as the same author subjoins, the progress of the new opinions, instead of being checked, was rather forwarded by these persecutions.

The members of your Honourable House cannot be ignorant of the persecutions suffered by the first Christians, who were denounced as a pack of Atheists, the professors of a diabolical and malignant superstition, and pests to society.

They were flung to wild beasts, torn asunder by horses, in short, all the torments that the most fiendish cruelty could devise, were inflicted upon them; and yet Christianity flourished, and hence it has passed into a proverb that the blood of the martyrs is the seed of the church.

This persecution seems to have been expected by Jesus Christ, who warns his followers that they (the priests) shall put them out of their synagogues, yea, the time cometh that whosoever killeth you, will think that he doeth God service.

All persecution for opinion's sake is the consequence of a savage and bigoted spirit, fatal alike to public as to private liberty. The principle of persecution is in itself to be reprehended, and the slightest kind of punishment would be equally a violation of public liberty. Persecution is the weapon of cowards, who strive to put down by brute force what they have not the courage or capacity to subdue by reason. It was asserted by the advisers of cruelty during Mary's reign, that if persecution of any kind be admitted, the most bloody and violent will surely be allowed the most justifiable, as the most effectual. Imprisonment, said they, fines, confiscations, whippings, serve only to irritate the sect, without disabling them from resistance; but the stake, the wheel, and the gibbet, must soon terminate in the extirpation or banishment of all the heretics inclined to give disturbance, and in the entire silence and submission of the rest. The fallacy of this monstrous opinion has been already shown in the opposite effects of the severities practised by Charles the Fifth, who, after he resigned his crown, seems to have acquired much sense and saw the gross absurdity of attempting by force to make men think alike. It is said that having amused himself with the construction of clocks and watches, he thence remarked how impracticable the object was in which he had so much employed himself during his grandeur, and how impossible that he who never could frame two machines that would go exactly alike, could ever be able to make all mankind concur in the same belief and opinion.

It cannot fail to appear, that if Charles, in all his glory, could not even check heresy, but only inflamed and increased it by his savage persecution, it would be madness for any modern authority, however high, to attempt to fetter opinion, or check infidelity by imprisonment or fine. These persecutions are a disgrace to the age, a scandal to that civilization which should protect the rights of men, not destroy liberty of conscience, be the presiding genius of harmonious liberty, not the champion of an impracticable spiritual unity.

As opinion precedes all voluntary action, and sound opinions induce just and proper action; it cannot be denied that speculative opinions should be carefully watched by those who are in authority, lest they run wild and throw the country into disorder. But let those who would govern well be careful how they meddle with opinion or attack the liberty of the press. Opinions, like trade, a wise minister or parliament will endeavour as far as possible to let alone, and the strong arm of the law will never be raised against them. Speculative opinions lead to physical consequences, says Burke, agreed, and for that very reason they should not be coerced, for the coerced error only grows more corrupt, deadly and powerful. Certain speculative opinions are undoubtedly evil, but he who would crush them by any other force than that derived from argument and reason, is a cruel and most foolish tyrant! who by his rash, ill-advised measures increases the evil he desires to extirpate. The proper business of authority, as said by an American writer, is to protect all opinions, to dictate none.

Outrageous attacks on individual liberty, under colour of regard for religion, are common in this country. The British people who should be foremost in the great work of emancipating the human mind, have been far outstripped in this glorious race by the nations of the continent, and the republic of America, where any parties may publish their opinions (for the doing which your petitioner is cruelly punished), without fear or restraint.

EXAMINATION OF BUTLER'S ANALOGY.

To the Editor of the Movement.

SIR,—You ask, in a recent number of your journal, if some one will "pour out Butlerian philosophy in your pages." I do not think that it would do you or your readers much good, if some one should. Much cannot be thought of the shrewdness or intelligence even of a Deist who could not answer such an argument as Butler's, when produced to prove a particular revealed religion from the apparent revelations of nature. Because there is something cruel, something bad in the present disposition of things—it is a reason that something should be given additionally cruel and wicked. The argument of Butler, whilst it can be indirectly used against the Deist, comes directly in support of the Atheist. I have often thought it would be a good thing to give a clear abridgment of Butler's Analogy as an Atheistical work. A greater than the Oxford barrister, in his profession, Sir James Mackintosh, admits the almost hopeless unintelligibility of Butler's writings, and therefore what are we to think of the reported shrewdness and intelligence of the artizan who could interpret the bishop? We must suppose "Mr. Loombes'" complete ignorance of the book in question which settled his faith and struck him, by analogy, with conviction of the superior claims of revelation—that Butler was not to be understood and therefore to be believed. Mackintosh, it is apparent, determined the character of Butler's performance, by a glance at the title page, without wading through the whole details. And I am convinced that any impartial person who reads Butler, must give it as his opinion that Butler became so impressed with his principle of Analogy, that he thought the more unintelligible was his way of writing, the better proof was it of his reasoning. In the first article on "*Oxford Theology*," in the *Oracle of Reason*, there are these observations on the Butler school of polemical theology." Mackintosh said he had learnt all his philosophy from Butler's three first sermons. Butler was amongst the best thinkers and worst writers, being in the latter respect *particularly dark and obscure*. His Analogy is not his best work; it is not philosophical but religious. The whole of it is contained in a single passage of Quinctilian, which he had honesty enough to give as his motto to the work; the subject of which is the development of the argument, that as imperfections are perceived in the natural world and allowed, apparent imperfections ought to be no objection to the religious government. *Now this can only be an answer to Deists, Atheists might make use of his objections, and have done so.*

Atheists stand on vantage ground, and such arrows as Butler shot at Deists, fall harmlessly at Atheists' feet. The Butlerians must recast their arts of war before they can hope to make an impression on your readers. To show you that I am not in error respecting Butler's mode of reasoning, I subjoin a brief analysis of it by Burdon, a man quite as respectable for his learning and talents as Master Loombes, Mr. Grinfield, or the *Bristol Mercury*. Burdon says—

"Butler in his Analogy—a book more remarkable for metaphysical refinement than sound reasoning—rests his whole argument upon the divine origin of the system of nature: and taking that for granted, he infers, that revelation coming from the same author, is liable to the same defects, and that they who believe the one must of consequence believe the other, because its defects are not greater; but this is taking two things for granted which ought to be proved independently of each other. His arguments for a future life are composed of equally gratuitous assumptions; his two first are utterly destitute of foundation. The first is, 'That having already undergone many changes from our birth to maturity, we should naturally infer that we shall exist hereafter :' but he forgets that these changes are gradual and imperceptible, and that there is no gulf between them like that of death: he argues also from the changes of animals, viz., worms into butterflies, &c.; and, to be candid, is forced to allow them also a future state of existence. This may be orthodoxy, but it is not argument."

If you think what precedes likely to throw light upon the subject to which it relates, it is at your service. W. J. B.

MR. J. M'NEIL.

Sir,—I write, according to promise, to inform you of the Campsie affair. It appears to me that I shall not be called upon this time. The judge arrives in Stirling on the 23rd inst., and as yet I have not been served with any indictment. Perhaps they may call me up before the Sheriffs' Court after the Stirling trials are over. If they do I will let you know. JOHN M'NEIL.
To G. J. H., Sec. A. P. U.

MR. KNOX'S CASE.
(*To the Editor of the Movement.*)

Sir,—As I was not explicit enough in my communication respecting Mr. Knox's case, I now inform you that the trial took place in the Police Court, Town Hall, Leicester. The persons who committed the assault were John and Lawrence Kind. The police officer assaulted, P.C. 15; and the magistrate, John Biggs, Esq.; and the date Monday, March 2nd, 1844. In addition, Mr. Knox received several kicks in assisting the police, besides taking care of the police constable's lamp, which he found in the street and took to the Police Station next day. I may also mention that about three weeks ago I memorialised the Secretary of State on behalf of Mr. Paterson; I received an answer, signifying that Mr. P. must submit to the prison rules, and that any application on his account must be made to the Prison Board, Scotland. I thereupon memorialised the Prison Board for an amelioration of those privations mentioned in his letter in the *Movement*, and received an answer from the Secretary of the Prison Board acquainting me that he would lay my memorial before the Prison Board on the first opportunity. A. Q. C.

LETTERS OF J. PIERREPONT GREAVES. *Parts II and III.—Concordium Press, Watson.*—We may liken the world to an ocean, society to a wreck on it, and Mr. Greaves's work to a boat launched to save the sufferers, but the work is so lightly built, being freighted only with spiritualisms, that it is no sooner grasped than it slips away or sinks under the weight it should support. In nautical phraseology, it carries no ballast. This is a fair estimate of the *Letters*, as accurately as one can guess, for it is impossible to do more than conjecture upon books written in an unknown tongue. Mr. Greaves ought to be styled *Irving Redivivus*. The "*Letters*" are about as intelligible as an electioneering speech, in the Arabic language, would be to a country constituency. Mr. Greaves may have truth in him, but it lies so deep in the wells of spirituality that he who should descend to fetch it up would infallibly be drowned. After a patient and earnest attempt to understand what these "*Letters*" teach, I am compelled to give them up in despair. The writer lays it down, that he who is to comprehend them must be familiar with *consociations*, possess a *triple organization*—live in a *sphered sphere*, and deliver himself of *spontaneities, instinctivities,* and *premonitions*—he must be *esthetic, beinged and wholed*, rejoice in *heaven fibres*, know *what is the* IS *that he is*, and *how the is is related to the I*, and *re-re-related to the spirit*—understand in what way the *absolute maker includes the 45, without the 45 including the maker*. And, finally, should he fall into a ditch he must not fail to remember, as an axiom, that *self-preservation is the first offence against the divine laws.* Candidly I confess myself without any of these unique qualifications, and consequently unable to speak of the value of these "*Letters.*" To enquire of others for information would be idle, for Mr. G.'s injunction to his disciples is—"debate with no one, dispute with no one." The Concordists are therefore to imitate the wisdom of those who call all men irrational for not adopting their views, at the same time declaring that not one man in the world is able to understand them. I, therefore, leave these "*Letters,*" whose purpose seems as far removed from the business of life, as they are from the common language of mankind. If any one like Themistocles would learn the art of forgetting, he may read Concordian writings with a fair chance of losing in oblivion the plain teachings of nature. Mr. Greaves's productions are a kind of metaphysical Lethe, in which any lesson of experience may be dipped, that is to be forgotten.

VEGETABLE DIET DEFENDED, *by Dr. W. A. Alcott,—Chapman.*—This Essay commences with a motto from Daniel, talks of "Love Holiness," attempts to make men "god-like," pretends to supply us from spirit, and arrays a tolerable file of creators and Christians, and does many other things not likely to influence us—but it is still a useful book and deserves perusal. The introduction disgustingly parades, as nearly all these performances do, bleatings, bellowings, and slaughterings — convulsed limbs and muscles, dissection smells, wounds, humours and clotted blood. One would think that these vegetarians were butchers, and wrote their books in the stews and slaughter-houses of Smithfield. This is wantoning in abominations. These writers will next, if they are consistent, inveigh against all eating and drinking. It matters little what may be the *kind* of food, if it will yield health and long life. We take medicine irrespective of the delicacy of the drugs. Food is to be tested by its utility, not by its nature. Mr. Bell is brought forward to prove that teeth were "originally formed for frugiverous offices." What matters it to us what teeth were formed for? our business is to use them for the most profitable purposes. If somebody should prove that "teeth were originally formed" to masticate baked clay, would the vegetarian dine off a plate of brickbats? This essay is not what it professes to be— Dr. Alcott's production. It has been altered greatly from the American edition by somebody—this is not fair without explanation. A table is given to show the nutritious nature of vegetables; but it oddly enough happens, that those which are declared most nutritious are also most earthy, which the author of "Biology," and many chemists affirm to be fatal to long life. Who are right—the Biologists or the Vegetarians? The Essay says that all attempts to heal society are superficial until vegetable diet is recommended. This is extravagant. The propriety and possibility of living on vegetable food depends on habit, convenience, constitution and duties. Still the discussion of the subject will do immense good, and lead to the adoption of simpler and purer diets than those which now shorten life and multiply diseases.

DR. KALLEY AND RELIGIOUS LIBERTY IN PORTUGAL.—The case of Dr. Kalley, a Scotch physician, who was, last autumn, illegally imprisoned at Madeira, on a charge of "blasphemy and heresy," and "abetting apostacy and heresy," has been tried at Lisbon and Funchal. On the 24th February, the Judge Conservator at the latter place passed the following sentence:—" Supposing the British subject, Dr. Kalley, to have disturbed the public order of this island by preaching doctrines opposed to its religion, as is sworn by the witnesses; and considering this preaching an abuse which degenerates into crime ; nevertheless, the said Dr. Kalley, as a Protestant, which he is, is not punishable, seeing that there does not exist a law to punish in the person of the accused the act charged. I, therefore, declare the accusation given against the said Dr. Kalley irrelevant, and order him to be held clear of guilt." Baffled on the religious question, Dr. Kalley's prosecutors, we understand, are going to institute proceedings against him as a disturber of the public peace. On the other hand, Dr. Kalley, at the suggestion of Lord Aberdeen, is about to petition the government at Lisbon, for compensation for the loss of his professional income during his illegal imprisonment. In the course of the proceedings before the tribunal of Rellaçae at Lisbon, the public prosecutor, acting as counsel against Dr. Kalley, gave a very lucid exposition of the existing law of religious liberty in Portugal, wherein he clearly showed that the supremacy of the Romish Church is no more, but that Portuguese subjects enjoy the same liberty as Englishmen do in all religious matters. He says, "I do not characterise the accusation as blasphemy, nor as heresy, because these crimes are only considered such when committed by followers of the Roman Catholic apostolic religion, and not by those who, like the appellant, follow a different faith, and therefore, being *extra ecclesiam*, are beyond all censure, civil and ecclesiastical. Nor can I characterise it as apostacy, because I understand that the crime of apostacy ceased to exist among us in virtue of Article 145 of the Constitutional Charter; in which ample religious liberty is guaranteed to Portuguese citizens in the following terms:—' No one shall be prosecuted for motives of religion ; ' wherein the absolute term ' *no one* ' excludes all exception of persons, and the very broad expression ' *for motives of religion* ' embraces all that relates to the religious creed of every one; and, therefore if citizens apostatized from our religion, though they did great injury to their souls, yet they did not commit any civil crime for which they can be punished."

CHRISTIANITY'S LIBERALITY.—It was stated by W. J. Fox in one of his recent lectures, that King Pomare, the father of the present Queen Pomare, was converted by the British missionaries in 1797, and that, at the suggestion and under the direction of the missionaries, he passed a law, still in force, to the effect that whoever shall attempt to introduce or teach any other religion than the *true* one taught by the missionaries, shall, if found guilty, be sentenced to banishment —or to hard labour on the roads !!!—and this shall be their award of whatever rank or station the offenders may be.

CHURCHMEN ABROAD.—It appears from the *Overland Herald* that Colombo has been in a complete ferment in consequence of the Catholic priest—the Rev. Caytano Rosayro, refusing to bury a little child because the poor thing had not been properly baptised. The *Herald* styles this, "inhuman conduct" and "a contemptible quibble." The Ceylon authorities were in requisition, mandamuses were issued, affidavits made, and the whole police and the Fiscal finally compelled the burial. This insolence of Rosayro, so much condemned in the priest, is practised daily by the churchman. The influence of creeds steps in to prevent even the performance of decency to the dead. No consequences deter the pious from carrying out the vile requirements of religion. Baptism had not been duly attended to and the child must go unburied, although in the climate of Ceylon the effects might afflict, with mortal disease, the whole inhabitants. Piety is incompatible with health, decency and civilization. It has been aptly said that "among the religious there are some good men, and so there are some tame panthers, but they are panthers still, and ready upon every occasion to show their ferocity."

MAGISTERIAL COURTESY TO AN ATHEIST.—A short time since, Mr. Joseph Allen, a bookseller, residing at 14, Chichester Place, Gray's Inn Road, was called upon at Clerkenwell Police Office, to prosecute a man who had stolen a book from him. On being tendered the Testament to be sworn, he objected to be sworn.—Mr. Combe: What is your objection?—Prosecutor: I do not respect that book or its contents, and without being sworn I feel it equally binding on my conscience to speak the truth. Then you deny the truth of the gospel?—I do. What do you profess?—I am an Atheist.—Mr. Combe, (peremptorily, and with much indignation): Then stand down, stand down, sir; I will not hear you. The evidence of the other witnesses was then taken, and upon that evidence the prisoner was committed, but Mr. Combe directed the clerk to bind over the prosecutor in the sum of £100 to appear at the Old Bailey and prosecute the case. When the recognizance paper, was handed to him the prosecutor refused to sign it, saying he objected to sign anything. Clerk: You must sign it; you are bound over in £100 to prosecute at the Old Bailey. Prosecutor: But I do not press the charge. I think——. Clerk: Oh, we don't care what you think. We won't have your thinkings here. Mr. Combe: No, certainly not; we don't want the thoughts of such a man here. If he does not appear at the Old Bailey an Exchequer process will be issued against him for the amount of his recognizance. He is bound over; let him attend according to the terms of his recognizance, or it may be worse for him.

In this case Mr. Combe forgot the proper impartiality of a magistrate, and for the sake of annoying a prosecutor, because of his belief, or rather disbelief, bound him over in a £100 bond to give evidence, which he (Mr. C.) declared he would not receive. This disgraceful conduct was not carried out. Mr. Allen shortly after received a polite note, informing him that his presence would not be required at the Old Bailey.

L' ABBE MAURETTE.—A heterodox work of his, "The Gospel and the Popes, or Good Bye to Rome," has, it appears from the letter of a private correspondent, been seized by the procurator-general in Paris. We will thank any of our readers for any particulars that may meet his eye. Our query about *Michel* is still unanswered.

NOW READY—"The Scotch Trials," complete, in stiff wrappers, price One Shilling.

ERRATUM.—In the article "Protean Goddittes," the following passage occurs—" in which [the milk of] all the more honourable traits of character. — Reject the words enclosed in brackets.

TO CORRESPONDENTS.

J. H.—Mr. Oldham's papers will speedily be brought to a close, to afford us a fair opportunity of comment. Many sentiments in his last article cannot be long allowed to pass unchallenged.

W. B.—We make no apology for the numerous errors of typography in recent numbers—we will take care that they shall be the last. The proof must have been read by a blind man, but we will open his eyes without the assistance of Jesus Christ. Censure as much as you please, we never complain of what is deserved.

SUBSCRIPTIONS TO THE ANTI-PERSECUTION UNION.

W. J. B. "for the exertions of our Secretary"	£0 10	0
Mr. D. Palmer	0 1	0
Mr. Bidwell, Col. 6	0 1	6
Per Col. 117	0 6	0
S. B., Vauxhall, per Mrs. Martin	0 2	6
W. H. Bennett, first subscription	0 2	6
A. H. Ham	0 1	0
J. Reddey, Jun.	0 1	0
H. Shaw	0 1	0
C. Woods	0 2	6
A. Hammon	0 1	0
W. J. Hammon	0 1	6
Per Mr. G. Adams, Cheltenham	0 5	0
Mr. T. A. Marrs, Coventry	0 2	0

G. J. H., *Sec.*

Printed and Published by G. J. HOLYOAKE, 40, Holywell-street, Strand, Saturday, April 27, 1844.

THE MOVEMENT

And Anti=Persecution Gazette.

"Maximize morals, minimize religion."—BENTHAM.

No. 21.   EDITED BY G. JACOB HOLYOAKE, ASSISTED BY M. Q. RYALL.   PRICE 1½d

THIRD LETTER FROM DR. KALLEY,
TO MR. G. JACOB HOLYOAKE.

Madeira, March 6, 1844.

DEAR SIR,—I received yesterday your note of the 16th ult. enclosing a printed copy of my last to you, and of the reply of the Anti-Persecution Union. I entirely acquit you of any intention to deceive me by the plausible name of your society or the official expression of sympathy; I thank you for the honorable manner in which my letter is copied, and as you sent to the *Voluntary* on the 16th January a copy of my first letter to you, I shall feel obliged by your forwarding to me a printed copy of it also.

When I wrote, returning you the £5 which you so kindly sent me, I did not know that any Christian in Great Britain had been informed of our correspondence, much less had I any idea of ought regarding it having appeared in the public journals. Being independent both of the journals and of the public, I desire to pursue what I believe to be duty, uninfluenced by the threats or the approbation of man. The remission of your money was irrespective of either. I knew of no reason to suppose that you sent it to me from any other motive than because you supposed that I was in want of such assistance, and this not being the case, I consider that my conduct would have been dishonest towards you had I retained it. In returning the money I had no intention of treating you with disrespect. I know that Infidels and Atheists are men and have feelings like other men. My religion teaches me to love all men, even mine enemies, not in word only but in truth, and my conduct would have been inconsistent with the Christian name, had I requited with disrespect the kindness you showed me. I do not mean to insinuate in any way that I look with less abhorrence than other Christians on all attempts to spread atheism and infidelity — I regard them as insulting to the benefactor of the universe, and destructive to the happiness of man; and, therefore, I desire openly to declare my unqualified abhorrence of them. But as a father may hate the evil conduct of his son while his soul yearns over him with intense affection, so while the Christian hates, or should hate, all pernicious doctrines. and all evil practices, he should also entertain unlimited benevolence towards those who are guilty of spreading the former and practising the latter. By the term unlimited benevolence, I do not mean such softness as to prevent the adoption of proper measures for hindering the progress of the evil, nor indifference as to whether it gather strength or not, for that would be like a soft hearted physician letting his patient die because he could not bear the idea of inflicting the pain of a blister, or a foolish father allowing his child to precipitate himself into an abyss of misery because he could not bear to correct him. By unlimited benevolence towards those guilty of such things, I mean such a feeling as the father entertains towards his erring children—a sincere desire for their welfare—dictating the most reasonable measures for its attainment consistent with a true and enlarged philanthrophy towards all mankind.

Endeavouring humbly to follow up such views in my life, I am sorry to find that you felt as if I stabbed you while desiring for you that which I believe to be the greatest and best of man's enjoyments on earth. I did not write with any feeling of unkindness—I have no reason to suppose you insincere, and did not mean to charge you with hypocrisy by using the words "ungratefully wish to forget God." My desire was to write as if writing to a brother who was in danger of suffering much throughout the duration of his existence, by erroneous views on a subject most deeply affecting his best interests.

Suppose a poor family were to find clothes ready made for each member of the family whenever they were required, and food prepared for every meal, and all their wants supplied without their care, and then while enjoying these good things they should maintain that all these kindnesses were *undesigned*, and that they were indebted to no kind friend for them. I think we might, without much impropriety, say that they ungratefully wished to forget their benefactor, even though they had never seen him, and by shutting their eyes against those proofs of his existence were able to disbelieve it. Now were your body left without a cuticle life would be agony—a covering is provided without care on your part—it is most skillfully fitted to your body, and formed of the most proper texture;—such is the clothing. All the food on earth, or any portion of it, would not avail for the support of your life for a single day unless your food were changed into blood, and your blood itself, instead of nourishing your body, would poison you unless constantly purified. In order to be purified so as to be fitted for your nourishment, the whole of your blood (probably about thirty pounds) requires to pass about five hundred times per day through millions of canals in your lungs, and be cleansed by air introduced into the millions of other canals in the same organs. Such is a small part of the preparation of your nourishment, over which you have no superintendence, and which is carried on even when you are asleep. Among the most essential necessaries for your life may be mentioned a guard over the entrance to the air passages in your lungs, were it to remain open when you swallow you would probably die suffocated during the first meal—and were it to be closed for a few minutes at any term, for instance when asleep, you must inevitably die; you cannot by any act of your will either open or close that entrance: yet it closes at the proper instant, and is kept open when required. That want is most efficiently supplied, and this is the case with regard to thousands of wants, and the performance of innumerable operations within your frame every day. Now the combination of such a vast number of most complicated and astounding operations within so small a space as the dimensions of your frame, all conducive to, and necessary for the production of, a certain effect—namely, your enjoyment of life and health, and the continued production of that effect amidst elements whose action on your body, if unrestrained would make it putrify, are to me irresistible proofs that you are indebted for all your comfort every moment to a wisdom incomparable superior to that of man. If there be in *any piece of mechanism invented by man*, ENOUGH *to prove intention or design*, surely in the *mechanism of our bodies* there is *superabundance* of proof of it. I have no hesitation in affirming that in one human body there is more proof of design than in all the machinery yet employed by man.

You object that "if these be assumed as evidences of wisdom, goodness, and power, which would imply that I thought them things intended or designed, then *must* we also assume that the inadaptibility, disadvantages, and miseries seen in nature are evidences of folly, malice, or impotence." I do not think that this necessarily follows. You yourself start the idea which *may* set aside your *must*. You acknowledge that your faculties are limited and cannot comprehend all; now what would you think of a man who, while confessing that he did not understand all about !a chronometer, or a steam engine, should shut his eyes to the accuracy of the one, and the action of the other; deny that there is any proof of wisdom, power, or design about them—attribute one part to folly, and another to impotence, and when asked why he did so? should reply, "when I have infinite knowledge I shall draw infinite conclusions." I would answer such a one,—"what you have to decide is whether, notwithstanding your ignorance of much respecting the machinery, there be enough exhibited and known to prove design. Follow the plain and humble course of judging according to the evidence you see and know, and do not suffer your ignorance of the rest of the universe to prevent your coming to a decision respecting so plain and easy a matter."

And with respect to the charge of malice, it seems enough to remark farther, that a father who tenderly loves his child, and eagerly desires that child's welfare may be induced, by that very desire, to chastise his child; and the child may hurt himself, and if he do so by neglecting the father's counsel, he has little reason to deny the father's benevolence. I do many things every day which an unprofessional, unintelligent observer might declare to be indubitably malicious, and yet they are acts of kindness. You have far, far less reason to doubt the benevolence of the wisdom and power displayed in the construction and support of your body, than the child would have to doubt his father's, or the patient to doubt the physician's kindness. Let me appeal, then, to your own heart, whether or not you have felt towards that fountain of all your enjoyment the gratitude you owe. I know that I have not: and when you question whether all the good things you enjoy are intended for your good, and whether all these operations within you are conducted by benevolent wisdom; pardon my frankness when I tell you, that I cannot regard your conduct in this respect otherwise than as exceedingly ungrateful to the author of your being. If he had not great patience and long-suffering with the ungrateful, neither you nor I would be to-day in the enjoyment of those good things, in return for which we have thanked and loved him so little.

I now turn to that part of your letter where you maintain that "I do *not know*, I *only suppose* I am right." This must be the case with the Atheist. After all his endeavours to fortify himself in Atheism, he must confess that he has no certainty in it—he cannot get further than to say, " I *suppose* that there is no God—I *doubt* the existence of such a being —but that there *may* be a God, I admit."

The believer in God draws proof from every member of his body, the operations within it —the formation of every plant and every animal—the adaptation of all to their respective elements—the movements of the planets,— in short, he cannot open his eyes without finding *positive facts* in proof of his belief in a great, wise, powerful, and living God. If in any case a man can be so convinced by evidence, as to be warranted to say, " I do not only suppose this to be true, I know it;" it is with regard to the being of a God, for there is more evidence in proof of this one fact than the whole amount of all evidence in proof of other facts.

The Infidel also must confess that he *only supposes*, and *does not know* that he is right. I have conversed with many Infidels, and read many of their works. Some of them have been men of much study, to whom science is deeply indebted, men of strong intellect, powerful eloquence, and keen wit. But with respect to religion and the evidences of Christianity, it is really astonishing what ignorance they display, and with what *flimsy answers* they seem to satisfy themselves in reply to the *facts* adduced by Christians.

I will for argument sake, however, suppose that we have found a man of talent, who, feeling the importance of the subject, has sat down to examine the proofs of Christianity: we will suppose him to have sought out carefully the arguments of Christians, and that on strict scrutiny before the bar of unprejudiced reason, he has been able to set aside every argument which has come before him, would he then be warranted to say, " I do not only suppose, I know that Christianity is not true, I know that it is not supported by rational evidence?" By no means. He might then say, " I *suppose* that Chistianity is unfounded—I *have not found evidence that is true* —but there *may exist somewhere proofs* of which I have not heard, *which*, therefore, *I have not examined*—consequently I have not *rational certainty* in Infidelity, and *must admit that Christianity may be true*."

The Romanists also, in reference to whom you say, that it may in the end be proven that their higher pretensions to the possession of true religion were well-founded. They also, I affirm, if they act rationally, must confess that *they do not know*, they *only suppose* they are right; for it is a dogma of their church, that it is meritorious to believe without proof —and whosoever believes anything in that way, can have no rational certainty respecting it. They do not profess to give rational proof of their peculiar tenets to those on whom they are imposed.

After showing that the Atheist, the Infidel, and the Romanist cannot have reasonable certainty in their opinions, you may think it presumptuous in me to profess that I can attain it. I do, however, unhesitatingly maintain, that the Christian has such an amount of *positive* evidence in proof of his religion, that he is fully warranted after examining it, to say, " I do not only suppose, I know that my religion is true." Christianity seeks investigation. — It openly says, " Prove all things." It exhibits its proofs, and asks from us no irrational credence.

I find that I must still further trespass on your patience with a few sentences respecting my persecutors. You seem to regard with suspicion my assertion, that the instigators and principal supporters of the persecution against me are avowed Infidels and Atheists. You think this " strange !" You say, they " Cannot persecute for their own glory, and they have not, like believers, the glory of God to do it for." You think it strange, because I " said in a former letter, that the true reason of my imprisonment was, that I had endeavoured to show, that the Great Creator of all cannot sell his favour or barter his mercy." And you cannot imagine how Atheists should care about this. And further, you think it strange that " Atheists should in this conntry enjoy immunity and power to instigate and support proceedings" against me. The fact is, that avowed Infidels and Atheists have power; and while they may not " persecute for their own glory," nor " care whether the Creator barters his favour" or not, you will easily understand that they may lend themselves as tools to Popery—*for their own gain.* You need not think it strange that they should act in direct opposition to their avowed opinions, and support superstition. Only bear in mind that it is *impossible* to attain *rational certainty* in Atheism, and you will not be surprised that men decline losing the prospect of gain for uncertain opinions. Few do so,—fewer go to prison for them, and fewer still would die for opinions, respecting which they cannot be certain.

Should you feel inclined to continue this correspondence, it will give me much pleasure to hear from you. I would willingly prepay my letters to you, but there is an order against the consul, who is our postmaster, receiving any sum, either for assurance or prepayment of letters. Should there be any expression which may appear unkind, I beg you will pardon it, and believe that no unkind feeling dictated. I am, most sincerely yours,

Rob. R. Kalley.

TO Dr. KALLEY IN REPLY.

London, 5, Paul's-alley, Paternoster-row.
April 26, 1844.

DEAR DR.—Your letter inspires us with gratification. After the vituperations of the press, the anathemas of the pulpit, and the brutality of the law, your generous expostulations and earnest arguments are quite refreshing—and if they have failed to produce conviction, they have won our esteem, given us delight, and furnished us with instruction.

A printed copy of your former letter shall be enclosed with this. Your explanation relative to returning our remittance is perfectly satisfactory, and now we *more* admire your intentions, than we before suspected them. That you should "look with abhorrence on the spread of Atheism," is perhaps natural—I often regret the perversity with which Christianity continues to be disseminated, notwithstanding the discoveries of science and the progress of philosophy. But, differing, as I thus do on this point, I cordially agree with you in "hating pernicious doctrines and evil practices," and in the propriety of "hindering their progress by the most reasonable measures consistent with a true and enlarged philanthrophy towards mankind. But I am reminded, that though we both agree to prevent the spread of pernicious doctrines by the employment of "reasonable measures," we may not be agreed as to what *are* "reasonable measures." You instance the paternal government in illustration of your views, but I should be sorry to be subjected, in matters of opinion, to government upon such principles, whether of a father, or of a god. As you would chastise the perverse child, would you chastise the perverse unbeliever? If so, I must disclaim any sympathy with such "reasonable measures," for though I could submit to the blister of the physician, I could never tolerate the blister of the saint. In my opinion, there is no opinion, so "pernicious" as the opinion that coercion may in any case, or by anybody, be employed to check opinion.

I perceive now, that you intended me no unkindness by what you said respecting my "ungratefully wishing to forget God." In applying the common interpretation to your language, it appears that I mistook your sentiments. The language of religion is the language of arrogance, and though you employ its verbiage, I am glad to find that you renounce its meaning.

The "poor family who found all their wants supplied without care of their own," would very naturally think that all such kindnesses *were* "undesigned," unless they had some good reason to think otherwise, and certainly they could not be deemed as "ungratefully wishing to forget a benefactor," whose existence they did not suspect. This is my own case. You say that the supposed "care and kindnesses" are proofs of the existence of the benefactor in question. I do not think so. You tell me as Dr. Paley does, that the admirable contrivances manifested in my own frame, are "irresistible proofs that I am indebted to a wisdom incomparably superior to that of man." That your argument may lose nothing of its weight, I will, at this point of its progress, admit it. But permit me to enquire where it will lead, and to ask you a few questions? Why is design said to imply a designer? Perhaps as you reason from Paley's premises, you will permit me to use his responses. Paley says that design implies a designer, because our *experience* tells us so. What is this designer? A person, answers Paley. But why a person? Because, continues Paley, the *same experience* which informs us that design implies a designer, informs us that that designer must be a person. Here Dr. Paley stops, but his argument is susceptible of continuation. Has this "person" an organized frame? Of course it has—the *same experience*, of which we have just availed ourselves to prove that design implies a designer, is our proof that no person was ever yet unorganized. But organization is designed. The "cuticle, lungs, and millions of blood canals of a person"—*you* assure me "are irresistible proofs of design, and that the person in whom they are manifested is indebted for them to a wisdom incomparably superior to his own." Then by your own reasoning, the person of God, which you say made me, was itself made—and the same is true of an endless succession of gods. I must now beg leave to retract my admission made a few minutes ago, and confess that "God is past finding out." For by reasoning from the argument of design, I am led, not to the discovery of one true God, but to a greater number of Gods than ever entered into the imagination of a Polytheist, and none of them the first cause, the supreme we seek. I enclose you a copy of "Paley Refuted," wherein I have pursued this argument at length, and should you be able to overturn my conclusion, you will find, me as willing to recant its correctness as I am now earnest in proclaiming it.

Do not contract my disbelief into want of appreciation. I question not the exquisite complexity which you have described in the structure of my own frame, I ever admit and admire it, but I cannot thence deduce the existence of Deity, as you do, and erect my admiration into an article of faith. Upon what do I fall back then, you will ask. Upon nature! which has peopled space with glittering worlds, given to earth its capabilities, to foliage its magnificence, to flowers their tints, that fills land and sea with joyous life, and sustains man in his proud dominion over all. I fall back on nature, from which man derives so much—of which he acknowledges so little, and which, when religious, he delights to subordinate to the vague and poor chimeras of his own imagination, which he has the vanity to set over nature, as though that which is self-existent, may not be self-operating, as though powers coeval with eternity, and that conquer both time and destruction require a parent or benefactor—or that nature, from which we learn wisdom, and order, and government, needs direction like a straggling army, or a wayward child.

I agree with you that he would answer absurdly who should require "infinite knowledge" to judge of a "steam engine," but I did not take the universe to be Watt's or Savary's invention! I think I said that infinite knowledge was requisite to draw conclusions in favour of the perfection of an infinite universe. If I am to suppose the deity in the situation of "a father who must chastise his children," I must also suppose the deity unable, like the father, to prevent the refractoriness he has to correct. If like the "physician," the deity must perform painful operations for our benefit, it can only be because, as in the case of the physician, the necessity for them has arisen in spite of himself. This mode of reasoning is still inconclusive, for though it leaves deity with benevolence, it still invests it with impotence. If by your appeal to me you wish to know whether the beauties of nature never give me emotions of joy—I answer *yes*; but one thing is wanted to justify me in calling such emotions gratitude, — the conviction of the existence of that personal intelligence whence you suppose they flow.

We may promote the better understanding of the points we discuss by ceasing to regard Theism and Atheism, as questions of "supposition," and considering them as questions of *probability* or *improbability*. If you think that I take any advantage of you by this proposal, I am willing that you shall still consider your own opinions to be *certain* truths, while I do not require you to regard mine as more than probable. I pretend to no certainty, in the strict sense of that term. It is the probability in favour of Atheism which wins my conviction—that probability may be little, but it decides me, because I think that in Theism I find less.

You tell me of the "*positive facts*," which you say everywhere abound, "in proof of a great, wise, powerful and living god." Whether they are historical, scientific, or philosophic facts, I know not, but if you will be kind enough to suggest them to me I will endeavour not to return you "flimsy answers," but will confess my sentiments honestly and unreservedly.

In your opinion "the man who has examined and answered every argument that has come before him in favour of Christianity, *must still admit that Christianity may be true.*" Be it so. But you also say that though such an Infidel "*had not found evidence that Christianity was true,*" yet proofs of it, which he had neither heard nor examined *might exist somewhere*, and consequently he could not have *rational certainty in his Infidelity.*" But have you not forgotten, that though the Infidel might find no evidence in favour of Christianity—that he might possess evidence in favour of his Infidelity? I am sure you would not be so disingenuous as to assume that the Infidel was an Infidel, without any evidence in favour of his infidelity, and would not the evidence which *he had* in favour of his infidelity, outweigh the evidence which he *had not* in favour of his Christianity, and give him a *rational* certainty in his opinion? But I can afford to pass this by, and will simply invert your own argument, and take your own opinion upon its merits. I will suppose that you, as a Christian have not evidence that Atheism is true, yet "proofs of it *may somewhere exist* of which you have not heard and therefore not examined. and consequently you have not *rational certainty* in your Christianity." I think, Doctor, that you will agree with me, that some more satisfactory test than this must be found of determining the certainty of our respective opinions. I am far from supposing that all the evidence is on my side, and none on yours. There are reasons in favour of Christianity as well as Atheism, and theological like legal differences must finally be adjusted as Burlamaqui directs—an account must be drawn up after balancing all the arguments, in order to see on which side the advantage lies.

Your eulogium on Christianity's liberality is that which its best friends frequently pronounce. You assure me that "it seeks investigation," and *I* believed it, until Mr. Justice Erskine undeceived me. You will remind me that this being but one instance, proves little, but I must refer you to passages in my former letters wherein I have treated this point fully, and I believe accurately.

The Infidels and Atheists whom you mention as having "lent themselves as tools of popery," and instruments of persecution, will find no sympathy with the avowed Infidels and Atheists of Great Britain, and I am sorry that you have not complied with my request, and furnished me with some clue whereby I might convey to them the abhorrence entertained here of their disgraceful conduct.

You are doubtless aware that persons are found attached to all parties, who have little in common with the majority save the name they bear. Men of this stamp may be found in Madeira, avowing themselves Infidels and Atheists, but they are no more to be esteemed as determining the character of their denomination, than Dr. Dodd, Lane Fox, and Herbert Marsh, are to be considered as deciding the character of British Christians. To account for the conduct of the parties you allude to, you beg me to bear in mind, the *impossibility* of attaining *rational certainty* in Infidelity or Atheism. I might answer you by asking whether believing Christians, who, in your opinion, have all "rational certainty" on their side, *never* "lent themselves as tools for gain"? I might remind you of the candid declaration of Bishop Kidder, that " were a wise man to choose a religion by the practices of its professors, perhaps Christianity would be the last he would select." But this would be recriminatory, unworthy ground for you and me to debate upon.

Adjacent to this is the more useful question—is not morality independent of belief in a deity? In my opinion, the courtesy we have received at your hands, as well as the usefulness of your medical life, are owing to more enduring principles than those which theism furnishes. I shall never expect you to tell me that you are a faithful friend or an honourable citizen, because such virtues are written in your bible or included in your creed, and that if, when you cease to believe in a god, you shall no longer be an affectionate husband or a kind father. The attractions of loveliness and truth were antecedent to the fabled precepts of Christ, or the commandments of Moses; and the principles of morality were understood irrespective of the speculations of piety which have so needlessly disturbed the world.

It is of no consequence that you are precluded from prepaying your communications —the pleasure we derive from this correspondence is not to be estimated by the postage of the letters.

If it was not an unofficial expression, I should subscribe myself—yours affectionately

G. JACOB HOLYOAKE,
Sec. to the Anti-Persecution Union.

P.S.—We must not omit to congratulate you on the defeat of your persecutors and your return to liberty. We sincerely trust that your application to the Lisbon government for compensation will be successful.

G. J. H.

REVIEW.

A SMALL pamphlet has just issued from the press, entitled *Law Breaking Justified,* by *Matilda Roalfe.* As this is the incipient effort of this writer, it would not be fair to expect great merit. But it may be said in this pamphlet's praise, that it exhibits a vivacity of expression not usual in a first performance. It treats an important and exciting subject, and communicates information respecting the opinions of many of the ancients upon "law-breaking," which will both interest and instruct. It compares the conduct of Infidels and the Free Church people of Scotland relative to law-breaking, where conscience is concerned, with excellent effect. Several detached parts of the pamphlet are good, but as a whole it is defective in precision. It is not sufficiently clear whether it is law breaking in general, or particular, which is justified. The reader can guess what is intended, but this is too much to leave to conjecture. Law breaking, like lying, if permissable, must be regarded as exceptional, and should be specified, defined, and limited in words of marble. Miss Roalfe really writes only in favour of breaking those laws which it is degrading to observe—laws which interfere with the respect which all men owe to conscience and to truth. It is almost unnecessary to say, that these laws, wherever they exist, have been made by Christian men, and are enforced for Christian purposes.

In treating her subject, Miss Roalfe has relied too little on herself—she is characterised both by propriety and plain good sense, and she will find these a better foundation both of usefulness and reputation, than the most brilliant adscititious aids.

Next we have a pamphlet by *Mrs. Martin,* entitled *A Few Reasons for Renouncing Christianity,* alike distinguished by judicious arrangement and persuasive talent. The history of her religious experience, the rise and growth of her scepticism, is told in a manner that cannot fail to win believers to her opinions. Mrs. Martin writes *to* believers, and *for* believers, and being intimately acquainted with their thoughts and conduct, she is well fitted to succeed with them.

Her objections to the bible and to christianity are strikingly arranged, and put with that regard to brevity and precision so essential to a complete essay, which is designed not only to excite curiosity but to satisfy it. The subject treated under the head " what is christianity?" is really *christianity's mythological origin,* a section which contains a curious table of *all* the Jesus Christs which have appeared in the world, their fathers and mothers, and other particulars of their histories. The coincidences of Christian and Heathen mythology are by this means set forth, in an instructive and convincing manner. At the conclusion of the book, a list of the Personal and Social Duties is given—thus, after inducing the renunciation of christianity, its better substitute, the practice of morality, is very properly supplied. The Social Duties named are *Forbearance, Instruction* and *Benevolence.* But should not Justice be written in the place of forbearance? Justice is a nobler virtue, and often renders forbearance unnecessary.

Forbearance is defined as "neither inflicting, nor vindictively resenting an injury." But if forbearance is a virtue it can only be when we have a right to *bear on*, when we refrain from inflicting what we are justified in inflicting. Now we have no right to inflict an injury or *vindictively* resent one. Genuine forbearance is not precisely of the nature ascribed to it here.

A forcible contrast to Mrs. Martin's placid and argumentative *Reasons* is—"*I am an Infidel; why are you a Christian?* by C. Southwell." This is an eccentric book—full of bold assertions, dashing criticisms, and unconnected arguments, better calculated to create sensation than conviction. An expression such as "More power to 'em, I say, with all my heart and liver to boot," only requires a little *lights* thrown upon it to make it a flower of rhetoric worthy of the shambles. This is careless—especially as *another* may have to defend such expressions—and not unlikely, as Miss Roalfe is the publisher, it may fall to her lot. The criticisms on Emerson, Watson, and others are in Mr. Southwell's cogent style. To the dogma of Emerson that "the aim of all science is, to find a theory of nature," Mr. Southwell correctly replies, "the aim of all science is, *dominion over natural things and not a theory which will account for them.*" The manner in which Emerson, in his erroneous admiration of christianity, "degrades nature by establishing its dependencies on spirit," is exposed with equal ability. Such smart things are spread over every page, that it should, when it reaches a second edition, be entitled *Part I of the "Katterfelto,"* as more appropriate than its present title.

Christianity Proved Idolatry is a larger work by the same author, and contains a useful digest of the Diegesis, and the concentrated essence of Paine. He would be a Diogenes, who should desire to exclude sprightliness and wit from argument, but the greatest patron of vivacity would suspect some expressions in this book of too great flippancy. Some critics have thought that a succinct arrangement by which the reader might easily find his way through the mazes of mythological christianity would have been a great improvement in the book. Undoubtedly it would—but Mr. Southwel is not to be judged with severity on this account—unless he pretends to the rigid precision of logic, rigidity is not to be expected from him. He has this rare merit, that the vivacity and good sense of his remarks, generally atone for the want of method. His excellence consists rather in what he says, than the order in which he says it. There is a freshness and an effectiveness in his style which belongs to no other Infidel writer of the day. It cannot be denied, however, that in both Mr. Southwell's last works he has relied more on his reputation than his talents for their success —but that they will well repay perusal is beyond question.

Probably some persons will regard the preceding remarks as cynical, rather than as unbiassed. To such, we say read and judge for yourselves. The reviewer, like a magistrate, is bound to decide by the evidence presented, and by the evidence alone. Like Aristides, he must, when justice requires it, decide against his interest; or like Brutus declare against his affections. This may seem like parading exalted virtues for trifling purposes, but unless an impartial spirit is found in criticism, we shall never improve each other nor will the public respect our opinions, or profit by our exertions. To the writers it may become one's duty to censure, I commend the consolation of Hume, that "the good fortune of a book and a man are not the same, and that it is a great unhappiness for an author who is never blamed or censured."

G. J. H.

SLOW ADVANCES OF REASON.—A methodistical sermon about heaven and hell and damnation, may make a dozen converts in an hour; but a sober address to the reasoning faculties of man, though it may convince him, will not always influence his conduct, nor impel him to attempt the conversion of others. Truth makes few proselytes compared to error. Imagination has a wide dominion, that of reason is very limited. Ten thousand believe in the inventions of the one, for ten that rely on the deductions of the other. Hence it is that I have very small hopes of living to see morality get rid of religion; though I am convinced that religion reconciles some men to the evils of this world by the hopes of a better, and thus becomes the foe of morality.—*Burdon.*

RELIGION'S EFFECTS.—The wretched man who, a few days ago, hammered in the brains of three of his children and drowned the fourth, was a preacher of Christ's blessed gospel, and accomplished his bloody tragedy in the *hope of going to heaven.* When committed to take his trial for his revolting murders, he went to jail *singing psalms,* and no doubt he will "die in the sure and certain hope of a glorious resurrection." Yet people exclaim against us as extravagant for denouncing religion!

Is it extravagant to denounce the murder of helpless children, and that system of horrid faith which makes men monsters?

NOTICE TO ATHEISTS.

The Atheistical Society will hold its next monthly meeting on Tuesday evening the 8th, at eight o'clock, at the Parthenium, St. Martin's-lane, to discuss the following question:— "Whether Atheists ought to take the usual oath administered in our Courts of Law;" to admit members, and to receive subscriptions and donations.

The rules of the society are printed in No. 2 of the *Beacon.*

THOS. POWELL, *Sec.,*
40, Holywell-street, Strand.

A MEETING of the Committee of the Anti-Persecution Union will be held on Monday evening, May 6th, at half-past eight, in Hudson's coffee-house, Upper Wellington-street, Covent-garden.

A FRIEND has Vols. I and II of the *Oracle of Reason* complete, but not bound, which he will dispose of for 10s., and give the price to the funds of the Anti-Persecution Union.

COMMON sense cannot enable men to judge, where the experience of common life cannot be applied.—*Drummond.*

TO CORRESPONDENTS.

M. A. L.—Unless an agent can be found in Bath, there is no way of supplying Mr. M. except by post.

JAS. MONK is thanked for his extract—it may be hereafter available.

H. COOK.—It would not be good taste to insert in the *Movement* anything so complimentary as his enclosure.

ENQUIRER.—The "Essay on Superstition," by Plutarchus, is by the same author as "Plutarch's Lives."

M. R.—His reply to A. T. has saved us some trouble.

D. MAC DONALD.—No order has yet been obtained from the Prison Board for permission to see Mr. Paterson. The parties in Perth should apply at the Gaol, and if refused memorialize the Prison Board for permission.

W. BROOM.—A friend has informed us that he is the author of two unintelligible letters at our office, moreover, we are told they are interesting. We wish those who say so were obliged to prove it by disciphering them.

INQUISITIVE. — The lines he refers to have never appeared in their complete state. They were written by our old friend Allen Davenport, and are as follows:—

GOD AND NATURE.

You ask me what is God? and I
Am no wise puzzled to reply;
My inward lights so clearly shine,
That heavenly things I can define;
And can, though but a finite creature,
Tell what is God, and what is Nature.
Whatever can be seen and felt,
Whatever can be heard and smelt,
Whatever can be tasted, and
All that the mind can understand,
All that our wisdom can conceive,
All that in which we can believe,
All o'er which fancy ever trod
Is Nature! all besides is God!
This solves at once the mighty riddle,
And breaks the metaphysic fiddle,
On which the priest performs so clever,
And settles what is God for ever. A. D.

A PHILALETHEAN.— Mr. Gillespie has informed us that his reply to Mr. Southwell's "Fallacies," like Mr. S.'s "Refutation," will be in two parts, and that the first will occupy a *Movement.* It will doubtless be an able article, and though it will inconvenience us to insert it whole we shall endeavour to do so.

Since writing this answer, Part I of Mr. Gillespie's "Reply" has arrived, but it will not fill a *Movement.* It is a perfect gem of terseness and order.

For M. Q. R. from "W. J." . £0 5 0
For Mr. Finlay from "W. J." . 0 3 0

SUBSCRIPTIONS TO THE ANTI-PERSECUTION UNION.

Mr. Yeomans and Friends .	£0	1 6
J. G. Hibbard, Mansfield .	0	1 0
H., per Mr. Watson . .	0	1 0
Per Mr. Ivory, card 34:—		
Spinoza	0	5 0
H. E. J.	0	2 6
H. Ivory	0	1 0
Several	0	1 6
Per Mr. Mellor, Oldham:—		
Friends by John Harrop .	0	3 4
Do. by James Mellor . .	0	3 0
Ambrose Wright . .	0	1 0
Alexander Boyd . .	0	2 6
A. T., Edinburgh . .	1	0 0
A Friend, per G. J. H. . .	0	6 0

G. J. H., *Sec.*

Printed and Published by G. J. HOLYOAKE, 40, Holywell-street, Strand, Saturday, May 4, 1844.

THE MOVEMENT

And Anti=Persecution Gazette.

"Maximize morals, minimize religion."—BENTHAM.

| No. 22. | EDITED BY G. JACOB HOLYOAKE, ASSISTED BY M. Q. RYALL. | PRICE 1½d |

ABERNETHY'S DEMONSTRATION OF THE EXISTENCE OF GOD.

A BOOK frequently put into the hands of Atheists for the purpose of their conversion, is "Abernethy's Discourses on God." This rev. gentleman was a Master of Arts, and, on the title page of his work, professes to do no less a thing than "demonstrate, *plainly*, the existence of a Deity." His "Discourses" are in high repute among the clergy of the established church, and though his performance is not deficient in ability of a theological cast, it is difficult to believe that the man was not "cracked"—he writes with such simplicity as justifies the suspicion that he either did not know what a demonstration was, or that he believed that Atheists did not.

When in Gloucester Gaol, the Rev. Mr. Cooper the chaplain, with many eulogiums on its value and erudition, put this same work into my hands, 1 can, therefore, if I can find my extracts and remember my impressions, comply with the wishes of some theological correspondents, who desire, for some reason or other, my opinion of Mr. Abernethy's production.

A choice specimen of the artlessness of which I have spoken occurs in page 3, Sermon 2. He says—"Some mechanic philosophers, even who profess to believe a Deity, have made too near approaches to Atheism; at least, too much served its cause by pretending to explain all the phenomena of the external world, without any divine interposition."

One of the grand and most often repeated objections of divines to the Atheistic scheme, is what they term its inability to explain the phenomena of nature—they say "without our theology all is cimmerian darkness;" but here we have one of the cloth letting out the secret, that they conserve the darkness that they may complain of it. What is dark must be kept dark, that theology may appear light. If philosophers would illuminate the world with science and reason, they must not do it because Atheists will not then feel the want of "divine interposition." The theologian resembles the man who should come into a brilliantly lighted saloon and exclaim—"Turn off that gas that you may see what a light my taper will make."

The next display of our Master of Arts is in these words in Ser. 7, p. 217-18.

"But least of all can we form any adequate notion of the Supreme Being himself. Not only the absolute perfections of his nature cannot be thoroughly understood by us, but we have no immediate perception of them, as we have of other objects. We have distinct ideas of sensible qualities, such as the figure and magnitude of bodies, and a direct intuitive knowledge of our rational faculties and operations, we have, also, very clear apprehensions of moral qualities, as of *goodness, justice, and gratitude. But of the divine, peculiar, and incommunicable attributes, necessary existence, eternity and immensity, we have not, nor are capable of forming any positive idea.*"

Was there ever ignorant presumption equal to this of the Rev. J. Abernethy, in pretending on the title pages of three volumes, to "demonstrate the existence of God to the plainest comprehension," when he knew that he should have to write the passage just quoted. If men are "least of all able to form an adequate notion of the Supreme Being himself," if neither "his perfections nor his nature can be understood by us"—if his "attributes are wholly incommunicable"—if "of his exisence we are incapable of forming any positive idea"—in the name of all the "Arts" of which Mr. Abernethy is "Master," how can he *demonstrate* God's existence? Not only does this confuter of Atheists confess himself, and convince us, of his own utter inability to do what he pretends, but he admits that which proves, that could he establish his dogmas, they would be of no use. If "we have sensible ideas of all sensible things" —if we "possess direct knowledge of our rational faculties and their *operations*"—if we have "*very clear* apprehensions of goodness, justice, and gratitude"—what need we possess or know more? If we can be "good, and grateful, and just," without the gods— what can they add to our virtue, our knowledge, or our usefulness? Why need we perplex ourselves about their "incommunicable attributes and eternally contested existence?"

I shall conclude this brief critique, by one other short quotation from Master Abernethy, of which, by way of introduction, it is unnecessary to say more than that it is worthy to bear company with those that have gone before, and worthy of Mr. Abernethy. He concludes one of his sermons with these words:— "We must abandon the Atheistic scheme, and have recourse to an intelligent cause which has deeply interwoven into the human constitution a sense of things entirely independent of matter and all its properties and powers."

We may well abandon "Atheistic schemes" after what Mr. Abernethy has propounded of Theologic schemes! An "intelligent cause" —of which, according to Mr. Abernethy, we have no intelligence whatever—"has interwoven into our constitution a sense of things entirely independent of matter"—that is a sense of *things* entirely independent of *things.* After this notable revelation, nothing remains but that we pack up our atheistical knapsacks and start on a pilgrimage to the tomb of the Rev. J. Abernethy, M.A., and do penance for the oblivion in which we have lived.

G. J. H.

SUPPLEMENTARY OBSERVATIONS ON THE DUTY OF THE CONGRESS FOR 1844.

(*To the Editor of the Movement.*)

SIR,—On looking over my letter as it appears in print, I think I may, without impropriety, hazard a few additional remarks on the duty of the Rationalist Congress for the present year, and therefore, in this letter, I shall apply myself to the consideration of the intellectual and pecuniary means of the working classes for the establishment of co-operating Home Colonies.

No one, who is at all acquainted with Mr. Owen's life, can suppose that he has anything of the miser about him, but on the contrary, must know that he is a complete spendthrift when forwarding his own plans of human regeneration, and for this reason, he is not the man to be trusted with the expenditure of the money of the poorer classes. He seems to overlook the cost of anything he requires as though it were a matter of no moment, hence the loss of his own large fortune, hence the social panic of 1842, and hence his anxiety to enlist in the cause the capitalist portion of British society, and hence also his depreciation of the powers (intellectual and otherwise,) of the working class, and his declarations of their incapability of emancipating themselves from competition's thraldom. I maintain that the working classes of this country are not only more likely to carry out the Rational System than any other class, but that they are the best qualified to do so from their past and present position. They are more likely to do so because they have a greater interest in the change, and because they are the only parties to any considerable extent, who have paid any attention to the subject; they are better qualified to realise the practices of the Rational System because they have had, with few exceptions, all that experience that Mr. Owen usually places to the account of those who have the profits of their labour. Should this be disputed by any of your readers, I beg them to consider for a moment, who are the parties that practically manage all the large productive operations of this country. Are they those who receive the profits of capital at the rate of five to one hundred per cent? Not they indeed; the profit is not gained *by* them, but *for* them by the "foremen" they employ. And who are these "foremen" but the most experienced among the despised and oppressed working men? Nor do the capitalists select their managers from their *own* skill in the business, for they are guided in their decisions by the opinions of the *favourite* men in their employ. A man gets "a character from his last place" and chooses or recommends those employed under him, this is the way things are generally managed. I say, therefore, to the self-sufficient theorist, despise not the skill of the working class, for to them are the capitalists of Britain indebted for becoming the commercial Alexanders of the world. It will no doubt be gravely asked, if the working classes have such qualifications as I contend for, how is it that they have not done anything for themselves? to which I answer, that it is the *multiplicity* of their qualifications that has prevented it, for these acquirements have created amongst them a fierce competition for employment, unequalled in the history of society. Besides it is not a fact that nearly all the measures of progressive reform originate with *them,* and that none are carried out without their aid? I say again, let no man despise them, for it is adding insult to injustice. But it will be urged, look at the manners of the working classes; I grant that there is room for improvement in this and many other respects, but the same may be said of every other class in society. Does any one in his senses suppose that the Irish fighting Attorney-General was any the better man because he sent a polite note to his adversary, informing him that he wished for a *polite*, a *polished* opportunity of shooting him through the head? Was he any better than the Irish brawler who drags his coat along the ground at fairs, asking some one to tread upon it that he may fight him for it? I should think not. For myself, I would rather endure the momentary outbursts of passion from the working classes, than have to do with the cool, "polished," smothered, but lasting, malignity of the higher class. Let us not be led away by appearances—all is not gold that glitters—all is not refined in manners that appears to be so. Rest assured that a *polished* phraseology often hides a malignant heart; besides this, the wealthy classes of society require no change—they know but little of, and *care* still less for, the misery that surrounds them—they have the monetary means, but not the moral will to do anything for mankind. By some, it will be said that this is a libel upon their character, because they give a good deal away to the societies established for the relief and improvement of the poor; but what are these gifts after all, but a return of a very small portion of that which ought never to have been taken away? If a large portion of the working classes of this country were fully convinced of the necessity for, and the advantages of, the Rational System, they, in my opinion, could find the means to carry out the *moderate plans* of the Rational Society; but as yet they are not so convinced, nor has the founder of the system done anything of late years to gain their confidence, but rather the reverse. The pecuniary resources of the industrious classes are not to be despised, for though they may not amount to much per individual, still their numbers enables them to command a large amount of the £ s. d. argument. The working classes are the worst treated members of society, and for them therefore ought the rationalist first to provide. No loss need attend this beginning at the right end, for communities might be established on the self-supporting and self-extending principle. I do not say to the wealthy, give the working classes anything, but *lend* them the means of obtaining something for themselves. In concluding this subject, allow me to say that I think you misunderstand Mr. Owen, when you suppose he intended the £700,000 plan of community for the working class. The development plans are addressed, both as regards the collection and expenditure of funds, to those who are already well to do in the world, and not for those who labour for their daily bread. These, of necessity, from the *expensiveness* of the plans, play but a very subordinate part, and for this reason I conclude that your pecuniary argument in the *Movement*, No. 18, does not deal justly with the question; be that as it may, I am, yours fraternally in the cause of human happiness,

A LECTURER OF SEVEN YEARS STANDING.

[It is like this "lecturer's" impudence to suppose that I can "misunderstand" anything. But has it not been an understood thing that Tytherly is to be moulded into a home colony of the development's dimensions? A million of money has been asked for that purpose. The Home Colonization Company take the Development as their building bible, and this same company has long had the affairs of the society in their hands, and no humbler object than £700,000 communities has yet been avowed. The buildings at Harmony have not been designed for "foremen" and the "working classes." Mr. Owen never dreams of anything less than the home colonies I cited, and never will, and he is president of the society and invested with powers which cannot be called in question with impunity. That colonies less expensive than those of the Development, can be established, and made better to answer all necessary purposes, I believe with the "lecturer," and my aim in instancing the calculations I did, was to induce Congress to adopt such as their objects.—ED. of M.]

PRACTICAL DIRECTIONS ON PETITIONS.

DEAR SIR,—I have been reading over what you say respecting petitions and petitioning, and as I consider the subject of the utmost importance I shall take the liberty of making a remark or two. In the first place, I do not think that presenting petitions will effect much more than serve to enlighten our legislators and the public in general, and if it does even this, a great object will be attained. Every opportunity that offers must, therefore, be taken to get up petitions, and if any one is neglected it will shew that we have not done our duty to ourselves and others. It is not necessary that a petition should be numerously signed, as it is not the number of signatures that will avail, but the number of petitions presented. At the time of petitioning for the abolition of slavery, I saw lots of them brought up, written upon half a sheet of common foolscap paper, with very few signatures attached, and these answered the purpose as well as if they had been written on parchment, and signed by thousands, they increased the number, and that was all that was required to go forth to the public; they were then thrown under the table and no more was heard of them. This first opened my eyes to the delusion of petitioning, and saved me a great deal of time and money, which otherwise would have been expended on them. In our case I would advise you to publish a short form of a petition, such as Cobbett did for a reform in Parliament, *something in this style,* headed in the *usual* form, and in *no other,* for "what's in a name;" we must *humble ourselves* if we wish our prayer granted. It's no use "cutting off our nose to vex our face," and, if in doing so we considered we *degraded* ourselves in the slightest degree, I should be the last man on earth to submit to it; but when so much *good* may arise to our fellow-creatures for only following a *settled form,* I do not think we are acting wrong in complying in matters of so trivial a nature. "To the Honourable the Commons of the United Kingdom of Great Britain and Ireland in Parliament assembled. The petition of the undersigned inhabitants of the parish of ———, Humbly Sheweth, That, your petitioners consider that every man ought to enjoy civil and religious liberty in its fullest extent without the fear of being fined and imprisoned.

"That your petitioners are of opinion that the recent convictions of Messrs. Paterson, Finlay, and Miss Roalfe, in Scotland, for blasphemy, are an infringement on the liberty of conscience and the rights of man, and that your petitioners under this conviction, pray that your Honourable House may abrogate all laws interfering with the freedom of opinion, and all enactments or regulations relative to blasphemy.

"And, your petitioners, as in duty bound, will ever pray."

This, or a similar petition, must be signed on the same sheet by more or less of the petitioners, and if necessary, an additional sheet may be attached for any additional names. It can be forwarded by post, if under, I believe, eight ounces, (which you can know at the post office,) and put under cover like a newspaper, both ends open, and addressed to some liberal member of Parliament, who will present it; and then it's *your part* to copy it in the *Movement,* and mention its having been presented by such a member. It is no use sending one to the Lords, as no notice is ever taken of such petitions by *their* reporters. I would fain hope if this plan be adopted, that many petitions will be forwarded before this session is over. I would recommend you and all those who have been imprisoned to forward *individual* petitions, signed by *each* of you, mentioning that having suffered imprisonment you pray for the abolition of the blasphemy laws in consequence.

You will find it will be of no use applying for remission of punishment to poor Paterson, &c., therefore, it is loss of time to wait long in expectation of it. I am so impressed with the importance of petitioning, that I would let this be the petitioning year, as O'Connell would say the Repeal year. Your remarks in a late number will surely have some effect on the Socialists, and induce them to alter their plans. You have demonstrated the necessity of their doing so in a manner that I think likely to carry conviction to every one.

I have received the last number of the "Trials," which will do much good if put into the hands of the community at large, and this can be done by reducing the price as low as possible; I would willingly contribute my mite, say 20s., for this purpose, if it would contribute to so desirable an end. Could money be sent to any one except yourself? if so, let me know. Your name must be well known to the post office authorities; and I know it was said, in 1798, that government opened letters and sealed them again.

N.B.—Keep the "Trials" out of the way for fear of being carried off. What a loss the cause sustained by Carlile's works being taken away, and left to the world.

A DISTANT FRIEND.

[With respect to reducing the price of the "Scotch Trials," the suggestion has been tried before with Mr. Paterson's Trial for Placard Blasphemy in London, which is now sold at 6d., but the effect has been to injure the sale of the "Scotch Trials." Purchasers have said, on seeing the numbers—"O, wait a bit, they will reduce the price when they are complete." But these gentry will be disappointed for once. The Anti-Persecution Union will have no objection to give copies away if enabled to do so, and our "Distant Friend" will be pleased to hear that parcels have been sent to the Scottish Union to be distributed among the editors, judges, procurators, sheriffs, and other functionaries that they may see that somebody makes these matters public, and that no one does an infamous thing to a conscientious blasphemer without the Anti-Persecution Union letting posterity know of it. —ED. of M.]

A VOICE FROM THE CHRISTIANS' DEN.
General Prison, Perth,
April, 1844.

DEAR HOLYOAKE.—Should have written before, but having sent a note to the "Board," requesting liberty to purchase other books, I waited their answer. The governor says that I am at liberty to communicate with you as often as is necessary on business connected with petitioning, &c., but his time would not allow of him examining letters of a trifling description, so that *now* you may avail yourself of it, if need be.

These two weeks back I have felt myself unable to think, and can hardly bear to write this letter. You are not to suppose me melancholy, for that would be incorrect; but my body being much weaker, has produced a corresponding frame of thought, so that, when my work is over, I am more inclined to lie down than read, unless it was some trifling tale. I see it is April *from the dates on the letters*, and by deep and much sagacious reasoning, I have concluded it to be spring, the time when people set oaks in black tea-pots, and turnips in green tin boxes; but, alas! how am I to get on suitably to the season? I have been trying botany, but I could not succeed for want of something *green*, an indispensible requisite in that science; however, I did the best in my power, I took *myself* as a specimen of the " ever-green," although differing in trivial points from the plant of that name, still, there appeared a general resemblance sufficiently strong to enable me to class myself as one of the *genus*. I am now settled down into a regular zoophyte, without any, or much locomotion, or much circulation of blood; hence my antipathy to write or think—or whether I am at present only in a caterpillar state, and may yet emerge like a butterfly, Chilton and his " Theory of Regular Gradation" only can determine.

I sent my " Petition" off the very day the form arrived here, but as accidents, may, and do happen to letters here at times, you had better make direct application to Mr. Hume on the subject.

Your letter to the " Board" is very good, so far as I am concerned, but I cannot think your " application for my alleviation" placed on such high grounds as it might have been; personal pity never goes far. This is only my notion, and I must thank you and the Union for the great trouble you have taken in the matter, but as I have myself written again to the " Board," and they have refused all but books—(they have allowed me to purchase *any* of Chambers' works); it will, I think, be of no use troubling *them* farther on the matter. Please yourself, however, as I cannot tell how things stand.

Talbert says, he " should like me to find out a cousin of his somewhere in Perth, but forgot the address." I would run into the town some day for him, but it looks so vulgar, inquiring for a person without an address.

Sorry to hear of " Frederick's" death—often think of that Sunday last spring, when we were all together,—pity, poor fellow!

Enclose a list of what books the governor has purchased for me; you will perceive I am in his debt considerably.

As I have now a stock of books and paper, should you think well to address the board again, abstinence from labour is the greatest request they could now grant. Books without that, they must surely see, is condemning me to the fate of Tantalus. T. P.

P.S. Letters received from 10th March. Mr. Liddle, 4.—Merrin, 2. — Chilton, 1 Emery, 1.—Hammond, 4.—G. J. H., 6.— Palfreyman,1.—Campbell, Ham, 1.—Clark, 1 —Talbert, 1.—Mrs. Adams, 1.—Harral,1.

INSANITY.
Manchester.

MR. EDITOR.—In No. 16 of the *Movement*, is an article signed " Arthur Trevelyan," the object of which is to prove that the whole human race are afflicted with *Insanity*, and lest it should be taken for granted that Atheists necessarily hold such opinions, I beg to offer a few remarks in opposition to A. T's. theory. I take the liberty of doing so, not having as yet seen any refutation in the *Movement*.

The individual who ventures to assert that the whole of the human race are in a state of insanity, although he will be unable to convince mankind of their madness, will find few who will have any doubts of his folly. To invent new meanings for old words to support some favourite doctrine, is a trick more worthy of a priest than a philosopher.

Insanity, as the word is generally understood, means a loss of that mental capacity once possessed by the individual; therefore no one can be insane who has not at some former period been sane.

The assertion of the *Phrenological Journal*, viz. "No human mind is in its right state," is not the language of philosophy but of superstition—Christianity asserts the same thing in the doctrine of original sin—we do not hear the professors of any other science talk such nonsense. The astronomer, the chemist in his study of nature, draws conclusions solely from his knowledge, *but for an individual to know that the human mind is not in its right state, he must have had experience of mind existing in a right state.*

Perfection is no more than ideal, hence not applicable to the operations of nature; there is no definite idea of perfection, no fixed scale for discovering its identity.

It would indeed be a lamentable fact that the world was a mad-house, and that human beings were its inmates. This is decidedly inferior to the ideas of christian writers, when they proclaim man a crawling worm, a walking hospital, or trodden grass.

Although my opinion may be ascribed to ignorance, still I cannot admit the soundness of the assertion contained in the concluding paragraph; the phrenologist can by an examination of the head, form a pretty correct estimate of the strength of an individual's passions, and his capacity to receive moral and intellectual cultivation, but it is absurd to say that his opinions, (or his morals, which in a great degree depend upon his opinions,) can be known by any examination of the head, both opinions and morals are formed and altered without any change of the appearance of the skull, consequently rendering it impossible to form any judgment by an examination of it. I myself am an illustration in point—twelve months ago, I was a firm believer in the christian religion, and now not only reject christianity, but am as fully convinced that there is no God as I once felt certain there was such an existence. I am, your respectfully, M. R.

CHRISTIANITY A BARRIER TO POLITICAL LIBERTY.

Some persons have fallen into the very great mistake of supposing christianity to have had a favourable effect in the promotion of political liberty. Though Guizot advocates this opinion, it is not on that account any nearer the truth. This writer argues that christianity—by its representing all men as equal before God—by its levelling all worldly distinctions with reference to the eternity before us — has had a tendency to elevate the political condition of the masses. But whether we look at what this religion has done, or view its doctrines to ascertain what it was likely to do, and free our minds from prejudice, we shall see that it has been, and from its nature must be, the friend of despots. Whenever tyrants wanted a justification of their evil doings, the word of God, and the ministers of that word, were at hand to defend their proceedings. Can it be forgotten, that until a comparatively recent period, the doctrine of the divine right of kings was deemed an indisputable portion of the teachings of the sacred volume? Can any one be ignorant of the fact that, at this day in the nations of Europe, where absolute monarchy is the form of government, the same odious principle is inculcated from the Bible. Can we be oblivious to the fact, that the people have, in every age, been discouraged in their efforts for political and social emancipation, by the threats of priests. The Bible, by its delineations of the character of deity—by its narrations of his arbitrary and capricious controul of the affairs of his dominion, and the government of the kingdom of heaven—by its precepts of unconditional submission to the powers that be, of non-resistance to rulers, however vile, does most assuredly constitute a prop and strong support to the enslavers of the millions of our race. Am I not borne out in the opinion I have advanced, by what orthodox christianity tells us regarding human nature? We are all wicked, says orthodoxy, at birth, we come into existence full of uncleanness, and as soon as we have breathed one breath we stand in the need of a redeemer—all the tendencies of our being are towards evil—our activity is the activity of depravity,—for, "man is born to evil as the sparks fly upwards;" hence it is inferred that it would be madness to give beings, so constituted, any degree of liberty. They are fitted only for a strong government, and to be kept down. To give them the privilege of acting in accordance with the dictates of their own nature would be to let loose licentiousness and scatter every imaginable mischief. A wise and good individual requires not to be placed under an iron dispensation, for he is a law unto himself, and the wider the sphere of his activity the greater the distribution of benefits. Now religion treats us all as inherently wicked, and, consequent"y, freedom is not for us— and God has shown his wisdom in appointing rulers and authorities over us, with power to act in opposition to the will of the people. Commend me not to the Bible, or to the creeds of churches, from whence to draw any argument for pleading in behalf of prostrate humanity.

Ye friends and advocates of human rights stake not the success of your generous cause upon the unstable basis of religion! Confine not your efforts to the destruction of political corruption, but aim also at that by which it is chiefly supported. If we would be really free—if we would see earth an abode of real dignity, virtue, and smiling happiness, we must despise the reproaches of friends, and the contumely of enemies— break superstition's crosses, and blot out the authority of the tyrant's text book. Religion's red banner has waved too long over a suffering world—now is the time for tearing down the emblem of discord, and of placing in its stead the white flag of peace and cooperation; and then every wind that blows shall convey to men a sign and a message of approaching and hitherto unknown joy.

HENRY COOK.

PRO BONO PUBLICO!—The Society for the Investigation of Truth.—The above society will hold a Meeting at 48, Henry-street East, Portland-town, on Monday evening next, 15th of April, and on every succeeding Monday. The chair to be taken at eight o'clock precisely. All classes are respectfully invited to attend.

MRS. MARTIN writes to say that the writer of the Review last week, was in error in saying that she had given a table of *all* the Jesus Christs—she considers her table only a sample of them, and it hardly embraces a fortieth part of the Jesuses who have afflicted the world with their divinity.

PAUPER RANK.—If ordinary beggars are whipped, the daily beggars in fine clothes, out of proportionate respect to their quality, ought to be hanged.—*Saville.*

BALANCE SHEET OF THE ANTI-PERSECUTION UNION.

For the Quarter ending March 26, 1844.

RECEIPTS.	£	s.	d.		EXPENDITURE.	£	s.	d.
Dec. 26. To Balance in hand	11	2	1	Jan. 10 To Miss Roalfe		5	0	0
Movement No. 5, to Subscriptions	8	4	7	Mar. 23 Ditto		3	0	0
Do. 6, do.	0	3	0	Jan. 16 To Scottish Union		3	0	0
Do. 7, do.	0	19	6	Mar. 15 To ditto, for Mr. Finlay		3	0	0
Do. 8, do.	0	6	6	To Mr. Paterson		2	0	0
Do. 9, do.	2	8	6	The Assignee of Lee and Haddock, in settlement of claim for Machining and Wrappering Trial (of Mr. Paterson in London)		1	10	0
Do. 10, do.	1	17	9	Mar. 4 200 Subscription Cards, 300 Members' Tickets		0	12	6
Do. 11, do.	6	17	8	Mar. 30 100 Card Cases, lettered		1	10	0
Do. 12, do.	0	5	0	Jan. 15 To assistant Secretary, for services of past Quarter		2	0	0
Do. 13, do.	2	15	0	Mar. 30 To do. present Quarter		3	0	0
Do. 14, do.	6	13	2	Mar. 8 Carriage of *Oracles*, (presented by W. J. B.)		0	6	9
Do. 15, do.	1	11	6	Expences of Printing Weekly Acknowledgments, Reports of Meeting, and General Correspondence of Anti-Persecution Union		1	10	0
Do. 16, do.	2	7	4	Expenses of Petitions, Memorials, &c. on behalf of the Scottish victims		1	0	0
Do. 17, do.	0	10	0	To Papers and *Movements* for circulation, containing Special Articles, Circulars, Post Orders, Parcels to Institutions, Members of Parliament, to America, Editors of Papers, &c.		1	5	0
To Sale of "Scotch Trials"	9	0	0	Miscellanies at the desire of Mr. Paterson, copying Articles, &c.		0	6	6
Do. Members' Tickets	0	13	0	To Purchase of Newspapers, containing matters of interest for the Union		0	5	0
Balance due to Treasurer	1	3	8	General Correspondence, Transmissions of Cards, Cases, Members' Tickets, &c.		1	11	0
				Printing and Publishing 1250 copies of "Scotch Trials," wrappers, bills, advertisements, &c. &c.		28	4	6
	£57	1	3		£57	1	3

Audited by us, and } ALLEN DAVENPORT, } Auditors.
found correct,   } JOSHUA HOPKINS.   }

NOTE.—Properly this Balance Sheet should have appeared early in April, but it has been delayed in order to get in the printer's bills, that the "Scotch Trials" account might appear complete. Though only a limited number have been struck off if the sale equals anticipation, a profit will accrue to the Union.

Some have thought that the sole object of the Union is the support and defence of victims. This, though the principal, is not the only object. The Union also endeavours to create a better public opinion, and by means of public meetings, reports of trials, and diffusing "addresses," to establish in the thoughts of men a sense of the utility of free discussion. The expenditure of a portion of the Union's funds for this purpose is a wise economy, for by so doing we attack and eradicate the *causes* of prosecutions, and take the shortest course to the "fulfilment of our mission." Only to relieve victims would keep persecution under, but to enlighten the bigot and awaken in him a sense of justice, is to destroy it.

The item of Members' Tickets does not show the amount really received, as many tickets have been included in the remittances from various places, and are incorporated with sums acknowledged in the *Movement.*

G. JACOB HOLYOAKE, *Secretary.*

POST AND PROVIDENCE.
THEOLOGICAL JIM-CROWISM.

WHAT nice alliteration. Could anything run more glibly and come off more trippingly from the tongue than "Post and Providence ;" not the door post, nor a street post, nor a sign post, nor the general post—no, but the *Morning Post*—Jenkins's post, which is anything on earth but a general, being on the contrary, a very particular and exclusive *Post.* Well, this nice, exclusive, priggish, pious, and godly compound of a Mantalini, a Jenkins, a saint and a politician, has positively turned round upon its friend Providence, whom it had always stood by and defended through thick and thin. Thus it says—

"Lord Brougham admits the sufferings and privations of the working classes; but looking from the calm heights of his sublime philosophy, he declares that such misfortunes are the inevitable lot of human nature in all civilized society. He considers it quite absurd to expect that, by human means or by human laws, the legislature should mitigate or alter that condition and those hardships which are the inevitable consequences of the mysterious dispensations of an all-ruling Providence! Who can hear without disgust such sentiments as these from such a man ? Who can be without a feeling of regret and shame in beholding a man of such range of thought, and such energy of expression as Lord Brougham, addressing himself to the task of asserting the inevitableness of human toil, and suffering, and poverty, in the richest kingdom of the world? It is most disgraceful in a man circumstanced as he is to utter such sentiments. Will he have the effrontery to tell us next that, owing to 'the mysterious dispensations of an all-ruling Providence,' he must have £5,000 a-year out of the public treasury? That he must have a noble mansion in London, and give sumptuous entertainments there, suitable for the wealthiest aristocracy in the world?—that he must have a "hall" in the north, to soothe him in the hot weather of the summer, and a chateau in the south of France, to which he may betake himself in our early winter, lest haply the winds of heaven should visit his delicate face too roughly ? Must all these things, too, be thrown upon 'the mysterious dispensations of Providence,' bringing about these 'inevitable consequences?' Away with such monstrous and disgusting profanation of awful words! Let Lord Brougham strip himself of the wealth derived from the taxes—of the wealth which would comfortably support 100 labouring families, and which is spent by him in luxurious indulgence—let him do this, and then let him speak as calmly as he may of the inevitable hardships and sufferings of the poor."

Vaux left off his philosophy, and God was all the go,
The *Morning Post* turned tail, d'ye see,
And loudly called out—No—
Then wheel about and turn about and say just so,
Vaux Brougham took up Providence and Posty let him go.

LEGAL OPPRESSION—Of all injustice, that is the greatest which goes under the name of law, and of all sorts of tyranny, the forcing of the letter of the law against the equity is the most unsupportable.—*L'Estrange.*

MAHOMETAN, VERSUS CHRISTIAN THEOLOGY.—The Turks tell their people of a heaven where there are sensible pleasures, and of a hell where they shall suffer what they do not know. The Christians quite invert this order, they tell us of a hell where we shall suffer sensible pain, but of a heaven where we shall enjoy we cannot tell what. —*Selden.*

POLICY.—We find in Machiavel and Cardau, that Pope Gregory VII. caused most of the valuable works of the ancients to be burned. It was this Pope who burned the works of the learned Varro, to prevent St. Augustine from being accused of plagiarism, the saint having stolen from him the greater part of his treatise De Civitate Dei.—*Gabriel Vaude*, 1650.

IF we create imaginary wants, why do we not create imaginary satisfaction?—*Bulstrode.*

ATHEISTS.—Although Atheists do not believe in a Providence, yet do they not cease to follow, in very many cases, the rules of honesty. They neither steal, nor murder; they abhor lying; they keep their promises; they detest unjust wars, and love peace.— *The Jesuit Martinus Becanus.*

THE HEIGHT OF CREDULITY.—Listening to the ravings of a parson about Christ's sermon on the mount—of the injunction— "when a man has taken your coat give him your cloak also," and expecting that *he* will act on it.

TO CORRESPONDENTS.

GEORGE ATKINSON.—We cannot undertake to answer his question. Our attention has not been directed that way.

A SUBSCRIBER.— If the *Times* ascribes the ruin of the Dorey family to Carlile, we may, with equal propriety, ascribe the forgery of Dr. Dodd to Jesus Christ.

E.—Not able to attend.

Printed and Published by G. J. HOLYOAKE,
40, Holywell-street, Strand,
Saturday, May 11, 1844.

THE MOVEMENT
And Anti=Persecution Gazette.

"Maximize morals, minimize religion."—BENTHAM.

No. 23.　　　EDITED BY G. JACOB HOLYOAKE,　　　PRICE 1½d
　　　　　　　ASSISTED BY M. Q. RYALL.

MAN, THE GOD OF THE ANIMALCULÆ.

Is there a God? is the question so often asked, and so often attempted to be answered in the affirmative. But few know what they ask, and as few know what they answer. How wide is the question—Are there any other living beings besides those we are made acquainted with by our senses? What *is* a *living* being, would be almost as difficult to define as what is a god; there may be many beings inferior to us, and there may be as many superior to us whose existence we do not know; it is, however, easier to look below than it is above us. I will not say there are not superior creatures to man in the other planets. It appears to me that this world is a superior being to me; it is a creature, and I know it has a longer existence than I have, if that is life; but whether it is intelligent I cannot tell. Perhaps it may be intelligent, and I have as much speculation about it and the stars, as the dog has in looking into our faces and watching our movements; or perhaps ourselves and the world resemble more nearly the animalculæ on our bodies. What observations they take of us we cannot tell. Perhaps they may live on us quite unacquainted with the fact that we are locomotive beings. If the world be not intelligent, then is an unintelligent body, a being, an existence that has motion vastly superior to mine, which is said to be gifted with mind, soul, and intellect. There are many things which surround us very superior to our intelligence. Some animals may be aware of human intelligence, even children acquiesce in the mental superiority of their parents. But there are many existences which cannot be aware of our intelligence, I doubt whether the flies and insects are, and most probably lesser beings do not know any thing about our intelligence. Analogy, therefore, would warrant us in supposing that there are beings intelligent, such as the world and stars, whom we do not know as such. This analogy may have made the savages personify all appearances, and believe that the sun, moon and stars, rain and wind, and the elements in whatever way they presented themselves, really lived and thought. The animalculæ on our bodies may have a very reverend idea of us, and think the flesh they are eating, and all the unknown properties and accidents which may affect them very surprising. They may be all worshipping away of idols and idolaters, there may be no end belonging to us. Some may be wiser, jump to first causes, talk of the all-wise, omnipotent, benevolent spirit of a great infusoria, that by its superintending providence manages all the concerns of such mortals as themselves. " This perfect one made us," they would say, " and it is not possible, that having given us so wonderful a life, such a place of existence so wonderfully adapted to our natures, such countless benefits and reverses, that he will not give our disembodied spirits eternal rest and happiness in a superior creation." They could not think that a man made animalculæ any more than we think the world made us; they propagate each other as we do each other, and therefore by induction, they must suppose some " great one" of their species made them all, as we suppose one " great being," whose image we are, made us all. If they became fully acquainted with the nature of the men and world they live on, and the rest of men and worlds moving about, they would not trouble their heads much about their mythologies, and religions. They would at once see their worship and their prayers had been in vain, their secondary causes and their first cause, their reason and their faith. It would be of no use addressing man, for he had not power over his own body, he only lived, and he died like them over a little more extent of time and space. He was mortal, nor did he know what was immortal, except the matter common to both; he lived on a world, the nature of which he did not know more than they did of the body which they had conceived to be their world. They would find they had been exactly bounded where we had been, we knew nothing beyond ourselves, and they knew nothing. Both might believe in superior beings without knowing anything more about them. One of the animalculæ supposing he had this revelation, would believe in the life and intellect of man, the life of beasts and their reason and instinct, he would be acquainted with the flight of birds and the diving of fishes, and all crawling things from the man to the worm, he that had before thought all had been dead matter, merely made for him to live upon, would come to this supernatural knowledge. Still we doubt whether he would be the happier, or we if we saw all the universe brought near to our senses, and full of life, motion, and intelligence—life, motion, and intelligence, which forebode danger to us every moment, and which caused our coming in and going out of the world—life and intelligence in us which act upon all existence below, voluntarily and involuntarily, without their knowing it, and without our knowing what acts upon us from above. Yet all animate creation below are certain that they have in their hands life and death, as we have a certain proportion of free-will overruled by higher causes and by necessity. Knowledge in both cases, whether by reason or revelation, would only prove that as the wiser went from immediate to more distant causes, so the wisest could only come to the conclusion there is no god, if that means a first principle, a beginning, an intelligence, a man creator, a power, an identity, a separate existence from matter.

It will not suffice to say that as the animalculæ know nothing of us, but may suppose man on which they live to be a first cause, as the atheist supposes the universe to be—yet had the animalculæ more knowledge they would be obliged to admit that man was but an effect of something superior—as the atheist may find the universe to be. The argument is this, that supposing the animalculæ from their nature cannot know that man is an effect, they are not warranted in inferring anything superior—therefore man being in the same situation, is not warranted in supposing anything superior to the universe. We are not justified in inferring conclusions from what we *may* know, but from what we *do* know. W. J. B.

THE GOD OF NATURE AND THE GOD OF THE BIBLE IDENTICAL.

The perusal of "A few Reasons for Renouncing Christianity, and Professing and Disseminating Infidel Opinions, by Emma Martin," has suggested to me sundry considerations which may prove useful to the readers of the *Movement*, generally—or at least tend to promote a better understanding than now exists, of the identity of the God of Nature and the God of the Bible.

Emma Martin is an unfeminine thinker, whose productions exhibit a happy mixture of self-relying talent and energy, which if infused into one tithe of the "weaker sex," would falsify the text—"her desire shall be towards her husband, who *shall rule over her*," or at least that portion of it we have italicized. She writes Infidel tracts as few can write them, they literally teem with point—every paragraph *tells*. Indeed, if they have a fault it consists in an apparent straining after effect. Hit follows hit so closely that the reader (whether friend or foe) is bewildered by them, and, moreover, apt to suspect his clever author planned to astonish him by a rapid succession of dazzling passages. But

"Many lights will not be seen,
If there be nothing else between,"

as Cowley said, and everyone will admit the "Reasons for Renouncing Christianity" is less continuously brilliant than any preceding pamphlet by the same author; and by so much *I* think the better—in other respects it is inferior, though bearing many "precious marks" of her skilful hand. The following passage, as regards intrinsic excellence and general usefulness, could scarcely be overmatched by any other equal number of words.

"I contend, further, that the whole principle on which christianity is founded, and without which it is perfect nonsense—is utterly false in philosophy. This assumption is, that man is capable of choosing his belief; but a little investigation will show that we have no power over this important article of religion. We believe a certain creed only because certain evidence has been presented to our minds. Time passes —new evidence is offered, in some minds of a candid and reasonable turn—the new truths sweep out the new falsehoods, while others are so brimful of prejudices, that the cup of their understanding has no room for the purest drop of truth that men may attempt to pour into it. Some minds, naturally inquisitive, cannot forbear enquiry, and enquiry leads them to new views, while others cannot bear the labour of thinking, and take their faith, as they would be glad to take their bread, from the sweat of other mens brows."

Our author's statement of "Reasons for Renouncing Christianity" carries the stamp of sincerity—is well put and very interesting —but to some opinions, interwoven therewith, I must demur; as for example, the opinion that "a beneficent ruler cannot be unjust," which experience flatly contradicts. There is no *necessary* connection between beneficence and wisdom. The individual in whom both are united will undoubtedly square his conduct by the rules of justice; but all know that sometimes fools, with the best intentions, act more unjustly than knaves with the worst. The Spanish philosopher, who said good intentions formed hell's pavement had, without doubt, caught a glimpse of that truth. The argument of our author is, that supposing an intelligent God to exist— other suppositions are inevitable, namely —that " he must have SUFFICIENT power to be supreme ruler" — that he "must not be frivolous, nor his recorded acts ridiculous " — that he " cannot be cruel "—and that neither " caprice " nor "injustice" can belong to him.

With submission, however, I think there is no warrant in nature for this argument— every part of it is unsound. Our author has made a serious mistake, and, on that mistake, has built a serious argument, which being founded in mistake, is, of course, a mistake altogether. She has done what Paine did throughout his " Age of Reason," assumed that nature teaches (supposing Deity's existence) one kind of God, and the Bible another; whereas, according to my view, the Bible·God's attributes do not antagonize, but perfectly harmonize, with any consistently imagined "intelligent ruler" of the universe. For nature, there is good and evil. The Bible proclaims the existence of a God, with good and evil attributes. Here is harmony — no clashing, no antagonism, but perfect harmony. Those who, like the Deist, suppose nature an *effect*, are bound to infer from it the attributes of its *cause.* Now nature bears a two-fold aspect —the aspect of justice and of injustice—of beauty and of ugliness—of truth and of falsehood—of constancy and of fickleness—of love and of hate—of happiness and of misery. If then we amuse ourselves by looking "through nature up to nature's God," we shall clearly see, by the eye of imagination, a Janus-faced Jehovah.

Either nature is compounded of contradictory qualities, or it is not. If it is, the study thereof cannot warrant belief in any other "intelligent ruler" than one with contradictory attributes. If, on the other hand, it is not, what can be thought of our author's *dicta,* that every believer in the existence of God is constrained to admit " that he must be just and merciful, and wise and good; and that a revelation from him must represent him as possessed of, and actuated by, these qualities.

Our author is also at fault when considering the *potency* of a possible " supreme ruler"—she has confounded power to do all things, the doing of which involve not a contradiction, with power to regulate nature. It is evident that nature has limits, in other words, cannot be *boundless* if ruled by an intelligent existence apart from itself. It is also evident that the regulations, or even creation of a *bounded* universe cannot prove its creator and ruler " so powerful that he can do all things which involve not a contradiction," as our author asserts. Were the creation of nature satisfactorily established, the existence of a being who had power to create it would likewise be established, but that is infinitely short of establishing that " he must be so powerful that he can do all things which involve not a contradiction." While therefore atheists allow a "supreme ruler" must have *sufficient* power to be supreme ruler, we demur to the conclusion that he has *more* than *sufficient,* which shows that E. M's. estimate of nature is *toto cœlo* different from ours, or rather it indicates that atheists *view* nature and argue *from* nature *as a whole,* whereas she clearly sees *one half only*—that the atheist's view embraces nature's *dark* as well as its *bright* side, whereas her's confines its range to the latter—Hence her mistake with respect to God as revealed in the bible, which bishops Watson, Butler, and others have established, is exactly the same God as the deist's natural bible warrants belief in. Our author thus addresses the reader in the 7th page of her pamphlet, " Has it never struck you as strange, that a God so powerful as he (Jehovah) is said to be, should have made or suffered man to become so bad, that 'he' repented that he had made him, and determined to drown the whole earth with a flood." Now the answer to this is, that though Jehovah is described in the bible as *powerful* and *wise,* he is also described in the same bible as *weak* and *silly,* in short, a being with contradictory attributes such as " nature teaches," is its intelligent ruler, supposing it to have one. Our author ought to have known this before she wrote her pamphlet, which unfortunately abounds with evidence, that she knew it not.

These remarks do not prevent me saying that I strongly recommend the pamphlet to "*savage,* saint, or sage," to Christians and Infidels as well as those who are neither Christians nor Infidels, because well assured that none can peruse it without the *chance* of being well pleased and much profited.

As to the freedom of my observations, it is unnecessary to say anything. Emma Martin is a woman of excellent sense, and doubtless as little values indiscriminate *praise* as indiscriminate *censure.* To one who admires her talent, her industry, and her rare courage, it may be permitted to point out what he considers erroneous, and being erroneous, may, when enforced with such ability, be said to be dangerous. C. S.

DR. MACNAB ON MORALS.

AMONG the more prominent personages who visited New Lanark at the period when Mr. Owen had made it so highly interesting and attractive, was Dr. M'Nab, the Duke of Kent's chaplain. The result of his visit was, a work written by him, entitled, "The New Views of Mr. Owen Impartially Examined." In that work the plans of Mr. Owen are extolled and recommended, but his principles of moral action are most unequivocally and unsuccessfully opposed.

On re-perusal of the Dr's. book, it has appeared to me that his arguments are deserving the special attention of those interested—and who of us are not interested?—in moral speculation.

In page 177 Dr. Macnab commences his animadversion upon Mr. O's. opinion concerning the primary and secret origin of moral action. He (Dr. M.) maintains, that a sense of duty is the directing power of all the virtuous movements of the hearts of man, and denies that utility, or enlarged self-interest, or a sense of pleasure constitutes the foundation of virtuous motives. But in disclosing the principle upon which rests the sense of duty, he undermines the basis on which he erects his argument and founds his opposition to Mr. Owen. It is stated by the Dr. that this moral sense "is built on the universal principles of the unity, consistency and dignity of truth." Now, the literal interpretation of this, amounts to what he at the onset repudiates. For "unity and consistency" are the attributes of truth which render it so useful to man, and from its subserviency to man's happiness truth derives its "dignity." Thus, in the very effort to get at the farthest remove from the vulgar ground of utility, he has thrown himself upon it. He has gone round a circle and arrived next the starting point.

I have used the word *literal*, above, because the phraseology "unity, consistency, dignity," by its pompous sound, appeared to verge on the figurative. Unless we take its literal meaning, we shall build on an abstraction—an ideality. Do virtuous men act truthfully or love truth because she is an honest and consistent personage, very dignified in her demeanour? If any persons do, or think they do, they appear not to found their sense of duty upon what the Doctor insists they should, "on the rational principle," but rather on poetical imagery. Whereas, taking this " unity, consistency and dignity" of truth on the concrete, we are dealing with the realities which the words figure forth. We then perceive that these realities are real advantages, —that these three points derive their importance from their practical bearing,—that they are three points of the utility of truth. Truth as a statement of facts, and the universal principles deduced from such statements or premises—necessarily characterized by " unity and consistency"—must bear upon man's interests, by preserving him from error, and the repetition of painful experience, and leading to conclusions correct and salutary.

Something of the "dignity of truth" may appear attending that sense of duty which is grounded on a benevolent and an enlightened perception of the useful—of that which brings the greatest amount of permanent good to the greatest number. For what real dignity attaches to the profitless? What course of conduct can be duty that yields good to no one? What can be more imperatively our duty than that which enhances the happiness of the greatest number? If we suppose the existence of a patriot or a philanthropist free from the desire of fame or emolument, urged on by a sense of justice alone, it is to a clear and forcible perception of the universal benefits which justice would confer, that we trace the source whence that sense of justice arose. The renunciation of self-indulgence for the advancement of general good, would afford, to a character thus constituted, the highest enjoyment he is capable of receiving. Hence, in order to raise the dignity of man, it is requisite that he be moulded by nature and society, to derive his minor pleasure from the exercise of his subordinate, and his chief pleasure from that of his higher faculties.

Dr. Macnab cannot conceive that happiness has such close alliance with excellence, he says—"The hope of eternal bliss, even as a motive to act, is too weak to prevent mankind from turning occasionally to the right hand or to the left in their religious passages through life." But might we not assert the same with reference to a "sense of duty," which, at the period of moral declension, is in the same condition as the "hope of eternal bliss?"—both for the time are inactive, or inadequate. What decoys the wanderer to the right hand or to the left? The doctor will readily allow that the desire of pleasure is the lure from the path of rectitude, but never the guide to a virtuous life. Our remarks, however, have tended to show, that which way soever earth's traveller goes, he is in quest of happiness, or as Dr. Jonathan Edwards has it—"*the determining motive is always the greatest apparent good.*"

Dr. Macnab delineates utilitarianism in the most selfish, contracted, and grovelling manner. He opposes the principle as one which regards nothing higher than the allurements of present pleasure, acquisition of wealth or laurels to be reaped. But we imagine something enlarged, lofty, and benevolent, when we speak of self-interest as the basis of virtue. It is not supposed that the virtuous man in his deliberations is continually proposing to himself, the amount of self-gratification to be enjoyed, or exclusive advantages to be gained; nevertheless, we do contend that that secret and recondite prompting—so remote from the result, that it may exist unperceived by the being whom it urges, yet so becoming of the moral philosopher to trace to its recess—is "happiness, our being's end and aim."

That man can be moved to the attainment of moral excellence by the desire of pleasure only, may be a view unsuited to the taste of some; but what if it is the exact view? How little correct action do we witness, that is not in a very marked and decided manner, connected with personal and exclusive interest! Let us then not be unwilling to elevate and expand self-interest by identifying it with that of the community or the world at large; let us cease to built ethics ar theology upon suppositions, because they are flattering to vanity, or expedient in politics. H. T.

BYRON AND SHELLEY,
To the Editor of The Movement.

Sir—As it has been frequently preached from the pulpit, by our soul-savers and body-destroyers, and as I have been frequently told myself by pseudo liberals of the deistical school, that "atheism has a demoralizing tendency, and that few, if any, of the writers of the atheistical school ever lived a good moral life." I feel happy in forwarding you the following extract from a sermon entitled "The Abuse of Talent," which appears to me a complete refutation to the above opinions. I do so the more willingly because it comes not from any friend to atheism, but from an orthodox clergyman. If the writings of priests in general would breath the same spirit of liberality, persecution for opinions' sake would not rage as it has hitherto done, and atheistical opinions would be more tolerated than they have hitherto been.

The author (the Rev. George Gilfillan, minister of the first Associate Congregation, Dundee,) published the sermon from which this extract is taken, along with some others in a small pamphlet in 1839; and, considering the craft which he belongs to, you will, I trust, deem it worthy of a place in the *Movement*. After noticing in his discourse several of the French philosophers, he introduces Byron in the following manner, and well reproves the petty meanness of many of his brethren.

"To speak of the present age on such a subject may seem to trespass upon delicate ground; but, if not of the living, may I not discourse of the dead? No motive of delicacy, surely, need prevent me from lifting up the shroud of Byron, and inviting you to look and wonder at the strange anatomy, and dark disarrangement which lie below. Far be it from me to trample on his tomb; far be it from me to heap harsh names and foul epithets upon any one of the mighty dead, however great may have been his errors —however tremendous may be his doom! This is the way, indeed, in which many low and malignant minds would avenge, and do daily avenge their hopeless and immeasurable inferiority."

I would willingly quote here all that Mr. Gilfillan says of Byron, but I am afraid of trespassing too much on your space, so I will proceed at once to his character of Shelley,—

"Or shall I clench the statement by an allusion to the case of another sublime unfortunate, whose character is to me a more perplexing and tantalizing puzzle still. No profligate, indeed, was he—no worldling— tinged with no selfish or sinister motives—a pure, shy, and lofty enthusiast—he lived out of, and beyond, and above, this present evil world; and yet looked down upon it with a mild and tearful eye, like the moon shining through a golden mist, upon the stir, and din, and blasphemy, and angry passions of this 'dim spot which men call earth.' And yet this man was an unbeliever, and an Atheist! He had realized the tremendous dream of the great German genius in his own imaginary experience—he had lifted up himself through the starry splendours of the universe—he had raised himself above their suns, and found no God—he had descended to the lowest limits of space—he had looked down into the abyss, and heard the rain descending, and the everlasting storm raging, but found no God! And he had come back to the world, and cried out, 'We are all orphans, neither I nor you have any father.' And even amid the glories of Alpine scenery —the sun shining above like the eye of Deity —the earth in bride-like beauty stretching below—the glaciers, like oceans, gleaming around, and every feature of the landscape eloquent with God — he did not hesitate to write himself down 'Atheist;' and long after the ink of that dire declaration was dry, he, throughout a long series of agonies, and sufferings, and persecutions, and woes, might be said to write it down again in his own life's blood. Strange and fearful infatuation!

'Oh, star-eyed' Shelley, 'didst thou wander there,
To waft us home the message of despair?'

"To think of a man like this, with an intellect of such grasp and amplitude—with acquirements so stupendous—with imagination, as yet unequalled by the sons of men —with a heart so warm, and benevolence so pure—with so much, in short, of the divinity about him, denying the existence of a God, and, with frantic earnestness, assailing the religion of his son, affects us with emotions of awful sorrow, tinged with unbounded surprise. What ailest thee, O great, but misled spirit, against him who had so bountifully enriched thee? What ailest thee against his holy child Jesus, with his pure and perfect character, and his bleeding love? Why didst thou not just reverse thine own first principle, which would have brought thee to the first principle—the life and essence of the Christian faith? Thou saidst 'Love is God.' Why didst thou not change it into 'God is love?" Thou didst deify a vague though beautiful principle of benevolence. Oh! why didst thou not turn and see that principle in a purer, loftier form, condensed in the countenance, illustrated in the character, and sealed by the blood of Jesus?"

"Thou wert sepulchred amid the waters. The sea is thine everlasting mourner. Let us hope that it wails not over the ruin of thy gifted spirit. Let charity hope, that space for repentance was granted; that a flash of final illumination darted on thee from the lightnings of the fearful midnight amid which thou went down; and, that in that dark hour, he whom thou hadst blindly and ignorantly abused, remembered, forgave, and saved thee!"

From the splendour of style I need scarcely assure you that the sentences quoted are all the author's own.

DONALD MACDONALD.

DOCTRINE OF THE CONCORDISTS.
IV.

IN our preceding papers we have glanced at man, and his antecedent and consequent relations generally; we now proceed to notice some *particulars* as exhibited in the usual course of human development, and the first in order of time and importance appears to be his educative relationships. What these *generally are*, is too well known to need repetition; what they *should be*, we will endeavour briefly to declare. We have said in our second article that man stands between the infinite and the finite; in this position he is acted upon on either side; he is constantly undergoing a creative process within by the infinite spirit, and a modifying process without by the finite conditions or circumstances. If he submits quickly to the creative spirit within, he becomes well-informed respecting all the required conditions, and is assisted to present to the spirit such as are the most facilitating to effect his real good, and is thereby early brought into the path of goodness, wisdom, and happiness. If on the contrary he yields to external circumstances, he becomes their slave, and is evil, ignorant, and wretched. He presents to the creative law the worst conditions, and consequently receives the worst results.

The generating, regenerating, governing or overruling work, is always proceeding in the best manner possible with the conditions man presents; when man is better and wiser, he will offer himself to the working power in better and purer conditions, and more happy consequences will follow. It is as though the Creator said to man "If you will obey my laws, the only condition in which I can effect your perfect good, my creative action shall never cease; your well-being shall ever be in proportion to your willing obedience to my conditions, and these shall be further made known to you, as fast as you obey those you already know."

He is the best educator who is the most conscious of, and obedient to, the divine laws in his own being; such an one will carefully watch the operations of these laws in his pupils, and be guided by them in all his educative measures. Genius, the spontaneous nature in the pupil, must not be checked; it is the voice, the act of deity. The pupil must not be allowed to pervert the inwrought impulses by his own self-willed activity. The pure exotic implanted in each human breast should have the watchful care of the divinely disciplined educator.

By the degenerate life-birth in which we are all at present involved, the divine image or inner man, enters this world thickly enveloped in the evil consequences of self-love, self-conceit, and self-activity, and the office of the educator is to clear away this accumulated corruption, and to prevent other evil appetites, prejudices, and inclinations being received. By careful attention to this, he provides for the second and third birth to which man's perfect destiny leads, viz., the light-birth, and the love-birth, to be added to the life-birth already partially received; these he must carefully and abundantly supply the conditions for, in a gradual and watchful opening of the intelligent and affectionate faculties, constantly directing the attention of the expanding mind to essential truth and love, with which all its perceptions and affections must be perpetually associated, as the one end for which it lives, sees, and feels.

The educator who does not regard the operations of the spirit in the pupil, as his living and guiding law, but goes on according to book rules and human authorities, adding lesson to lesson, and task to task, until the memory of the pupil is filled with much verbal knowledge of theories and facts, and perhaps at last makes a learned fool, is like a gardener, who disregarding the vegetable spirit and its conditions as his guide, considers it needless to follow the successive seasons for preparing, planting, pruning, &c., but ties a quantity of artificial fruit upon the trees and plants, and persuades himself and others that they look very beautiful, and answer his purpose as well as waiting for the natural periods for every movement, and with presumptuous pride exhibits his garden as a specimen of superior culture, *completed in half the time of the natural mode.*

The human soul is like the soil, into which the creative spirit sows the divine human germ. It supplies the vitality, the germs, the seeds, the seasons, and the fruitful crop. The educator, although the highest re-agent in the universe, can only conditionate; he he can only prepare the soil, train, and prune. and vigilantly tend the growing plant. This is all he can do. or ought to attempt; when he aims at more than this ne abstracts the creative process, and deforms the fair plant of heaven. But where are the new order of educators to be found? this is the great difficulty. Where are the beings to commence the work? scarcely a man or woman is to be found who is devoted in heart, head, and energies, to conditionate the spirit for its own creative manifestations, for its own end in the rising generation. For hire or preferment only, educators like other hirelings will work; so long as this is the case, they must exhibit just such results as the parties paying them demand; altogether regardless of what is required by the universal laws. The object of the educator should be to unite the faculties of the pupils with the universal origin, and let it connect them as intended, with the divine end. The being that is merely physically natured cannot by any educative means be made into a spiritual or spirit-born man. The benevolent and intelligent faculties being deficient at birth, we may place the pupil under the most skilful educator, and he can only make of him a moralized and intellectualized ape.

The universal characteristics of a truly human being are benevolence and intelligence, these being wanting man is deficient of all that designates humanity. The more physical man is, indeed, in a hopeless state, if there be nothing better for him, than what the best education or instruction can afford. He may, by education, learn notions, names, things, and their causes; but with all his acquired knowledge he is but a civilized fractional existence, still needing the natures to be born in him, which alone can elevate him in the scale of being, and entitle him to the rank of a whole human maturity. These he can only receive by submitting to the spirit in its own manner, for the regenerating work needful to engraft in his defective constitution the light and love essences. In short, whatever education may do for the physical man, he must depend entirely upon the regenerator for the universal benevolence, and the universal intelligence, which alone can constitute him a human being. The tutor who conditionates not for the birth of the benevolent and intelligent essences in the pupil, but who goes on to develope only the life faculties, and fill these with notional and learned acquisitions, is doing all that is possible to increase the misery of the educated, and the unhappiness of those with whom he associates in after life. The various acquirements of the merely natural man are so many doors through which evil is poured into the world. The well educated, life natured man is greatly more capable of misery than the uneducated man. Being defectively natured, he is rendered immensely unhappy in his efforts at intelligent and benevolent conduct. Without the natures, out of which such conduct must proceed, disappointment and distress must continually attend him. Benevolence and intelligence are needed to complete the physical man, and no education, however refined, can add these to him. Regeneration in a three-fold order must as necessarily precede happiness, as generation must precede existence. Man can only have the happiness of his complete destiny by being natured of love, of light, and of life. Without this triad nature he is in disharmonic relation with *that* which alone can render him permanently happy.

Education is at best only a conditionating work, and must not be confounded with a regenerating or creating work; the former gives modes and forms, the latter essences and natures. When man is triunely born he will no longer need regeneration. Man in his whole triune birth will as to essence be perfect, and will only have to be gradually developed in the divine order.

Education therefore, we affirm, is not the one thing needful; regeneration is the great panacea that is to put generation on its right basis, viz., in direct unity with love, wisdom, and power, which alone can rectify or justify the human race, and render it eternally good, wise, and happy. W. O.

"RUM, GUNPOWDER, AND MISSIONARIES."—Our readers may recollect an article under this head which appeared in our paper a few weeks since, stating that a vessel was about to sail to Africa from this port with a cargo consisting in part of rum and gunpowder, and that several missionaries were to go out in her as passengers. The *New York Regenerator*, in copying the article, adds the following proof that the missionaries to that country, *have* dealt in these commodities, inasmuch as in their treaties with the Africans for land, they gave them *rum, guns* and *gunpowder*, in payment; and not only this, but in their subsequent intercourse with the Africans, when they found themselves unable to "*convert*" some of the more stubborn, these same pious missionaries, as if determined to subdue the poor natives at some rate or other, brought a long nine-pounder to bear upon them, and, for the glory of God and the good of their souls, blew their brains out!—But to the remarks from the *Regenerator*:—

" Whoever will take the trouble to look over the files of *Niles's Register* will find in a number issued, I think, during the month of September 1821, a narrative of the treaty ratified between Ayers and Stockton for the American Colonization Society on the one part, and several African chiefs an the other part, by which was ceded to the former the land which has been the theatre of these missionary operations from that time to this. Among other articles paid for the land, will be found beads, pipes, canes, looking-glasses, *guns*, *gunpowder*, and *rum*! When the purchasers went on to take possession of their property a difficulty arose from some misunderstanding between the parties, and the missionaries mounted their brass cannon to settle it. In the second volume of the African Repository will be found a narrative of the early proceedings of this missionary establishment, from the pen of Jehudi Ashmun president of the colony and missionary from some board on this side of the Atlantic. In the course of the narrative, he alludes to a battle fought between the missionaries and the natives, in an early part of their intercourse. He describes the natives—in their greater ignorance of the tactics of more refined human butchery—as congregated so densely that a child could have walked on the tops of their heads. Thus crowded together, and situated only at a distance of about fifty yards, the missionaries brought their long nine-pounder to bear upon them. Now hear Ashmun's description of its awful destructiveness. He says—' *every shot literally spent its force in a solid mass of living human flesh*!' This work of slaughter has gone on from time to time until Rev. George S. Brown, Methodist missionary, on a Sunday morning, three or four years since, in a battle with the natives on the mission ground, with his victims at the distance of a few yards only, on his own cold-blooded story for it, personally 'taking deliberate aim at fifties of them,' 'shot out their hearts, bowels and brains like a tornado!' He is still continued the denomination's missionary, and has received no rebuke from the missionary world generally, for his work of wholesale murder."—*Boston Investigator.*

THE NORTHAMPTON HERALD.—The editor of this journal in reply to our article in No. 17, on the Rev. Herbert Marsh, calls the *Movement* a "profligate *five farthing* publication." This man will ruin us—we get *six* farthings for it.

EDINBURGH.—During the past week the city has been placarded, (and the police bu in removing the placards,) announcing three nights' discussion between Dr. Green and C. Southwell. First night, "Is there a God?" Second night, "Did Jesus Christ represent God?" Third night, "Is such belief philosophic? It is needless to add who takes the affirmative and who the negative.

He is unfit to rule others who cannot rule himself.—*Plato*.

VOTES OF THE HOUSE OF COMMONS, 29th APRIL.—" Blasphemy "—Petition of the chairman of a meeting of Inhabitants of Aberdeen, for amendment of Law relating thereto," to lie on the table.

FOREIGN PROGRESS.—Moreover, infidelity had never put forth such efforts as were now employed to instil its doctrines into the minds of the millions of India. The works of Voltaire, Paine, and Owen were translated, printed, and circulated by thousands over that vast continent. Idolatry was fast waning in that country. In the presidency of Madras, eight out of every ten, and in the presidency of Calcutta, six out of every ten of its temples were in ruins or deserted, and there existed a popular belief that their system was about to be abolished, and all the efforts of their priests were fruitless to prevail on the people to repair their temples.—*Speech of the Rev. Mr. Saffery, Baptist Public Meeting, Bristol, May, 1st, 1844.*

For G. J. H. from W. B. B. .	£0 10	0
For M. Q. R. from W. B. B. .	0 10	0
For Miss Roalfe from W. B. B.	0 10	0
To purchase the 2 vols. of the Oracle of Reason for Mr. Finlay, from W. B. B. . .	0 10	0
For Mr. Paterson from " W. W."	1 0	0

SUBSCRIPTIONS TO THE ANTI-PERSECUTION UNION.

T. Rose, J. C. Savage . .	£0 1	0
J. Cook, Infidel Repository, Ipswich	0 1	0
Bristol Subscription for April:—		
Per card 11.	0 9	0
13.	0 2	0
12.	0 1	0
16.	0 5	0

G. J. H. *Sec.*

Printed and Published by G. J. HOLYOAKE, 40, Holywell-street, Strand, Saturday, May 18, 1844.

THE MOVEMENT

And Anti=Persecution Gazette.

"Maximise morals, minimize religion."—BENTHAM.

No. 24.	EDITED BY G. JACOB HOLYOAKE, ASSISTED BY M. Q. RYALL.	PRICE 1½d

THE METAPHYSICAL ORIGIN OF THE GOD IDEA.

THE objects of our ideas are real or ideal, and there is a certain rule for judging the reality or ideality of these objects. In order to judge we must know the nature of an idea, of which there are two classes, sensible ideas and abstract ideas. A sensible idea is the pure result of the action of an object upon the organs of sense; the object of the sensible ideas is then a real being, a being who has an individual existence, for in order for anything to act, it must exist. An abstract idea is formed from the comparison of sensible ideas by reflection; the object of an abstract idea is necessarily an ideal being; the idea does not result anymore from the action of the object, but from the comparison we make between our sensible ideas. In this comparison we perceive the relation that these sensible ideas have between themselves. This relation we arrive at by an act of our attention in separating it from compared ideas, and representing it by a sign, or expressing it by a term. This relation thus separated from sensible ideas, represented by a sign or expressed by a word, is the object of the abstract idea. It is evident that the relation, to which the sign or the term which represents it gives a sort of existence, cannot really exist, except in the understanding. The abstract idea then consists in the perception and expression of the relation that two or several sensible ideas have amongst themselves; the object of such an idea then must be in ideal being, the example of which does not exist in nature. The existence of god hence ceases to be a problem. That the idea of god is an abstract idea, it is impossible to deny, and here we have the origin and formation of it. When we arrive at the end of analysis, the idea of god is that of a being that we believe to be cause of all things which are. The idea of God then is only the idea of being, united to that of cause. The idea of god then is a complete abstract idea, or compound of two general ideas. The relations which are the objects of these ideas are easy to discover. The first of these relations is the quality of *being*, common to all things which exist, and there is no relation more general among divers beings. By force of attention, this relation among objects is separated; by the term being, is designed the perception of this quality common to all existing things, and the idea general of being, remains in the mind. The second relation is that of *cause*. We express by this term, the capacity of acting we observe to be common to all bodies. We separate from bodies this common quality, we express it by the word *cause*, which becomes the representative sign of it, and thereby we arrive at fixing in our understanding the idea of cause in general. The general idea of cause, as well as that of being, are only two abstract ideas; but it is from the reunion of these two ideas, that the complete idea is formed, which we say is the idea of god. This idea then, only represents an ideal being, composed of two general relations, that the understanding discovers in the divers beings which act upon the organs of sense. The mind does not acquire these abstract ideas except by the comparison it makes between its sensible ideas. The objects of these ideas are only the relations which exist between them. The objects of these ideas are not then real being, but only ideal being. Now the idea of god, as has just been seen, is of the class of abstract ideas. If any one should doubt of it, let him compare this idea with some of those sensible ideas from which it is drawn. It is easy to see, I should tell him, that all the objects which surround him have a common quality —that of being. Direct attention only to this general relation that different objects have amongst themselves; separate this relation from objects—express it by the term being, and you will have the idea of being in general. Afterwards observe that all bodies present to the eyes, in acting one upon the other, produce different effects. The property then of producing certain effects is a property common to all bodies. Separate, by an act of your attention, this general relation which exists between all bodies— designate it by the term cause—and then you will have in the mind the abstract idea of cause, or the idea of cause in general.

We comprehend then how we rise from the consideration of a particular body, to the general ideas of being and cause. Now it being from the re-union of these two ideas that the idea of god is formed, we are forced to acknowledge that the idea of god is an abstract idea—that the notion of god is the object of that abstraction. Therefore god has no individual existence, but is a perfect ideality.

Further it can be shown that the real existence of such a being is impossible, for the conclusive reason that the same being cannot be at once real and ideal. It is to that which we arrive in respect to god. On supposition this being would be a reality—and this same being, being the object of an abstract idea, would be, by the nature of things, only an ideality. God then must be, and must not be, at the same time, which implies a contradiction. It is then demonstrated that god is not a being who has an individual existence. Philosophers, who have had the idea of god, have not realized the object of this abstract idea because they have not paid attention to the origin and generation of this idea. They have not seen what it is in the nature of things—but they thought they saw it, and they had only a dream.

W. J. B.

GOD'S INSTRUMENTS.

THE SENSITIVE SERGEANT—Plaintiff's principal witness in the great Bow-street case—"God *versus* PATERSON."

The notorious police informer, Weston, (as the *Dispatch* of May 5th spells it,) whose delicate nerves were so dreadfully shattered by the Holywell-street profanities, has been most consistently conniving and drinking with the brothel keepers, and permitting the gentle persuasive of an occasional half-guinea to shut his ears and eyes to *their* peccadilloes. This immaculate officer, who was sentenced by *our* Twyford last week to a month's imprisonment for taking bribes from brothel keepers, (and who after having had his uniform stripped, luckily for him got off through the magistrate's subsequent discovery that he could not inflict the punishment after a six month's committal of the offence,) is the actual serjeant who was most vigilant and active in the cases against Paterson. Doubtless, half-a-guinea from "the man," had he stooped to the act, would have prevailed as easily in winning over the serjeant from being God's witness in the great case, God v. Paterson, as similar fees have been in the cases of the bagnio proprietors. This is the serjeant with the convenient vision, between whom and Mr. Paterson's counsel the following question and answer took place:—

Mr. Thomas.—"Do you mean to tell us that at these picture shops at the corner of Southampton street and adjacent, there are not twice as many persons as at Paterson's door?"

Serjeant Western.—"I have not seen it myself, there might be, but I *have not seen it.*"

Truly it may be said of this meritorious officer, "None are so blind as those who won't see."

This is the actual serjeant in relation to whom, and the vile features of Paterson's case, Mr. Thomas made the following severe animadversions:—

"It really is coming to a pretty pass that the inside of a shop is to be construed to mean in a thoroughfare, and that every book or every line of writing in a shop, which can be seen from without, which, from its tendency or character, may annoy somebody, shall be construed to be in a thoroughfare, and within policemen's jurisdiction. I believe, that by these policemen going to this shop so continuously, they were sent there by the parties who are instituting this prosecution, until they could get up crowds and cases of offence. I say, that by two policemen going there and two coming by and stopping, which created in this narrow pass, a stoppage, the passengers were induced to stop also, and see what was upon the placards these policemen were copying. Do you doubt this? Can any one doubt that this Western and the other policeman, copying for hours and reading documents, and comparing them, would not attract the attention of passengers? If you see a man with a pencil in his hand looking at a mark, you stop at once—seeing him copying from a shop window, who would not stop? It is they then who committed the offence, for which you are punishing this man—the paid, hired policemen for the purpose, and the plotting bigots who, doubtless, have urged on this prosecution. This reminds me of offences created by bad men in bad times, who lived on bread purchased with blood money; monsters hired for the purpose of entrapping their fellow creatures, and betraying the unwary into their hellish net. I am here as an advocate to comment on the evidence which has been adduced before you, and I say, addressing you as an experienced lawyer, that it appears to me, from the evidence, that these men were employed by the government to create the very evil and crime which they call upon you to punish. Here two of them go to the shop, and two of them stop as they go by; there they are then, four of them at this little shop which is not more than a yard wide; four, as the witness swears, and Tyler instigating the crowd of ten to noise, in the presence of four policemen, and how many more government spies for the purpose, who knows? These were enough to arrest the attention of persons passing by? If there really had been passengers complaining, then something might have been said; but here they are sent to the shop, not accidentally there, but there with the design of making up an offence. Are there not objects enough for punishment in this metropolis, are there not offences enough arising in the course of the passage of life, without creating more for the pleasure of punishing them. I say naturally and necessarily, there are enough, without making them up by efforts of this sort. I must say, I think the public should know what work the police is required for; policemen going to the goverment office daily, seeing the government solicitor, getting his instructions, so as to make sure of their victim, is more, I think, than is required by the public. I cross-examined these men; they are paid out of the public earnings, for the performane of a duty for the public good, and it would appear, that they are hired for the government services, and their time wasted in going about to create offences, and then calling upon you to punish them, to get the fines you impose; for what are they but paid spies ? It appears to me, to be a thing so gross, that the public must mark it, and I hope the public will mark it—with reprobation. I do not think people are aware for what objects they are rated.

" These cases seem to grow less and less as we go on; we have now got to just one witness; only one! that one a paid policeman, hoping to get the fines, and perhaps promotion; (for who goes constantly to the government offices, without such hopes for services) he goes to a shop in plain clothes, creates an obstruction on the pavement, and asks you to punish the defendant, for that annoyance which he had planned and effected. Did he not create a disturbance and an obstruction ? Here he was every night, like some lurid night-mare bestriding his victim, grinning at and jeering the defendant in his shop, tolerating and countenancing noise and disturbance, and constantly tempting him to commit some offence, but yielding no assistance when an insult or robbery was committed upon him, expecting immunity here. Such a witness makes out this case alone; not a neighbour, not one passenger, not brother policemen to make a case of annoyance to passengers or neighbours—oh, ridiculous; Is absurdity to prevail? Is argument to be futile. Is common sense to be discarded ? or is terror of the government, and the influence of a bad portion of the public press, to govern these decisions ?"

This Western is the identical sergeant, who, I heard, expressed himself in his ex-officio zeal, so sorry that he had not been present when I forced myself in to regain possession of Paterson's shop, after the machinations of the landlords, or some low devilry had succeeded in ejecting the "boy Clarke," and cheating Paterson out of a month's rent in advance, and who boasted he would have seized me *at all hazards*, had he been there. Doubtless he knew the leanings of a Bow-street magistrate, who interpreted a thoroughfare to mean the inside of a shop, and who, even behind the legislature, wrested a class of cases into his own jurisdiction which Parliament only meant to come before the higher courts. This God defending and officially approved policeman would have ventured, trusting to the sympathies of a magistrate to bear him harmless—to do that which the officer at the time on duty, perhaps less hackneyed in the ways of justice's justice, did not presume or attempt.

Of a verity, some who "bear witness for the Lord," are truly worthy of their employer. M. Q. R.

IMPORTANT PUBLIC DISCUSSION.

The placards which you noticed in your last *Movement*, relative to a pending discussion between Mr. C. Southwell and Dr. Greer, excited, as you may imagine, a great deal of interest with all parties—most persons expected the authorities would have interfered. One of our bill-stickers was *told* he would be apprehended if he persisted; however we got another in his stead, in case of accident, but he was not molested. All of us looked forward to Tuesday night, as all felt that that night might determine the fate of Infidelity, or rather its progress in this city, for should the *question of questions,* " Is there a God," be allowed to be discussed without legal interference, we felt that a grand triumph would be achieved, it being a question which had never before been so publicly asked of the "Gude People of Modern Athens."

When the hour for discussion arrived, Whitfield Chapel was literally crammed, about 800 persons being present, and hundreds anxious to be admitted went away disappointed. Dr. Greer opened the debate, but did not advance anything in our opinion like an argument. When Mr. Southwell followed, he enunciated atheism, and materialism, and denounced the belief in a supernatural existence as rank folly, vile superstition, and most ably dissected the god idea. The audience listened with moderate attention, some at times seemed disposed to be noisy, but upon the whole they were very well behaved.

Dr. Greer did not satisfy the christian part of the audience, for they seemed as much displeased with what he advanced as they did with what Mr. Southwell said in reply, and when the debate terminated for the night, all parties were pretty much of one opinion respecting Dr. Greer.

Wednesday evening came the question, "Did Jesus represent God?" The chapel was filled, and all felt that this question could not be discussed until such time as the "existence of a God" had been proved. The Doctor beat about the bushes the whole night, nothing whatever being advanced to the purpose, and as a proof that the Doctor felt he could do nothing with his opponent, in the course of his last speech he offered *to prove Mr. Southwell's belief in a God if he would allow himself to be mesmerised, and he would make him pray to God before the whole audience.* Of course this proposal was treated by the audience and Mr. Southwell with contempt, and so dissatisfied were they, that many of them wished the Doctor to decline coming forward on Thursday evening.

Thursday night, "*Is this belief philosophic?*" was the question for discussion; but, until the two prior questions had been settled, this one could not be legitimately considered.

The same farce as was played on Tuesday and Wednesday was repeated by Dr. Greer; for in each of his speeches he took the greatest care imaginable to avoid saying anything whatever about the question at issue. The discontent on the part of the Christians was more manifest than ever; they all heartily regretted that such a man should put himself forward to defend christianity.

In his last speech the offer to *mesmerise* Mr. Southwell was repeated. The only proof he had of the existence of a God was that man was the only animal that had the organ, or bump of veneration, and if there was nothing to be venerated or adored, how did they think man came to have the organ? As a proof of the state of the feelings of those present, at the conclusion of the discussion the following resolution was put and carried by an immense majority:—

RESOLVED:—"That it is the opinion of this meeting that the subject of the existence of God has not been duly handled by the affirmer in this debate; we desire that a deputation be appointed to wait on the Rev. George O. Campbell requesting him, in the name of this meeting, to meet Mr. Charles Southwell on that all important topic."

Accordingly a deputation of six persons were appointed from the meeting to wait on Mr. Campbell, four of whom were Christians. An amendment was moved to the effect "That a deputation be appointed for the purpose of procuring better advocates on both sides, which was lost by an immense majority.

After this we may, with propriety, say that something has been done by the late agitations. But a few months ago you could scarcely whisper about atheism in a public meeting; now we can dispute the existence of a God in a crowded meeting, and be listened to with the greatest attention.

All things considered, this is a complete triumph, not over Dr. Greer, but over the authorities and public predjudices; we may now very properly infer, if this is passed over unnoticed, that free discussion is not altogether unattainable even in this psalm-singing-city. A large number of addresses of the Anti-Persecution Union, printed for the occasion, were distributed at the doors, which I have no doubt did a great deal to allay the feelings of the more noisy persons present—a copy of which I send you.

I will let you know shortly the result of the deputation. W. BAKER.

[We insert this report, it being the fullest we have received. The character of the discussion seems sufficiently attested by the resolution of the audience on the last night. And the report is at least negatively corroborated by the fact that we have received no contradictions of the statements from any of Dr. Greer's friends. Our correspondents would always oblige us by reporting the *new* arguments adduced by either speaker. The best reports are those in which each speaker's best sayings are stated, and the public left to judge, as the audience did, for themselves. Such reports we always desire to present, and they will alway be welcome either from friends or foes.—ED of M.]

LIBRARY TALK.
MEN AND CREEDS.

MANDEVILLE has a good remark on the mode in which current religious opinions are taken for granted without examination. "The generality of men are so wedded to, and so obstinately fond of, their own opinion and the doctrine they have been imbued with from their cradle, that they cannot think any one sincere who, being acquainted with it, refuses to embrace it. This holds in all religions, the Mahometan and most absurd of the Pagan not excepted." These remarks, intended to apply to the fanatics of the religious world, are no less pertinent to those of the sceptics or infidels who think that all men must be either fools or knaves who believe, or profess to believe in, absurdities. I think there are two rather prevalent mistakes among our irreligious friends; one, that of a disbelief in the sincerity of a large mass of professing religious believers; another, that sincere believers in certain dogmas, appearing to them eminently absurd, must be men of weak intellect. There is doubtless a large mass of insincerity among professed believers of every creed and shade of creed; but the sweeping condemnation of the supporters and propagators of sectarian shades of difference appears to me unjust. Interest alone is not the guide to all superstitious creeds.

The early recollections of many of the most acute infidels may teach them this. The position in which they once were, others may still retain, and what appears to them the most arrant nonsense, may be invested with a dignity and importance in the eyes of others. The author just quoted cites the following curious instances.—" As there is nothing humane minds may more widely differ in than in what concerns religious matters, so, there is no opinion so monstrously despicable, but some may adhere to it with zeal and sincerity, whilst others with the same sincerity may have sentiments not perfectly agreeing with any opinion that is known. About the middle of the last century, whilst the trinitarians were accusing one another of believing tritheism; and the unity of God was strenuously asserted among the Protestants, the Chevalier Borri (who was burnt in effigy, together with his writings, in Rome) started a notion among the Roman Catholics that the Virgin Mary was a real goddess, and a fourth person in the divinity. The emperor Alexander had in his palace an oratory where he went early in the morning to practise religious ceremonies in honour of the patrons he had mode choice of. Here he had, with the effigies of his ancestors, those of very good princes who had been deified, and other holy men, and among them Apollonius Tyanæus, Jesus Christ, Abraham, Orpheus, and such like gods, says my author. Nothing can be more unaccountable than the mixed worship of that emperor or the notion he must have had of the deity; yet Lampridius who wrote his life, and informs us of this, speaks of him as of a virtuous, sincere, and devout prince." Now these two persons, the Chevalier Borri and the Emperor Alexander only require to be looked upon through a somewhat different medium from that of the generality of the Christian religious world, to put them at least on the same footing of sanity as most other belivers.

It seems now to the unreligionised judgment but a very small grade of difference between interceeding with Mary the mother of God, praying to her, and accounting her a divinity. The piety of Alexander, too, would appear but a practical commentary on the " safest-to-believe" doctrine, urged to us infidels by atmost all Christian sects. " If your opinions should be right," quoth the creedest, " it may be well; but suppose them to be wrong, (and there is that awful possibility, he says, with elongated face and dismayed expression,) how will you meet the dread alternative of being cast into hell flames, which, my bible tells me, is the fate of him who believeth not."

The worthy emperor solves this difficulty at once, and all others of a similar stamp, by believing in every thing and every body. And this is, after all, the only way of complying with the " safest-to-believe" view of religion, therefore—Mandeville's opinion to the contrary notwithstanding—many things might be much " more accountable than the mixed worship of that emperor." Our author stated the case well, but his citations to illustrate co-mingled worth and absurdity were not, to my thinking, so conclusive as he deemed them. This happens from the different aspect in which opinions are viewed. If his illustrations do not prove his position, his failure may do something towards it in showing the different value that may be attached, by men of a philosophic turn, to the peculiarities of religious belief. These reflections and comparisons are, in truth, the best teachers; they do not tell us, " go and be charitable to the failings or misconceptions of others—bear and forbear," with a string of other preceptoral maxims, they show us by comparison, analysis and self-examination, the tendency to error from the universality of credal teaching, and lead us, by the just, natural, and impressive process of induction and discovery on our own parts, to that proper frame of thought and propriety of sentiment which distinguishes the sincere enquirer from the bigot, be he of whatever denomination he may, or of no denomination at all. M. Q. R.

JEWS AND GENTILES—
AT HOME AND ABROAD.
I.

THE condition of the Jews is interesting to the Free-thinker. The good or bad treatment of this people is one of the indications of the prevalence of liberty or despotism among the nations with whom they are located. It is with painful interest that all lovers of freedom have observed the recent events in connection with them—the barbarities and oppressions to which they have been subject, not only in the east, but in the west. The Jews are pointed to triumphantly by the Christians, as a living confutation of the errors of septicism. If, owing such a debt of gratitude to this truly unfortunate people, the Christian world was to foster, cherish, and tenderly guard them, they would do no more than bare justice to the props, so called, of their system. To us, the Infidel public, the Jews are interesting as a persecuted people and have claims on our regard, through the attack constantly sustained in their persons on the liberty we so dearly prize, and determinedly defend. The "delenda est Carthago," the unextinguishable war we wage against oppression, inequality of condition, and of religious right, incline us to all who are wronged.

Between the Jew, and the Infidel, as the term is understood in modern parlance, there is, if not a community of sentiment, at least a community of wrong and suffering, and were it not so, the persecuted Israelites should be no less objects of our surveillance and regard. "Standing monuments," as the Christian disputants call them, of "the truth as it is in Jesus," they are melancholy mementos of the implacability of their religious foes. So powerful a hold has Christian fanaticism on its votaries that even a cessation of open hostilities is but a prelude to more insidious attacks. While the opposition is being weakened year by year to the Jews' eligibility to offices of trust—evidenced in the election of Sir Moses Montefiore and others to important public offices in the city—a movement has been going on, essentially Christian,—because furtive and grasping,—in which an attempt has been made, through the instrumentality of the mongrel bishop Alexander, to establish a sort of judaico-church-of-Englandism in the east—the centre of the radii, being Jerusalem. Without any present means of tracing the operation of this ill-timed and ill-placed movement, a conjecture may be hazarded, that the exasperation produced by the measure may have some connection with the recent jewish persecutions. Of a piece with this church-planting is the proselitizing fancies of some Christian worthies. "These proselyte-mongers," as *Punch* says, "have their special pets; among them the Hebrew people bear a great price. Hence, as was shown at a late meeting, upwards of 25,000*l.* are annually subscribed for the conversion of the Jews at Jerusalem, Hebron, Beyrout, Constantinople, Smyrna, and we know not at how many other places promising in apostacy. We must confess we should like to see a fair balance-sheet of this account. We should like to know the exact number of converted Hebrews, that we might arrive at something like the market price of a renegade Jew. We own it; we more than fear that he is a great luxury, a bird of Paradise of exceeding cost. Hence, we confess it, we would have our gentle countrywomen retrench their outlay on the foreign curiosity, that they might better afford to buy up somewhat of the misery produced at home.

"Allowing, however, that it is necessary to the apoplectic philanthropy of some folks to bleed their purses for the Heathen, we think that at least the Jews might be left as they are until every other unbeliever should be converted.

"——— Here, madam,—you who at the last meeting invested 5*l.* in apostate Jews,—here is the map of the world. Cast your eye over it. Here is the poor Esquimaux doomed to whale blubber and a soul-blighting creed—here the Red Man—here the Hottentot—here the New Zealander—here people on people, and tribe on tribe, all in the uttermost darkness. Enlighten them, and then, if you will, begin with the Hebrew. Meanwhile, for ourselves—we confess it—we have more than a sneaking respect for a people who had Moses for a leader and a law-giver. We rarely meet a long-bearded Rabbi that he does not carry our thoughts to the plains of Mamre—to the first patriarchs of the first nation.

"And ye, who would convert the Jews, first copy the Jews' great virtue: first take care of your own poor; feed and clothe them, and then if you will, with the superfluity make proselytes of the Hebrew. Meanwhile, with misery wasting thousands of our fellow-Christians at our very doors, we hold the subscription of large sums of money for, at best, the questionable conversion of the Jew, as the offering of a miserable, morbid egotism; and should still think so of the purpose, though the whole bench of bishops wagged their silver tongues in aid of it."

If christianity's abettors have the hardihood to deny that the Jews have suffered, and do suffer, through the instrumentality of Christians, at least they must admit that these sufferings have been with their permission. In Christian countries — our's among the number — have not Christians the sway? Do they not perform the legislative, administrative and judicial functions? In autocratic countries is not christianity the reigning religion, the court religion? In electoral countries is not christianity the religion of the electors. Will they have the brazen impudence to tell us that the sectarians who could clamour down the educational clause in the factories' bill, could not, by an exercise of the same influence, gain some instalment of civil and religious liberty for both Jew and Infidel? But those who are not stultified by the Christian cant and who do not suffer interests, real or supposed, to warp their judgment, can clearly see that all civil disabilities and intolerant religious distinctions are not only permitted but enacted and perpetuated by Christian zealots of the various denominations, whether Church-of-Englandists as by law established, or congregationalists as by law opposed. The representatives of the dominant sect in our Commons House of Parliament—the bench of bishops—are notoriously the most rancorous opponents of liberty and equality, not only to Jew and Infidel, but to rival sects. It is but a fortnight since they gave all the opposition in their power, happily in this case ineffectual, to the bill brought before the House, for securing to the various sects the legacies they have had left them, and to prevent the alienation of their chapels and properties by a forced and illiberal interpretation of the law as at present existing. The Unitarians having been successfully robbed by recent law decisions, the dominant sect wished to retain all such nice chances as might turn up to cram to distension their insatiable maw. If "the people of the lord" were united, what would become of Jew and Gentile? It is, probably, to their enmity we owe our safety. If they were not always ready to tear each other to pieces, what would become of us? The "Anti-State-Church" move may be a "great blessing to Infidels" — who knows but we may catch some crumbs from the tables of the Christian Dives. It is only by such means—which they never intended and can't help, that we ever get anything. In the same way as the brutish multitude got some benefits never intended, through the opportune quarrels of the barons with the kings.

As pretty and characteristic a specimen of the Christian spirit towards the "jewish brethren," as I ever alighted upon, is exhibited in the following notable passage from the recent work of Guillon, catholic bishop, against the writings of Gibbon, Strauss and Salvador:—"While the son of Mary is adored as the saviour of the world, the people who reject him are punished by the most desolating and inexplicable ruin that ever existed; dispersed throughout every land, and every where strangers, without a country, a temple, an altar, continuing to live for themselves alone, still miserable, still subsisting to serve for ever as a testimony to the truth of the prophets; the rigour, and if I may so express myself, the uniqueness of the punishment in attesting the enormity of the transgression, attest at the same time *the justice and mercy of him who thus avenges himself.*" Was there ever a more revolting passage? Can impudence, folly, and rancour be carried further? The ravings of a M'Neile, an O'Sullivan, or a Stowell—the vaporings of a Brindley, or a Barker—the spleen and malevolence of a Philpot or a Bloomfield could scarcely produce an example that would exceed this choice morceau. Truly, prelate, preacher, and pastor, Romish, Anglican, Lutheran, Prebyterian, or any other erian are—minor differences apart—all imbued with the blessed gospel spirit. The Nazarene kicked up a row, so they say in Judæa, headed disaffected mobs and *blasphemed*, yes blasphemed, according to their own showing—for which purely religious-made vice, the Roman authorities, with the sanction of the Jews, whose "feelings were hurt," and whose institutions, doctrine, and church discipline were attacked—subjected the delinquent to the ordinary punishment of the day for an extraordinary fault. Have not the Christians served every Messiah in the same way as long as the law leaned to the hanging side, and do they not inflict upon similar delinquents, all that the law, made by themselves and softened by a few infidel legislators, will permit. From Mrs. *Shiloh*, to *Zion Ward*, *Thom* of Canterbury to the *White Quakers*, do they not "prosecute to the utmost rigour of the law," and fine and imprison to the fullest extent. Will not the lapse of eighteen hundred years abate a jot of the bitterness against an oppressed, calumniated, and down-trodden people, who but acted then as their christian oppressors act now? Will they make no allowance for errors of judgment or false zeal, which the less benighted among them would urge for their own sects? Seeing that they make a standing use of the Jews as a monument of evidence in their own favour, will they never hang the flag of peace upon this monument? Or supposing that their God *is* continually displeased (how arrogant to assume his pleasure or his displeasure with anybody of men) with the Israelites, and continually punishing them, must they add to those torments as though they were appointed God's special torturers and Jack Ketches? Do they doubt their Deity's power to avenge itself? or do they not really doubt the fact of God Almighty's temper and conduct to the Jews, and themselves set about performing what they feared would never be accomplished did they not "put their own shoulder to the whe l" of persecution? But what stupidly gross brutality in the idea of the Jews being continually preserved as afflicted outcasts for the sake of attesting the truth of *their* doctrines! How well it accords with their own apple story, original sin, and the punishment of Eve's ninety times removed great-grandchildren for *her* peccadillo! What vile slavering mockery, that of God Almighty showing his *justice* and *mercy* by thus avenging himself! Be true to your vocation, Christians! rake up old prophecies, turn them, twist them, pick and choose, strain, warp, garble, misconstrue, literalize, alegorize or apocryphize books, chapters, passages, texts—set forth God Almighty's thoughts, words, intentions—give it attributes of justice and mercy, and make justice and mercy consist in horribly severe and incessant oppressions—failing any of these in the uncontrolled order of events —invest yourselves with the office of God's avengers—then taunt your victims with the signal and unique nature of the punishment —conjure up prophecies as pretexts for ill-using them, and boast of the ill-usage as a fulfilment of the prophecies. Thus are *our* people kept in ignorance that they may remain in bondage, and are retained in bondage that they may remain ignorant. Education and the suffrage are governed by the same rules as christian prophecyings and oppresions—You have 'got the Jews down, keep them down, most meek and lowly christians—as long as you can. But that you need not be told—Rationalism will bring about all that the quarrelings and strivings of rival christian sects shall leave undone, for Jew and Gentile, in the establishment of liberty and and equality. M. Q. R.

Peel, Providence, & Co.—A pious professor of the knife, at the bottom of Liquorpond-street, announces that he has plenty of meat for sale—" thanks to Providence and Sir Robert Peel." We thought that Sir Robert was in business on his own account, but it appears that he has taken a partner—From the manner in which our friend the sheep-killer displays his notice, by putting Providence in small capitals, and Sir Robert Peel in large, we still conclude that Sir Robert is the principal member of the firm.

NOTICES.

Mr. Gillespie's Reply.—The first part of Mr. Gillespie's Reply to Mr. Southwell's Strictures will appear in the next number of the *Movement*. It is due to this gentleman to state that a notice to correspondents, which appeared in No. 21, was written in misapprehension of his meaning. The explanation will be best given in Mr. Gillespie's words, who writes thus:—

" Your first notice in No. 21, astonished me. I never contemplated writing you, that my first part would occupy a *Movement*. What I meant by the sentence (in my letter of the 9th ult.) which misled you, was, that my first part would be as much as I could expect to get into one *Movement*. You must really think us Theists, and Christians, to be all without any shamefacedness. I admired your goodness in agreeing to my (*supposed*) proposal."

Petitions.—We must unceasingly draw attention to the importance of petitioning for the release or amelioration of the treatment of Mr. Paterson. It is hoped that the recent articles on this subject from a valuable correspondent will excite to active exertion. A petition lay at John-street Hall on Sunday evening for signatures, got up by the Chartists of Marylebone; it will be gratifying if every district follows such example. We shall be obliged by receiving copies of every petition sent for presentation, with all subsequent particulars.

On Sunday evening, at half-past seven, Mr. Holyoake will Lecture at the Cityroad Hall of Science, near Featherstonesteet. Subject—"A New Estimate of Christianity's Historical Evidences."

Edinburgh.—The question, "Is there a God?" is again to be discussed in this city the week after next. The Rev. John Elliot Hudlow, late of St. George's Chapel, Dumferline, Fife, is to be Mr. Southwell's opponent on this occasion. Whether this is an arrangement made by the deputation mentioned in another page, we are not informed.

Just Published, *cloth, lettered—Price* 1s. 6d.

The first of a *Short Series on Practical Instruction*, intended for the use of Schools, Mechanics' Institutions, and Literary Classes.

PRACTICAL GRAMMAR,

or

COMPOSITION

Divested of Difficulties,

WITH SELECT EXAMPLES FROM THE WRITINGS OF ELEGANT AUTHORS.

Containing all that is necessary for ordinary purposes, and no more; and intended for the use of those who have little time to study.

BY G. JACOB HOLYOAKE.

No department of knowledge is like grammar A person may conceal his ignorance of any other art—but every time he speaks, he publishes his ignorance of this. There can be no greater imputation on the intelligence of any man, than that he should talk from the cradle to the tomb, and never talk well.—G. J. H.

LONDON:

J. Watson, 5, Paul's-alley, Paternosterrow; E. Nicholls, 61, Broad-street, Birmingham; and M. Roalfe & Co., 105, Nicolson-street, Edinburgh.

TO CORRESPONDENTS.

W. Mereer will see that the 2 vols of the *Oracle* have been purchased by "W. W. B." therefore we need not give an opinion on his suggestion. The most convenient way of sending small sums to the A. P. Union is by enclosing postage stamps.

E. N.—" The Morality of Atheism," will receive our attention.

H. Roche.—His enquiry will be answered.

For T. Paterson from W. W.	£0	5	0
For C. S. from W. W.	0	5	0
For Miss Roalfe from W. W.	0	5	0
For G. J. H. from W. J.	0	5	0

G. J. H. Sec.

Printed and Published by G. J. Holyoake, 40, Holywell-street, Strand, Saturday, May 25, 1844.

THE MOVEMENT
And Anti=Persecution Gazette.

"Maximize morals, minimize religion."—BENTHAM.

No. 25.   EDITED BY G. JACOB HOLYOAKE, ASSISTED BY M. Q. RYALL.   PRICE 1½d

REPLY TO CHARLES SOUTHWELL'S "FALLACY OF THE ARGUMENT A PRIORI, FOR THE BEING AND ATTRIBUTES OF GOD, AS THAT ARGUMENT IS STATED BY WILLIAM GILLESPIE," published in numbers 14 and 15 of *The Movement*.

By William Gillespie

IN TWO PARTS.

Contents of Part First.
1. Introduction.
3. Plan of Mr. Southwell's Answer.
4. Dissection of that Plan.
5. (1.) Mr. S. insists on the connection between Proposition I., and all the rest, of the "Argument."
7. (2.) Mr. S. denies Prop. I.
9. (*First.*) Promising to prove the falsity thereof.
11. (*Secondly.*) And giving three things *in lieu* of proof.
12. The first thing.
14. The second. And
15. The third.
17. 18. The reason why Mr. S. gives no proof. Mr. S. changes sides, and admits the truth conveyed in Prop. I.
22. Proof that Mr. S. does so.
26. Application.

1. THE Philalethean Society's challenge, which was applicable to "any one connected with the *Oracle of Reason*," (the organ, formerly, of the Atheists of London), to answer my Argument, *à priori*, by showing "that in any part of it there is A SUBSTANTIAL FALLACY";[*] the Philalethean Society's challenge, I say, was accepted in February 1843. Mr. Southwell, the Choryphæus of the London Atheists, having prepared an answer, the answer appeared in the *Movement* (the successor of the atheistical organ above-mentioned) in the month of March last. The answer in question fills two papers, which together are comprised in about *four* pages. The long interval which elapsed between the acceptance of the challenge and the publication of the answer, entitled us to expect better things. *There was great cry, and there is little wool.* But perhaps what the Philaletheans have at length been presented with is very precious, though meager?

2. Certain it is, that Mr. Southwell tells his readers, at the close of his performance, that he takes leave of my "grand argument" "in the confident expectation" that his Philalethean *challengers* "will, with all convenient speed, either answer what is" written in his *Fallacy*, "or acknowledge it unanswerable." These Philalethean challengers choose to answer what Mr. Southwell has written, as the *easy* alternative. To say that Mr. Southwell's *Fallacy* is unanswerable, would require a *face of brass*. And on the score of *speed*, there is small scope for my opponent finding any fault.

3. Distinguishing between the strictures in general, and the *answer* in particular, of Mr. Southwell; the plan pursued in the *answer* is this: The author grants—to my "great joy, and perhaps surprise"[*]—that the whole of my demonstration is a logical sequence from my first Proposition; of which, therefore, he denies the truth. Proposition I. is: "Infinity of Extension is necessarily existing." Mr. Southwell allows, that the necessary consequence of the admission of that truth would be—A GOD. And *therefore*, argues Mr. Southwell, it is *not* true, that infinite extension necessarily exists.

4. In the *first* place, then, Mr. Southwell grants, yea—which is very surprising—strenuously contends, that all the Propositions of the "Argument" are true, *if* the initial proposition be true.

5. "Every atom of the 'grand' argument "MUST," maintains my answerer, "SURVIVE or perish with" the admission of Proposition I.[†] This proposition is said to the "proposition every other proposition in his (Mr. Gillespie's) book rests upon." In accordance with which, my conclusions are "conclusions logically flowing" from my assumptions or premises.[‡] And, lastly: "Our author is not only sure that infinity of extension necessarily exists, but also that none can help having an idea thereof, for, says he, even when the

---
[*] Oracle of Reason, No. 61, p. 66-67.
[*] Mr. S's 1st paper, paragraph 11.
[†] Paper 1st, par. 14. [‡] Paper, 1. par. 1.

mind endeavours to remove from it the idea of infinity of extension, it cannot, after all its efforts, avoid leaving still there the idea of such infinity.

" If this were so, why, then indeed"—He means that all the rest would follow.*

6. I wish the reader to dwell on that close connection, which Mr. Southwell states so forcibly, between my premiss,—the necessary existence of infinite extension, and my conclusion,—the necessary existence of GOD. Great is the complacency with which I see my opponent do what he can to render the connection indissoluble. The cause of my complacency will not long be any secret.

7. In the *second* place,—Mr. Southwell denies the truth of the proposition affirming, " Infinity of Extension is necessarily existing." He classes it with " absurd assumptions."† He calls it " that unproved, unprovable, and most idle assertion."‡ He calls it, by an elegant *idiom*, " the *rotten* proposition."§ He insinuates, it constitutes " the most ridiculous of metaphysical fallacies."‖

8. Not only this: My answerer is to *prove* is too. He positively sets himself to show the falsity of the proposition in hand.

9. He says he shall be excused " by readers in general, and Gillespie's admirers in particular, for taking some pains *to prove* that there is no such *thing* as infinity of extension."¶ In another place, he speaks of something he is to do, " before proceeding *to prove* that the ' grand' argument's fundamental proposition is a fundamental fallacy."** And towards the conclusion of his first paper, he promises " *to demonstrate* in the next *Movement* that there is no such *thing*, and consequently no such *existence* as extension." Accordingly, the second paper commences thus : " That infinity of extension necessarily exists, is the first and fundamental proposition of our author—that there is no such a thing as extension I have engaged, and shall now attempt to demonstrate."

10. The promise of the proof occurs, we see, often enough. No want of parade either. But as for the proof itself—the proof itself, to be sure, never comes. And should any one of Southwell's admirers (for there is nothing impossible in the supposition, he has admirers) allege that the proof referred to ever came, the least he can do is, to put his finger on the place.

11. Is there not, then, at least something given *in lieu* of proof? There is : but you will not think much of it. Much or little, you shall have the whole of what is given *in lieu* of a proof of the falsity of the position which affirms, *that infinite extension necessarily exists*.

12. First, then: " The truth is, (and that it is the truth, any one may convince himself by five minutes' *wholesome reflection*) that the only thing, *i.e,*, re**a**l existence of which it is possible to think at all, is matter."* Here an appeal to our Reflection, or Consciousness, is instituted by Mr. Southwell, who, of course, gives honestly the result of his own Reflection, when he teaches, that it is *not possible* so much as *to think* of a vacuum, or of aught else than body, as *in rerum natura.* Alongside the dictum of Charles Southwell's Consciousness, I shall lay the decision of John Locke's, which perhaps, will be granted to be as honestly reported as is the other. " This solid thinker believed the material universe to be finite. ' If,' he says, ' body be not supposed infinite, *which I think no one will affirm*,' &c. Essay, B. II. ch. xiii. § 21. And the like in numerous places. And as he believed matter to be finite, so he believed, and could not but believe, space to be infinite. ' This,' he declares, ' is c rtain, that WHOEVER pursues his own thoughts, will find them sometimes launch out beyond the extent of body, into *the infinity of space or expansion.' Ibid*, ch. xv. § 4. To the same effect he speaks in many passages." (" Examination" of Antitheos, part viii. § 11.)

13. I must not forget to notice, that Mr. Southwell's appeal to human consciousness, even were it sure of a favourable response, would not serve the purpose for which it is introduced. Were the appeal entitled to a favourable answer, it would be *instead of, and for want of,* a proof.

14. Secondly : " Our author ought to know that *extension*, oftener called *space*, is a word philosophers have agreed shall represent a certain class of ideas, generated in us by *the order of things existing*."† By the way :—I ought to know, were it not the case that I have long known, *all* that my answerer can tell me, as to what philosophers are agreed in. It happens, too, that I know more than my answerer knows. For it is not all philosophers, but only some philosophers, these the followers of *Leibnitz*, who hold that *Space* is just the order of *co-existing bodies.* A position which such great authorities as Dr. Isaac Watts, and Professor Dugald Stewart, pronounced to be *not even intelligible.* But the dogma has received a full consideration, and, I may add, exp sure, in my ' Examination" of *Antitheos*, part ix. § 32, &c.

15. The third and the last *substitute* for a proof is as follows :—" If extension is ideal, and who in his senses can doubt it ?)"‡ The

---

* Paper 2nd, par. 3-4.
† Paper 2nd, par. 1. ‡ Paper 1. par. 3.
§ Paper 1, par. 14. ‖ Paper 2, par. 22.
¶ Paper 1. par. 3. **Paper 1, par. 11.

---

* Paper 2, par. 4.
† Paper 2, par. 14. ‡ paper 2, par. 23.

non-ideality of extension we touch, we confess with fear. For just observe the penalty hanging over all those who, with Sir Isaac Newton, and his disciples and followers, hold the existence of *vacuum*, or of pure space.

16. If any one can point out in Mr. Southwell's strictures, aught else—we shall not say proving, or tending, in the most distant way, to prove, but—so much as professing to prove, the falsity of my first Proposition; I must have read those strictures to little purpose. A thing not to be credited

17. But, after all, it is not so much to be wondered at, that, of proof of the kind in question, there was none, and, of a substitute for proof, but little. The reason is convincing: In this world there never was, and there never will be any proof of the kind. And to evince this, what were necessary but that Mr. Southwell should change sides, and admit, and again admit, in the broadest and "*grossest*" manner, the truth of the proposition he would prove the falsity of?

18. The Proposition which my answerer would prove untrue is, be it remembered, the following,—" Infinity of Extension is necessarily existing." And I shall evince to the heart's content of every reader of this periodical, that Mr. Southwell admits, ay, and maintains, the truth conveyed in that proposition; so soon as ever I quote one or two passages from those works of mine which were in that gentleman's hands, when he set himself to the penning of his unhappy strictures.

19. The first of those works cited by Mr. Southwell, from which I shall quote, is the old edition of my "Argument *à priori*." The Appendix relative to my first Proposition says, " Let the extension be of space *merely*, or of matter *merely*, or of space and matter *together*. The proposition affirms that there is Infinity of Extension, but affirms nothing more."

20. The next work is, the "Examination" of *Antitheos*. In a note to § 88 of part ix. of this performance, the following important information occurs. " It did not suit our purpose *to take for granted* (even so little—or, if you please—so much, as) the separate existence of pure space, *i.e.*, space without matter. The 'Argument' sets out from the thing denoted by the unambiguous word *extension*, infinite extension; not caring (at the first stage of the demonstration) of what nature the extension is. That there is expansion, or pure space, *distinct* from the extension of matter; it is the business of the second (or general) scholium under Prop. iv. Part I. to demonstrate.

" In fact, had the first Proposition in the demonstration (in place of being ' Infinity of EXTENSION is necessarily existing,') been in these terms—*Infinity of* SPACE *is necessarily existing*; it *might* have been objected: That it was—unwarrantably, for without proof—assumed that in nature there is space where there is no matter. A position, without doubt, of vast consequence, as against atheism: and by no means to be laid hold of, before right to possession be established."—A right to possession is established in the first Sub-Proposition,* where it is proved that the Material Universe is finite in extension. And the same truth is touched on in other portions of the demonstration.

21. And now for Mr. Southwell's admission of the truth conveyed in my first Proposition:—which being granted, all the rest of the demonstration becomes undeniable; which being true, all the rest is necessarily true also. The connection between the initial step and the whole of what follows, I would not for the world call in question. How fortunate that my answerer—in this, not my opponent—does what he can to establish, or confirm, that connection!

22. " I tell our author that it is not infinity of extension, but *infinity of matter*, we cannot *but believe*, which we *always suppose*, even though we *would not*."† Again: Not only is matter necessarily infinite in extension; "Matter is the *only* infinite."‡ These passages are sufficiently express, and, without quoting additional ones, I simply refer to others, of similar import, scattered through my answerer's second paper. That Mr. Southwell holds matter's extension to be infinite, may be considered a point sufficiently notorious to the readers of this periodical.

23. Matter is infinite, necessarily infinite; this Mr. Southwell holds. And as matter unquestionably is extended, or has extension; with Mr. Southwell, extension is necessarily infinite. Now I say (in accordance with the passages in my works quoted above), while I consider myself, in point of logical progress, at Proposition I., I am perfectly satisfied with the assertion, that the extension which matter has is infinite, and necessarily existing. The proposition in question lays down no more than this, that extension, *of some kind or other*—of matter, if you will—or no-matter, if any other will—is infinite, and necessarily so. Thus my answerer, the redoubtable Atheist Charles Southwell, joins me cordially in upholding, in his own way, that grand primary truth, which, if my answerer is to be credited, —and I credit him—leads infallibly to Theism. Mr. Southwell, I say, joins me in contending, " Infinity of Extension is necessarily existing,"—if he be only allowed to add, There is no extension but the extension of matter.

---

* I have here the *new edition* in my eye.
† Paper 2, par. 4. ‡ Paper 2, par. 16.

As an affair of dialectics, or, as the phrase is, *for argument's sake*, I allow him to add that, and as much more as he chooses to add, even everything but a retractation of what he has already granted; *so long as* he and I, and our readers, are at this stage of the journey—*But no longer*, for when we arrive at the subsequent propositions of the " Argument," it will be found that they can speak for themselves.

24. For instance: To go no further on than Proposition II., which runs thus, " Infinity of Extension is necessarily indivisible," and is to the effect, that the parts of what is infinite in extension are necessarily indivisible from each other, either by any operation of nature, or by any supposition of man's mind. The demonstration of this second Proposition shows, that by the very nature of *infinite* extension, divisibility, or the possibility of division, is excluded. If infinite extension were divisible really or mentally, it would not be infinite extension.

25. A *necessary consequence*, which is glanced at in a remark under Prop. II, and is brought out expressly and more fully afterwards, is that the Material Universe, the parts of which are divisible from each other, is not infinite in extension.

26. Thus, on the whole: According to Mr. Southwell, all the " Argument" is true, *if* proposition I. be true. According to Mr. Southwell, Proposition I, *is* true. Therefore—but I need not draw out the conclusion. Were my answerer consistent, he would cease to keep company with Atheists: he would become one of the glorious company of Theists. And I invite him—and I hope "that he will cheerfully accept the invitation—to become *one of us*." Or shall we say, keeping a paragraph of his own in view: Our author stands proved a dishonest Theist, or a Theist so stupid as not to know he is one? One may be a Theist by all the rules of logic, though by none of the graces which suit the character of a believer.

End of Part First of Reply.

SCIENCE AND RELIGION.

SCIENCE and religion are natural enemies. They may appear to assimilate, may enter into a hollow confederacy, or assume each other's character. The relationship is not hearty, genuine, real. It is contracted either through ignorance of each other's nature, or for sinister purposes. Science investigates, religion dogmatizes. Science applies itself to things and existences, searches to discover the rules according to which they move and are moved, are changed, combined, and re-combined, and teaches us "dominion over nature." Religion invents speculations, and promulgates suppositions; seeks not for information, because it pre-supposes infallibility, and substitutes for the properties of things, the attributes of nothings. Instead of directing and improving the instincts and faculties, it tries to abolish them or subjugate them to arbitrary rules of its own ignorant imaginings, and would make us the sport of the elements by diverting our attention from the causes of natural phenomena to the fictions of unnatural idealities. Religion consistently followed up would teach us a "pater noster" in a hurricane; science would point to the compass and the helm. Religion would pray for deliverance from plague, pestilence and famine; science would adopt the means, physiologically, economically, and politically to avoid them. The spirit of science is shown in an unpretending yet dignified bearing; that of religion is displayed in overbearing pride or debasing humility. The religionist proclaims himself as one in communication direct, handed down, or inspired, with an invented cause, and controller of all things, itself no thing. The man of science considers himself as " an infant picking up pebbles on the sea-shore of knowledge, while the great ocean of truth lies unexplored before him." The religionist shows the spirit of exclusiveism in founding a sacerdotal order whose privileges are to dictate, controul, and command. The man of science shows the liberalizing tendency of his studies by an invitation to, and ready acceptance of, fraternization with all parties, countries, and sects, among whom barriers had been raised by religious prejudices.

The arrogant pretensions of religionists are no where more strikingly illustrated than in the conduct pursued towards men of science, which has always been bitterly oppressive or deceitfully encouraging. The early dawnings of science, when in the treacherous embrace of religion, have been associated or identical with the vilest imposture or charlatanery. In proportion as religion was mixed up with it, have chains been, through religious agency, forged for the manacling of the human intellect. Thus sorcery, magic, divination, charms, astrology, alchemy, were the early quackeries that theology imposed on the infant efforts of science, and which so long kept them from developing their beneficial and delightful uses, when directed into the channel of mechanical, astronomical, and scientific investigations.

The East has been supposed the birthplace of religion—it is reputed the hot-bed of tyranny, and the most inaccessible to science. From the rank luxuriance of Eastern religionism has the more frigid West imported the religion of the cross, and the deadly upas plant shows continual evidence of its origin.

The custom of orientalism to immure the children of the reigning prince during his lifetime, has been familiarised to most readers, in Johnson's "Rasselas." The brutish and degrading practice aptly exemplifies the spirit of religion towards science, and the relationship subsisting between them, whether we delineate the feebleness of infancy or the strength of maturity. Nursed like the younger progeny of Asiatic despots, in obscure, ignoble, and lethargic content, while under the prevailing dominancy, it is, like them, pursued, attacked, and if possible destroyed, whenever the attempt is made to substitute liberty of thought and action for the crippling bonds of slavery. From the moment that science at any time made the attempt to emancipate itself from the poisonous contact of religion, it was pursued with relentless oppression, or chilled by contemptuous neglect. When sufficient advances have been made by science to command attention, the fury of religion has been invariably poured out to subdue and overwhelm it. As science has progressed, as open repudiation, or opposition, and the sacrifice of victims have failed in effecting the object, religion has assumed a different attitude—it has recognised the claims of science and offered its protection and patronage. This is the most critical period of its progress. The fabled allurements of the Syrens who decoyed but to destroy, the dalliance of a Delilah to lure to betrayal, the slimy embrace of the boa are not more dangerous nor deadly than the nursing and fostering of religion. From the time when the great Bacon, first casting his brilliant light upon the intellectual horizon, stepped aside to pay homage to religion—throughout the tribe of theological philosophers of the Butler, Clarke, and Paley schools—amid the fashionable reign of Bridgewater treatises, down to the rational religionizing of "the Universal Community Society of Rational Religionists"—even to the revival of the Aristotelian machinery of terms, forms, and logical chicane for the inductive processes of right reason—throughout this comparatively short, brilliant, yet chequered era—to trace the advances made by science, when in the road of rationalism, and its difficulties, dangers, and obscurations when swerving among the fogs and quagmires of religion, is signally instructive and interesting.

Religious faith, the prime evil, engendering the monstrous progeny of revelations, multitudinous in crimes and follies, with infamous doctrines, stolid worship, and undelegated authority, had received a terrible blow from the moment that science had begun to emancipate itself from the god trammels, and to become free to the approaches of the many. But with the tenacious gripe and crafty shiftiness of all bodies, become powerful through a career of fraud, and depending for existence upon the perpetuity of their misdeeds, the sacred tribe endeavour to make it appear that the interests of the scientific world were bound up with their own. If the antagonist principles could not be reconciled, the antagonist persons have been seduced, or attempted, by cajolery, bribes, or intimidation.

Science and religion, then, in whatever close or distant relationship they may have appeared to subsist, are, when brought to the test of analysis, essentially irreconcileable.

To do full justice to the subject, a master-spirit should arise. To accomplish for the history of science what Gibbon has for that of a nation, would be a noble work. To display the true causes of, and obstacles to, progress, to lay bare the springs of action, to analyze real motives and false professions, to tear the mask of hypocrisy from the sactified scoundrelism that has duped and swayed the world, would be a great achievement. The industrious research, patient investigation, critical acumen, and shrewd penetration, set forth in all the stately pomp of diction, the prodigal graces of style, and withering, yet dignified irony in which the great historian so eminently excelled, would be worthily employed on so grand a theme as "the progress of science in its disenthralment from religion."

If from a study of science—of that science most repugnant to religion, and most friendly to humanity—of that science for whose sake its prime elucidator abdicated the throne of popularity by an emphatic declaration against all religions—if, through the benign philosophy of the Social Science, we are disposed to make all possible allowances for those of the scientific world who ignominiously betray their trust of expounders of truth—all honor to those, who like the Phrenological Association and projectors of the *Zoist* esteeming the dignity of their vocation beyond the applause and patronage of the vulgar great, guided by rectitude, and sustained by self respect—refuse to succomb to the wiles or threats of religionism, and follow science whithersoever it leads. M. Q. R.

MISS FRANCES WRIGHT.

I BELIEVE it may be safely asserted that less is known with respect to the personal history, origin, and family connections of Miss Frances Wright, or Madam D'Aursmont, than of any other character of existing notoriety. This has doubtless been caused by the fact, that when not impelled by the hope of achieving some great public good, she has lived in retirement, bordering on absolute seclusion. Many and various surmises have consequently run current relative to the life and character of that distinguished and eloquent lady, and singular to relate, few, if any of these surmises have had any foundation in fact.

As the reader may be curious to know by what means I arrived at that knowledge which her numerous admirers in this country seem altogether destitute of, I may briefly state that Madam D'Aursmont lately visited Dundee for the settlement of important business connected with property she has inherited from a cousin of her father—the last of the name. The news of her arrival soon spread through the town. Feeling anxious to see a woman whose eloquence has gone so far to effect a revolution in the mind of America, I embraced the earliest opportunity of soliciting an interview; I was received with the greatest kindness.

Madame D'Aursmont is amongst the tallest of women; being about 5ft. 5 inches high; she walks erect, and is remarkably handsome. Her brow is broad, and, phrenologically speaking, magnificent; her eyes are large; her face is masculine, but well formed.

In the course of our conversation I mentioned to her that certainly little was known of her life, as I had seen it stated in an Edinburgh Magazine that she belonged to Glasgow.

She replied, that was not surprising; she had seen biographical notices of herself which did not contain a single fact. Adding, "The reason is obvious. I have always avoided speaking about myself; and of course, no one knows where I belong to, or anything about me."

After a desultory conversation, and a promise from her to call at my abode; we separated.

After waiting a few days, and finding that Madame D'Aursmont did not call, I wrote to her, stating that my views in calling upon her were to obtain from her such facts of her life as she might think proper to favour me with, to be published in some Liberal newspaper or magazine, for the information and gratification of her numerous admirers in this country.

On the same day this was posted, Madame D'Aursmont called at my residence, with the following note, remarking that she intended to leave it if she had not found me at home :—

"DEAR SIR—Should I not find you at home, let this line, which I shall leave in that case, in token of ready sympathy with your wishes, satisfy you, that I did not, that I could not, misinterpret your only too flattering enthusiasm. So far as this may have been inspired by those principles of truth and liberty which it has ever been the effort of my mind to interpret correctly, and the object of my life to advance—that enthusiasm can only meet with an echo in my own breast. So far again as in the ardour of youthful feeling, you may have apostrophized the advocate of those principles, instead of purely and entirely those principles themselves, my censure cannot and will not be too severe, since I can recall the time when I was prone to err in the same manner and in equal excess.

I beg that you will dismiss all fears of intrusion, and call on me as frequently and as freely as inclination may dictate. I look for my husband and daughter by the next London Steam Packet.

Your's, dear Sir, with much respect,
F. W.D' AURSMONT."

The reader will now perceive that my opportunities of ascertaining the information so much wished for, were of the best description. In my next article, I will endeavour to give a lucid and succinct biography of a woman who is unquestionably the most intellectual female defender of liberty in the present age. T. MYLES.

Northern Star—Dundee, May, 1844.

CHRISTIAN ADMINISTRATION OF LAW.

I GIVE this title to my animadversions, and I think very appropriately so, on account of the very palpable connection between christianity and the interpretation of the laws by our law-administrators. The case of Serjeant Western, last week, reminded me of, not only a gross injustice, but a gross violation of law, or a most palpable straining and wresting of the law, by the Bow-street functionaries. The explanation to this case is, that the offence was one against christianity, and that the prosecution was instituted by government; and when christianity and government hunt in couples after victims, once marked out by them, the game is pretty sure of being run down, whether fairly or unfairly—in accordance with, or in spite of their own rules. The alleged guilt or innocence in the case quoted—namely, that of Paterson, for displaying profane placards—hinged (as far as police magistrates could determine) upon the exhibition taking place, in a *thoroughfare or not*—the former class of cases coming within, the latter being excluded from, the jurisdiction of the police magistrate—The decision is familiar to all of us—it was in favour of himself—that is in favour of his competency to try a case which the legislature had determined to place, and passed acts to confine, within higher jurisdiction. But god's christianity, backed by government Maule, gained the day, as it always does, against such as Paterson, reason and justice. Now, how would the matter stand, should the "thoroughfare" question enter into the merits of any other case in which offence to christianity was a conspicuous ground of accusation? Would the even tenor of the law be disturbed, and worse than informality—absolute illegality—be practised? No instance of such forced and perverted misinterpretations have come within my knowledge in cases apart from heterodoxy. Misreadings and perversions are cooked up expressly for such occasions. Scores of instances could be adduced of the vilest and grossest offenders against humanity or decency, escaping scatheless because the magistrates, confessed their inability to act, from insufficient powers. The most unmanly violation of decency and atrocious ruffianism has escaped punishment from this plea of the magistrates.

It is not a fortnight since, Mr. Long of Marylebone-street, announced his incapacity to deal with a case of disgusting indecency, reported in the *Times* of the 11th, because not committed in a thoroughfare; these are his words—"He could not punish the prisoner, inasmuch as the offence alleged against him had not been committed in a street or public place." Had this been a god almighty, cross, or gospel case — we are seriously justified in asking—would the same decision have been given? I say not this with reference to Mr. Long—I do not desire to individualize—but the common course of heterodox trials, and the general tendency of the system—the Christian-based, or Christian-interwoven, system—shows us what we have to expect in the way either of law or justice by their sworn administrators. Mark the singular parellelism of the two cases.

Mr. Jardine—In the profane placard case —" I do not say that I consider the question, whether the exhibition to public view in a thoroughfare, *is so clear as I could wish in a penal act of Parliament.*" [Notwithstanding which confession, he *convicted*.]

Mr. Long—In the indecent exposure case —" He could not punish the prisoner, inasas the offence alleged against him had not been committed in a street or public place; and he must, therefore, be *discharged.*

Let us mark all such instances of gross partiality. The one-sidedness of the legislature is bad enough, but when added to this, is the still grosser and more unscrupulous bias of those who are intrusted with the judicial functions, it becomes a more crying evil. It would be highly useful to our cause and the "Union," that all cases, both of legislative and judicial injustice, should be recorded. Those who would transmit to us—especially when the local press will not expose the criminality—authentic accounts of such particulars would be doing good service to the interests of liberty.

The Central Board of the "Rationalists," promptly, judiciously, and boldly interfered in a case of local judicial tyranny, and with eminent success. And though they dropt the Whitechapel case—as we learn from the last *New Moral World*—it may be hoped that not only their first example may be followed by all whose means may enable them to adopt a similar course, but that, by all the public reprehension and petitioning that may be in our power, we may hasten the march of freedom. M. Q. R.

MORALITY SUPERIOR TO RELIGION.

The moral principles which have been supposed to require the aid of religion, are in all countries nearly the same, which is a proof that they are fixed and indispensible in their nature; while the religions which support them are various as the climates of the globe, and extravagant as their different authors. Morality is founded on the reason of mankind, and has for its object the general advantage. Religion is founded on their folly, in pretending to dive into that which they can never comprehend, and is converted into a gainful trade, for a particular set of individuals; the one is simple and uniform, the other is various, mutable, and confused. We neither know, nor can know, the intentions of the Supreme Being, because we are ignorant of his nature, and unless he is a man like ourselves, which the ignorant generally conceive him, there can be no such a thing as a revelation of his will; for we have not faculties to comprehend a divine intelligence. We talk of inspiration, and yet know nothing about the nature of spirit, or how it acts upon matter; a revelation, therefore, from a Being whose nature we are acquainted with, is a contradiction in terms. There can be no evidence of a supernatural agency acting upon the mind of man, unless it enables him to tell with certainty things which could not otherwise be known, and there is nothing in either the Old or New Testament which can bear such a test, for all that is there declared to be foretold, is dark and ambiguous, and capable of almost any interpretation, and all that is said to have happened contrary to the established laws of nature is incapable of proof, because it contradicts the experience of our senses, which are the only medium of knowledge or evidence. *Burdon.*

VALUE OF MAHOMETANS.

Whenever we abuse the Mahometans we should remember the benefits we have arceived from them. They were for years almost the only people who wrote and possessed any considerable portion of knowledge. There is a book of the lives of their Poets in no less than fifty volumes. Astronomy, chemistry, arithmetic, medicine, mathematics owe much to the Arabs; our notation we have entirely from them, and through these they have largely contributed to civilize the human race. A degree of the earth was several times measured in Chaldea by them. Cordova, when they had it, possessed a library of nearly 300,000 volumes, and in the kingdom of Andalusia alone there were nearly one hundred public libraries. Grenada was nearly as well supplied; six successive authors took up 115 years in writing a history of Spain. The Alif lita wa lilin, or One Thousand and One Tales, is by no means an unfavourable specimen of their lighter labours, and after the lapse of years does not now convey a bad idea of the customs of the Arabians. Al Bathani, or Albathenius as he is called, drew up the Sabian Tables in the ninth century, after forty years observations, and they were for many years the standard authority in astronomical matters. The Arabian architecture was magnificent: there are still standing in Spain splendid specimens of this delightful art; monuments which would astonish those only familiar with the edifices of London or Paris. We know less about these things than we ought, from the ridiculous way we distort their writer's names. An European, if he was to ask in Mocha or Cairo for any author who had been studied by him in Europe, would not be understood, and, of course, *vice versa*. Who would recognise, under our name of Avicenna, their well-known and famous physician Abdallah ibn Sina? We have done the same with most of the celebrated Rabbins.   Dr. P. Y.

NOTICE.

On Tuesday Evening next, at 8 o'clock, the London Society of Atheists will hold their next Monthly Meeting, at the Parthenium, St. Martin's Lane, to receive Subscriptions, admit Members, and discuss the following adjourned question, "Ought Atheists to take the usual oath administered in our Courts of Law."   T. Powell, *Secretary*,
40, Holywell-street.

Now Ready, in a neat wrapper, price Sevenpence, part 6 of the *Movement*.

Did you ever know a settled minister to have a 'call' to preach to a poorer congregation?

On Sunday evening, June 9th, at half-past seven o'clock, will be delivered, at the City Road Hall of Science, a Lecture by M. Q. Ryall, on Bible Interpretations.

Mr. Paterson acknowledges the receipt of the following letters. Mrs. B. I—Mr. Liddle 2—Messrs. Birch, Adams, Jeffery, Sharp and Hammond, 1 each. He desires a few small articles and some books of travels, which will be sent to him. One of Emerson's finest orations, which had been copied and sent to him by a young lady of piety, residing in London, has been objected to by the chaplain.

Just Published, Tracts for the People, by Emma Martin. No. 1—A Conversation on Being and Attributes of God. No. 2 —Religion Superseded, or the Moral Code of Nature sufficient for the Guidance of Man.

MR. PATERSON'S PETITION.

Bryanstone Square, May 11, 1844.
Mr. Hume begs to acknowledge the receipt of Mr. Holyoake's note respecting Mr. Paterson, and regrets to inform him that he has received a positive refusal from Sir James Graham to do any thing in his behalf.

Mr. Hume will present the petition next week, but would wish to see Mr. Holyoake on the subject previously to his doing so, and will write again to name the day when it will be most convenient.

[The Anti-Persecution Union on the receipt of this information, at once determined on holding a public meeting, as the answer of the Home Secretary was only necessary to enable them to do so consistently with the course, which on the calmest consideration, they had marked out for themselves. The public meeting will be duly announced the moment arrangements are completed.

Ed. of M.]

TO CORRESPONDENTS.

H. Roche.—His suggestions will be taken into consideration. M. Q. R. received the remittance.

A. M. W. will see that the *Grammar* is at length published. It has been unexpectedly delayed in the printer's hands.

SUBSCRIPTIONS TO THE ANTI-PERSECUTION UNION.

H. Roche, Derby £0 1 0
G. Dixon, Stratford, for Member's
   Tickets 0 3 0
                              G. J. H., *Sec.*

Printed and Published by G. J. Holyoake,
40, Holywell-street, Strand,
Saturday, June 1 1844.

THE MOVEMENT

And Anti=Persecution Gazette.

"Maximize morals, minimize religion."—BENTHAM.

No. 26.   EDITED BY G. JACOB HOLYOAKE, ASSISTED BY M. Q. RYALL.   PRICE 1½d

JEWS AND GENTILES,
AT HOME AND ABROAD
II.

WHERE sceptical philosophy and rationalism most extensively prevail, and with the high sanction of authority—where the Academy and ministers of public instruction are included in the reproach—where the epithets *Pantheist* or *Universalist* have been attempted to be affixed by Christian bigots, as opprobriums to the highest names in science and letters—there a degree of toleration has been reached, which, poor as the word is, marches in advance of all other continental powers. In France, where sectarian dominancy has had its talons cut, though the poison fangs of the old state religion have not been as yet entirely extracted, reputable citizens, respected functionaries, military chiefs, philosophers, literati, and artists adorn its annals from among the generally despised and oppressed race of Israel. In a few liberalized states where such characteristics are more or less prevalent, similar results may be observed. Here these Jews, whose very name has been a proverb and a byeword, who, as Dr. P. Y. would say, are scorned at and stigmatised as the old-clothesmen and pedlars of the world—where noble attempts have been made by the philosophic and unchristian to unsectarianize their country—here the downcast, the lowly, the despised have arisen in the strength of manhood, vindicated their common claims to brotherhood, and stood forth as the scholars, the gentlemen, the emancipators and publicists of their æra. With deep gratification must all lovers of their species perceive how the alien, the slave, and the outcast have given the lie to the foulest aspersions on their moral and intellectual capabilities, when once humanity has been suffered to have fair play. Many of the continental journals pleasingly illustrate this exhilarating fact, not only chronicling such instances of progression, but edited by members of the Hebrew church. Les *Archives Israelites de France*, whose conductors and contributors are Jews, from the manner in which it is sustained, and the liberal tenor of its pages, is a gratifying evidence of what is now adduced. Much of the information now published is from some of its recent numbers.

M. Crémieux, who ably and successfully pleaded the cause of the editors of the Paris Journal, the *Gazette de France*, refused any remuneration for his services, saying, " I never accepted a fee for the defence of the opposition journals, and I will accept no other terms from those who differ from me in opinion." M. Crémieux exhibits an admirable disinterestedness and nice propriety of judgment on the subject of freedom of opinion, which would do honour to the most liberal among the members of the British bar. His conduct might also furnish a hint for a re-consideration of what is called the etiquette of the bar.

The editor of the *Archives Israelites de France* claims the above gentleman as a co-religionist. In the ranks of those of the members of the Jewish church who have distinguished themselves among the notables of the continent, is mentioned " M. Edmond Halphen, a just magistrate, paternal in the administration of his official business, and zealous in the discharge of his duties." He has been elected, all political influence having been disregarded, as mayor of the second arrondissement of Paris. It continues, " this should afford an example to our intolerant adversaries; here is an instance of the most populous, rich, and enlightened department of the first city in the world, by a sweeping majority, electing an Israelite for its chief officer. This is not all; in the same arrondissement, one of our most honourable fellow-religionists, M. Michael Goudchaux, has also obtained a great number of votes, and thus is presented the rare example of a mayor and his two colleagues in perfect agreement, and exchanging fraternal services, of whom one is Protestant, the second an Israelite, and the third a Roman Catholic. M. Franck, also a Hebrew, and professor of philosophy, has been chosen a member of the Academy, and professor of the sciences of morals and political economy."

The *Democratie Pacifique* of Berlin, thus writes:—" Notwithstanding the representations of the French, English, and German press, the Emperor Nicholas persists in his projects of persecution of the Jews. By a ukase, recently published, he forbids the Jews to show themselves in the city of Kiew, under penalty of hard labour. The emperor is deaf to the remonstrances which reach him on all sides. He is beset by the idea of a national unity, having for its basis the Greco-Russian religion, and he desires to abolish all that is opposed to it, whether Judaism or Catholicism. It appears that the King of Prussia, brother-in-law to the Emperor, far from dissuading him, encourages him in his intentions. A new law against the Jews is now being considered in the state council, which is to place the Jews in the position of a body isolated and entirely out of the state. They are to be excluded from the army, from the administration, and the masonic lodges. The King of Prussia has no affection for the Jews, he regards them as the principal propagators of Spinosism, and the philosophy of Hégel. Almost all the German journals sympathising with France are edited by Jews or Jewish converts; hence the hatred of the Jews, fomented by the pietists and attachés of the court of Berlin, thence the edict against the Jews. A great number of these unfortunate persons are about to emigrate to France and England. Meyerbeer has had a private audience of the King to offer his resignation, which has not been accepted; Mendelsohn, who is a converted Jew, an old favourite of the king, has to struggle against a fanatical clergy. The king had instructed him to compose psalms to be sung in church during divine service. These psalms were rejected by the clergy, who discovered in them worldly tendencies."

Mendelsohn, says the same journal, was to return to Leipsic, and Meyerbeer once in Paris was not expected to set his foot again in Berlin.

It is remarkable what a coincidence there is in this account and some passages in "Coningsby, or the New Generation," D'Israeli's last work, which must surely be a work of some merit, seeing how heartily it is praised and abused by the press. One of his characters says, "It has been much the fashion of the day to express an absurd wonder that the Jews possess so much influence in so many European cabinets. Why, they possess this influence in all, for show me the cabinet in which one at least of the privy councillors is not a Jew. A few years ago I went to negociate a public loan to St. Petersburg. On my arrival I had an immediate interview with the Russian minister of finance, Count Cancrin: I found him the son of a Lithuanian Jew. I afterwards went to Madrid on a like errand, and I had to transact business with the Spanish minister Mendizibal, the son of a Spanish Jew. Something connected with this loan required me to proceed straight to Paris to consult the president of the French Council, Marshal Soult, in whom I found another Jew. Marshal Massena was also a Jew, his real name being Manasseh. Nor did my experience end here. Having a short time afterwards to go to Prussia, I was attending the council of ministers when Count Arnim entered the cabinet, and I beheld a Prussian Jew."

In another place, musical Europe is claimed as belonging to the Jews. "There is not a company of singers, not an orchestra in a single capital, that are not crowded with our children under the feigned name which they adopt to conciliate the dark aversion which your posterity will some day disclaim with shame and disgust. Almost every great composer, skilled musician, almost every voice that ravishes you with its transporting strains, springs from our tribes. The catalogue is too vast to enumerate—too illustrious to dwell for a moment on secondary names, however eminent. Enough for us that the great creative minds to whose exquisite inventions all nations at this moment yield, Rossini, Meyerbeer, Mendelsohn are of Hebrew race? and little do your men of fashion, your 'muscadins' of Paris, and your dandies of London, as they thrill into raptures at the notes of a Pasta or Grisi, little do they suspect that they are offering their homage to the sweet singers of Israel!"

The jew, Sidonia, is a singularly delineated character. The *Times* in its review, thus describes him, and the peculiar opinions which D'Israeli puts into his mouth. " Had we not already quoted so largely from the novel, we would give at full length the ingenious and eloquent illustrations by which Sidonia, is represented as maintaining the final superiority of generic organization over the political power, and the sectarian persecution of inferior races. The mixed persecuting races, he contends, disappear—the pure persecuted race survives, not only does it survive, but exercises an insensible but momentous influence over the fortunes of its nominal masters. There is not, says Sidonia, a kingdom or a state of Europe, Protestant or Catholic, where the wealth of the Jew, and more than his wealth, his penetrative intelligence, his supple adroitness, his impulsive genius, is not giving an indirect but powerful momentum to the course of public events." The critic gives the following in the words of the author. "The first Jesuits were Jews; that mysterious Russian diplomacy, which so alarms Western Europe is organized, and principally carried on by Jews; that mighty revolution which is at this moment preparing in Germany, and which will be in fact a second reformation, is entirely developing under the auspices of the Jews, who almost monopolize the professorial chairs of Germany. Neander, the founder of spiritual christianity, and who is regius professor of divinity in the university of Berlin, is a Jew. Benary, equally famous, and in the same university, is a Jew. Wehl, the Arabic professor of Heidelberg, is a Jew. Years ago, when I was in Palestine, I met a German student who was accumulating materials for the History of Christianity, and studying the genius of the place, a modest and learned man. It was Wehl, then unknown, since become the first Arabic scholar of the day, and the author of the Life of Mahomet. But for the German professors of that race, their name is Legion. I think there are more than ten in Berlin alone." These are high words—but be they true, false, or exaggerated, it is fitting that we should not be behind the reading public of the orthodox world—such statements are worth deeper enquiry and investigation, involving as they do, considerations of a moral, political, and physiological character. That part of the assertion respecting Jewish concoction of Russian diplomacy certainly requires explanation. Russian diplomacy by Jews, and Russian persecution of Jews, are irreconcileable on ordinary principles.

On the subject of the brutal Russian proscriptions against Polish Jews, a letter from the Grand Duchy of Posen says, " Every day brings us intelligence of fresh persecution of the Israelites; their humble attitude, their black costume, their flowing beard and hair, show these unfortunates to be in much the same abject condition in which they were in the middle ages. They dare not speak, but with hat in hand, and for the most trivial service testify the liveliest gratitude."

" If it were needed," says the *Constitutionel*, "to demonstrate the advantages of a free over an absolute government, it would suffice to direct the attention to the tyrannical measures to which the unfortunate Israelites of Poland are subjected. The will of one man invested with power is sufficient to condemn to exile and to misery a numerous and inoffensive population. No law which this unfortunate people can invoke, no tribunal to hear their complaints, no justice to expect from a government whose barbarity is hardly concealed by a flimsy cloak of civilization."

Is it credible, in reading the details of this persecution, that we are in the nineteenth century, an epoch of progress and humanity?"

Israelites of England! the Autocrat is now on your shores—will you let him depart without a remonstrance on behalf of your brethren?

M. Q. R.

THOUGHTS on READING Mr OWEN'S FOURTH PART OF THE "BOOK OF THE NEW MORAL WORLD," EXPLANATORY OF THE RATIONAL RELIGION.
(*For the Movement.*)

I BELIEVE that the Socialists are generally aware of Mr. Owen's intentions respecting the completion of the above book, as he has long since announced that it will when completed, contain a full, correct, and complete exposition of the rational system as propounded by him. Such being the case, the completion of it will form an epoch in the history of rationalism, whence may be known what he intends it to be, and what his followers may make of it after he has passed away.

With reference to that part of it now under notice, I may safely say that the public has for some years been in possession of all it contains. It differs in no respect whatever from his former statements upon the same subject, except in phraseology, which every reader of it will admit is in some places much more severe than is usual with Mr. Owen. If this increased severity of language was likely to produce conviction in a shorter period of time, it would be a matter for rejoicing; but this is not the case, for it leaves all unsettled questions in precisely the same state as before.

I certainly did expect something *new* upon the *old* subject, but I have been disappointed, except in some minor particulars. Mr. Owen's subject naturally divides itself into two parts, first, the defects of the old, second, the beauties of the new religion. But Mr. O. so confounds them in his method of treating the subject, as to leave the reader to infer, that if he rejects one he must inevitably adopt the other. To such a view of the matter I, for one, decidedly object. Mr. Owen, when advancing a series of naked, unsupported propositions, overlooks some important considerations. He takes for granted that a number of facts have occurred to prove that he is right, and all others wrong; he also takes for granted that all his readers are acquainted with the aforesaid facts, whilst the truth really is that those of his readers who are in any considerable degree tainted with the opinions of the old world, are like the " Humphrey Hawkins" of *Tait's Magazine*, a fellow who " *could never see things in that light.*" I should like to know from the most inveterate Owenite what facts prove Mr. O's. novel proposition "that true religion is truth, and truth true religion." It is true that I am now writing for *the Movement*, but how that can be a part of true religion I am at a loss to divine.

In the first part of the work we are told that " truth is nature and nature god, that god is truth and truth is god," a definition manifestly at variance with that given in the fourth part, so that for consistency's sake we must apply to the *unique* lexicographers of Ham Common, who will no doubt help us out of the dilemma, by defining the meaning of this to be " the truth—nature—god—religion." Joking apart, such attempts to retain the name and not the substance of religion, can do no good whatever.

If the progress of truth mainly depends upon policy, as so many professing rationalists affirm, the best plan would have been to have commenced in a moderate way at first, and giving more and more as the mind became " prepared to receive it ;" it should have been done on the principle laid down in the holy scriptures, " milk for babes, but meat for men ;" for myself I know of no reason why truth should at any period be withheld, if a knowledge of it concerned the human race.

I by no means wish to detract from the assumed value of Mr. Owen's writings, any more than strict justice demands. On the contrary, there is perhaps no man in existence upon whose defects I could look with so lenient an eye; but I cannot help thinking, nevertheless, that Mr. Owen's works are not explicit enough to convince the world, even if they were universally read, for although he is a capital hand at the manufacture of abstract propositions, he often fails in carrying them out in an argumentative point of view—not, I admit, because he cannot do so, but because he seems to have contempt for all minor considerations. He is reported to have said in Stockport that all the gods in the world were in his way. I believe such to be the fact, and well would it have been for rationalism had this subject been entirely omitted, or that this statement had always been clearly made, that it was no matter, so far as the adoption of Owenian rationalism was concerned, whether there was a god or not, as the people living under the influence of the system could do either with or without one.

But first, to lead people into religious controversy and guarantee them liberty to pursue it, and then find fault with them for it, is rather too bad.

Your readers will no doubt begin to inquire after they have read what I have written, what is to be inferred from all this? To *me* the inference is very plain ; it is, that the *general* character of Mr. Owen's writings is not very likely of itself to cause the adoption of his system. I take pleasure, however, in saying that Mr. Owen can write differently and more effectually when he chooses to depart from his usual course. His address to the Congress of 1837, in my opinion, proves this most satisfactorily; he there in a few words gives materials for a vast amount of thought, compelling even believers to think. Let the reader compare the following propositions taken from the address I have just alluded to, with those that are usually found in the other works of the author—take, for example, the first and eighth articles of the rational religion. These, though not perhaps the best for my purpose, will from their being generally known answer tolerably well for the object I have in view. These are the

Propositions given by Mr. Owen in 1837 for the first time, and I believe never repeated since, at all events not in his printed works, he says, that they (the religionists) now *gravely* propound as divine truth**s**,

" I. That there is a being who made, and who governs the universe, and all within it; and that without him (for they represent him as a male existence,) nothing was made. That this being is infinite in knowledge, in power, and in goodness, that he knows all things, does all things, and can do anything that he wishes or desires.

II. That he made all things at first perfect, in heaven, on the earth, and throughout the universe ; that he had the power, if he chose, to keep all things, eternally in this perfect state, and that he alone made angels in heaven, and men on earth.

III. That, yet through some other power or influence, an angel, although first made perfect by infinite wisdom and goodness, became, or by some unaccountable process, made himself a devil, and then seduced other angels that had also been made perfect, to follow his example; and that this party, with the devil at their head, seduced man to become the irrational being that he has been, and now is in, over part of the world, and to act continually in opposition to his own happiness, and to the will of his own creator.

IV. That there is eternal enmity between these two opposing parties, the first god and his angels always desiring to make men wise and happy, while the second power, that is the devil and his angels, are equally intent upon keeping men ignorant, wicked, and miserable.

[As men are at this day ignorant, wicked, and miserable, the unavoidable conclusion is that the devil and his angels are more powerful than the first deity or god, assisted by his angels.]

V. That this eternal, infinitely wise, and good being, who made human nature so perfect and happy, yet so made it that the devil and his angels could so corrupt it, in the first man and woman as to render it for ever afterwards corrupt and sinful.

VI. That human corruption and sinfulness can be overcome and removed only by the most unaccountable proceedings of a being, said to be the son of this first being, and at the same time to be the first being or god himself, that this being, son and father in one, took upon himself the human form, suffering human misery, and an ignominious death; and even then, that a part only of the human race are to be saved from everlasting perdition by this supernatural and most mysterious agency of this all-wise and all-good being, who desires the happiness of the universe."

The reader will find this quotation appended to the Six Lectures delivered in Manchester, previous to the discussion with Mr. Roebuck, and they will find, also, that these lectures contain the best exposition of rationalism that has been given to the world, either before or since their publication.

I know no reason why Mr. Owen should not, in all his works—or attempt, to say the least of it—lay down his data after the fashion of 1837. Certain I am it would save a world of uncertain disputes as to what he means. The simplicity of truth, as distinguished from the complexity of error, has been so much eulogised by the founder of the rational system that it is somewhat surprising that he has not always contrived to state his views of right and wrong in a way that could not be mistaken by friend or foe.

Trusting that the succeeding parts of the work here reviewed will compensate for the defects spoken of, I leave the subject to the consideration of your readers.   J. C. F.

MR. T. RYLEY PERRY'S PETITION.

(*To the Editor of the Movement.*)

DEAR SIR,— The article on "Practical Directions on Petitions," in *Movement* No. 22, I much approve of, and have thought it might be of service to publish the enclosed Petition to the House of Commons, which has been entrusted to Mr. Hume, in order that it might operate as an example in cases of individual petitioning on the subject of blasphemy.

Many timid but well-meaning people have an idea that a fearless course would be attended with danger to the interests of individuals in trade, more particularly when unpopular opinions are broached publicly; this has been the case heretofore, but I rely much upon the effects of moral temerity when numbers are brought to bear upon this all-important subject, in our day, for be sure of it, the sledge hammer is beginning to tell slowly but surely, and I accordingly agree with you that it is not the numbers of signatures presented that will so much prevail, as the number of petitions.

I am much pleased with the spirit displayed in Paterson's last letter in the *Movement*. It is more than probable that he will have the high honour of being the last of "Christian Martyrs."   T. R. P.

"To the Honourable the Commons, &c.

"*The Petition of Thomas Ryley Perry, Chemist and Druggist, Market Street, in the Parish of St. Margaret, in the Borough of Leicester.*

"SHEWETH—That your petitioner is strongly of opinion that the recent convictions for blasphemy in Scotland, in reference to Thomas Paterson, Thomas Finlay, and Matilda Roalfe, is an infringement on the fundamental doctrines of Protestantism, the right of private judgement, the liberty of conscience, and the inalienable rights of mankind.

"That your petitioner is one among nearly thirty individuals, men and women, who have, since the year 1819, been convicted and imprisoned for various terms of incarceration, and whose sentences ranged from periods of six months, to three years, for the alleged crime of blasphemy.

"That in the year 1824 your petitioner was tried at the Old Bailey, London, before the then Recorder, Newman Knowlys, and a common jury, and sentenced to three years in Newgate. That your petitioner there defended himself on a charge of blasphemy, for selling " Palmer's Principles of Nature," in the shop of the late Richard Carlile, and that the judge, in passing sentence on your petitioner, stated that he doubted not ere the termination of your petitioner's' imprisonment, your petitioner would see cause for a recantation in your petitioner's views and feelings.

"That your petitioner, so far from seeing and feeling the force of the judge's observations, did experience, through all the dreadful period of such an imprisonment, and thence to the present moment of time, does more strongly and most conscientiously think, declare, proclaim, and publish these and similar opinions; and that out of nearly thirty persons who have been so imprisoned, but one individual has recanted, or been led to express opinions otherwise than they did before their trials.

"From the experience, therefore, of your petitioner, as well as from the experience of many thousands of good men and women in the United Kingdom, entertaining similar opinions; and, also, seeing the utter inefficiency of coercing the human mind for publishing speculations on the subject of religion, whether orally or through the medium of the printing press, your petitioner implores your Honourable House to abrogate all laws interfering with the freedom of opinion, and all enactments or regulations relating to blasphemy.

"And your petitioner as in duty bound will ever pray.

"THOMAS RYLEY PERRY."

REASONING WITH THE RELIGIOUS.

Remarks on a recent paper entitled "The God of Nature and of the Bible Identical."

(*To the Editor of the Movement.*)

Sir—You will perhaps allow me, through the pages of the *Movement*, to endeavour to correct a "mistake altogether" which your correspondent C. S. has fallen into, in his critique inserted in your paper recently, of my "Reasons for Renouncing Christianity."

Your correspondent supposes my book intended for atheists, and that I predicate from nature certain characteristics as belonging to god, if such a being exists; but I do not think there is a sentence in my pamphlet which can even look like an appeal to nature to settle such questions as the being of a god, or the attributes of a god. The *Reasons*, (and I may say the same of my writings generally) are addressed to those not yet within the pale of infidelity, and chiefly to the informed and thoughtful of the religious world. There is not one of that class who will dispute the position I have taken with regard to the possession of the attributes named, and if they can be made to see that the Bible represents god as doing that which is inconsistent with such attributes, they will be compelled to abandon the bible. To the rest of the world the whole pamphlet is useless, unless it may help them to arguments which may assist them in a similar controversy.

There is not a man in England who would worship a thing whom he believed "unjust, capricious, cruel, &c." nor call him god; nor would he believe the Bible to be a revelation from a god, could he see its consistency with the *character* he holds sacred.

C. S.'s grand mistake seems therefore in considering that I *affirmed* something respecting an intelligent ruler of the universe, whereas I only took the affirmations of the religionists to shew them that if they were right in these they must be wrong in other opinions, which are at present also dear to them.

The *design* of the "*Reasons*" is therefore mistaken. It may be my fault that it is so; I might possibly have limited the sense more, but I believe that nothing but such a critique could have convinced me that any person could possibly have mistaken my meaning.

Another mistake of C. S. seems to have arisen in like manner from not allowing the general tenor of the essay to fix the meaning of an isolated sentence. He demurs to my statement that "a beneficent ruler cannot be unjust," forgetting that the reading of the paragraph fixed the meaning to a *god-ruling*. It is not an ordinary individual in whom I am asked to believe, but a *wise* and immutable god, no one will have the effrontery to ask me to worship any *other*, and how then can his benevolence be rendered nugatory by want of wisdom?

I have made no attempt to lead my readers into deism; if they can read god in nature they are welcome to do so for me, so that they do not attempt to *make* me read him there too, for I fear I should find it even under coercion a very difficult if not an impossible task. Consequently C. S. has fallen into another mistake, that of answering me that, I ought to be content with the Bible's weak, silly, cruel god, because I read these things in nature also! What if they were true? It is only saying that god not only ordered a silly, cruel, bad book to be written, but that he did this that it may match an equally bad world which he had previously made, for those who believe in a god at all, believe him to be the author of nature.

I have no doubt of the correctness of the rebuke of C. S. that "I ought to have known what the Bible contained before I wrote the pamphlet," but may not critics need information on the subject on which they write as much as authors! and perhaps it may not be out of place to remark here, that the mistake is probably not in the "*Reasons*," but in the critique. The Bible nowhere describes Jehovah as *weak* or *silly*, as well as wise and powerful; if it had done so, it would have needed no lengthened controversy to overset its claims as a divine revelation. It everywhere *describes* its god as possessed of the attributes of wisdom, justice, holiness, mercy, &c., but it also narrates actions which common sense decides to be opposed to those excellent qualities, yet it never admits that those actions are evidences of the want of the qualities, but on the contrary excuses or approves them on some of the highest grounds it can take—at one time indignantly exclaiming, "Nay, but who art thou, oh man, that revilest (or criticises) god."—at another, "What! shall the potsherds of the earth, say unto him that made them, "Why hast thou made me thus?" alluding to the choice of Jacob and rejection of Esau, and generally to the doctrine of election.   Emma Martin.

Edinburgh Discussions.—In a recent letter I said that a second public debate on the "God Question," between myself and the Rev, John Elliot Hadlow, formerly officiating minister at the Episcopalian Chapel, Dumfermline, would soon come off in this most religious of cities; but alas, between the cup and our lip there *has* been a slip, for in consequence of discoveries made since the letter referred to was written, I fear it "*winna do*" to discuss any question with my would-be opponent, the said Rev. J. F. Hadlow. He stands accused of being a very pitchy kind of christian, and no one needs telling that we cannot come into close contact with such sort of folk "without being defiled." And now a few words with regard to another *reverend gentleman*. You are aware that at the close of my debate with Dr. Greer, it was resolved by an overwhelming majority of our hearers, that seeing the unsatisfactory manner in which the Doctor had proved a god, a deputation be appointed to wait on the Rev. G. D. Campbell of this city, who has signalized himself as an opponent of infidelity, and request him to meet me in public discussion so soon as mutually convenient. But this reverend gent. was not to be had; he told the deputation that nothing was to be feared from atheism, though many parties thought otherwise, and declared it quite ridiculous for any two individuals to mount platforms in order to discuss, which he likened to the action of two game cocks fighting on a dung heap. He said that Mr. Southwell might go on administering poison as long as he pleased; he, the reverend Mr. Campbell should be content to furnish the antidote. Whereupon a christian member of the deputation remarked, that he thought the antidote, to be at all antidotish should be given where the poison had been received, a remark the reverend gentleman evidently did not relish, though doubtless still convinced his antidote might be most safely and beneficially administered to "canny" christians, who never came within a mile of my poison. He then bowed out the deputation, who were thoroughly disgusted by his despicable conduct, and I am happy to add that the christian section of them were particularly indignant, and vowed never to rest till they had brought into the field *some* reverend christian warrior with courage sufficient to publicly prove there *is* a god. Truly yours,

C. S.

THE DECISION OF SIR PETER LAURIE.—We have not been unmindful of the wisdom recently displayed by this functionary, with regard to the picture exhibited for sale by Mr. Thomas of Finch-lane, which decision was justly the subject af animadversion by *Publicola*—but as we could not take notice of it in the way we wished, in this case we took none. Our desire was, had funds been at our command, to have the objectionable plate engraved, and to present a copy of it to each subscriber of the *Movement*.

The fruitful source of crime consists in one man's possessing in abundance, that of which another man is destitute.—*Godwin.*

THE VISIONS OF ETZLER.

IT would not only be an injustice to the individual, but it would discover a want of appreciation of the value of those who think, and toil, and act for the improvement of man's social condition, not to welcome among us with fervid cordiality so remarkable a man as J. A. Etzler. This distinguished engineer is now sojourning in this country, endeavouring, and we trust successfully, to awaken attention to his wonderful mechanical inventions. Mr. Etzler is eminent among that race of men whose high purpose it is to make art and science fulfil their destiny far man's benefit. It has been said, that "there is not an element or an object in material nature—not a science or art—not an event in history, or a condition of society, but what may be regarded as having a mission for human good." But it is useless that they have a mission unless they fulfil it. The world wanted some one with a mission to see that science performs its mission, and Etzler appears to be the man. His "Paradise within the reach of all men by the powers of nature and machinery," eminently evinces his mechanical genius, his original invention, and great earnestness for the fulfilment of this task.

The dawn of civilization is marked by the little masteries of man over the elements of nature, in making them work for him, and civilization is incomplete until science is the servant of man, and ministers to his every want, until he is sole lord of nature and of time. Etzler's writings breathe the poetry of mechanics—he looks on the world as Goëthe did on Switzerland, and sees in man's mechanical conquests, the means of emancipation from that thraldom which demands every hour for toil, and subjects the mass of mankind to be throughout life the slaves of their physical wants.

The "Two Visions" are a very improved production of the Ham Common press, and are intended to attract attention to Mr. Etzler's views. Such *visions* were never given to the world before. Had the prophets of old seen such, they would have "dreamed dreams" to better purpose than they did. It would be impossible to give a just idea of Mr. Etzler's "Visions," without quoting them entire, which as we cannot do, we must strenuously commend them to general attention. They tell how men have madly fed on each other, while the earth abounded with unused produce and unemployed powers—how the desert and morass may be converted into orchards and gardens, and filled with happy inhabitants—how poisonous vapours and dismal swamps may be exchanged for the pure breeze and the purling brook—how an acre may be made indefinitely productive, and labour reduced to nothing—how men may travel with the speed of birds in *houses* of comfort, traverse all lands, learn the language of nature, annihilate war, and perpetuate peace and joy for ever. This is not the dream of the saint but the dream of science, and facts, and figures, and models, and calculations, that ignorance cannot gainsay, nor ridicule put down, are the foundation on which all rests.

Mr. Etzler has left his "pleasant home in the West Indies," and is making his "last attempt" here. If unsuccessful, he will "retire either solitarily, or with means and friends to found a paradise in the tropical world." Let not England, this nursing place of fanatics, impostors, and demagogues, turn away from its shores this ardent herald of inventions, science, and plenty. G. J. H.

PAINE.—At the 107th Anniversary of this father of modern politicians held in Philadelphia this year, the Oration was delivered by Mr. Campbell. Among the sentiments given during the evening were the following—

Christian Persecution—Being derived from the Book of Abominations, [see 2 John, x. 11 —Gal. i. 6, 7, 8,] by them deemed Holy, and which contains doctrines of all sizes, shapes, colours—to suit all times and tastes, it is not to be wondered at that the spirit of persecution should enter so strongly into the sheepfold.

Woman—Traduced and vilified by the Bible and its supporters,—made by them a menial instead of a companion for man,—robbed of her rights by assumed spiritual authority—yet Reason and Justice shall, ere long, enlighten the minds of mankind, the fetters of Superstition and Injustice be burst asunder, and Woman shall gloriously arise from the ashes of her degradation, to be the companion, the comforter, and the joy of the opposite sex.

VIEWING MATTERS IN THE RIGHT LIGHT. —The *Pawtucket Chronicle* says that William H. Hammett, one of the Mississippi representatives in Congress, was a preacher of the gospel several years ago. During the canvass preceding his election, in a discussion of political topics before the people, his opponent made allusion to the fact of his having been a minister of the gospel; to which allusion Mr. H., in his reply, referred, and characterized it as an ungenerous arraignment of the *indiscretions of his early youth!*

NICHOLAS OF RUSSIA.—It is a singular coincidence, that while the recommendation at the end of the article, "Jews and Gentiles," was in the press, a meeting at the *National Hall* was being convened, corresponding with it—Placards have been torn down, and boardman seized.

A BONE FOR THEOLOGIANS.

If God a *perfect* being is,
How did he form the plan,
To spoil with evil his own work,
And make imperfect man?

If God did *perfect* make the man,
Who made his imperfections?
For man could no more make the thing
Than make the whole creation.

If God *imperfect* made the man—
Made him a sinful creature;
Where is the justice of his plan
To *damn* him for his nature?
Regenerator.

NOTICES.

A PUBLIC MEETING

Of the Members and Friends of the ANTI-PERSECUTION UNION will be held in the LITERARY & SCIENTIFIC INSTITUTION, John Street, Fitzroy Square, ON MONDAY EVENING, JUNE 10th, To Memorialize Parliament for the Amelioration of Mr. Paterson's Condition, And the abrogation of all laws affecting the free expression of theological opinions. The Chair to be taken at Eight o'clock, by MR. ROBERT CLARK.

This meeting is called in consequence of Sir James Graham refusing to interfere on Mr. Paterson's behalf. The meeting will be addressed by Messrs. HOLYOAKE, FLEMING, HETHERINGTON, and ELLIS. G. J. H., Sec.

CHAMBERS' JOURNAL, No. 21, present series of this periodical, contains an interesting description of the Central Prison, Perth, where Mr. Paterson is imprisoned.

NATIONAL HALL.—The friends of eloquence and progress will be pleased to learn that W. J. Fox Esq. will deliver Sunday Evening Lectures in this place throughout the year. The second course is just announced, embracing two on that compound of political and fashionable novelty—"Young England."

From I. I. for G. J. H., to be appropriated to the general objects of the *Movement* £1 0 0

SUBSCRIPTIONS TO THE ANTI-PERSECUTION UNION.

T. Bidwell, (the price of the 2 vols of *Oracle*) for Mr. Paterson . £0 10 0
T. Dent, Members' Tickets . £0 1 0

Bristol Subscription for April inserted in Number 23, instead of Card 11, 9s., should have been Card 11, 4s., W. H. per C. S. 5s.
G. J. H., Sec.

Printed and Published by G. J. HOLYOAKE, 40, Holywell-street, Strand, Saturday, June 8, 1844.

THE MOVEMENT
And Anti=Persecution Gazette.

"Maximize morals, minimize religion."—BENTHAM.

No. 27.   EDITED BY G. JACOB HOLYOAKE, ASSISTED BY M. Q. RYALL.   PRICE 1½d

THE SOCIALIST PARLIAMENT.

THE rectification of social wrong and the triumph of the rights of industry are bound up in some modification or other of socialism. Solidity in politics, and liberalism in theology, will yet come out of it. It is a proud and important element of human progress, whose fresh phases are full of hope and interest.

No one word will designate the result of the recent Congress. It will not do to call it merely surprising, for though it is something that was not expected, it is also something that was not desired.

With more precision than *Punch* predicts the result of the Derby-day, might any one, familiar with social tactics, have predicted the results of the Congresses of 1842 and 1843. One knew that Mr. Owen would announce another "crisis." That some unfortunate delegate, believing it, and thinking something should be done, would rise to move a resolution. That Mr. Owen would politely remind him that they were at *Harmony Hall*, and their proceedings must be conducted *harmoniously*. Mr. Fleming would intimate that they must set an example of *unity*, and that any difference of opinion would look like the old world proceedings. "We don't discuss," "We don't discuss," would exclaim Mr. Galpin. Mr. Jones would blandly deprecate one party finding fault with another party, and end himself by finding fault with both parties. *Nem. Con.* would then be the order of the day, and resolutions, cut and dried months before, would be passed unquestioned by this meeting of mutes—this Congress of dumb delegates. Thus the worst of cant would arise out of the best of principles, and the new world act far less reasonably than the old.

At the recent Congress much of this folly took wing. Whatever may be said as to the members deciding discreetly, no one will deny that they acted with spirit. But before estimating the value of the results they arrived at, a few words upon one part of the debates.

Mr. Fleming made some remarks in a style of discussion, more fashionable than candid, respecting "attacks made in several periodicals because of the refusal of the Socialists to advocate atheism in their corporate capacity "—" He wished to keep clear of individuals," (I quote *New Moral World* No. 49), while his remarks by implication involved them. I only refer to his observations for the purpose of showing how slender were the reasons he had to offer in opposition to the course the *Movement* has recommended.

"Mr. F. referred to the policy necessary for the society to pursue in putting the principles before the public. How would it look if any of the lecturers of the Anti-Corn-Law League were to commence lecturing on Atheism?" Very badly, Mr. Fleming. But is there no difference between the Anti-Corn-Law League and the Rational Society? Is the principle of the formation of character by *material* agency, precisely the same thing as "buying cheap and selling dear?" Does the explosion of man's free will, and the denial of human depravity, leave us with the same theological reputation as the demand for free trade? Is the philosophy of Robert Owen and Richard Cobden identical, that you lay down for us one identical policy? If they are not so, Mr. Fleming's arguments are invalid.

It is due to Mr. Fleming to say that he professed "to look at the question altogether as a matter of practical *policy*." But the request put to Congress in the *Movement*, was to look at it as a matter of *principle*. If atheism flows from the principles of socialism, the Congress had only to say so, and this discussion had terminated for ever. If atheism is not deducible from socialism, the fact only had to be shortly and simply proved to set the question at rest. It is no fault of ours that the controversy is prolonged. It has been reduced to a narrow compass. *Yes* or *no* would decide it. Why did not Mr. Fleming answer *yes*?—echo answers. Why did he not answer *no*?—Because he could not prove it.

A far more agreeable subject of comment is the conduct of the executive capitalists. The capitalists are the kings of the working classes, and will be the governors of every community, and any sudden improvement in the condition of the industrious depends upon them, and their sentiments are of just importance. We—speaking for those who think with me—differ from Mr. Galpin on many points, but a thousand differences would not weigh against our admiration of his generous statement—"I would not take 19s. 11d. in the pound for my money unless the society can pay the same to every other party." For the working classes not to hold in lasting remembrance such disinterestedness as that exhibited by Messrs. Bate, Galpin, and others, would prove them to be fitted only for the portion of poverty.

It is not within the province of the *Movement* to discuss the diplomatic ingenuity of Congress—or rather the total want of it. The delegates separated without asking what was wanted, and the old executive did not offer it. Indeed they did not appear to understand it—if they had they would have been in office now. The experience gained by the late rulers is so much valuable capital belonging to the society of which it should have availed itself. Such men as Mr. Buxton should have been added to them. It was not necessary that he should, nor does he appear to have, desired to, supersede them.

A call had been made upon the executive to communicate candidly their real position. This is the hinge on which confidence only can turn. They exhibited no notion of doing this. On the whole it was interpreted to mean that if Mrs. A. differed with Mrs. B., that all the *pros*. and *cons*. were to be published in the *New Moral World*, with a full, true, and particular account of the purchase of every pennyworth of cheese, and every pot of blacking. Never did candour fall into such unhappy hands before.

These errors may delay, but they will not prevent, Socialists achieving their objects. Socialism is amphibious, and can exist in water or on dry land. It resembles those animals that when cut in two still live on with no other inconvenience than that of being a little less. But at this moment severance is less to be apprehended than before, and with what of vitality has lately been added to its movements, it may, more speedily than was expected, achieve consistency and success. G. J. H.

PROSELYTISM AT MADEIRA.

A DEPUTATION consisting of the following persons, had yesterday (May 30) an interview with the Earl of Aberdeen, at the Foreign-office:—Mr. P. M. Stewart, M.P., the Hon. Arthur Kinnaird, the Rev. John Sym, Free Church of Scotland, Edinburgh; the Rev. Dr. Henderson, Highbury College; the Rev. Charles Prest, secretary of the Wesleyan Committee of Privileges; the Rev. James Hamilton, Scotch Church, Regent-square; Mr. James Lord of the Inner Temple, barrister-at-law; Mr. William Hamilton, Mr. Nathaniel Wathen, and Mr. George Matthews. The object of the deputation was to lay certain facts before his Lordship, recently communicated from Madeira, relative to the case of Maria Joaquina, who had been condemned to death by a Portuguese judge there (who is also British Judge Conservator), for the crimes of heresy and blasphemy. The result of the interview was highly satisfactory, and we trust that the Portuguese Government, for its own sake, will refrain from carrying into execution so cruel a sentence.

On Tuesday last a meeting of the town-council of Edinburgh was held in the council hall, the Lord Provost in the chair. After some routine business had been transacted, Mr. Macfarlane, a councillor, called the attention of the council to the case of a woman, named Maria Joaquina, who had been sentenced to death in the island of Madeira for denying the worship of the Virgin and the doctrine of transubstantiation, and moved that the council transmit the following memorial to Lord Aberdeen, Secretary for Foreign Affairs:—The memorial of the Lord Provost, Magistrates, and Council of the city of Edinburgh, humbly sheweth,—That your memorialists have heard with the utmost surprise and horror, that a Portuguese woman, in the island of Madeira, named Maria Joaquina, has been condemned to suffer death, solely on account of her having embraced the doctrines of the Protestant faith, nothing else having been brought against her than her denial of worship to images, and of the doctrine of transubstantiation. That viewing with the utmost abhorrence and alarm this recurrence to the practice of the dark ages, of propagating religious belief by persecution unto death—a practice which was believed to be entirely abandoned on all hands—your memorialists cannot but express in the strongest manner the feelings they entertain regarding this most atrocious proceeding, as an interference with the sacred rights of conscience, and a most alarming encroachment on the rights of mankind. That holding such sentiments, they would most respectfully urge upon Her Majesty's Government the propriety of using such influence as they might be able to exert to produce a reversal of this sentence, and your memorialists shall, &c." Mr. James Duncan (who lived for some time in Madeira) seconded the motion, which was unanimously agreed to. The council, at the same time, directed copies to be sent to Lord Howard de Walden, our Ambassador at the Court of Portugal, and to Mr. Stoddart, the British Consul at Funchal, in Madeira.

ADDRESS OF THE SCOTTISH ANTI-PERSECUTION UNION TO THE PEOPLE OF EDINBURGH.

Fellow Citizens,—The people of Scotland have been taught to think conscience-coercion at an end. They have been cajoled into the belief that *their* rulers would scorn to dishonour themselves, or damage their religion, by alliance with mental despotism. But they are deceived—grossly, miserably deceived. Scotland is still disgraced by persecutors: state hirelings who would "bring to one dead level every mind," and instead of conceding to all equal rights, as regards questions of conscience, endeavour by the infliction of merciless punishments, to awe dissenters into silence.

We ask, is it fitting, is it just, that *any* individual should be denied the right to express what he thinks true; be either bribed or terrified into silence when conscience bids him speak? To freely speak what we think is the most valuable of all human privileges. It is a privilege all demand, and surely it is a privilege for which all should struggle. Then rally round the Scottish Anti-Persecution Union! Sink minor differences and come to the support of a great principle. You love sincerity; then, why stand idly by and see fellow-creatures goaded into the practice of hypocrisy? Why, in the name of consistency, laud sincerity as the first of virtues, while permitting your rules to punish the sincere as the vilest of criminals?

In America men not only babble about "the right of private judgment," but realize the right of expression; and so essentially practical is that right now become, that the Atheist may just as safely avow his *disbelief*, as the Christian his *belief* in a God. And why should he not here? Why should a country like Scotland be dishonoured by the fact, that thousands daily parade its streets, who dare not publicly express those opinions, the force of evidence has compelled them to entertain? By punishments you may succeed in making men hypocrites, and obliterate from their breasts every vestige of self-respect: to convince their judgment by such means is impossible.

It is ridiculous to suppose any individual *wilfully* mistakes error for truth. Men often cheat each other, but they cannot desire to cheat themselves. "None," said Plato, are *willingly* deprived of truth," and by parity of reasoning, none are willingly the recipients of falsehood. Clearly, therefore, either to badger or to burn men into this or that belief, is the act of those worse than madhouse lunatics, who affect much zeal in the extirpation of heresy, as a blind for their ambitious projects.

Protestantism in this nation, has assumed the Presbyterian form. Here Presbyterians may protest against Church of Englandism, Popery, and Atheism, not only in safety but with honour. If, however, they take to themselves the privilege of railing against Episcopalians, Papists, and Atheists, why should Atheists, Papists, and Episcopalians, be denied the right to rail against them? If Presbyterians were true to their avowed principles they would as freely allow the Atheist to express his Atheism, as they are allowed to express their Presbyterianism: they would not only acknowledge his *right* to do so, but *guarantee him in the complete exercise thereof*. This, however, they have not done. This they will not do, until a sufficient number of energetic individuals unite to put down persecution, or, failing that, to encourage, sustain, and protect the persecuted.

The time has arrived when friends of mental liberty must crush, or be crushed: when neutrality is criminality, and not to act *for* freedom is in effect to act *against* it. Bigots in high places are crowding our prisons with honest unbelievers. They are anxious it would seem to emulate the brutal intolerance of their ancestors, who, in the name of a merciful God, made scaffolds reek with heretical gore. Like those ancestors they are eager to crush every individual who has the manliness to publish opinions hostile to the established creeds and systems. Instead of confuting as the readiest mode of suppressing, they suppress as the readiest mode of confuting. They answer books by seizing them, and establish the truth of their religion by locking up, or knocking down its rejectors.

And what is the cry that has been raised in extenuation of such arbitrary proceedings? Why, the very comtemptible one of "*danger to public morals.*" But people of Edinburgh, you should know the cry of "*danger to public morals*" is oftenest used by those who are the most insidious corruptors of those morals, and that like the state cry of "*Church in danger,*" or the once-fashionable one of "*No Popery and wooden shoes,*" alarms none save ignorantly timid persons who stand in the same relation to such open-mouthed imposters as carrion does to hungry crows. The fact is, crafty persecutors must have *some* plea for their despicable conduct, and the danger of allowing all opinions a free course is the most convenient one they can find.

Arouse then from your lethargy, and aid us in the glorious work of Emancipating Mind!

Letters, money-orders, &c., to be addressed to Mr. W. Baker, Secretary, 105, Nicholson-street.

THE SOUL IN PARLIAMENT.

DURING the recent debate on the Ecclesiastical Court's Bill, in the House of Commons, Dr. Nicholl contended for the power of the church to punish " brawling," although it is an offence cognizable at common law. Any person who should attempt discussion in a church would be charged with "brawling," and the clergy are not content that the civil magistrate should punish this *offence?* but they must do it themselves in their own way —which never yet was a lenient one. Upon this Mr. Roebuck made the following excellent remarks, as reported in the *Times*. Mr. Roebuck said—It was a base superstition that any one could take care of his soul (hear, hear, and a laugh,) or of any other person's soul. Let a man take care of his own soul, and he was a lucky fellow who could do that. They pretended that they could take care of what they called the soul's health. He knew what that meant—it meant dipping into the pockets of the people. (Hear, hear.) In one expressive word it meant " costs." (Hear, hear.) He remembered going to a learned man in the early days of his life, and saying to him, " Excommunication? What care I for excommunication?" "I know you don't," was the reply," but I know what you do care for, and I'll whisper that word in your ear—*costs!"* It was by means of these courts that lawyers got larger fees than they could get by common law process. That was the use of the courts—the only use of them. " The soul's health" meant " costs "—" taking care of the soul's health," meant *" getting larger costs."* That was the long and the short of the matter. If he treated it all as a farce, it was not because he was insensible of the seriousness of the subject. A soul was too important a matter for a laugh. (Hear, hear.) In the fourteenth century, the hon. member opposite, (Dr. Nicholl,) might have rendered him a very unhappy subject by talking about " his soul's health," but in the present day of enlightenment his soul was under his own jurisdiction, and not, happily, in the power either of the hon. member or of his bishop. As for crimes affecting the soul's health, why should it be a greater offence to brawl in a churchyard than upon a highway? Why; at any rate, should the offence be 'tried by a different tribunal? What, he should like to ask, constituted the hon. gentleman opposite an ecclesiastical judge? He had none of the properties of the priest in him. (A laugh.) He was a layman. He had no right to act as an ecclesiastical judge, save upon this understanding—that all ecclesiastical law was abrogated and that this was only another way of administering the law upon the same matter. The truth was that these courts were simply a bad form, devoid of the sanction which the ordinary administration of the law possessed, and devoid also of all those ingredients which gave the law authority in the eyes of the public.

MR. PERRY'S PETITION.

Bryanstone Square, May 29, 1844.
SIR—I presented your petition as soon as I received it, and I delayed an answer in hopes I should be able to inform you of some modification of the punishment of Mr. Paterson in Perth Jail; but my application has been unsuccessful.

I disapprove of all prosecution for opinions, and consider such conduct as contrary to the principle on which the Protestant church is founded, and it shows a fear of their own principles, lest by discussion, they could not stand the test of truth.

I at the same time think that those who differ from their society should do so in the least offensive manner.

I remain, your obedient servant,
JOSEPH HUME.

P. S. — I find that I presented another petition to the same effect. But yours will be presented to-morrow.

THE SUPREMACY OF MAN EXAMINED.

THE argument from design, in favor of a god, is one of analogy. As a proof drawn from comparison, it is exhibited in its weakest form, when it would endeavour to support a deity. It would draw a comparison between the works of our hands and the forms of matter, between which there is not the slightest real resemblance; but with regard to man, analogy is capable of throwing considerable light upon his relation to the animal world. We, indeed, try to imitate nature by some petty combinations of its powers, but we act in obedience to its laws, we cannot create matter, we cannot infuse life, we cannot avoid change, we cannot prevent dissolution. We are as much makers as the beasts and the same blind instruments of other agency. There is every similarity between us and animal and vegetable life, we share powers in common, all tending to the general purpose of existence, all subservient to the same decay, and experiencing the same revolutions. There may be great apparent differences between us and the rest of animated nature, magnified as they are by being brought so near to our inspection, but we agree in many more things than we differ; and whilst the points of distinction are mere details, those of resemblance are general rules and universal laws which bear no exceptions. There are some properties we possess which we may think superior; but every other race of living beings, and every other kind of animated nature, have some advantage over us, which might entitle them to think themselves an higher order in the scale of creation. Many of their senses seem to be finer than ours, or they have faculties of which we do not know the nature; the very differences in organization may seem a benefit to them, and often must be admitted to be an advantage on their side; their modes of propagating their species is better than our way, which, according to the religionist, is an exclusive curse on our race. Their relish and digest of some sorts of food which would leave man to die, is a convenience, and their indifference to external circumstances, which exercise a mastery over us, confer a superiority on them. Besides, we cannot fly like birds, nor swim like fishes, nor breathe under the earth, which seems to warrant a sentiment of pity in animated nature, above and below, who contemplate such a miserable, impotent, intermediate, crawling fixture, as humanity. We cannot, like the Polypi, if we loose one head furnish a dozen. In formation and destruction, we are equal—we feed upon others, and we are fed upon by others; if some have no power of resisting us, others have an invisible dominion over us, and we all go to the worm. If it were our duty to give a meaning to what a noted individual uttered, we should say, that respecting the worm that never dieth, and the fire that is never quenched, was only a figure of speech to speak of this perpetual formation and destruction taking place in the universe. Fire being supposed to be, by those eastern nations, whence christianity was stolen, the revivifying principle, as the worm, the heir of death, typified that constant succession of life. We are all equal in this particular, that from earth we come, and to earth we go; the geologists have found out no strata peculiar to man, which might serve as clay in the pottery of some future maker. Whilst we live, and directly we die, we go to form other beings; instead of rising to the skies, and having the wings of birds, or fins of fishes, the dead body may be seen by those who survive, fattening animals, or enriching vegetation. But we possess reason, says mankind, and on that sole assumption we claim a vast superiority over the brute and the rest of nature. It is curious, if we alone possess that faculty, that all philosophers who have written on the subject, have not been able to refuse it to the animal. We see the results, but it has always been found difficult to draw the distinction between the reason of man and of brutes, and few could answer the question as to the exhibition of a separate faculty in man, who have always taken it for granted, that they had reason, but the beast none. We make this one difference between man and the rest of nature of greater consequence than all its conformity, and an overbalance to any preponderating qualities on the other side. But if it be so very slight a difference that it cannot be clearly shown to exist—surely on such a very narrow foundation we cannot build for ourselves such a wide superstructure of distinctions. We must recollect that if we think our mental superiority leaves behind so immeasurably distant, the animals — there are those amongst them much more highly endowed than others. The dog and the elephant are as far before other living things as we are before them, and the same reasoning on their own superiority, and other's inferiority, would give them as just title to be heirs of immortality, and images of a creator, as those above them, and the same right to exclude all others from a share in their expectancies, who did not come up to their own standard of excellence. Besides, as far as matter is concerned, we are all the same, we all enjoy the same properties and qualities in turn, if from matter we come and to matter we go, and vice versa. We see matter descend, and we see it ascend, and every particle that goes away, goes to form other vegetable, animal, and intelligent life. Every part has touched the highest as well as the lowest on the scale: therefore, everything has a fair claim to the immunities apparently sought to be established for one class, composed, decomposed, recomposed, of all and from all, it would be impossible, as unfair, to confer on one classification of matter a superiority over the rest.

In consequence of this difficulty some philosophers and some divines have given souls to all animal life, and some have preached the transmigration of souls. Solomon, if we take his word literally, drew from analogy what he was warranted by fact, "I said in mine heart concerning the estate of the sons of men, that God might manifest them, and that they might see that they themselves are beasts. For that which befalleth the sons of men, befalleth beasts, even one thing befalleth them; as the one dieth, so dieth the other; yea, they have all one breath, so that a man hath no pre-eminence above a beast, for all is vanity. All go unto one place—all are of the dust—and all turn to dust again. Who knoweth the spirit of man that goeth upward, and the spirit of the beast that goeth downward to the earth?" W. J. B.

[We are expressly desired by "W. J. B." to say that the article entitled the "Metaphysical Origin of the God-Idea," bore his initials by some accident of our own, as, when he furnished the article, he stated in a note (that never came to hand) that he had translated the paper for us from the French of Fréville. Fréville was a political economist, and translator of English works. He professed atheism in private society and in coffee-houses, and the argument in the paper referred to, was the celebrated one which he always adduced.—Eds. of M.]

THE CHINESE AND THEIR RELIGION.
NO. I.

LARGE as has been the issue of tracts and works, and extended as the information of late on this subject, the curiosity of the public as to this interesting people, would appear to be rather stimulated than satisfied. The new fields of enterprise also, which have been opened by recent events, having brought us as it were, into closer proximity, increase the interest, already sufficiently great on account of the peculiarities of the people.

The Chinese claim a national existence, coeval with the most remote antiquity. Much that is recorded in their annals, however, is admitted even by their own historians, to be doubtful; while the authors of every other nation who have written upon the subject, pronounce the earliest so-called history of China as absolutely fabulous. Good authorities name Fuh-he, who flourished about 2247 years before Christ, as the first Emperor. Yaou, a virtuous sovereign, some centuries after, reigned 102 years. The empire then floated down the stream of time without any extraordinary event or national convulsion, while the morals of the people were greatly improved by the precepts and writings of their great philosopher, Confucius, who was born 550 years before Christ. In the twelfth century of the Christian era, the Chinese used a paper currency founded on government security, being the earliest record we have of paper money. It has, however, been long discontinued, and its place supplied by the present metal coin, previous to which the shell of the tortoise and pearl oyster were used as a circulating medium in exchange for commodities. A. D. 1246, Marco Polo, a Venetian, visited China, and shortly after, his brother joined him. They were received with favour by the Imperial Sovereigns. Catholic, and particularly Jesuit missionaries, were afterwards permitted to reside in China for several ages, but were at length expelled on the pretext, real or assumed, that they interfered with the government. In the thirteenth century, China was invaded by Genghis Khan, who put millions to the sword; and the nation finally submitted to the Mongul Tartar Sovereigns, A. D. 1280. In 1368, however, the Tartars were driven out, and a native dynasty continued until 1644. In that year the Mwan-chow Tartars invaded the empire, and placed their chief upon the throne, and the present monarch, Taou Kwang, is descended from that successful warrior. The Portuguese were the first European traders to China; and they were soon followed by the British, French, American, and other nations.

The religious doctrines and observances of the Chinese, are particularly interesting. The principal religion of China is Buddhism or Boodhism, which also prevails over Birmah, Siam, Ceylon, Japan, and Cochin-China. It is stated by Ward, that Boodh, the founder of this religion, is described in Burmese books to have been a son of the King of Benares, that he flourished about 600 years before Christ, and that he had in various ages, ten incarnations. The Buddhists do not believe in a First Cause; they think matter eternal; that every portion of animated existence has its own rise, tendency, and destiny, *in itself;* that the condition of creatures on earth is regulated by works of merit and demerit; that works of merit raise us to happiness and the world to prosperity; while those of vice and demerit degenerate the world, until the universe itself is dissolved. They suppose a superior deity, raised to that rank by his merit; but he is not governor of the world. The Buddhists believe that persons who obtain a knowledge of things past, present, and to come, have the power of rendering themselves invisible, and are ABSORBED into the Deity. They all consider their adoration as paid to a being or beings of exalted merit—*not to a Creator.*

"The God, "Fuh," so much revered in China, as the founder of a religion introduced from India into the empire, in the first century of the Christian era, was miraculously born in Cashmere, 1027, before Christ. He was deified at thirty years of age, and his priests are called Lamas, Sang, Talapoins, or Bonzes. He died at the age of 79, declaring to his disciples, " Know then, that there is no other principle of all things, but nothing. From nothing all things have sprung, and to nothing all must return. There all our hopes must end.' Such is the atheistical philosophy and belief of Fuh, whose followers recognise "the three precious ones," as the object of their supreme worship—the past, the present, and the future; but the doctrines taught in his name are divided into *exoteric* and *esoteric*—the former distinguishing actions into good and evil, with rewards and punishments after death, and recognising the five precepts or commands of Boodh, already noticed; while the latter teach the belief that all things sprang from nothing, and to nothing all things will return; but in so returning will be absorbed into a pure essence, and become a part of the Deity."

The doctrines or philosophy of Confucius have obtained a reputation, not merely national. They have been long celebrated among the literati of Europe, as evidencing a high state of intellectual and moral progress, and the precept on which christians mainly rest their moral code, " do unto others, as you would they should do unto you," has been traced to the still higher antiquity of the school of philosophy, instituted by *Kung-foo-tsze*, popularly Confucius.

The Taou, or rational religion, is indigenous in China.

This religio-philosophic sect is numerous, and consists of the followers of the doctrines of Laou-Keun-tsze, who lived 560 before Christ. The founder of this system has been called the Epicurus of China; and, in some points, there would seem to be a resemblance between the doctrines of the Chinese sage and the Grecian philosopher.

He inculcated a contempt for riches and honours, and all worldly distinctions, and aimed like Epicurus, at subduing every passion that could interfere with personal tranquility and self-enjoyment. According to Mr. Davis, however, they could not even pretend to despise death, and, therefore, studied magic and alchymy, in the hope of discovering some elixir or other means of prolonging life. In this they failed, of course. Some of the leaders of this sect, are called, "Doctors of reason," and many of their tenets and traditions are of an extremely fanciful and absurd character. M. Q. R.

MODESTY OF CHRISTIANITY.

WHENEVER any new and valuable enterprise for the improvement and happiness of mankind, is presented to the world, it is almost always put down to the credit of christianity. It is a manifestation, say the pious, of the blessed influence of our holy religion, when the fact is, that nine times in ten, the project was originated by an Infidel. We have a striking proof of this remark in what is called socialism. This system having become somewhat popular, and being found to inculcate principles of benevolence and equality, is claimed by certain christians as the doctrine of the New Testament. Its oldest and most faithful and disinterested advocate, if not its founder, ROBERT OWEN, is overlooked: and the origin of socialism is attributed to Jesus. Now we have no disposition to deny the Nazarene the credit of any good deed or precept he may have done or taught; but we do not believe that his doctrines, either as practised by the world, or even as he taught them, can in truth be said to be identical with those of Robert Owen. If we look to the practical operations of christianity, we behold a system destitute of charity and benevolence. We shall be told, however, that the teachings of the New Testament inculcate charity; but it is not sufficient to tell us this. It does not prove that charity is practised by those who call themselves Christians. We wish to see charity in practice; but we do not believe we ever shall, so long as christianity rests its foundations on a dogmatical belief; for this promotes sectarianism and strife, and hence christianity, as carried out, is directly opposed to socialism. But will the precepts that Jesus taught bring about an improved social system, and are they the precepts upon which Robert Owen has acted and now acts in the regulation of his social communities? If we can understand the meaning and spirit of language, we say No! But let us enumerate some of his precepts and acts, and see if our conclusion is not a correct one.

Was it social to *drive* the money-changers out of the temple, to *drown* the swine, or to *curse* a fig-tree? Was it social to *refuse* a man permission *to bury his father*, and to "let the dead bury the dead?" Was it social to say that "he (Jesus) came not on earth to send peace, *but a sword?*"—Was it social to say to his mother, "Woman, what have I to do with thee?" Was it social to say that he should be rewarded who should forsake *father and mother*, and sisters, and houses, and lands, for his (Jesus's) sake? Was it social to say, "he that believeth shall be saved, and he that believeth not *shall be damned?*" Was it social to call those who differed from him in belief, fools, blind guides, serpents, hypocrites, &c., and threaten them with hell fire? In all these, and many other cases, where was the good feeling and sociability of Jesus? Or where have been the social consequences arising from his system? Have they been hanging, drowning, quartering, roasting, &c.? Let the Inquisition, St. Bartholomew's day, Smithfield, the numerous long and bloody wars against the "Infidels," answer. The man who can say that the christian system is a social system, must either be ignorant of facts, or possess a bold face.—*Boston Investigator.*

THE CONFEDERACY OF PRIESTS AND LAWYERS.—On Sunday evening next, at the Hall of Science, City Road, M. Q. Ryall will adduce some arguments and instances to expose the continual system of plunder of which the heterodox are victims.

The recent case of the Girard Will in the United States—in which Daniel Webster, the lawyer and law-maker, is retained on behalf of the spoliators—will be cited among other instances.

[We extract the following glowing effusion from "Studies of Sensation and Event" by Ebenezer Jones. Its appropriateness to the present state of popular feeling on the visit of the Autocrat of Russia, and the forcible manner in which it suggests the inutility of gods, if there are any, to permit the breed of the "Kings of Gold" to flourish, have been the reasons of its selection.—ED. of M.]

SONG OF THE KINGS OF GOLD.

Ours all are marble halls,
Amid untrodden groves,
Where music ever calls,
Where faintest perfume roves;
And thousands toiling, moan,
That gorgeous robes may fold,
The haughty forms alone
Of us—the Kings of Gold.

Chorus.
We cannot count our slaves,
Nothing bounds our sway,
Our will destroys and saves,
We let, we create, we slay.
Ha! ha! who are Gods?

Purple, and crimson, and blue,
Jewels, and silks, and pearl,
All splendours of form and hue,
Our charmed existence furl;
When dared shadow dim
The glow in our winecups rolled!
When drooped the banquet-hymn
Raised for the Kings of Gold!

The earth, the earth, is ours!
Its corn, its fruits, its wine,
Its sun, its rain, its flowers,
Ours, all, all!—cannot shine
One sunlight ray, but where
Our mighty titles hold;
Wherever life is, there
Possess the Kings of Gold!

And all on earth that lives,
Woman, and man, and child,
Us trembling homage gives;
Aye trampled, sport-defiled,
None dareth raise one frown,
Or slightest questioning hold;
Our scorn but strikes them down
To adore the Kings of Gold.

On beds of azure down,
In halls of torturing light,
Our poisoned harlots moan,
And burning, toss to sight;
They are ours—for us they burn;
They are ours, to reject, to hold;
We taste—we exult—we spurn—
For we are the Kings of Gold.

The father writhes a smile,
As we seize his red-lipped girl,
His white-loined wife; aye, while
Fierce millions burn, to hurl
Rocks on our regal brows,
Knives in our hearts to hold—
They pale, prepare them bows
At the step of the Kings of Gold.

In a glorious sea of hate,
Eternal rocks we stand;
Our joy is our lonely state;
And our trust, our own right hand;
We frown, and nations shrink;
They curse, but our swords are old;.
And the wine of their rage, deep drink
The dauntless Kings of Gold.

Chorus.
We cannot count our slaves,
Nothing bounds our sway,
Our will destroys and saves,
We let, we create, we slay.
Ha! ha! who are Gods?

NOTICE.

A society has lately been formed for the gratuitous distribution of Infidel Tracts. It meets every Sunday morning, from 10 till 12, at No. 1, Acorn-street, Camberwell, to admit members and transact business. Brief Infidel articles for the press will be thankfully received. Communications addressed to Mr. W. Broom, Secretary of the Infidel Tract Society, 1, Acorn-street, Camberwell, will receive attention.

ERRATUM.—In page 206, par. 3, for "consistency," read *inconsistency.*

TO CORRESPONDENTS.

W. B. C.—Received; but there are many objections to inserting his paper at the present stage of the discussion to which it refers. It shall receive attention as early as possible. The extracts he promises will oblige us.

H. WATKINS.—Very much obliged to him.

B. J. with enclosure received, and the requested communication made.

C. J. S.—Received.

SUBSCRIPTIONS TO THE ANTI-PERSECUTION UNION.

Bristol Subscriptions for May, per W. C.:—

Card 11	£0	4 0
12	0	2 0
14	0	1 6
16	0	5 0
Various Subscriptions	0	3 6

Next week will appear a report of the public meeting held on last Monday.

At a special meeting of the Union Mr. Thomas Powell was appointed Secretary, *pro. tem.,* during the absence of Mr. Holyoake in Manchester.   G. J. H., *Sec.*

Printed and Published by G. J. HOLYOAKE,
40, Holywell-street, Strand,
Saturday, June 15, 1844.

THE MOVEMENT

And Anti=Persecution Gazette.

"Maximize morals, minimize religion."—BENTHAM.

No. 28.   EDITED BY G. JACOB HOLYOAKE, ASSISTED BY M. Q. RYALL.   PRICE 1½d

FREEDOM OF EXPRESSION.

ON Monday evening, June 10, pursuant to announcement, a Public Meeting of the Anti-Persecution Union was held in the Literary and Scientific Institution, John Street, Fitzroy Square, in consequence of the refusal of Sir James Graham to order the amelioration of Mr. Paterson's condition. ROBERT CLARKE, Esq., in the chair.

Mr. HOLYOAKE moved the first resolution. He said, the chairman had called on him first because, as secretary of the *Anti-Persecution Union*, he could state the circumstances which had led to that meeting. Of these the Memmorial he held in his hand was somewhat explanatory. He would read it, and afterwards move that it be adopted by that meeting.

"The memorial sheweth, I. That Mr. Thomas Paterson was sentenced in the High Court of Justiciary, Edinburgh, on Nov. 9, 1843, to 15 months' imprisonment, for the publication of Atheistical sentiments, and, in the opinion of your memorialists, such sentence was an unwise exercise of the powers of the law, for the public utility cannot, in this age, be promoted by visiting with legal penalties the conscientious convictions of any man. Your memorialists, therefore, pray your Hon. House to take such steps as will lead to the immediate release of the aforesaid Thomas Paterson, and to the repeal of all laws affecting the unrestricted publication of theological opinions.

"II. That the said Thomas Paterson is subjected to all the horrors of solitary confinement, from which your memorialists fear that insanity will result. That he is only permitted to write to his friends once in three months. That he is not permitted to see visitors, nor allowed leisure time for study and improvement—in the event, therefore, of your Hon. House not seeing sufficient reason to adopt measures for his liberation, your memorialists earnestly pray that you will advise that the said Thomas Paterson be removed at once from solitary confinement, have the privilege of seeing friends, and be permitted to purchase food, when he is inclined to spend a portion of that time in study which must now be occupied with work before food is supplied him."

Upon the sentence being passed, referred to in the memorial, Mr. Paterson was removed to the General Prison, Perth, and placed as a felon in solitary confinement. Not until one or two months had elapsed did he commence applying to the authorities at the gaol for an amelioration of his condition. No redress being afforded him, he memorialised the Board of Prison Directors at Edinburgh—a body of judges and gentlemen in whom is vested, by act of parliament, the entire controul of the prisons of Scotland. His application was refused. Then the Anti-Persecution Union respectfully represented his case to the Board. To this was returned an official answer, which, as official answers generally do, signified nothing. Then Mr. Paterson forwarded a petition to the House of Commons, which Mr. Hume kindly consented to present. It was agreed that the petition should first be laid before Sir James Graham, to ascertain if he would step in between bigotry and its victim, as on former occasions, to his honour, he had done. But he had refused to interfere. Hence that meeting to consider the propriety of memorialising parliament on the subject. (Hear.)

Public bodies are composed of men who, differing greatly on little subjects, and on the details of great ones, are yet agreed on a broad principle. Such is the Anti-Persecution Union. It does not identify itself with this man's sentiments, nor that man's mode of advocating them, but it claims the right for all men of being heard in their own way and in their own words, unhindered by the law. That meeting was not called upon to approve Mr. Paterson's atheism, or his mode of publishing it, but it was called upon to see that there was fair play in the religious world, and that policemen were not appointed to decide questions in theology—that the Atheist and the Christian, the Infidel and the Churchman. Robert Kalley of Madeira and Thomas Paterson of Perth met together in the enjoyment of the common privilege of unrestricted speech, and none but public opinion daring to make them afraid. (Cheers.)

Propably some persons might be disposed

to think that what *they* would call the violent manner, of the persons who had been prosecuted, exempted them from public sympathy and support. This charge he might meet, as the Hon. and Rev. Baptist Noel had met a short time since in Exeter Hall, a similar charge against the Free Church party of Scotland. His words were—"Repeatedly have I met this charge against them. In Scotland, and here, I have heard it said, 'That cannot be right which is maintained with so much violence.' Was Luther guilty of no violence? Did Wickliffe never indulge in violent language? Was there no violent language even in the homilies of our Church? Did those persons who carried on the Calvinistic controversy in the days of Whitefield and Wesley, indulge in no angry recrimination? And yet, who would venture to say they were not Christian men after all? If, in moments of great excitement, —I am sure those who are present are ready to make allowances for the men who have made sacrifices which we could not have imagined, who have shown resolution and constancy to which we, perhaps, are not equal,—if they have, in the defence of these principles, allowed a few angry words to escape them, this ought not to condemn them, much less their cause, in our eyes. Whatever they were, their principles remained the same." That language, which on the whole, was precisely applicable to the Scotch victims, would doubtless be admitted by the most fastidious Christian as extenuative of their case, unless they refused to Atheists those allowances, which, under similar circumstances, they made for Christians. (Hear, hear.) But he (Mr. H.) would not put the case of his friends on that ground. Their manner did not proceed from mere "excitement," but from conviction. Violent or not, men were no more to be punished for their manner than their opinions. Manner, like speech, was an exponent of thought, and must not be regulated by any man's dictation. He had never denied the interest of theological speculation. Two views were presented to the Atheist. The best men among Christians represented religion as the golden link which connects humanity to the future, and invests life with poetry, hope, and joy. The opposite representation was that of torments in which humanity was to be engulphed because of heretical opinions. As a mere matter of policy—when the Atheists turned from the gloomy picture of one party and regarded but as delusive dreaming the speculations of the other—what was gained by his imprisonment, but to make him justly suspect the sincerity of both parties, and grow harder in his unbelief? (Cheers.)

The memorial raised no question as to the propriety of prosecutions, for opinion, in past time. It might not be right then, but, reference was made only to the present time, and the existing order of things. If, after 18 centuries of action, christianity was unable to meet its opponents on equal ground —could not array on its side argument and evidence, talent and truth, sufficient for victory, but must strike down the conscientious—send the Atheist forth as a moral cipher in the world—reduce him to the shadow of a man, with aspirations he could never realise, and sentiments he dare never utter—if christianity must do this, then will it justify the conclusion that it has grown impotent with age, and retains nothing vital about it but malevolence. (Cheers.)

While our present blasphemy laws existed the meanest man in a public meeting had the liberty of every speaker at his disposal by lodging a charge of blasphemy before some priest who had a pious friend on the bench. At Cheltenham, in his (Mr. H.'s) case, a witness was brought from the cock-pit to give evidence on behalf of the "Lord of Hosts." (*Laughter.*) In the placard agitation in Holywell-street, and during the blasphemy war in Scotland, policemen, who were professionally familiar with every species of vice and crime, and bailiffs, who were saturated with inhumanity, and in whom every moral feeling is deadened before they are qualified for their wretched calling—these moral abortions of society had only to lodge a charge of blasphemy before some Jardine or Chief Justice, and they could subject reputable citizens to long and horrid imprisonment. Would not the meeting agree under these circumstances to demand the repeal of all blasphemy laws? (Cheers.)

At that hour Mr. Paterson was sitting down in his silent cell, weak and weary, and listless after the hard labour of the day. For eight months he had scarcely seen a human face, nor heard a human voice, certainly no friendly one during all that long period. If no amelioration was procured for him, at some distant day he would probably be set at liberty deprived of health and of reason. (Sensation.) Then let them be unwearied in their memorials. They might not be effective, but they could be earnest. Let them make up in perseverance what they wanted in power—and if their applications were not efficacious, at least let them be incessant. The Union knew the difficulties in the way, but, for the right of free speech, they were content to struggle hard, and to struggle long. (Cheers.) He would formally move that the memorial read, be adopted by that meeting, and that it lie for signature, at convenient places throughout the metropolis.

Mr. G. A. FLEMING seconded the adoption of the memorial. He would take advantage of the neutral principle of the Anti-Persecution Union which enabled him or any other person to speak to a resolution without being identified with the atheistical or other sentiments that might be held by particular individuals. There were two reasons why he came forward on that occasion. First, he had great faith in the power of truth and the efficacy of free discussion; and, second, he had a deep-rooted dislike of any proceeding which tended to discourage free enquiry, and prevented investigation by the strong arm of the law. (Cheers.)

Upon the truth of the principles at issue, connected with the prosecutions to which the memorial related, he had thought and read much, and the only conclusion at which he had been able to arrive was, that as yet nothing certain was known on the subject, and therefore, in his opinion, that constituted an additional reason for the utmost freedom of enquiry, in order, if possible, to arrive at more unimpeachable conclusions than those now prevalent. He disliked persecution for opinion-sake in any shape. Even when that persecution applied to political opinions, it was an unwise and injurious interference with mental freedom. The law ought to take cognizance of acts, not opinions. But if this was true in the case of political opinions it was much more applicable to heterodox views in theology. Political opinions frequently led to overt acts, to sedition, and social disorder—but long experience had assured them theological heresy was of a very different nature, and did not lead to such results. O'Connell had broached opinions which, if carried out, might lead to the severance of the empire, and materially affect the security of the government of Sir Robert Peel, and the comfort of Queen Victoria of Great Britain and Ireland, and Defender of the Faith! (Laughter.) But would the same results follow the dissemination of the principles of Thomas Paterson? (Hear, hear.) If God existed, it could not matter what Thomas Paterson thought or said on the subject.—The fact did not rest on his belief. (Laughter.) So long as the believers in the Trinity and similar dogmas only *believed* and did not *know*, he did not see why those who proclaimed their inability to assent to such doctrines should be subjected to persecution. (Cheers.) Contrast the difference between the political and religious offender. O'Connell, for offences much more serious than Mr. Paterson's, was lodged in the governor's own house in Richmond Gaol—a place so conveniently fitted up, that Mr. O'Connell's own party, some time ago, complained of the expences attendant upon it. Here he enjoyed luxuries, had the unrestricted use of splendid gardens, and held levees at will; while Mr. Paterson, as had been well described by Mr. Holyoake, was shut up in a narrow cell, without society, without comforts, without communion with his friends, and compelled to labour. What was the inference? why, that it was better to fall into the hands of the devil of the state than into those of the demon of the church! (Cheers.) The whole army of the clergy, dissenters and churchmen, numbered some 28,000! Surely they were numerous enough to take care of their doctrines. (Cheers.) They had wealth and influence, and their sons—he was going to say the young goslings! (Laughter.) were distributed in all places of power. Now, it was too bad that 28,000 well paid, well fed, stout, able-bodied parsons could not stand on their own legs without the aid of the policeman and jailer. (Roars of laughter.) It was no easy thing to oppose popular opinions. The scrupulous could not get on. The men of capacious and easy consciences, they who could swallow the 39 articles without wincing; (Laughter) they were the men whose lines were fallen in pleasant places, and who sat in the easy chairs of society. (Cheers.) Mr. Paterson was fed upon gruel and his hair had been cut. Really he could no see how feeding a man on gruel could prove the existence of God, or how cropping hair could prove the existence of the Holy Ghost. (Laughter.) There was no logical sequence here, at all events that the parsons should be obliged to call in the aid of policemen was rank cowardice, and that they should proceed to such cruelties in defence of their dogmas, as in the case of Mr. Paterson, was enough to make a man question for ever their sincerity. He cordially supported the adoption of the memorial. (Loud cheers).

Mr. M'CULLOUGH rose to support the resolution, and made some general remarks on the value of free speech. Tacitus, he said, related that while the Roman commonwealth was free that it had numerous authors, but upon its enslavement they vanished. That Pliny the Younger apologised for the want of spirit in a literary performance, on the ground that it was written in the reign of Nero. Milton had happily likened the enemies to free discussion to a man who erected a wall around his garden to keep the crows out! He, Mr. M'C., regarded the necessity for an Anti-Persecution Union as a black spot on the history of our times. Upon the discussion which had followed Mr. Petitt's motion in the American Congress relative to the abolition of a paid clergy class, some of the pious had styled the motion an attempt to banish God Almighty out of the republic. They did not say for how long a period this banishment was to last. If the language of Christians was looked to, it would be found calculated to bring god into contempt more than the language of Infidels. Why then should Infidels be prosecuted? He made no hesitation in avowing himself an Atheist, and unless persecution was put an end to, all would be entitled to blaspheme as a right. The case of Joaquina, mentioned by Dr. Kalley in a letter recently published, was an awful instance to what length religious fanaticism ran when unchecked by public opinion and Anti-Persecution Unions. (Cheers).

Mr. HARTNETT desired leave to say a few words at that stage of the proceedings. He feared that the meeting had exhausted its applause on preceding speakers, and that he placed himself in an unpleasant predicament. He would not oppose the memorial on Mr. Paterson's behalf, but he thought those speakers who had just preceded him had attacked christianity out of place, as they were not met for that purpose. The law—he thought the law was binding, and that the imprisonment alluded to was not persecution, but punishment for the violation of the law. But what were they to expect; when one gentleman who had sat down, had been all his life learning nothing. (Laughter.) But learned men and scholars did know something about god.

Mr. FLEMING.—The preceding speaker had made various remarks which had ended in very much like nothing. (Laughter.) He had endeavoured to identify him (Mr. F.) and that meeting with the advocacy of atheism. It was his duty to correct that mis-statement. Mr. McCullough had avowed his belief in atheism, and had a right to do so, but that only proved his belief. The previous speaker avowed his belief in the existence of god, very good, he had a right to do so, but it only proved his belief, it did not prove the point at issue. Neither had *demonstrated* his opinions, and, if he understood the object of that meeting it was to proclaim its partizanship with neither, but to demand fair play for both. (Cheers.) Those scholars and learned men who had been alluded to, had been all their lives labouring, and had *proved* nothing. (Laughter.) When these worthies could prove that God existed as much to human satisfaction as the mathematician did his theorems, the chemist or the geologist his leading views, then would they settle the question of atheism for ever. (Cheers.) It was a fact that his hearers were present—when the existence of God was made equally evident learned men need not trouble themselves—there would be no Atheists. (Cheers.) The speaker did not seem to know the difference between *Knowledge* and *Belief*.

Mr. R. RIDLEY spoke with great earnestness in support of the resolution. Who made the law to prevent freedom of speech? —the Christians. Who shed the blood of those who differed from them?—the Christians. It was priestcraft which enabled kingcraft to bind the chains of servitude on the people.

The chairman put the resolution, and it was carried unanimously.

Mr. HETHERINGTON said that the resolution in his hand would strictly prevent any general remarks from him, but he thought, after the discussion they had heard, that he should not be wholly irrelevant in saying a few words. He congratulated Mr. Hartnett on his appearance in opposition. He was glad to see such persons come forward. We could never disabuse our fellow-men of erroneous prejudice unless we could induce them to express their views. How beside common sense were these prosecutions! Locke had proved the necessary nature of our ideas, and it was wanton cruelty to punish differences we could not help, and a sincerity which did us honour. There could be no infidelity to truth—all men desire to be true to their own convictions. Priests were the only persons who promoted this infidelity to truth by the prosecution of sincere conviction. But there was a reason for it—

They stand on peril's brink
If for themselves, the flock presume to
    think. (Laughter).

He was bred a good churchman. But he must say, that his parish priest, the rector of St. Giles-in-the-Field, since the bishop of Chichester, was the worst parson he ever knew. Cobbett used to say, that we had no occasion to think for ourselves, as we paid the parsons to do that. Now his mother was of that religion, and brought him up in it. But on one occasion he found, by accident, in a book of pictures, the thirty-nine articles in which he had been believing all his life, and he thought that he would see what they were. There he found out they were all to be damned, (laughter) and that they were all conceived in sin. (Roars of laughter.) Then he went to his mother and said. "Mother, do you believe that?" (Peals of laughter.) Next I found out that good works were bad; (laughter) that they went for nothing. (Laughter.) He assured them, that it was so. It was in the 11th article. He must give the full particulars or they would not believe it. (Laughter.)

The connection of these remarks and their present meeting was, that if any doubted these things, and expressed their doubts, they had a blasphemy law to shut them up in jail. (Cheers.) After all, he liked the church-clergy better than the dissenting—

they were more honest. They said at once that they wanted the tithes, and they did not care what people believed, provided they got them. Dissenters were not less fond of this world, but they made a greater fuss about the next. It was odd that parsons were always called *one way.* Nobody was ever known to have a "call" to receive £200 a-year, when he was pocketing £400. (Laughter.) Their calls were all *upwards.* (Laughter.) A body of American Christians once sent to Priestly to find them a preacher, but when the doctor heard what salary they could afford to give, he frankly answered, that he could not get one at that price. (Laughter.) They had heard of Sambo, who was all tears when his pastor was delivering his farewell sermon. "Massa," said he, "why you go leave us?" "I have had a call, Sambo." "Very sorry," said Sambo; "but what you *have,* Massa, now?" "£100, Sambo." "What you have then, Massa?" "£200, Sambo." "Ah! Massa, Massa, god almighty not found you someting more, he might a called till he black in de face 'fore you come."{(Laughter.) Yet are we to be subjected to blasphemy prosecutions for expressing our opinions concerning the dogmas of such men.

On his own (Mr. H.'s) trial Lord Campbell told him, if he would plead guilty, he would not be called up for judgment — but how could he plead guilty when he was not guilty? When he spoke of honesty in the matter, a lawyer of considerable eminence asked him if he had not been vitiating his understanding by reading novels. Lord Campbell said, that Mr. Hetherington might entertain what opinions he pleased, but not express them. Now if it was not criminal to differ from a lord, he could shew that that was all nonsense. (Laughter.) What should we think if a physician, who, by long study had discovered cures for many serious complaints, should be told that he might believe what he pleased of these discoveries, but must not express them? Lord Campbell, by his long experience, had been enabled to suggest many improvements in the law. But what would he say if he was told to keep his opinions to himself? (Cheers). His lordship would not agree to this. Then why should we not be allowed to make known our discoveries or reflections on theology? There were some men who were kept in order by red coats, and some by blue coats, and some by black coats. The grown-up children were kept in awe by the *black* coats. This was the case with his friend Hartnett. They told him that he must not hear anything against christianity, if he did he was "done for;" and that was sufficient to keep him in order. (Laughter.) Sir Robert Peel was liberal enough to release Carlile and he might do it in Paterson's case. Paterson ought not to be neglected; he was one of those men to whom he would ever acknowledge the deepest obligations. He (Mr. H.) was growing old, and fond of retirement, and was thankful to those young fellows who would battle for liberty for him. But if the government interfered with his right of free speech, old as he was, and ruinous as it might be to have his home broken up again, he would submit to it, and endure any kind of imprisonment rather than give up that right. (Protracted cheers.) Mr. Roebuck was a man of talent and integrity, and he had no doubt that he would do justice to the memorial. He should, therefore, move that that gentleman be requested to present it in the House of Commons.

Mr. ELLIS seconded the resolution. It was unnecessary, after what had been said that night, to dwell at length on the case before them. He felt that his country should arouse itself and put an end, by one great struggle, to such atrocious proceedings as those connected with the imprisonment of such men as Mr. Paterson. He hoped the time was not far distant when the persecutor would sink into the tomb of oblivion. (Cheers.)

Mr. HYDE desired leave to say a few words. He believed that the Union was open to all. He regretted the introduction of any theological topics at such meetings. He would rather that no discussion of the 39 articles had taken place. The great endeavour should be to unite all differences, and induce all to join the ranks of the Union. (Cheers.)

Mr. HOLYOAKE — the resolution being carried unanimously—moved that the meeting express its appreciation of the valuable services rendered that night by their chairman. The circumstances under which Mr. Clarke took the chair very much enhanced the value which always attached to his generous and willing services. (Cheers.) Perhaps he might say that the petition lay at the doors for signature. Also, persons were in attendance to receive subscriptions. The recent Whitechapel case had been abandoned because of the want of funds to obtain a reversal of Mr. Norton's decision. The right for which they contended was worth any price. They would be as much trampled on if they were poor, as they could be if they were servile. To return— he moved for an expression of their appreciation of the services of their excellent chairman.

Mr. HETHERINGTON would bear testimony to Mr. Clarke's zeal, ability, and devotion, to all good objects, and with great pleasure seconded the resolution, which being carried with acclamations, and Mr. Clarke having acknowledged the compliment, the meeting separated at eleven o'clock.

THE CHINESE AND THEIR RELIGION.
NO. II.

The doctrines of the Confucians are embodied in nine classical or sacred books, called "The Four Books," and "The Five Canonical Works." These contain a complete body of rules, first, for the government of one's self, and the regulation of social intercourse, secondly for the government of a family, and the education of a community; and, thirdly, for the government of an empire and the management of its complex machinery. The sententious brevity of style that characterises these celebrated productions, renders the meaning often obscure, and has induced a mass of commentaries of formidable bulk; but it cannot be doubted that they contain many maxims just in sentiment, wise in policy, and admirably suited to the genius of the people,—maxims which have conferred merited immortality upon the memory of their author, and done more for the stability of the empire than all other causes combined. Confucius, however, avoided, almost entirely, strictly *religious* subjects. Dr. Morrison says, that he did not understand much concerning the gods; and he adds, that his most celebrated contemporary, Choo-foo-tsze, affirmed that sufficient knowledge was not possessed to say positively that they existed.

Thus, it will be seen, that the three religions of China are by no means uniform; and are much blended one with the other—that a species of Epicurean philosophy prevails, that atheistical doctrines are derived from Fuh, and that their idolatry is accompanied by the most debasing, absurd, and superstitious bigotry, both in precept and practice, notwithstanding the wholesome restraints and sound ethics inculcated in the writings of Confucius.

And yet, on the other hand, it is but justice to admit that the Chinese, with all their faults, the metaphysical difficulties, contradictions and absurdities of their religion, have entirely divested their worship of the cruelties and other abominations that deform the rites of the gods of Hindostan, and add a still deeper dye to the crimes of idolatry. Their mythology is perhaps quite as ridiculous as those of the Greeks and Romans, though certainly not so offensive to good morals as some parts of those systems.

No Sabbath is observed by the Chinese, nor is it intimated in their divisions of time, It will, however, be interesting to the Christian world to learn that by some of the Chinese, our Saviour, Ya-soo, is ranked among the number of the gods; while all the better informed classes, consider Him as a just and perfect man. The Virgin Mary (Ma-le-ya, or Maria) being placed by them in the same class.

One of the most remarkable features in the above epitomes is the strong Atheistic tendency, which is attributed both to the religion and philosophy prevalent among the Chinese. It might appear not a little remarkable that the total disbelief of a god, or gods, should co-exist with any religion; the very essence of which, in whatever form or variety we find it, is a foundation of god-belief. It may, however, be accounted for, by the peculiarities of the *esoteric* and *exoteric* doctrines, the former of which being intended for the priests and the initiated only, the latter for the common herd, were by a very ordinary priestly juggle contrived to exist and be taught simultaneously. The morals and philosophy too, by the same accounts, seem similarly tinctured with atheism. The saying of one of the most learned and celebrated writers of the Confucian school, that "sufficient knowledge was not possessed to say positively that the gods existed," sufficiently indicates this bias. It must, however, be conceded that no eastern nation had surpassed this people for polite accomplishments, decorum, and the courtesies of life. It may be appropriately left to those who have deeply studied the human heart, and the origin and progress of doctrines and opinions, both true and false, to pursue these enquiries to their foundation. It is only fair, that we should speak of men and nations as we find them. We can never go wrong, in recording with care and accuracy every contribution, however slight, to historical and national information. M. Q. R.

CONSERVATISM AND REFORM.

THERE is always a certain meanness in the argument of conservatism, joined with a certain superiority in its fact. It affirms *because it holds*. Its fingers clutch the fact, and it will not open its eyes to see a better fact. The castle which conservatism is set to defend is the actual state of things, good and bad. The project of innovation is the best possible state of things. Of course conservatism always has the worst of the argument, is always apologizing, pleading a necessity, pleading that to change would be to deteriorate; it must saddle itself with the mountainous load of all the violence and vice of society, must deny the possibility of good, deny ideas, and suspect and stone the prophet; whilst innovation is always in the right, triumphant, attacking, and sure of success. Conservatism stands on man's incontestable limitations, reform on his indisputable infinitude; conservatism on circumstance, liberalism on power; conservatism is debonnair and social, reform is individual and imperious. Reform is affirmative, conservatism negative; conservatism goes for comfort, reform for truth. Conservatism makes no poetry, breathes no prayer, has no invention; it is all memory. Reform has no gratitude, no prudence, no husbandry. It makes a great difference to your figure and to your thought, whether your foot is advancing or receding. Conservatism never puts its foot forward, in the hour when it does that, it is no establishment but reform.—*Emerson.*

LETTERS TO PERTH GAOL.

Mr. Paterson desires to acknowledge the receipt of letters from Messrs. Liddle, Ryall, and Dent. Some persons have addressed letters to the gaol, containing much personal abuse of the governor. This, besides being unjust to that gentleman, is calculated to operate in a manner highly injurious to Mr. Paterson, and may probably cause an abridgement of the few privileges he enjoys. As Mr. Paterson's address has been made public in the *Movement*, it is probable that enemies have taken advantage of it, to add still more to the severity of his punishment. Our readers will oblige us by forwarding any information in their power that may lead to the detection and exposure of the authors of these letters.

EXTENSION OF THE FRANCHISE.

A movement has commenced in the extensive and populous parish of Islington, and, we believe, in some few other places, to carry out the late decision in the Court of Common Pleas, on an appeal from the Revising Barrister's Court, viz: that all lodgers and occupiers of small tenements, although not paying the parochial rates, are entitled to the franchise, if they pay a rent of not less than £10 a year or 4s. per week. If means were taken generally to make this decision known, and to assist the parties entitled to make their claim, there cannot be a doubt that in many places the popular constituency would be more than doubled. The association that has been formed in Islington for this purpose have already forwarded above 550 claims to the overseers.

[This important decision concerns our readers. Let all to whom it applies send in their claims to their respective parishes or boroughs, if they have not already done so. Those who complain of the injury of religion should lose no prospective opportunity of lessening its influence. An infidel electoral body would soon purge the country of fanaticism. Candidates are asked all sorts of questions at elections, why should they not be asked to vote for the repeal of the blasphemy laws? Ed. of M.]

[The following excellent satire on conventional expediency is extracted from the same work, "Studies of Sensation and Event," from which we recently borrowed—a volume of poems recently published, which has been hailed with satisfaction by the lovers of genius and poetry. Ed. of M.]

SONG OF THE GOLD GETTERS.

"The essence of trade is to buy cheap and sell dear."—*House of Commons, England*, 1843.

Oh! truth may have suited the knights of old,
   And have royally crowned the barbarian's brow ;
And the Hottentot's mother his grave may have scrolled,
With " He never once lied ;" but Utopia now,
In our civilized world, is the only land
Where truth could be worshipped, where truth could live ;
For from statesman to tradesman, all utterance is planned,
Any meanings but true ones to hint at or give.
   Lie! let us lie! make the lies fit;
    It's the only way mortals their fortunes can knit.

If the minister orders war ships at a foe,
He pretends they are bound quite a different way ;
And where is the man that shall dare to throw
Disdain on the lie, or the truth to say ;
The traveller, hearing the lion's roar,
Lies to the lion by feigning death,
And lives by the lie ; and what can there be more
In the minister's lie to the enemy's teeth !
   Lie! let us lie! make the lies fit;
    It's the only way mortals their fortunes can knit.

" The best policy's honesty," horn-books tell,
Though we know who lies best gets the best of the pelf ;—
'Tis the sire for his children the axiom likes well,
For the lie's an advantage he wants all himself;
For the same cunning reason, your pulpits, your thrones,
Your senates, your judges, the axiom repeat ;
Each wants to monopolise lying, and moans
That he can't with this lie, truth from other men cheat.
   Lie! let us lie! make the lies fit;
    It's the only way mortals their fortunes can knit.

Truth now starves in garrets, or rots in a gaol,
Whate'er may have been in the times gone by;
And supremacy national, "cakes and ale,"
Honour, and station, reward the lie;
Let us lie then like statesmen, like fathers,
    and gold
We shall heap and keep;—the world is war
And out of war's articles, none will uphold
The virtue of truth when a falsehood gains
    more.
            Chorus.
Lie! let us lie! Oh! we'll make the
    lies fit;
It's the only way mortals their fortunes
    can knit.
                    Eben. Jones.

THE ROSHERVILLE GARDENS.—On sunday last, the Socialists of the Metropolis made their annual excursion, and the Rosherville Gardens was the point of attraction. Beautiful, delightful, fine, being terms which express our highest perceptions of the agreeable, a due regard to the best understood proprieties of speech would forbid their employment on any but extraordinary occasions, but it may be said of this occasion—all were pleased with the weather, with their accommodations, with the gardens and each other. The party was numerous, and it would have been a happy thought to have taken the petition adopted at John-street on Monday for signature. Among so much gaiety and beauty persons would have felt a generous pleasure in remembering the contemporaneous desolation of others. But it is not too late for those who have not affixed their names to do so.

AN IMPROVEMENT IN VERDICTS—SUBMITTED TO MR. WAKLEY.— A coroner's jury having sat on the body of a young lady in Baltimore, America, who had hung herself in a fit of *love frenzy*, brought in their verdict—*Died by the visitation of Cupid.*

ATHEISTICAL RELICS.—Miss Roalfe has forwarded a copy of the "Spirit of Bonner," and various curiosities of atheistical literature, which were seized by the Procurator Fiscal on her premises, and now bear interesting marks indicative of having been in his custody. These relics are intended to enrich the Atheistical Museum.

WISE men have always been inclined to look with great suspicion on the angels and demons of the multitude.—*Macaulay.*

"DIDEROT, on his death-bed, was urged by the curate of St. Sulpice to recant his opinions. 'I know,' said Diderot, 'but will it do to tell a downright lie?'"

Received for Mrs. M. from "W. J." 0 5 0

NOTICE.

MR. HOLYOAKE'S address until July 18 will be Hall of Science, Campfield, Manchester.

TO CORRESPONDENTS.

"A YOUNG ENQUIRER" has addressed to me a series of sixteen queries under the title "Phrenology versus Godology." Their main purpose is, by directing attention to the phrenological organs, natural adaptations, and some other phenomena, to prove the existence of a god and design. I have given them a careful perusal. The arguments are worth consideration in the *Movement*. To be properly noticed they should be quoted entire. This, I submit, would render necessary re-perusal and revision on the part of the writer. Is he willing to comply with this suggestion? If so, a line addressed as before will obtain attention.
                    M. Q. R.

Received.— "Naamanism" by Dr. P. Y. Defence of a recent paper entitled "The God of Nature and the Bible Identical," by C. S.—we will guard against the errata of which he justly complains. — The *Belfast Commercial Chronicle.*

J. B. complains that the discussion on Monday Evenings, at No. 48, Henry-street East, Portland town, is not attended by atheistical disputants. What is the Atheistical Society doing? Our young friends should attend to these opportunities of explaining their views. We cannot be everywhere. It would be useful if they would put themselves in possession of all the places where debates are held on atheism:—distribute themselves among them — and report to us the results, as often as is convenient. We should be happy to record their exertions in the *Movement.*

SUBSCRIPTIONS TO THE ANTI-PERSECUTION UNION.

Mr. Hill for Mr. Paterson .	£0 2 6
Mr. Armfield do. . . .	0 1 0
Do. Subscription . . .	0 0 0
Per Public Meeting, John-street	0 17 2
Per Mr. Geo. Dixon, Stratford—	
For Members' Tickets .	0 6 0

All communications for the Anti-Persecution to be addressed to Thomas Powell, Secretary, *pro. tem.*, 40, Holywell-street, Strand, until further notice. Money orders to be made payable at the Post Office in the Strand.
                    G. J. H., *Sec.*

Printed and Published by G. J. HOLYOAKE,
40, Holywell-street, Strand,
Saturday, June 22, 1844.

THE MOVEMENT

And Anti=Persecution Gazette.

"Maximize morals, minimize religion."—BENTHAM.

No. 29.   EDITED BY G. JACOB HOLYOAKE, ASSISTED BY M. Q. RYALL.   PRICE 1½d

THE ABROGATION OF BLASPHEMY LAWS.

THE recommendations of the *Movement* to petition the Government relative to these laws has not been made in vain, as the petition of Mr. Ryley, a former colleague of Carlile, and an old veteran in the cause, evidences. The committee of the Anti-Persecution Union have adopted the following form, to be addressed by themselves individually to the House of Commons, and by all members of the Union, and other persons who may find it expressive of their sentiments.

"The Petition to the Hon. the House of Commons, of A. B., of—(*such profession, place, &c.*)

"That your petitioner is of opinion that the recent convictions of Messrs. Paterson, Finlay, and Miss Roalfe, in Scotland, for blasphemy, are an infringement on the liberty of conscience, and that your petitioner under this conviction, prays that your lHonourable House may abrogate all laws interfering with the freedom of opinion, and all enactments or regulations relative to blasphemy."

Hundreds of these petitions ought to be forwarded every sessions until the object is achieved. Let every liberal voter, or to-be-voter according to the recent decision in the Court of Common Pleas, at once send one through his borough member. Both in town and country throughout Great Britain and Ireland, this should be done. Petitions as above, properly written out, can be had on application to the Secretary of the Union. They will only require filling up, signing, and sending.

"The Memorial to the House of Commons of George Jacob Holyoake, Mathematical Teacher, of 4, Wellington-street, Goswell-street, parish of St. Luke, Middlesex.

"SHEWETH—That your memorialist respectfully solicits your House to annul all laws, and all practises of courts relative to blasphemy on the ground that they are of iniquitous operation.

"A short time ago your memorialist had the misfortune to be charged with blasphemy at the Gloucester Summer Assizes of 1842. His offence consisted in a brief answer given in discussion, which answer, the witness for the crown, admitted to be conscientious and provoked. Yet your memorialist was sentenced by Mr. Justice Erskine to six months imprisonment. Of that which was true, your memorialist spoke that which he deemed most appropriate, and although he has no pleasure in imprisonment, and takes no pride in breaking the law, yet, under the same circumstances, he could not now do other than give a similar answer.

"Your memorialist prays your House to advise the Queen to order the release of Thomas Paterson, now confined in the General Prison, Perth, for the publication of atheistical sentiments, or at least to remove him from his solitary confinement, and generally ameliorate his severe treatment.

"For why is he sever'd from all we hold dear?
Why is he apart, like a corpse on its bier?
What—what is his crime? Hath he taken
    away
The widow's, the orphan's, the destitute's
    stay?
Has he taxed the distressed? has he taken
    the bread
From those who were starving, to pamper
    the fed?
And, at last when all famished and hopeless
    they lay,
Has he dragg'd from them dying their pallet
    away?
Oh, no! the sole crime that hate can make
    clear,
Is this—that he has been, and still is—*sincere*!"

"Finding the existing laws and practices of courts relative to blasphemy, only calculated to encourage dissimulation, your memorialist believes them to be both unwise and iniquitous, and, therefore, earnestly prays for their immediate abrogation.

Signed, *George Jacob Holyoake.*"

THE FATAL SENTENCE OF MARIA JOAQUINA, FOR BLASPHEMY.

THE following is a letter from Dr. Kalley referred to in the speech of Mr. M'Cullough reported in last *Movement*. It tells its own horrid tale to every one, of the fearful nature of religion. We are not safe from a return to the same practices in our own age if once the determined opposition to religion is relaxed. Hibbert most truly declared, that to attack religion is but a well understood system of self-defence. The letter is extracted from the *Belfast Protestant Journal*.

"My dear Sir,—Although very hurried I cannot allow the steamer to go without communicating to you the state of matters here.

"Last Sabbath two persons, when going home from my house, were taken prisoners and committed to gaol, where they now lie, for not kneeling to the host as it passed. On Monday a third was imprisoned on the same charge. On Wednesday several were mauled with sticks, and some taken by hands and feet, as in procession, and carried into the church, and made to kneel before the images. On the 2nd of May, a girl brought me some leaves of the New Testament, telling me, with tears, that her own father had taken two and beat them with a great stick, and then burnt them. On the same day, Maria Joaquina, wife of Manuel Alves, who had been in prison nearly a year, was condemned to death. The counts against her were, that she denied the doctrine of the Trinity and the virginity of Mary, and maintained that the sacramental bread is bread, and that images should not be venerated. A gentleman, who was present during the whole trial, assured me that, respecting the Trinity and the virginity, there was no proof adduced. Respecting the sacrament, only one witness swore that he heard her say that the host is bread. And respecting the images, all declared that she did not say that they should not be venerated, but that she did say that the holy Scripture forbids the adoration of them. My informant was astonished that the country people should have known the difference, and given so clear evidence before a prosecutor, who put leading questions and tried to confound them. It will hardly be credited in our fatherland, that such a sentence could have been given in this century; but the mother of seven children, the youngest of whom was at the breast when the mother was cast into prison, is now a prisoner in the gaol of Funchal, condemned to be hanged, for having said that images should not be adored; and, under such circumstances, she is forbidden the use of the holy scriptures, or any part of them. It is as likely that she will be actually executed, as it was that she would be condemned to death. We suppose it impossible to perpetrate such an act. We also supposed it impossible that such a sentence should have been given in any part of Christian Europe in 1844.

"Yesterday a young man, a father of two or three little children, came to speak about the rage of the enemies of truth in his parish, and the danger in which he found himself. On the way home a large company—among them, as ringleaders, the nephews of a priest, belaboured him. He went on quietly—that is, without answering or striking, but as fast as could, to be free of them. He is to-day in bed, all black and blue, and his brother had to flee for safety. What is done to those who perpetuate such things? Nothing. Not one is taken up for them—they are said to be encouraged. I understand that the object is to make it appear that I am exciting a commotion; but I always urge those who hear me to follow the command of Christ, 'Love your enemies,' and that they resist not evil, but remember that they are sheep, and that their safety consists in keeping close to the shepherd Jesus, and calling on and committing themselves to him.

"The sentence having just arrived, I translate and send it, which will speak for itself:—

"QUESTIONS AND ANSWERS OF THE JURY, AND SENTENCE OF THE JUDGE, NEGRAO.

"I. Is the crime of heresy, of which Maria Joaquina is accused in the libel, proved or not?

"Answer, by the majority,—The crime of heresy, of which M. J. is accused, is proven.

"II. Is the crime of blasphemy against the images of Christ and Mother of God, against the mystery of the most holy Trinity, and the immaculate conception of the Virgin Mary, of which M. J. is accused in the libel, proved or not?

"Answer unanimously—The crime of blasphemy against the images of Christ and Mother of God, against the mystery of the most holy Trinity, and the immaculate conception of the Virgin Mary, of which M. J. is accused in the libel, is proved.

"III. Is the extenuating circumstance that the witness, Antonia Maria, is an enemy of the accused, and has not spoken with her for three years, proved or not, Funchal Oriental, 2nd May, 1844. Signed Joze Sereira Leito Pitta Ortagueira Negrao.

"Answer unanimously—The extenuating circumstance that the witness, Antonia Maria, is an enemy of the accused, and has not spoken with her for three years, is not proved:—Luis Antonio de Freitas, Felisbesto Bittancourt Miranda, Licio d'Athoguia Freitas Uzel, Sebastiao Leal, Manoel d'Oliveira, Filippe Constantino Silva, Antonio Jose Gonzalves de Ornellas, Joze Joaquim la Costa, P. Jorge Monteiro, Francisco Pedro Olival, Christovao Augusto Perreira, Gaspar Ignacio Eonies.

"SENTENCE.

"In view of the answers of the jury, and discussion of the cause, &c., it is proved that the accused Maria Joaquina, perhaps forgetful of the principles of the holy religion which she received in her first years, and to which she still belongs, has maintained conversations and arguments condemned by the church, maintaining that veneration should not be given to images, denying the real existence of Jesus Christ in the sacred host, the mystery of the most holy Trinity, blaspheming against the most holy virgin, mother of God, and advancing other expressions against the doctrines received and followed by the Catholic Apostolic Roman Church, expounding these condemned doctrines to different persons, thus committing the crime of heresy and blasphemy, punished by the laws of the kingdom; and although it be affirmed that nobody can be prosecuted for motives of religion, as a principle truly constitutional, it is necessary that the religion of the state be respected, and public morals be not perverted by words or acts that are condemned, as it is expressly established in the fundamental laws of the state, art. 145, sec. 4; which the accused, in truth, did not do; on the contrary, blasphemy against God and his saints, she gave over respecting the religion of the state to which she belongs, seeking to associate to her party those who nourished principles different from hers. This accusation cannot be eluded by the defence to which she has recourse, because it consists only in sustaining the illegality of the action, and the incompetency of the court to condemn in the penalties decreed by the ordinanca, book 5th, title 1st. It appears that it belongs only to the tribunal *ad quem* to decide a question on all accounts delicate. Attending, then, to the fact, that the crimes of which the prisoner is accused are found proven in the form decreed by the law of 15th of December, 1774, and ordinanca of book 5th. title 2nd, sec. 1, which says thus—"And if he be a peasant, let him recive thirty strokes at the foot of the pillory, with a cord and proclamation, and let him pay two dollars, observing, moreover, that the foresaid law of the 15th of December imposes on those guilty of the crimes of heresy the penalty of death with infamy; observing, likewise, that now is abolished the said penalty of infamy and strokes, and that the greater punishment always includes the lesser, I condemn the accused, Maria Joaquina, to suffer death, as declared in the said law, and in the costs of the process, which she shall pay with her goods. Funchal Oriental, in public court, 2nd of May, 1844. Joze Pereira Leito Pitta Ortegueira Negrao."

"The signal gun is fired for the steamer to be off. Pray for us, and believe me ever your sincere friend,

ROBERT R. KALLEY.

"The condemned believes in the doctrine of the Trinity, and never said a word against it. She is a most clear-minded, intelligent Christian woman, and quite willing to die if the Lord will.

"May 4, 1844."

ADDRESS
TO MADAME D'AURSMONT,

From the Conductors of the MOVEMENT *and Anti-Persecution Gazette;*

(a Weekly Journal of Republican Politics, Anti-Theology, and Utilitarian Morals.)

DEEMING your visit to be as fleeting as it has been silent, the promptings of respect, which would have induced us to address you earlier, were restrained, but finding from your communication to the *Northern Star* that it is not yet too late, we hasten to congratulate you on your presence in Europe, where your writings have long been admired, and your memory held in esteem.

It is not more objectionable to your own pure taste, than foreign to our dispositions to address you in the language of adulation. We coin no eulogies—the facts of your history are eloquent praise. The celebrity of your works, the frankness with which you have spoken, and the risks you have incurred, bespeak talent, courage, and integrity. To this recital attaches no suspicion since it is not the testimony of a party, but of the public.

We speak for many, who, could their names be promptly appended to this address, would rejoice to join in it. It may assure you of the interest felt, that we, from whom conquerors elicit no welcome, wealth no reverence, and royalty no attention, are anxious to testify to Frances Wright our admiration and esteem.

Your writings have done much to promote free discussion, to exalt morality, and to rationalize the popular notions of religion—a task which genius might always well commence, but which on the whole is best performed by a lady. For when women see through popular delusions, and free themselves from conventional trammels, men will no longer be found weak enough to defend such, and civilisation will advance by equally steady steps.

Subjoining our best wishes for the welfare

of Mons. D'Aursmont and your son, we subscribe ourselves respectfully,
G. Jacob Holyoake,
M. Questell Ryall.

WORKS OF WILLIAM GILLESPIE.

As great numbers of our readers have taken an interest in the controversy in the *à priori* argument for the existence of deity, it may serve them to direct their attention to the works of Mr. Gillespie on this subject, without a knowledge of which the controversy will be but partially understood. Whatever may be thought of Mr. Gillespie's Arguments, all will admire the industry with which he has arranged them. His productions will please the methodical, and instruct the diffuse. We cannot say they will afford the same satisfaction, but the study of them will afford the same kind of discipline as the elements of Euclid.

Mr. Gillespie's principal works are—

"An Inquiry into the Defects of mere *à posteriori* Arguments for a God."

"Reviews of the Demonstrations by *Mr. Locke, Dr. Samuel Clarke*, the *Rev. Moses Lournan*, and *Bishop Hamilton*, of the Existence and Attributes of a Deity."

"Necessary Existence implies Infinite Extension."

"The Argument, *à priori* for the Being and Attributes of A First Cause."

"An Examination of Antitheos's "Refutation of the Argument *à priori* for the Being and Attributes of God."

All these works are issued by the Philalethean Society for peaceably repressing Infidelity—and can be had of all booksellers.

105, Nicolson Street, Edinburgh,
June 6th, 1844.

REPORT OF GENERAL PROGRESS.

Miss Roalfe has, since her liberation, made several applications to the Procurator Fiscal for the books that were seized prior to her imprisonment, and on May 29th she waited on the Procurator at his request per note, when the whole of the books not prosecuted were given up to her.

Those I send you are a copy of each of the bills seized and returned. I have enclosed you a list of the books returned:—

436 Nos. of the *Oracle of Reason*; 57 *Investigator*; 19 Nos. *Existence of Christ Disproved*; 16 Nos. *Strauss's Life of Jesus*; 8 Nos. *Palmer's Principles of Nature*; 14 *Freethinker's Information*; 8 *Devil's Pulpit*; 1 copy *Great Dragon*; 1 No. *Yahoo*; 2 Parts *Library of Reason*; 1 *Galileo and the Inquisition*; 1 on the *Character of Prayer*; 1 *Spirit of Bonner*; 10 bills of *Oracle of Reason*, 26 of *Freethinker's Information*, 58 other bills of various publications; 1 *Atheism Justified*; 1 *Atheism for the Million*.

A board which had one of Miss Roalfe's Manifestos, they refused to give up; but two or three hours afterwards sent it home by one of the officers of the court, the manifesto having been removed.

You will find by looking to the report of Miss Rolfe's trial, that one of the witnesses against her is called John Colquhoun; of this man I quote the following from the *Edinburgh Weekly Chronicle and Scottish Pilot* of May 25th.

Police Court.—On Saturday, John Colquhoun, a police constable, was placed at the bar by Capt. Haining, for stealing a pound note from the person of a man in Highstreet. Three witnesses were examined for the prosecution, when the charge of theft was found not proven, but from the suspicious circumstances connected with the case, the magistrates dismissed him from the establishment. Colquhoun has been nine years in the service, and has been till lately an assistant criminal officer, from which duty he was removed by the superintendent a few weeks ago.

I have been on a fortnight's tour in the south of Scotland selling infidelity. I found a considerable number of friends, but in all cases they were afraid to openly express their opinions, lest they should lose their employment. Some time ago Mr. Southwell lectured at Galashiels, 32 miles hence, and one poor man with a family of five children lost his employment in consequence of his being active on the occasion. In Selkirk, 38 miles from here, I found a similar case. In Hawick I found one poor man with a family who has been several months out of work—many other minor cases came under my notice.

The object of my tour was to satisfy all that might want books, that they could be supplied by writing to our depôt, Nicolsonstreet. Many labour under the impression that the shop was only opened for a while in opposition to the authorities, whereas we want to make it a centre for infidelity in Scotland, but without direct support from friends we probably shall be unable to go on —our expenses are so heavy. If you can give this any publicity in the *Movement* do so. All the Nos. of the *Oracle* seized, and now returned, are for sale as before. A large number of the *Bible, an Improper Book for Youth*.

J. W. Baker.

NOTABLE THINGS.

Parliamentary Senses.—Not parliamentary *sense*, but *senses*, are worth a passing notice. Another of those peculiarly parliamentary phenomena only displayed in the regions of the collective wisdom recently took place. It was on occasion of the discussion of a very delicate matter in the "Lords." On the Bishop of Exeter rising to move the second reading of his "Brothels' Bill"—Lord Campbell stopt him short by suggesting that strangers should be excluded —but as the bishop did not happen to intend saying anything that could not be "placed on the most delicate breakfast table next morning—he thought their lordships should know nothing of strangers being present; they *could not conceive such a thing.*" No sooner was this said than up starts Lord Brougham — *Punch's* own Brougham —exclaiming with his peculiar energy, and vehement extension of his right arm — "I cannot allow this to go any farther. It is contrary to all order that we should ever *talk* about strangers being here, (and this the very instant after the reverend prelate declaring their lordships could not *conceive* of their being there), because the moment you *know* they are here, the standing order of the house *removes them* of course. Either do it in the ordinary way, or let it alone altogether." The ordinary way we should have thought the last on earth for this extraordinary lord to recommend.

The Lord Chancellor—If I *am told* that strangers are present, I must enforce the standing order.

The Bishop of Exeter—I have *no eye* for strangers.

Lord Brougham—THERE ARE NO STRANGERS PRESENT.

Thus ran the round of Parliamentary Senses, which seem a sort of composite order, partly composed of external or everyday senses, partly of internal or spiritual senses, partly of a new order which can receive no appropriate name but that of *Parliamentary.* How funny this would sound anywhere else but in Parliament or Bedlam.

A.—Strangers! strangers! turn 'em out
B.—Don't tell of 'em, or they must go.
C. — Don't talk of them, or they must.
D.—Can't see 'em. E.—There an't any.

PROGRESS OF RELIGIOUS FREEDOM IN FRANCE.—A weekly journal states that the chief consistory of the Jews at Paris have addressed a letter to the minister of public worship, expressing gratitude for the royal ordonnance regulating the mode of forming the Israelite consistories in the different towns of France, and thus extending to them an equal protection of the law.

MAGISTERIAL LIBERALITY.—It is pleasing to be able to record an instance of fellow-feeling for the poor on the part of a magistrate. On application by a police inspector to Mr. Painter, the Wandsworth magistrate, for putting down some humble and cheap Sunday amusements under the name of "nuisances," Mr. Painter is reported by the *Dispatch* to have said—" The Police Act gives me no power to interfere, and I do not see why I should. In no other country than this are the working-classes restricted in their Sunday amusements, and I do not see, as long as those amusements are harmless in their character, that they should do so in this. The gentry throng the park on Sunday in their carriages, and as equestrians, then why should not the humble mechanic ride on a donkey?" The inspector said it was the gentry who made the complaints. "Then let the gentry, before they make these complaints, set the example of abstemiousness in their own persons," said Mr. Painter.

INFIDEL REVIVALS.—At the Richmond Court Chapel, on Sunday, 23rd June curt., and three following Sundays. Infidel Sermons on Popular Fallacies, will be delivered by Mr. Southwell, in the following order :— Sunday, 23, Morning, God—Evening, Devil. Sunday, 30, Morning, Heaven—Evening, Hell. Sunday, July 7, Morning, Angels— Evening, Witches. Sunday, July 14, Morning, Ghosts—Evening, Goblins. Morning, Sermons will commence at half-past 11, and evening at 7 precisely.

Take notice!—The committee appointed to get up Infidel Revivals, earnestly recommend the public to attend at an *early hour,* if they desire to hear these extraordinary Sermons delivered, as the Chapel (they are sorry to say) will not well accommodate more than 500 persons. The committee have also made arrangements for the delivery of Lectures by Mr. Southwell in the above named Chapel, every Wednesday Evening till further notice. The lectures will commence at half-past 8, and conclude at 10 o'clock precisely.

THE STATUE OF BYRON.

THE exclusion of the statue of Lord Byron fiom Westminster Abbey, was a national disgrace, and he could not help regretting that the Dean and Chapter had pursued such a course.—*Lord Brougham.*

He hoped the erection of Byron's statue would never be allowed in Westminster Abbey.—*Bishop of London.*

Such statues were not proper to be placed in religious edifices.—*Bishop of Exeter.*

(*Lines written in the Album kept in Hucknell Church, where Byron is interred.*)

He lies not in obscurity, though here
This humble dwelling gives his dust a home,
For Byron has not — ne'er shall have — a tomb;

That name—the spirit's blaze—will flash it
  dear,
And animated light for ever there,
Where thought can roam, where mind can
  mock the doom,
Of mouldering mortality—the wing
Of time will fan into a brighter ray,
That glory as he passes on his way,
And o'er that name a lustred record fling,
More strongly splendid, wider radiating
Through cloudless and interminable day.

But if on earth a spot were chosen meet
For his earthly part to rest in, well
Mighty Niagara, and that alone should tell
The traveller who yearns that grave to greet—
That ever rolling stream, his winding sheet!
That deep-toned thunder voice his endless
  knell.

C. R. Pemberton.

DEMOCRATIC AND ATHEISTICAL EMIGRATION.

WE should be wanting in our duty did we not draw attention to this unique Co-operative Society for emigrating to the Western States of North America. This Society is established on the basis of " pure democratic communism, self governing and self dependant." It is the first association of the kind which has made the rejection of religion one of its principles of union. With so much foresight and good sense as this step evidences, the association deserves success. An "Address" has been published from which we gather that an extensive combination is contemplated, or has been entered into with various continental "sections," who look forward with high hope to the formation of a democratic and irreligious world in the Arkansas or N. W. districts. Their excellent objects are thus set forth:—

" It is proposed that our sections may be looked upon as an assured asylum for the veterans of political and mental freedom, where they may enjoy a haven of honourable and honoured rest, after having struggled for the good cause to their own hindrance and injury; and that they may not fear the tender mercies of a poor law union, the poverty stricken old age of St. Simon, or the solitary death bed of Fourrier."

From the "Address" we subjoin the " Fundamental Laws," to which for the sake of insuring unity of principles, all the members will be required to assent; and in accordance with which to insure unity of action, the laws of all the sections must be founded.

1st. That no money qualification, or any other qualification than that of personal utility, shall be received as ground of admission to the society.

2nd. Since we conceive all religious creeds to be the inventions of men, and not, as is pretended, the revelations of the will of a deity,—but that they are, and always have been, only intended for, and adapted to, the subjugation of the credulous to the power of the crafty, and to the maintenance of that power;—that they are utterly incompetent to produce a better conduct than the faithful would otherwise lead, as many ancient and modern philosophers have taught—and if competent on this point the good effect would be the result of evil means;—we are therefore prepare to defend, and determined to assert, the dignity of that truth whose beauty we admire, and to denounce all such pretended revelations as the offspring of knavery and credulity.

3rd. The maintenance of Fraternity, Equality, and Liberty, as the basis of Democracy. 4th. The abnegation of individuality before the community, and the duty of sacrificing self-interest to that of the public; such sacrifice, if properly appreciated, would be claimed as a right. 5th. The duties generally considered as degrading, or which are in reality disagreeable from hardship, exposure, or other causes, to be performed as follows. Those of each individual by him or herself. Those of each family by itself. Those of the community by all the members, regard being had to sex, age and the power of performing them. 6th. The education of the youth in common. 7th. The maintainance of the domestic circle. 8th. Submission in all disputes to Arbitrators forming part of the Section. 9th. The sick and infirm to be provided for under all circumstances. 10th. The children to become equal proprietors on coming of age. 11th. The widow and orphans of a deceased member to enjoy the same rights as they would have done had the husband and father lived. 12th. The will of the majority to be in all cases, the law; but not to interfere with these fundamental laws, except by rendering them more progressive."

" All who hold our opinions, and wish to carry out the ideas above suggested, will be met by the society in that spirit of fraternity which alone can ensure the success of such an enterprise; and are invited to to attend our meetings which are held at Hudson's Coffee House, Upper Wellington Street, Covent Garden, every Sunday Evening at 8 o'clock, or to correspond with the Secretary, Charles Sully, 11, Roll's Buildings, Fetter Lane."

THE DEVIL AT COURT.

THE plain-speaking worthies of the "National Hall" who got up the meeting—perhaps the only honest demonstration—to notify their estimation of his autocratic Majesty of the

Russias, were indignant with the press in general for the part they took on the occasion. Have not the newsmongers, court people, and the like, got stereotype arrivals, departures, receptions, acclamations, and all that sort of thing, concerning royalty, varied to suit names, places, and times.

Certainly the last affair of the kind possessed some peculiarities which had to be artfully insinuated among the stereotyped compliments in the most delicate way imaginable. Besides, in this particular case, there had been such lots of abuse heaped on the " Northern Despot," that simple people could hardly divine how a tolerable reception could be accorded when he had become a " Royal Visitor." But look at the difference. —The other day when we were horrified by the dark doings of confiscations, banishment and murders by thousands and tens of thousands—the perpetrator was at a distance; since then we have been dazzled by the effulgence of his presence, and he looks so very like other human beings, or rather, it is discovered he looks so much superior to most other human beings, that the case is altered. There's his noble bearing (perhaps he hasn't got round shoulders)—his majestic appearance, (our little Queen can walk under his arm) his erect mien, (he hasn't a hump) his noble expression, (he doesn't squint) his princely aspect (he has a star stitched to his coat), his martial air, (he wears a sword, a belt, and a feather)—all this would do for a foot soldier, the very first you see in the ranks—but you must then dub him prince, king, or emperor. The *Times* began " to turn about, and twist about, and do just so," even before the time of the " august presence." The smaller sort of sycophants waited till he came—when his sun arose in our horizon—Poland and Circassia were enveloped in darkness—the darkness of oblivion.

If the Autocrat of all the Hades, instead of the Autocrat of all the Russias was to pay the Britannic court a visit,

Provided he came in pomp and state,
Had lots of serf-devils upon him to wait,
And threw about gold with a plentiful hand,
He'd be fawned, cringed, and " glozed upon" over the land.

Poor and humble he musn't appear,
Friendless and cheerless—he " can't lodge here,"
Let him come with an air that's " genteel and respectable,"
Country and town he'll then find most delectable.

If old Nick came to court he must be full dress'd,
Of course he'd put on his Sunday best—

" Jacket of red and breeches of blue,
And a little hole behind for his tail to peep through."

—Or if monkey fashion to ape's give place,
The tail he'll tuck in with devilish grace,
The hoofs in Wellingtons he'd insert,
Cocked hat and feathers the horns would girt.

Young Nick more modest than *Times* or *Post*,
Bull, Herald, Standard, and all the host,
Would fain have hidden from public scan,
And come and gone like a common man.

Scarce dared he to hope that for love or pay,
A newspaper hack could be found to say
How he looked—how he spake—but the hireling slave
Let the secret out when he told how he *gave*.

Siberia's horrors, and Poland's pains,
Circassia's groans — knouts, gibbets, and chains,
In his memory lived—and he thought in these climes,
No place but a Court will gild my crimes.

M. Q. R.

WORKING-CLASS CAPACITY FOR GOVERNMENT.

" *A Lecturer of Seven Years standing* " contends, in opposition to the recent remarks of an ex-officer of the " Rationalists," that the opulent and leisurely are not the only classes capable of conducting extensive operations in which *Government* is a leading division. It is not the absence of intelligence—as was before set forth in a valuable paper wherein the managerial departments were stated to be filled by working-men—but "the dependent position of the working-classes that prevents them from doing anything for themselves." — If working-men's communities were impossible, why did the founder of the system " delay the declaration of incapacity till hope had been created only to be blasted and destroyed ?"—The working-classes in our correspondent's opinion " have as much useful knowledge and practical experience as any other class, and a great deal more, progression, on a national scale, is never affected without their aid." He congratulates the Rationalists on the resolution of Congress, that " the society shall adhere to the objects it originally had in view, to test the great principle of co-operation in the production of wealth, and its equal distribution amongst those who produce it, and to erect the structure of universal liberty on the basis of universal equality. I now both hope and expect from the working-class a greater degree of support for the Rationalists' cause than they yet have given."

A NEW PHENOMENON.

Another effect resulting from the denunciation of reason is this. Among the thinking portion of the lower classes of this country, there has arisen a sort of anti-christian fanaticism. A class of persons has sprung up, who have a hatred of every thing connected with christianity, and who differ from each other only in the latitude within which they exercise this feeling. Dealing with the subject unconventionally, bringing to it the light of their untutored common sense—when told to bow down to the Bible without question, in a natural revulsion of feeling, they fly to the other extreme; and wronged by persecution, and irritated by the hurling of opprobrious epithets and social obloquy, they wage eternal war with all that bears the christian name. (Here came something about the light which might be thrown on the subject by better education and maturer judgment). There needed the combination of church bigotry and social persecution to produce such a result;—they *have* combined—it *is* produced — and the church and state of England have called from the abyss of chaos the portentous phenomenon of an Infidel Martyrology.—*W. J. Fox.*

Hint to Persecutors.—There happened a quarrel one day among some brickmakers I had occasion to employ, and two of them fell to boxing. One of the two, whose name was Peter, had the other down, and beat him unmercifully. The fellow that lay under him cried out, and, as I was at some distance, I ran with some servants to separate them, thinking he had cried murder; but, coming nearer, I understood him better, and found he cried out, " Pay me, Peter; 't will be my turn by and by!" Peter did his best, and being a strong fellow, mauled him sufficiently. But at last, when Peter had beaten him till he was out of breath, the fellow's turn came; he got up, and Peter was undermost, and the other used him accordingly. I make no applications; I would have nobody undermost; I would have all love, peace, charity, and union; but, if ye will be mad, —if you will be all persecution and conformity, or nothing,—dragoon them into it at once, gentlemen; show yourselves fairly; set up gallows and galleys; send the parents to goal, confiscate their estates; take their children from them, and educate them in your own blessed principles; affront the Queen, dissolve the settlement, restore King James, and declare your minds; but then, I beseech you, do not forget the story of Peter and his fellow.—*De Foe.*

The Chameleon. — Eventually Christianity arose. It gathered the polished Greek, the restless Roman, the barbarous Saxon, around its standard; it spoke soft words of peace and pity; but it was a thing for an *age*,—not for eternity, and therefore was suitable only for the era for which it grew. it had anathemas for the bitter-hearted to hurl at those they chose to designate " God's enemies;" it had promises for me hopeful; cautions for the prudent, charity for the good. It " was all things to all men, that by all means it might win some." It became the grand *leader*—of the ascetic, to the convent—of the chivalrous, to the crusade —of the cruel, to the Star Chamber—of the scholar, to the secret midnight cell, there to feed on knowledge, but not impart it.— *Emma Martin.*

The London Atheistical Society will hold its next meeting at the Parthenium, St. Martin's lane, on Tuesday evening next, July 2 to admit members and discuss, " What will be the most efficient means to spread the principles of Atheism." T. Powell, *Sec.*

A Memorial to the House of Commons for the release of Thomas Paterson, lies at the following places for signature:—Social Institution, 23, John-street, Tottenham-court-road. Social Hall, 26, Frederick's-place, Goswell-street-road. Mr. Watson's 5, Paul's-alley. Mr. Hetherington's, 40, Holywell-street, Strand. Mr. Marshall's, 29, Great Garden-street, High-street, Whitechapel, and 57, Judd-street, Brunswick-square.

TO CORRESPONDENTS.

M. R.—It is no fault of ours that Mr. Gillespie's second paper has not appeared. Mr. G. informs us that " he will let us have it very soon. Other matters have prevented him looking Mr. Southwell's way since forwarding Part I."

"Observer."—It was own own Jardine who made the very gracious allowance for the outrage of the drunken soldier, but who strained the law to oppress an Atheist. The *Examiner* reminded him of Mr. Paterson's case as one which had apprised the public of his peculiar aptitudes.

Will *Mr. Miles* please to transmit the " *Reminiscences ?*"

SUBSCRIPTIONS TO THE ANTI-PERSECUTION UNION.

Sale of Trials, for Placard Blasphemy, per Mr. Stewart	£0 4 6
John Cook, Ipswich	0 1 0

G. J. H., *Sec.*

Printed and Published by G. J. Holyoake, 40, Holywell-street, Strand, Saturday, June 29, 1844.

THE MOVEMENT
And Anti=Persecution Gazette.

"Maximize morals, minimize religion."—BENTHAM.

No. 30.   EDITED BY G. JACOB HOLYOAKE, ASSISTED BY M. Q. RYALL.   PRICE 1½d

THE SOCIAL REFORMERS OF HARMONY, HAMPSHIRE.

No one, be he a mere friend to freedom of expression, Freethinker, or Atheist, can view without interest and gratification, an experiment in the practical workings of social science, in which the leading departments of progress have their appointed place. A scheme of societarian arrangements which professes to effect gradually, steadily, but surely, all that the various agitating bodies are striving for with great sacrifice of wealth, the accompaniment of much anxiety and the wear and tear of brain, must awaken curiosity, even though its pretentions might be deemed high and arrogant. To the friend of free intercourse throughout the world, it holds out, according to the avowed organ of the society, the accomplishment of his favourite hopes in providing the means, not merely for the free and beneficial interchange of material and manufactured commodities between nations, but of that more valuable wealth—*free thought*—leading to indefinite moral, social and physical improvement. To those who regard the diffusion of enjoyment among the population more than the multiplication of manufactures, or the heaping of wealth upon wealth, the expositor of socialism says; "by its medium the discoveries of science, now too often made the cause of home misery and destitution, the source of foreign arrangement and suffering, would become a blessing to mankind everywhere, and multiply leisure and wealth for all, instead of, as at present, producing the contrary results." The equalitarian is told that "every human being under the arrangements proposed to be carried out in communities based on the principles of Robert Owen, will be in turn a producer, a distributor, an educator, and a governor; and this not as a matter of favour, or by election or selection, but as a right—a duty. Equality will, by the Rational System, be based upon the only substantial or enduring foundation, namely, equality in position, education, and training; and the individual varieties of character which would necessarily arise under such circumstances, be only an agreeable element of general society." Thus speaks the *New Moral World*; and though the sceptical should consider the picture overcharged, and that the separate benefits from diverse associative efforts are, without sufficient grounds, claimed for the "Rationalists" alone—the circumstances of their practical operations on the land, the nature of their tenure of it, the liberal terms on which they have had capital from members of the association, conjoined with that which they have raised by weekly contributions from middle class and working members—the incipient community arrangements, their important commencement of an educational establishment and the expected new draught of members to increase the production and facilitate the distribution of wealth, and the element of self-goverment which it is part of the system to carry out on new and improved principles—all these interesting facts cannot fail to make a vivid impression on a thoughtful spectator.

Recent events which have taken place within the society wear the present appearance of having infused fresh confidence and impelled them with a new and powerful stimulus. Without the necessity of entering here upon an enquiry into the causes of such impetus or the desirability of the events which have brought it about, it is sufficiently gratifying to perceive that there is a cheering earnestness, a hearty vigor and a glow of enthusiasm both in the proceedings of the constituencies and of the executive head. One of the reporters paints this glowing picture of recent proceedings of the Manchester branch.—" The sum of £65 8s. 8d. was laid at the feet of the apostles, for the good cause, upwards of £10 of which were donations, and the rest loans. At the close of the scene there was a regular clearing out, and a shower of the useful, almost like a hail-storm, was poured upon the stage, amidst the cheers and shouts of an audience truly delighted at the sight of the good work which was being done in good earnest and for a good purpose, all seeming to compete with each other which could clear out their stray coppers first; this is as it should be—this is as it must be throughout the Society. We must have a *revival*, and return to the energy of our youthful zeal, and the object for which we have long struggled will be within our reach. Make Harmony self-supporting, and then, like the Liverpool and Manchester Railway, when it first opened, it will give an impetus to the establishment of communities in various parts of the country; and for my own part, I despair not of seeing half a dozen at work before I leave this stage of existence. Be of good cheer, despair not, doubt not, but have faith in the principles, and prove your faith by doing your duty. Nay, why need I say be of *good cheer*, when I look to the tree of life which is found in the middle column of the 420th page of last weeks' *New Moral World*? (about £200 subscriptions.) Let this tree be well watered *every week*—keep it well supplied with the *dust* of the earth; yea, verily, the *gold dust*, the dust of silver, and *copper dust*, all are good in their places, and from this time, you will know the proper place to keep the tree growing."

The last address of the President to the members, dated on the 23rd from Harmony Hall, breaths the spirit—as that of a delegate elected by universal suffrage should—of the society.

There is a plainness of purpose, a candor and a healthy ardor in the following, which promises well:—

" It was my intention, immediately after appointment, to return to my business, believing that I could perform the duties of President, even at a distance, by keeping up a continual correspondence with the Board in London and the Harmony establishment; that I should merely hold the office of Governor nominally, and that the Acting-Governor would retain his position. I have, however, been mistaken in one instance, and disappointed in the other. The weight of business appertaining to the Presidency soon convinced me of the impossibility of its being dispatched with the readiness required in an office of such magnitude, and I soon discovered that to do it efficiently, my whole individual attention must be given.

" After the decisions of Congress were known, the Acting Governor handed his resignation to the Secretary of Harmony, which was, at the request of the Board, subsequently forwarded to Manchester. Although I had received private intimation of it, I entertained a hope that he (the Acting Governor) might be induced to continue to hold the office, were I to request him to do so; but when I received the letter containing the resignation, I perceived the avowal of a belief that ' the resolutions of Congress could not be carried out,' that we were exciting hopes that could not be realized; and further, that in justice to himself, and justice to the Society, he could not hold the office under such circumstances. In reply, I expressed my regret that the service of one I so much respected should be thus withdrawn; but much as I lamented this step—much as I deplored the loss of the late Acting Governor's services—I was not prepared to ask any individual, be he the wisest or best, to hold any office at the expense of justice; and resolved (if unable to procure an Acting Governor, or Deputy, who had the good wishes of the members, both in the establishment and the branches) to devote the whole of my time to the duties, whatever might be the risk, the sacrifice, or the personal inconvenience; and, rather than abandon the position taken at the recent Congress, I would dedicate my humble services, my undivided attention, to the performance of a sacred duty; and, if necessary, would hasten to the scene of operations, and devise the most speedy means of giving effect to the measures adopted by Congress.

* * * * *

" It is needlees to say I met with the most cordial reception from the members, and I am now more than ever satisfied, that, despite the doubts and fears of those who estimate man's governing powers by the weight of his purse, I shall be enabled, with the hearty co-operation of all who think with me, to convince even the most sceptical, in less than twelve months from this time, that the changes effected by Congress were necessary to complete our incipient community. But there must be no disunion amongst us,— no counteracting agencies,—no duplicity,—no tergiversation. All must work together for the welfare of the Society; and those who cannot conscientiously do so, will see the necessity of standing aloof; if they do not concur in the future policy of the Society, they ought not—must not —and I hope they will not throw any impediment in the way of those whose whole energies are directed to the attainment of our objects. Let but support be given freely, unhesitatingly, and unreservedly, and the happiest moments of my life will be those employed in completing the experiment, and in promoting the regeneration of the human race.

"'In perusing the *New Moral World* of last week, I am much gratified at the manner in which you have already responded to the various calls that have been made, for the purpose of aiding the Executive in extending the operations of the Society. If evidence were before wanting to prove that you had confidence in your present officers, it has been abundantly supplied in the cash receipts for the week ending June 15; it proves that enthusiasm, the distinguishing characteristic of infant Socialism, has not become extinct.

* * * * *

"During my sojourn here it will be my duty as it is my intention; to commence a searching inquiry into every department of our operations, so that I may be prepared, not only to supply the necessary information to those who are interested in our proceedings; but for the purpose of devising such measures as are likely to contribute to the success of the experiment."

There is nothing of the "king's speech" about these words, however *presidential* they may be. Let them only be carried out, and as the free choice of the entire constituency of the Rational Society, the results should show of what metal the association is made, and what hopefulness there may be in their "New Views of Human Nature and Society."

M. Q. R.

THE GOD OF NATURE AND OF THE BIBLE IDENTICAL.

II.

SCORES, nay thousands, of men would worship a devil with sincerity, as heartfelt as they now worship a God, if priests took some pains to convince them more might be expected in "kingdom come" from the former than from the latter. All worship has its root in vulgar and thoroughly brutal selfishness. Without doubt devil-worship would universally prevail if men everywhere believed more could be got by *diabolism* than *divinity*. With rare exceptions, the temper of religionists is the temper of slaves. Almost every "man in England," who worships at all, feels towards his God just as slaves do towards a tyrant task-master.

I am clearly of opinion that if men really thought their divine idol, essentially and necessarily *good*, they would cease to worship him. The fact is, what they call God, they imagine a devil, that is to say a being fully as unjust, capricious, and cruel, as themselves. Did not Romans deify Nero? Did not Romans worship, as "very gods," Caligula and Heliogabulus? Unquestionably they did. But will it be maintained that in so doing they acted upon principles and from motives less pure or admirable than those which animate the breasts of fanatical religionists?—I fancy not. The Romans who worshipped Nero knew he was a tyrant, and detested while they worshipped. The English who worship God have no more respect or love for *him*, than *they* had for *Nero*. There are few *real* religionists who do not dread their deity; and why do they dread him? The answer is plain;—they think him an omnipotent tyrant, and make a merit of seeming to adore what they sincerely detest. Were human brains purged from the disgraceful fear of being pitchforked into hell by *good* Jehovah, his worshippers would mightily diminish in number and fervour. Such purgation would infallibly be followed by the important discovery that there are comparatively few who do not call God, aye, and worship too as God—"a thing whom they believe unjust, cruel, and capricious."

In my previous paper I noticed an argument, *not* derived from the affirmation of the existence of an intelligent ruler of the universe—*not* derived from the assertion or even admission of the reality of a universal ruler —but from the hypothetical datum that *if* God exists he must possess certain attributes, such as mercifulness, justness, wisdom, and goodness, or, that *supposing* the existence of God we cannot deny him these attributes, and a revelation from him must represent him as possessed of, and actuated by, these qualities and attributes. The *hypothetical* datum which I cited was not mistaken by me for an *assumed* datum—neither did I contend against an argument because drawn from a hypothetic datum — but against *erroneous argumentation from the hypothetic datum laid down.*

Were it true that if an intelligent ruler of the universe exist, he *must* possess the attributes of justness, mercifulness, wisdom, and goodness—were it true that every one who supposes the existence of God, will admit that he must be so powerful that he can do everything which does not involve a contradiction—my remarks would have been pointless—but the hypothesis is the opposite of true. It is positively false to say that every one who supposes the existence of God will admit that he must be so powerful that he can do everything which does not involve a contradiction; that he must be just, and merciful, and wise, and good; and that a revelation from him must represent him as possessed of, and actuated by, these qualities. The falsity of this reasoning was made manifest in my previous paper, where it was shown that the potency of a possible supreme ruler, or the power to do all things which involve not a contradiction, had been confounded with power to regulate nature—that, granting the existence of a Being capable of creating nature to be satisfactorily established, the admission fell infinitely short of establishing the existence of a Being who "must be so powerful that he can do all things which involve not a contradiction—that in nature there is good and evil; and, therefore, a revelation from its author must represent him as possessed of, and actuated by, *contradictory or opposing qualities.*

But, better, far better, perhaps, than all imaginable *arguments*, is the *fact* that many eminent believers in God deny that nature teaches, and admit that revelation does not represent him possessed of the "certain attributes which, it has been asserted, every believer in the existence of an intelligent ruler of the universe will allow he possesses."

Bishop Butler in his "Analogy of Religion, Natural and Revealed," observes that nature and revelation teach an *identical* God; and bitterly derides those who reject Jehovah because of his horrid attributes, while adoring "an intelligent ruler of nature." The bishop maintained that he who denies that god wrote scripture, because of the atrocities there detailed; "*for the very same reason* might deny the world to have been formed by him.

Bishop Watson, in his famous "Apology for the Bible," strives to make out that it is highly inconsistent to reject the Pentateuch god, and accept nature's god. Nay, the learned bishop fairly takes the bull (*deistic*) by the horns, in the sensible and really brave declaration that "God has a right to punish wicked nations by the infliction of judgments—such as pestilence, or famine, or by employing the sword of enemies—because we see that he does so *in the course of his providence*.

In my recently published pamphlet, entitled "I am an Infidel—Why are you a Christian?" *these two bishops are cited as authorities against deism*. At page 14, are these words:—

"And what is the defence of that divine being (Jehovah) set up by Bishops Butler and Watson? Why just this—The Pentateuch god is a shocking monster we admit, but then, the god of nature is as shocking a monster; and, seeing that you believe in nature's god, notwithstanding the wholesale atrocities committed by him in the course of his providence, you cannot consistently reject the god of the Pentateuch on the ground of his cruelty or other vices.

That the "sacred volume" everywhere describes its god as possessed of the attributes of wisdom, justice, and so forth—are assertions of such bulk and quality, as a "charity brat', could easily overset, by showing from the Bible itself that the Bible god is *devil as well as god*—in short, an imaginary being, with every conceivable attribute. Our modern universalists, at the head of whom stands the Rev. J. E. Smith, (better known as Shepherd Smith), tell us the scriptures are a confused image of universal existence itself, and contain the two extremes, as well of doctrine as of practice, blended, however, in such a way as to appear absurd and contradictory. They are right so far, at all events. By them *the Bible god and Bible devil are placed on the same footing*. If asked whether it was god or devil who inspired the scriptures, they *seriously* answer, "both." Hence, say they, we may presume there is a mixture of truth and error in them, and consequently they are not to be relied upon. Bravo, universalists. You are capital fellows—Not Atheists—By no means; only pantheistic philosophers, who make of Jehovah, and Satan, and Nature, a trinity in unity—*three* in *one universal being*.

C. S.

SENSIBLE IDEAS AND GOD-NOTIONS—WHENCE DERIVED?

Mr. Editor—Permit me through the medium of the *Movement* to make a few remarks upon an article signed W. J. B., which appeared in No 24, entitled "The Metaphysical Origin of the God-idea," in which I think is to be found much false philosophy—much unsound reasoning.

W. J. B. says, "there are two classes of ideas, sensible and *abstract*. A sensible idea is the pure result of the action of an object upon the organs of sense; the object of the sensible ideas is then a *real* being, a being who has an individual existence, for in order for anything to act, it must exist. An abstract idea is formed from the comparison of sensible ideas by reflection, the object of an abstract idea is necessarily an ideal being; the idea does not result any more from the action of the object, but from the *comparison* we make between our sensible ideas."

W. J. B. must pardon me when I say that I can perfectly understand what he means by a "sensible idea," but that I am consummately ignorant of what he means by an *abstract* idea. But let us take the continuous arguments which W. J. B. has given and see if they will at all elucidate the principle he wishes to establish; here they are: —"in the comparison we perceived the *relation* that these sensible ideas have between themselves. This *relation* we arrive at by an act of our attention in separating *it* from compared ideas, and representing *it* by a term." Further on we have the following:— "The *abstract* idea then consists in the *perception* and *expression* of the *relation* that two or several ideas have amongst themselves, the object of such an idea then must be an ideal being, the *example of which does not exist in nature*."

This seems to me to be most extraordinary to suppose we have the power of possessing ideas, the prototypes of which are not to be found in nature. W. J. B. himself says, "that for a thing to *act* it must *exist*, and if this be true, and I think it is, how can we have an idea without the action of some entity in nature, if it be necessary to have a real existence to produce an idea, surely W. J. B's. "ideal being," will not be sufficient to produce one? I am quite willing to admit with W. J. B. that *it* is by *comparison* we perceive the relation between two objects, but that we possess the power to *separate or abstract* such relation from the things compared I deny. The classification of ideas into sensible and abstract seems to me to be more fanciful then real; for all our ideas I presume must come through the senses, all such ideas having their prototypes in nature. Suppose an individual were to ask me what idea I had of "*truth*," I could only reply that in its substantive sense I had none at all; for truth being only a *property* of proposition I could only have an *idea* of the *proposition*, that being the *existence*,—the *prototype* of the idea possessed by me. It would perhaps not be amiss to state what I understand by the term idea. An idea I consider to be the action upon the brain of any existence in nature. If this definition be correct, the veriest trio in physics must see the inaccuracy of W. J. B's. conclusions; for, I suppose no one will contend that the *relation* of an object to another constitutes an existence.

The word *being* and *cause* are called in to assist in supporting the power of abstraction, but if I mistake not with no better success. Let us substitute the word *existing*, for *being*, and speak about an existing house, an existing horse, man, or anything else, and I have an idea of the *things* mentioned; but abstract the adjective *existing* and change it into the noun *existence* and I have no idea whatever. Take away the substratum of the *quality*, existence, and you have taken away everything that can produce an idea in the brain. If W. J. B. or the reader can under such circumstances have an idea I confess that they are constituted differently to what I am.

It is the same with cause. The word *cause* is a relative term, and is used in reference to antecedent and succeeding phenomena. Let us take an example, when carbonate of soda and tartaric acid in solution are brought in contact, the phenomenon called effervescence is produced. This result called effervescence *uniformly* succeeding the contact of the before mentioned solutions, the contact of them is said to be the *cause* of effervescence. Now what ideas are excited in the brain by these phenomena? The ideas of the two fluids before contact, and the motion of the one fluid after contact. And this is the only idea we can have of cause and effect. The *things* spoken of as *causing* the effect, together with the phenomenon called the *effect* produce ideas in the brain, but the mere *relation* of these things one to another cannot effect any such result.

W. J. B. concludes that the word God, represents an *abstract* idea, but I can assure W. J. B. that I, though once a strong believer in the existence of a God, never had any ideas generated by the three letters G, O, D, except those excited by them in their shape and form as letters. I remember that my *carnal* mind was very prone to set up an image of myself—a man in the clouds, and that the orthodox principle "that God is a being without parts and passion," used to chase away that impious idea ; but I also remember that when that *idea* was annihilated nothing was left behind in the shape of being, or the ideas of any existing being, excepting those generated by the characters G, O, D.　　J. P.

CHRISTIAN RESPONSIBILITY AND CHRISTIANITY'S INFLUENCES.

I.

Is there any one rule of doctrine or action which christians as a body apply to themselves in common with others? The query may sound strangely in the ears [of christianity's professors, but let us proceed to consider it. We all recollect their reception of the doctrine of moral necessity, first published at large by Mr. Owen. It is familiar to all, that the denial of the philosophical propriety of moral responsibility, and its consequences, the attributing of merit and demerit, and recourse to rewards and punishments, were received with general execration on their being first broached to the christian world. Let us make this principle the touch-stone of their justice, and enquire if they are content to submit themselves to the standard which they set up to determine upon others. Are Christians, according to themselves, responsible? Is christianity influential in anything?

Who killed three hundred thousand people to settle the question of transubstantiation and consubstantiation, and left it after all just as they found it? Who put to the sword a hundred thousand Manicheans? Who carried on the crusades which carried off by fire and sword countless myriads? By whom were one hundred and fifty thousand Hussites put to death? Who scourged Europe for a succession of appalling years with slaughter and devastation, partially depopulating Flanders, Holland, Germany, France, England; massacred the victims of St. Bartholomew's eve, the Valdenses, Cevanni, the miserable Irish, to the amount of millions more? By whom were tens of thousands ruined, tortured, burnt by the dreadful horrors of the Inquisition?

Who slaughtered millions, extirpating whole populations of the least offensive people in the world, the miserable inhabitants of South America? Who murdered one portion, spoiliated another portion, and ground down all that were left of the miserable inhabitants of the East Indies? Who have filled the prisons in our own country with suffocating crowds of their fellow-men, of whom eight thousand have perished in a single reign? Who have plundered their own countrymen during the compass of a half-a-dozen years, by seizures, escheatments, confiscations, and a host of other such machinations, of no less than two million's worth of money and property? Who have continually inflicted on each other, "every imaginable species of outrage and insult, petty vexation and agonizing suffering, every species of legal and illegal plunder, loss of estates, friends, liberty, and life itself?" Who have carried on, and are carrying on the very same iniquity in sort, but minor in degree, and are only curbed by the anti-christian philanthropy of the age?—CHRISTIANS!

This is the answer which the whole world would give if it could be constituted into an impartial tribunal—upon christians would be thrown the responsiblity. Yet christians, who are earnest in fastening the heaviest responsibility upon others, endeavour to shake it from themselves. They will tell us they were not christians who did these things. Who are christians? Are they not to be recognised by their professions, by their doctrines, by their acceptance of one set of scriptures for their guide, and exposition of their creed and worship? Will they tell us that by acts alone shall you know the true christian—what sort of acts; good acts or bad? good. Then the moralist and atheist may be a christian according to that showing. This, when pressed, a christian was never known to concede. Are churchmen denied to be christians? This it would appear to be the aim of very many to assert, or at least insinuate; and when the churchmen, who are infinitely the more numerous in almost all christian countries, deny this point blank, the assertors are further off from shirking this responsibility than before. Howitt would have us believe that it is not christians who ever persecute, but christian churchmen, or christians turned churchmen. The christian, however, is so peculiarly conformed, or endoctrinated, or whatever you like, that—even according to Howitt and all the christian journalist organs of the non-churchmen order—they never can get the chance of being made churchmen without at the same time being made persecutors or plunderers. He recites that "England, after William III., afforded no further scope for imprisonment, the martyr's flaming pile, or the bloody axe of the executioner." If England has not afforded scope, a pretty deal has been done without scope. In the imprisonment line they have scarcely ever stopped from that time to this, all on account of christianity. Mr. Howitt says, that "while power was left to the church, it persecuted and would have continued to persecute." All the anathemas used to be hurled at one church, the church of Rome. When it was discovered that another church—the church of England, or church of Scotland, or church of any-where else—did the very same sort of thing whenever "power was left" to it, and that it would never be harmless till impotent,—a sort of moral legerdemain was attributed not to christianity, but to church-christianity.

Thus, notwithstanding the poor compliment this theory pays to the stability of christians when made church-christians of, they of course are unexceptionable and irreprehensible when out of this magic circle of the grand demoralizer. The church is the wizard of the world, and does stranger feats and wonders, in the way of transformation, than the far famed Wizard of the North. Herr Döbler must be a mere pretender to the Archbishop of Canterbury—and the thimble-rig men, whom Sir James Graham has so unceremoniously banished from the scenes of their ancient glories, might have been left to the fair field of competition—their changes and juggleries would have been eclipsed by the superior prowess of a Philpot of Exeter, or a Bloomfield of London. Mr. Howitt tells us that the Act of William III, "put an end to the church's power to persecute." Terms, some people call matters of taste; the opposition christian journals—the outs would, methinks, give him a different version—no matter—he tells us to "henceforth look for the spirit of priestcraft," (not the spirit of christianity or religionism, or goddism,) "in a different shape — this wily spirit has conformed itself to circumstances." Christianity then is convertible into churchism, and this is no greater, nor more uncongenial, metamorphosis than other christianity is prepared to undergo—when it has the chance. Then priestcraft is brought forward as another designation for church. "Its wily spirit conforms itself to circumstances"— what "spirit," and what "circumstances?" We have got a long way off from christianity now, according to this style of reasoning. But what remarkable adaptation there must be in christianity towards churchism and the "wily spirit of priestcraft." Something so evidently and facilely adaptible hurries us to the suspicion of intention. It seems but another "christian evidence" of what *Square* would call the "eternal fitness of things."

In the language of Paley "the question, which irresistibly presses itself upon our thoughts, is, whence this *contrivance* and *design?*" We will see on the one hand what spirit it was that pervaded the church, and on the other, what circumstances moulded it to a different course of action—not to a cessation from persecuting, but to an altered mode of persecution. "Where unlimited power was within its grasp, it seized it without hesitation, and exercised it without mercy. Egypt, India, all ancient Asia and feudal Europe, are witnesses of this. Where it could not act so freely, it submitted to the spirit of the people." Now we have got to the point of antagonism—what was it that opposed the church and mitigated its ferocity? *The spirit of the people!* Does that sound anything like christianity? Is there anything of the sense of christianity in it? Yes; it might be rejoined, because the people are christians—But the churchmen are christians. Here is christianity against christianity. This remarkable difference subsists between an established church and a people;—the former well knit, compact, disciplined, and constituted for religious purposes, can show, and does show, its religious nature at every turn. The people being so diversely christianized or religionized can rarely bring their christianity to bear upon a national object — they could do so in small bodies, sections, or churches; but as nations, something else appears, essentially differently from christianity. It is the same with smaller bodies of the people, made up of various denominations of christians, and brought together, or otherwise influenced to act with a national or comprehensive purpose. This kind of action is the furthest removed from anything that has relation to christianity. Religion disappears, in large combined efforts, *though those efforts may be made by religionized men.* In these cases religion is kept in the back ground for the sake of acting in concert, and politics engross the attention. The spirit of the people is then, not that of their christianity, but of their pantings after civil liberty. The case is not altered when men rise up to defend their rights in the name of religion or of a religion. A religious watch-word does not alter the nature of the thing contended for — political freedom. Neither—when the religious or christian motive is denied to religious or christian men, when contending for liberty—is it to be conversely said, that, therefore, religious or christian men, when contending for persecution, are not influenced by a religious or christian motive. When men fight for religious or or christian persecution, domination, or proselytizing, their war is a religious war.

When they fight to rid themselves of such persecution, domination, or proselytizing, it is a political war, or war of liberty. In the former case religious sentiments are attempted to be inforced, in the latter religious sentiments are not so much defended as the right to entertain what sentiments they please. The former is aggressive, the latter defensive. Religion, when made corporate —*that is when made potent*—is ever aggressive—political liberty averse from interfering with the rights of others, is essentially defensive.

How then shall christians avert the responsibility they are so eager to fasten on others? How shall christianity be held innocent of the doings of its disciples?

M. Q. R.

EMMA MARTIN'S SERIALS.

THE third of the series of "Tracts for the People," has just appeared. These are the titles and order of the publications,—No. 1. "A Conversation on the Being of God." No. 2. "Religion Superseded, or the moral code of nature sufficient for the guidance of man." No. 3. "The Bible no Revelation, or the inadequacy of language to convey a message from God to man." There is a stamp of individuality about Mrs. Martin's published as well as oral discourses, which distinguishes them from most contemporaneous productions of the present infidel school It would not be fairly characterising them to represent them as deficient in boldness, plainness, or out-spokenness—to say so would be to misrepresent them. There is no truth blinked, no cloak of vagueness thrown over the phraseology in order to smuggle in a little truth with a great deal of mystification. They will probably make better "calls to the unconverted" than others of more formidable calibre or more energetic antagonism. There is throughout an air of earnestness—a tone of mellowed soberness prevails—a desire to confer benefit by instruction is made apparent, by which a corresponding condition is prepared on the part of the reader to give heed to the arguments according to their merits, which rise above the ordinary level. From the startling *Jew Book* article, the *Broadsides, Thrusts* and *Placards* of the *Holywell Street* epoch—the paradoxical and daring flights of *Christ Disproofs* and *Christian Idolatries,* it may be gravely doubted if a single effort has been thrown away, or been even unrequited— the non-repellants of Mrs. Martin do not the less perform most high and useful functions. To put into the hands of Christian worshippers they are excellently adapted.

FACTITIOUS GRIEFS.—The great source of calamity lies in regret or anticipation. — *Goldsmith.*

A VETERAN PUBLICIST!

Mr. ALLEN DAVENPORT takes a benefit at the Hall of Science, (near Featherstone-street) City-road, on Tuesday evening the 9th. A vocal entertainment—tickets 3d. each—commences at 8 o'clock. Mr. Davenport will deliver an address.

Those who know Allen Davenport will be present. To those who do not, we say—go, on our recommendation—you will by your presence and support, gratify and assist a worthy man—a tried and courageous advocate and defender of freedom in dangerous times. As a popularizer of the *Spencean* theory of Agrarian justice in the teeth of parson and landlord persecution—grown grey in opposition to priestcraft and tyrannocraft of all kinds, his sight dimmed by years, and honourably poor—he appeals irresistibly to the friends of the *Movement* to smooth his declining years.—Those who would be disposed to bring their families or acquaintances, as a matter of entertainment, need not, we are told, fear the result, popular favorites having volunteered their services. Hyams of the Pavilion—the comic singer Sadler, Hill and Family the glee singers, G. Wells being announced in the programme.—Tickets at the Hall of Science, and Hetherington's, Holywell-street, &c.

EMIGRATION TO THE TROPICS.

Mr. ETZLER has issued a practical pamphlet on this question. It does not come within the scope of our general objects to dilate on emigration, but we will take the liberty of recommending to notice Mr. Etzler's views relative to it. On this, as on other subjects, the reader may rely on receiving really practical information from him. He disabuses the public of the false and crude notions gathered in classical books respecting the torrid zone. His calculations and facts relative to the means of subsistence and enjoyment in the tropics will be found of a novel nature. A list of valuable books is appended to the pamphlet to which the reader is desired to refer, and which corroborate the views presented. Persons desirous of information on the subject can obtain it by letter addressed to Etzler & Co., 266, Strand, London.

THE FRANCHISE.

The importance of prompt attention to the obtainment of electoral privileges cannot be too strongly urged on all the friends and supporters of our periodical and the opinions it represents.

Recollect that any body who lives in any thing worth £10 a-year, is qualified to vote, *whether he pays rates or not.*

Register at once!—which you do by getting your name placed on the poors-rates, whether *you pay them or not.*

You may get forms and any more particular information of the Anti-Corn-Law people, Reform Secretaries, &c.

NOTICES.

RECEIVED the admirable circular of the "Society of Propagandists," which we will transfer to our columns.

A copy of the Prospectus of the "Theological Association" has been looked out as kindred with the spirit of this Society. Will the Secretary direct us where to send it?

EDITORIAL COMMUNICATIONS are to be addressed to the office of the *Movement*.

Received the *Dublin Monitor* and *Evening Sun*.

SUNDAY SLAVERY.—Mr. Bibliophil has "blown" on this custom. He has sent forth the "*First Blast of his Trumpet*" against *Sabbath Slavery*. He treats the origin of the day historically, but not satisfactorily. The continental journalists, he informs us, say that "the English nation dies every seventh day;" but the Trumpet must blow us another note before we shall understand what he desires us to do. We should like some practical observations relative to the evils of observing the day religiously. No matter what its origin was—to what purpose can we put it? is the question.

WE have received from Mr. Gillespie three copies of his principal work, entitled the "*Necessary Existence of Deity*," issued by the Philalethean Society. As Mr. Gillespie has placed these works at our disposal for public purposes, we have presented one to the "London Atheistical Society," and shall cause the others to be circulated in those quarters where they will be attentively studied.

DISCUSSION.—Sunday, 7th July, half-past Eight, P.M., Parthenium, St. Martin's Lane, —"Being of a God."—Ryall.

TO CORRESPONDENTS.

I. L.—The name of *Deist* is said to have been first assumed about the middle of the 16th century, by some gentlemen in France and Italy. Leland pretends that it was adopted to cover opposition to christianity by a more honourable name than that of Atheist. Viret speaks of Deists in his *Instruction Chretienne*, which was published in 1563.

SUBSCRIPTIONS TO THE ANTI-PERSECUTION UNION.

Collector, 117 . . .	£0	2 6
„ 19 . . .	0	0 6
„ 5 . . .	0	4 3
Mr. Watts, Islington . .	0	2 6
„ „ „ for Paterson	0	2 6
W. M., Glasgow . .	0	1 0

T. POWELL, *Sec. pro tem.*

Printed and Published by G. J. HOLYOAKE,
40, Holywell-street, Strand,
Saturday, July 6, 1844.

THE MOVEMENT
And Anti=Persecution Gazette.

"Maximize morals, minimize religion."—BENTHAM.

No. 31.   EDITED BY G. JACOB HOLYOAKE, ASSISTED BY M. Q. RYALL.   PRICE 1½d

PROGRESS; MORE PARTICULARLY MANCHESTER PROGRESS.

IN Manchester everything is dingy, the streets, commerce and morality. The streets are dingy with smoke, commerce with competition's cunning, and morality is dingy with religion. Here a thousand chimneys like one vast volcano, incessantly throw up soots against the fair skies, darken the face of nature, and descending begrime the human wretchedness below. Here the beautiful productions of art sadly contrast with the bony, haggard and deformed producers—the capitalist spins humanity up in his mills, weaves into his calico the hopes, affections and aspirations of the poor, and then "moves heaven and earth" for foreign markets to sell them in. In this melancholy struggle, Socialism is lifting up its voice with new vigour, teaching the artizan how to guard his industry, how to enjoy its fruits, to breath the balmy air and be free. But religion, as ever, only turns its dim visage on the sad scene—saying to the poor man "in whatsoever state it has pleased God to call ye, be ye therewith content."

This is a thoroughly theological district. The people have quite an appetite for pickled saints. I who regard my atheistical wares as a thrifty housewife does her silver service, who brings it out only on special occasions, have had already to display sundry specimens for the gratification of our heterodox friends. On all sides I have been told "you must be theological or you will be nothing," of course I accommodate them.

But justly as our friends despise religion's cant, they have an eagle's eye on the practical. They estimate religion lightly—they push it out of the way because they find it to be a barrier to substantial good. Had not the recent congress made the changes it did, there would have been a *new* Harmony here. I have been with Mr. Samuel Ingham of Castle Hill, and Mr. Joseph Smith over the contemplated estate. We climbed on the top of a glorious old structure of the ancient days which stands in the centre covered by time's own hands with antiquity's glories. All around is redolent of commercial advantages, fertility and sylvan beauty. Our friends at Harmony do not want the stimulus of competition to spur them forward, but if we do not soon have—what is now said we always were to have,—" a working man's community," our friends here will establish one, and afford the Harmony directors the benefit of comparison.

The letters in the *New Moral World* which bear Mr. Vines' name—for no one supposes that the old gentleman has made himself so ridiculous—are often the subject of comment. The pressing enquiries about potatoes, turnips, mangel wurzel, and reports, it is thought should have been made twelve months earlier. A little wholesome discussion upon these letters would have been productive of benefit, and should have been allowed in the *New Moral World*, for they were calculated to allay those angry feelings which should be as far from our practice as they are from our profession. Nothing can be more fatal to Socialist success than that party feeling of any kind should be fermented among us.

A resurrection of the dead is expected in this quarter. Mr. Finch delivered a funeral oration over our late excellent friend Mr. Lowe, from these words, " For this purpose the Son of God was manifested, that he might deliver them who, through fear of death, have all their lifetime been subjected to bondage." By all to whom I have spoken on the subject, it is agreed that if there is any coming back, friend Lowe will come back. Poor fellow! how uneasy he must feel to be dismissed from the world with such language!

One evening after I had descanted on christianity's historical evidences, and proved that they were unworthy attention and good for nothing, a christian rose up, and with much smartness contended that he had heard nothing *new*. I suppose he has always known that. I shall have to show before I return, that religion is without reasonable foundation, and shall be delighted to find that Manchester christians in general are of the same opinion.

There is little probability that the hall here will be sold. The discussion of the question by the shareholders seems to have arisen, so far as I can learn, from a desire to place the trustees in a position to protect themselves from liabilities. So far this is laudable. This power is usually conceded in the trust deeds of public buildings.

I have placed the necessity of sending the petitions of the *Anti-Persecution Union* before the audiences in every town in which I have lectured. A favourable feeling has prevailed. The Socialist public which I have addressed seem not less friendly to the largest measure of liberty, than they are enthusiastically attached to community. G. J. H.

REPLY OF MADAME D'ARUSMONT.
To G. Jacob Holyoake and Maltus Q. Ryall, conductors of the *Movement and Anti-Persecution Gazette*, London.

Dundee, 1st July, 1844.

GENTLEMEN,—I thank you from the heart for your welcome to my native island, and your invitation to visit the friends of liberty in London. I need not say that all my sympathies are with you, or that my services are sworn for life to the cause of truth and justice. But, seeing the narrow limits prescribed to individual strength and existence, and the immensity of the field open to individual exertion, the soldiers of the great army of the universal "movement" have to divide the work, and to select each his post of attack and defence. Having selected mine in early youth, I feel pledged by honour and commanded by prudence not to exchange it for any other, until the strongholds of error and misrule shall be there carried, and a first example of wisdom and justice in the administration of human affairs shall be there opened by a people master, in principle, of the soil, and sovereign to will and to execute the emancipation and salvation of the human race.

Having recently declined an invitation from Glasgow, and equally declined to meet the wishes of many friends of liberty in this, my native city, the conductors of the *Movement* will not fail correctly and kindly to interpret this reply to their generous and eloquent invitation.

Receive, Gentlemen, the assurance of my my most respectful consideration.

FRANCES WRIGHT D'ARUSMONT.

My husband and daughter acknowledge and most kindly return your respects and good wishes.

CHRISTIAN RESPONSIBILITY, AND CRISTIANITY'S INFLUENCES.
II.

IN the previous paper was shown how christian bodies of men have systematically oppressed all who have differed from them whenever it has been in their power. The argument—that it was not their christianity that did this, but a powerful hierarchical system, invested with vast temporal powers—was treated at length. It was attempted to be shown that it was the inalienable intolerance of religion's self, of which christianity is so important a branch, that played the conspicuous part in the world's drama, and not the particular sort of corporation into which christians might form themselves. To say that christians would not unjustly interfere with the religious rights of others, unless when associated in a state establishment, is only to say that they would not do so while they could not—and to say that they would act unjustly, when invested with authority, amounts to this—that they would where they could. This, however, is not a gratuitous but a forced concession from christians, upon whom the facts press too notoriously for denial, but who make a desperate effort to explain them away, to save their system from utter condemnation. As was before remarked, any and every weight of responsibility may be laid on others' shoulders provided not the slightest share is borne by themselves. But let us push the inquiry still further. Suppose that peculiarly favouring circumstances, such as those which the Roman church early enjoyed from the immunities and privileges at first voluntarily conceded to her, led to the possession of great temporal influence, thence to the demand and enforcement of what were first volunteered as gifts—suppose it progressing from its modest spiritual communion of believers to the enormously dominant power which it wielded in after years—you will only trace, say christianity's defenders and the church's accusers, what may take place on every occasion when you place christian men in such positions. The point is given up of christianity protecting men, aye, any set of men, from unworldly influences of such a nature. What should we predicate of those but recently admitted, even partially, or locally, into state preference?—who have not, like the church of Rome, nor even that which is its proper offspring and inheritor of its powers and dignities — the church of England—been cradled in power and authority? What shall we expect to be the behaviour of such a christian church? What should we anticipate from a body of christians schooled in adversity, and who had passed through many "sore trials and tribulations?" What says James Abbot, A.B. on this point? "No reasoning could not restrain churchmen, orthodox or heterodox, when they were invested with power, or with the direction of power, from using it violently." This is a pretty explicit answer of the general question. The gradual growth of power and ages of its irresponsible exercise are not even hinted at. But our author says, give churchmen power, or the direction of it, and they will use it with violence. What is this but saying, their abstinence from violence occurs only where they can't use it, and whenever they can, they do. But from opinion let us turn to facts. "The presbyterians justly exclaimed against the violence and tyranny of Laud and his brethren for harrassing, imprisoning, fining and persecuting them; and even driving them from their native homes to seek peace and shelter, and the quiet worship of God in the woods of America. He had converted the High Commission Court into an Inquisition; indeed, every bishops' court was become an Inquisition; and many of the best churchmen were silenced, fined and even deprived, for adhering honestly to the doctrines of the Reformation, to primitive strictness of manners, and to the observation of the Sabbath.

"Did the presbyterians afterwards—these presbyterians, who had thus groaned and smarted under persecution, and bitterly complained of its injustice and fury, exercise charity and forbearance towards others who dissented from them when they became masters of ecclesiastical rule? No! never was a more bitter and intolerant race, or more vigorous exactors of conformity. Every man who differed from them was an enemy to the state, an innovator, forsooth, whom it behoved the state to suppress. They had forgotten that Laud had brought the same charge against them but a little before, and how unmercifully they had been used as public incendiaries, enemies and innovators. Thus it is, no set of priests fail to draw down if they can, the anger of the crown upon any man who has merited theirs. Disaffection to civil authorities is a charge which all domineering priests in the world have ever brought, and will ever bring, against all who offend them, and against all who withdraw from their power, and disown their systems. The presbyterians, both before and after they attained the predominancy, felt this to be true, and exclaimed against it; but did not forget to reiterate the charges without blushing, at soon as they tasted of dominion.

"The churchmen, who had persecuted the presbyterians without mercy, the moment they found themselves persecuted by parliaments, made heavy outcries against persecution, and preached and wrote for toleration. It was then that Dr. Taylor published his book, entitled "The Liberty of Prophecying," an excellent book, and one that was extremely applauded by his brethren of the episcopal profession. But let me ask did these churchmen, did even Dr. Taylor, after the restoration, act upon its own reasoning and writing for indulgence to dissenters? No. It was the great business of the churchmen, when they had resumed their old seats and revenues, to preach, to write, to solicit severe laws, and to urge the execution of those laws against their protestant brethren, during a long reign." Thus, the more we inquire, the more proofs accumulate, and the stronger they become, of christian *causation*. If christians could for the time divest themselves of their faith-instilled, time-hallowed predelictions, they would clearly perceive, and concede this point. Some progress would then be made towards the confession of universal justice. They would find that it is not old, indurated, wrinkled, worldly, worn-down christian churches alone that thus oppress their fellow man. Young stripling churches, vigorous, energetic, but just out of their strugglings against the oppressions of their elder disciplined brethren—escaped but now from the fangs of old *established* persecutors—still fresh from all their anti-church christianity—straightway fall into the practices of the hacknied offenders, whose iniquities they had been loudly proclaiming as emanating not from their *system*, but their *dominancy*. Oh! what a little short-lived dominancy can — by christian showing — preponderate over centuries of system!

How, I again ask, will you shift off this incubus of responsibility from yourselves? How will you repudiate the influences legitimately deducible from the system you uphold?   M. Q. R.

POPULAR OUTBREAKS IN GERMANY.
[*From a Correspondent.*]

THE dastardly and shameful neglect, which for centuries past, the humbler (working) classes of society have met at the hands of those, who call themselves the higher ones — government — although it seems, that they have not taken the pains of *governing* anything; the effects of this, as I said dastardly and shameful neglect begin to bear fruit, even in quiet—in so called patriarchal Germany. About four months ago, on the price of beer being raised in Munich, the populace at once took to arms, as it were, houses and breweries were ransacked, and the military, with some pieces of ordnance, (loaded with the usual *quietus* for the people, namely grape-shot) were put into requisition to assuage the coming storm. His gracious majesty, the king, appeared at first in a very fighting mood, but when (ominous to say) some of the monarch's horse guards had joined the people, he grew alarmed and the usual temporary and worthless concessions were made to the latter.

Outbreaks of a more important nature— and strongly bearing on the chronic ones, in *this* country—have lately taken place in Austrian and Prussian Silesia. The people —the *working* classes, neglected, borne down, ground down in their pitiful earnings, by a stolid, self-conceited, more than empty-headed aristocracy, and would-be aristocracy—also betook themselves to arms, seeking redress, somehow, somewhere! The usual cycle of events—troops charge—defeat! Still it was found out that this outbreak was not an isolated event—but one resulting from the German *people* (the working classes) also beginning to talk, to think, to act. It is impossible to conceive, that with all the *paternal* solicitude of the German rulers towards their subjects, in the shape of censorship, constant opening of letters and so on—the great Revelation of the nineteenth century could have been concealed from them! Still, the names and efforts of those benevolent (be they right or wrong) men, like St. Simon, Fourier, Owen, have reached—aye and penetrated even the thick ears of our German fellow men. It is even asserted that there exist wide-spread and energetic secret associations, for infusing communist and socialist ideas into the mind of the German masses, but toward such I have always observed a position of neutrality; believing as I do, that grand, obvious truths require no secret propagation—as soon as stated, they are evident as the sun at noonday. However, the greatest proof, that the great Revelation of the nineteenth century is piercing every where, peeping out every where, are the late outbreaks (19th June) at Prague in Austria—in the land of the eminently paternal government. At the latter place, thousands of working men turned out, complaining in despair about the scanty wages, to which a grasping, mean and lowly luxuriating clique of employers had reduced them. They hid themselves first and congregated in the extensive quarries adjoining the above city, whence they finally burst forth, and burnt the manufactories of their brutish oppressors. The sequel as usual. A whole regiment (*en ordre de bataille*) was drawn up against these helpless, despairing sons of toil—battering down and slaughtering those whose wives and children were craving at home for a morsel of bread.—These are strange times indeed; but I believe that HE—the ancient of days, will finally also interfere in this instance. The hand of fate is (perhaps) on the curtain, about to bring the scene to light.

[Who the devil is HE?—ED. of M.]

POST OFFICE REVELATIONS.

The Parliament—the Press—the People.

"A NEW and monstrous thing has been done in the land"—such at least is the popular feeling since the great Post-office revelations. A few people all the time have had a tolerable notion of the Post-office practices, and many are well aware of the Post-office powers, or rather the Home Secretary's powers, in connection with the letter department. However limited the general information on the subject, it is gratifying to be persuaded that universal England has started up in alarm and indignation at this "new, monstrous and un-English" inroad on our rights, and invasion of the domestic privacy which was supposed to be guarded with the same scrupulous delicacy as one gentleman would show towards another. That the utterly abhorrent and revolting practice of private letter-spying has been carried on, we too well and too certainly know—that it has been carried on to a vast extent we have reason to believe; but that it is new, or out of the common course of government procedure—that it is un-English, or illegal—or not permitted or contemplated by parliament or constitution, is wholly, or almost wholly, a mistake. If there is one thing more than another peculiarly *English*, it is *secret* letter opening. In most of the continental countries letters are known to be regularly opened, or subject to opening; in some states, we are told, it is usual to give a summary of contents on the outside, and the name of the writer, which usually ensures a safe and punctual transit; elsewhere the letters are uniformly opened and stamped. There the people know what they are about, and act accordingly; no one is dolt enough to trust the Post-offices with any thing he does not want exposed—here on the contrary, suspicion has been so completely lulled, or perhaps rather so entirely nonexistent—that Post-office espionage has been maintained with the most profound secrecy. The outcry, though in itself so salutary an indication of revolted feelings, and intense hostility to a *seemingly new* attack on public liberty, is ignorant, misdirected, and uncertain. It is ignorant of the origin and duration of the grievance, misdirected as to the objects of attack, and uncertain of the mode or extent to which it would have the grievance remedied.

Thus the public indignation, just in nature, is wrong in kind, quality, and intensity. It is erroneously based—it is grounded on the supposition that the Post-office outrages are unprecedented, transient, accidental, personal—not of old standing, permanent, systematic and official. It can be hardly yet known, that previous administrations have had this power and exercised it—or if known, it has certainly not been dwelt upon with the same energy of vituperation which has been bestowed upon the partisan or personal view of the subject.

Party considerations may be deemed insepa rable from all public topics—but if ever there was one which should be an exception, this is unquestionably that one. The prime mover in the legislature—the uncompromising foe to the ministry, Mr. Duncombe, with his usual clear and sound judgment, repudiated the party aspect of the question, and in order that it might be sifted on its merits, renounced all intention of making it a "no-confidence" measure.

How stands the case thus far?—the *personelle* of the matter has actually taken the lead throughout the journalist animadversions, not even excepting the *hitherto* ministerialist *Times*. This phenomenon of the newspaper world—uniting in itself the two most opposite qualities, power and inconsistency, to an unexampled extent—has directed the fiercest of its attacks against the *Jonas* of the ministry. Not a shred, a miserable tatter of principle has been left to this great "constitutional" question. Sir James Graham is censured for *his* having done the deed, instead of some more *respected* or *fitting* functionary—Aberdeen, for instance—and for not having told us what he did it for. It is accepted as ample excuse that Mr. Mazzini's or Stolzman's, or any other foreigner's letters should be broken open for the sake of obliging, and quieting the subjects of, a friendly foreign power. What virtuous bile has been stirred up against this miserable minister, before and beyond all others—and why?—*because he was found out!* Though the writers who are mis-directing public opinion know, or ought to know, that the present opposition ranks, and late ministry—the Melbourne cabinet—were as deep in the mire as the Peel cabinet in the mud. How many letters of disaffected radicals and chartists contributed to their wholesale accusations, trials, and convictions under the whig administration? To one portion of the press it is convenient to speculate on this aspect of the case, to another, to affix the stigma to the tories or conservatives as parties, instead of scape-goat Graham.

The position of both parties was clearly enough exposed by Sir James Graham's readiness to submit to a committee of five whigs and four tories, to the exclusion of Duncombe, Hume, or any independent member. The secrecy for which he stipulated he thought would not be broken in form or substance by those who through publicity would expose themselves. If this precious, secret, and pre-guilty committee "satisfy John Bull," heaven help Johnny for a easy old fool!—his ready, gulping credulity would even surpass his reputation.

What shall be the remedy? Is it possible for the public to arrive at a fair understanding of this subject in the midst of the prevailing journalist mis-directions? Is it credible that the dismissal of Sir James Graham has been a prominent recommendation? We should have to memorialise the Queen to dismiss the government itself—to rid ourselves of perpetrators and connivers of post-office iniquities. We should desire also the exclusion of Lord John Russell and his party from the cabinet, to exclude letter-violators from the administration. We should have a general election, and pledge the candidates not merely to oppose a letter-opening government, but a letter-breaking parliament.

If the journalists speak the public sentiments, there seems an admirable confusion as to remedial measures. Schemes of gradation have been advocated, from the little, miserable, peddling recommendation of not letting the *present* Home Secretary do the business, to that of preventing clandestine and secret opening by *any one*. The utter, total, unconditional abolition of letter-burglary, open or secret, has not, that I am aware of, been once advocated. Are we to be legally subject to this enormity—sometimes—by some functionaries—and under some circumstances? Yes; seems the general, if not universal, answer of the press. Is this the right answer? or is the general, almost universal press incapable of judging rightly as to principle ?

Do their petty, sectional, localised associations cast up obstacles insuperable for throwing off party trammels on great questions affecting universal freedom?

I invite attention to this subject, and appeal to the equalitarian publicist to aid in the enquiry.
M. Q. R.

THE GOD OF NATURE AND THE GOD OF THE BIBLE IDENTICAL.

III.

THOUGH the age of reason school of theologists is virtually extinct, many actual infidels, and those too of the first water, may be ranked among the adopters of its most important, as well as most obvious errors. With strange inconsistency they avow themselves Atheists and occasionally argue like Deists. Paine was a Deist, his attack on the Bible was grounded on the unlucky assumption that the God of Nature could not have played the monstrous part ascribed to Jehovah—the assumption was unlucky, because false—its author never could have made it the primary principle of his Age of Reason, had he mastered the term nature, on the doing of which Coleridge rightly said all theology depends. That Paine did not succeed in "mastering the term nature," is plain from the fact that though a believer in one God and a hoper for happiness beyond this life, he rejected the God of revelation. He seemed to have no idea that an author of nature must be held accountable for ALL; for defects as well as beauties, for vice as well as virtue, for misery as well as happiness. He admitted the existence of God and yet denied the Bible was from him; which is about as reasonable as the logic of those who declare God the auther of everything, and in the same breath deny he is or was, or can be the author of *sin*—nay Paine's logic and their logic are the very same. He was satisfied that God made man and woman, and gave them the earth for an inheritance, but revolted at the idea of his "good author of all," making rich and poor. While sure God caused cabbages to grow, he was as sure he did not cause revelations to be written. Oh, no; the God of the cabbage could not be the God of the Bible: nor the God of the earthquake or pestilence, the "God of battles." A good deity might cause millions of innocent creatures to perish by pestilence or famine, but, would be blasphemy to think he could or rather would say "sword go through the land and purge it of inhabitants." "Whenever," observes Paine at page 13 of the Age of Reason, "whenever we read the obscene stories, the voluptuous debaucheries, the cruel and torturous executions, the unrelenting vindictiveness, with which more than half the Bible is filled, it would be more consistent that we call it the word of a Demon than the word of God." But, why so? Why should a God who 'in the course of his providence' betrays innocence, protects guilt, and winks at or actually perpetrates all imaginable deeds of cruelty and injustice, be deemed incapable of *anthorizing* obscene stories, voluptuous debaucheries, or cruel and torturous executions. Why should a God who is unrelentingly vindictive enough to permit the wholesale starvation of human beings, be incapable of the most fiendish act of cruelty, detailed in our Bible. Ruffians thrust a red hot iron into the living bowels of Edward II. Is MONSTER a term too strong for application to the God who with power to prevent, yet permitted, nay, *caused* the horrid act. Seneca, speaking of Sylla, says, *Deorum crimen, Sylla tam felix*; (the gods were criminal, in allowing Scylla to be so fortunate,) and Cicero declared that the lasting good fortune of Harpalus, a successful pirate, bore testimony against the gods; *they*, it seems wrote upon the principle, that "where the offence is, let the great axe fall"—even though it fell upon the neck of divinity itself.

Jew and christian moralists shrink with detestation from the man who tells them that if there is a God who created and now rules the world, all crimes are of his commission, all lies of his telling, all injustice of his perpetration. Less wise or less bold than heathen philosophers, they credit God with the authorship of good *only*. Evil they place to Satan's account. To him they ascribe whatever parts of divine providence no God, pervious to shame, would like laid at his door.

The ancients treated Jove much less gingerly than moderns do Jehovah. His thunderership, though reputed father as well of gods, as men, met with sorry treatment at the hands of Homer, Æschylus, and other Greek poets, who taught that "immortal Jove" was dispenser of evil. All *good* it is true they placed to the credit side of his godship's ledger; but as true it is they feared not to debit him with all *evil*. Homer, for example, assures us—

" Two vessels on Jove's threshold ever stand,
The source of evil one, and one of good.
The man whose lot Jove mingles out of both
By good and ill alternately is ruled ;
But he whose portion is unmingled ill,
O'er sacred earth by famine dire is driven."

If our Homer, marvellous Milton, had represented the functions of Jehovah, as these lines of his more marvellous prototype represent the functions of Jove, 'tis probable his head would have been compelled to part company with his shoulders. Milton took a safer, because orthodox course. His great poem, the " Paradise Lost," was designed to " vindicate the ways of god to man." That he was a believer in " one god and no more " is probable; but that he failed to "vindicate" him in the "Paradise Lost" is certain. Indeed, viewed as a defence of Deity, it is supremely ridiculous. Its author could not have been fool enough to believe a verse of it. But, as already observed, there is reason to think he was a Deist who had a notion that the god of nature and the god of the Bible are very different beings, whereas it can easily be shown, from scripture itself, that the god of Moses and the god of Paine are similar, or rather *the same* in character. " I form the darkness, and create light; I make peace, and create evil ; I, the lord, do *all* these things." So reads verse vii. from chapter 45, of " prophet " Isaiah. How clear it is that the Deist's god does *all* things. Sin no less than holiness—war no less than peace —darkness no less than light—are his work ; in short, *all* proceeded *from* him, and is governed by him. I may be told that though scripture affirms this doctrine, it also denies it, and to be sure there are texts which make Jehovah " a god of truth, and without iniquity;" a god whose spirit wrestles with evil, is grieved by evil, and, of course, is evil's bitter enemy. But the two-fold, or, as some call it, *bipolar*, character of Jehovah is precisely what I insist upon. Hence, my expression "Janus-faced Jehovah," an expression fully justified by the Bible which describes a two-faced god; in other words, *a god with contradictory attributes.* Surely Jehovah cannot be, and not be, the author of evil; yet the foregoing texts prove that the scripture declares that he is—"He causes men to hate and deceive each other"—Psalm cv., 25. "He sends lying spirits to deceive men"—I Kings, xxii. 33. "He hardens men's hearts, and makes them obstinate that he may destroy them"—Deutronomy, ii, 30. Could the devil do more? Yet in the face of texts like these divines dare tell us God never lies, never tempts, never deceives. Oh, no; Satan manages all that. To him belongs the wicked department of universal business; Jehovah looks to *all* the rest. Queer doctrine that, which makes his devilship lord-low every thing below, and his godship lord-high every thing above; but 'tis the doctrine of our respectable priests, who tell us it is "inconsistent with the nature and government of god to stir up sin in the human mind." They denounce as "worst imaginable impiety," the belief that Jehovah sent lying spirits to deceive men, or did evil of any sort, though their Bible plainly tells them so.

There is now before me a short poem on the devil, written by one David Millar, where we are assured,—

"The devil did our first parents at the beginning deceive,
When tempting them for the forbidden fruit also to receive.
The eating of that did god grieve,
When sinning against his holy leave.
The devil is going about seeking whom he may devour,
And tempting all the people in the world to their last hour.
The devil was once an angel of light,
When dwelling into the heavenly height.
And he was cast down for rebellion and pride,
And sent into the bottomless pit to bide.
Hell is a place of real torment and woe,
Where the devil is the wicked's foe.
The devil was a liar from the beginning,
Which caused our first parents to be sinning.
Satan seeks the human race to destroy,
And that is all his damnable employ.
The devil is an invisible spirit,
Tempting people to destruction for it.
He cannot go farther than the length of his chain,
Although that he should rage across the whole ocean's main.
Lord save us from the devil's devices,
For he is full of deceiving advices.

Satan tempts many people with riches,
Trying to get them into his clutches.
People have need to beware of his pranks,
For all his riches are but cursed blanks.
The devil lays in the world for a snare,
When he is flying about through the air.
Satan's riches will us nothing avail,
For they all unto distruction fail.

The critical may sneer at these lines, but the orthodox will rejoice over them. When they first appeared, in connection with a score or two of "poetical pieces" equally meritorious, they were declared by a local editor productions superior, in their way, to anything that had seen the light since Noah was a sailor. Not myself being a good judge of poesy, I will not pretend to say whether his opinion of Mr. Millar's "poetical pieces" is right or wrong, but I hesitate not to declare that *the* piece before us is "a gem of terseness and order." Where can be found in fewer words the grand doctrine of our priests? Nowhere. "Paradise Lost" teaches that doctrine, but oh how differently! A man might read Milton for a month without knowing what he means, but who can mistake David Millar? No one. He is, or rather his poem is, lucidity itself. There we learn that the devil "did god grieve, when sinning against his holy leave."

There, too, we learn who the devil was, where he was, where he is, and what his "damnable employ" is, in short all 'tis possible to learn regarding him. But though David Millar gives a full and popular account of the Devil, Scripture, as already shewn, is against him. Scripture makes *god* "a liar from the beginning." Scripture says *God* hardens men's hearts and makes them obstinate, that he may destroy them. Scripture expressly declares *God* the author of *all* things; if so, God is Devil and Devil God, or (as I think) there is neither the one nor the other. Both are one, if the Bible may be relied on. I am supported in this opinion by the Rev. J. E. Smith,* who says, such a conclusion exactly corresponds with the science of Nature which divides nature into two extremes—yet these extremes are one, though diametrically opposite. Nothing is more opposed to love than hatred, yet one mind contains them both. God and Devil, continues Mr. Smith, are the two extremes of nature, which it is now the business of men to regard as one mind. The Bible, therefore, is the joint production of both, and is strictly correct when it says, God is *not* the author of evil, and equally correct when it says he is the author of evil. For if you call one of the two extremes God, then he only does one half of the work—the Devil

---

* See *The Shepherd*, No. 18.

does the other; but if you call the two extremes God, then God does all the work. It manifestly appears from all this that in one sense God and Devil are *one*, in another sense that they are *two*, and in a third sense that they are *neither*. "Extremes of nature," the last quoted writer calls them, and as by extremes he merely means darkness and light, good and evil, it is plain they are his God, his devil, his every thing. The Bible he views as the joint production of nature's two extremes—so do I. It's God and Devil he views as a personification of those two extremes—so do I. He thinks that the God of Nature and the God of the Bible are identical—so do I. Our opinions on these topics are within less than a hair's breadth of each other.

C. S.

TRADE MYSTERIES. — Provincial booksellers who do business with the liberal London publishers, generally act on the good old axiom that "brevity is the soul of wit," as the following curious extract from "an order" will demonstrate. Though apparently mysterious to those unacquainted with the trade, yet it is perfectly intelligible to the publisher.

12 Brains.
6 Almighty Gods.
4 Devils.
2 Eternal Hells.
12 Lakes of Fire.
24 Immortal Souls.
18 Priests.
35 Worlds.
"And a Lot of Pulpits."

If we could fancy this astoundingly heterogeneous order literally supplied, it would certainly *beat all nature* by chalks, as the Yankees say. It would be a realization of the compound title that astonished the *Movement* pages a while back—*Celestio-inferno-super-humano-mundanities!*

GUIDANCE OF THE FEELINGS.—Unless the conscience of a man be directed by better guides than his own *feelings*, it may render him the most destructive being on the face of the earth.—*Cogan*.

CHRISTIANITY BEWITCHED. — Mr. Fox spoke of the decay of faith in miracles and witchcraft. "The majority of christians, however, still believe in *one* witch—and the woman of Endor stands her ground the last of her race."—He then read an extract from a recently commenced periodical, the *North British Quarterly Review*, an accredited organs of the Free Church of Scotland, giving a full, true and particular account of the character and habits of Satan, and the wiles he practised in order to entrap human souls. Mr. Fox asks why, if all were so well known, were not some means of prevention taken? Why is not A. 1. sent after him? Why does not Lord Ashley bring in a ten hours' bill to restrict his labours, confining him to the day-light, and no longer permitting him to prowl about in the darkness. If this account had appeared in a daily paper, people would think that the writer had gone mad! The time will come when it will seem equally absurd in a Quarterly review.—*W. J. Fox's recent lecture at South Place*.

NOTICES.

TO ACTIVE FRIENDS.—SPECIAL.— Our provincial friends, more especially those inhabiting large towns, can materially forward our common views and objects, and the interests of the *Movement* publication in two ways—by taking charge of copies of our periodical, or papers from it, to deliver to the most suitable journals in their locality; and by acquainting us with any notices of the same which may be inserted. Those who are sufficiently friendly and warm in the cause to charge themselves with these commissions, are requested to communicate with us at their earliest convenience.

WOULD some friend favor us with Mr. Webster's speech on the Girard will case, lately tried in America? He is reported to have made a "magnificent defence of christianity."

TO CORRESPONDENTS.

RECEIVED Mr. Macdonald's letter respecting Mr. Paterson, and the kind application of Mr. Cathels. The letter has been forwarded to Mr. Holyoake, who will at once send the form required.

WE have received a short report of the Discussion at John Street; but it is not sufficiently complete to warrant us in giving it insertion—we suspect that it wants impartiality. To correspondents who favor us with reports of discussions we are obliged. We shall be glad of reports, though written without pretensions to elegance of diction—but they should contain the principal features of the debate on both sides.

THE contribution on "Phrenology *versus* Godology" will receive early attention.

RECEIVED.—The *Regenerator* (American paper.)

SUBSCRIPTIONS TO THE ANTI-PERSECUTION UNION.

Mr. Haxton £0 2 6

T. POWELL, *Sec. pro tem.*

Printed and Published by G. J. HOLYOAKE, 40, Holywell-street, Strand, Saturday, July 13, 1844.

THE MOVEMENT

And Anti=Persecution Gazette.

"Maximize morals, minimize religion."—BENTHAM.

No. 32.   EDITED BY G. JACOB HOLYOAKE, ASSISTED BY M. Q. RYALL.   PRICE 1½d

AMENDMENT OF THE LAW.

SOME years ago, an "Association" was formed "for Promoting Humane Legislation," of which Ralph Thomas, Esq., (the same barrister, we believe, who so ably conducted Mr. Paterson's Bow-street case,) was chairman. The committee of management numbered some of the best names in law, literature and art. The laudable aim of the association was "to bring into discussion those objects of justice, toleration, and truth, which the good and wise in all ages have deemed most excellent." The prospectus of the association expressed this valuable sentiment—" To *individual* exertions a lasting debt of gratitude is due ; every age, almost every clime, has produced a martyr to the cause of mankind—a voluntary sacrifice in the gulph of prejudice or tyranny ; and these have not fallen in vain if they have made the path clear for those who follow in their course." This is an important sentiment, uttered by men nearly all distinguished for their individual exertion. It is valuable as coming from men who had honourably and nobly proved its worth—it is valuable in all times as bearing testimony against that inanity by which the multitude excuse their apathy—it is valuable as exposing the flimsy plea of those who say that individual exertion can do little against the mass of wrong and prejudice, who, sinking back into the sluggish ranks of custom's servile slave, make one more for the friend of liberty to battle against, and swell the very tide which they confess is overwhelming young enterprise and improvement. To return to our prospectus,—we are reminded that the present improvement of our penal code is chiefly owing to the *individual* exertions of such men as BECCARIA, HOWARD, ERSKINE, ROMILLY, and BENTHAM, so that in law as in politics and theology and all great professions, individuals have worked out striking reformations. Out of this excellent association has arisen a "Society for Promoting the Amendment of the Law," at the head of which is Lord Brougham. This society comprises among its members persons of the greatest legal distinction in the world. Guizot, Dupin, Savigny, Mr. Justice Story, and Professor Mittermaice are among the number, and, to our surprise and satisfaction, Mr. Hall of Bow-street and our own Jardine. "This society," according to its advertisement in the *Times*, "is fully impressed with the conviction that it is of the greatest importance to the community, that safe and expedient alterations in the law should be proposed and investigated, that all information as to them should be brought before the legislature and the public, and that they should be encouraged and supported by all legitimate means.

It has, therefore, been thought useful that an association should be established (without reference to any political party) to assist and carry forward these great objects. It seemed most proper that it should be commenced by persons acquainted with the administration of the law in various departments. But, in addition to the present members, the co-operation, not only of other members of Parliament and of the legal profession, but of all other classes, and more especially of the *trading* and mercantile classes, is earnestly invited. The principal objects of the society will be—

1st. To bring into co-operation individuals who have already taken, or desire to take, active steps towards the amendment of the law, and thus render their efforts more systematic and effectual.

2d. To collect and diffuse information with a view to the objects of the society.

3d. To undertake a communication with the proper authorities in foreign countries, on subjects connected with the amendment of the law. And

4th. To publish from time to time, under the sanction of the society, such suggestions as may seem to deserve more than ordinary consideration.

Communications may be addressed to Lord Brougham, at 4, Grafton-street; or to the Treasurer, James Stewart, Esq., 13, Southwick-crescent, Hyde-park; or to the Honorary Secretary, William Vizard, Esq., 16, New-street, Spring-gardens ; or to any other Member of the Society."

As this society appears to prefer the co-operation of "individuals" desirous of taking active steps towards the amendment of the law, the Anti-Persecution Union has requested its secretary to represent to the chairman of the above society, the anomaly and injustice of the blasphemy laws of Great Britain, with a view to their amendment or abolition. In compliance with such request, the following communication has been forwarded to Lord Brougham, and a copy to the principal members of the Society, for their individual consideration.—

TO LORD BROUGHAM,
(President of the Society for Promoting the Amendment of the Law).

My Lord,

I take the liberty of soliciting the attention of the "Society for Promoting the Amendment of the Law" to the propriety of recommending the abrogation of the Blasphemy Laws, or perhaps, more correctly to the practices of the courts relative to the publication of heterodox opinions, for the judges do not profess to cite statutes so much as to follow an understood practice, which they style the common law.

A society has for some time existed, under the title of the *Anti-Persecution Union*, whose object is to obtain the repeal of all laws or practices affecting the conscientious expression of theological opinion. This object could be more efficiently entertained by the society of which your lordship is the head, as the far greater influence and the professional knowledge of that society would, if exercised, speedily effect the abolition of the disgraceful practice of punishing men for the alleged offence of blasphemy.

The operation of blasphemy laws is resolvable into a question of equal justice. One portion of the community is permitted to express sentiments without limitation upon the interesting topic of religion, while the other portion is punished for exercising the same privilege. Abolish the blasphemy laws, and this gross anomaly ceases. The history of irreligion proves that the publication of theological opinions may be left free, not only with safety, but with advantage to the public interests. Experience proves that not only has the public security not been endangered by the heterodox, but that on the whole, those views uniformly condemned as blasphemous, have advanced civilization in all countries.

So long as the blasphemy laws are unrepealed, bigots may take advantage of them, and when cases are carried into courts, judges, as your lordship well knows, must administer the law, although, from superior enlightenment they may, as did Lord Denman, regret its exercise. Europe has been revolted by the sentence of Judge O'Neall, of South Carolina, on a person who assisted in setting a slave at liberty, and the *Times* has made light of that judge's defence of his sentence, wherein he has reminded the Scottish public that he acted only as the administrator of a law passed a *hundred* years ago, and yet remaining on their statute book. But at the Gloucester Summer Assizes of 1842, a young man was tried for an attempt to set an Englishman free from (in his opinion) the degrading slavery of religion, and he was sentenced to six months' imprisonment by virtue of a law which was passed *two thousand years* ago—for Mr. Justice Erskine assured him that it had descended to us from time immemorial. The conduct of Judge O'Neall is but a parallel case to that of Mr. Justice Erskine, and we can only be saved from the national disgrace of repetitions of the same proceeding by annulling the blasphemy laws.

Should your lordship see reason to direct to this subject the attention of the "Society for Promoting the Amendment of the Law," it would generally gratify the friends of civilization.

I am, most respectfully,
Your Lordship's obedient servant,
G. JACOB HOLYOAKE.

5, Paul's-alley, Paternoster-row,
London, July 13, 1844.

CHRISTIAN RESPONSIBILITY AND CHRISTIANITY'S INFLUENCES.

III.

A REVIEW has been taken of the conduct of christians, when combined and consolidated into a church acknowledged as spiritual head, disposer of realms, kings, and subjects. We have seen how christians have acted under various circumstances of dominancy and state preference, old and newly acquired power, spiritual and worldly prosperity and power—so striking has been the similitude, modified and bounded only by means and opportunities, that the conclusion was forced upon us of the existence of something in the men themselves, their doctrine and system, actuative and preponderative beyond the accidental circumstances of more or less actual state-government and dominion. It remains to view the followers of the cross as less successful adventurers, as mere aspirants after the solid privileges, immunities, place, dignities and advantages, realized by their brother winners of the race. Shall we speak of some, even, who profess no desire for civil and ecclesiastical domination, who even repudiate the idea, and who protest they would have no state-endowed and privileged church, though that church should be centered in their sect and theirs only? It must be confessed that it is a large concession for us to be called upon to admit. We should like first to have seen an example of refusal of state protection, favour and preference, to an absolute *bona fide* offer, which would put the offerees in a positively better position by state endowment than they previously were by congregational collections and allowances. A case is on record of a large portion of a church voluntarily seceding and calling itself the " Free Church," trusting for support to the uncompelled and free subscriptions of the body. True, and the spiritual heads—for they also have spiritual heads—have found the solid support fall very short of their expectations or wishes. Something far beyond this is more than hinted by those who are not absolutely interested in the affairs of the seceders; it is strongly asserted that regretful manifestations are already displayed, and that the affair is to be characterized by Guizot's late emphatic and remarkable word, in allusion to a political proceeding—*regretable*—in the estimation of the principal movers.

But let this pass—let it be a moot point; let us even suppose there are christian churches,—I speak in the large and congregational, not ecclesiastical sense,—not desirous of any preference, might, power, and dominion for others or themselves. Will it be affirmed that there co-exists with this spirit, that if the concession, or rather desire for, and advocacy of, perfect freedom to all others? I unhesitatingly say NO; and that this damning negative does not apply peculiarly to christian churches, dominant or most influential sects, but to christians and christianism generally. Have not the non-church christians, aye, the anti-church christians entered upon persecution with as high zest and as keen a relish, whenever the opportunity has been afforded, as their endowed and envied brethren? Who have stood by and permitted the assaults against the heterodox? Whence have the infidel persecutions received countenance and support? I am told it is the church which has committed these injustices. Who have encouraged them? Who have dropped the strife and animosity, till then raging among them, and patched up a hollow truce for a common onslaught on the infidel? Hypocrites! in the richly vituperative language of your incarnate deity, hypocrites, who " compass sea and land to make one proselyte, and when he is made, ye make him ten-fold more the child of hell than yourselves." Hypocrites! whited sepulchres! ye " generation of vipers!" was it through church and state influence that the dissenting christians of Bristol set upon Southwell for infidelity, that they incited and set to work the beagles of the law, that they hounded them on, acclaiming, yelling, and exulting? If they were English or Scotch Church christians who pounced upon Holyoake, Paterson, Finlay, O'Neil, Matilda Roalfe and the rest, were they not non-churchists and anti-churchists who approved or looked on? Or, if this be impudently and barefacedly denied, were they not unheard, *non-remonstrant*, *unprotestant*, conforming and assenting, instead of *non-conforming* and *dissenting* to these villanies? The commotion they made on the factories' education clause has scarcely died away, and the influence they brought to bear is notorious and acknowledged by a powerful government, confessedly defeated. The clamour of dissenters against the dissenters' chapels bill (because it went to equalize the rights of *Socinian* christians) still rings in our ears. When did they petition, when did they meet to express disapproval, when did they stir, raise their voices, or make a poor solitary effort to stay the christian persecution of infidels?

The subject could be pursued with the same damnatory evidence and overwhelming demonstration, throughout every instance in which christians as a body exercise influence over the destinies of liberty. Active, passive, or permissive—intolerance and partiality in the framing and application of the laws is attachable to the christian professors, whether orthodox or heterodox, in power, shut out from power, or expectant of power. Not only do they, while they can, prevent us expressing our sentiments, they would prevent us using our own means for our own objects. From out of their conventicles have they denounced those of infidels, and striven to prevent the raising of structures and assembling in edifices raised by "voluntary" efforts, while they have been exalting voluntaryism for themselves to the seventh heaven. The *ins* robbed us of property willed to us, (Mr. Thompson's), declaring that being for infidelism it was for immorality, and the *outs* rubbed their hands and chuckled over it. Whenever practical equality has been attempted by us, we have been, as far as in their power, opposed and frustrated by christians votaries.

Will it be argued that not merely state-church privileges, but state-church contact or propinquity pollutes those who are exposed to it? Is there nowhere in the wide world that the so easily perverted christian can get out of the way of his wicked big brother church? Does he forget there is such a place as America?—that he can there jog on without an atom of preferment, not a doit of state salary, not a bit of government patronage. place, pension, or preference one over another? Oh! then here christianity has a chance, here it can develop its capabilities, exercise its legitimate influences. The " blessed influences of the gospel," the mercy, the love, equity and "moral suasion" which the panegyrists affirm to be its essence and the ruling guides of gospel-believers, will be seen in all the plenitude of their purity and beauty, and majesty and might.

Is it credible that men can argue thus in the teeth of a monstrous and atrociously criminal slave system, which its very supporters presume not to defend out of republican institutions, but uphold most confidently on the authority of the Bible?

From what cause spring the most insensate and implacable divisions, party arrays, mobbings and murderings in an anti-state church continent? From christian hates and strives. "The shibboleths of 'down with the papists!' 'down with the orangemen!'" which would have been cherished for a state church grievance, and that alone, are pronounced with the most fatal results in the land of voluntary christianity. Did the soil of "free and energetic, and vital christianity" prove ungenial? No where do the weeds of dissention flourish with ranker luxuriance than in the land of "revivals and voluntaryism" in christianity. But is not the person and the property of the unbeliever more respected? Hitherto the sectaries have been too well balanced, there has been too slight a preponderance of one over the rest to permit exactly the same results. We must not anticipate, we must watch and record results as they occur.—As vile a conspiracy for plundering of the most approved orthodox character, is now being attempted or actually perpetrated, as we could possibly find, in the mother country. We have an anti-state church parliament of christians here, nursed and fostered and trained by the *Non-conformist* organ of the party. Let us present them with a picture of trans-atlantic anti-state church christianity. Will they permit us to judge of these by those? We will not imitate illiberality—conjecture, speculate, and anticipate—but only cite our experience. Hear the *Herald of Freedom*, American journal, on this matter.

"Daniel Webster is trying for a fee of some 50,000 dollars to break old Stephen Girard's will, because he bequeathed money to erect a college, into which he forbade the intrusion of priests. Webster argues that it couldn't be a legal *charity*, therefore, I think he'll succeed, and is right. You can't have a charity without a priest, any more than you can a "church without a bishop." Nor a college without a clergy, any more than a monastery without monks. The law will not countenance the erection of a seminary of learning, unless it is consigned to the management of the clergy. The clergy are the pray-hounds of the law, and law as a system of regulated violence cannot be maintained among men without them, nor can they be kept up without military law. They will blow old Girard's will to the moon.

"Henry Wood calls the Girard college an infidel one, because it was intended to be free of the wizards, and says—'the project is blasted under divine providence.' Does he really think so at this time of day? or is it a sly, monkish remark?

"*Our christianity is a mere matter of civil law, the whole of it.* It is as unlike the christianity taught by Christ, as a gun and bayonet are unlike an olive branch. I don't care if Webster blows up the college, although it is interdicted to the wizard clergy. I don't like to see these tyrant piles of marble, looming up amid a population, one-third houseless, and without the lowest necessaries of life. The world is every where too much deformed with them. I wish they were all *gently* dismantled, and their massy materials laid up into cottages, and their sites planted with potatoes. But the court will *piously* defeat the Girard will, I predict, because of its committing the college, founded at the pleasure of the testator, to the charge of the people, instead of the ordained monkhood. Learning is not allowed the people in this country, under the administration of the clergy. Webster is justifiable for pleading the doctrine—for he is to be tremendously paid for it. Justifiable as an attorney. But I point the people to the fact as indicative of the power of the priesthood.—A college under the management of the people is an illegality and a nuisance, and the courts of law will abate it.

"Wood's journal says the infidel 'will required a plain building,' and they have departed from it and built a "magnificent structure, which is yet incomplete." He then lays the failure of its completion to the infidelity of the will, and the consequent anger of providence. So absurdly may a priest talk in solemn matters. — *Boston Journal.*"

Here then the anti-state church christianity is self-confessed as great a culprit as the state church christianity—"a mere matter of civil law!" Oh, unhappy, bewildered wight that goes to look for "real christianity."—"Unlike the christianity taught by Christ too!" Oh, most god-like—that is, inexplicable, incomprehensible, inexpressible christianity—most labyrinthine system! Where shall we look for thy proper interpretation? Where shall we seek thy true manifestation?

Do not WE alone afford the solution? Is not christianity—true christianity—seen and exemplified every where that a christian church is congregated, and a christian bible read and acknowledged as a rule of faith and direction of conduct?

Say now, christians—Is not your responsibility, doctrine—if valid, fastened on yourselves? Is not your christianity influential in the shaping of prevalent conduct, and consequently in the promotion of existing injustice? M. Q. R.

HONEST CONFESSIONS.

Honest christians are rarities in these days. General information and the growing popularity of common sense have rendered christians shy in confessing their real sentiments, but in a few cases, where they are bold in their badness, as is the Rev. Mr. Close of Cheltenham, or where they are somewhat removed from critical observation, as they are in some parts of Ireland, they let out a little wholesome character-indicating truth. This has lately been done in Belfast. A meeting of the Church Education Society has been held there. It was precided over by the Lord Bishop of Down and Connor, and Dromore, and attended by vicars, archdeacons, reverends, and M.P's. The Rev. Thomas Walker, who moved the first resolution, "called on the meeting to withhold their contributions to the National Board of Education, if the Bible was not used in the schools. He differed with every system of instruction that did not unite a scriptural with a secular education, and considered it an insult to that meeting to discuss the question." The Rev. W. M'Ilwaine said "his motto was '*No Bible no Board*.' He said deliberately that were the choice between *entire ignorance, and knowledge without religion, he would prefer entire ignorance.*"

Professor Stevelly "cordially agreed with every word uttered by those who had spoken before him. No man who had any regard for religion could have anything to do with the National Board. (Hear, hear.) It separated religion altogether from education, and a system of National Education which did so was only suited for a nation of infidels. (Applause.) He would just as soon let lunatics out of an asylum with weapons in their hands to enable them to destroy every one they would meet, as educate the people without instructing them in the principles of religion, the duty they owe to god and their fellow-man. (Hear, hear.) Education without this would only be enabling men to carry out bad purposes, and he fully agreed with the last speaker when he said he would rather have no education, than an education without religion. (Hear, hear.)

The Rev. J. S. Monsell objected to the Educational Board because it decided when, where, and in what parts the scripture should be read. He denied the right of any man or set of men to lay restrictions on the word of god. He would be far from wishing to inculcate disobedience to parents, but he would not allow the right of the parent to keep out of the hands of his children the word of god. The rev. gentleman then pointed out that in one version of the Bible which he had seen, it was stated that Jacob adored the top of his rod, which was a contradiction of the second commandment—now, continued the rev. gentleman, a man might very justly say, *where there is contradiction there can be no truth.*"

These clergymen of the Irish church prefer to keep the peasantry of Ireland, to whom knowledge is so necessary, without knowledge entirely, unless it is mixed up with their own dogmas. True to their order, they hesitate not, their resolution is expressed in a few words—" No religion no knowledge." And the knowledge then to be had is to be vitiated with religion. It is generally admitted that a parent may keep from his children's hands obscene books, just as he would keep an enemy from them who sought to destroy their peace. The Bible is of this character; Mr. Shiel declares that its voluptuous images are unfit for presentation to youth. Its narratives, we know, are calculated both to debase and debauch, yet these christians would *compel* the parent to place this book in the hands of his unsuspecting and confiding child.

According to the Rev. Mr. Monsell's admission, " where there are contradictions we may justly conclude that there is no truth." Let this rule be applied to the Bible honestly, and nine parents out of every ten will come to the conclusion that it is not a book of truth, and must be a dangerous guide of life. Yet, argues the rev. gentleman, I would not allow the parent the right of withholding this. To support their religion these men find it necessary to strike at knowledge, at the innocence of children, and the moral right of parents to preserve them from degradation and impurity, and finding it necessary, they boldly do it. The only difference between Belfast piety and that nearer home is that Irish religion is less restrained by surrounding intelligence, and consequently ventures to speak a little more plainly. These clerical admissions, which are chronicled by a Belfast paper, are not without their value. Since contradictions, according to orthodox christian authority, warrant a rejection of the word of god, many a weak believer, and almost disbeliever, whose infirmity of purpose and fears kept him in godly bondage, finding no version of the Bible in which contradictions do not appear, might " very justly say " there "can be no truth " in any of them. It would go hard with him, if after this, he did not " better the instruction," and, bursting his chains, emancipate himself entirely.

G. J. H.

THE GOVERNMENT OF HARMONY.

Our attention has been drawn to the letter in the last *New Moral World* from the "Late Acting Governor" of Harmony. Deep as is the interest we profess and feel in the success of Tytherly, neither our space nor our objects will permit us to discuss the minor questions which will occasionally agitate that society. The proper place for the facts to be given in answer to the L. A. G.'s letter is the *New Moral World*. As far as we are able, we will notice all points of main importance. We are not afraid of giving opposition or support to any party, so soon as we are convinced that the public interest (as accurately as we can understand it) may be promoted thereby. For the honor of the order of industry the present executive of the socialists must have a fair trial. At present they labour under disadvantages from which all former executives have been exempted. The talent and editorial influences of the *New Moral World* are conscientiously in opposition to them. The letter of the L. A. G. might be passed by. At least we hope that the president will not be diverted from his course at this early period by unnecessary controversy. The letter of the L. A. G., upon cursory reflection, resolves itself into a few plain statements. It says that "some remarks made by the present president are calculated to convey an erroneous impression to those at a distance, who have no opportunity of knowing all the circumstances as which induced the policy of the L. A. G." The meaning of this is that "those at a distance" would approve of the "policy" in question, did they know all the circumstances which induced it. But there is the fact, that the late Congress—all persons from "a distance" *were* made acquainted with "all the circumstances" of the case, and yet were not satisfied, as the changes they made prove. The L. A. G. says that in two years certain "new departments of school, boarders, and visitors," were introduced, which produced £2,000 per annum." But, if I remember rightly, the impression of the late Congress was that the expenditure of these departments exceeded their income. Consequently the society only gained a loss. The introduction of these departments is unquestionably meritorious, but perhaps they may be improved. The letter says it was one of the L. A. G.'s principles "that all must produce as much as they and their families consumed." The value of this rule depends on its application. Mr. Owen would give £1,000 for the good opinion of a neighbouring squire, and think it productive expenditure. It is to be hoped that the new executive will not think so. The L. A. G. says he is "at a loss to discover any substantial difference in the intentions of the new executive and the old." But this remark only leaves lookers on "at a loss to discover any substantial reason" for the L. A. G. and other members of the old executive refusing to act with the new. If there is not great difference in the intentions of these parties the late Congress was a farce, and the delegates were mad. The letter in question says "it will be impossible to carry out the objects agreed, as desirable, in anything like the time *impatient* friends expect. Half this is true. Every body knows that Harmony cannot progress rapidly. It was fixed in a frost twelve months ago. It is in debt £1,000. The new executive have taken the office like heroes under the most disadvantageous circumstances. The usual enemies, cool friends, and an empty treasury surrounded them. It is not true that socialists are "*impatient*"—men who have sat quietly during two years under the paternal forms of government are social *Jobs*. Lastly, the L. A. G. turns waggish and "counsels the new executive to make good what *now is* before taking a step in advance." Of course every retiring governor thinks that his successor should do just as he has done. If Mr. Cobden was made premier to day, Sir Robert Peel would "counsel" him to carry out his sliding scale "before taking one step in advance" —if fact "to make good what *now is*." But Mr. Buxton has been called to the presidency because what "*now is*" does not suit us. *We* "counsel" him to carry out the resolutions of Congress—to this duty he has rightly addressed himself. We want to see what our collective wisdom has done for us. Need it be added that the preceding remarks are penned in no unfriendly spirit towards the late Acting Governor of Harmony? whose suavity, integrity, and general abilities, have never been disputed. We are not bound— because we think him estimable to think him infallible. To analyse his letters, or question his policy, is not to impugn his honour.
G. J. H.

A MANCHESTER MATTER IN A NEW LIGHT.

My colleague's (G. J. H.) letter from Manchester, in last week's number, had the following:

"A resurrection of the dead is expected in this quarter. Mr. Finch delivered a funeral oration over our late excellent friend Mr. Lowe, from these words, 'For this purpose the Son of God was manifested, that he might deliver them who, through fear of death, have all their lifetime been subjected to bondage.' By all to whom I have spoken on the subject, it is agreed that if there is any coming back, friend Lowe will come b·ck. Poor fellow! how uneasy he must feel to be dismissed from the world with such language."

It is right that Mr. Finch should be heard in reply. In his absence I will call up counsel for the defence. Hear the Manchester correspondent of a Kilkenny paper—no descendant apparently of the "Kilkenny cats," as he seems more lackrymose than fightable.

"SHOCKING DEMORALIZATION OF THE ENGLISH—FUNERAL OF AN INFIDEL.—On Sunday I attended the burial of an Owenite; they proceeded from the Hall of Science, at the camp-field, celebrated for its battle-ground during the civil wars. They marched three deep, men and women; they mustered about one thousand strong. On their arrival at Christ's Church, a Mr. Smith addressed them in the most anti-Christian style for about ten minutes, and summed up his discourse by singing the Owenite hymns, joined by his party, commencing with the words "what's death but the shadow of a dream;" on the conclusion they marched in the same order back to their hall. I was forcibly struck at the contrast when I thought of old Mr. Potter's funeral at Mary's Church, when Mr. Caulfield prevented the Catholic service being read. Good God! when I thought of the Christian character of that good old man, and the service of his church being denied to his remains, and saw before me the remains of an infidel interred within five yards of the principal entrance of a Protestant church here, and then the blasphemous oration that followed it; it made a lasting impression on me. Oh! poor, virtuous, faithful, Christian Ireland, what treatment you patiently suffer from your Saxon taskmasters. I went back to see the result of the affair at the Hall of Science, a beautiful and spacious building; a Mr. Finch, an iron master, then addressed them, contending that there might or might not be such a place as Heaven, and that such a place of punishment as hell he completely denied, and then taxed the scriptures with many contradictions, and strove, with the most fiendish industry of misconstruction, to turn them into the greatest burlesque, completely showing, as he said, that it was a hoax got up by witty churchmen, and in the coarsest manner ridiculed the notion of Christ! In fact, it was a pitiful picture of depraved humanity. After the address they all had a tea party, but I was so thoroughly disgusted with them, that I did not wait to see the conclusion. Let Ireland suffer what she will, there is this satisfaction, that God has not withdrawn his grace; on the contrary, he has firmly planted the faith of the saints in her people, and will, in his own good time, for her patience to other nations, raise her up as an example of his grace.—*Private Correspondent of the Kilkenny Journal.*"

IRRELIGION IN THE AMERICAN CONGRESS.

GREAT excitement has lately prevailed in America in consequence of the motion of Mr. Petitt, member from Indiana, to abolish the payment of chaplains by the treasury of the United States. We have only seen the christian side of this subject. The *Christian Guardian* published at Toronto, under the direction of the Wesleyan Methodist Conference in Canada, gives a portion of the debate, but suppresses Mr. Petitt's speech. According to the speech of Mr. Hardin, in opposition, Mr. Petitt's intention was to bring christianity into disgrace. "He asserted that the doctrines of Christ taught us that if Great Britain took Maine, we must return good for evil by returning her Oregon. He said that if Congress sent chaplains among its soldiers, and they believed what they were taught; when they were attacked by an enemy, and struck in the face, they must turn their backs and let them strike again. What did he? what could he mean? except that the christian religion degraded the army, and made both soldiers and officers cowards." Mr. H. then asks if Mr. Petitt "supposed that the people of Indiana were sufficiently infused with *Fanny Wrightism* to sanction such an attack on the religion of their forefathers.

The *News* newspaper, published in Kingston, Canada, has a long article on Mr. Petitt's motion. "It will be seen," says the *News*, "that a member of Congress of the United States has solemnly declared from his place, that the *principles of the christian religion are incompatible with the spirit of our political institutions*, giving earnest of his belief by a motion to abolish the office of chaplain in the public service; and sustaining his proposition by a grave and formal argument."

ANNIVERSARY OF THE STORMING OF THE BASTILE.
[*For the Movement.*]

THE sixth commemoration in London of the above event—one which has been always honoured by such re-unions in every town in France—took place at the Crown and Anchor Tavern, on Monday, 14th July.

The meeting, which was in the large room, and numerously attended, was remarkable for the perfect harmony which subsisted, in an assembly composed of such various elements as the natives of different European nations thus brought together. A new and peculiar characteristic was exhibited by this festival, in the cordiality and fraternity of sentiment displayed by the natives of nations but recently considering themselves enemies. A gratifying and unanswerable proof was thus exhibited, that a people who are guided solely by their genuine feelings, and alive to their true interests, have no difficulty in understanding one another, in effacing the prejudices which have separated them, and which governments have basely endeavoured to perpetuate among them.

The numerous patriotic addresses pronounced in the principal European languages, and especially those sentiments which invoked the union of all nations in the same bonds of morality and fraternity, were received with the highest enthusiasm and reiterated plaudits. Patriotic songs and hymns were also sung, in which all present joined in chorus. So many working-men— the representatives it may be said, of the chief continental nations—thus united, as it were in one family meeting, and in whom amity and cordiality were displayed no less in words than in looks, tones, and gestures, formed a truly delightful and exhilarating spectacle. The evening's proceedings redound to the honor of those true cosmopolitans, who have too much good sense and humanity to permit their governments and a corrupt press to foment strives and jealousies among them, and who have shown evidences of a universality of feeling, which appeared to make the natives of each particular country think he had found his home. It was an evidence of no ordinary liberality and delicacy of sentiment, that the president, elected by the conductors of the meeting— themselves Frenchmen, and assembled on a French anniversary—was a native of another nation.

A collection was made in the course of the evening for the Spanish refugees.

It was also unanimously decided that an association be formed for the assistance of foreigners in distress in all countries.

A VICTIM TO RELIGION.—Mrs. Electa, wife of Mr. Oratio Stratton, aged 21 years, put a period to her existence at Northfield Farms, August 15, by drowning herself in the Connecticut river, during a fit of insanity caused by Millerism.—*Pawtucket Chronicle.*

NOTICES.

NEWSPAPERS containing local matters illustrative of the workings of the system, theological, political, or social, we are glad to receive; as if not sent, they are very unlikely to come under our observation. They would be doubly acceptable if marked (which is not prohibited by the post office, provided writing is avoided,) at the noticeable passages —much valuable time is by this means saved.

RECEIVED—The *Vindicator* (Belfast paper), the *Sheffield Iris.*

ISLINGTON MEETING.—We are anxious for an authentic account of this affair, the subsequent action at law, and donation to the Anti Persecution Union.

MR. SOUTHWELL lectures at the Hall of Science, City-road, on Sunday the 28th.

TO CORRESPONDENTS.

C. S. S.—Yes, Mr. Montgomery the poet, is covered with fanaticism. He is always performing some freak at the Mechanics' Library in Sheffield. The pretty little thing on prayer, for which he has been so lauded, I do not believe to be original. I have seen the same thought in a book published 200 years ago, and one very likely to have fallen in Mr. Montgomery's way. Mr. John Saltmarsh, who was chap'ain to Fairfax's army, and who died Dec. 4, 1647, was the author of "Sparkles of Glory," and "Holy Discoveries and Flames," adorned with emblems. In his work the "Sparkles of Glory," originally dedicated to Parliament, and reprinted in 1811, he gives a chapter on the *Discoveries of Prayer*, in which may be found nearly word for word, the whole of Montgomery's hymn, beginning "Prayer is the soul's sincere desire," &c.   G. J. H.

As singularly corroborative of the above, the *Sheffield Iris* of the 4th gives an instance of this reverend interference, on the discussion "upon the admission of works of fiction, (the Life of Pemberton seems to be the sore point with the saints,) into the Mechanic's library." Instead of coming to the discussion, the author of " Satan" sent a note, which Mr. Ironside protested against being read at such a period as to forestall the debate, and which a gentleman of the name of Beal said was an attempt to prejudge the question, and asked why did not Mr. Montgomery come and manfully meet them in discussion, like any other member of the library?"   M. Q. R.

G. Hammond; R. Lazarus; W. B.; J. Macara received.

SUBSCRIPTIONS TO THE ANTI-PERSECUTION UNION.

J. Cook	£0	1	0
Card 11	0	4	6
„ 12	0	1	0
„ 16	0	5	0

T. POWELL, *Sec. pro tem.*

Printed and Published by G. J. HOLYOAKE, 40, Holywell-street, Strand, Saturday, July 20, 1844.

THE MOVEMENT

And Anti=Persecution Gazette.

"Maximize morals, minimize religion."—BENTHAM.

No. 33.   EDITED BY G. JACOB HOLYOAKE, ASSISTED BY M. Q. RYALL.   PRICE 1½d

INSTRUCTION. — RATIONAL AND SCHOLASTIC.
EDUCATIVE CONVENTIONALITY. — THE SCHOOLS — GRAMMAR IN GENERAL— HOLYOAKE'S GRAMMAR IN PARTICULAR.

PREAMBLE—*dogmatic and erudite.*

As "autocrat of all the *pages*"—invested with supreme authority for the time being—in the absence of the 'titular head'—my high-will and pleasure is to treat of the subject hereunto set forth — all supposed personal considerations influential thereto, notwithstanding.—Asketh any for a reason? With the great Falstaff, say I, 'what upon compulsion?' * * * If reasons were as plentiful as blackberries I would give no man a reason upon compulsion.' The 'sic volo, sic jubeo, stat pro ratione voluntas'— the will without reason, of all despots, is my answer.—Pretty well, I ween, for a month's editorial autocracy."

How much is lost to the thinking world and progressionists, through ignorance of the art of using words is beyond the power of speculation to surmise. To trace many of these barriers against enlightenment to the "workings of the system" would appear to many, far-fetched—to some almost monomaniacal—not unlike the *one-idead* projects of the currency men, free traders, piety propagators, and other panaceists. A moment's reflection will, however, show that the vile and tinsel conventionality, which sneers down the man who does not speak or write according to the fashionable standard, has exerted and continues to exert a widely-spread influence for evil.

Many a tyranny would have been overset which yet rides rampant—many a fraudulent political devise exposed, which now furtively, yet effectually, operates—many an improvement widely influencing society would have been introduced, which has been checked, postponed, or set aside, had men been as capable of expressing what they were able and honest enough to execute. None knows, and has reason to deplore, these facts more than the reformer, moral, political, social, religious, or scientific. Ill-constructed, ill-expressed hobbling nonsense, evincing the utmost ignorance of grammar, may be tolerated or passed over in the orthodox—but the progressionist must pick his words as the coxcomb picks his way, if he would not have every *lapsus linguæ* pointed out with the most relentless perseverance. Although grammar does not necessarily give effectiveness either in speaking or writing, it enables the student to obtain these qualifications— and without it he cannot expect them. As illustrative of the license which the orthodox are permitted to have, or at any rate take, nothing can be more striking than the quotation from the "Christian Institutes" of the Rev. Christopher Wordsworth, D.D., formerly master of Trinity College, Cambridge, appended to the work under notice, and aptly characterised as a first-rate sample of "loose, complicated, ill-arranged, long-drawn sentences."

" First, then, I think that something— not a great deal, (nothing more, indeed, than is already required in some of the individual colleges,)— something ought to be enacted and insisted on under this head, as subject matter for the regular employment of *all* our students, *during* their under-graduate years. And, secondly, I am equally convinced that much of this nature neither *can* or *ought* to be reserved till *after* that under-graduate season,—so, I mean, as to be carried on here, prosecuted within our own walls, and conducted by the university itself; excepting always, in case of such— confessedly in the highest degree important, but, in point of numbers, comparative diminutive portion—as shall have occasion to prolong their stay as members on the foundation, connected with the education of the place, or otherwise engaged officially by the university itself, or the particular societies to which they respectively belong."

Where is the grammarian from Priscian to Doherty that will venture to *parse* this syntactical prodigy ? To disentangle such a gordian knot of involved verbosity would baffle a grammatical Alexander, and his plan alone would succeed, of cutting through, instead of untying the difficulty. Suppose this precious morçeau, which is a sample of all that is original in the four mortal volumes had been pounced upon in an anti-tyranny, anti-tax, anti-religious, or *Movement* publication, would not the jeering have been interminable? How Hunt was persecuted in the "house of the deliberatives" is notorious. How eagerly the small wits of the press would fasten on the least inaccuracy in any of the blasphemy trials, to stigmatise the accused as illiterate, is well known to us all. The career of Mr. Stevenson, the eminent engineer, persevering and energetic as he has proved, exemplifies the difficulties which uninstructed or self-instructed talent encounters, and the rebuff which men of progress experience in the *upper* circles. He thus artlessly relates one of these instances:—

"After planning the line, I had to go to London to give evidence before a committee of the House of Commons. I soon found that a witness-box in Parliament was one of the most disagreeable situations I had ever been placed in. I could not easily find words to make the committee understand my meaning. Some said he's a foreigner.' 'No,' others replied, 'he's mad.'"

A less resolute man would have been put down by these little great people—these wits among lords and lords among wits. There is not a more pestilent fellow than your genteel blackguard, ill-mannered lordling;—the vulgar great, who make up the mob that do the shuffling, coughing, stamping, yelling, hooting, cock-crowing, braying, and other bear-garden practices to *burke* the man who tells truth in rough, homely, unpolished, and uncourtly phraseology. We could afford to pass them over unnoticed did they not prove seriously obstructive in deterring the anti-corruptionist from his most useful exertions. We have then to fortify the struggling reformer with the most effective means of resistance or attack. We may recommend the avoidance of, and teach how to avoid these sneers, or the causes of them, while we reprobate the sneerers. The topic of grammar is not one on which we are to talk of resisting or upsetting, this stupid, yet cunning, conventionality and fashionable domination. We can talk of opposing verbal conventionality when we are prepared to advise, or adopt, the giving up of hats, stocks, shoes and stockings, long-tailed, tight-cut coats, skimping waistcoats, pinched in trousers, and other such inconveniences and inelegancies to which custom has reconciled us. Meantime there is something reasonable, as well as consistent with polite usage, in speaking grammatically—and this of itself is sufficient inducement for the acquisition of the art. The author of "Practical Grammar" goes the length of saying that "that there can be no greater imputation on the intelligence of any man, than that he should talk from the cradle to the tomb, and never talk well." That he should rub on too, without exposing his deficiences is a hopeless expectation, for it is well added—"A person may conceal his ignorance of any other art—but every time he speaks he publishes his ignorance of this."

The propriety, policy, and reasonableness then of the acquisition of grammatical knowledge being assumed as a point fairly established — if it was not even superfluous to support such a view by argument—it remains to state what experience and observation teach—to describe and contrast plans prevalent, and plans desirable.

M. Q. R.

NOTES FROM THE NORTH.

ALL my lectures in the north have been designed to enforce what for two years has been with me a favorite idea—the capability of socialism to build up individual as well as general character, to serve as a complete body of moral, political, and social philosophy; in fine, in the words of Milton, to enable a man 'to perform justly, skilfully, and *magnanimously* all the offices, both public and private, of peace and war." I have been in earnest about this, for seeing the many hindrances that would lie in the way of the wisest of us in carrying out our community projects, and desiring to induce our friends to regard, as they justly may, socialism's benign and practical philosophy as something in itself worthy of esteem, even though ulterior intentions should never be realised.

During half my stay in Manchester I occupied a room in which a former inmate hung himself It was hinted by a pious friend that I, having no religious restraints, should probably follow the same example. But I quieted all apprehension on this score by the assurance that, in my profession, I did not like to be *tied* to any particular *line* of practice.

On Sunday morning inquisitive parties made their appearance at the Hall of Science to satisfy themselves that I do not wear horns, nor carry eyes in my elbows—and little troops of *Oracle* and *Movement* readers, who had travelled from the surrounding towns, presented themselves to talk over the prospects of the *Anti-Persecution Union* and the dissemination of atheism. It was a pleasing sight to behold these humble and hardy men, with whom I had so often shaken hands by letter as Secretary of the Union, and who are accustomed to diminish their hard earnings to help and succour the imprisoned, and to fight the battle of liberty in distant towns.

In Manchester I was introduced to Mrs. A——, the sister of James Bartram, the witness against me at Gloucester. His sister is now, and was then, a very good socialist and member of the branch. She felt acutely the disgrace which her brother brought upon her family through being religious. If this unfortunate man is consistent with his principles, his own sister will become the victim of his piety, another verification of religion's melancholy influence in neutralizing social affections and setting " brother against sister."

I delivered lectures in Stockport, Rochdale and Oldham. At these places I enquired, among other things, how stood religion in the estimation of the usual frequenters of the halls? The answer was, " you may guess that from the kind of lectures you have been desired to deliver." Those relating to the necessary divorce of religion from morality, satisfied me that there existed a very creditable appreciation of the utility of atheism, and that it was believed to be the practical ally of social improvement. When I wrote in recent *Movements* against the *New Moral World's* erroneous views of the bearings of atheism, I did it under the impression that such views were general among socialists, but I am now satisfied that the mistaken sentiments to which I then replied, were far from being reciprocated by the earnest and plain dealing socialists of the north.

I was told by Mr. Kincaid of Rochdale, who was with Mr. M'Neill when apprehended in Campsie, that the Rev. Mr. Lee who occasioned it, had left Campsie in disgrace arising out of that affair. That a meeting of the inhabitants was held, and a resolution passed censuring his conduct in prosecuting the opinions he ought to have answered. This is very interesting. Could Mr. Jeffery transmit to us a copy of the resolution passed, and would he send any other particulars with which he may be acquainted?

The audiences of Oldham were the most crowded and eager of all I addressed. The Oldham people must be descendants of Korah, Dathan and Abiram whom Moses caused to be swallowed up because of their unbelief. The first lecture was, by their own choice, the " Refutation of the Great Argument for the Existence of God, as laid down by Archdeacon Paley, and illustrated in the celebrated Bridgwater Treatises." Three policemen graced the assembly by order of the magistrates, and there is hope that before this time the whole bench have been benefited by my labours. I was taken into some of the factories where men, women and children work 14 and 15 hours a-day in *hot air*, and I thought I discovered the secret of SWING. Some of the poor things are so parched and dried by the heat, that they are reduced to the condition of lucifer matches, till at last when they rub against the door they ignite and set fire to the building. *Swing* is of local origin—of purely home manufacture.

I visited an old lady in this district who, though eighty-two, looks for the weekly arrival of the *Movement* with the regularity and eagerness of a young devotee. She is the oldest atheist of her sex that I have met with. She is still hale, abounds in lively humour, and manifests quite a motherly solicitude for the welfare of young unbelievers. I took farewell of the north at a supper given by a coterie of hearty friends in Oldham on July 18.

G. J. H.

PATERSON'S "PRISON THOUGHTS."

[*Extracts from Correspondence.*]

General Prison, Perth.

" DEAR HOLYOAKE,

" Your parcel was duly received by the chaplain. It is now riding quarantine in the office, and will be given to me at my resurrection. The governor has brought me some works of a less objectionable character than those you sent; so you are now relieved from further anxiety.

" Every ' dog has its day ' was the remark of some extraordinary wise-acre, now for mine; — the *Spectator* puffs your ' Grammar,' and you are lifted up about that. What think you is the opinion of the chaplain on that production? ' That it is an utterly worthless book.' How do you feel now—cut?

" My health, which several enquire after, is tolerable—how could it be otherwise, when the winds of heaven are not allowed to visit me too roughly? Unlike ' Alfred,' my time is divided into two great portions—one to sleep, another to work, and a small trifle to eat and read in.

" P. S. — Very temperate in all my habits.

" Could you not say what is likely to be the result of the prosecution?—whether the law is likely to be altered, or whether there must be a few more victims? Am I likely to be sent back here shortly after my liberation, &c.? These matters are now becoming interesting as I am beginning to build ' castles ' for the future.

" Letters.—G. J. Holyoake . 2
Liddle 1
Emery, Leicester . 1
Finlay, ditto . . . 1
Ryall 2
M. Roalfe 2

" DEAR RYALL,

" My friend ' Western's ' misfortunes affect me. I can never forget, that when all London stood aloof, he stuck by me like a brick to the last, and when I was a stranger he took me in. I gave him a knife for a keepsake; will he send me a lock of his hair?

"Why am I, in my cell, like the Bishop of Exeter in Parliament? Because 'I have no eye for strangers.' Without detracting from my old friend the Bishop, I think my saying is the most literal.

"The half of my time is now up—held a little *levee* that day, presented myself—made a neat speech on the occasion, which I encored—drank all your healths in a cup of water, felt rather giddy, fell, head first in conformity to the law of gravity, jumped up again—so 'don't be alarmed, I'm not hurt.'

"My health keeps good, my spirits better, and look forward to the time when I shall mix amongst you all, and help to kick up a row. I have lately been reading some of 'Keith's Prophecies,' and should like, if it is not already done, to go a tour through the land of Edom, which he says, '*never can be done.*' Will you speak to W. J. B. on this subject?

"Regards to all,
"I am, yours truly,
"T. PATERSON."

ANALOGICAL SPECULATIONS.

On the analogy doctrine which makes us so much superior to the beast here, and therefore hereafter, an argument might be engrafted, that as there is as much difference between the wise and the foolish as between man and the beast, the unseen prerogatives of the one human sort must be higher than those of the other.

The world's grandees—the rich, the noble, the powerful, the learned—might draw similar conclusions from the superiority of their condition and the immeasurable distance between them and the common herd. Are our more refined sensations, higher powers, and more comprehensive faculties and knowledge given us for nothing? Shall they not distinguish us hereafter as well as here. Are the rulers and controllers of earth's affairs to meet no more fitting and discriminating destiny than that of the slaves, serfs, and peasants who vegetate on its surface? We live like gods, they might say—the rest of the world like brutes—can our fates be alike? No! the finer order of sensations, those mental refinements have not been given us for nothing here, but will be eternally prolonged and perfected elsewhere. The rich and luxurious, those who have enjoyed the dignities on earth, unwearied of good things, have only their appetite sharpened for that eternity which depicts them as never ceasing and always increasing. While the laborious part may look forward to the end of life, as rest from toil. Death brings them certain advantages here, if it has nothing to give beyond the grave. The higher classes have everything to lose, and therefore it is that acted upon by hope and despair, they uphold religion and attend churches. Though in youth they may have doubted the exalted nature of one part of the human species over the other, their subsequent attainment of greatness, honours, and homage would foster the doctrine of the endless progression of individualism instead of that of mankind at large. They might be as much blinded to the common characteristics between man and man, as others are to those which approximate man and the brutes; and might with no less impropriety give to a part only of animated nature—themselves—a perpetuity of blessings or a redress of wrongs, denying these privileges to all besides.

The materialist's acquiescence in the facts of nature, if too infinite for his elucidation, dispenses equality and justice amongst all life. All matter as far as he can see, is in common, and therefore in the eternally multiplied forms of animated life, the same conditions seem proportionably dealt out to all. His benevolence, as far as he can exert its influence, not only extends to the futurity of all of his own species, but the greatest amount of happiness and least misery of all animated nature. These materialistic notions seem to have had their effect amongst eastern nations, who in all their systems of religion and jurisprudence, have made provisions for the animal as much as for the man. Christians impressed with the belief of a future state, reserved it for themselves alone; one life for the beast, and another for man. God in their opinion having lived amongst them, taken their nature upon him, and omitted to mention the brute creation, they treat the rest of animated matter with much greater indifference than they showed to them before they came to a knowledge of their own souls. It is notorious that in Europe, and all Christian countries, the greatest cruelty, and unnecessary torture, is exercised upon the brute creation. To "do as you would be done unto" is confined to those who have a monopoly of a future life, the boasted christian maxim that was extended to all, was restricted, by the coming of a God, to a part of animated nature. He was a curse for us, says St. Paul, but he forgot to take off the curse from the rest of matter, and perhaps it is necessary that he come back and take the nature of the beast upon him. He himself did not know what it was "to do as one would be done unto," until he had thrown off his own immortal, and taken the mortal nature upon him, until he had experienced life and death in its worst features, and found the common lot of mortality which he himself was said to have imposed upon human existence, was not so agreeable. He was glad to hurry off to his father in heaven, and promised soon to return to raise up all dead bodies from the grave, as exhibited in his own resurrection. He has forgotten his promise to "do as he would be done unto," he has neither come himself, nor raised up others. Probably he had not consulted with his anatomical and chemical councillors, who would tell him that the fact as he had represented it, was impossible, and the expectation of his coming must remain a point of "faith with the foolish," or he might be told that he had forgotten his commission, and that not having in his memory the rest of animated nature, he had left the condition of the world worse than he found it, unless he would return and take upon himself all the fortunes of animal and vegetable existence. Probably he declined becoming a cab or hackney coach horse, tender lamb or veal, with a chance of descending into the stomachs instead of the tombs of our Arimatheans.

Much of our information in morals depepends upon analogy, and there is no good reason why it should not be applied to religion, but, if it was applied in spiritual, with the same honesty as in temporal matters, the firmness of religious faith would often suffer. Perhaps it was forseeing this which induced Lord Brougham in the dialogues introduced into his Natural Theology, to warn religious disputants against climbing the dangerous heights of analogy. W. J. B.

PETITIONING.
[*Extract from a Letter.*]

I AM glad you do not forget the petitions; every petition presented to the House of Commons is recorded in the votes which are sent to each member for his perusal; it also appears in the weekly report of petitions classed under heads. Those documents are received in all public rooms and come very high, say £19 or £20 per annum. This will shew you the advantage of petitioning for the purpose of giving publicity, which is a great point gained if nothing more is attained. I would say, then, get up as many petitions as possible, if it only serves to make poor *Paterson's case* known to every member of parliament. But it will do more, it will enlighten every individual who is in the habit of attending reading rooms, and in Belfast alone there are 500 to 1000 individuals, in Ireland 100,000. It is advisable that each petition should be given to different members and presented separately, in order to bring the question as often as possible before the public, and it is the number of petitions that will avail and not the number of signatures to the petitions. It was a sad mistake in Feargus O'Connor presenting all the universal suffrage petitions at one time, instead of annoying parliament by frequently bringing the subject before their eyes at different times. It was by doing this that the Catholics succeeded in getting emancipation, and it is by proceeding in this manner that we will make our way in a perverse and stubborn generation. W. B. B.

SOCIETY OF PROPAGANDISTS, ESTABLISHED FOR PROMOTING THE CAUSE OF ABSOLUTE FREEDOM OF EXPRESSION.
"Ceci tuera cela."

THAT the great obstacle to free enquiry, and to the consequent improvement, progression, and emancipation of the human intellect—is superstition, the offspring of ignorance.

It is this truism that has suggested the formation of a society for the purpose of removing the incubus which priests, of all creeds and ages, have imposed upon mankind as the means whereby to thwart and prostrate the progressive energies of the human understanding.

The committee of formation of this society feel no disparagement as to the limited sphere of its direct action, but rather calculate upon its indirect influence.

The object they have in view, is to incite a free and unbiassed investigation of those principles which are deemed the *natural* basis of morality, rather by exciting doubt in the mind, than by propounding any ultimate doctrine as the true result of reason.

The committee, in pursuing this, the course pointed out by the school of scepticism, do so from a firm conviction, that the excitement of doubt gives birth to free inquiry; and, relying on the salutary influence of free investigation, they hope to awaken the slaves of superstition from the lethargy into which they are plunged; to rouse their dormant faculties to a knowledge of their true position as thinking, intelligent beings; to unloose the chains by which poor degraded humanity is fettered; and, by a promulgation of morals derived from nature's materialities, to perform their part in the overthrow of despotism and priestcraft. They employ these means as the surer policy to further the dissemination and adoption of principles, which, though for the present veiled, will ultimately appear as the regenerating ones of man's social and moral condition

The committee consider the sudden removal of those restraints which ignorance and superstition have necessarily imposed upon men, as the means to keep him within the pale of moral action, a course highly to be deprecated, *unless* a substitute more simple and just in its operation and more in accordance with reason be found; they feel confident, however, such a substitute does exist; and, therefore, it will be their constant endeavour to instil into the minds of those who come within the sphere of their operations, ideas and principles which, when duly reflected upon, will give to their converts an appetite for other rules of morals than those laid down in the traditional records which form the bases of all supernatural religions.

For the carrying out of the objects stated in the preceding, the committee of formation determine on employing the following means.

1. The collécting of the works of authors who have written in favour of freedom of opinion and expression, for the purpose of forming a library for gratuitous circulation among individuals who may from time to time be recommended to the society by its agents.

II. The encouraging and aiding the formation of discussion-classes, and for giving tone to the sentiments there expressed, and the principles investigated.

III. The publication, at intervals, and distribution of tracts and circulars intended for the promulgation of the universal principles of nature, upon which should be founded those laws which govern man, as a moral, social, and intellectual being. These publications will consist either of original matter, or comprise selections from expensive and voluminous works.

IV. The co-operating with other societies having the same objects in view; so, by affording and demanding mutual succour, to accelerate in every expedient way the dawn of a new age, characterised by the dethronement of that monster trinity — *Superstition, priestcraft, tyranny;* the domination of liberty; and the universal spread of knowledge and philosophy.

London, 16th June, 1844.

PUBLICATION OF OPINION.—If an opinion which contradicts the most important institutions of society should not be promulgated, we shall sanctify the inquisition of Spain, and every crime hallowed by public institution all over the world; human thought, according to such notions, is irredeemably enslaved by civil, religious, and domestic institutions, and is only to be emancipated in affairs of little moment.—*Stewart.*

PROVIDENTIAL INTERPOSITION. — The *Liverpool Journal* tells us that Mr. William Backhouse of Darlington, who died so suddenly in the meeting-house of the Society of Friends, had arranged to go out to Hamburgh in the Manchester steamer, which was lost on the voyage, and that there is every reason to believe that his sudden death was the means of saving him from being—drowned!

HINT TO THE HEAVEN-BOUND.
THE following we would rather have named *Christian* rapacity, seeing that the practice came in and was introduced not by the nation, but the system.

ANGLICAN RAPACITY.—On the 22nd June, the coat of the Catholic priest of Morpeth, Northumberland (the Rev. G. A. Lowe), was sold publicly, by auction, at the Market-cross, for 25s., amount of church rates due by him, with costs, on their recovery. The Protestant rector of Morpeth, in whose name this violence was committed, is son of Earl Grey, the brother of Lord Howick, whose living is upwards of £1,600 in value, although two-thirds of his parishioners are the flock of other shepherds. He it is who takes the coat off the back of the Catholic priest, whose annual income is under £100, and who, out of that mite, spends much upon the poor.—*Tablet.*

[Will the *Tablet* please to inform us if the skinned priest obeyed the instructions in his master's sermon on the mount—" And if any man will sue thee at the law, and take away thy coat, let him have thy cloak also." What a splendid opportunity of pegging on a notch for heaven! "Blessed are those which are persecuted for righteousness-sake, for theirs is the kingdom of heaven." How singularly fortunate then are these martyrs, since their sprats of martyrdom enable them to catch such fat salmon of recompence. We'd be stript to the skin on the same calculation.] M. Q. R.

DR. FOSSATI'S ADDRESS
To the Phrenological Society of Paris.

MY attention has been drawn to the able address of Dr. Fossati of Paris, on "Education, and the Contest between the French Clergy and the University," which appears in the *Zoist* for this month. A cautious friend asks me whether the doctor does not adopt a more effective and a less objectionable mode of winning over the christian world than our plain way of inculcating atheism. The passage which gratifies our friend is this:—

"Who dare to maintain that god is impotent? And if he is not impotent, how can we believe that he requires from man an exclusive worship? If man on earth adores and venerates god with different forms of worship, it is because god wills it, and because it enters into his impenetrable views that things should be so. Do we not see that the same god who sees it good to be worshipped according to the forms of the Israelites, raised up amongst them another faith, which is established upon the ruins of the former? And who shall say, that in the great course of progress upon which we are entered, it does not form part of his plan to establish a new one upon the ruins of that one which exists? The symptoms of such transformation have already manifested themselves clearly to the reflecting observer. For christianity, such as it has been made for us at the present day, is very different from what it was at its origin, and no longer resembles, in any respect, what it was in the first ages of its institution."

My opinion is, that the doctor is joking, and intends by sly irony to drive the religious to the conclusion that their god is "impotent." Supposing the doctor to be serious, his reasoning stands thus:—god is worshipped now in a different manner to what he was. Christianity is a more rational religion than Israelism. Men have set up new creeds and improved systems of faith. If god does not approve these they must be supposed to exist in spite of god, and against his will, which makes god to be "impotent." But what is this but relapsing into the pernicious doctrine of Pope—that "whatever is, is right? If "to venerate god with different forms of worship" is right because it is permitted—then is the daily triumph of villany right because it is permitted. According to this reasoning the christian may go on as if no god existed. He may attempt what he pleases, and if he succeeds with some new freak of faith, he may be sure it is right, for success is made the test of its propriety. If it succeeds, and is supposed to be wrong, it proves that god is "impotent." Sophistry, such as this, will impose but upon few. It would be far less inconsistent to believe that god is impotent, or that there is no god, than to take such a rule as a moral guide. We must reiterate our perpetual sentiment, that from no theory of religion can satisfactory rules of moral action be drawn. Dr. Fossati tells us in one line of god's "impenetrable views," and in the next, that "god sees it good to be worshipped according to the forms of the Israelites." Unless the doctor penetrates what he tells us is *impenetrable*, how does he know that "god sees it good to be worshipped according to Israelitism" or Fossatism?

My objection relates solely to that part of Dr. Fossati's address which I have quoted—the other portions are powerful contributions to the cause of irreligious humanity, and command high appreciation. G. J. H.

SOCIAL AND POLITICAL PARELLEL.—Society is produced by our wants—Government by our folly.—*Law of Reason.*

THOUGHT IN BONDAGE.—To offend nobody, we should have no ideas but those of the world.—*Helvetius.*

THE SCEPTIC'S DEATH.—Mr. Montgomery describes the death-bed of a Sceptic with what we suppose is meant for energy:—

"See how he shudders at the thought of death!
What doubt and horror hang upon his breath,
The gibbering teeth, glazed eye, and marble limb.
Shades from the tomb stalk out and stare at him."

A man as stiff as marble, shuddering and gibbering violently, would certainly present so curious a spectacle that the shades, if they came in his way, might well stare.—*Edinburgh Review.*

NOTICES.

OUR weekly half-sheet is inadequate to our purposes—we are quite unable, in the space, to do justice to our correspondents as well as to our cause. We expect that until we are enabled to extend our arrangements, we shall be credited with a just appreciation of the numerous favours received. Until we can double the present size our correspondents must accept intentions for performances.—We are obliged at present to resort to a most ruthless process of condensation.

THE remainder of Mr. Gillespie's Reply to Mr. Southwell's Papers is in hand, and will (the first portion of it) appear in the next or subsequent number.

FOR the convenience of Lancashire friends who applied in several places to Mr. Holyoake for back numbers of the *Oracle of Reason*, a quantity of all the numbers not yet out of print have been forwarded to Mr. George Smith, 11, Greengate, Salford. All parties in those districts desiring to complete volumes or obtain particular numbers for distribution, can be supplied by Mr. Smith as readily as at the *Movement* office. Mr. Smith has kindly undertaken this duty for Lancashire. The proceeds of the *Oracles* sold go to the funds of the Anti-Persecution Union.

RECEIVED.

FROM Mr. Macara of Edinburgh a M.S., purporting to be his opening speech in the discussion with Mr. Southwell.

THE Conclusion of the Critique by H. T. on Dr. Macnab's Review of Robert Owen's system.

THE *Northern Star*, which contains a spirited and excellent debate raised by Mr. Councillor Hobson, on the right of FREE DISCUSSION, in the public market-place.

THE *Cheltenham Free Press*, containing, in extracts from the Irish *Monitor* and English *Churchman*, an exposé and condemnation of the Rev. Mr. Nangle for vending obscene prints. The scribe of the latter journal has some impertinences about the Holywell-street operations, concerning which he is either a libeller or an ignoramus.

THE *Scotch Reformer's Gazette*, of July 13 and 20.

FROM Mr. King a series of pamphlets, tracts, cards, &c. on *Currency*, a subject now occupying a large share of public attention, and to which this gentleman has indefatigably devoted himself on ultra principles.—We must look into this branch of reform.

" A Letter to the Rev. John C. Barrett," of Birmingham—by S. Kempson.

GEORGE ADAM'S Letter to T. S. Duncombe, M.P., and Petition to Parliament to abrogate the Blasphemy Laws and release Thomas Paterson, with Mr. Duncombe's Reply that he has presented the petition.

A FRAGMENT about " Staggering an Infidel," of which we can make neither head nor tail.

TO CORRESPONDENTS.

THE *Movement* can be obtained of Mr. Heywood, Oldham-street, and of Mr. J. R. Cooper, 72, Bridge-street, Manchester; of Mr. George Smith, Salford; of Mr. Ephraim Moss, Brookbottom, Mossley; in Rochdale, Stockport, Oldham, indeed in every town in the north, unless we are wrongly informed. Some one liberal agent can be found in every place. Readers who find any difficulty in procuring it will oblige us by sending word.

J. H. is entitled to be heard, sharp as he is upon our correspondent—but he must first drop the incognito. No doubt he is sharp enough to understand this—*verbum sat.*

Mr. P. makes an ingenious proposition for lithographing and publishing biblical indelicacies, for which he would assist with funds. We put it to him—are indecencies to pass current because sacred? Shall those who say " Maximise Morals, Minimise Religion " lend themselves to corruption, however sanctified and authorised? In *thus* bringing sacred things into contempt do we not do irreparable injury to the young, by blunting the fine edge of early susceptibilities, rudely destroying the freshness and bloom of that rational innocence, which has been uncontaminated by holy horrors and pious prefanities?

W. KING says—before we can destroy *Priestcraft* we must destroy the influence of *Gold* that feeds it. " Banks of Industry," he thinks, alone capable of destroying the " Kings of Gold." We will not quarrel about precedence. If he can show us a better way we'll follow him.

R. LAZARUS, a Jew, relates some discreditable instances of persecutions by his family and tribe, on account of his change of opinion from theism to atheism. Can bigotted jews be expected to be superior to bigotted christians? Is not the contaminating god-belief common to both. R. L. must set off the self-satisfaction against the social penalty for honesty.

MR. SOUTHWELL informs us that in his discussion on the *god question* with Mr. Malcolm M'Neil he is the challenged, not challenger—he lays stress on this—saying that from the incompetency of previous disputants it has been insinuated that he has *hired his opponents.*

THE correspondent (we cannot decipher the signature) who quotes from the *Cork Examiner*, a vile instance of oppression by the guardians of a Poor-union, will oblige us by communicating name and address. We can explain how he can serve the *Movement* still more effectively.

G. HAMMOND severely animadverts on the " Eye of Superstition " of the " Old Friends "—in fact he goes near to poking it quite out. Will try what room we can make for him.

QUITE agree with T. A. B. Will he look us out some more, *according to sample,* that we may make a batch of them?

Subscription to the Funds of the *Movement*, by Cosmopolite . 1 10 0

SUBSCRIPTIONS TO THE ANTI-PERSECUTION UNION.

Per Mr. G. Smith, Salford.

Messrs. E. Hyde, H. Walker	1	0
" C. C., S. Walker .	1	0
" J. Wells, J. Dodd .	1	0
" G. Osbaldiston, Mr. Sanders, and M. Wright	1	6
C. C., per Card 23 . . .	7	6
Edward Hyde, per Card 20	2	0
H. S., Mr. Hyde, per Cards	1	0
Thomas Walch . . .	1	0

To Sale of Scotch Trials, per G. Smith, Salford 2 8

Mr. Ward, per Mr. Thomas Martin, Stockport 1 0

Per Mr. Kincaid, Rochdale.

Malcolm Kincaid . . .	1	0
Thomas Moorcroft . . .	1	0
Edward Waff	1	0
Joseph Etherington . .	0	6

G. J. H., *Sec.*

Printed and Published by G. J. HOLYOAKE, 40, Holywell-street, Strand, Saturday, July 27, 1844.

THE MOVEMENT
And Anti=Persecution Gazette.

"Maximize morals, minimize religion."—BENTHAM.

No. 34.   EDITED BY G. JACOB HOLYOAKE, ASSISTED BY M. Q. RYALL.   PRICE 1½d

INSTRUCTION — RATIONAL AND SCHOLASTIC.
II.

GRAMMAR is the art, or science, or both, which has to do with WORDS—being grammarians, we know how to write, utter and put together our words with correctness. When we talk, as some do, of grammar teaching us *things* we get into a rigmarole —when we expatiate on the elegancies of grammatical construction, we are beyond the mark. In either case we are out of the sphere of grammar—the one of the above branches of knowledge is *natural philosophy*, the other is *style*, in literary composition. A man may be an excellent grammarian and yet firmly believe that Joshua stopt the moon in its race round the earth—he may believe in "the four corners of the earth," and that air, earth, fire, and water, are elements; he may, on the other hand, also predict an eclipse, measure the distances and track the orbits of the planets; he may analyze, decompose, and trace to their simplest constituents, the mineral, vegetable, and animal worlds, and yet not know how to put a dozen words together in an accurate and intelligible manner. So, also, he may be an excellent grammarian, and write a dry, correct, and technical sentence without force, beauty, or vivacity, barren of point and sentiment, disconnected, involved, without a scintillation of wit, one felicity of expression, or the adornment of a single grace. Grammar is, nevertheless, the stepping-stone to all these acquirements—the instrument by which they are to be reached, when the tongue and the pen are prompted by the requisite knowledge, and improved by the requisite practice.

These introductory remarks might appear to some superfluous—I think otherwise. The author of "Practical Grammar"—who is now as fairly liable to critical animadversion from me as any other author—assists in giving currency to this over-rating of grammar, the claiming for it more than is its due. He quotes, approvingly, the observations of an acute and able man, the author of that admirable work *the School-master*, which go to identify grammar with natural philosophy or physics. He also infers that grammar will teach good and elegant writing—I deny both positions. As already said, grammar treats not of the nature of things, but words —it teaches not effective or elegant, but correct speaking or writing.

How, now, is grammar to be acquired. If I were asked by the Hampshire "Harmony" people, for example, who are professing to instruct rationally, how shall we teach our little embryo community to speak grammatically? This would be my first dictum— Throw away all the "Grammars." What then? Let the pupils hear nothing but grammatical speaking and read nothing but grammatical diction — their speaking and composition will follow their models. Is this too plain, simple, and easy? Is there too little "mystery, mixture of error, and fear of *grammarians*" in this, to please the educationalists? Whether or not, it can't be helped—it is the way of things, and schools will not alter them, although they may send out parrots, and ninnies, and dullards. Children, I say it advisedly, are practically either grammatical proficients or ignoramuses, beween their sucking and their lollipop days. Their mothers and companions are their teachers, and their proper and legitimate teachers too. Children do not learn from being told, dogmatised or preceptorised—they learn from seeing and hearing—to imitate what they see and hear they need no telling. To prevent them imitating what they see and hear no telling will suffice—nothing short of putting out their eyes, and stopping up their ears. The instincts of curiosity and imitation, which we have to work upon, are stronger than our preceptoral nonsense. Children become *artists* while we are making sciences to teach them. Art ever has, and ever will, precede science in the most important business of life—in that which every body learns. They learn to do it first, and the rules for doing it after. If children had to wait for our rules before they walked and talked, a very pretty set of cerebral and bodily cripples we should have in the world. The most difficult and important acquisitions in life — those of walking and talking are acquired without our rules—and yet we can never sufficiently overload, with arbitrary complications of rules, those little unfortunates who are placed under our sway to be taught far more easily-acquired arts.

Knowing the infernal drudgery of the thing—my horror is so great of a school book—that I would almost as soon pitch it out of the window as I would a Bible or a Prayer-book — if I found it among children who could read.

The French pronounce studied *éloges* or panegyrics on their great men—were I to compose an *éloge* upon literature, I would say some *school-boys* have become proficients in it. So powerfully attractive has it been to some that in spite of school scourging, school drudgery, and school brutalization, they have become members of the republic of letters! How thoroughly Milton knew the wretched routine—else how should he have described it so faithfully? Even after the new scenes and associations, which his travels had opened—after years and experience had ripened his judgment — with all his impressiveness of manner, and gorgeousness of diction, he thus pours forth his sentiments:—" I deem it to be an old error of universities, not yet well recovered from the scholastic grossness of barbarous ages, that instead of beginning with arts most easy, and those be such as are most obvious to the sense, they present their young immatriculated novices, at first coming, with the most intellective abstractions of logic and metaphysics; so that they, having but newly left those grammatic flats and shallows, where they stuck unreasonably to learn a few words with lamentable construction, and now, on the sudden, transported under another climate, to be tossed and turmoiled by their unballasted wits, in fathomless and unquiet deeps of controversy, do for the most part grow into hatred and contempt of learning, mocked and deluded all this while with ragged notions and babblements, while they expected worthy and delightful knowledge."

Old Montaigne, the father of the celebrated essayist, though no scholar himself, knew, or was wise enough to learn from able men, how scholars were made. He wished his son to have the advantages without the drudgery of a liberal education, and instead of sending him to be stultified at school, there to have drifted on "grammatical flats and shallows, and to have stuck unreasonably to learn a few words with miserable construction;" he engaged the most qualified persons to *talk* Latin with the young Montaigne. No scholastic "grammar rules and exercises" here—no fruitless attempts to drive in Latin—the young scholar took to it as he did to leap-frog or peg-top. In the practice and theory of the Montaignes, father and son, we may partly trace a rough draft of the sytem Rousseau elaborated so well, more than a century after.

Are "grammars" then utterly useless? I may be asked by some who have had but a glance at this subject. By no means. A grammar is an absolutely needful *book of reference*. A comprehensive grammar contains model-groups, and classifies the words with whose use we *are already familiar*—and gives model examples of the words in our language, which change when in new positions, and under different relations, with respect to each other—which changes we *had already learned to make*. These processes are technically called *Etymology* and *Syntax*, the first of which treats of the various sorts of words, as *nouns, pronouns, adjectives, verbs, adverbs*—their changes, as *declensions* and *conjugations*, and their arrangement into sentences. All these processes we had performed over our cakes and sugar-sticks, our dolls and hoops, before we knew or heard of, the soon to be dreaded sound— "grammar," and the beauty of it is, that like the *bourgeois gentilhomme* in Molière. who had been talking prose all his life without knowing it we had been declining, and conjugating, and performing all sorts of grammatical operations, so delightfully technicalised for the utter obfuscation of the young brain—all through our childish days, without knowing it.

We, then, find a grammar a capital book to tell us what we have been doing—and how to do the same sort of thing in instances where we may be at a loss—and if it is rationally and philosophically written, it will tell us why we say such and such a thing in preference to any thing else; but for mercy's sake save the innocent child from learning *grammatical* speaking and writing—from a "grammar."

Another use of a grammar—not one of the school sort—is to give young fellows, or grown persons, who have been ungrammatically brought up, examples of the appropriate changes in words, and their proper distribution in sentences, *during and after* careful observation of correct speaking and writing in others, and continuous practice of both themselves—without these two contemporaneous courses, I tell them, they may as well shut up the grammar book, even though the most rational and least scholastic in the world.

I like Holyoake's Grammar, though differing very much as to the propriety of some of his terms and classifications — it is so completely the anti-pode of a school-book. The abominable old pedantry—the endless prolixity—the multitudinous exceptions out-numbering the rules—the pedagogueish sententiousness—the intricate subdivisions—and irrational technical jargon are absent from this "Practical Grammar," and by so much the more likely is it to be practical, or rather to approach, or further, facilitate the practical. For, be it remembered, the truly practical is what the student does *without* the grammar, on reference to, or by direction of, the grammar if you please—since we have got hold of a rationalised grammar—but by all means through individual effort in the way of speaking and writing first — leaving the rules till afterwards.

A great number of common errors are pointed out in "Practical Grammar;" condensation, brevity, and simplifiation, are discernible in every page, and the hints and suggestions for literary composition are particularly valuable to inexperienced writers. Some good counsel is interspersed for the promotion of self-improvement.

I would add, that a tolerably safe guide for study is afforded by the school-grammars, if you only take the trouble of *reversing* them. Thus you are told to make yourself perfect master of all their rules and examples before you attempt composition. I tell you to *compose first*, beginning with the most simple forms of expression. They direct you to commit their rules to memory; I specially counsel you *never to commit* a rule to memory—whatever you want thoroughly to understand, master *in your own terms.* You are presented with vocabularies or spelling list of words from one syllable to seven syllables, I specially caution every body against these abominable vocabularies—the little miserables who have the slavery to perform of thumbing these vile lists by the inch from page to page daily, are commonly spoilt for life as to spelling. If they should happen to escape early enough from this infliction, they may hit upon the simple expedient of practising the spelling, taken *as it comes*, from any favourite book, by spelling aloud from it—also by copying first; afterwards, writing the same from dictation, then referring to the original—as well as by short, simple, and familiar essays and letters, looking out the spelling in the dictionary.

M. Q. R.

PROGRESSION.—The true wisdom of all ages hath been to review at fit periods those errors, defects, or excesses, that have insensibly crept into the public administration; to brush the dust off the wheels, and oil them again, or, if it be found advisable, to choose a set of new ones.—*Marvell.*

INSTRUCTIONS OF THE CHIEF OF THE CAPUCHINS AT RAGUSA, TO BROTHER PEDICULOSO, ON HIS DEPARTURE FOR THE HOLY LAND. BY VOLTAIRE.

I.

[These "Instructions," though originally translated for an American paper, and thence transferred to Mr. Carlyle's *Lion*, are sufficiently valuable to bear re-publication, especially as it is nearly twenty years since they appeared in print in this country, and the rising generation—not of "Infidels," but of divines, "tractarian, evangelical" or others —may derive some excellent hints from their perusal. Though written for Romish, they will be found equally serviceable by all other Christians.]

THE first thing you do, brother Pediculoso, will be to visit Paradise, where God created Adam and Eve, so well known among the ancient Greeks and Romans, the Persians, the Medes, the Egyptians, and the Syrians, that not a single writer of all those people has ever mentioned it. It will not be difficult to find; for it is situated at the sources of the Euphrates, the Tigres, the Araxes, and the Nile; and though the sources of the Nile and the Euphrates are 1000 leagues from each other, that is nothing; you have only to ask the way of the Capuchins at Jerusalem, and you cannot possibly miss it.

Do not forget to eat some of the fruit of the tree of knowledge of good and evil; for it must be confessed that you are a little stupid and somewhat ill natured; when you shall have eaten of that fruit, you will become a very good and a very wise man. Perhaps you may be uneasy respecting the consequences; for in the book of Genesis it is said expressly, "*In the day that thou eatest thereof, thou shalt surely die.*" Never fear, my dear brother, but eat away; Adam ate, and lived 930 years afterwards.

As to the serpent, which was "the most subtle of all the beasts of the field," he is chained, you know, somewhere in Upper Egypt; several of our missionaries have seen him. Bochart will tell you what language he spoke in, and the song with which he seduced Eve; but take care that you are not seduced too. Then you will find out the ox that guarded the gate of the garden, for you are of course aware that *cherub* in Hebrew signifies an ox; and that is the reason why Ezekiel calls the king of Tyre a cherub. Vide St. Ambrose, the abbe Rupert, and, above all, the cherub Calmet.

Examine carefully the mark which the Lord put upon Cain. See whether it is upon the cheek or the shoulder. He deserved to be branded for killing his brother; but, inasmuch as Romulus, Richard III., Lous XI, and hundreds of others have done the same, it is a matter of no great consequence whether the murderer is pardoned or not, especially as the whole race is damned for an apple.

As you intend to push on as far as the city of Enoch, which Cain founded in the land of Nod, you will be particular in ascertaining the exact number of masons, carpenters, blacksmiths, weavers, hat makers, painters, wool carders, labourers, herdsmen and shepherds, handicraftsmen, judges, and jailors he had in his employ, when there were but four or five persons on the face of the earth.

Enoch was buried in that city which his grandfather Cain built; but he is still alive. Find him out; ask him how he does, and give him our compliments.

From thence you will pass between the legs of the giants who were begotten of the angels upon the daughters of men, and you will present to them the works of the reverend father Don Calmet; but be careful to speak civilly to them, for they don't understand raillery.

You will go to the top of Mount Ararat to see the remains of the Ark. Ascertain the correctness of its dimensions, as given by the illustrious Le Pelletier. Measure the mountain carefully, and then measure St. Gothard and the Pichincha in Peru. Calculate, with Woodward and Whiston, how many oceans it would take to cover them, and to rise fifteen cubits above. You will also have the goodness to bring us, in the original Hebrew, the text which places the deluge in the year of the creation of the world 1656; in the Samaritan, that which says the year 2309, and that of the Septuagint which makes it 2262; and to reconcile these three texts.

Present our respects to our father Noah, who planted the vine. The Greeks and the Asiatics were so unfortunate as to know nothing of him, but the Jews could boast of their descent from him in a right line. Ask him to let you see the covenant which God made with him and the beasts. We are grieved that he should get drunk, and warn you not to follow his example. Above all, get a memorandum of the precise time when Gomer, the grandson of Japhet, began to reign in Europe, which he found thickly peopled. This is a historical fact to verify.

Find out, if you can, what has become of Cainan, the Son of Arphaxad, so celebrated by Septuagint, and of whom the Vulgate says nothing. Beg of him to conduct you to the Tower of Babel, and see if the remains of that tower correspond with the dimensions given by the reverend father Kircher.

From the Tower of Babel you will go to Ur in Chaldea, and you will inquire of the descendants of Abraham the potter, why he left that fertile country to go in search of a tomb at Hebron, and to buy corn at Memphis, why he made his wife pass for his sister, and what he got by that contrivance; but, above all, learn, if you can, what cosmetics she used to make her look handsome at the age of ninety. Ascertain whether she made use of rose or lavender water as a perfume, when she arrived at the courts of the king of Egypt and of the king of Gerar; for these things are essential to our salvation.

You know that the Lord made a contract with Abraham to give to him and his descendants all the countries from the Nile to the Euphrates. Ascertain the exact reasons why that contract has not been fulfilled.

While you are in Egypt, find out where the horses came from which Pharoah sent into the Red Sea in pursuit of the Hebrews; for, all those animals having perished in the sixth and seventh plagues, certain infidels have pretended that Pharoah had no cavalry. See the book of Exodus, of which Heredotus, Thucydides, Xenophon, Polybius, Livy, and all the Egyptian writers make such particular mention.

We will say nothing of the exploits of Joshua the successor of Moses, nor the moon which he made to stop at mid-day in the valley of Ajalon, and the sun which stood still upon Gibeon. These are trifles which happen every day, and not worth taking any trouble about.

But there is a matter of infinitely more consequence to morals, and which would contribute essentially to our improvement in honesty, humanity, and justice—I mean the history of the Jewish kings. Ascertain exactly how many assassinations they committed. Some fathers of the church compute them at 580; others at 970; it is important to know the true amount. You will understand me to allude only to those cases where the murdered were near relatives of the murderers, for, as to the others, they are innumerable. Nothing can be more edifying than a true account of all the murders committed in the name of the Lord: it would serve as an excellent commentary upon the sermons on brotherly love.

TO THE RIGHT HON. SIR JAMES GRAHAM, Bart., AND HER MAJESTY'S MINISTERS.

[Arguments drawn from christianity are by no means *Movement* favourites. They are never certain. What one man interprets to be christianity another utterly denies. But, since so indefatigable a reformer as Mr. Trevelyan is disposed to think christian logic useful, it would almost imply intolerance not to permit him to reason in his own way, therefore for once we present our readers with the following letter from his pen. The article is already in the hands of the government.—Ed. of M.]

Newcastle, Tyne, July 22.
"We should say to every individual, remember thy dignity as a man."

GENTLEMEN.—I do not ask as a favour, but I demand as an *act of justice*, the immediate liberation of Thomas Paterson, at present confined in the Penitentiary, Perth, for the *unintelligible* crime of blasphemy; an *imaginary* crime more severely dealt with than the crime of murder is to the duellist, when his brother christian meets death by his revengeful hand.

Christianity, according to the opinion of the judges appointed by you, is the "law of the land," but the conduct of the men composing the government of Britain, is in direct variance to what we are told are the commands of Christ, therefore you set the lamentable example of being the greatest law-breakers.

Does Christ command you to risk the chances of murder and suicide by fighting duels? Some of the members of the government are duellists.

Does Christ command you to countenance gambling, and other vices consequent on the encouragement given to horse-racing?

Does Christ command you to manufacture drunkards, by using alcoholic liquors and licensing the sale of them, and thus making such poisons appear to be a necessary, and the use of them respectable? Emphatically has it been said that "the moderate drinkers are the drunkard manufacturers." Alcohol, a dreadful poison, which, by its use, leads to such direful consequences; cruel men! and you put this engine of destruction within reach of the ignorant, miserable, vicious and insane, and thus cause suicide, vice, and crime. Your brother christians do what you wish, that is, drink to the prosperity of the revenue, and then you punish them for the results of the extra insanity actually caused by your laws; you know, and I state it without fear of contradiction, and the parliamentary returns prove that all crimes are committed when the individuals committing such crimes are under the influence of christian made intoxicating drink. But, by the bye, I nearly forgot, if it was not for the use of christian-made drink, there would be no business for the lawyers, and no need for jails or other lunatic asylums, and you would not be able to enlist men for soldiers (alias men-butchers), and the priests and parsons could not pray and preach for want of *spiritual* influence—the latter would be a lamentable loss, forsooth!

Does Christ command you to make dear the necessaries of life by heavy taxation and high duties, yea, even while thousands of your fellow christians are on the brink of starvation, and numbers actually die from that cause—very many within these last three years?

Does Christ command you to punish poverty as a crime? I suppose you do unto others as you wish to be treated yourselves. Aristocrats generally care more for the comfort of their canine friends than they do either for the honest or distressed poor.

Does Christ command you to hire men, and after training them as men-butchers, send them into foreign lands or employ them at home to massacre their fellow countrymen, yea, even fellow christians, and rob the poor Indians, and ravish their females, deeds even perpetrated by christians on christians during the late war, headed by those miscreants Napoleon and Wellington.

And as to any glory in your Indian wars, you are conquerors only by reason of being better armed than the natives, place them on an equal footing with your troops in that respect, and the British forces would be easily beaten.

Does christianity allow you to perpetrate in any way revenge for so called national insults, often imaginary, (and too often trumped up as an excuse for an opportunity to plunder a nation or city) and making millions of innocent people suffer unheard of miseries, for the offence of only perhaps a contemptible crowned head?

Does christianity permit you to force the Chinese by murder to pay for poison—opium, and rob them in the shape of a ransom, to save their city from christian brutalities; what an idea of honesty you must have—please to define it?

Does Christ command you go to law against your brother, or in any way to revenge yourself for private wrongs, also often imaginary?

Does christianity permit you to drive your fellow creatures extra-insane by solitary confinement in christian jails?

What sort of animals are christians, who revenge themselves on a brother because he destroyed a hare or a partridge, &c., denominated game, or for trespassing across a field; verily I think such revengers make the game of Christ's precepts and example?

Does Christ command you to take by force money from those individuals who are unwilling to support a blood-stained-established-religion, falsely called national?

Does Christ command you to take the life you cannot give for any crime? and you wretches allow such laws to exist, even when we have almost annual experience of the execution of the innocent under circumstantial evidence.

Does christianity intend you to encourage the worship of the idol Juggernaut by a grant of £6000 per annum; and then punish a *poor* individual for blasphemy.

An honest government have no need for secret-service money, or to *open letters*, and then have them reclosed with great nicety to prevent detection ; men who commit such acts are possessed of feelings equally degraded with the banished felon.

If there is any truth in christianity as taught, you and the rest of the men constituting the British government are unfaithful to the religion you profess to believe in, therefore are infidels.

It appears that you allow all the above deeds to harmonize with christianity, for this reason, that a part of the government are christ's bishops, (who are associated with duelists). and they never lift up their voices in heavy denunciations against what are unjust acts and immoral laws. Then I say it is a worthless religion, unworthy even of savages, a disgrace to humanity, and none but the ignorant, mean, extra-insane and dishonest uphold it as truth.

After the above statements which we know to be facts, can there be a particle of honour in the brain of any one of Her Majesty's ministers? no, impossible; therefore the only conclusion to be drawn, and the only excuse we have for you, (and a fact that can be phrenologically proved), is, that you are MORAL LUNATICS, and I really believe that the feelings of conscientiousness and benevolence are unknown to you. *No honest man* could be a member of the British government as at present constituted.

Wishing you a speedy reformation,
I am, your well wisher,
ARTHUR TREVELYAN.

ATHEISTICAL PREACHING.

On Monday Mr. J. Savage, Jun., was brought up at the Guildhall, charged with resisting a police officer who attempted his removal on the preceding Sunday from Smithfield market, while addressing an assembly. The policemen witnesses talked of blasphemy and disturbance. Mr. Savage insisted on knowing the precise charge which was settled down into " resistance." Mr. Cooper was a witness on Mr. Savage's behalf. " It is of no use swearing persons who do not believe in religion," said the clerk, and Mr. Cooper gave his evidence unsworn. His statements went to disprove that Mr. Savage offered any resistance whatever. Mr. Savage was fined 10s. or to be imprisoned for seven days.

While this was being done, a Mr. West, a preacher, patronized by the police (discriminating souls) because he was godly, asked entrance at Guildhall. He was holding forth on the ground at Smithfield, and was mixed up in the dispute. He asked if Mr. Alderman Hunter presided—said he was his friend —sent in a note, and was admitted, while Mr. Savage's father, with witnesses on his son's behalf, were refused admission. The case was tried, or mock tried, while Mr. Savage, Sen. and friends were kept outside.

Afterwards Mr. Savage sent in a note to the magistrate, and then was permitted an audience. Policemen stated that admission was denied because the court was full and the day was hot. It is false that the court was full. It was thinly peopled, and to refuse a prisoner's friends and witnesses because of the heat, is to condemn a man not because of any crime, but because the day is hot.

Mr. Savage, Jun., was taken to gaol, giving orders that no one should pay the fine. But a few of his friends knowing that his absence from his employment would be of serious consequence, liberated him the same morning.

The real reason of Mr. Savage's apprehension was that he was preaching Atheism. Mr. Broom has been ill-treated for the same reason. A policeman complained of Mr Savage that he talked of brothels. His real remark was that our moral clergy ought not to be found deriving an income from such places as were the Dean and Chapter of Westminster.

THEOSOPHERS. — THE GODLY-WISE.

HAVE " NATURAL THEOLOGIANS," MORE THAN PROFESSED REVELATIONISTS, PRECISE NOTIONS OF THE ORIGIN, NATURE AND TENDENCIES OF THEIR GOD-BELIEFS?

IT would be difficult for a reasonable enquirer to account for the one-sided belief in a good omnipotent being, did he not call to his aid the reflection that men in their creeds are apt to be guided the rather by what they wish than what they know. The desire for what is good and for its prevalence, and the dislike to what is evil and for its success, and not reflection on the nature of things, incite men to endow the objects of their worship with admirable attributes. It is, also, probably from glimpses of the nature of things being occasionally presented to worshippers, that we detect actual, if not professed acknowledgment of evil mixed with good in the qualities of the worshipped. I quite agree with that view of Southwell which he broached in his "God of Nature and the Bible Identical," that if a god is supposed who does all the work that is done in nature, as distinguished from the operations of man, then must he be called evil as well as good. The only alternative for avoiding this difficulty, for those who do not like worshipping compound beings, is to suppose another god, or devil if they will, whose business it is to manufacture all the evil—in short, to do all the dirty work. I cannot help thinking, that those who call themselves deists entertain speculations of the least sustainable kind. A curious old writer of the sixteenth century, Behmen, who would seem throughout his speculations, to have anticipated the views of Swedenborg in many respects, thus replies to one who had taken upon himself the office of critic.

"My Sir libeller,—Whence will you then take the original of the devil? you will not allow the devil to be a *great part* of the *deity according to the father's nature*, whereas yet *Lucifer*, is by Christ himself called a great prince; now, if you will not allow that, then show me *another* nature, out of which the devil was created, than out of the *divine?*

"You must necessarily allow that the devils *were angels*, now, these angels are children of god, out of god's *substance;* they are creatures, and a creature must needs be out of or from nature; now if they be eternal creatures, then they are also proceeded out of the *eternal nature*, and that is god the father's in the first principle.

"For if you, indeed, know that the *devils* have the properties of god's anger, and of the dark world, and so, also, have all wicked *souls* of men; from whence else will they have their properties, than from *their mother* which hath generated them? If here you *will not* understand, then god help you."

Now Sir deist, as quaint old Behmen would say, if having concocted a supernatural power, you do not make one supernaturally evil as well as supernaturally good—if you will not understand that for the production of good and evil, an infinitely good intelligence is inadequate—that there must either be a bad one in addition, cr a compound of good and bad. If, I say, you will not understand, then god help you—I can't. I can give you argument, as the dogmatical doctor said, but I cannot give you understanding.

The Magi, and probably many who preceded them, ancient as their doctrines are, could see these philosophical difficulties, and boldly met them by creating two principal gods, Oromazes, absolutely good—the other, Ahrimanes, absolutely bad. What is the jewish, what the christian, doctrines of god and devil, but a modification under different names of the same ideas? The Persian Oromazes was of purest light, Ahrimanes of profoundest darkness—and these two continually war against each other—though from the desire inherent in sentient nature—for good to be predominant, arising from the universal organic preference to agreeable sensations, the absolute good was eventually to overcome the absolute evil. The same is seen in the construction of epics, tales, romances, in which the creator, the poet, fictionist, or romancist, has it all his own way. He fabricates according to what he sees, and hears, and knows, a multitude of good and evil incidents or events affecting his heroes and heroines, pleasurably and painfully, and ends by making them supremely happy. The tragedy—a particular kind of fiction, is but an exception to this general rule—the most greedy devourer of the wonderful and horrible, who won't read a romance without, at least, three murders, four ghosts, and "cutting" love adventures without limit must, still have it end well. It is in conformity with nature, human as well as brute, to seek pleasurable sensations, it is characteristic of rational nature, while forced to acknowledge the miseries of evil, to look fondly forward towards universal progress, dwell over the description of it by the poet, and enjoy it in anticipation.

As no theological speculation, from the grossest to the most subtle, is without a foundation in the nature of things so those "longings after immortality" which have puzzled so many wise heads—Shakespere's among the number—have originated in those sensations and perceptions which are part of our being. Capable of high pleasure, yet frequent and intense sufferers, men have sometime persuaded themselves, sometimes been persuaded by others, that a recompense would be awarded hereafter for sufferings here. The higher exercise of reason has not taught all —counteracted as it has been by the baneful influence of interested governors, religious or political—that their miseries here are to be remedied here. The one great, and eminently potent obstacle to progress has been in looking beyond self, and beyond realities, for reparation and recompense, instead of to self and to realities for advancement and improvement.

To return to the god-varieties—Zoroaster is thus quoted:—Oramazes made six gods, the first of benevolence, the second of truth, the third of equity, the rest of riches, wisdom, and pleasure. Correspondent deities were the handy work of Ahrimanes. Oromazes made twenty-four gods, and put them in an egg—Ahrimanes made as many more. The egg was broken, whence it comes that good is intermingled with ill. The time is to come in which Ahrimanes shall be utterly destroyed, when there shall be one life, and one city—or common society—for all men living, and one language. What is the temporal government of the messiah according to the ancient jewish doctrine, or the period of the millenium, according to the modern or reformed jewish, or christian doctrine, but a modification or reproduction of the Chaldaic or Persian theosophy—this perhaps of another, and so forth?

Accursed theology in any or all of its varieties, however deadening to the faculties cannot do away with the hankering after improvement—but its maleficent influence has been horribly successful in destroying and preventing efforts towards its accomplishment. M. Q. R.

THE LATE EDINBURGH DISCUSSION ON THE BIBLE.

34, London St., Edinburgh,
6th July, 1844.

Sir.—In terms of a previous engagement and arrangement, Mr. Southwell, the social and infidel preacher here, and I, had on the evenings of the 1st and 2nd curt., a Public Discussion in Richmond Court Chapel, on the question, "Is the Bible a Divine Revelation?" I maintained the affirmative, and Mr. Southwell the negative. My opening speech was the only written one on either side, and as it, generally speaking, embraced the whole views taken of the subject, I feel desirous that it be printed in your periodical, *the Movement*. It will, with the introductory notice, take up I believe nearly six of your pages. If you agree to its insertion, I will send you a copy of it on hearing from you.

I am, Sir,
Your very obedient, humble servant,
JAMES MACARA.

From your name *Holy*oake, and the name of your street, *Holy*well, one would expect something very good.

Mr. G. J. Holyoake, London.

ANSWER.

Holywell-street, Strand, London,
8th July, 1844.

Sir.—Your letter of the 6th came duly to hand. Would be glad to receive the communication, which will doubtless be acceptable. It cannot, however, be promised insertion unconditionally If you will do us the favour to submit it, we will determine after perusal upon using or returning it.

We rejoice in being able to say that we have nothing *holy* about us but the name.

Respectfully yours,
M. Q. RYALL.

Since the preceding correspondence, Mr. Macara's speech has arrived, but really it cannot be inserted, it is too pointless, inconsecutive, and tame. We may as well be killed by persecution as killed by tedium. No wonder that Mr. Southwell has left Scotland, if Mr. Macara is a fair specimen of his opponents. Mr. Macara has a design upon us —but we are not so simple as he thinks—he knows that if he prevails on us to insert his speeches, he will save the government a world of trouble. There would be no occasion for the Attorney General to put us down, we should by afflicting our readers with Macaraism, put ourselves down.—ED. of M.

From the Votes of the House of Commons, July 10th—Petition of George Adams for for release of Thomas Paterson, now confined in the General Prison, at Perth. To lie on the table!

NOTICE.

The London Atheistical Society will hold its next Monthly Meeting on Tuesday evening next, August 6th, at half-past 8 o'clock, at the Northampton Coffee-house, Newton-street, High Holborn, when the question "What is Atheism?" will be publicly discussed, and elect a secretary.

THOMAS POWELL, *Sec.*

Just Published, *cloth, lettered—Price* 1s. 6d.

THE SECOND EDITION OF
PRACTICAL GRAMMAR,
OR
COMPOSITION
Divested of Difficulties,
BY G. JACOB HOLYOAKE.

TO CORRESPONDENTS.

R. B.—His "Remarks on the Character of Byron" are not of sufficient merit to warrant us in entering on the discussion of such an often-handled topic. If R. B. had written something new we could not allow him to "edify" any one in the way of controversy, unless he informed us of his name and address.

A PHILOSOPHICAL ENQUIRER.—Mirabeau disposed us to regard theories like his favourably. If he will send the remaining paper we will decide upon them.

SUBSCRIPTIONS TO THE ANTI-PERSECUTION UNION.

Mr. Watts, Islington £10 0 0
(Full particulars of this donation will be given next week. They are in press, but are obliged to stand over.)
From W. B. B. for G. J. H.,
to be appropriated to the general objects of the Anti-Persecution Union. £1 0 0

All persons having charge of petition sheets are requested to hasten their return.

ALL communications for the Anti-Persecution Union to be addressed as before, to the Secretary, G. J. Holyoake, 5, Paul's-alley. Paternoster-row.

All money orders to be made payable at the Post-office, Strand. G. J. H., *Sec.*

Printed and Published by G. J. HOLYOAKE,
40, Holywell-street, Strand,
Saturday, August 3, 1844.

THE MOVEMENT

And Anti=Persecution Gazette.

"Maximize morals, minimize religion."—BENTHAM.

No. 35.   EDITED BY G. JACOB HOLYOAKE,
ASSISTED BY M. Q. RYALL.   PRICE 1½d

THE RIGHT OF PUBLIC MEETINGS.

A SHORT time since various mock public meetings were called in London, by religious bodies, to oppose the "Dissenters' Chapels Bill." I attended one held on April 25th, in the Freemasons' Hall, which was conducted in the grossest violation of a well understood public right. The meeting was called a public one, but the moment Mr. Green, the unitarian, and Mr. Watson, publisher, requested permission to address the meeting, the chairman put them down, because they were not a certain description of persons set forth on a card in his hand. Against this conduct both these gentlemen, in the name of the public, protested At a public meeting *every* description of persons have a right to be heard. But these pietists wanted to blazon forth that a public meeting had seconded their views, when in reality it was but a private meeting of their own friends. They meanly essayed to usurp the public's sanction, while they denied the public's right of questioning and discussing. At one of the many meetings of this kind Mr. Watts of Islington was present. He demanded to be heard. A rev. gentleman gave him in charge of the police, but he was not a man to be put down unjustly, and he still insisted on his right to be heard, as a member of the public, and amid the blows and thronging of rev. gentlemen and their abettors, he was conveyed to the stationhouse. Being well known and respected he was directly bailed out — the next day the charge was heard. The rev. prosecutor affirmed that Mr. Watts had resisted the police, in order to give a legal colouring to the charge of which he was ashamed. This point was flatly contradicted by one of the clerical gent.'s own witnesses, who nobly said that, though he differed from Mr. Watts, he would not tell a lie to injure him. The rev. accuser then informed the magistrate that Mr. Watts was a notorious chartist, and well known to the police. Mr. Watts at once protested against the reflection upon his character, that "he was well known to the police." He had been twenty-five years in business, and no man had ever yet impugned his probity. The magistrate enquired if he was a house-keeper—which was at once answered in the affirmative, and he dismissed the case. Thus owing to the accident of a just witness appearing against him, and to his being a respectable house-keeper, Mr. Watts owed his escape from this reckless attempt to traduce his character, and deprive him of his right to address a public meeting. This right, Mr. Watts, being a man of public spirit, resolved still farther to establish, and entered an action against the rev. gent. for the injustice done him. The face of affairs was altered, and the solicitor of the rev. accuser was instucted to seek a compromise. Mr. Watts, entertaining no personal ill-feeling towards the party, but only anxious to protect a public right, consented to drop proceedings on condition that ten pounds was paid into the funds of the Anti-Persecution Union which was accordingly done a few days after.

Every man is indebted to Mr. Watts for risking his liberty and money in establishing a right of so much importance. This is the first time christian injustice has been made tributary to the funds of the Anti-Persecution Union. Verily, a christian would say Providence smiles upon us.

The names and addresses of all parties concerned in this transaction would appear, but from a laudable delicacy on the part of Mr. Watts not to cause any pain or annoyance to persons, who, though they wronged him, have since apologised. But it would be unjust to the public to state less than is here related for the encouragement of our friends and warning to our enemies.   G. J. H.

RELIGIONISM.—Professed religionists have much to answer for: they have often aimed at preventing reasoning, which is to crush the power of reasoning. Many dislike freethinking, because they love subserviency to their own judgments: all this is vicious. As we should bring a plant to the full growth of its stem, and expansion of its leaves, and beauty of its blossoms, so should we subserve and delight in the cherishing of every faculty of thought, until human intelligence shall generally attain and exhibit its full proportions.

REPLY TO CHARLES SOUTHWELL'S "FALLACY OF THE ARGUMENT A PRIORI," &c.

Contents of Part Second.

1—11. The Champion of the Scotch Atheists and the Champion of the English Atheists, at variance internecine.
12. The Argument, the grand Argument.
13—16. Mr. Gillespie uses, and Mr. Southwell abuses, the evidence of two great philosophers.
17, 18. A challenge of Mr. S's. disposed of.
19—29. The grossest falsehood in the "Fallacy" displayed.
30—34. Style of "Fallacy."
35. Conclusion.

1. Having discussed Mr. Southwell's "Fallacy," so far as it can be viewed in the light of an answer—*good or bad*—to my "Argument, *a priori;*" it remains that I offer some remarks connected with each other. I must now address myself to particular portions of Mr. Southwell's answer, which, as a whole, was replied to in my former Part.

2. Several years ago, the Atheists of Glasgow, being resolved to answer, and to refute (if they could), the "Argument, *a priori*," fixed upon a champion to do their work, who, in the face of "high Heaven," designated himself "Antitheos." The champion of those Scottish Atheists, in his "*Refutation* of the Argument," (for *such, and so forth*, is the title of his work,) proved himself to be a man of talent—if not of taste too—and tolerably well acquainted with his subject. The author of the "Fallacy," himself, intimates that Antitheos is a "very clever person," *a shrewd thinker*, "a talented opponent;"* and concerning his performance we are assured, "ably written" "it certainly is."†

3. But now that we are dealing with London Atheists, and *their* champion, we discover, and cannot help discovering, that *his* performance is different from the others, as to

Both matter, form, and style.‡

From *Antitheos* to Charles Southwell, is a descent indeed.

4. It might appear exceedingly strange that, at the very outset, the spokesman for the English Atheists should fall foul of the representative of the Scotch ones; did not the strangeness of the *reason* of the fact throw the strangeness of the *fact itself* into complete shade.

5. "It seems to me," says Mr. Southwell, "the author of the 'Refutation' has not ex-

actly overturned the 'Argument, *a priori*, for the Being and Attributes of GOD,' as laid down by Gillespie; nay, his 'Refutation' * * * has in nowise damaged, but rather lent an appearance of strength to that 'Argument.'"§ All this one can readily believe, and 'tis evinced, at length, in the "Examination," aforementioned.

6. Of course, my readers will be desirous to know why Mr. Southwell thinks, that Antitheos has strengthened the "Argument *a priori*." The reason may be briefly stated: *Antitheos* admits the truth of the first proposition in the "Argument." But to be more particular, the champion of Scotch atheism declares:—

"The first Proposition,—'*Infinity of Extension is necessarily existing,*'—it would be absurd in the extreme to deny. No more can we imagine any limit prescribable to extension, than we can imagine the outside of a house to be the inside of it."‖

7. This is the declaration of Antitheos, and such has been the declaration of every man writing upon the subject, till the present champion of English atheism, in an evil hour, blurted out a counter-declaration.—Verily, the London Atheists pitched on a singular champion.

8. But I must to the proof of the counter declaration. The unqualified assent accorded by Antitheos to Prop. 1, Southwell terms "a very foolish admission."¶—"which," Southwell goes on, "Gillespie has turned to excellent account, in his 'Examination.'" Again: "Antitheos, in admitting the assumption," [of "the basis" of my "Argument"—Prop. 1,] "did foolishly."** Once more: Antitheos's admission we are told, is, "of all admissions that could be made to such an antagonist" [as Gillespie] "at once the most silly and important:"††—*silly*, in poor Antitheos, *important* to Mr. Gillespie. So important, that "I marvel not," says Southwell, "that Gillespie should *make much* of the 'most important admission.'"‡‡ Lastly: Antitheos's conduct is spoken of as being the consequence of a "mistake."§§

9. If any reflection can lessen Antitheos's *folly*, and render his mistake not so odious, in

---

* Paper 1, par. 2, 14. † *Ib.* par. 2.
‡ Milton.

§ Paper 1, par. 2.
‖ "Refutation," chap. 6.
¶ Paper 1, par. 2.   ** *Ib.* par. 3.
†† Paper 1, par. 14.
‡‡ *Ibid.*—"To me, *this is a most important admission.* For if that Proposition (Prop. 1,) is granted (and who can rationally deny it?) I undertake to make out all the rest *by necessary consequence.*"—Examination, part. 2, § 11.
§§ Paper 1, par. 14.

our eyes, it must surely be this,—that Antitheos has a Southwell to join in the folly, and fall into the same mistake—with a grace peculiar, indeed, to the latter gentleman.*

10. Did such a question as the following never once occur to my answerer's mind: since both Gillespie, the theist, and his "talented and skilful" opponent, the anti-theist, are so entirely agreed as to the truth that *Infinity of Extension is necessarily existing;* should not a Charles Southwell pause before dissenting? 'Tis wholly unnecessary that we here enter into the merits of the topic; these having been sufficiently weighed in the preceding portion of this reply: still one may be permitted to hint, that, as a Southwell has been the first, even of Atheists, to deny the necessary existence of infinite extension, so this Alpha shall be the Omega too. Hitherto, the truth alluded to has been considered to be a fundamental position in Atheism of every species and modification.† The disturber of the universal harmony has embarked in a desperate undertaking. If his laurels be not tarnished, inconsistency and genuine Atheism may long flourish together.

11.—Thus, Atheists, like *Doctors*, can disagree.

12. Since I have been led to speak of the author of the "Refutation," there is another thing deserving of notice. The reader of Mr. Southwell's strictures must have been struck with the frequency with which allusion is made to the "Argument," as being the "*grand* Argument." The first line of the "Fallacy" contains "this grand Argument;" the last paragraph is not without my "grand Argument;" and the "grand Argument"

* See Part 1 of this reply—par. 17, 18, 22, &c.
† The following sentences occur in the challenge accepted by the Glasgow Atheists:—
"You challenge the world to prove, to you, that there exists an *Intelligent Great First Cause*. The work in question (the Argument, *a priori*) professes to demonstrate that matter by the *most rigid* ratiocination. It asks you to grant no proposition but those propositions which constitute *the starting points* of your Atheism, to wit, *that* there is infinity of duration, *and that* there is *infinity of extension*,—be that extension of matter *merely*, or of space *merely*, or of matter and space *together*. How plain must those truths be which are insisted on by all sound Theists, (I might have said by all men sound in their minds,) and are THE PRIMARY ASSUMPTIONS *in atheism itself*."
The Atheists of Glasgow were not the men to aim a blow at one of the props on which they leaned.

makes its appearance I don't know how often in the course of the performance. What is the reason of all this (may I call it?) grandeur. The secret lies here, that, in spite of anything which may be said to the contrary, Southwell has a sneaking admiration of Antitheos's whole method of procedure, and Antitheos has named my work the "grand Argument."* I take the name for a good omen.

13. A great portion of my opponent's strictures is wide of the mark—wide, very wide, of any mark. At the present stage of the business, my readers might take my word for the perfect *inapplicability* to the point in hand of I know not what number of my antagonist's paragraphs; but I have a reason for not leaving the truth of what I have advanced to be taken for granted. However, I shall give but a single instance: more would needlessly annoy my readers.

14. "Infinity of Extension is necessarily existing, according to the 'Argument'" [and according to the 'Fallacy' too, unless I forget what it says, in several places,†] "and as my desire is to give this *decisive* proposition‡ all the advantage it can derive from the authority of great names, I gladly take this opportunity of mentioning that Locke declared it 'near as hard to conceive any existence, or to have an idea of any real being, with a perfect negation of all manner of expansion, as it is to have the idea of any real existence with a perfect negation of all manner of duration.'

"Dr. Samuel Clarke, another 'great name,' observes that 'extension does not belong to thought, because thought is not a being. But there is *need* of extension to the existence of every being, to a being which has or has not thought, or any other quality whatsoever.'

"Here are two first-rate authorities, of whom, it must be confessed, Gillespie has sufficient reason to boast, as giving respectability (in appearance), to the 'infinity of extension' dogma. Many other authorities, almost equally respectable, might be adduced on the *same* side, but what availeth it though *all* authority were on that side, if *truth* is on. the other.

"Gillespie, in the 'Introduction' to his 'Argument,' says 'if reason can with certainty pronounce anything, it may pronounce this decision, that extension and existence are so necessary to each other, that there can be no existence without extension. Talk of a substance which has no extension, you present

* See "Refutation," chap. 6.
† See Part 1 hereof, par. 22, 23.
‡ This reminds me of Mr. Southwell's declaration, that "every atom of the 'grand' Argument must survive" with the admission of Prop. 1. See Part 1, par. 5.

us with words of amusement.'" Paper 1st, par. 16, 17, 18, 19.

15. Now, in all this, the author of the "Fallacy" does not understand himself. He quotes my "authorities," without comprehending the reason why they are *authorities* with me. The gist of the affair is this. I brought forward those two great authorities, Locke and Clarke—" as great authorities, in speculations of this nature, as can anywhere be found" "in behalf of the position, *that* existence cannot be without extension"—in other words, *that* the human mind cannot conceive a Being or Substance destitute of extension: while Mr. Southwell drags in Mr. Locke, and Dr. Samuel Clarke, on the plea that I had borrowed their aid " as giving respectability (in appearance) to the 'infinity of extension' dogma"—in plainer language, as witnessing to the truth, that *Infinity of Extension is necessarily existing.* I sought the assistance of those philosophers to establish the *connection* between extension and existence: extension is a true *sine qua non* of everything that exists. Mr. Southwell has me seeking their assistance to establish the *fact* of the necessary existence of infinite extension: a totally different matter. I had one reason for introducing the philosophers: but when I fall into Mr. Southwell's hands I am made to have another altogether. True, Mr. Southwell was not aware of the circumstance. But that was no fault of mine; 'twas entirely owing to his own stupidity.

16. Will my readers believe, that, hard on the back of those *inapplicable* paragraphs, the author of the "Fallacy" should have the confidence to deliver himself in the following remarkable manner? "These words are in the 'Introduction,' followed by those quotations from Locke and Clarke given above. They are 'most important,' and (without offence, be it said,) furnish as pretty a specimen of the *self-damnatory* mode of reasoning, as any of the very many pretty specimens I have had the 'great good fortune' to cast my eye upon, though a tolerably industrious reader. But"—but enough of the precious stuff. If there be any *reasoning* in the matter, on whose side the *pretty specimen* of "the *self damnatory*" reasoning is to be found; I am quite content to leave to the decision of every sensible reader of the passages borrowed, for inspection, from the "Fallacy"— which a "Fallacy" will continue till the "crack of doom."

17. I cannot find a better place than this to consider a challenge which the doughty champion I am engaged with has seen fit to give me.

—" Save in the sense of *partial consideration* only (to borrow a sentence," or, at least, a phrase, " himself [Mr. Gillespie] so *freely uses*) the parts of matter are necessarily *indivisible:*" this, the atheistic champion calls a "*fact.*" " (Except in the sense of partial consideration only) the parts of the material universe are NOT *moveable among themselves.*" This also, and as a thing of course, our anti-Newtonian calls a "*fact.*"* " The parts of infinity of matter (save in the sense of partial consideration only) are necessarily indivisible from each other, really or mentally. This conclusion is inevitable—it is ' the conclusion to which the rules of philosophy entitle us to come,' and our author is *challenged* to prove it fallacious."† Here I am challenged to prove fallacious the position which lays down, that the parts of matter are *not* divisible from each other: If they be *in*-divisible from each other, they must be *im*-moveable among themselves—Just as, if they be moveable, they are, *a fortiori,* divisible. Challenged to prove fallacious the proposition affirming, that the parts of matter are *not* divisible, *not* moveable! Why, we know of matter only as divisible and moveable, where not already divided and moved. Mr. Southwell, surely, must be jesting with his readers, when he assures them, it is a *fact* that the parts of matter are not moveable, not divisible? But no —a jest would have been too strikingly ill-timed. What are we to think then? For all bodies not in motion are moveable, and all bodies not divided are divisible. Nothing less deniable. After all, who could have expected to find a dogmatic Atheist sitting in the seat of the Sceptic—setting aside the evidence of his senses—denying what every individual sense testifies? Truly, there is no end to human inconsistency.

18. As to the *freely used* phrase which Charles Southwell has condescended to borrow from me: before he borrowed it from me, why was not he at the pains to understand the sense in which I used it? To comprehend— at last—this sense, let him ponder to good purpose a sentence in the "Examination"— to which, indeed, he alludes,‡ tho' without mastering its contents.

" When Mr. Gillespie speaks of parts in the sense of partial consideration only, he has something in his view very different from the parts of matter, which all, so far as not already divided, are divisible, or may be considered as divisible, from each other, which, therefore, are parts in another sense than by partial consideration *only;* he has in his view the parts of the extension which is of infinity, which parts, both really and mentally, are necessarily indivisible, and, so, are parts *only*

---

* Paper 2, par. 15.   † *Ib.* par. 16.
‡ Paper 2, par. 16.

THE MINER'S STRUGGLE.

Mr. MITCHELL draws our attention to the condition of the miners of Northumberland and Durham, who have been sixteen weeks on strike against the avarice and inhumanity of their employers. He is right in supposing us deeply interested in the brave struggles of humble industry, and although we cannot insert his narrative — our objects being advisedly specific—yet we gladly notice a case so well deserving of sympathy, support, and attention. The miners exhibit unexpected and laudable coolness in their proceedings. From Mr. Mitchell's statements they appear to have done what all trusty men should do—measured their patient endurance against the power opposed to them, and have prepared themselves for suffering. These men merit victory. A subscription list for their support lies at our office, and we hope this notice of it will not be in vain.

"TO THE EDITOR OF THE DERBY MERCURY.

SIR,—The enclosed publication was put into my hand at a short distance from the Mechanics' Hall last night, just after I left the Meeting of the Protestant Association held there. Something ought to be done to prevent such horrible blasphemy from being circulated among the people.

Hoping you will not lose sight of the matter, I am, Sir, yours respectfully,

A PROTESTANT."

Derby, July 25, 1844.

"[The publication to which our correspondent alludes is No. 1 of a weekly paper, printed at Bristol, called " *The Oracle of Reason, or Philosophy Vindicated*," and is edited by a person named Charles Southwell, who proclaims himself to be " a perfect atheist." It is one of the most disgusting exhibitions of a depraved mind which we have seen, and renders, we have no doubt, both writer and publisher liable to a prosecution. We have a pretty shrewd guess as to the source of its circulation in Derby.—ED. D. M.]"

The editor is shrewder than we take him to be if he guesses rightly. Where has this simple editor been? The "horrible blasphemy" he speaks of, is two years and a half old. We must send him one of the pattern cards issued at our blasphemy establishments, with specimens of all sizes, shapes and shades, manufactured since the *Oracle of Reason* was first patronised by Sir Charles Wetherall. If none of our samples should suit the fastidious editor, by writing to our office, or to the Atheistical Depôt, 105, Nicolson-steet, Edinburgh, he can have any quantity prepared on the "shortest notice," and on very reasonable terms.—ED. of M.

THE BIBLE-GOD.

(*To the Editor of the Movement.*)

[The following communication would have appeared earlier but for the absence of the name and address of the writer. These being furnished upon our request, the article is inserted.—ED. of M.]

SIR,—Your correspondent, C. S., page 235, must have taken a view of the christian body generally, from a point of observation, so distant and unfortunate, as to lead him to very erroneous conclusions respecting the opinions held by christians on the essential attributes of their god. All christians invariably represent god as all powerful, wise, holy, just. C. S. has brought forward two witnesses to prove the contrary, Bishops Butler and Watson; but then he has brought them into court, saddled with his own *extraordinary* construction of their language. Christians on hearing C. S. cite Butler and Watson, in proof of their deity's possessing "horrid attributes," would be inclined to recommend his friends to take care of him.

Will C. S. allow the two bishops to speak their own words, and give us from each a passage, verbatum, in proof of their describing god as possessed of " horrid attributes?"

Many a "charity-brat," to use C. S.'s courteous phraseology, would find no difficulty in disproving his assertion, that the Bible represents god and the devil as identical—or in shewing that the Bible everywhere describes god as possessed of the attributes of power, wisdom, justice—which all christians believe.

The assertion that all christians "detest their god as an omnipotent tyrant," is one of such " bulk and quality "—so pregnant with good sense, discrimination, and candour, that I will give C. S. its counterpart, that he may read the qualities of the one in the light of the other. Almost every atheist is a man so revelling in vice and crime that he rejects religion to escape the restraints it would impose upon his evil passions. Here is a declaration worthy to stand abreast of C. S.'s—displaying about as much knowledge of those whom it pretends to characterize, with an equal amount of candour and discrimination.

I am sorry to find C. S. stumble so awkwardly in his progress through the Bible—he would travel much easier by applying the same principle of interpretation that is usually employed in the investigation of other books. The Bible lays down a few first principles, which are the keys to all its passages, in which the sense is not governed by the context; it represents god as the alone author of all moral good, and of all retributive evil. Satan as the antagonist of all moral good, and the author of all moral evil; so that whenever C. S. reads of god being the author of evil in parts where the context governs the sense, such passages are invariably governed in harmony with our first principle, and retributive evil is the sense determined; and where the sense is not determined by the context, surely I need not remind even C. S. that the first principle being never contradicted, must be ever obeyed.

I would thank C. S. for a passage from the Bible, *describin* god as possessed of "horrid attributes, (*describing.*) I shall not be content with any of his random inferences; other minds might draw an inference from the passage very different to his, and, indeed, a great many minds would differ from C. S. in their mode of inferential reasoning. Fancy, too flippant for rule, governed by prejudice, overbearing all method, is an unsatisfactory test for any book worthy of investigation.

J. HYDE.

APPLICATIONS TO PARLIAMENT.
"To the Hon. the Commons—
"*The Petition of George Adams, Cabinet-maker, 21, King-street, Cheltenham, in the county of Gloucester.*
"SHEWETH—That your petitioner is one who, having suffered imprisonment from the laws relating to blasphemy, considers such laws to be in opposition to the spirit of Protestantism, said to be founded upon the right of private judgment, liberty of conscience and *free* expression of opinion.

"That your petitioner respectfully solicits your hon. house to abrogate all laws interfering with the freedom of opinion, and all enactments and regulations relative to blasphemy.

"That your petitioner prays your house to advise the Queen to order the release of Thomas Paterson, now confined in the General Prison, Perth, Scotland, for the publication of Atheistical sentiments—or at least to remove him from his solitary confinement, and generally ameliorate his severe treatment.

"Signed GEORGE ADAMS."

Copy of letter accompanying petition.
"To T. S. DUNCOMBE, ESQ.
"Honoured Sir,
"You will oblige one of that class of whom you are the acknowledged representative in the House of Commons, by presenting the accompanying petition as soon as convenient.

"I was confined in the county gaol for publishing a work containing, what a jury decided, was blasphemous; this jury, composed not of my peers, but of hucksters, butchers, and gaziers, sitting in judgment on a question requiring the most mature and deliberative investigation. The evidence upon which I was convicted—was that of a man who could neither read or write.

"I complain of being put to ruinous expenses in defending myself against laws that are partially administered, for if the laws by which I suffered were impartially put in force, there is not a publisher in the kingdom but would share the same fate.

"Yours respectfully,
"GEORGE ADAMS."

MR. DUNCOMBE'S REPLY.
"3, F. Albany, July 11th, 1844.
"Sir,
"I beg to inform you that I presented to the House of Commons, yesterday evening, the petition which you did me the honour to transmit to me for that purpose.

"I have the honour to be, Sir,
"Your obedient servant,
"THOMAS DUNCOMBE.
"George Adams."

INSTRUCTIONS OF THE CHIEF OF THE CAPUCHINS AT RAGUSA, TO BROTHER PEDICULOSO, ON HIS DEPARTURE FOR THE HOLY LAND. BY VOLTAIRE.
II.

WHEN, from the history of the kings, you enter upon that of the prophets, you will enjoy, and cause us to enjoy ineffable pleasures. You will have many inquiries to make, and many explanations to receive; but, when you come to Ezekiel, then will your very soul dilate with joy. First of all you will see the four animals with the faces of a lion, an ox, an eagle, and a man; then the wheel with four faces, like unto the waters of the sea, (each face having more eyes than Argus,) going upon its four sides and not turning as it went. You know that God commanded the prophet to swallow a whole book of parchment; inquire carefully of all the prophets you meet, what were the contents of that book.

Get Ezekiel to show you the tile upon which he drew a plan of Jerusalem, while he was bound with the bands which the Lord gave him; and to tell you why he was commanded to lie upon his left side 380 days, and then 40 days upon the right.

In reporting your conversations with Ezekiel, be careful, my dear brother, not to alter his words as you have done: that is a sin against the Holy Ghost. You have said that God commanded the prophet to bake his bread with cow dung; but the vulgate says, (Ezekiel, chap. iv. v. 12.) " Thou shalt eat it, thou shalt cover it with the ordure which comes from the body of man." The prophet ate and cried out, " Pouah! Pouah! Pouah! Oh, Lord God, I never made such a breakfast in my life." Always be careful to preserve the purity of the text, my dear brother, and do not change it in the least tittle.

If the breakfast of Ezekiel was rather filthy the dinner of the Jews of which he speaks is somewhat cannibalish: " The fathers shall eat their sons, and the sons shall eat their fathers." It is well enough, perhaps, for the fathers to eat their children who are plump and tender, but for the children to eat their tough, old, stringy fathers, that is a new fashioned cookery.

There is great dispute among the learned respecting the 39th chapter of that same Ezekiel. The question is whether it is to the Jews or the beasts of the field that the Lord promises to give the blood of the princes and the flesh of the warriors for food. We are of opinion that it is to both: the 17th verse is incontestibly in favour of the beasts; but the 18th, 19th, and the following are for the Jews. " You shall eat the horse and his rider." Not only are they to devour the horses, like the Scythians, but also the riders like worthy Jews as they were. See what it is to have a thorough knowledge of the holy scriptures.

The most essential passages of Ezekiel, the most advantageous to morals, the best adapted for the edification of the people, and the most efficacious in inspiring the youth of both sexes with modesty and a love of chastity, are those in which the Lord speaks of Aholah and Aholibah, chap. 23, these admirable texts cannot be read too often.

After a careful examination of these inimitable passages, we would have you lightly to look into Jeremiah, who ran naked throughout Jerusalem, loaded with a pack saddle: but we beg of you not to neglect the prophet Hosea, whom the Lord commanded " to take unto him a wife of whoredoms and children of whoredoms;" and, some time after, to love an adultress, and he bought an adultress for fifteen pieces of silver, and a homer of barley, and half a homer of barley, chap. 3.

Nothing will contribute more, my dear brother, to form the minds of young persons than able commentaries on these texts. Do not forget to calculate the value of the fifteen pieces of money: we are of opinion that they will amount to at least seven livres and a half, and you know that the Capuchins get girls much cheaper than that.

ENLARGEMENT OF THE MOVEMENT.

THE Reply of Dr. Kalley, to which we have immediately to attend, and Mr. Gillespie's papers now appearing, which we are pledged to insert, will compel us to exclude various articles specially connected with *Movement* objects unless we make more room, therefore for the present at least, the *Movement* will be enlarged to twelve pages, and charge one half-penny extra.

WHITECHAPEL.—Mr. Southwell is delivering a course of four lectures on Monday evenings at this Institution. On Tuesday evening, August 13th, he will debate the question of the " Existence of God," with the Rev. G. Hill, in the same place—the Hall of Science.

On Sunday evening next, Mr. Holyoake will Lecture.

MR. ROBERT OWEN.

ON Sunday morning next a public breakfast will be given to Mr. Owen in order to testify to him the respect of his numerous friends previous to his departure to America on a visit to his family. The breakfast will be taken in the John-street Institution. No word need be said by way of urging the friends of Socialism to be present on this interesting occasion. No friend to liberality of sentiment will think of being absent. In the evening Mr. OWEN WILL LECTURE.

Mr. T. Paterson, from W. W.		15	0
Do. do. from W. J.		2	6
Miss Roalfe, from W. W.		5	0
Do. do. from W. J.		2	6
C. S. from W. W.		5	0
G. J. H. from W. W.		5	0

LEGENDS.—Until mankind shall overcome the repugnance to saying " I do not know," we shall be infested with false, foolish, and misguided theories. The ignorant are ever ready to credit legends connected with any remarkable physical fact. The position of a large stone, a peculiarly shaped rock, a deep ravine, a fissure, or a cave serve to hang a supernatural story upon, and cannot be suffered to remain unexplained: any thing, with weak minds, is preferable to acknowledging they do not know the cause. It is characteristic of mankind, in their present religious teaching, to substitute errors for facts of which they are ignorant.

Dr. Kalley.—Something effectual seems likely to be done for the protection of Dr. Kalley and the British protestants in Madeira. Lord Aberdeen has made a claim of £1,200 in favour of the Doctor, by way of compensation for his losses during his illegal imprisonment in the goal of Funchal. We hope this demand will be not merely made, but *vigorously enforced.*

Votes of the House of Commons, June 3—Blasphemy, Petition from St. Marylebone for amendment of law relating thereto. To lie on the Table !

June 13.—Blasphemy, Petition from Leicester for amendment of the law relating thereto. To lie on the Table !

July 22, 1844.—Political and Religious Opinions, Petition of John Marshall against the infliction of penalties for the free expression thereof. To lie on the Table !

Just Published by Matilda Roalfe & Co., Edinburgh, price 2d.—The EXISTENCE of GOD DISPROVED by BELIEVERS in God. "*Magna est veritas et prævalebit.*"

NOTICE.

Vol. I. and II. of *Oracle of Reason,* with Trials of Paterson, Southwell, Holyoake, and all the numbers of the Deist, elegantly bound and lettered, £1. Application to be made at the office, 40, Holywell-street.

TO CORRESPONDENTS.

Received from Dr. Kalley of Madeira, an elaborate letter.

Mr. Hindle of Ashton-under-Line requests half-a-dozen copies of the Petition adopted by the Anti Persecution Union, which he can get sent for presentation by as many Electors of his town. Could not other active friends follow his example ?

Received the *Belfast News Letter,* containing the article on the Scripture Evidence of Miracles, by J. R. Young, Esq., Professor of Mathematics in the Royal Belfast Institution. It shall receive attention.

S. D.—We don't quote scripture. True, there are some good remarks in it, but we do not use them, because the book has such a bad reputation that we should not like to be known to be acquainted with it.

SUBSCRIPTIONS TO THE ANTI-PERSECUTION UNION.

To sale of Members' Tickets . 4 6
Mr. B. G. Lewis, for Mr. Paterson 8 0
Mr. Cousins for Mr. Paterson . 16 0
                        G. J. H., *Sec.*

Just Published, the Second Edition,
Cloth, lettered—Price 1s. 6d.

[The first of a *Short Series of Works on Practical Instruction,* intended for the use of Schools, Mechanics' Institutions, and Literary Classe .]

PRACTICAL GRAMMAR,
OR
COMPOSITION
Divested of Difficulties,
WITH SELECT EXAMPLES FROM THE WRITINGS OF ELEGANT AUTHORS.
Containing all that is necessary for ordinary purposes, and no more; and intended for the use of those who have little time to study.

BY G. JACOB HOLYOAKE.

London :—J. Watson, 5 Paul's-alley, Paternoster-row, and all Booksellers.

OPINIONS OF THE PRESS.

A series of smart remarks, expounding science in the conjoint style of *Punch,* and an Ultra Radical setting the world to rights —*Spectator.*

Mr. Holyoake's vein is singularly cheerful, and without a spice of dogmatism or pedantry. We commend "Practical Grammar" to the patronage of parents and teachers —*Critic.*

The author has evidently *studied* grammar—his work will be a favourite—and well deserved—will be the success which it may receive.—*Nouveau Beau Monde.*

This book might have been entitled "Grammar made easy and entertaining." The author has imparted a spirit and vivacity to the subject which we do not remember to have met with previously in any other book of the class.—*New Moral World.*

It is a very readable book; which is more than can be said of grammars in general.—Mr. H.'s grammar will be found very useful for learners.—*Penny Satirist.*

Lowth, Horne Tooke, Cobbett, Doherty, Priestley, Hazlitt, Hine, Brenan, and others do not appear with this author, as names quoted merely for display. The valuable ore with which they have enriched the treasures of the science of language seems to have been refined in the crucible of the author's brain. By a skilful condensing process their respective contributions have been pressed into the service, and familiarised to the reader. The philosophy of chapters is dashed off in a few tersely phrased sentences.—*Sentinel.*

In his "Composition" there are some very good remarks—but—the Practical Grammar contains neither rules, nor reasons, and, therefore, is not a rational grammar.—*Lloyd's Weekly London Newspaper.*

More than a mere compilation—a simple but strictly philosophical analysis of the English language.—We cordially recommend it.—*Sheffield Iris.*

"Practical Grammar" is specially likely to be a favourite with those who desire to teach themselves. It is plainly written, it is agreeably worded, tersely expressed, impressive for the memory, and highly suggestive of thought.—*Northern Star.*

The author of this little treatise is a young man of considerable ability. His ideas are communicated in a pleasing style, by means of clear intelligible language —*Cheltenham Free Press.*

Printed and Published by G. J. Holyoake, 40, Holywell-street, Strand, Saturday, August 10, 1844.

THE MOVEMENT
And Anti=Persecution Gazette.

"Maximize morals, minimize religion."—BENTHAM.

No. 36.   EDITED BY G. JACOB HOLYOAKE, ASSISTED BY M. Q. RYALL.   PRICE 2d.

A NEW ESTIMATE OF CHRISTIANITY'S HISTORICAL EVIDENCES.

WHATEVER expedites the business of reasoning expedites the common business of life, and hastens the adjustment of that great question—the relation of man to the external world—in which human happiness is involved. Therefore a new estimate of christianity's historical evidences, including a shorter mode that any in use of determining their value, may not be without interest nor utility.

I do not subscribe to the opinion of those persons who say that theological discussion is a waste of time. In one sense all discussions are wastes of time, since it would be more economical to seize upon truth before we commenced the investigation of it. But the order of things is otherwise. The attainment of truth is a contest, and though it is of that nature that those who lose to-day may win to-morrow—yet all must contest who win. Truth is a prize for which the racer must run, and the warrior fight, and he who is too lazy for the one, or has not courage for the other, will go without it. In debating a question details may be entered upon before principles are settled, or the question itself may be of minor importance—but these are incidents belonging to all discussions. When properly understood and properly conducted, theological controversy is no more a waste of time than any other controversy.

If the topics of theology are the inventions of knavery still it is necessary that we expose them. But the religious questions, agitated by intelligent persons, had their origin in the limited powers of man, contemplating the marvels of nature. They arose out of the insatiable longings of men to fathom the mysteries of life, and time, and death. These are questions which are not answered by being passed by—they are not to be stifled by supercillious contempt. They are questions which man, in solemn moments, puts to nature and to himself, and he must be satisfied that they can or cannot be solved. Christianity pretends to furnish us with the proper solution, and if a doubt is raised as to its competency to do so, we are triumphantly referred to its historical evidences—the value of which may be variously estimated.

Many centuries ago, long before the age of books, certain manuscripts were given to the world, but by whom, or for what motives, little is now satisfactorily known. Some centuries after their supposed first appearance portions of them began to be called the Bible, and the remainder corroborations of the Bible, or the historical evidences of christianity. These papers in numberless years have descended through innumerable hands, and undergone countless changes—inculcating obedience to the "powers that be," they were soon in requisition in various countries, and being translated into different languages, many variations of meaning unavoidably crept in. Copied sometimes, as they doubtless were, by careless writers, important alterations would be made, which, though by no means intended, they would be alterations nevertheless—and if copied by a scribe badly paid for his work, no unlikely occurrence, he would be induced to abridge his performance to shorten his labour, and thus, instead of the truth according to the apostles, we probably have the truth according to his pay! Besides, the Bible becoming the common text book of tyrants, priests, and politicans, what ignorance might not do interest would doubtless perform, and if no abridgements were made by poverty they would be by cunning—and amplifications and interpolations. Dr. Lardner admits that something like this was among christians, the great fault of the times. Dr. Henry Moore shows that every church in Christendom was guilty of intruding falsehoods in the word of God. Daille says that the early christians were in the habit of forging whole books; and father Hermas admits that lying was the besetting sin of a christian. Thus all historical evidence is enveloped in collusion, falsehood, and uncertainty; and yet we have the Bishop of Chester's word for it, that christianity can never be efficiently understood except through the media of its historical evidences.

The documents composing these evidences are gathered from ruined cities, ancient cloisters, and obscure libraries — and to oppose them, such as they are, or those portions put forth by christians, historian has to be opposed to historian, document to document, and passage to passage. And care has been taken that on the unbelieving side these shall not be easily found. Theodosius issued "The decree, that all writings whatever, which Porphyry, or any one else hath written against the christian religion, in the possession of whomsoever they may be found, should be committed to the fire; or we should not suffer any of those things so much as to come to men's ears, which tend to provoke god to wrath, and to offend the minds of the pious."

So soon as this prudent measure had taken effect christians began to taunt infidels with the lack of that argument and authority which they had taken such effectual care to destroy; and in modern times sceptics are reproached with having little to adduce on questions on which nothing has been left. The literature of the Jews being a prolific source of objections to christianity, the catholic divines of the 16th century condemned all Jewish books, without exception, to be burned. But supposing that nothing of this kind has taken place, and that historically, the contest is an equal one; before authorities corroborate or destroy the evidence of the Bible, the interpretation of the Bible itself is to be settled. The church of Rome says she has the clue to the mystery. The Protestant church claims the right of private judgment. Swedenborg declares in favour of science, and Strauss of mythos. Here we commence a war with churches, divines, translators, and grammarians—mouldy record is matched against musty parchment—the Talmud against the Bible—Celsus against Josephus—and Drummond against Lardner; and he who has most opportunities and most research, is most successful, since it is parchment, and not truth, which decides the victory.

Shortly after I had settled down with this view of this subject, I met with the following characteristic corroboration of it from a speech of Mr. Whiting, a shrewd thinker of some reputation in America. The passage transcribed is quoted approvingly in the *Dial.*

"The book from which christians professedly 'extract' their faith, may not inaptly be compared to the common law of England and America. This law consists of precedents and decisions of courts, running through many centuries, and as various and diverse in character as the individuals by whom, and the circumstances under which, they were given. When a question comes before the courts it is settled, not by justice alone, but by an appeal to the authority of precedents. So the counsel upon the different sides search the old records to find what the courts have done before, which may be made favourable to the cause they have in charge. Thus they respectively quote from my Lord Mansfield, or my Lord Coke, or Sir William Blackstone; and he who can produce the greatest number of these so called precedents, is considered entitled to judgment in his behalf. It is of very little consequence what the naked right of the matter is; what do the books say?—these are points of enquiry. Occasionally these tribunals are found giving righteous judgment; but they dare not do it on the simple equity of the case. They search the books and bring the case of 'Hobson v. Snobson' to shew that their decision is in accordance with the law, as expounded in other courts."

Enough is said to justify an estimate of christianity's historical evidences much lower than the one received. Such evidences may amaze, they may serve to display erudition, or gratify the taste for research, but they can never satisfy the practical understanding of men of the world. Christianity exercises an influence of which our daily experience can inform us whether it is good or bad. Youth is cradled in its faith, manhood matured, and old age saturated with its prejudices, and with few exceptions we find them credulous, effeminate, and bigotted. Society is covered with the mantle of christianity so that few rays of truth can penetrate the gloom. It not only darkens but it lowers human nature. Then "what matters" it to us if historical evidence *is* in its favour—experience is against it. Christianity talks of the existence of god, of future states—these are no matters of history—the crotchets of the old schoolmen are no proofs of these propositions, unless they repose on ever present facts, men of sense will never repose in them their confidence. Christianity, historically, is nothing to us—it is with christianity practically that we are concerned, and of this we can judge by experience and by facts. To investigate christianity by its historical evidences, is like going down to a distant town by the canal conveyance instead of travelling by the railway. It is as though in journeying through Italy, we should forsake the high road or open plain, for bye ways and mountain passes, where every step we may slip into a ravine, be crushed by a falling avalanche, or perish by the dagger of a bandit.

Very transient reflection establishes the superiority of the evidence of facts over the evidence of history. Up till a certain time the world was drowned, according to historical evidence, but geology disproved the fable—there was no America, according to historians, until Columbus crossed the ocean to see if they told the truth—this planet is fixed and the sun dances round it, if books are to be believed in preference to Gallileo's scientific teachings—the earth is flat and our geographies are false, unless observation and experiment are worth more than the evidence of rolls and records. We have only to bring history and experience side by side, and where they are opposed to each other, all men feel at once that one fact is worth a hundred authorities, and that the actual evidence of a single hour will weigh down volumes of history.

There is higher ground on which to debate christianity than that of its historical evidences, and which should be taken before time is wasted on minor questions. To the atheist, who believes nothing of the gods on whose existence christianity rests, its historical evidence is of no consequence. Prophets and prophecies are nothing to those who do not believe in prophet senders. It is not worth while that I dispute with my neighbour whether the people in the moon hop on their heads and have eyes in their heels, if I do not believe that there *are* people in the moon. When Mr. Paterson was challanged in Birmingham to discuss the existence of Jesus Christ, he properly replied, " it is not worth my while to discuss the existence of the Son, when I do not believe in the existence of the Father."

The moralist cares nothing for historical evidence. Is christianity compatible with human duty and dignity? is his first question. If he believes, as he well may, that christianity is a serious moral evil, no authority or argument about the existence of Christ will disturb such conclusions. If Christ did live, so much the worse. It proves that he spent his time to little purpose and his power to a worse, and that the errors of his religion have the sanction of history.

Mrs. Martin has lately written a tract upon the question, "The Bible no Revelation." People who take her view of the subject—and able writers agree with her, that in the order of things there cannot have been a revelation—of course pass by all historical evidence in favour of the infallibility of what to them is but an ordinary—and judged by ordinary rules—not a very excellent book.

Mr. Babbage, in a work which is numbered as the Ninth Bridgewater Treatise, labours to prove mathematically that Hume was in error in his famous argument against Miracles. Professor Young, of the Royal Belfast College, has lately carried Mr. Babbage's reasoning more plainly out, and the theory of Probabilities has been wrested from the Annuitants' Office in the vain attempt of overthrowing, or at least mystifying the subtle logic of Hume. But why all this trouble and parade? What cares the man of common sense whether or no Moses saw a burning bush? Sinai may have thundered and the dead have risen at the crucifixion of Christ. Be it so, these unnatural occurrences do not make christianity a whit more moral, or useful, or rational. No man who has tasted its bad feeling in a court of law, or witnessed its pernicious operation on society, but will exclaim with the Bishop of Salisbury, " so long as christianity does not comport to the light of nature and the moral obligations of reason, all the evidence in the world cannot declare in its favour."

Discussions on the authenticity and genuineness of the Bible—the mythologic origin of christianity—whether Jesus Christ was a reality or an allegory, are, if the reasons herein advanced are substantial, rather fitted for amusement and display than to be used by atheists or moralists. Christian with mere infidel may debate such points, but the atheist who labours in earnest for the settlement of religious questions, will on all occasions adhere to the great practical points before alluded to, on which men of plain sense can join a determined issue, and which involve those minor questions which have so long occupied a large share of attention, and so little hastened the termination of theological controversy. G. J. H.

REPLY TO CHARLES SOUTHWELL'S
" FALLACY OF THE ARGUMENT A PRIORI,"
&c.

PART II.
(*Continued and concluded.*)

19. I shall now turn my reader's attention to what is perhaps the most shameful literary falsehood* in Mr. Southwell's performance. Where there are so many reckless assertions, 'twere not easy to determine the point of precedency in extravagance;—but there is one false affirmation which, even in the " Fallacy," has no second in shamelessness.

20. " Our author's entire work might *easily* be converted," writes my most indiscreet antagonist, "into one of the *very best* Atheistical books extant." Such is the assertion which is pre-eminent among all Charles Southwell's impudent untruths. And next comes the proof which the gentleman pleases to give of its *correctness*. " *So soon as convenient*, I propose to *atheise* the WHOLE Argument, by the *cheap* process of substituting about a score of proper words for an

* I beg that the full force of the qualifying *adjective* may be borne in mind. It is only in a sense akin to a Parliamentary sense, I use the *substantive*. I am far from charging Mr. S. with giving birth to a falsehood: I charge his literary progeny only.

equal number of improper ones. Thus in the new edition:

"*Infinity of* MATTER *is necessarily existing*, will stand Proposition 1.—*Infinity of* MATTER *is necessarily indivisible*, will stand Proposition 2.—*Infinity of* MATTER *is necessarily immovable*, will stand Proposition 3.—*There is necessarily a* BEING *of infinity of* MATTER, will stand Proposition 4."

21. In passing, let me just ask—In what respect do the *first* and *fourth* Propositions of this atheised theism differ? The "*Being* of Infinity of matter," of Proposition 4, is distinguished (by no less than two intermediate propositions) from the "Infinity of *matter*," of Proposition 1. They are distinguished, but what is the difference? What is the difference between the necessarily existing infinite matter, and the necessarily existing being of infinite matter? Tell us that, Sir, and we shall be aware of your progress in *atheising* the "Argument"—which, so far as we have yet advanced, does certainly not seem to be so very *easily convertible* as one could have supposed, after the assurance held out. But the best part of the "*process*" *of substitution* may be to come?

"*The Being of Infinity of* MATTER *is necessarily of unity and simplicity*, will stand Proposition 5."

"Here are five" [and no more, and why no more we shall soon perceive] "of our author's propositions stated atheistically, *i. e.* as they ought to be stated, by the simple substitution in every case of *matter* for *extension*, and in like manner *all* his *other* propositions may be altered to the full stretch of 'grossest' atheism; aye, and they shall be too, in due time."*

22. But no time like the present. Let us therefore proceed to observe how some of the "other propositions" look after being duly "altered." After being cast in the new mould, whether they shall be good *atheism* or no, we at least have some right to expect that they shall be good *sense*.

23. To pass over the sub-proposition in Part 1,—viz., "The material universe is finite in extension"—As to which, "the simple substitution of "*matter* for *extension*," will not do, seeing *matter* (in the shape of "the Material Universe") is, as ill luck will have it, the subject of the sub-proposition already. To pass over Part 2, which relates to *duration*, and could not be at all managed by the "simple substitution" "of matter for extension," for this simple reason, that "extension" is in no case there to be substituted—To pass over, I say, Part 2 altogether. To pass over Part 3, in the same wholesale manner, and for equally potent reasons; we arrive at Division 2 :* the first proposition in which is—"The Simple, Sole, Being of Infinity of Expansion and of Duration, is, necessarily, *Intelligent* and *All-knowing*."

24. This is the theistic, or old, dress: now for the new. 'The Simple, Sole, Being of Infinity of—matter—and of—matter—is necessarily Intelligent, and All-knowing.' Matter, or the material universe, intelligent and all-knowing—necessarily intelligent and all-knowing! Verily, verily, there is a *substitution here*—a substitution. for theism, of nonsense. Or, should it not be allowed to be nonsense, 'tis no better than a strange unaccountable species of theism. Be the proposition, in its new guise, nonsense, I make Mr. Southwell welcome to it. Be it but bad theism, I welcome it myself. Better a Stoical or Heraclitical sort of God than none.

25. To take a second from among the "other propositions," which "all," urges my adversary, " may be altered," by the "cheap process of substituting" atheistic, for theistic elements. The third Proposition in Division 2, runs thus: "The Simple, Sole, Being of Infinity of Expansion and of Duration, who is All-knowing and All-powerful, is, necessarily, *entirely Free*." This proposition, no introduction of corporal elements could fit for the use of Stoical philosophers; since the God of the Stoics' system, if not fate, is *fated*. The God of the Stoic is as much acted on by fate as is the Stoic himself.

26. But tho' unfit for Stoics, may not the metamorphosed proposition turn out to be fit for atheists? The proposition, metamorphosed, is to the following effect: 'the Simple, Sole, Being of Infinity of—matter, and of—matter—who *is* All-knowing, and All-powerful, is, necessarily, entirely Free.' Now the truth is, that Freeness is of all things that which is most abhorrent to your thoroughpaced atheist. He hates anything having the form of free agency, more, perhaps, than he hates all the other theistic attributes together. And the predication, regarding matter, of freedom of the will—much as the atheist presently loves and respects matter—were enough to sow the seeds of a dangerous animosity in the mind of every true atheist. And it would never do for your atheist to cast off his only solid friend.

27. As Division 2 of the "Argument" is concerned with the Natural Attributes, so Division 3 advances to the Moral Attributes—in especial, to the great Moral Attribute of Goodness. And if it be absurd to invest body, as body, with Liberty of the Will, it were much more absurd (if there can be degrees in impossibility) to clothe the merely corporeal

---

* Paper 2, par. 18, 19, 20, 21.

* Called, in the preceding edition, Book 2.

with consummate Happiness, and the most perfect Goodness.

28. In fine, neither Division 2, nor Division 3, will submit to be *atheised*. Atheise such propositions as we have instanced, and meaning vanishes, nonsense ensues—So far from their being capable of being "altered to the full stretch of ' grossest' atheism."

29. I now leave it to every impartial reader to pass proper sentence on Mr. Southwell for his excess in effrontery, in burthening the *Movement* with so impudent an assertion as this, that my "*entire* work might *easily* be converted into one of the very best Atheistical books extant." The "Argument" may be metamorphosed, not only into good Atheism, but into the best: only think of that! Can I be wrong in prophesying, that Charles Southwell's "convenient season," for atheising "the whole Argument," will come with Felix and Drusilla's, for doing something else?

30. It would be injudicious, to close this criticism on Mr. Southwell's strictures, without remarking a certain peculiarity in the *style* in which they are written.

31. What reason had my answerer for introducing into such a discussion so much low vulgarity? Why does he indulge so freely in a *figure of speech* which (having Warburton in view) I may denominate the *lewd sneer*?—The GOD whose existence the London Atheists were *challenged* to disprove;—whether is that God, asks their champion, "not the most comical of deities?" "Infinite extension, infinite expansion, and infinite duration——can," writes the same gentleman, "neither be bottled off by the pint like wine, or [grammatically, nor] cut and eaten by the pound like cheese—no."* My readers have had a specimen: in mercy, I refrain from "That strain again."

After what *writers*—I nearly wrote *speakers*—did this Charles Southwell form his style? Who were his models? or is the style strictly original?

32. Is there one word in all the "Argument. *à priori*," that could give my adversary a handle for seizing on such offensive weapons as he brandishes, to the injury of—not the cause he opposes, but—his unfortunate readers? Mr. Southwell's instruments of offence put one irresistibly in mind of the attack made on Gulliver by the Yahoos, who, for want of better arms, discharged their excrement upon him.

33. The truth is, the weapons Mr. Southwell rejoices in wielding hurt only himself. A good cause is not that which can be furthered by scurrile mirth.

34. One thing is especially to be regretted.

---

* Paper 2, par. 13.

The *style* which my antagonist has seen fit to employ will, in all likelihood, have the effect of repelling the approach of many excellent persons, who, otherwise, might have dipped seriously into the controversy. May a sense of duty overcome a repugnance to come into contact with coarse ribaldry!

35. To bring my *Reply* to a conclusion, by returning to what, after all, is the point of greatest moment in this discussion. The *first* Proposition of the "Argument"—the proposition affirming, that "*Infinity of Extension is necessarily existing*"—has, indeed, turned out "an Atheist-confounding *truth*;"† Mr. Southwell having contradicted his own denial of the truth, and pledged the subject-matter of his whole philosophy for its veracity.‡ It turned out an Atheist-confounding-truth, not "under Gillespie's wonder-working hand,"§ but under Southwell's own hand, which worked no wonder, altho' it dealt in contradictions. The man who denies, that there is necessarily infinite extension, must, sometime or other, yea before long, contradict himself.

P. S. I may mention to those of my readers who perused Mr. Southwell's strictures, that I have in no case taken any advantage of the *errata* (and consequent nonsense) which they contain. I may have been too indulgent in particular instances: supposing a meaning, not brought out by the printer, had been intended by the author, where no meaning would have appeared had the printer employed all the resources of his art. But truth, not victory unaccompanied by truth, was the quarry I aimed at.

THE NEW SOCIALIST EXECUTIVE.

I.

WE take advantage of our temporarily enlarged space to offer a few remarks on Socialists affairs, at home and abroad.

On Sunday week Mr. Buxton was honoured with a public breakfast in the Branch A1 Hall. The party was presided over by Mr. Robert Clark, and addressed by Mr. Buxton, Messrs. Ellis, Southwell, Holyoake, and Fleming. Mr. Buxton's history of his position and outline of his policy was received with marked satisfaction and applause. At the conclusion one opinion was, by resolution, unanimously expressed, as to the soundness of the President's view, and of "confidence in his integrity and judgment." This is as gratifying as it is important. An opinion prevailed among the socialists of the provinces, that the socialists of the metropolis were proud, respectable, and cold

---

† "Fallacy," Paper 1, par. 3.
‡ See Part 1 of this Reply, par. 18, 22.
§ "Fallacy," Paper 1, par. 3.

in their bearing towards the new executive which has been borne to power by provincial suffrages, and supported by greater enthusiasm, and plainer and bolder purposes than their predecessors. But this impression will now be happily dissipated—the socialists of the metropolis without one dissentient voice, intimated their approval, and awarded their confidence to the new executive. Mr. Buxton asked only for one year's fair trial. Mr. Fleming, in a speech which promised something like cordial co-operation for the future, hoped that Mr. Buxton might not enjoy one year only of office, but many.

The struggle out of door is now over. Our hopes now depend on what may be accomplished within. We have been told that "it was always the intention of the late Board to have a working man's community." But our new board must do something more than *intend* it—a little, if they please, towards realising it. The present executive is a working man's executive—if it is not that it is nothing. To that idea they owe their position, and upon the triumph of that idea depends the triumph of socialism. Let them not be deterred by sayings about "party names," or "charity for all," or "universal interests." We have an excess of philanthropic pretensions, arising no doubt in benevolent error, but it is error nevertheless. Socialists, priding themselves on being an influential party, have decried party and all its necessary appendages of practical distinctions, until they have nearly extinguished themselves as a party. "Charity for all" has been with them—not intentionally—but practically, charity for nobody in particular. "It is not our intention," said recently, an authority on socialism, "to establish a *working man's*, or a *capitalists'* community — but a community of united interests." But a "community of united interests" is at present but a watch-word, a pole star idea, like that of human perfection, indicative of ultimate object, pointing out the course to be steered in, but expressive of nothing practically realizable. The only practicable thing that can now be done is to establish the working man's interests—to give to the order of industry the power and independance of a party. The attempts to blend all interests at Tytherly, by the late board, ended in promoting nobody's. The old executive hovered blandly and childishly over all interests, and touched none. The result was that they lived without popular sympathy, and died without regret. They had not half wealth enough to make an attractive home for the rich, and it was all expended on buildings unfitted for the poor. Establish a working man's community, and take all the care you please that his interests injure no other interests—make them promote other interests if you can, but attend chiefly to his emancipation—give him position, self-reliance, independance—and when he is elevated socially, then the union of hearts and interests will be easy, solid, lasting, and complete. In the history of society, wealth never yet cordially united with poverty, and in the nature of things it cannot. Men cannot in the mass descend —but poverty may be raised—working men *can* be made rich men, and he is the truest friend to equality who aims directly, exclusively and solely at industy's emancipation. Such men may make little noise as universal philanthropists, they may not be credited with enlarged views, but they are working at philanthrophy's true foundation, they are doing its first' work—*raising the lowest*. Others are dreaming—they are doing.

The true province of the moral reformer is not to waste time and energy in the vain endeavour to blend rich and poor interests —but to devote all his energies to the elevation of the law. Burke gave it as the result of much parliamentary experience, that it was "idle to attempt the pleasing of those who were not willing to be pleased." The rich are not willing to be pleased with our equalitarian notions, and it more becomes us, as men of sense and spirit, to confine our exertions to pleasing ourselves, in all good feeling and fellowship toward our more fortunate fellow-men—envying them not, dispising them not—accepting any co-operation they are willing to render—but still chiefly, earnestly, and resolutely bent on achieving our class independence. In this way, and in this way only, can working-men command the esteem of the wealthy, and at the same time surely and firmly promote their own welfare.

Permit me to quote the honest and sound advice of a writer in *Chambers' Journal* a few weeks ago. "We would only fear that there is some danger of leading the humbler classes to trust too much to those above them. It is a law of nature that each man must look chiefly to himself for the protection and advancement of his own interests; for no other can do it so well. Each person is bound to take some care of his own conduct, for it is impossible that he can be safely conducted in moral leading strings all his days. Are the millions of brains among the working classes to take no active or independant part in these respects, but to trust entirely to the smaller number of superior rank? There is surely some absurdity here?"

This language of actual, not theoretical experience, we commend it to the consideration of our new executive. A thousand points of importance crowd forward for expression. We must devote a series of papers to their discussion, for this week we must leave this subject—insisting as a primary principle of action that our new socialist directors display singleness of purpose, and that that purpose be the raising of the wretched and the low. Then may the glorious sympathies of former times be revived, and their days be long in the land.

G. J. H.

ADDRESS TO ROBERT OWEN.

(*On his departure for America.*)

FROM THE CONDUCTORS OF THE MOVEMENT.
Read by Mr. Holyoake at the Public Breakfast, August 11, 1844.

THE persons whose names are appended to this address may be taken as representing a party, who, though belonging to the society of which you are the acknowledged head, are considered somewhat in the light of dissentients, for *this* reason they have sought this opportunity of assuring you that whatever may be their difference of opinion, there is no difference in the affection they bear you.

In you they recognise the benevolent sculptor, who, out of the misshapen block of society, has hewn the beautiful and breathing statue of co-operative humanity. A moral Euclid, you have done for society what that mathematician did for geometry—collected the scattered wisdom of earth's sages, and given to it order, system, and practical utility. Other philosophers have pointed to what *should* be done—it remained for Robert Owen to propose *to do it*. For half a century humanity has known you as its friend. In both hemispheres you have borne witness against societarian error, and in the retreats of grandeur, and the humble haunts of poverty, you have gone like the herald of happiness, and pointed to the equality of mankind. By your writings wealth has been taught its true office, and enslaved industry the means of emancipation—human nature has been made the popular study of the multitude, and thought, both in the old world and the new, has received a lasting impetus. On all these accounts we naturally congratulate you, because in whatever adds to the independance of humanity, perhaps more than other men, we are deeply interested.

As recipients of those great metaphysical truths, which you have been instrumental in disseminating to the world, we are your debtors. That it is our good fortune to seek the fabled blessings of religion only in the practice of morality, and the supposed guardianship of a providence, in the triumphs of science, were first owing to your instruction and example. It is, therefore, no less our duty than our pleasure to bear testimony to the advantages of having lived within the sphere of your influence.

It would be to impugn the high philosophy both of your writings and your life, were we to deem it necessary to excuse ourselves for having, on some particulars, dissented from yourself. Your usefulness has emanated from independance of thought—and to respect individuality of sentiment is the proud characteristic of Socialism. To have broken in the blindness and bigotry of the age, and stimulated a nation to practical and liberal thinking, will ever be reckoned among your most honourable triumphs.

It is not necessary that we wish that your visit to your family, to whom we desire our regards, may be a happy one. Whatever pertains to the province of affection, is, in your case, no subject of anxiety. But if fortune can be influenced by our hopes you will not only reach them in safety, but return in health, to witness the realization of those plans of human progression, with which the name of Robert Owen, will, through future time be associated.

Signed } G. JACOB HOLYOAKE,
M. QUESTELL RYALL.

London, August 11, 1844.

THE PUBLIC BREAKFAST TO MR. OWEN.

THE public breakfast to Mr. Owen, at John Street on Sunday morning, August 11, previously to his departure to America, was crowded and enthusiastic. Mr. Owen was in excellent health and spirits. Gratifying addresses were presented to him, appropriate without being fulsome, and full of feeling without compromise of principle. Public men often suffer more from their friends than enemies, but Mr. Owen on this occasion had reason to be gratified with the discreet eulogy, the honest and honourable appreciation expressed of his long and useful life. Mr. Clarke, Mr. Fleming, Mrs. Chappelsmith, Mr. Ellis, Mr. Campbell, and Mr. Southwell spoke on the occasion.

Mr. Owen sustained his high character by the feeling and good sense which he displayed on the occasion. He spoke of the changes of the government and the New Executive like a philosopher. His bearing on these topics was of a superior order. He said, "let the New Executive be tried, let them have fair, honest, and ardent support. Let every man help them. He thought they attempted what greater experience would convince them was impracticable, still his plan was, let them try—let them gain the experience. It would be of great worth, and if they succeeded, glorious would be their triumph. It would be a cheering lesson to the world." There was no coldness, no semi-praise and semi-censure, so impartially combined as to neutralise each other—it was honest, warm, disingenuous, philosophic encouragement.

He spoke of Mr. Bate, who is unfortunately labouring under an attack of ill health which threatens his life. "It was necessary that he should seek the sea breezes and perhaps a warmer climate. But as he had advanced the whole of his ample fortune towards the Harmony experiment, it was necessary that a portion of it should be placed at his disposal again, that he might command all the means nature afforded of recovering his health." The deep sympathy with which mention of Mr. Bate was received, evinced the intense and honourable appreciation with which his generous and noble sacrifices were regarded. Upon this we must express our opinion that the Executive must be put into immediate possession of the means of placing Mr. Bates' property at his own disposal. We shall ourselves at once commence assisting in this object, and call upon every body who reads this paper, or takes the slightest interest in socialist proceedings and reputation, to do likewise. From those who can assist with pounds, to those who can only pay in pence, all must at once join in this object. Better by far that Tytherly fail an hundred times over, than that one honourable and generous man should suffer by his generosity to us. No faith, no tittle of faith expressed, implied or understood with any capitalist, high or low, must be broken. I would rather that Harmony be sold by auction to-morrow, than that one subscriber or loan lender be the wronged of one farthing. Let those who pretend to regard Mr. Owen with affection or veneration show their sincerity by responding at once to this, his parting appeal, and show to such excellent friends as Mr. Bate, that we are not unmindful of their worth.

G. J. H.

THE INFIDEL TRACT SOCIETY.

[The following is an extract from a letter of a member of this society to a gentleman, informing him of the society's plans and constitution. Having fallen in our way we have taken the liberty of using it. The intentions of our young friends are so cool and, apparently, so soberly matured, that we are happy in soliciting attention to the proceedings. They will do themselves credit, and society good if they fulfil their fair promise.—ED. of M.]

"DEAR SIR,—The Infidel Tract Society is as yet in its infancy, and lacks consolidated strength sufficient to enable it to withstand the attacks, and interference of our blessed politic-religious government and "Old Mother Church," assisted as they will be by the dissenters. We shall supply, as far as our means will allow, friends in the country towns, as we wish our sphere of operations to be as extensive as possible.

"The society is not a mere bubble of the day—it is no idle or thoughtless speculation —it is not a mushroom affair, which springs up one day and is cut down the next—it will not be *dependent* on extraneous aid, although such aid will at all times be gladly accepted. It has within itself the means to conserve its existence—those means are boldness, honesty, integrity, and when necessary and called for, self-sacrifice — pecuniary and otherwise. We have a straight forward course to pursue—we shall avoid all cowardly, deviating, tortuous lines of policy, and while, abiding by principle alone, and acting out our determination to exert all our power in the attempt to overthrow and extirpate the present system of tyranny, slavery, cheating, and credulity; the aid of any party will be gratefully accepted. But should others not think fit to assist us, we shall still pursue the (probably not even) tenor of our way—and instead of asking or begging for assistance (I scorn the begging system) we will rely on our own strength, and "e'en go on without their aid." Apathy will not retard, and persecution will facilitate, its operations, as Mr. Owen would say.

Religion has been an incubus on human society for ages upon ages, stretching back into the distant, dim, obscure past, far beyond human ken or power of observation. Let ultra-infidels then, boldly act up to their convictions and professions, and lend a helping hand to redeem humanity from its degraded condition, to deliver man from the cunning, cruelty, and delusion of priestcraft, to subvert monarchy—that scourge of the world which is built upon the bones, and cemented together with the blood, of its victims. Let them put forth their mighty energies, and never cease their efforts until they have utterly destroyed the belief in the god of theology, and the christian scheme of revelation.

RICHARD DOYLE.

MAKING THE BEST OF IT.—A procession was taking place to the church of St. Genevieve, for the purpose of obtaining dry weather. The pious people had scarcely reached the square when it began to rain with great violence. "Never mind that," said the bishop, "the saint mistakes us entirely—she thinks we have been praying for wet weather!"

INSTRUCTIONS OF THE CHIEF OF THE CAPUCHINS AT RAGUSA, TO BROTHER PEDICULOSO, ON HIS DEPARTURE FOR THE HOLY LAND. BY VOLTAIRE.

III.

We will now turn your attention to the New Testament. First you will reconcile the two genealogies of Christ, which you will find the easiest thing in the world to do, for the one is totally different from the other, and it is evident that this is a holy and admirable mystery. The good Calmet says very candidly, in speaking of the two genealogies of Melchesidech, "*As falsehood always betrays itself, some give his genealogy in one way and some in another.*" "He owns then," the unbelievers say, "that this enormous difference is an evident proof that the whole story is a lie." Very true, so far as Melchisedech is concerned, for he was only a man; but Jesus Christ was both man and God! of course, therefore, he must have two genealogies.

You will see how it happened that Mary and Joseph took their child into Egypt, according to Matthew, whereas Luke says they remained at Bethlehem; and explain all the other sacred contradictions. Some very pretty things may be said respecting the water changed into wine at the wedding of Cana when the guests were all drunk, for John, the only one of the apostles who speaks of it, says, expressly that they were: "*et cum inebriatate fuerint,*" says the Vulgate. You had better read the "*Questions of Zapata,*" upon the massacre of the innocents by Herod; upon the star of the three kings; and upon the fig-tree that was blasted for not bearing fruit, " when it was not the time for figs," as the text says. The ham curers of 'Westphalia are surprised that Jesus should have sent the devil into the bodies of 2,000 swine, particularly as there were no swine in Judea; they say that if he had given them the swine, instead of sending the devil to them, they would have made more than 20,000 florins by them, that is supposing they were fat.

When you shall have made these things all clear, we recommend to you, most earnestly, to set about a vindication of Luke, who, having been the last among the evangelists who wrote, and of course better informed than the rest of them, as he says, ought to be received with great respect. This respectable Luke assures us that when Mary was ready to lie in, Cæsar Augustus commanded (in order that the prophecies might be fulfilled) a census to be taken of all the inhabitants of the world, and that Quirinus, governor of Syria, published that edict in Judea. Certain infidels, who unluckily are learned men, pretend that there is not a word of truth in this story; that Agustus never issued so ridiculous and extravagant an order; that Quirinus was not governor of Syria until ten years after the confinement of Mary; and that Luke was in all likelihood a blockhead, who having heard that a census of Rome was made in the time of Augustus, and that Quirinus was governor of Syria after Varus, confounds events and dates; that he talks like a country booby, ignorant of what passes in the capital, and yet has the vanity to say that he is better informed than other people.

This is what the impious say; but do not heed them: think and speak only as the pious think and speak, and above all, do not forget to read those questions I have mentioned; they will clear up these difficulties, as well as all others; perhaps there is not one of them that might not puzzle a Capuchin; but, with the grace of God for help, every thing may be explained.

Do not fail to inform us, if you meet in your travels with any of those wretches who think lightly of the transubstantiation, of the ascension, the assumption, the annunciation, and the inquisition, and who satisfy themselves with believing in God, with worshipping him in spirit and in truth, and with acting uprightly. You will easily recognize these monsters; they only aim at being good subjects, good sons, good husbands, and good fathers; they give alms to the poor, and none to the Capuchins. There is no true religion but that which gives millions to the Pope, and abundant alms to the Capuchins. Finally I commend myself to your prayers, and to those of the sacred little people who inhabit your beard.

THE END.

TESTIMONIAL TO MR. PATERSON.

At a meeting of the Committee of the Anti-Persecution Union, held last week, the secretary reported that the Union's ancient friend W. J. B. had sent £1 to be appropriated to the "Paterson Testimonial;" it was resolved that £5 be added to it from the Union's funds, and that the friends of liberty be called upon to augment this Testimonial to be presented to Mr. Paterson on his liberation, as some token of the estimation in which his services and sufferings are held. Subscriptions to be addressed to the Secretary of the Anti-Persecution Union.

PERSECUTION FOR OPINION. — No one but the religious persecutor, a mischievous and overgrown child, wreaks his vengeance on involuntary, inevitable, compulsory acts or states of the understanding, which are no more affected by blame than the stone which the foolish child beats for hurting him.—*Sir James Mackintosh.*

ARMOUR FOR ATHEISTS.

A LITTLE tract from the pen of Mr. Southwell, and published by Miss Roalfe of Edinburgh, has just made its appearance, under the title of "The Existence of God Disproved by Believers in God." It is a capital idea. By it the atheist will be put upon extending his observations over a far wider field—he will be put in possession of arguments, probably of far greater efficacy with the christian world, than those by which he might have reasoned himself into his present sentiments. Many god-believers might suffer this tract to be put into their hands, and be stimulated to peruse it by the weight of the authority. We may then fairly leave them to the operation of the weight of the arguments.

Mr. Southwell has thus divided the subject:—

"There are five, and *only* five, methods of proving the existence of God—the *scriptural*, the *miraculous*, the *a priori*, the *à posteriori*, and the *sentimental*. All these methods of satisfying the thoughtful that ' God is,' were invented by believers; and the design of this tract is to show, that, by believers, they are proved essentially defective.

"The *sentimental* method of establishing the reality of an imagined Author of Nature, is very simple; consisting in an appeal to the *feelings*, or what the admirers of that method designate the 'light within.' They deny that God can be ' found out' by way of reason. Feeling or sentiment, *not* reason, is their guide in all that concerns the existence and providence of ' Spiritual Being.' They say, that unless a voice from within proclaim the existence of something *more* than Nature, it never can be proclaimed."

The " five, and only five methods" above, by the way, are as assumptive and probably as baseless as the celebrated " five facts and twenty laws"—*that is as to number and classification.* But let that pass; they are valuable, instructive, and suggestive; that is, the so called " five, and five only methods," (no disparagement also to the " five facts and twenty laws" as aforesaid,) in the way they are carried out in the book. Oregen Bacheler's argument I take to be the least cogent as against the sentimentalists, it seems rather to defend reason than to attack sentimentalism. Lord Brougham's is far the most crushing. It is so well put that I cannot resist transferring it to our columns. Mr. Southwell classes this argument as antagonistic to his "First and Second Methods," that is adverse to the " scriptural and miraculous" methods of proving the existence of God.

" Suppose it were shown by incontestible proofs that a messsenger sent immediately from heaven had appeared on the earth; suppose, to make the case more strong against our argument, that this messenger arrived in our own days, nay, appeared before our eyes, and showed his divine title to have his message believed, by performing miracles in our presence, no one can by possibility imagine a stronger case; for it excludes all arguments upon the weight or the possibility of its testimony; it assumes all the ordinary difficulties in the way of revelation to be got over. Now even this strong evidence would not at all establish the truth of the doctrine promulgated by the messenger; for it would not show that the story he brought was worthy of belief in any one particular except his supernatural power. This would be demonstrated by his working miracles, all the rest of his statement would rest on his assertion. But a being capable of working miracles might very well be capable of deceiving us. The possession of power does not of necessity exclude either fraud or malice. This messenger might come from an evil as well as good being; he might come from more beings than one; or he might come from one being of many existing in the universe. When christianity was first promulgated, the miracles of Jesus were not denied by the ancients; but it was asserted that they came from evil beings, and that he was a magician. Such an explanation was consistent with the kind of belief to which the votaries of polytheism were accustomed. They were habitually credulous of miracles and of divine interpositions. But their argument was not at all unphilosophical. There is nothing whatever inconsistent in the power to work miracles being conferred upon a man, or a monster, by a supernatural being, who is either of limited power himself, or of great malignity, or who is one of many such beings. Yet it is certain that no means can be devised for attesting the supernatural agency of any one, except such a power of working miracles, therefore it is plain, that none sufficient can ever be given by direct revelation alone in favour of the great truths of religion. The messenger in question might have power to work miracles without end, and yet it would remain unproved, either that God was omnipotent, and one, and benevolent; or that he destined his creatures to a future state, or that he made them such as they are in their present state."

The other god-believers pitted against each other are Mr. Gillespie and the Rev. J. Smith, and if like the Kilkenny cats, they have fairly devoured one another body and bones, why the less trouble is left to us the ungodly—we have nothing to do but to pitch the tails after them.

M. Q. R.

BALANCE SHEET OF THE ANTI-PERSECUTION UNION,

For the Fourth Quarter, ending June 29, 1844.

RECEIPTS.

	£	s.	d.
Subscriptions, as per *Movement* No. 19	1	14	11
Do. do. 20	1	18	6
Do. do. 21	2	9	4
Do. do. 23	0	19	0
Do. do. 25	0	4	0
Do. do. 26	0	11	0
Do. do. 27	0	16	0
Do. do. 28	1	7	5
Do. do. 29	0	5	6
From W. B. B. for Miss Roalfe	0	10	0
Do to purchase 2 vols. *Oracles* for Mr. Finlay	0	10	0
To Sale of Scotch Trials	2	0	0
To Balance due to Treasurer	1	11	9
TOTAL	**£14**	**17**	**5**

EXPENDITURE.

	£	s.	d.
Balance due to Treasurer	1	3	8
To Secretary from W. J. B.	0	10	0
To payment of Mr. Whiting	1	12	6
To Printing in Gazette	1	9	0
To 2,000 Bills of "Trials."	1	10	0
To Mr. Paterson, Perth	0	3	6
To do. as per Subscription	0	7	4½
To Parcel of Brushes, Books, &c.	0	10	0
To Mr. P. from Mr. Bidwell	1	18	6
To Expences of Public Meeting at John Street, Advertisement, &c.	0	10	0
To Purchase of 2 vols. of *Oracles* for Mr. Finlay	0	10	0
To Miss Roalfe	0	11	3
Gazettes distributed to Journals, &c.	0	1	6
Printed Petitions	0	2	0
Distributing "Trials," for review	0	0	8
Post Orders deducted in remittances	0	0	7
Letter to Dr. Kalley	0	0	4
Two Acts of Parliament	0	0	10½
To General Correspondence	1	4	9
Collector's Card Cases for Scottish Union	0	7	6
To Assistant Secretary	1	10	0
TOTAL	**£14**	**17**	**5**

Audited by us, and found correct,

JOSHUA HOPKINS, } Auditors.
ALLEN DAVENPORT,

POLITICAL VIRTUE.—Moral obligation is without a meaning, if the faithful discharge of the electoral duties is not among the highest.

NOTICE.

DEPARTURE OF MR. OWEN.—On Sunday, at three o'clock, the Socialists of the Metropolis and friends of Mr. Owen will, if the weather is fine, meet him at the Duke of York's Column, and accompany him to the railway terminus.

THE SECOND ANNUAL MEETING of the Anti-Persecution Union will be held in the Hall of Science, City-road, on Tuesday evening, August 27th.

MEMBERS TICKETS.—The Members and friends of the Anti-Persecution Union are informed that the new quarterly tickets of membership are now ready to be issued; to be had on application to the secretary, or of the collectors in town and country.

THE GILLESPIEAN DISCUSSION.—Mr. Southwell's Rejoinder to Mr. Gillespie will appear in our next.

Mr. Gillespie's Comment on the Remarks of G. J. H., in No. 16 of the *Movement*, entitled the " A Priori God," will appear also, if possible, in the same number.

A REPORT of the Public Breakfast to Mr. Owen and his Evening Lecture, will be published this day by Mr. MERRIMAN, Barbican.

TO CORRESPONDENTS.

RECEIVED—The *National*—*Boston Investigator*, from W. B. B—The Second Quarterly Report of the Leicester Branch of the Anti-Persecution Union duly audited.

Mr. G. ADAMS informs us, with reference to the allusion to Saltmarsh's opinion on prayer in *Movement* No. 32, that that writer declares " that if a man prays he is in a state of pupilage, and not yet brought into the liberty of Christ—that while christians pray for anything, they are in the dark and in bondage," which Mr. Adams says he does not doubt. Mr. S. does express more rational notions on prayer than any christian writer with which we are acquainted. No doubt but Mr. Montgomery was indebted to Mr. Saltmarsh for the best idea he has expressed on prayer.

Mr. IRONNSIDES says, with reference to the notice of Sheffield proceedings in No. 32, " Our Montgomery's christian name is James. It is Robert Montgomery who is the author of Satan. M. Q. R. was wrong in supposing that the life of Pemberton was the sore point with the saints. That work is in, but the fact was used as an illustration of the inconsistency of the party opposing the admission of novels and plays, and admitting a work containing plays.

T. A. B.—Will he tell us who is the author of that description of angels with which he favours us ?

T. P.—We believe that Mr. Watts of Manchester obtained his title from the same German University that Dr. Beard, the Unitarian, obtained his. Dr. Watts' degree is from Giessen, Hessen Daunstadt, the University where the celebrated Liebeg teaches. The title was obtained by transmitting one of Mr. Watts' own books, " Facts and Fictions," and an Autobiography written in German. We do not admire these foreign diplomas, unless voluntarily conferred, but our taste need not be everybody's standard.

H. R., DERBY.—We are greatly indebted to our excellent friend. His suggestions shall not be lost sight of.

M. R.—We did by accident see the paper, signed an " Enemy to Cant and Humbug." It would be well if the writer was also an enemy to " Calumny and Scurrility." The degraded author of the production has long been the public disgrace of the town in which he resides. To the palpable malignity in which he writes, is added the cowardice of the assassin who stabs in the dark. Let the writer put his name to his attack, and the persons calumniated would quickly visit him. The good sense of mankind has long consigned the anonymous slanderer to execration.

FROM W. J. B., for the editor of the *Movement* and Secretary of the Anti-Persecution Union 1 0 0

SUBSCRIPTIONS TO THE ANTI-PERSECUTION UNION.

W. J. B. to the Paterson Testimonial £1 0 0
The Balance of the Second Quarter's Subscription of the Leicester Branch of the Union . 0 18 4
Bristol Subscriptions for July, per Mr. Chilton:—
Card 11 . . . . 0 4 0
12 . . . . 0 0 6
13 . . . . 0 1 0
16 . . . . 0 4 0
G. J. H., *See.*

Printed and Published by G. J. HOLYOAKE, 40, Holywell-street, Strand, Saturday, August 17, 1844.

THE MOVEMENT
And Anti=Persecution Gazette.

"Maximize morals, minimize religion."—BENTHAM.

No. 37.   EDITED BY G. JACOB HOLYOAKE, ASSISTED BY M. Q. RYALL.   PRICE 2d

THE BATTLE OF THE CHORYPHÆI.

"It is evident that if time be succession and space be extension, man needs for the formation of these two ideas a third idea—the idea of movement.—Now the idea of movement pre-supposes the idea of something moving, consequently the idea of time and space is neither original nor primitive, but one derived—first from the idea of something given, and secondly from the idea of something moving."—*The Rev. J. E. Smith.*

To the Editor of the Movement.

SIR,—I perceive that William Gillespie in ignorance or contempt of the sage admonition—*Waste not thy time in attempting impossibilities*, has replied in numbers 25, 35, and 36 of the *Movement*, to certain Strictures of mine which appeared in numbers 14 and 15 of that periodical. I wrote them by particular request of some modern Athenian "feelosophers," known to fame as Philatheans, who for many years have been "peaceably suppressing infidelity," so very peaceably, that themselves excepted, no one knew anything about it. However, they seem desperately bent *now* on making a considerable noise in order to effect the peaceable work they stand pledged to perform, and about twelve months ago were by admiration of Mr. Gillespie's "Argument," so far transported beyond discretion's bounds as to challenge everybody or anybody to overturn it—Of course under such circumstances we poor "London Atheists" could find no loop-hole through which an escape from the great Northern Wizard's terrible logic might honorably be made. The upshot was my "Strictures," which penned as Mr. Gillespie did me the felicity of declaring "by the Choryphæus of the London Atheists" have had the happy effect of drawing out the Choryphæus of the Edinburgh Philatheans:

    When Greek meets Greek
    Then comes the tug of war

every one will admit, and the Reply clearly establishes, that when Choryphæus meets Choryphæus a like result ensues. It also illustrates the old truth, that replies are not always answers.

But though the Reply is no Answer to the Strictures, it undoubtedly is a *curiosity*. Anything so studiedly impudent, so logically indefinite, and so little to the purpose I do not remember to have met with. Viewed as a case of complete and very systematic *felo de se*, it is unmatched and perhaps unmatchable. With propriety perfectly mathematical —it is printed in two Parts, which taken together fill no fewer than seventeen *Movement* columns, so that the "Reply" cannot justly be called "meagre," and I hope, sir, to demonstrate its claim to be considered a "very precious" production.[*]

The saints forefend that Mr. Gillespie entertain any such foolish horror of candid friends as was expressed by George Canning, because in dissecting his Reply my resolve is most *mercilessly* to act the part of one.

That Reply proves nothing save and except only its author's ability to sneer at, to misrepresent, and thus to *evade* atheistical arguments. As however I am "an Atheistic Propagandist," and Mr. Gillespie's printed judgement of all such persons is that they

[*] Our author has thought proper in a recent edition of "*The* Argument to the exclusion, as it were, of all other *a priori* methods," to displace "God" by "a great First Cause." —Those who are curious to know his reasons for such displacement may satisfy their curiosity by turning to an "Address to the Third Edition." Had I seen the edition in question before penning the Strictures, "Great First Cause" would have been uniformly used in lieu of "God," but seeing no good end to be achieved by substituting at *this stage of the controversy*, the former long and inconvenient term for the latter short and very convenient one, I shall (under favour of my antagonist) adhere to it—Of course, however, throughout this "Battle," all quotations not made from the Reply itself will be faithful extracts from the last, that is to say the *third* edition of our author's performance. This I mention to obviate mistake or confusion.

are* "nondescript monsters created by nature in a moment of madness;" I cannot reasonably expect him to highly esteem my arguments, especially when those arguments happen to strike at that renowned fallacy on which he has so strenuously laboured to build up a philosophical reputation.

It would of course be worse than futile for either of us to drag into the present controversy any *secondary* question until we have settled the *primary* one. Mr. Gillespie *affirms* I *deny* the existence of Infininity of Extension, and it will be time enough for him to chuckle about my admission that "if Proposition 1 of his Argument is sound, the whole Argument is sound," *when* Proposition 1 is proved sound. But Mr. Gillespie should take the trouble to *prove it sound* before shouting as though a victory had been obtained. To halloo before out of the wood is a species of childishness, children should be left to practice.

Mr. Gillespie labours hard in the First Part of "Reply" to make it appear that I *admit* the existence of extension. Now those who have watched this controversy are aware that over and over again I have *denied* the existence of extension; and how 'tis possible for any one, wise or simple, to admit while denying the existence of extension Mr. Gillespie is bound to explain.

In No. 14 of the *Movement* are these words:—

"I promise to demonstrate in the next *Movement* that there is no such *thing*, and consequently no such *existence* as extension, and that Gillespie is *quite right* when he asserts there can be no existence without extension, though *quite wrong* when he calls extension an existence, for as already remarked, and as shall be clearly shown, extension no more exists than time or motion.

In the next *Movement* I said:—

"If extension is real, it is matter, and our author (Gillespie) stands proved a dishonest Atheist, or an Atheist so stupid as not to know he is one—Atheism claiming for matter precisely what he claims for extension.

"If extension is not matter, it is nothing, for matter and something being convertible terms, to somethingize extension is to materialize it—a demonstration that the infinite extension of our author is just an infinite nothing, the parts of which are without doubt, necessarily indivisible from each other.

"It is no more possible to have an idea of extension where there is nothing extended,

---

* See page 10 of general Preface to the Necessary Existence of God, by William Gillespie.

than to have an idea of motion where there is nothing moved.

"Matter is the only existence properly so called, and without denying that our author has an idea of extension, I assert the non‚ existence of extension in the same way tha‾ without denying he has a distinct idea of duration, I distinc:ly assert the non-existence of duration."

Now I put it to readers of the *Movement*, whether in the face of these explicit statements, Mr. Gillespie can fairly charge me with *admitting* the existence of extension. The language of my Strictures is plainness itself—none can mistake its import who have capacity to understand any propositions whatever, and assuredly none would *pretend* to mistake it save some of our logical swindlers who are not ashamed to *misrepresent* when unable to *answer* an opponent.

For saying his entire work might "easily be converted into one of the very best Atheistical books extant," Mr. Gillespie charges me with "most shameful literary falsehood," whether justly or not remains to be seen, but (as he says) no time like the present for exhibiting *his* literary falsehood. It is only in a "parliamentary sense" he accuses *me* of literary lying, but I accuse *him* of lying in every sense. The Reply contains a literary falsehood of the most barefaced character— that falsehood moreover, was *wilfully* told, for it cannot be credited that Mr. Gillespie supposed I really did admit the existence of extension after I had so often denied its existence. Surely he read the Strictures before he ventured a reply to them, and if he read them he must have seen that I allowed extension to be an attribute of existence *not* existence itself.

Whatever exists (I declared) exists in *some* form, *some* where; we are sure too, it has *some* weight, *some* density; in short, *some* of all those properties or attributes which *cannot even in thought* be separated from realities.

The Reply is silent about this declaration. My "discreet antagonist" makes no attempt to show that extension has *some* form, *some* weight, *some* density—in sort, *some* EXISTENCE. Why, instead of misrepresenting my opinions did he not honestly grapple with such declarations as the one just quoted? Most likely my "unhappy Strictures" demonstrated that only two paths were open to him—one was to confess himself thrashed; the other to play "artful dodger," which latter was preferred as the "*easy* alternative."

Having convicted Mr. Gillespie of "impudent untruth," I will now briefly expose his ridiculous inconsistency.—Were not the fact in print it would not be believed, that in Part 1 of his Reply (par. 3) he says "Mr.

Southwell allows that the necessary consequence of the admission of that truth (infinity of extension is necessarily existing) would be a god—and therefore argues Mr. Southwell it is *not* true that that infinite extension necessarily exists; while at paragraph 26 he says "according to Mr. Southwell all the Argument is true, *if* proposition 1 (infinity of extension is necessarily existing) is true— According to Mr. Southwell Proposition 1 *is* true.—So, sir, it seems from the contents of one paragraph in Reply that I argue " it is *not* true that infinity of extension necessarily exists ; and from the contents of another paragraph that I argue it *is* true that infinity of extension necessarily exists. Mr. Gillespie *may* be able to reconcile these conflicting statements, which assurealy I am not.

Again : at paragraph 23, Part 1 of Reply, we are told " matter is infinite, necessarily infinite; this Mr. Southwell holds. And as matter is extended or has extension, *with Mr. Southwell extension is necessarily infinite;* while at paragraph 10, Part Second, we are assured " Southwell has been the first even among Atheists *to deny the necessary existence of infinite extension;* so the Alpha shall be the Omega too—Hitherto the truth (?) alluded to has been considered to be a fundamental position in Atheism of every species and modification. The disturber of the universal harmony has embarked in a desperate undertaking. If his laurels be not tarnished inconsistency and genuine Atheism may long flourish together."

These contradictory statements of *accurate* Mr. Gillespie can with difficulty be accounted for, on any other than the Phillip drunk and Phillip sober principle. I am driven to the hard necessity of supposing that when he wrote the paragraph in which I am made to admit the existence of infinity of extension he was " half seas over," and when he wrote the paragraphs in which I am made to deny the existence of infinity of extension, he was sober as every Christian ought to be; but whether sober or the reverse when these *irreconcileable* paragraphs were penned, friend Gillespie must arouse his heavy energies, or all the world (feelosophers included,) will be compelled to conclude that though possessing "a mind well skilled to find or *forge* a fault," he is a forger not by any means skilful enough to *conceal* his forgeries—as the "fault" of admitting the existence of infinity of extension which he thought proper to *"forge"* for me amply testifies. To a certainty, never was controversial trick so clumsily played off. Here it is not a question of verbal *errata*, but of palpable contradictions and barefaced fraud. The Strictures though brief, contain at least half a dozen distinct denials of extension's existence. Yet in the face of those denials Mr. Gillespie has the matchless effrontery to declare in *some* parts of the Reply that I admit the truth of Proposition 1, and the matchless folly to declare in *other* parts of the same Reply that I deny the truth of Proposition 1. In Part 1, Mr. Gillespie boasts his ability to " evince to the heart's content of every reader of this periodical (*Movement*) that Mr. Southwell admits—aye, and maintains the truth conveyed in that proposition." In Part 2, he affects to be much astonished at my impudence in daring to " blurt out a counter declaration," and warns me to " pause before dissenting" from such excellent authorities as himself and Antitheos who "are so entirely agreed as to the truth that infinity of extension is necessarily existing." So that according to this profound logician, I have ruined the cause of Atheism by *admitting* the existence of infinity of extension, and at the same time have proved myselt an insolent, ignorant, presumptuous elf, by *denying* the existence of infinity of extension. Hitherto, quoth he, " the truth alluded to (that infinity of extension exists) has been considered to be a fundamental position in Atheism of every species and modification;" and then proceeds to take me roundly to task for disturbing "universal harmony." Here I cannot forbear exclaiming in the *elegant* language of my antagonist—"verily the Edinburgh Philatheans pitched on a singular champion." What his feelosophical friends will think of so interesting a case of suicide I can't say; but assuredly better things might have been expected from one

" Who is in logic a great critic,
Profoundly skilled in analytic ;
And can distinguish and divide,
A hair, twixt south and south-west side."

If so disposed, I could here lay down the pen without fearing an adverse verdict from competent judges of this controversy, who cannot fail to conclude that when Mr. Gillespie said, "According to Mr. Southwell, Proposition I. is true ; he said what he himself *knew* and has *declared* to be false ; but having promised to dissect his Reply, I will do it thoroughly. It has been seen that at paragraph 26 of that Reply, Part 1., are these words: "According to Mr. Southwell, all the Argument is true if Proposition 1. be true. According to Mr. Southwell, Proposition 1 *is* true ; therefore, &c." It has also been seen that I deny and have denied the truth of Proposition 1. Mr. Gillespie himself admits the fact, as if forgetful at one time of what he wrote at another. Well has it been said that persons of a certain class should have good memories. If friend Gillespie's memory had been good, controversy would not have been scandalized, nor Philalethean " feelosophers" put to the blush by a

Reply in which an opponent is in the same breath sneered at for admitting, and abused for denying a fundamental proposition. Such wretched subterfuge may, however, for ought I know, take rank among " the graces which suit the character of a believer."

Any one who attentively examines the Reply will perceive that though its author may be an excellent " joker of heavy jokes," he is quite incompetent to deal with my objections to his "Argument." Readers who would detect the confused and confusing sophistry of Mr. Gillespie, should carefully remember that he pretends to the singular honour of demonstrating the existence of " one infinite and eternal being, the cause of all the phenomena and of all the matter in the universe:" as by keeping this pretension in view, we also keep clearly before us the extravagant genius of him who made it, and are less likely than, under other circumstances we might be, to lose ourselves in that wilderness of nonsense he modestly declares irrefragable demonstration of the " Being and Attributes of a Great First Cause."

Indeed, no individual with sagacity equal to that of "the learned pig," can fail to observe that infinity of extension could not have created the very matter without which even Mr. Gillespie must know none of us could exist, far less have an idea of extension, finite or infinite, real or unreal.

I agree with Locke—it is " very hard to conceive any real being with a perfect negation of all manner of extension;" but methinks a tougher task (if that be possible), would be to conceive any real extension with a perfect negation of all manner of being.

If, as Mr. Gillespie asserts, extension is an infinite *thing*, there can be no other *thing*; it being manifestly impossible to conceive two infinite *things*.

To say matter is extended, is one thing—to say, extension is matter, or something, is another. The first I admit, the second I of course deny; and yet Mr. Gillespie has taken a vast deal of pains to twist my phrases so as to make the unwary believe I do *not* deny that extension is a thing.

Extension no more exists than motion. We see matter move—hence the idea of motion. We see matter extended—hence the idea of extension. But will my antagonist venture to say motion is a *thing*. Certainly not. Why not, though? Answer, ye Philalethean "feelosophers." There is just as evidently infinity of motion as infinity of extension; and if Gillespie is resolved to make an existence of extension, to be consistent he should do the same for motion.

In the Reply (Part Secoud, par. 15), he talks about establishing " the connection between extension and existence," and assures us " monsters" whom nature produced when out of her wits, that extension is a true *sine qua non* of every thing that exists.

Anything more preposterously dogmatical than this never was put to paper. Extension is not the *sine qua non* of any thing, for this excellent reason—it is not itself anything. Mr. Gillespie confounds extension, which is merely an attribute of existence with existence itself. Extension is the god of his idolatry; but how extension, which is an *attribute*, can be reasoned into a *being*, it is for him to make manifest. Had he studied Spinoza in any other spirit than that of a god-inventing sophist, he would have understood that extension, like thought, is an attribute of existence, not itself existence, If he persist in asserting the reality—*i. e.* existence of infinity of extension—at least an effort should be made to show it an infinite something, and having pushed so far on the right road, he is bound not to stop till he has shown how the infinite something he calls extension can coexist with either the finite or infinite something called matter. *There cannot be two infinite existences in one universe.* Either matter exists or it does not. If it exist finitely, that is to say, if it have bounds, still it must destroy the infinity of aught beside itself. Suppose, as some curious supposers have supposed, that the parts of the material world if brought close together might be crammed into a nut-shell—still it is evident no other existence could be infinite so long as bounded by that walnut-shell full of matter. Nothing can properly be called infinite the dimensions of which we know, or the boundaries of which we distinctly conceive. Infinite is a word of solely *negative* meaning; hence the folly of those hot-brained persons who fancy they understand, or at all events believe in, a God of infinite this, infinite that, and infinite t'other. All such persons are infinite simpletons—*i. e.*, so simple that no one can say how simple they are.

Mr. Gillespie has written a great deal about the parts of extension and their infinite divisibility. Why, he might as well concoct " gems of terseness and order," and call them demonstrations of the parts of nothing and *their* infinite divisibility. A well paragraphed, logically written piece of that kind would take uncommonly, and would do to bind up with " *the* Argument *a priori.*" In truth nothing is the basis of that argument; for what *more* than nothing is extension? Answer—Nothing.

Extension is a quality. Of what? Matter to be sure. What else can it be a quality of? What else can be imagined to have quality. Nothing—is again the answer.

(*To be continued in our next.*)

WORDS AND DEEDS.

ESSENTIAL difference — opinion, however objectionable, not to be met by acts.—Illustrations of fanaticism—to be opposed only by refutation.—Active interference not sufferable.—Aggression, legal or otherwise, to be resisted to the utmost.—Organized efforts for this purpose worthy of most strenuous support.—No means of subduing persecution to be neglected.

Many people still do not seem to understand this grand and important subject; urgent, eloquent, and well-reasoned appeals have been repeatedly made—a few very plain words, with homely illustrations may not be thrown away.

" Strike, but hear!" has been often quoted, and often admired. I had rather say hear, but don't strike—leaving, with all my heart, to the "turn-the-other-cheek" people to stand and be drubbed as long as they like. " Words break no bones," says an old English proverb, and though some words may be confoundedly annoying, law and reason conjointly agree in drawing a very marked line of distinction between them and actions. *Noli me tangere*, then, touch me not, I say, suits my notions, as well as the practice of those who preach it, much better than taking a second slap in the face without value returned for the first. I say, hands off, and I'll hear you. The measure of the endurance of the rough handling of law-ruffians, by such as are attacked for speaking their thoughts, is only to be computed by the amount of their capacity to resist.

Doctrine and acts, then, are essentially different. A different mode of consideration is due to each. The legitimate treatment of each accords with its nature. Doctrine may be treated with the pen and the tongue. Acts may be treated with the right hand—no matter if a man has nothing in the said hand but his fist. A man may tell me he's a miserable sinner, or that I am a miserable sinner, that he, through the blood of the lamb, the grace of the ghost, the merits of the mediator, and the cross of Christ, shall jump up in a glorious resurrection, shall have all his miserable sins scratched out of his offence-sheet, and fly into Abraham's bosom, never to leave him, except to pray, shout, and trumpet, hosannahs to the highest — while I, being no respecter of lambs, ghosts, crosses, and mediators, will have all my miserable sinship sticking to me like bird-lime, and, having made no interest for spiritual soap-suds, hanging about me like filthy rags. The spiritually-minded man, the regenerate man, he who has put off the old Adam and stands spick-span, fresh, and innocent, like a new born babe, who proclaims himself as the predetermined, and appointed and selected, and elected of " god, the father almighty, maker of heaven and earth, and Jesus Christ, his only son, our lord," and all that sort of thing—he, I say, who made out all these nice arrangements for himself, may poke me outside, or thrust me into the coal hole, or give me nothing but a stoker's place, to stir up the brimstone and blazes underneath poor miserable spitted souls, or other more evil-disposed person or persons than myself. But what does all this amount to? Words! Words!! Words!!! He neither spits, grills, roasts, boils or fries me, he leaves the devil to do all that, and only "wishes I may get it." While his piety rests here, here let it rest; and if he contented himself with *serving* me up in imagination—I could be well content to be thus toasted or roasted, or dished for the whole term of my natural or unnatural life.

Now, if the godly, pious, and most christian spirit, which pervades those who have " cast off the old man and put on the new," only prompted them to endoctrinate and not to operate, to talk and not to act, to pray, preach, and swell like bull-frogs, sacredly inflated with the divine breath of the holy ghost, the comforter—not to "meddle or make" with what belongs to me, nor handle, touch, or concern themselves with my person or property—it would be well, excellently well; and right welcome would they be to shout, and puff, and blow, here and hereafter to all eternity.

Mine may be " awful opinions " — the " spirit of evil may indwell " with me, my words may be the words of " the graceless " —I may be " given up by a merciful and long suffering-god, to a reprobate mind," or my writings may be the " cold philosophy of the infidel." All this, and ten thousand times more to the end of it, may the mawworms blatter forth like gospel phrased parrots.—Let them but rant and rave, keep to the tub or the pulpit, and meddle not with me or mine, and they might set up shop wherever they could get custom—*out of a thoroughfare.*

It would not concern me that they denounced my opinions, as long as when calumniated, I could defend them. I would not mind being termed graceless, as long as they contented themselves with showing that their " grace did the more abound," nor how frigid my philosophy was termed, if they tried to warm it by arguments and not by faggots. They could well dispense with any other than tongue-combat, if they thought their own preachments of any avail. Do they not let off red-hot biblical bombshells, enough to blaze up a never-dying flame among each other? If their divine heat was more than " sound and fury signifying nothing"—if it was actuative beyond the circle of crack-brained zealots—if it signified as much as it soundeth, they might fire the North Pole, melt the heart of a poor-law commissioner, or kindle an atheist into saving grace.

Their preachments and tract system is cheerfully conceded to them. We have, in fact, no business to call this propagation of opinion into question: we have nothing to do with its tendencies, mischievous or otherwise. What right should we have to set up a judgment of what they shall tell and others will hear. Further: their schemes of tract distribution, subscriptions, bible-diffusion collections, and missionary gatherings are no affairs of ours. Are we to dictate to them or their audiences what to support or what to do with their money? What concernment is it of ours that the people of the Thames think they can teach theology to the people of the Ganges and the Indus, and a deal better theology than the poor benighted Indians know? What more is it to us if they send British money to wean people from the crescent to the cross? Would the money be applied to a purpose a whit more useful here if it did not go there. But, be that as it may, it is only by talking and persuading that we would divert it into any channel.

The offences and crimes of the christians against us infidels are not, in doing things which they would prevent us doing, and which we would not interfere to prevent their doing. Our charges against them are not for their prayings, nor dogmas, nor delusions, nor proselytisms, nor swelling their purses by public appeals, nor increasing their power, wealth, and influence in any way they can, consistently with the voluntary principle. Our quarrel is for their *actual interference* with us—with their prevention of us exercising the same liberty which they enjoy. All that deters or may deter an infidel from striking down the first who interferes with this just and equal liberty, is his powerlessness, or the difficulty of getting at the first or instigating parties through the entanglement of the law, of which "christianity is part and parcel," and the shuffling, shirking, covert way in which christians deal their blows, through series of deputies and subordinates!

You utter in public your sentiments, antagonistic to the stereotyped inanities which are drawled forth from the nearest church, or the hell-fire denunciations which are bellowed forth in the neighbouring conventicle, and straightway you are assailed by a vile, officious functionary with a staff, a bull's eye and a rattle, who, at the least resistance, can call forth other accomplices, and who perhaps is just enriched with the last half guinea, or heated by the last glass of brandy and water which, Weston-like, he had received from a brothel keeper. This is the first *deed, not word*, to which we object—next comes the deed of locking you up in a miserable den—of keeping you fast till you get bail, and till assize time if you do not get bail—of hiring lawyers to plead against you—of judges turning counsel against, and misleading stupid juries against you—of condemning you to fine, imprisonment, and espionage through a rigorous term—and inflicting these with all the brutality, or more than the brutality which the law allows.

Are these not deeds, distinguishable from words? Are they not deeds we should never cease our efforts to place among the blank catalogue of history's most revolting recitals, instead of remaining living instances of atrocious tyranny and infamous inflictions?

"Words and deeds"—the pen and the purse—meeting, petitioning—the attainment and right use of the suffrage—active support of the present useful "Union" against persecution for opinion, may and should all be put into requisition to exterminate interference with freedom of expression.

M. Q. R.

INSTRUCTION—RATIONAL AND SCHOLASTIC.

III.

I PURPOSE still to enlarge upon a department of the subject which was treated before. It is one not commonly presented. A proper development is not pretended—space will not permit, but the few additional thoughts here thrown together will be found suggestive.

The special province of grammar was in the last paper declared, and its precise limits defined. The claims set up in its behalf for philosophical teaching, and instruction in elegant diction were repudiated. In reference to the "Practical Grammar," its author was stated, though otherwise original and not trammeled by authority, to have fallen into the error of over-estimating and over-stating the subject he had in hand. An example occurs in the seventh page:—"How severe is the reproach of Shelley, in the following passage in his letters from Rome: 'I have seen women here of the highest beauty; their brows and lips and the moulding of the face modeled with sculptural exactness, and the dark luxuriance of their hair floating over their fine complexions—and their *lips—you must hear the common places which escape from them before they cease to be dangerous.*'" Now, this is not saying they were bad grammarians; people may talk "common places" from morning till night in the most unexceptionable grammar. It is not grammar's province as already contended, to teach elegant, fine, or impressive, but correct speaking.

A singular instance occurs of confounding grammar with a subject foreign to it, by the author before named as quoted in the "Practical Grammar." "The most ignorant can know grammar in its primitive state; for all that he sees, hears, and understands, all that we have been speaking of, is grammar in its original state. * * * *
All this simplicity and grandeur of nature being set before men, all men are prepared to begin the study of SECONDARY grammar. As in primary grammar there are different sorts of animals, as men, horses, dogs, cows, lions, whales—and different sorts of actions as talking, trotting, barking, flying, roaring, swimming—so in secondary grammar there a e different sorts of words, or parts of speech to express these different things." With all respect and deference to the author of "the Schoolmaster," this is a jumble of error, confusion, and valuable explanation. None would have more keenly detected these fallacies, or Cobbet-like, crushed them in others than the writer. How preposterous to talk of *primitive, primary,* and *secondary* grammar, and grammar in its *original* state. What confusion worse confounded, in attempting to identify grammar—the art and science of words—with philosophy which teaches the nature of things. A little reflection would tell anybody, not only that "all we see, hear, and understand," is *not* grammar, but that the knowledge of what we hear, see, and understand, is *not* grammar. The knowledge of the agreement and arrangement of the words that express what we see, hear, and understand, may stand very well as a definition of grammar.

Let me be permitted to recapitulate. It is no less an error to confound the right and correct use of words—which alone is a grammatical use of them—with power or pomp of language, and the adornments of style—nor to confound words, which are but instruments to confess our knowledge or sensations of things, with their particular knowledge on those sensations—nor, again and lastly, to confound words with the things themselves. Such extreme of absurdity as this last would be incredible in a reasonable writer, were we not accustomed to remark the lengths to which a smart notion may sometimes lead a precipitate thinker, or the mystification in which a particular turn of phraseology will enwrap an idea.

The "error and confusion" in the above paragraphs are doubtless now clearly made out—if anything clear can come of error and confusion. It remains to point out the "valuable explanation" of the elements of grammar. A careful consideration of the last sentence of the above-quoted paragraph will give the first plain outline view of the theory of grammar—it forms part of the alphabet, as it were, of the subject. It is not complete, nor does it pretend to completeness. Prominent and easily intelligible examples of two large classes of words are presented—the "different sorts of animals, as men, horses, dogs, cows, lions, whales, and different sorts of actions, as talking, trotting, barking, flying, roaring, swimming," immediately acquaint the uninstructed, in a manner impossible to be misunderstood, with the nature and character—properly founded on a knowledge of the nature of things—if a vast multitude of words. —I lay aside now the rubbish of styling animals and their actions primary grammar, and the words representing our ideas of them as secondary grammar—Nouns and verbs—the principal words in all language—and those which are designated by the above examples, are not asserted to be thus completely defined—scarcely can they be said to be defined at all in the proper acceptation of the term. I doubt greatly if definitions, properly so termed, are fitted for elementary learners.—A definition should explain the thing defined—all the thing—and nothing else than the thing—in such a way as to be impossible to be mistaken for anything else. Among the grammarians who have racked their brains for these thousand years, to define a noun, those who have come nearest to the true definition would not by that definition convey to the uninstructed an idea of the word defined—Tell a child or uninformed adult that "a noun is the name of anything that exists or of which we have any notion," and that "a verb is a word which signifies to be, to do, or to suffer," and he will know as much about the matter as before you gave the definition—Repeat to him the previously quoted sentence—and though only touching on a small proportion of examples—it will at once put him in possession of the grammatical names, and prepare him for understanding the function of many thousands of words.

It is this quality of seizing the most obvious and striking functions of the large classes of words which grammarians have called "parts of speech," and presenting them briefly and lucidly, which makes Holyoake's Grammar so practically useful to those who have neglected the technical study of language. I differ with him considerably in details, consider that there are grave defects of systematization and arrangement which I would point out in numerous instances did our space permit—these defects however do but disfigure, they cannot efface the peculiar merits of the vivid, forcible, and expressive explanations which abound. The following instance gives the greatest possible amount of information, with a trifling exception, in the fewest words; but not only this, it explains enough at a time—just what a tyro could well understand:—" We require *nouns*, because there are things—*descriptives*, because of the qualities of things—*verbs*, because of the existence of motion—we must have *pronouns*, because of unpleasant repetitions, *connectives*, to continue discourse—and *adjectives* to express certain relations."— To the word *objective*, I demur, as having no proper relation to the meaning, but only to an occasional variation, depending on the action of another word. The old term *preposition* may be objectionable, but it is not mended by that of *objective*—The term *descriptive* is perhaps far better than *adjective*—the old term—and may take its place with advantage—but it should not stand for the *adverb*, which performs entirely different functions—I would recommend a correction of this defect in another edition.

The reader has the author's word for it, that he is fresh enough from his studies *not* to have "forgotten the difficulties which delay a student's progress." He recollects then, how many unavoidable difficulties have to be surmounted. Teachers of maturer scholarship than one who is but "fresh from a difficult journey," have retained a painful recollection of the tedium and barrenness of school drudgery. The scrupulous accuracy of the schools need not, on this account, be wholly disregarded.

"Practical Grammar" has its merits and defects—both its own, for wherever it is bad, it is "bold in its badness"—vigour, originality, conciseness and pleasantry characterise it—carelessness, mal-arrangement, lightly considered innovations, and other disorderliness sprinkle its pages—On the merit side however we may rank the essentials, on the demerit side the details.—This judgment though differing from that of the critic of *Lloyd's*, accords with that of the *Spectator* whose generally icy-cold strictures have been turned into tolerably warm approval in its condescending *bracketed* note on the "Grammar." All the rest of the formidable force of critics ranges itself on the *pro* side. G. J. H. has been treated by M. Q. R. with far less ceremony than censors of the press generally.

As a criticism, this paper is extremely incomplete—to do justice to the topic, far more space would have been necessary than the scope and objects. together with the limited size of the *Movement*, would permit.

My estimate is stated in the following brief summary:—

On the whole it might be that the schoolmartinet, who values order, arrangement, strict classification, punctilious accuracy, and long accepted formulæ as prime and indispensible requisites, will reject this book—some gentlemen of grave deportment, with square caps, and a great many letters of the alphabet attached to their names, might pronounce it an abominable and arrogant innovation. The young mechanic, tradesman, or clerk—he who has had bad schooling or no schooling—whoever is deficient in time or means for long and expensive studies—whoever eschewing elaborate technicalities, refined subtilties, or hair-drawn distinctions, requires practical information conveyed in the briefest and pleasantest manner—or he, even, who would adopt an agreeable mode of preparing the way for more solid studies will be delighted with "Practical Grammar," and deem it a valuable acquisition.

M. Q. R.

[One of the fruits of the Atheistical agitation in Scotland is the formation of an Infidel association in Galashiels. We subjoin below an abstract of their first address to the public, which has been handsomely placarded in the Galashiels district.]

ADDRESS OF THE GALASHIELS INFIDEL ASSOCIATION.

CHRISTIANS,—If you believe your religion to be divine, as you say you do, why all this tumult about the spread of infidelity? You seem to have lost all confidence in the power of truth, and the promises of the gospel. If you have *not*, then why recoil with so much horror at every thing which bears upon it the name of Infidel? Why, as Protestants, do you defend the right of private judgment, while upon those who exercise that right, and arrive at a conclusion different from your own, you encourage the infliction of the most degrading punishments, for propagating what they believe to be truth?

And why, as Christians, do you profess to *love your enemies*, while towards those who merely *differ from you* in matters of opinion, you cherish the most rancorous malignity, and manifest the most deadly hatred? Even while boasting that "the weapons of our warfare are not carnal, but spiritual," do we not find you rejoicing with savage delight, when bigots in authority are tearing men (aye, gentle woman not excepted,) from their families and their homes, casting them into loathsome dismal cells, for daring to exercise that right to which every religious sect lays claim, namely, the right of propagating their own opinions, unmolested and uncontrolled by ANY LAW.

How much longer then will you disgrace yourselves? Talk not to us of the rampant spirit of bigotry, and the persecutions of

Catholicism. Talk not to us of the horrors of Paganism, and the tearful character of blind superstition—*Worse by far is the spirit manifested by you, the followers of the meek and lowly Jesus.*

And again, why, we ask, do you persecute us? Have we committed any crime? Have we violated the rights of property? Have we taken from any man that which did not belong to us? As fathers, husbands, and citizens, are we less honest or moral, than yourselves? We earnestly call upon you for a candid and honest answer to all these questions, and feel satisfied *you cannot answer* YES. And if such be the case, why do you act the part of ignorant and bigoted fanatics? Ponder well on these things, and remember, that GREAT IS TRUTH AND WILL PREVAIL!

THE NEW SOCIALIST EXECUTIVE.
II

A FEW years ago the Socialists of Birmingham in the exubriance of inexperienced philanthropy, determined to erect a "Hall for the People." *All* parties were to have equal access to it. They invested some £400 in the project. But when the chances of their using the "Hall of the People" were calmly considered, it became very questionable whether such opportunities would often fall to their share. They were but a fraction of the people, and if the religious parties only put in their several claims to have the use of the "People's Hall," the turns of the Socialists were likely to be but "few and far between." The Birmingham Socialists for the first time found out that universal philanthropy required universal means. They then set about subscribing new money, and selfish though it was, procured a hall for their own exclusive use. They then were able to weekly diffuse their views in the town, which otherwise could seldom have been done. To help themselves was found, to a certain extent, the only possible mode of effectually helping others.

Something like this is true of the Socialist party generally. If they attempt to establish a community for all parties, they will soon discover the inadequacy of their means, and the impossibility of providing for their own order. The conception is generous, but we must not forget that generosity requires a full purse. The rich man enjoys more comfort in one day than falls to the poor man's lot in a year. He who would provide a happy home for the rich, must be able to produce a world. But give the poor man healthy employment, simple competence, leisure, education and the means of certain advancement, and he is at once happy, and on the high road to social, moral, and political prosperity. Let the working classes attend to their own interests and they will do well enough. I say it not selfishly, but advisedly. The rich can take care of themselves, and they will never believe that the working classes can provide communities for their wealthy neighbours, until they have provided communities for themselves. Public opinion, experience, good sense, as well as private interest, say to the working classes, take care of yourselves. Gentlemen of our new executive, first emancipate the poorer members, and then you may talk of reforming society, of providing for the well-doing of all interests. Then the government will credit you with wisdom, and the world cease to think you visionary, and not till then.

Poverty has claims—let it have a voice! Don't be deterred by that proud but spurious philosophy which affects to despise you as being a party. Party is the soul of action. Party sometimes exhibits a bad spirit—that avoid—but in avoiding do not go to the suicidal extent of abandoning the energy, the activity, the singleness of purpose which mark a bold and decided party. Take your stand, avow your principles, elect sides, hoist your colours, declare whether you are for oppressed humanity or against it. The men of no party are men of no principles, of no decided purpose. They are cavillers but not helpers. Humanity, freedom, progression, owe them nothing. If any one says, " you declare for one phasis of humanity, but I, rejoicing in 'more enlarged views,' declare for all phases." Never mind this doctrine—it is larger in view but weaker in practice. Sober men know that this is chiefly pretension. It is either the language of folly or knavery. Utter it who may, we must deduct from his sagacity or impugn his integrity. *All* phases of humanity are not worth declaring for. Many phases are happy phases, and want no help. Let it be your pride to declare for the oppressed phasis. Let indigence, trampled virtue, and struggling industry have your chief sympathies. Abjure party!—why we are misgoverned by party, crushed by party, the fruits of our toil enjoyed by party, and we must be redeemed by party. Shall wrong have the engine of party and right never employ that power? Let it be your honest glory and pride to be of the party of poverty. Never mind the cant of philosophy—let the world, if it will, benefit the world,—be you distinct, have an idea of your own, a will, a plan, a purpose—work it out, and stand like true soldiers at the post you are called to defend.

G. J. H.

POWER OF CIRCUMSTANCES.—It is probable that complete change of their respective circumstances in infancy and in youth, *would have placed the criminal on the bench and the judge at the bar.—The Ponderer.*

EXAMINATION OF THE DOCTRINES OF THE CONCORDISTS.

NO. I.

When we commenced inserting in *Movement* No. 3, the articles of Mr. Oldham entitled the "Doctrines of the Concordists," it was stated that "comment would be dispensed with until those views were sufficiently developed to enable our readers to form a judgment of their meaning and value." But when that time should arrive, it was understood that "comment," according to our usual custom, would be freely indulged in. Of that understanding I shall now avail myself.

In consequence of some very questionable, and in my opinion, dangerous sentiments in Mr. Oldham's third article, it was intimated in No. 20 that "his papers must be brought to a close, as some of his views could not longer be allowed to pass unchallenged." With this intimation Mr. Oldham at once and willingly complied, and in No. 23 the series terminated. The earnestness with which I desired the opportunity of comment, and the long time suffered to elapse before making it, must have appeared, to Mr. Oldham and readers, as an imputation on the sincerity of the request, but absence from town and pressing duties have compelled the delay. It is due to that gentleman and them to offer this explanation.

A radical objection to Mr. Oldham's "Exposition" is its palpable uncertainty. His principles are fleeting as clouds, gliding as eels, and changing as Proteus. His first article, in *Movement*, No. 3, commences by affirming positively and unhesitatingly many things, of that of which *he* assures us "we can affirm nothing." His affirmations separately set forth are as follows:—

1. "We affirm, first as an indispensable axiom, that prior to all motion there must be a primary mover."
2. "Which (primary mover) is never moved."
3. "Before all manifestation there *is* that which can be never manifested."
4. "Antecedent to all creation, the creator *is*."
5. "And (the creator) is ever creating."
6. "Itself (the creator) being the only uncreated."

Thus, of a "mover," an "*un*-manifested *is*," a "creator," we have six distinct assertions. The prince of affirmation could not be more positive or dogmatic concerning them than is Mr. Oldham. Yet the very sentence following these six affirmations, gravely informs the reader, "of this (the 'mover,' or the *un*-'manifested *is*,' or 'creator,') we can affirm nothing." But two conclusions can be arrived at from these contradictory, changing statements. Either Mr. Oldham has written plain nonsense, or he has some secret esoteric signification of his words, and is mocking his unfortunate reader with phantoms.

His affirmations, such as they are, are defective. Take the first: Allowing, for the sake of argument, that "prior to all motion there must be a primary mover," it is also true, that prior to all motion there must be something to be moved, and since we cannot conceive of immateriality being in motion, we fall back on matter as the something to be moved, which existed "prior to motion." All we certainly know from this first affirmation is, that "prior to all motion there must be" matter to be moved. Whether matter's motion was not self-originated, or if it had a "primary mover," whether that "mover" came into operation before matter or after, Mr. Oldham has yet to inform us.

Next we are enlightened to the effect that this "primary mover" "is never moved." But how that "which is (or was) never moved," ever contrived to set anything in "motion," is yet locked up in the treasury of Concordian secrets.

The third thing told us by Mr Oldham—wonderful man! who affirms of what we can't affirm—is, that "before to all manifestation *is* that which can never be manifested"—"that we are obliged to admit it although it be ineffable, and can only proceed to speak of its appearances, its outbirths, its masks, clothings or operations." How Mr. Oldham discovered the "appearances, outbirths, masks, clothings and operations" of that which "can never be manifested," can only be made known by some exoteric echo of the esoteric speech. His "antecedents to all creation the creator is," is rhapsody. We know nothing of "creation" in the legitimate sense of that term, and though we live on raw potatoes from July to eternity, we never shall.

Without entering farther into these affirmations, I submit, that judged by common reason, they bear upon them the broad stamp of absurdity. If Mr. Oldham does not mean that his language should bear the common interpretation, then is he trifling with the good sense of the public, and wantonly disappointing those who read his papers with the humble hope of understanding his meaning and benefiting thereby. If he pretends that the public cannot understand his language, why does he write? Has he superior light? let him shew it. To talk in mystical language is to play fantastic tricks with humanity, it is mocking at endeavours after improvement, for the poor vanity—seeming if not real—of setting up a fictitious superiority over the unfortunate who may confide in such instruction.

It won't do to tell us that these principles are not to be discussed. To those who will not explain their principles, we cannot listen.

The affirmations I have examined lie at the root of Concordianism. They are put forth as the first principles. If these remain mysterious, all that follows must remain unintelligible. From the "unmoved mover," the unmanifested is," and "uncreated creator," Mr. Oldham deduces—the inventor of secrets only knows how, but he does deduce—a "triad exhibition of physical, psychical, or spiritual primary universe manifestations," which have the felicity of being the "substratum, the pervader, permeater, and very radix of the essential I." This is his god, a "threefold category," under which all things may be "classified." Whatever can induce people who profess to lead mankind a better way, to adopt this forbidding and unintelligible jargon? Self reform is with Concordists a favourite idea—could not they begin by reforming their language?

I am anxious to regard the Concordists as well meaning men—but well meaning men are always plain men. I have esteemed them as desirous of relieving the evils of society, not as adding to them, as they certainly do by their mysticism. If they have light, or help, or wisdom, humanity has need of it. Its lacerated and bleeding form, blinded by ignorance, misled by error, torn by passion, and goaded by oppression, cries to all good men for assistance, and to answer it by "permeaters, pervaders, and radixes," is very much like laughing at it. I can assure these gentlemen, for their future guidance, in the feeling words of Judge Haliburton, that " misery is keen enough without poking fun at it."

G. J. H.

EFFECTS OF RELIGION ON NATIONS.

PERSECUTION of religious opponents is at present the order of the day in Philadelphia. This is not the fault of Republicanism. On the contrary, the misfortune for Republicanism is, that it has, in the states, still to contend with the fanatical creeds and systems imported from priest-ridden Europe. In every age and every clime superstition has been the bane of mankind, and the prime cause of their slavery and misery. Behold the workings of the fell monster even at the present time! In France, we see the priests struggling for the restoration of that power wrested from them at the Revolution, and conspiring with all their ancient craftiness and energy to affect once more the subjugation of the mind of France to their unhallowed sway. Switzerland, the oldest Republic in the world, is threatened with a speedy disorganization and dissolution, because her children, as Catholics and Protestants, unmindful of the patriotism of TELL, turn their arms *against each other*, instead of against the jealous tyrants who surround them, and who hail those disunions with joy; *and this is the work of priestcraft.* Rome, the once mistress of the world, and Italy, the paradise of Europe, withers and perishes under a bloody and gloomy tyranny: *and this is the work of priestcraft.* Spain is reduced to the lowest state of crime, slavery, and misery: *and this is the work of priestcraft.* Ireland has suffered wrong and tyranny for centuries, because her children were, and are yet, fiercely arrayed against each other, through differences of religious belief: *and this is the work of priestcraft.* Lastly, we have now to lament over these Philadelphian outrages, disgracing the fair fame of the freest land under heaven, because the black-slugs of fraud and superstition will not let men live as they might do, in amity and fraternity: *and this is the work of priestcraft.*

While priestcraft continues to exist, there can be no real freedom for mankind; no hope of the stability of free institutions. Priestcraft has for centuries kept the whole world in subjection to kings and aristocrats; and unless rooted out of America, will yet poison all that is good and glorious in her institutions. *There should be no peace, no truce with this arch pest of the world.* Its existence is intolerable; and no matter under what mask, cloak, or name it exhibits itself, it should be warred with to the death. *Delenda est Carthago.—Northern Star.*

PRIESTCRAFT.

(*Copy of a paper lately exhibited by Mr. Finlay before his door.*)

MR. HUME in the House of Commons lately remarked, "the church might be said to be at enmity with the people, unfortunately the whole of the clergy might be said to be leagued against the people."

Perhaps Mr. Hume's remarks were too severe, for there seems to be some liberal priests, the Reverend Charles Berry for instance, who at a meeting held in Leicester, in England, said, " I verily believe that priests of all denominations are the most inveterate and most implacable foes that the liberties of mankind have to contend with."

But perhaps it is not their fault, for the Reverend Robert Taylor says, "If the office of priest does not find a man a knave, it very seldom fails to make him one."

Then let us beware of the craftiness of priestcraft, let us watch its motion, let us observe its manœuvring with deluded congregations to oppose the running of railway coaches on Sunday.

Why do these gentlemen of the black corps call Jesus Christ their commander in chief, and yet set at naught his example?—Did he not take a walk into the country with his disciples on the Sabbath, and no doubt he would have taken a ride in a railway carriage, from Dan to Beersheba, had railways been invented in his time?

Let us hold fast our Holy-days or Sundays, but let them not be days to afflict our souls, which we shall do if we listen to priests' nonsense.

Let us make Sunday what it ought to be, a day of recreation, mental enjoyment, and rest from labour, such as the people in France and other countries make it.

The working class should have two such days a week, instead of one, considering how hard and long they work on other days.

Mark the inconsistency of these holy men and the deluded saints, who join them in their schemes against railway riding and other cheap Sunday pleasures. They do not raise their voices against the many hackney coaches and gigs of all descriptions that are seen running in all directions, and standing in rows in the streets on Sundays waiting for hire.

So it seems it is only what they call the souls of the working people that priestcraft is so anxious about.

Priests seem to have very little sympathy for their bodies; only think of the hard working people who toil six days in the week in close unwholesome workshops, and think of a parcel of selfish, and bigoted priests, with sanctified simpletons laying their heads together to prevent the poor mechanic from having a cheap ride to the country on Sunday, his only breathing day, to enjoy the fresh air, or visit his friends.

Truly the poor owe much to priestcraft.

Mr. Owen's Departure.—On Sunday afternoon the Socialists of the metropolis and friends of Mr. Owen assembled in the Park to greet him once again before his final departure. The president and several members of the ladies' class, Mr. Robert Clark and other gentlemen proceeded in carriages to the residence of Mr. Owen, and accompanied him to his friends in the park. The assembly was numerous beyond expectation, sanguine as expectation was. Near to Vauxhall Bridge Mr. Owen and Mr. Fleming delivered short addresses to the multitude, and Mr. Owen bidding them farewell, parted at the railway terminus, with the fervent and friendly wishes of thousands.

Conventionalism.—An honest man, to appear sensible in the eyes of the world, must become a scoundrel in his own.—*Pemberton.*

NOTICE.

The Annual Public Meeting of the Anti-Persecution Union will be held on Tuesday evening next, August 27th, at the Hall of Science, City-road, seven doors from Featherstone-street. The Annual Report will be presented, and new officers elected for the ensuing year. It is hoped that all friends of the Union will make this notice as widely known as possible. The chair will be taken at half-past eight.

Whitechapel.—On Monday, August 26, Mr. Southwell will deliver in the Hall of Science, his second Lecture "To the Socialists of England." Tuesday Evening, August 20, Discussion between Professor Burns and Mr. C. Southwell, on the Existence of God.

Branch A1.—On Sunday Evening, May 25, Mr. Holyoake will Lecture on "Policy, private and public—its character and rules."

TO CORRESPONDENTS.

J. R. Mr. Buxton explained at the John-street breakfast that the Halifax report gave a wrong impression, making it appear that Mr. Jones corrected him as to important points, when in fact Mr. Jones's interruptions related to dates.

Received.—*Birmingham Advertiser.* R. B. T. Emery. H. Cook—will he send his present address. Peter Gray.

G. A. We believe that Mr. Campbell *has* separated from the Concordium, but yet adheres to the "faith," as he understands it. The cause of the separation, as we are rightly informed, was that Mr. Campbell was of opinion that "two could make a circle," while his colleagues thought that "only three could make a circle." Mr. Campbell inclined to the opinion that "two could be at one," while his friends were satisfied that only "three could be at one." This was deemed an alarming heresy, and they separated—we wonder that they ever joined.

Received T. Emery's enclosures respecting the Leicester branch of the A. P. U.

SUBSCRIPTIONS TO THE ANTI-PERSECUTION UNION.

T. Bidwell	£0 1 0
S. B. per Mr. Skelton . .	0 2 6
Per Mr. Hindle, Ashton-under-Lyne:—	
W. Aitken . . .	0 1 0
W. Robinson . . .	0 1 0
W. Meadowcroft . .	0 1 0
J. Hindle . . .	0 1 0
Several persons . .	0 4 0

G. J. H., *Sec.*

Printed and Published by G. J. Holyoake, 40, Holywell-street, Strand, Saturday, August 24, 1844.

THE MOVEMENT
And Anti=Persecution Gazette.

"Maximize morals, minimize religion."—BENTHAM.

No. 38.	EDITED BY G. JACOB HOLYOAKE, ASSISTED BY M. Q. RYALL.	PRICE 2d

THE SECOND ANNUAL REPORT OF THE ANTI-PERSECUTION UNION,
(Presented at the Public Meeting on Tuesday last.)

THE Anti-Persecution Union has at length become a publicly recognized confederation for defending the free publication of theological opinions whether by tongue or pen, by Christian or Atheist.

Since its formation, two years ago, it has steadily progressed in efficiency and usefulness—its principles have been defined, its constitution settled, its organization matured. It has its weekly paper, the *Anti-Persecution Gazette*, and in the principal towns of the nation it has collectors.

The actual cash receipts of the Union during the year have been—

First quarter	..	..	..	..	10	18	4
Second ditto	..	..	..	..	33	16	7½
Third ditto	..	..	..	..	45	19	2
Fourth ditto	..	..	..	..	14	17	5

£105 11 6½

During the past year the Union has assisted Mr. Finlay, Mr. Paterson, Mr. M'Neil, and Miss Roalfe, who have severally suffered imprisonment for the publication of their theological sentiments. These cases the Union has weekly urged on public attention. It has published reports of their trials, held public meetings, distributed papers and pamphlets, and appealed to Parliament both against the principles and practice of persecution. But for such exertions the persons named would have been subjected to longer imprisonment and greater severities, and such prosecutions would have been multiplied.

Following the example of this union a similar one has been formed in Scotland, which has already rendered good service to the cause of free discussion. In England a branch of this union has been established in Leicester, by a few enterprising friends of liberty, and it is expected that other towns will follow their example until in every district in which persecution may rear its head, there will be an established society ready to challenge its right and attack its power.

The introduction of the new libel law, by Lord Campbell, is a gratifying incident of the past year. It is now provided that the truth of an alleged libel and the good intentions of the alleged libeller shall be received in extenuation of the offence. If these pleas are permitted in the case of blasphemous libels, it will no doubt very much modify the verdict of the next jury, who shall try an indictment for blasphemy.

In the course of the past year applications have been made to the Union by various political persons to extend the operations of the Union to the defence of persons indicted for the free expression of political opinions. Upon so large a question your committee have not felt justified in taking the initiative until they could see the achievement of their avowed object—the freedom of theological sentiment. However, should any feasible plan be devised whereby both objects could progress simultaneously, it should receive immediate attention.

Inquiries were instituted by your committee into the case of Michel, lately convicted of blasphemy in Paris, who appears to have fallen a victim to the struggle between the clergy and the university, but owing either to accident or miscarriage the particulars required have not yet been furnished. The persecution of the Jews of Ancona, engaged the active attention of the Union for some time, but as it appeared to have arisen from mixed political and religious causes, it was abandoned as not falling quite within the Union's legitimate objects. It is possible that little pecuniary assistance could have been rendered to these parties, but publicity could have been given to their cases, and it is something that a bond of sympathy should be established between those who struggle for liberty in every clime, and that the victim of bigotry in the remotest land may be assured that his efforts and sufferings will be honored in England, and that the intolerant may be apprised that their conduct is being handed down to the execration of posterity.

The successful exertions made by the Union's excellent friend, Mr. Watts, of Islington, in defence of the right of public meetings, as recorded in a recent *Movement*, are properly a subject of congratulation. It will be recollected that that gentleman attended a public meeting concerning the Dissenters' Chapels Bill—he attempted to speak on the occasion, as any member of the public had an undoubted right to do, and for this he was given into custody. Determined to test the legality of this step, he entered an action against the parties who took it, and obtained £10 in compensation. This sum he directed to be paid over to this Union. Handsome as was this conduct of Mr. Watts, of far more value is the right he established.

Acting on its professed principle of knowing no distinction of persons or opinions, the Union made a remittance to Dr. Kalley, of Madeira, to aid his defence against charges brought by the Portuguese government. Happily the Doctor has been set at liberty, and a friendly correspondence has grown up between him and the secretary of the Union upon the merits of their respective views, and the dogmas of persecution.

The account paid to G. Hinton, solicitor, of Bristol, for services in the case Queen v. Southwell, and the balance commenced to be paid to Mr. Whiting, of Bristol, for the maintenance of Mr. Southwell while imprisoned, were not originally incurred by the Union, though now inserted in the list of its liabilities. These contracts were entered into by active individuals before the Union, was in existence, but the purpose in view was so identical with the objects of the Union, that it has appeared to the committee just to discharge those accounts. Mr. Whitaker, of London, and a number of gentlemen for whom he acted as treasurer, paid £30 or more of the original bill. The friends in Bristol have for some time past sent in subscriptions for the payment of the remainder, and the committee hope to be shortly able to liquidate the whole of Mr. Whiting's claim, and then no account, either direct or indirect, will be due from the Anti-Persecution Union.

It will be seen that the Union has on hand a stock of "Trials," and " Reports," worth £32 besides perhaps 100 dozen of back Nos. of *Oracle of Reason*—all calculated to diffuse information respecting the principles on which free discussion should be based. Such friends as will subscribe for the gratuitous distribution of these works, or promote their sale, will at once increase both the funds and the efficiency of the Union.

Your present committee, who resign office with the presentation of this report, take the liberty of urging on their successors the prosecution of the Union's objects until liberty of speech shall be achieved. The presentation of memorials to the legislature require to be persevered in, and some member of Parliament induced to move—every session —that all blasphemy laws or regulations be repealed. Until this is done, effects only will be attacked when causes should be eradicated. Though no man may be molested, yet until the blasphemy laws be repealed, no man will be safe. We trust this will be generally agitated, and whenever a candidate for a seat in Parliament presents himself, that our friends among the electors will rise and request him to support the abolition of the blasphemy laws.

In closing their report, your committee feel it their duty to urge on the consideration of the Union the augmentation of the " Paterson Testimonial," founded by the Union's generous friend, W. J. B. Mr. Paterson has suffered much, and long, and well. The conclusion of his severe and lengthened imprisonment may leave him without health and energy to mix, at least for a time, in the active pursuits of life. His exertions and sufferings constitute a claim on the public, and its being one that *he* will never urge makes it more a duty in men of honour to promptly acknowledge, and your committee trust that it is one to which the opponents of persecution will liberally respond.

G. JACOB HOLYOAKE, *Sec.*

ANOTHER MELANCHOLY INSTANCE.— Mrs. Betsey Libbey, wife of Major Josiah Libbey, of Scarboro', (Me.,) aged 68, during a temporary fit of derangement, on Saturday morning week, cut her throat with a razor in three different places. She was still alive on Saturday night, but the physician in attendance stated that it was impossible that she could recover, as a piece had been severed from her wind-pipe. She had always sustained the character of a kind, active, and intelligent woman, until a recent period, when owing to undue religious excitement, she became subject to fits of partial insanity, fancying that all the promises in the Bible were against her, and that she was a doomed being.—*Portland Bulletin.*

WE appeal once more to the people :—How long will ye sanction those systems of faith which drive your fellows around you by scores to madness and self-destruction.— *Boston Investigator.*

A BIGOT IN GRAIN.—Origin Bacheler, in a letter to the editor of the *Herald of Freedom*, says—" I care not whether a thing be *good* or bad in itself, if it be infidel; its infidelity is enough to condemn it." If this be the spirit of Christianity, the less the people have of it the better for the cause of truth.— *Boston Investigator.*

THE BATTLE OF THE CHORYPHÆI.

II.

Sugar produces in us the idea of sweetness, but there is no sweetness in sugar. In like manner matter produces in us the idea of extension, but there is no extension in matter. Sweetness is an attribute, not an existence—so is extension; and as rationally might Mr. Gillespie deify the former as the latter. Of extension he makes an omnipresent, omnipotent, all wise, *all free*, and benevolent God, that is to say, *he attributes to an attribute all these attributes!!!* Cool-headed readers of the *Movement* will probably allow that the "feelosopher" who is not ashamed to publish such extravagant absurdities would be fit company for those queer people of whom 'tis gravely related, that their tongues occupy all the space where their brains *ought* to be.

Extension is nothing more than one of matter's primary attributes. Metaphysicians have thought fit to make a division between what they called primary and secondary qualities. With the former they ranked solidity, figure, and *extension;* with the latter, smell, taste, colour, &c. Now, though without matter there could not possibly be any idea of qualities, who will assert that qualities are matter?—Will Mr. Gillespie? If he will I have mistaken my man " a wee bittee," as the Scotch say, and he is not *so* artful a dodger as I supposed. No—*even he* will not go the length of declaring the materiality of qualities. But if he dare not assert the materiality of qualities or attributes (remember, sir, these two words are one in meaning), will he have the goodness to explain how the primary quality called extension can be an existence without being anything? Throughout the "Argument," extension is invariably dealt with as *anything you like—not matter.* Now what is not matter is nothing, and I call upon Mr. Gillespie to demonstrate; first, that infinite extension is not infinite matter; and secondly, that though not infinite something, it is not infinite nothing.

Mr. Gillespie affects to believe it is of slight consequence if we will but acknowledge that "extension is necessarily infinite," whether it be considered matter or not matter. "I am perfectly satisfied* (says he) with the assertion, that the extension which matter has is infinite, and necessarily existing. The proposition in question (Proposition 1.) lays down no more than this—that extension, of some kind or other, of matter if you will—or no matter if any other will—is infinite and necessarily so.

Before commenting upon this singular piece of philosophy, which is equally singular considered as a piece of smooth composition, I will give Mr. Gillespie a Roland for his Oliver, by asking,—after what *speakers,* I nearly wrote *writers,* did he form his style—who were his models? or is the style strictly original?

Passing from the *style* to the *matter* of the passage here quoted, I must take the liberty to remark, that Mr. Gillespie cannot be permitted to deal so loosely with important words as he seems inclined to do. It is perfectly ridiculous to write as though extensions materiality or immateriality were a point of no moment in this controversy. His cavalier announcement that 'tis no matter whether extension is matter or no (grammatically *not*) matter, amounts to a piece of sheer and arrogant absurdity. Has he yet to learn there is no *media res*—no half way house between something and nothing, any more than between truth and falsehood? Has he yet to learn that extension must be something *or* nothing, that it cannot be both, and that it cannot be neither? If a being or existence, it is something; if a mere attribute or quality, it is nothing. Matter is an existence and evidently the only one; all being it, and it being all. As to such words as time, space, attraction, repulsion, inertia, heat, cold, colour, life, and death, every one knows, or at least should know, that they do not represent *existence,* simple or compounded; but ideas generated in us by the *motions* and consequent *phenomena* exhibited by *existence.*

Bodies exhibit the phenomenon called inertia; but few *Movement* readers need be told that inertia is not an existence. Bodies attract and repel, but neither attraction nor repulsion exist. We have agreed to call heat certain sensations often experienced in nearly all climates. We have agreed to call cold certain other sensations of a different description; but neither heat nor cold is an existence. "Little children" would laugh at us were we to erect heat and cold into beings who do the business of warming or cooling, just as pious people imagine some mysterious being called mind, soul, spirit, and other pretty names, does the business of thinking. Life means nothing more than the sum total of individual sensations, and only God-struck lunatics ever amuse themselves by trying to believe, sensations can be experienced without body to experience them. Life is a name we have agreed shall represent a certain state of body or bodies. Death is a name we have agreed shall represent a state of body or bodies the very opposite of life. " Death (said my Lord Rochester) is

---

* Paragraph 23, Part 1.

nothing, and nothing death;" and as verily it may be added—life is nothing and nothing life; inertia is nothing, and nothing inertia; attraction is nothing, and nothing attraction; repulsion is nothing, and nothing repulsion; heat is nothing, and nothing heat; cold is nothing, and nothing cold. The short is, all attributes (extension of course included) are nothing, and assuredly, in the paradoxic sense of Rochester, *nothing* are all attributes.

Right or wrong, there is no mystery about my philosophical creed. That creed is ultra-materialist. Whatever exists acts, and that which acts I call matter: others may call it other names if they choose. What we call that which acts is of no consequence if we do but understand ourselves and each other. Nothing cannot act. The reasoner who is not sure of *that* is unfit to reason, but quite fit to believe in the God Mr. Gillespie or any other Nihilist may choose to set up. Any attempt to prove nothing can't act, would be thoroughly absurd. The Cheshire clowns who set about raking the moon from the bottom of a pond, would advantageously compare, as regards practical sense, with our learned logicians, who try their heads at demonstrating how divinely *nothing created, acts upon, and regulates everything*. But if nothing cannot act, that which acts must be something. Now something is matter, and matter is evidently something. What can be all and in all but matter? Mr. Gillespie writes about attributes as if they were "sensible to feeling and to sight;" as if we could measure, handle, and taste them; in brief, *as if they were realities*. Never man dealt more absurdly with an attribute than he has with extension. If that "necessary" attribute could, it should chant his praises, for he has made, not a reality merely, but a most "potent, grave and reverend" God, of it. Mr. Gillespie charges me with "low vulgarity," chiefly, it would seem, because I spoke of that God as "the most comical of deities;" which shows that ridicule is the weapon he most dreads—and with reason; for of all the Gods to whom metaphysicians have introduced us, by far the nearest to ridiculousness in perfection is He of "the Argument *a priori*." All other Gods must henceforth "hide their diminished heads;" for he is, as it were, by fits and starts, infinity of expansion as well as infinity of extension, and though not matter or aught so grossly substantial, "unquestionably is" the simple, sole being of infinity of extension, of expansion, and of duration; who is all knowing, all powerful, entirely free, and necessarily completely happy, and necessarily perfectly good.*

---

* See page 34 of the "Argument *a priori*," &c.

I am a plain man, and want plain arguments. Hair splitting I hate. A wordy warfare is my aversion. Words without signification, however high-sounding, learned, and logical, are, to my thinking, sheer nonsense. If Mr. Gillespie is disposed for an honest war of ideas, I will (as Hamlet says) "fight with him upon this theme till my eyelids can no longer wag!" But he is much deceived if he expect to snatch a victory by any such trick as that of perverting my meaning, or by any such shallow policy as that of attempting to bother me out of my propriety by wild stuff about infinite chimeras, or by a cunning substitution "for the properties of things the attributes of nothing." At the eminent risk of maintaining my character for "low vulgarity" and "lewd sneering," I will remind *friend* Gillespie that old birds are not to be caught with chaff." This I do in the hope (a vain one perhaps) of convincing him that "London Atheists" are not to be caught by such "chaff" as the Reply.

That "very precious" production, which cost so many weeks in the concoction, leaves untouched every part of the Strictures except a few verbal inaccuracies, which will, I am sure, be excused by every candid reader who knows how wretched a scrawl I write, and that I did not see a single proof. It was certainly careless in me not to make arrangements for the correction of proofs, especially when dealing with an impertinent antagonist, who loves to make a parade of his logical and grammatical acquirements. But, apart from verbal inaccuracies, such, for example, as (see *Movement*, No. 15, page 115), "a million identical nothings wo'n't amount to a single *non*-identical something;" which should have been "a million of identical nothings wo'n't amount to a single identical something;" there is not a single line of the Strictures I could wish had not appeared. That Mr. Gillespie is sadly annoyed by them is manifest from the Reply, which abounds in evidences that its author's tender leaves of vanity have been nipped by a frost, "a killing frost." From beginning to end of that Reply there is little else than either triumphant conclusions drawn from admissions I never made; personalities the most contemptible I ever saw in print; virtuously indignant denunciation of my "impudent untruth" in daring to say "our author's entire work might *easily* be converted into one of the very best atheistical books extant;" stale jests about my "figures of speech," and, by way of conclusion, my poor *style* comes in for a large share of that "scurrile mirth" and "coarse ribaldry" Mr. Gillespie is so desirous *I* would not indulge in.

Such, sir, is the substance of that Reply, from which so much was expected, and which its author thought so severe that, before its appearance in print, he wrote to condole with me thereupon; probably fearing I should cut my throat from sheer vexation, and himself suffer the agonizing reflection arising from a consciousness of having caused me to commit the rash act. But luckily for my *throat* and my antagonist's *peace*, the mountain in labour only brought forth a very small mouse. In truth, the noise made about the Reply and its subsequent *entrée* reminds one of that startling flourish of trumpets which in " Bombastes Furioso announces "mighty Thomas Thumb."

Evident it is that Mr. Gillespie's mortified self-love dictates to his discretion. He *was*, perhaps, a tolerably prudent disputant, but the Strictures seem to have unduly excited his poor brains. One specimen of the Reply's self-contradictions has already been furnished; another almost equally glaring shall now be given.

You, sir, have read the Strictures, and, of course, are aware, that while freely admitting the great talent of Antitheos, I declared he " did foolishly" in saying it would be absurd in the extreme to deny the existence of infinity of extension. My words were,* " the Refutation by Antitheos of Mr. Gillespie's ' Argument *a priori*,' for the Being and Attributes of God," ably written, though it certainly is, has in no wise damaged, but rather lent an appearance of strength to that Argument, because containing a very foolish admission (that infinity of extension exists), which Gillespie has turned to excellent account, &c. Again—" I shall, without doubt, be excused by readers in general, and Gillespie's admirers in particular, for taking some pains to prove that there is no such *thing* as infinity of extension, and *consequently* that Gillespie, in assuming as the basis of his Argument that there *is*, has assumed unwarrantably, and Antitheos, in admitting the assumption, did foolishly."

Elegant or inelegant, these words are perfectly explicit. They involve an express condemnation of Antitheos for being so "daft" as to admit the *existence* of an attribute!! Now it is quite natural that Mr. Gillespie should in the Reply abuse me for not following the "daft" example, because as very candidly stated in the Refutation " Antitheos's admission is a most important one," but methinks 'tis a little too bad, rather beyond a joke, to charge me in par. 10, Part 2 of Reply, with something like ignorant presumption for venturing to dissent (in a fundamental point too) from Antitheos; and in paragraph 12 of the same Part, to declare that " in spite of anything which may be said to the contrary, Southwell *has a sneaking admiration of Antitheos's* WHOLE METHOD OF PROCEDURE. One paragraph makes out that I object in *toto*—to " a method of procedure," for " the whole of which," according to another paragraph I have " a sneaking admiration!!!" From all which *logical* sort of reasoning the conclusion is inevitable that I admired the whole method of procedure, adopted by Antitheos in his dealings with Mr. Gillespie's " Argument," though sure he acted foolishly in admitting the truth of a notorious falsehood, which forms the basis—the very foundation of that Argument. Oh, how wonderful is the power of that logic which reconciles impossibilities, and demonstrates the verity of opposing propositions. Who but the logician of *supernatural* merit could have discovered that while differing fundamentally with Antitheos's " whole method of procedure," I do nevertheless *admire* that " whole method of procedure."

But though so astonishingly subtle a logician, Mr. Gillespie appears to be an uncommonly dull sort of individual. So dull, so utterly stupid, I may say, as to be incapable of distinguishing the difference (which is infinite) between *my* proposition that matter is infinitely extended, and *his* proposition that extension is an Infinite Being—no two propositions can be more distinct; and yet in the Reply they are treated as identical!!

At paragraph 23, Part 1 of the Reply, Mr. Gillespie declares himself perfectly satisfied with the assertion that the extension which matter has is infinite, and necessarily existing; an expression of satisfaction no one would have a right to quarrel with, if I had asserted anything so " nonsensically false." The assertion is however placed to my account by Mr. Gillespie, who don't stick at trifles when trying to make out a good case. I never asserted, never thought of asserting that matter has extension. Let any one consult the Strictures and he will find that matter is declared " the only existence;" he will find infinity of extension placed in the same category with infinity of time, infinity of motion, and other *nonentities*; he will find Gillespie declared *quite right* when he asserts there cannot be existence without extension, though *quite wrong* when he calls extension an existence; in short *he will find that those Strictures were entitled and considered by me a demonstration that there is no such thing as extension*. How enormous then must be the stupidity, the dishonesty, or both, of that man who publishes sixteen mortal columns of what he aptly calls Reply, more than one half of which refers to and is built upon my admission of the existence, yea, the necessary existence of infinity of extension.

---

* See No. 14 of the *Movement*.

" It would be no more ridiculous to declare motion an infinite and necessarily existing* being than to assert as does our author that extension is an infinite and necessarily existing being.

When he (Gillespie) succeeds in proving motion an infinite being, he may possibly succeed in proving extension an infinite being, duration an infinite being, expansion an infinite being, and all three infinite beings, but one infinite being. After getting thus far with his " Argument," he may venture a step further, and demonstrate upon principles strictly mathematical, that the " one infinite being is simple, unique, necessarily intelligent, necessarily all-knowing, necessarily all-powerful, and necessarily all-free."

These two passages are from the Strictures, an l Philalethean " feelosophers" excepted, I do not think any individual or individuals can be found so thoroughly stupid as to fancy that he who penned them " joined in the folly" of admitting the being or existence of extension, finite or infinite.

Throughout the Strictures I have argued that matter is all. Now if matter is all, all is matter; and it unquestionably follows *there is nothing else.*

The idea of matter's universality once embraced, excludes the idea of any other than material existence. Atheists think matter universal, *i. e.* everywhere and everything. If asked why—they answer, *because its nonexistence is inconceivable.* Not to employ our thoughts about something is to cease thinking —" Even when the mind† (Mr. Gillespie will I hope excuse my making such good use of all but the *nonsense* in Proposition 1, Part 1, Division 1 of " *the* Argument") endeavours to remove from it the idea of infinity of matter, it cannot, after all its efforts, avoid leaving still there, the idea of such infinity. Let there be ever so much endeavour to displace this idea, that is, conceive infinity of matter non-existent; everyone, by a reflex examination of his own thoughts, will find it utterly beyond his power to do so.

" Now since even when we would remove the notion of infinity of matter out of our minds, we cannot but leave the notion of it behind; from this, it is manifest, infinity of matter is necessarily existing; for, *everything the existence of which we cannot but believe, is necessarily existing.*

" To deny, therefore, that infinity of matter necessarily exists, is to utter a downright contradiction: infinity of matter is, then, necessarily existing."

Nihilists may write about their no (grammatically *not*) matter infinity till " the crack of doom ;" but the fact is, they neither conceive such infinity themselves, nor enable others to do so—and at best are learned dolts who display all sorts of sense but good sense. It is difficult to enter fully into the spirit of their productions without thinking aloud—

' Nothing, how great art thou, stupendous, nought."

The *nothingness* of space or extension* is admirably exhibited in the following sentences from No. 8, vol. 3 of " The Shepherd," which appear as a Transcendentalist's answer to his Universalist correspondent:—

" If U. reflects on the meaning of the word " space," he will find *it is merely the form in which outward things appear,* and that it is by no means a thing, or *even an appearance.* If we look at the sky and call it a large space, we mean that *we see an extended blue surface.* At night we say we see the stars floating in space; we mean that we see little bright spheres bounded all round by a little dusky surface. Let U. only try to imagine a circle without picturing to himself the surrounding surface and that of a different colour. * * Admitting that space is external to the body, what is mere space ? Is it of any colour ? Has it any properties whatever, unless the mere absence of body be called a property ? How then shall we distinguish it from nothing ?"

How, indeed !

But if we will only be so courteous as to admit extension's necessary existence, Mr. Gillespie don't care a fig whether its name be nothing or something. Nothing, *i. e.* that which is not matter—he considers a most capital foundation for rational Theism. Only give him " extension *of some kind or other,* and lo a God *of some kind or other,* is immediately *à votre service.* With this *expressive* fact before them, the bulk of *Movement* readers will be at no loss to account for the otherwise unaccountable trouble taken by

---

* By some mishap " indivisible," instead of " existing," appeared in the Strictures.

† See " The Necessary Existence of God," by William Gillespie—new edition.

* Space just means extension or expansion. " The words space, extension, amplitude, and expansion are," says the author of the Impartial Enquiry, " nothing different, neither in their general significations, nor in their original use"—" whatever distinction is wont to be assigned is merely arbitrary." See his discourse concerning the nature of space.

Space then, is merely another term for extension—See Part 7, page 149 of an Examination of Antitheos's Refutation, by William Gillespie.

Mr. Gillespie *to make it appear* I had given my principles the lie by admitting the existence of that infinite HUMBUG, which he calls Proposition 1 of "*the* Argument *a priori.*"

Indeed, Mr. Gillespie has throughout his "Reply" battled upon the principle that all's fair in war time." Perhaps the annals of controversy do not furnish a more flagrant instance of paltry manœuvring than is to be met with at paragraph 14, Part 1 of that Reply. They who have read the Strictures will remember the following passage :—

Our author ought to know that *extension*, oftener called *space*, is a word philosophers have agreed shall represent a certain class of ideas, generated in us *by the order of things existing.* Our author ought to know that *duration* oftener called *time*, is a word philosophers have agreed shall represent a certain class of ideas generated in us by *the order of things successive.*

Just to show off, I presume, his critical talent, Mr. Gillespie *affects* to believe that by the term "philosophers," I meant *all* philosophers, and gravely asures me "it is not all philosophers, but only some philosophers, these the followers of Leibnitz—who holy that space is just the order of *co-existing bodies.*"† For which piece of information, I ought to feel deeply obliged to him. Never till he condescended to instruct me could I conceive the possibility of philosophers disagreeing about anything. But now, thanks to him, I see clearly that all philosophers don't entirely agree upon all topics. Verily, I do so far emulate a noted sage of antiquity as to "grow old learning many things."

Having relieved myself very considerably by this outburst of grateful feeling, I will say a little about the *some* philosophers who hold that space is "just the order of co-existing bodies." It happens in truth that the only *some* philosophers, amount to the great majority of philosophers, both in Germany and in France, if the authority of Dugald Stewart be worth anything; who tells us in a note at the foot of page 142 of Dissertation First, prefixed to the Encyclopædia Brittanica—it always appeared to him "*a thing quite inexplicable that the great majority of philosophers both in Germany and in France have on the above question* (concerning the the necessary existence of space and time,) *decided in favour of Leibnitz*—so that after all Mr. Gillespie's *crowing* about authorities, it seems the best as well as the most numerous are against him. To poor Dugald Stewart it appeared "a thing quite inexplicable"—*but he admits the fact*, which is all I have at present to do with. And really it does at once amuse and astonish me to find Mr. Gillespie quoting Stewart and Dr. Isaac Watts as "great authorities." But for taste there *is* no accounting.

Without presumption it may be affirmed that none can possibly conceive the non-existence of matter, and as the conception of matter's annihilation, or at least annihilability is *implied* in the conception of what fanciful people call pure space, it follows that to conceive the existence of pure space is impossible. Locke thought otherwise; so did Newton and Edwards, and Reid and Dugald Stewart, and (oh, marvellous) Antitheos, as shown by Gillespie in the Examination of that gentleman's "Refutation ;" but these philosophers have proved themselves absurdly fallible—Indeed the single authority of Leibnitz concerning this question of extension or space, backed as it is by *unanswered* reasonings, is of far more weight with me than that of all other philosophers lumped together.

In a note to page 142 of the Dissertation above referred to, Mr. Dugald Stewart says, "The question concerning the necessary existence of time and space formed one of the principal subjects of discussion between Clarke and Leibnitz. According to the former, space and time are both of them infinite, immutable, and indestructive. According to his antagonist, '*Space is nothing but the order of things coexisting*,' and '*time nothing but the order of things successive.*' The notion of real absolute space in particular, he pronounces to be '*a mere chimera and superficial imagination*;' classing it with those prejudices which Bacon called *idola tribus.*"

Bailly, a writer by no means partial to D'Alembert, in his "*Eloge de Leibnitz,*" quotes, *with entire approbation*, the foregoing observations, subjoining to them, in the following terms, his own judgment on the merits of this branch of the controversy between Clarke and Leibnitz: '*La notion du temps et de l'espace, est un des points sur les quels Leibnitz a combattu contra Clarke ; mais il nous semble qu'Anglais n'a rien opposé de satisfaisant aux raisons de Leibnitz.*"*

So much for authority with regard to the fundamental point of difference between myself and Mr. Gillespie, to which, methinks, had be been *discreet*, he would not have appealed. A disputant should never appeal to authority unless quite sure it preponderates on his own side of the question. In the for-

---

† Query—Can bodies exist *without* co-existing?

* The notion of time and of space is one of the points regarding which Leibnitz has combatted against Clarke, but it seems to us that the Englishman *has not opposed anything satisfactory to the reasons of Leibnitz.*

mer part of my Strictures I had *generously* admitted that my antagonist had reason to boast of "two first-rate authorities." If wise, he would have been satisfied with that admission. If wise he would have been particularly well satisfied with me for dismissing the question of authority with the remark that "though *all* authority were on that (his) side; it availeth nothing if *truth* is on the other." But being the opposite of wise, he took the foolish course of forcing me to discuss this question of authority, and by good authority to establish the fact that "the great majority of philosophers, both in Germany and in France," denied the existence of space or extension, and thought it what I think it—*a mere chimera and superficial imagination.*

Before passing from this part of the Reply, I will merely observe, that pure space, about which our Lockes and Clarkes have written so much, is allowed by Mr. Gillespie to be the same as pure extension or pure expansion. According to him, "*space* just means *extension* or *expansion*," and of course, according to him, pure space just means pure extension or pure expansion. But, in point of fact, pure space is inconceivable, and *therefore* to talk about it is pure *blockheadism*. This I write deliberately and with the knowledge that Locke demanded of any one to remove any part of pure space from another, even so much as in thought; for though my respect for him is great, my respect for the "truth of things" is much greater. If an angel from "high heaven" were to prate about the *parts of pure space*, I should not hesitate to say he prated like a blockhead.

D'Alembert—a rather better authority than Dugald Stewart, or Dr. Isaac Watts—shrewdly asked, "Would there be space if there were no bodies, and duration if nothing existed?" These questions (continued he), seem to spring from the opinion *that time and space possess a reality which they have not.* * * * * * * Children who say a vacuum is nothing have reason, because they cling to the simple notions of common sense; and philosophers who fain would realize a vacuum, *loose themselves in their speculations.* The vacuum was brought forth (*enfanté*) by abstractions, and in it we may behold the abuse of a method useful in so many regards. If there were no *body, or succession, space and time would be possible, but they would not exist.*"

Thus D'Alembert,—but a greater than he is Gillespie, who *perhaps* will tell us, " some day or other," how space and time, alias extension and duration, would be possible without body or succession. According to his "Argument," the material universe is finite in extension.* Now it is manifest that if the material universe is finite (the difference between the finite and infinite being infinite) there must be an infinite *bodiless* extent beyond it — a conclusion reason rejects.

But Mr. Gillespie's reason don't reject it —nay, he positively asserts "that in nature there is space where there is no matter."† A position, quoth he, without doubt of vast consequence, as against Atheism; and by no means to be laid hold of before right to possession is established—so far good; but let us see how he contrives to establish his right to possess this *impregnable* position. The Reply (paragraph 20) assures us "a right to possession is established in the first sub-proposition, where it is proved that the material universe is finite in extension."

Now I beg your attention to so much of the said sub-proposition as need be quoted in order to convey the gist of my antagonist's reasoning.

" If then (says he) it should be maintained that the material universe is the substratum of infinity of extension; (which will be maintained, as is most evident if it be contended that the material universe is a thorough *plenum* of infinity of extension) to put to proof whether or not the material universe can be such substratum, we have but to ask, are the parts of the material divisible from each other? and are they moveable among themselves? For if they be so divisible, if so moveable, then the material universe cannot be the substratum of infinity of extension.

" We know of a certainty that some parts of the material universe are *divisible from each other;* and, as far as we know, every part of it, to which our minds could be directed, is as divisible as are the parts which we certainly know are divisible; and this is the conclusion, to which, by the rules of philosophy, we are entitled to come.

" Therefore the material universe cannot be the substratum of infinity of extension."

This is what Mr. Gillespie considers conclusive reasoning in support of his *much needed* assertion, that " the material universe is finite." The whole of it, however, is "wide of the mark—wide, very wide of any mark." Indeed, a lamer or more impotent attempt to *circumscribe the boundless* and establish *the truth of an impossibility,* is not to be met with even in his " Necessary Existence of Deity."

(*To be concluded in our next.*)

---

* See page 14 of the " Argument *a priori,*" &c., new edition.

† See paragraph 20, Part First of the Reply.

RELIGION versus SCEPTICISM.

If the effects of scepticism were as bad and as self-evident as the effects of intemperance; one could readily understand and *feel* the advantages of religion, and the folly and wickedness of unbelief. This has never, to my knowledge, been shown to be the fact. I know that religious people will say, and contend that it is true, that they have only to pray to their deity to obtain whatever they may desire. An acquaintance of mine, who keeps a huckster's shop, and who has got rich by the profits of his trade, has often told me the same thing. I have represented to him that the means whereby he lives are far from honest—that he buys cheap and sells dear—and that, too, to the poorest and most hard-worked class — that he is frequently applying to the local courts to compel those who are in arrears to make good their engagements. I have urged upon him that it would be much better, in order to avoid such practices, to pray to his deity to give him the additional wealth which he still thinks he wants—and thus escape the danger which he incurs of being cast out at the last day, for his extortion and usury towards those who, it is said, shall inherit the kingdom of heaven. To this he replies, that I mistake the meaning and object of prayer—that it is absurd to expect that god will give us material wealth and material comforts—that we were sent here to labour for our means of sustenance, and that if we are holy and righteous god will *help* us to get it, but that he wont give it to us unless we first exert ourselves to obtain it without him. This appears to me exceedingly absurd. If we can support ourselves without god's help, there is no call for placing ourselves under an obligation to him—and if we cannot support ourselves, it appears he will not assist us. For my own part, I shall not call upon him so long as I have health and strength to work—and when these fail me, should I feel inclined to call, I expect "he will not answer." Religious people tell me that I cannot expect god's blessing and protection unless I obey his commands, and conduct myself lowly and reverently before him. I never did expect his blessing, and have never been disappointed, as a consequence. Now, in this, I am better off than many of my neighbours, for I have seen the righteous begging their bread, although I believe it is said that they never should have occasion to do so. When I was in Birmingham, some time since, I often remarked groups of poor miserable creatures singing in the principal streets and in the most piteous strain—"I love Jesus—yes, I do." But I always observed that those who were singing what are called profane songs, had the largest audience, and received more remuneration for their trouble than those who were making open profession of their faith and love for the Saviour. In the street in which I lived thousands of persons passed to and fro daily, and many of them were members of the various religious congregations of the town, and some of them parsons with large incomes, but I never observed them stop and give out of their abundance to those who were steeped in poverty, and yet would declare that they "loved Jesus." I never missed these wretched specimens of christianity in my accustomed walk—I never had reason to believe that their more fortunate or more favoured fellow-christians, had given them the means wherewith to live, and that they were established in comfortable homes, with cheerful fire-sides, where they could read their Bible, sheltered from the inclement weather, and give god thanks for all his goodness to them. No, this I never saw, for as every succeeding day began to wane, there they were again singing their plaintive ditty, and reiterating their oft-told affection for one who never appeared to heed their grief, nor care aught about their woe—and his followers, as in duty bound, acted upon his example. If these are the *gains* of godliness, what is lost by scepticism?

W. C.

THE LEICESTER BRANCH
(Of the Union.)

THE friends of anti-persecution in Leicester, who held a public meeting some time ago to memorialise the Prison Board of Scotland on behalf of Mr. Paterson, have obtained from the Secretary the following acknowledgement:—

"Chambers of the General Board of Directors of Prisons.

"Edinburgh, 16th April, 1844.

"SIR,—I am directed by the Viscount Melville, Chairman of the General Prisons, Board, to acknowledge receipt of your letter of the 6th instant, with its inclosure; and I am to acquaint you that I shall lay these papers before the General Board at their next ensuing meeting.

"I am, sir, your obedient Servant,
"LUD. COLQUHOUN.

"Mr. Thomas Emery,
No. 11, Neale-street, Leicester."

Next our indefatigable friends adopted the following petition, which received 1650 signatures:—

"To the Commons of Great Britain and Ireland in Parliament assembled.

"The Petition of the undersigned inhabitants of Leicester.

"SHEWETH—That your petitioners have

learned with sorrow that legal proceedings have been instituted against various parties in different parts of Great Britain, for the free publication of opinions.

"That no less than nine persons have been imprisoned within the last three years.

"That two persons, to wit, Thomas Paterson and Henry Robinson are now suffering imprisonment in Scotland.

"Your Petitioners submit, that these proceedings are directly opposed to the first principles of Protestantism, which profess to guarantee to every individual the right of private judgment in matters of religion, they therefore request that you will take the aforesaid cases of Thomas Paterson and Henry Robinson into your immediate consideration, and request Her Majesty to order their release.

"And further, that you will pass such a measure as shall have the effect of abrogating all laws which prohibit the free publication of opinions."

This petition is printed word for word as sent to Mr. Duncombe for presentation. It was drawn up in accordance with the suggestions in *Movement* 17, and though denuded of all conventional compliment, and phaseology, it was presented by Mr. Duncombe—as he writes to notify—and was "ordered to lie on the table," as was stated in *Movement* 35. We thank our friends for trying this question. It was thought we had o'er stepped discretion's bounds, in recommending the course we did. But we had confidence in plain honest language, and thought our House of Commons would allow it, and are rejoiced to find that they have. No "honourable" House—no "humble" petition—no, "and your petitioners will ever pray," were employed, and yet the petition was ordered to "lie on the table" as other petitions are, and there it does lie, the proudest, most independent, and perhaps the honestest of them all. It is worth going to the House of Commons to see that petition lie there. When other petitions "lie on the table," they generally do *lie* there. But the Leicester petition reclines there in truthfulness. Marry we may all be honest if we only have courage!

Religion would be beneath notice, were it not made the great handle for bad purposes, and the engine for extortion and tyranny. While so many believe the tale to be true, or are so ignorant as to say they believe in the absurd fable, while thousands of priests uphold the glaring falsehood, and are paid or exact millions annually for maintaining falsity to be truth—surely the greatest duty of knowledge and philanthropy is to use means for rescuing society from such a state of abasement and subserviency.

Chartist Liberality.—The annexed resolutions were unanimously passed, some time since, at two public meetings convened in the Chartist Hall, Bristol. They should have reached us at the time, but have been delayed by the omission of the person in whose hands they were left. It is due to our political friends to give them publicity, and we have pleasure in doing it:—

1. Resolved, "That as the free expression of opinion is the natural right of all men, this meeting is of opinion that any attempt to prevent its free utterance is unsocial, antichristian, and impolitic; and this meeting is further of opinion that all the victims of such persecutions merit the commisseration of true lovers of liberty.

2. "That, in the opinion of this meeting, the principles of democracy recognise the full right of thought and speech in all men of all creeds and opinions; we therefore express our heartfelt sympathy with Messrs. Robinson, Finlay, and Paterson, of Edinburgh, in their present persecution for the supposed crime of blasphemy."

CORRESPONDENCE.
(*To the Editor of the Movement.*)
Brighton.

Dear Sir,—In responding to your appeal for help from those who can assist, I have enclosed an order for £2 5s. Will you pay to the Central Board £2 as a deposit for one share in my name, and to the Paterson Testimonial appropriate 5s. John Ransom.

Dear Sir,—My present object is to request that you will put down in the next *Movement* W. B. B. £1 to the Paterson Testimonial. The example being set by that *true* friend, W. J. B., I wish to lose no time in following it. W. B. B.

MRS. MARTIN'S TRACTS.

Prayer—is the title of the Fourth of the Tracts for the People by Emma Martin, which sustains the useful character we have before given to these serials. The whole having been re-issued (No. 1 having reached the fourth thousand) in a very improved style. No. 3 has been dedicated to the Rev. J. Burder of Bristol, in consequence of that gentleman having thought fit to designate No. 1, horrid blasphemy. Mrs. Martin offers strong temptation to the rev. gent. to come out of his shell either on the platform or on paper in defence of his opinions. But we suspect he knows better than to trust his cause to free discussion.

Still to be Achieved!—An absolute freedom in religious discussions has never yet existed in any age or country. It is one of the dreams of the new philosophy.—*Booth*

WITCHCRAFT.—A doubt has been raised by some writers on this subject as to what the witchcraft mentioned and denounced in holy writ consisted in. To us this appears a mere cavil. The scripture expressly talks of persons who had familiar spirits; and what the particular connection of such persons with such beings was, it can be of small moment to inquire. We would willingly have abstained from allusion to this part of the subject; but it is necessary, in order to show on what grounds the reality of instances of witchcraft was admitted in former ages. To this admission, the belief in the existence of evil spirits and in their power of interference with the human race, would naturally lead. This belief was founded on scripture. ¡ It is true there are many persons, professing to believe in christianity, who endeavour to explain away those texts, which assert the being and attributes of evil spirits. Can such texts be so explained ? Clearly not, except by a process, which, in the interpretation of any other book, would involve the most monstrous solecisms in rhetoric and verbal criticism. According to this mode of construction, when it is said, over and over again, that devils possessed human bodies, what is meant is, that they did not possess them; when they are represented as entering into those of animals, that they did not enter into them; when we are told that they spoke, that they did not speak; when we read that they believe and tremble, that they neither tremble nor believe. Commentators who adopt these views, must, we should think, at least admit that they are questionable; and that the scriptures appear, at any rate, to assert the existence of evil spirits. But whether they assert it or not, certain it is, that their apparently doing so impressed a corresponding belief on the early christians.—*Illuminated Magazine.*

FANCY ENVELOPE.— Mr. Merriman has published a pretty envelope covered with various devices and sentiments. The engraving is a little too heavy. The many judicious sentiments upon it will make it a general favourite. The use of such an envelope is a very genteel mode of proselytising.

PROGRESS. — Philosophy may be safely backed in these times against Christianity. Ready money is more potent than religion. Malthus and Co. have floored the Bible; their precepts have smothered those of the New Testament.—*Times.*

[We have only, by the co-operative views, " to floor money and Malthus," then moral and social improvement will have a free course.—ED, of M.]

PETITIONS.— Petitions have been forwarded by Messrs. Aitken, Orme, Broadbent, Pollitt, Bedford, and Hindle, from Ashton-Under-Line, against the blasphemy laws. J. Brotherton, M.P., has written acknowledging the receipt and presentation of that from Mr. Hindle. It is probable that the others are presented, but no official notice of them has reached us.

MRS. MARTIN'S TOUR.—Mrs. Martin has delivered a course of three lectures in Leicester which were well attended. In Nottingham she announced a sermon on the execution of Saville, from the text, " Their feet are swift to shed blood, destruction and misery are in their path, and the way of peace they have not known." She engaged the " Assembly Rooms" for its delivery, but that being held by parsons and magistrates, its use was refused. Not to be prevented fulfilling her object, she delivered her sermon in the market place, where she had the satisfaction of addressing 5000 people, and the mayor, who was present, and who we believe is a liberal man, had the gratification of seeing that although the brutal exhibition of a *public murder*, attended by priestly teachers, may bring together a multitude, that there are other and better who for wiser purposes can gather the people together, and turn their thoughts into nobler channels. Mrs. M. lectured in the evening in the same place. A tea party was held in honour of Mrs. Martin, at which the affair of the market place was described as " the best thing which had happened for socialism there." Two pounds were presented to her by way of compensation for losses through being deprived of the Assembly Rooms, Mrs. M. next lectured in Derby, and on Sunday last in Manchester. On Sunday, Sept. 1, she lectures in Preston, and on Monday and Tuesday, Sept. 2, 3. On Wednesday, Sept. 4, she lectures in Bolton. Mrs. Martin's address is Hall of Science, Manchester, to which place applications can be made by Branches desiring her services.

CHRISTIAN MORALITY?—What an unendurable oddity in any class of society would be a man of thorough christian sincerity—a man, I mean, who should think freely as well as speak freely. How every little circle of society fixes bounds of opinions and manners! Here the Dissenter is proscribed, there the Unitarian. Most nominal christians act as if they thought that infidelity was greatly improved by hypocrisy.—*W. J. Fox.*

STRONG OWENISM.—It is as absurd to entertain an abhorrence of intellectual inferiority or error, as it would be to cherish a warm indignation against earthquakes or hurricanes.—*Sir James Mackintosh.*

TOTAL ASSETS AND LIABILITIES OF THE ANTI-PERSECUTION UNION.
(At the Present Time.)

ASSETS.	£	s.	d.	LIABILITIES.	£	s.	d.
To 774 Copies of Paterson's London Trial	11	3	5	To Balance of Mr. Whiting's bill for maintenance of Mr. Southwell while in Bristol Gaol	25	3	11
To Scotch Trials in Wrappers and Sheets	14	0	0				
4 Southwell's Trial	0	2	6	To Payments by Bristol Subscription last Quarter £1 7 0			
93 dozen in Sheets	5	17	3¼	Present Quarter 1 0 0			
Oracles	1	0	0	Per Remittance 1 0 0	3	7	0
Balance due from Mr. Hetherington	1	3	7				
	£33	6	9¼	Balance due £21 16 11			

LECTURES.

WHITECHAPEL.—On Sunday Evening, September 1, Mr. Holyoake will lecture. On Monday Evening, September 2, Mr. Southwell delivers his second lecture "To the Socialists of England." Tuesday Evening a discussion between the Rev. G. Hill and Mr. C. Southwell.

SEPTEMBER 1.—Social Institution, Goswell-road.—On Galvanism and Electrotype, with illustrative experiments, by Mr. Stanton.

SEPTEMBER 5.—Hall of Science, City-road. — Lecture on Phrenology, by Mr. Hamilton.

MANCHESTER.—Hall of Science, Campfield, on Wednesday, September 4, Mr. Robert Cooper will deliver the third of his Course of Twelve Lectures on the BIBLE. Subject —"The Characters of the Christian Fathers and Apostles." To commence at 8 o'clock.

DISCUSSIONS.

AUGUST 29.—At Mr. Cartwright's Coffee Rooms, 80, Red Cross Street,—Question, "Is there any evidence in the universe of the existence of a Deity and his providence?"

AUGUST 30.—At Mr. Wisedell's Coffee Rooms, 7, Long Lane, Smithfield—Question, "Which has been most beneficial, Christianity or Infidelity, to civilize and improve nations?"

AUGUST 31.—At Mr. Cornish's Coffee Rooms, Bunhill Row, St. Luke,—Question, "Is Atheism more reasonable than a belief in a God—separate from and independent of the material universe!"

SEPTEMBER 1.—At the Social Institution, Goswell Road, after the lecture,—Question, "Will the advance of science ultimately extinguish poverty?"

SEPTEMBER 2.—Cartwright's, 80, Red Cross Street, Adjourned Dissussion from Thursday.

SEPTEMBER 3.—Wisedell's, Long Lane, Adjourned Discussion.

SEPTEMBER 4.—Bunhill Row,—Discussion on the Corn Laws.

THE members of Branch 53, late of the Rotunda, meet at the St. George's Temperance Hall, corner of Webber Street, Blackfriars Road, on Thursday and Friday, for Conversation, Amusement and Instruction.

PLAIN PREACHING.—A clergyman in the north of Scotland, very homely in his address, chose for his text the following passage in Psalms:—"I said in my haste all men are liars." "Ay," premised his Reverence, "ye said it in your haste, David, did ye? Gin ye had been here, ye might hae said it at your leisure, my mon!"

NOTICE.

ANTI-PERSECUTION UNION.—The committee hold their Monthly Meeting on Tuesday Evening, September 3, in the Coffee Room, John-street Institution, Tottenham-court-road.

THE Monthly Meeting of the Atheistical Society will take place on Tuesday Evening next, September 3, at the Northampton Coffee-house, Newton-street, High Holborn, when the Discussion of "What is Atheism" will be opened by Mr. Powell.

TO CORRESPONDENTS.

RECEIVED.—T Paterson. R. B.—we have written to him. J. P. on design. T. Finlay. Letter from Alexander Campbell respecting our notice of his separation from the "Concordists."

SUBSCRIPTIONS TO THE ANTI-PERSECUTION UNION.

	£	s.	d.
W. B. B., for the Paterson Testimonial	1	0	0
J. Ransom, Brighton, for ditto	0	5	0
Card 19	0	1	6

G. J. H., *Sec.*

Printed and Published by G. J. HOLYOAKE, 40, Holywell-street, Strand, Saturday, August 31, 1844.

THE MOVEMENT
And Anti=Persecution Gazette.

"Maximize morals, minimize religion."—BENTHAM.

No. 39. — EDITED BY G. JACOB HOLYOAKE, ASSISTED BY M. Q. RYALL. — PRICE 2d

EXAMINATION OF THE DOCTRINES OF THE CONCORDISTS.
II.

IN Mr. Oldham's second article, to be found in *Movement* 9, if we may attach to them the common meaning, are some very pretty thoughts. "We can conceive," says Mr. O., "of a being of kindly feeling, of clear intellect, and of certain and successful action." This "perfect man," if I guess rightly at that chameleon thing, Concordian meaning, the Concordians desire to realise. After much bewildering mystery about "universe generative laws," it is said that "when man's antecedent relations are correct, his consequent associations will be happy." Probably so, but what the world has wanted since the days of Chilo is some one who would have the kindness to explain these "antecedent relations." But the Concordists act the part of the priests of Egypt, who only enlighten the world by hieroglyphics which make their knowledge a more formidable mystery than before. The next time, after the sentence quoted, that Mr. Oldham is intelligible, he echoes the grave truth ejaculated long ago by the melancholy Pestalozzi, when passing in review the French Revolution, of glorious memory—" No modification of man's external circumstances can permanently alleviate his internal disquiet."

The only remaining sentiment in article No. 2, which I am able to comprehend is that "Man is unhappy from what he *is*, not from what he does." This is not true. Man is unhappy from both. The sober hypocrite and the thoughtful trimmer are unhappy from what they *do*, as well as from what they are. It is not well to represent that men's actions are immaterial in their consequences to themselves. It not only is not true, but it would be unfortunate if it was. It is greatly moral to proclaim to the human race that the doings, both of the oppressor and cheat, will recoil on their own heads, and generate their unhappiness.

The actions of to-day will, in the common order of time, become antecedent relations to-morrow—and if consequent happiness depends on antecedent relations, as we have just been told, why, even according to Mr. Oldham, man will be unhappy from what he *does* as well as from what he *is*.

In article No. 3, *Movement* 14, Mr. Oldham proceeds to speak of the relationships of man to man—there the sentiments, I thought so questionable, first appear in all their spiritual deformity. Mr. Oldham hastens to tell us that *"He who is intensively natured in unity with the creator, will attach but little importance to the relations in human society — his individual attachments will be held lightly, and but little regarded."* Either the cloven foot of mysticism is exhibited in these sentiments, or the Concordian expositor has chosen an unfortunate way of explaining his views. To "attach little importance to the relations of human society" is to act immorally, and this is what Mr. Oldham's words predict, as the consequence of his doctrines. The beauty of life consists in perfecting "individual attachments." Mr. O. says that "benevolence and integrity will mark all the conduct on earth" of the person "who holds individual attachments lightly," but this cannot be—that is spurious philanthropy, which sheds not a strong influence over home and friends. "Being actuated by the universal," says our expositor, the Concordist "feels but little in common with the *merely* individul being." When the bigot Abolitionist came to Emerson, melting with his last news of the state of the Barbadoes slave, Emerson replied to him " Go, love thy infant; love thy woodchopper ; be good-natured and modest; have those graces ; and never varnish your hard uncharitable ambition with this incredible tenderness for black folk a thousand miles off." So it might be replied to Mr. Oldham —" go, cultivate the pure affections of home, and the 'attachments' of private life— make yourself a human being—and study human relationships before you attempt to teach universal man his duties." It is very probable that the benevolence of the man, solely "actuated by the universal," has such an extent of surface to cover that it is spread out like gold-beaters' skin, and so precious thin as to be unfelt by those whom it touches. At the conclusion of article No. 3, we are informed "that in all a Concordist's most active life a perfect passivity to universal laws is his highest duty." What kind of "most *active* life" that is, in which the Concordist is "*perfectly passive*" I cannot stay to determine, but if these "universal laws" should howl out the old monkish mandate of celibacy, the Concordists, in perfect "passivity" thereto, will at once discard the wife of his youth and affection; for — "benevolent universal man," has learned "to regard the relations of human society as of little importance"—and on this point Concordian history could say something. A man is imprisoned by the priesthood, a Concordist would, as a common lover of liberty, protest against this violation of right and justice—he might, as a man, feel some "individual attachment to those who struggled according to *their* "being" for man's enlightenment, but as a Concordist, he can raise no voice in favour of the oppressed, he is "perfectly passive to the universal laws" that teach him "to hold individual attachments lightly." Let Mr. Oldham declare, if he can, that it is not so. Christ said, that when his doctrines spread, a man's foes should be those of his own household, and Concordianism comes to verify the diabolical prediction, and teach, if Mr. Oldham is to be believed, that human relations are to be little regarded. This sentiment of genuine Concordianism is a black drop of mysticism, into which all the streams of base unmanly submission may run, until one foul pool of fanaticism is generated. What could the priests say more? What more have they said than that we must submit faith, reason, actions, and integrity to spiritual dictation? "In whatsoever circumstances a man may find himself placed it is his *duty to submit* at all times to the universal laws (even) whether they militate or not against the laws established by man." These are Mr. Oldham's words. What are these universal laws? Who is to proclaim them? Are we to take the rule of submission from the mouth of mysticism's high priest, Pater Oldham? I have dreamed that the favourite idea of the Concordists was the perfectability of man as an individual. But it seems that the fatal love of the mystical has poisoned noble intention. According to our "Exposition" man is first evaporated in universal laws, and then condensed into degrading submission. "And this is the process of their love and wisdom." The authoress of "Vivia Perpetua" exclaims—

"Never yet
Found I true dignity in any one
Who let the world's opinion cripple thought."

And whether it be the world's opinion or Mysticism's latest born—" universal laws," the evil is the same to man, and dignity is lost to those who profess such principles.

In these representations of Mr. Oldham's Exposition I have inclined to that version of his views which belongs to plain interpretation, and to actual Concordian practice. His sentiments are less injurious to his own sect than most erroneous sentiments are to others, in the particular that they are not likely to affect posterity, for if they carry out their newly adopted Shakerism, it is plain they will have no posterity to affect.

The second and third paragraphs of article 3, the one just considered, contains some useful thoughts on education, at least I humbly think so. But in such doubt am I as to the correct interpretation of Mr. Oldham's language that when I find a beautiful thought I expect to be blamed the next moment for my incapacity to perceive that in "true spirit being" exactly the opposite is intended.

When I look at what Concordists have endeavoured to realise in practice, I make large allowances for their fantastic tricks with humanity. To simplify diet,—diminish care,—practice self-reliance in active, if not in thoughtful life, to realise co-operation and reform generation are ideas of cardinal value, and one cannot but sincerely regret that men of so much intelligence and courage should be seduced into a strange jargon, vile mysticism, and humiliating submission. I am far from thinking that Mr. Oldham is aware that his sentiments are of the tendency I have pointed out. In his mystical dogmas he probably sees some dim vision of human beatitude, although his views are but the revival in a new form of spiritual pride and human subjugation, mixed up with commendable intention and an extreme tincture of stoical practice.

In Mr. Oldham's 4th article, in *Movement* 23, we are told that "genius is the spontaneous nature of a pupil." It therefore is probably found among the Concordists. Let us hope that it may be developed in the ability to speak plainly when next they present to the world an exposition of their doctrines.

But what a strange mixture are even the Concordist's notions of education! Well regulated egoism is the foundation of self-respect, of honour, and man's noblest qualities. But a primary office of the "re-agent educator," is to eradicate "self-love." Passing by the folly of the task, the dogma comes with infinite grace from a man who stands forth as a Pater, and who, according to the tenor of his papers, would rule with a rod of spiritual iron the thoughts of men, who like another Nebuchadnezzar would set up the golden image of "triune laws," for all men to bow down to, on pain of being cast into the fiery furnace of his pity. Pestalozzi cultivated the independance of his pupils' nature, Jacotot proclaimed all intelligences equal in order to promote the strong cultivation of individual energy, and glorious Emerson says, " Trust thy self; every heart vibrates to that iron string;" but Emerson knew nothing of Concordian hearts. Mr. Oldham directs the educator to clear away the " corruption of *self-activity*." Whatever of beauty dwelt in Concordianism, Mr. Oldham contrives to blast or obscure.

Sometimes Mr. Oldham does the poetical, and then the scintillations of his spiritual fancy are dazzling. " The object of the educator," says he, " should be to *unite* the faculties of the pupils to the divine *end*." Just fancy this " highest re-agent" " connecting" the faculties of his pupils like so many strings to the " divine end," just as a boy ties haf-a-dozen tails to his kite. This must be vegetable imagination.

Atheism delights in plain reasoning on religious matters. It reduces faith to the rules of common experience. On anything above or below reason it looks suspiciously. Plain judgment is atheism's characteristic. Every system presented in the *Movement* will be subjected to that test, and whatever refuses to submit to it does not come within the pale of our operations. If Concordianism declines to be so analysed, we must make a wholesale present of its doctrines to its founders. Concordianism comes to us in the name of goodness, therefore we treat it gently—but we must examine it. " Whoso," says Emerson, " would be a man, must not be hindered by the name of goodness, but must explore if it be goodness. Nothing is at last sacred but the integrity of our own minds." G. J. H.

FRENCH DEMOCRATIC SOCIETY.—On Monday evening a deputation from the Chartist body waited upon this society, for the purpose of making arrangements for a dinner in commemoration of the FRENCH REVOLUTION. A value, beyond ordinary celebrations of this kind, is attached to this *reunion*, particularly at the present period, when the aristocracies and middle classes of the two countries are encouraging the ancient spirit of national animosity. The meeting together of the Chartists and other English democrats with the foreign Republican Societies to make a common declaration of sympathy with revolutionary objects and actors, will form the commencement of a new epoch in popular progress. We hope to meet all our *Movement* friends, atheistical, republican, and communistic on the 23rd.; the place of meeting and other particulars will be announced next week.

THE BATTLE OF THE CHORYPHÆI.
III.

Only three paragraphs of this marvellous sub-proposition are here given, because the remaining four are either mere repetitions of, or conclusions drawn from, those paragraphs, where, " in *lieu* of proof" that the material universe is finite, we are helped to very amusing *assurance* and *assumption*. We are assured the material universe cannot be the substratum of infinity of extension, before a shadow of *proof* appears that infinity of extension *has* a substratum, *or even an existence*. A substratum I take to be something which *stands under* some other thing. Will Mr. Gillespie condescend to tell us how the infinite attribute he calls infinite extension can *stand under* that everything or universe, without which there could neither be existence nor attribute. To tell me the material universe cannot be the substratum of infinity of extension is waste of breath, for the simple reason that *I deny the possibility of a universe having a substratum*, and incline to the opinion that Mr. Gillespie can no more prove his assertion, that *all* is propped up by an infinite something, not anything, but the attribute of everything, than could the famous Spallanzani *his* assertion, that the spermatic particle of a toad, designed to fecundate a tadpole, has the 2,994,687,500th part of a grain.

The *admitted* motion of parts, is *relative* not *absolute* motion. Absolutely speaking, there are no " parts of the material universe." In the sense of partial consideration only," can that which has neither beginning, nor middle, nor end, have parts. To say everything moves is equivalent to saying *the whole moves out of itself!!* It may be all very well for Mr. Gillespie to make merry with my assertion, that " the parts of the material universe are *not* (except in the sense given) moveable among themselves;" but heavy wit is lightness itself when weighed against undeniable fact. To *his* assertion, that " we know of matter only as divisible and moveable," I have no objection to make, *if* he mean *relative* moveableness and *relative* divisibility. What I maintain is, that " save in the sense of partial consideration only," matter, under which term I include *all*, is neither moveable nor divisible. While, then, admitting the *fact* of motion, I assert a plenum, in which *absolute* motion or *absolute* division is impossible. True it is, that the idea of a *plenum* involves much that is *inexplicable*, but as true it is that the idea of a *vacuum* is *inconceivable*. He who affects to have it, does in the very act " set aside the evidence of his senses—denying what every individual sense testifies," namely, that *nothing is the only thing with respect to which everything can be truly denied, and nothing can be truly affirmed.*

At paragraph 17, Part 2 of the Reply, a good deal of *indignant* astonishment is expressed with respect to my denial that the parts of matter are either moveable or divisible. Its author's first impression was that I " surely must be jesting;" but his first impression seems to have been succeeded with lightning-like celerity by a second, that " a jest would have been too strikingly ill-timed," and then follows the ill-feigned burst of scornful surprise in the " after all, who could have expected to find a dogmatic atheist sitting in the seat of the sceptic, &c. &c."

Now, sir, a plain tale will put an extinguisher upon all this fanfarronade. It is only necessary for me to make quite clear the meaning I attach to the words divisibility and motion, in order to show that the particles of *everything*, though not "*immoveable among themselves,*" are certainly " *indivisible from each other.*"

I presume it will be granted that the universe cannot move, because if Philalethean or any other "feelosophers" refuse to admit there is no absolute motion in the universe, in other words, that the universe cannot move out of itself, I will call upon them to tell us, if the *whole* moves, *where it moves to.*

It is clear, that where there is no absolute motion there cannot, by possibility, be an absolute division of parts. Bodies undoubtedly change situations relatively to us and each other. Their can be no doubt of their moveableness, but so far from *admitting* their divisibility or separation, I cannot so much as *conceive* it. The notion of matter's divisibility involves *nihilism;* for how, unless there be *gaps of nothing between parts of that universe which in reality has ¦no parts, can matter be divisible ?*

In answer then to the question, " Are the parts of the material universe divisible from each other ?—I say no; for *the whole* is not incapable of division. And in answer to the question, " Are the parts of the material world moveable among themselves ?—I say yes, to be sure they are; I do not, however pretend to *explain* their moveableness; *motion* is not to be *explained ;*† but the *fact* that matter moves, it were idle to doubt, and madness to deny.

---

* A dogma of Dr. Samuel Clarke's.

† There is nothing more mysterious than motion: he who unriddles that mystery, may call himself divine."—*The Rev. J. E. Smith.*

Mr. Gillespie fancies that if the parts of matter are moveable relatively TO each other, they must be divisible absolutely FROM each other, which evidences, that though he unquestionably is a wizard as regards superfine logic, he is no conjurer as regards shrewd sense. "We know of a certainty (quoth he) that some parts of the material universe are divisible from each other ;"—and how do you suppose, sir, he makes out that we *know* this "*unknowable*" truth ?—Why, by the clever process of assuming that if any given parts of the universe are moveable among themselves, they must be divisible from each other !! *If we know anything of a certainty, it is that no part of what includes ALL can be absolutely and actually separated from any other part.* It follows that Mr. Gillespie " draws the long bow" when he declares* the material universe cannot be the substratum of infinity of extension, *because* the parts of the material universe *are divisible from* each other, even if the proposition that infinity of extension has a substratum, were *true* instead of *false.*

An aphorism of the late matter of fact, Sir Richard Phillips is so pertinent to this part of my argument, that I will quote it.

" As animal senses (says he) and perceptions take cognizance only of matter or body, so the varieties of matter, as presented to the senses, in all relations, are the sole instruments of sensible phenomena, and the sole subjects of philosophical investigation."

Mr. Gillespie is challenged to point out a defect in this aphorism, *which however must be proved defective* before it is possible to establish the existence of infinity of extension ; for if our animal (query—can there be any other ?) senses and perceptions take cognizance only of matter or body, and if the varieties of matter, as presented to the senses, in all relations are the *sole* instruments of sensible phenomena, and the *sole* subjects of philosophical investigation, infinity of extension is *figuratively* an immaterial existence, and *literally* no existence at all. Now, no existence amounts to nothing, and, Philaletheans excepted, all the world will allow, that nothing is a queer, unsolid sort of *substratum*, on which to rest " *the* Argument *a priori* for the Being and Attributes of God."

Without doubt it may be, for it has been objected to the aphorism in question, that properly speaking it is not matter, but the *qualities* of matter that are the subjects of philosophical investigation ; to which I say—agreed; but can there be *qualities* without matter or body ?—that is the ques-

---

* See sub-Proposition—"The material universe is finite in extension,"—page 14 of the " Argument *a priori.*"

tion our "cute" genuises who write by the yard to convince us there is bodiless or immaterial being, in whom converges, and from whom diverges, all existence, though itself an existence which exists independently of all existence,—are called upon intelligibly and satisfactorily to answer. Mr. Gillespie may say, " 'tis entirely owing to his own stupidity" that Mr. Southwell can't make top or tail of an existence so shadowy as one of this unsubstantial class; but the fact is so, and, to a certainty, my conviction is that "a face of brass" is needful for him who, if only [allowed infinity of extension to begin with, undertakes "to make out, by necessary consequence," an immense somebody equal to an immense nobody; *to* whom he *denies* materiality, and *for* whom he *claims* simple existence, sole existence, necessary existence, infinity of extension, infinity of expansion, infinity of duration, all knowingness, all powerfulness, complete happiness, and—oh! shade of Minerva!—perfect goodness. Behold, ye "feelosophers," the God whose existence, yea, necessary existence, is demonstrated by *the* Argument to the exclusion of as it were of all other *a priori* methods, and after taking a good look at him, declare if you can that he is NOT the most comical of deities, or that believers therein are NOT

———— phrenzied by disease or woe,
To that worst pitch of all which wears the reasoning show.

That Mr. Gillespie himself believes in this strange god of his own fabrication, I cannot presume to say; but I can venture to assert on the strength of intimate and thorough acquaintance with all he has written in demonstration of his divine idol, that no metaphysician of our age has so profoundly studied, or so ably illustrated orator Henley's famous work on "The Philosophy, History, and Great Use of *Nonsense*." But I must not go on praising him at this rate or mayhap he will think aloud in the elegant *idiom* of Mrs. Slipslop—"Southwell is '*ironing*' me," which I certainly am neither doing nor desirous to be doing.

And now a few serious words about *style*. To find fault with my style is much easier than to detect flaws in my reasoning. Mr. Southwell is not logical—Mr. Southwell indulges in coarse ribaldry—Mr. Southwell is wanting in precision and elegance—are sentences any blockhead who chooses to set up critic can scribble. Indeed that is just what blockheads of all kinds do scribble. Friends and foes of the wooden-pated tribe, have from the day I published the *Oracle of Reason*, made a dead set at my *style*; but I laugh at, and really have cause to be much obliged to them, as the "intelligent public" cannot fail to see, that a *style* so provoking to such a race of critics must have considerable virtue in it.

Mr. Gillespie has not been ashamed to join this "common cry of curs." The Reply states (par. 34, Part 2,) as "one thing to be especially regretted," that "the *style* in (query—ought not the *in* to be *out*) which my antagonist has seen fit to employ will in all likelihood have the effect of repelling the approach of many excellent persons who would otherwise have dipped seriously into this controversy—May a sense of duty overcome repugnance to coarse ribaldry." In other paragraphs of the same "Part," Mr. Gillespie expresses most amiable ignorance of my reason " for introducing into such a discussion so much low vulgarity ;" and by way (I suppose), of apology for his own, declares "it would be injudicious to close this criticism on Mr. Southwell's Strictures without remarking a certain peculiarity in the *style* in which they are written."

The self-complacent and perfectly cool impudence of these " remarks" will be duly appreciated by readers of the Reply—*especially* if they keep in view that their author assured me *sub rosa* that he "strictly avoided in all his controversies, personalities or the use of words too personal," and thoroughly disliked "all ungentlemanly performances!" Though it may seem incredible that any one reputed sane should write a "Reply" in which vulgarest personal vituperation is freely used, and at the same time *privately* assure the individual vituperated, he (the vituperator) strictly avoided personalities, or the use of words too personal; I pledge myself, if called upon, to "demonstrate" its truth.

There is an old maxim and just as old, that men should come into court with clean hands —in other terms that they should take care not to be themselves guilty of the delinquences they charge upon others. Mr. Gillespie sets at naught this maxim in the Reply, which literally teems with the "low vulgarity" and " scurrile mirth" it so harshly deprecates. Can anything be more inconsistent than to indulge in abuse while deprecating it, or to make a parade of morbid sensitiveness about personalities, while in the very act of *trying* to outrage personal feelings—such epithets, for example as "*doughty champion*," "*impudent untruth teller*," &c., ill become the mouth of one who shrinks with horror from personalities—nor are such phrases as "*blurted out*" "*dipped seriously into*," "*hard on the back of*," "*the spokesman for*," "*should fall foul of*," "*discharge their excrement upon*;" at all creditable to a person who like Gillespie feels such a Miss Carolina Wilelmina Skeggs kind of admiration for "fine writings and fine peoples." It might have been expected that phrases so "*gross*" would have been left to "vulgar Atheists." But no, my "doughty" antagonist's Reply cannot fail to beget a suspicion that he aimed at a complete monopoly of them. There, however, he greatly erred, and upon the strength of my candid friendship, I will pause a while, just to read him a short but useful lesson.

A pugnacious young man ('tis said) asked a noted pugilist which was the best attitude of defence? Oh, as to that, replied the fistic Solon, the best attitude of defence is *to keep a civil tongue in your head.*

Mr. Gillespie should take to heart the *moral* of this lesson. He may rely upon it that in a contest of this nature, it is by far the safest to be moderately civil. Verily, verily, they who tenant houses of glass should not be forward to throw stones. Of all controversialists, believers in such a god as William Gillespie's, can least afford to be witty, sarcastic, or abusive. These admonitory sentences are dictated by the purest spirit of atheistic benevolence. If "too severe," my antagonist has the consolation to know the fault is "all his own." I am "cruel" to be sure, but then 'tis "only to be kind," and have no inclination to prepare for him a fate so dismal as that of Lelande the antiquarian. Besides, if *very* hard upon him, he might like Jerry Sneak when unceremoniously ejected from the drawing room, pluck up courage to say "I would have you know, sir, I will not allow myself to be *too much* kicked. It may nevertheless be quite prudent and proper to add that "if Mr. Southwell's instruments of offence put Mr. Gillespie irresistably in mind of the attack made on Gulliver by the Yahoos;* I can vouch for it that Mr. Gillespie's instruments of offence, put Mr. Southwell irresistibly in mind of a foreign animal well known to sailors, and by them called *Stinkard*, on account of its habit when hotly pursued of voiding in the face of its pursuer, an excrementitious substance whose stench is intolerable.

Though not quite done, sir, with the Choryphœus of the Edinburgh Philalethians, I must draw to a close. His " shameless literary falsehoods," obvious self-contradictions; pedantic allusions to immaterial verbal errors, and "forcible feeble" attempt to interpret my words in the sense they were not intended to convey, have been pointed out, and I trust satisfactorily exposed. Nor has his "style" been neglected, from a conviction that in dealing with unscrupulous opponents there is nothing more just than giving "measure for measure."

* See page 32, Part 2 of Reply.

But then the grand Mistake has yet to be transformed into a grand Truth. The Reply furnishes amusing evidence of its author's astonishment that I should have the "effrontery" to assert my ability and intention to atheize his Argument, *not* as he would have it believed by the substitution of *matter* for *extension*, but by the substitution of "about a score of *proper* words for an equal number of *improper* ones." He prophesies at par. 29 of Reply, that the "convenient season" for doing this, "will come with Felix and Drusella, for doing something else." I can, nevertheless, assure him that however wishful to prove true prophet in this instance, he will certainly prove a false one. Of course, after the peppering already given, I am not anxious to be at all severe, but palpable it is, he should not have committed himself to any such prophecy. By the boldly imprudent denial that his "*entire* work might *easily* be converted into one of the very best atheistical books extant;" he has in point of fact abused the privilege of being foolish, just as another distinguished individual is said to have abused the privilege of being ugly. Life and health permitting, *he shall see* that his " Argument" *can* be atheised, and that too by the "cheap process" of word substitution just mentioned. He may again, if so disposed, call this assertion "impudent"—but time and I against any two. We are quite equal to the task of showing that as regards my promise to atheise "*the* Argument *a priori*," assertive impudence is all on the side of Mr. Gillespie, who is strongly recommended to possess his soul in patience for a while. He may rely upon it, the grand Mistake may and shall be "metamorphosed not only into good Atheism, but into the best—only think of that!" If space and leisure were at my disposal, I should at once set about the work —as, however, they are not, a little delay ought to be excused. But lest certain suspicious characters, north of Tweed, should think this a mere *put off*, I hereby promise that if you, sir, are agreeable, an atheised version of the Philalethean Choryphœus's "*entire*" work shall appear in Nos. 42, 43, and 44 of your paper.

CHARLES SOUTHWELL.

P. S.—As thoughout this Battle, a victory for TRUTH was the object sought, no advantage has been taken of the verbal blunders (and consequent absurdities) which abound in the Reply. While duly castigating its author, I made large allowance for such slips of the pen, as proverbially involve no fault of the mind. Perhaps this kind of indulgence has been carried to excess, but the weakness is amiable, and will surely be excused, nay admired by all who love to see justice highly seasoned with mercy. Notwithstanding, however, this profusion of good-nature on my part, I venture to predict—in the first place, that my Philalethean "challengers" will be very ill-pleased with our "Battle," and this I do on the strength of an old conviction, that 'tis hard to please people who won't be pleased ;— in the second place, that Mr. Gillespie will be no better pleased than his " backers," and again cudgel his poor brains in the vain hope of battering therefrom another proof of his own wisdom and my stupidity which proof will only prove that " your dull ass will not mend his pace by beating ;"—in the third and last place, that his discreet friends (if any such he have) will not be at all anxious to renew " THE BATTLE OF THE CHORYPHÆI.

THE SECOND ANNUAL MEETING
OF THE
ANTI-PERSECUTION UNION.
(BRIEF REPORT.)

THE Second Annual Meeting of the Anti-Persecution Union was held in the Coffee-room of the Hall of Science, City-road, on Tuesday evening, August 27, G. KNAPP, Esq. in the chair.

The Chairman said he considered it a bold step to establish an Anti-Superstition Union, the power of fanaticism was yet so great in Europe and throughout the world. The friends of philosophy had a hard task before them in battling for a free course for the dissemination of their views, and in the Anti-Persecution Union they found an able auxiliary. There was a consolation in the fact that the propagation of religion was not so rapid as was represented. When a rich man was drawn over to religion, it was said that his whole household was converted—of course they went by right of patronage, or by virtue of serfdom. Philosophy and reason gave liberty and independence, and would progress surely. He rejoiced in assisting the Union to remove obstacles out of the way. He should call on the Secretary to read the Annual Report.

Mr. HOLYOAKE then read the Report printed in last week's number.

Mr. HETHERINGTON moved that the Report be adopted. He had been gratified with it. Contrast (said he) the state of things now with the state when the Union was started. Persecution had signally failed. The flame of liberty could not be put out in Scotland. Persecution was dead at present. But he would remind them of the boy in the " Children of the Wood." " Is the man dead ? (asked the boy). Yes (answered the person questioned), I've killed him. Then go and kill him again (rejoined the boy) for such a wretch cannot be too dead." So he would say of persecution—go on killing it, for the wretch could not be too dead. He gloried in the struggle of Mr. Watts, mentioned in the Report. His triumph was truly valuable. Why should there be such an outcry against the heterodox opinion respecting future states. If there was error, expose it. Nobody profited by error except those who lived by error ;—

The foolish seek a world of bliss,
The wise seek happiness in this.

It was true, priests said the labourer is worthy of his hire. But then they only meant themselves, for they were the only labourers who got it. He approved free discussion, and wished that priests would indulge them with a little more of it. Infidels would all be clever fellows if they could have better opportunities of exercising themselves. After some satirical remarks in Mr. H.'s usual humour, he recommended the adoption of the Report.

Mr. J. B. LEAR seconded the adoption of the Report. He thought the Report should be adopted, because it was a correct statement of bona fide transactions. That these transactions were strictly legitimate, tending to further the objects of the Union, and indeed just such as, under the circumstances, ought to have been done. That the suggestions of the retiring committee were very desirable, and strictly within the scope of the Union's operations. He thought that if, in eighteen centuries Christianity had, by mere declamation as to its kindness and forbearance, attained its present height, but a few years would be required for Atheists, by their acts, to place the Anti-Persecution Union in a much more commanding position.

The Report was adopted unanimously.

Mr. HOLYOAKE moved—"That this meeting pledge itself to renewed exertions in furtherance of the objects of the Anti-Persecution Union." He said, that as he spoke on these occasions officially, he should speak but briefly. It was easy to pledge themselves to renewed exertions, because it was now comparatively easy to make them. Besides, they had greater means: the Gazette of the Union had been enlarged, and would probably be soon permanently enlarged again. They had given their words when they commenced that they would extirpate legal persecution, and he was sure he was addressing men who would never forego that noble pledge. The public understood such to be their pretension, and that pretension they would fully support. The *Border Watch* was one instance of many that proved that the Union's principles were advancing. Persecution has been made to recoil on the head of religion.

He was instructed to say that Mr. Paterson's condition had been much improved. He was glad to state this, and more glad that Mr. Paterson desired it stated; for it proved that while they complained of severities, so long as they lasted they were prompt to acknowledge the justice which relaxed them. The Union would prepare to welcome Mr. Paterson to liberty, and he (Mr. H.) trusted that the " Testimonial" would amount to £50. They would renew their exertions till the right to publish opinion was conceded. Burke had said, that a right on sufferance was a right condemned. They would never rest until the right was acknowledged. He approved Mr. Paterson's sentiment, that they could never trust their liberty into the hands of priests. While the church retained the power of prohibiting opinion, they possessed a dangerous monopoly. The Anti-Persecution Union sought to promote a healthy equality in this respect. Their objects pointed to the pole star of democracy — humanity's brightest hope.

Mr. M. Q. RYALL said that some few Christians would profess to allow to all persons the right of free expression. There were white crows, but very few; and so there were of these liberal Christians. But even of the few who allowed, how few supported, the right! He knew many journalists, men who ranked high in public estimation as liberals— they would concede this right, but how miserably did they support it in their papers—at most damning it with faint praise. These facts should teach them self-reliance, and to pledge themselves to renewed exertions. It was wished to stamp the *Movement*, but £400 security was required that nothing libellous should be inserted; but while the blasphemy laws existed, they could be charged with a libel every week. He rejoiced at the founding of the Paterson Testimonial; if they did not see that those who were victimised were placed in a higher position than before, they would be unworthy of the liberty earned for them. He seconded the resolution.

Mr. J. C. SAVAGE, jun., thought the good done by the Anti-Persecution Union demanded a cordial pledge of renewance. He trusted that the Paterson Testimonial would not only be £50 but £100. There were minor cases of persecution continually occurring which demanded attention. Gross injustice was experienced by persons who attempted to preach Atheism. A person was invited by the inhabitants of Thorall-square, Bethnal-green, to speak his sentiments—but no sooner did he attempt than the police were instructed to remove him, on the ground of his irreligion. Yet at the same time (only a Sunday ago) the Christian Instruction Society pitched their tent in the square, and included the public pump, so that the inhabitants could not obtain water, yet these persons were protected by the police. After reciting a case recorded in the *Watchman*, he concluded by supporting the resolution.

Mr. SAVAGE, senior, said—that the reason why we had not more persecution was owing to the *Movement* and Union. He agreed with the picture of fanaticism drawn by their Chairman. He, too, was of opinion that a right tolerated was a right condemned. He was not disposed to interfere with the quarrel of Christian with Christian, as had been recommended to the Union;—

Let dogs delight to bark and bite,
For God had made them so.

There was too much reverence paid to persons in authority, and referred to a case of Mr. Broughton and the recent decision of Alderman Hunter against his son, and spoke with warmth against the clergy. He advised determination in all dealings with them;—

Soft and easy touch a nettle,
And it stings you for your pains,
Grasp it like a man of mettle,
And it soft as silk remains.

The resolution was then put and carried unanimously.

Mr. HOLYOAKE then moved that Messrs. Powell, Ridley, Lear, Brittain, Ivory, Palmer, Cooper, White, Merriman, Ross, and Allen be Committee for the ensuing year, with power to add to their number. The motion was seconded and agreed to unanimously, Mr. Hetherington and other gentlemen bearing testimony to the efficiency of the services of the retiring committee.

Mr. HOLYOAKE moved that the thanks of the meeting were presented to their excellent friend Mr. Bendall for the gratuitous use of his hall. He had declined any remuneration even for gas or the attendance of his servants, and in that manner which placed beyond doubt his disinterestedness. The resolution was cordially agreed to.

Mr. J. THORNE rose and charged the Chairman with having called the Union an Anti-Superstition Union. Complained that the priests had not been fairly treated, and asserted that the *Movement* contained language insulting to its readers. The discussion between Mr. Gillespie and Mr. Southwell was disgraced on both sides by low scurrility.

The Chairman explained.

Mr. HOLYOAKE said it was not far from the truth to call the Union an Anti-Superstition Society. The Chairman had not inaptly designated it. If it was not for superstition there would need no Union. It was very well for people who had never fallen into the hands of the clergy to be wonderfully tender of them. Such persons knew little of c'ergy nature. Mr. H. defended Mr. Savages's warmth. He had witnessed the treatment he received a few days ago at Guidhall, when he was forcibly kept out of court, and his witnesses on his son's behalf. And his son was marched out to gaol before his eyes. It was maddening. Respecting the *Movement* its pages were open to Mr. Thorne's strictures, and if he would appear there, he would meet with satisfaction.

Mr. MERRIMAN remarked that whatever of the objectionable there might be in the discussion referred to, it was plain that Mr. Gillespie had set the example.

Mr. HETHERINGTON addressed some waggish observations to Mr. Thorne, and begged he would consider their case, and not come down on them with such terrible broadsides!

Mr. ALLEN moved that Messrs. Ellis and Skelton be auditors of the Union's accounts. Carried unanimously.

Mr. HETHERINGTON said he had had the honour of working with Mr. Knapp for many years, and knew his worth. He rejoiced that a man of his station and abilities was found sanctioning their excellent cause by his presence. He should move the thanks of that meeting to that gentleman for his services in the chair, which was unanimously agreed to, and afterwards the chairman suitably acknowledged the compliment, the meeting separated.

CORRESPONDENCE.

LETTER FROM MR. PATERSON.

General Prison, Perth,

DEAR HOLYOAKE,

Solitude and silence are very far from being vexatious now, whatever they may have been, let this, therefore, be borne in mind—your own convenience for the future, in correspondence, will be the most agreeable to me.

To Ryall I am deeply indebted for his last two letters, with advice as to voting, registry, &c. My rental, however, does not come within the statute, could I dispose of my vote in this place to any advantage—I am too much of a patriot to give it for nothing. Perhaps it may be gratifying to Ryall to know, that in three months more I shall be able to claim a parish here, so should I be fortunate enough to lose a leg or arm in the " good fight," 9d. a week will be secured to me, free from all incumbrances—so you will observe my case is not so hopeless as some may have been led to think.

You will not credit the pleasure your remark, that there " were likely to be no more prosecutions," gave me; proud, positively proud, shall I be if my trifling exertions have assisted in bringing that desirable end about, as you well know my sphere is not noise and turmoil, but *seclusion*, which, henceforth, I will the more complacently enjoy in the reflection that it will be more extended. But I beg of you not to relax in your exertions till that boon, freedom of expression, is declared by edict—for I never can put my trust in priests, nor my liberty in their keeping. My experience here has been nothing favourable either to their candour or veracity, and as men know and feel so must they speak.

I shall be gratified to know if any steps can be taken, and what they are, for the recovery of my seized property, *before* my liberation, so that it might be ready for my disposal without loss of time; a little reflectiod will convince you of the necessity of this step, whether or not there is likely to be further prosecutions.

I forgot to mention, you ought to send to Chambers' a biographical account of Pemberton and his Literature—I hope you have.

You, who are toiling amidst the strife of life, will no doubt be too much occupied with its cares and troubles to survey the scenes of other times; but I, who have had so few happy hours, look back with delight upon many of our wanderings on the Don and Severn, with our conversations, aspirations, and mutual friendships. All these events are things that *were*, and I enjoy them even more *now* than then, as only the sweets are remembered, and the bitters forgot. Best regards to Mrs. H., whose presence flits so often in my day-dreams of the past.

THOMAS PATERSON.

Letters received:—
    Mrs. Adams, Cheltenham;
    William Harral, Leicester;
    G. J. Holyoake, 3.

MR. CAMPBELL AND THE CONCORDISTS.
(*To the Editors of the Movement.*)

FRIENDS to the freedom of expressing human thoughts and ideas on all subjects.

In the 37th number of the periodical under your management, I have read and laughed at your *eccentric* reply to " G. A." relative to my withdrawal as a member of the Concordium. I cannot think that your reply was meant to be a serious one, but rather given either with the intention of ridiculing the whole proceedings at the Concordium, or inducing me to put the readers of the *Movement* in possession of the true state of the case.

Presuming the latter to be your wish, I shall, with your permission, first give a statement of the terms on which I was admitted the first member of the Concordium by Mr. Oldham, its founder, and should the statement satisfy your "wonder," I shall in a subsequent communication state my reasons for withdrawing from the Concordium, and trust that these reasons will be satisfactory to all who may feel interested.

After some correspondence and a personal interview with Mr. Oldham, it was mutually arranged that I should join him with my family, which I did on the 4th of November, 1842. From that time till the first of January, 1843, the residents then at Alcott House, who intended to become members of the first Concordium, were principally occupied in garden operations, repairing the premises, for future proceedings.

On the 23rd of December, 1842, I addressed the following letter to Mr. Oldham. On the 1st of January it was read to the residents, and accepted by Mr. Oldham as the expressed principles on which the society should be formed; in testimony thereof he gave me a card certifying on it that I had been admitted No. 1, member of the First Concordium, and signed his name to his testimonial:—

"Mr. W. Oldham.

"My dear Sir,—In applying to become a member of the first Concordium, it is requisite that every person should clearly express the principles inducing them to become associated.

"That no misunderstanding may exist on this important subject, I now proceed to state my present feelings and convictions in order that those with whom I may be associated may fully understand why I desire their co-operation, and that this document may afterwards be referred to relative to my conduct, as a member of the society.

In the first place I have been made to feel and understand that I am an agent or instrument of *that power* which animates all sentient beings, and manifests its laws in all things. I am also deeply impressed with the idea that there is a divine end to be accomplished with man by this power which I call LOVE, and that the instinctive inspirations of a higher and better state of humanity, for the furtherance of which the Concordium is commenced is an indication of the reality.

"Under this divine feeling and conviction, I am quite prepared to submit myself entirely to LOVE, relinquish all private property in persons or things, and place all my disposable effects along with that of others to form a common stock to be used for the maintainance of all the members of the society, and universal extension of similar principles and institutions.

"I am also prepared to labour with my heart, head, and hands, for the same end, and to assist, as far as practicable, all the human family without regard to their creed, country, or colour, and in so doing abide by such regulations as the expressed WILL of the society, by their executive council may from time to time determine to adopt.

"In the event of wishing to retire from the society, or being requested to withdraw from the Concordium, by the proper constituted authority, I shall do so without any other claim whatever except for such property as may be registered as my portion in the books of the society.

"For the performance of these duties, all I wish for in return is a sympathetic response from my associates, and an equal share of the requisites and conveniences of life, to be furnished by the united capital, skill, and labour of all the members, and a full right to express my thoughts and feelings on all subjects.

"With a full and sincere reliance on LOVE to make me submissive to its laws, by which alone the nature that gives happiness can be realized in the being of—A. CAMPBELL.

"Alcott House, Dec. 23rd, 1842."

[We deny that our "reply" to G. A. was "eccentric," it was perfectly *circular*. We would not think of saying anything "eccentric." We did not "ridicule," but stated the reasons of Mr. C's. withdrawal word for word as they fell from the lips of a great authority at Ham—Mr. Galpin. Has such a man of plain sober sense as Mr. Campbell been at Ham all this time without knowing that to appear to ridicule them it is only necessary to repeat their own words. The *Times* used to satirise Hunt by printing his speeches verbatim, and the present Concordists may be satirised pretty much in the same way. We shall be glad to hear Mr. Campbell's "reasons for withdrawing," and can promise him on the part of ourselves and readers a ready and pleasant hearing..

EDS. of M.]

LETTER FROM MR. GILLESPIE.
Forbanehill, near Bathgate, N. B.
27th August, 1844.

SIR,—You have neglected to send me a copy of No. 37, in which you engaged to insert Mr. Southwell's "Rejoinder" to my "Reply."

Not having yet seen Mr. Southwell's "Rejoinder," I may mention, that I do not think I shall see it to be my duty to write any formal full article in reference thereto; I having, as I conceive, evinced, in the completest way, Mr. Southwell's incompetency for the task taken in hand by him, when he engaged to answer and refute the "Argument, *a priori.*" To follow one who writes to unwrite what he has written (and I cannot conceive, I own, what Mr. Southwell, in his "Rejoinder," can do else than write to write down himself) is an employment which I shall endeavour to avoid, as being altogether superfluous, if not unbecoming.

As a measure of *precaution* I pen this, which would not come from me with so much force had I had an opportunity of perusing Mr. Southwell's new piece, or of knowing the nature of its contents.

I shall make up my mind on becoming acquainted with Mr. Southwell's performance. It is possible, that the course pursued may be different from that which I have anticipated.

I am, sir, &c.
WILLIAM GILLESPIE.

ANTI-PERSECUTION PUBLICATIONS.

I HAVE written to Edinburgh for Southwell's Tract reviewed by M. Q. R. The Scotch Trials are selling slowly, I wish the price had been lower *at first;* the sooner it is done the better. The subscription for Paterson would be benefitted by so doing, and I know no single publication so well calculated to make Atheists as those trials, particularly *Paterson's* trial. If they had been sold separately, more would have been distributed through the country; it is well, however, you got leave to send so many copies gratis to particular individuals, be assured it is no loss to the Anti-Persecution Union, when they assist in putting tracts into the hands of the community. They may suffer in a pecuniary point of view, but one convert made to the cause will recompense them more than any loss they think they sustain. It was by the distribution of tracts *in bales* that brought about the French Revolution. This fact should stimulate the Union to act upon the same principle, and urge them to follow an example which will produce similar effects. It is astonishing to think what effect may be produced on the mind when it is in a frame to receive an impression without being prejudiced in a particular manner; truth is, in such a case, sure to prevail over error and superstition, and the individual becomes a new creature, never more to be made the tool of priestcraft and kingcraft. With this consideration, I never despair of doing good by distributing tracts and publications of an atheistical nature, and I think I am performing a duty by urging others to go and do likewise. W. B. B.

Dumfries.
DEAR SIR,—You will, doubtless, by this time suppose me gone to the Father, or, having taken up the cross, burnt the collecting card with which you entrusted me—so late, I am ashamed to confess as April last—the more so as this is accompanied by no remittance. Indeed, until I set about it, I had no idea of the uphill work in this part those have to undertake who solicit for the commission of his satanic majesty, as I was charged with doing lately. The fact is, that those who have the means dare hardly own their unbelief, and the consequence is, that I have received but five shillings for the Anti-Persecution Union. This I should send, but I delay doing so in the hope that—as the fact of my being ready to receive subscriptions to the Union gets known to the parties to whom I have alluded—and they are not few—a sum may be placed in my hands worth sending.

We have had some good Nos. of the *Movement* of late. By the way, we do not receive it in Dumfries until a week after the day of publication; although *Cleaves' Gazette* and other cheap London publications arrive two days old only.

On Tuesday month, I went with two young fellows on a boating excursion. The craft upset, fortunately in a shallow part of the river. On feeling her go over, I sprang out—my companions sat still, and she capsized on the top of them. When we had scrambled to the bank, I pulled out a copy of your journal to dry it, and my friends jocularly attributed the ducking to the lord in the first instance, and to the fact of the *Movement* having been on board—one of them at the same time taking a New Testament out of *his* pocket. I said—"but you forget that while you went completely over head and ears, I was only immersed to the neck; and if my partial escape is not to be attributed to the *movement* I made in the boat, I have a right to infer that it should be to the one in my pocket."

We expect Bronterre O'Brien here on Friday and Saturday. He is at present on a political tour through Scotland.

I had almost forgot to thank you for the honour conferred by the card of membership sent. I assure you I value it highly.
PETER GRAY.

[There is no valid reason why the *Movement* should not reach Dumfries with the other papers. It is published in London on Wednesday night. Through what London publisher is the *Movement* obtained? Answer, and we will call upon him.—ED. of M.]

Burnley,
DEAR SIR,—You will find enclosed, for the benefit of the *Movement*, the sum of ten shillings, which trifle I give for a peace offering to *truth*, to enable you to continue

the *Movement* at the present enlarged size and price, two-pence. I have not the least doubt but if that could be done you would be able to sell a greater quantity.
H. UTTLEY.

[Friend Uttley takes the most likely means in the world to keep the *Movement* enlarged, as he wishes it. If a few more persons should wish after the same manner we shall enlarge it to sixteen pages, without increasing the price.—ED. of M.]

WEITLING.—All our friends will be delighted to hear that Weitling is safe out of the clutches of his continental persecutors, and *now among us*. Steps must be taken to give him a cordial welcome.

LECTURES.

[*Any omission of announcement observed in the following list is owing to the neglect of the Secetary of the Institution not writing to us.*]

SEPTEMBER 8.—Social Institution, Goswell-road.—W. D. Saull, Esq., on " British Antiquities." After which a discussion on the question—" Is the evidence of Facts to be preferred to Written Testimony ?"

SEPTEMBER 8.—Hall of Science, City-road.—Mr. Southwell's first of a series of lectures on " Popular Fallacies."

SEPTEMBER 8. — Turnagain-lane, Snow-hill.—Mr. Cheer, on the " Effects of War."

SEPTEMBER 8, at 8 o'clock, in the Assembly Rooms, Circus-street, New Road, Marylebone—Mr. A. Campbell, late of the Concordium, on the " Uselessness of the Charter as a means for removing the evils of society." Free Discussion invited.

SEPTEMBER 11. — Manchester Hall of Science.—Mr. R. Cooper on the " External Evidence of the Bible."

DISCUSSIONS.

SEPTEMBER 7.—Social Institution, Whitechapel.—Question : " The comparative merits of Socialism and Christianity."

SEPTEMBER 7.—Coffee-rooms, 66, Bunhill-row.— Question : " Would the general belief in Atheism tend to moralize or demoralize Society ?"

SEPTEMBER 8.— Political and Scientific Institution, Turnagain-lane, Snow-hill, at 11 a.m.— Question: " The Policy of the Repealers."

SEPTEMBER 9.—Coffee Rooms, 80, Red-Cross-street, Barbican. — Adjourned from Thursday.

SEPTEMBER 10.—Social Institution Whitechapel.—"On the Existence of God," between the Rev. G. Hill and Mr. C. Southwell.

SEPTEMBER 11—Bunhill-row—Adjourned discussion on the " Corn Laws."

The Society for the Investigation of Truth, 49, Henry-street East, Portland-town, has changed its time of meeting from Monday to Tuesday. Chair taken at eight o'clock.—Subject of enquiry—" The Existence of God."

THE members of Branch 53, late of the Rotunda, have succeeded in getting possesion of a small but commodious room for an institution. We need scarcely add, that at such time heads and hands are wanted, Socialists do not require to be told *how* they may assist. Besides donations and services, personal attendance alone will be valuable.

TO CORRESPONDENTS.

RECEIVED.—*Edinburgh Weekly Register, Brighton Herald, Northern Star* (2 Nos.) J. M'Neil.

WE regret that Miss Roalfe's communication on the Progress of Infidelity in Scotland, is obliged to be delayed until next week.

OBSERVER.—Of course the word in par. 1, page 268, was wrong ; it should be *ingenuous*.

J. L.—We have seen an article from the *Movement* in *La Reforme*, a French paper. Other journals have been mentioned, but they have not fallen in our way. We will thank J. L. for any information respecting them.

J. B.—Mr. Firmin's school is flourishing under the title of the Surrey Edueational Institute, No. 131, Blackfriars-road, opposite the Surrey Theatre. On the close of the Rotunda Mr. Firmin took the above eligible premises, which, with much expense and care, he has fitted up for his schools. He promises to have a flourishing establishment. A day boarders' department has been added to the day schools, and evening classes for youths and adults has been opened.

SUBSCRIPTIONS TO THE ANTI-PERSECUTION UNION.

J. Cook, Ipswick . . .	£0	1	0
Friends at Northampton, per J. G.	0	5	0
J. R., Paisely, per Mr. Motherwell	0	2	6
At the Hall of Science, City-road :—			
Mr. Pemberton . .	0	2	6
Per Members' Tickets, &c.	0	7	0
Members' Tickets, Whitechapel	0	2	6

PATERSON TESTIMONIAL.

D. P. 0 2 6

G. J. H., *Sec.*

Printed and Published by G. J. HOLYOAKE, 40, Holywell-street, Strand, Saturday, September 7, 1844.

THE MOVEMENT
And Anti=Persecution Gazette.

"Maximize morals, minimize religion."—BENTHAM.

No. 40.   EDITED BY G. JACOB HOLYOAKE, ASSISTED BY M. Q. RYALL.   PRICE 2d

DR. KALLEY TO G. J. HOLYOAKE.

LETTER IV.

Funchal, Madeira, 12th June, 1844.

DEAR SIR,—1. On the 24th ult. I received your favour of the 26th April, along with your little volume, for which I thank you.

2. Allow me to remind you of the difference between proving a negative and proving an affirmative. A few credible witnesses suffice to give rational certainty respecting an affirmative, but much investigation is necessary before we can have rational certainty respecting a negative. Were six credible witnesses, for instance, to swear that they saw an arch of rock in the ocean, between the 30° and 40° of lat. N., and 10° and 20° of long. W., their evidence could give rational certainty of its existence; but there could be no rational certainty of its non-existence unless that portion of the ocean were all surveyed, and no such arch discovered.

3. Atheism is negative; it declares that there is no god. In order, however, to have rational certainty of this negative, the atheist would require to have searched the universe, to know all things, (as stated in par. 13 of my 2nd to you), and be himself the omniscient whose existence he denies. I cannot imagine how anything short of this could give rational certainty in atheism. Pardon, then, my proposing the question whether it be reasonable to maintain (as in par. 4 of my 2nd to me) that " atheism is true," and that it " is most precious truth, worth suffering for even unto death."

4. Infidelity is also negative. The negative is embodied in the term. It declares that christianity is not true. In order to establish his negative, the Infidel would require to shew that the whole field of evidence was fully surveyed, otherwise (as stated in par. 10 of my 3rd to you) he must confess that there may exist somewhere proofs of which he has not heard, which, therefore, he has not examined, and which if known would convince even him.

5. In par. 9 of your last, you seek to invert this argument. You suppose me not to have evidence that atheism is true, yet you say proofs of it may exist somewhere, of which I have not heard, which, therefore, I have not examined, and consequently that I cannot have rational certainty in christianity. The argument, however, cannot bear inversion on account of the difference between proving a negative and proving an affirmative. After hearing the testimony of a few credible witnesses in favour of the existence of the arch referred to, I have rational certainty regarding it, without waiting for the survey of all the rest of that part of the ocean, but as already said, the survey of the whole is necessary to prove the negative.

6. In the said par. 9, you ask whether the evidence which the Infidel has in favour of his infidelity may not outweigh the evidence which he has not in favour of christianity?

7. To simplify this question, let us return to that respecting the existence of the arch in the ocean. Suppose 200 ships to pass through the portion of ocean named, and that all the crews come to the Admiralty and swear that they saw no such object. This would be evidence (like the Infidel's) in favour of *not* believing. Suppose that 200 more, or 200,000 more should do the same, would that set aside the evidence of six credible witnesses? By no means; for within such an extent of surface each successively might have passed without seeing the arch, *though it existed*. In point of fact, the non-existence of certain rocks within the space named is still uncertain, although thousands of crews have passed through that space without seeing them. Rational certainty of this non-existence can only be obtained by actual particular survey, and in the same way the Infidel can have rational certainty of his negative only after the actual particular survey of the whole ground on which proof of christianity *can* exist. How could the Infidel's evidence in proof of his negative be known to outweigh the unknown amount of affirmative proof which might be found in what he has not examined? If not *known* to outweigh it, how could he have certainty?

8. Christianity is affirmative. It rests on facts; it adduces its witnesses. In its standards it claimed investigation 1800 years ago, and it does so still. If like atheism and in-

fidelity it had no standards, the conduct of its professors might be a fair criterion as to whether or not it seeks investigation; but having acknowledged standards, it is to be judged of by them, and not by the conduct of any one of its professors. I repeat that it seeks from us no irrational credence, that the Christian after the most careful and scrupulous examination can say, I do not only suppose, I know that my religion is true, and that neither the Atheist nor the Infidel can have rational certainty in his opinions.

9. While, however, I decidedly hold and openly avow these opinions, I am quite ready to comply with the proposal in par. 7 of your last, and to consider the question of deism or atheism as a question of probability or improbability. I must, however, premise, that on either side there subsists " a problem without solution," " a knot still tied," " a labyrinth untrod," a mystery which neither deism, atheism nor christianity professes to solve. Its existence, therefore, affords no probability in favour of atheism any more than of either of the other sytems. The mystery to which I refer is the existence of something which had no beginning. Had there ever been absolutely utter nothing, no power, no life, no wisdom, nor matter, there must have continued to be absolutely utter nothing *for ever*. Your existence, mine, that of any being, proves that something must have existed without a beginning. If atheism could solve that mystery, which no other system has solved, I grant you that it would have something wherewith to "press natural theology."—But atheism solves it not. Indeed, as far as I can understand atheism, it solves nothing. Its language is—" Ingenuity has not been able to show more than that nothing can be known." "Theology exceeds human comprehension." " It is wise to set down in quiet ignorance." " The incomprehensible is god's name;" therefore, I will not seek to know any thing about him. While atheism thus DISSUADES IN VESTIGATION and *recommends ignorance*, it can hardly be expected that it should solve any thing. Were it proved that "every thing supposed to be known" of astronomy or any other science, was only " unsatisfactory," not false, would that be a reason for throwing it aside in contented ignorance? Should it not rather excite the philosopher to deeper search?

10. The question between us is not whether there be or be not something which never had a beginning — but *what* exists without having ever begun to be. You use the term self-existent, I will use it also, and the meaning which I attach to it is that, the being to whom, or what (for I do not wish to beg the question) it is applicable, possesses existence underived, independent, inherent in itself. Let us bear in mind that it is not *self-created*—which would be absurd —but self-existent.

11. Granting then that something is self-existent, is it more probable that the self-existent is a god or not god? You tell me you think that the probability is in favour of atheism, and that you fall back on nature. I ask, then, what is nature? In your third letter to me, par. 12, you seem to say that it is the life, animation, and materiality which you see around you; and in your last, par. 5, you say that from nature we learn wisdom, order, and government, that it has powers coeval with eternity, and that conquer both time and destruction—that it has given to foliage its magnificence, to flowers their tints, to earth its capabilities, fills land and sea with joyous life, has peopled space with glittering worlds, and sustains man in his proud dominion over all.

12. Allow me to remark, that if nature be the life and animation which you see around, and fills land and sea with joyous life, it would seem to be not self-existent merely, but self-created.

13. Again, if nature be matter, and the glittering worlds you mention matter also, and nature peopled space with them, surely this seems to imply self-creation.

14. Is nature not merly life, and animation, nor merely matter, but a combination of life, animation, and materiality? Then are there as many kinds of nature as there are kinds of matter? or is there only one nature pervading all matter? If the former, then we must have a countless crowd of self-existents. Self-existence is, however, " the knot still tied, the problem unsolved." Does reason or probability recommend our choosing to receive that which has so many knots and unsolved problems, or that which has but one?

15. If there be as many self-existent natures as there are kinds of matter, how can you account for the arrangement and harmonious adaptation of such a multitude of self-existents? What has become of the self-existence of those genera which are made known to us only by their ossific remains? Farther, the existence of each individual of a race, being dependent, what degree of probability is there in favour of that of the whole being independent? I may add, if each genus be in its own nature self-existent, how can it be said that nature *has given* to foliage its magnificence, to flowers their tints, and to earth its capabilities? Is the self-existence of each communicated?

16. If it be said that there is only one self-existent nature which does all the glorious things that you enumerate, then the

question between us resolves itself into an inquiry respecting the qualities of the self-existent. Respecting one quality of it we agreed, namely—that it exists, independent of any thing else, and never had a beginning. Have we, however, any adequate conception of this mysterious property? The mind may look back on the years of which it has had experience, and taking these for a kind of measure, may attain some idea of 100, 1,000, or 10,000 years; but what are 10,000 times 10,000 years to that which had no beginning? We struggle hard to grasp the idea of unbegun existence; but however strenuous our efforts, we struggle in vain. Beyond the utmost stretch of our faculties extends the duration of *that which had no beginning*, and inscribed upon it we read the mysterious, confounding words "coeval with eternity." Impatient at being foiled, the mind would fain deny that there is any such existence; but it is checked by the reflection, that had there ever been absolutely utter nothing, there must have continued to be absolutely utter nothing forever, and it is compelled to acknowledge a self-existent.

17. Is there *a priori* any probability of, or against, the presence of any other quality in the self-existent? I will suppose you to say that *a priori* we know nothing at all about it, and, without disputing this for the present, only reply—"Let there be no prejudice either for or against the existence of any other attribute in it." You will perhaps allow, that if there be any other quality in the self-existent, it probably corresponds and harmonises with that incomprehensibly sublime attribute already acknowledged; and that, in the event of any other quality being discovered in it, there is more likelihood of its proving noble and stupendous than mean and little. If, however, you be unwilling to concede even this, still you must grant that immensity in any quality will not *alone* be a sufficient reason for denying its existence in the self-existent. If it were, then the unmeasurable duration of self-existence would be a sufficient reason for denying it also.

18. What is the extent of the self-existent? If it peopled space with glittering worlds, and by these glittering worlds be meant only the planets of this system and their satellites, even then that which peopled space with them would require to be many hundred millions of miles in diameter. But if the fixed stars be included among the glittering worlds, then where are the limits of the self-existent? We can see far into the abyss of space, but the most powerful telescope does not discover to us the boundary beyond which there lies no glittering world. If those things with which the self-existent peopled space exist in every direction, at distances altogether immeasurable to man, then what is the vastness of that which peopled space with them? The extent of the self-existent, like its duration, is a quality which we confess that we cannot comprehend fully—but we know something about it—it is overwhelmingly great.

19. Speaking of the self-existent you refer to "powers coeval with eternity," and that conquer time and destruction. If these powers, then, are coeval with the self-existent, are they co-extensive also? If coeval and co-extensive with the self-existent, are they inherent in nothing? Are such powers self-existent? Then how many knots have we to untie? Is it more probable that each power is self-existent, or that the powers you mention are inherent qualities of that with which they are coeval and co-extensive? Like the qualities already referred to, such power is incomprehensible to our finite minds, but we see its operations and must confess its being.

20. If, however, there be powers of which we cannot conceive the limits either in respect of their duration or extent, upon what principles of reason are we warranted to conclude that they must be incapable of creating? How shall we establish that negative? Nay, on the supposition that there is only one self-existent nature, how can the variety of beings be explained except by acknowledging a creation? The immensity of such power (or of any other quality, as already mentioned) is not *alone* a sufficient reason for denying its presence in the self-existent.

21. Let me further ask if "we learn wisdom, order, and government" from a teacher that has none? Could the self-existent be self-regulative without knowledge or discretion? If man have wisdom and nature, none then the tiny man is a nobler being than that which "fills land and sea with joyous life—peoples space with glittering worlds, and sustains man in his proud dominion over all." If, however, you grant that nature has wisdom as well as power, then what probabilities are there against the opinion that all the wonderful mechanism and strange adaptations in our frames were designed? You think that the poor family, whose every want was supplied by an unseen benefactor, might very naturally suppose that the benefits were undesigned. Were there as many suits provided as there are leaves on a tree, and had they to choose from such a number each a suit for himself, then they might be less inexcusable in supposing that they were not intended for them. But there being only one suit for each individual, and that an exact fit, not selected by him, but actually put upon his body, and of texture

varying according to the situation; thick and tough on the soles of the feet, horny on the points of the fingers, elastic over the joints, and transparent over the eyes—surely the balance of probabilities is in favour of its being designed for him, more especially as the suit is given to him before he feels his want of it, lasts as long as he needs it, and goes to pieces as soon as he has done with it.

22. If, however, design be not proved by such adaptation of our clothing to the skin, let us look within it. Suppose that there be subjected to your inspection a machine in which you can easily discover the skilful employment of the lever, the wedge, and the pulley in a manner which appears so perfect that man cannot suggest any improvement on it, and that you are asked to say whether the probability is in favour of or against the idea that it had an intelligent designer— what would you reply? Still further suppose that within the dimensions of a human body you should find an extensive hydraulic apparatus—(the tubes of which, if all put together so as to form a straight line, would be miles in length)—perfect locomotive machinery— a telescope— a microscope—an acoustic instrument—a mill—a large pneumonic apparatus—an extensive chemical apparatus, &c., &c., &c., all most intimately and yet harmoniously combined on scientific principles in one system—and that you are asked whether the probabilities are in favour of, or against the opinion that they had an intelligent designer—what would you reply? If such a machine were at rest, the proof would be strong in favour of a designer; but we see it in motion, and find life, intelligence, and reason added, being as it were a workman boxed up in the machine to look after the supply of fuel and attend to part of the machinery which is under his controul. Shall this set aside all the other proofs of design? Does it not rather rivet them for ever?

23. If the self-existent be not wise, instead of one problem unsolved there remain millions unsolved and insolvable. If it be wise, then its wisdom as displayed in the universe is like its duration, extent, and power too vast for the human mind to form any adequate idea of its greatness; but if such duration, extent, power, and wisdom be united in one being, is it a God or not a God?

24. This letter has already grown so long that I must not now enter on the consideration of any other quality of the self-existent, but desire to reply to an appeal which you make to me in the end of your lettter. You ask me whether morality be not irrespective of the existence of a God. Even if by the term morality you mean only our duty to our fellow-men, excluding from the term our duty to any other being—yet it is not altogether irrespective of God, inasmuch as men have not known the proper standard of their duties to their fellow-men, except as revealed by [God. The proof of what morality is without God must be taken in those regions where Christianity is unknown, and not from systems formed by the Deists of England, who draw largely from the Christianity they despise. I may add, that he who denies the existence of a God and his relations to him wants the highest motives to morality that exist—namely, gratitude towards such a generous benefactor, and the desire of gaining the approbation of that glorious being whose unmeasurable superiority makes the approbation incomparably more desirable than that of all creatures.

25. If, however, you take morality as including *all* the duties of life, then it is not irrespective of God. Were a man to maintain that morality referred only to his conduct towards his dog, and was irrespective of his parents, how ignoble would his ideas of morality be? But to exclude from the code of our duties that towards our parents, and to recognise only what we owe to the inferior creation is rectitude compared with the denial of our duties to God. The highest morality respects the eternal. Gratitude, love, and adoration are rational towards him, and they ennoble man.

Sympathising with you in your illness, and sincerely desiring for you every good,
Believe me, very truly yours,
ROBERT R. KALLEY.

CHRISTIAN PORTRAITURE OF CHRISTIANS.
"FRUITS" OF THE SYSTEM.

WITH the rare consistency which distinguishes the motley patchwork called Bible, and the heterogeneous throng called Christians—the commonest thing in the whole *binding* is the rich vein of vituperation running through it — and the commonest thing among christians is their recurrence to the denunciatory passages. A smart rebuke is nuts to your genuine biblist. A good round of abuse is a perfect relish. The constant use of all this sort of high-seasoned stuff by antagonist sectarian, testifies both of the plentifulness of the commodity, and of the aptness of the disputants in employing it.

There is another species of offensive texts furnishing admirably effective missives to christians militant. With the doctrinal texts, they may thrust and parry till absolutely weary with harmless fencing. Not so with that class of texts which points to the workings of the system. Some of these give very hard hits. If the petty victories of sectarianism did not weigh more with these belligerents that the propping up of christianity as a system, they would abstain from hurling such texts at one another as would damage the whole christian citadel. For *forms of faith* they might fight on for ever— but the lord Jesus should be imprecated to preserve them from allusion to the *works of faith*— the "fruits" of doctrine. These fruits, indeed, are regular biblical bombshells. When all other ammunition has failed, these come in to do real execution. Thus, after all sorts of stir, and dust, and babblement of doctrinal disputations, without breach effected, or damage done — after grand tilting and jousting of Armenians against Calvinists, Baptists against Ana-Baptists, Libertarians against Necessarians, Sublapsarians against Supralapsarians, Trinitarians against Unitarians, *cum multis aliis*—after all the harmlessness of dogmatical engagement—see what desperate damage and slaughterous destruction ensues from directing the attack against actual conduct. In vain have old church and new church, or Papist or Protestant, Presbyterian and Seceder, assailed each other in credal contests—the fatal conflict was reserved for the occasion when they came to speak of practice instead of theory, results instead of anticipations, fruits instead of seeds of christianity—" Ye shall know them by their fruits." And when they thus came to close quarters to judge of the tree by its fruits, and to expose the tender mercies of christian for christian—what an utter levelling—what a fell-swoop and devastating destruction of christian anticipations, promises, avowals, pretensions, and pretences! To hear them tell of christian vociferations over christian discomfiture, of christian exultation over christian persecution, of christian yellings over christian endungeonings and gibbetings —oh! surely " by their fruits ye shall know them !"

To come to still more actual, practical, present and every-day exemplifications of the fruits of christianity as graphically displayed by christians—what an accurate and well-pencilled portraiture is here of their leading factions. — " Persons who make a principle, or at least a practice, of never entering those walls at any other time, feel no scruple, and find no inconvenience, in coming when a church-rate is to be opposed, or some 'religious luxury' to be lopped off. On these occasions they will sometimes express themselves without much delicacy or reserve, and *show* as *little respect for the feelings* of church-people, as they do for the sanctity of the place. They will use language *unnecessarily irritating*, and introduce topics which have *no other reference to the question* than that they are likely to *give pain* and *promote disagreement*, besides what may be called the interjections of debate, viz.— cheering, hissing, hooting, cat-calling, stamping, ' oh, oh '-ing, ' turn him out,' ' question,' and the rest—all admirable in their place, which, however, the church does not seem quite to be. These gentlemen, also, not unfrequently manifest their conscientious objections to the doctrine of sacred places by other more visible forms of protest. They keep on their hats, climb the pulpit, mob'the reading-desk, squat about the communion-table, spit about upon the chancel carpet, wipe their boots upon the pew-cushions, and dim the lustre of the newly painted panels." Here's "respect to the sentiments and feelings of others"—and those others, co-religionists, and co-christians. Here's regard to the sanctified and holy ground—or ground at any rate so considered by fellow-christians, specially devoted to the worship of the blessed lamb. Here's desecration of that awful sanctuary, where the word of the lord is read, his body is eaten, and his blood drunk! But this paints only the dissenting, non-conforming, congregational, or mob-gregational christians. Now for the orthodox, protestant, church-as-by-law-established christians — the portraits are taken by a member of the latter con-fraternity.—" To this it is painful to add, that even the best church-goers do not universally keep their temper on these occasions. Notwithstanding what might be expected from the superior tone of their religion, (—now for its fruits—) they cannot always resist opportunities of recrimination. In fact, we have heard it intimated that, owing to the greater zeal, or to some misapprehension, as to the reputed force of truth, *they are quite as violent as their opponents*, excepting, of course certain demonstrations of irreverence, which it would suit their purpose as little as their feelings to indulge in." The fact is—and they cannot apply the *argumentum ad hominem* without revealing it—there are the very elements of discord unalterably fixed in the compound thing christianity—churches, say some, produce this disreverence, distraction, and mutual crimination—but the churches have produced christianity according to their showing—christianity has produced churches and a very congenial Caliban progeny she has given birth to.

But what, say they, shall be done with these christian "strivings and fightings?"— how shall we prevent our respective congregations being a "scandal to religion," and a scoff and a bye word to the infidel!?

"Upset the church—down with it—utterly abolish it," say one of the contending factions.—Expel the mal-contents. "Introduce some compendious machinery of fines from five shillings to five pounds." Bring in a bill into the house "to prohibit the holding of vestries in churches"—say two divisions of the other faction.

How faithfully they can depict one another and sometimes, as above, sit to themselves for their own portraits—"when it would suit their purpose." How admirably the "fruits of the system" are exhibited in christian practice by christian demonstration. How abundantly efficacious the system itself is, "under Providence" to bring about the "communion of saints," when they must brawl and fight over the "communion-table." How all-sufficient when on the one hand, nothing but destruction is raised to the church-system of the opponents—on the other nothing but resort to ex-ecclesiastical expulsion or the strong arm of the law.

M. Q. R.

PROGRESS OF INFIDELITY IN SCOTLAND.
I.

Sir,—I shall feel obliged by your inserting in the *Movement* the following paragraph from the *Border Watch*, a Free Church paper, as it will no doubt be gratifying to your readers to learn that our labour has not been in vain.

It is worthy of remark, that at the time Mr. Paterson was arrested, the editor of the same paper congratulated the authorities for having stopped his career, and incarcerated the "awful blasphemer." But since we have convinced our opponents that all their attempts to stop the progress of free enquiry are futile, this very christian editor has changed his tone, and illustrates the "alarming progress" of what he is pleased to term the "Socialist delusion," as a proof of the "deplorable effects in all cases of whatever savours of persecution."

Surely such a circumstance should stimulate to exertion all who are engaged in the glorious cause of mental freedom. It is only by a steady perseverance, and a determined opposition to the Goliah of superstition, that we can hope to gain the victory. The weapons of our warfare may be likened to the *sling* and *stone* of the shepherd youth; yet I trust ere long we shall not only disarm, but finally overthrow that giant which has in all ages been the curse and oppressor of the nations.

M. Roalfe.

TO THE EDITOR OF THE BORDER WATCH.
Galashiels, August 11, 1844.

Mr. Editor,—I beg to call your attention to the fearful spread of Atheism and Infidelity in this locality, which, to every one at all interested in the eternal welfare of the rising generation, must appear truly alarming; and I do think that some *rational* means ought to be adopted,—not persecution, which is too often resorted to by ignorant, but well-meaning Christians,—but something addressed to the understanding and the judgment, which may tend to arrest the progress of this dread calamity. The enclosed "Address," which has just been issued by the "Galashiels Infidel Association," sufficiently indicates that there is no lack of moral courage amongst its members, in thus bringing themselves so prominently before the public, and every true Christian cannot but regret that that courage, so useful in itself, has not been applied by them to a purpose not only more useful to themselves, but more beneficial to the world.

It is confidently asserted by some that this "Association" numbers upwards of 350 individuals; now, Mr. Editor, only think of such an immense number in a place like this, looking upon the Bible as being "an old wife's fable;" and some are of opinion that even the very idea of a God is a pernicious delusion. All this in a country village, with a population of 3000 inhabitants!!—and a church almost at every door!!! They are also making great exertions to draw others into their ranks. The walls of the town are almost continually placarded with advertisements of books for sale, such as the following:—"Christianity proved Idolatry;" "A few reasons for renouncing Christianity;" "The Bible an improper book for Youth;" "The existence of God disproved by believers in God;" and "Paley refuted in his own words."

Such, Mr. Editor, is the state of things here at present, and unless ministers of the Gospel, and private Christians as well, use every legitimate means in their power to combat and overcome what every one at all impressed with the truths of our holy religion must look upon as dangerous and fatal errors, they cannot but expect (judging from the past) that, ere long, the great majority of our once pious and industrious population will, like Tacitus of old, look upon Christianity as a "pernicious superstition." Let them, then, be up and doing;—let them never cease their labours till truth shall cover the earth as the waters cover the channel of the mighty deep.

Mr. Editor, by inserting the above in your paper you will oblige, yours truly,

A Constant Reader.

[Although scarcely disposed to go the length of thinking, with our Correspondent, that ere long the majority of our population will become avowedly infidel, it is not that we think such an event impossible,—for we remember France,—or that we despise the present audacious efforts of the Spirit of Evil to overthrow all that we hold sacred,—for the signs of the times are in many respects similar to those that preceded the French Revolution,—but we cannot forego the hope that the Almighty, who has so many thousands of faithful worshippers in this land, will enable them, through his grace, skilfully and successfully to ward off the threatened calamity. We pity the poor individuals who are insulting God and man with their mad ebullitions, which we would not pollute our columns by quoting; but they are not the only guilty parties. Our unfaithful clergy, "dumb dogs that bark not," "saying, Peace, peace, when there is no peace,"—our wanton, unprincipled, frivolous, fox-hunting, game-preserving gentry, —our purse-proud votaries of Mammon, wringing the life-blood out of their pitiful slaves, without regard either to their souls or bodies,—these are the real culprits. Who that judges of Christianity only by the lives of the majority of its professors can be anything but an infidel? Let him who would understand the mystery of the present times study the inspired prophetic writings and the discourses of our Saviour. He will see there what made the Jewish nation infidel, and precipitated the Divine vengeance upon Jerusalem. Let the Christian learn also, from the alarming progress of the Socialist delusion, the deplorable effects, in all cases, of *whatever savours of persecution.* Let us have *no more odious imprisonments—no confiscations of goods—no legal interdicts*—grounded on the alleged insult offered by these men to the Church or to Christianity. If they break the civil law, let them make due satisfaction! if they outrage common decency, let them be restrained by the proper officers, but let not the high and holy cause of Jesus be mixed up, in the mind even of the most ignorant, with the idea of intolerance or persecution. It was not so much because she was a corrupt, as because she was a persecuting church, that Rome fell. "Great is truth, and it will prevail!" " The weapons of our warfare are not carnal, but spiritual."—ED. B. W.]

CHRISTIAN EVIDENCE.

(*Copy of Hand-bill circulated by Mr. Savage.*)

IT is a common practice with christians to appeal to the *evidences* of their religion when any objection is made, and to challenge an array of evidence of a similar nature for *other* religions. The following report of a police case, at Guildhall, will afford some information as to the peculiar kind of evidence upon which the christian superstition founds its claims on the intellect and respect of the human race:—

On Sunday, the 28th of July, 1844, I happened to be in Smithfield, and perceiving several persons expressing *their* sentiments of religion, I was ignorant enough to suppose that I had a right to express *mine,* but was soon told that I had not; for Mr. West, of No. 17, Red Lion street, Clerkenwell, who was preaching to support christianity, fearing it might be seriously injured by the efforts of a humble individual like myself, and being conscious that it was unable to stand against the breath of scepticism and inquiry, sent over to the police station for some one to remove me from the place; and the call was promptly responded to by the inspector, Joseph Martin, (one of the livery servants of Christ,) who came up and *insolently* ordered me to go away, which I respectfully declined doing; at the same time promising to desist when the other preachers did; whereupon the *lacquey* of Jesus rejoined,—"Then I'll make the others go away, and will also take care that *you* shall *not* go." Accordingly I was removed to the *store room of christianity* — the station house.

At the examination at Guildhall the next day, Mr. West, instead of appearing in his *true character*, as the prosecutor, shrunk back from the infamy of the affair, in the guise of a *witness*, and by some arrangement of Mr. Martin's or Mr. West's, the whole of the witnesses for the prosecution were admitted into court at once, Mr. West claiming admission as the *intimate acquaintance* of Alderman Hunter, the presiding magistrate. He immediately obtained admission, and the charge, which stood the 9th in succession on the police sheet, was called on before the 7th, for the convenience of Mr. West, while the whole of my witnesses and friends (between twenty and thirty in number) were forcibly prevented from entering the court, and the door-keeper of the Guildhall Inquisition Court threatened to lock my father up for demanding admission; and Mr. Alderman Hunter, without allowing one of my witnesses to be called, decided that I should pay a fine of 10s. or be imprisoned seven days. Upon this decision being made known to my friends, who were waiting outside, my father wrote to the magistrate, demanding admission, which was then given, and some of my witnesses were examined, *after I was safely lodged in Giltspur-street Compter.*

Mr. Alderman Hunter disclaims the honor of Mr. West's acquaintance, and, therefore, I am bound to suppose that the christian preacher has spoken falsely, or that falsehood has disgraced the Aldermanic character. This, however, is certain—if Mr.

West be the *intimate friend* of the Alderman, roguery has usurped the seat of justice. If he be not, then the Alderman has allowed the balance to be taken from his hand, and the magisterial authority has been guided and directed in its decision by the policeman and the Methodist parson; and the Alderman, by convicting first, and examining the witnesses afterwards, has fully exemplified the character of the UNJUST JUDGE, ascribed to the christian god in Mr. Luke's parable. One of the witnesses thought it very improper of me to say that christianity had spead solely through the protection of the law; and so, to prove that it needed not the protection of CIVIL power, I was removed to be punished *according* to law, for impugning the religion of EVIDENCE. Yet this is only one more link in the long chain of such evidence, the only substantial evidence upon which christianity is founded. The superstition of Christ has ever been a persecuting superstition, from the time of its establishment by the holy cut-throat Constantine, through all ages to the present time. Let the deeds of the Inquisition, the Massacre of St. Bartholomew—the murders, the torturings, and the hatred that have *sprung from christianity*, tell their tale; let the names of Paine, Carlile, Taylor, Southwell, Holyoake, Paterson, and others be remembered; all, all attest, that PERSECUTION IS THE ONLY EVIDENCE OF CHRISTIANITY.

CHARLES JOHN SAVAGE.
27, Mape Street.

The fine was subsequently paid by some of my friends, to my great surprise and regret.

MRS. MARTIN'S TOUR.
(*From a Correspondent.*)

CONSIDERING that the *Movement* should be made more the recorder of the doings of infidels all over the country than it has been, I will trouble you with a remark or two relative to Mrs. Martin's doings in these parts. Being at Nottingham when Mrs. Martin was there, I was cognizant of the proceedings relative to her sermon on "Capital Punishments" noticed in a recent number of your journal. The room was taken and paid for—no questions being asked as to the class of persons intended to be admitted, but on placing a board, on which was a placard stating the admission to be *one-penny*, at the door, the shareholders, in the person of a priest, who is one of them, declared the sermon should not be delivered, as such a price would admit all the "scum of the town," "the sweepings of the streets"—such was the classic language with which one of *god's own* chosed to honour those whom kingly tyranny and priestly delusion had made poor. Well might Mr. Owen say "the mere theological made mind is not only the most useless and irrational, but it is also the most injurious upon earth." At the time of meeting the people collected in hundreds, and loud murmurs of disappointment were heard in all directions, until some one in the crowd proposed that Mrs. Martin be requested to write an address on the subject. The subscription was immediately made. She agreed. The address was written and issued immediately, calling upon the people to attend in the Market-place, on Sunday, at three o'clock, at which time Mrs. Martin made her appearance in an open carriage, and delivered her sermon to an audience of at least five times the number that could have obtained admission to the room that had been taken for the purpose. I hardly need say the sermon was of the right sort, and went to the very root of the evil, whence has originated the crimes that have rendered capital punishments apparently necessary. Kingcraft and priestcraft, and the Bible as the text book of both, were denounced as the great obstacles to the improvement of the people. Christianity was shewn to be the best apology for crime, while it was the most decided opponent of every thing that could elevate, enlighten, and improve mankind. These sentiments were received with the most evident satisfaction—a proof that the people are prepared to hear the whole truth on such subjects. Anti-Theological sentiments are not so frightful to the great mass of the people, as some of our *half* "theologically made minds" (which half Mr. Owen tells us is so much insanity,) would have us believe. Finding her sentiments so favourably received, Mrs. Martin announced her intention of delivering another address in the evening. The people assembled in the evening in numbers at least equal to—some say greater —than in the afternoon. The subject was "The Bible and Missionary Societies"— exposing their follies and crimes; a fruitful theme, which I assure you had justice done it, with perfect satisfaction to the audience, who were heard inquiring in all directions at the close, "when will she come again?"

Afterwards we had four lectures in Derby, at the Old Assembly Room, at which nothing unusual occurred. With the exception of an attempt, by a well-dressed drunken christian, to create a disturbance on the fourth night, the lectures have passed off well.

H. ROCHE.

PRESCRIPTION.—There is a time when men will not suffer bad things because their ancestors have suffered worse.—*Burke.*

THE CRITICISMS ON "PRACTICAL GRAMMAR."

SEVERAL readers interested in the question of grammar have desired my opinion on the criticisms of my friend M. Q. R. To these I *therefore* briefly advert. Mr. Ryall choosed to deprecate some parts of my book. To do this he had a right. The book is on trial before the jury of the public, and every man is free to give in his verdict. Burke has told us, that " when the trial is by friends, if the decision should happen to be favourable, the honour of the acquittal is lessened; if adverse, the condemnation is exceedingly embittered." But this is a small evil when one is sure of an honest opinion, as every man is from M. Q. R. When Mr. Ryall praises my work, some persons would suppose that I had influenced his opinion, and when he condemns it others would regard my inserting the adverse view as a species of mock modesty. But deeming his opinions useful, I was obliged to disregard what that fastidious old dame Mrs. Grundy may say.

M. Q. R.'s first paper, in *Movement* 33, abounds in valuable hints. But he seems rather to apologise for the "*lapsus linguæ* of progressionist" by calling the perseverance "relentless" with which they are pointed out. True, educated and respectable people may sneer unwarrantably at the blunders of ignorance—but it is a small evil, because it is one that every person, in these days, can remedy. We ought not to complain of that arrogance which exists through our supineness.

Mr. Ryall's second paper, in *Movement* 34, treats of grammar with that enviable aptness of phraseology for which Mr. R. is remarkable. If I have, as he says, "confounded grammar," either directly or indirectly, "with natural philosophy or physic," my language has failed to convey my perception of grammar's true province. To "over rate" any subject is the vice of enthusiasm against which I perpetually guard. But grammar, as I have endeavoured, in my treatise to expound it, is a *thinking* system. Every step throws the student back on himself. There are two classes of arts—arts of the hand and arts of the head. Grammar is an art of the head. M. Q. R. makes no distinction of this kind, but reasons as though wielding a pen involved but the same intellectual exercise as wielding a pike—as though talking correctly did no more to refine thought than walking correctly. The *study* of grammar is not "imitation," but a perpetual exercise of logical and metaphysical thought. It may not teach the parallax of the stars, or the age of stones—I have not supposed that it would—but grammar being the art whereby we express all knowledge, it more than any other art serves to familiarise us with *all* knowledge. On these grounds I estimate its influence more highly than M. Q. R.

Mr. Ryall happily depicts the true course to follow in the education of children, but expresses no little " horror of a school book." It is strange that ten of my critics have taken care to explain that " Practical Grammar" is not calculated for children. It never was intended for *children*, but for boys and girls, and young men and young women who can think. In a school it must be accompanied by the teacher. With this appendage it has been found useful and entertaining. Several schoolmasters have done me the honour to introduce it into their schools. " Practical Grammar" has been a school book, since the first day of its publication, in the Surrey Educational Institute. Years ago, to boys and girls able to reason, I taught its principles, and in a few weeks made them little grammarians.

In M. Q. R.'s third paper, *Movement* 37, he reiterates the charge of " over estimating" my subject. As a general rule, it will be found that persons who take the thoughtful care of their expressions which " Practical Grammar" recommends will not often be found uttering the " common places" which Shelley satirised. Exceptions there may and will be, but the *majority* of persons who have studied what Samuel Bailey designated the " niceties of arrangement," that " lucid and orderly dependance of ideas" which implies " consummate skill," and that force and elegance of style which the " practised eye of taste instantly appreciates," would never fall into the manufacture of puerile " common places." Upon this point M. Q. R. and I do not differ, but he has restricted grammar to Syntax, while under that name I have included Composition. Hence his apparent difference of opinion. To refer to the *nature of things* as the foundation of grammar, although styled by M. Q. R. *preposterous, confusion, extreme absurdity*, and *rubbish*, will amazingly help the pupil on the right road. Between words and the ideas which prompt them, there exists a closer connection than my friendly critic perceives, or allows. Snowdon the name, I grant, is distinct from Snowdon the mountain, for I could put the name in my pocket, but could hardly put the mountain there. Yet Snowdon the mountain was the origin of Snowdon the name. To refer the pupil to " the class of things" for which names stand, is as M. Q. R. confesses " at once to prepare him for understanding the function of many thousand of words." There is no mode known among men whereby we can correctly comprehend the true grammatical definitions of words, but by reference to the nature of things for which the words stand.

Of the critic in *Lloyd's Weekly London Newspaper* I only care to say that the strongest cases made out against me were made out by suppressing part of my words. In some particulars he is right. But the principal points adverse to me are effected by putting his objections in the shape of questions, which, though a common, is not a just way of criticising, because literary etiquette forbids me to answer. His queries look unanswerable only because I cannot be heard.   G. J. H.

CHEMICAL DESIGN.

It has often occurred to me as very singular, that the religious world should be so confident and dogmatic upon the existence of a god, and yet be at so much pains and exercise such a vast amount of ingenuity in showing the *reasonableness* of a belief in such existence. If there can be no doubt upon the subject, it is not only a waste of energy and time, but is also highly ridiculous to be continually endeavouring to show that scepticism is foolish. I have my doubts that religious folk are so thoroughly convinced of the rationality of their belief as they would wish to make appear.

In *Chambers's Journal* of Aug. 3, is a notice of a work by Mr. Fownes, Chemical Lecturer in Middlesex Hospital, on " Chemistry," as exemplifying the wisdom and benificence of God," a prize essay, springing from a private endowment, under the care of the Royal Institution. *Chambers* remarks, " We are now familiar with books tracing divine wisdom and benificence in physics, physiology, and the mental constitution of man. Mr. Babbage has called even the unpromising subject of mathematics into the same field. But this, as far as we are aware, is the first systematic attempt to draw inferences of design from the chemical constitution of the earth and its inhabitants. The book is a very able one, and *has a virtue*, which we know will be a great further recommendation, *it is short.*" This is but doubtful praise at the best—in fact, were I the author, I would not say " thankee" for it. The subject of the wisdom and benificence of God is generally considered by the religious world to be of the first importance, and when handled in a proper manner, could not have too much said upon it, I should think. *Chambers* evidently thinks otherwise, and is of opinion that the least said upon the matter the better, for they say Mr. Fownes' book has a virtue, viz., it is short. I shall not dispute the point with the Messrs. Chambers, who are much better able to form an opinion upon the question than I am, seeing that I have never had the good, or it may be ill luck, to read the various works that have been written in support of the goodness and beneficence of god in the creation.

If this essay of Mr. Fownes is the first attempt to prove god's goodness and wisdom from chemistry, I think society will not lose by its being the last. I do not think a more unfortunate illustration could have been chosen, for if chemistry under some of its phasis can be supposed to prove wisdom and goodness, there are a multitude of cases in which the same science can be proved to evidence malignity and folly. Contemporaneously with the article in *Chambers* appeared the discussion in the House of Lords upon the subject of the sanatory regulations of towns and cities, in which it was stated by the Marquis of Normanby that *fifty thousand* persons perished annually in England through bad drainage, a lack of water, air, and light. *Chambers* say, " The chemistry of the atmosphere presents a very striking example of what can *scarcely be considered in any other light than design.*" This is curious reasoning, — a " striking example" is said to admit of a doubt. If it can be questioned, I *may* be right in my scepticism and Mr. Fownes and the Messrs. Chambers may be wrong in their belief.—Who is to decide? No one can decide. Then why should either party dogmatize where there can be no proof? The atheist does not affirm that there is no design observable in the operations of natural causes, he only declares his inability to perceive it; there is no crime in this. The folly is on the side that positively declares *there is* design clearly apparent in the constitution of the earth and its inhabitants, without being prepared with *proof* to substantiate the assertion.

Mr. Fownes argues that the atmosphere of our earth is evidently designed, in its pure state, to support vegetable and animal life. For the sake of argument I will grant it. The Marquis of Normanby declares, upon the best of all possible grounds, the fact, that the atmosphere of many towns in England is so impure that fifty thousand persons die annually, whose lives may be saved were known healthy regulations to be established. If the purity of the atmosphere be evidence of wisdom and goodness, the unhealthiness of the same atmosphere must equally be evidence of folly and wickedness. If one proves a god, the other proves a demon, for both the healthy and the unhealthy are said to be subject to the same power.

The atheist does not assign the evils of life to demoniacal influence, but the religious man is compelled to admit that his god could remove all evils if he would. The atheist feels convinced that there is an adequate cause for effect, and that whatever is, is from necessity, and that if there be a god, he deserves neither praise nor blame for the good or evil which exists. The god of the religious world is either an imbecile or a tyrant—he cannot act if he would, or he can act but will not.

If the gentlemen who are so fond of displaying their talents in endeavouring to prove wisdom and beneficence in the beautiful phenomena of this earth, would employ their pens upon the many seeming anomalies and monstrosities so plentifully distributed over the face of our globe, there would be some sense in it, it would shew they were not afraid of the question, which at present to me it seems they are. When they have done this, we shall be better able to determine to what order their god belongs. W. C.

TO WELL-WISHERS TO THE MOVEMENT.

(*From a Committee of its Friends.*)

To "Maximize Morals and Minimize Religion" has become essentially the principle of the times. Every reform has professedly for its object the improvement of the moral code of nations, but in doing so it is found that sacred enclosures must be broken into, and vested rights in conscience exploded. The very necessity for reform shows a demoralizing cause, and the struggle for freedom must be opposed to some tangible *bone fide* oppression. This demoralizing cause we take to be religion; whose faith generates immorality, and whose books support injustice. The contest against religion is not a mere struggle in the legislature, nor a battle in the vestry, not an uproarious meeting, private wrangle or public chat, but a battle fought for a principle, and which in one point of view may be called *par excellence*, a "condition of England question."

The *Movement* is the only paper which goes at once to religion's influences as the root of all reform, and endeavours to engraft such advanced views on the best minds, to make it the corrective principle of all parties—the clue in the maze of opinions. And it is conceived that without attempting the amalgamation of all systems, or the uniformity of all creeds, the adoption of this principle will keep their measures open to investigation and amendment.

Atheistic, democratic, and communistic in sentiment; it has been highly instrumental as Gazette of the Anti-Persecution Union, in protecting freedom of expression, and supporting the victim of oppression.

Its influence on the most important social reform of the day has led to the purification of the society, and its restoration to healthy action, from a state of progressive extinction.

Its pages have ever been open to opposing sentiments, when supported by argument—the important controversies carried on in its columns, which in no other papers would be presented to the public—the general tenor of the *Movement's* articles require no other commendation than the influences they are known to have exercised.

Taking the past as the surest guarantee for the future, a few friends, seeing how much may be effected by a proper combination, have determined, if possible, to obtain for the *Movement* a wider circulation, and for its conductors increased means for effecting their objects—many of which are at present scarcely entered upon. Hence they appeal to the friends, in confident anticipation, that when they know so much has been effected with such limited means—no obstacle to greater good shall remain.

Possessed of funds, a first step will be to bring the paper more frequently before the public by sending it round to reading-rooms, club-rooms, and houses of public resort, by presenting it to the press for review, and hand-bills and other means of advertisement will be resorted to; the co-operation of friends in all parts of the kingdom, being solicited to aid in their distribution.

To friends—no opportunity will now be wanting to enable them to assist. The more affluent will know how their contributions are needed, and will be appropriated. Those whose leisure will permit, may effectually assist by taking charge of *Movements* for gratuitous distribution in their locality, to papers, reading-rooms, &c.

Persons anxious to co-operate are desired to send in their names and addresses, with a statement of what they are disposed to do, to the Secretary at the *Movement* office.

J. TONGE, *Sec. pro. tem.*

REPORT OF THE FAREWELL BREAKFAST TO MR. OWEN.—Mr. Merriman has published in a convenient form—the size of the *Movement*—a report of the interesting proceedings on the above occasion, and being in a separate form, it is a great convenience. Our friends in the country can now keep it at hand as an antidote to those libellous reports, which will probably be raised so soon as it is generally known that Mr. Owen has left England.

THE ELECTION OF ROBERT DALE OWEN.—The *Indiana Statesman*, remarking upon this event says:—" It is one of no ordinary value to the lover of republican liberty. It ranks far higher than a mere party triumph. The question whether it is necessary for a candidate to *profess* religion in order to secure the suffrages of his fellow citizens, has been set for ever at rest. The people have uttered a most decided negative to this, as well as on the question whether it is necessary to be a citizen by *birth* alone, to fill any office provided for by the Constitution. Both these issues were forced upon the democratic party by their opponents. Boldly have they been met, and nobly have we triumphed. In spite of every appeal to the passions and prejudices of men on these points, the principles of political and religious liberty have been warmly sustained by the voice of an intelligent and thinking people. The victory on these grounds alone is of inestimable value. It will be hailed throughout the Union as a death-blow to hypocrisy, religious as well as political, from which it can never hope to recover."

A PHYSICIAN.—Voltaire defines a physician to be an unfortunate gentleman who is every day required to perform a miracle—to reconcile health with intemperance.

In cloth, lettered, price 1s. 6d.,
PRACTICAL GRAMMAR,
OR
COMPOSITION DIVESTED OF DIFFICULTIES.
By G. Jacob Holyoake.

" WE have to mention with approbation, 'Practical Grammar, by G. J. Holyoake,' an odd performance and a strange medley, which has, we confess, entertained us more than it has informed us."—*Literary Gazette.*

LECTURES.

[*Any omission of announcement observed in the following list is owing to the neglect of the Secretary of the Institution not writing to us.*]

SEPTEMBER 15.—Hall of Science, City-road.—Mr. Southwell on " Popular Fallacies."

SEPTEMBER 15.—Whitechapel Social Institution.—Mr. Ellis.

SEPTEMBER 15.—Oldham Hall of Science. —Mrs. Martin, in the afternoon and evening.

SEPTEMBER 16, Do., Mrs. Martin.

SEPTEMBER 18. — Manchester Hall of Science.—Mr. R. Cooper on the " Genuineness of the Bible."

SEPTEMBER 19.—Do., Mrs. Martin will lecture.

DISCUSSIONS.

SEPTEMBER 10.—Social Institution, Whitechapel.

SEPTEMBER 17.—Do., between Mr. C. Southwell and the Rev. G. Hill,—Subject, " The Existence of God."

Votes House of Commons.—July 30, Petition from William Carr, for Abrogating all laws interfering with the freedom of opinion. To lie on the table!

EVERY Thursday evening at 8 o'clock, Mr. Holyoake's " Select Class" meets at the North London Schools, No. 8, George-street, New-road.

ERRATUM.—At page 320, par. 5 of our last No., for " *incapable*" read *capable.*

NOTICE.

LIBERTY, EQUALITY, AND FRATERNITY! —The grand fraternal Democratic Banquet, to which we alluded last week, to celebrate the Anniversary of the French Republic, and the declaration of Equality between citizens of all nations, will take place on Monday, September 23rd, at Highbury Barn Tavern, Islington. P. M. Mc. Douall, Esq., will preside. Tickets 2s. each. Dinner on table at 7 o'clock precisely. Several distinguished English, French, German, Spanish, Italian, Swiss, and Polish advocates of liberty, are pledged to attend. Tickets to be obtained, an early application for which is necessary, at the *Movement* office, and all the Social Institutions.

THOMAS M. WHEELER, *Sec.*

TO CORRESPONDENTS.

W. BROOM.—We will insert the notices of the Infidel Tract Society and the balance sheets if possible.

RECEIVED from " An Old Reader" a valuable letter on the state of liberty in Italy. The Border Watch. J. A. B.

THE Report of the " INVESTIGATORS" is unavoidably postponed until next week.

For Movement, W. B. B.	.	0	18	0
Do. do. T. Ironside	.	1	0	0

SUBSCRIPTIONS TO THE ANTI-PERSECUTION UNION.

A friend in Milan per Mr. Holyoake	0	10	0
8 working men in Whitehaven, per Mr. Wilson	.	.	0	4	0
Members' Tickets per Mr. Dixon, Stratford	.	.	.	0	8	0
Do., Whitechapel	.	.	0	1	0

PATERSON TESTIMONIAL.
Cosmopolite 1 0 0

G. J. H., *Sec.*

Printed and Published by G. J. HOLYOAKE, 40, Holywell-street, Strand, Saturday, September 14, 1844.

THE MOVEMENT

And Anti=Persecution Gazette.

"Maximize morals, minimize religion."—BENTHAM.

No. 41.   EDITED BY G. JACOB HOLYOAKE, ASSISTED BY M. Q. RYALL.   PRICE 2d

TO DR. KALLEY.
LETTER V.

DEAR DOCTOR,—If "six credible witnesses" swore to having seen an arch of rock in a certain part of the ocean, it might be necessary to survey that part, and have occular demonstration of the non-existence of the arch before we could have rational certainty in our denial of it — but when we had made the survey required, under the same circumstances as our witnesses made their observation, and failed in finding what they affirmed—might we not be very reasonably in doubt about the existence of the "arch of rock" in question? This arch of rock is deity, the universe is the ocean in which theistical witnesses affirm they have discovered it. But atheistical observers, living in the identical place, with the same interest in making the discovery, and the same opportunities of knowing the truth, are yet unable to see what theistical witnesses aver, and I suppose that these observers may credit *their* senses just as theistical "witnesses" credit theirs. Still you contend that until the atheist "has examined all space and found no proofs of the existence of a God," he can have no "rational certainty" in his denial of the object affirmed. But has he not the same certainty as the theist? His "field" of observation is the same, his means of observing the same, his powers the same, his interest in exercising them is the same, and his researches are as extensive. How then can you fairly, under circumstances of such close affinity, and under the operation of equal evidence, allow rational certainty on one side, and deny it to the other? What inherent virtue is there in an affirmation that rationality must belong to it independently of evidence? You will insist that there *may be* evidence which the atheist has not examined. But by what patent is the *may be* of the theist made of considerable importance, and the *may not be* of the atheist of none? This stage of the argument being one where no proof can be adduced, one conjecture is as good as another. The atheist may not have "searched through the universe," but he has searched as far as the theist, and all beyond their equal investigation is alike unknown to both, and I do not see why, when evidence can no farther go, the theist alone should be allowed to add the weight of his ignorance to the weight of his argument.

If atheism is necessarily devoid of "rational certainty" because it is a negative—no negative is rationally certain, and mankind who have quietly given up belief in witches, sylphs and fairies, need now to arouse themselves from their slumber, and at once scramble over bog, brake, marsh and moor,

On hill, in dale, forest and mead,
By paved fountain, and by rushy brook,

in search of these fantastic beings—for a "survey of the whole is necessary to prove the negative" of their existence. We question the evidence in favour of witches—we answer the arguments brought forward in proof of them, and, so far as we know, no weighty evidence is found—but the *Wise Wives of Keith* MAY *somewhere* exist. Every old woman should undergo the ancient ordeal. "We must confess that their may be proofs of which we have not heard, and consequently not examined, and which would convince even" the infidel to witchcraft. "Credible witnesses" without number have borne testimony to the actuality of witches. Good people of England! lulled in false security by your fire sides, bestir yourselves —at this moment the "weird sisters" may be at your doors—for, according to Dr. Kalley, there is no "rational certainty" of the non-existence of these wiry ladies!

At every step we are reminded how imperfect are human analogies when employed to illustrate this nonpareil question. The search through the ocean is définite, the longitude and latitude of the arch of rock can be given, but where shall we find the latitude and longitude of the locality of deity? If the arch of rock is still of "uncertain" existence, although "credible witnesses" have named the space where it is situated, how much greater "uncertainty" must pertain to the existence of deity, whose latitude no man has surmised, and whose retreat defies the powers of the telescope and the penetration of thought.

The non-existence of certain rocks within the space you name, may still be uncertain. But if "thousands of crews" continue to pass over the place and see nothing of them, navigators will cease to believe in that which is never found. The report will sink into a tradition, and, being unsupported, die away. So it will be with the affirmation of the existence of a deity—should it remain uncorroborated by experience—the "uncertainty" concerning it may linger long, but ultimately Jehovah, like Jupiter, will become a dead tradition.

Need I press this example farther? Suppose, instead of an arch of rock, a likely and natural object, the witnesses had affirmed the existence of a rock without body or parts, in fact an immaterial rock, an inconceivable existence, such as deity is affirmed to be, how few navigators would be at the trouble of searching for it, and how little and of what transient duration, would be the credence reposed in it?

You say, again, that " christianity rests on facts, adduces witnesses, and possesses standards by which it is to be judged," If not troubling you too much, you will oblige me by briefly defining what christianity is, as *you* understand it, and formally setting forth its fundamental "facts and standards" of appeal.

Christianity is comparatively modest in your hands. In the remark that "neither atheism *nor christianity* professes to solve the existence of something which had no beginning," christianity resigns one of its principal pretensions. It is not quite true that "Atheism solves nothing." It solves theology. It proves it, in the words of the French priest, to be ignorance of natural causes reduced to a system. "Atheism," you say disparagingly, " sets up nothing." It sets up humanity in moral health. Just as the physician sets up the health of his patient by removing disease and leaving him free to the restoratives of nature, so Atheism by removing the malady of religion leaves a man, as Bacon admits, to sense, to reputation, to philosophy, and the laws—those restoratives of morality.

Often have I admitted that the solemn mysteries of life, and time, and death demand, and whether we will or not, will occupy attention. They are questions which every thoughtful man has pondered over. So far from denying the importance, I would insist on the duty of investigating these thrilling topics. All reasonable attention let them have—but when that has been given, may we not pause? Our philosophers in the *Encyclopædia Britannica* tell us that "it does not appear from any true history or experience of the mind's progress, that any man by formal deductions of his discursive powers, ever reasoned himself into the belief of a god," and as formal deductions are the only safe deductions, what would you have the Atheist do?

" Man," observes Dr. Clarke, " without the assistance of revelation, did not attain to a right knowledge of God in any considerable degree. Some argued themselves out of the belief of the very being of God." And without these systems of argument, Lord Brougham emphatically contends that " revelation is no better than mere tradition." What can more powerfully " dissuade " from this investigation than this hopeless picture drawn by Theists in their calmer moments ? Nor is this all. The idea of God has baffled plain penetration through all recorded time until there seems between it and human intelligence an established unsuitability. " None but a God," said Vanini, "can understand a God," and Goëthe admonishes us that " they who enquire into God must persist in believing the incomprehensible to be comprehensible, otherwise they inquire into nothing." Thus from this investigation both our incapacity and inconsistency warn us to retreat, and we sit down not only in " quiet " but *necessary* "ignorance." The crime is but trivial of " dissuading investigation" where nothing can be known.

Two centuries ago mathematicians revived the puzzled problem of the quadrature of the circle. While professed solutions were teeming from the press, a sober Friar sat down and *demonstrated* the impossibility of solving the question. *His* performance remained unanswered, and geometers went on to weariness with their fruitless labour, necessarily leaving, at last, the question where they found it. Atheism performs a part analogous to that of this wary Friar, and insists on the impossibility, while human nature remains as it is, of solving theology's great question. It treats the subject of deity's existence as the good sense of mankind now treats the long agitated question of the *Philosopher's Stone*. The interesting *Elixir of Life* has not been proved to be " false." The grand secret may yet be evolved from our laboratories, and it might be remarked in your own words, that " were it proved that 'every thing supposed to be known' of it was 'unsatisfactory,' would that be a reason for throwing it aside in contented ignorance? Should it not rather excite the philosopher to deeper research?" Such observation would be full of plausibility, but Dr. Kalley would hardly sit down in these days to investigate that famous chimera.

I thank you for the delight you have given

me by the eloquent precision with which you have put the question of the one "self-existent, unbegan being." You rightly state the question of our enquiry. "We agree that there is something which never had a beginning, and *what* that something is," whether immateriality or matter, is the problem to be solved. If when I represented nature as "peopling" land, sea, and space with sentient existences, I gave you the impression that I regarded nature as a distinct entity from those existences, I must have tinctured reality with fancy, and unwittingly as unwarrantably trespassed on the poetical precincts of personification. I used the term nature in the sense of Dr. Paley, as signifying the aggregate of material objects with which our senses are conversant. Some of these objects, which are organised, are found in a state of "life and joy," others, which are inanimate, in a state of "glittering beauty." Many of the processes are known by which these formations are effected. "Every day," in the elegant language of Dr. Reid, "nature is put to the test of experiment and made to confess its secrets." The offices fabled of providence are happily being fulfilled by science, and men begin to walk in dignity under the guardianship of conscious intelligence which knows no prostration of thought, and brooks no dictation. The relation of man to the external world is being established — the uses of things discovered—herein I see the line of human duty and progress, and herein let me say in passing, that the Atheist encourages all investigation. That the essences of things are hidden retards not this study. It is the knowledge of the use rather than the origin of things which is necessary to man. Whether necessary or not, beyond the uses of parts of materiality he knows nothing. What matter is—whether "divisible into kinds"—whether "composed of innumerable self-existences"— "whence its properties," or its "harmonious arrangements." I must answer again as I have answered you before, I know not. To engage you with conjectures—to refer you to astronomy for the formation of planets like our own, to enlist geology in explanation of the origin of animal life—or expatiate on theories of regular gradation, would only be delaying the real answer. You would properly press me to explain *whence* came, or what is the property of matter producing these changes? My answer is before you: I have no interest in, and no taste for, evasion. However, let me add, that, admitting Nature to be a marvel, or if you would rather, a series of marvels, I do not see how the difficulty is lessened by Theism adding the marvel of a deity to the number.

The self-existent into whose individuality we enquire, "we are agreed is independent of anything else, and never had a beginning." This self-existent being I take to be matter. The human powers can conceive of no other "independent" existence. A self-existent immateriality is nothing. The idea mocks at words. It is a solecism to say that immateriality exists. But we are sensible of the existence of matter. It is the plainest of all propositions. Now matter is a self-existent being. Matter always was. "Had there ever been absolutely utter nothing, there must have continued to be absolutely utter nothing for ever." If you refuse to allow this, matter must have been created, which is an absurdity—for out of nothing, as you have stated, nothing could come. To start the hypothesis of a creator is to make the origin of matter, already confessedly mysterious, an absurdity. "Does reason or probability recommend our choosing that which has two unsolved problems, or that which has but one?"

True, I cannot understand the age of matter, nor could I the age of deity. The theory of matter being *the* self-existent unbegan being involves no more of difficulty, and less of absurdity, than the hypothesis of deity. The existence of matter is a fact, the palpability of which no one in his senses doubts, and finite or infinite, consciousness tells us it is eternal. Moreover, until matter is annihilated, no infinite being can exist, and in less than an infinite we cannot trust.

You remind me that I speak of "powers coeval with eternity, and that conquer time and destruction," and ask if "these powers are inherent in nothing? Let me ask, could they be inherent in immateriality? Of course I take them to be inherent in matter. I spoke of nature *alias* matter. Powers are matter's properties. Disassociated from matter powers were never known. The age of matter is the measure of eternity. The only conceivable "power coeval with eternity" are matter's attributes. If we suppose these powers independent and not to inhere in matter, they must be self-existent, and in your own words I might ask, "then how many knots have we to untie?"

If the idea of an immaterial deity did not baffle human comprehension, what do we gain by it? If, by taking refuge in the absurdity of creation, we suppose matter's origin to be cleared up, what more know we about its properties? its principles of harmonious arrangements? Are we less confounded than before? We may, such is the weakness or vanity of human nature, feel better contented, but are we better informed?

If matter be not the self-existent being we seek, what is? If matter be not self-existent, it had a creator. But whence came the creator? If we cannot allow matter to be self-existent, why do we allow the creator to be self-existent? If matter was created, why not deity? If we admit the idea of creation, we must ever admit it. In courtesy we might assume deity to be the self-existent. But this is not a point to be settled by courtesy, but by evidence. We have this evidence in favour of matter. We are warranted in denying that it was created, because the contrary involves the absurdity of something having been produced of nothing. But once admit that matter was so produced, and it must be admitted that deity *may have* been so produced. The difficulty is removed but one step farther. We have now to discover whence came deity. If matter cannot be maintained as the self-existent unbegan being, what can? It was the wise apothegm of Newton, that whatever was not founded on phenomena could have no place in philosophy. The hypothesis of Atheism is thus founded, but that of Theism, with its immaterial self-existence, is without phenomena to rest upon.

Taking as I do matter to be the "self-existent unbegan being" no difficulty arises from the consideration of its powers being altogether "immeasurable," since we necessarily expect to find them co-extensive with that in which they inhere. Matter being all-extensive, its properties must be so. But you ask "if there be powers of which we cannot conceive the limits, either in respect of their duration or extent, upon what principles of reason are we warranted to conclude that they must be incapable of creating? How shall we establish that negative?" Just as we prove that a deity cannot make a circle in the form of a triangle, or a straight line without two extremities. No power, however extensive, can be conceived as performing physical impossibilities. Creation is a contradiction. You rightly remark that "the immensity of any power is not alone a sufficient reason for denying its presence;" but does not the stated quality of the power being such as involves a contradiction justify us in its rejection? The wants of the human understanding force us to take up the idea of a self-existent unbegan being, and probability inclines to matter as that individuality, for no other hypothesis is so consistent with itself.

Human wisdom, knowledge, and discretion come only of observation, study, and intercourse with men. It does not follow, because man owes his best acquisitions to these sources, that he is "nobler than nature," unless he reason that the river is superior to the source whence it flows, or the effect superior to the cause whence it proceeds.

You return to the argument of design, but only to amplify your positions, not to answer my objections. You embellish the principle, but do not strengthen it. In par. 4 of my fourth to you, I showed how a designer of nature only leads to a designer of deity. It may not be warrantable to carry out the argument of design in the manner I do, or, being carried out, it may not, as I represented, destroy itself. These positions you assail not, but leaving the argument unquestioned, present new illustrations of design, mistaking in this instance reiteration for new evidence.

You tell me of the skin's remarkable adaptation and the body's wonderful structure, and ask me "if they are not the production of an intelligent designer?" To this question I gave you before the common answer of the thoughtless and the superficial —yes. This reply satisfied me before I thought on the subject and saw to what it leads. The intelligent designer involves a material personality, the personality includes an organization, this implies the presence of contrivance, which again leads to a contriver, —a second deity, personal, material, and vast—greater immeasurably than the first. This second involves the existence of a third —the third of a fourth, until we are compelled to admit the monstrous hypothesis of an infinite series of huge beings, disporting in boundless space, rising in awful gradation one above another.

In the words of Emerson, that prince of modern thinkers, I regard "morality as a system of human duties proceeding from man," and "irrespective of God" morality must be, until it is known what deity is and what the duties it requires a e. The duties you say God has revealed, are at present hidden from me. Is any thing worthy of the name of revelation extant? If we are in possession of any useful and unquestionable truth which could not have been discovered by man, we may suspect a revelation, but scarcely otherwise. Refer we to regions where Christianity is unknown, we find the Hottentot, the Tartar, and the Affghan acquainted with justice and injustice. Integrity has place among them. Instinctively they prefer that which promises to be useful, to that which threatens their pleasure. They may not have reached our refinements or philosophy, but they are naturally, and without knowing it, disciples of Bentham. The Deists who have drawn morality largely from Christianity excite my curiosity. Their skill in extracting ethics from that source greatly exceeds mine. Among ethical writers it is agreed that morality is that conduct which best and ultimately tends to promote man's felicity here. Christianity respects that chiefly which it is supposed tends to man's felicity hereafter. Herein Christianity and morality clash. The practice of Christianity is expressed in the reply of Mrs. Judson, the celebrated missionary lady, to Mong Shwa-gong, a sceptical Boodist, — "A true disciple enquires not whether the fact is agreeable to his own reason, but whether it is in the book." What is written in the book may happen to be useful—the interpretation put upon it may happen to accord with human progress, but this depends on accident, and morality should have a surer foundation. They who are guided by a book rather than by reason, will often be found acting contrary to reason, and men who square their conduct chiefly with reference to another world, will continually sacrifice their chances of happiness in this. Guided by faith instead of that wisdom born of human experience, Christianity has warred against sound morality like Briareus with fifty heads and a hundred hands.

Gratitude is a noble emotion, but can it only find scope when directed to ideal existence? Has it no home and no exercise among men? So far from it having no place in the moral code, when a deity is out of the question, it would exist in double energy, as one of those virtues necessary to dignify life. But now, under christianity's effeminating sway, when the patient thought of our fellow-man has achieved some new triumph, or his humanity in some particular case has saved life, we are taught to "give God the glory," and that emotion of thankfulness and joy which should concentre in our brother, and make him afresh the object of our love, is evaporated in the skies. O'Connell has just been liberated from Richmond Gaol—this *he* ascribes to the Virgin, and others, less Catholic than he, render heaven all the praise—but had it not been for the greatness, courage and independence of Lord Denman, he would still be a prisoner in spite of heaven and all the virgins in it. For thus exalting the national character for equity, vindicating the uprightness of the bench, and enabling men to repose confidence in its high impartiality, to whom can we best be grateful—to a real or an imaginary being — to Lord Denman or to a metaphysical abstraction.?

Yours very sincerely,

G. JACOB HOLYOAKE.

"WHAT I admire in Christopher Columbus," says Turgot, "is not his having discovered the new world, but his having gone to search for it on the faith of an opinion."

REMARKS ON MR. HOLYOAKE'S ARTICLE, ENTITLED "THE A PRIORI GOD," PUBLISHED IN No. 16 OF *The Movement*.

BY WILLIAM GILLESPIE.

I. Besides the Criticism of Mr. Charles Southwell, there has appeared a Criticism, on the ",Argument, *a priori*," by the Editor of the *Movement* himself. As a sequel to the reply to the one, a reply to the other will be in *good keeping:* the reason whereof will be obvious enough. Mr. Holyoake's criticism is short; and in commenting upon it, I, too, shall be brief.

2. Mr. Holyoake's performance does not profess to concern itself with the "logical relevancy" of the "Argument." To examine, to refute (if possible), the Argument's logic: that was Mr. Southwell's business. Mr. Holyoake comments upon the *manner*, rather than the *matter*, of the piece.

3. " Mr. Gillespie's god is," asserts Mr. Holyoake, "the driest god in the world. The way of the Lord was never so arid before."

4. In other words, the "Argument, *a priori*," is a logical, as contradistinguished from a rhetorical piece. It endeavours to reach, by "the *most rigid* ratiocination," the most rigorous demonstration: Admitting not one superfluous word; far less, " attributes of honor and compliment only, and nothing but the religious nonsense of astonished minds, expressing their devotion towards what they fear."* The work in question aims at being a strict logical argumentation, and Mr. Holyoake suggests, by his words, that it may have succeeded in its aim.

5.—What Mr. Holyoake holds up to notice as faulty, many others, they not second-rate men, have praised, as one of the greatest beauties connected with the performance.

6. " This *Argument* is buried beneath the weight of *Prolegomenas, Scholiums, a, b,* and *c, propositions, divisions, corollaries,* and *subpropositions.*" " It is a modern mummy in metaphysical wrappers. Its meaning is hermetically sealed in learned jargon. Job and Mr. Gillespie must have been twins."—Sorry objections! One would have thought that the employment of *a, b,* and *c,* in place of the star (*), dagger (†), and double dagger (‡), of the printers, could not have been represented as a very serious delinquency. Mr. Holyoake, however, thinks otherwise, and Mr. Holyoake is entitled to his own opinion.—Even though Job were my brother, and, in consequence of a transmigration of

* Cudworth's System, p, 652.

my soul, this were my second appearance on the present theatre, (a thing, by the bye, far from impossible); still, the demonstration—however "choked with the pedantry of the schools" of the Arabians of the desert, Job's congeners—may be a perfectly valid one; and the validity of the demonstration is, after all, the grand affair. In fine, there might be a more damning fact in relation to the "Argument," than its author having the good old patriarch for so near a relation.

7. But though *manner* be Mr. Holyoake's, he trenches on Mr Southwell's, province: the *matter* really comes under the lash too. "A 'great cause' or a little cause, no cause so obscure as Mr. Gillespie's ever yet peered in the twilight of theology." "Let him who doubts that god is past finding out, read Mr. Gillespie's demonstrations of his existence, and he will be sceptical of the fact no more." If all this be really so——"The Argument" is a sad dialectical failure. But this is not the place to expose the *untruthfulness* of Mr. Holyoake's representation.

8. As a consequence of those imperfections in relation to the *manner*, and of that defect in relation to the *matter*: "To all practical and popular purposes it is dead." Nothing could more convincingly demolish (in an expeditious way) the premises, and the conclusion, above set forth, than a history of two or three of those cases in which my book has been *instrumental* in bringing back, from the path of atheism, to God, and, thus, to the Bible, persons who had strayed into, and in, that path, found, by them, to be so "gloomy," and full of "horrors."

9. Notwithstanding all that Mr. Holyoake urges against the *style* and the *substance* of my proof, he does not say that I have not been fortunate with the same. His words are:— "I do not here declare that Mr. Gillespie has not succeeded, but if he has, his performance is a wonderful work, not more calculated to surprise us, than to astonish his own brethren"—the Arabians?

10. And this leads me to notice the very important circumstance, that Mr. Holyoake quite agrees with Mr. Southwell, touching the close connection which exists between the truth of the first Proposition, and the truth of all the rest, of the "Argument."* "If by 'infinity of extension,' the abstraction with which Mr. Gillespie sets out, the reader suspected that it was put for what the pulpits proclaim as 'God over all, blessed for ever more,' he would narrowly inspect such an artful premise. What Christian ever dreamed in his most frantic moments that his 'crucified Saviour,' is 'infinity of extension'! and the holy spirit that guides him is an 'immovable being'!!† Yet these are the *literal results* which Mr. Gillespie by Aristotelian," *i.e.* syllogistic, that is, irrefragable, unimpeachable, "ratiocination, brings *out of his* FUNDAMENTAL *proposition.*"

11. If Mr. Holyoake's "criticism and comment" had borne much harder on my production than it has done, I might have found a source of consolation in the opinion expressed, so poetically and even passionately, concernig the Prince of pure Geometricians. Nothing could be more injurious to Euclid than what Mr. Holyoake asserts, were this gentleman able to make good his assertion. "When Euclid and Tacquet descant on a mathematical theorem, they favour their reader with axioms, definitions, and postulates—they place before him points, lines, and angles, surfaces, and SOLIDS, and with these SUBSTANTIAL *auxiliaries* to meaning, one hangs with delightful rapture over their lucid arguments." Here is a *bodily* mathematician for you! a *material* geome-

----

† 1. *Infinity of Extension* is not put, by Mr. Gillespie, for *God over all;* though it accords with Mr. Gillespie's reasoning, that *God over all* is of *Infinity of Extension* (See "Examination" of Antitheos, part viii, § 8, 9, 10, &c.)—In other words, is Infinite, Immense, Omnipresent; as the Bible, and orthodox believers, maintain. 2. No Christian ever thought, that his once *crucified Saviour* is *infinity of extension.* But He who, in order that he might become our Saviour to the uttermost, took upon him, in assuming human nature 'in all respects,' that material *body* which was *crucified;* He, I say, is likewise *infinite in extension*, or 'in all places:' being, as he is, the very Son of God. 3. *The Holy Spirit*, the third in order of the I AM, who guides every Christian, is indeed, because *infinitely extended, an immovable Being.*—Motion cannot," says a master-spirit in philosophy, "be attributed to God,——because HE is an infinite spirit." (Locke's Essay: as quoted, more fully, in *Examination*, part viii, § 12.)

For the satisfaction of Mr. Holyoake, who seems to be struck with peculiar amazement (else, why that modern truly expressive *figure of speech*, the *two* points of admiration?) on starting the topic, I may mention that no less a philosopher, no more a Christian, than Aristotle, contended that the origin of motion is itself immovable. "There is one numerically first immovable mover, and no more." (Met. b. 14, ch. 8.) Thus Aristotle: The thing, therefore, commends itself to right reason at all times.

----

* See my Reply to Mr. Southwell, part I, in No, 25 of *Movement.*

trician verily! a marriage-maker between mathesis and matter, with a vengeance! What Mr. Holyoake esteems the beauty of the science, would, with others, they no second-rate philosophers either, constitute its falsity or impossibility. Were the lines and figures of the geometrician such as his diagrams represent, *mathematical demonstration would vanish: geometry would be destroyed by giving external existence to its subjects.* "There is no mathematician," affirms David Hume, " who will not refuse to be judged by the diagrams he describes upon paper." It is quite true, that " Mr. Gillespie disdains to perform *so* kind an office for his reader" as to furnish him with "SUBSTANTIAL *auxiliaries to meaning.*" With Mr. Holyoake, " great truths are *solid,*" and mathematical theorems are descanted on by means of auxiliary *substances*—"*solids*"—placed before the reader. But with Mr. Gillespie, Mr. Holyoake's *solids*, and very *substantial auxiliaries* to mathematical studies, bring forcibly to mind the *auxiliary substances* and *solids*, of one '· whose disposition to the mathematics was discovered very early, by his drawing parallel lines on his *bread and butter*, and by intersecting them at equal angles, so as to form the whole" [in this case, solid and substantial] *"* superficies into squares."

——" What most conduced to his easy attainment of *the Greek* language, was his love of *ginger-bread*,"—[Observe, with the change of *study*, the change of *auxiliary*] "which his father observing, caused it to be stamped with the letters of the Greek alphabet; and the child, the very first day, eat as far as Iôta." — *Memoirs of Martinus Scriblerus.*

PROGRESS OF INFIDELITY IN SCOTLAND.
II.

OUR Galashiels friends are luxuriating just now in agitation. An association has sprung up in that district for the express purpose of declaiming Infidelity out of existence. This promises well. From a communication of Mr. Sanderson, an active member of the Infidel Society, it appears that a discourse of the extinguishing association, lately delivered, ended with this felicitous peroration:—" We charge upon Infidelity the perpetration of every dark and awful crime, villany, assassination, robbery, murder—if there is anything worse, it is the parent of them all. A nation of Infidels would be a nation of fiends." Atheistical violence has been paraded with ostentations, but in all its exaggerations it sinks into insignificance, compared with this specimen of Christian virulence.

Next we have an elaborate article in the *Border Watch* on the "*Rapid Spread of Infidelity*," "from the pen of an operative," and compared with the lucubration of the priest, it is philosophy itself. Our operative's opening remarks presents us with the modern history of the progress of irreligion in Galashiels:—

" Men of the present age are characterised by boldness of action. Opinions, whether true or false, are propagated with zeal regardless of consequences. If Christianity has come forth in apostolic life and vigour from the cold grave of Moderatism, Infidelity has also broken the bars laid upon it by former controversies, and sprung into renewed existence. Christianity is no longer secretly attacked or made the subject of jest amid the excitements of festive mirth; it is now openly and systematically opposed, and its bulwarks are attempted to be overthrown in the face of an intelligent universe. 'The *Oracle of Reason* wars not with the Church, but with the altar,—not with the forms of worship, but with the worship itself,—not with the attributes, but with the existence of God.' The cry is ' away with the atrocious Trinity, a God whose reasons would disgrace an idiot—whose laws would shock a savage.' Such is the language of Infidelity as it is now fearlessly spoken out in Hawick and Galashiels. In the latter place an Infidel association has been organised, and impious documents are now frequently to be seen posted upon the most public parts of the streets. The members of this society are chiefly young men, disciples of a Mr. Southwell, who lectured against the Bible in Galashiels some months past."

Our operative tells us that Infidelity has " renewed its existence," as though " it had never fallen beneath the weight of argument, or fled into dark obscurity before the blaze of truth." What does he mean? Does he refer to the time when Paterson fell with a broken head at the Waterloo Rooms, " beneath the weight" of policemen's staffs? Are the sombre cells of Tolbooth, Calton, Perth, and Stirling gaols the "dark obscurity" to which he alludes, as the places of Infidelity's retreat " before the blaze of Christian truth." If so, decency should have taught him to restrain such an exultation. If our operative really means that Christianity has both "argument and truth" on her side, why did he not bring it forth twelve months ago, when the Atheistical agitation was at its zenith? It is not prosperity, but adversity that tries friends—and in that day of Christian adversity, what friend sought Christians in confidence—" the weight of moral argument " — the now vaunted " blaze of Christian truth?"—or the brute terrors of the dungeon? Let aged Thomas

Finlay—let Miss Roalfe—let Thomas Paterson answer! Not too fast, our good operative! argue, if you please, and if you are not intolerant we shall respect you—but don't parade Christianity's moral power before those who have so lately proved its falsity, and tasted its utter cruelty.

Next our operative is complimentary, and tells us that "the ideas" he holds "of God, the soul, and the Bible—are above the Infidels' puny comprehension." But if these ideas are, as the Infidel contends, contradictory and impossible to be entertained, no comprehension, puny nor capacious, can reasonably entertain them. He demands "whence came man? and calls on the Atheist to believe in God because he cannot understand inanimate nature." Great faith must our operative have in human weakness and credulity, to think that others will accept additional mysteries by way of solving those they already have. He assumes that Atheists "refuse to believe in the existence of the soul, because it cannot be seen," and contends that for the same reason "they must refuse to believe in the phenomena of life and ideas." The truth is that the philosophy of materialism teaches that there is insufficient reason to believe in the existence of the soul, as a distinct entity, and on the same ground it is justly denied that life and ideas are distinct beings. Our operative calls the Bible a "splendid novel"—what does he think of the Lamentations of Jeremiah? He says "nothing can be *grander* than the Bible—what thinks he of Ezekiel's dinner of dung? He says "nothing can be *comlier*"—what thinks he of Lot's seduction of his daughters? He says "nothing can be *holier*"—how does he estimate David's adultery with Bathsheba, and the murder of Uriah? True, these are but special instances, the book *may* be good on the whole, but a book with such cases on its pages as those just cited can only be palmed off as "a paragon of sublimity" in some moment when the writer is demented. Let our operative carry such another "splendid novel" to Colburn or Constable and test its value by endeavouring to get a penny a sheet for such a miserable immoral and incoherent rhapsody. This indiscreet operative "challenges infidels to make good the charge that the Bible teaches vice." Why slavery, war, intemperance, licentiousness, and frauds of all kinds are sustained by an appeal to its pages. If the Bible does not teach vice, how are these facts to be got over—and facts they are, blazing in open day, in every Christian land.

"The morality of the Bible," says our operative, "is to do good"—what, as Paul did when he struck Elymas blind for disputing his statements? "Its morality (says he), "is to seek peace"—we suppose after the fashion of that Biblical discourse whose words we have quoted at the opening of these remarks. "The Bible (he remarks) says love mercy—who believes it?—what Christian in Scotland loves *justice?*—does our operative, let him look to Perth? Does he condemn persecution? Let us have proof of it in a contribution to the Anti-Persecution Union for the benefit of Mr. Paterson. He continues—"the Bible says love your enemies." But what says Paul?—"if any man preach another gospel to you than that which I have preached, (whether enemy or friend) let him be accursed." But the subject is sickening. It is of no use to give us precepts of morality from one page, which are contradicted on the next, and those which contradict the precepts our operative puts forth, are those which are interwoven into the Christian practice of the whole world. What our operative quotes are in the book only, the others are both in the book and in the life. Which set Christians believe their practice decides.

Our *Border Watch* penman gets rid of the "Bible's contradictions" by putting them down as "sublime mysteries." The idea of annihilation he says would kill rational creatures. Has he never heard of the idea of hell killing people and sending hundreds to mad-houses? And what is the Christian heaven? David will be there, and Paul will be there, and *Christ* will be there—who said, he who believes not, whether he can or no, shall be damned—Bonner, Pitt, and Castlereagh will be there. *Wellington* will be there—Sir C. Wetherall, and Justice Clerk, and the jury who sent Paterson to solitary confinement in Perth, will be there. All who have cursed mankind by their creeds—drank the blood of the martyrs—trampled on the liberty of the poor, or waded through blood to increase our taxes and enslave nations, or have struck down truth with a savage hand—all have died or will die, in the sure and certain hope of a glorious resurrection, and *all will be there*. Annihilation is an anodyne falling on the parched spirit compared with an eternity with such saints.

Space will not allow the discussion of every point of our operative's paper. If not better employed, we should recommend our Galashiels friends to get out a small pamphlet in reply to it, and circulate the reply widely. His paper being free from much of that asperity and ill-nature, which usually characterises the attacks of Christians on Atheists, it merits respectful attention.

G. J. H.

PARSONS, PUMPS, AND POLICEMEN.

THE inhabitants of Thorold Square have, as was noticed in *Movement* 39, for some time past been annoyed every Sunday by the erection of a tent, belonging to the Christian Instruction Society. This tent, besides occupying upwards of two-thirds of the square, actually enclosed the pump that supplied the inhabitants with water. This, of course, was considered a serious inconvenience, and application was made to the society to discontinue the erection of the tent, the inhabitants assuring them that if they did so, they were welcome to preach there. This offer they arrogantly declined, and as several accidents happened in consequence of the tent being left standing, an application was made at Worship-street for the removal of the nuisance. Mr. Bingham decided that the erection of the tent was an illegal act. On the next Sunday the inhabitants assembled to prevent the pitching of the tent, but the Christian Society, with the assistance of five policemen, again obstructed the thoroughfare and set the inhabitants at defiance. In consequence of these occurrences, myself, my father, and Mr. SPENCER were invited by the inhabitants to lecture in opposition to the maw-worms. On Sunday, Sep. 1, we took our stand and delivered six lectures during the day. In the evening, H. 103, promised to send policemen in plain clothes to take notes of our speeches. Mr. Bingham being a second time applied to, again declared the erection of the tent to be illegal; still the Christian Instruction Society had the assistance of the police. In the afternoon of Sep. 8, we attended and preached the " True Gospel." However, in the evening, but not till then, we were left alone, the Philistines had struck their tent and departed.

C. J. SAVAGE.

LECTURE TO THE SOCIALISTS OF ENGLAND.

[I have been able but very briefly to fulfil your request of reporting Mr. Southwell's lecture at Whitechapel to the "Socialists of England." But as with you any performance is esteemed more highly than none, brief as my report is, I enclose it. Mr. Southwell was as usual, very effective and happy in the delivery of his sentiments,—these can only be heard, not written.—J. B. L.]

Mr. Southwell began by expressing his abhorrence of partizanship, and then very happily exposed the conceit of the socialists in supposing their doctrines to be new, or their measures the only practical ones. Co-operation, he said, was but a rational mode of conducting competition, which last he thought never ought and never could be eradicated. All that Socialists should do is to carry out old principles in the new spirit. He ridiculed the idea of supposing that the New Moral World could be realized in a day, or that the mere knowledge of some truths could effect it; knowledge without action was a dead letter. On discipline his remarks were very lively, and illustrated by a short account of his recent visit to Harmony. The coldness and apparent apathy there manifested, was an example of how the world may be reformed "by rule and compass," certainly very different from the way in which Luther and other great men had effected their reforms. He thought grave errors had been committed by Mr. Robert Owen and the old Executive in their estimate of human nature, by neglecting to cultivate the feelings as well as the intellect. These errors he thought still existed in the management of the Branches, referring to Roman Catholicism, its ceremonies, &c., as an example of what should be done. To the old Executive he charged the almost utter extinction of the enthusiasm that once animated the Socialists, and conceived that any twelve old women, whether Billingsgate or apple-women, would have managed affairs much better. From the new executive he hoped much, believing their head to be a man of great determination and honest purpose. But it would be found a gigantic, if not impossible task, to renew the old feelings of ardour. In conclusion he thought Socialists had two duties to perform: 1st. To support the experiment at Harmony: 2nd. To diffuse abroad a knowledge of their principles, and thus remove the fearful obstacles in the way to further progression,—these obstacles being the popular prejudices, viz., politics, morality, and religion. To accomplish these it should be remembered, that great truths were only so when greatly told. Hence, honesty and universality were the two guides by which to steer their path.

" THE INVESTIGATORS."
(*Report.*)

WE (not the "people of England" but a few friends in the neighbourhood of Whitechapel) have established an association for the discovery of truth, through the means of fair and unrestricted investigation, and have taken a comfortable little room at No. 6, Charlotte-street, Fieldgate-street, Whitchapel, about two minutes' walk from the church, where we at present meet on Monday and Thursday evenings. The former we devote to debate upon *any subject* chosen by the majority, the latter to study and conversation. It is in contemplation to establish several classes for the study of Gurney's system of short hand, chymistry, logic and grammar, and to get up for the use of the association a monthly or quarterly manuscript work, to consist of essays, reviews, &c., written by the members.

The terms of membership are 2s. 6d. per quarter. Any person desirous of truth, and friendly to the unshackled exercise of reason, being admissable if introduced by a member.

We provide pens, ink, and paper, and members will be *supplied with them as required;* this we hold to be essential, for it frequently happens that persons would comment upon and reply to what they read, but that they have not the *free* and *convenient* use of these articles.

The publications we have at present resolved upon taking in are, the *Zoist*, the *Wesleyan Magazine*, and the *Movement;* our means will not just now admit of our doing more, but we shall be very happy to lay before our members any other publications, should any kind friend feel disposed to supply them, and to accept any donations in books, maps, or apparatus, to increase our facilities for discovering truth. It will be seen by this that we are liberal in our proceedings, and inclined to examine evidence both *pro* and *con* —which, by the bye, is that only upon which any claim to the title of " INVESTIGATOR" can be legitimately based.

We shall do our best to encourage in each other a rectitude of conduct, determination of purpose, and a strict adherence to principle, without which an attachment to truth cannot be securely established.

All letters for the " *Investigators*" to be directed to the Secretary at their place of meeting as above. S. T. C. *Sec.*

ABNER KNEELAND.

[The following letter, addressed to the editor of the *Boston Investigator*, from the venerable infidel martyr, Abner Kneeland, wi'l be read with interest by his European friends. The "Infidel Convention" alluded to is one which has been earnestly proposed to the American Infidels. The *Investigator*, an excellent atheistical paper, has completed its fourteenth volume.—ED. of M.]

" Salubria, (I. T.,) April 2, 1844.
MR. EDITOR,—I went off South last fall to get away from the cold weather, and I spent the winter in Helena, (Ark.,) and as I did not wish to be idle, I opened a school there. I have enjoyed my health extremely well, and I now weigh *two hundred*, which is more than I ever weighed before in all my life.

" The idea of an Infidel Convention fully meets my approbation, and I am glad to perceive that it still gains ground; and if the first one should not, I hope there will be one ultimately at either Pittsburgh or Cincinnati, at either of which places I should try, if possible, to attend. One great object of a Convention is to call out men of like or similar views, and to fix some rallying point, around which they can concentrate and unite for self-defence, self-protection, and general good.—There are thousands, I presume, who are real Infidels at heart, but who still think it expedient for them to glide along in the general current of superstition; although they are aware that it is both expensive and unpleasant, who, if they only knew the great and increasing number of Infidels that are spead out all over the country, and were equally know by them, would join heart and hand in promoting the good cause of moral philosophy, unmixed with any religious or superstitious dogmas. I am too old now to start any new plan whatever, being, on the 7th instant, three score years and ten; yet, if I still have any influence, I wish to throw it into the right scale, if possible.

" The following may be considered as axioms, viz :—

" 1. We are just as certain that something must have existed from all past eternity, as we are certain that any thing now exists.

" 2. The organization or composition of matter, so as to form bodies which are obvious to our senses, does not create a single particle of matter more than what existed before the organization or composition took place; hence the same matter, however invisible it might have been, must have existed, in some state or other, before.

" 3. Prior to organization, if we can conceive of such a period, there could have been no such thing as mind in the universe, that is, in space; because what we call mind is the effect, and not the cause, of organization.

" 4. Where there is no sense, there is no mind; where there are no organs of sense, there is no sense.

" 5. The three following expressions— 'God and his works,' 'Nature and her phenomena,' 'Matter and its operations,' if they have any meaning at all, are perfectly synonymous.

" 6. If it be true that the time will ever come when God shall be 'all in all,' and equally true that 'he is the same, yesterday, to-day, and for ever, without the least variableness or shadow of turning;' then God is ALL IN ALL now, ever was, and ever will be; and this is the doctrine of PANTHEISM; that is, that all, and nothing short of the whole of existence, is God.

" Yours very respectfully,

" ABNER KNEELAND."

HOW IS MAN's CHARACTER FORMED?— *by Edward Walter.*—The second edition is just issued of this lively letter to the Rev. Dr. Redford of Worcester.

LETTER FROM FATHER PINELLO TO FATHER BACASS.—This is another pamphlet just issued by M. Roalfe & Co., which ought to be dedicated to the Missionary Societies of England. Indeed the preface very properly draws the attention of those worthy bodies to it. The "Letter" is a translation from a rare Portuguese MS., by a gentleman who met with it in the "Transactions of the Jesuits." It gives an account of Father Pinello's unlucky attempt to convert the natives of Pariboo. To the lovers of irony it will be a treat.

THE LIBRARY OF REASON.—All doubt respecting the reappearance of this much-enquired-after work, was ended by the publication of No. 7, under the auspices of Mr. Hetherington, on Saturday last. The No. contains the completion of the "Fallen Star,"—that star is really down now—"The Three Rings," one of Boccacio's elegant, amusing, and instructive tales, valuable facts from the Bible of Reason, and Lord Bacon's admirable remarks on "Superstition."

WORCESTER.—Our friends in this charming little city are quite revived again. Mr. Walters is engaging the clergy, another gentleman some time since engaged the attention of the press. The Hall of Science has been re-decorated, and lastly, 10s. has been forwarded to the Anti-Persecution Union. A little persecution has lately sprung up there, which has suggested the propriety of assisting in the extinction of that great bar to progression. It would not be amiss when the Anti-Persecution Union sends a subscription card to any supine place, to send at the same time a note to the parish priest, desiring him to give his neighbours a slight proof of the powers vested in him by law, of annoying non-conformists. It would stir up our friends to the exertions necessary to put an end to that persecution which can now, at any hour, be brought to bear upon them.

DERBY.—Our industrious friend, Horace Roche with a few others of similar views, we are glad to find contemplate forming a branch of the Anti-Persecution Union in that town. They have some intention of carrying the principle of the division of labour into morals as well as manufactures, by establishing a class for theological discussion.

HAWICK.—We have reason to know that the number of individuals at Hawick professing Infidelity and Deism has increased very considerably of late. Many of them are zealous in propagating their opinions; and we think the ministers of the town ought to consider the propriety of delivering a course of lectures upon "Natural and Revealed Religion," "The Evidences of Christianity," &c. —*Edin. W. Register.* Of course they ought.

IPSWICH.—I have not been visited of late by any links of the *dragchain to improvement.* So myself, with two or tree others, have taken it in hand to ask the *Street Preachers* questions. One of them while expatiating on the *Bible* said, that among other *good* things it contained "the *purest* morality," so when he had done I asked him to read the 38*th chapter of Genesis,* instead of which he shook his *pious finger* at me, and with a look that none but the *truly godly* can assume, told me that he was a *licensed preacher,* and would not be annoyed; whereupon I told him that I would discuss the subject publicly with him. He replied he knew (which I did not doubt) where I lived, and that he would call and hold a discussion with me, but particularly requested me to keep quiet *then.* I desisted, as I could not appeal so strongly to his feelings as £75 per year, and having nothing else I gave a lot of Social tract away. Hurrah for Atheism.—J. COOK, *Infidel Repository.*

THE THOROUGHFARE LAW.—"A. Mr. Hedges, a Primitive Methodist preacher, was on Saturday last, Aug. 24, committed for three weeks' hard labour to Oxford Gaol, in default of paying 15s. fine, for a pretended obstruction of the highway, while preaching to five persons on religious topics. Anything more infamous and outrageous can scarcely be imagined. It looks like one of the bloody records of the Star Chamber. But as bad if not worse than this, is, that while Mr. Hedges was in gaol, he suffered one of his friends to pay the fine without even a protest. By this he has betrayed the interests of English freedom and Christian liberty. He has not done his duty as a man or a Christian." Thus talks the *Wesleyan Chronicle.* Were we disposed to be vain-glorious, we might point the editor of the *Wesleyan Chronicle* to our friend Paterson who so resolutely bore the brunt of the battle in London respecting the *thoroughfare* question, when raised by Mr. Jardine. Evidently our Methodist Propagandists may profit by the example of an Atheist. The Wesleyans have wealth—let the case of Hedges be enquired into, and if the decision is unjust, appealed against.

GERMAN STUDENTS.—Amongst the whole number of German students whom I have known, it would be difficult to select a dozen who were not confirmed deists. Let those who doubt the extent to which this philosophical pestilence is spread, go and judge for themselves; but let none send out solitary youths to study in German Universities who do not wish to see them return very clever, very learned, and very completely *unchristianised.* —*W. Howitt.*

WELCOME TO WEITLING.

Assembly of English and Foreign Socialists at the John Street Institution.

Next Sunday Afternoon is appointed for assembling English and Foreign Communists to express the cordiality of our sympathy with a fellow reformer, who has undergone severe sufferings through his untiring zeal and energy in advancing social and political reform, as well as to draw more closely the bonds of brotherhood between those whom language, habits, and craftily-fomented national antipathies had hitherto kept apart, but whom identity of sentiment and principle now irresistibly draw together. Fleming, Ryall, Holyoake, Chilman, Moll will be among those who will address the meeting; others are invited and expected. Tea on the table at five o'clock. Tickets 9d. each.

LECTURES.

[*Any omission of announcement observed in the following list is owing to the neglect of the Secretary of the Institution not writing to us.*]

September 22.—Branch A1.— Mr. A. Campbell 2nd lecture on the "Rise and Fall of the Orbiston Community."

September 22.—(In the morning) Mr. Southwell, in Assembly Rooms, 29, Circus-street, Bryanstone-square, Subject,—" Was Jesus Christ an Actual or Fictitious Being?"

September 22.—Hall of Science, City-road.—Mr. Southwell on "Popular Fallacies."

September 23.—Oldham Hall of Science. —Mrs. Martin.

September 24.—Branch A1.— Mr. A. Campbell on "Hamism."

September 25. — Manchester Hall of Science.—Mr. R. Cooper (7th of the course) on "Prophecy."

September 30.—Mutual Instruction Society, 66, Bunhill-row Finsbury, Mr. W. Cooper on the "Struggles of Genius."

DISCUSSIONS.

September 24.—Social Institution, Whitechapel.—Mr. C. Southwell and the Rev. G. Hill.

September 24.—49, Henry-street, East Portland-town,—on the "Existence of God."

NOTICE.

In the list of the New Committee of the Anti-Persecution Union, printed on page 324, the name of Mr. W. H. Bennett was omitted by accident. That gentleman was duly elected.

Just Published — elegantly printed, and suitable for framing, Lines by Emma Martin, entitled the "LAST OF THE MARTYRS," price 1d. The profits to go to the Paterson Testimonial Fund.

H. Hetherington announces that he has made arrangements with the proprietors of the *Library of Reason* for resuming the publication. The work will, in future, be regularly publishes every alternate week. No. 8 will contain The Condition of Morality Examined, by W. Burdon.

Rare and curious works will, from time to time, appear on Theology and Politics, and suggestions from friends and readers in furtherance of the object will be esteemed as favours.

The Rev. Mr. Lee of Campsie.— With reference to a statement in No. 33, respecting this gentleman, Mr. Mc. Neil writes, that it was known six months before he was taken to Stirling Gaol, that the rev. gent. had "a call" to Greyfriars' Church, Edinburgh. But that the Chartists held a meeting in their hall on the subject of persecution, and speeches of ability were delivered on both sides; and a great majority passed a resolution to the effect that persecution for opinion sake is impolitic and unjust, and that they sympathized with John Mc. Neil and all others of whatsoever opinion, who are on such grounds persecuted, by which conduct the rev. gent. was publicly and justly condemned.

TO CORRESPONDENTS.

Received.—H. H. D.'s Notices (too late), H. J. Williams and J. Mellor, Q in the corner—Report of "Mr. Southwell's Second Lecture to the Socialists of England"—Socialism in France, from *Le Populaire*— *Boston Investigator*—"Letter from Mr. Gillespie to Mr. Charles Southwell."

SUBSCRIPTIONS TO THE ANTI-PERSECUTION UNION.

Worcester per Mr. Allen:—

W. Weaver and J. Wilks . .	0	1	0
W. Wilks	0	1	0
F. Stinton	0	1	0
W. Allen and T. Allen . .	0	1	0
G. Cracroft	0	1	0
H. Southan, Esq. . . .	0	5	0

Bristol Subscriptions for August.

Card 11	0	3	0
„ 14	0	1	0
„ 16	0	5	0
Per Mr. Truman, Coll. 44. .	0	2	0

G. J. H., *Sec.*

Printed and Published by G. J. Holyoake, 40, Holywell-street, Strand, Saturday, September 21, 1844.

THE MOVEMENT

And Anti=Persecution Gazette.

"Maximize morals, minimize religion."—BENTHAM.

No. 42.   EDITED BY G. JACOB HOLYOAKE, ASSISTED BY M. Q. RYALL.   PRICE 1½d.

SPEECH OF WEITLING.

(*To the English and Foreign Socialists assembled at Branch A1.*)

FRIENDS,—" All's well that ends well ." I am again free—free in action and in word—I am among you according to your invitation, and I feel I am welcome.

I—a stranger, a German, and called a dangerous Communist—here find hospitable and sympathising friends, such as generally wait only on the great, the learned, and the rich. But you warmly greet a stranger who is not one of these; showing thus to the world that liberty of speech among you is not " as sounding brass or a tinkling cymbal," but a reality which leads you to the recognition of Communist principles, and the practice of their consequences. A sympathy springing from the principles that mutually animate us has induced you to welcome me; this welcome will be a message of gladness to our friends on the Continent, and a brand of shame for our bigoted persecutors, if, indeed, the smallest feeling of shame still slumbers in their breasts. What have we asked of them?—what have we to expect? Freedom of speech, free discussion, a public refutation of our principles, with arguments to prove that the present state of things is based on truth, while our ideas and propositions for its amelioration are utterly erroneous. Instead of this, what have they done? They have in a cowardly manner avoided this great question, and introduced plans for hindering liberty of speech and writing, by means of threats, imprisonment, fine, and banishment. They have partly executed their plans, but what have they gained? They have tried to blow out the spark of liberty, but they have only kindled it into a blaze.

Some time ago the doctrine of Communism was, in literature but a small uncultivated plant in a barren wilderness. But what see we now? The journals which heretofore found no interest in admitting the subject in their columns, or dared not discuss it, have advanced by degrees till they teem with criticisms and reports of Communists and Communism. Our philosophical and political literature, which can no longer avoid the contact, we now find becoming more and more imbued with it. Our philosophers of the new school are consequently Communists: yes, even a party of our adversaries begin to call themselves Socialists to hide from the public, in more pleasing garb, the one-sidedness of their ideas of political reform. Is not this joyful progress? and have we not to thank our enemies—the monkeys for throwing heavy nuts to injure weary travellers, who, smiling and refreshed, pursue their journey with renewed vigour. Even the people from whom the literary language of our philosophers and politicians is hidden, who seldom understand the terms they use, the people who have no money for books, and no leisure for reading, have thought deeply on that immeasurable world of ideas which lies in that, to them, strange sounding word Communism. " To have all things in common would be right," is whispered from mouth to mouth, from Berlin to Vienna, from Köln to Köningsburgh, from Prague to Langenbielau.

We will not burn their houses, said the infuriated weavers, for the proprietors would be indemnified by the insurance companies, but we will pull them down—Let them also feel what it is to be poor.

The blind rage of persecution, the arrogant scoff, the unnatural hardening of all tender feelings have brought us to this state of things. The oppressed, the pursued, the victims find everywhere a helper or avenger. And how can it be otherwise, when even animals sympathise with the oppressed among them. Observe a little dog bitten by a larger one, how often other little dogs run indignantly to attack the oppressor; and if animals have such feelings to whose dictates they must bend, how can *men* resist their influence? These deep and irresistible feelings are natural, and their demands constitute our rights. Our rights, therefore, are not matters of science, but feeling; they are not to be calculated mathematically, nor by a money standard, nor are they to be measured by fine and imprisonment. Feeling alone is the accurate barometer of our rights; if different degrees are occasionally shown, it is because some are pressed to the earth, others elevated to the clouds. What now in the language of lawyers is called our right, is a sophism, a deceitful play upon words, mere jugglery for making white black, or the contrary. It is a fishing-hook which provides food for men of useless and even pernicious professions, and which the satiated glutton passes by with impunity, while the half-starved and diseased bleed to death upon it. You know they have many rights, had they also a right to banish me? No; according to the mathematical scheme of Prussian rights they had none. I said to them, I have a right—but they answered, we have the might; such might is that of brute-force by which an ox has more right than a man. You see that if in such circumstances we depend upon our rights, it will be necessary at last to connect the feeling of our right with the recollection of our power. Our physical power is hired and turned against us by the gold of our adversaries. If it is to be used for our own benefit, no one will offer one farthing for it. But we have still our intellect, which is the creator of all that is and can be done by us. How shall we so develop this intellectual power as to conquer and triumph? Not by Captain Warner's invention of destructive engines; not by the extensive financial operations of Rothschild and company; not by the cunning manœuvres of diplomatists; not by the dogmatism of useless and slavish erudition—no, it must be by freedom of expression that fears no contradiction, but, on the contrary, expects it—by freedom of expression, proved and measured by opposition—the power alone of free expression, that in explaining the interests of individuals as the necessary, the useful, the beautiful, and agreeable, finds in each man's breast a natural defender!

Here, it is said, we have freedom of expression; if so, welcome England, asylum of liberty of speech in Europe!—oh! why art thou only that? Why art thou also the residence of Mammon our material god? Thy innumerable ships cross all waters, accumulating and exchanging the products of labour, from the sweat of many millions of workmen of different countries! Why, like a cruel stepmother, dost thou suffer thy most diligent children to sit by their hearths empty-handed, whilst, capricious to others, thou fillest their pockets with useless toys and sweatmeats. Thou art great in thy dominion over the seas; thou hast devised and partly accomplished the emancipation of the black slaves; why, England, dost thou nothing for the emancipation of the white? Canst thou be indifferent whilst thy magazines and warehouses are over-stocked with the wealth of the globe—whilst thou seest the producers ragged and and hungry strolling through thy streets.—See the winter approaches—the destitute crowd in unhealthy holes, or are exposed, without shelter, to bitter frosts and chilling damps, whilst the idle consumers fly to the south, their warm nests left empty. The swallows also fly to the south, leaving their nests empty, which the sparrows take possession of for their own comfort. Why should houseless, naked creatures, in sight of splendour and luxury, be frozen to death? Have not the people built and furnished all these nests? Have they not a better right to them than the sparrows, who have not built those of the swallows? Proud England, who hast diffused among the most distant nations the light of knowledge, improvement, and Christianity, who givest to whole nations thy language—see the ignorance and wretchedness of thine own children. See the female in the period of childhood, the image of death depicted in her countenance—see her on the slippery brink of corruption—see her earning her bread by the most degrading debauchery—look, England—behold and help thine own children. How long, England, wilt thou beg for what thou hast a right to demand?—so long as the energies of the many are employed for the exclusive interests and enjoyments of the few, and laws are made and punishments enforced to preserve such a state of things—SO LONG AS THOSE WHO LABOUR ARE POORER THAN THOSE WHO GOVERN.

A beautiful and excellent thing is freedom of expression—a powerful call in the mouth of the oppressed—an indescribable sound of rejoicing from the lips of the mighty;—but it is nothing and falls inoperative if the ideas it involves are of an impracticable nature; therefore we see all ideas occupied with that which is essential to all, which can be proved, compared, explained, fear no discussion, for they are the life-blood of freedom of expression. These have created that sympathy which has animated the phalanges of all European Communists. Our power lies therefore in the power of our principles; it is developed by their propagation—the best propaganda is then the best means of attaining our ends. If we approve them, we shall look for men with the principles of Owen, and with the resolution and generosity of Oscar, the young King of Sweden, who gave at once voluntarily to his people what millions have here many years vainly demanded.

Thus I end, having freely expressed myself, and hoping, though a stranger, you will not banish me for it, as the republican government in Zurich and the *liberal* government in Prussia have done.

ANOTHER SPECIMEN OF RELIGIOUS SWINDLING.

THE frauds practised by the believers of the Christian religion, and the crimes which they have perpetrated are so numerous, that a whole life spent in diligent compilation would not be sufficient merely to catalogue them. Well may the followers of the faith deprecate the drawing of any inference as to the character of their creed, from the character of its adherents. Point to the crimes, vices, and persecutions of the christian world in all ages, and we are then informed that the criminal, vicious and persecuting are not christians, and that the true followers of Christ are but few among the many professors. If such is the case, surely we may ask in return, where then has been the glorious triumph of the gospel? Where are the evidences of its being backed by almighty power, seeing that its real influence has been small indeed, and that it has made so few *genuine* converts, who alone, according to the saints themselves, are worthy of being called after their divine lord and master? If the belief of the christian dogmas, the hope of heaven and the fear of hell, do not make the believer a good man, then is christianity impotent, its agencies and motive powers have been exhausted and have failed. It is certain, however, that neither heaven nor hell have been sufficient to make honest men of the actors in the piece of roguery we are about briefly to relate.

On Wednesday evening, the 4th inst., a public meeting of the inhabitants of Glasgow, called by public advertisement, was held in the Trades' Hall, Glassford-street, for the purpose of " hearing a deputation of the Catholic clergy, from the diocese of Down and Connor, make some startling disclosures regarding the Irish Presbyterian Home Mission and the Irish schools, under the patronage of the Synod of Ulster." The hall was filled to overflowing and the addresses of the deputation seemed to leave a powerful impression upon the audience. On the motion of Dr. M'Donnell, the Rev. Mr. Gordon was called to the chair.

After a few remarks from the chairman, the Rev. Mr. Fitzsimons, in a long speech, in the course of which he entered into ample details, exposed the " Mission" above referred to. He was followed by the Rev. Luke Walsh to the same purpose. It appears that the persons calling themselves the Irish Presbyterian Home Mission, have for some years been collecting large sums of money to promote, as they professed, the establishing of schools in Ireland, for teaching the holy scriptures in the Irish language, and for reclaiming the young from Popish darkness and abomination. For several years they have collected in Scotland about £1200 per annum, upon the average, by means of collections at church doors and ladies' auxiliary societies. Annual reports were published, containing flourishing accounts of their doings, how schools were rising on all sides, how popery was being overcome, and further explaining how those who supported the " missions" were " lending to the Lord." The last report stated that this society has 600 schools in Ireland, attended by about 14,000 pupils. Now, from evidence adduced at the meeting, it seems that this statement *is an enormous lie, that the schools have no existence save in the imaginations of the framers of the report.* But we will quote on this a short passage from the speech of the Rev. Mr. Fitzsimons, as reported in the Glasgow papers:—

" Now, gentlemen, documentary evidence will this night be laid before you, to prove that there is no actual *bona fide* school of the kind in all Ireland. With regard especially to that district of the country called the Glens of Antrim, in which we are placed, and with which we are well acquainted, we are prepared to prove that there is not a single school in existence, though the annual reports of the Home Mission state that, for the last four or six years, there were twenty-six schools, attended by 600 scholars. We at once admit that there are a number of unprincipled individuals who are receiving salaries, and making a return of schools and scholars that are altogeter fictitious, and this is done with the knowledge and concurrence of the Inspectors of the Home Mission Society. In the summer of 1842, a number of these so called teachers, stung by remorse of conscience at the imposition they were practising, came before me, and voluntarily signed a document to the following effect, and which afterwards appeared in one of the Belfast newspapers. — ' We, the undersigned, who were receiving money from the Synod of Ulster, under the plea of teaching the Irish language, do hereby declare that we have not taught any for the last four years, neither has there been any school in this parish (which comprises that portion of the county Antrim denominated the Glens) during that period, nor, as a matter of course, has any school under us been inspected during that time, by any officer belonging to the synod; and we considered it no harm to take the money which the synod gave us for doing nothing : Patrick Macauley, Patrick Loughran, Patrick Quin, John M'Kessick,—June 20, 1842.' Here then is a complete exposure of the system, of the working of which I have a perfect knowledge. A person who has the name of being a teacher, and another, who is an inspector of schools in a certain district, have both an interest in getting their salaries; but you perceive they cannot get their money unless they return their school and a certain number of scholars. Well, the master sits down and writes a number of fictitious names of persons who had never an existence, and when his imagination fails him, he sets down some of his neighbours as attending the school. Then the inspector comes round and sets it down as a school, seen and inspected by him, and thus the two gentlemen get their salaries."

In the course of the evening several declarations from teachers who had made reports of schools which had no existence, (and with the connivance of the inspector,) were read. Surely it must strike the subscribers to the "mission" who have been thus duped, that if they can be so easily imposed upon in matters near at home, how much more easy it is for canting vagabonds to deceive them with reference to missions among the heathen in far distant lands where the means of detection are not so close at hand, and the opportunities of fraud far more abundant. Let the priests and teachers of religion go on exposing each other, for according to the old proverb, "when rogues fall out honest men come by their own."

HENRY JEFFERY.
Glasgow, 27, Charlotte St.,
12th September, 1844.

SOCIALISM IN FRANCE.

Le Populaire, of 1844, Journal of Re-organization Social and Political, edited by M. Cabet, Ancient Deputy, published monthly at Paris.

[Translated for the *Movement*.]

LE POPULAIRE, a journal of Social and Political Re-organization, is the organ of a class of French Socialists known as the Icarian Communists. They take this title from a work called "Travels in Icaria," written by M. Cabet, their leader, with whose sentiments they identify themselves. The broad line of distinction which they draw between themselves and the other social reformers of France is, in their own words, as follows:—
"The reason we have adopted the title of Icarian Communists, is to be distinguished thereby from that faction of Communists who, although not very numerous, compromise all, in demanding the abolition of marriage and family connections, and in involving violence and constraint. The title *Icarian* signifies merely the adoption of the general principles laid down in "Travels in Icaria," and has no other end than to protect us from persecution. It has been our safeguard as it is still our shield."

Their household gods—if we may be allowed the term, or rather those words—of which every system possesses some, and are supposed to contain in themselves the essence of thought, the gems of progress—their watch-words are equality, fraternity, liberty, unity, education, morality, labour, and order.

In an article headed "Communist Doctrines," their principles are thus briefly set forth:—

"This is the principal and essential character of Communism:—the national territory is indivisible and belongs to the community or the people at large, which is the the great proprietor, agriculturist, and manufacturer. It employs all the citizens as workers. It so directs agriculture and industry as to produce every article of food, clothing, lodging, and amusement. It collects together a l the produce, and distributes it equally among the citizens according to their wants, so that all may be amply and equally well fed, clothed, lodged, and instructed.

"Communism is the antipode of Agrarian law. It is order, justice, fraternity, concord, and peace. It is the realization of democracy and Christianism.

"For its establishment Communism demands electoral reform, the establishment of democracy, and the reduction to practice of the principle of fraternity consecrated by Christianism.

"After the establishment of democracy it claims not the spoliation of any person's property for the purposes of community, but solely that the popular representation would allow a transition state of decreasing inequality or increasing equality, and above all that it will protect all those who desire to go into community.

"For a further exposition of our system of community and the doctrines of Communism it will be necessary to read the "Travels in Icaria."

Under the head of "Foreign Review" we find the following:—

"What troubles everywhere!
"Ireland—Is *always* agitated.
"England.—The ravages of the incendiary are ever being perpetrated there.
"Germany.—The troubles of Silesia and Bohemia have extended to Saxony.
"Greece.—The sudden outbreaks, provoked perhaps by some foreign power, have often led to bloody collisions.
"Italy.—Fifty Italian refugees set out from Corfu and disembarked in Calabria in in the hope of its rising in revolt. But, deceived in their expectations, they were arrested and condemned; nine were shot, and among them the two young BAN-

DIERI, sons of an Austrian vice-admiral. What blindness among the revolutionists! What noble blood shed to the great injury of liberty!"

We are also told, in a paragraph headed " Progress of Social Reform," that — " Social questions attract more and more public attention: *La Démocratic Pacifique* inserts extracts from an immense number of journals from the provinces and foreign parts who seek a remedy in Socialism. The *National* itself advocates Social reform. Louis Napoleon in his prison at Ham, the new king of Sweden in his speech to the legislature of his country, and the King of Prussia in a public circular to his great officers, all recommend the study of Social reform.

The difficulties which oppose the path of the reformer in France are almost inconceivable to us living under institutions of apparently illimitable freedom, when compared to the espionage and extreme watchfulness of continental governments. The immense ramifications of their spy systems, and the shameless means adopted for the implication of any party considered obnoxious, makes it wonderful that reform is ever heard of in those countries. And yet these are the places where their influences are most felt — their numbers greatest — their doctrines more expansive—their devotion most intense. As a sample of the nature of the thorny path through which they have to pick their way, take the following, truly called an *infernal snare :*—

"A man enters the shop of a wine merchant, Mr. Z——, well known for his democratic opinions, and whose lady is behind the counter. 'Is your husband at home, madam?' 'No, sir.' 'Ah, I am very sorry for that; I want to speak to him on business of great importance.' 'He will be in in about two hours.' 'Indeed; I will walk a little further, and then return. Desire him to wait for me. Good day, madam.' 'Good day, sir.' '*A propos*, I have a parcel which incommodes me, would you have the goodness to allow me to leave it with you till my return?' 'Most willingly, sir.' 'Take care of it, if you please, that no one may take it.' '*I will put it in the desk.*'

"Shortly after, the husband returns, but instead of the stranger, a commissioner of police enters the house, commences a strict search, finds the packet in the desk, and opens it. 'What have we here? cartridges!' Of course the cartridges are seized, and the wine merchant dragged off to prison. After a long *preventive detention* he is at length brought up before the court. He has a good witness as to his innocence, and who relates the preceding circumstances, but still he is condemned to *one year's imprisonment*, and 1,000 francs (£42) fine. The fact is that the cartridges were left by some infernal agent, or some infamous enemy, who then lost no time in denouncing him to the police. Beware, then, how you receive anything from a stranger!"

We have in the same paper another scheme of some barber who incited the people to insurrection at Lyons; and no wonder that, from such accounts as the above, there are many impatient to revolt. This barber was considered to be the hero of his party; and to render his empire the more complete he engaged to head an attack upon the barricades. In this onslaught he was killed, and his body secured and carried off by his followers. On searching his papers to ascertain his name and family, " they discovered with horror that he was an infamous agent" and tool of the government. The *Populaire* adds—" It is these infamous men, this credulity and blind confidence of a small body of the labourers, which caused the catastrophe at Lyons in April last—at Paris, and throughout France, and which furnishes such desirable pretexts to government to erect bastiles at Lyons, and facilitate still more those now proceeding at Paris. Examples are also given of how the Carlists seek to entrap the workmen, and two others of attempts on the editors and correspondents of the *Populaire* by means of anonymous letters, &c.

The editor very ably exposes the folly of secret societies—shows that they are powerless for good but almost omnipotent for harm, and compares them to a bird in a cage, while the police interested in their formation, takes the pigeon whenever it is convenient to them.

To attain their ends " the golden key " is used to a tune that appears almost incredible. The editor says that when it is necessary to buy any one, if 1,000, 2,000, or 10,000 francs won't accomplish it, they do not hesitate to give if necessary 50,000 or even 100,000; indeed it is well known that "all the prefects of police have boasted that they have *all* the reports they desired from any committee either the least numerous or the most secret."

But this appears but a small item in the vast scheme of oppression and grinding tyranny more especially affecting the working classes.

At a slight disturbance of the working tailors of Grenoble, nine were arrested and sent before a jury at the court of assize. Their innocence becoming manifest, the procuror of the king desisted from pressing the case, and they were liberated after *four months preventive detention.*

The labourers of Lyons not being Communists, desired to associate for mutual support. Many were authorised so to do, others were in the act of obtaining the necessary license, and others were preparing their articles for submission to the proper quarter to make them legal. In March last, a commissioner of police by some means got information of their meetings, penetrated into a room where eighteen were assembled, and seized thirteen in another. He found them discussing some propositions contained in a written sheet placed before them. It was in vain that they maintained it to be the outline of a plan to be submitted for legalization. The commissioner pretended that they were a society already formed and consequently illegal. Four months after three foremen were condemned to fifteen days imprisonment; three tavern keepers thirty francs fine; and seven labourers to a fine of sixteen francs. At the same time five others were condemned for a combination, two to fifteen days' imprisonment, and three to a fine of sixteen francs.

And all these sentences enforced against honest, hard-working men, who only asked to work that they might live! *Some workers in stained papers* were tried on the 20th of August, after three months preventive detention, on a charge of combination. They affirmed and demonstrated that the manufacturers had combined, but the court would know nothing of the coalition of *their patrons*. The labourers then proved that *they* had not combined, but the court contended that they had, and passed the following sentences on seventeen of them:—one to eight months imprisonment; four to three months; five to two months; one to one month; three to fifteen days; three to eight days; and all to great expences. All were arrested *three months ago*. Three women, two children, and five labourers have been declared innocent and set at liberty. But even these were detained as prisoners for three months! What a barbarity is this preventive detention! What a state of society! Oh, unhappy working men!

The above are the tangible difficulties opposed to the societarian reformer. Of course there are many others more hidden, but not a whit less obstructive, and almost overpowering from their existence everywhere. These are the prejudices of the people, their ignorance and vanity, the underhand trickery of the priesthood, and lastly, more powerful than all, the divisions among themselves, and the sneers, jealousies, and oppositions of so-called friends. These unfortunately abound among the French Socialists, of which the paper before us bears ample testimony. Let us hope that the sentiments of fraternity so much lauded among them will not much longer remain a dead letter; and that if it is found that they cannot of themselves amalgamate, the stepping in of the English Socialists will serve as a medium through which this desirable end may be attained.

J. B. L.

THE MOVEMENT TO ITS READERS.

(*Private and Confidential.*)

This week the *Movement* returns to its former size and price. The discussion with Dr. Kalley has for the present terminated, and that between Mr. Gillespie and Mr. Southwell was apparently brought to a close in the 39th No. As it was understood that the enlargement was to be temporary, to continue it longer would be a breach of that good faith we ever maintain with our readers.

Some have desired that the enlargement should be permanent, and others that it should be increased to sixteen pages, but neither of these proposals can be listened to at present. The enlargement, besides entailing much greater labour, has entailed an expence which has not been met by the usual returns. Time, attentions, exertions, are at our controul, but debts no man is always sure of paying, therefore on *no account* do we ever incur them. Every bill of the *Movement* has always been paid as soon as the No. owing it has been issued, and from this rule we will never consent to depart. The first day it is necessary to incur a debt, on that day the *Movement* will cease. Better not to be, than to be under obligation.

The perfection of the *Movement* at its present size must take place before an enlargement. A little well done is more satisfactory than much done indifferently, and the *much* must never be attempted until the *little* has been well performed.

All the means at our disposal will be employed in improvements. The last page will be printed in nonpareil, to admit of a greater number of notices, and the *Movement* will in future be published on Wednesday, the same day as the *Non-conformist*, by which arrangement it will be earlier ready for country parcels, present fresher intelligence, and of some kinds a greater quantity.

Complaints have occasionally reached us of the inaccuracies which have appeared in our pages. Had we not been more enthusiastic than pedantic, we should, from this cause, have given up the *Movement* long ago. But would it not have been ridiculous to have allowed an organ, which has defied the powers of the Attorney-General, to be put down by the blunders of a printer's boy? Once for all, readers may be reminded that the *Movement* has to be written and revised in the intervals of business, as it is (the assistance of friends included) but slightly remunerative. The last thirty Nos. of the *Oracle of Reason* cost £30, besides being gratuitously edited.

Since our publications were in the hands of Mr. Chilton, they have not been with any printer who has taken a gratuitous pride in their correctness. Not being able to bribe skill, or spare the required time for revisals, errors have necessarily gone forth. But these are daily growing less, and will shortly disappear. For a long time the prosecutions to which the *Oracle* was subjected, prevented a single copy of any atheistical work being any where exposed publicly for sale, except by the few persons who were imprisoned—but spite of these difficulties the *Movement* has made its way. It is the acknowledged expounder of the most heterodox sentiments of the day, it has taken its place among our periodical literature—either it was wanted or it has made itself necessary, until it may fairly be considered as *established*.

RUSTIC RUMINATIONS.

I

I TAKE, or intended to take, advantage of your temporary enlarged space to comply with your request of writing you. Is it an axiom in philosophy that "nothing can come of nothing?" Well, this is sheer absurdity, as your extracting this letter from me proves.

At this moment I am gazing on a regiment of "bold peasantry," who are making heroic attacks on a field of bristling corn, near Halifax, in Yorkshire. This twenty-shilling work of Englands pride," (for ten of them are working for 4d. a day, which makes £1 a week for the lot), look as though they would be very glad if he who said " by the sweat of his brow man shall eat" would have the kindness to see that they who do " sweat " have a chance of eating after.

Sometimes I sit down and hold dialogues with idealized humanity, and muse over man's better destiny. These are all very pleasant operations till one looks round on the realities of life—then comes the reaction. Being one of three in a bed, and the other two porcupines, is nothing to it. One feels like a disjointed and broken up anatomy—like an asphyxiated cat issuing out of a lime pit. A man with his head upon the block of a guillotine—with his nose in unpleasant proximity with the "basket" which will shortly contain his head — when he grinds his teeth—when he contracts every muscle in his body, in expectation of feeling the "knife" dig into his neck—when he hears the knife sliddering down the frame the feelings of a man in such a situation are enviable — it is perfect beatitude— extatic bliss—it is a realization of the Mahometan paradise, when contrasted with the feelings and situation of a man emerging from a day dream.

Something like determination possessed me when I began, but the hot weather has volatised it all, and now I can scarcely endure the excitement of watching the growth of a mushroom, or the digging of a ditch.

On Sunday last I came down here for the purpose of latitudinarianizing and rusticating among nature's glories, whieh the saints would define as being but a pleasurable method of stuffing, seasoning, and preparing one's soul for hell-fire, so that it may roast, frizzle, crisp, and brown upon the most approved principles and according to the utmost wishes of omnipotent malignity. But I must not proceed in this strain, or I shall be reminded by my friend the rector, who is crossing the next field, that I shall be called to account on that day when the angel will perform upon the cornet à piston, and the dead kick off their shrouds in their eagerness to dance the Real Polka.

W. P. J.

GALASHIELS.—We read in a local paper that there is a society here, consisting of 350 persons, entitled the "Galashiels Infidel Association; and that the walls of the town, the population of which is about 3000, are constantly placarded with the announcements of profane and irreligious publications. Surely there must be something wrong in the spiritual government of this place, or the example of the wealthy classes must be anything but a wholesome one.—*Edinburgh Weekly Register.*

[350 associated Infidels in a population of 3000, is a satisfactory proportion. If there is "something wrong in the spiritual government of the place," there "must be" something right in the people, who have taken so wise a course as the dissemination of "irreligious sentiments.—ED. of M.]

LOVE ONE ANOTHER.—Let us consider a razzia by the French—one of those interludes which, to the employment, if not the delight of the recording angel, they are every day enacting in Africa. These Christian men come swoop upon an unarmed village. They cut the throats of the men—bayonet their wives and children, if at all troublesome—set fire to the growing crops—and drive off every head of cattle. Consider the scene — the heroes with another sprig of laurel marched away—and say if it be not a place for devils to revel in ? Consider the blackened earth, the smouldering ruins, the human form divine gashed and stabbed, and worse than all, outraged beyond the decency of words to tell; and what is there in the spectacle that Beelzebub himself might not feel a diabolic pleasure to claim as his own especial handiwork —his own doing? albeit committed by men whose creed it is to "love one another!"— *Punch.*

SECOND EDITION—Price 1s. 6d.
PRACTICAL GRAMMAR,
By G. Jacob Holyoake.

Watson, 5, *Paul's Alley, Paternoster Row.*

This is a shrewd, common-sense, practical treatise on English Grammar, and the Art of Composition. It is written in a highly interesting style—terse, pithy, and epigrammatic—and we have no doubt will be found extremely useful to a numerous class of students. Many persons will not go to work without rule and compass before them; and to all such we can confidently recommend the Practical Grammar of Mr. Holyoake.—*Leeds Times.*

One of the numerous works undertaken to "divest" their specific subjects of "difficulties;" this proposes to relieve "Composition" of them. It has the merit of being readable and anecdotal. For the rest its claims are modest, professing to contain "all that is necessary for ordinary purposes and no more.—*Athenæum.*

NOTICES.

The Welcome to Weitling.—We have presented in another part of our paper the speech of M. Weitling, at Branch A 1., on Sunday last. A full report of this interesting meeting appears in the *New Moral World.* We shall present a general notice of the speeches next week.

Anti-Persecution Union.—The next Meeting of the Committee of the Anti-Persecution Union will be held in the Coffee-rooms, 23, John-street, Tottenham-court-road, on Monday Evening, September 30.

Atheistical Society.—The Monthly Meeting of the Atheistical Society will be held on Tuesday Evening, October 1, at the Northampton Coffee-house, Newton-street, High-Holborn.

Caution.—On Friday, August 31st, a vessel, entitled the "Breadalbane," was launched from the Bay of Quick, containing a cargo of Religious Freebooters, destined to the Highlands of Scotland. This vessel is vulgarly known as the "Free Church Yatch," and has been built at the expence of the credulous, costing £800 or £1000. The cargo is composed of preachers intended to cruise round the shores of the Western Hebrides after the manner, says the Rev. Dr. Mackay in the *Greenock Advertiser,* of Christ and his Apostles. But instead of these worthies filling the nets of the fishers there, it is expected they chiefly intend to fill their own. All her Majesty's lieges, who have any regard for purse or sense, are advised to keep out of the way of these religious marauders, who are sailing about "like roaring lions seeking whom they may devour." These parties are known, not only to attack the pockets, but, what is worse, the reason of those who happen unfortunately to fall in their way. Persons having business on the shore, will find it necessary to go well-armed with common sense as the best protective in case of attack—women and children, unless such as are accustomed to think for themselves, should keep within doors.

Wanted.—The following odd numbers of periodicals, published by the late *Richard Carlile.*—*Gauntlet,* No. 49 and 51; *The Iris,* No 14, 15, 16. Full price will be given for copies, by post or otherwise. Apply, R. Carlile, 2, Lovell's-court, Paternoster-row.

The New Institution of the Rotunda friends (which will be shortly opened) is situated in Union-street, almost adjoining the Rev. Mr. Sherman's Chapel. This rev. gent. is reported to have boasted that he had extinguished the Socialists on the Surrey side. He will probably be convinced of his mistake now that the Socialists have become his next door neighbours.

Missing, from the neighbourhood of Colne and Burnley in Lancashire, one Mr. Grubb, who, a short time ago, manifested prodigious anxiety to discuss questions of the Existence of God. and the authenticity of the Bible—until it was known that a gentleman from London was engaged to accommodate him. Since that time he has not been heard of. He had, when last seen, an air of the most approved Christian bluster. He is supposed to be concealed in some vestry or pulpit. Any parties delivering the gentleman up will be handsomely rewarded for their trouble.

LECTURES.

September 29.—Branch A 1.—Mr. A. Campbell on the "Rise and Fall of the Orbiston Community."

September 29.—Whitechapel Institution.—Mr. Fleming on the "Life and Writings of R. Owen."

September 29.—Assembly Rooms, 29, Circus-street, Bryanstone-square.—(Morning), Mr. Southwell—subject, "Is it rational to believe that the Universe was created and is governed by a Being or Beings independent of itself?"

September 29.—Assembly Rooms, 29, Circus-street, Bryanstone-sq., —(Evening), Mr. O'Brien—subject, "The Doctrine of Christianity not opposed to the principles of Democracy."

September 29.—Hall of Science, City Road—Mr. Southwell.

September 30.—66, Bunhill-row, Finsbury.—Mr. Cooper on the "Struggles of Genius."

October 2.—Hall of Science, Manchester.—Mr. R. Cooper on "Miracles."

DISCUSSIONS.

September 27.—Branch A1.—On "Phrenology as the Philosophy of the Mind.

September 28.—Social. Institution, Whitechapel, —Public Discussion.

September 30.—By the "Investigators," 6, Charlotte-street, Field-gate, Whitechapel.

October 1. — Social Institution, Whitechapel—between Mr. C. Southwell and the Rev. George Hill, on the "Existence of God"

October 1.—47, Henry-street East, Portland town.—(This Society has removed from No. 49.)—Subject, the "Existence of God."

TO CORRESPONDENTS.

Received.—*Greenock Advertiser. Belfast Commercial Chronicle.* Letter from Mr. Paterson. J. Thorne.

The Speech of Mr. Southwell to the Investigators arrived too late for insertion.

SUBSCRIPTIONS
TO THE ANTI-PERSECUTION UNION.

Chillman and Logan	..	..	£0 1 3
J. G. Hornblower	..	..	0 1 0
Mr. Watts of Islington	..	..	0 5 0
W. J. P.	..	..	0 5 0

A P U.—The collectors of the Anti-Persecution Union who have funds in hand are respectfully requested to forward them, as the quarterly account is about to be made up.

Paterson Testimonial.

W. J. B. Second Subscription	0 10 0
Mr. Henry Walker, per Mr. George Smith, Salford	0 3 0
Mr. R. Thomas, per Mr. Kincard, Rochdale..	0 1 0

G. J. H., *Sec.*

Printed and Published by G. J. Holyoake,
40, Holywell-street, Strand,
Wednesday, September 25, 1844.

THE MOVEMENT
And Anti-Persecution Gazette.

"Maximize morals, minimize religion."—BENTHAM.

No. 43. EDITED BY G. JACOB HOLYOAKE, ASSISTED BY M. Q. RYALL. PRICE 1½d.

CHRISTIAN PRESUMPTION.

WITH sincere persons, the transition from one system of belief to another is generally, if not always, a vital struggle. To make the transition completely, and act upon it consistently, is ever honourable and pleasing. Christians frequently do this—why should not Atheists generally follow the example? The reason probably is, that in them it would be deemed presumption. A bold and consistent convert is held in honour among believers—let the same be done among unbelievers. If the Atheist frankly avows his atheism, he is said, as the *Monthly Repository* said of Julian Hibbert, to be seeking notoriety. That course which in the Christian is respected as a duty, in the Atheist is held to be vanity. If a Catholic abjures his faith and becomes Protestant, or *vice versa*, to publicly recant his error, is a common and tolerated occurrence. If the Atheist in a similarly open manner, recants christianity, and denies God as a Protestant denies the Virgin, it is deemed daring presumption. Yet where is the difference? Moral courage, consistency and frankness are as beautiful in the Atheist as in the Christian.

In a Dramatic Poem, in five acts, entitled *Vivia Perpetua*, by Sarah Flower Adams, is a speech of Vivia's which illustrates these views. Vivia Perpetua was a noble Roman lady who lived in the third century. But being converted from the Pagan to the Christian religion, and making public her new sentiments in what was then deemed an offensive manner, just as our Unitarian magistrate, David Jardine, saw fit to deem Mr. Paterson's proceedings in London offensive. The result to Vivia Perpetua was that she, gentle, lovely creature, was publicly put to death. So unresisting was she

When the swordsman,
For youth—or shame to pierce such willingness.
All mastery of his hands to guide his weapon lost,
Herself did turn the point against her throat.

Before this melancholy occurrence, she went into the temple of Jupiter Olympus, walked up to an altar burning before a statue of her former God, and thus spake—

Lo! where all trembling, I have knelt and pray'd;
Where vow and sacrifice, at morn and eve,
Shrouded in incense dim, have risen to appease
The wrath, great Jove, of thy once-dreaded thunder,—
Up to the might of thy majestic brows,
Yet terrible with anger, thus I utter,—
I am no longer worshipper of thine!
Witness the firm farewell these steadfast eyes
For ever grave upon thy marble front;
Witness these hands—their trembling is not fear—
That on thine altar set for ever mo e
A firm renouncing seal—*I am a Christian!*

The shadows blacken, and the altar flame
Troubles them into motion. God of stone,
For the last time, farewell! and farewell ye,
The altar where my childhood's wreath was flung,
Frail as the faith that claim'd its dedication!
Yon niche, where an apart was sought, alone—
Unconscious treasury of tears! that oft
Fell, like fast rain, upon those senseless stones,
That, like yon image, then a deity,
Sent no returning pity. Jove! *give back*—
Give back those tears were shed in vain to thee:
Give back those trembling vows were made to thee;
Give back the sacrifice was paid to thee.

Bear witness all ye myriads of angels
That, like the radiant stars, cluster in heav'n;
Thus, on my knees,—thus—thus, before the Lord,
I solemn vow,—record it all ye hosts,—
Never again to come within this temple,
Whate'er the penalty, or death to me,
Or agony—worse death—to those I love.
Upon my head so let it come, O, God!

When it is remembered that Vivia Perpetua had to abandon a fondly loved child as one of the "penalties" of her conduct, the sincerity and courage of this recantation, including, as it did, "agony—worse death to those she loved," will be deeply evident. The italicized words are not so in the original. Just read again those daring lines. Mark! she died with willingness."

"Herself did turn the (sword's) point against her throat."

Let an Atheist do this and all would cry out that he *courted* martyrdom. It is wrong thus, or in any way, to court martyrdom. But let not that be extolled in your Vivia Perpetuas, which would be censured without measure in our Matilda Roalfes.

Mark how boldly she looks up on the "majesty brows" of her quondam God, "*yet* terrible with anger," and declares—

"I am no longer worshipper of thine!"

Why should not the consientious unbeliever

thus act, and before the very "front" of deity,

"————— Set for ever more
A firm renouncing seal—*I am an Atheist!*"

The language of truth and deep conviction ought to be as welcome from the lips of Atheists as from Christians.

Vivia Perpetua was no timid Christian—no mere lip service did she render to her new belief. On Paganism's altar was "flung her childhood's wreath." In its temple's 'niche" she had prayed " alone," but now looking back, as thousands may do, on the waste of worship, she resolutely demands—

"JOVE! *give back.*
Give back, those tears were shed in vain to thee;
Give back those trembling vows were made to thee;
Give back the sacrifice was paid to thee."

And then she properly and solemnly vows

"*Never* again to come within his temple."

All honor to Vivia Perpetua—and Christian though she was, may she find, among Atheists, many an imitator—courage like hers should adorn a nobler cause than that in which she engaged. G. J. H.

THE BISHOP OF DOWN AND CONNOR AND DROMORE.

THIS reverend of many names has addressed a letter to Sir Robert Peel, with reference to "National Education" in Ireland. It has had an immense circulation, and we suppose has met with general approval among the class of his Lordship's supporters. The letter again evidences the pernicious influence of religion. The Bishop is an excellent soldier in the army of *anti-progressives.* Fearless and undaunted, he refuses to step aside from the course marked out for him, from complaisance to reason, philosophy or the spirit of the age.

His Lordship declares that "the education of the poor ought to be regarded not as the instrument of political, civil, or merely moral improvement, but of *religious improvement*"—another instance of the distinction, which exists in practice among the most influential of Christians, between religion and morality. Thus are the solid interests of humanity openly sacrificed at the shrine of a stultifying creed. His Grace admits that " efforts to improve the condition of the poor" may be "well-intentioned," but if such effort should cause the poor to make "shipwreck of faith," it must be abandoned,—again evincing that there is no security for the poor while religion lasts.

The Bishop is of opinion that National Education would " leave place for error in religion or viciousness in life ;" meaning, that where the doctrines of the church are not inculcated, viciousness of life must follow. Thus strengthening the destructive prejudice, that he who does not believe as the church believes, is to be regarded as of inferior virtue.

Philosophers judge of systems by their effects—they are guided by facts, by reason, by experience. Our Bishop despises such vulgar rules of judgment, his sole question is— is the proposed education "calculated to promote the end of his ministry towards the children of God, and the spouse and body of Christ ?" Thus religion ever perverts man's reasoning powers, and converts him into a passive automaton, pulled by the wires of ancient creeds and obsolete dogmas.

Like the Revs. Walker, M'Illwaine, Monsell and Professor Stevelly, whose sentiments we criticised in *Movement* 32, under the head of "Honest Confessions," the insane cry of the Bishop is, " No Bible, no Board." His Grace will have the whole Bible, "not in detached, selected, accomodated passages." The opinion may be safely hazarded, that a more unfit book for general circulation does not exist than the *whole* Bible. In its present state, its absurd and immoral tales are only calculated to vitiate both morality and sound sense. Not only will it blight the buoyant feelings of childhood, but it will surely nip the opening buds of intelligence.

Poor men! who feel the evils of ignorance, remember to whom you owe it—to such men as the Bishop of Down and Connor and Dromore! Politicians justly complain of the tardiness of government to promote the improvement of the people, and when our rulers are somewhat disposed to diffuse among the many that knowledge which, emphatically, is power—remember, ye Christian Repealers, Suffragists, and Chartists, remember that the opposition comes from your Bishops, and your Bishops are influenced by religion !
G. J. H.

RELIGIOUS ENTHUSIASM.—During the whole of the week special services were appointed to be observed daily at the Wesleyan chapel at Holmfirth, amongst the congregation was the wife of a respectable general shopkeeper in the neighbourhood, named Joshua Mosely, a woman noted for her activity in the Methodist cause, and for her regular attendance at the chapel. On this particular occasion, however, she prayed with more than ordinary zeal, and ultimately worked herself up to such a pitch of imaginary and extravagant inspiration or delirium, as to produce a decided state of insanity, in which state, lamentable to relate, the unfortunate woman still remains.—*Leeds Intelligencer.*

LECTURE TO THE SOCIALISTS OF ENGLAND, DELIVERED AT THE SOCIAL INSTITUTION, WHITECHAPEL, SEP. 2, 1844. BY CHARLES SOUTHWELL.

II.

THE Lecturer commenced by reading some extracts from a letter in the New Moral World, by Mr. Finch, predicting the speedy advent of the millennium, from the facts of the readiness of the poor and the fitness for paradise, while the rich, according to accounts, were anxiously awaiting an opportunity of investing their funds in the attempt, in perfect confidence of the result, and because certain old prophecies could not be otherwise accomplished, so that Millennium must necessarily be, because they (the prophecies) had said so. The letter was, of course, dedicated and written to the governments of the world. The lecturer thought such language at the present time, not only contemptible, but injurious, tending to create in the public mind an impression of the visionary and futile plans of the Socialists. He thought Mr. Finch must be mad to suppose the people fit for community. This was but an offshoot of the conceit in which the Socialists were wrapped—a conceit that led them to believe themselves the possessors of all knowledge worthy the consideration of man, or necessary for his happiness. This conceit kept them ignorant, for, in the words of Bacon, the reason we know so little is because we think we know so much. It prevents their holding the mirror up to nature, and scares from them those friends who would tell the truth. It was but a repetition of the old game at church, where the rule is to tell just such truths as are pleasing and no others. Truth required a better advocacy than this. Indeed, he thought the principles had done more for the Socialists than they had done for the principles. That superior advocacy they once had, many years ago, long before the agitation was known under the name of Socialism. Then Mr. Owen was truly eloquent—the most eloquent speaker of the day—the eloquence whose beauty lay in truth and effectiveness, in plainness, and simplicity. But times had changed—Mr. Owen had altered—Socialism had become standstillism, and their leader had kept them back, for of late he had done more harm than good. The disciples had imitated the master in all his faults, as imitators always do, and here we found them applauding to the very echo those who told them only what they wanted to hear. These disastrous effects were elucidated in the conduct of Mr. Galpin, at the Congress in 1841, who did not scruple to declare that though he might have formed an opinion on the most mature consideration of a question, yet if Mr. Owen expressed a different opinion he should not hesitate to abandon *his* in deference to Mr. Owen. Again, while Mr. Owen was at Harmony he lectured twice, sometimes three times a-week, and it was frequently his delight to select those most ill-mannered or least educated, and, addressing them personally, proceed to dwell on the impossibility of their ever becoming fit associates for the aristocrats.

These examples, said the lecturer, would induce in the minds of the disciples a supposition of the infallibility of their leader. But he that would palm such a doctrine on mankind was either the most deceived of all men, or the most daring deceiver.

The lecturer then proceeded to combat the notion that human nature was to be cut and fashioned to a new standard, omitting some ingredients and inserting others. Ambition many thought was bad, and should be eradicated. But no propensity was bad, and never could cease to belong to human nature. We seem to forget that all crimes are relative, and are induced by previous treatment — severity attended by vicious feelings—kindness by generous ones. Less racking of the brain was wanted, but more good feeling. We could dispense with a little intellect if its place was amply filled with generous warm hearted emotions.

The broad path of duty lay before us to help on all reform guarding against narrow-minded conceit. But above all it was of first importance to prepare ourselves for the noblest individual exertions.

J. B. L

USEFUL INFORMATION.—The angels are all pure spirits; that is, they are uncompounded, immaterial substances, or subsisting as simple beings which have no parts, as bodies and matter have. In them nothing is to be found of colour, shape, extension, or any other quality of matter. They are by a property of their nature immortal, as every spirit is. For a simple entity, or what has no parts, can only perish by annihilation, which is a supernatural act of divine omnipotence, no less than creation.—*Andrew's Weekly Orthodox Journal.*

A CORRESPONDENT'S WISH.—May the good you have at heart protect you in danger, and the purity of your motives encourage and cheer you in difficulties—and may you go down to the grave, at a good old age, hated by tyrants, and cursed by priests—with the sighs and blessings of the despised and lowly, as your only requiem, is the hearty and sincere wish of one whom you know too well to suspect of flattery.

LETTER FROM MR. GILLESPIE TO MR. SOUTHWELL.

To Mr. Charles Southwell,

Sir.—I have seen your *rejoinder*, in three parts, which you are pleased to term "The Battle of the Choryphæi." The course pursued by you, in your *Battles*, is different from that which I anticipated. I must do you the justice to say, that you have *not* as yet written to unwrite what you wrote.

You do not, I am happy to say, in any of your Battles, call in question the connection between the truth of the *first* Proposition of "The Argument," and the truth of all the rest of the Propositions, down to the very last one. You began by *assuring* your readers of the *existence* of such a connection,* and you do not evince the least disposition to retract, by a hair's-breadth, the *assurance* given in your "*Fallacy*"—no *Fallacy* in that. This, manifesting as it does a consistency which I did not, I own, look for, augurs well for our debate reaching a definite conclusion: The connection spoken of may *now* be held as *a settled point*. A connection which (if I dare say it here) bids so fair for my final palpably triumphant success in the present controversy.

But—to my signal astonishment—you call in question, as much as ever you did, the truth of that first, and "fundamental Proposition."†

In short, you still follow your old course.

I must take some notice, therefore, of your Rejoinder to my Reply. But the present communication is by no means to be considered as my answer to your Rejoinder: 'Tis merely preparatory to my answer. This letter is a mere preliminary.

To answer your Rejoinder, would imply that I *understood* it. Now, there are some things in it which I cannot at all understand, or make sense of. And as (if I may hazard a conjecture) they would have an important signification and bearing, if light were thrown upon their real character, I am led to address this letter to you, Sir, in order that you may accord the requisite explanation.

In Battle II., par. 14, you have these words: *My* "proposition that matter is infinitely extended."

But, in the next paragraph, you write thus: "Mr. Gillespie declares himself perfectly satisfied with the assertion that the extension which matter has is infinite, and necessarily existing: an expression of satisfaction no one would have a right to quarrel with, if I had asserted any thing so 'nonsensically false.'"

These two statements seem to me to be perfectly irreconcilable with each other: but if not, I wish for a clew to a method whereby I may reconcile them.

Again: In the same Battle, par. 2, you say—"Extension is nothing more than one of matter's primary attributes."

While in par. 1, you had alleged: "There is no extension in matter."

And, in Battle I., not far from the end, you say; "We see matter extended—hence the idea of extension."

But, in Battle II., par. 15, you allege: "I never asserted, never thought of asserting, that matter has extension."

These passages parallel — in place — are presented as a specimen which might be very much enlarged, were there any necessity for loading the page with such passages. The parallel assertions seem to me—and, I fancy, will seem to every person but one—to be nothing less than *flat contradictions*. I declare, upon my word of honour, I do not know how to reconcile them; that is, I do not know what you mean. Whether it be your intention to deny, with the partizans of *Leibnitzian* or *Wolffian* monads ("things which made so much noise in their day,")* that matter, or body, is extended,—allowing matter, or body, only a *quasi* extension—or whether you mean to admit, with the great mass of mankind throughout all ages, that matter is something which is long, broad, and deep, or extended in three dimensions, viz., length, breadth, and depth; I really do not know.

But it is of the very utmost importance, as far as this controversy is concerned, that I should know. For, should it turn out, that, after all, you mean to side with the overwhelming majority of men, and to contend that matter *is extended*, or *has extension* (two expressions denoting the same thing); then, the great dispute between us will be easily settled. Because, if you contend, that matter is extended, or has extension,—seeing that you make matter infinite, you must make matter's extension infinite. And the infinity of extension—of some kind or other, of matter for example—is all that Proposition 1 maintains.† The Proposition having been framed with the *express view* of being in unison with the tenets of all Atheists—of Atheists of every class; in order that the advantage of a *common* foundation might be obtained.‡ It is the business of certain succeeding portions (not, assuredly, of the very first Proposition) of the demonstration, in "The Argument," to prove the existence in the universe of *pure space, or expansion*;§ that is, space or expansion void.

---

* See passages quoted in Part 1 of my "Reply," par 5.
† "Fallacy" 1, par. 11.

* See "Examination" of Antitheos, Part 3, § 46, also § 29.
† See Part 1 of "Reply," par. 19, 20.
‡ See Part 2 of "Reply," note to § 10.
§ You are aware, that, after I have proved

of body or matter. Not void of everything—because filled with God.*

I have to beg that you will bestow attention on the affair brought before you in this letter. Give me to understand what it is you mean to say, and to *abide by*, as touching *matter*. Is matter extended, or un-extended? One of the two it must be. I want no arguing in your answer: I want simply a categorical answer, with a reference to the parallel passages above set down. This letter, as I have already informed you, is not by any means to be regarded as in answer to your Rejoinder: this letter being a mere prelude to my answer. I call upon you to afford me that explanation regarding your meaning, without which, as must be evident to all our readers, it is impossible to advance.

I shall not conclude this letter without stating, that should you, at any time, desire to put a question to me, an *explicit* answer from me would be immediately returned. Sould you, for instance, ask such a question as the following—and there are abundant materials for raising such a question in Battle 1, page 295, to refer to no other place: How do you, Mr. Gillespie, come to say, that Mr. Southwell denies, and yet that Mr. Southwell admits, the *first* Proposition in " The Argument ? My answer would instantly be: You, Mr. Southwell, in some places deny that Proposition *in words ;*† while, in other places, you virtually, or (as I may say) in deed, admit the truth, or, at least, what in reality implies the truth thereof.‡ There is, verily, a contradiction ; but the contradiction is Mr. Southwell's. All that I, Mr. Gillespie, did was *to point out* the contradiction.

I trust, that you will never find it necessary to ask what is the meaning of anything I may write. I remain, Sir,

Your obedient servant,
WILLIAM GILLESPIE.
Torbanehill, 11th September, 1844.

the existence of pure space, or expansion, I confine to *matter* the use of the name *extension :* for, Sir, *surely you read the Argument before you ventured an answer to it.* See " General Scholium" § 2.

* See " Examination," Part 8, § 5.
† See passages quoted in Part 1 of " Reply" par. 7.
‡ See passages quoted *Ibid.*, par. 22.

you during six weeks ; however, on enquiry, the Governor informs me that he has detained several of yours of late, as well as those of others, which no doubt accounts for me not receiving *one this last month*. Surely you have become outrageous lately ! Your blood is up. Have the dog-days affected you ? Be cautious, I beg of you, until I am liberated, that I may take the " Paper" out of your hands again.

In case of my demise, I bequeath to you the balance of an account due to the Governor, for books, paper, &c., purchased for me, £1 8s. The stock of books are yours and welcome. It is all I have to bequeath.

You know, and the *Herald* knows, my hobby for fashionable resorts, both, therefore, will be delighted to hear, that Perth is a *locale* for Scottish gentles, *retired* ones, I grant you, but that's in keeping ; this is so that it might be fulfilled which was spoken by " W. J. B.," " that although I suffered a political death with the poor, yet I made my bed with the rich." Strange coincidence with my great prototype ! ! Still more so should I re-appear on the first day of a week. Birds of a feather will flock together.

My days creep on with grave serenity ; no elbowing nor jostling my way through the bustling throng of society, but in the shade, out of harm's way, I contemplate the ignoble strife, glad to be out of the crowd. True, there is one day in the week, and one hour of that day, in which my gravity is effectually dispelled, one hour in which my cachinnatory muscles have fair play—one hour is allowed for the empire of tirade, verbiage, and ideal dulness—the hour when I hear the sermon. I am preserving you some choice specimens of inspired elocution, or logic run mad.

One letter came to hand from Miss Roalfe, another from W. Paterson, Edinburgh. Recollect I always acknowledge *all letters* I receive. Neither friends nor others can be admitted to see me. This is in answer to Paterson's query. T PATERSON.

IS THE BIBLE TRUE? *A Letter from the Bishop of Worcester, by Edward Walker.*—This is a very important question, put with becoming earnestness, and deserving, as we hope it will receive, a satisfactory reply from his Grace. It is not " the base of a right-angled triangle which is equal to the two sides," but the square of the base which is equal to the squares of the two sides containing the right angle. The hypothenuse is notoriously incommensurable by the sides of its triangle. Illustrations drawn from science (and indeed drawn from where you will) should be scrupulously correct, or a crafty opponent may take advantage of them to throw discredit on the whole argument. A man cannot be too cautious with a Bishop.

LETTER FROM MR. PATERSON.
General Prison, Perth,
Sep. 14, 1844.

DEAR H.—I take the pen in hand to break the monotony of a month—and to blow you up. On Aug. 17, I sent you a letter complaining of your unfrequency of communication, as I had received but one letter from

CONTROVERSIES.

(To the Editor of the New Moral World.)

[The following letter was addressed to the editor of the *New Moral World* by Mr. Southwell, in consequence of anonymous reflections on him in that paper. The editor having declined to insert it, is our reason for publishing—not the whole of it, that our space will not permit—but as much of it as enables Mr. Southwell to do himself justice. This is a duty, as "A very old Member" ought to know better than to write, and the editor of the *Rational Gazette* than to publish, *anonymous attacks.*—ED. of M.]

SIR,—I claim the right to relieve myself from the imputation cast upon me by that flippant person who prudently writes himself "A Very Old Member." You published his attack, and, of course, will be no less liberal as regards my defence.

Est ars etiam maladecendi (pray excuse this "show of learning,") there is an art in slandering; those who are ignorant of it do not so much defame their enemies as exhibit their willingness to defame them. My anonymous assailant's ill-natured remarks about "ill-natured controversies" prove him well fitted to play "first fiddle" among the rather disreputable class of self-damaging villifiers.

Far be it from me to say anything "offensive," but I must say that if A Very Old Member turn out to be some unprincipled renegade, some *sworn* preacher and teacher of infidel congregations, some once popular controversalist who, having fallen into the abyss of contempt, is anxious to drag me down after him, I shall not be at all surprised, for such persons usually ally folly with shrewdness; ostentatious charity with practical intolerance; high flown notions of respectability and decency with vulgarest baseness; "meanness that soars" with "pride that licks the dust."

"Beyond a doubt" to "the stranger's mind," A very old Member's childish cant about controversy will seem satisfactory evidence that he is in his dotage, or that pitiable state significantly denominated second childhood. It amounts to this—" I, a very old member, have no objection to controversies if they are conducted just as I think they ought to be conducted. When *I* think a controversy is not carried on for truth's sake, or dexterous arguments employed rather than forcible ones, *I* think it ought to be stopped. When *I* and you, dear Mr. Editor, open our mouths let no dog bark. Our journal finds its way into the hands of strangers, and what I ask would be the result if our opinions were called in question by such fellows as Southwell, and others, who are ever on the watch to pick up every straw of difference from whatever quarter it may float. Never let us allow these restless, dissatisfied, fault-finding fellows (who really desire nothing else than to show learning and puzzle the vulgar,) to press all languages under heaven into the service of open rebellion against our infallibility."

Good Mr. Editor! pray put an end then, by all means, to the nuisance of which I complain.

When the spirit of faction, said Swift, enters into a man it sweeps the house clean, my judgment may be unrighteous, but I cannot help judging that a spirit compounded of faction and cant has swept clean the earthly tabernacle of A Very Old Member.

Don't, for pity's sake, Mr. Editor, take the advice of A Very Old Member. Let me intreat you to have mercy upon those heterodox "nuisances," of whom I am the chief. In charity's name I conjure you to throw over us the broad strong shield of editorial protection. Despise and set at nought the wisper of discontended, because discomfited faction, whose anonymous defenders are always on the look out for "small reasons" why "a stop should be put" to every kind of controversy disagreeable to themselves.

If Socialists are only liberal to those who echo their opinions, and humour their prejudices, in what respect do they excel the most contemptible of sectaries? If they cannot tolerate the freest measure of controversy, in what consists their superiority to the most grovelling fanatics? Parties, like trees, are known by their fruits, and perish, say I, every party whose fruit is intolerance. A party whose principles are true, whose cause is just, and whose practice is honest, can gain much, but lose nothing, by controversy.

That "wordy strife," of which such vehement complaint is now made, was once the delight and glory of Socialists. Cervante's immortal hero never manifested greater eagerness to engage giants or other monstrosities than did A Very Old Member and other Socialist missionaries five years ago, to fight the parsons. At that time their appetite for controversy was quite equal to the famous Dragon of Wantley's. At that time bitter were the complaints made against Old World teachers, who refused to "come out." At that time even a third or forth-rate antagonist was welcomed as a regular God-send. At that time motives were not at all minutely scanned; nor did the lucky missionaries, into whose hands an antagonist fell, very particularly wish to know whether he intended to use forcible or merely dexterous arguments. All they cared to know was a succession of fair stand-up fights. Like the Irishman in a row, they were "any body's customer." The *New Moral World* was no less warlike in theory than were New

Moral Missionaries in practice. It columns were not "stained by such petulant matter" as A Very Old Member's, but week by week contained words of comfort and encouragement to those engaged in the "wordy strife." Its columns were not at the disposal of anonymous writers, who "stabbed in the dark" men whom they feared openly and fairly to meet.

Whenever worsted in argument these Pecksniffs and Joseph Surfaces' loudly complained of being abused. A Very Old Member has signalized himself in this pitiful kind of work. He rushed to to the rescue of othodox Mr. Walter, and did for that gentleman what any gentlemen would be ashamed to do for himself. Dear Sir, quoth he, you should step in and separate them, at the risk of having your own person covered with the dirt that one or both may be in the act of dealing out. But my advice is that you leave such dirty work to be done by "A Very Old Member," who, without doubt, would set about it *con amore*, and if not successful will deserve to succeed.

As to the charge of being abusive, I utterly and emphatically deny its truth. There is not an abusive sentence in the letter, A Very Old Member has thought proper to condemn. I presume that it contains nothing you deemed unfit for publication in the "journal of the Rational Society."

I cannot persuade myself to conclude without expressing a hope that you, Mr. but Editor, will put a stop not to controversy *cant*. Though dubious as regards the truth of Sterne's opinion that of all the cants in this canting world, the cant of criticism is the worst; assuredly nothing disgusts me so much as the "decency" "charitable," "without-any-desire-to-offend" "cant of lady and gentlemen Reformers," who call *abuse* all language which wounds their vanity without swelling their gains.

CHARLES SOUTHWELL.
London, Sept. 16, 1844.

THE WEITLING WELCOME.—Mr. Weitling's speech, was the speech of the evening. The manly address of Schapper, and the shrewd eloquence of Chillman were specially admired. Upon Weitling's nervous address, and happy, fervid conceptions, we need not now descant, as a critique on his writings and views generally, translated expressly for us, from an able foreign contemporary, will put our readers in possession, next week, of interesting facts on this subject. The news of the John-street Meeting, by friends and spies, was the next morning posted to every part of Europe. To English Socialists it will, if the intentions of the few who originated the meeting be carried out, be productive of great and beneficial consequences. Not only will the interchange of valuable ideas, hitherto finding no vent, necessarily work important changes, but the refined ardour of our German friend will infuse a spirit of poetry over the hitherto dull and tame character of English Communism.

THE DEMOCRATIC BANQUET.—The Dinner at Highbury Barn, on September 23, was well attended. As many sat down to dine as could be conveniently accommodated. Such an assembly of parties so politically and socially distinct, perhaps has not met for years, and with such an object never here. That night promises to be an epoch in political progress. The elements of fraternization were gathered together, and crude as was its first developement, it will spread itself and revivify the atmosphere of party strife. Before the assembly separated the following resolution, suggested by M. Chillman, was proposed by Mr. Hetherington, at the request of Mr. Holyoake, Mr. Hetherington having first approved it, and passed :—

"That this meeting resolve, that each of the Democratic sections taking part in, or approving of, the present meeting, be requested to appoint one individual to form a Committee for promoting the principle of National Fraternization."

It was then agreed, "That the Chairman, P. M. M'Douall, be requested to present the resolution to each of the sections." What steps follow we shall be prompt to announce, and as early as possible present some practical observations on the great principle of National Fraternization.

KOHL ON BIBLES.—The remarks of this shrewd foreigner on England and the English are sometimes not only pleasingly instructive, but amusingly quaint. The *Examiner*, no less quaint, thus quotes and comments on him: "His occasional comparisons of us with his experiences of other countries have the most interest, and often not a small share of significance. The first fact of the sort is perhaps worth naming. In the great show houses, the Warwick Castles, the Trenthams, and so forth, he observed a bible and prayer book in every bed-room. Yet he was not moved by envy. 'With us there is seldom more than one Bible in a house,' says this contented German. He does not think us likely to be better for our greater pretences, he does not moralize our condition in the least, but it strikes him ' there must be an immense consumption in the country for this class of books!'"

CHURCH CONSECRATION FEES. — The number of consecrations during 1840—43, according to recent parliamentary returns, are 432, and the fees £9,533 : 6 : 11d.—*Wesleyan Chronicle*.

DEVIL CHEATED.—The devil is a very extraordinary fellow. Scarcely a thing is done wrong but this unfortunate being has to bear all the shame.

Squire Slick made a fortune in a country village by selling liquor, consequently he ruined some of his neighbours. After making a fortune, and during a temperance revival, he came to the conclusion not to sell any more liquor, and abandoned the practice altogether, and became an ardent and warm supporter of temperance. One day a sort of a vagabond, who had not yet left off the habits of drinking, accosted the "squire" and wanted to know why he had given up selling liquor.

"Why it was wrong," said the squire.

"Wrong, ha;" was the reply, "but who set you to doing this wrong?"

"The devil, I suppose."

"The devil, indeed—was he your partner, theh?"

"He was in selling liquor."

"Well, look here, squire, I've just seen him, and he wants you to send him *his share of the profits.*"

The squire marvelled very quick, and the devil was cheated out of his share of the gains.—*The Illinois Wasp.*

IMPROVEMENT CLASS, *North London Schools, No.* 8, *George-street.*—Mr. Holyoake has been induced to commence his Select Class for the improvment of persons of both sexes in *Grammar, Composition, Logic,* and *Oral Investigation.* At the Theological Institute and the Rotunda, where it previously was held, the best results followed. The design of the class is, to give a higher tone to instruction than is now common, and to revive the ancient spirit of the Academies. Every species of knowledge in the power of the teacher to communicate is, in the course of instruction, imparted, and each pupil is fitted for active life and public usefulness. Many members are not so much desired as earnest members. Terms, 5s. per Quarter, or 6d. per Week, if paid weekly. The Class meets every Thursday Evening at half-past Eight.

Subjects for Thursday evening, Oct. 3, Critique of Exercises; Questions Answered; Model Sentences of pronouns; Syntax's First Rule; Value of Habit and Purpose Illustrated; Summary of Discussions of previous night.

NOTICES.

A PRIORI ATHEISM—Mr. Gillespie's "Argument, a priori, for the Being and Attributes of a Great First Cause," Atheised by Charles Southwell, will appear in No. 10 of the *Library of Reason.* It has been found impossible to find space for it in the *Movement's* pages. Ample justice can now be done to this unique production.

HUMAN PHYSIOLOGY.—On Tuesday Evening, October 8, Dr. Epps has kindly consented to deliver the Introductory Lecture of the Anatomical Class, at Branch A 1.

TRACT SOCIETY.—The Annual Ball for the benefit of this Society, will take place on October 21, at Branch A 1.

NEXT week we shall present a list of places where the *Movement* lies for reading.

MONTHLY PARTS of the *Movement.*—The *Movements* of every month can be had in neat WRAPPERS. Arrangements are being made to answer such correspondents, whose queries lead to lengthened replies of interest, on the *monthly wrappers.*

Preparing for Press.—An Inquiry into the value of Christian Missions, by Emma Martin.

LECTURES.

[*From the lists of Lectures and Discussions furnished us, our rule is to select those which pertain to the general objects of our paper. Our aim is to present a weekly synopsis of the public agitation relative to the general principles we advocate.*]

October 2.—Hall of Science, Manchester—Mr. R. Cooper on the "Consistency of the Bible."

October 3.—Hall of Science—Mrs Martin.

October 6.—Hall of Science—(Afternoon and Evening,) Mrs. Martin.

October 6.—Hall of Science, City-road—Mr. Southwell.

October 6.—Branch A 1—Mr. Ellis.

October 6.—Finsbury Institution, Goswell-road—Mr. Simpkins on the "Formation of Character."

DISCUSSIONS.

October 4.—Branch A 1.

October 5.—Social Institution, Whitechapel.

October 6.—Finsbury Institution, Goswell-road—subject, "Is Man responsible to God for his opinions and actions?"

TO CORRESPONDENTS.

RECEIVED.—G. Begg. H. Uttley. H. R. on "Atheism and Free Agency." The work commented upon is hardly worth such distinction. M. Jenneson. "A Friend to the *Movement*," confounds grammar with metaphysics. A name may be taken grammatically but not metaphysically—because grammatically it is a word of so many letters—metaphysically an idea. The *Glasgow Examiner.*—D. P.—The Kalley correspondence has "terminated" for no longer a period than that necessary for the transmission of letters to and from Madeira.

T. A.—Mr. William Goddard, of Southampton, has been elected Secretary to Branch A 1. Mr. Truelove retires in consequence of a call to Harmony.

Will Correspondents please to remember that reports of proceedings, interesting to us, should be forwarded the earliest moment after their occurrence.

W. J. B., for *Movement* £0 10 0

ERRATUM.—The subscription of "5s. from Mr. Watts, of Islington," should have been placed to the "Paterson Testimonial".

Paterson Testimonial.

W. B. B., Second Subscription .. £0 10 0

ANTI-PERSECUTION UNION.—Any person who may perchance, owing to some unforeseen mishap, not find his remittance acknowledged within a fortnight of forwarding it will much oblige the Secretary by writing respecting it. The more promptly an omission is enquired after the greater the facility of rectifying it. G. J. H., *Sec.*

Printed and Published by G. J. HOLYOAKE,
40, Holywell-street, Strand,
Wednesday, October 2, 1844.

THE MOVEMENT
And Anti=Persecution Gazette.

"Maximize morals, minimize religion."—BENTHAM.

No. 44.   EDITED BY G. JACOB HOLYOAKE, ASSISTED BY M. Q. RYALL.   PRICE 1½d.

CONTINENTAL COMMUNISM, AND ITS REPORTERS.

A VARIETY of concurrent circumstances contribute to render the subject of Continental Communism one of deep interest to all men of progress. The advance of social science, its identity with, or the variations it exhibits from, the same class of opinions prevailing in our own country — the fierce prosecutions of its adherents—the immense spread of socialistic sentiments—the tendency of political and other democratic reforms towards societarian changes—the gathering together of extreme reformers of all nations in our metropolis, and the presence of Weitling among us, afford peculiar inducements to a more intimate acquaintance with the views and condition of our brethren abroad—foreign they might be called, but that they can hardly be said to be such, in any thing but language. Nationality and dialect are but slight tokens of approximation and identity, compared with similarity of sentiment on the subject of political, social, and moral science.

The resolution passed at the recent great public meeting of revolutionary reformers, recommending the formation of a conference or committee of the different sections is calculated also to give the cause of extreme progression an impulse which more than ever necessitates, on the part of all, reciprocal knowledge. What appears to be a candid and able exposition of "Communism in Germany," just published in that country, and reviewed by the Paris Journal, La Presse, will help many to a better acquaintance with the things thought, and said, and done on the subject than they have hitherto had.

The author of the work "Communism in Germany" (Der Communism in Deutschland;—Carlsruhe; 1844,) is represented by the critic of La Presse as a man of progress, one who appears to have been intimately concerned with the leading political and social movements of magnitude in Europe; and to have derived his information partly from the official documents connected with the Zurich prosecutions, partly from some communistic documents which were saved from seizure, and partly from his personal knowledge. The French reviewer is a mere politician, or rather political partizan of the Molé ministry; and although he has acquitted himself with decent propriety, as one representing opponents' sentiments it would be too much to expect that he should enter into their opinions and ideas. His representations, when correct and untinged with partizanship, serve the cause of communism—due allowances being made for his colouring.

From all this it would be inferred that the comments of La Presse, which seem to enter very fully, and generally pretty accurately, into the matter, and in which a sort of analysis or resumé is given of the contents, would be presented to the reading world for the first time; but it is a singular fact that not only the substance of the critique in the Paris newspaper, but the bulk of the article verbatim et literatim is taken—of course with the substitution of French for English words—from an English newspaper published nearly a year back, and about the period of the Swiss prosecutions. Whether there are those of the genus penny-a-liner among the French newspaper scribes, or that the conductors of the Paris journal knowingly give as new an article which had first appeared in the London Times and subsequently in the New Moral World; certain it is that the whole narrative connected with Weitling, his doctrine, imprisonment, position, numbers and influence of his co-labourers and followers are given with the same circumstantiality, the same amount of correctness, and the same mistakes. We may take it for granted, perhaps, that the readers of the Presse would not be very much more enlightened than its conductors about the staleness of its intelligence, therefore it may all go down as new gospel.

This is not all, however, in connection with this nine months' birth of the Socialist intelligence; certain mistakes were pointed out a fortnight after its appearance in the English newspapers, by a correspondent of the New Moral World. If the editor of the Presse is equally active in his "foreign correspondence," we may expect to see Mr. Engel's corrections transferred to the French columns in about nine months more.

Next we have the critic criticised—his accuracy having been called in question just as unceremoneously as he had previously done that of the *Times'* correspondent.

The *Communist Chronicle* next makes its appearance with a *resumé* compiled from official Swiss documents and Socialist publications. Fresh and more detailed matter is here introduced, about the order of proceedings and the works belonging to the various communist societies. Last comes the little tract published by *Watson*, containing a reprint of the account of the highly interesting meeting, to welcome Weitling, at John-street, and an introductory " Memoir of Wilhelm Weitling." It is very opportunely brought out, and from the intrinsically interesting and important nature of the assemblage, whose proceedings it records, cannot fail to attain, as it merits, extensive circulation.

Now for the historical features of these accounts. Every *New Moral World* reader knows how its informant tell foul of the *Times'* correspondent ; he " hardly knew where to begin in exposing the blunders" of a sentence where the Hambach and Steinhölzli meetings were mentioned. The *Times* seems to mention them together, though some hundred miles apart—one being a village in Bavaria, the other a place of resort, like Highbury-barn, Islington—and our Social informant named them as though but *one* meeting had taken place in each locality.

Nothing, however, beats friend Barmby's capital notions about Hambach and Steinhölzli, of which he innocently says, " but Hambach and Steinhölzli, *two persons of a progressive tendency!"* as though one should speak of Blair Athol and Rosherville Gardens as two of the right sort of fellows, walking into the Goat and Compasses—making a couple of their best speeches, and being enthusiastically received by their devoted adherents.

Not content with this ludicrous *propaganda* (a smartish lady the other day gave a new reading—*proper gander*), the blunder has been pertinaciously adhered to in the little tract " Young Germany," with the account of the meeting. Several minor errors are also retained, which should another edition be struck off, I should be happy to point out.

We may learn something, after all, from all this :—the difficulty of obtaining trustworthy information — the great care that should be taken by public writers in disseminating it—and the scrutiny with which it should be examined by readers.

M. Q. R.

QUESTIONS FOR CHRISTIANS TO ANSWER.

Allowing that there exists in the community a certain number of honest Infidels, who believe that all errors, and Christianity of course, are injurious to the well-being of society, what ought these Infidels to do? We put this question to honest and intelligent Christians. The usual answer to this question is no more nor less than an evasive one. They tell us, for instance, that the honest Infidel will make a re-examination of the proofs of Christianity; and that he ought to do this before he undertakes to make proselytes to his own unbelief. Well, allowing that he has made this re-examination, and doubted and repeated this re-examination many times, what then ought he to do ? Again we should hear an evasive answer of this sort:—Are there not some excellent authors on the evidences that have been overlooked by you? Have you perused the whole works of Dr. Lardner, of Dr. Adam Clark, of Bishop Butler, and many others? Or, if you have, which is very doubtful, read all the standard works of this description in the English language, have you read any of the still greater works on the Evidences of Natural and Revealed Religion, which have been written in the German Language? If not, you have a task and a duty to perform, which, if you are sincerely desirous of knowing the truth, you will not neglect.

By such replies, these cunning theologians get an Infidel completely cornered; as there is no man, however learned he may be, who has or could have read the whole of these works. Ask these Christians when you may reasonably stop your reading and investigation, and rest satisfied, if you are still an unbeliever, that you have read as much as the cause of truth requires ? Their answer is still evasive. They would still keep you reading the evidences in one everlasting circle, so that if you had read them twelve hours a day, for fifty years, so numerous are the works on this subject, there would still be left unread some one which they would consider important to be read, before you could reasonably rest satisfied with your unbelief. Such answers, therefore, being evasive in their nature, are not such as we demand to our question— What ought the Infidel to do? There are limits to the amount of reading and investigation on the subject of the truth of Christianity, which ought to satisfy any sound and intelligent mind, before they have extended through a whole Encyclopedia of Divinity and Philology. Some minds of strong metaphysical powers are often confirmed in their Infidelity by the simple perusal of the Bible, without looking into the books which have been written to prove it or to disprove it. Will any men presume to say that an individual cannot be honest in his Infidelity, who has arrived at such a conclusion by an examination of the Bible alone, with his unaided, and, of course, untrammelled reason. We think not many.

Granting, then, that there are Infidels, who having made as thorough an investigation of Christianity as they believe to be necessary, are satisfied and confirmed in their unbelief, we ask again—What ought they to do? Shall they be honest and sincere, or dishonest and hypocritical? Most Christians would be willing to give a general answer to this question in favour of honesty and sincerity. But an Infidel who is honest and sincere will openly avow his opinions, and inasmuch as he believes error to be injurious to society, he will endeavour to proselyte others to his unbelief. The same Christians, however, who acknowledge in general terms that an Infidel ought to be honest and sincere, will condemn the very actions which are the fruits of honesty and sincerity; and the community will prosecute him for the same.—Again, therefore, we put our question to Christians, and we politely ask our brethren of the press who are believers in Christianity, to favour us with a full and direct answer to our question—*What ought the Infidel to do in relation to his opinions on the subject of religion?*—*Boston Investigator.*

NAPOLEON BUONAPARTE.

"THE glory of a nation is its intelligence. Look at Buonaparte. He was a man of giant intellect, who seemed to gain knowledge without those steps which are requisite in most men. But where has lived a greater foe to freedom? [!!] Nothwithstanding all his fair promises, and his professions of devotion to man, he directed all his power to aggrandize himself, and secure dominion over the earth. His lonely situation on St. Helena; his mighty mind curbed and humbled, and his noble frame wasting away under the confinement to which he was subjected, were peculiarly calculated to excite the sympathy of the humane; but justice will silence compassion's voice, and ask whether one had not better suffer justly, than millions unjustly?" —[O. A. Skinner.—*The Symbol.*]

Poor Bona! Has it come to this? that a free-born Yankee, a liberalized Universalist preacher, should denounce thee as "a great foe to freedom." Buonaparte destroyed one of the greatest obstacles in the path of human progress that history ever recorded. The same obstacle still exists in England, and opposes Briton, Irish and Scot, in their warmest wishes for elevation and political liberty. It was the corrupt and vapid old aristocracy of France that stood in the way of reform. This aristocracy was the support of the throne, and when it fell, the throne went with it. All the privileges which the masses should be left free to combat and strive for, were monopolized by this aristocracy. They went down in the Revolution; the stalks were cut off, bound up and " cast into the fire!" But the root and seed were still there, deeply imbedded in the institutions of France. Buonaparte came forward, and ran his sub-soil plough of reform through the nation; he found that the soil would produce an aristocracy, and he made it one of talent—one of genuine merit. And thus, almost the last vestige of the lifeless aristocracy of Louis XVI. was eradicated. The new seed was frightfully prolific, certainly; but with all its weight of sin, taxes, and blood and glory, it has passed, and has left France in a situation to lead in the work of political reform, the latest republic of the nineteenth century. Where are the ancestral dignities of the present French aristocracy? In bakers', butchers', tailors', and painters' shops. " Where has lived a greater foe to freedom?" asks Mr. Skinner! The old, rotten rubbish of a thousand years' increase was removed by the mighty genius of one man; the restrictive and tyrannical governments of Europe modified, and the most revolting laws eradicated from the statute books of Europe by this man, and still he is called a foe to freedom!

But,—but,—*but!* Mr. Skinner, Bona's mind was never *humbled*, if you please, and as to his " noble frame's wasting away," as you assert, the report of the physicians, after a *post mortem* examination of his body, informs us that he died of dyspepsia and of— FAT!!—*Montgarnier.*

MILAN—ITS RELIGION & POLICE.

[The following communication is from a friend, a short time since sojourning in Italy. He was requested to furnish a few traits of Italian life and institutions, and this is his first report. His being a foreigner will acccount for the peculiarities of style.]

Milan, Aug. 10, 1844.

DEAR H.—When we parted we agreed to write to one another. I trust that my silence has not misled you to suspect me of having the intention to apply the proverb, "out of sight, out of mind." You would in this case have done me the more wrong, as almost every thing here conspires to make my stay in Italy unsupportable, and to make me strongly regret London. I should have written to you ere now, had it not been for the hope that some more experience of Italian life might temper the first disagreeable and discouraging impressions it made on me. I am almost totally deprived of every rational mental supply, and my mind threatens to die away of inanition. It is true, like certain animals who, during hibernation, feed on their own substance, so do I ruminate on those mental stores which I brought over with me from London, and of which, indeed, many were not digested. But at last their nutritive principle is consumed.

You know the institutions I frequented in London, the lectures I heard, the rational friends with whom I often associated. With the exception of a dear German friend of my age here is nothing of that kind, and, indeed, had 1 not been able to baffle the watchfulness of the custom-house officers in getting my small rational library through, I should almost be in a state of mental starvation. Add to all that, the entire independance I enjoyed in London when out of the office, and the liberty of communicating my thoughts. But here an arbitrary police is informed, so to speak, of every word you utter. You understand my regrets.

To them who are not deceived by an outward shining, but penetrate into the interior of the object under consideration, Milanese, and I venture to say, all Italian life presents a gloomy, gloomy aspect. When I consider the state of things here, I might despair of every possible progress; and unsurmountable barries seem to me to rise up against the introduction of any of those great philanthropical schemes for the reform of society, which emerge now, however imperfect yet, out of the more advanced nations. That the impulse should come from within Italy herself, is still less possible. Like those swarms of locusts, who in certain climes lay waste whole tracts of well cultivated land, so do priests and soldiers here destroy all mental vegetation. The soil is good—the Italian is happily gifted by nature; he perceives quickly, he feels warmly, and the best results might be expected if those qualities were given the right direction. But by the subjugation under which he sighs, and by the miserable education he receives, his sagacity becomes cunningness and deceit; his warm heart the focus of passion.

Priests and soldiers are active in finding out and rooting up the seeds of which emancipation might spring forth. All are beset by innumerable spies, who insinuate themselves everywhere. The confessional and the prostitute are alike in the hire of government; the former for worming out servants about their masters, and the company these keep; the latter for reporting the "propos," when having been in some "orgie," where, perhaps, under the influence of the intoxicating liquors, some one might reveal some conspiracy. Your shoemaker, your tailor, your servant, your own friend—if you have not good reasons for doubting it—may be bribed; and it is this mistrust which every one has in the other which is perhaps the safest preventive for government of any secret design against them, more so than the 7,000 or 8,000 soldiers we have here.

"Grahaming" letters (I know the expression from the *Gazette d' Augsburgh*) has for long been a common practice here, and will probably continue to be so. How careful people must become of what they write, since the infamous practices of the English government, with regard to the post-secretness, have been known, and at which I particularly was astonished. I remember, however, that you once mentioned a suspicion of your government doing so, which I then could not share, but which I find now but too clearly justified. It is not without the most disagreeable sensation that I confide now my letters to the post. I would relate many facts concerning Italy did I not know that you are to well *au fait* of the doings of governments, not to think them capable of anything that suits their purpose. Some time ago a student of the academy of painting of this town came in for a passport in order to go to Switzerland, where he intended to continue his studies under his brother, who was then painting *al fresco* in one of the Seigneurial Villas of the Lake Major. After having been inquisited in all ways about his motives for going there, whether he belonged to any political body, what society he frequented in Milan, &c., &c., all which he answered in a manner which could not in the least commit him, even had he been implicated in some such affair, (which he was not), he was told to call again in a few days, which he did, quite confident to obtain his passport. But how great was his astonishment and disappointment when it was refused to him. He naturally inquired on what grounds, and here is the answer he received, *"Know, sir that the police of Milan never give their reasons for what they do."* This is Austrian discipline. I abstain from all further reflection on it in this letter. One fact more, and then I shall not weary you much longer by the enumeration of provoking truths; this one illustrates the power of the priests.

Last year a person here entered into an agreement with one of the silk spinners of the environs for spinning silks for him. After a few days' regular work, all the women employed (silk is almost exclusively spun by women in this kingdom) staid out, and could not be caused to work again, however great their loss and that of their employers was— and why? Were they ill-treated or ill-paid? No; they were perhaps better treated than they would have been in any other spinnery, and their wages were those which it then was usual to pay everywhere. They staid out because their employers were Protestants, because their priest had awed into fear the credulous women by telling them they would run alive into the devil's arms if they went on working for those heretics! Whether this has been the effect of a manœuvre of some other competing spinner who was in an understanding with the priest or that of real fanaticism, I am unable to decide. Enough it was done in the name and through the influence of religion, though good Christians may say that it was from the want of religion. The English rationalists are in the error when they fancy that John Bull is more humbugged than any other nation by their clergy. If they could view the religious practices of this place, where, besides extra ceremonies than those which the Catholic church in general prescribes, the Ambrosian rites being fashionable here, they are performed; they would think the English on the climax of rationalism.

(*To be continued.*)

MEN OF BUSINESS.

PERSONS in the country have a prodigious opinion of London men of business, but it may be useful to remark, that belonging to London does not necessarily constitute a man of business. Some time ago, the *New Moral World* essayed to bring discussion into contempt, and to prohibit the agitation of Atheism on the ground that such pursuits were not " business-like" in Social branches. That despotism in disguise — the paternal form of government—came recommended in the name of "business." Among the Socialists, if a man put pertinent objections to some finality scheme of capital, or ask some awkward question respecting adherence to principle, he is put down on the ground of inexperience and want of business habits, until the really useful sentiment of business has degenerated almost into a cant.

During the last two years, a class of persons have sprung up in the Social branches who listen to no argument adverse to their views, who regard as so much rashness any enthusiasm they happen not to understand, and who treat with a respectable kind of contempt those who find it necessary to depart from their somewhat supercilious dicta,—these are " men of business."

When the Atheistical agitation was being pursued with just intent and singleness of purpose, Mr. Owen waved his hand in deprecation; Mr. Galpin talked cautions in his own solemn and inimitable way; and the Central Board wrapped themselves up in orthodox propriety, the better to frown at such unbusiness-like propensity, until even, in self protection, it has become necessary, now and then, to take a passing glance at those pieces of propriety — those orderly, methodical, judicious model machines, known to fame as Social " men of business."

There are two halls in London of more than common pretension—the National Association and the John-street Halls. These places are so wisely constructed that the persons who lecture have to force their way to the rostrum through all the people who may be assembled, and on the occasion of holding a public meeting, when many speakers are required, some of them never find their way there—and if they succeed, when all is over, the felicity is theirs of forcing their way back again under the same favourable circumstances. At the latter place the lady or gentleman who has lectured has, upon arriving at the door, to encounter, in the cold blast rushing in from the street, a stream of persons descending from the gallery—and up three pair of stairs thus thronged with people, against a hundred toes and knees in impatient agitation, the ascendants must stsuggle—for the committee room, by the happiest combination of forethought and convenience, is placed at the top of the building. The reader need not be told that that this felicitous arrangement was the work of " men of business."

No Ranter in the three kingdoms who who ever had a barn repaired for holding forth in, nor poor Chartist who ever fitted up a room for lectures, but knows that double his calculated sum will be required for the purpose; but when this latter hall was erected in the neighbourhood of Fitzroy-square, the managers fixed a sum of £1000 less than their requirements, and when the building was to be finished, an appeal and mortgages had to be made for £1,200 or £1,300 more, and a debt incurred not yet liquidated. Need it be added, that the " primest minds" were the persons who superintended this affair. In Manchester or Liverpool we expect these errors, the people in those districts being " inexperienced," but in Branch A1. the world looked for better things.

The branches are the strongholds of Communism: they are moral castles spread over the country to defend humanity against the attacks of error and bigotry. Two or three years ago the branch halls began to be invested in the hand of Congress, Birmingham setting the example—and soon Socialism, like Methodism, would have covered the land and deeply seated itself in the hearts and interests of the people. Who nipped this wide propagandism in the bud, and systematically and on principle dissevered the branches?—the " men of business " of the old board.

In the year 1841 Mr. Owen selected no less notorious a place than the Egyptian

Hall, Piccadilly, in which to proclaim that—" Hitherto the public have acquired but little correct knowledge of the system which I advocate; indeed the subject has been so misconceived and misrepresented both by friends and opponents, that I should myself have much difficulty in recognising it under the distorted forms in which it has been made to appear." These were his exact words, and, *if true*, are an imputation on his own capacity to explain, and that of his friends to comprehend what he would be at. Who published to the world this wholesale proclamation of the inability of the Founder of the Rational Society and the stupidity of his followers?—the "men of business" of the Home Colonization Society! and they did this at great expense, and in all publicity, in Reports of Mr. Owen's lectures. If Mr. Owen's vain remark was false—to publish it was the sheerest folly, as it misled the public and made us contemptible. If true— that Home Colonization Society and the whole Social body ought to have shut up their halls and offices, stopped their *New Moral World*, and Mr. Fleming, Lloyd Jones, Mr. Galpin, and Mr. Cuddon, with the Central Board, ought to have joined hands, thrown their satchels over their shoulders, and, like other children, quietly walked to school again.

Later than this, in 1843, the President of the Rational Society publicly addressed a letter to no less a personage than DANIEL O'CONNELL, LIBERATOR OF IRELAND—in which he thus described himself and those whom he officially represented:— "I am the President of the Rational Society—a *poor, despised*, calumniated, persecuted body of men." Did such a pitiable description ever before appear? Why, it would be a libel on a body of Norwegian rats! To be "*despised*" is to be *contemptible*. To be hated, or calumniated, or persecuted, no man can help, but if he is brave and earnest he will take care *not* to be "despised." Who did this spicy recommendation of the Rationalists, at which I never look without blushing?—need I add—a "man of business."

Of vast importance is the accession of capital—this has always been acknowledged; but capital requires to be satisfied by bonds and agreements of repayal—this is natural, and everybody knows it. Yet the largest sum ever lent to the Queenwood experiment was found by the present general secretary, Mr. Simpson, entered only in pencil. A mere pencil memorandum that £10,000 were lent by Mr. so and so, being deemed quite sufficient—it is almost idle to add that this was the work of "men of business." None but the "primest minds" are privileged to talk so much and to do so little.

I do not underrate the sentiment of business, but only point out its inconsistencies, that it may learn modesty. It is not belonging to London, or this or that place, but in sagacity that its best feature lies. It is of unquestioned importance that the working classes should acquire business habits, but such habits should pertain to the true sentiment of business, which uses up the intellect around it, not imposes on it—which is unpretending, incessant, generous, prompt, sober-sighted, and sedate.

Out of many cases fitted to bear company with those already cited, only one more can be given, but that one is both recent and rich. At the *Weitling Welcome* I went into the John-street committee-room and presented the card of the reporter of the *Movement* for a free admission, expecting from people who talk of the desirability of public opinion being on their side, and to whom publicity of their views is everything, that it would be instantly honoured. But the secretary looked at the president, and the president looked at the secretary—"What's the matter?" I asked, "the reporter from the *Movement* has the same right of admission here as the reporter of the *Times*." "Must we pay for his tea?" said the president. I felt half choked at the indignity offered and the parsimony displayed. I am far from thinking that this was other than an accidental exhibition arising from want of thought and knowledge of the value of the public press. The admission *was* made out, but of course declined. Here were "men of business," estimating the labours of a gentleman in a profession requiring considerable talent, during five or six mortal hours in a crowded room, besides the occupancy of the same time the next day transcribing notes—at *sevenpence!*—the sum they pay per head for tea. Any of the usual members of the press would, on such an intimation, at once have retired with disgust. Here was a risking of the chance of that important meeting not being known for the sake of *sevenpence*. No Chartist, despised as he may be for want of tact, would exhibit such suicidal economy.

I mention this incident with pain, but it ought to be related, I am assured by long experience, to prevent the recurrence of such cases. It was one of those things which have often turned ardour cold, and given good but weak friends lasting disgust. Upon us it had no such effect—we have been used to them so often, and I and M. Q. R. quietly went down and reported ourselves—(no pleasant thing, by the way to have to make speeches and act as reporters),—and when we found that Mr. Fleming was disposed to give a good report in the *New Moral World*, we supplied him with such transcripts of our notes and remarks as he desired.

Bronterre O'Brien tells us that in the West Indies the name of liberal is a nickname for a screw. The tide of public feeling has flown to Toryism only because it recognises the value of a real service with more promptitude than Whig or Radical bodies. Let us hope that Communism will preserve or obtain a fair reputation for the exercise of as wise a spirit.

The little incident last mentioned is one of those against which the heads of branches should warily guard. Private expostulation should have been used by me, in this case, but the error is so widely spread as to need public reproof. I could name many once distinguished friends of Socialism, in every town in the kingdom, who have grown cool through similar trifles. It is weakness thus to desert a just cause—but all men are not able to bear up against contumelies. What a true friend sees wrong he will endeavour to amend, and will still do all in his power to advance his chosen cause—just the same, whether praised, or slighted, or censured for his pains.   G. J. H.

ATHEISTIC DEMONSTRATION IN GLASGOW.

On Tuesday evening the 24th of September, a supper was held in the Crow Tavern, George's-square, Glasgow, in honour of the principles of Atheism. The meeting was not in any way made public, the committee intending it as a sort of experiment of the practicability of commencing regular anniversaries in favour of the non-belief of a deity or deities. Had it been announced in the Social Institution or otherwise noised abroad, many times the number would no doubt have attended; but as it was, all the tickets issued were disposed of, and between forty and fifty gentlemen sat down at table. Mr. Jeffery, social missionary, occupied the chair, and Mr. Simpson acted as croupier. After the removal of the cloth and an address from the chairman, the following toasts were proposed, in neat and appropriate speeches, by the gentlemen whose names are annexed.

Mr. Bruce—The progress of Atheism.
Mr. Granger—The memory of Shelley.
Mr. Ferguson—The memory of David Hume.
Mr. M'Donald—Epicurus and the Atheists of antiquity.
Mr. Jeffery—Robert Owen, the world's philanthropist, and success to his mission in America.
Mr. Ferguson—The memory of the late respected "Antitheos" of Glasgow.
Mr. Bruce—Robert Dale Owen the amiable and talented opponent of Origen Bachelor.
Mr. M'Haffie—Miss Frances Wright, and all female advocates of civil and religious liberty.
Mr. Ruddoch—"The Man Paterson" and all sufferers for the cause of freedom of expression.

The above toasts were heartily responded to by all present. The company was very enthusiastic, and before separating, expressed a determination of meeting again another year, when means will be taken to make the demonstration public, and to secure a large attendance of the Atheists of Glasgow. Perhaps the above meeting being decidedly and unequivocally Atheistic, is unparalleled in the past history of hitherto pious Scotland. These are signs of the times. Priests! take note of them and learn a significant lesson!   H. J.

CONTINENTAL PROGRESS.

In Paris, on my way home, I visited a Communist Club of the mystic school. I was introduced by a Russian who speaks French and German perfectly, and who very cleverly opposed Feinbach's* reasoning to them. They mean just as much by the term God as the Ham Common folks by *Love-Spirit*. They however declared this a secondary question, and to all practical intents agreed with us, and said " *enfin, l'atheisme c'est votre religion :*"—In the end Atheism is your religion. Religion, in French, means *conviction, feeling*, not worship. They affirmed, that the noise and hubbub of the *Bourgeois*, or middle class, against England, is all nonsense; and they were very anxious to convince us that they had not the slightest national prejudice, that the working men of France care nothing about Morocco, but know that the *ouvriers* (workers) of all countries are allies, having the same interests. The French middle class are quite as egotistical, as avaricious, and quite as insupportable in society as the English, but the French *ouvriers* are fine fellows. We have much progress among the Russians at Paris. There are three or four noblemen and proprietors of serfs now at Paris who are radical Communists and Atheists. We have in Paris a German Communist paper, the *Vorwärts*, published twice a week. In Belgium there is an active Communist agitation going on, and a paper, the *Débat Social*, published at Brussels. In Paris there are about half a dozen Communist papers. *Socialiste, Socialitaire*, are very fashionable names in France ; and Louis Philippe, the

---

* The resolution of the God-idea into *man*.

arch-*bourgeois*, supports the "*Democracie Pacifique*" with money and protection. The religious exterior of the French Socialists is mostly hypocritical; the people are thoroughly irreligious, and the first victims of the next revolution will be the parsons. The Cologne folks have made enormous progress. When we assembled in a public house we filled a good room with our company, mostly lawyers, medical men, artists, &c.. also three or four lieutenants in the artillery, one of whom is a very clever fellow. In Dusseldorf we have a few men, amongst them a very talented poet. In Elberfeld, about half a dozen of my friends and some others are Communists. In fact there is scarcely a town in Northern Germany where we have not some radical Anti-Proprietarians and Atheists. Edgar Bauer, of Berlin, has just been sentenced to three years imprisonment for his last book.—*Correspondent of the New Moral World.*

COMING ROUND.—The *Glasgow Examiner* in a recent review of a "Short System of Theology," on that part (page 30 of the work) where the author states that "the existence of God may be proved," says, "We should prefer the word *assumed* instead of 'proved,' as the existence of God is a primary self-evident fact, which admits *not of proof*, though his perfections do."

A CHRISTIAN'S ESTIMATE OF HUMAN NATURE.—The paper just referred to in the same review furnishes an example of the degrading idea entertained by the religious respecting mankind. Alexander Smith Paterson, the author of the "Concise System of Theology," defines belief—"To assent or to give credit to truth upon the authority of another." No, says the reviewer, "this is a most unfortunate definition; a man more readily believes a *lie* than the truth, and more readily on his own authority than that of another." With regard to the assertion that "men more readily believe lies than the truth," it is only fair to enquire whether the *Glasgow Examiner* speaks from its own experience or authority, or on that of others. If, indeed, it be true that "men do more readily believe lies than truth," then are we enabled by a new and truly religious hypothesis to account for the general prevalence of belief in the Christian religion.

WOODBRIDGE.—Here in this little country town every one submits so quietly to the dominion and the routine of religion and the customs which accompany it, that there are no wars or rumours of wars of which I could send you notices, testifying that the end of superstition is at hand. The policy of the wealthy is still to use every device to bow the poor to their will, and the policy of the poor is still to cringe to the hand of power. This is the dull, tame history of Woodbridge and its neighbourhood as far as I am acquainted with it.

IMPROVEMENT CLASS, *No.* 8, *George-street, New-road,* Thursday evening, half-past Eight —*Subjects*, Model Example of Composition; Critique on Emerson, First Department—Thought; Dr. Paley's Plan of Instruction in the University; The *Times'* Critique on the "Lowell Offering;" Value of Taking Notes.

OPENING of the Social Institution, 5, Charlotte-street, Blackfriars-road, near Rowland Hill's Chapel. —The above Institution will be opened on Sunday next, Oct. 13, at half-past Three in the afternoon, with an Address by Mr. Charles Southwell. Mr. Southwell will lecture in the evening at Seven, in answer to the question, "What is Socialism?"

LECTURES.

October 9.—Hall of Science, Manchester—Mr. R. Cooper on the "Morality of the Bible."
October 10.—Do. Do.—Mrs Martin.
October 13.—National Hall, 242, High Holborn—W. J. Fox, "On the Moral Principles implied in the 'People's Charter,' and the application of those principles to the concerns of daily life."
October 13.—Finsbury Institution, Goswell-road, near the New River—A Friend on the "Principles and Objects of the Rational Society."
October 13.—Hall of Science, City-road—Mr. Southwell.
October 13.—Branch A 1—Mr. John Ellis on Education.

DISCUSSIONS.

October 11.—Branch A1.
October 12.—Social Institution, Whitechapel
October 13.—Finsbury Institution, Goswell-street, near the New River,—Subject, "Is Socialism Practicable?" (After the Lecture).
PUBLIC Discussions are about to be commenced at the Association Hall on Thursday nights.

TO CORRESPONDENTS.

RECEIVED "Reasons for Leaving the Concordian Society," by Alexander Campbell. *Dublin Monitor*. "*The Dying Testimony* of Abram Combe." A Galashiels Operative. Richard Doyle. 'Wedge.' The Saints. Defence by the *Nonconformist*,

R. R.—We have not been apprised of Mr. Owen's arrival in America yet, but we have seen the address from the conductors of the *Movement* to him, copied from the *Sun* in the *Working Man's Advocate*, published in New York on Sep. 14, and we suppose that sufficient time has elapsed for the news to arrive. It may be expected this week.

An article on "O'Connell on Persecution" has been written, but is obliged to stand over. Also List respecting *Movement*, J. Thorne and J. Perriur, and Persecution in Hull.

SUBSCRIPTIONS
TO THE ANTI-PERSECUTION UNION.

From the Cathedral City, per "Wedge" 0 2 0

Paterson Testimonial.

Per Mr. E. Johnson 0 6 3
J. Renton 0 2 6
R. R., First Subscription . . . 0 5 0
J. M. C., First Subscription . . . 0 5 0

G. J. H., *Sec.*

Printed and Published by G. J. HOLYOAKE, 40, Holywell-street, Strand, Wednesday, October 9, 1844.

THE MOVEMENT
And Anti=Persecution Gazette.

"Maximise morals, minimise religion."---BENTHAM.

No. 45.   EDITED BY G. JACOB HOLYOAKE, ASSISTED BY M. Q. RYALL.   Price 1½d.

MILAN—ITS RELIGION & POLICE.
(*Continued from page* 373.)

LAST Sunday, I was on the Lake of Licco, the environs of which present one of the finest sceneries in Italy. Passionately sensible of nature's beauties, I abandoned myself to my feelings—I was in extacy. But where religion exists, nothing is without an intermixture of sorrow. Human wretchedness and feebleness meet us at every step, and not only in our human concerns, but they find their way even into those darling places of nature, where one most expects unmixed delight. Rambling on, absorbed in the enjoyment of the surrounding scenery, I arrived on a spot whence I had a view which was before hidden from my eye by vineyards and chesnut wood. I saw on the top of a near hill, numerous people going to a chapel, called San Gerolamo, from the name of a saint who had lived there in the year 1511, and taught the orphans of the environs. He had formerly been a warrior, and when made a prisoner, fervently prayed to the Virgin Mary, who, on hearing his prayers, came down from heaven, broke his fetters, and led him by the hand through the midst of her guardians, out of the enemy's camp; after which he became an hermit, and then a saint. It was not, however, this childish story which made me melancholy, but it was the sight of the mood in which the credulous pilgrims obtained their indulgence. Not far from this chapel, somewhat higher on the mountain, there is a grotto, in which an image of marble of the saint is kneeling before a cross. Up to this grotto, lead hundred steps, formed by irregularly-paved, feet-hurting stones; and beneath this stair is the inscription of which the following is the verbal translation : " Indulgence of 200 days to all those faithful, who, with at least a contrite heart, walk up this stair, and kneeling down at every degree, pray according to the intention of Highest Priest (sonimo pontefice). The said indulgence is also applicable to the holy souls of the purgatory." I staid but about half an hour in the place, but counted more than twenty persons, men and women, who were flaying their knees in this atrocious manner, bare-headed, under the scorching rays of an Italian sun. It was a heartrending sight, which greatly damped the happy trance in which I was lost at the aspect of the surrounding scenery.

Coffee-houses and theatres are the poles on which turns the social life of Milan. Actors, carriages, eating and drinking, and their amours, are the chief topics of conversation of the Milanese. Even with regard to music, I have been deceived in them; and think the English their superiors. The Italians, I own, have the greatest composers; but, in speaking of a people, we must call that the most musical among whom this art is most practised, it matters not whether from a natural disposition, taste, or fashion. Here you never hear any of those sweet, homely, native airs sung or whistled by the people, such as you do in England, France, Germany, and Switzerland; and besides a few middling operas— the grand opera not being open yet—there are neither concerts nor any other musical entertainments here; while in England, even in provincial towns, there is scarcely ever a season in which there is a want of them. I am a passionate friend of music, and therefore miss this enjoyment very much.

The English are generally thought, and often modestly think themselves, to be the most calculating, money-eager, shopkeeping nation of all. But in this I cannot agree. The Italians, in chaffering, fail not to do the greatest honour to the country in which Mercury, the god of merchants and theives, once was worshiped. The English, at least, like fair-play, and, under the present arrangement of society, cheat honestly, if I may so express it; while with the Italians, it is all trickery and acknowledged deception. Cheating is done systematically, and the better a merchant knows how to take you in, the more prudent he is thought be, and the surer his credit is. Foreigners, before they are acquainted with this system of dealing, are always the dupes of it. Even in their games, down to the amusements of the children, this taking advantage of the other's unsuspiciousness, is predominant among the Italians.

Prostitution is very prevalent here, and married life is not spared by it. A wife who has not her paramour besides her husband, or a husband who has no other female connections, are phenomena. The Milanese are ignorant of the charms of domestic life. Women are considered good for nothing but sexual companions, and it is to this end that the so called homages are conferred on them. Before marriage, they are kept strictly within doors, not allowed to go out alone even during daytime. In their retirement, their imagination is inflamed by romances; they long for marriage, and accept the hand of the first suitor who presents himself, and whom they may perhaps have never seen before; and hence the unhappy marriages and the ensuing promiscuous intercourse.

Churches are generally the places of rendezvous. There is an immense number of them here, which is a very good thing, not only for those who have sweet-hearts to meet or prayers to make, but also for those whom ill-luck calls out of the house in the middle of the day, and who thus find for a moment shelter from the roasting sun, those places being always nicely cool. This applies particularly to the dome, a majestic monument of architecture, under the lofty vault of which you enjoy an agreeable freshness, and gratify, at the same time, your taste for objects of painting, sculpture, and architecture. While lost in contemplation, the sunbeams shine through the beautifully coloured arched windows, and tinge, with rainbow hues, the opposite walls and colonnades. The remainder of the edifice is in comparative darkness, and the resounding organ begins the solemn choral, while the ever-burning incense intoxicates you—produces an elysium impression which overpowers with raptures, until the tasteless lamenting songs of the priests disagreeably awake you out of this revery, and chase the reflecting mind out of this magnificent harbour of ignorance and bigotry.

Of the journalism of this place, I have nothing to say. Besides a few local papers, devoted almost exclusively to theatrical criticism and commercial interests, we have but the "*Gazetta Privilegiata*," whose political colour and tendency you may guess from its name. I only read the "*Gazette d'Augsberg*. As you will have perceived in the newspapers, the two expeditions of the Italian refugees were defeated and they made prisoners or killed. It was a foolish enterprise, which injures the cause of emancipation more than it serves it. Had they even succeeded in bringing about a resurrection, it would have had for result nothing but anarchy and complete dissolution. *The Italians cannot yet govern themselves. They must be prepared for it by a free press, by education. Nobody could take the lead. Ignorance is too predominant, even among the higher classes.*

My dear Holyoake, excuse my chat. I very likely have tired you with it, the more so as not being quite conversant with the English language, I must be pretty turgid; but, whose heart is full, his mouth flows over. I have now still many things to add.

It seems you don't have your trip to the Continent this year, else you had written to me. How goes the "*Movement*" and the Anti-Persecution Union? has the latter become numerous? I enclose an order for 10s. as my subscription. Have Paterson and Miss Roalfe been released? What news have you from your friend, Dr. Kalley, in Madeira? By these details you will not satisfy a mere idle curiosity, but the lively interest that I take in these matters. Be so kind as to inform me of the present state of the socialists in England, and of what is your opinion of their affairs. Does the establishment of Harmony still prosper?

CENSORSHIP.

Mr. J. Thorn has transmitted an admonitory epistle. The objects of his strictures are, the Report of the last Anti-Persecution Union Meeting, the Remarks of atheistical speakers at that meeting, and some of the matter which has been admitted into the *Movement*. Always more accessible to censure than to praise, as shown by the critical animadversions admitted, and the eulogiums rejected. There is yet a limit to the endurance of even a *Movement* publication. That limit is passed since the receipt of our correspondent's communication. We never take in ill part, a little blame, any more than we do a little advice, let it be as sharp and strong as may be; but when blame attains such appalling proportions as the case before us, when, in fact, it becomes a sort of homily, containing a new version of the old theme—*the whole duty of man*—our customary complacency vanished our editorial elasticity is done away; we look ruefully at the ten mortal pages, and then despairingly at the narrow limits of our little circumscribed columns and say, "the thing's impossible." And it *is* impossible for us to make room by the side of essentially current matter, for ten bath-post pages of monitory and exhortatory matter, with necessary comments, although addressed with more than maternal solicitude. A few samples, the best we can select, must suffice for both contributor and reader. Our correspondent complains thus:—" your report was so short and erroneous that I am compelled, contrary to my wishes, to ask you to print what I *did* say." The report's shortness must be ascribed to iron-hard necessity, not voluntary curtailment by our reporter. Were all the good things, said at such meetings, to be reported, verily, many *Movements* would not suffice to hold them. The erroneousness, if any, of the report would have been cheerfully corrected; but, singularly enough, in the nine and a half following pages, J. T. has totally forgotten to say what he " did say." In the present communication, he only says what he thinks. Of the meeting itself, J. T. says, " I thought there were other times and places where the tyrannies of priests, and religion's foul promptings should be the theme of the harrangue." An ordinary person would innocently marvel, where on earth could a fitter place and occasion be found than an Anti-persecution Union meeting to make "priest's tyrannies and religion's foul promptings the theme of the harrangue." St. Paul's, or Westminster Abbey? He continues, " I had pictured to myself, that there might be some poor being, nay more than one, hated, tortured by his fellow man, for that he had cherished other notions of a God, of religion, or perchance had fearlessly denied a god's existence, or a religion's usefulness; methought those men, whate'er their creed, deserved at least my sympathy, and claimed my best support, I cared not that it was Christian Kalley or Atheist Paterson."

So good an Artist is J. T. that what he " pictured " to himself is just the very thing that occurred. When he " thought" that all the persecuted for creed's sake deserved sympathy, he thought like the common every-day members of the Union, and in caring nothing whether it was Kalley or Paterson, he just cared, as the Union cared, who alike protected both.

J. T. next idealizes. In a bold fancy sketch, he traces what such a meeting might be. " That meeting would have been perfect could we have had there representatives of many opinions, and many creeds, to see there christians of many sects, Greek and Roman christians, followers of Calvin, or of Luther; christians of English or of Scottish churches, Mahometans, followers of Ali, or of Abm Bekr, Budhist, Sol worshippers; the Brahmin and Pariah working together for a common good, and mingled with them the man who knew no god, who owned no religlion." This is almost as daring a vision, in its way, as Volney's famous conference of nations. Simple matter-of-fact people would be apt to oppose this little difficulty—that if such a Babel-like assembly could be got together, in an in-door, or open-air meeting, without hanging, bowstringing, roasting, or otherwise butchering each other; if they ceased to thirst for each others' destruction—for what purpose would an anti-persecution union assemble? A little further on he says " But think you, sir, this bright consummation of an undying hope will e'er be realized, that the slightest approximation to it can be while men, when ostensibly engaged in a work of love and charity, should so far forget their high vocation, and descend to retort and recrimination. The numbers attending the meeting of the Anti-persecution Union, are enough in themselves to testify that there is room for conciliation. Why were the numbers less than on the year preceeding, when increased success would predicate increased numbers, but that those meetings are made the vehicles of accusation against parties whose religion we dislike; meeting which would have been fitly named, ' meeting to hear decried in the most unmeasured terms christianity and christians.' "

Now, as to decrying of christians when christians are persecutors, where is the impropriety in that. The same would be consistently spoken, if atheists had turned persecutors, and was so on the representation of Dr. Kalley, *assuming it to be true* that there was an atheistical persecution of dissenting christians in Madeira. That christianity itself was so decried by the generality of speakers none but J. T. deposes. It has been studiously avoided by the generality of speakers, and the most prominent among them by many grave thinkers deemed too much avoided. Something of the warm glow of imagination which tinted the picture of J. T.'s " perfect meeting" must surely have been infused into this representation. He notes elsewhere, this passage from a speaker at a previous meeting, ' Let dogs delight to bark and bite, let the parsons imprison and persecute each other, I will not interfere.' Perish such opinions, and that society (if any), which would foster them, calculated as they are to strike at the root of all human love and good."

Is not here a raking up of an inadvertent expression, in the warmth of speaking, and overlooking its practical disavowal by the Union. Did not the Union do all in their power to protect parson from parson. Did they not send succour to dissenting parson when hunted down by orthodox parson. But J. T. answers himself further on. "But 'tis refreshing to look from opinions so grounded in the want of catholic charity, to the example you have set, and to read again the words you have written, in connection with the affairs of the Union. Such as in writing to Dr. Kalley — 'the distance between you and them makes no diminution in their sympathy. They condole with the victims of religious persecution in every clime. It is enough for the Union to know that you are imprisoned for expressing theological opinions to establish your claim to their protection.' Again, 'your disagreement with many of them in opinion by no means diminished the interest with which they perused its contents, &c..'" All these commendable sentiments, accompanied by equally commendable actions, remittance of 5*l.* and letters of condolence and sympathy, are said by the secretary of the Union, as the authorised mouth-piece of the Union. A still stronger passage is quoted "'They have nothing to do with the sentiments of any party, christian or atheist, Dr. Kalley or Thomas Paterson are alike to them.'" What says J. T.—"These are good, kind, and cheering words, well worthy of remembrance by every member of the Union." Why they are the Union's. What more practically, extensively, comprehensively, consistently liberal and liberty-loving Union can you find?

The following is extremely well put, and deserves attention from every atheist. "The peculiar position which atheism now holds, in relation to the world's creeds, most forcibly inculcates the lesson, that our object ought to be to make our fellow man respect our opinions, through the respect they have for us as individuals; to show by our lives that our opinions hinder us not from being as good members of the human family as men professing any creed. Do we not say to christians, 'the tree is known by its fruits,' and behold the fruits which christianity has produced for the last 1800 years, and then, from the dark scene of christian doing, could we turn and say, behold these are the fruits of atheism·'" J T. follows up this train of ideas in another part of the following judiciously expressed observations. In examining the pretensions of atheists we are led to expect from them a mode of life superior to those who are not degraded by the debasing rites and dogmas of religion. The atheist is either the possessor of better principles, which should lead him to perform better actions, then he should be marked out from among his fellow men, as a good man, pre-eminent in noble deeds, or of what avail are his better principles? Or, the atheist is at least free from influences which tend to degrade his fellow man, and therefore should be free from those failings caused by these evil influences."

The third ground of complaint, that connected with contributions to the Movement, is thus laid down. "These observations lead me to a remark on articles which have appeared at various times in the pages of the Movement, particularly those portions of a discussion, which has displaced much more useful matter, between Messrs. Gillespie and Southwell. Each of these gentlemen lay claim to superior principles, or, at least, to being free from the pernicious opinions of the other, and oh, what a falling off of the good effect of their principles is there. If half [which I can scarce believe] be true which they have said of each other, what company can they be fit for, but that of the lowest of the low. The 'you're a liar, sir, and you're another,' is but one actual specimen of language used in this debate. What to me is it, that Mr. Gillespie said liar first, or last, ought not Mr. S. to have shewn the superiority of his atheism, by neglecting to return wrong for wrong; but they have both made the pages of the MOVEMENT a record of their shame, and proved that the principles of either are insufficient to make them respect the opinions of their fellow man."

Comment on these last strictures is more properly the province of the parties immediately concerned. It has been our general plan to let men speak in their own way, fair play has demanded this of us; we do the same in the instance of J. T. Brevity we must stipulate for, by the nature of the "surrounding circumstances" of the small diameter of our margin.

J. T. cannot complain that we have destroyed the force or blunted the severity of a single remark, or that we have omitted anything accusatory connected with the Report, the Union, or ourselves. We give his parting advice, on which we will reflect, —and benediction.

"Stop these defaming controversialists, and make, if possible, the members of the Union remember the old proverb, that 'fair words break no bones, foul ones many.' A bright future will then await the exertions of the Union, and its organ, the Movement. That such fortune will be attendant is the sincere wish of J. T."

M. Q. R.

O'CONNELL ON PERSECUTION.

At a recent meeting of the Repeal Association, in the Conciliation Hall, Mr. O'Connell took occasion to declare, but on what authority we know not, "the *day of persecution is gone by*. In, I believe, almost every country on the face of the globe, with the exception of two, *persecution for religion is at an end.* Sweden and Denmark are the only two countries where the persecution law exists (hear). It was said the other day at Edinburgh, at a meeting of some Dissenters of one kind or the other, that a woman was persecuted at Modena for professing Protestant opinions. We instantly wrote to make the inquiry—the inquiry has been made; and we find it was a mere lie (hear, hear). I call on the Protestant governments of Sweden and Denmark to vindicate their Christianity from the *foul blot which persecution throws upon it*, and, by adopting a different course, do honour to their common faith, on the basis of benevolence, the emantion of that benevolence being acts of Christian charity (hear, hear, and loud cheering)."

Thus is Mr. O'Connell reported in the *Dublin Monitor*, of September 25th, and the same version is given in the *Nation*, the *Times*, and other papers. " Persecution for religion is at an end in all countries except Sweden and Denmark?" What does Mr. O'Connell think of the recent Imprisonment of Messrs. Southwell, Holyoake, and Paterson, in Bristol. Gloucester, and London? Is not England a country of Europe? What does he think of the recent cases of Messrs. Finlay, Paterson, McNeil, and Miss Roalfe, who were Imprisoned in Edinburgh, Perth, and Stirling Goals? Is not Scotland a country of Europe? Either Mr. O'Connell's knowledge is very limited, or his geography is very defective. We know nothing of *Modena*, but we do know something of Madeira, and there, in a *Catholic* country; Dr. Kalley, as is known to Lord Aberdeen, to every Member of Her Majesty's Government, to the readers of the *Movement*, and almost every journal in Europe, has been recently imprisoned for impugning the divinity of the virgin. In the same Catholic Madeira ; one poor woman, Maria Joaquina, a mother of seven children, with the youngest at the breast, was lately sentenced to *death*, for blasphemy against the Mother of God and the Images of her Son, as was recorded in the *Belfast Protestant Journal* a short time ago. The information was communicated in a letter from Dr. Kalley, who is incapable of reporting falsely, and the letter (published in *Movement*, 29) bore internal marks of being genuine. And Mr. O'Connell can procure, if he pleases, a copy of the original sentence, dated, Funchal Oriental, 2nd May, 1844, and signed by the Judge Joze Pereira Leito Pitta Ortagueira Negrao. We should be happy if it was as Mr. O'Connell states, but facts will not permit christianity to be credited as yet free from the damning imputation of living by persecution. Nevertheless, we heartily rejoice at Mr. O'Connell's denunciation of persecution : it proves that we are fast bringing it into contempt. We do not expect Mr. O'Connell, or any other christian, to act up to his declaration, yet that they find it necessary to proclaim " persecution a foul blot upon christianity," is proof that christians at last are sensible of its destructive effects on themselves. It is scarcely a year and half ago since Mr. O'Connell made a speech at the Corn Exchange, in which he denominated the infidel as a miscreant, and significantly hinted at the uses of the Liffey, as a receptacle for unbelievers. Latterly the *Belfast Vindicator*, made a call upon the Police to put down the dissemination of infidel views. These cases *rather* resemble persecution, and they are proceeding from Mr. O'Connell's lips and occuring under his eyes. But consistency was never the attribute of christianity; we will not look for this, but content ourselves that even persecuting christians are compelled to disclaim persecution.

G. J. H.

THE DESIGN ARGUMENT.

J. P. writes to draw our attention to another line of argument which he recommends in dealing with the Design question. He observes, " the work entitled ' Paley Refuted in his own words' has, I think, clearly shown that Paley's argument proves too much, and consequently, nothing. But though this has been done, still I think there is a shorter and more expeditious mode of dealing with this argument. Paley says, design must have had a designer, and I think he was right, too; once admit design, and depend on it you must also admit a designer. Now it is clear that by admitting the existence of design, we admit that which involves a *petitio principii*, as logicians call it ; an admission as unnecessary as it is fraught with danger to the cause of truth, and with danger to those who admit it."

J. P. proceeds to show, that "what is *called* design is to be found in results flowing from a fortuitous combination of events." He instances the formation of a perfectly delineated balloon from the falling of a drop of ink; a perfect outline of a human face from the shadow produced by clothes hung on a bedstead, and infers that, since *apparent design* can be produced from a series of circumstances known not to be really designed, therefore that which is called design in the universe *may be* but apparent design, flowing from a combination of fortuitous events. He concludes, that "upon the bare *possibility* of apparent design resulting from any other cause than a sentient entity, may be obtained a lever powerful enough to overturn the whole of this voluminous argument of theologians and theistical philosophers."

This subject would afford a good exercise to some thinking reader. The working out the ratiocinative process, to try the validity of J. P.'s argument, will not fail to sharpen one's wits. Owen and Bacheler's Discussion will help this investigation.

PERSECUTION IN HULL.

Persecution of the meanest and most despicable kind has been commenced in Hull. Mrs. Martin lately delivered a lecture in that town, on the Crimes and Follies of Christian Missions; Mr. Watson, who let his room for the purpose, has been fined by the Magistrates, (on summons) 1*l.*, and 9*s.* costs for doing so; and Mr. Johnson, Bookseller, who, it appears took twopence of one James Freeman, has been fined in the same way, 20*l.* and costs, for the same offence. There is something manly in prosecutions for blasphemy, compared with this petty malignity. A man indicted is heard in his own defence, but in this case, with scarcely a hearing, a man is ruined for doing only that which other public parties, Dissenters and Churchmen, are doing daily with impunity. The Police were immediately in possession of Mr. Johnson's house and property, and on Monday the sale of his property was to take place. One result of this persecution, is, the determination of the people of Hull, to have a Hall of their own. Now that religion has peeped out on the good people of Hull in its native form, they will deserve to live for ever under its curse, if they do not bestir themselves to strike it down. Mrs. Martin is agitating the town, and we call on the friends of the Anti-Persecution Union, to immediately send in subscriptions, to enable the Union to act as may seem most fitting.

The Life and Testimony of Abram Combe.—Abram Combe was the brother of the now well-known George Combe, to whom we shall shortly have occasion to refer. Mr. Campbell has lately returned to life and usefulness, and this "Life and Testimony" is one of his new labours. Mr. C.'s pamphlet is calculated to be very useful, and we hope will be extensively circulated among the misinformed, respecting the influence of the social views on life and conduct.

MRS. MARTIN.

This lady who has been lecturing on the "Missionary Imposture," has created marvellous excitement in this town of piety and spinning jennies; one of the great missionary meetings was announced to be held in Mosely Street Chapel, Sept. 30, and Mrs. M. placarded her intention of being present, which seems to have brought thousands there. Just as the first resolution was about being put to the meeting Mrs. Martin rose, in one of the pews, and desired permission to speak; upon this she was assailed with yells from all parts of the Chapel, which were answered by vehement cheering from more than half the persons present, who seemed friendly to Mrs. M. being heard. One female saint, near Mrs. Martin, threatened "to poke her umbrella through Mrs. M.'s bonnet." The whole Police Corps appear to have been sent for by the Chairman, and entered the meeting; but a number of sturdy mechanics belonging to one of the principal firms in the town, surrounded Mrs. M. and protected her from arrest. Placards we are told have since been put out headed something to this effect, "send for the Police—the Missionaries are in want of the Police!" and Mrs. Martin has delivered a lecture on her "Adventures at the Missionary Meeting." Mr. Geo. Smith, of Salford, has been threatened with prosecution for selling blasphemy, and the religious world of Manchester seems turning up side down, poor thing!

Since writing the preceding, we have had a very warm letter from Mr. Smith of Salford, fully corroborating the preceding statements. From his letter it appears that the meeting was opened with prayer, but when Mrs. M. appeared, instead of calling upon God the preacher called upon the Police, they knew who was most likely to help them. Mrs. M. was struck at with sticks, and it was an elegantly dressed lady who actually poked her precious parasol at Mrs. M.'s head.

We understand that the Inhabitants of Colne, where Mrs. Martin has visited, have erected a tent for her accommodation.

At Hull, Mrs. Martin has held a discussion within these few days, with a Rev. Pulsford, at which high prices were offered for Tickets of Admission. "The subject of discussion was "the Evidences of Christianity."

EDINBURGH.

I think we may consider that we have won the battle of mental freedom in this city, as I have the place regularly placarded with bills, advertising the sale of the "Existence of God Disproved," "The Bible an Improper Book," &c., and not the slightest notice taken, except that *I* am looked upon as a sort of *she devil*, by the saints. I received a letter from a Clergyman the other day, in which was enclosed a Tract entitled, "The Unanswerable Question." I propose answering the Rev. Gent.'s letter, and shall enclose one of Mrs. Martin's "Few Reasons," for his perusal.

M. ROALFE

THE LATE FRATERNAL MEETING.

I am told, Chillman and Schapper consider the *Star's* report not only defective, but seriously erroneous, amounting to misrepresentation. You may perceive that the really important act of the evening, the resolution, is not mentioned. However disposed to make great allowances for the paper, on account of its notice of poor men's movements, advocacy of poor men's interests, a duty is forced on honest democrats, to expose *intentional negligence*. Should it prove to be the case, that the *Star* intentionally suppressed Lovett's and Hetherington's observations, and the mention of an important public determination to sanction a mutual understanding between all real publicists, it should be made known. It would not be doing justice to the *Movement* party to conceal such untrustworthiness, though the exposure should prove inimical to our particular interests. I had an interview with Mr. McDouall, who expressed willingness to take the necessary measures for acquainting the "section," with the public request that they appoint delegates for a general conference. The French and German delegates are already appointed. He suggested that the meeting should have ostensibly, a benevolent or some other legal object; to prevent prosecution. Avoiding or evading the force of the law, would be good, if not accomplished by the sacrifice of truth or principle; this will have to be discussed. Weitling and Moll agree with me, that the first, or one of the first things, should be a general exposition, clearly and comprehensively of each delegate, of the views and objects of his party or association, distinguishing the essential, the debateable, and the indifferent.

Note from M. Q. R.

GALASHIELS.

A letter, from Mr. Walter Sanderson, has appeared on the walls of Galashiel, challenging on behalf of the "Infidel Association," the Rev. Mr. Blair, to a public discussion, "On the comparative merits of Religion and Infidelity;' but the Rev. defamer cannot be brought out. This Rev. Mr. Blair, is the author of that passage quoted at the commencement of Article II., on the progress of infidelity in Scotland, *Movement*, No. 41.

ANTI-PERSECUTION UNION.

At the first meeting of the new committee, held on Monday, Sept. 30, Mr. Holyoake was added to the committee, and re-elected general secretary. The members and friends of the Union are informed, that the member's tickets for the ensuing quarter, are now ready for issue. The payment of sixpence, on the receipt of one of the tickets, constitutes the holder a member for the quarter.

The *Auditors* of the Union, appointed at the last annual meeting, are, Mr. John Ellis, No. 8, George-street, New-road; and, Mr. John Skelton, 24, Cecil-court, St. Martin's-lane, London. The reason of publishing the addresses is to enable subscribers to apprize the auditors of any error or omission that may remain uncorrected, after proper representations have been made to the officer of the Union concerned. Of course the Auditors will, in such case, refuse to certify the account until the complaint has been attended to.

Phrenological Repartee.—As the late Professor Hamilton was one day walking near Aberdeen, he met a well-known individual of weak intellect, "Pray," said the Professor, accosting him, "how long, can a person live without brains?" "I dinna ken," replied Jemmy, scratching his head; "how old are ye yourself?"

WEITLING'S WELCOME IN ENGLAND.—After his arrival in England, the "Movement" announced that he had at last escaped the fangs of his persecutors, and that he ought to be welcomed. This welcome was fixed for Sunday, September 22. The large Social Hall (the Meeting-house of the Socialists), was so filled with persons of both sexes, that the saloon and galleries were found insufficient. Vocal and instrumental entertainment (by choirs of young male and female singers) alternated with speeches, was the order of the evening. In one of these, an English Socialist thus expressed himself, "That they certainly praised or blamed no one (a known socialist principle), however, the circumstances were of such a kind that in regard to Weitling they required an exception, for they welcomed in his person, not merely a martyr, but rather the representative of the Communists of the Continent."—THE VORWAERTS.

M. Weitling's speech is then given at length. The quotation is given quite correctly, the mistakes being those of the foreign journalist.

THE SOCIALISTS IN ENGLAND.—M. Weitling, arrested and imprisoned in Switzerland for publishing Socialist Works, then delivered to Prussia, his native country, has been most cordially welcomed by the Socialists in England. The "Movement," and and the "Vorwaerts" give an account of the reception of the German workman.—LA REFORME.

REVERENCE FOR THE REVERENDS.—Our Paris contemporary, La Reforme, thus compliments the Exeter Hallians, who have taken upon themselves to patronise the "Reverend Pritchard." "On Tuesday, at a meeting presided over by George Wilson, Esq., divers of these grave personages made speeches to demonstrate the incomparable superiority of their society over all other societies of the kind. The principal object of the meeting appears to have been, to congratulate the Reverend Pritchard on the European success obtained through his patriotic intrigues at Tahiti. * * * The French blood spilled for Christianity's sake, in this virtuous quarrel, well merited so high a mark of distinction by these traders in bibles and calicos, who mingle with their dealings and their piety so much hypocrisy.

CIRCULATION OF THE MOVEMENT.—Copies of the Movement are supplied gratuitously, on application at the Office, to keepers of Public Rooms, Coffee Houses, Saloons, &c, who will lay them in convenient places for reading. Every week, a quantity of numbers are put in neat wrappers, and delivered by active friends in different districts. One or two friends are wanted for this purpose in Marylebone and Westminster. The following is a list of the places where it is now left for reading by one friend residing in Islington.—

Lunt's, Middleton-street.—Kirton's Coffee-house, City-road.—Morgan's Commercial-place, City-road. —Gallop's, Milton-street, Beech-street.—Cornish's, Bunhill-row.—Cartwright's, 60, Red Cross-street.— Wisedell's, 7, Long-lane.—Gully's, 85, Long-lane. Kirtland's, 40, St. John-street.—Wright's, St. John-square,—and Wilson's, Clerkenwell-green.

TO CORRESPONDENTS.

A NEWCASTLE CORRESPONDENT, who wrote on the demonstrability of the Existence of Matter, will think himself and friends who have been occupied with the subject, greatly neglected—and he will think right. His correspondence was handed to INVESTIGATOR, whose able critical animadversions, in the early numbers of the "Oracle of Reason," may be remembered with much satisfaction by its readers. Few men would bring more clear-headed discrimination to bear upon a subject that has been made so obstruse by learned disputation, or ingenious paradox. The papers in question are still in the hands of Investigator, whom it is hoped this appeal will induce to illuminate our pages.

"THE HOLY TRINITY" had better put the question to Mr. Begg.

W. BROOM. However willing, we cannot commence a discussion on Philology in the "Movement."

H. COOK.—Will he send his authority on which his statement respecting the Egyptian Gods are founded.

H. J.—We do not feel called upon to express an opinion, either way, respecting Mr. Southwell's lectures, reported in the "Movement." They were reported as news, not inserted as articles.

"THE SAINTS,"—The thoughts in these lines are spread through too many stanzas.

A Correspondent, no doubt unthinkingly, has forwarded us a newspaper with some written remarks on the wrapper, in violation of the Post Office rules. We protest against this. The Post Office operations are one of the few public boons we enjoy, and it should be a point of honour never to violate its regulations.

MR. GRAY.—Walter Sanderson, Galashiels.

NOTICES.

THE FOURTH ANNIVERSARY in aid of the Rational Tract Society will take place at the John St. Institution, on Monday, October 21. Tea at half-past six, Dancing at Ten. Sentiments will be spoken to by various friends.

IMPROVEMENT CLASS, No. 8, George-street, New-road, Thursday Evening, at half-past 8 o'clock, will be superintended by Mr. Ryall, Mr. Holyoake being absent from town.

LECTURES.

Oct. 16.—Hall of Science, Manchester, Mr. R. Cooper,—The Philosophy of the Bible.
Oct. 20.— Social Institution, Surrey-streei, Blackfriars-road, Mr. Holyoake,—Socialism as in Code of Moral practice.
Oct. 20.—Hall of Science, City-road, Mr. C. Southwell,—The French Revolution.
Oct. 20.—Assembly Rooms, 29, Circus-street, New-road, Mr. Southwell (in the morning),—The second lecture on Lord Wharncliffe's recent Speech on Education.
Oct. 20.—Finsbury Institution, Goswell-road, A Friend,—The Objections to Socialism.
Oct. 20.—National Hall, 242, High Holborn, W. J. Fox,—The Moral Principles implied in the "PEOPLE'S CHARTER," and the application of those principles to the concerns of daily life.

DISCUSSIONS.

Oct. 18.—Branch A 1.
Oct. 20.—Finsbury Institution, Goswell-road,—Subject, Is opposition to Mr. Owen, by priests and others, justifiable ?

SUBSCRIPTIONS
TO THE ANTI-PERSECUTION UNION.

Mr. John Ellis............................ 1 0
Per Mrs. B............................. 1 0
                         G. J. H., Sec.

M. Q. R., from W. J. 5 0

Printed and Published by G. J. HOLYOAKE, 40, Holywell-street, Strand.
Wednesday, October 16, 1844.

THE MOVEMENT

And Anti=Persecution Gazette.

"Maximise morals, minimise religion."—BENTHAM.

No. 46.   EDITED BY G. JACOB HOLYOAKE, ASSISTED BY M. Q. RYALL.   Price 1½d.

ADMIRABLE DEFENCE
OF
Messrs. SOUTHWELL, HOLYOAKE, PATERSON, FINLAY, M'NEIL, AND MISS ROALFE.

IN the *Nonconformist* for Sep. 25, under the head of "Ethics of Nonconformity," I find the following remarks, which though really written in defence of dissent from established religions, are admirably suited to those who dissent from religious creeds and dogmas *in toto*. If it be not only right but a primary duty for the religious nonconformist to be continually "under arms," to be entirely regardless of consequences which may result from his avowal and advocacy of the truth as it is in him—to care for no abuse, and to pause not through any annoyance his own conduct may be calculated to produce—to break in pieces the favourite idols of those to whom he is opposed, and to wage perpetual war with error—if this be the sacred duty of the religious nonconformist, is it not the duty also of the infidel and the atheist dissenter? The *Nonconformist* declares that they who wink at delusions are traitors to truth. Have not reformers of all ages and all classes been neglected, sold, and betrayed by winkers and blinkers at truth? Men who pretend to worship it in their closets, when none are by to attack, but who deny it, or use mean evasions, with unblushing fronts, when charged in public with being its apostle. Did not Southwell suffer from such—was not Holyoake reviled as rash, and Paterson fled from as from a pestilence, because they took up arms in the cause of truth, and boldly defended, and endeavoured to spread what they conceived to be right, and what hundreds who blamed them and who refused to aid them had all their lives, *in private*, believed also to be right?

The extract is somewhat long for your limited space, but such is its importance, in my eyes, that I should advise your making a twopenny number for its accommodation, rather than reject it.

"The doctrine is a remarkably comfortable one, by the aid of which we may contrive to get through the world without the disagreeable necessity of having the countenance ploughed up with wrinkles. To be reputed as a man of moderation, singularly discreet, amiable, and courteous—to be well spoken of by all parties, in return for a word of commendation judiciously administered to all—to be known for earnest attachment to nothing, save to that kind of neutrality which shrinks from the ill-will of any - to be quiet when action would expose to reproach, and active when activity would secure general praise—to speak nothing which by possibility may give offence—to do nothing which might create an unpleasant stir—to tread the very ground with an affected meekness, and smile upon everything, and shake hands with everybody, and utter every sentence in a tone of fond endearment and familiarity—all this may suit some men's natural tastes, but we are apt to suspect that this is not precisely the vocation nor the bearing of the betrothed to truth.

"It may startle some, but we give it as our deliberate judgment, that the first duty of a nonconformist, occupying the high position we have assigned to him, is to be "under arms." Let him not dream of peace. In a world crammed full of errors, many of them morally pernicious to a most deplorable extent—in which conventional falsehoods pass current in all circles—the greater proportion of whose inhabitants are laboriously practising delusion upon themselves and others—where hypocrisy is as common as masked faces at a carnival—and where all, with an extremely insignificant exception, are pursuing self under some guise of virtue—*it is impossible to stand up a sincere and courageous servant of truth, without having all classes at your throat.* You might as well expect to drive a ploughshare through a wasps' nest in open day, and not be stung, as to be truthful without giving offence. There needs nothing of a blustering air, or a moody brow, or a coarse tongue, or a forward presumption, to provoke people to rise up in arms against you. You have but to speak of things as they are, to estimate them at their proper value, to thrust at error because it is error, and to treat sin as sin wherever you meet with it—all of which you are bound to do by your profession as a dissenter – and you may bid farewell to that comfortable life, which some men identify with Christian peace.

"' *Offences must needs come,*' then, at least when men faithfully deliver themselves of the truth that is in them. This is a settled thing—and equally settled is it that the offence will be deep, virulent, and active just in proportion to the greatness, vitality, and energy of the truth which excites it. It follows that *to suppress truth with a view to avoid giving offence, is merely transferring to other shoulders the responsibility which we are too cowardly to take upon ourselves.* We have no license to ground our arms and stand at ease. We can plead no warrant for winking at delusion. We have never received permission to chat affably with falsehood. We ought to be iconoclasts—image-breakers, wherever we go. *Some men must do the work —or the world will never be rid of error.* And whenever it is done, as done it must be, a dust will be raised about the ears of those who perform it. *But that which a man knows, he is, by the very fact that he knows it, laid under obligation to communicate. It is the primary duty of a nonconformist,* consequently, *to preach his principles whatever may come of it.* The stir that he will make in doing so is to be no part of his consideration. He may be told that he will be always in hot water. Well, he was born to be in hot water, and he must make the best of it. *What business had he to profess dissent, if he had not previously made up his mind to hot water?* He live at peace with all men. It may be, it ought to be, in his heart to do so. The ill-will must not be on his part—the malice must not be his—he must be no party to the enmity he may provoke ; but assuredly, unless he is at peace with all systems of delusion and of falsehood, the men who profit by them, or who cling to them, will not be at peace with him.

" For our parts, we are free to confess that we like to hear a man well spoken against. It is a presumption in his favour. It proves that he is doing some work, and work of a kind which society does not like. Now, society is especially fond of its knickknacks and gew gaws; and when a man wields truth with a vigorous arm, he is sure to disturb some of them. Then bursts forth an outcry which rings through every circle of hollowness—' *Oh! the violence, the hotheadedness, the sour temperedness, the arrogance, the all-conceivable and inconceivable badness of that man!* Well, if he be a true man, and working for truth, he will just go on heedless of the buzz.* Then, possibly, bickerings about him among those who had previously agreed in condemning, will follow. Party will range itself against party, and house be divided against house. He will regret it, but *he is not responsible for it. He must go on, leaving these things to adjust themselves.* By the time this man has finished his career he will have done something for the world ; and if his name should live for future generations, which, however is no part of his bargain, the common gratitude of mankind will be considered his due. Such has been the history of all the heroes for truth's sake ; and such will be an epitome of the history of every soldier who girds on his armour in this moral warfare. He ought to be calumny-proof, for he will have enough of it before he has done.

" What, then, is the law binding upon the dissenter as such ? Simply this. That as he has professed his adherence to truth for truth's sake, and has renounced an error, although gilded with worldly attractions, and authorised by worldly power, because, in his opinion, it is an error, he takes, by so doing, his sword and spurs and vouches himself to be a faithful knight in the service of that mistress to whom he has sworn allegiance. *It is his special vocation to drive falsehood out of the earth—to give it no quarter— to fall upon it wherever he meets with it—and to make his whole life tell in the advancement of right principles all the world over.* He is, of course, to exercise his wisdom as to the likeliest mode of doing this ; but he must do it all events. He will not irritate where irritation can be avoided, but he will not consider it consistent with his duty to let error live in order that peace may be maintained. In short, he will set his face as a flint towards one object, and steadily pursue it, undistracted by the clamours of professed friends, and undaunted by the opposition of open foes." W. C.

GEOLOGY AND THE BIBLE.

Our friend, Mr. Gray was kind enough to forward an abridgement of the interesting fracas at the Meeting of the British Association, between Science and the Bible, occasioned by the Dean of York reading a paper entitled, " Critical remarks on certain passages of Dr. Buckland's Bridgewater Treatise." The Dean directed his observations entirely to Dr. Buckland's theory of cosmogany, and he attempted to reconcile ob-

* Shade of my friend Paterson, would thou couldst see this!

served geological facts with the Mosaic account of the creation. The reply was by Professor Sedgwick, and though the whole recontre is generally known, we must preserve an epitome. Mr. Gray correctly thinks it is, when taken in connection with Dr. Engledue's chivalrous onslaught in another quarter, a cheering trait of progress. We just quote the *Spectator*, which always tells a story with felicity.

"Among public meetings of the season, must not be forgotten the British Association, to whom, this year, the public are indebted for many interesting matters, and not the least so for a pitched battle between Dogma and Experimental Philosophy. Dogma was personated by the Dean of York, who (as a member of the Association we presume) assailed Dr. Buckland's Theory of the creation, and his antagonist was Professor Sedgwick, who with a speech stronger in practical knowledge of the subject than in form or courtesy, so discomfited the Dean that Dogma was utterly routed. The Dean, however, did not know when he was beaten, his discourse having been held so utterly valueless, that an apology was made for permission having been given to read it. He determined to " shame the fools and print it," which he did the same afternoon, in a pamphlet, entitled, " The Bible Defended against the British Association," not very honestly implying that the British Association had attacked the sacred volume. Still not content with that costly resort of damned authors, he mounted the pulpit, " drum-ecclesiastic," and breathed holy war against his antagonist in the Minster! A sly fellow the Dean! he knew where to have his opponent without risk of a reply."

The *Globe* says, " In making this assault on the Dean of York's theory, the Rev. Professor was not sparing in disparaging expressions. He spoke of the inconvenience of allowing " addle-pated " individuals to occupy the time of the Association with their crude speculations; he said the Dean had shewn himself to be quite ignorant of facts; that he should have come there to learn, and not to presume to teach geological truths, *and that such indigested notions were merely " tales for the nursery,"* and not fitted for a scientific assembly. Alluding to the fossil remains of the great megatherion, which, according to the Dean's hypothesis, must have been caught up and deposited with other animals of a former creation, Professor Sedgwick said, ' the Dean of York had altogether mistaken the age of the animal, he had forgotten to look the megatherion in the mouth.' This objection, and many others of the salient points of the Professor's speech, were received with great laughter, and when he concluded he was greeted with several rounds of applause.

" The Dean of York, who sat with an unperturbed countenance through the whole of Professor Sedgwick's cutting speech, said he and the Professor did not differ as to the facts, they only differed in their modes of accounting for them.

" Professor Sedgwick's speech created a great sensation, as it is quite unusual in the proceedings of the Association, to make such a sledge-hammer attack, especially on a person holding a position like that of the Dean of York. The Council offered very meagre reasons for allowing the paper to be read; for if they had not collectively the moral courage to reject it, it was rather too hard on Professor Sedgwick to appoint him single-handed to extinguish the Dean's theory.

" The Minster was crowded on Sunday to hear the Dean of York, who, it was understood, would repeat from the pulpit his attack on the British Association. He took for his text the third chapter of the first epistle to the Corinthians, the nineteenth verse, " The wisdom of this world is foolishness;" and on this sentiment he enlarged, asserting *that the tendency of worldly knowledge is to render ' pigmy man' wise in his own conceits, and to produce infidelity.* Professor Sedgwick sat near the pulpit, and, though there were no personal allusions in the discourse, yet the significant glances and smiles of the congregation showed their application of expressions to the members of the Association. The 'affair' between the Dean and the Professor has created a great sensation, and will probably give rise to future paper warfare."

MIRABEAU'S EROTICA BIBLION.

[This work is not by MIRABEAUD, the author of "The System of Nature," but by Mirabeau the famous French orator. The " Erotica Biblion" was his only atheistical work, and the only work we know of devoted to an exposition of the obscenities of the Bible. *This* Mirabeau is the only author who has systematically treated this department.]

PEIGNOT in his dictionary of books condemned to the flames, says, "this work was so severely proscribed by the Police when it appeared, that only fourteen copies of the first edition got abroad. It is a production in which the author pretends to prove, that spite of the dissolution of our own morals, the ancients and *especially* the Jews were much more corrupt than ourselves."

Another edition of this work was published, which became alike scarce; the copy of it from which I have made my observations has the manuscript note of some purchaser, mentioning that he paid tenpence a page for the book, or 250 francs.

We cannot do more in the pages of the *Movement* than point to some of the passages in the Bible, which Mirabeau has introduced with his usual wit and some apparent novelty. Having occasion to mention the eradication of the marks of Judaism by the Philistines—II Macabees, c. i., v. 16, he adds in a note that the Jansenists pretended that the words used in the Bible could not be spoken by young girls.—the Jesuits on the contrary, asserted that it was a crime to alter a single word. Kings, book the seventh, c. vi., v. 17, is referred to, as curing a disorder by a golden imitation of the part which stands the least honored among us, but has been thought worthy of the highest esteem among the Jews. From Genesis, c. i., v. 27, which Mirabeau renders thus "God created *man* after his own image, male and female created he *him*," and from the succeeding verse, the 27, "increase and multiply, and replenish the earth;" he infers that God created Adam hermaphrodite, with the power of propagating his species and being created after God's own image, God himself must be in similarly organized predicament. Mirabeau says that his conclusion was supported by some Rabbis.

In speaking of Leviticus, Mirabean says, the Jews had enough of real impurities without creating so many imaginary ones. The Hebrews he says, in their commerce with goats; Leviticus, c. xvii., v. 7, thought they had intercourse with demons under the form of those animals. Mirabeau remarks of Leviticus, c. xviii. v. 7; "we do not carry to this degree filial love." The obscene rites practised before the statue of Moloch, mentioned Leviticus, c. xviii. v, 21., Mirabeau by very rational interpretation, shows to have degenerated into the sacrifice of infants. Leviticus, c. xviii., v. 22, he gives as an instance of the most subtle refinement of licentiousness practised by men towards women and the extraordinary interdiction found necessary in their laws. Not only of some animals mentioned, and not to be supposed agreeable to women, but of all animals—whence it evidently results, says Mirabeau, from Leviticus, c. xx., v. 16, that the Jewish women, prostituted themselves to every kind of beast without distinction. Still more remarkable does he consider the fact, that they must have brought to light the offspring of some of the ill-sorted alliances, when there is a law sentencing to be burnt the consequence as well as the actors in the crime.* After speaking of the amputation which was so singular a communion to be established between God and man, and which according to St. Paul, I Cor. c. 7., v. 18., Jews converted to christianity, were desirous of effacing: after giving a history of this delight to God and in the eyes of the Princess Royal, Michel who required it of David for a dowry, Mirabeau in apologising for going through with such a subject, says, for mere dirtiness there are other passages infinitely stronger than those already cited, and he instances the example of King Saul, who going in a cave at the bottom of which David was concealed, who coming up gently behind cuts off the shirt tail of Saul; then immediately the king leaves, runs after him to show him that he could easily have transfixed him, but he was too brave to kill him behind, I Kings, c. iv., v. 4. When one sees this, says Mirabeau, one is astonished; but when passing from astonishment to astonishment, on this vast and holy theatre, we meet with such passages as, 1 Sam. xviii, 27,—Tobri ii. 10,— Esth. xiv, 2,—Eccles. xxii, 2,—Isaiah xxxvii, Lamen. iv, 5,—Mal. ii, 3,—Ezech. iv, 12, we are astonished no longer at anything.

It is necessary to say, that Mirabeau quotes from the Latin Bible. Unpleasant as is the subject, it is a chapter in the history of God's chosen people that cannot be wholly passed over by the candid enquirer. It makes us wonder the more at the infatuation of men of intelligence who extol such a book as the Bible. W. J. B.

THE BORDER WATCH ON INFIDELITY.

To the Editor of the Movement.

Sir,—In No. 41, of your Journal, there are a few remarks made upon an article, entitled "The Rapid Spread of Infidelity," which appeared in "The Border Watch" sometime ago. In these you have, no doubt inadvertently, made statements totally destitute of truth, and glaring evasions, which require animadversion. To these I beg to call your attention, believing that truth and argument will be acceptable, from whatever quarter they may come. I may here state, that you have been misled by your correspondent, as to 'an association having sprung up in this town, for the

* In the language of scripture, it is always fornicating with sorcerers, &c., as if the religious principle of the Jews was mixed up with licentiousness in morals. Jeremiah, c. xxxix. speaks of satyrs as existing.

express purpose of declaiming infidelity out of existence;" for what I have published on that subject, I am solely responsible. I, nowhere in the article alluded to, call the Bible a "splendid novel" or in complimentary (ironical) terms state that "*my* ideas of God, the soul, and a divine revelation, are above the, "puny comprehension of infidels," what I stated was, that if there is no God, the Bible must be a "splendid novel," from the pen of a soulless being Thus, it is infidels denying the existence of God, and not I, who make the Bible to be nothing but a "splendid novel; and if so, the Bible being the best book in the world, practising bookmaking and knowledge derived from other books, has only tended to lower the character of books. In reference to the "ideas of God, the human soul," &c.; what I stated, was upon infidel authority. Certainly these ideas must be above their "puny comprehensions;" when to them they are contradictory, irreconcilable, and impossible to be believed. Thus there was nothing complimentary in the statement; and if the above ideas are to be rejected, because they are irreconcilable by men, for the same reason the book of nature must be discarded. I nowhere *assume* that Atheists refuse to believe in the existence of the soul because it cannot be seen. Instead of that being an assumption, it is a reason which I have heard advanced against the existence of the soul; and my *argument* was the following. If the soul's existence is denied because it is invisible, on the same ground deny the "phenomena of life and ideas." Is it an answer to the question - whence came man? to be told that it requires great faith on my part, " in human weakness and credulity, to think that others will accept additional mysteries, by way of solving those they have." Now Sir, this answer to the question—whence came man? And you are still called upon to shew whence had he his origin? If called into being by some agency in nature, apart from God? *How, and when, did that agency become inoperative?* And if there has been an eternal succession of human beings, give something like rational grounds upon which to form such an idea, and besides, show that self-existent beings can die. The idea of self existence is inseparably associated with an eternal succession of beings.

The history of man is a long history of mortality, consequently life in man must always be dependent, and not underived. And the only answer to the question "whence came man" is to be found in the Bible, *God created him*. In sound philosophy find another, and we will compare the two. The indiscreet operative (you say), " challenges infidels to make good the charge, that the Bible teaches vice;" Yes!—and he fearlessly repeats the challenge, because the Bible speaks in plain terms of the vices of David, Lot, and others, does it follow that it teaches vice? If so, then *you* are a persecutor, because that blackest of vices is frequently mentioned in your writings. To prove that the Bible *teaches vice*, you are bound to show that *God* blessed David and Lot for their *guilty actions*, or that there are precepts and commands of universal obligation in *it* of an immoral character. Because bad or *deluded* men have "appealed" to the *Bible* in support of their traffic in human blood, and other deeds of darkness, proves nothing either for or against its morality. That Miss Roalfe, Mr. Finlay, and Mr. Paterson have been incarcerated for blasphemy, what argument is that against the Bible, its every precept is as much opposed to persecution as to blasphemy. Because the executors of the law, have seen fit to imprison these characters, is christianity to be implicated? No, to their master, the judges of the land, stand or fall. Christianity and enlightened Christians unite in condemning every act of injustice, " and all who have cursed mankind by their creed, drunk the blood of the martyrs, and waded through blood to increase our taxes, and enslave nations;" are just the very characters, upon Bible testimony, who, as such, shall never inherit the kingdom of heaven, but have their portion throughout eternity, with *atheists* and *unbelievers* in the place of unmitigated torment. Hoping that you will insert the above, and see the necessity of dealing manfully with an argument, as misrepresentations and evasions are, hurtful to any cause.

A Galashiels Operative.

THE DEMOCRATIC FRIENDS OF ALL NATIONS,

Meeting at 20, *Gt. Windmill-street, Haymarket, on the first Wednesday of every month, at Eight o'clock in the evening.*

The Democratic Friends of all Nations being deeply impressed with the importance of cultivating a brotherly feeling among the people of all countries, and of advancing their social and political rights, conceive that those desirable objects would be promoted if a few democratic friends belonging to different nations could be brought together monthly, for the purpose of friendly conversation; for reading such newspapers of different countries as may be desirable; for affording som-assistance to such political offenders as may be driven from their country for advancing the cause of human liberty; as well as for calling Public Meetings, from time to time, for hearing the democratic opinions of different countries; and for adopting all legal means to create a public opinion in favour of the great principle of human brotherhood. They therefore invite the democrats of all countries to aid them in promoting those benevolent objects, and where practicable, to send a friend from their different bodies, to attend their monthly, and public meetings, and to afford them every information and assistance in furtherance of their objects.

That with a view of conducting the proceedings with order and harmony, the following regulations be observed.—

That a chairman be chosen at the usual monthly meeting to preserve order, to see that the proceedings are conducted in conformity with the above objects, and that no irrelevant matter is introduced calculated to produce division, or frustrate the principle of national fraternity.

That an honorary secretary be chosen every six months, who shall take minutes of all proceedings, and perform all other duties appertaining to the office of secretary. He shall be eligible to be re-chosen.

That a treasurer be chosen every six months, who shall receive all subscriptions or donations that may be given in aid of the objects stated; and keep regular accounts of all receipts and expenditure; nor shall he pay any monies except by a resolution, agreed to at the monthly meeting, and the order be signed by the secretary and two others.

That committees be appointed (whenever necessary) for getting up public meetings, obtaining newspapers, collecting subscriptions, and promoting the general objects herein described.

That in promoting the object of fraternity, the democratic friends of all countries shall be publicly introduced to the chairman; and in order that there shall be no secrecy or illegality in the proceedings, such persons shall give in their names and addresses to the secretary, who shall enter them in the minute-book, the same to be open to all persons who attend.

That as many of the public be admitted, to witness the proceedings of the monthly meetings, as the room will accommodate.

That any of the above regulations may be altered or amended by a notice of the same being given at one monthly meeting, and decided at a subsequent one.

C. *Schapper*, Hon. Sec. pro tem.
Oct. 19, 1844.

MR. JOHNSON'S CASE.

We are happy to be able to refer our readers to the *New Moral World* of last Saturday for a more lengthened report than we could give of the proceedings in Hull, in Mr. Johnson's case. The *Hull Packet* thus states the causes of the prosecution.

"A few weeks since, no ordinary excitement was created in this town by an announcement that Mrs. MARTIN would deliver lectures at the large room of the Cross Keys Hotel, 'to prove the evils and falsehood of Christianity,' and to 'expose the follies and impostures of Christian missionaries.' This startling proposition was met in a *proper* spirit by the Mayor, who caused it to be intimated to the person who had let the room for an *illegal* as well as pernicious purpose, that should he persist in opening the room, he would be made answerable for his conduct. This intimidation had its effect. It, however, did not prevent the delivery of the lectures, as Mr. Watson, landlord of the White Horse Inn, Carr-lane, permitted Mrs. Martin to have the use of his room. The lectures were well attended, the extraordinary powers of eloquence possessed by the lecturer obtaining for her increasingly large audiences. She at length left Hull for Manchester, having, previously to her departure, agreed with Mr. Pulsford, the resident Baptist Minister of this town, to meet him in the Temperance Hall. Paragon-street, on the seventh of October, there publicly to discuss the principles of Christianity, As regards Mrs. Martin, steps were taken, through a communication with the Home Secretary, to afford the Attorney-General the option of prosecuting her for the open dissemination of her principles; and in order to reach the offences of her adherents, informations were ordered to be laid against Watson, the landlord of the White Horse, and against Johnson, a printer and bookseller, in Savile-street, who took money at the doors for admission to the lectures.'

Then follows the trial, before Messrs. *Cookman, Burkworth,* and *Firbank,* the Magistrates, and the excellent and spirited defence of Mr. B. L. Johnson, the Solicitor on behalf of Mr. Johnson, the defendant. Mr. B. L. Johnson, after pointing out how the case had been got up by the pettiest feelings of persecution, and could only be sustained by gagging acts of 1799, which had long lain obsolete and in odium. He asked, what was to be said respecting the Chartists, and Free Trade meetings, for which the authorities had granted the use of the Town Hall? Political and religious discussions would be at an end, if a conviction in this instance took place. Similar lectures were allowed to be given in London and other parts of the kingdom, and reminded the bench that not only those who too money for admission to the lecture, but also those who paid, were liable to the penalties; so that 400 persons, including Baptist ministers, and members of the Town Council, might be proceeded against, and the town be half bankruptized. What was sauce for the goose was sauce for the gander.

The magistrates retired to their private room, with their clerk; and on their return to court, Mr. Cookman announced that the defendant was convicted in the full penalty of £20. his goods to be distrained upon in case of non-payment of the fine. He was further told, that he was liable to *six months imprisonment*, in case there were no goods or chattels to be distrained.

Mr. Watson, the landlord indicted pleaded guilty, and in consideration of that was fined only one pound and costs. Mr. Johnson pursuing a different course, the police were put in immediate possession of his house, with orders to strictly carry out the law; and a bill of sale, a copy of which we intend to preserve in our columns, as a relic, was soon after placarded over the town.

Mr. Johnson writes to a friend, "We had little competition at the sale. The people were disgusted—all was bought in at home, and will be at the shop. I shall commence business again as soon as the sale is over. And we trust a good trade he will be able to command, after the manly stand he has made. Mr. Johnson has issued an excellent address, setting forth the infamous law under which his conviction was ordered. Some of them should be procured, and cirrculated in every town. Mrs. Martin is preparing a small pamphlet, with a statement of the whole case. This is as it should be. These proceedings must be published everywhere. Let those Hull Christians become infamous everywhere, and for ever.

On Sunday evening October 13, a collection was made at the Hall of Science, Manchester, by the direction of the managers, on Mr. Johnson's behalf. Mrs. Martin made the appeal, and nearly Six Pounds were given. We trust that this example will be followed by the London and provincial Branches generally. Nothing can be more to the purpose than the remarks of the *New Moral World*, "We trust that the manner in which Mr. Johnson fights the battle of free speech, will induce all to rally round and support him. This is at once the true way to recompense a public benefactor, and disappoint bigotry and intolerance of its triumph. If it is discovered that popular support follows the steps of the victim selected to endure the penalty of laws alien to the genius of the times, we apprehend that persecution will quickly cease."

Subscriptions may be sent to the Secretary of the Hull Branch, and those to whom it is more convenient, may forward them to the care of the Anti-Persecution Union, addressed to G. J. Holyoake, 5, Paul's Alley, Paternoster Row, London. Mr. Johnson should be enabled to present Mr. L. B. Johnson, the Solicitor who so generously stepped forward to defend him, with the usual fee.

Meanwhile, the agitation goes bravely on. Mrs. Martin is determined that despite of Paul, the "voice of women *shall* be heard in the churches." We have seen bills both from Manchester and Hull, announcing Lectures on Infidelity, by various rev. gents. who are waxing—in their pulpits, in policemen and acts of parliament—very valiant, but in the God very weak.

Christianity Weighed and found Wanting.—This is the title of a "Rejoiner" by Mrs. Martin, to one L. Beckwith, of Hull, who thought fit to write some strictures on her Lectures, in that town.—a benefit for Mr. L. Beckwith.

Baptism.—This is a new pamphlet by the same author, designed to prove Baptism a pagan rite, and contains rare and curious remarks on this famous but idle mythological ceremony.

Etzler's Tropical Emigration Society. The next meeting of this society will take place at the Parthenium Coffee House, St. St. Martin's-lane, on Sunday Afternoon, at 2 o'Clock, and not 266, Strand.

Beneficial Influence of Infidelity.—A pious Scotch Journal, the Glasgow Examiner, lately administered to its readers this warning: "narrow-minded bigotry to every right-thinking mind is alike despicable and detestable. The times in which we live demand that *minor differences should be entirely forgotten*, and that where parties are agreed in the main essentials of christianity they should maintain a *friendly intercourse* with each other, and make it appear to the infidel, that though not united in name, they have, at least, "one faith, one hope, one baptism."

PUBLIC DISCUSSION, BETWEEN MRS. MARTIN AND THE BAPTIST MINISTER.—This proceeding excited great interest. Much anxiety was manifested to procure tickets, some of which were passed from hand to hand for as much as seven shillings. Mrs. Martin and Mr. Pulsford were cheered by their respective friends, on their coming upon the platform. Each party made many speeches. It was quite evident the infidel, as a debater, was an overmatch for the Baptist; her tact was unbounded, and thus was afforded additional EVIDENCE OF THE FOLLY OF ACCEPTING THE CHALLENGE FOR PUBLIC DISCUSSION. Mr. Pulsford's addresses, were beautiful and heartfelt evidences of the great truths of Christianity, in a declamatory style. To these were opposed the most subtle and specious arguments, supported by eloquence of the highest order. The meeting did not break up until a late hour.—HULL PACKET.

MR. HOLYOAKE'S CLASS, North London Schools, No. 8, George-street, New-road, Thursday Evenings, at half-past 8 o'clock, Subjects,—Verbs, ; natural table of them—laws—Critique on Emerson. 2nd Department, Style—Analysis of Method according to the Encyclopædia Britannica—Principles of Composition.

Leicester.—The Magistrate here are intimidating the Vendors of Infidel Publications.

Manchester.—Mrs. Martin still attracts crowded audiences to the Hall of Science, by reporting the visits she pays to the unhappy clergy of the town.

Hull.—Subscriptions for Mr. Johnson to be addressed to Dr. Loudon, Anti-Persecution Committee Rooms, Sackvile-street, Hull. A new Blasphemy Depot, has been opened there. Well done Magistrates !

Worcester.—Lectures are being delivered here by a Mr. Huggins, Lecturer on Theology and Elocution of Edinburgh, on Creation and Atheism. Mr. Walter has fired the city. Why don't Mr. Huggins stay at home—he is much wanted there. Has that prophet no honor in his own country?

NEXT WEEK will be commenced, Chap I. of a *Visit to Harmony Hall*, by the Editor.

B. 2, for Movement........................ 10s.

TO CORRESPONDENTS.

RECEIVED the *Ayr Advertiser*, *The Witness*, *Hull Packet*, The *Statesman*, etc., etc., *Boston Journal*, *People's Rights.* Letter from Mr. Southwell to Mr. Gillespie. J. Cook. T. Allen. T. Bidwell.

Enquirer.—The recent newspaper report respecting Mr. G. Barmby, was but one of those cases to which many men have been subjected to, who have been conspicuous in dissenting from society's iron opinion. The case was one got up to extort money—overtures of compromise were made in court to Mr. B. by the party, which he indignantly rejected. Mr. Barmby's peculiar opinions would not permit him to avail himself of the services of a lawyer, or the charge would have been instantly crushed. He refused to give money to the reporters, and therefore they gave the worst colouring they could. The Grand Jury returned *no Bill.* This at once rebuts the imputation and clears Mr. Barmby. That gentleman has published a statement of his case to which we direct attention.

The Committee for the defence of Mr. Johnson, beg to acknowledge from the friends at Manchester, the sum of 5*l*. 18s. and to say they have effectually prevented the christians rom ruining Mr. Johnson.

T. B. Loudon, Sec.

LECTURES.

Oct. 23.—Hall of Science, Manchester, Mr. R. Cooper,—On the Influence of the Bible on Society
Oct. 27.—Ditto, ditto, Mrs. Martin will lecture Afternoon and Evening.
Oct. 27.—Hall of Science, City-road, Mr. C. Southwell,—On Shakspeare's Opinions on Religion, as developed in his Dramatic writings, at 7, P.M
Oct. 27.—National Hall, 242, High Holborn, W. J. Fox,—On Moral Power and Money Power ; and their collisions in the present state of society, at 8, P. M.
Oct. 27.—Finsbury Institution, Goswell-road, Mr. Cooper,—On Marriage and Divorce, at 7, P. M.
Oct. 27.—Social Institution, Surrey-street, Blackfriars-road, Mr. A. Campbell,—Are the Principles and Practice of Socialism calculated to satisfy the rational desires of man in active life, and support him in death ? at 7, A. M.
Oct. 27.—Social Institution, Whitechapel, Mr. G. Edwards will lecture.
Oct 27.—Branch A 1, John-street, Tottenhamcourt-road, Mr. J. Ellis,—On Late Proceedings in the British Association.
Oct. 28.—Mutual Instruction Society, 66, Bunhillrow, A Member,—On the Beauties of Dickens, at 8½, P. M.

DISCUSSIONS.

Oct. 23 & 30.—Public Hall, Temple-street, Bristol, —Subject, Has Religion a tendency to benefit the human race ? The Affirmative by G. Powell,—Negative by H. Cook.
Oct. 25.—John's Street Institution.—On the Immortality of the Soul.
Oct. 26.—Social Institution, Whitechapel,—Public Discussion.
Oct 27.—Finsbury Institution, Goswell Road,—Would a Law permitting Divorce to the Poor have an immoral tendency ? After the Evening Lecture.
Oct. 20.—Social Institution, Whitechapel, — The Rev. G. Hill and Mr. Southwell,—Question, Is Materialism true ?

SUBSCRIPTIONS
TO THE ANTI-PERSECUTION UNION.

Per M. G. Smith, Salford
  To Sale of ORACLES 1 0
  J. Jones........................... 2 6
  Several Friends.................... 2 2
At City Road, Oct. 13, per Mr. H.
  D. Murphy......................... 1 0
  Jas. Betts 1 0
  E. Well, and J. Rough 1 0
  C. Davis, W. Day 1 0
Bristol Subscriptions, for Sept.
  Card 16 .... 5 0
  J. Cook, Ipswich 1 0
  Card 39, W. F...................... 2 6
  T. Bidwell......................... 1
                    G. J. H., Sec.

Opening of Investigation Hall.—This neat, convenient, and commodious Hall, situate 29, Circusstreet, near St. Mary's Church, Marylebone, will be opened on Sunday next, Oct. 27, under the auspices of Mr. Bendall, jun., son of the well-known and respected proprietor of the Hall of Science, City-road. J. B. jun. has lately taken possession of Investigation Hall, and is prepared to conduct it in a manner worthy of the great purposes to which it will be henceforth devoted—the pursuit of truth, the recreation and elevation of the industrious classes. C. Southwell will deliver the opening address at 11, a.m. and G. J. Holyoake will deliver the Evening Lecture, at p. m.

Printed and Published by G. J. HOLYOAKE,
40, Holywell-street, Strand.
Wednesday, October 23, 1844.

THE MOVEMENT

And Anti=Persecution Gazette.

" Maximise morals, minimise religion."—BENTHAM.

No. 47.   EDITED BY G. JACOB HOLYOAKE, ASSISTED BY M. Q. RYALL.   Price 1½d.

A VISIT TO HARMONY HALL

BY G. J. H.

I

It is a perfect pilgrimage to visit Harmony, so remotely is it situated from any of the socialist branches. Really, those who have the hardihood to make the journey ought to be enabled thereby to ensure their social salvation. Catholic redemption has often been purchased on easier terms.

Reader, if you set out from the provinces, and your road to Harmony Hall lies through London, ask before you leave home where the Nine Elms Terminus is situated. Nobody in London knows it. I asked twenty people before I found one who had the slightest notion of its whereabouts. The *New Moral World* says, go to the *Nine* Elms Terminus, at *nine* o'clock in the morning, and book yourself for the *nine* mile water — but there are *nine* chances to one against a stranger doing this.

On Monday morning, October 14, I "wended my way," as the novelists have it, down by Parliament House and over Vauxhall Bridge on my visit to Harmony Hall. At nine o'clock, to a minute, at the Nine Elms Terminus, I demanded a ticket for nine mile water, Harmony Hall. "Oh" said the official in the railway office, "you must take a ticket to Farnboro'! that's the station." Taking it for granted that he knew all about it, in five minutes I was on my way to Farnboro'—the rain pelting down as though it was half an hour too late, and the wind blowing as though they were trying a new pair of bellows up above. In about an hour I alighted at Farnboro' station, and thought — "well, after all, Harmony is not so far off as people have said," and I looked about for friend Buxton and one of the Harmony vehicles. But I found myself surrounded by a crowd of Frenchmen, gabbling like mad, and I thought surely these people can't belong to Harmony Hall, unless they are the "hired labourers" of the old Executive. I enquired at once for Queenwood, "Queenwood?" said the marvelling superintendent, "there was a gentleman who once before came here asking for that place. It is forty or fifty miles below. You had better take the next train to Winchester, and then enquire again." I gave up all ideas of seeing Harmony that day, and expected only to find my way there in the course of the week. I had nothing to do but to turn myself to the fire and the Frenchmen, in the hopes of finding either warmth or amusement. In a few minutes I found that the Frenchmen were king's attendants, waiting for the arrival of Louis Philippe and the Queen, who were expected from Windsor at one o'clock. Before long I observed some strange looking men darting off at all angles, without any apparent reason, and pushing people about I could not tell why. But soon I discovered their movements followed on the nod and beck of a marble eyed elderly gentleman, who was, if I mistake not, one of Sir James Graham's special commissioners, whom I saw at Gloucester Gaol, and I saw I was surrounded by the famous A Division of Police from Scotland Yard, who darted about at every roll of the official orbs before mentioned. I immediately called in all external signs of curiosity, and looked as much like nobody as possible, by which means I noticed everybody in security. When the royal party arrived from Windsor, even the gaping gentry of the neighbourhood were thrust to the back of the building at every avenue policemen brandished their batons – a poor Frenchman looking over a gate was rudely thrust back and given in charge of the police, and none but officials and the Editor of the *Movement* stood in the narrow passage made for their majesties to pass. I inserted myself in the midst of the police, deeming that the best place for not being seen by them—and I was right. Guizot first interested me. His half military dress detracted from his philosophical character, but his well moulded head and firm features, resting upon his iron looking shoulders, gave him, though rather a short man, an appearance of majesty, which none of their Majesties possessed. He looked one of the princes of what the Chambers style, the "intellectual aristocracy." Many a Frenchman will envy me. Louis Philippe I could have shot half a dozen times, had I been so disposed. There is nothing inviting about him. His cheeks hang like collapsed pudding bags. His frontispiece struck me as resembling Jupiter's with the brains out. His head baffled all my phrenology—it is something between facetiæ and mathematics—half comical and half conical. The only thing to which I can compare it, is an inverted humming top.* Perhaps his conduct had prejudiced me, for I gladly turned away from the odious restrictor of the French press.

Prince Albert has a right princely appearance. His large German eyes are singularly full and glaring. He looks as though he was very well fed, and never thought where it came from. None of these I had seen before. The Queen I had not seen since she was a girl, and I wondered how the cooped up, swaddled thing I saw in Birmingham had become so nice a young woman—I was agreeably surprised at her. The breezes of Blair Athol have left her quite blooming, and her pretty Saxon face beaming both with maternal affection and thought,† quite prepossessed me in her favour. I don't think that she means us any harm, though she does us no good. The royal party passed on to Gosport, for Louis Philippe was going home.

By three o'clock I was again on the line, making another violent attempt to get to Harmony Hall. O Æolus, how the wind blows on the Southampton railway! Those who travel there this weather, should tie caps on their heads, and to ligature their heads on their shoulders will be found no superfluous precaution. My cap, which had seen some service—having had six months' imprisonment, was almost blown into its original fleece, and was near taking up its old abode on the backs of the neighbouring sheep.

* The people of France, I have since learned, nick-named him *Louis le poire*—or the pear-headed, from the resemblance they discovered in his face and head to an inverted pear. And Paris—until he interfered—used to be placarded with pictures of pears, bearing his face, with the words annexed, "When the pear is rotten it will fall." An event not deemed unlikely to happen.

* The people of Belgium, during the Queen's visit there, thought her affected with the malady of her grandfather, George III., from the vacancy of her laugh, and it is sa'd that her repeated excursions are ordered by her physicians, to keep away a melancholy with which she is threatened. At times she sobs and cries much. I should say she is improving now.

At last I reached Winchester, having paid 12s. for my ride in the 2nd class. It was half past four, and Stockbridge was nine miles off. No conveyance being to be had, and the rain abating, I walked the distanc

The *New Moral World* directs that persons visiting Harmony should "book themselves at Noyce's coach office, to go by the nine o'clock morning train." Those who do so are taken by the second class to Winchester, and then on Noyce's coach to Nine mile water, thirteen miles farther on, for 10s. But not being able to understand what booking at a coach office had to do with the morning railway train, I took my ticket in the railway instead of the coach office. The railway people have an arrangement whereby those who only travel to Winchester pay 12s., but if they go thirteen miles farther on, they pay only 10s. The farther you go the less they charge. The road from Winchester to Stockbridge lies over bleak hills and barren dales. Here and there a solitary tree or bush raises its disconsolate head and looks half alarmed at its own temerity in getting out of the earth in that bald district. Before I reached Stockbridge

The gloomy night was gathering fast,
Loud roar'd the wild inconstant blast,
The murky clouds were big with rain,
I saw them driving o'er the plain.

At last, regular Egyptian darkness—such as could be felt, set in, but where Stockbridge lay, whether near or far, on hill or in hollow, I knew not. At last, poking my way with my umbrella, I ran against something that proved to be a ploughman, from whom I learned that I was on the verge of the village, that I must turn by the "Ship," ask for the "Queen's Head," and tell "Stone" that I was one of the "*Zozialites*," and I should be all right. There I found a pretty kind creature of a landlady, and in due time, (by half past seven), I was munching toast and listening to one of those organised funguses, which seem to vegetate about Stockbridge in the shape of farmers' labourers, singing for the amusement of his companions—

If I had a wife wot blow'd me up,
I'd get a gal and make her jealous.

For supper, bed, and song, having paid 1s. 6d., next morning found me on my way to Harmony Hall. It rained then like it did when Noah took the fish into the Ark to prevent them being drowned.

My directions were to pass through the village, and at a mile and half onwards turn off to the left, by a gentleman's house, which would lead me (somehow) to Broughton. I was now fairly in the land of flint and chalk. Everywhere lay flanks of earth, dressed in nature's shabbiest attire—not unlike a man in threadbare hose, and the mounds of white chalk, peeping up here and there, presented the picture of nature out at the elbows. While the hills, presenting their raw noses around, with only an old dark brown coat on their backs, flabbing in rags over their slough covered feet, looked like vegetable swells out of luck.

When high on the road that "lay by the gentleman's house," I asked my way of an old villager, who, unfortunately for me, "knew the road well." He sent me along this field, over that, by a stile, "which I should be sure to see," (but be sure not to know), and after turning here and turning there, I should come out somewhere in Broughton.

Reader! let me entreat you to take warning by my fate. Men who "know the way" have nearly been the ruin of me. In every town they have been my greatest bores and most dreaded persecutors. If I was going to be hanged, the first thing I should warn young persons against would be all those "people who knew the way." If all the misfortunes of my life, from other causes, were gathered together, they would fall far short of the miseries heaped upon me by these officious tormentors. Every week of my life I have walked five times farther than my real way, through following the directions of people who sent me "the nearest way." When a stranger asks his road, instead of being directed straight forward, through high-ways or well known streets, which he could not miss—somebody who knows all the lanes and bye-ways, courts, and alleys, will direct him through them. The moment a stranger enters the first of these, he knows not where he is, and has to spend more time in making enquiries than would take him ten times the actual distance. Some plain person, who knows little about a place, is the man to seek as a guide. In Bristol, I had the good luck on my entrance, to be taken to Bristol Bridge. This became my centre — everywhere I went I started from Bristol Bridge. I was never so happy in any other town. In London, through always being directed "the nearest way," I am sure I have walked 1000 unnecessary miles. After travelling until I thought it was dinner time, I happily discovered the road I had left, and soon came in sight of Broughton, which is scarcely four miles from Stockbridge. But what with the weather and bad guides, I shall hardly be able to reach Harmony Hall in this chapter.

Broughton is a pleasant village to look at, but all its pleasantness is outside—it is plain and dull enough within. But as it is the first relief from barrenness and stones, one is glad to see it. About a mile through it, over a chalk hill, is the next road to be taken, and as the traveller descends the hill's brow, he comes suddenly upon Harmony Hall. It is a very respectable looking building—imbedded in a mountain—half red half blue—a compound of brick and slate, of no conceivable shape, with two spires in front, and two glass chimneys, apparently intended to let people see the smoke come up, but farther examination tells you they are skylights over the corridors, leading to the dormitories. C. M. 1844, are observable at one end of the building, which informed me, for the first time, that the Millenium had commenced *three years* ago.

Verdure and beauty first make their appearance in the neighbourhood of the Hall. Around, pleasant prospects arise. But it was a place to look at rather than to live on. The soil has *now* been made productive, at great expense, but the flints which cover the land, point out the place as one intended by nature, not for a colony of socialists, but for a colony of gunsmiths, before percussion caps sprung up. Such a colony might have made their fortunes by gathering the flints. The more a stranger gazes on that estate, the more he wonders at the sagacity which first selected it, and he comes to the conclusion that it was chosen with an eye to insolvency, under the impression that the chalk pits in the neighbourhood would be convenient for "white washing."

(*To be continued next week*).

THE GALASHIELS OPERATIVE.

The following brief remarks were intended to be appended to the letter of the Galashiels Operative last week, but space did not permit:

Respecting the "association," concerning which our friend the operative declares I have been misled, it will be sufficient to remark that a placard has been posted in Galashiels, headed "Exposure," stating that "the clergy and others have formed themselves into a "*society for the suppression of Infidelity.*" Do the christians of Galashiels intend taking a less honorable way than "declaiming"—and will they do, as they have done elsewhere, bludgeon it as the easier method of putting "infidelity out of existence?" These are the operative's words respecting the "splendid novel"—"taking it for granted that there is no God, it follows that the Bible is—a splendid novel from the pen of a material soulless being." Is *not* this giving the Bible credit for being a splendid novel? But if the operative thinks now that it is not a "splendid novel" he agrees with us, who think it, with or "without God," anything but a "splendid novel."

The next passage in the article in question from the pen of the operative, which I quote is this—" the ideas of a self-existent eternal God, the human soul, another world, and a Divine revelation, are above their (the infidels') puny comprehension." Now these ideas of "God," "soul," "world," and "revelation," are the operative's ideas, and is not the sentence in which they are, a plain assertion that *his* ideas are above the puny comprehension of the infidel?" I need not spend more words in proving that I did not even "inadvertently" make statements totally destitute of truth." Just mark the simplicity of our operative, he says, "thus you see there was nothing *complimentary* in the statement." The innocent doesn't know when he is laughed at. We never thought he did compliment us by his talk of "puny intellect."

Of course both "the Book of Nature," as well as the "ideas," I questioned, must be "rejected" if found "irreconcilable;" no sane man believes in contradictions, whether born of God or nature. I do not know "where man came from," and am no wiser by being told that "God created him." This is the old trick of putting one difficulty forward to account for another.

If we would throw a veil over the obscenities and immoralities of the Bible, "indiscreet" christians would not let us. Such records as those of Lot, Noah, David, and others teach vice by the example they set. To go at once to Christ the "master" of our operative, he taught vice—his diabolical sentiment that "he who believed should be saved and he who did not should be damned,"— taught a vicious faith and practice to all succeeding ages. The Bible teaches human depravity. This is vice. The words of Paul, that he who taught a doctrine different from his should be accursed, teach vice. It is idle in our operative to set himself up as the sole decider of what is christianity. The judges of Scotland are more competent authorities than he. The Clergy know christianity better than an operative, be he who he may, and they support persecutions as altogether christian. All christians, save a few bold ones, deny persecution to be christian in argument but support it in practice. Did our operative ever subscribe a penny for those victims who were sacrificed in the name of Christ? Has he sent a single petition against prosecutions for blasphemy? He does not answer these questions. Works are better than faith.

We have published our operative's paper, and answered frankly his interrogatories. The *Border Watch*, his own christian paper, that published his attack on infidelity has refused to insert the answers sent by our Galashiels' friend. Is this the way *christians* " deal manfully with arguments?"— *Ed. of M.*

MR. JOHNSON'S SECOND ADDRESS.

Mr. Johnson has issued a "Second Address" to the inhabitants of Hull. Its manly spirit and temperate firmness, merits high approval. The following are two paragraphs—

"The rumour that it was my intention to lay informations against a number of persons who attended Mrs. Martin's lecture, on the 20th of September, has widely circulated, and in candour I must admit that, from the flagrant injustice done me, and under the impulse of painful excitement, I did entertain something like a notion of retaliation, by subjecting the police informant to similar proceedings, with a view of testing the impartiality of the magistrates. But on making myself acquainted with Act under which I was convicted—and on more mature consideration, finding I had been, according to my understanding of it, ILLEGALLY PUNISHED, I could not longer entertain the idea of being the means of inflicting that injustice upon others, which I had myself been subjected to."

"It being considered that as I was but a poor man, and in indifferent circumstances, probably the magistrates thought the matter would pass without further comment, except perhaps so far as my being held up as a terror to evil doers, but in this, they will find they have been deceived—for although I am not able to boast of the magnitude of my means, yet, I possess the feelings of a man, and as such, know when they are *unjustly* outraged, and I consider myself bound to bring their decision—which to me appears a gross infringement on the rights of an Englishman—under the revisal of a higher tribunal, and I doubt not that public feeling will go along with my endeavour to attain justice and to secure the right of free discussion. I now cease to look at the matter as a private and personal one, but as a subject to which the attention of the public of every sect and party ought to be directed, with a view to this Act being more clearly defined, so that if found to be so obnoxious, as our magistrates have rendered it, means may be taken to have it erased from the Statute Book."

We need only add how sincerely we call on friends, far and near, to aid Mr. Johnson in this excellent and spirited undertaking. On Sunday morning, Mr. Holyoake, by permission of the president, brought the matter before the members of Branch A 1. And soon we shall probably be able to report some assistance determined to be rendered.

LETTER FROM MR. SOUTHWELL TO MR. GILLESPIE.

Sir,—I am sorry that you are dissatisfied with " The Battle," nevertheless, your frank admission that I have *not* written to unwrite what I wrote, is consoling, genuine balm in Gilead.

Assure yourself of my being no less " happy " to repeat than you are " to say," that if the first proposition of your grand *Mistake* can be proved true, all the rest of its propositions cannot be proved false. No more, then, in Job's name, about that " settled point," lest you should unsettle the equanimity of our very patient friend, the Editor of the *Movement.* If, instead of again and again referring to points of agreement, you would set about settling *our only material point of difference,* it occurs to me, that less might be *said* but more to the purpose be *meant* in your pieces.

That I should " call in question as much as ever," the truth of proposition 1, is an " old course," you were not, it seems, prepared to expect I should " still follow." In short, my " consistency," though it ' augurs well for our debate reaching a definite conclusion," has filled you with " signal astonishment "—as if (upon the principle of measuring other men's grain by your own bushel) you thus reasoned with yourself:—I am far from consistent, and am unable to understand how anybody can hesitate to be inconsistent, at a pinch.

Some parts of " The Battle " seem to have signally *confused* you. To answer what I have written, you properly say would imply that you *understood* it. Then follows a confession that there are things therein " which you cannot at all understand or make sense of." After which, you furnish " passages parallel," which seem perfectly irreconcilable with each other; but if not, you " wish for a clue to a method " whereby they may be reconciled.

Sir, you shall have the desired " clue " in the tangible shape of some two or three plain sentences.

Is matter extended or unextended is *the* question. A categorical answer to which you require. You want no argument, but simply an *explicit* answer.—Here it is.

Matter is extended, *but* extension is not matter, and, of course, nowhere exists. What is not matter is not anything. Extension is no more *in* matter than *out* of it. Nothing exists but matter, all being it, and it being all. This, sir, I say, and am prepared to *abide by* as touching *matter.*

The " passages parallel " which seem to you, and which you *fancy* will seem to every body else but me, " *flat contradictions,*" are all true, and may easily be reconciled by any one who is capable of understanding that *all* matter is extended, or, if you like the words better, has extension in the same way *and no other.* That some matter (wormwood, for example) is bitter, or has bitterness. I object to the words, " matter has extension," *if understood to mean an existence— a something not matter—not otherwise.*

With a view to your satisfaction, I conclude by observing, that the uncaused cause of all causes and effects, which I call matter, undoubtedly " is something which is long, broad, and deep, or extended in three dimensions, viz., length, breadth, and depth."

I beg to be considered, sir, your well-wisher,

CHARLES SOUTHWELL.
London, 18th Oct., 1844.

ZEAL.—" What a noble fellow is that subscriber to the Anti-Persecution Union, whose one shilling monthly is sure to be forthcoming, though he is only a hard-working man ! What an incentive to others to follow his example. If all atheists were like him, how the cause would progress. Give me those who say little and do much. I could not refrain from writing to tell him that there was one man who appreciates his zeal in supporting infidelity ; and in reply, he says, " I willingly subscribe my mite to the funds of the Anti-Persecution Union, because I know that the more support is given to a society of that sort, the more confidence is created in persons situated as I am, being only a working-man. My wife used to say to me, ' you'll get yourself into a mess, and then what will become of us, the *religious* people would like to see us starving and would say, it was *God's* doing.' That was before the establishment of the Union; now, she says nothing to me, but rather assists me in the good work. For myself, I fear nothing that the minions of priestcraft can do, but I have them that have claims upon me which makes me less useful than I like to be to the Union, but I *determined* o do all that I can.'—*From a Correspondent.*

We have requested permission to insert this extract, scarcely knowing which to admire the more, the devotion of our humble friend, or the thoughtful discrimination of our correspondent, who has singled him out, and been at the trouble to write him to express that appreciation which all must feel at his conduct. Goodness often pines because it is never assured of the esteem it wins. We have no reason to think this of our friend, the artisan, but all men are not strong in their own resolves. Some virtue, like the oak, stands firm in its own strength, other, like the ivy, clings to good opinion for support.

INFIDEL TRACT SOCIETY.—We have received a long report from Mr. Doyle, addressed to the " Infidel Public," respecting this association. The Report states, that " limited means " and " difficulty of procuring a printer to print their works, are as yet obstacles in the society' sway." The Report urges " the necessity of an Infidel Tract Society, at a time when the Religious Tract Society is exerting its pestiferous influences over the intellectual energy of the people."

" The medium through which the funds of the society may be supported is by donations. Twopence per week is the amount of subscription. Any member sending three weeks' subscription, with a stamp, will have a member's card forwarded by return of post. The address of the secretary is—*Richard Doyle, 10, Alfred Place, Old Kent Road.*

OBITUARIES.

WILLIAM WATTS, of Hoxton, a constant and indefatigable friend and Collector of the Anti-Persecution Union, died August 7th. We have but lately been apprised of the fact. We have had the gratification of learning from his widow, (whose name appears this week in our list of subscriptions) " that he died as he should have died—stedfast in the cause to which he was so warmly attached—thereby giving proof that Materialism is as well to die with as to live with."

THE REV. ROBERT TAYLOR.—This celebrated Deist died on the 5th of June, at least so writes Mr. Richard Carlile, in the *Northern Star.* Beyond this nothing is certainly known. Mr. Carlile assures the public that the newspaper paragraphs concerning him are wholly incorrect.

JOSEPH WALKER.—A Biographical Sketch of this eccentric democrat appeared in No. 100, of *Lloyd's Weekly London Newspaper*, from the pen of Mr. H. Sculthorp. Mr. Walker died in Dublin, in September. He prided himself on his acquaintance with the late Richard Carlile, and Julian Hibbert. The public have been indebted to the exertions of the author of " Political Touchwood," and his memory deserves to be preserved as a benefactor of his species who laboured and suffered for the popular advancement.

A SPICEY BIT OF PROGRESS.—I am happy to inform you that we are likely to have a revolution in our Edinburgh Hall; at least, it was purchased by Mr. Grant the other week for £150. It is to be painted and decorated, the pulpit is to be removed, and a platform erected in its place. The entrance from the court is to be stopped up, and, in fact, I dont know what is not to be done.

At the request of Mr. L. Jones, there was a meeting of the friends on Friday evening last, which was very thinly attended. Mr. J. addressed us in his usual style, about offending " public prejudices," and thought we had too openly professed infidelity; and it was principally owing to this that our Branch was in such a condition as he found it : he told us it was *our own fault* if we allowed our lecturers to speak in such a manner as to drive the public from the hall.

Mr. Brown, thinking this a side blow at Mr. Southwell, rose and defended him. He said Mr. S. was an uncompromising advocate of truth, and that during his stay amongst them, he believed he had acted consistently and conscientiously. That he had never delivered a course of lectures without first consulting the Committee, and although, when he first came here, he was not a member of the social body, yet he would affirm, without fear of contradiction, that the best lectures ever delivered on Socialism, in Edinburgh, had been delivered by Mr. Southwell.

There was a meeting of the members on the last Sunday evening that Mr. Jones lectured, to consider the advisability of engaging another lecturer, and it was unanimously agreed on that another should be engaged ; and in the presence of Mr. J., several declared that they would not give their vote for any but an " out and out atheist," but they were at a loss to know who to get. Hamilton, with the *curly hair* was one of the members who declared that it was useless for any but an atheist to lecture to us after being accustomed to hear Mr. Southwell. Mr. J. replied, " I tell you what, young man, had I the power, I would cut you off altogether from the society." Hamilton told him he might do it and welcome, if he could, as we could soon form ourselves into a society of infidels. " It is useless," he continued, " for any *half-and-half* fellow to come among us now." You can easily imagine how Mr. Jones looked at this speech.—*M. R.*

Mr. Owen.—Files of American papers have arrived in this country, announcing the presence of Mr. Owen in that country. Journals that disagree with Mr. Owen on every point, have yet published his addresses and welcomed him among them. This speaks well for republican liberality. He won't meet this respect from our monarchical journals, when he returns even to his own land.

The Recent Discussion.—The Rev. J. Pulsford and Mrs. Martin, having read over the Report of the Discussion now circulating have decided that it is very incorrect and deficient, and that the heading and comment attached to the pamphlet, is unjust and highly reprehensible.

A corrected Report will be published as soon as possible, in which *Mrs. Martin's* speeches will be revised by herself, and an *Appendix* will be furnished, containing additional illustrations of the great subject in dispute.

Mr. J. Bronterre O'Brien respectfully informs Landlords, Capitalists, the League, his friends, and the Public, that on *Saturday*, 16*th* November, 1844, will appear, No. 1 of
THE NATIONAL REFORMER,
and Manx British and Foreign Review. A weekly journal of politics, literature, and science, devoted to the instruction and emancipation of the industrious orders.

The *National Reformer* will belong to no party, sect, or faction. It will be the deadly foe of class legislation and class distinctions. It will advocate equal rights and equal laws for all. Its columns will be always open to reports or notices of public proceedings useful to the million. It will contain ample and faithful reviews of Standard Works and new Publications, friendly to the the rights of man. It will have able correspondents in all the principal towns in the United Kingdom, through whom, as well as from other sources; it will collect early intelligence and useful information on all subjects likely to instruct or to interest the People.

The *National Reformer* will be conducted by gentlemen of tried character and ability. It will be neatly printed on good paper, with new type, cast expressly for the occasion. It will be on a large sheet, its form quarto, and to make it accessible to the poor, *its price will be only twopence-halfpenny.* Thus constituting it the cheapest weekly newspaper in the kingdom.

As the *National Reformer* is established for the benefit of the three kingdoms alike, —it will be printed and published in the centre of all three—viz :—in Douglas, Isle of Man, where it will enjoy equal facilities of intercourse with each, and whence the post will convey it carriage-free to all parts of the kingdom.

Agents: Watson, Cleave, Hetherington, and Berger, London. Heywood, Manchester. Guest, Birmingham. Robinson, Cranston Edinburgh. Love, Glasgow, Smith, (Scotland Place) Liverpool. O'Brien, Dublin. Woodward, Brighton. Leggett, Portsmouth. Chappel, Bristol. Sidwell, Bath. Horn, France and Co., Newcastle-upon-Tyne. Arthur, Carlisle. Ottley, Sheffield. Williams, Sunderland. Lingard, Barnsley. Clayton, Huddersfield, and Hobson, Ashton-under-Lyne, &c., &c.

Letters and communications for the editor to be addressed, post-paid, to Post-office, Douglas, Isle of Man—till furthernotice.

"*The Last of the Martyrs.*"—These spirited lines, addressed to Mr. Paterson, by Mrs. Martin, can yet be had, price 1d., elegantly printed on stiff paper. Only 1000 were struck off, so that those who desire to preserve them, must do so early. It ought to be known, that Mrs. Martin, besides presenting the M.S. of the lines to the Anti-Persecution Union, took 300 *copies at full price*, which nearly paid all expenses, and the profits of the remainder she desired to be paid to the *Paterson Testimonial.*

Just published, price One Penny, The Doctrine of the Human Soul a Fiction ; in answer to a Lecture, delivered by the Rev. J. Pulsford, of Hull,—By Matthew Tate.

For Mr. Paterson, from " W. W."			0	15	0
For Miss Roalfe,	do.	do.	0	5	0
For C. S.,	do.	do.	0	5	0
For G. J. H.,	do.	do.	0	5	0
For Mrs. Martin,	do.	W. T.	0	7	6
For Mr. Finlay,	do.	do.	0	2	0

PATERSON TESTIMONIAL.

W. J. B., third subscription	1	0	0
J. M. C., second subscription	0	5	0
R. R. C., second subscription	0	5	0
Mr. Kincaid, Rochdale, per Mrs. Martin	0	4	0
From Preston, per Mrs. Martin	0	1	0
Mr. Credder, per Mr. Marshal	0	0	6

BALANCE SHEET OF THE ANTI-PERSECUTION UNION,
For the Quarter ending September 29, 1844.

RECEIPTS.					EXPENDITURE.			
To Subscriptions, per *Movement* No. 30		0	13	3	Balance due to Treasurer last quarter	1	11	9
Do.	do. — 31	0	2	6	Paid to Mr. Whiting, Bristol, on account	2	9	0
Do.	do. — 32	0	11	6	To Miss Roalfe	1	0	0
Do.	do. — 33	1	3	2	To Mr. Paterson, as per subscriptions	1	6	6
Do.	do. — 34	10	0	0	To do., as per vote of committee, (Sep. 30)	2	0	0
Do.	do. — 35	1	8	6	To "Paterson Testimonial," per vote of			
Do.	do. — 36	2	7	10	committee	5	0	0
Do.	do. — 37	0	11	6	To do. do., as per subscriptions	*4	16	0
Do.	do. — 38	1	6	6	500 Members' Tickets	0	12	6
Do.	do. — 39	1	3	0	Bills and expences of Annual Meeting	0	10	0
Do.	do. — 40	2	3	0	Printing Weekly Receipts, Balance Sheets,			
Do.	do. — 41	1	1	0	Notices, Reports of Meetings, Progress,			
Do.	do. — 42	1	6	3	&c.	1	12	0
To Balance due to Treasurer		0	13	3	Assistant Secretary	1	10	0
					Eleven dozen of *Movements*, containing special Anti-Persecution Union matter, circulated, &c.	0	15	0
Audited by us and found correct,					To general correspondence parcels, deductions of Money Orders, Newspapers for			
JOHN ELLIS, JOHN SKELTON.					use, Petition Sheets, etc., etc.	1	7	6
		£24	11	3		£24	11	3

G. JACOB HOLYOAKE, *Secretary*

* Thus the total amount of the "Paterson Testimonial" in the hands of the Treasurer, at the date of this account, September 29, was 9*l*. 16*s*. It still increases.

NOTICES.

The Committee of the Anti-Persecution Union will meet in the Coffee Room of John Street Institution, Tottenham Court Road, on Monday evening, Nov. 4, at half-past eight o'clock. Important business will be brought forward.

Now READY, the 11th Monthly Part, price 7d.

MR. LEAR meets his Latin Class every Sunday morning at eleven o'clock. For particulars, apply to Mr. J. Perrin, Jun., George Street, Trafalgar Street, Walworth.

Tropical Emigration Society.—A lecture will be delivered on Thursday evening next, at the Parthenium, No. 7½, St. Martin's Lane, by Mr. Etzler—when the Models of his Satellite and Automaton will be exhibited. To begin at half-past eight o'clock—admission free.

Gillespie's argument Atheised, by Charles Southwell, will appear in No. 10 of the *Library of Reason*.

TO CORRESPONDENTS.

WALTER SANDERSON.—We published the Operative's letter a week ago. It can matter little whether we publish his letter or not, if the *Movement* never reaches—as it appears not to do—Galashiels.
RECEIVED.—"A Methodist Sermon." T. Emery (we can only transfer the theological part of his letter to our columns). *A Mover* is thanked for his trouble. Mill's Human Soul. "Report of Baptist Home Missionary Society." J. Trueman. Notes on the Jesuits, by W. J. B.

LECTURES.

Nov. 3.—Branch A 1, Fitzroy Square, Mr. G. J. Holyoake, subject,—Some reflections on popular attempts at the elevation of woman, with a new proposal on the subject. At 7, P.M.
Nov. 3.—Social Institution, 5, Charlotte Street, Blackfriars Road (afternoon), Mr. Southwell,—On the Biblical, Moral, and Religious speculations of the Communists of Germany. (Evening at 7), Mr. Campbell,—What is Religion, and how far has its practice benefited man?

Nov. 3.—Investigation Hall, 29, Circus Street, Marylebone, (morning), Mr. Southwell. An evening lecture at 7 o'clock by Mr. Ellis.
Nov. 3.—City Road Hall of Science, Mr. Southwell, —On the Religious opinions of Shakspere. At 7, P.M.
Nov. 3.—Finsbury Institution, Goswell Road, Mr. Cooper,—On the Religion of the New Moral World. Doors open at 7. Discussion after.
Nov. 4.—Finsbury Mutual Instruction Society, 66, Bunhill Row, Mr. J. Merriman,—On the French Revolution. At half-past 8, P.M.

Mr. Johnson desires to acknowledge 25s. received from Stockport, namely—Thomas Goulden, Esq., 10s.—Mr. D. Bowlas, 10s.—Mr. R. Cooper, 2s. 6d. —Mr. S. Ingham, 2s. 6d.

W. J. B., for the Secretary of the Anti-Persecution Union, and our Editor, 1l. For *Movement*, a friend, Coventry, 10s. For *Movement*, W. D. Saul, 2s. 6d. For M. Q. R., from W. B. B., 10s. For G. J. H., from W. B. B., 10s.

SUBSCRIPTIONS
TO THE ANTI-PERSECUTION UNION.

	£	s.	d.
W. J. B., for Johnson of Hull	2	0	0
Mrs. Katherine Watts	0	2	6
Mrs. Martin, 100 "Last of the Martyrs,"	0	8	4
A friend, Coventry, second annual subscription	0	10	0
Mr. E. Nicholls, Birmingham	0	1	0
Mr. Clements, per do.	0	1	0
Per Mr. Holyoak, Secretary of Leicester Branch of Anti-Persecution Union—			
Mr. Mansfield and Nottingham friend	0	2	6
Subscriptions of Leicester Branch	0	12	3
J. Rough, for Mr. Johnson, Hull	0	1	0
Mr. Page, for Mr. Trueman	0	0	6
At the Hall of Science, City Road, after Mr. Southwell's lecture, October 27, for Mr. Johnson of Hull	1	8	6

G. J. H., *Sec.*

Printed and Published by G. J. HOLYOAKE, 40, Holywell-street, Strand.
Wednesday, October 30, 1844.

THE MOVEMENT
And Anti=Persecution Gazette.
"Maximise morals, minimise religion."—BENTHAM.

No. 48.　　　EDITED BY G. JACOB HOLYOAKE,　　　Price 1½d
　　　　　　　ASSISTED BY M. Q. RYALL.

A VISIT TO HARMONY HALL
BY G. J. H.
II.

YES, reader! in a remote part of Britain, down in Hampshire's very heart, as far as possible from any seat of manufacture or commerce, and out of the way of every body concerned, is situated the famous Socialist's experiment. Had it been near Manchester or Birmingham, it would have commanded, in its own friends, without expense of conveyance, a ready and unfailing market for all its produce. Had it been near some coal district, and contiguous to some river, manufactures might have formed, as was always intended, a part of its operations. But it has neither natural nor artificial advantage as a trading community. As an agricultural colony only can it, for a long time, succeed, and for this species of success nature has done little, and its directors less. Their first care was to erect normal schools when they wanted farmsteads.

Among the inmates of Harmony Hall and its dependencies, I found numerous old friends and acquaintances, from all parts of the country. The Hall itself more resembles Drayton Manor, the residence of Sir R. Peel, than the home of pioneers. Everything has been provided in the most expensive way. Economy appears to have been laughed at in its erection. During that panic of pride, a pretty infants' school, erected under Mr. Joseph Smith's superintendance, was contemptuously termed a "shed." The cellars of the Hall, now used as a dining room, have a costly range of windows tastefully pannelled, the sides of the whole room ribbed with mahogany, and all the tables, neither few nor small, of the same costly material. Of the kitchen, it has been reported, that there are few in London so completely and expensively fitted up, and with "One who has whistled at the plough, I am sorry to say, that such is to all appearance the case." No objection can be held against having everything that is really useful and of good quality. It is the profusion of contrivances and vessels that strike the observer as being only necessary in the higher stage of epicureanism. The ball room and class rooms, on the basement story, have ceilings richly finished, and everywhere are elegance and splendour. The Hall is a monument of *ill-timed* magnificence. At first, nothing was wanted but utility, convenience, and economy. The Hall was not intended for a community but for a normal school, and in this the Directors appear to have departed from the socialist's original, most necessary, and most cherished intention. They aimed at a conquest of the world when they should have been achieving the independence of the young community, and giving, in the words of Mr. Hunt, " a practical demonstration to the working classes, that any given number of them possess the means within themselves, to effect a similar change in their own condition."

Under the credulous ideas entertained by Messrs. Owen and Galpin, and so readily swallowed by their coadjutors, that Sir Robert Peel and the Queen's Cabinet, were coming to embrace them, the oddest things were done. Instead of colonization it appears to have been squanderization. Books of Mr. Owen were reprinted which nobody read—and *New Moral Worlds* amassed which nobody bought, and prospectuses issued to which nobody attended. To ask for less than a million of money was thought mean and beggarly. When the garden was laid out, Mr. Owen instructed Mr. Scott to make arrangements for two thousand people, before two hundred had a chance of coming. The late Acting Governor had walks laid out, when the land wanted sowing, and such walks they promised to be! The old Roman roads, made for two thousand years, were not more deeply trenched, nor more wastefully bedded with flints—and thus hundreds of pounds were expended while the landlord's rent was accumulating in arrears. They talked of "experience," indeed, but talk was all. The *New Moral World* rang with their sagacity, but the visitor to Harmony Hall will seek in vain for proofs of it. They went on until their coffers were exhausted—till debts were thicker than their crops—and their walks and fountains still unfinished, corroborated the truth of the

Spaniard's proverb, that "knowledge will become folly unless good sense take care of it." The intensely sublimated imaginations of those Directors told them of capital half crazy to be spent by them, and continually crying "Come, use me." Public opinion they deemed absolutely impatient to be theirs. Really, these strange expectations make one think there can not be a breathing man who knows so little of human nature as Robert Owen. No objections can be urged to speculations, even the wildest, when the speculators spend their own money —but in this case the money of others went in expensive schemes, and security and self-support were forgotten in the dreams of grandeur. They seemed to believe that the more they asked the more they would have. On capital, instead of on the land, these Home Colonization people fixed their precious eyes. With them a prime mind meant a full purse. Their policy was that of a spendthrift—their wisdom that of a gamester. A long vine wall was erected, which probably cost a guinea a yard. When Mr. Southwell was there with a friend, it was debated with them, whether the wall was erected to support the vine or the vine planted to support the wall. It scarcely need be added, that be this as it may, the grapes at present are mortal few. I do not doubt or insinuate that the Directors of this community did not intend the best of things, but carried away by Mr. Owen, they fancied all the world was coming to their arms, while, in fact, they were coming fast to the Gazette. Some of them, like Mr. Ironside, were not really blinded, but were determined to carry out the spirit of the paternal form of government, and in doing so they carried themselves, and nearly the society, out along with it. Had not the last Congress made the present changes the experiment would ere this have passed for ever from the dreams of hope. "What has all this to do with the present state of the establishment?" some will ask. It has this: Heavy debts were accumulated which the present executive have had to pay, by which their efforts have been crippled, and the thousands of pounds untimely expended on the building, not only now lie producing nothing —but are heaping up unpaid interest which presses like an incubus on the young energies of the household—and, though it may not be demanded, it is *expected*—if it is not asked for, it is owing—and the capitalists are rendered nervous, angry, fretful, and often threatening, till the wheels of the executive government roll on through unknown obstacles and unknown anxieties. "Why rake up old grievances—better bury the past," will cry some sapient soul, whose chief wisdom consists in crying peace, peace, when there is no peace. I tell the past as a warning for the future. It is not good to blunder in vain. Let failure tell its tale and teach its lesson. Let us have the means of judging principles by their product. The more is known of the truth of the case the less surprise we shall feel at the declaration of Mr. Southwell, at the public breakfast to Mr. Buxton, at Branch A 1,—"The old executive are dead and buried, and may they never suffer a resurrection." If the true position of the present executive is not told, at next congress their failure, should they fail, will be ascribed to their policy, when it will have resulted from their position, and a position made for them by the very men who will then so blandly blame the results.

It will be said, but do not railway and canal companies expend immense sums of money, and erect their termini and arches in elegant and durable forms—in what respect did these old directors differ from railway and such like people? But do railway people lay out their lines, or do canal companies commence expensively to erect their works before they know where the capital is to come from to finish the whole with? More than this, they neither attempt to cut line nor dig river, until they have seen their boats swim and their carriages run. It should be so with communities. With us communities are but experiments, and we can't too cheaply try whether co-operative life can be made to accord with the genius of the English people, and the communities at the same time be self-supporting establishments. When this has been proved it will be time enough for socialists to engage the architect of the Birmingham Town Hall to erect their farm houses.

I was surprised at the estate's extent. A day is insufficient to walk round it. Stretching far over hill, dale, and entangled woodland, lie the Great and Little Bentley farms, with their rosy orchards, venerable homesteads, and antique wainscotted rooms. But, reader, I could never forget for a single moment that the rent was unpaid.

As I walked over that estate and its glorious undulations of hill and dale, through its broad expanse and woodland relief, and down its gorgeous yew tree avenues, with its long aisles of vernal glory, colonnades of venerable firs and gothic ceiling of fretted trellis work, and bright sky bursting in at the bottom, like a silver lamp lighting the whole, making a palace scene which no picture has exaggerated and no language done justice—I could not do as some have done, bound along exclaiming, brethren, "*This is ours.*"—I could not, like the *New Moral World* of last week, talk of "breathing the air of freedom—of listening to the melody of *our own* birds in *our own* woods." I could not forget the madness which had perilled to us that splendid place—the unpaid rent gave its beauty the air of desolation. I could not even stand upright under its gothic arches, where a bailiff might next walk. Those men who favoured us with their paternal wisdom could have had no love of nature left amid their vast dreamings or they would have clung with a lover's fondness to those sunny scenes, and by economy, foresight, and care, have secured that place from every liability. So soon as the welcome day arrives when that experiment shall be declared free, and standing on its own pillars of support, no longer be dependent on casual bounty, on accidental subscription or the tremblingly lent loan of the timid capitalist, then could I walk from England's remotest bound to mingle again with those devoted communists, and stroll once more up that glorious avenue—when no claim is unmet, and every capitalist has deep down in his pocket the last cent. of stipulated interest, then could I exult with any one—but not till then. Till then the very blades of grass would reproach me; nor could I reciprocate the dasies' smile, or the buttercups' glow.

When the last congress met, hopeless were the prospects, and when it separated matters were, in its immediate neighbourhood, worse. The news spread like wildfire that the establishment would be broken up. £1000 of debts were owing, exchequers were empty, confidence was low, capitalists looked iron things, and professed friends were cold as ice. Under such circumstances Mr. Buxton took office, and deep is the debt of gratitude due to him for the responsibility he assumed and the sacrifices he has made. Persons who had let their debts stand over for years then threatened legal proceedings unless instant payment was made—loans lent for short terms were demanded, and for weeks after taking office, sleepless nights were passed by the Governor—and well it might he so—a man might rather "coin his heart for drachmas" than live so besought.

An agreeable fiction has been received of Mr. Owen being on visiting terms with Sir Isaac Lyon Goldsmid, and some dream'd of favours to flow, or thence have flowed. Those that have flowed, so far as I can learn, belong to the region of dreams. Aristocratic friendship is not worth much when rent is unpaid. Socialists, don't forget that your landlord would as soon lay his hands on your broad acres as on any one else's,—and rather, as they are of more worth—if you leave them in his power. You are not safe, you ought not to be safe while under obligation. If I lived at Harmony, I am sure I should sleep, as Cooke declared the Bristol people do, with one eye open, that I might miss no chance until every stiver of rent was paid.

To remedy this state of things Mr. Buxton, and his excellent coadjutor, Mr. Simpson, have done everything economy and self-denial could do. During his short term of office he has paid £800 of bad debts. All useless expenditure has been nipped in the bud. All salaries abolished. The land is being made productive. Every soul is usefully employed, and the experiment is at last on the high road to be self-supporting.

In the hall, contentment and equality reign. The fare is wholesome, good and sufficient. All eat and drink alike. The Governor sits at the same table as the members, and Mrs. Buxton does the same share of labour as any other woman. No private tables are spread. No lady in velvet frowns for the benefit of good order, and no friend Galpin prohibits laughing in the name of propriety.

The family meetings are family parliaments. There are no secrets, no mysteries, no private carousings of heads of departments, no listening at office doors. All is open and above board. Every member knows every thing. Upon everything all deliberate, all advise. All seem to feel that the experiment depends upon each. The result is that they make all conceivable sacrifices; they toil early and late—the 1s. a week, allowed them by law, they give up. Knowing the difficulties of the establishment, they work like heroes and heroines, and endure like devotees.

Those who join the family, are with few exceptions, at first disappointed. The duty of a pioneer is no sinecure, and the new habits are hard to put on. Those who have been well to do seem sooner to conform to the new associations than those who have been less happily placed. The reason is, the comfortable expect to make personal sacrafices while the others anticipate immediate advantages. Had I space for details, I have many to tell, but I must hasten to treat of the hinges on which success or failure hang. It seemed easy to see in this new and improved state of the family feeling, the reason of the anticipated failure of the democratic form of government by the old executive. They said it would not do because they never tried it. They could not descend to the same equality—they had few feelings, few sympathies, in common. How could there be democracy where the rulers had a contempt for the ruled. The old executive said the mere members could not understand their views—this was the secret, they could not trust them to them, as many a tale could tell.

Rude may be the endeavours, many may be the mistakes made, slow may be the progress of a democratic society, but without such principle and practice only negative will be the progress made. Working men must work out their own freedom ere they can have it. I have never known a poor man's institution that was began to be conducted on respectable principles that was not at once seized with the agonies of death, and that did not expire in the most polished torments. *Cæteris paribus*, the vulgarest democracy is preferable to the paternal presidency of an almighty-god. Democracy may be vulgar but its frankness is to be cherished. It is the only government of equality; and its perpetual demand on individual perfection, makes it the only government of true progression. It is only under its influence that the vision of QUARLES is realised—

There proud disdain, and every evil lust,
And two-faced fraud, and heavy brow'd distrust,
And boiling rage, and troubled state sedition,
And faithless doubt, and evil-eyed suspicion;
And stupid sorrow and ungenerous fear,
Are banished quite.

Marvellous was the wisdom employed in building up the paternal form of government, in insisting on the wholesale subjugation of the understanding, and the long exploded doctrines of despotism were to be for ever popularised among us—but most signal has been the failure of these principles in practice. Mr. Owen must have "heads of departments" by which means he lost all head over his own. If anything was wanted, "Oh," he would say, "you must ask Mr. So-and-so, it belongs to his department." But when you reached Mr. So-and-so he did not think so, and another and another Mr. So-and-so had to be found, until the unhappy applicant had at last to sit down very "so so" himself, without what he wanted being done. Then these heads of departments (at Ham Common they have more departments than heads) were little demi-gods in their several districts, and a thing was right in Mr. Owen's eyes, not because of its fitness, for about that he never troubled himself, but because the heads of departments ordered it. Now the governor superintends and judges all.

To generalise was another point of the new philosophy; and, O, Mother of God, how they did generalise! Mr. Reid said at the London Mechanics' Institution, with some truth, that Mr. Owen was so anxious for the good of the whole community that when one member had a fever, to specially attend to him would be contrary to his principles, he could not conscientiously trouble himself unless they *all* had a fever.

Talk of men of business—shade of Walkingame, what specimens those prime minds were! Congress after congress owned, as Dr. Reid did of Clarke's "A priori argument," that their book-keeping might be very sublime but they could not understand it. What was borrowed they did not know, what was spent they could not tell. Even the late Acting Governor made, on Mr. Buxton's accession to office, a demand of £500, but voucher, receipt, or entry could not by him be produced, nor any where be found. To ask what they were doing was deemed proof positive that the questioner was beside himself. Friend Rigby, or Galpin, or Fleming, or Jones, would shake his head, and ask how a localised inexperienced mind could understand such magnificient operations, as digging the precious earth and keeping an account of what was got by it. Simple as it was, they might well ask who could understand it, for I don't believe they could themselves. Sometimes our government seizes the documents of a society and discovers all its secrets, but often have I prayed that the government might seize ours, for could they discover the state of affairs they would do more than we could.

At Harmony 1 lighted on one or two remnants of the old wisdom, who said that twelve months would be too little to understand what was going on there, until I had the impression that that mysticism which had crept into their morality pervaded their works, and that Harmony resembled nothing so much as theology, where all we know is that nothing can be known. But being accustomed to such repulses, I contented myself with humbly hoping that I might at least be able to discover that nothing could be discovered.

But luckily, there is a clear headed man at the secretary's desk now. In Mr. Simpson's hands I saw books that by next congress will tell many a tale. Take one book as a specimen. On one side of a folio, every field is entered, its acres, yards and inches; its present condition and value—with every day and hour's labour upon it, whether of man or horse, with whatever of seed and compost are laid upon it, that field is *debited*.

On the opposite folio it is *credited* with all the produce it is found to yield. Side by side stands the gain or loss upon that field during the year. So plain is all this that a child may understand it. Thus in every depar ment mystery is dissipated, and if the executive are enabled to continue their labours, by next congress they will have matters in such genuine business like order, that a plain man may tell in an hour what will become of his money if he invest it there.

(*To be concluded next week*).

THEORY OF REGULAR GRADATION.

I will trouble you to allow me to call the attention of those subscribers to the *Oracl of Reason* who read the "Theory of Regula Gradation," to arguments of mine contained in Nos. 15 and 16, where it is contended that the recent discoveries in astronomy warranted the supposition that the earth was formed from a process similar to what astronomers declare is at present going on in our system. This view, it will be found, is supported by De la Beche; and in the *Athenæum* for October 5, in Professor Sedgwick's reply to the Dean of York, at the meeting of the British Association, is the following:—" With regard to Dr. Buckland's 'Bridgwater Treatise,' I believe that his account of the successive changes by which the earth has been brought to its present state, substantially represents facts. His account of the original nebulous condition of the earth, is not a wild conjecture, but a probability, suggested by the phenomena of the heavens." We may now consider it as established that the formation of the world was entirely different to the revealed (?) account of it given in Genesis, upon which the fact of its creation entirely rested. Upon this, Genesis, the same veracious authority, rests the *fact* of the creation of men and other animals, which is still insisted upon by the *same men*, who have so effectually disproved the creation of the world—the formation of myriads of species by natural causes, is considered perfectly rational by philosophers of the present day; but the formation of a zoophyte by like means is declared to be the hypothesis of a fool, the dogma of a madman, or the blasphemy of an unholy wretch, so enamoured of error, that he wilfully wrests truth to his own destruction. Let those only who are more in love with truth than they are with creeds and systems decide between the creationist and the supporter of the hypothesis of the transmutation of species.

I cannot help thinking that philosophers of Professor Sedgwick's school see clearly enough that the facts related of the formation of the world bear equally upon the animals and plants on its surface, for without any apparent reason, except to put inquirers upon a false scent, we find him closing his reply as follows:—

"In determining the succession of the strata, or any other problem in our science, we must be content to ascend, step by step, from small assemblages of facts, to higher generalisations, until we obtain the whole sequence." This is very good, but we shall see how soon the professor forgets his own position when it is likely, if acted upon, to overturn a pet theory. He continues—"With regard to the succession of animal life, *the evidence is so conclusive that no materialist or competent observer will now deny that new species have continually appeared*"— [and yet the Bible states that *all* living things, from the lowest to the highest, were created in *one day;* if new species have continually appeared, why may not other new species *yet* appear?]—"not by the transmutation of those before existing—but by the repeated operation of creative power." How does he know this—has the learned professor ascended "step by step from a small assemblage of facts to a higher generalisation" in coming to this conclusion? If he has, I think he must have very carefully hid his light under a bushel, instead of setting it on a hill, that the world might be illumined by it; for I have neither heard of nor seen any of the *facts* which would warrant such a generalisation. But there is yet some further information of God's handy work exclusively possessed by Professor Sedgwick, who is, I presume, God's "own reporter," which I should be sorry to keep from my readers, even if I should not be charged with cowardice were I to do so. He thus concludes—"In his *ordinary dealings* with the natural world (that is his week day work) God works by second causes—*so that one natural phenomena may be said to flow directly from another.* But when we see successive orders of animal existence, and successive organic types, which once ministered to the functions of animal life, *we can only say* a living spirit had been breathed into dead matter, few differing from the mere causative of natural laws, and that the beings, of whatever order, were the effect of a direct creative will."

This is a specimen of "cool, easy assurance," after the "step by step" declaration. The professor must be understood as speaking for himself alone when he says, "we can only say," etc., for most assuredly

myself and many others hold a different opinion. But the very expression, "we can only say" proves it to be a mere unsupported hypothesis—a conclusion jumped at to hide his ignorance or to mislead the unwary. The learned professor, though very clear and conclusive in his refutation of the fallacies of the Dean of York's paper, "The Bible defended against the British Association," because he argued from known facts, is by no means so clear in his refutation of the fallacies of materialism.
W. C.

PROPAGANDISM AND PATERSON.
To the Editor of the Movement.

MUCH has been written, and that earnestly, in the pages of our paper, to urge men to more energetic, decided, and useful actions—that much good has been effected and many added to our numbers, even the orthodox will not deny. Yet, with all this in our favour, there remains much to be accomplished. The Hydra-headed Goliath of bigotry may have been wounded, but if we have pretentions to liberty, it remains for us to direct the fatal blow. There may be many good men on our side, who, from a want of spirit, are only silent observers—let me urge them to arouse themselves, for he alone is the true lover of wisdom who scorns to submit his reason to the standard of custom, education, or interest. When there is more of honesty there will be less room for fear; reformations of any kind, religious in particular, are attended with discouragements and difficulties, and the man who enters upon a work so dangerously good, must arm himself to support persecution and calumny. But shall this tame us into submission? Shall we boast ourselves friends to freedom while, by our silence, we remain abettors to oppression? Reason forbids. Let the cringing subterfuges of the Hull Christians arouse us into action. Such goddism shows this is no time to be wavering, for while we are sparing these dogmatists, their heaven learnt love recoils upon us in the shape of fresh persecution. Let all learn a lesson. "Go-a-head" we must if progress is our aim. Every step we advance is a nail clenched in christianity's overthrow. Let us shake off half fearful scepticism, arouse ourselves in name, and follow out in practice decided and uncompromising atheism.

I think, sir, a good opportunity is at hand to prove our strength and show our determination. The well tried friend to our cause will soon be among us again, and I think it should be made the time for a move in the right direction. A demonstration similar to that held in Glasgow on the 24th ult., would have a threefold tendency to unite us more together, make many friends to our cause, and the Union necessarily more substantial. Paterson has claims upon us that must not be disregarded, and I hope every lover of freedom will rally around him on his liberation. His return to society should be marked by a hearty reception. The tyrannical would then see, that while he has been immured in one of christianity's slaughterhouses, we have ever been mindful of him who has suffered so much in our cause. I think, sir, if a general weekly subscription was immediately commenced, it would be the means of augmenting very much the present testimonial. There are numbers, I am sure, who would be glad to respond to such a call, that cannot pay crowns or half crowns at once, in forwarding so laudable an object. Every liberal bookseller would receive subscriptions—it only remains for you to devise a plan.
T. BIDWELL.

We are happy that our constant friend T. B. has drawn attention to the duty of publicly welcoming Mr Paterson to liberty. Upon the course to be pursued we have already thought, and shall in due time introduce the subject. But the augmentation of the Testimonial is very judiciously pressed upon the attention of our friends at this time. The machinery of the Anti-Persecution Union is perfect for collecting. This T. B. can employ as far as he is able. If he will apply for subscriptions and make known other persons willing to do the same, the state of the Testimonial will soon be improved.—*Ed. of M.*

MR. CAMPBELL'S REASONS FOR LEAVING THE CONCORDIUM.
To the Editor of the Movement.

SIR,—In my former letter I stated the principles on which I proposed to become a member of the Concordium, and according to which Mr. Oldham, the Pater, agreed to accept me as his first Concordium brother.

A few weeks after my admittance as a member, a constitution and rules, based on the same principles, were unanimously agreed to by the other candidates, presented by them to Mr. Oldham, and by him also accepted as the standard for future operations. In accordance therewith, an elective government was adopted, consisting of Pater, Elder, and Superintendents of Departments, who, as far as the *natures* of the individuals and the conditions in which they were placed at the commencement of the experiment, enabled them, conducted the family affairs according to their conception of justice, or modified them as it appeared expedient for the time being. Various causes had, however, contributed to make the condition of the members very uncomfortable, and consequently there was a constant uneasiness and unsteadiness in all their proceedings, which gradually led to a change in the government, from being an *Elective Pater and Council* to that of an *Absolute Pater,* "who considered himself under the Divine appointment, alone in the position he now occupies."

The Pater also considered that those who furnished the money capital should always have the power of governing. Mr. Oldham being thus absolute "*under the Divine appointment*," selected Mr. Galpin to act with him as his secretary and adviser, who also took upon himself the power of regulating the whole business of the establishment. These two gentlemen soon began to propose to the family such alterations, theoretically and practically at variance with the principles and mode of proceeding which appeared right to me, that I could not quietly acquiesce with them; and therefore, as opportunities were offered, I expressed my dissent.

The following are some of the propositions introduced under the *Absolute Patership*, to which I objected, and which are now the rules of the society:—

1st.—That all persons being admitted members must subscribe a declaration, or affirm that they *believe in a universal spirit.*

2nd.—That those who had acquired property before becoming members of the society, should be allowed to use it in any manner they thought proper, but that no person should be allowed to acquire any private property after becoming a member of the society.

3rd.—That in the event of any member leaving the society, every article of clothing, &c., which he had received from the family store should again be returned to the Pater, who alone determines what should be given or retained.

4th.—That *entire celibacy* should be the declared principle and practice of the society.

5th.—And lastly, because the treatment towards some of the members, candidates, and children, and other transactions were in direct contradiction to their declared principles and professions.

It is not requisite for me to state my reasons for opposing these new "new views," it is sufficient to state that I did so, and for so doing I was considered an obstruction to their progress, and as Mr. Galpin said, " evidently not *at-one-ment* with them, without which it would be impossible for him (Mr. G.) to remain as a member of the family."

To avoid further opposition, it was suggested to me by Messrs. Oldham and Galpin that I might try to form another Concordium according to my own views in a distant part of the country. When I saw and felt that my presence was an obstruction in working out their NOTIONS, I intimated my intention to retire as soon as the requisite arrangements could be made for that purpose, which have since been effected. I have now given you my reasons for withdrawing from the Concordium, and whether they may be satisfactory to others or not, they were sufficient to cause the separation.

In conclusion, I shall add, that although I could not be "at-one-ment" with friends Oldham and Galpin in the course they were pursuing, yet I believe their intentions are good, and it is possible they may be made agents in the development of good in others.

A. CAMPBELL.

[It is not necessary to comment on Mr. C.'s "Reasons." They speak for themselves, and to us are quite satisfactory Mr. Oldham has a *capital* conception of the Divine appointment. His " Divine authority" is cash authority. He considered that " capital should always have the power of governing." Of course—all " Divine authority" says so. We can understand and are at "one-ment" on this point.]—*Ed. of M.*

DR. KALLEY.—A Correspondent in the *Times*, Oct. 23rd, writes from Lisbon, Oct. 16th, " That the case of Dr. Kalley appears now to have arrived at something of a crisis. The Portuguese government has proposed to Lord Aberdeen to give pecuniary compensation (about 800*l.*) for the Dr's imprisonment of 170 days, admitting the illegality of the proceedings against him; but upon the condition that he will immediately withdraw from Madeira and the Portuguese dominions. Lord Aberdeen's answer has not yet been received; but in the meantime, by a late arrival from Madeira, we learn that Dr. Kalley has again proceeded to preach publicly against the Roman Catholic religion, in Funchal, and that a great ferment has been the result. The Charter tolerates every form of religion in private, or within the confines of heterodox churches erected within the Portuguese dominions, but it most distinctly announces the Roman Catholic to be the established religion of the place. If, therefore, Dr. Kalley will not consent to retire, he will certainly be put down by a special law, which no effort of British diplomacy can prevent from passing.

BRONTERRE O'BRIEN'S NEW PAPER.

I insert a few lines,—although our journal is full to overflowing, with matter of varied interest, and papers of my own will again give way to some valued friends, already too long excluded—to recommend to all movement men the perusal of the forthcoming *National Reformer*. Need our friends be reminded what powerful aid was given to the popular cause by Bronterre's earliest writings. How much they contributed, as the Editor of the *New Moral World* last week justly observed, to popularise political knowledge. The *Poor Man's Guardian* was foremost in the arduous and admirable struggle of the "unstamped." A large number of the most active aud influential political reformers, in the true sense, at this moment can date their enlightenment from the day when they became recipients of Mr. O'Brien's teachings.

There is a feature in this new project specially deserving of attention. We may recollect that though the brave champions of the "unstamped," vendors as well as writers, through their persevering energy and unyielding endurance, triumphed over the powerful conspiracy of legislator, priest, and lawyer, backed by the constabulary army of ready tools—they were beaten in detail. The Whig government of that day, coerced by the superior power and resolution of the contrabandists to make an alteration in the laws affecting the stamp upon knowledge, contrived, through the most damnable policy, by reducing them instead of abolishing them—making them one penny instead of fourpence, to effect just that amount of reduction which, in destroying the great disparity of prices, destroyed the successful competition of the people's papers. Had the same stamp been maintained, the contraband popular papers would have been continued—had the tax been entirely abolished, the same result would have been attained—the twopenny press would have maintained its place—the crafty, underhand, juste-milieu policy effected that which the utmost efforts of a powerful government, rigorously enforced, could not accomplish.

Now O'Brien's paper will, if rightly supported, re-commence the existence of a people's press. This may be said without disparagement to any existing popular organ. Its price Twopence Half-penny, and its circulation, post free, through being a Manx paper, sufficiently guard this recommendation from being considered invidious.

Mr. O'Brien would be greatly assisted by the receipt at once of half yearly or quarterly subscriptions in advance. Let those who can afford five shillings or half a crown remit it without delay, as directed in the circular in last week's number.

M. Q. R.

DEATH OF ABNER KNEELAND.—Abner Kneeland, formerly editor and founder of the *Boston Investigator*, died at his residence in Salubria, I.T., on the 27th ult., in the 71st year of his age. His complaint was common bilious fever, and his sickness was only of eight days duration. Mr. Kneeland was ultra in his opinions on religion, but was a man of pure moral character, and much respected by a large circle of acquaintances. The *Investigator*, which contains a long obituary notice of the deceased, is clad in mourning for the event.—*Working Man's Advocate.*

A NEW BOOK WANTED.—On Wednesday an officer called at Mr. Hetherington's and asked for a book "*about no God*," no book of that title being on sale, the "Existence of God disproved, &c." was handed to him. These gentlemen must be accomodated with the kind of books they want, even if we have to give a special order for them. On Friday, Mr. Hetherington read in the *Post* that "Hetherington of Holywell Street, the notorious Radical, was fined £25 (by the Court Leet) for blasphemy." This was the first Mr. Hetherington had heard of it. Should they come for the fine, somebody else will hear of it. Mr. H. supposes it to have been done by the parson of the parish, because of Mr. H's refusal of the church rate.

MR. ROBINSON will be liberated on Saturday, November 9.

IMPORTANT PUBLIC MEETING will be held in the Literary and Scientific Institution, John Street, Tottenham Court Road, on Friday evening, November 15, to consider the conduct of Messrs. *Cookman*, *Barkworth*, and *Firbank*, Magistrates of Hull, who have lately seized and sold the goods of Mr. Johnson, bookseller of that town, in payment of a fine of £20, inflicted for receiving 2d. admission money to a public lecture. Chair to be taken at half-past eight o'clock — admission free. The managers have granted the use of the Hall gratuitously. G. J. HOLYOAKE, Sec. A. P. U.

The friends at the Roan Street Hall, Greenwich, announce that they have made arrangements for a course of Theological Lectures, to be delivered on alternate Sunday evenings, by G. J. Holyoake and M. Q. Ryall, (Editors of the *Movement*), commencing at half-past six o'clock. Equal time allowed to lay or clerical gentlemen who may feel disposed to engage in discussion.

LECTURES.

Nov. 6.—Social Institution, 5, Charlotte Street, Blackfriars Road, Mr. Ellis, subject,—Bible education irrational and immoral. At half-past 8, P.M.

Nov. 10.———Mr. Ellis, (late Baptist preacher), —on the causes of his conversion to Socialism.

Nov. 11.———Mr. Southwell, — On the Life, Character, and Genius of Byron. At half-past 8, P.M.

Nov. 10.—No. 4, Roan Street, Greenwich, Mr. Holyoake, subject,—Refutation of Archdeacon Paley's grand design argument for the Existence of God. At half-past 6, P.M.

Nov. 10.—Investigation Hall, 29, Circus Street, Marylebone, Mr. Southwell. At 11, A.M. Mr. Ryall,—On the "Pursuit of Religion under Difficulties." At 7, P.M.

Nov. 10.—Hall of Science, City Road, Mr. Southwell,—On the Religious opinions of Shakspeare.

Nov. 10.—Finsbury Institution, Goswell Road, Mr. Peter Jones,— On phrenology. At half-past 7, P.M. Discussion after, "Can the immortality of the soul be proved."

DISCUSSIONS.

Nov. 7.—National Hall, 242, High Holborn, (adjourned),—Would the enfranchisement of the people occasion the overthrow of the good institutions of the country?

Nov. 7.—Globe Tavern, Titchfield Street,—What has most advanced civilisation?

Nov. 8.—Branch A 1, (adjourned),—Immortality of the soul. At half-past 8, P.M.

Nov. 13.—Investigation Hall, 29, Circus Street, Marylebone,—Between Mr. Southwell and Mr. Alexander Campbell.

SUBSCRIPTIONS
TO THE ANTI-PERSECUTION UNION.

S. B. Vauxhall	0	2	6
Second 100 of Mrs. Martin's "Last of the Martyrs"	0	8	4
Per Mr. G., Dumfries,—A friend	0	2	6
An acquaintance	0	1	0
Mr. G.	0	2	0
Per Card	0	1	1

G. J. H., Sec.

Printed and Published by G. J. HOLYOAKE,
40, Holywell street, Strand.
Wednesday, November 6, 1844.

THE MOVEMENT
And Anti-Persecution Gazette.

"Maximise morals, minimise religion."—BENTHAM.

No. 49.   EDITED BY G. JACOB HOLYOAKE, ASSISTED BY M. Q. RYALL.   Price 1½d

A VISIT TO HARMONY HALL
By G. J. H.
III.

THE tendency to diminish expenditure is in every department of Harmony Community, observable. Twenty-five shillings a-week were paid for hired labour in the laundry two or three weeks ago—now all is done by the wives of the members. Hired labour on the farm is being rapidly dispensed with. The well furnished orchard, the property everywhere exposed, naturally, to an unknown extent, fall a prey to people having no common interest in its preservation. While I was there, twenty-four yards of new cloth, which lay out bleaching, walked off. Not even a policeman was spoken to, lest some poor devil should have his hard lot made hopelessly harder. So much as £21 were paid to hired labourers as wages, the week prior to my visit. Much more economical, besides much more consistent and agreeable, would be the employment of our own members. In proof of this, it may be stated, that Mr. Buxton has been able to increase the number of hands on the estate, and decrease the expenditure. Yet Mr. Finch protests against the dismissal of this functionary, and Mr. B. exclaims, " my property will be ruined if members are brought down "—but what says facts. Mr. Thompson of Manchester was three times nominated by his Branch, and three times objected to by the Central Board, on account of his family. Mr. Buxton had him brought down, and this is the result. He displaces 18s. per week, Mrs. T. 9s., one son 14s., and another 11s. Thus, this one family saves the establishment 52s. weekly in wages, probably not costing themselves more than a third of the sum. I do not desire to obscure the fact, that the labourer is to be regarded as indigenous to the soil—that he may justly expect to live on the land on which he was found living, that if he is not retained as a labourer, he may become chargeable as a pauper, and that the estate must either pay wages or poor rates—these points may be admitted, and it may still be true that the Community's best servants are its own members.

Take an example of how much a little cash is needed at this juncture. Sixty sheep are feeding in the fields, worth about £75. During the next six weeks they will eat up produce without being worth more. But if £20 could be expended on them in linseed oil cake, they would, at the end of the same six weeks, be worth some £130, and the fields on which they pastured be worth £20 more, through their being fed on the oil cake. Moreover, the land not being thus manured, will prevent ten acres of wheat from being sown, the produce of which would yield some thirty quarters, worth about £70 or £75. Who that had £20 to spare would not send it down?

In telling how communists live in community, I must not omit to add how strangers live there, which is by paying 2s. per day, less than half the former charge—which 2s. entitles them to three meals, wholesome, excellent, varied, and substantial, and a capital snoose at night in a nice room, a wide bed, and friend Cotterell's trumpet to wake them with in the morning.

One reason why the accounts of the society are not farther on the way to intelligibility is, that too many people are doing one work. To wit, the Central Board receive Community funds and school fees, which, as they belong to Harmony, ought to be sent there direct. As it is, double accounts have to be kept, and sundry official transmissions of money have weekly to be made, by which confusion sometimes, jealousy often, unavoidably spring up. Whether the Community fund is not being appropriated as Mr. Newall appropriated it —to the support of Missionaries, nobody certainly knows—there may or may not be large arrears of school fees, but as some are paid at Harmony and others in London— until those two accounts can be compared, it remains a mystery, and it is with bookkeeping as with bipeds in general—whoever or whatever sits on two stools, has a seat somewhere on the ground. Thus, the society is pretty much in the condition of

Elwes the miser, who, when he had one servant he had his work always done, when he had two it was only half done, and when he had three, he had to do it himself. The duties of the Central Board would be best restricted to the management of the General Fund, and propagandism in general, and Harmony should be suffered to take its own affairs into its own hands.

Of the schools at Harmony I am the most puzzled to speak. The class rooms are fine, the conveniences of education are many, and the children are rubicund and happy. Staying but for a short time, and having many things to see, it was impossible to make that examination that a school requires. The children keep no register of their acquisitions, because it is thought likely to deceive parents—but such indexes never deceive teachers, and had such a record been in existence, I could have satisfied myself respecting them. As a principal is just now wanting, no general system can be expected to prevail. From all I heard, the future may be promising. The past career of the schools has left few indications of that wisdom that belongs to our philosophy, and is expected from our professions. The former appointments were unhappy ones. Mr. Reid publicly established, in London, his utter inefficiency for his office, and Mr. Ostriecher, in my opinion, did pretty much the same thing in the *New Moral World*. Mr. R. failing in morals, and Mr. O. through mysticism. Both appointments were such only as Mr. Owen could make. It appears not to have been known at Harmony that the grand problem of Education has been solved by Phiquepal d'Arusmont, namely—"that instruction may be so judiciously calculated as to develope, simultaneously, the moral, intellectual, physical, and industrial faculties of children, and cover all its own expences, together with those of the preceding state of infancy." An experiment of this kind, under the intelligent management named, was found fully adequate to its own support in *six months*. But it is impossible that the Harmony schools, with their vast advantages, will not share in the common impetus, and some day revive the spirit of the ancient academies, and rival the best efforts of Heldenmaier.

When I set out for Harmony, I had no confidence whatever in the success of the experiment. I did not doubt the industry of the members, but I much questioned the fertility of their soil. I had no fears for the judgment or integrity of the new Executive, but I expected the difficulties in which they were placed would be too great for them. Some persons holding back their money for fear it should not answer, and some for fear it should, some because the new Executive had taken office, and some through fear they would not be kept there, had made funds a very scarce article. But finding the land better than expectation, witnessing the devotion of the Communists there, the prudence, and economy of the Governor, and the efforts made to get out of debt, quite satisfied me that they will succeed if they meet with support during their years of office, and that by next Congress that experiment will be on safer and more satisfactory grounds than it ever yet was, and nearly, if not quite, self-supporting.

The true predicament at this time of the Harmony experiment deserves investigation, because all sorts of persons will judge, by its success or failure, the ability of the working classes to manage their own affairs. Even Mr. Owen, the last thing he said was, " I doubt the power of the working classes (from their necessarily contracted knowledge of things) to manage beneficially their own affairs, or to carry on the Harmony experiment successfully." Now it will be to libel the working classes to ascribe the failure of Harmony to them. If fail it should, it will not be through the " contracted knowledge of the working classes" so much as through the distracted condition in which the capitalists have left it, who not only expended, in a nearly useless manner, all the money the working classes subscribed, but mortgaged all they can now raise in the shape of debts, they, the capitalists, left unpaid. The reproaches of the President of Branch A 1, addressed to the Northern Branches, have no application, because those Branches have contributed what would have amply carried on one of their own experiments, but as it is they have to extricate a capitalist's experiment from difficulty. Strenuously have Mr. Owen and his coadjutors inculcated the slavish doctrine of the absolute dependence of the working classes on capitalists. Behold, Socialists! in your hour of need, what assistance you get from them ! The letter just addressed by your Central Board to all members and friends, respecting the day's wages to be presented to Harmony, has this passage

"We are informed there are monied parties watching our proceedings, who believe Harmony cannot be carried on in accordance with the resolutions of Congress, and *therefore will not assist us with their capital.*"

Precious men to depend on are these capitalists! When you are safe through all your difficulties they will run to your assistance, and credit themselves with all the wisdom and all the success. Miserable imitators of God Almighty! who helps only those who can help themselves, and takes all the glory.

The governing party of Socialists have erred chiefly in extremes. At first they were all talk, and at last they were all bustle. Those who would coolly enquire into what they intended at the beginning, and what they were at in the end met with no little contempt. The only reply would be, " we are past that point now, we can't stop to dispute. We have had enough of talking, we must be *doing*." Forgetful that *doing* without the talking, which explains our intention and informs our friends, is but the blind thumping of ignorance, without a plan and without an advantage.

To very different causes than those usually assigned, will the judicious commentator on Socialism ascribe the apathy of friends and the disorganization of Branches. Mr. Lloyd Jones lately had the hardihood to tell the people of Edinburgh that their paralyzed state is owing to their having engaged an heterodox lecturer. Although it is a fact, that hardly a year since, when the old Executive were in power, the President of the Edinburgh Branch came to London, and handed over to the Central Board £60, saying, that had the people of Edinburgh confidence in that Board's proceedings, of which Board Mr. Jones was one, he should have had £130 to pay into their hands—thus proving that it was not to heterodoxy so much as to orthodoxy that the Edinburgh Branch owes its inactivity. When Mr. Owen was last in Birmingham, some two years ago, he wrote in the *New Moral World*, March 18, 1842, that theological discussions had ruined that Branch. Passing through Birmingham at that time, I made enquiries respecting this statement, and found that the very two lectures which followed his, and which were upon Atheism, proved far more attractive than his own, aided as his were by large placards and the popularity of his name. And it is conceded that Mr. Southwell always drew better audiences than the preacher of the most sedate namby pambyism the society ever patronized. It was what is now tolerably well known as "back-bone Owenism" that ruined the Birmingham Branch. They grew respectable and they grew dead, and the finest set of fellows, in the finest town in the kingdom, shrunk into utter inanity.

The great difficulty under which the present managers at Harmony have lain — a difficulty not to be overlooked in any just estimate to be formed of the value of their policy and exertions, as it is a difficulty under which no former Executive laboured —the want of an organ at their command, in which themselves and friends could be heard. The paper of the society has not been the paper of the Executive—the *New Moral World* has been notoriously in the interests of the old party. In my reply to the late Acting Governor, in No. 32 of the *Movement*, I drew attention to this fact, and it will not be invidious in me to notice it again. Mr. Buxton, from a desire to conciliate, was anxious to retain all the officers he found appointed. But in my opinion, his chief error has been in not taking the *New Moral World* into his own hands. It was of immense importance that the organ of the society should express the opinions and represent the wishes of the society. To its not doing so may be ascribed the inefficient assistance yet rendered to the new Executive. In other respects the result has been disastrous. Letters like those of Mr. Vines, and the late Acting Governor, have appeared, and the friends of the new Executive denied the chance of reply. Indeed, Mr. Buxton himself has not enjoyed the privilege always conceded to the humblest correspondent of the *Movement*, that of being heard in his own words and in his own way. Whole paragraphs of great importance have been struck out of his letters. His communications have been carried to the Central Board by the Editor, and they induced (Mr. Buxton being absent) to consent to their suppression, until he has ceased to write at all, or only on general, unimportant topics. Who can learn the true situation of the new Executive, with the hands of the old Executive on its mouth?

The old Executive, with all their faults, would not have committed the mistake of not securing the *New Moral World*. They would have dismissed Mr. Fleming again, as they did before. Mr. Galpin, with all his extravagances, was brave. Why, Mr. Fleming would have dismissed any man who was half as much an obstacle as himself. When I published the "Spirit of Bonner," in defence of Mr. Southwell, Mr. Fleming came down to Sheffield, and told the Branch that I was an obstacle in the society's way, and as such, would be removed. Then Mr. Lloyd Jones came and, while I was sent to Bradford, delivered a lecture, in which he recommended the Branch to dismiss me.

To all this I made no objection then, nor since, nor now. At any time that my exertions in favour of free discussion, or any other cause shall render me an obstacle in the progress of my chosen party, I say with Atrides—

> Let me be deem'd the hateful cause of all,
> And suffer, rather than my people fall.

In these reflections, the most malevolent will hardly ascribe to me envious motives, or suppose that I personally disparage the parties to whom I have referred. Mr. Fleming and Mr. Jones may be conceded to be able men, without at the same time being exactly suited to advance a cause, with which they have little sympathy, and that has become a cause in spite of them. At Congress they declined to act on the Central Board, and how can they advocate what they could not advise? How can they recommend that to which they are conscientiously opposed? They cannot even wish success, much less promote the new policy. It is not in human nature—it would be building up an imputation on their own wisdom. Let readers of the *New Moral World* think even better of present doings than that paper may pourtray. It can be but negatively favourable. It rather tolerates the present Executive than supports it, and seems to write in its favour rather from a sense of decency than a feeling of enthusiasm. The Editor resembles an old servant, who has been taken to among the other fixtures of a forfeited estate, and who is rather respectful than affectionate to his new masters, who renders his services—not his heart, and who has sworn never to say any thing in favour of his new protectors that will be likely to compromise his old ones.

As I have neither time nor space to detail elaborately all I saw and learned during my visit to Harmony Hall, it may be that my recitals will want something of fullness, but brief as the picture is, it wants nothing of truth, and the fact that all discussion of the conduct of the late Executive has been purposely suppressed in the *New Moral World* is presumptive evidence in favour of this opinion. There must have been a reason for such conduct. No man avoids discussion when his cause will bear it. Reflecting men will not hesitate a moment in coming to the conclusion that a case to which no reference is to be made is a case condemned.

Some will suspect my criticism as being vastly too free—

> Where I must speak what wisdom would conceal,
> And truths, invidious to the great, reveal—

but I stay not to weigh the scruples of Calchas. I value private friendship much, but public duty more. Then I cannot attack as is the socialists' fashion—speak of an opponent as "an unfavourable circumstance,"—conceal a sting under charitable regards, and stab while I pity. I do not shelter myself under bland generalities, but step out, tap the men I mean on the shoulder, call them by their names, tell them who strikes, and leave them free to do their mightiest.

Charity, that bastard son of justice, in the person of some piece of neutrality whose sole virtue consists in doing nothing and averting nothing, will admonish me that I had better not moot the topics of this chapter—"they only irritate," or "at least they had better be delayed to the next congress." Reader, if you can endure such a formal procedure, permit me to tell an anecdote on this point.

When confined in Gloucester Gaol, I commenced to address applications and memorials to the authorities there for an amelioration of my treatment. Upon this, Captain Mason, the Governor, took occasion to say, "It is of no use, Holyoake, that you address these applications. I have no power to grant your request—the Magistrates will not listen to your memorials, and Sir James Graham will reject that to which they have refused to attend. You have discretion, and you had better not pursue a course which can only annoy those who may otherwise be favourably disposed." "My dear sir," I replied, for I had grown familiar with indignation, "though you should burn every memorial I draw up, before my eyes, the moment it is finished, yet will I continue to do them in the best and most fitting manner, and address one to every official over me. I would tell those stone walls my wants, and shout my requests through those iron bars—for when I leave this place, if leave it I shall, and complain to the public of my treatment here and at your hands, you will be the first person to say, 'Well, why did you not complain?' and the magistrates will re-echo, 'Why did not Holyoake apply to us?' and the public will remark, 'if Holyoake had grievances it is only natural that he should have made them known.' Captain, it is my place to apply—yours to refuse, if you please." Wily devils were those gaol people! they thought to discourage my complaints that thereafter they might swear there could have been no occasion for them. But I did apply, and I need scarcely add, that my applications were not burnt, and that my condition was soon improved. So if such matters as I have recited are not published now by some one, at the next social Congress the argument will leap to the mouths of men there, " Why were not these evils, if they existed, made known before?" For this reason, without enquiring Mr. Buxton's views, or consulting the taste of persons averse to him, I determined to make known, on my own responsibility, such facts as to me appeared to bear upon the future existence of our young Community.

The opinions on many points which I have given in these papers on Harmony, differ from those I formerly held. When in the provinces, I had few opportunities of knowing the truth, and being, in common with others, guided chiefly by the *New Moral World*, I was in the simple condition of Burns's ploughman, who could not conceive how a lord could be a fool, or a godly man a knave. Overwhelmed by the cant of prime minds I could not believe in the deficiency of common sense, but piercing the veil of all this orthodoxy and vanity, I confess to having arrived at opinions somewhat different from those expressed in my review of the "Socialist Parliament," in *Movement* 27, in which I characterised its changes as "something that was not expected, and also something that was not desired."

As I turned to gaze on Queenwood for the last time a thousand thoughts thronged for utterance. It seemed as if the spirit of progression, first refulgent in the gardens of Plato, had sent its genial rays down time's broad stream, to nurture a young republic in the nineteenth century. What proud efforts were making within for its success—what hopes without were concentrated there! Probably no spot on this unconquered land, sacred to antiquity, poetry, or political struggle, is more full of interest to humanity than that place on which industry has fixed to work out its emancipation. Even wretchedness smiles as community is named, and out of the otherwise pathless desert of life a way opens there to independence. Toil-worn men, at the anvil and the loom, turn to that place as the happy land where the craven spirit will no longer submit, nor the Jew spirit torture industry for gain, nor the scoundrel spirit longer laugh at the mortal agony of the poor. Onwards, Communists! to success or failure, that we may the sooner know whether the creed of labour is to be peaceful or sanguinary—for the iron maxim of those who rule is, that *no man suffers while he endures*.

A PHŒNIX!—Strenuous efforts have been frequently made, and may be by well intentioned persons, to bring about what is termed " the reconciliation of the middle and working classes." Among those who look most deeply into the nature of class-distinctions, such designs seldom meet with more than a smile, or a shake of the head. The total impossibility of an unanimity of sympathy and sentiment between employer and employed, as *claasses*, is laid down as axiomatic. It does not not on that account follow, that sincere attempts on the part of portions of these interests, irreconcilable as a whole, shall not earn our respect and good will. An instance of this kind has recently occurred, and which will hardly fail to be appreciated by the most uncompromising of our adherents. Towards the subscriptions for the Public Walks and Gardens, about to be opened in Manchester, the *Phœnix* Fire Office of London has contributed £200. Surely, the sordid genius of trade must have deserted their board room, and the lofty spirit of fraternity presided in its place, when they determined on such an act, accompanied by such words as the following, acknowledging, too, in such handsome terms, the spontaneous good offices of the working classes:—"The board feeling that during its long and extensive connection with the trade of Manchester, the Phœnix Company has had frequent experience of the good disposition of the labouring classes, when their personal services have been required, in cases of fire, are desirous to avail themselves of the opportunity which the measure alluded to presents, of adding their assistance towards the success of a measure so well calculated to effect the object contemplated."

M. Q. R.

THE MORALITY OF THE BIBLE.— In *Movement* 46, "A Galashiels Operative" contends that the Bible does not inculcate persecution nor immorality. I hope some of you *Movement* people or your correspondents will stick fast by that operative and show him how much he is mistaken in regard to the character of the Bible—if not, I am his man—he is just such a one as I like to grapple with. Is it not immoral to command people not to eat unwholesome meat, but sell it to a foreigner or give it to a stranger that he may eat it, Deut. xiv, 21. The butchers in Edinburgh are fined from £5 to £20 for acting up to that divine command. What does the temperance society think of Deut. xiv, 26, "Spend your money on strong drink, or whatever your soul *lusts after."* Of authority for persecution, I will be bound to point out plenty in the *New* Testament—for instance, Gal. i, 8. With regard to bloody work, hear what the Lord says, according to Jeremiah xlviii, 10, "Cursed be he that doeth the work of the Lord deceitfully, and cursed be he that keepeth back his sword from *blood."* And see Pslams cxxxix, 5, to the end.

T. FINLAY.

THE HOME MISSION.—The deceptions practised by this society, and to which Mr. Jeffrey drew attention in No. 42 of the *Movement,* still excites investigation. In the *Belfast Vindicator,* No. 571, is a startling letter from the Rev. Luke Walsh, in which the affair is spoken of as the "Home Mission Humbug," and Dr. Edgar and the Rev. Mr. Allen, who have stepped forward to defend it, are proved to have been able to discover only one miserable place behind a "hallan wall," which they called a Home Mission School, when they had asserted that those glens contained twenty-six schools and 700 pupils. The Rev Luke Walsh calls it "a scandalous humbug, *one great monstrous swindle* from beginning to end. The masters are cheating the Inspectors, *with their own consent;* the Superintendents are cheating the Directors, *with their own consent;* and the Directors are gulling and swindling the public."

Some curious revelations are made in this letter of the Rev. Luke Walsh, from which we must some day borrow. Now we can only add the manner in which Dr. Edgar is introduced to the reader as the narrator of one of the neatest miracles that ever came in our way.

"About ten years ago, the Rev. John Edgar, now ycleped D.D., Professor of Theology, and calumniator of the priests of the Glens, asserted, at a public Biblical meeting in the Commercial Buildings, Belfast, that one of the officiating Catholic clergymen there had expelled the devil out of a man, in the *shape of an eel, and laid him on a plate!"*

NEW DEFINITION OF GOD.—Asking a Christian a short time since, to explain what he meant by the term "God," he replied, "O, I cannot define what God is, but I believe him to be an *indefinable, inconceivable concern."* I thought this the best *definition* of deity I ever heard. "God help" God-a-mighty, what a figure he'd cut in St. Athanasius's creed as a *"concern"—* but really the introduction of this term would render the creed much more comprehensible; for instance, "So the Father is God, and the Son is God, and the Holy Ghost is God, and yet there are not three Gods, but one *"Concern."* So, likewise, the Father is Lord, the Son is Lord, and the Holy Ghost is Lord, and yet not three Lords, but one *"Concren."* Would not this be an improvement upon the old version of the creed?

M. A. L.

MR. J. BRONTERRE O'BRIEN respectfully informs Landlords, Capitalists, the League, his Friends, and the Public, that on *Saturday, 16th November,* 1844, will appear, No. I of

THE NATIONAL REFORMER,

and Manx British and Foreign Review. A weekly journal of politics, literature, and science, devoted to the instruction and emancipation of the industrious orders.

PRICE ONLY TWOPENCE HALF-PENNY.

Thus constituting it the *cheapest weekly newspaper in the kingdom.* Quarterly Subscriptions, 2s. 6d. Half yearly, 5s. Yearly, 10s.

OATH TAKING.—A woman, deaf and dumb, was brought before the bench to swear a child. Her father acted as interpreter. A Rev. on the bench asked " does she know that there is a God?" Her father replied "he did not think that she did, for she had never made any signs to that effect." "What, you a *father,"* said the Rev. gent, "and have not taught your daughter that there is a God?" Her attorney enquired, " does she know that there is a heaven and hell?" Still the answer was in the negative. (Query, might it not have puzzled both the Rev. and attorney to have answered with reason either of the questions in the affirmative?) The case was to have been deferred, that the learned bench might have time to make inquiries into such a monstrous case, but the man on whom she should have sworn the child, had the honesty to come forward and acknowledge that he was the father— so that the bench were saved further trouble. Under the present law, if the man had not acknowledged himself the father, the poor woman would have been compelled to have born the entire burden of maintaining her child, *because* she had not acquired the usual theological nonsense about a God, a heaven, and hell. H. UTTLEY, Burnley.

[What sign could the woman have made had she received the notion of a deity? Perhaps some one experienced in deaf and dumb languages could enlighten us on the matter. Perhaps there may be virtue in signs, since words fail to convey any fixed idea. The most likely sign to be guessed is that of the thumb pointing over the left shoulder.]—*Ed. of M.*

BIOGRAPHY, ETC., OF FRANCES WRIGHT D'ARUSMONT.—*J. Myles, Dundee.* Whatever relates to Madame D'Arusmont is of interest to the reformer. During many years the eye of curiosity has been dilated in searching for the history of Frances Wright. On her recent arrival in Europe, she witnessed an attempt to present her biography to the British public, and she happily stepped forward and presented a sketch herself. Hastily as the sketch was necessarily written, and brief as haste necessarily made it—though only just what the occasion required and no more, yet it is characterised by that—not masculine thought, for thought and sense have no sex—but by that high purpose which has ever distinguished its amiable authoress. Unlike those who when asked for a fish give a stone, now that public curiosity asks her for a toy she gives them wisdom—they seek her personal history, to amuse them, she presents her political history, which will greatly instruct them. With just as much personal narrative as connects, and as much characteristic anecdote as enlivens, we have a contribution of rare facts and philosophical reflections. Her brief remarks on the Americans form the most striking defence of them anywhere to be found—her views on the extirpation of slavery go, in a greater degree than any others, to the root of the evil, and are sound, comprehensive, and magnificient. Perhaps the best history extant of the failure of the New Harmony Community is to be found in this Biography, and many secrets its authoress could tell, had more time been at her disposal. Upon her recorded experience with her Tennessee experiment, Socialists should ponder. They would learn enlarged views of politics and grow less contemptful of political labourers. It would be an injustice not to quote the following important note from the Biography. "It is truly difficult in this age to know what to believe. It is not two years since there appeared in the *Gazette des Tribunaux* (the organ of the French law courts), and also in the *Times*, a civil case, in which M. Phiquepal d'Arusmont was made (himself absent and confined by sickness) to plead his own cause, in the sense of his adversary, by the mouth of an attorney speaking in his name; in consequence of which M. Phiquepal lost his suit. And yet this again, not in consequence of any argument or any evidence, however foreign to the truth, which appeared in the official account of the trial, but upon the strength of a violent tirade from the Advocate for the Crown, against the public course pursued by his wife in the United States; which tirade, astounding to those who heard it, was not even alluded to in the published record. The sentence of the Bench—as given in consequence of this (to say the least of it) irrelevant attack upon a person entirely foreign to the case—not content with refusal of justice to M. Phiquepal d'Arusmont, pronounced, in addition, a stigma upon his honour. At a second hearing of the cause, when M. Marie, the head of the French bar, appeared as the duly appointed counsel of M. Phiquepal d'Arusmont, and appeared with credentials in hand from the most distinguished characters of France, substantiating, at one and the same time, the justice of his claim and the disinterested, as well as enlightened, nature of his unremitting labours in the cause of juvenile education. At this second hearing of a most interesting cause, M. Marie was interrupted, silenced, and seated by the Presiding Judge at the opening of his speech, and before he had concluded the perusal of a very flattering letter (given in the Biography) from the Duc de Plaisance to Baron Cuvier, on behalf of M. Phiquepal d'Arusmont.

"Let not the public accuse those who shrink from rendering it disinterested service. At the time present, there is no prudence that can ward off vengeance from those who bear the reputation of serving humanity for herself. M. and Madame Phiquepal d'Arusmont thus outraged in a case which presented in itself no one political feature, were residing in all but absolute seclusion from the world."

The most important fact given to the world on education is that of the grand instructional problem, solved by Phiquepal d'Aursmont, some few particulars of which are given in this sketch. But reader, it is unnecessary to say more than that this book is the political autobiography of *Frances Wright*—whom nature long preserve and mankind honor !

The "Political Letters and Observations on Religion and Civilization," from the same pen, and re-published from the *Northern Star* in a complete form, by Mr. Myles, demand from us the fullest attention, and that we shall hasten to give them.

REVIVAL OF PERSECUTION IN HULL.

An Important Public Meeting

Will be held in the Literary and Scientific Institution, John Street, Tottenham Court Road, on FRIDAY EVENING, NOVEMBER 15, to consider the conduct of Messrs. *Cookman, Barkworth,* and *Firbank,* Magistrates of Hull, who have lately seized and sold the goods of Mr. Johnson, bookseller of that town, in payment of a fine of £20, inflicted for receiving 2d. admission money to a public lecture. Chair to be taken at Half-past Eight o'clock—admission free. The managers have granted the use of the Hall gratuitously. G. J. HOLYOAKE, Sec. A. P. U.

Mrs. Martin has consented to delay her departure from London that she may be present at the meeting.

THE WHITE QUAKERS.—The community of these eccentric people has lately been partly burnt down, through a fire breaking out in Usher's Quay. They were unwilling that the engines should play, as they trusted in Providence. We expect they will find heaven a poor insurance office.

On the first of December, will be published, No. 1 of THE PLEBEIAN; or Poor Man's Advocate, and journal of progress. Its leading principles will be "Morality without Religion, Politics without Party." Edited by Matilda Roalfe.

Why does not the Bishop answer the Question "is the Bible True?" A letter to the Right Rev. Father in God, the Bishop of Worcester. By Edward Walter. Price three half-pence.

An Important and Serious Investigation as to whether the Scriptures support the Separate Existence and Immortality of the Human Soul. By H. Mills. Price Twopence.

PROGRESS OF MISSIONS.—A meeting held last week in Belfast, in favour of Missions, was only attended by about a dozen of friends, when formerly hundreds mustered on a similar occasion.

LEGAL CRITIQUES.—The "Home Thrust" of M. Q. R., and Law Breaking Justified by Miss Roalfe, having been submitted to the Magistrates of Leicester by the Vicar, the same were duly declared to be "awful."

DEITY.—W. J. Fox is now delivering an excellent course of Sunday morning lectures, at Finsbury Chapel, South Place, "On the History of Opinions concerning Deity."

MR. L. BECKWITH.—This gentleman has issued another pamphlet, entitled "Infidelity Exposed," being an answer to Mrs. Martin's rejoinder. The people of Hull are being kept in an agreeable ferment.

PRESTON.—The lectures of Mrs. Martin in this town did not fail to produce their usual fruit. Since their delivery, public discussions have been held, one between Mr. Brooks and Mr. Hamilton, on the question, "Is there a God." Mr. Hamilton has published a smart critique on a lecture by Mr. Brooks.

Errata.—In the first list of subscriptions, on page 407, for W. T. read W. J. In paragraph 8 of Mr. Southwell's letter, page 405, the first full stop is an error, and all that follows to the next full stop belongs to the first sentence.

LECTURES.

Nov. 17.—Finsbury Chapel, South Place, W. J. Fox,—The Monotheism of Moses. At 11, A.M.
Nov. 17.—4, Roan Street, Greenwich, M. Q. Ryall, —Origin and Pretensions of the Book called Bible. At 7, P.M.
Nov. 17.—Social Institution, 5, Charlotte Street, Blackfriars Road, Mr. G. J. Holyoake,—On Political Policy. At 7, P.M.
Nov. 18.————— Mr. Southwell,—On the Life, Character, and Genius of Lord Byron, illustrated by copious quotations from the works of that distinguished poet.
Nov. 17.—Hall of Science, City Road, Mr. C. Southwell,—On the Religious Opinions of Shakspeare, so far as those opinions may be inferred from his dramatic writings, 4th lecture. At 7, P.M.
Nov. 17.—Investigation Hall, 29, Circus Street, Marylebone, Mr. Southwell,—Is man a Free Agent? At 11, A.M. Mr. Lear,—In Vindication of the French Revolution. At 7, P.M.
Nov. 17.—National Hall, High Holborn, W. J. Fox, —On Suicide.
Nov. 17.—Finsbury Institution, Goswell Road, W. D. Saul, Esq.,— On British Antiquities. At half-past 7, P.M. After lecture, discussion, "Will Antiquarian researches remove Traditionary Superstition?

DISCUSSIONS.

Nov. 13.—Investigation Hall, 29, Circus Street, Marylebone,—On the Nature of Man. Between Mr. Southwell and Mr. A. Campbell.
Nov. 14.—National Hall, 242, High Holborn.

NOTICES.

LATIN.—The Committee of the Latin Class, superintended by Mr. Lear, at George Street, Trafalgar Street, Walworth, begs to state that they can receive a few more pupils at 6d. per lesson.

MRS. MARTIN.—This lady is at present in London, on a visit to her family, previously to making a tour in Scotland.

Mrs. Martin will be in Glasgow on the 24th, and will lecture, morning and evening, in the Social Institution, on Sundays, and twice during the week. Any communications for Mrs. Martin may be addressed to the Social Institution, Glasgow—until the end of the year.

SUBSCRIPTIONS
TO THE ANTI-PERSECUTION UNION.

From friend in Coventry, for Mr. Johnson,
Mr. Leavesley 0 10 0
.. Roe 0 3 0
.. Aston 0 1 0
.. Barnes 0 1 0
.. Robinson 0 1 0
.. Morris, May 0 1 0
.. Keen, Lynes 0 1 0
.. Brown, Griffin 0 1 0
.. Moore, Clary 0 1 0
Per Mr. Truman—Members' Tickets 0 1 0
A. P. U. Box, Investigation Hall 0 1 2½

PATERSON TESTIMONIAL.

W. B. B., 3rd subscription 0 10 0
G. J. H., Sec.

The Committee for the defence of Mr. Johnson of Hull, acknowledge the receipt of £1, per Mr. Mc Arthur, Halifax—Mr. William Saling, Leith, 5s.— Per Mr. Richard Dickinson, Burnley £1 0s. 6d.

Printed and Published by G. J. HOLYOAKE,
40, Holywell-street, Strand.
Wednesday, November 13, 1844.

THE MOVEMENT
And Anti-Persecution Gazette.
"Maximise morals, minimise religion."—BENTHAM.

No. 50.   EDITED BY G. JACOB HOLYOAKE, ASSISTED BY M. Q. RYALL.   Price 1½d

OUR FRIENDS ABROAD.

How extremely desirable it is that we should be informed authentically of the movements of democratic friends in different parts of the world is signally exemplified by the miserably defective, erroneous, one-sided or meagre intelligence afforded by the newspaper press in general. The great democratical effort in Sweden has before been alluded to—almost all we hear is through the distorted medium of the *Times* or some such reporter. This is not as it should be. When the columns of a single English print are open to the recital of humanity's struggles, to record their failures as warnings, or rejoice over their successes as triumphs, no friend perfectly acquainted with a single fact should withhold it. The growing intimacy, and substitution of fraternal sympathy for mutual antipathy, exemplified in the recent gatherings of Continental and English Political and Social Revolutionists at the Crown and Anchor, the Socialist Hall, and Highbury Barn Banquet, together with that most important of movements, the Conference of Friends from the democratical sections, without exclusion of party or nation, impart to such intelligence value and interest surprisingly great. While we have the *Northern Star*, the *New Moral World*, the *Movement*, and even Friend Barmby's paper, the friends of Progress abroad will be afforded the opportunity of enlightening us at home. The *Star* for the labourer and artizan's wrongs, electoral and agrarian advancement, the *New Moral World* and *Communist Chronicle* for intelligence of societarian progress in general, the *Movement* more particularly for anti-religious, anti-persecution, revolutionary, and other thorough communistic progress—all these form so many channels for the *diffusion* of such truly *useful knowledge* into the most genial soils—or rather, they form the only medium we know of, for the communication in England of such facts. But the power to communicate, through these organs alone, such momentous facts and opinions, to the most honest, ardent, *public spirited*, energetic and intelligent reformer should be amply sufficient to stimulate all progressionists to aid the common cause by contributing all of which they have *positive* knowledge. In publishing those of the press willing to give currency to progressive movements, it would be unfair to withhold the name of the *Nonconformist*, which, albeit hoisting the standard of the cross, bloody and persecuting as we deem this symbol, has shown itself a bold opponent of privilege, pseudo-respectability, and conventionalism. The best outline of practical ethics has appeared in its pages. So congenial as to warrant transference to our columns. To it we are indebted also for the best account of the political revolution in Sweden.

To contrast the drivelling details of the puppet-show puerilities of royal visits with the bald, partial, and fragmental notices of popular progress, must be enough to induce all who can, to impart full and truthful information. First, if not worn out by the wearisomeness and disgustfulness of the task, cast your eyes over the crowded columns teeming with the frivolous inanities, or vapid fripperies of the court, or solemn fooleries of local lickspittles—how the little queen put on the big king's garter, when they played at making "knight of the garter" at the old castle of Windsor—how the Common Council-men fell to loggerheads about which of the Smiths, or Browns, or Robinsons, should associate his ignoble patronymic by means of a slavering address, with that of the royal Louis Philippe, who got and kept his crown by schemes as graspingly mean, trickish, and dishonest as some have their gowns, —how a squad of waddling, turtle-headed, sycophantic citizens and aldermen, plethoric in paunch and turtle, who rejected a Harmer and elected a Gibbs—left their miserable clerks and shopmen in dire and dingy counting-houses, or glaring tinsel show-shops, while they struggle, stare, sweat and sprawl before the man whom they would have spurned from their doors a score of years back, when engaged in the honorable avocation of mathematical teacher—how the penny-a-line-panderers to long-eared curiosity, twaddle and prattle about the way the queen sneezes, and the prince blows his nose, and all the little princes and princesses suck their thumbs or lick their pap-spoons—how, too, " not the least precaution was taken" to guard the precious person of royalty—that " there was neither police nor guard" while all the time the smartest and stoutest fellows in the A division of police constables were stationed, in livery and out of livery, in every sort of dress and device, filling up every available cranny—and all thrown into a transport of solicitude and phrenzy of alertness, at the apparition of a stranger Frenchman within pistol-shot of the portly potentate. After all this, or a tythe of it, which would be more than the rationalist could peruse with patience, let him look for an appeal to popular principle, a denouncement of popular prejudice, the inculcation of a great truth, the relation of a great event connected with the people's liberty and security—what will be found but a pert turn off—a contemptuous sneer—a dry and curt remark—a distorted statement —a wholesale libel or total concealment. In the *Times'* report, of a month back, the affairs of young Sweden were represented in so garbled a manner, in a way meant to be discouraging to the popular party and their sympathisers here, as to call for special animadversion. See how they deal with the event in their last notice. Into the following compass do they reduce all the foreign intelligence connected with this eventful struggle : " The Swedish journals state that the Chamber of Nobles has rejected the proposal of having the proceedings of the houses of parliament and the speeches of the members published."

Behold the sum total of what the *Times* deems it necessary to transfer from all that " the Swedish journals state,"— its own reporter has nothing to add, or it has no " own reporter" on a field where a people's regeneration is attempted to be worked out. In Blair Athol, this broad-sheet must have, along with nearly a dozen others, a special reporter to chronicle every nod, wink, or hiccup, of masculine, feminine, or infantile royalty.

Again I say it becomes us to keep a watchful eye on progressive events of which we are enabled to speak with accuracy, and make it a point of duty faithfully to transmit trustworthy intelligence to such organs of progression as will give it publicity. If we, who are so deeply interested in these things, do not attend to them, who will? The friends of progress must be evrything to themselves. M. Q. R.

ANTI-CLERICAL ARTILLERY.

Pamphlets thick as hail-stones darken the intellectual horizon—darken did I say?—illumine should be the word, no matter though the figure be a little defective.

The Reverend Newman Hall—reverends are always at the bottom of mischief—has made a *pulpit* attack on infidels and socialists. By the way, the pulpit is the most approved place for all sorts of dirty work which can't bear exposure, seeing that licensed declaimers have a patent for uttering calumnies without incurring the danger of reprisals, at least on the spot. A rare case is it for these sacred personages to venture out of their skulking-holes upon an open platform, for it is only here they find their level. I had the good fortune to catch the Bishop of Norwich at such tricks when he had not the walls of a sacred edifice to protect him, with portly fellow in gold-laced hat, or smart young constable, bludgeon in pocket, at his command, to arrest a malcontent. This worthy, reputed the most liberal among the lawn-sleeves, become partly the patron, partly the tool, of the notorious itinerant buffoon, Brindley, dared, at the Hanover Square Rooms, to vent the most infamous aspersions on the socialists, particularly the socialist women, of Norwich. A vote of strong disapprobation which I proposed, was seconded, and immediately passed, and this pillar of the church had the delightful satisfaction of seeing himself proclaimed in the columns of the *Morning Chronicle*, as a publicly pronounced slanderer. Mitred and " surpliced ruffianism," as well as the insidious malevolence of puritanical *Cantwells*, has been too long triumphant. It has been too long met with tremulous tones, abashed looks, and faltering footsteps. It is time to deal with it after a different fashion, and our infidel friends, from the platforms of People's Halls, in the Public Meetings, through the pages of *Oracles* and *Movements*, and with the artillery of Tracts and Pamphlets, have begun to show that they are both willing and able thus to deal with it.

The aforesaid Newman Hall, having professionally adopted the clerical routine-course of vilification towards infidels and socialists, on Sunday the 3rd, could scarcely have got from the vestry room into his arm-chair and slippers, ere the active Secretary of " Hull Branch, No. 39," must have gone to work to take him to task—and hardly could he have swallowed, or at all events digested, three dinners, before the publisher, Johnson, with equal alacrity, had printed, folded, wrappered, and stitched, the *Review of the Sermon*.

Profundity and erudition would not be expected to characterise this pamphlet,— " rough and ready," might be its motto. Mr. Begg has certainly crammed into a twelve-page pamphlet, as long a catalogue of stock anti-religionisms as are usually scattered over half a dozen. Triteness, rudeness, and a worse sin with the literati— ungrammaticalness, would be a sufficient reason for casting this Review aside by the fastidious. But it is well that plain, unclassical men should be found to take in hand these scholiasts. A more extensive spread of those valuable qualities, self-reliance, independence, and undauntedness, is indicated by such occurences. And again, plain-spoken men will commonly convey to those of all others whom it is most desirable to impress, a conviction of the clerical and other fashionable chicanery by which they have been imposed on.

Most of the topics in Mr. Begg's pamphlet are sufficiently familiar, to our readers to supersede repetition. But the following is so well introduced that it is worth extracting, " He next raised a quibble about the passage ' be subject to the powers that be ; ' and told us that in the original it was ' authorities ' and not ' powers ; ' and ambiguously attempted to soften down the construction. This is the way to convince sceptics of the ' truth of scripture.' Point out to them the parts that are wrong, and damn all those that will not believe ! Let it be understood after this, that where the book tells us that ALL the cattle in Egypt were killed, it does not mean that they were ALL killed, but only those that were in the fields; Mr. Hall has made this very important discovery. ' God is no respecter of persons,' and although we are told that he loved Jacob and hated Esau, yet hated is a Hebrew idiom, and does not mean *hated*, but only *loving a little less !* Perhaps Mr. Hall will take an early opportunity of shewing what we ought to read instead of what we do read, concerning Judas and his doings and deaths, for we find that—

The Judas of the Gospels repented.
The Judas of the Acts did not repent.
The Judas of the Gospel despaired in his iniquity.
The Judas of the Acts triumphed in his iniquity.
The Judas of the Gospel returned the money.
The Judas of the Acts kept the money.
The Judas of the Gospel bore an honorable testimony to the innocence of Christ.

The Judas of the Acts bore no such testimony.
The Judas of the Gospel gave back the whole sum he had received, to the priests, who put it into the treasury.
The Judas of the Acts bought a field with it.
The Judas of the Gospel hanged himself.
The Judas of the Acts died by an accident.
The Judas of the Gospel met a death that was entirely natural.
The Judas of the Acts met a death that was entirely miraculous.
These are all easily reconcilable, according to Mr. Hall's method of reading and understanding, for what ever it may *say*, it does not *mean* what it says."

In the social part of his defence, Mr. Begg gives a very fair little epitome of the spirit of Socialism, allowing for his very contracted limits. The *New Moral World* will give him credit for this at all events.

I know not if this is Mr. Begg's first brush with the clergy—but with time and care, and friendly criticism, he may produce what may be formidable to them. Our friends should patronise this young effort.

M. Q. R.

LETTER FROM MR. PATERSON.

General Prison, November 6th.

DEAR H.—Glad you have news in store for me. Quite dead to the world and all its dear little vanities.

I should be pleased could you or Ryall come to Scotland. Under one or other of your auspices I should be prepared to do wonders, for we ought to follow up our success by extra exertions, this in-coming summer.

Twelve months nearly elapsed since the night birds of society, in solemn conclave, doomed me to tease oakum and divinity for fifteen months ! The result is, that to day, sweeter in my ear is the clanking prison door, with a conscience, than a comfortable fire-side with submission. I am still prepared to write or speak, as truth dictates, and not to cozen or lie merely to please those who have themselves no conscience. I am not yet frightened from my duty because the animal sensitiveness of theological porcupines is awakened, and their volleys of abuse, opprobrium, and tyranny are in full play. For the future I shall go on my way rejoicing, despite of the fury of bigots, the howls of demoniac fire-brands, or the canting whine of selfish knaves. When I cry *pecavi* it shall be to arguments, not blows—to syllogisms, not courts—to dilemmas, not prisons. I know the difference between civility and sycophancy—civility does not consist in licking the hand that smites, or thanking the vultures for abuse.

As there is nothing in any of your letters which prompts replies that would be "passed," I will conclude by giving my regards to Mrs. H. and R., and soon will do myself the honour to wait on them.

I must not omit a word on Hull. You said lately that I was probably the last martyr to cant, but as a prophet you will never be thought much of in your own country. Give my card to the Hull persecutors, and promise, on my word, that I shall be in that town on the 12th of February, and if matters are not then altered, I shall open a Depot. I have a notion that Hull would give a good business, and it should be a rule always to "open a place" whenever persecution commences in any considerable town. I am truly happy that our efforts in Edinburgh are not without fail, and I will be too happy in assisting to finish what it is our duty to attempt.

I would recommend your Union to provide copies of the English and Scottish Law, so that they might be able to afford *victims* some salutary advice as to their proceedings. Had I been thus furnished, I could have stood my ground with better effect than I did.

Regards to Messrs. W. J. B. and Ryall.
Yours truly,
T. PATERSON.

Letters received—1 Campbell, Leicester, 1 Siddle, 2 Miss Roalfe.

Mr. Paterson's Card.

Mr. PATERSON respectfully presents his Compliments to the Magistrates of Hull, and begs to say, that on the 9th of February he shall be at liberty, and on the 12th he will be in Hull, if they are at all disposed to patronise him, and open another Blasphemy Depot there. In variety and quality of his Goods, Mr. Paterson defies competition.

HARMONY HALL.
To the Editor of the Movement.

SIR,—My attention has been directed to a paragraph in a recent article in your paper on the above subject, in which you say—

"Even the late Acting Governor made, on Mr. Buxton's accession to office, a demand for £500, but voucher, receipt, or entry, could not by him be produced, nor anywhere be found."

This, sir, is erroneous, and I exceedingly regret that you should have made such a statement except upon the highest authority. There is a regular entry made of the transaction in the books of the society, and this was pointed out by me to the present Executive, the transaction itself is well known to all the previous officers, and to all the Delegates of the Special Congress in July, 1842, two months after the money was lent *as a temporary loan for one month only.* At present I refrain from saying more, except that I had a right to expect that the Executive, on seeing the paragraph in question, would, for the credit of the society, if not in justice to myself, have set you right in the matter.

Trusting that you will make this public,
I remain, Sir, Yours, &c.,
The Late Acting Governor of Harmony.
London, November 14, 1844.

[The remarks on the above gentleman, in my "Visit to Harmony" were made with more pleasure than any comment on other persons, as I felt assured, from ancient knowledge of the Late Acting Governor, that he would have the frankness to speak out if he was displeased—and without waiting to make any enquiry respecting the correctness of his allegation, I at once insert his letter. He questions *one third* only of my remark. He says he pointed out "a regular entry in the Society's Books," but he does not deny that neither "receipt nor voucher was produced." *Two thirds* of my statement are therefore unquestioned. But the Late Acting Governor makes a martyr of himself, and pretends that I have done him an injury, which was not only not designed, but *not inflicted.* As he demands the "highest authority," for my statement, and tells us that "Delegates to the Special Congress knew of the loan he made," he assumes that I have called his integrity in question. This will not do. My criticisms shall not be turned into a petty personal controversy. Not a single line of my three papers impugns any man's honour. I *did not* deny that the Late Acting Governor lent the money, I only cited the unbusiness like manner in which the transaction was conducted. Perhaps it is to the credit of the Late Acting Governor that he procured no voucher, but if it proves that he had generous confidence in those to whom he lent his money, (which I believe he had) still it proves their negligence. Further, if the Late Acting Governor thinks I insinuated want of honour against him, he wrongs me. I should despise myself if I could stoop so low—no! had I thought him dishonest, and chosen to have noticed him, I would have *branded* him with it in a moment. But one word more. The Late Acting Governor says that he "*refrains from saying more at present.*" But does he pretend to say that he witholds something in mercy to me. I won't have it, let him out with it—I'll print it, every line, if I have to pay for a supplement to the *Movement*. When the Bishop of Exeter treated the Late Acting Governor in this way, he at once defied the Bishop to do his worst—I admired his conduct, and beg leave to imitate it. I will consult the "highest authority" on the point called in question, and in the next *Movement*—if the post permits, will adduce proof of my statement, or amply retract the error.]—*Ed. of M.*

INFIDEL TRACTS.

Sir,—I perceive by a recent number of the *Movement* that the Infidel Tract Society have complained of the difficulty in getting a printer to print the Society's works. That this is a serious obstacle, few persons in the least acquainted with the subject will doubt. The difficulties which we have had to contend with on this score, have been immense, in fact so great, that it has been with considerable difficulty that we could get printed, things of the most trifling nature. But this is not the most serious difficulty under which the Infidel world labours, for having found a person willing to print our works, we are under the necessity of paying him his own price, and that is not very often a moderate one, for knowing the difficulty we labour under in getting such things done, they charge accordingly.

But we hope ere long, to be enabled to say "we have a press which shall be devoted to the cause of Infidelity," and then an earnest effort must be made to put the public in possession of works at a much cheaper rate than they have ever yet had them. The high price of Infidelity is unquestionably a serious obstacle to the successful propagation of our views. The advantages to be derived from the possession of a press, are not to be calculated. Fully satisfied that no great advance can be made until we can wield a press with the same chance of success as our opponents.

To prevent such case as our friend complains of, has been our anxious desire, and should the same difficulty occur again, it may be obviated by writing here, enclosing copy, and stating the size of the article required, and as to cheapness, we hope to be able to do it as cheap as any that has been yet done. The *Plebeian*, which will appear on the first of December, will be, in every sense of the word, a practical proof of our intentions as to printing.

We hope, therefore, that our friends will no longer allow the difficulty to retard their progress, but at once avail themselves of the opportunity that now presents itself, and should we meet with that support which our intentions deserve, we promise the Infidel public that ere twelve months more we will have stereotyped some useful and valuable tracts, that may be as widely distributed as are the tracts of the Religious Society in Paternoster Row.

W. Baker.

105, Nicolson Street, Edinburgh.

THE PATERSON TESTIMONIAL.

On Sunday afternoon, October 27, 1844, a few friends of small means, met at a private house in Leicester, to sympathise with, and assist Mr. Paterson, on account of his sufferings in the cause of liberty. The means they employed were the holding a tea party, to which each one paid sixpence, and as several of them made little presents of the *essentials*, a considerable portion of the cash received was clear. As soon as tea was over, Mr. T. Ryley Perry was called to the chair, who briefly stated the object of the meeting. Mr. Campbell made a few remarks, during which he informed the meeting of the amount of imprisonment their chairman had endured for the cause they were now met to assist—which was received with evident feeling. The remainder of the evening was spent in conversation with the chairman, upon points of interest, interspersed with songs and recitations. The amount announced as profit was 7s., and considered satisfactory, from the private nature and limited means of the parties present.   Thomas Emery.

[We trust this excellent example will be followed in many places. We are happy to learn that the Social Branch in Leicester will hold a public tea party for the benefit of Mr. Paterson, on the first Sunday in December.]—*Ed. of M.*

THE PLEBEIAN;

Or Poor Man's Advocate, and Journal of progress.

Its leading principles will be

"*Morality without Religion, Politics without Party.*"

Edited by Matilda Roalfe.

No apology is necessary for ushering into the world this periodical, as at the present time there is not a publication of any kind in existence, to which the working classes of Scotland can refer, and learn what exertions their fellow-men are making for the benefit of the class to which they belong, or what steps are taken to arrest their progress, by those who are especially interested in so doing.

The possession of such knowledge would be of the utmost importance to the working classes. Nothing would tend more to advance the poor man's cause; as by knowing what progress his fellow-man was making in other parts of the country, he would be stimulated to greater exertion; and by knowing what his enemies were doing, he would be on his guard, and better able to defend himself against the machinations of those who live not by the sweat of their brow.

To accomplish so desirable an end is the object of the *Plebeian*, and for which it has been especially projected. To be enabled to present the public with the necessary information, arrangements have been made with some of the most zealous and active among the working classes, in the principal towns throughout Scotland, for correct reports of all that transpires in their immediate localities, either of a religious or political nature.

Religion will first engage the attention of the *Plebeian*, being fully satisfied that from that source proceed all the injustice and misery that at present afflicts the human race. Few persons indeed, can be ignorant of the fact, that religion is made the test of the accuracy and usefulness of every principle promulgated; and should a principle not square with it, it is at once denounced, not only as useless, but highly injurious; hence the *Plebeian* will narrowly watch the proceedings of the various religious parties throughout Scotland, and hold up to public scorn any act of injustice or oppression on the part of those who profess to watch over the interests of their fellow beings.

The *Plebeian* will not be personal, but should it have occasion to comment upon the doings of public men, it will not be scrupulous in exposing either hypocrisy or dishonesty in matters of opinion, for it is only by directing public attention to such parties that it can be known whom to trust.

Politics will form another feature of the *Plebeian*; it will endeavour to promulgate and defend such measures as seem best calculated to do the most good, and will comment upon all schemes false in theory or likely to be pernicious in practice.

The *Plebeian* will contain occasional extracts of importance from the newspapers and other sources; also short and useful articles on *Science*, with correct accounts of any new and important discovery.

The pages of the *Plebeian* will be open to all parties on all subjects, either for the communication of general news, or the discussion of religious or political questions.

The *Plebeian* will appear on the First of every Month, and contain twelve 8vo pages of closely printed matter, double columns, Price One Penny.

Agents:—Edinburgh: Roalfe, Baker, & Co., 105, Nicolson Street; London: Merriman, Red Cross Street; Glasgow: Love, Nelson Street; Dundee: Myles, Overgate, and all Booksellers.

No. 1 will be published on the First of December.

RAISING RELIGIOUS WIND.—A good example of the flash manner in which this is attempted, where there is reason to suppose that sufficient credulity exists to work upon, will be found in the following extract from speeches lately delivered at a Baptist Missionary Meeting in Bristol:—" The Rev. E. Williams, of Aberystwith, in proposing the adoption of the report, said, *there was a principle of self-love implanted in every man's nature*, and that principle ought to lead them to aid that society, because they knew that God would repay every one, in this world, ten-fold for all that they did for his glory. The Rev. speaker illustrated this part of his argument by relating an anecdote of a poor old woman, of pious feeling, at Merthyr. There was a missionary meeting there some time since, and as no chapel was capable of holding the people, it was held in a field. The collection, also, was so large that they could get no vessel large enough to contain it, except a bucket. When the bucket was handed round to poor Ruth, she had nothing to give but her prayers. As she was going away from the meeting she met a gentleman who gave her a sixpence, and she immediately hastened back, and calling for the bucket exclaimed, " light come, light go." and threw in the sixpence. The news of the pious offering soon spread, and some young ladies who heard of it, gave her a shilling, which poor Ruth was unable to keep to herself, and which she also threw into the bucket. God did not suffer her to be a loser by her liberality in his service, for some good people of Merthyr hearing of it subscribed and bought her a suit of clothes. They might all depend upon it that they would never lose anything by serving God. His was the silver and his the gold; and he would bestow upon them all they wanted. The Rev. G. H. Davis seconded the resolution. The Rev. gent. then followed out the train of argument pursued by the last speaker, and explained that, from principles of piety, love to man, and self-love, every person present was bound to lend his support to the society. God would bless those who served him, and he never knew an individual to suffer on account of his liberality in God's service—indeed, their benevolence never came near to that; they never gave so freely as to injure themselves; they consecrated to God nothing but the surplus of their means. When they emulated the example of the poor widow, and, like her, cast all they had into the treasury of the Lord, then might they expect a reward like hers—they had no right to look for her recompence till they had acted upon a similar principle, and in a similar manner."

Character of the General Assembly of Scotland.—Swift used to say that he would be very much obliged to the Pope, when he was weeding his garden, not to throw the weeds over *his wall.* In his day, there was a great rage for Popish converts to the Church of England, but they boldly and openly bought them in by the head. Like the Assembly, they never inquired whether they were convinced of the truth of Protestantism, but whether they would declare against the "errors of Popery;" but such was the character and complexion of their converts, that they soon got ashamed of them, and gave up the system; and, to her credit be it said, the Church of England is now very circumspect in receiving any of those pretended converts. But it appears that the weeds, the very dregs and scum of the Catholic population, are snatched up by the General Assembly; and the more immoral, profligate, and abandoned they are, the greater favourites they become, and are paraded as the glorious trophies of Presbyterianism. Suspended and immoral priests, who have broken their vows, and steeped their souls in sacrilege and perjury—disappointed, irreligious candidates for the ministry—mercenary, abandoned, and profligate wretches among the laity, who would sell themselves to the devil, every day in the week, for money—these be the worthy converts that are to recruit the ranks of the General Assembly. This Assembly *of ours* must be a most cleanly animal, she has such a voracious appetite for every *vomit* of the Church of Rome. And here I would ask the rational and intelligent Presbyterians, are those precious converts worth what they cost? If they be, they must value them highly, for there is not one of them that does not cost them one hundred pounds —too high a price for such renegades, even supposing them sincere, which is often problematical.—*The Rev. Luke Walsh—Belfast Vindicator.*

GALASHIELS.—Mr. Blair, with his wonted virulence, still continues to lecture on Sunday evenings, either on the "awful nature of Infidelity and the immorality of Socialism," or the "evidences of Christianity, external and internal." But with all his shallowness, he is dupe enough to refuse having anything to do with discussions. He sets up an opponent of his own imagination, knocks him down with great skill, then raises a shout of victory, and with an impudence peculiarly his own, not unfrequently exclaims, "Where now are the Infidels." W. S.

W. J. Fox.—This gentleman was written to by the Secretary of the Anti-Persecution Union, to request that he would announce to his audience at the National Hall, on Sunday, November 10, the Public Meeting to be held at John Street on the Friday following, respecting the persecution in Hull. It is of no use having liberal men if we do not make use of them. There is no other public man, reputedly religious, to whom such a request could have been made without it being deemed insulting. Well, Mr. Fox, *actually* would have announced it had it not been for a rule at the Association Hall, not to give out notices, because if they did, so we are told, they must make a selection, and that would be invidious. So *they* reason. To select announcements with regard to their importance is not invidious but wise. To be invidious is to slight parties on grounds of personal dislike, or interest. Do not the National Hall people find fault with the Chartists who refuse all reform because they cannot have the Charter? But is not the saying, we can't give out all notices, so we won't give out any, the same thing? It means because we can't do all the good we wish, we will do none.

THE PUBLIC MEETING ON FRIDAY.—A full report of this highly important meeting will appear in the next number of the *Movement.*

ANTI-PERSECUTION UNION.—It has been determined by the Union, for reasons stated at the public meeting, to at once assist Mr. Johnson to enter and sustain an action against the Magistrates of Hull, for the recovery of his fine. His conviction having been plainly illegal.

WORTH PRESERVING.—The following is a copy of the bill of sale of Mr. Johnson's property—

To Furniture Brokers, Booksellers, and Others.

TO BE SOLD BY AUCTION,

By J. Waite, on Monday, October 14th, 1844, at ten o'clock in the forenoon, on the premises of Mr. Johnson, 13, Ann Street, Osborne Street, under a Warrant of Distress, the whole of the genteel

HOUSEHOLD FURNITURE,

Comprising one set of mahogany chairs, pillar and claw Pembroke and card tables, carpet, fender and fire irons; a clock, pier and swing glasses, camp bedstead, feather beds, mattresses, and bedding, dressing tables and bason stands, kitchen furniture, culinary utensils, &c. Also at two o'clock, at the shop, Saville Street, the

STOCK-IN-TRADE

Of General Stationery, and Books in great variety, a Circulating Library of about 600 volumes, being chiefly the works of the most esteemed authors.

W. L. Anderson, Printer, Hull.

VISIT TO HARMONY.—We have received a rather scolding letter from Mr. Morgan of Worcester, respecting the "Visit to Harmony," but as Mr. Morgan's remarks are written on papers No. 1 and 2, we wait to see if he has anything to add or retract, now that No. 3 has appeared. Once, when a juryman had inspected a bond, in the early part of a cause tried before Lord Kenyon, the jury-man exclaimed, "Oh, my Lord, I am quite satisfied the bond is forged, you need not proceed further." "There cannot be," said his Lordship gravely, "a greater misfortune than that a man should make up his mind before he has heard half the case." "A misfortune? my Lord," said a counsellor, "there cannot be a greater *fault*." This fault our friend Mr. Morgan commits. He decides of the wrong before he reads all—he strikes before he hears. This is only half our misfortune. Mr. Morgan is a bookseller. Now we never like to hold disputes with booksellers, because if we don't happen to please them, they won't sell any more *Movements*. But if Mr. Morgan particularly desires to appear in print on this subject, we shall be sure to accommodate him.

"THE HOME MISSION HUMBUG.—The *Belfast Vindicator* of November 13, has a long report of a public dinner, given to Messrs. Walsh and Fitzsimons, to celebrate their triumph over what they style the "Missions Humbug." At the conclusion they drank the memory of the Missions in solemn silence. We hope the day is not remote when the memory of all Christian missions will be received in a similar manner. A pamphlet has just appeared of the following attractive and instructive title—

The Priest flogging the Minister; or, a salutary chastisement inflicted on the Rev. JOHN EDGAR, D.D., Professor of Theology, for his falsehoods, misrepresentations, and calumnies, on the subject of the *Home Mission*: being a complete refutation of "The Priest's Curse," in two letters, by the Rev. LUKE WALSH, P.P., Culfeightrin, Co. Antrim.

Belfast: Printed by Robert and Daniel Read, Crown-Entry.

RELIGIOUS LIGHT DEFINED.—The *Hull Advertiser* of November 8, says, that at the opening lecture for the season, at the Driffield Mechanics' Institute, was given on Tuesday evening last, by Mr. Stead, the librarian, on the Wonders of Nature. The lecture-room was brilliantly lighted on the occasion, for the first time with gas, and was a pleasing improvement over the "*dim religious light*," shed by *drowsy penny candles*. From which it follows religious light is penny candle light. We always thought it was a rather dull affair.

For *Movement*, from Atheistical Society.... 1 0 0

BRANCH A 1.—On Sunday morning, at the Members' meeting, the third paper of the Visit to Harmony Hall was read and canvassed. A disposition is manifesting itself to enquire into the subjects to which the papers relate. A message of some kind relative to it is reported to have been delivered from Mr. Lloyd Jones.

THE PAPERS ON HARMONY HALL.—Mr. Edwards, formerly a Vice President of the Socialists, sends a challenge to a public discussion, of a formal a priori proposition, respecting the views taken in the "Visit." It is to be read on Sunday evening next, after the lecture, at John Street. We shall publish this curious challenge next week.

LECTURES.

Nov. 24.—Finsbury Chapel, South Place, W. J. Fox,—The Oriental Doctrine of Two Principles. At 11, A.M.

Nov. 24.—4, Roan Street Greenwich, Mr. Holyoake, —Morality distinguished from Religion. At 7, P.M.

Nov. 24.—29, Circus Street, Bryanstone Square, Mr. Southwell,—On the White Quakers. At 11, A.M. Mr. Ryall,—On the Origin and Pretensions of the book called Bible. At 7, P.M.

Nov. 24.—Social Institution, Leicester, J. N. Bailey, —The Bible—is it true? At 8, P.M.

Nov. 24.—5, Charlotte Street, Blackfriars Road, Mr. Campbell,—Jesus Christ *rationally* (?) explained. At 7, P.M.

Nov. 25.————Mr. Southwell,—On the Life, Character, and Genius of Lord Byron.

Nov. 24.—Hall of Science, City Road, Mr. Southwell. At 7, P.M.

Nov. 24.—Finsbury Institution, Goswell Road, Mr. Taylor,—Prophets and Priestcraft. At 7, P.M.

TO CORRESPONDENTS.

Received—*Le Populaire, Hull Advertiser*, God's word and God's works, by W. C., Geology and the Bible, by P. G.

J. Wells, Boston—a copy of any report we are expected to notice should at least have been sent to us. An age may elapse before it may come to hand.

Errata.—Page 413, article "Theory of Regular Gradation," 13th line from bottom of first column, for *species* read *spheres*. Second column, 9th line from bottom, for *few* read *far*.

SUBSCRIPTIONS
TO THE ANTI-PERSECUTION UNION.

Brittain, Chubb	0	1	0
Skendall, Drew	0	1	0
For Mr. Johnson, from friends at Leicester	0	7	4
Trueman, T. Bidwell	0	1	0
Collector 44	0	1	6
Per Public Meeting. John Street	2	17	10½
Per Mr. Friend, Collector 44,			
Members' Tickets	0	2	6
Subscriptions, per Card	0	3	9
J. P., Halifax	0	1	0

PATERSON TESTIMONIAL.

Atheistical Society	0	10	0
Per J. Renton, from Berwick on Tweed,			
W. Black	0	1	0
R. Mathison, do.	0	2	0
T. Bidwell	0	1	0

G. J. H., *Sec*.

MR. G. BEGG of Hull, acknowledges 6s., from the Investigators of Whitechapel, for Mr. R. Johnson.

Printed and Published by G. J. HOLYOAKE, 40, Holywell-street, Strand.
Wednesday, November 20, 1844.

THE MOVEMENT
And Anti=Persecution Gazette.
" Maximise morals, minimise religion."—BENTHAM.

No. 51.   EDITED BY G. JACOB HOLYOAKE,   Price 1½d
           ASSISTED BY M. Q. RYALL.

REVIVAL OF PERSECUTION IN HULL.

PUBLIC MEETING.

[This meeting was not expected to be more than an expression of public feeling at the conduct of the Hull Magistrates, and it was not known what the exertions of Mr. Hetherington and other friends would lead to, until an hour before the meeting assembled, or arrangements would have been made to present this report in our last number.]

BRANCH A 1 having granted the free use of their Hall to the Anti-Persecution Union, a numerous public meeting assembled in the Literary and Scientific Institution, Fitzroy Square, pursuant to announcement, on Friday, Nov. 15, and at the appointed hour the members and friends of the Anti-Persecution Union took their seats on the platform, and Mrs. Martin, on her appearance, was welcomed by several rounds of enthusiastic applause. Mr. Alexander Campbell, who was to preside, having been suddenly called to Ham, George Bird, Esq., was unanimously elected chairman.

The CHAIRMAN briefly opened the business of the meeting, and said, though unexpectedly called to occupy that important position, he gladly rendered his aid on such an occasion. It gave him pleasure to find so numerous an assembly, prepared to express their sentiments on the proceedings to be brought under notice. He would not delay the discussion of those topics by lengthened remarks, but at once call on Mr. Hetherington to move the first resolution.

Mr. HETHERINGTON—That meeting had been assembled to consider the conduct of Messrs. Cookman, Barkworth, and Firbank, Magistrates of Hull, who had fined a bookseller in that town £20, for taking admission money at a public lecture. (Cries of shame). Those magistrates thought thereby to strike a blow at free discussion, but he hoped they would be taught differently. The case arose out of Mrs. Martin's Lectures in that town. The magistrates having found that they could not put that lady down by arguments, meanly had recourse to force. They all knew when a woman took anything into her head, how hard it was to get it out, and all of them who were married knew that when a lady lectures it is the proper duty of gentlemen to listen patiently. But the Magistrates of Hull not understanding their duty, had proceeded to very ungallant extremities. Mr. H. referred to the assistance rendered by the clergy in these infamous cases, and quoted the satirical remarks of Mandeville, on the habits and character of that pernicious profession. He spoke of the notorious and justly detested gagging act, the 79th of Geo. III., under which the Hull Magistrates had convicted Mr. Johnson. His, Mr. H.'s property, had been seized under the clauses of that iniquitous statute, and nothing had been left him but the bare walls. However, a few years ago, informers who fed on such laws, had lain 300 indictments against booksellers, and it was found that all Mr. Knight's works of the Society for the Diffusion of Useful Knowledge were liable in common with others. Then a deputation, of which he (Mr. H.) was one, waited on Lord John Russell, and he was so struck with the baseness of that law, which the Hull Magistrates had not scrupled to employ against a woman, that he passed a law, making for ever illegal all convictions procured by other parties than the Attorney General, and no doubt but that the conviction of Mr. Johnson was entirely illegal. Let them then take measures accordingly. He was no admirer of Christ's precious precept, if struck on one cheek turn the other also. His maxim was to return the blow. The clergy were afraid of Mrs. Martin—that was the truth. She dragged them out whether they would or not. They ought not to be trampled on by religionists. He believed they acted on the principle of Foster, who, when asked by the Lord Mayor, some years ago, why he, a respectable man, so imposed on the people, answered, " the truth is my Lord, there are such a number of damned fools, that it would be a pity not to cheat them." Let them not be the fools to be cheated—he called on them as a veteran in that cause to support Johnson in obtaining justice.— After a speech of great ability, Mr. Hetherington proposed

"That the Metropolitan meeting, after deliberating upon the discreditable notoriety which the town of Hull, through its public functionaries, Messrs. Cookman, Barkworth, and Firbank, has achieved, deems it an imperative duty to declare that the above named Magistrates, by the persecutions instituted against, and the fines levied upon, Messrs. Johnson and Watson, for simply letting a room for a lecture, and receiving admission money, have manifested a bigotry and barbarism which the country had reason to hope were obsolete, and buried in the infamy of the Sidmouth and Castlereagh administrations, and that the revival of such unjust, arbitrary, and impolitic proceedings, emphatically calls for the severest and most indignant repudiation on the part of all honest men."

Mr. SOUTHWELL rose with great pleasure to second the resolution. He liked the latter part of Mr. H.'s speech as regards the non-passive doctrine. He thought the people should let their rulers see that however willing they may be to play the tyrant, the nation would not consent to act the slave. He fully agreed with the truth of the observation, that it was slaves who made tyrants and not tyrants who created slaves. The Magistrates of Hull had made a halter for their own necks, and he hoped they would not be allowed to withdraw without placing their heads in it. He thought that in Mrs. Martin they had caught a tartar, and like the Paddy, could neither get away with it nor get from it. Jacks in office must be taught that they cannot play fantastical tricks with the free expression of opinion, except at their own expense. That was the question of questions. They boasted of their freedom, but distinguished as they were by the arts and sciences, were they really free? At the bottom of these proceedings were the clergy, who, in their own estimation, were "Dogberries most terrible." Those men created mischief everywhere from their position—maintained falsehood while it was to the interest of the public to have truth. They dreaded discussion, for the fact was, that with fair discussion, with competent opponents, Christianity could not maintain its position twelve months. The enlightened among the clergy were to the last degree hypocritical—Christianity did not deceive *them*—they were not to be caught by such chaff. There was a notion abroad that the people could not bear the truth—that it must be administered relatively to their follies—hence the hollow system of humbug which everywhere abounded. The people neglected their own interests, in allowing men to suffer unaided. The noble minds were turned against them. Another mischievous error was the notion of woman's dependence. That, too, was the doing of the priest, who thereby made a readier tool of mankind. But it must never be forgotten, that till woman is free and enlightened, a fearful barrier is opposed to all true progression. When he reflected on the way in which people allowed themselves to be cajoled, he almost despaired. But they should look into themselves—find the causes of failure in misapplication of talents, and laying their plans more wisely, should unite on grand indisputable principles, for the working out of grand practical reforms. Freedom must be allowed to all, and universality of principle sought for as the basis —the only basis from which good could spring. But instead of this, even among reformers, among Socialists, bigotry and intolerance were rampant. Among the wise reformers there were boobies. In enlightened, liberal London, constraint was severely felt. There was an intolerance as to style—one must write and think in a certain way—he must balance his sentiments in another's scale, and if this was not done, vast was the outcry, incessant and powerful the efforts made by bigotry to put down what it deems offensive. He liked to praise where praise was due. For two years Mrs. Martin had nobly stood to her post—had done her duty while the Socialists had shrunk from theirs. Their duty lay plain and open before them, having chosen an honorable course, they must follow it out manfully, not looking too narrowly to the consequences, but ever prepared to maintain their rights, exhibiting a bold front,— teaching Christians their duty. Those Hull Dogberries must be made to disgorge their spoil. There was every encouragement for reformers to hold on. They knew the nursery rhyme—

Umpty Dumpty sat on a wall,
But Umpty Dumpty had a great fall,
Not all the king's horses nor all his men,
Could set Umpty Dumpty up again.

And he would say let but the priests carry on their present game, and they might soon sing

Superstition sat on a wall,
But Superstition had a great fall,
Not all the Queen's horses nor all her men,
Could set Superstition up again.

Mr. Southwell having seconded the resolution, it was put and carried unanimously.

Mr. PUDDEFORD here presented himself, and executed one of his weekly performaances on Christianity, with the usual effect, which having subsided,

Mr. HOLYOAKE came forward and moved the second resolution. He desired that Mr. Puddeford might stand excused, as that gent. appeared to have a commission to make a speech on Friday nights, and no matter where he was or what was the business of the meeting, speak Mr. P. must. They were met that night because certain wise men of Hull had attacked that principle of free discussion which the Anti-Persecution Union was formed to defend. This was proved by the fact, that the magistrates had passed by various societies in Hull, whose officers were equally liable with Messrs. Johnson and Watson—the magistrates had attacked but one set of views and one class of reformers. These magistrates would prate to that meeting of a day of judgment, but would those magistrates, according to their own dogmas, answer for any one present? Not they. Then was it not monstrous that they should interfere were they would not be responsible? No! that meeting would resolve, that since they are fabled to answer in heaven, they would be heard on earth. Some one would perhaps appear and censure speakers for alluding to Christianity. But were it not for Christians, that meeting need not have been called. Did not parsons prompt every infamy? Who was at the bottom of Mr. Hetherington's prosecution but parsons? Who committed Mr. Southwell but James Wood, the Methodist of Bristol? There was Francis Close in Mr. H's case. Who sentenced Mr. Paterson to barbarous punishment in Tothil Fields, but David Jardine, one of their philosophical Unitarians? And two of the Hull Magistrates were dissenting preachers. It was glorious to witness their miserable success. The *Hull Advertiser* of Nov. 8, could now "consider the persecution ill-advised." He would read a letter just received from Mr. Paterson. (Here Mr. H. read the letter inserted in last week's *Movement*, which was rapturously received). Some one said that those whom God intended to destroy he first hardened. He (Mr. H.) thought that, if God there be, he was taking that course with his servants, who were burying Christianity in contempt. The Hull Magistrates aimed at Mrs. Martin, but not being able to reach her, they had the meanness to strike at those less able to defend themselves. Mankind had ever detested those despicable men who fled from the enemy in the field but returned when the battle was over and stabbed the dead, whom they feared to face when living. So had the Christian magistrates of Hull acted —not daring to meet by argument the doctrines of Mrs. Martin, they had wreaked their miserable vengeance on an obscure publican and a defenceless bookseller. But luckily the 39, Geo. III., c. 79, on which they had proceeded, had been so amended by 2 Victoria, c. 12, as to make their conviction illegal. Mr. Johnson had stood by the right of free discussion in a manly, uncompromising spirit, and he (Mr. H.) doubted not that that meeting, and the country at large, would see that he had justice. He would therefore propose

"That in the opinion of this meeting, the prosecutions instituted against Messrs. Johnson and Watson of Hull, are not only immoral, but illegal, and that steps should be immediately taken to compel the magistrates to refund the fines levied."

Mr. PARKER seconded the resolution with considerable fervour—he thought all should rally around the victims, and therein show the glory of free men. The resolution was then put and carried unanimously.

Mr. ELLIS said he should have addressed the meeting, but he was anxious not to disappoint them in their anxiety to hear Mrs. Martin, he would therefore briefly propose —That the preceding resolutions be advertised in the Hull newspapers, and otherwise made public.

MRS. MARTIN said, that in seconding it she could not but feel delighted in hearing so many eloquent defenders of a case, so peculiarly her own. She, if any one, was the offending party. But she was above the power of the persecutors, being exempted by her sex, and protected by the enlightenment of the people, whose warm sympathies in her behalf were not to be mistaken, or lightly opposed. Nothing could be more injurious than the union, in one and the same person, of the offices of magistrate and priest. The magistrate, to enforce the laws, is endowed with immense powers, and when the priest comes in with his hobby, it becomes necessarily his duty, as well as his wish, to use those powers for the assistance of his fell schemes. So was it with the Mayor of Hull, his hobby, religion, would be endangered by her lectures, hence he determined to stop them. Attended by the police, he went in person to put the pad-lock on the door of the lecture room, so that when she arrived in Hull, in the evening, she found herself and intended audience shut out, and the good people of Hull in a state of delightful commotion. Another room was procured, when the

Mayor again interfered, threatening the Innkeeper with the loss of his license, &c. To this a spirited answer was returned, "that the Mayor had no right to interfere, and that before he became chief magistrate, he should have made himself better acquainted with the duties of his office, and with English law." However, subsequently, the innkeeper, Mr. Watson, knowing the damage that would occur to his landlord's property by the loss of the license, when the informations were laid, made a promise of future refusal of his room, and was therefore only called on for a mitigated fine. Neither the Mayor nor lawyers of Hull were very well acquainted with the law of this case, and she believed that her mentioning the infamous act, under which the proceedings were afterwards instituted, in her lecture, might have given the hint for their prosecutions. This she did not however regret, since she was persuaded every step taken in the attempted suppression of freedom, will be only one really in advance So informal were the proceedings, that the statute was not mentioned in the warrant, and several hours were spent in searching through the statutes at large to ascertain the probable Act which would be appealed to. Johnson was convicted in the penalty of £20, and the police instantly put in possession. His friends made strenuous efforts to save him. Manchester alone subscribed nearly £7, and friends in other parts being also generous, he was enabled to buy in all his goods and stock, with the exception of one small lot, which was knocked down to another bidder, the *only one*, she believed, who at all interfered. The people of Hull were ashamed of the proceedings, and their indignation was widely and warmly expressed. The result had been highly beneficial. The Mayor's term of office has since expired, and a gentleman elected to fulfil his place, who probably owes his return, in no small degree, to the interest he took in these proceedings. Some members of the Town Council are also among our friends, so that it is impossible to say what a glorious future may yet await this spirited affair. There are now *two* Blasphemy Depots at Hull. She had held a public discussion in the town, with the Rev. Mr. Pulsford, Baptist Minister, which had been published, and which she was then reprinting. Several pamphlets had been issued on the various subjects agitated, all showing how lively an interest was awakened.

Mrs. M. then alluded to her proceedings at the Missionary Jubilee, in Manchester, as being one of the indirect causes of the Hull prosecution—as it would not have done to have attacked her in Manchester, where she had so many friends. Our limits will not allow us to insert her remarks on the subject, but we refer the curious to the "Missionary Jubilee Panic," by this lady, for full particulars.

Mrs. M. continued—There are many obstacles in our way. Perhaps the greatest is the half-hearted policy—the backwardness of men, and women too—in standing nobly by the cause of truth. There should be no preference of policy to principle. Socialists think some of us go too far, that we run madly in the face of prejudices. It is thought we ought to bow to their (the Socialists') standard. Procrustes of old would fit all men to his standard bed, those too short were stretched, and the tall cut to its size. There are some who would do the same with our minds, and fashion all modes of advocacy of the principles of truth, to what they think it should be. And what is the result? Mr. Lloyd Jones's "highly respectable" lectures in Hull, passed off unprosecuted it is true, but then so quietly and gently did he agitate his social reforms, that the *public* of Hull were scarcely aware of his presence. The prosecutions have been amply counter-balanced by the attention which has been excited. Had we been aware of the existence of the Act which has been read by Mr. Hetherington this evening, the convictions could not have taken place. How is it we are ignorant of such important matters? If the *New Moral World* was that which it should be, ignorance would not be so prevalent as to the laws, liabilities for infraction, or the means of avoiding them. For my part I am determined, in spite of friends or foes, to pursue the path before me. My plan is to speak out. To rouse Christians you must goad them. Shout in their ears truths that touch highest interests, and should persecution come, it must come and welcome. We must suffer before we enjoy. Would we burst our fetters we must twist and wring them. Tell me not then of hurting prejudices. Have we not a right to free opinions? Are they not as essential a part of the organism as the colour of the eyes? Therefore should we protest strenuously against any man, be he the Attorney-General, or whoever else, having the power to arraign them for their opinions. Against the law on this point all must protest, and cease not our endeavours till it is expunged from the Statute Books. Odious and abominable is such a law. By this Act the lecturer or manager may be fined £100, the check-taker, and each and all of the audience £20, and even coffee and reading rooms are equally liable.

Mrs. Martin concluded with an earnest appeal to the audience to subscribe the requisite funds for the Anti-Persecution Union, to compel the magistrates to account for this illegal stretch of authority. She was warmly and enthusiastically received throughout the whole of her speech. Messrs. Callow and Smith here presented themselves with a resolution to the effect, "that Christianity, professing to be the truth and basis of moral action, would, in the opinion of that meeting, be better supported by reason than by force." They effectually supported their position, but it was decided by the chairman, that as the proposition could not be considered in the character of an amendment, the resolution previously before the meeting should take precedence. It was accordingly carried unanimously, and after a vote of thanks to the chairman, the meeting separated, manifesting a lively interest in the proceedings.

GOD-BELIEF AND GOD-BELIEVERS.

A " Second Conversation on the Being of a God," has been brought out in a Penny Pamphlet by Mrs. Martin.

A new edition of No. 3 of " Tracts for the People," before noticed, has appeared with the addition of a letter to Dr. Conquest, reputed editor of a newly amended Bible. The 2nd edition of " God's Gifts and Man's Duties " has been sold off, and the sixth thousand is reprinted, and a new Tract is just issued under the portentous title of " The Missionary Jubilee Panic, and the Hypocrite's Prayer, addressed to the supporters of Christian Missions."

This lady's activity is incessant. One day she sends all Hull into convulsions by an attack on the missions, next she upsets a missionary society in Manchester, she hurls a pamphlet-missive against the theists one day, incontinently projects another against the mission-money seekers, and ere this be well dry from the press will have a fresh paper pellet in readiness for active service.

The " Conversation" forms the fifth of the series of " Tracts for the people." The dialogue form is one which is very apt to be abused by those who undertake to frame arguments for both sides. There is an old book extant in which opposite views are taken by two disputants on the god-question. It is a capital specimen of all-on-one-sidedness. The theist is made to preach little sermons every time he opes his oracular mouth, while the unfortunate atheist is allowed but a few words in edgewise, used as a sort of a link to connect the godist's long-winded speeches.

The dialogues comprising Mrs. Martin's tracts are not liable to such imputations, the respective arguments are pretty equally and fairly sustained, but they are susceptible of improvement. For instance, in making her " theist " say, " I confess you beat me in this logical sort of disputation, the fault must be in the reasoner, not, I think, in the creed." The lady-writer will not be much thanked by the godists for putting into the mouth of a champion such an admission.

A singular trait in the character of this " theist " places him or her among the animal curiosities. Fancy a theological disputant giving utterance to the following, " though I cannot think my talent or information sufficient to do justice to so great a subject, I hope the cause will not suffer through the inefficiency of the advocate. The proofs of the being of God seem to me unquestionable, yet I do not know that I can prove them to be so,"—and a few lines further on, we have the god-defender's confession of " being foiled in one line of argument." Why, if ever that half-virtue, toleration, was a result of god-belief, instead of this extraordinary and, indeed, undesirable stretch of diffidence and puerility, we might almost venture to let them believe till all's blue before we need trouble our heads about proselytism. But we all know the currently-prevailing fact to be—that theistic disputants of the Christian stamp have an assumption and arrogance in their tone in the highest degree incompatible with such hyper-modest expressions. For the most part, when believers reason on the god-topic, they do so, if not imperiously and dogmatically, at least condescendingly—not to discover what is right, nor whether they are right, but to prove themselves right.

This peculiar tone and bearing known to be characteristic and prevalent among theists, or at least christian theists—as one of Mrs. Martin's interlocutors is—might well be represented to keep up the *vraisemblance*. If departed from so widely as in this instance, a new genus is represented not hitherto known to the theological zoologist. Meekness, lowliness, and humility is the christian cant—it does very well to preach —all that such folks do in the way of humility with atheistical oponents, is to recommend it—all that they practice is the pride that apes it.

(*To be Continued*.)

LETTER FROM MR. LLOYD JONES.

60, Seymour-street, Euston-square.
Nov, 23rd, 1844.

Sir,—In No. 47 of your paper there is an article in which my name is introduced, headed, " A Spicy bit of Progress." I beg to state that it is a tissue of falsehoods from one end to the other.

In No. 49, you yourself " state that when I was at Sheffield, and you were absent at Bradford, I delivered a lecture in which I recommended the Branch to dismiss you ; " I never spoke a word in my life, publicly or privately, directly or indirectly, at Sheffield nor anywhere else, with any such meaning or intention.

I make these corrections as a caution to your readers, should you think proper to introduce my name again into your paper. Permit me to state in conclusion, that it is quite possible for you and your correspondents to be imaginative without being malignant.

I remain,
LLOYD JONES.

[It is true persons may be imaginative without being malignant, and Mr. Jones's letter proves that persons may be malignant without being satisfactory. Did I desire a triumph over Mr. Jones, his letter would afford me an ample one. Nothing could be more wanting, than this letter, in that respect which is due to himself.

The manner in which he uses the privilege which he knew I should grant him, of making *any* corrections he pleased in the *Movement*, to " *caution* " the readers against me and my correspondents is a piece of contemptuous effrontery unsurpassed in the annals of controversy. The assumption he makes that my remarks on himself proceeded only from malignancy, exhibits a taste which I do not care to characterise, as such imputations can only injure those who make them. Mr. Jones knows the author of the report he alludes to, and who will no doubt render him justice. But it can hardly fail to strike the reader that whatever the fact may prove to be, the tone of Mr. Jones's letter gives an air of probability to the report he questions. *My* statement respecting Mr. Jones in Sheffield makes no reflection on his character. If he did do what I state, it is only what a conscientious man may at any time do who would remove his friend rather than injure a public cause. As I brought no charge, made no complaint, and designed no imputation, it will hardly be believed that I wrote through malignancy. Before leaving for Bradford, I desired my quondam " Curate," Mr. Paterson, to take notes of Mr. Jones's lecture, as I expected it would contain some allusions to my conduct at that time. On my return Mr. Paterson put into my hand a paper, from which I copy verbatim, and it being in Mr. Paterson's hand-writing, can be no fabrication got up for the occasion, seeing that Mr. Paterson has now been twelve months in prison. The paper contains the following words:—

Extracts from Lloyd Jones's Evening Lecture.

" We have been charged with apathy.

" Our society has never shrunk from principle.

" We never associated for any other purpose than community, never for disputing religion.

" We are not to be thwarted by false friends, or led by the nose by interested persons, who have joined with Socialism for the purpose of combating religion. Any one acting thus, *dismiss him*. Elect your own leaders,

" It is not worth our while to discuss about religion. We have done more good at Tytherly than ever was done by lecturing on nonsense.

" By obeying our executive we have done more in 5 years than politicians or priests in 500."

Let it be known that about this time Mr. Galpin was charging me (untruly) with " giving a prominence to theological topics in my lectures to the Branch,"—that Mr. Ironside, the President, was in correspondence with the central Board on the subject, and that Mr. Jerison, a member, publicly charged me with designing to break up the society by my theology—with these facts before him, and remembering that Mr. Southwell was in prison, Mr. Hollick not known to be the Editor of the *Atheist and Republican*, and no one but me to be alluded to, who will say I drew a strained conclusion from Mr. Jones's words on that night ? The members drew the same conclusion, and significantly hinted to me during the following week, that I " had better look out for a new situation."

Does any one fail to recognise the extracts from Mr. Jones's lecture ? Mr. Paterson scarcely knew Lloyd Jones at that time, and certainly had not heard him for two years, and could hardly have invented sentences so peculiarly Lloyd Jones's. The allusions to " apathy," " principle," and the non discussion of religion " are known to be stock topics with Mr. Jones. The structure of the language, the sentiments throughout, imperious and decided, are so Lloyd *Jones-ish*, that there is no mistaking their identity.

Having cited the authority for my statement, so emphatically denied by Mr. Jones, it becomes me to leave the matter to the judgment of readers. I only beg it to be understood that I do not reciprocate the spirit of Mr. Jones's note. I have often differed from him in opinion, but I have always admired his talents, acknowledged his services to our common cause, rejoiced in his good fortune, and valued his friendship—nor will his present letter diminish the good will I bear him. In my "Visit to Harmony Hall" I wrote to reason—not to quarrel with my co-labourers, and though others, in moments of excitement, may overlook my intentions, I shall not be found forgetting them myself.]   G. J. H.

CHALLENGE TO MR. HOLYOAKE.

"I, I. J. Edwards, challenge Mr. G. J. Holyoake to a public discussion, in any of the Halls of the Social Institutions in London, in which I will undertake to prove the following proposition:—

"That the three letters, published in Nos. 47, 48, and 49 of the *Movement*, headed 'A Visit to Harmony Hall,' and signed G. J. H., bear evidence that the writer has not a knowledge of the 'Practical Formation of Character'—and, consequently, that several of the conclusions which he there draws, are erroneous."

[The writer of this challenge is a good natured harmless man. But if I did not know something of him I should think him demented. His proposition is to this effect —"G. J. H. does not understand the Formation of Character, therefore G. J. H. did not see what he did see at Harmony." What can my knowledge or ignorance of Mr. Owen's *Book of the New Moral World* have to do with the principles of the Old Executive, or the difficulties of the New?— points which I principally discussed. Next I shall be told that because I happen not to have read De Lolme on the Constitution of England, that I did not see Prince Albert, or for want of a "practical knowledge" of Dupin, I could not perceive that Louis Philippe had a pear-head. But what can I say to friend Edwards! Whether I understand the formation of character as he understands it I do not care one jot. How can I accommodate him? A much valued friend of mine always advises me "to do nothing rashly, but first sleep on my resolves." I'll take his advice, and of course a nap too, and if I should happen to awake in time, I will answer Mr. Edwards in the next number. I am sure that gentleman will admire this piece of prudence in an inexperienced young man "who does not understand the practical formation of character."   G. J. H.

Mrs. Morrison.—This lady, the widow of the much respected editor of the "*Pioneer*," has lately been lecturing in Manchester, in answer to Mrs. Martin. Mrs. Morrison formerly lectured to the Socialists. In a recent lecture she promised her audience to display cases of Infidel immorality, and cited Mr. Holyoake as a first example. She declared that his conduct when in Gloucester Gaol, in refusing to go to chapel, was highly *discourteous* and improper. Gravely, this was the charge—well it was too bad. Seeing that the state so kindly provided for him—Christians giving him his daily bread and keeping him out of harm's way—refusing to go to chapel where there was a nice parson kept to preach to him—was ungrateful. He must behave better next time.

German Atheism.—The Rationalists of Germany boldly preach the abandonment of all positive belief, and predict the speedy downfall of Christianity. Forty years ago they only expressed their *doubts* of the meaning of the Bible, and their questionings as to the Trinity, the Divinity of Christ, and other great doctrines of evangelical religion; but these doubts and questionings have already given way to a philosophy that openly contemns the whole Bible as an antiquated volume, not suited to the improved condition of man. As face answereth to face in water, so does the *heart* of Rationalism in America to the Rationalism of Germany.—*Boston Recorder*.

The Right of Admission to Public Lectures.—The Anti-Persecution Union, determined to ascertain whether our public institutions are to be in continual danger from heavy penalties, for taking admission money at public lectures, at the will of every base informer, or bigoted magistrates, have commenced legal proceedings against the Magistrates of Hull, in pursuance of the resolution at the public meeting. Efficient Counsel have been engaged. The Committee of the Union trust that the Managers, Presidents, and Directors of all Literary, Social, and Political Institutions, will endeavour to assist them, forthwith, with subscriptions to defray the expences attendant on this step. All subscriptions to be addressed to the care of G. J. Holyoake, General Secretary, at the Office of the Anti-Persecution Union, 5, Paul's Alley, Paternoster-row, London.

Back Numbers of the Oracle.—We receive occasional applications from the Lancashire district for back numbers of the *Oracle*. We again refer such friends to Mr. George Smith, of 11, Greengate, Salford, in whose hands are, as we recently stated, du ⟨ ⟩ ⟨ ⟩ of all the numbers of the *Oracle* that are extant, or that can be had for love or money.

SONG OF THE SOIL.
BY J. H. R. BAYLEY.

I start the bulb of the beautiful flower,
And feed the bloom of the wild-wood bower;
I rear the blade of the tender herb,
And the trunk of the stalwart oak I curb;
I force the sap of the mountain pine,
Aun curl the tendrils of the vine;
I robe the forest and clothe the plain,
With the ripest of fruit and the richest of grain.

The cheek of the peasant I flush with health,
And yield to the sturdy yeoman wealth,
I give the Spirit of Commerce wings,
And prop the tottering thrones of kings.
The gorgeous palace and humble cot
Owe every atom to me they've got—
And the prince at his banquet, and hind at his board,
Alike must depend on the fare I afford.

Man may boast of his creature might—
His talents in peace, and his prowess in fight;
And lord it over both beast and bird,
By the charm of his touch, and the spell of his word;
But I am the sole and mighty source
Whence flows the tide of his boasted force—
Whatever his right and whoever he be,
His pomp and dominion must come from *me*!

I am the giver of all that's good,
And have been since the world hath stood;
Where's there wealth on ocean or land,
But sprung from the warmth of my fostering hand?
Or where the object fair or free,
That claims a being, but's traced to me?
Cherish! then cherish, ye sons of toil,
The wonderful might of the fruitful soil!

"VISIT TO HARMONY HALL."—No. 2 of these unhappy papers was read on Sunday moning, at the Branch A 1 meeting of members. Considerable excitement prevailed. Mr. Jones, who attended, threatened the Society with his withdrawal, and other "moving accidents by flood and field."

ATHEISTICAL SOCIETY.—Mr. Holyoake will meet the members of this society on Tuesday evening, December 3, at half-past 8 o'clock, in the Northampton Coffee House, No. 2, Newton Street, High Holborn.

LATIN.—Mr. Lear's Class for the study of this tongue, now meets at the Social Institution, 5, Charlotte Street, Blackfriars Road—at 11, A.M., on Sundays.

THE REV. MR. PHILLIPS.—This gentleman, whose name appears this week in the list of subscriptions for the Anti-Persecution Union, from Northampton, is a regularly ordained minister, and is the first of the clergy ordained, or unordained, who has done himself the justice, or us the honour, to rank among the practical enemies of persecution.

THE LATE ACTING GOVERNOR.—Next week we shall be able to publish a letter from Harmony Hall, by Mr. George Simpson, the new General Secretary, respecting the communication from the Late Acting Governor.

SEASONABLE.—The Rev. Mr. Eastmead of Bristol has announced a lecture on the *First Moment in Hell.* We suppose this to be the first of a winter course.

DR. KEENAN.—We are happy to find that this gentleman is still lecturing on his new views of life, at the Western Literary and Scientific Institute, Leicester Square. But for a perpetual press of matter, we should present a summary of his new theory, as we did before.

Mr. GILLESPIE.—Next week will appear, from the pen of this gentlemen, the close of the controversy on the argument on the a priori on the Being and Attributes of God.

LECTURES.

Dec. 1.—Finsbury Chapel, South Place, W. J. Fox,—The Oriental Doctrine of Two Principles. At 11, A.M.

Dec. 1.—Finsbury Institution, Goswell Road, Mr. H. Hetherington,—On the Theological Writings of Thomas Paine. At 7, P.M. Discussion after lecture,—Is Deism likely to become Universal?

Dec. 1.—Branch A 1, Mr. Lloyd Jones. At 7, P.M.

Dec. 1.— Social Institution, 5, Charlotte Street, Blackfriars Road, Mr. Ellis,—The Effects of his Conversion. At 7, P.M.

Dec. 2.————Mr. Southwell,—On the Life and Genius of Lord Byron.

Dec. 1.—Hall of Science, City Road, Mr. Southwell. At 7, P.M.

Dec. 1.—Investigation Hall, Circus Street, Mr. Southwell,—On the Punishment of Death. At 11, A.M. Mr. Holyoake,—On the Right Interpretation of the Bible. At 7, P.M.

Dec. 1.—4, Roan Steet, Greenwich, Mr. Ryall,—An Inquiry into the Nature of the God-Idea. At 7, P.M.

TO CORRESPONDENTS.

Received.—*Hull Herald*, Irish papers. The conclusion of the controversy, from Mr. Gillespie.

W. C.—We cannot find room for the excellent address of G. Powell, which he sends.

R. C., Stockport.—We have written to Mr. Heywood, but have no reason to suppose that gentleman unwilling to supply the *Movement*. Our friends who are in earnest about procuring it, can do so, we are informed, if they will be at the trouble of repeatedly ordering it of their booksellers. A channel will soon be opened for it.

"Critical Examination of *Dwight*," &c., Inadmissible.—The writer should nevertheless persevere. He might—notwithstanding "the friends in his neighbourhood wishing to see it in print"—improve it, and by so doing, improve himself. Several of the arguments on the "attributes" are misplaced—for instance, illustrations of malevolence are cited for illustrations of power—the same of arguments on other attributes. Some reasonings are too hacknied—and there is too large a proportion borrowed, although the quotations are excellent and most happily selected. His judgment is not yet sufficiently matured to work up skilfully such rich materials. If he would at first aim at less, he would soon produce what would be more valuable. We shall re-post it as desired.

SUBSCRIPTIONS TO THE ANTI-PERSECUTION UNION.

J. M. C., for Counsel	0	3	0
For Mr. Johnson's case, per Mr. Gurney, Northampton,			
Joseph Gurney	0	1	6
Richard Foster	0	1	0
W. Inwood, W. Willis	0	1	0
Mansfield, B. of Broughton	0	1	0
W. Jones	0	1	0
J. Watts, Mrs. Mellows	0	1	0
Lewis Harris	0	1	0
J. Johnson, J. Rabbit	0	1	0
Several	0	0	5
Rev. Thomas Phillips	0	0	6

G. J. H., Sec.

Printed and Published by G. J. HOLYOAKE, 40, Holywell-street, Strand.
Wednesday, November 27, 1844.

THE MOVEMENT
And Anti=Persecution Gazette.
" Maximise morals, minimise religion."—BENTHAM.

No. 52.   EDITED BY G. JACOB HOLYOAKE,   Price 1½d
                ASSISTED BY M. Q. RYALL.

THE JESUITS AND JESUS.

LATELY meeting with a very curious work, purporting to be the Code of the Jesuits, I have extracted a few of their rules, and contrasted them with the practices of Jesus, upon which they are professedly founded. Whether such wide-awake fellows as the Jesuits could really have been guided by the dicta of such a problematical fanatic as the Nazarene parable-monger, may very well be questioned. But though the Jesus of the Bible is thought to have had a dash of the radical dissenter in his composition, so doubtful were his doings that the Jesuits had no difficulty, as history informs us, of persuading mankind that their own subtle order was founded on his doctrines. But to the extracts.

The Jesuits were careful to inculcate "that they were not an incumbrance upon the people, as other religious orders were." Jesus came with the advantage which every founder of a new sect has over an old religion, he professed to be supported by voluntary contributions and to be no burden upon the poor, he inveighed against an establishment which looked for regular means of support alike from all orders of society. " The Jesuits were commanded to pay the greatest attentions to widows, that they might give to their necessities; and to inculcate upon them the recommendations of St. Paul, that they should continue in celibacy, in order that they might have more to bestow upon Jesuits, and might remain faithful to them." Jesus was ministered unto by many women, and the examples given happen to have been men's wives, or to have stood to them in a still less respectable relation. The principle of pardoning sins, or the power of absolution, claimed by Jesus and his disciples, gave a superiority to his religion over every other. The Jesuits, who understood and carried out this principle of Christianity, establishing upon its foundations the superstructure of their system, made it a maxim of their policy, "that the notion should be instilled into the people that their society was entrusted with a far greater power of absolving than any other religious order."

In their behaviour towards princes, noblemen, and the magistrates of every place, it was a fundamental maxim of the Jesuits to gain such an ascendant over them, that "they should be ready to exert themselves even against their nearest relations and most intimate friends, when for Jesuit interest and advantage."

Those worthy of Jesus who took up their cross and followed him, were told by him that they must hate father, mother, brother, and sister. This principle which made them know no obstacle to their views, was the great secret of their success.

Jesuits were to pretend that they declined all interference in public affairs, whilst they drew within the influence of their society the whole machinery of state. In order to effect their object, they were to affirm "that the duty of their office obliged them to speak such truths as they would otherwise omit." Jesus proclaimed that his business was with another world, and affected indifference to mundane matters, whilst his preaching and his works tended to produce a revolution, which, continued by his followers, terminated in favour of Christianity. This opposition to all authority left it no choice but to succumb to him, or let the law take its course, and be fulfilled in his destruction.

"The Jesuits were seldom or never to accept of small presents for their own private use, but were rather to recommend the common necessities of their province or college." By which means they could receive gifts with an air of disinterestedness. Jesus said sell all that you have and give to the poor; he was said not to ask for or accept of anything for himself—except the box of ointment, but the money was entrusted to the stewardship of Judas, and was shared amongst themselves.

"They were to represent themselves as containing the perfection of all other societies, only not having their cant and outward austerity." Jesus assumed superiority over the Pharisees and other sects of Jews condemning their language and observances.

It was made incumbent on Jesuits to point out the defects of other societies, as Jesus was ever pointing out the faults of his neighbours.

"Widows were not to be rigorously treated by Jesuits in confession, and all indulgences were to be represented to women as at the discretion of their society." How kind was Jesus to the errors of Magdalene and the woman taken in adultery. The Jesuits were always to represent to those they wished to join them, the easiness of their yoke, as Jesus said his yoke was easy and his burden was light, and he compared the profession of his faith to the more weighty observances imposed upon people by the Jewish religion.

Thus it is evident that none of the deceptive proceedings of the famous order of the Jesuits—and no religious body, save them, ever carried the art of imposing on mankind to such perfection; they reduced deception to a science—but have parallels in our villainously protean holy writ. W. J. B.

GOD'S WORDS versus GOD'S WORKS.

"The Bible defended against the Dean of York," is the title of a paper in the *Athenæum* of October 12, by Isaac Cullimore, in which it is stated, "'That the highest discoveries of science will ever be found to be in perfect harmony and accordance with the *language* and meaning of *revelation*, as inferred by Professor Sedgwick in his judicious comment on the above mentioned communication*; that the language of the WORKS and *word* of the Creator *can never be at issue*, and that the friends of science are, consequently, the friends of revelation.'"

This appears very reasonable, at first sight, but a little thought shows it to be full of errors.

If there be a Creator, and man has a revelation from him, then the discoveries of science *ought* to be in harmony with revelation. It is reasonable to presume that the language of God's *works*, as brought to light by science, must be in harmony with God's *words*, as found in any revelation emanating from him. Again, whilst the language of God's *works*, through the imperfections of man's knowledge or science, may be sometimes, or for sometime, obscure —the language of God's *word*—ought never to be so—if really intended for a revelation. Where words are obscure there can clearly

* "The Bible Defended against the British Association."

be no revelation—for an obscure or concealed thing can never be a clear or revealed thing.

And, further, the ignorance of MAN upon any particular point cannot be an argument against his correctness upon other points, upon which he has had more information— whilst the incorrectness of the language of a DEITY, *in any one case*, in a supposed revelation from him, invalidates the whole *as a revelation*—for man is fallible, a Deity infallible. In a supposed revelation, containing inaccuracies, we must either imagine that the Deity did not know his own works, or wilfully intended to mislead his creatures, by giving them for a revelation of his acts that which was no revelation, but, on the contrary, a falsehood. Or, we must come to the conclusion that that which is supposed, or asserted to be a revelation from a Deity, is no such thing, but rather the work of men ignorant of the truth, who sought to cover their ignorance with the mantle of revelation. Or, that it is the production of men who, firmly believing what they wrote to be truth, thought that they could not have become possessed of such knowledge without the assistance of Deity, and that, therefore, it was specially revealed to them for the guidance of others.

It is of no consequence which hypothesis we adopt—they are all equally fatal to revelation. And here the old argument on this subject applies with the same force as ever—that if man, by means of his senses, and the appliances he employs to aid his senses, can discover the same truths as are said to be revealed, a revelation was unnecessary. For, as cleverly and clearly shown by Mr. Southwell, in his "Letters to the Archbishop of Canterbury," in the *Investigator*, REASON must always determine the *truth* of revelation. Reasons are conclusions evolved from experience--science is the aggregate of man's experience from age to age, collated with great care, and placed in consecutive order, divided and subdivided, to suit his limited capacities, and to render it easy of application for his numerous wants and pleasures. From this it follows, that until we have acquired experience, and learnt to compare things and ideas, and deduce reasons, revelation is of no use - and when we have arrived at this point, revelation is not wanted, for we have obtained all that revelation could teach. In fact, wanting experience, revelation is worse than useless, for it states, things *we are not warranted in believing*, and which reason rejects as absurd. It has been stated over and over again, by competent theological authority, that to test revelation by reason is to destroy it—it was (they say) never intended to be reasoned upon, but to be received as true through *faith* in the unerring nature of the being who gave it to man for his assistance—for if the same information could have been obtained by investigation, it would never have been specially revealed.

This at once upsets the assumption that the language of God's *works* will *always* be found to harmonise with the language of his *word;* it, on the contrary, affirms that the language of his *word* will *never* be found to harmonise with the language of his *works* —a view of the matter which science *has* proved and is daily proving to be the *true* view.

It is a favourite argument with God defenders, that the Deity never does anything in vain; that he always goes the shortest way to work. But if he has given us certain words to explain his works, which works we are subsequently compelled to examine with great care and labour, in order to satisfy ourselves that they will harmonise with and justify his words, there was clearly a deal of unnecessary labour expended in giving man a revelation, and a great quantity of good paper and ink uselessly wasted, to say nothing of the millions of money subscribed, from first to last, in distributing such supererogatory information.

If I am correct in the view which I take of the inutility of a revelation to man in the *maturity* of science, then I think the writer I have quoted clearly shows its inutility in the *infancy* of science for he distinctly declares that, in the infancy of man's knowledge, he was *misled* by revelation, and that he misinterpreted it—explaining it by his then narrow conceptions and limited experience, which philosophers *now* declare to be incorrect.

Mr. Cullimore thus proceeds:—" It is, perhaps, not surprising, that in the infancy of science, when the earth was *supposed* to be the centre and primary body, not only of our solar system, but of the universe itself, there should have been no distinction made between *solar* and *præ-solar* time of the Hexaëmeron, or the six evening-mornings of creation; and that the whole should have been understood as representing six of our present solar days; *although this view could never explain the sacred text,* STILL A BETTER WAS, PERHAPS, IMPOSSIBLE UNDER THE CIRCUMSTANCES. But, in an age when the true system *is* understood; when not only the earth, but the system in which it moves are known to perform a secondary part in the great system of creation, that such ideas should be still prevalent in any educated minds, and that we should still continue to measure the præ-solar time of the Bible by our solar standard, so as to make the biblical state of the *beginning,* identical with that of Adam, is inexplicable, *and as much opposed to the* VERY WORDS *of divine record, as to the results of scientific investigation.*"

This is all very well for Isaac Cullimore and men of his class, who appear to be determined to make science and revelation agree, however discordant the declarations and premises of the two might be. Isaac Cullimore should, however, recollect, that at a time not *very* distant, in comparison with the Mosaic account even of man's first appearance upon the earth, " the *very words* of [the] divine record" were considered to mean something entirely different to that which he now says is the only true meaning. Galileo was persecuted almost to death for asserting that the sun was fixed, and that the earth went round it—*only because* the " divine record" warrants no such conclusion, but, on the contrary, expressly leaves it to be inferred that the sun *does* go round the earth. The generations of 6000 years have passed away in entire ignorance of the true meaning of a supposed revelation, and we have only just now discovered what is *said* to be its correct interpretation.

Can that be a revelation which requires interpretation?

In conclusion, we have no security that the interpretations of the biblical revelation *now* assumed by scientific men to be the correct one, is really the only true one— seeing that we are but now on the verge of a vast ocean of facts, which lies unexplored before us. I think it reasonable to suppose that the information yet to be obtained by subsequent experiment and by future ages, is as much superior to our *present* information, as is our present knowledge to the knowledge of the age when man first became an inhabitant of the earth—and that we are just as likely now to misinterpret the language of revelation as he was then. If our present knowledge proves man's early interpretation of revelation to be incorrect —why may not future ages prove our interpretation to be equally incorrect?

After the quotations I have given, Isaac Cullimore enters into a very learned argument, through which I am wholly unable to follow him. and I beg to refer my readers to the article, if they are curious on the matter. I. C. states, with regret, that La Place " was no friend to revelation," and that he "proposed to supersede the Christian era by a universal astronomical one"—preferring, I presume, science to religion, a circumstance, truly, *very much to be deplored.* W. C.

THE PRIEST FLOGGING THE MINISTER ; OR, SOUL SAVING AT A DISCOUNT.

In No. 42 of the *Movement*, a Correspondent drew attention to a specimen of "swindling" by the Irish Presbyterian Home Missions. This swindle, as our readers are aware, consists in the Home Mission collecting some £1200. per annum, for the reputed support of twenty-six schools, with 600 scholars, in the Glens, County of Antrim, Ireland, to teach the Bible in the Irish language, while the Roman Catholic Clergy of that district, headed by Messrs. Walsh and Fitzsimons, deny that the Mission have a single school there, or throughout Ireland, and charge the Mission with forging fictitious class rolls. These charges are supported by the public declaration of the whole parish, by the public confession of fourteen individuals that they had been paid as teachers and inspectors for false reports and forged lists, and lastly, by the confidential letters of the officials of the Mission, which were put into the hands of the Rev, Mr. Walsh for use against it.

These facts, with their corroborating circumstances, and all that had been said for or against the Mission were published in a pamphlet by the Rev. Mr. Walsh, six months ago. Mr. Allen, the then superintendent, attempted a weak defence, which implicated him and his colleagues still more. Then the silent system was tried, and little allusion made to the case. At length, however, a noise was made. Mr. Allen was displaced by the Rev. J. Edgar, who lost no time in repairing to the Glens. There, after a stay of ten days, to search a district of twenty-five miles in circumference to discover schools, he at length surprised "*one* Irish school, with *sixteen* scholars, at full work, in a miserable hut of a single apartment, behind a halan wall, under a cloud of intolerable smoke, and round a farthing candle, some reading, some spelling, some translating, under the supervision of an old man of 60, with spectacles on his nose. All this, too, at the dread hour of midnight." Instant upon this discovery, out came a report with this fact, a good deal about "respectable Protestants ready to attest," but more on the "terrible power of the priests," with interlardings of the "Priests'

curse," and other set-offs to their own defalcations, or intended concealments of their own duplicity.

To this report, the pamphlet entitled the " Priest flogging the Minister," which we advertised in a recent *Movement*, has been issued as a reply. It is from the pen of the Rev. Luke Walsh, who severely castigates the principal of the Home Mission. The Rev. Dr. Edgar is treated mercilessly. Rev. Walsh is a rude and savage opponent, but no one can acquaint himself with the doings, or rather pretensions and frauds of the Home Missions, without feeling that their duplicity has fallen into proper hands, and has only met, from the Rev. Mr. Walsh, with its due reward.

A deputation of six preachers has been sent to Scotland, and another deputation is spoken of to follow, to counteract, if they can, the effect of Walsh's exposure. We trust that Mrs. Martin will be able to give particular attention to these gentry. The Walsh pamphlet should be extensively circulated. The character of the Home Mission is irretrievably ruined ; except upon true Christians, they will never be able to impose again. Let this case be a public warning. Let the character of Missions be more closely looked to. The manner in which missionary money is publicly collected, is the least open to objection of any, and if people choose to be gulled in the name of Christ, plenty of people will be found to accommodate them. We hope the enquiry, began so well, into *what* Missions *do* with their money, will be carried further —into what it is *collected for*. J. B. L.

CONCLUDING LETTER FROM MR. GILLESPIE.

Edinburgh, November 18, 1844.

To the Editor of *The Movement*.

SIR, In no way, could it be incumbent on me to answer Mr. Southwell's Rejoinder, till the Rejoinder be completely finished. In the last of Mr. S.'s *Battles*, Mr. S. intimates, that an " atheised version " of the " *entire*" " Argument, *a priori*," should appear, as a sequel to those *Battles*. And in No. 47 of your periodical, the following announcement occurs:— " *Gillespie's Argument Atheised*, by Charles Southwell, will appear in No. 10 of the *Library of Reason*." A longer notice, to the same effect, having appeared in No. 43.— I wait, then, for the publication of No. 10 of the " Library of Reason" which shall be commented on by me, *unless* " The Argument," after all Mr.

S.'s *possible* atheising of it shall appear to be more forwarded by Mr. S.'s preposterous labours to make it speak the language of atheism than it could, by any possibility, be by aught in the shape of remarks upon Mr. S.'s *nonsense*. I confidently prophesy, that the Proposition and Demonstrations of "The Argument" will be found to be a terrible *experimentum crucis* respecting the possibility of giving expression at once to orderly atheism and good sense.

But—meantime—Mr. Southwell having, in the aforesaid 47th No., answered my Letter, inserted in No. 43, one of the Epicurean mathematicians' asses might comprehend how the controversy stands.

" Is matter extended or unextended," is my question. "MATTER IS EXTENDED," is Mr. Southwell's answer. And this answer, he declares, he is " prepared to *abide by* as touching *matter*."*

In Mr. Southwell's Letter, in answer to mine, it is maintained, for the tenth or twelfth time, (as if the Atheist were impelled, by an irresistible Fate, to write the condemnation of his own system)—" If the *first* Proposition," of the " Argument, *a priori,*" " can be proved true, all the rest of its Propositions cannot be proved false." And at length, after all Mr. Southwell's turnings and windings, shifts and evasions, looking away from the point, and looking as if he did not know what the point was—after all these, here we have Mr. S. unequivocally, undisguisedly, proving the *first* Proposition to be true. " Matter *is* extended," declares Mr. Southwell. I " am prepared to *abide* by " this declaration, he says. And having, " many a time and oft," affirmed matter to be *infinite*, even the blindest atheist of them all must perceive, that the Champion of London Atheism is so hemmed in to a corner, so tied and chained there, by ligatures of his own providing, that release and escape appear to be evident impossibilities. " If " (I quote from my Letter to the gentleman standing, before our minds' eye, in *durance vile*—"a pitiful spectacle "!) " If you (Mr. Southwell) contend, that matter is extended"—and I " am prepared," breaks in Mr. Southwell, " to *abide by* " the position, that " matter *is extended*"—" Seeing that you (Mr. S.) make matter infinite, you must make matter's extension infinite. And the infinity of extension—of some kind or other, of matter, for example —is all that Proposition I. maintains."*

——So true is it that one cannot deny, even in words, a single Proposition of " The Argument *a priori,*" without stultifying himself. To quote, from a letter received by me *only the other day*, the language of one who has been converted from Atheism, to genuine Theism, by means of my volume —for which (as I am not arguing with an atheist, at this precise moment) I would give GOD the glory—" You have fully demonstrated the existence of the Divine Being, so that no well constituted—no *honest, minds* need longer remain in doubt if they read your excellent work."——

Mr. Southwell has been obliged to admit what involves the truth of Proposition I. All the rest logically follow. Mr. Southwell, therefore, is a Theist, *if* right reason were to determine the point. But, alas! it is to be feared, that Mr. S., in his present mental condition, would think nothing of eschewing right reason, if it sought to lead him within the portals of belief in GOD. Atheism must be hailed by him, though all the laws of logic, though eternal reason and eternal morality, were to be never so grossly outraged. Mr. S. has *substantial* reasons for his atheism.

And now, Mr. Editor, as THE *subject in dispute* between me and my antagonist must be, in the apprehensions of all your readers, be they Theists or Atheists, *perfectly exhausted ;* I trust, that you will see the propriety of inserting nothing more from Mr. Southwell's pen, in reference to *that subject.* —Mr. S. could write further, only for writ-

---

* It is true, that Mr. S. follows up his declaration by such stuff as this : " Extension is no more *in* matter than *out* of it." Who ever said, that it was? Who ever said, that matter's extension is *within*, or *without*, matter? Nobody, I am sure, ever said so—except, perhaps, some disciple of the same white-is-black school to which a certain atheist belongs. But Mr. S. required to say something, to distract attention, as much as possible, from his disgraceful defeat; like an eel, apprehensive of danger, raising all the mud about it, as it seeks to shrink from sight.

* See my Letter, in No. 43., and the places referred to in it. The following important words are appended to Proposition I, as I have before noticed, in The Movement (No. 25). " Let the extension [of Prop. I.] be of space *merely*, OR OF MATTER MERELY, or of space and matter *together*. The Proposition I. affirms, that there is Infinity of Extension, but affirms *nothing more*."

ing's sake—and no one knows better than yourself that he can

———Write about it, Goddess* and about it,

without writing aught but a sort of tautological verbiage. All the Propositions in "The Argument, *a priori*, for the Being and the Attributes of GOD," are true, if Proposition I. is true. And if Mr. Southwell, by contending that matter—which, with him, is extended—is necessarily infinite, have not established the truth of that Proposition, which affirms that extension (matter's extension, be it) is necessarily infinite; it is not in the power of human language to affirm, that extension, of some kind or other, is necessarily infinite. Were Mr. Southwell entitled to the dignified appellation of *Philosopher* (a term his worst enemy would not apply to him) I should hereafter cite him as one of my *strong* authorities for the truth of my *first*, and, as you have well called it, "*fundamental*" Proposition. As for me, should Mr. S. write on, heaping verbiage upon nonsense, I shall notice nothing which he may write further in regard to a topic *so very evidently* exhausted. I shall notice nothing which he may write further, unless he now proceed to unwrite what he has written, and, admitting Proposition I., deny some one or other of the remaining Propositions. But I do hope, that he, even he, will not be guilty of additional self-stultification. Fortunately for my great cause, he has too often admitted, that the truth of the *first* proposition involves the truth of all the rest. Fortunately, even the most besotted atheist must now see, that, according to Mr. Southwell, the *first* Proposition stands on a basis as *solid* as the grand *Numen* of every atheist—*brute-matter.*

I am, Sir, yours, &c.,
WILLIAM GILLESPIE.

THE LATE ACTING GOVERNOR.

To the Editor of the Movement.

SIR,—Having read your "Visit to Harmony," and also a letter by "The Late Acting Governor," in Movement 50, I feel that I am called upon to give you what information I have upon the subject of the temporary loan of £500.

I was chairman of the Committee appointed at the last Congress, to examine the Accounts of the Home Colonization Society,

* To wit, the Goddess of *Dulness*—" the mighty mother of the Dunciad "—At whose altar Mr. S. tho' no polytheist, often sacrifices.

and the impressions I now have respecting those accounts are, that the amount in question is not entered in the books farther than as a Loan through the H. C. S., that being the case it would be scarcely possible for the Executive to know from THEIR Books, anything of the amount owing to the Late Acting Governor. I must also state, that at the examination of the accounts, I was informed by Mr. Galpin that it was an error in placing £500 of the Late Acting Governor's to the account of the Home Colonization Society, as he lent it to the Rational Society, temporarily. Mr. Galpin was the Secretary to both Societies at the time, so he would be acquainted with the whole matter. In the report I gave in to the Congress, I pointed out this mistake, and recommended that this £500 should be deducted from the amount due to the H. C. S., and be placed among the ordinary Loans of the Society, to the credit of the Late Acting Governor.

I am not aware whether this was done, but I rather think not, as one or two members of the late Central Board refused to give the Scrip of the Society to only a portion of the H. C. S. All were to agree to accept the Scrip or give none to any.

With respect to the Late A. G. having *voucher* or *receipt*, I know nothing, therefore can say nothing.

The reason I have taken up your space in giving the above explanation is to clear away any doubt that might be raised, that the Late Acting Governor DID NOT ADVANCE THE MONEY, which doubt I feel assured you had no intention of causing, yet if a stranger read the remarks, I think he would fall into that error. GEORGE SIMPSON.

Harmony Hall, Nov. 21st, 1844.

[That third of my statement questioned by the Late Acting Governor, stands slightly corrected. There *is* an "entry" of some kind. But if instead of the letter, the spirit of my assertion be taken into account, as it will be by impartial lookers on, my statement stands exactly where I left it. I only questioned the business pretensions of the late Executive, and this letter from the "highest authority" assures us there was no proper entry, accurately informing the new Secretary from whom came the Late Acting Governor's loan, and no distinct understanding as to whom it should be credited. This corroborates the only impression I intended to convey. In a moral point of view I believe the whole transaction to be excusable, but the parties concerned made other and rather arrogant pretensions, and those pretensions I deemed it useful to question, and what has been elicited shows that this has been done successfully.]—*Ed. of M.*

MR. LLOYD JONES'S DENIAL.

Sir,—Miss Roalfe has shewn me a letter, addressed by you to her, in which you request to know if the report contained in No. 47 of the *Movement*, headed "A spicy bit of Progress," can be corroborated.

I hereby, most willingly, bear testimony to the truth of the Report, for I was standing within one yard of Mr. Jones's elbow at the time, and, if there is any occasion, I can procure the testimony of at least one dozen persons who heard the remarks about the failure of the Branch being ascribed to heterodox lecturers.

I have called on Mr. Hamilton, referred to in the report, and he most willingly bears testimony to the truth of it, and hereby adds his name.
ROBERT HAMILTON,
81, Nicolson-street
W. BAKER,
105, Nicolson-street.

From Miss Roalfe.

My dear Sir,—You are at liberty to make what use you please of Mr. Baker's letter, and if the evidence of the individuals who have signed their names is not sufficient, I can procure at least a dozen others. My letter, as you are aware, was not intended for insertion in the *Movement*, but what I wrote is, nevertheless, *strictly correct.* MATILDA ROALFE.
Edinburgh, Nov. 27, 1844.

The Cant of Authority and Abjectness of Servility.—Make but a man an overseer, or bishop, or prime-minister, and you'll have plenty of *hero-worship.* Your Cromwell tells his listener, in the true Pecksniff vein, that he wishes to God he had remained by his wood-side and tended a flock of sheep; and there are plenty to beseech him to stay and trample on them where he is, rather than go and attend to his sheep.—*Examiner.*

THE MADEIRA PEOPLE.—One of their favourite amusements at night was imitating the noises and cries of different animals. They alternately crow like cocks, roar like bulls, and gobble like fiery-turkeys. Their imitations, I must say, were correct, but the effect was anything but pleasing. There appears to be but little religious feeling among them; indeed, their priests seem to be almost objects of contempt, and their places of worship to be nearly neglected. The squalid poverty you everywhere meet with is pitiable and revolting; the children run about almost in a state of nudity, and are the ugliest little set of wretches, except, perhaps, the diminutive old women, I ever saw.—*Mrs. Houstoun's Yacht Voyage.*

A CARD OF CHARACTER.—The Atheist and the Republican, the Destructive of every grade, is busily at work, sapping the foundations at once of our religious and our political institutions. He thinks no labour too great to obtain one convert. He thinks no sacrifice too costly to obtain even a small instalment of the object he has in view. With untiring, with indomitable energy he toils in the work of destruction, and supports with undeviating oneness of purpose the public advocates of his views. With a liberality, which in any other cause might well be termed magnanimity, he subscribes, according to his means, for the support and inculcation of "Destructive" sentiments.—*Birmingham Advertiser.*

MAKING THE BEST OF IT.—A procession was taking place to the church of St. Genevieve, for the purpose of obtaining dry weather. The pious people had scarcely reached the square when it began to rain with great violence. "Never mind that," said the Bishop, "the Saint mistakes us entirely—she thinks we have been praying for wet weather!"

MRS. MARTIN IN GLASGOW.—This lady, who left London on her Scottish tour as the accredited representative of the Rational Society, (one proof of the better feeling the wise policy of the present Executive is producing) has already commenced her labours in Glasgow. She has issued two addresses to the Scottish public. The first asks the following searching questions:—In England I have met with no answer to the charges which I have brought against Missionary Societies. Will they find a defender in Scotland? The charges to which I challenge reply are the following—(I have *Christian authority* for all my statements). 1st.—The Missionary Societies promulgate gross falsehoods respecting the condition, religion, and morals of foreign countries, in order to excite pity and obtain funds. 2nd.—Their translations of the Bible are miserable and hastily concocted disgraces to literature—calculated to mislead the unfortunate reader.

THE HULL MAGISTRATES.—The following has appeared as an advertisement in three of the Hull Newspapers—it was ordered to be inserted that the people and gentry of Hull might know what opinion was formed, in London, of their proceedings :—
"At a numerous Public Meeting, held on Nov. 15th, in the Literary and Scientific Institution, Fitzroy-Square, London, convened to consider the conduct of the Magistrates of Hull, respecting the recent prosecutions in that town, Geo. Bird, Esq., in the chair; the following resolution, amongst others, was passed unanimously :—
RESOLVED—"'That this Metropolitan Meeting, after deliberating upon the discreditable notoriety which the town of Hull, through its public functionaries, Messrs. Cookman, Barkworth, and Firbank, has achieved—deems it an imperative duty to declare that the above-named Magistrates, by the prosecutions instituted against, and the fines levied upon, Messrs. Johnson and Watson, for simply letting a room for a lecture, and receiving admission money, have manifested a bigotry and a barbarism which the country had reason to hope were obsolete, and buried in the infamy of the Sidmouth and Castlereagh administrations, and that the revival of such unjust, arbitrary, and impolitic proceedings, emphatically calls for the severest and most indignant repudiation on the part of all honest men.'"

GEO. BIRD, Chairman.

LITERARY AND SCIENTIFIC INSTITUTION, JOHN STREET.—*Resolved*—That the Secretary be instructed to acquaint the President of Branch A 1, of the acknowledgment of this Committee for his kindness in granting the use of the Hall for the public meeting, relative to persecution in Hull, and that a copy be sent to the *New Moral World* and *Movement*.—*Extract from the Minutes of the Committee Meeting of the Anti-Persecution Union, of Nov.* 20, 1844.

BRANCH A 1.—The debates on the Letters on Harmony Hall still continue at the Sunday morning meetings. Mr. Lloyd Jones moved the adjournment on Sunday last. Friends from a distance may attend without reference to a cold morning, as the discussions are very warm.

In the Press, and will shortly be published, Price 2d., a Lecture on the Value of Biography in the Formation of Individual Character—delivered to Branch A 1. By G. Jacob Holyoake. Watson, Paul's Alley, Paternoster Row.

Next week we shall publish a review of Mr. Watson's new and important pamphlet on *Post Office Disclosures*.

ILLNESS OF W. J. FOX.—We are sorry to announce that the lectures of this gentleman are at present discontinued through his ill health.

THE NORTHERN STAR IN LONDON.—On Tuesday, Dec. 10, a Tea Party will be held in the Literary and Scientific Institution, John Street, Tottenham Court Road, in honour of the conductors of the *Northern Star*. Feargus O'Connor, Esq., Mr. Joshua Hobson, and Mr. George Julian Harney have been invited, and will attend.

POPULAR CONCERTS.— We are desired to announce that on Monday evening, Dec. 9, a *Vocal and Instrumental Concert* will be held in John Street Institution, Fitzroy Square. The celebrated American Buffo Singer is engaged, and a host of favourites These efforts of the Managers to place such treats within the reach of the industrious classes, deserve popular support. Hall, 6d. Gallery 1s. Commencing at Half-past 8.

LECTURES.
Dec. 8.—Branch A 1, Mr. G. A. Fleming.
Dec. 8.—Hall of Science, City Road, Mr. Southwell.
Dec. 8.—Investigation Hall, 29, Circus Street, Bryanston Square, Mr. Southwell,—On the Jew Book text, "Canst thou by Searching find out God?" At a quarter-past 11, A.M.
Dec. 8.—————Mr. Watkins,—On the way to get the Charter. At 7, P.M.—Free admission.
Dec. 8.—Social Institution, 5, Charlotte Street, Blackfriars Road, Mr. Ellis,—On the Fear of Death. At 7, P.M.
Dec. 8.—4, Roan Street, Greenwich, Mr. Holyoake, —Anticipations of what Society would be without God in the World. At 7, P.M.
Dec. 8.—Finsbury Institution, Goswell Road, Mr. Jenneson,—On a plan to effect a Social Revolution. At 7, P.M. Discussion after,—Have the American and French Revolutions promoted human happiness?

DISCUSSIONS.
Dec. 4.—29, Circus Street,— Is there a God. By two well known disputants.
Dec. 10.————The weekly discussion in the Coffee Room.
Dec. 6.—John Street, Mr. Ellis and the Rev. Mr. Hill.

MR. JOHNSON, bookseller, lately fined the sum of £20, for receiving money paid for admission to Mrs. Martin's (the Socialist) lectures, applied on Monday for a copy of the ground of his conviction, but Mr. Ayre said that he was not entitled to one, and the application was refused.

SOCIALIST LECTURES.—Mr. M'Manus applied on Monday to the Magistrates to know how he was to act under the following circumstances :—It appears that for some time past, Matthew Tate, a Socialist lecturer, has been in the habit of giving discourses on his creed in the open air. On Sunday last, while "holding forth" on the pier, the vast mob by whom he was surrounded became infuriated, and Tate was obliged to run for his life, followed by a mob of two or three hundred people. At length, assisted by the police, he managed to avoid their fury by taking refuge in a house in Blanket Row. Mr. Carrick said he should grant no protection to the man, as his lectures were clearly illegal.— *Eastern Counties Herald.*

For Mrs. Martin, from W. J............ 0 5 0

Errata.—The letter signed T. Finlay, page 422, for Psalm cxxxix—5, to the end, read Psalm cxlix—5, to the end. Collector 44, in list of Anti-Persecution Union subscriptions, in *Movement* No. 50, should have been Collector 4.

SUBSCRIPTIONS
TO THE ANTI-PERSECUTION UNION.
R. Mellville, W. Duncan................. 0 1 0
H. Mills.................................. 0 1 0
J. Cook, Theological Depot, Ipswich...... 0 1 0
Mr. George Bird, for Legal Fund........ 0 5 0
Cosmopolite, do. do..................... 1 0 0
Mr. Pickford, do. do.................... 0 10 0
C. Dent.................................. 0 1 0
T. Walsh, Mr. Mather................... 0 1 4

PATERSON TESTIMONIAL.
Cosmopolite 0 10 0
C. Dent 0 5 0
G. J. H., Sec.

Printed and Published by G. J. HOLYOAKE,
40, Holywell-street, Strand.
Wednesday, December 4, 1844.

THE MOVEMENT
And Anti-Persecution Gazette.

"Maximise morals, minimise religion."—BENTHAM.

No. 53.   EDITED BY G. JACOB HOLYOAKE, ASSISTED BY M. Q. RYALL.   Price 1½d

ALPHABET OF MATERIALISM.

A.

[The following is the first of a series of papers, occasionally to appear, from the pen of Mr. Southwell, in which will be brought into the foreground, certain curious opinions pertaining to the philosophy of Materialism, expressed by old and new remarkable authors who have hitherto remained by neglect, or have been thrust by design, into the background.]

ARTHUR COLLIER, who wrote during the seventeenth century, endeavoured, by "dry reason, and metaphysical demonstration," to establish the rather startling hypothesis, that what is commonly called *matter*, though *visible*, is not *real*. His famous " Clavis Universalis, or a New Inquiry after Truth," was written to prove " the non-existence or impossibility of an External World." To guard against misconception on this point, he was so laudably anxious that in " the Introduction" to his book he explains as follows :

" The question I am concerned about is in general this, whether there be any such thing as an external world. And my title will suffice to inform my reader, that the *negative* of this question is the point I am to demonstrate."

He then proceeds to define, "world " as " whatsoever is usually understood by the terms body, extension, space, matter, quantity, &c." and " external " as what is " usually understood by the words absolute, self-existent, independent, &c.

There are theists so superficial, as to sneer at and deride all attempts to demonstrate the impossibility of an external world—not considering that if it *does* exist a God *does not*. Collier saw, and had the courage to avow that belief in *matter* is incompatible with belief in *God*, and consequently, that one or other of those beliefs must give way. That I have not misrepresented him the subjoined passages from his book furnish full and satisfactory evidence. *

------

* Clavis Universalis : or a New Inquiry after Truth, pages 68, 69, 70, and 71.

" Consider it (the external world) in its whole, and it has the unity of infinity. It is one alone, and absolutely incapable of being multiplied by any power whatsoever; which is as much as can be said of God, and even more than they have a right to say, who consider him, not as universal, but some particular being. Consider it in its several parts, or bodies included in it, and each particle of matter has such a unity in, or identity with itself, as I think should not be ascribed to anything but God, who alone is the same yesterday, to-day, and for ever. Again, I consider that an external world is independent on the will of God, considered in its expansion, which will and must be infinite, whenever God pleases to make, or will it to be so or not, supposing only that he wills to produce or make any the least extent, or that any the least part or extent is made or in being.

" As for instance, let God be supposed to will the being of a certain cubical part of matter or extension, about the bigness of a common die. This, I say, is impossible in fact, and this draws another impossibility after it, which is that by this the will of God is overruled or frustrated by the work of his own hands. For what should bound this cubical extent ? It must be something or nothing. If nothing, it is plainly infinite ; if something, it must be matter or extension ; and then the same question returns, and will infinitely return, or be never satisfied under an extent actually infinite. But this has an independency of being, which I think can belong to no creature, it being the same with that which we use to call necessary existence—*I conclude, therefore, that there is no such creature as an external world*.

" Much the same sort of difficulty occurs if we consider it in not being, after it has been supposed to exist. That God can annihilate every creature which he has made, is I think, a maxim undisputed by any ; if so, I think it plainly follows that that which in its idea implies an utter impossibility of being annihilated, is a thing, in fact, impossible. But this, I say, is the case or implica-

tion of an external world. This is evident from the foregoing article, which shews the absolute necessity of its being infinite, or the supposition of the being of but the least part of it, for certainly if nothing less than infinite can exist, or be made, no part of this infinite can be unmade or annihilated. And therefore, though in words we may say that God can annihilate any part of it, yet we utter that in words of which we can have no conception, but rather the contrary to it For annihilate it in supposition as often as you will, yet still it returns upon you; and while you would conceive it as nothing. it becomes something against your will; and it is impossible to think otherwise, whatever we may say.

"Another difficulty which still attends the notion of an external world, is, that if any such world exists, there seems to be no possibility of conceiving, but that God himself must be extended with it.

"This I take to be absurdity enough in reason, to hinder us from supposing any such world. But so unfortunate are the stars of *this idol of our imagination*, that it is as much impossible, on another account that it should exist, though this were no absurdity,— or though it were supposed and allowed that God himself were extended.

"I suppose, then, in the first place, that God is not extended. If so, I say there can be no external world. For if there be an external world, and if it be a creature, we must suppose that God is everywhere present in and with it; for he is supposed to preserve and do every thing that is done in it. *To deny this is to shut him out of the universe, even altogether to deny his being.* On the contrary, to affirm that he is thus present with every part and particle of it, is to make him co extended, which is contrary to the supposition.

"Yes, it may be said, God is extended, and consequently, there may be an external world, notwithstanding this dilemma, I answer,—secondly, be it so, that he is extended, (to humour a corrupt and absurd itch of argumentation)—yet this avails nothing towards the being of an external world, but directly towards the non-existence of it. For if God be extended, where shall we find room for an external world ? Can two extensions, infinite extensions, co-exist ? This is evidently impossible. So that all the choice we are left is to acknowledge God or an external world; which I think is a choice we need not long be deliberating upon. *I conclude, therefore, that if God is, there is no external world.*"

Thus Arthur Collier, whose reasoning reduces orthodox Theists to the uncommonly disagreeable necessity of choosing between *God* and *Matter.* They must abandon one or other of these as an "idol of our imagination." To be sure there is a highly intellectual but not very consistent class of heterodox theists, who affirm that God and matter are the same one, uncreated, everlasting thing, though, as Collier expresses it, "that an *external* world is God himself, and not a creature of God." These persons who properly call themselves Pantheists,— in course believe in nothing more than the universe. "*If*" (said one of their ablest expounders) "*we name heaven and earth, the stars and elements, and all that is above all heavens, we by so doing name the whole God.*"* If so, atheists may reasonably say, your "whole God" is exactly our whole *matter*, and Pantheism amounts to Atheism. The omnipresence of matter can only be accepted as an article of faith by those who believe there is nothing else but matter; and as to talk about matter being God, it means, *there is no God.*

The reader would do well to remember that one reason for denying the existence of an external world, advanced by Arthur Collier, was the manifest and absolute impossibility implied in the idea that God is *everywhere* though matter is *somewhere.* Now, we know that all Theists declare omnipresence an attribute of deity. God, say they, "moves the atom and controuls the aggregate of nature." Having satisfied themselves upon that point, they unavoidably concluded he must be "present in and with" atoms as atoms, and aggregates as aggregates. That *nothing can act where it is not*, no argument is necessary to prove, and equally superfluous would be any attempt to convince the reader, that if nothing can act where it is not, God, to act everywhere must be present everywhere. Collier very properly reminds us, that "if there be an external world" we are bound to conclude that God does "everything that is done in it." In short, he must be in all places at all times, not by his *virtue* (so called) merely, but by his *essence*, which word essence (if it mean anything) means the sum total or totality of that which constitutes a being what it is. By *essence* of deity, I understand the material or sub-

---

* So man nennt Himmel und Erde, Sterne und Elemente, und Alles was darin ist, und alles, was über allen Himmeln ist, so nennt man hiemit den ganzen Gott."— Böhme.

stance of which, if he exist, he undoubtedly is composed. That Newton believed his God acts upon and preserves *in propria persona*, any one may satisfy himself by looking into the *Principia*, at the end of which we are told, " *Deus est omnipresens non per virtutem solam, sed per substantiam, nam virtus sine substantia subsistere non potest* * By what process of reasoning he arrived at belief in a *substantially omnipresent God*, while admitting the reality of matter, I confess myself quite unable to comprehend. To me it seems *certain* that if God is present *everywhere* matter is present *nowhere*, unless like Pantheists, we say Matter and God are not two but *one*, which, I repeat, is equivalent to denying the existence of God. If, then, it is true, as Newton and other orthodox Theists assert, that †" Even the Deity knows all things, and acts upon all things, *only by being present with all things*." There cannot be an external world, or God operates universally, without a particle of body to operate with. The latter conclusion involves the idea that impossibilities are possible; for as Tertullian, in his treatise, *De Anima*, wisely said, *What is not a body is nothing*, and nothing we all are sure can no more be present in or act upon everything than everything be present in or act upon nothing. The other conclusion involves the idea that *nothing is but what is not*—which idea, if true, demonstrates that we, ourselves, no more exist than the external world.

CHARLES SOUTHWELL.

GEOLOGY AND THE BIBLE.

SINCE I sent you the abridged account of the discussion between the Dean of York and Professor Sedgwick, I have read a more ample report of the affair in the *Athenæum*, as well as perused an article of considerable length in the Edinburgh *Witness*, the chief organ of the Free Church party. The article in question is, I presume, from the pen of the editor, Mr. Hugh Millar, originally a working man in Cromarty, and an accomplished geologist.

A perusal of the Professor's speech, in its extended form, fully bears out my strictures on the miserable theory he so unmercifully demolished, and I would fain extract a few

---

* God is omnipresent, not by *virtue* only, but by *substance*, since virtue without substance is not able to subsist.

† See p. 11 of Dr. Price's Second Communication to Dr. Priestly, respecting the nature of Matter.

---

quotations here in support of my position, but, as most of your readers might doubtless have seen the original, and as the size of your sheet counsels brevity, I will pass on to the article of the *Witness*, merely noticing that the Professor, in his concluding remarks, asserted that " he had no fear of the results of an attempt (if soberly made on right evidence and in the simple love of truth) to reconcile the phenomena of geology with the word of God—not doubting that the highest discoveries of science would ever be found in perfect harmony and accordance with the meaning and language of revelation." We shall see.

Some of the out-and-out champions of the book, have however, gone farther than the Dean of York, with all his ignorance dared to venture. For example, the *Record* arrives at the sage conclusion that, " for aught which appears in the bowels of the earth, the world might have been called into existence yesterday." This assumption brought out the *Witness*; and I shall briefly recapitulate the leading features of his argument.

It is a general truth that—

Philosophy will clip an angel's wings,
Conquer all mysteries by rule and line,
Empty the haunted air, the gnomed mine;

but this is peculiarly opposite when applied to experimental, as distinguished from speculative philosophy. If ever put down, what old Pliny termed the "new superstition," mut perish by and in the name of science. Many things, (such as the existence of Gods, the eternity of matter, and other hypotheses of a like nature), broached in the various religious systems, cannot, to my thinking, be rigidly determined for lack of facts. But along with these there are statements advanced which can be brought to the touchstone ; and if we are able to prove those false, it necessarily damages the remainder, more or less, according as they are fundamental or otherwise. That is the reason why I attach so much importance to a controversy like the present. This, however, is a digression.

The *Witness* sets out thus :—" Let us examine whether the opinion of the *Record*, regarding the inferences by which geologists conclude that there existed creations anterior to the one described by Moses, is not an opinion objectionable on this score, and whether it can be safely held that for aught which appears in the bowels of the earth, the world might have been called into existence yesterday." He then conducts his readers into " an ancient burying ground, in a northern district." " We dig," says he, "into the soil below—here is a human skull, and there numerous other well known bones of the human skeleton. We dis-inter portions, not of one but of many of them—some comparatively fresh, some in a state of extreme decay, and with the bones there mingle fragments of coffins, with the tinsel mountings, in some instances, still attached, and the rusted nails sticking in the joints. We continue to dig, and at a depth to which the sexton almost never penetrates, find a stratum of pure sea sand, and then a stratum of the sea-shells, common on the neighbouring coast. We dig a little farther and reach a thick bed of red sand-stone, (the old red) which we penetrate, and beneath which we find a bed of impure lime, richly charged with the remains of fish of strange and antique forms." "Do appearances such as these," he triumphantly asks, warrant the inference that the earth may have been made yesterday? Do these human skeletons, in all their various stages of decay, appear as if they had been made yesterday? Was that bit of coffin, with the soiled tinsel on the one side, and the corroded nail sticking out of the other, made yesterday? Was yonder skull, instead of having ever formed part of a human head, created yesterday exactly the repulsive sort of thing you see it? Indisputably not. But can we stop in the process of inferences at the mouldering remains in the church yard? Can we hold that the skull was not created a mere skull, and yet hold that the shells beneath are not the remains of molluscous animals, but things created in exactly their present state, as empty shells? The supposition is absurd. And if we cannot stop at the skeletons, why stop at the shells—why not pass on to the fish? We cannot stop short at the shells. If the human skull was not created a mere skull, not the shell a mere dead shell, then the fossil fish could not have been created a mere fossil. Were we compelled to take our stand anywhere, it would be rather before we had recognized as human remains the remains of the church yard, than at any subsequent step. Ere entering on this first stage in our progress, we could at least be consistent, but not at any after stage. He winds up in the following significant strain:—"We have accomplished our end if we have succeeded in indicating the danger of arraying against presumed deductions of religion, the laws which regulate and control human belief. The infidelity of France arose not out of the mysteries of religion (?), but out of the monstrous absurdities which Popery had tacked to it; and how incalculable the loss and damage to human souls which that infidelity occasioned (!) We would fain urge on those traversers of the laws of credulity who unwittingly foster the scepticism of a country, and unknowingly but powerfully seconds its proselytizing infidel in their proper work," &c., &c.

The vulgar notion that the universe was created out of nothing, about 6000 years since, and in the space of seven days, of twenty-four hours each, is, then, given up by every person whose opinion is entitled to any weight. But several theories have been propounded, with the view of "reconciling," in the words of Professor Sedgwick, "the phenomena of geology and the word of God." With only two of these am I at present acquainted. One is that the six days of Moses refer to the same number of indefinite periods of time corresponding with geological epochs. That requires no refutation—its absurdity must be apparent to the meanest tyro in geology. But the favourite one appears to be that evidently hinted at by Mr. Millar, in the concluding words of the first sentence I have quoted from his able article—namely, that "*there existed creations anterior to the one described by Moses.*" This is by far the most tenable one, at first sight—and in my opinion forms the cardinal point upon which all future controversy must hinge. It must also be speedily disposed of; and to that task I shall now address myself.

These anterior creations are supposed to have taken place in the period between that indicated in the first verse of the first chapter of Genesis, (which is disconnected from the contest, and presumed to announce the general fact that "in the beginning God created the heaven and the earth.") The remaining portion of the chapter is in the same way held to be a description of the creation of the races that now people the world. Yet, although the vegetable kingdom is said to have sprung into existence on the third day, the sun, which performs so important a part in relation to that great division of nature, was not made until the fourth. How the existing races of plants, or previous ones could either exist without the sun, surpasses my comprehension. And the trunks of some of the vegetable relics of these presumed "anterior creations," too, are composed of concentric rings, showing periods of alternate repose and growth, such as is now caused by the alternation of summer and winter. Besides, in the same verse, after stating that "God made two great lights—the greater light to rule the day, and the lesser light to rule the night," Moses adds—he made the stars also. This obviously upsets the hypothesis in hand, not to speak of the "nebulous theory" of Herschel, as taken in connection with the first verse. Here can be no doubt the idea is intended to be conveyed that our earth, and the sky above it, was first created out of nothing, covered with vegetable life, after the former being fitted for its reception; and then the sun, moon, and stars, or every thing else. This I do think, after a dispassionate consideration, will be the conclusion at which every unprejudiced mind will arrive. What strikes one forcibly here is, the fact that Moses appears to have no notion of what the fixed stars, and our own sun, are now ascertained to be—the centre of systems; he never alludes to one of their chief offices, that of keeping the lesser bodies in their orbits; they were "set up" he says—not the sun and moon only, but the *stars* likewise, "to *give light* on the earth, and to rule over the day and the night." According to the Dean of York's text, "the wisdom of man is foolishness with God; but, truly, the wisdom of Moses's God is the very acme of ignorance and blundering stupidity.

It is told of Sir Charles Napier, that in giving an account of the attack on Acre, he praised the marines highly. "I knew them" he said, "to be a very pious corps, so I touched them on their religious feelings, and brought them into action like men." "But how did you bring their religious feelings into play," enquired a bystander, "what did you say to them?" "Gad," replied he, "when they were coming on I cried, now, at 'em, you infernal rascals, *and fulfil the prophecies.*" When Jesus rode on a jackass into Jerusalem he did so, "that the Scriptures might be fulfilled," and historians have palmed distortions upon mankind as truths, for the same holy end; but there is one agent and one historian to whom falsehood and trickery are alike unknown—nature. The truth of this was forcibly impressed upon my mind while reading the veracious legend of the Jewish prophet, which we have now been considering. The 30th verse, of the first of Genesis, is as follows:—"And to every beast of the earth, and to every fowl of the air, and to every thing that creepeth on the earth, wherein there is life, have I given every green thing for meat." Upon the strength of this, and some others of a like tendency, theologians tell us that all the animals, of whatever kind, behaved themselves—that the big ones refrained from eating the little ones, until Eve shook the apple-tree.

"'That forbidden tree, whose mortal fruit brought death into the world and all its woe;" and one of the prophets raves about the time when "the lion shall eat straw like the ass." The whole structure, internal and external, of beasts and birds of prey, gives the lie direct to Moses and the prophets. Who would believe that the curious web of the spider was intended by a "wise creator,' not for the purpose to which we daily see it applied, but to snare, perchance, the seeds of the dandelion, or some such plant. The "sacred historian" takes particular care, however, that the fishes get no flies, at least for the first day of their existence. A young friend of mine, a devoted disciple of Isaac Walton, to whom I mentioned this circumstance, remarked, "that it would have been a glorious time for the angler, who would have had no opposition in the shape of natural flies." But I must cut my story short; although, in the meantime, with your permission, I shall be happy to enter more fully into this subject on some future occasion. P. G.

GOD-BELIEF AND GOD-BELIEVERS.

(*Concluded from page* 437.)

In constructing Theological Dialogues, on the Socratic model, we do ill to abate a jot of force from the antagonist's arguments, but let us not fall into an error of another kind, that of investing the religious dogmatist with the diffidence only exemplified by the philosophical investigator. The revelationist may be constitutionally, and even in ordinary personal intercourse, gentle, courteous, and unassuming, but he is doctrinally arrogant, overbearing, and intolerant. It is in consequence of the assumption of a merely speculative or conjectural belief for a proven and authoritative truth. His reasonings, therefore, when he condescends to reason, like those of the *Faber*, and *Irons*, and *Puseyite* school, are employed not to discover unknown truth, but to support assumed truth. He will thus accept any reasons that support, or reject any that may subvert his notions; or, as these gentry have already done, reason to show that reason may be dispensed with on occasion—that is when its use militates against pre-accepted dogmas.

Of dialogue in general, it may be said with Hume, that, while the dialogue-writer desires, by departing from the direct style of composition, to give a freer air to his performance, and avoid the appearance of *Author* and *Reader*, he is apt to run into a worse inconvenience, and convey the image of *Pedagogue* and *Pupil*. This defect may be slightly perceived in the tract under notice—but it must be remarked that nothing savouring so strongly of school-boy deference occurs throughout the whole as the extracts here quoted.

Of dialogue in particular, or that specially treating of Natural Religion, we have from the same source these excellent remarks. Any question of philosophy, so *obscure* and *uncertain*, that human reason can reach no fixed determination with regard to it; if it should be treated at all, seems to lead us naturally into the style of dialogue and conversation. Reasonable men may be allowed to differ where *no one can reasonably be positive.*"

In the dialogue under review, some striking points are well put on both sides, and it cannot be said that the fair, legitimate inferences to which the line of argumentation should lead, is evaded. The tract cannot repel by its lengthiness; it is so brief as to be readily perused by the least studious reader. The following is as much in the way of extract as can be given without transferring too large a portion of its contents.

" If there is that in the universe which beholds our miseries and could remove them, and yet looks tamely on, what shall we say of him? what shall we offer to him? Prayer! If you should make me kneel, I'd say, " Oh thou that sittest on the throne of thine unapproachable loneliness! Who mad'st but regardest not the highest of thy created things! Shall I thank thee for a life full of danger and distress, or for the prospect of future interminable agonies? Shall I thank thee for the Serpent? thou didst make it. For the fever and the famine? thou hast sent them; for the tyrant and tormentor? thou permittest them, they come from thee!

" I do not pray thy will be done, for tigers and tornados, and pestilence are in it! I pray not for thy kingdom—even in thy Eden there was a betrayer—but if thou wilt bestow on man one boon which will be his highest and fullest happiness, Oh, leave him to the universe around him and within him, and torment him no longer with a name and worship which has profitted him so little."

The tract named by Mrs. Martin " The Missionary Jubilee Panic," gives an account of the Manchester Missionary Meeting, of which a notice has already appeared in our column.

Some will object, those whose cool discretion, or respectable fears, overbalance their enthusiasm, that there is over-much frowardness in the action, and egotism in the description of Mrs. Martin's anti-missionary expedition in Manchester. It may be rejoined, that such undauntedness as is here displayed, even according to the shewing of avowed opponents, is of itself something worthy our admiration,—but from Mrs. Martin's statement, we learn that the Manchester Meeting was announced on the bills to be a PUBLIC one—a stock religious trick—while the Chairman, Massie, endeavoured to shield the missionary functionaries from criticism or amendment, by assuming the meeting to be one only of " *Christians*—of *members of* Missionary Societies." The noted *Cummings*, the anticatholic disputant, affected contempt, a week or two since, at the Course of Lectures by G. J.H. and M. Q R., at Greenwich, when asked to attend it, the moment after he had been valiantly challenging all the papistical world, attempted to play off this prank at a meeting in Lambeth, where a friend and myself were present. When about to put a question to him, he hastily rose, pretending that the meeting was one of a limited character, not free to public animadversion. My friend, who had provided himself with the actual bill, put forth by the conveners of the meeting, proved in his teeth, to the persons present, that public debate had been solicited. The only way in which the Reverend Cummings sneaked out of it was the making some trivial excuse about time.

The similar conduct pursued by the chairman in Manchester, is thus described in the pamphlet:—" A Socialist, opposite to where a man had been just turned out by the police, shouted out, 'It's my cause as well as yours: we have a right to be heard.' —Mr. Massie : ' no, sir, it is not your cause : are you a subscriber to this society ?'— Socialist: ' no.'—Mr. Massie : ' then you have nothing whatever to do with it.'— Socialist: ' it's a public meeting.'—Mr. Massie : ' no, it is not a public meeting : it's a meeting of Christians—of members of the Missionary Societies.'" To which Mrs. Martin appends the following as a note: " Mr. Massie here legitimatized his claim to the Christian character by uttering a premeditated and palpable LIE !! As the advertisements in the *Guardian*, and other announcements of the meeting will testify. It was explicitly termed in the advertisement a PUBLIC MEETING." The newspaper report continues in this strain:

"After the Revds. Francis Tucker and Mr. Fletcher had addressed the meeting, the Rev. J. W. Massie spoke at some length in support of the resolution, and in conclusion said, in reference to Mrs. Martin: 'Could you have imagined a more pitiful, a more painful object than that which presented its claim of a hearing from the chair this evening. There could not be a more humiliating spectacle of human form—(Hear, hear), and of woman's character—(Hear, hear), than was exhibited there.'

To this Mrs. Martin retorts, and however much of the *I* there appears, is amply warranted by the previous truely priestly personality:

"*I* saw a more pitiful object than myself that night. I saw cowards and bullies, imposters and dupes, each of these was more 'pitiful' than I. I saw *you*, Mr. Massie, and hundreds thought you looked wondrous 'pitiful,' when you said, 'I expect Mr. Livingstone to take Mrs. Martin away,' and 'that woman' defied him and you to do it. Hundreds thought you looked most 'pitiful,' when the policeman's staff was your only answer to such charges as those which I had brought."

There is one thing pretty clear, that Mrs. Martin's flagellations do not please—like the drummer boy, let her lay on how and where she will, there is no satisfaction, they don't like to be flogged at all—who does?

M. Q. R.

CORRESPONDENCE.

To the Editor of the Movement.

SIR,—I send you the enclosed Letter for insertion in the next number of the *Movement.*   LLOYD JONES.

Bank Street, Sheffield.
Dec. 2nd, 1844.

Mr. Lloyd Jones,

DEAR SIR,—I forward you an extract from the minutes of the Sheffield Branch of the Rational Society.

"*General Meeting, Dec.* 1, 1844.—The attention of the members having been called to Nos. 49 and 50 of the *Movement*, in which certain statements are made and reiterated, relative to a lecture delivered by Mr. Lloyd Jones at Sheffield, in which he is stated by Mr. Holyoake to have recommended the Branch to dismiss him (Mr. H.) It was unanimously agreed that it be recorded in the minutes that no member of the Branch has any recollection of any thing of the kind having taken place. At the same time, the members think that the sooner all these matters are buried in oblivion the better, as their only tendency is to distract and divide the ignorant—the wise and the good never noticing them.

Signed,
ISAAC IRONSIDE, President."

[I pass over the vagueness of this minute—the doubt we are left in as to what proportion of the present members of the Branch were members at the time of the lecture, nearly three years ago, and what number of *them* remember ever being at the lecture—the unlikelihood that the few who might be there would retain an impression, at this distance of time, of what did not concern them—the absence of my friend Mr. Paterson to point out *who* were there and direct me to parties who might corroborate his report—I pass over these important particulars, which certainly deserve consideration, and leave the resolution for what it is worth. All I care to say is, that these Sheffield people make peace as they make their knives, with a sharpe edge. When they recommend my notice of Mr. Jones to "oblivion," they assume it to have been made to his injury, in spite of my earnest declaimer, then before them, of any thing of the kind. While pretending to advise peace, they invent the *fresh* accusation that I have written what has a "tendency to distract and divide." They knew they were making this resolution for the *Movement,* for it was asked for for that purpose. Why should I be included in a common censure with Mr. Jones? I proved my determination to have nothing to do with "matters," fitted only to be "buried in oblivion," when I disclaimed every thing disrespectful to Mr. Jones—and for the Sheffield Branch to step out as a body, overlook this fact, and still treat me as an accuser, is to treat me unjustly. Let me tell them that they who would make peace should learn to discriminate. However, I suppose I may console myself by their assurance that "the wise and good never notice these matters," consequently, if I happen to be adjudged not "wise and good," by those who appear as my censors, Mr. Lloyd Jones is proclaimed, by his own friends, to be "not wise and good," and the Sheffield Branch, who really *do* "notice" these "matters," confess themselves to be in the same disreputable condition—without wisdom and goodness. If they mean thus to characterise themselves, they real cast a suspicion on the testimony they bear.—G. J. H.]

PREPARING FOR PUBLICATION, in a separate form, the "Visit to Harmony Hall," with emendations, and a new and curious Vindicatory Chapter. Dedicated to the Socialists of England and Scotland. By G. J. H.

Look closer to't ; you make the evil first ;
A base, then pile a heap of censures on it.
'Tis your own sin supplies the scaffolding
And mason work, you skilful, rear the grim
Unsightly fabric ; and there point, and say
' How ugly is it.' You meanwhile forget
'Tis your own handy work. I could say more ;
But there's a check within ; 'tis such an one,
As you I trow, have banished from its birthplace.
Old Play.

London : Hetherington, 40, Holywell Street.

LETTER-OPENING.—Every man who would know the morality of the Government, into whose hands he trusts his private thoughts, should read a pamphlet just issued by Mr. Watson—price 4d., entitled —Letter-Opening at the Post Office. The article on this subject, from No. lxxxii of the *Westminster Review*, for September, 1844, entitled Mazzini and the Ethics of Politicians. To which is added some account of the Brothers Bandiera: by J. Mazzini. London: J. Watson, 5, Paul's Alley, Paternoster-row.

THE PLEBIAN.—No. 1, consisting of twelve pages the size of the *Movement*, price one penny, of this promising periodical, Edited by Miss Roalfe, is now ready. Among other interesting features we are glad to see the Scottish Anti-Persecution Union making its appearance in its pages.

MR. EDWARDS'S CHALLENGE.—Mr. Holyoake's time has been so much engrossed by various parties respecting his "Visit to Harmony Hall," that he can ill spare time for a public discussion, with all its attendant pre-arrangements, but if Mr. Edwards will make his appearance in the *New Moral World*, Mr. Holyoake will answer him there at his leisure.

RECOVERY OF W. J. FOX.—The Committee of South Place Chapel announce that Mr. Fox is expected to resume the morning services next Sunday, December 15.

BRANCH A 1 DEBATES.—The discussion on the Harmony Hall letters was continued on Sunday morning, Mr. Lloyd Jones and Mr. Holyoake as on the preceding Sunday, were the principal speakers. Mr. Holyoake produced the authorities on which his statements were founded, and Mr. Jones criticised and explained. We should present a full report of what was said, but so much of our space has been monopolised by these matters, as to render such a step too great a tax on the good nature of our readers. If an opportunity should arise of discussing the question in the *New Moral World*, we shall enter fully into the facts of the case. In the meantime we refer readers to the new edition of the "Visit," advertised above.

DR. KALLEY.—The affair of Dr. Kalley, and the disturbances connected with his missionary labours, have been productive of the greatest ferment throughout the island. The question has now been set at rest by negociations, between Lord Aberdeen and the Portuguese Government. The Dr. is to be paid £650 immediately, as compensation for his illegal arrest, and a special law will be at once introduced into the Cortes, authorizing the Government to remove from the country, at its pleasure, any promulgator of doctrines pronounced heterodox. The *Im. parciel* of Funchal states that Dr. Kalley has resolved upon leaving the island.

MR. SOUTHWELL leaves London the first week in January, to fulfil an engagement of five months in Manchester.

MISSIONARY HUMBUGS.—Several persons, who were said to have become converts to Presbyterianism in Kerry, through the labours of "The Presbyterian Mission" in that county, have published a solemn denial of the statement, and also allege that some names mentioned among the converts are totally unknown in the locality—*Pilot.*

DEMOCRACY.—Messrs. Ryall and Holyoake will deliver a course of lectures at the Chartist Hall, No. 1, Turnagain-lane, Skinner-street, Snow Hill, on the following subjects :—Mr. Ryall, on Sunday, Dec. 15th, 1844, The two great Leagues—that of Property against the Poor. And on Sunday, Dec. 22nd, The League of the Government against the Governed. Mr. Holyoake, on Sunday, Dec. 29th 1844, Popular Errors respecting Popular Rights. Chair to be taken each evening at seven o'clock.

TO CORRESPONDENTS.

Received.—Review of the "Vestiges of Creation," by W. C.
The Jews, by J. B. L.
Mr. Morgan next week.
POST OFFICE DISCLOSURES (review) is again postponed, to give place to the letter sent by Mr. Lloyd Jones. If we did not insert Mr. Ironside's letter Mr. Jones might think us loath to afford him the means of justification.
J. M. C.—The answer to Mr. Edwards was sent for insertion last week, but the printer could not find room for it.

LECTURES.

Dec. 15.—Social Institution, 5, Charlotte Street, Blackfriars Road, Mr. Ellis,—On Hell. At 7, P.M.
Dec. 15.—Branch A 1, John Street, Tottenham Court Road, Mr. Jones. At 7, P.M. (First of a Course of three Lectures).
Dec. 20.——————Discussion between the Rev. Mr. Hill and Mr. Ellis. At Half-past 8, P.M.
Dec. 15.—Finsbury Institution, Goswell Road, Mr. Savage,—Astronomy, illustrated by Diagrams. At 7, P.M. Discussion after,—Is the Universe eternal ?
Dec. 15.—Hall of Science, City Road, Mr. Southwell. At 7, P.M.
Dec. 15.—Investigation Hall, 29, Circus Street, Marylebone, Mr. Southwell. At a quarter past 11, A.M. Mr. Holyoake. At 7, P.M.

SUBSCRIPTIONS
TO THE ANTI-PERSECUTION UNION.

Per Collector 22—A. Park 0 5 0
A. Park 0 2 0
Bowman 0 2 0
Brown 0 2 0
E. Strickland 0 2 0
T. Pocock 0 2 0
J. Gradwell, D. Ross 0 1 0
C... 0 1 0
Mr. Watts, Islington, Mr. Johnson's case 0 5 0
K., Bury St. Edmunds 0 5 0
Do.   do.   Mr. Johnson's case 0 1 3

PATERSON TESTIMONIAL.

W. J. B. 0 5 0
K., Bury St. Edmunds 0 1 3
Miss Haywood, do 0 1 0
Geo. Anderson, per Miss Roalfe 0 1 0

G. J. H., *Sec.*

Printed and Published by G. J. HOLYOAKE,
40, Holywell-street, Strand.
Wednesday, December 11, 1844.

THE MOVEMENT
And Anti-Persecution Gazette.

"Maximise morals, minimise religion."—BENTHAM.

No. 54.   EDITED BY G. JACOB HOLYOAKE, ASSISTED BY M. Q. RYALL.   Price 1½d

STATE MORALS,
ILLUSTRATED BY THE POST OFFICE DISCLOSURES.

THERE is a morality of the governing, and a morality of the governed—a morality for public, and a morality for private use. The distinctions thus set up have complicated and confused the subject of morals, as much probably as the divisions which were of old arbitrarily assigned to practitioners on the human frame retarded progress in the "healing art." The science of conduct in its simplest aspect, that is, when public, political and national considerations are for the most part excluded, has been too little understood. How to act individually and socially, in accordance with our nature, instead of conforming to supposed authoritative precepts, has but lately found open expounders and advocates. Puffendorf, Grotius and the like are consigned to the schools, or grow musty on the shelves of the colleges—Franklin, Mirabaud, Volney, Rousseau, Helvetius, are the the text books of the liberal student, following in whose wake come our Bentham, Owen, Southwood Smith, Combe, and others, who as moralists, physiologists and natural philosophers have mightily helped to place morals, and consequently happiness, on a sure foundation. They are teaching us to study for ourselves, and without the intervention or dictation of priests.

In what regards governmental or international morality the people at large are greatly at fault. One of the last mentioned philosophers, Bentham, has, it is true, laboured assiduously to abolish political and legislatorial "chicane," and to establish right rules for future guidance. But government functionaries will not, and private individuals cannot avail themselves of his teachings. The former are enveloped in an atmosphere of corruption which effectually dims their moral vision, the latter, except among those highly favored persons having rare opportunities and leisure, are excluded from access to these most valuable sources of knowledge and codes of conduct. Thus while the delinquencies of governments are known and felt—known perhaps only by being felt—the secret springs of their criminalities are utterly concealed from the public at large, and the well rounded and plausible sophisms with which false doctrine is represented and criminal actions defended, continue the delusion. The warped and crooked party views with which the acts of governments have been regarded, sedulously fomented as they have always been by the venal aristocracies, have also materially tended to throw dust into the eyes of the lookers on.

Any earnest and vigorous efforts to make the workings of state frauds hideously manifest to the dullest vision, without the tinsel drapery of frothy orators, is a real and worthy deed. The British public are deeply indebted to Mazzini for the energetic and persevering course he has pursued in tracing out and making known to them a moral canker eating into the very vitals of the body politic. The Post office frauds which he discovered, and by the aid of that steadiest of people's friends, Duncombe, disclosed and made public, opened the eyes of the people of England to a new, unparalleled and unsuspected source of criminality. Numerous must have been the partizans for the first time directed to the fallacy of party tests of political and public virtne. The consecutive and systematic delinquencies of successive administrations, tory, whig, conservative, or whig-radical, proved the existence of a more deeply seated disease.

It becomes then a grave duty to ascertain whether official, public or state morality can be put on the same footing, low though it be, as that commonly recognized by everyday conventionalism, and to what we shall attribute the greater laxity of government officials—public men.

In our thirty-first number, a paper on "Post office Revelations" was concluded in words so applicable to the present mode of considering this topic that it may perhaps form a sufficient excuse for reproducing them here.

"If the journalists speak the public sentiments, there seems an admirable confusion as to remedial measures. Schemes of gradation have been advocated, from the little, miserable, peddling recommendation of not letting the *present* Home Secretary do the business, to that of preventing clandestine and secret opening by *any one*. The utter, total, unconditional abolition of letter-burglary, open or secret, has not, that I am aware of, been once advocated Are we to be legally subject to this enormity—sometimes - by same functionaries—and under some circumstances ? Yes; seems the general, if not the universal, answer of the press. Is this the right answer ? or is the general, almost universal press incapable of judging rightly as to principle ?

"Do their petty, sectional, localized associations cast up obstacles insuperable for throwing off party trammels on great questions affecting universal freedom ?

"I invite attention to this subject, and appeal to the equalitarian publicist to aid in the enquiry."

A reply has been at length afforded by an intelligent writer in the last number of the *Westminster Review*, in an article entitled "Ethics of Politicians*," and he introduces the subject in the following emphatic words:—"We feel it incumbent upon us to denounce, in the strongest language we can command, a principle of administration, which, if carried out, would be found subversive of all the moral obligations of society ; and yet a principle now openly advocated, not merely by political opponents, but in some instances by men with whom we have been accustomed to act, and a class of politicians standing well in the world's regard for public character and private worth.

"We have long considered the state of our academical and university education to be the cause of half the errors committed in legislation ; but of all the evils to be traced to this fruitful source, none are greater than the moral canker they occasion. The ethics of Archdeacon Paley and Professor Sewel,— political expediency on the one hand, and blind submission to authority on the other,— the transformations of Ovid and the history of Punic Wars, leave no place for the decalogue, or any sound interpretation of its meaning ; and the result in after life, when our high-born university graduates appear at the council board, is, as the world has seen with astonishment, a formal recognition of PETTY LARCENY as a fundamental maxim of state policy."

* Reprinted by Mr. Watson in a four penny pamphlet, under the title of "Letter opening at the Post Office," with the addition of "An account of the Brothers Bandiera, by Mazzini."

Passing over "the decalogue," knowing that by it the writer *means* the first principles of morality—college morality, whether of the Paley or the Sewel order, whether based on the despotism of authority, or the meanness of expediency, whether productive of an obstinate orthodox Inglis, or a wily temporising Peel, can directly influence but few politicians, and indirectly no very extensive circle. What then shall we say of those who have never come within the sphere of such influences ? How shall we account for the prevailing absence of a fixed and inflexible opposition on the part, at least of no official politicians, and the majority of journalists to official letter burglary ? The *Westminster Review*, after quoting from the Commons' Committee Report the names of a long series of successive cabinet ministers, down to Graham and Aberdeen, implicated in letter-opening practices, considers that "the only apology for them must be sought in the tendency of the mind, especially when trained as we have described, to confound principle with precedent, moral law with legal custom. We doubt whether there has been any Secretary of State, or Lord-Lieutenant of Ireland, who, if he had not found on coming into office the custom of prying into letters sanctioned by long usage as a part of the ordinary routine of office business, but, instead, had been asked for the first time to violate the sanctity of a seal, would not have exclaimed in effect, and perhaps in the words of Haman, ' Is thy servant a dog, that he should do this thing ?' " The " especially when trained as we have described " will of course only apply to college men, or those under university influences—the custom " sanctioned by usage "—the confounding of " principle with precedent, moral law with legal custom" may be set down as far more potent and widely actuating motives.

May we not add, as the most extensive cause of the false reasoning of parliamentary men, and the absence, on the part of the public, of one loud, indignant, and universal remonstrance against this deep political criminality, that unfounded and fatal separation, propounded or tacitly affirmed, between public and private morality, and the facility thus afforded by this false basis for the deceptions and delusions of designing rulers and quack politicians.

Let us help to record the estimate of the political course already described, by one who has not learnt to make these artificial distinctions— who emphatically expresses his disgust that conduct should be held becoming and right in governments, " which if practised between private gentlemen, or between a common clerk and his employers, would be punished with a horse-pond or the treadmill." This is the Reviewer's bold out-spoken language.

" We are fully aware that those who prepared it [the report], and those who signed it, so bewildered themselves by their own sophistries, that they did not, in fact, well know what they were about; but we feel not the less necessity of stripping the principle advocated of all disguise, and we would present it to the reader in its naked hideousness.

———— ' A monster of such frightful mien,
As to be hated needs but to be seen.'

" Here, then, is the moral creed of English statesmen in the 19th century; or more correctly speaking, a portion of that craft of government which sets itself above all laws, human and divine.

" 1. THEFT is permissible, when information important to the public interest can only be obtained by STEALING it from a letter.

" 2. LYING is permissible to conceal theft; in the tacit form of resealing a letter, so that the fact of its having been opened may never be detected.

" 3. FORGERY is permissible for the same object; in the form of counterfeiting seals and imitating Post office stamps.

" 4. TREACHERY is permissible in ' cases of emergency.' The servant may betray his master for the ' public good;' the confidential agent may act as a secret spy. The bearer of a written communication, compromising, perhaps, the lives and fortunes of individuals, may carry it direct to their bitterest enemies, and be honourably commended for his breach of trust.

" 5. ROGUE-MAKING is also permissible; for the arts of knavery are somewhat distasteful to honest men, and forgery, in particular, is a SKILLED profession, which cannot be thoroughly acquired without many opportunities of practice.

" 6. TYRANNOUS INJUSTICE is permissible: in the form of secret accusations, and secret tribunals for trying a man in the dark, upon the evidence of STOLEN documents, of which the purport may be wholly misunderstood.

" In using the word PERMISSIBLE, we have put the case less forcibly than we should have done, to place it upon its true merits. The business of a public office, like that of the Secretary of State, does not consist in the exercise of optional privileges. Sir James Graham, or Lord Aberdeen, when they opened Mazzini's letters, did so, not, of course, from motives of idle curiosity, but from a sentiment of duty. Observe, then, where our moral legislators are leading us, It is the DUTY, say they, of a minister, in certain " cases of emergency," affecting " important public interests," TO STEAL, TO LIE, TO COMMIT FORGERY, TREACHERY, and TYRANNOUS INJUSTICE; and to keep in constant training, a staff of knaves fit for similar acts of public servic, when not convenient to perform them personally.

Startling as this mode of putting the case is—hideous as is this picture of the conduct of government functionaries, there is yet another aspect presented by the reviewer, perhaps still more revolting because carrying corruption into wider and hitherto uncontaminated channels. The Melbourne, Russell, Mulgrave of one administration, or the Peel, Aberdeen, Graham of another may concoct, among themselves, all sorts of diableries, and bad enough is it for a nation to be over-ridden by so unscrupulous a set of men, but when in addition to these snug iniquities, they become, from the moment of their installation in office, the source whence continually flows a stream of moral pollution, how great a self-condemnation is it to a country that should be compelled to acknowledge the existence of such things. How fearfully demonstrable is this melancholy truth, the following passages on the Commons' Letter-opening Committee will fully bear out.

" If letters from abroad were habitually opened at the Foreign office in 1782, as the committee admit; if the same clerks or their successors, have had from that period to the present the same class of letters, day by day, laid upon their desks, with a power of inspection, as the Lords' committee tell us, we take upon ourselves boldly to assert that foreign letters have been habitually opened up to June 1844; opened, not perhaps, by ministers, or with their cognizance, but opened, at all events, by other persons than the parties to whom the letters were addressed.

" The extent to which the practice of opening letters has been carried, depends, not upon the number of warrants issued, but the *modus operandi* of their execution. The public want to know what securities were taken that the ingenious men employed to counterfeit seals should never transact a *little private business on their own account*—whether warrants have not in practice been regarded as mere forms (the public knowing nothing of their existence), and so sometimes filled up before, sometimes after, the occasion for their use, and sometimes omitted altogether; as commonly happens in the case of all other matters of mere office routine?

The committee tell us, that upon an average the letters of one person per month, or twelve persons per year, are opened and resealed at the Post office. Of how many more is that the true indication? We have heard it said, and not lightly, but by well-informed persons, that within the memory of many now living, the contents of any letter passing through the Post office *might be obtained for a consideration*, by a person interested in the matter, and making a judicious application to the proper parties. We can readily believe it: for in complete contradiction to the present report Colonel Maberly, in his examination a few months back before the Post office committee, has described this department of Government as thoroughly demoralized. He says, 'there has been enormous plunder and robbery' (1163); nay, that 'the plunder is terrific' (1176), and that 'a letter posted with money in it might as well be thrown down in the street as put into the Post office' (1178) These are strong expressions from a Secretary of the Post office, and it is quite clear that Colonel Maberly never thought of their *possible application to the Home Secretary* when he made use of them. The subordinates of the Post office thus harshly described have done nothing more than *imitate the conduct of their chiefs*. The plundering of letters by the state from motives of expediency was a state secret to the public, but not to Post office officials: when Lord Aberdeen determined to steal the contents of Mazzini's letters, he was necessarily obliged to make *all the sorters and receivers* of St. Martin's-le-Grand a party to the theft.

"Let this fact be well weighed by the public. Letters directed to Mazzini did not present themselves of their own accord in Downing-street. They had to be *searched for by human hands*, and carefully selected from a pile of perhaps many thousands, and then to be sent about by *different messengers* from one office to another. Or, supposing the fact to have been that the Devonshire-street bag was sent to the inner office and searched by Colonel Maberly himself, the notoriety of the object for which the bag was required would still be the same. 'Why,' it would of course be asked, 'does Colonel Maberly always require, every day and every month for four months in succession, to count the letters contained in the Devonshire-street bag?' The general fact of the detention and opening of letters must therefore have been known to some hundreds of persons, including common letter-carriers; and what wonder is it that poor ignorant men should convert public expediency into private expediency, and keep their own counsel when abstracting a bank note, as safely as they had been taught to do the political felonies of their employers. Twelve months ago the newspapers were filled with the case of a Government clerk, who forged exchequer bills to the amount of several hundred thousand pounds. It is not at all an unlikely fact that the initiative step in his career of fraud was the instruction he possibly received in the art of counterfeiting seals for state purposes. Think of forgery in this form being *systematically taught in a Government department*, and of the probabilities of its stopping there; an apt pupil never becoming too expert for his own teacher!"

The italics are our own, intended to draw attention to the deeply important import of these penetrating and acute remarks. To the unsuspecting and confiding, the Post office exposures carried consternation or disgust, but they were put upon their guard. Those who esteemed this great public department, with its thousands of subordinates, in the administration of which every individual in the country is interested, as faithfully managed, have now learned this great secret, that our rulers are no more to be trusted than a gang of swindlers. We have been unsuspecting victims. If we now trust them with a confidential communication we care to have examined and revealed, we do it with our eyes open, and can only blame ourselves.

The pernicious effects of government training are sufficiently obvious in the well drilled and well flogged automata of the army, the semi-savageism of the navy, the brutality and anti-citizenship of the Revenue, Police, and Excise service, with the prying and spying incidental to numerous departments—these leading features of Government influence are notorious, but that there should be something so direfully infectious in Government conduct as to spread foul contamination throughout a department like that of the Post office, was incredible till the mist of our ignorance was dissipated by the light of these unexpected disclosures.

A vast scheme of demoralization is here exposed through the exertions of Mazzini, the Parliamentary Committees—despite of their gross neglect of duty and laxity of morals—the able and acute strictures of the Westminster Reviewer, still more cheaply and popularly disseminated through Mr. Watson's reprint—a vast scheme of iniquity is disclosed in a new quarter, and honest, intelligent men become dismayed at the communication of the lamentable fact that the Post office under Government management, has become *a Training School of Demoralization*, in which fraud is systematically taught, and promotion or appointment to the upper and most privileged classes is dependent on the superior ingenuity with which it is perpetrated. The slight memoir of Mazzini, which forms the conclusion of the paper, will be perused with the highest interest by all who sympathise with the democratic movement abroad as well as at home. The villainous machinations of governments who cut each others' throats—or rather their peoples'—openly, and conspire in secret—are for the first time popularly made known by indisputble facts The despicable part our own Government have played is exposed, and some of the machinery is exhibited by which, through diplomatic conspiracy, the nascent efforts of national struggles for liberty are suppressed.

The account of the political *murder* of the noble brothers of the family of *Bandiera*, and their devoted associates in their chivalric enterprise for the deliverance of Italy, which Mr. Watson obtained from Mazzini, and appended to his reprint, though stated as a simple recital, is of stirring interest. The appendix by Mazzini makes known how the Italian patriots were *entrapped and shot* by the Austrian government, and *through the instrumentality of the spies, letter breakers, and informers of the English government.*

Our pages have already been too much encroached upon by the length of this paper. further extract—though the best remains behind—would be inappropriate and disproportionate to the limits of the tract and of our columns. I am informed that a considerable number of copies still lie upon the publisher's shelves. How is this? If there were not one individual besides, interested in so great a theme, are there not *Movement* readers numerous enough to clear off an entire edition, without reckoning those of the *Northern Star*, *New Moral World*, *Communist Chronicle*, and *National Reformer*, as well as the new candidate for democratic favour, the *Plebian*? Our thousand subscribers alone could do so at a copy each. Well-timed, watchful attention to the public interests and advancement, by the issue of these damning revelations, should meet with corresponding encouragement. This class of undertakings, too bold, startling, and *uncertain in the production of profits* to be taken up by the mere trading publisher, should never be suffered by the true friends of progress to become losing speculations.

M. Q. R.

CORRESPONDENCE.

To the Editor of the Movement.

Sir,—I have carefully perused the articles respecting your visit to Harmony, which appeared in the *Movement* of the 2nd and 9th inst., and as I feel an interest in the establishment, and a desire that correct principles should be known, I feel induced to offer a few remarks upon the subject.

It has appeared to me that wrong notions respecting Harmony have lately been gaining ground—notions that are not consistent with the Social principles. No one will dispute that in society, as at present constituted, there are great and deplorable inequalities of condition as regards wealth. That these inequalities are injurious *to all*. It is likewise true that these inequalities do not exist to the same extent as regards *happiness*. Working people, taking them in the mass, live as long, are as healthy and as active as their more wealthy brethren. There are evils suffered by the poor from want, and the fear of it, but there are also evils peculiar to the rich, suffered by them from the artificial situation in which they are placed. Without being able to assert, as Mr. Owen has done, that the poor are happier than the very rich, still a trifling insight into the formation of character is sufficient to show that all grievously suffer from the present social system; hence the folly of having what is called a working man's community.

The grandest discovery of the present age is undoubtedly the knowledge that man forms not his own character—from that discovery we shall have to date the existence of a science, the results of which will be difficult to over estimate. It is Mr. Owen's practical knowledge of this new science which gives that peculiar value to him, his exertions, and writings, it being probably not possessed by any other man.

A community should be established, not for the purpose of appealing to one portion only of the people, the working class, but to all; for all classes suffer. Mr. Owen has been blamed for not commencing with cottages, but however prudent some might think it, we know it would have been the most expensive, because, before those superior, economical, and social arrangements could be made, necessary for the formation of a superior character, the superior buildings must have been erected and the cottages abandoned. It is not having in abundance the necessaries of life, such as food and clothing, nor is it having a community of the American stamp which will satisfy those that have reflected on the sublime principles discovered by Mr. Owen, or appealing to the feelings of any but those that are engaged in a struggle to live, even if such communities were practicable, which is very doubtful. At Harmony there are no superstitions to govern by as in the American societies. No, a community such as Socialists aspire after must not only be self-supporting, but must, in every respect, bend to the grand principle of creating as perfect and noble specimens of the man divine as human nature, knowledge, and institutions can be made to produce. I believe that reflection will show that the truest, the quickest, and the most selfish plan (in its rational sense) for we the working class to advocate, is the most perfect community that can be formed. We have had too much of this appealing to class, we are *all* in the vale of tears. 'Tis unity that is wanting, and we shall have the good and the intelligent from every class. What have the working classes ever achieved when disunited from the more influential? Nothing. After these years of agitation amongst them, how small the amount of money subscribed. A great part of the capital spent at Harmony has not come out of their pockets. Do I blame them for this? No, far from it, for I do not think there is one in twenty among them that can give, without debarring himself from some of the necessaries of life.

It is possible that those things in relation to Harmony you hold up as samples of the want of wisdom in Mr. Owen and the party who acted with him, others may think differently upon. I allude to its distance from the manufacturing districts, poorness of the soil, &c. The distance of New Lanark from any large town was a circumstance that made Mr. Owen value it, as although prejudicial in a commercial sense, was highly important in not interfering with his arrangements for the formation of a superior character for the population. Did you never hear of such a thing as a mob, urged on by priests, for the destruction of any thing prejudicial to their interests; look to the persecutions of the Mormonites, by the liberty-loving Americans. With respect to the land being poor, it should be recollected the rent is not one quarter what it would be if good, and situated in the heart of the manufacturing districts, and if successful, will be the greater monument of what can be effected by manure, labour, and skill.

There is nothing easier than to find fault and divide mankind. Is it not better to teach principles, and leave these personalities alone. The *Movement*, and the *Oracle* before it, have been continually finding fault with Mr. Owen, and sometimes even holding him up to ridicule—a man who conducted an establishment, where thousands had to be governed, for upwards of thirty years, and that he did this most successfully, we have Government documents to prove. Truly, when we look at these things we must have a clear head to see the wisdom that should get rid of him, and put a youth, in comparison, in his place, whom no one knows, and then think that the public will support him better than a man who, in his person and writings, has been before them for twenty years. I repeat, you may write up the present Executive, and decry the old party as often as you choose, but the reflecting part of our body must have some practical proof of the wisdom of the present leaders before their confidence will be gained. Trusting to your love of fair play to insert this. I remain, yours, &c., G. MORGAN.

[No! no! Mr. Morgan, it is not true practically, that the inequalities of wealth are injurious to all. I agree with Mr. Bronterre O'Brien, that the rich villain enjoys more happiness in one month than falls to the poor man's lot in his life time. I leave Mr. Morgan's comments on old Socialism—they have been urged and answered to satiety before. Mr. M. affects to censure fault-finding, but with what consistency does *he* "find fault" with the *Oracle* and *Movement?* Upon his own principle he has no right to "find fault" with my *Visit to Harmony.* He flagrantly contradicts himself by writing his present letter. It will be time enough to attend to Mr. M. when he is found observing his own precepts. With what grace does Mr. M. disparage Mr. Buxton in the same letter in which he takes credit to himself for condemning " personalities?" If Mr. M. really laments party bickerings, why does he impute base motives to me? I have written neither to raise one executive, nor to lower another, but to advance the general interests of Socialism by promoting a better practice, which cannot fail to arise from a manly, frank review of former, perhaps unavoidable mistakes. In these discussions I have found but too many persons, who, like Mr. Morgan, cannot conceive how any one can differ from them without being actuated by mere party feelings. Since Mr. M. appears as the unqualified defender of the old executive, by what right does he demand of me "fair play?" Let him first teach his own friends " fair play." If I had sent such an epistle of condemnation to the *New Moral World*, as this of Mr. M's to the *Movement*, would it be inserted ? Mr. M. knows better. If Mr. M. wishes to put an end to the criticisms I have written, I commend his own friends to his correction, and if he should happen to succeed with them, *I* shall have less occasion to comment upon them.—G. J. H.]

BRANCH A 1 REPORT.

At the last Sunday morning's meeting Mr. HOLYOAKE complained of the Report of the Branch in the *New Moral World*, which charged him with having written "letters of an evil tendency," with " maligning the characters of others"—with making " statements *undigested and not altogether founded upon truth*," " and derogatory to the *honesty* of individuals once in power." Mr. Holyoake denied having done any thing of the kind, and wondered, after the facts he had adduced on the previous sunday morning, that such a statement should be sent forth. He (Mr. H.) had refrained from giving any colouring to that discussion in the *Movement*, because that paper was too small to afford Mr. Jones an opportunity of presenting his own case, should he think that he was misrepresented, he (Mr. H.) should deem it decidedly unjust to make, or permit to be made, any reflection upon another, without being first prepared to allow the person reflected upon an equal chance of justifying himself. He (Mr. H.) regretted that Mr. Bailey, the reporter of the Branch, should have sat in judgment on their discussion without giving the facts on which his opinions were founded, and that too in a place—the *New Moral World*—where there was so little chance of a person being heard in his own defence. He hoped that the report would be retracted, or that the Branch would order their reporter to present a digest of the discussion, that the readers of the *New Moral World* might be acquainted with the facts on which the imputations published in the last report were founded. He (Mr. H.) did not care *what* they said when they had given a fair report of the debates on both sides. He was quite content to be judged by any who had the facts of the case before them. He therefore hoped, that as a matter of justice and fair dealing to him, as a member of the Branch, that they would order the retraction of the report, or send a digest of the facts on which it was founded. The Branch determined to do neither and the matter dropped.

ADVENTURES WITH THE HOME MISSION MEN.—Mrs. Martin has caught these gentry in the Old Low Church, Paisley. She hastened from a lecture of her own on the evening of December 4, to the Low Church, where Dr. Edgar and others were to speak, on behalf of the Irish Home Missions. On Mrs. Martin and her friends entering (for part of her audience were with her) the old Kirk seemed shocked from its propriety. The Rev. McNaughten, who was in the chair, immediately gave out announcements of other meetings, and pronounced a blessing on the meeting. Mrs. Martin directly rose, and begged to know whether Dr. Edgar had answered Luke Walsh's pamphlet, and proved the existence of the 26 schools, for whose pretended support the public had been " swindled." The chairman turned to Paul to help out his friends, and declared that they "never allowed women to speak in the churches." Thereupon up rose a gentleman, who exclaimed, " well then, I am a man, will ye hear me ?" The Rev. chairman answered, " the meeting is dismissed." Mr. Baker of Edinburgh, who had been desired by Mrs. Martin to watch the proceedings, here asked Dr. Edgar why he had not answered the charges brought against the Home Missions, by the Catholic priests.—" He had done so." Where was a copy to be obtained.—" Oh, anywhere, they had been distributed through the town." But *where*, said Mr. Baker, can I go and obtain one?—" He would give him one "—and THE pamphlet was given. But instead of the pamphlet pretended, it was the the wretched, miserable production which the Rev. Luke Walsh has lashed so unmercifully, in his pamphlet entitled the " Priest flogging the Minister." Oh Dr. Edgar!

MEETING OF THE FRIENDS OF THE MOVEMENT, at the rooms of the French and German associations —the Tavern, 20, Great Windmill Street, Haymarket.

On Friday evening, December 20, at 8 o'clock, the friends and supporters of the *Movement* will meet to receive a report of the balance sheet of the receipts and disbursements of the sums sent for its promotion and circulation, and the propriety and possibility of the *Movement* being enlarged to an octavo sheet of 16 pages will be considered and determined on.

THE LEGAL proceedings of the Anti-Persecution Union are in the hands of the proper parties, and are progressing as rapidly as the forms of law allow.

WILL BE PUBLISHED, ON CHRISTMAS DAY, (a Christmas box for Socialists) price 2d., twenty-four pages,

A VISIT TO HARMONY HALL,

(Reprinted from the *Movement*) with Emendations, a new and curious Vindicatory Chapter, and a Digest of the Suppressed Discussions at Branch A 1. Dedicated to the Socialists of England and Scotland. By G. J. H.

In thy halls
Let faction so convolve her serpent councils
That art may ne'er untwist them : let them in
Perplexed entanglement, unravelled rot,
And so be buried in forgetfulness.
Leagued friendship clip thy people in one bond
Of compact guard, for very lack of cunning
To plot a mischievous division—so farewell.
Pemberton's Podesta.

London: Hetherington, 40, Holywell Street, Strand.

WILL BE PUBLISHED, next week, price 2d., The Value of Biography in the Formation of *Individual* Character. Illustrated by the Life and Writings of Charles Reece Pemberton.—A Lecture delivered May 14, 1844, to Branch A 1 of the London Communists. By G. Jacob Holyoake.

Man is his own star—and the soul that can
Render an honest and a perfect man,
Commands all light, all influence and all fate,
Nothing to him comes early or too late.
Our acts our angels are and good or ill,
Our fatal shadows that walk by us still.
Old Epilogue.

London : J. Watson, Paul's Alley, Paternoster Row.

END OF THE VOLUME.—The first volume of the *Movement* will close with the present number. Next week the index will be issued, and the first number of the second volume will appear on New Year's Day. The present title and form will still be employed. As the *Movement* has been quoted in the French and German papers, and is known among our brethren on the other side the Atlantic, it seems advisable to retain the name of *Movement*. The *Atheon*, of which the prospectus will appear in No. 1, Vol. 2, is indicative of practical intention, and may serve to give new features to the struggle in which we have embarked. Copies of the prospectus are being circulated that other persons may be induced to take up the leading idea and carry it out.

GRAMMAR AND LOGIC CLASS.—This Class, originated by the Lambeth Branch, has determined on meeting every Sunday afternoon at the Social Institution, 5, Charlotte Street, Blackfriars Road—conductor, Mr. G. J. Holyoake. Terms—5s. per quarter. Early application must be made by those who intend joining, as the meetings are just commencing. Apply to Mr. Friend, Secretary of the Class, at the Institution, personally or by letter.

MR. SOUTHWELL.—This gentleman, whose intended visit to the manufacturing districts we last week noticed, has, we learn, confirmed his engagemen for three months only—not five, as we stated, and as was at first proposed.

MR. HOLYOAKE will lecture at the Social Institution, Leicester, during the month of January, commencing on the 5th. All letters for him after that date must be directed to Mr. Holyoake, 61, Conduit Street, Leicester.

THE MONTHLY PARTS will be ready for delivery next week, with index and title page complete.

A COMMITTEE meeting of the Anti-Persecution Union will be held on Monday, December 30, in the Coffee House, Rathbone Place, at half-past 8, P.M., to make arrangements for welcoming Mr. Paterson on his return to London, and hearing the report of the Hull proceedings.

NATIONAL HALL.—The managers of this place have, we are informed, agreed to promote the subscriptions of the Anti-Persecution Union, for carrying on legal proceedings against the Magistrates of Hull. They will hang up a Subscription List in their Hall.

TO CORRESPONDENTS.

A Hater of Priestcraft.—His suggestion is a good one, but it properly belongs to the Tract Society. The province of the Anti-Persecution Union is protection, and the Union cannot interfere in the propagandism of any other principle.

M. T.—No enclosure was found in his letter.

Received.—The "Alphabet of Materialism," article B, by C. S. "Cuvier and Gradation," by W. C.

J. P.—We shall do ourselves the honour of publishing thy letter.

LECTURES.

Dec. 22.—Branch A 1, John Street, Tottenham Court Road, Mr. Lloyd Jones,—On Christianity. At 7, P.M.

Dec. 22.—Hall of Science, City Road, Mr. Southwell. At 7, P.M.

Dec. 22.—Finsbury Institution, Goswell Road, Mr. Cooper,—On War agitating Protestant Missionary Christianity. At half-past 7, P.M. Discussion after,—Ought Missionaries to the South Seas to be encouraged ?

Dec. 22.— Investigation Hall, 29, Circus Street, Marylebone, Mr. Savage,—On Moloch. In the morning, at a quarter-past 11, Mr. Southwell,—On Witchcraft.

Dec. 22.— Social Institution, 5, Charlotte Street, Blackfriars Road, Mr. G. J. Holyoake,—The Scholar of Society.

Dec. 22. — Political Institute, Turnagain Lane, Skinner Street, Mr. Ryall,—The League of the Governors against the Governed. At 8, P.M.

THIS DAY, Mr. Miall, Editor of the *Nonconformist*, lectures at 7, in the public lecture room, Great Suffolk Street, Borough—subject,—State Establishments incompatible with the rights of Citizenship.

ERRATUM.—In paragraph 2, column 2, page 450, for "agregates as agregates," read *agregate as agregate.*

SUBSCRIPTIONS
TO THE ANTI-PERSECUTION UNION.

Mr. Coltman, piano-forte tuner, Leicester	0	4	6
A hater of priestcraft, Canterbury	0	0	11
Neal, Balls, per Mr. McCullough	0	1	0
Aliqus	0	10	0

PATERSON TESTIMONIAL.

Aliqus 1 0 0
G. J. H., *Sec.*

Printed and Published by G. J. HOLYOAKE,
40, Holywell-street, Strand.
Wednesday, December 18, 1844.

THE MOVEMENT
And Anti=Persecution Gazette.

"Maximise morals, minimise religion."—BENTHAM.

No. 55.   EDITED BY G. JACOB HOLYOAKE, AND M. Q. RYALL.   Price 1½d

ON THE COMMENCEMENT OF OUR SECOND VOLUME.

To our Readers.

It is not necessary to renew in this place, protestations with which we commenced our first Volume. It is for those who have broken promises to repeat them. The volume we have just concluded exonerates us, we trust, from this formality.

THE DESTRUCTION OF	THE SUBSTITUTION OF
RELIGION	MORALITY
AND	AND
CLASS RULE	REPUBLICANISM
AND	AND
PRIVATE PROPERTY.	COMMUNISM.

These, reader, including of course *freedom of expression* are the plain, undisguised objects of our little revolutionary Journal, which we have never concealed, nor diluted, nor mystified, and we want them now to be distinctly recognised.

Some persons have been so disconcerted by our proceedings as not to know what to say of us, and others so reckless that they have said anything. Their joint and general charge is, that we pull down everything but build up nothing. We suppose, in mercy, that these gentlemen are too agitated to speak the truth. But henious as the offence is painted, in the face of stigma and deprecation, we plead guilty to a good deal of pulling down. There is much, by far too much, of folly, cant and crime that demands extirpation. There are targets at which every man should shoot—moral Bastiles which should be forthwith and for ever felled to the ground. It would seem as if our critics regarded nature as a nervous, rickety child, who will, if startled, fall into fits, and must be bandaged and braced in order to keep it on its deformed and feeble legs. We love rather to regard humanity as full-grown, vigorous and brave—as an impatient captive struggling to be free, who only needs a few active friends to break his fetters, and who, when that service is done him, and a few infernal obstacles knooked out of his way, will bound on—onwards and for ever. It is only vanity that pretends to *so much* building up. The best services we can render to nature are negative—in removing impediments lies our *great* task—this task we boast has been and is still ours.

Our building, if in any true sense the term can be employed, consists in advising facilities for nature to exert itself in, rather than in imposing foolish conditions to bind it. We have no faith in creeds, but perhaps more confidence in humanity than those who have, and think that the morality, republicanism, and communism (this is their natural order) we would substitute or introduce, would spring spontaneously up, were piety (the doctrine of prostration), class government, and individual competition out of the way. Greater exemplification would be here out of place; we beg only the public patience, and in our future numbers we shall further develope and demonstrate these sentiments.

THE EDITORS.

ALPHABET OF MATERIALISM.

B.

"Bishop Berkeley's doctrine approaches Pantheism, while he denies there is any matter. His God is the substratum of all our sensations, in short, is a kind of intelligent matter. Nature with him is no cold dead thing, with an indolent divinity at repose in one corner—every being he meets is a manifestation of an ever active, an ever present Deity. So far he agrees with the Pantheists—but when he gives man a mind totally independent of Deity, making him quite a distinct being, and in fact the only being who is not God, he differs from the Pantheist, who, with his divinity would embody man also. He requires a step further into idealism, he has to seek an identity of himself with the things he perceives, and I am far from thinking Berkeley has gone too far, he finds on investigation that he has not gone far enough.

This account of Berkeley's speculative notions about "airy nothings," in the shape of *substratum of all our sensations*, is taken from No. 3, Vol. 2, of The Shepherd. Its author is Mr. Oxendorf, who we are assured by the very ingenious editor of that periodical[*] "is well known as a dramatic writer, is an excellent classical scholar, and intimately conversant with German philosophy." From a *pantheistic* transcendentalist of such reputation, we could hardly have expected such palpable nonsense to proceed as is worked up in the above quoted paragraph. Did any one attempt its reconcilement with sense and reason, in all probability his fate would be analogous to that of blessed Virgin-struck Peter D'Alva, who, after writing forty-seven volumes, folio, in explanation of "The Mysteries of the Holy Conception," was thought to have left the subject a greater mystery than he found it. With Mr. Oxendorf's exposition of idealism, as it was in Berkeley, I find no fault, for though brief, it is full, clear, and essentially accurate; but some opinions he has mixed up therein are indeed extraordinary.

According to him, Berkeley would have been a pattern philosopher had he done *more* than deny the existence of matter, and by taking the "step further" in the direction of idealism, have plunged (on paper) into the vortex of absolute nothingness.

According to him, Berkeley did infinitely less than deny the existence of matter, for he believed in a God, the subject or substratum of all our sensations, which subject or substratum *is a kind of intelligent matter*

According to him, Berkeley blundered radically in making man a being totally distinct from Deity, in fact the only being who is not God—and therein he so much *differs from the Pantheist, who, with his divinity would embody man also.*

The plain, *unavoidable* inference from all this verbiage seems to be that its author rejects Berkeley's idealism as not sufficiently ideal, and sees nothing repugnant to right reason in the notion of embodying man with his bodiless divinity. But stay, I am wrong, Mr. Oxendorf's God *has* a body, of a very substantial kind. In the article from whence his account of Berkeley's doctrine was drawn he says—

"To those who like a dead nature we leave the pleasure of imagining Deity, who has hung the firmament with a parcel of gewgaws, and has retired; but let us rather consider every star, every flower, every green tree to be animated by the great Soul of the world, then we shall contemplate the field of nature with feelings really sublime; and though the stars of heaven use neither speech nor language, voices shall be heard among them."

This is simple Pantheism. But how the *opinion* that Berkeley's idealism is not sufficiently ideal, can be reconciled with the belief that nature is real, and "all alive, O!" the most acute of Pantheists may safely be defied to tell. If there are such things as stars, flowers, and green trees, an omnipresent God is an impossibility. To say with Berkeley, *God is the substratum of all our sensations*, is just an idealistic way of denying God's existence, for we have *experience from fact* that the substratum of souls, or aggregate of sensations, is matter. It is idle to talk about the Pantheist, who, *with his divinity would embody man also*, for embodied divinity is exactly equivalent to no divinity at all—make God material and from Atheism there is no escape—make him "the great Soul of the world" and at once you warrant the conclusion that he no more exists than the *small* soul of man. Materialism teaches "that the mind (soul) does not contemplate forms as the eye sees them, that the mind is not apart from its perceptions, but that it *is the perceptions*— that a percipient being is a state of the percipient, and that mind is the collective unity of these various states."[*] If so, the soul of man is not an entity or existence, but the state of an entity or existence, and by parity of reasoning the soul of nature is not an entity or existence, but the state of all entities and all existencies. Let it be granted that individual mind is merely a state of the individual percipient, and then avoid who can the conclusion that universal mind is merely a state of the universal percipient Materialists call Matter, and Idealists call God.

To the reader who has *examined* the first letter of this Alphabet, it will doubtless

---

[*] See No. 4, Vol. 3, of "The Shepherd."

See page 30 of an elaborate paper on Spinoza's Life and Works—republished from the *Westminster Review*, No. lxxvii, for May, 1843.

occur, that Arthur Collier was Berkeley's forerunner in the wilderness of metaphysics; which is the truth, and I am no less astonished than Dugald Stewart declared himself to be, that a writer so learned, acute, and philosophical, should have been almost entirely neglected, while Berkeley, who published nothing new about the non-existence of the external world, is extravagantly lauded and generally thought the first to attempt the formal disproof of matter's existence. Not only were Collier and Berkeley " at one" as regards disbelief of an external world's reality, but also as regards the impracticability of reconciling the existence of an *anywhere* present matter with an *everywhere* present Deity. Both hated Materialism, and both agreed that by far the most *free and easy method* of compassing its destruction was, without remorse or dread, *to expel matter out of nature** Their object was the same, their reasonings similar, and their general doctrines concerning Matter, God, &c. differ about as considerably as six differs from half-a-dozen. They wrote well if not wisely, and it must be allowed that they improved upon the philosophy of Norris, and at the same time exhibited in glaring colours the deplorably miserable shifts to which Materialism's ablest antagonists are put. We find a Collier and a Berkeley *imaginers* of a Deity, for whom they could not otherwise *find room* than by the *annihilation* of matter. Strong-headed enough to perceive that Materialism fairly followed out terminates in Atheism, they struck at its fundamental assumption by boldly denying the reality of anything but God and ourselves,—*i. e. our own minds*. Matter, quoth they, exists nowhere but in the mind of him who perceives it. Vulgar people are apt to suppose the block against which *they* may be unfortunate enough to knock their heads, is a reality with which real *sconces* come in contact. But that is quite a mistake. Collier and Berkeley (if themselves may be credited) have demonstrated that the only reality is *mind*, and when we dash our heads against a post, or other hard substance, the conclusion should be *not* that we do actually come in contact with anything but that it is *the will of God* we should seem to do so. Now, philosophers have agreed that the actor must have one property in common with what is acted upon. If so, *nothing* can neither act nor be acted upon, for it is minus *all* properties, and therefore talk about pain or any effect whatever *caused by the action of God* is idle, unless God be something having properties in common with the something on which he is imagined to act. He merits to be accounted a *visionary* who pretends to solve the mysteries of causation by reference to a Universal Cause who being confessedly immaterial, must be without properties of any kind, and consequently be incapable of performing any operations whatever. And if with a view to avoid this difficulty such *visionary* persons make their *Soul of the world* consist of, viz.—a *highly attenuated kind of matter*, they do so at the price of another difficulty equally formidable. For attenuated matter is still matter, and to make a God of it would be mere heathenism, without its reasons, use or consistency. A material God, however thin or unsubstantial, must in common with every conceivable existence, be subject to what are popularly called *the laws of matter.* It may be as well also to remind these *visionary* people that pain being confessedly nothing but a series of sensations, it must have a substratum of living matter: in other terms, attributes, properties and effects, presuppose causes. Now we have experience from fact, that all causes are material. Any immaterial post would be no post at all, and as no head, real or imaginary, could come in contact with what does not exist, it follows either that *the will of God* is nothing at all, and therefore incapable of action, or it is matter, the existence of which we have seen Collier and Berkeley expressly deny. The last named writer may occasionlly have reasoned as though the substratum of all our sensations, or what he called God is *a kind of intelligent matter,* but he could not have intended that any such conclusion should be arrived at, seeing the utter and palpable contradiction involved in the hypothesis that matter is a phantom of the mind, and yet God, the only real existence, is nevertheless a mere mass of intelligent matter. No, no, the philosopher who like Berkeley labours to argue us out of belief in matter cannot fairly be supposed to believe in a material Deity, or a material anything.

But what are the consequences of demonstrating the non-existence of matter. One, and a highly important consequence, presents

---

* The great object of Berkeley, in publishing his system of Idealism, it may be proper to remark in passing, was to nip up by the root the scheme of Materialism. " Matter," he tells us himself, " being once expelled out of nature, drags after it many sceptical and impious notions." " Without it your Epicureans, Hobbists, and the like, have not even the shadow of a pretence, but become the most cheap and easy triumph in the world." Page 168 of Dugald Stewart's Dissertation, first prefixed to the Encyclopædia Brittanica.

itself in the shape of *conviction* that there never was such production from nothing as is recorded in the Bible. The interpreters of Genesis gravely assert that in the beginning God *created* the heavens and the earth; if, however, as Norris, Collier, Berkeley, and their followers contend, the earth and the heavens, with all that in them is, have no actual being but are *mere creatures of the mind*, which God *wills* that we should *fancy* exist, it follows that there is no heaven, no earth, in a word, no external world, and of consequence, that there never was either beginning or creation. In another letter of this alphabet, I will notice the attempt made by Collier, in a "Discourse on Genesis," to harmonise popular belief of an actual creation rather more than six thousand years ago with his own disbelief in the reality of an external world. It is curious but far from satisfactory, our church and chapel going Theists will assuredly deem it so, for independent of the difficulty they must find in believing matter exists nowhere but in mind, their entire education has tended to breed and root in them *orthodox opinions* concerning the production of man from *the dust of the ground*, and the dust of the ground from nothing. Preachers tell them the very day on which it happened. Chevreau was even more precise for in his "History of the World," he tells us that it was created the 6th of September, on a Friday, a little after four o'clock in the afternoon.*
C. S.

* Precisely 5844 years, and three hundred and sixty three days and 17 hours before this article went to press.—*Eds. of M.*

PROSPECTUS OF THE ATHEON.

EVEN those who do not care to insist on the practical truth of Atheism yet allow that its dissemination, as a mere matter of policy, is attended with beneficial results. It alarms bigotry, checks persecution, teaches religionists modesty, and establishes freedom of discussion in theology—just as republicanism has done it in politics, and communism in social science—not so much by asking for the liberty as by taking it—not so much by merely showing that extreme opinions ought to be expressed, as by expressing them. To further these useful objects, and better promote personal improvement, and public fraternity, the friends of Atheism in London propose to establish a small *Atheon*. As the Pantheon was the place of all the Gods, the *Atheon* will be the place of none. At first it will consist of one or a few convenient rooms, centrally situated, under the superintendence of Mr. Holyoake, serving the following purposes :—

FRATERNAL INTELLIGENCE. — Though loud have been the professions of universal love, with which Europe has rang during the last half century, little has been manifested by popular parties among themselves. Go to which section one may, it knows nothing of the doings of its neighbour if it happen to bear a different name and hold a different opinion. Thus the professions of brotherhood are belied, each party grows torpid within the frozen circle of its own selfish sympathies, and the great sentiment of fraternity is little more than a name. But in the *Atheon*, lists will be kept of the names and addresses of all progressive parties in London, political or social, whether English or Foreign—so that strangers coming to London from the provinces or foreign countries, may, on calling there, learn when and where they may find persons of congenial opinions. Also, a record will be kept of all places in Europe, America, and indeed in every accessible part of the globe where men of progress, atheistic or communistic, republican bands, or emigrant sections— meet. So that persons going to the Continent, or to any quarter of the globe, may learn the exact spot where to find the friends of humanity, by which means it is thought that friendly intercourse will be promoted— fraternity established, and good men in all climes become knit together. Skeleton maps will be prepared, marking the locality of the different societies in each country.

A LIST OF TRADES, Wants, and Professions of friendly persons, known by whatever name, or belonging to whatever party, will be made, so that co-operative intercourse may be as much as possible be promoted among co-labourers.

ATHEISTICAL SOCIETY.—The Atheon will be the place where this Society will date its communications, where its meetings will be held, and whence its declaration of principles will be issued. Here Theological Classes will be formed, in which young persons will be trained for the dissemination of Atheism by tongue and pen—to watch public meetings and the press—and otherwise establish the influence of the Society in a way that shall command respect and secure co-operation.

MOVEMENT OFFICE.—Another department will bear this name, that the *Movement* may have the advantage of a regular office for the transaction of its business and the necessary publicity resulting therefrom. It has seemed no unsuitable alliance of the

Movement paper with an Institute specially devoted to the interests of the Movement party and of Movement progress generally.

ANTI-PERSECUTION UNION.—It is proposed that a portion of the *Atheon* shall be at the disposal of the *Union* as a place in which its Committees can met, where its letters can be addressed — Subscriptions paid, and where every information respecting its proceedings shall be publicly known to be always obtainable.

THEOLOGICAL MUSEUM.—It has long been desired by the curious, that an assemblage should be made of diagrams and models, setting forth the various sensible shapes in which, from earliest time, the god idea has appeared. Such an exhibition will be attempted, as there is reason to think that it will be very instructive. Added to this will be the *Blasphemy relics*, collected during the various prosecutions. This will form a unique treat for the student of Christianity.

ATHEISTICAL LIBRARY.—It is thought that a Library, composed of the choicest Atheistical books extant, in all countries, would be of great value to lend out to known enquirers, that they may become acquainted with all the excellent things which have been given to the world on Atheism. Such a public collection of books, scarcely yet attempted, would be of great interest.

READING ROOM.—The large room will be open daily to members and their friends, and in addition to the Library, will be, as soon as possible, supplied with the best papers and magazines, English and foreign. Refreshments will be supplied, so that the best facilities will be afforded for making it a place of reading and study, appointment and pleasure.

Should this project not succeed, it will serve the cause of progress and be creditable to have attempted it. But as many of its features are general and not sectarian, and as the *Atheon* does not clash with the operations of any existing institution, it is expected that it will meet with some countenance. Many of the objects sought to be accomplished have long been felt to be eminently desirable, by persons who have no sympathy with Atheistical opinions.

Books presented to the Library will be considered the property of the donors, in case the establishment is given up.

The expenses of the *Atheon* will be met by donations, by yearly subscriptions of 10s. to members in London, and of 5s. annually to members in the country, who will be entitled to the free use of the Institute whenever in town, and may transfer their tickets to friends visiting town, who will enjoy the same advantages as the original holders. Subscriptions can be paid in advance, half-yearly or quarterly.

The *Atheon* will be open so soon as this prospectus has received the attention of friends, who will please to make their intentions *early* known, addressed to G. J. Holyoake, to the office of the *Movement*, 40, Holywell Street, Strand, London.

In order to secure immunity from annoyance it is intended to take an entire premises.

A Balance Sheet of the accounts of the *Atheon* will be presented annually in the *Movement*.

THE NEW MORAL WORLD.

THE following letter was handed personally by the writer to Mr. Fleming for insertion in the Rational Society's—I had nearly said *his*—paper. No promise could be given of its insertion, but an answer was to be made, either by post or the paper, but two reports from Branch A 1 have been admitted into the *New Moral World* since, without the appearance of my letter or any intimation of its fate—unless the current number should happen to bear it. If the New Moral World we seek to establish can no better bear discussion than its representative, we shall have to live in blankets where nothing can come between the wind and our susceptibility.

To the Editor of the New Moral World.

SIR,—In your Gazette of Dec. 13, 1844, Branch A 1, in a report which that branch has since adopted, charges me with having " maligned the character of others," with " retailing statements ill-digested (or undigested) not altogether founded on truth," and " derogating from the judgment and honesty of individuals once in power." This I believe is the substance of the imputation (for the *New Moral World* is not before me). Now, Sir, permit me to say, in the most quiet and passionless way in which pen and ink can say it, that this is not true.

It is due to the Branch to say that they give the imputation as opinion and not as the fact—but the difference is only in words, for their opinions are assumed to be founded on fact, unless I am at liberty to suppose that their charges have no foundation whatever.

The report speaks of discussions in which these opinions were arrived at, and the charges implied established. Nothing can be easier than for the persons who established such allegations against me in Branch A 1 to do so in the *New Moral World*. That they will attempt this, Mr. Editor, is all I ask.

It may be said—it has been said—that I made charges and must expect charges to be made against me in return.* But when I made charges I said *why* I made them, and I made them *where* they could be met, and I have a right to expect treatment equally fair. The readers of the *New Moral World* have heard judgment pronounced upon me. Let them also hear the witnesses against me and my reply. Attack me if you please, lay on and spare not—I ask no mercy, no forbearance, no charity—only evidence and a hearing, and if these cannot be granted, at least let me be heard to ask them.

Yours, respectfully,
G. J. H.

PETITIONS.

Sir,—Allow me to call your attention to the Companion to the Almanack for the year 1845. In the list of public petitions you may find,

"Petitions for alteration of Blasphemy Laws 8, Signatures 1639."

This is encouraging, but still far short of what it might and should be.   C.

Present to the Ham Commonists.—Those who, in their admiration of the fine arts have ever been led into Wild Street, Drury Lane, (not a very favourite resort of the fine arts) have seen hanging out for sale a painting of a pig—painted as pig was never painted before—dead, hung up, gambrelled, open, and the clotted blood all dripping through his nostrils. What vile Dutch fancy executed such an object on canvass we know not, but there it is, and we propose its purchase and presentation to our friends at Ham, whose more than Jewish horror of pork is notorious. To convert some epicure to their anti-pig creed, it will be only necessary to place this picture in some room to be called, *a la* Madame Tussaud, the "Chamber of [Swinish] Horrors," and introduce the Gentile to it—his conversion will be complete. Over the painting let there be suspended this distich, altered from Pope,

Pigs are monsters of such frightful mien
That to be hated need but to be seen,
But seen too oft, familiar with their face,
We first endure, then pity, then we *ate*!

* Note, *not attached to Mr. Fleming's letter.* The President of Branch A 1, when I applied to have the report supported by evidence, replied in open meeting, " You have kicked us and you must expect to be kicked again."

Prince Albert a Pig-feeder.—All the papers in giving particulars of the late Cattle Show, in Baker-street, have the following:—

"Pigs, Class XVI.—Pigs of any breed, about 13 and under 26 weeks old. His Royal Highness Prince Albert, of Windsor Castle, a pen of three 25 weeks and 4 days old Suffolk and Bedfordshire pigs, bred by his Royal Highness, and fed on milk, barley meal, and pea meal.—2nd prize, £5."

Probably this is the first honest penny our Prince has earned since he has been among us. Pig feeding is a rather uncourtly pursuit, but it may not be without its uses. The Lion and Unicorn of the royal arms will give place, we suppose, to the Lion and the Pig—but this may be endured if our right royal Prince will just turn his hand from fattening his pigs to fattening his subjects—many of which would be all the better for the process.

Disinterestedness of the French Republicans.—Lord Brougham in his "Sketches," says of these reformers, "As to corruption, it was attributable to few or none of them; indeed, the generally received phrase was, that they had all vices save this. The men who had, unwatched, the distribution of the whole revenues of France, distributed among themselves monthly the sum of 360 francs for all their expences; and when Robespierre was put to death, the whole property found in his possession was thirty-six francs of the last supply thus issued to him. Carnot, in like manner, never received a farthing of the public money for his official services; but in a different respect, his singular disinterestedness was truly striking; it was peculiar to himself, and it proved to a demonstration how entirely every selfish feeling was absorbed in his zeal for the public service. Though at the head of all military affairs, he never received his own promotion in the army more rapidly than the most friendless subaltern. He was only a lieutenant when he came into office. He was only a captain while directing the operations of fourteen armies, and bestowing all ranks, all commands, upon his brother officers. It was not till the latter part of his directorship that he became colonel, and he remained colonel only while king of the country."

Religious Persecution.— If experience has taught us anything, it is the absurdity of controlling men's notions of eternity by act of Parliament.—*Rev. Sidney Smith.*

THE THEOLOGY OF THE OLD TESTAMENT.

As Mirabeau in his Erotica took up the Jewish idea of decency, so Georg Lorenz Bauer took up and traced out in a separate work the Jewish idea of Deity. His object was, and his learned research in pursuing it has rendered his work famous among Biblical critics, " to examine the opinions of the Ancient Hebrews of the relation of God to man and of man to his [supposed] maker—their ideas of God and notions of his Providence: to trace the history of their religion, as it is collected from the Books of the sacred writers through each successive stage of its developement."

There is always something striking in a new case well put, or an old topic placed in a novel and clear point of sight, revealing some important feature scarcely before noticed or dimly seen. The Theology of the Bible is no new topic, but its selection from the multifarious matters with which it is blended, and presentation as a whole by Bauer, is certainly a new idea and an acceptable performance. In his progress through his work, he occasionally stumbled over such gross errors in the English authorised version that he found it necessary to have recourse to Eichorn's translation. One remarkable instance, worth citing here, is found in those well known words of Job,

" I know that my *Redeemer* liveth and that he shall stand at the *latter day* upon the earth; and though after my skin *worms destroy this body*, yet in my flesh shall I see God; whom I shall see for myself, and mine eyes shall behold, and not another; though my veins shall be consumed within me."

Thus runs the English Bible, but according to Eichorn, as translated by Bauer, these are the words of Job in the original,

" For I know that my *Vindicator* liveth, and at last he will stand forth on the field of combat. And although my skin and this body are corroded by diseases, still out of this body shall I see God. As I am I shall look upon him as my defender, and my eyes shall behold him but no longer as an opponent."

It has been triumphantly pretended that Job spoke of " Christ crucified," but we find in the actual words of Job, as reported in the original text, not one word about a *redeemer*, or a *latter* day, or *worms*, or the *destruction of his body*. Instead of foretelling to the resurrection, he simply referred to the time when he should be cured of the scurvy.

The conclusions of Bauer's work cannot be overrated in importance. These are what we desired to present. Bauer thus states them.

" Our investigation has led us to the following conclusions:

1. " The historical Books of the Old Testament contain the most crude and unworthy notions of God and of his Providence. The human representations of Deity given in Genesis are quite in character with the mode of thinking which prevailed in the infancy of mankind. Jehovah is portrayed as the national—God of the Hebrews throughout the historical writings.

2. " The notions concerning God contained in the Books of the Prophets, particularly in those which were written after the captivity, though strictly Judaical, are certainly less limited, and less remote from truth.

3. " The purest and most elevated conceptions of God are to be found in those Books which were composed by private individuals; who either disregarded the peculiar national ideas and prejudices of their countrymen, or had raised themselves above them. It was not so much by the teaching of their priests and prophets, as by the studies and contemplations of their other wise men, that the religious principle was cultivated and developed among Jewish people."

From which we learn that the most religious and most extolled notions of the Bible are the most crude and unworthy, peculiar to the ignorance of the early ages. That those sentiments, recorded after the writers had mixed with mankind generally, as after their captivity, were more enlarged and reasonable, and that the most rational ideas, the best part of the religion of the Old Testament, were derived not from inspired but private men, not from priests and prophets, but from profane persons. G. J. H.

Religious Intelligence.—A few miles on the other side of *Cheltenham* the traveller may observe a church erected upon an eminence; it is called Churchdown, but the name is corrupted by the natives to " Chosen." The poor inhabitants of a neighbouring village resorted to it on Sundays for divine worship, having no church of their own; but hearing constantly this verse used in the prayers, " And make their chosen people joyful," they took offence, and came no more, saying, " *They din't see why the Chosen people should always be thought of, and they never mentioned.*"

SONG OF THE SILESIAN WEAVERS.

[The following sensible song by Heine is a prosaic translation from the German, given in an interesting report of communism in that country, in the Dec. 13 *New Moral World.* Could not Eben Jones do something of the kind for the English weavers?]

Without a tear in their grim eyes,
They sit at the loom, the rage of despair in their faces;
" We have suffered and hunger'd long enough;
Old Germany, we are weaving a shroud for thee,
And weaving it with a triple curse.
"We are weaving, weaving!
" The first curse to the God, the blind and deaf god,
Upon whom we relied, as children on their father;
In whom we hoped and trusted withal,
He has mocked us, he has cheated us nevertheless.
"We are weaving, weaving!
" The second curse for the King of the rich,
Whom our distress could not soften nor touch;
The King, who extorts the last penny from us,
And sends his soldiers, to shoot us like dogs.
"We are weaving, weaving!
" A curse to the false fatherland,
That has nothing for us but distress and shame,
Where we suffered hunger and misery—
We are weaving thy shroud, Old Germany!
"We are weaving, weaving!

PAINE.

" The day returns—friends of mankind rejoice—
On which was born to evey craft a foe;
The man who, with his powerful pen and voice,
Chased superstition to the shades below,
The immortal PAINE; 'twas he who first began
The ' Age of Reason ' and the ' Rights of Man.' "
The Gauntlet.

JUST PUBLISHED, 28 pages, closely printed, price two-pence,

A VISIT TO HARMONY HALL!
(Reprinted from the *Movement*) with Emendations, and a new and curious Vindicatory Chapter, containing a Digest of the Suppressed Discussions at Branch A 1. Dedicated to the Socialists of England and Scotland. By G. J. H.
In thy halls
Let faction so convolve her serpent councils
That art may ne'er untwist them: let them in
Perplexed entanglement, unravelled rot,
And so be buried in forgetfulness.
Leagued friendship clip thy people in one bond
Of compact guard, for very lack of cunning
To plot a mischievous division—so farewell.
Pemberton's Podesta.
London: Hetherington, 40, Holywell Street, Strand.

THE TITLE PAGE, Preface, and Index to the first Vol. of the *Movement* are now ready in one number, price 1½d.

LATIN.—The Class for the study of this language, conducted by Mr. J. Benson Lear, meets at the Institution, 5, Charlotte Street, Blackfriars Road, every Sunday morning at 11 o'clock—Lessons 6d. each.

TEA PARTY TO MR. FLEMING.—On Sunday afternoon a tea party will be held in the Social Institution, John Street, Tottenham Court Road, in honour of Mr. Fleming, Editor of the *New Moral World*, previously to his departure for Harmony. Tea 9d. each—admission after tea as usual. Many old and distinguished friends of communism have been invited and are expected to attend.

WILL BE READY FOR DELIVERY ON SATURDAY, the first Vol. of the *Movement*, complete—with the original Prospectus, cloth lettered, 8s.

A LA JESUS.—" Chartism," with its assumed omnipotence of numbers; " Socialism," with its *brute Atheism, swinish lust*, and *kindred manifestations of political debauchery* are all variously festering into bitterness, and fermenting into rebellion the habits and dispositions of the lower classes.—*From the Rev. R. Montgomery's* " GOSPEL BEFORE THE AGE."

ATHEISM IN BRISTOL.— A Mr. Higgins, who lately figured in Worcester as a lecturer on " Psalmmody and Stuttering," has been lecturing on Atheism in this city. A person who asked permission to reply at the time was refused, being told that " controversy led to no good."

EDINBURGH.—Mrs. Martin has arrived in this city and has issued an excellent challenge to the most respectable of the clergy there.

MR. HOLYOAKE.—All communications for Mr. Holyoake intended to reach him up to January 26, must be addressed to 61, *Conduit Street, Leicester.*

ROBERT NICOL.—On Tuesday, January 7, the friends of poetry and progress will hold a tea party at the National Hall, to celebrate the birth day of Nicol. Several of Nicol's songs will be sung during the evening, by Mr. Collett and others.

LECTURES.

Jan. 5.—Hall of Science, City Road, Lecture at 7, P.M.
Jan. 5.—Investigation Hall, 29, Circus Street, Bryanstone Square, Mr. Cooper,—On the Life and Writings of Paine.
Jan. 5.—Finsbury Institution, Goswell Road, Mr. Simpkins,—On the Philosophy of Socialism. Discussion after,—Is Socialism likely to become universal?

TO CORRESPONDENTS.

RECEIVED.—Letter from Dr. Kalley. J. Mellor. The " Devil." " Christian Advocate." " Authority of Scripture," by the Unknown. An Acrostic to the *Movement*, by Z. P. The Argument of Mr. Gillespie in a new light, by J. Alexander.
Report of the Meeting of the Subscribers to the *Movement*, and Balance Sheet, next week.

SUBSCRIPTIONS
TO THE ANTI-PERSECUTION UNION.

Collector 19	0	2	0
S. B., Vauxhall	0	2	6
G. Begg, Hull, (Members' tickets)	0	2	6
W. B. B	1	0	0
Friends at Nottingham, per Mr. Woodhouse	0	2	6

PATERSON TESTIMONIAL.

W. J. B., fifth subscription	0	10	0
T. Bidwell	0	1	0

THE friends of the Anti-Persecution Union are informed that Members' tickets (6d. each) are now ready for the new quarter, and can be had of the Collectors and Secretary.
G. J. H., *Sec.*

Printed and Published by G. J. HOLYOAKE,
40, Holywell-street, Strand.
Wednesday, January 1, 1845.

THE MOVEMENT

And Anti=Persecution Gazette.

"Maximise morals, minimise religion."—BENTHAM.

No. 56.   EDITED BY G. JACOB HOLYOAKE, AND M. Q. RYALL.   Price 1½d

"VESTIGES OF THE NATURAL HISTORY OF CREATION."

Theory of Regular Gradation.

SOME short time since I asked the favour of your publishing a few remarks of mine upon the above subject; and I then thought I should not have occasion again to draw upon your kindness. Neither would I now occupy your very valuable space, but that I conceive the matter of general, in fact, of vital, importance to the cause of materialism.

Little did I think when Southwell and myself first debated the propriety of the Theory of Gradation forming one of the articles in the *Oracle*, that so brief a period would elapse before the main features of the hypothesis we endeavoured to establish would be admitted as correct by one of the first serials of the orthodox party. Little did either of us imagine that a work would be published supporting, nay advocating, our views, of which the editor of a popular and erudite journal should say that it contains "So many great results of knowledge and reflection, *that we cannot too earnestly recommend it to the attention of thoughtful men.*" It is as true as strange, that Fonblanque, the editor of the *Examiner*, so expresses himself in reference to a volume that has lately appeared, having for its object the developement of an opinion identical with Southwell's and mine, namely, that vegetable and animal forms *have* resulted from purely *natural* causes.

Every day proves the truth of Byron's remark, as respects the majority of mankind, that

Truth is strange—stranger than fiction.

The complication of organs in animal forms —the seeming adaptation of every part for the particular functions it has to perform, has ever been considered an unanswerable argument to the scepticism of the Atheist But this, the *only* remaining ground left to the theologian, is sliding from beneath his feet, and all that will shortly be left the class will be to cry *peccavi*, and seek by more honest means to gain their " daily bread."

One portion of the religious world (the Puseyites) are endeavouring to regain the ground which has been lost through the advancement of knowledge, and seek to re-establish the christian religion upon its old foundations—the Mosaic cosmogony and the fall of man. Whilst another portion (of whom Dr. Buckland, Dr. Pye Smith, Professor Sedgwick, etc., might be considered members) are labouring to dovetail in with revelation the facts of modern science. Neither class will permanently succeed.

Several years ago I contended that the religious world were not so clever as they thought themselves—that their wisest course would be to argue that the deity originally gave certain properties to matter, and that all natural productions were the result of those properties. This view of the subject is precisely that taken by the author of the work of which I have spoken, and, I am inclined to think, will be the transition state at which the religious world will presently arrive. Then will follow Pantheism, or god everything and everything god—from which by " an easy mutation," men will glide into atheism, or god nothing and nothing god.

I have so many extracts to make, that I shall be obliged to confine myself to very brief remarks, and only where absolutely necessary. And so I proceed. After the extract quoted the *Examiner* proceeds: " It is the first attempt that has been made to connect the natural sciences into a history of creation." This may be true as respects " a history of creation," but not so as respects the history of the phenomena which certain men *assume to have been created*. He thus continues, " An attempt which presupposes learning, extensive and various; but not the large and liberal wisdom, the profound philosophical suggestion, the lofty spirit of beneficence, and the exquisite grace of manner, which make up the charm of *this extraordinary book.*" This high opinion of the book is valuable, and I quote it on that account.

I have not yet seen the work, and am necessarily confined to the extracts given by the *Examiner*. The author is reported to say, " We advance from law to the cause of law, and ask, What is that ? Whence come all these beautiful regulations? *Here Science leaves us.*" True; but the author contends i is "only to conclude, from other grounds, that there is a First Cause to which all others are secondary and ministrative,"—and here we leave the author, it not being to my purpose to discuss this point with him now.

The *Examiner* states that the book " opens with a chapter on the arrangement of the bodies of space, and on the wonderful relationships that exist between the constituents of our system. The result of the reasoning in this chapter would seem to be, that the formation of bodies in space is *still and at present in progress.*" The course pursued in the Theory articles in the *Oracle.* The description of the book is still proceeded with : "The formation of the earth is described in its various eras. We have the era of the primary rocks, and the commencement of organic life. The era of the old red sandstone and of the secondary rocks. We have the formation of land and the *commencement of land plants*; the new red sandstone era, and the *commencement of land animals*; the oolite era, and *commencement of mammalia*; and we have the various incidents which belong to the cretacious, tertiary, and superficial formations. The Geological revelations of the earth's wondrous history are thus laid succinctly before us: their narrative closing suddenly as man is about to enter on the scene." Thus far the reviewer, and the author states that the earliest living creatures on earth were "the unpretending forms of various Zoophites and Polypes, together with a few single and double-valved shell-fish (mollusks), all of them creatures of the sea," and he thus continues : " The fact of the *economical* arrangements being an effect of natural law, is a *powerful argument* for the *organic arrangement being so likewise* – [so Southwell and myself thought, and hence the "Theory" articles]—*for how can we suppose* that the august being who brought all these countless worlds into form by the simple establishment of a natural principle flowing from his mind, *was to interfere personally and specifically on every occasion when a new shell-fish or reptile was to be ushered into existence on* ONE *of these worlds ?*" The author, it is evident, saw clearly the puerility, the childishness of the popular dogma, and has here succinctly stated that which has been urged over and over again by the atheist, to be answered only by anathemas and revilings. The editor of the *Examiner,* however, in reference to this last quotation, clinches the nail which the author has so well driven home; he says, " But it is not a matter of general likelihood *simply ;* science supplies facts which bring the assumption more nearly home to nature." We are going on swimmingly when such *dangerous* truths are so fearlessly announced in the organs of orthodoxy.

Further on the reviewer states that the author " believes the whole train of animated beings to be *a series of advances of the principle of development*"—(the italics are his own)—and says it was "a system foreshadowed by Plato," and he might have added, elaborated by Lamark, White, and others, but denounced as visionary and blasphemous by all true god believers, and condemned as unphilosophical and inconsistent with facts by Lyell and Sedgwick. The author has applied the " step by step " system of Professor Sedgwick to organic as well as inorganic phenomena, and has arrived at a totally opposite conclusion to the learned gentleman.

The author next proceeds to describe the stages of organic life. An insect, standing at the head of the articulated animals, is, in the larva state, a true annelid, or worm, the annelida being the lowest in the same class. The embryo of a crab resembles the perfect animal of the inferior order myriapoda, and passes through all the forms of transition which characterise all the immediate tribes of crustacea. The frog, for some time after its birth, is a fish with external gills, and other organs fitting it for an aquatic life, all of which are changed as it advances to maturity, and becomes a land animal. *Nor is man himself exempt from this law.* His first form is that which is permanent in the animalcule. His organization gradually passes through conditions generally rasembling *a fish, a reptile, a bird,* and the *lower mammalia,* before it attains its specific maturity. At one of the last stages of the fœtal career he exhibits an intermaxillary bone which is characteristic of the perfect ape ; this is suppressed, and he may then be said to take leave of the simial (apish) type, and becomes a true human creature. Even, as we shall see, the varieties of his race are represented in the progressive developement of an individual of the highest, before we see an adult Caucasian, the highest point yet attained in the animal scale "

There is nothing new in all this ; all that the author states has been known to physiologists for many years—but the conclusions which he has drawn from these facts are new to the world at large, and will startle many a pedant from his slumbers, and awaken many a youthful mind to a sense of the bigotry and folly attempted to be crammed into the minds of the rising generation. The editor of the *Examiner* in allusion to the foregoing, says, " of these *truths* of physiology, strange as they may seem, *there is no doubt.*"

The strangeness appears to me to consist in the possibility of men doubting *the truths* of physiology, geology or any other branch of science.

The author next proceeds to combat the objection that there has been no change in the organization of man since his first appearance upon the earth, and says: "But the historical era is, as we know, only a small portion of the entire age of our globe. *We do not know what may have happened during the ages which preceded its commencement, as we do not know what may happen in ages yet in the distant future.* * * Is our race *but the initial* of the grand crowning type? *Are there yet to be species superior to us in organization,* purer in feeling, more powerful in device and act, and who shall take a rule over us! *There is in this nothing improbable* on other grounds. The present race, rude and impulsive as it is, is perhaps the best adapted to the present state of things in the world; but the external world goes through slow and gradual changes, which may leave it in time a much serener field of existence. There may then be occasion for *a nobler type of humanity,* which shall complete the zoological circle on this planet, aad realise some of the dreams of the purest spirits of the present race."

The book of Genesis says that man was made in the image of his creator—the author of the "Vestiges of the Natural History of Creation," thinks it probable the time might arrive when that " image " will be improved upon. Query, for theologians— *Will the creator share in the improvement of the creature?* if he do not, the creature will be superior, in form at least, to his creator ; and if he does, how will he reconcile his consistency, after his positive assertion that he is " without change or shadow (even) of turning," and that, as he " was in the beginning, is now, and ever shall be?" Verily, philosophers are sad plagues to divinity !

The reviewer says, " The writer seems but little cognizant of the notions of the Greek philosophers, and it is the more strange to what an unconscious and large extent he corroborates many of their most striking views. *This idea of a higher race was held by Pythagoras,* who connected it with that view of more consummate worlds in space, inhabited in their turn by beings more perfect and beautiful than those of earth, *which we have,* in an earlier part of this notice, *seen to be in some sort sanctioned* by the results of astronomical inquiry."

Wonder produces wonder! The editor of the *Examiner,* not content with peopling the earth by natural causes, is also for doing the same thing for the innumerable other spheres which exist in the universe. And yet, there is not a word in " the book of books " to warrant such an hypothesis—on the contrary, it is stated in Genesis that the sun, moon and stars were created to give light to this earth. Neither is there aught in the New Testament to warrant the conclusion that the " Son of God " went from hence to other worlds to expiate the sins of their inhabitants. Perhaps in accordance with the view of Pythagoras, they are so good as not to require such a sacrifice. Should this be the case, I envy them their good fortune, for they will be spared a world of controversy and ill-feeling, besides much misery and bloodshed.

Having now finished my extracts, I will briefly conclude this article.

Is it because I have been so long used to investigate the validity of the god question by an examination of natural phenomena, that I attach so much importance to arguments drawn from such source ? Has the love of my hobby blinded me to the superior value of other modes of discussion ? Are the arguments for the non-existence of deity evolved from nature of no more value or service than a metaphysical reason to the same effect ? I think not. *I* think that a disproof of god, drawn from the only tangible evidences of his existence, must at all times be superior to any abstract and abstruse reasons. It will certainly most readily address itself to the uninformed mind—and the tutored intellect can amuse itself in finding other objections in the nature of things if it so pleases. In fact, it is universally admitted, that the proof of god from god's works is the only foundation upon which *reason* can rest. If this mode be unsatisfactory, there is no help but *faith.* Here the theist has the atheist at an advantage—for the atheist cannot have *faith* in the non-existence of a god or of anything else. If a reply to that effect would satisfy the theist, it would not satisfy the atheist. Faith is an affirmative belief and not a negative one.

So long as men could be led to believe a god existed, and that all they saw was the work of his hands, simply upon the assertion of other men supposed to possess superior knowledge upon the subject—so long were priests content to look no further for proof of the truth of their dogma. But, in after ages, when daring men arose, who, unable to reconcile the incongruities by which they were surrounded, and who did not hesitate to avow their doubts, and declare their difficulties—then were the priests driven to the alternative of showing a *reason* from nature and natural objects " for the *faith* which was within them." If the atheist can contend to advantage with the theist upon *this* ground, we are quite certain he can defeat him upon the ground of blind belief. Atheists, I am afraid, have given themselves too much to the consideration of the metaphysical points of the question in dispute, from the circumstance of this mode of argument depending upon certain arbitrary propositions and generally admitted principles, which would be affirmed or denied without reference to objects, and not requiring the slow and cautious process inseparable from an investigation of the subject through the medium of scientific discoveries. The metaphysical mode whilst the most easy is the least satisfactory —the scientific or natural mode though necessarily slow is commensurately sure. A man may evade a syllogism but he cannot be blind to a fact—he may cut a metaphysical puzzle, but science will cut him. Let me earnestly recommend to Atheists a consideration of the physical arguments in their favour.

The author of the " Vestiges " says the *Examiner*, " Doubts the *reception* of his labours, and intimates that, for reasons connected with them, his *name* will in all probability never be generally known.' Verily, the man is wise in his generation.

Through the kindness of my very respected friend W. J. B., I expect to have the book in a few days, when it is probable I shall return to the subject.
W. C.

DREW ON THE IMMATERIALITY OF THE SOUL.

A friend has desired a notice of Drew's " Essay on the Human Soul." Mr. Drew was a man strong in piety and coarse in prejudice, one who stigmatized an Atheist as " a solitary meteor, wandering through a century, exciting mixed emotions of astonishment and contempt." But this shall not prevent a fair estimate of his performance in these pages.

Mr. Drew was a Methodist preacher, and of sober abilities as a reasoner, which, had his powers been cultivated, would have raised him to distinction.

The " Essay " commences by assuming the existence of matter and spirit. On the existence of matter it refers to Beattie's Essay on Truth, and is perfectly satisfactory.

" That matter or body has a real, separate, independent existence ; that there is a real sun above us, a real air around us, and a real earth under our feet, has been the belief of all men who were not mad, ever since the creation. This is believed, not because it is or can be proved by argument, but because the constitution of our nature is such that we must believe it. It is absurd, nay, it is impossible, to believe the contrary. I could as easily believe that 1 do not exist, that two and two are equal to ten, that whatever is, is not ; as that I have neither hands, nor feet, nor head, nor clothes, nor house, nor country, nor acquaintance ; that the sun, moon, and stars, and ocean, and tempest, thunder and lightning, &c., have no existence but as ideas or thoughts in my mind, and independent of me and my faculties, do not exist at all, and could not exist if I were to be annihilated ; &c. I affirm, that it is not in the power, either of wit or of madness, to contrive any conceit more absurd, or more nonsensical, than this, That the material world has no existence but in my mind."

But of the separate existence of a spirit, nothing clear is anywhere advanced. An omission unpardonable in such a work, and fatal to its efficiency. Mr. Drew argues very well that spirit *may be*, " though too remote for the human intellect to grasp." But the writer we want is he who will enable intellect to grasp, as it ought to do, whatever intellect pretends to believe in. The edition of Drew's Essay, under consideration, has very candid notes by Mr. J. R. Miles, who frequently points out serious defects in Drew's reasoning. For instance, (p. 35) Mr. Miles tells us that " Mr. Drew contradicts what he has before admitted. He has assumed Will as one of the principal powers of the mind, and shortly after asserts it to have no certain existence." This is often true of the Essay in essential chains of reasoning. Sometimes Mr. Drew sins against all logic, and sometimes against himself. Mr. Miles warns the reader in one place, that Mr. Drew " evidently draws a conclusion, fixing a limitation to God's power, and wholly inconsistent with the principles that ought to characterise a Christian philosopher,"—and in another place we are told that Mr. Drew " has assumed the very point which he ought to have established by a vigorous train of demonstration." But these candid admissions, for which the commentator deserves credit, should not deter from the careful weighing of what Mr. Drew is supposed to have left sound, did we not find Mr. Drew so little acquainted with what has been advanced, with greater ability, on the immateriality of thought by others. Mr. Drew was a man of great but uneducated powers, and hence he was unfitted, as his work proves, to satisfy or much instruct mankind on such a topic. It would be folly to enter a general objection to natural ability only, but on some points mere force of untutored thought can do little for a theme already in a highly advanced stage of inquiry. Mr. Drew rose from a shoe-maker to be a metaphysical writer. This is to his honour, but little to our advantage, as he was but little acquainted with the labours of others in the same field of inquiry. Consequently, his work is little more than what might have been produced in the infancy of metaphysics, and at that period would have deserved, and were we at that period now, would receive from us elaborate criticism. G. J. H.

SOCIALISM ACCORDING TO BRANCH A 1.

THROUGHOUT the provinces, and in the Metropolis too, Branch A 1 has long been suspected of inflation—of pride, pretence, and unsociality. This I hoped, when I joined it, was a misunderstanding—but its recent doings justify a worse opinion.

Had any one told me, that in any Branch or class in the kingdom, belonging to the Social body, however obscure or ill-informed, an earnest friend would have been deprecated, rudely treated in a members' meeting, severe reflections on his character published, and the slightest chance of redress refused, I should have indignantly—as I have done a hundred times—repelled the charge. That it could have been done in Branch A 1, which is said to contain the élite of our body, and at the instigation of our most esteemed leaders, I should never have believed—no, nor even have endured the supposition. However, Socialists must now plead guilty to the disgrace—and unless there is spirit enough in the body to wipe away the stain as publicly as it has been inflicted, they will suffer in public opinion as they never suffered before—for they have done themselves an injury no opponent has hitherto been able to accomplish.

Not long since we had John Brindley running round the country, slandering Socialists, and Mr. Jones was kept to run after him to dare him to the proof of his assertions—for inasmuch as John shrank from that, did he fall in public opinion, and at last retired in contempt. But now we have Branch A 1 publishing in the *New Moral World* of December 13, imputations à la John Brindley, and when openly called on to substantiate their assertions—(like John Brindley) refusing an answer—Let them take care that they do not share his fate.

From lands' end to lands' end have arisen execrations of the *Times*, for its one sided and calumnious reports. Every struggling body has had to lament its partial statements. Instead of giving the speeches delivered at Chartist or Social meetings, its reporter gives his own conservative comments on the party. Precisely this same course has been pursued by the Branch A 1 reporter—the Branch sanctioning it by resolution, and the *New Moral World* admitting it without compunction, and indeed refusing to correct the wrong done. Truly, Socialists are becoming a liberal body! Some time ago (*New Moral World*, October 12, 1844,) Mr. Fleming said that the time was come when " it was imperative that unfavourable constructions should be promptly met." The conduct of the *New Moral World* respecting my Visit to Harmony, justly subjects it to " unfavourable constructions." The Editor injures the party he represents by lying still under them. He should " promptly" meet them—if he can. It is due to himself—to his cause, to fair play, and to us.

In the last *Movement* appeared a letter addressed to the *New Moral World*, demanding what one would expect honourable men would gladly afford—proof of their assertions. These are refused, and in the *New Moral World* of January 4, appears a resolution to the effect that my " Visit" is but " a reiteration of falsehoods before exposed, and a mis-report of late proceedings in Branch A 1." A vestry meeting would not exhibit a greater contempt of decency, justice, or public opinion, than Branch A 1 has done in this instance. My consolation is that this was done by a respectable Branch, or a fragment of one, and under the paternal form of government—that it is the moral exhibition of " prime minds," and not of the " inexperienced, the crude and vulgar."

The *New Moral World* speaks of the resolution being come to after " considerable discussion." The discussion lasted about a quarter of an hour. *Twenty-one* members voted for it, and some 200 belong to the Branch. Mr. Jones and Mr. Bailey, the reporter, are said to have drawn the resolution up. Hence there is reason to fear that it originated in personal pique rather than from a sense of public duty. Mr. Ivory, a member, says that from the smallness of the meeting, the hasty nature of the transaction, no notice of it being sent to me, although I had requested it—and from the fact that several of the members whom he questioned after their voting, confessed they had not read the "Vindicatory Chapter" which they had censured—he never beheld such a farce enacted before in Branch A 1. Though a few have done this, unless the members generally refuse to be thus involved, the disgrace will rest upon them all. We shall see how they will act.* When the resolution was being proposed, one gentleman, I am informed, Mr. Colin Campbell, put it to Mr. Jones whether such an exhibition on his part was not very unbecoming—but Mr. Jones had too much committed himself to retrace his steps, and unless he has a stronger sense of honour than he has lately exhibited, will blindly persist in his present course.

I am far from supposing that Branch A 1 are to agree that my "Visit" is correct. Nothing of the kind. They are quite justified in censuring it—if they deem it to merit censure, but as honourable, fair dealing men, they are bound to give to the public the ground of their condemnation when called upon. I have deserved better treatment than I have received at their hands.

Since they have deliberately published me as "reiterating falsehoods," I can no longer appear as hitherto, as the defender of Socialism in public—unless the body shall cancel the opinion of Branch A 1. In all circumstances I have been true to my duty as an accredited lecturer, to which office a former Congress appointed me. Because I was a Socialist chiefly was I imprisoned in Cheltenham—I was better treated as an Atheist than as a Socialist—but in Court, before Justice Erskine, I for two hours, to the prejudice of my liberty, defended the principles—though at that time the *New Moral World* raised no voice in my favour, but left me to my enemies. But now for the first time am I ashamed of being a Socialist. I shall still continue a member, and wait better times and the dominion of better principles before I can own, without blushing, that I am a Socialist.

The "highest authority" of the body, as I have proved in my "Vindicatory Chapter," have pronounced my statements on the whole correct. Perhaps on this account I stand exonerated, but it is due to me that this resolution be publicly cancelled. One triumphant fact deserves notice. No principle involved in my "Visit" has been attacked anywhere. Mr. Jones and others have only dealt in personalities, or questioned minor details. Do they think that that which they have temporarily obscured, they will be supposed to have answered?

We have heard of "factious people who wish to introduce division," but what are we to think of Branch A 1, who in opposition to their regularly constituted authorities, call my "Visit to Harmony" *falsehoods*, when those best able to judge bear testimony in its favour? The public will think that Branch A 1 are anxious to stifle by slander what they cannot answer by argument. It was not be expected that Mr. Jones would incite the body he professes to defend, thus to traduce itself. I believe that those excellent, but somewhat mistaken men, of whom I have spoken in my "Visit," will be far more pained by Branch A 1's defence of them than by my honest, fair, and open strictures.

It would not be worth my while to formally notice this matter, had I not always prided myself in the hitherto unspotted reputation of Communism, whose name reverberates through Europe as the moral synonime of equality, truth, and justice. This transaction teaches, trumpet tongued, how effeminately unsound are those sentiments of " charity and forbearance," so long given currency to from social rostrums. The philosophy wanted in this age is one that will teach us to bear, *not forbear*. Wherever there is wrong and rottenness, we should out upon it—cry out who may. All my published sentiments bear witness that I shall never shrink from the sternest censure when it comes in the name of sincerity and fair play. Publicly or privately I would we were never charitable—it is such aristocratic cant it makes me sick—but I would that to each other and to all the world we were openly, strictly, sternly just.

G. J. H.

IMPORTANT RESOLUTION
RESPECTING THE PATERSON WELCOME.

The Committee of the Anti-Persecution Union, who have superintended the collection of the Paterson Testimonial, have come to the resolution of restricting the issue of tickets to the tea party at the "Paterson Welcome" to such persons as have bought his "Trials," or subscribed or assisted in some way or other the funds of the "Testimonial." Only to such persons will tickets be sold. We shall explain the reasons of this judicious step.

---

* I have since learned that before this can appear, Mr. Henry Hetherington will have given notice of a motion for rescinding the resolution under consideration.

MEETING OF THE SUBSCRIBERS OF THE "MOVEMENT."

Pursuant to our announcement, the Subscribers of the *Movement* met (December 20) in the rooms of the French and German Democratic Associations, Great Windmill Street, Haymarket, (kindly lent for the purpose) to receive the Annual Balance Sheet of receipts and expenditure.

Mr. Sully was called to the chair.

Mr. Holyoake being desired by the chairman to place the business before the friends assembled, said that the report to be presented by himself and his coadjutor Mr. Ryall, had not to be spoken—the labours of the year was its own report. It needed not to be read—he could hand it to them. He then laid on the table a complete volume of the *Movement*, with the extracts from the various English and Continental Journals into which its contents had found their way. Also all the tradesmen's bills, from first to last, duly *receipted*. He said the only item due would be found to be a small one to the Conductors. He then read the following—but at that time unaudited

FIRST ANNUAL BALANCE SHEET OF THE MOVEMENT.

RECEIPTS.	£	s.	d.	EXPENDITURE.	£	s.	d.
From Publisher	162	13	3	To Printers	141	14	5
R. R., yearly subscription	2	12	0	Editing 55 weeks	55	0	0
M. C. R., do. do.	2	12	0	Do. to 6 weeks enlarged Nos. extra	3	0	0
J.	2	0	0	Expences—Commencing, Circulars, Advertisements, Canvassing, etc., etc.	6	12	6
J., as per friend	5	0	0				
Mr. Hetherington, P. 1 & P. 2—£1 each	3	0	0	Library Subscription	0	15	6
W. J. B.	5	10	0	Prospectuses	2	0	0
Dr. E., Atheistical Society, and A. or Z.—£1 each	3	0	0	Posters	1	5	0
				Writing Paper	0	19	0
Anti-Persecution Union, for printing in 54 Gazettes	6	15	0	Small Bills	0	6	0
Mr. G. B. and Mr. Ironside—£2 each	4	0	0	Sundries—Newspapers, Postage of Letters, Reporting, etc.	15	9	11½
Mr. White	2	15	0	Disbursements, per direction of Mr. Ironside	1	0	0
Cosmopolite	2	2	0				
Mr. Gillespie, for *Movements* supplied	2	7	9				
Mr. Cooper	1	12	0				
Mr. M. A. Liddle	1	2	6				
Mr. H.	1	4	0				
Mr. Palmer	1	0	7½				
Mr. Brittain	0	18	4				
W. B. B.	0	18	0				
J. Powell	0	15	0				
W. D. Saul	0	12	6				
I. P., Mr. Lear, Thomas Powell, H., H. Uttley, Burnley, B. 2, A Friend, Coventry, Aliqus—10s. each	4	0	0				
Mr. Hindle, Ashton-Under-Lyne	1	2	6				
Mr. Wheelhouse	0	9	2				
J. W. Davis	0	7	6				
C. R. and G.—5s. each	0	10	0				
Messrs. Ivory, Plasto, Johnson, Spooner, Thompson—2s. 6d. each	0	12	6				
Mr. Sully	0	4	0				
Miscellanea	0	9	6				
	220	5	0½		228	2	4½
ASSETS.				LIABILITIES.			
Stock—Publisher's estimate, 45*l*. 8s. 5d—probably worth one fourth	10	0	0	Balance due to Conductors	7	17	4

Audited by us and found correct, December 24, 1844.

J. Benson Lear,
William Cooper, } Auditors.

———o-o———

After the reading of this statement, it was on the motions of Messrs. Dalrymple and Brittain ordered to be received, and at the request of Messrs. Holyoake and Ryall two auditors, Messrs. W. Cooper and J. B. Lear, were appointed by the meeting.

On the motion of Messrs. Bidwell and Cooper, it was then resolved unanimously—

"That in the opinion of this Meeting the subscriptions to the *Movement* should be continued as heretofore, and that for the forthcoming year they shall be devoted as far as possible, after the disbursement of the usual expences, to advertising the *Movement* in its present form—awaiting a more extensive acquaintance with it on the part of the public, before it shall be enlarged to a whole sheet at 2d."

The Meeting then adjourned until February.

JUST PUBLISHED, 28 pages, closely printed, price two-pence,
A VISIT TO HARMONY HALL!
(Reprinted from the *Movement*) with Emendations, and a new and curious Vindicatory Chapter, containing a Digest of the Suppressed Discussions at Branch A 1. Dedicated to the Socialists of England and Scotland. By G. J. H.

In thy halls
Let faction so convolve her serpent councils
That art may ne'er untwist them: let them in
Perplexed entanglement, unravelled rot,
And so be buried in forgetfulness.
Leagued friendship clip thy people in one bond
Of compact guard, for very lack of cunning
To plot a mischievous division—so farewell.
Pemberton's Podesta.

Opinion of the Press.
"Reiterated falsehoods."—*New Moral World.*
London: Hetherington, 40, Holywell Street, Strand.

Just Published, price Twopence,
THE VALUE OF BIOGRAPHY IN THE FORMATION OF INDIVIDUAL CHARACTER,
Illustrated by the Life and Writings of Charles Reece Pemberton. A Lecture delivered, May 12, 1844, to Branch A 1 of the London Communists. By G. JACOB HOLYOAKE.

Man is his own star, and the soul that can
Render an honest and a perfect man,
Commands all light, all influence, all fate,
Nothing to him falls early or too late.
Our acts our angels are, or good or ill,
Our fatal shadows that walk by us still.
Old Epilogue.

London: J. Watson, 5, Paul's Alley, Paternoster Row; Hetherington, 40, Holywell-street—Cleave, 1, Shoe Lane, Fleet-Street—J. Sharp, 47, Tabernacle Walk, Finsbury—Heywood, Manchester — Guest, Bull-street; and Taylor, Smallbrook-street, Birmingham—Stewart, Whitechapel, Liverpool—Paton and Love, Nelson-street, Glasgow—Robinson, Edinburgh—J. Brown, 4, Colliergate, York; and all Booksellers. 1845.

BRANCH A 1.—On Sunday morning last the "Visit" was again the subject of animadversion. No *reiterating* resolution was passed — but Mr. Hetherington gave notice that on next Sunday morning he would move the following resolution—and particularly urged the necessity of a full attendance on the occasion.
—"That the Resolution, passed at a thinly attended meeting of the members of Branch A 1, on Sunday morning, December 29, 1844, in reference to a pamphlet entitled "A Visit to Harmony Hall," be rescinded; inasmuch as the Resolution is founded on erroneous assumptions, being directly contrary to the facts elicited during the investigation into the truth of the statements contained in Mr. Holyoake's Visit to Harmony Hall; and that to pass a Resolution censuring the author, in his absence, without notice to the members, after refusing to publish the facts, or an abstract of the official documents which he laid before the Branch in justification of his published statements, is unjust in principle, unsound in policy, and has a tendency to lower the character of the Rational Society in public estimation."

PHRENOLOGICAL OBSERVATION. — A chap on passing an intelligence office recently, accosted the keeper thus: "Old Gripewell, I intend to start an opposition to your concern; I am going to set up a non-intelligence office." "If you do," was the reply, "you can save the expense of a sign, by thrusting your head out at the window."

In the Press, cloth lettered.—Price 1s. 6d.
THE THIRD EDITION OF
PRACTICAL GRAMMAR!
Or Composition divested of difficulties. With select examples from the writings of elegant authors. Containing all that is necessary for ordinary purposes and no more; and intended for the use of those who have little time to study. BY G. JACOB HOLYOAKE.

No department of knowledge is like grammar. A person may conceal his ignorance of any other art—but every time he speaks, he publishes his ignorance of this. There can be no greater imputation on the intelligence of any man, than that he should talk from the cradle to the tomb, and never talk well.—G. J. H.

"Mr. Holyoake, when engaged as a teacher in our late Mechanics' Institution, gave ample testimony of the superiority of his mind. We are glad that he has turned his talent to the production of a grammar to supply the deficiency of authors on the English tongue, in which he has been very successful. His style is very pithy and instructive, and shows he understands his subject. It is not crammed with technicalities and unmeaning phraseology, like most other works of the kind, that perplex the reader until he throws them aside in despair; but written in such a pleasing manner that it engages and rivets the attention of the learner, convincing him that success is certain if he will but persevere. He gives no rule without a reason, and allows full scope for the exercise of thought. Although some persons may not be induced to adopt the same course, yet they cannot peruse it without profit. It is an excellent auxiliary for those who have neglected this part of their studies, and should be in their possession."—*Birmingham Pilot.*

London: J. Watson, 5, Paul's Alley, Paternoster-row.

J. Griffin Hornblower, *for Movement* 0 5 0

LECTURES.
This evening (Wednesday) at the Hall of Commerce, Threadneedle Street—a Lecture by a member of the Peace Society, explanatory of the views of that association—admission free. Another will also be delivered at the same time and place next week.
Jan. 12.—Branch A 1, John Street, Tottenham Court Road,—A Lecture. At 7, P.M.
Jan. 12.—Finsbury Institution, Goswell Road, Mr. Shorter,—On the British Drama. Discussion after,—Has the Drama exercised a moral influence.

TO CORRESPONDENTS.
The "Devil" and the "Patriot" will receive early attention.
H. B.—We know all about the resolution. We could not have said that the Branch "refused" what was asked, unless they had *refused by resolution.*
RECEIVED.—Letters from Mr. Paterson, and Mr. Anderson, which will appear in next number.

PATERSON TESTIMONIAL.
W. J. B., sixth subscription.............. 0 15 0
Mr. Ivory................................. 0 2 6
Mrs. C. G. Holyoake Hornblower.......... 0 2 6
G. J. H., Sec.

Printed and Published by G. J. HOLYOAKE, 40, Holywell-street, Strand.
Wednesday, January 8, 1845.

THE MOVEMENT
And Anti-Persecution Gazette.

"Maximise morals, minimise religion."—BENTHAM.

No. 57. EDITED BY G. JACOB HOLYOAKE, AND M. Q. RYALL. Price 1½d

ALPHABET OF MATERIALISM.

C.

CICERO confessed he could far easier tell what he did not than what he did think of Deity. Modern expounders of divinity might, without wounding truth, make the very same confession; for, to a certainty, they are unable to furnish one jot more positive information concerning *their* God than the great Roman orator could about *his*. That God is they marvel any one should doubt, but what God is they are puzzled to teach, and deem it little short of impious to inquire. Nevertheless, the question, What is God? may pertinently be put to them who so oracularly declare the reality of God, as every body knows our divines are in the habit of doing. And they should be prepared to answer it by something better than positive information of a purely negative kind. But, assuredly they are not, nay, divines in general, so far from pretending to knowledge of God are forward to admit that of him they comprehend nothing except that he is incomprehensible. Their writings teem with evidence that they have no knowledge whatever of the Deity they profess to adore. When, for example, sceptical Robert Dale Owen, in his controversy with orthodox Origen Bacheler, quoted Arnobius, who in the celebrated Work " Adversus Gentes," addresses God as unseen and incomprehensible, Bacheler says that the quotation made from him (Arnobius) merely shows he considered God incomprehensible; and who does not so consider him? No one in his senses, is the answer suggested by the question whose author evidently put as evidence, pointed and palpable, that in his opinion utter and universal ignorance of Deity is a *fact* none save madmen would attempt to dispute. Admitting the soundness of that opinion, I naturally infer, that what our theologians call Revelation reveals absolutely nothing relative to the nature of its supposed unnatural author. Bacheler, the christian, Bible in hand, is no more knowing, or rather, no more ignorant on that point than Cicero, the heathen. So far, indeed, from teaching what God is, " Holy Scripture " expressly announces that to search for him is vain, for he *is past finding out*. To be sure, the suppposed creator, judge, preserver and governor of all things, is there spoken of as a *spirit*, but only fanatics are satisfied to explain one word which means nothing by another which means no more.* There are, in all modern languages, many words signifying merely the absence of signification, and spirit is one of them. I say, emphatically, modern languages, because we are told by Toland, in his " Letters to Serena," that " the most ancient Greek philosophers did not dream of any principle or actuating spirit in the universe itself, no more than in any of the parts thereof: but explained all the phenomena of nature by matter and local motion, levity and gravity, or the like, and rejected all that the poets said of god, dœmons, souls, ghosts, heaven, hell, visions, prophecies, and miracles, &c., as fables invented at pleasure, and fictions to divert their readers." All which, if true, may seem to warrant the inference that very *ancient* languages were not disfigured and disgraced, as every modern one is, by meaningless but most mischievous words, which, without doubt, were invented by traffickers in speculation for the twofold purpose of concealing their own ignorance of causes, and at the same time, appearing to explain them. In no other rational way can we account for the pollution of language by such words as god, devil, and angel, heaven, hell, &c., which stand for nothing but something each individual who hears them may imagine they stand for. Well has it been observed, that to shake the existence

---

* See page 120 of " Discussion on the Existence of God," and page 4, of ditto on the " Authenticity of the Bible," between Mr. Robert Dale Owen and Mr. Origen Bacheler.

* It explains nothing to say God is a spirit. Spirituality is an absurdity. To speak in the language of modern theology, a spirit is nothing more than the absence of an idea, which idea is yet without a model.—*Good Sense*.

of deity, we need only ask a theologian to speak of him. The same observation holds good with regard to spirit, which every body knows is only another " formidable name " for the same " nonentity." It may, however, be proper to observe, that Dr. Priestly took much, and I think successful, pains to prove that the word spirit is an obvious derivation from the Latin *spiritus*, (breath) was originally and for many ages, understood to mean *an extremely subtle kind of matter*. But since the advent of Christianity, human conceptions have spiritualised at such a rate that though God is still believed to be a spirit who likes to be worshipped " in spirit and in truth," a spirit is believed to be immaterial, in other words, not anything. The theology of our day revolts at the idea of a matter-god system, which, say they, is only atheism in disguise : and it must be confessed, not without good reason. For if deity is matter, he must, in common with every other material existence, be the subject of accidents. One property of matter is solidity, a property which no existence can be conceived without. Take away *attraction*, said Priestly,* which is a *power*, *solidity* itself vanishes. Which is tantamount to saying that unsolid matter is no matter at all. If so, a material deity must be solid; and as solidity involves the idea of length, breadth and thickness, it is plain that nothing can be more *impious* than belief in its reality. Our priests are evidently of that opinion. Something less than two centuries and a half ago, their worthy prototypes destroyed Giordano Bruno, for daring to call God *the monad of monads*, and it is by no means unlikely, notwithstanding their new-born zeal on the side of humanity, they would not scruple, if they had absolute power, to launch into eternity any one so far heretical as to assert that God is but *the atom of atoms*. But though so furiously bent on maintaining the opinion that God is a spirit, all they know about spirit is negative, *i. e.* no knowledge at all. God is a spirit and a spirit is not matter, *voilà* their whole stock of information respecting that " most sublime of subjects." I have often laughed at Sir Thomas Browne's *information* respecting those brilliant omens called letters in the candles, which he tells us †" only indicate a moist and pluvious air, which hinders the avotation of the light and favillous particles, whereupon they settle upon the mast." But far more provocative of laughter is the information about deity, vouchsafed by our grave teachers, of what no man comprehends. The foregoing account of letters in the candle, though rather obscure, may by the patient and laborious, be made to yield positive instruction, whereas, the account they give of deity is utterly void of all sense save that which is an outrage upon all sense, and either conveys no positive meaning, or a meaning which to well cultivated reason is a positive insult. Over anxious to explain everything, they confuse everything, and any one who has seen the *Critic* may well be expected, after listening to their *interpretation* of Nature's mystery, to say with Puff, " Egad, the interpreter is the harder to be understood of the two."

The priests usually distinguished as the early Christian Fathers, entertained very gross ideas of God; for though they called him a spirit they insisted that every spirit is a body, and has a form proper to it. Beausobre, whom learned Christians esteem very much, assures us " the most able and orthodox Christian Fathers always declare that God is a light and a sublime light, and that all the celestial powers which surround the deity, are lights of a second order, rays of the first light."* In the same high authority, we have it that " In general the idea of a substance absolutely incorporeal was not a common idea with Christians in the beginning. When I conisder (adds Beausobre) with what confidence Tertullian, who thought that God was corporeal and figured, speaks of his opinion, it makes me suspect that it must have been the general opinion of the Latin Church. Who can deny, says he, that God is a body, though he is a spirit ? Every spirit is a body, and has a form proper to it. Melitor, so much boasted of for his virtues and knowledge, composed a treatise to prove that God is corporeal."†

Dr. Priestly, after quoting these and many other passaages of similar import, observes that ‡passages of Scripture which speak of God as a spirit, were so far from deciding this controversy in favour of the immateriality of the divine essence, that those Christians who believed God to be corporeal, alleged in favour of their opinion, that very expression of our Saviour that God is a spirit. Can you, says Gregory Nazianzen, conceive of a spirit without conceiving *motion* and *diffusion*, properties

---

* Page 12 " Disquisition on Matter and Spirit."
† See his book entitled " Vulgar Errors."

* Vol. I., p. 468, " Histoire Critique de Manichée, et du Manicheisme.
† Ibid.—Vol. I., p. 474.
‡ " Disquisitions on Matter and Spirit," p. 227.

which agree only to body. Origen says that every spirit, according to the proper and simple notion of the word, signifies a body. This is confirmed by Chalcidius. The idea of a spirit according to the ancients, was nothing but an invisible, living, thinking, free and immortal being, which has within itself the principle of its actions and motions.

This idea of spirit is certainly less unreasonable than the one now in vogue, which, signifying the negative of everything, is not properly an idea at all, but as already said, the absence of one. The Anthropomorphites who not only maintained that God is figured, but a being *exactly human in appearance*, though despised by their brother Christians of the same spirit school, were the only people I ever read or heard of, who could talk intelligibly about Deity. They worshipped that of which they had a distinct conception, which is more than can be truly said of any modern believers in God. Beausobre tell us *the belief that God had a body, subtle like light, but with organs exactly like the human body, is an error so ancient that it is hardly possible to find the origin of it. But if to believe in a God with body is wrong, can it be right to believe in a God without one? Who is able " to conceive of a spirit without conceiving motion." If there be so marvellous a conceiver, no one will doubt his ability *also* to conceive of motion where nothing is moved. If God exists, he acts; if he acts, body is essential to him. The early Christian Fathers were of that opinion, and for my own part I do not see how it is possible to be of any other. With them the word spirit represented something figured, and of course bearing a relation to time and space. Unable to conceive the idea of immaterial existence they boldly asserted the materiality of God, an assertion which in a subsequent age when Christians had spiritualised themselves into belief of nonentities, Giordano Bruno and others were brought to the stake for little more than insinuating. At a period when God was not only believed material, but in all save attributes a human creature, any one might safely have defined him as the monad of monads. Men who made God after their own image, and thus, as said by a witty philosopher, returned the compliment to Deity who made *them* after *his* own image, can scarce be supposed over nice in such matters.

One of many serious objections to the matter-god conceit is that no wit can reconcile it

---

* Ibid.—p. 502.

with the notion of his infinitude. All figured bodies are bounded, and therefore not infinite. The whole is the only infinite: for only *that* can properly be called boundless. Now a God with organs exactly like the human body, or indeed any body, must be finite, inasmuch as his body is bounded by body. And as to an unbounded God I think it is demonstrated by letters A and B of this Alphabet, that his reality can only be imagined by persons who like Collier and Berkeley so far from agreeing with the early Christian Fathers that God is a spirit and spirit is matter are satisfied that matter exists nowhere but in mind, that mind exists nowhere but in God, and that God exists nowhere but in himself, which is a *place* the latitude and longitude of which has not yet been determined.

I am much out in my reckoning, or the candid believer in God who has proceeded thus far with this Alphabet, will at once admit (if hitherto a rejecter of the fact) that the nature of Deity is no better understood now than in the days of Cicero. And if any one argue that though the *nature* of God is still a mystery, his *attributes* are revealed in the Scriptures, to him I say the Scriptures being far from intelligible,* and very far from consistent upon the subject, any appeal to them as conclusive authority, is frivolous in the extreme.   C. S.

SOMERSET.—Intelligence is making a little progress in Somerset. Moral worth is supplanting external forms, gloomy faces, and antiquated ceremonies—but, alas! it is with a few compared with the many, and hardly with them as it ought to be. I know upwards of twenty who are Infidels, but dare not, or if they dare, do not own themselves as such. Can anything be done to make these Infidels men?

WHO SAYS THAT RELIGION DOES NOT PRODUCE INSANITY? - The fifth annual report of the directors and superintendent of the Ohio Lunatic Asylum, gives a table of the causes of insanity among the inmates of that institution, from which we learn that 57 of them were rendered insane by *Religion*; and by *Intemperance* only 35, plainly showi g that religion is here the principal cause of insanity.

---

* The Christians, says the same writer, (Beausobre), who were always unanimous with respect to the *unity* of God, were by no means so with res-to his *nature*. The Scriptures *not being explicit* on the subject each adopted what he thought the most probable opinion, or that of the philosophical school in which he had been educated.—*Disquisition on Matter and Spirit*, p. 223.

AN INFIDEL'S VIEW OF SO STYLED CHRISTIAN DEMOCRACY.

Respectfully submitted to the Editor and Supporters of the "Nonconformist."

"Deal with us, if you are so minded, as enemies—marvel at our presumption—suspect our motives, draw yourselves up into an attitude of stern defiance—but hear us out. Englishmen are wont to be manly, Christians are bidden to be courteous. We ask at your hands the manliness of the first, and the courtesy of the last. Shall we ask in vain?"

THE *Nonconformist*, in issuing its New Year's Address, suggests some serious reflections. There is a tone of healthy vigor and earnest sincerity in this journal, and an able exposition of democratic doctrine, which has gained a warm circle of admirers. Though a Christian writer, the editor of the *Nonconformist* has given utterance to such truly noble and thoroughly *unconventional* sentiments on the subject of social and political duties, that the conductors of the *Movement*, departing from their usual course of confining its pages to original papers, felt highly gratified in appropriating the splendid article "Ethics of Nonformity," convinced that nothing could have been said more thoroughly and ably embodying, to the extent that it went, their views and principles. With much propriety might it be asked—how comes it that having respectively started from two extremes of doctrine—one being a thorough belief in divine revelation—Christian revelation—the other a complete disbelief in all divine revelation and supernaturalism—you agree in one moral code. The Christian will reply that he draws his morality from the pure fount of Christianity, and that the Infidel, when a good moral teacher, is so in spite of his Infidelity—*mutatis mutandis*, the Infidel says the same—the Christian promulgates right views of morality, having drawn them from other sources than those of his creed, and in short, entertains them despite of his Christianity. Here then they are at issue. But the question can be put upon another footing, one on which there may be something like a mutual agreement, without compromise. May it not be supposed that the science of ethics can be studied without a preparatory creed or anti-creed. In putting this case the concession, if any, would come rather from us. Even religionists separate morality from religion. One can, according to this admission, be moral without being religious, however they may deny the possibility of being religious without being moral. Then whence are right sentiments and practice derived? From the common impulses and reason of our kind, unconnected with creeds and speculations, popular or anti-popular. Not that men may not progress in morals as a science, from having the foundations of knowledge more correctly laid, but that correct sentiments and practice may exist independently of such beliefs or speculations. The utility of such conclusions is to rid us of the prejudice that morality, in teaching or practice, can only emanate from our respective parties.

The following passages from the New Year's Address above alluded to, show how much more cordially we can adopt the temper and sentiments, and even acknowledge the similitude in position, of the writer, who assumes as a basis of his principles what we regard as a gross and pernicious superstition, rather than those emanating from the generality of the avowed liberal world, who are supposed to have escaped from the current religious prejudices.

"Upon what we *have* done, we shall comprise what we have to say in very few words. We have given our hearts to our work. We have spoken, in all cases, what we thought. We have made many enemies. We have, we hope, retained some friends. We have served no party, save as the untiring advocacy of broad principles may have served them. What we began to uphold and to enforce, we have continued to uphold and to enforce until the present day."

Does not every word tell? Are not our progress and position as faithfully described as if the sketch had been limned for us by ourselves. But now let us view the aspect of the case more peculiarly theirs; and here commences the gravest part of the subject in what concerns the revelationists of the Christian world.

The editor continues in the following strain—

"What we *shall* do, may best be learned from what we have done. With the same constancy, perseverance, and assiduity, we shall attempt to promote what we believe to be the cause of truth—*and we wish we could add, with increasing efficiency.* We are quite sensible of the defects of the *Nonconformist*—we know, too, how easily they might be supplied—but the supply of them depends upon what we do *not* command, and what a *considerable increase of subscribers alone* would enable us to command. *One* mind cannot make every department of a newspaper perfect. *Several* minds imply several bodies, and all the wants which bodies bring with them. *Double our present number of readers* would remedy a great many faults which at present we can do nothing but deplore."

I have italicised some passages in the above paragraph for the purpose of more easily indicating the points to which I now wish to direct attention.

Now what is the actual fact? that the ablest, sincerest, most honest, truth seeking, liberty-loving journal that the Christian ranks have ever had the high honour to call theirs, is comparatively inefficient, confessedly below par—in commanding the ordinary newspaper machinery for successful competition with the commonest hacks of the press. The entire weight of labour appears to devolve on one man—a labour that to be properly executed ought to be divided among several competent well paid literary men. Who have permitted this? The Christian world. Who fail in support? The Christian world. Among what affluent and very numerous body is it that pre-eminent political ability, integrity, and the healthiest democracy cannot obtain a merely paying support? The Christian world. Not the hierarchical Christians only, nor the church-and-state Christians —but the dissenting nonconformist Christians.

Without undue disparagement, without the desire of using one unnecessarily harsh expression, or coming to an unjust conclusion — is not the inference here forced upon us that Christianity is not the exponent of sincere, truth-seeking, liberty-loving sentiments and doctrine.

Is not the editor of the *Nonconformist* in advance of the Christian public, and by so much, in advance of Christianity? When he so forcibly and eloquently expatiates on the beauties, and pleasures, and duties of adherence to principle, the casting away of expediency, and contempt of the mere respectabilities, conventionalities, and authorities of ordinary routine, is he not rather drawing from the pure sources of a humanitarian rather than of a divine morality—of an ardent love of his species and an inextinguishable hatred of wrong and oppression, rather than from the dictates of credal dogma, or so styled revealed authority?

M. Q. R.

It is a common notion we believe among clever fellows, that the public is to be gulled, tickled, addressed as a child, and that the lower the tone assumed, they will be the more pleased. Our experience says quite the reverse.—*The Chambers.*

ANOTHER VICTIM TO RELIGIOUS INTOLERANCE.

We copy from the *Inquirer* of the 21st ult., the following statement of an atrocious act of persecution towards an individual, whose sole offence is, that he presumes to have a conscience in matters of religion. In the village of Long Sutton, Lincolnshire, there is a free school, endowed on the most liberal principles, and for a long time under the able direction of a Mr. James Newman, a Unitarian. In October, 1843, a new vicar came to reside in the village, and shortly after directed Mr. Newman to teach the church catechism in the schools, with which request he respectfully refused to comply. Mr. Newman was then summoned to London by the death of a relative, and on his return, after a week's absence, found that a new master had been procured by the vicar, who was then actually engaged in remodelling the school according to the rules of the National School Society, although a few years back the trustees had obtained from the British and Foreign School Society a loan of £168, on the understanding that the principles of this last mentioned society should be recognized in the management.

The evidence that a sectarian education was contrary to the intention of the founder, reinstated Mr. Newman as master, and save threats, no further annoyance was offered by the baffled vicar, until May last, when finding it necessary to be again absent for a few days, on his return he received regular notice to quit his situation, and was *forcibly* ejected by direction of the vicar and trustees, for which summary proceeding they have refused to furnish any definite reason, contented with the bare assertion that the master has been guilty of a neglect of duty by closing the schools for the short periods mentioned. But in the written regulations furnished to him by the trustees, it is stated that the master should be allowed twelve days in each year at his own discretion, as holidays in addition to the regular annual vacations.

It appears, however, that they have taken counsel's opinion whether a *Unitarian* could legally fill the office of master. They have been making inquiries also, whether Mr. Newman is a communicant among the Unitarians, and how often he has been in the habit of attending their place of worship. From these facts there can be no doubt regarding the real cause of the dismissal of this worthy man. It is to be hoped that he may yet have the means of baffling the bigotry of his cruel persecutors.—J. B. L.

POST-PRISON PROPOSALS FOR PATERSON.

Mr. George Anderson, in a letter from Arbroath, says—

"I perceive by Mr. Paterson's "Card," contained in *Movement* 50, that it is his intention to be in Hull immediately on his return from Perth Penitentiary—a place never to be forgotten by all friends to free inquiry.

"Be that as it may, I think, and others with whom I have conversed bear me out in my opinion, that it would be a pity for Mr. Paterson to leave for England without giving his Scottish Atheistical admirers the benefit of a *call*.

"You know after Christ's liberation from the *Arimathean cell*, that he appeared unto five hundred of his disciples at one time. Now, to carry out the arithmetical idea, if after 'three days' in the *bowels of the earth*, he, Christ, appeared unto five hundred, to how many should Paterson, after sixteen months, appear?

"Let all those who are enthusiastic in the regeneration of mankind from mental prostitution, come forward to the various Halls in which he may appear and answer the question."

Mr. Anderson earnestly calls on the Atheists of Scotland to "prove to the votaries of Christianity and persecution that honesty has yet its 'due reward,' and that however earnest the Lord Chief Justice Clerk may have been in his devotions to his god on the morning of Paterson's sentence, he has taken the name of the lord '*his*' god in vain, inasmuch as his prayers have not been heard.

He adds that "there are a whole host of towns favourable to the spread of free inquiry, and all within one day's—several within a few hours' coaching of Perth."

EXTRACTS FROM A LETTER OF MR. PATERSON.

Dec. 25th, 1844.

A "Merry Christmas" has no doubt been rung in your ears often enough to-day. Mine has been dull enough. "Patience and temper," said a celebrated Roman, "are the greatest of virtues, but the hardest to practise." So say I.

This letter must answer you and Holyoake both. The governor duly received his "order" for cash. I had expected he had this acknowledgment ere now, but *I just* find *my letter* to him was stopped. Sorry for that, as he has not written since, five weeks ago. The last I received from you was dated November 18th. You must be all dead. Surely you would not depart this life without letting me know? I have reason to think some of your letters to me may be detained. Should you write again, please put no *Extracts* in your letter.

I hope you make good use of your press and periodical. Perhaps you are so taken up with your *Plebeian*, that you can't devote much attention to a Patrician of my stamp. Just so, the way of the world. Fortune seems on good terms with you. Showers the right sort of favours in your lap. The Dame mistakes me for some one else surely, when hurling her brick-bats and tiles at my head. Perhaps she whips those she loves. If so, I am safe.

Happy to hear Mrs. Martin visits Auld Reekie. I should much like to welcome her there. In holy writ is the sage remark, "Pride was not made for man." It must have been made for the women then, which accounts for them doing their duty so well, when the *bold* and *prideless* sex are shrinking from theirs. Go on. Show in true colours that faction who befool and blind the people by parading before their eyes the forms of liberty, but keep them hard and fast in mental slavery—show that Protestantism differs only in *name* from Catholicity—that the one allows them to bustle and shake their chains *only;* that in both cases they are rivetted. Show that the word liberty is prostituted in their mouths—that it means the liberty to tyrannise—to debase. Show that the system that sent me to herd with felons, cannot ennoble, but rather degrade —it may contract the heart, stupify the mind, nurse the animal, but it embrutes the intellect. Talk of "humanising influences!" forsooth, talk of the gentle hug of the Polar bear—of the affectionate embrace of the rattlesnake—in short, talk of any improbable or impossible thing, but not of liberty of speech wherever the flag of bigotry waves.

By the bye, you never acknowledged my letter of September. I thought I had said some very pretty things in it. I wish you outside parties would at least acknowledge what I send. When I am long without communication, I think the world is going wrong with you, or that you are growing wrong to me. Letters are like gleams of sunshine in winter, they cheer the present and gild the past. I am not sorry that you have felt the bigot's arm. The mind untasked is worthless. You have risen with the gale, your energy has been roused by the conflict and collision. Had your path been strewn with roses, or fanned by vernal gales, why you would have been a mere hot house plant. Instead of which, qualities and powers have been called forth and unfolded none knew you possessed. The cause has been well succoured, for numbers must have been with you in feeling—if not in belief—and sympathy you know is the best preparation, and almost certain antecedent.

My health fairish. Want of sleep, through want of exercise. Lately got allowed eight ounces of *meat* weekly.

Send this to H., and give my regards to Mrs. M. Jeffery, Hill, Greer, Robinson, Finlay, and every body who values them, and you will oblige

Yours truly,
T. PATERSON.
To Miss Matilda Roalfe.

PROGRESS ABROAD.

IN Switzerland another periodical is by this time added to the Continental publications, which, more or less, advocate Social Reform. In name, and mainly in principles, as far as we can learn, it resembles the English Socialist organ, being called the *New World*. Thus, the fruits of the propagandism of Weitling, and the government prosecutions instituted against him, have not only appeared in the government reports, so widely circulated and commented on, but in renewed efforts on the part of his friends—an instance of which appears in the present publication.

The *Forvaerts*, German Communist paper, published in Paris, which we have before noticed and quoted, will henceforth appear monthly, instead of twice a week. This alteration has been forced upon the conductors in consequence of a government prosecution, by which a fine has been levied on them for having failed to furnish the security (75,000 francs) required from actual political papers appearing twice a week. The editors, however, propose to take advantage of this change in publication, by preparing expositions of communistic principles more carefully arranged and elaborately digested, and consequently of more permanent value than when it was their province to take cognizance of passing events.

In parts of Germany, theological stagnation no more prevails than with us. A modern Luther has arisen, and his doings have thus found their way into the English Journals—" A Roman Catholic priest, John Rouge, in Upper Silesia, excommunicated for having written his celebrated letter to the Bishop of Treves, in which he denounces the late exhibition of the holy garment, has addressed a pamphlet to the lower orders of the Roman clergy, calling upon them to unite their exertions with him in the pulpit and in the professional chair, against the Italian Catholics and the Pope, in order to found, by council and synod, a national German Catholic church, independent of Roman darkness. He wants to abolish auricular confession, the celebration of the mass in Latin, the making of proselytes by money, the stultification of the lower clergy by the commands of the higher hierarchy, and at the same time he asks for liberty to think and to investigate for every clergyman, and permission to marry for all priests. The police have seized the pamphlet."

When did a christian dissenting body not begin by demanding freedom of investigation for themselves, and end by refusing it for others? If admired, they must still be watched.

M. Q. R.

THE CARPENTERS.—At the Coffee Room, Literary and Scientific Institution, John Street, Tottenham Court Road, a number of carpenters, seeing the trade getting much depressed, have made a subscription, *weekly*, for forming a Carpenters' Society. The object is to procure a school, or workshop, and to make a provision for out of employment, old age, loss of tools, accidents, and for improving the children of members, and each other, in every way possible, giving men when out of employment 20s. per week, and employing such for the permanent good of the society by perpetual accumulation, enabling every society to make provision for its surplus hands, assisted by the children of its members, with many other advantages. Particulars may be obtained at the Institution on Sunday afternoons at three o'clock.

MR. DISON, Sec., pro tem.

SCHILLER ON POLICY.—All men are captivated by immediate advantages, great minds alone are excited by the prospect of distant good. When policy calculates on the prudence of others, or trusts to its own unsupported strength, its plans are chimerical, and it runs the risk of incurring the ridicule of the world; but it may assuredly calculate upon success, when it can enlist even barbarism, avarice, and superstition on its side, and render the interests and the passions of mankind the executors of its plans.—*History of the Thirty Years' War.*

MEETING AT BRISTOL FOR JOHNSON OF HULL.—A Public Meeting is announced at the Hall, Temple Street, Bristol, for January 15, (this day), at which resolutions will be proposed, condemnatory of the conduct of the Hull Magistrates in punishing Mr. Johnson for exercising the right of a citizen, and demanding the free expression of all opinions. The Meeting will be addressed by G. Powel, G. Reuvel, W. Barton, W. Bonnor, W. Canning, and W. Cook.

THE PATERSON TESTIMONIAL FUND.—On Sunday afternoon, January 19, a Public Tea Party, under the superintendence of the Leicester Branch of the Anti-Persecution Union, will be held in the Social Institution, Market Place, Leicester — the proceeds to go to the Paterson Testimonial Fund. Mr. Holyoake, Secretary of the London Anti-Persecution Union, will deliver an address on the occasion.

THE HOME MISSIONS.—We were gratified to find that our last notice of the Home Missions found its way into that active Catholic organ, the *Belfast Vindicator*, which honestly acknowledged the source whence it obtained the notice of Dr. Edgar's detection by Mrs. Martin.

IRELAND.—If an Atheist needs, which we hope is not often the case, reanimating with zeal to extirpate the fatal religious idea, let him turn to Ireland, and the scenes of bigotry and intellectual subjection which religion exhibits there. How little chance there is of their political emancipation, is evidenced in the fact that Mr. O'Connell has recently declared that no infidel should in that country enjoy the right of the suffrage. Do people deserve liberty who would refuse it to others because of a different opinion on religious points? But the exertions we make are not in vain. Ample evidence of this is now before us, and shall shortly be introduced to our readers.

HEAVENLY IDEALITY.—The rare edition of the *Biblica Germanica*, in two folio volumes, published in 1487, contains many coloured wood cuts, remarkable for the singularity of their designs; for instance, Bathsheba is represented washing her feet in a small tub of water, and Elias ascending to heaven in a four-wheeled waggon.—*Chambers' Journal*, Jan. 4, 1845.

GOD NO REPUBLICAN.—A London journal, remarking upon the weather vouchsafed to her Majesty when on her recent visit to the city, opens with the following:—"It has been remarked, as a gratifying and auspicious circumstance, that on every occasion of her Majesty's 'progress,' however threatening might be the previous aspect of the weather, and however lowering the first break of the morning, the seasons have suspended their menace, and the sun has continued to shine through the opposing mists, and smile upon the royal cavalcade." They tell us God is the friend of the poor—then he would not be found smiling on royalty and its expensive pageantry, which the children of toil and poverty furnish. We find out as well as the Silesian Weavers that God is neither of our interests nor our politics.

THE ATHEON.—Several letters have been received expressing approval of the proposed undertaking, and making offers of donations and subscriptions for membership. According to the number, value, and promptness of such communications, may a timely and just decision be determined on respecting the extent of the arrangements and the period of commencement.

BRANCH A 1 DISCUSSION.—On Sunday morning last the discussion took place in the Coffee Room of this Branch on Mr. Hetherington's resolution, the terms of which were announced last week, for rescinding a former resolution on the subject of Mr. Holyoake's "Visit to Harmony." Mr. Hetherington who entered fully into the question, Mr. Hornblower who supported him, and Mr. Lloyd Jones who opposed the proposal, were the principal speakers. The debate being prolonged till the usual time of departure, an adjournment proposed by Mr. Hornblower, opposed by Mr. Jones, was lost by a minority less by one only than the majority. The unfairness to Mr. Hetherington of not suffering him to be heard in reply, being strongly represented, Mr. Clark agreed to withdraw his opposition, which would reverse the decision. The adjournment was ultimately carried by a small majority of the meeting.

A SERIES of four lectures was commenced by Mr. Buchanan on Monday the 13th, at the Southwark Social Institution, on the "Philosophy of the Jewish Scriptures." The three following lectures will be given on the 20th and 27th of January, and the 3rd of February.

ON Wednesday the 15th, the Rev. J. Burnett lectures in the Weigh House Church, on "State Curches unsanctioned by Old Testament Analogy." This may be worth attending, to discover how the Anti-State Church case is made out from the priestly authority of a *theocratic* nation.

Mr. Coltman, piano-forte tuner, Leicester, for *Movement*........................ 0 3 6

TO CORRESPONDENTS.

RECEIVED. — Social Communities and Harmony Hall, by W. C. *A priori* argument for the Existence of God, by Freville, translated by J. B. L. Conversion of the Rev. J. Barker. A.C. E. HYDE, Salford.—His friendly complaints will not be lost upon us.

LECTURES.

Jan. 19.—Social Institution, Market Place, Leicester, Mr. G. J. Holyoake will lecture.
Jan. 19.—Branch A 1, John Street, Tottenham Court Road, A Lecture. At 7, P.M.
Jan. 19.—Social Institution, 5, Charlotte Street, Blackfriars Road, Mr. Hindle,—On Human Destiny.
Jan. 19.—Finsbury Institution, Goswell Road, Mr. Cooper,—On Christian Missionary Enterprise, its Dupes at Home and its Converts Abroad. Discussion after,—Ought the Missionaries to the South Seas to be encouraged?
Jan. 19.—National Hall, High Holborn, W. J. Fox,—The Birthday of Copernicus (1473), and of James Watt (1736).

SUBSCRIPTIONS
TO THE ANTI-PERSECUTION UNION.

Bristol Subscriptions— Card 16 for Oct., Nov., and Dec........................ 0 15 0

PATERSON TESTIMONIAL.

W. B. B., fourth subscription............ 0 10 0
G. J. H., *Sec.*

Printed and Published by G. J. HOLYOAKE, 40, Holywell street, Strand.
Wednesday, January 15, 1845.

THE MOVEMENT

And Anti=Persecution Gazette.

"Maximise morals, minimise religion."—BENTHAM.

No. 58.   EDITED BY G. JACOB HOLYOAKE, AND M. Q. RYALL,   Price 1½d

CUVIER AND GRADATION.

"We see organised beings *develope* themselves, but never *form* themselves. In all cases beings are found to derive their origin from a being of similar form, called generally a *parent*—the offspring termed a germ. It is a rule without a single exception, that the progeny must have originally formed a part of a being like itself."—*Cuvier.*

THE most competent person must approach with respect, and must feel great diffidence in venturing to oppose, any opinion of Cuvier on the subject of geology. Whilst the respect might not be less, the diffidence must be immeasurably increased of any one, like myself, who ventures to differ from that great man. The above quotation is in perfect keeping with the *expressed* opinions of, I believe, all geologists of the present day. Taken *literally*, the extract is unexceptionable, for it contains little else than a statement of self-evident truisms. To treat it thus would be to destroy it, and to imagine that Cuvier wrote for no other purpose than simply to declare what no one could dispute. Either through the difficulties of the French language, preventing the Baron being more explicit, or through ignorance on the part of the translator of the question discussed, I imagine the *intended* meaning is obscured. The last reason is most probably the true one. Cuvier, I take it, intended to *deny the natural production of animals and plants*—but *I* deny that the quotation will *fairly* bear that construction, or that it is clearly and philosophically expressed. Not expecting my *ipse dixit* will be taken, I will give my reasons.

There is nothing in the extract at the head of this article but *simple affirmations* of known truths, to deny which would involve an absurdity. It is one thing to assert that every *offspring* must have had a *parent*, which is clear to every one—but it is another to deny that animals and plants are *natural productions*, which is not so clear to some. There are but two theories to account for the existence of animals and plants: one, that they were created by some great powers; the other, that they are natural products, like rocks, water, air, and other inorganic substances. I incline to the latter opinion, but still readily admit that "it is a rule without a *single* exception that the progeny *must* have originally formed part of a living being like itself." The existence of progeny necessarily involves the previous existence of progenitors—the one could not be unless the other had preceded it. This does not touch the question—whether man *originally* was artificially or naturally formed. No one, to my knowledge, ever saw a man rise up out of the earth, without having first gone down into it; nor did I ever hear of a man dropping from the clouds, who had not previously gone up in a balloon. But gentle and simple, literate and illiterate think that the Atheist *must* hold some such ridiculous belief; because they do not know and will not inquire what he does believe. Cuvier would seem, by the first sentence, to hold even a more absurd opinion than this, and to be combating some real or imaginary article of faith, to the effect that men and animals *formed themselves.* I am but slightly read in either ancient or modern authors, but I never even heard that any one ever existed so irretrievably insane as to advocate such an idea. Fry indeed supposes that "The substances proceeding from the sun, in the form of light, united with those of a similar origin in the form of heat, gases, or air; electric, magnetic, or galvanic fluids, are constantly forming combinations, and producing not only mineral substances, but certain organic globules, *endowed with life and voluntary motion;* and these globules combining also in various circumstances, are the causes of all the genera and species in the animal, vegetable, and mineral kingdom." To these globules he ascribes the formation, at least, of the lower orders of plants and animals; although he imagines that, in favourable circumstances, they might even construct the body of an elephant, and organise all other species of animated bodies which inhabit the earth.*

---

* Dr. Jameson's "Essays on the Changes of the Human Body."

Here, however preposterous the idea might seem to be, it was the *organised* globules that formed the man, and not the man who formed himself—for man, as an organised being, could perform no act, in fact, was not a man, until perfectly formed. There is no more difficulty in conceiving a man swallowing himself, than there is in imagining a man making himself. Upon this opinion of Fry, Barclay remarks, " With all the motions, instincts, and volitions, and even the degree of intelligence and foresight with which our author has endowed his globules, it will be difficult to conceive the manner in which they can construct an animal or plant, without the aid of what Bacon has called the regal or political motion. Without such a political motion, whether it be the effect of a ruling part or a vital principle, or an archeus, how are the globules, with all their instincts, foresight, and intelligence, in proceeding to form a plant or an animal, to agree or come to a general understanding about the plan on which they are to operate? Suppose they are about to form an animal, as a man or a horse, how do they fix on the number of bones, their situations, their relative proportions, their forms, their connexions, their varieties of motion, and the number and adaptation of joints to each of these varieties?" He then proceeds to state that the globules must further agree as to which shall work on the right hand and which on the left; which shall form the bones, which the muscles, and which the veins, arteries, and lymphatics—and so on, throughout the whole body.

When I first read Barclay's objections, I thought them very fair, and I still think so for the time in which he wrote; but since I commenced this article I find that I am as liable to jump to unwarrantable conclusions as other men, and that Fry's opinions are far from being so improbable as I was inclined to conceive. In a lecture delivered in the Manchester Royal Institution, on November 22 of last year, by Professor T. R. Jones, of King's College, London, it is asked, " What is an animal? It is an aggregate of parts, of them composed of atoms. Now, Buffon broached a very startling theory—that *all animals were made of animalcules;* that these little monads, met with in such numbers in the waters around us, were the materials of which animals were made up. This theory was at once scouted as absurd; but strange to say, *we are coming round to the same point,* at least to the extent, not that animalcules are separate and distinct beings *merely,* but also that *every atom of the animal is alive.* The gigantic puff-ball found in the fields, that grew in a single night, examined under the microscope, was found to consist of an immense number of cells; each of which dividing, separates itself in two, as soon as it attains a certain degree of growth. Every one of these cells was able to nourish itself by absorbing food and to divide itself into two cells, similar to each other, as soon as it attained this state of maturity. *What more was necessary to constitute an animal?* Every one of the cells must be looked upon as *acting for itself,* and assisting to constitute the entire mass—an aggregate being composed of hundreds of millions of these component parts."

Why, the above is almost a literal corroboration of Fry's hypothesis, there being little or no difference between an " organic globule" and an animalcule. Professor Jones says that the same requisites which form a plant will also form an animal; and that inasmuch as each cell in the puff-ball, acting for itself, assists to constitute the entire mass, so each animalcule, acting for itself, would assist to form the entire mass of an animal.

According to Fenelon, it was the opinion of Epicurus, that men and other animals came up out of the earth ready formed, but imagines that nature made a great many futile attempts at first. Southwell, in the *Investigator,* article " Speculations on Man," would seem to approve of this notion, for he says, " I cannot but conclude that our earth, under certain circumstances, has produced perfect animals." This does not of course pledge him to the belief that men and horses ever came out of the earth direct, for a zoophite is a " perfect animal " as much as man, the only difference being in the complexity of the organisation. But if Southwell agrees with Epicurus so far as to believe that animals highly organised and of large growth have, at some time or other, been produced direct from the earth, through a combination of favourable circumstances, why I must beg leave to differ from him. If men, or animals of much less complex organisation, originally resulted from tumours on the face of the earth, or from any other mode independent of each other, there would not be that *regular gradation* of form which comparative anatomy has unquestionably established to exist now, and to have before existed. If all animals were produced in this way, whence comes the striking similarity of form which one animal bears to another? Why should the zoophyte be connected with man by a long chain of animal forms, not one link of which can be removed without leaving a visible gap? Is it not reasonable to suppose that under the hypothesis of Epicurus, there would be very great chasms and many links wanting? Comparative anatomy warrants the conclusion that *one form has grown out of another*, and that complex forms are developments of more simple ones. General science, in fact, is at issue with the idea that Nature performs any delicate operation suddenly—all changes are gradual, from the upheaving of mountains and the deposition of strata, to the formation of the fœtus and the decomposition of organisations; the rise and decay of all forms are by slow and almost imperceptible degrees. I can no more imagine that mammoths have been produced from globules or bubbles on the face of the earth, than I can conceive that mountains many thousands of feet high were formed upon its surface without the particles of which they are composed having previously been deposited at the bottom of waters. Mountains and men have, I imagine, resulted from the inherent properties of matter; should science ever establish as a fact, that stones and metals are *self-formed*, then I think we shall be right in conjecturing that animals are self-formed also—but not till then. W. C.

THE CONVERSION OF THE REV. JOSEPH BARKER.

I beg to inclose herewith a curious tract, now widely circulating in the Potteries, the production of Joseph Barker—it is producing a strong, strange sensation among his old followers, and most certainly would be considered a blasphemous production if it had been the effusion of "the Man Paterson," C. Southwell, G. J. Holyoake—or any of the members of the Rational Society. Perhaps you may deem it of sufficient value to give it a corner in the *Movement*, as an indication of the *change* of convictions and feelings which its author has undergone since I held the public discussions with him in the Potteries, Preston, Staley Bridge, Ashton, and latterly in the Odd Fellows' Hall, Halifax.

ALEX. CAMPBELL.

" SECTARIAN THEOLOGY AND EVANGELICAL REFORM.

"Nothing can be more absurd than many of the doctrines of sectarian theology. You may go round the world, you may collect the most foolish and ridiculous, the most horrible and monstrous, the most unnatural and impossible, the most preposterous and blasphemous notions to be found among all the idolatrous and superstitious nations of the earth—you may take in the wild men of New Holland, the savages of New Zealand, the Hottentots of Africa, the Indians of the American wilderness, the natives of the frozen North, or the multitudes that throng the unmeasured regions of China and India —you may go back to former ages, and collect the most absurd, unnatural, cruel, and impossible notions of the ancient inhabitants of Egypt and Babylon, of Greece and Rome, of Britain, Germany, and Gaul, and it is my conviction, that you will not, in all your wanderings, be able to glean, nor in all your researches, be able to discover, a set of more incredible, irrational, anti-christian, nonsensical, preposterous, unworthy, discreditable, barbarous, immoral, abominable, unaccountable, profane, ungodly notions, than many of the notions which form a part, a leading part, of the theology of the hireling priesthoods of the present day. What can be more absurd than the doctrine of the Trinity, as laid down in the Athanasian creed? What can be more absurd or impossible than the notion that a father can beget a son, that from the father and his son a third may spring or come forth, and that yet the father, the son, and the third one proceeding or springing from both, should all be the same age, none before or after the other? What more impossible than the notion that a person may be begotten by another, and yet be eternal, without beginning, an eternal son, eternally begotten? What can be more wild or monstrous than the notion that God should die, be buried, go down to hell, and rise from the dead the third day? What can be more blasphemous, more profane, more horrible than the doctrine that God, on account of one man's sin, causes all mankind to be born in the image of the devil and of the brute, utterly corrupt, depraved, full of all evil, empty of all good, irresistibly prone to sin, and utterly disabled, disinclined, averse to all righteousness, under God's wrath and curse, unfit for everlasting life in heaven, and liable to everlasting life in unutterable torments in hell? What can be more horrible or blasphemous than the doctrine that God from eternity did fore-ordain or predestinate, and render certain and inevitable whatsoever comes to pass—that he fore-ordained or rendered certain and unavoidable all the sins that were ever committed, and all the suffering that was ever endured—that he fore-ordained or rendered certain and inevitable the continual rebellion and impiety, and the final and eternal damnation of by far the greater part of the human race—that he fore-ordained the sin of Adam, and all its terrible and eternal consequences—that after he had done this, he wrote a Book, in which he said that he was good to all, and that his tender mercies were over all his works—that he was love itself—that he had no pleasure in the death of the wicked, but had rather that the wicked should turn from his evil ways and live—that he hated sin, and would have all men to repent and give up sinning—that he would have all to be saved—that he was no respecter of persons, but that he was the Father, the affectionate and kind hearted parent of all the human race ? What can be more unworthy than the doctrine that God cannot forgive sin, unless some innocent and infinite being bear the punishment of the sin, and that when God does forgive men's sins, it is not because they repent, and return to obedience, nor because he himself delighteth in mercy, but because, solely because, solely on account of Christ having borne the punishment of their sins, solely on account of Christ having satisfied his justice, solely on account of Christ's bloodshedding and merits ? What can be more nonsensical than the prevailing notions of the priesthoods about trusting in Christ's merits, or relying on Christ's blood, or recumbing, or reclining, or lying down on Christ for acceptance, forgiveness, and eternal life! What can be more irrational or licentious than the doctrine that men are justified and saved by faith alone? What can be more irrational or impossible than the doctrine of Transubstantiation or Consubstantiation, the doctrine that bread and wine are turned into the body and soul of Jesus Christ, and that in addition to the body and soul of Christ, the complete Godhead may be swallowed in a wafer? And what can be more horrible, or more contrary to the character of God, than the doctrine of eternal life in torments? And what can be more contrary to the sacred writings on this subject ? From Genesis to Jude the whole bible teaches, not that the wicked shall live for ever in unutterable torments, but that they shall *die, perish, be destroyed, consumed, burnt up*—that their 'everlasting punishment' will be 'everlasting destruction.' There wants an Evangelical Reform."

IMPROMPTU, on hearing a Lady praise a certain Reverend Gentleman's Eyes.—

I cannot praise the Doctor's eyes,
  I never saw his glance divine;
For when he prays, he shuts *his* eyes—
  And when he preaches, he shuts *mine*.
         Boston Investigator.

LETTER FROM A. TREVELYAN TO THE CENTRAL BOARD.

[The following Letter is inserted as indicative of the light in which some of the best friends to Socialism regard the " Visit to Harmony Hall." The writer of the letter from his wealth and station, might be expected to express very different feelings, but he is of an unsophisticated and earnest nature, and is one of the few who, whenever they entertain a sincere approval, make it a duty to express it. Mr. Trevelyan sent it to the Central Board with a view to its being inserted in the *New Moral World*. It might as well have been sent to the Carlton Club with a view to its being inserted in the *Globe* or the *Standard.*]

" TRUTH requires no tenderness of investigation,
    and scorns all subterfuges.
" It is, when displayed, divinely bright,
  One clear, unchanged, and universal light."

The greatest Philanthropists and Rationalists are those persons who publicly denounce, and practically renounce all religions.

I don't in any instance blame, their brains misguided them.

Newcastle-upon-Tyne, Jan. 10, 1845.

To JOHN BUXTON, and the Members of the Rational Society.

Brethren,

The thanks of the Society are due and ought to be given through you to one of our sincerest friends, namely, Mr. G. Jacob Holyoake, for the publication of the rational, useful, and truthful observations that resulted from his visit to Harmony,—but I regret to perceive that Lloyd Jones and several members of the Society, even after the truth of his account was most satisfactorily proved, at a Meeting of Branch A 1, should, owing to active secretiveness, self-esteem, &c., and inactive conscientiousness, &c., treat him most uncourteously, quite *à la* Christian, and wished to suppress the publication of what passed at their meeting, thus proving themselves enemies to our glorious cause, a cause founded on truth, and those who are friends to, or can appreciate its principles, never shrink at the truth being displayed,—and the editor of our Gazette, in not inserting among other articles, some that would militate against the management of the late Executive, also shews himself, owing to the formation of his brain, an enemy to the cause of human redemption.

The accounts of the Society, as kept by the late Executive, exhibit deficient order and conscientiousness in those who undertook the management of them,—and how comes it that on the retirement of R. Owen from office, so many of his colleagues should have followed his example, if they had possessed genuine social feelings, would they not have been too glad to have associated with the new Executive, in working out the glorious scheme to remove misery and vice from off the face of this beautiful world,—but the fact appears that R. Owen wished to make a Community of middle-class aristocrats, and after the unnecessary and harsh judgment of their social father, that the working classes were incompetent to carry through the Harmony experiment, we cannot be surprised that their self-esteem, &c., could not brook the idea of that class taking the management into their own hands.

The interests of the Society you manage, demand the exercise of the highest moral courage, in dismissing and in choosing those who are to assist you, and let your motto be—secretiveness we abhor.

Are there no pretended friends among the members who would like to see the attempt fail? I have not the least doubt of it, after the exhibition of the action of the inferior organs of the brain, at the late Holyoakean meeting of Branch A 1.

Believing friend Holyoake to be wronged by Lloyd Jones and other members of the Rational Society, I was induced to write this letter in his defence, which I trust will be inserted in the *New Moral World*,—and may it be our lot ever to be superior to the letter opening, moral-lunatic members of the aristocratic government of this country, who have exhibited for the last 300 years, men, idiots to the feeling of conscientiousness.

Wishing you happiness and success,

I remain, sincerely yours,

ARTHUR TREVELYAN.

A FACT FULL OF MEANING.—In a late religious excitement in Boston a person met a Christian neighbour, who took him by the hand and besought him to go to one of those meetings and become a Christian. "I have done so," said he, "and have got religion. I am at least a Christian."

"You are a Christian then all at once," said the other; "you profess to act strictly on Christian principles. I am glad of it. I congratulate you. Suppose we now have a settlement of our little accounts between us. Pay me what thou owest."

"No," said the new-born child of grace, turning on his heel, "*Religion is religion, and business is business.*"

THE PATERSON WELCOEM.

AND

TESTIMONIAL FUND.

WHEN it was proposed to erect a monument to the memory of the late C. R. Pemberton, and a few persons of rank and reputation (sincere friends of Pemberton) had put down their names on the Subscription List, many of the gentry of Birmingham were willing *then* to join in the honour of perpetuating the name of a man, whom in his lifetime and day of need, they had *neglected*. It was then that W. J. Fox recommended that only such persons as had subscribed to his "Illness Fund," or bought his pamphlets, etc., should be permitted to subscribe, for it would have been an ungracious thing to Pemberton to allow men who had denied or neglected to give him bread while living to offer him a stone when dead. It was well known that could Pemberton be conscious that such a thing had been done to him, he would lift the stone from his grave. In this spirit the Committee of the Paterson Testimonial Fund have been induced to limit the issue of Tickets to his Welcome to persons who have bought his "Trials," or subscribed to his Testimonial Fund, in some way or other. Mr. Paterson would regard it as a very indelicate thing to attempt to make a show of him to the curious, or to surround him, on the occasion of his return to the Metropolis, by any other than his tried and thoughtful friends.

It is intended that the Tea Party on his welcome, which will be attended by determined friends of liberty, English and foreign, who will take part in the proceedings, shall be held in the Hall of Science, City Road, which above all London Halls is *the* Hall of Anti-theology; and, moreover, has for its proprietor, that liberal friend of the Anti-Persecution Union, Mr. J. L. Bendall.

The tickets of admission to the Hall after the cloth is withdrawn, (when the Secretary of the Anti-Persecution Union will present the Testimonial, and various sentiments, etc., will be spoken to), will in like manner be only sold to such persons as above described. This procedure will probably restrict the amount of the Testimonial, but a small sum subscribed by undoubted friends will be more highly valued by Mr. Paterson and the Union, than a large one obtained by indirect, sordid, or clap-trap means.

By order of the Sub-Committee,

G. J. HOLYOAKE,

J. B. LEAR.

SOCIAL COMMUNITIES—HARMONY HALL.

I have read with some interest your "Visit to Harmony Hall,' as given in the *Movement*. Of the article, as a piece of composition, I highly approve, and I think none but an unfortunate bigot can mistake your motives. Your bluntness will startle, but your good temper will reconcile. Many of your statements surprised me, but I perfectly coincide with your conclusions generally. Altogether I am so well satisfied, that I leave to your discretion the propriety of publishing the following, which have been my opinions for years. From the limited space at your disposal, you were only able to glance at what I conceive to be the most essential of all requisites in the establishment of co-operative communities, namely, *that they should be made self-supporting in every stage of their existence*—and that whether they consisted of two thousand members, two hundred, or even of twenty only, they should ever be independent of external aid or assistance. These, I think, are your views, or I have mistaken your meaning when, in reference to Harmony, you say (p. 4(9) "They aimed at a conquest of the world *when they should have been achieving the independence of the young community.*" With the idea of an incipient community in England, with limited means, I have always associated the second epoch in the history of settlers in a new country. The land having been cleared, they set to work with might and main to make it as productive as possible; making shift, in the interim, with such social accommodation as circumstances will provide, without detriment to the first great object, the speedy and profitable cultivation of the estate. This I deem to be so reasonable, and a conclusion so evidently to be drawn from the premises, that I mentioned it in Bristol, in the course of a conversazione on Harmony, without the slightest conception that it would be disputed. One friend, however, remarked, that he should not like to see the communists of Hampshire "a mere colony of plodding farmers"— whilst another stated that the buildings at Tytherly would endure for a century or more. Now, there was no more necessity for the pioneers of Hampshire remaining all their lives, or any great portion of them, plodding farmers, than there was for the Shakers of America to remain all their days in the poverty with which they commenced their communitarian existence. The Shakers are now rolling in wealth, though they began in poverty—why was the example of these industrious men and women so often quoted by the Socialists as an unanswerable argument against their opponents, and yet their valuable experience given to the winds the very first time Socialists had a chance of proving its truth to millions of anxious and inquiring minds? Great things were predicated of a *successful* community in England—not more, I believe, than would have been realised—and those who engaged in the first experiment should have been far less careful of their lives than they were of its interests. What ever they did, they should not have gone too fast, but, like children, have *felt* their way for a few years, and not have attempted to run before they were able to stand *alone*. As to the durability of the edifices, I say now as I said when it was remarked to me, were I one of the communitarians I would not care if the buildings erected in the beginning crumbled to pieces in one quarter of the time the present ones are calculated to last. The result of five and twenty years intelligent labour on an indefinitely improvable estate, would have been very discouraging indeed if it did not furnish an ample surplus for building new dwellings. But, how is the case bettered by expending all available means on substantial buildings and handsome walks—and leaving the principal source of existence and comfort to chance? If the estate is worthy of cultivation, the buildings that are on it will not affect the crops. Further, is it not probable that long anterior to 1945 the present buildings, admirable as they may now be, will be found to be very inadequate for the wants of the generation of that day? Habitations are amongst the first class of things to advance with a truly civilised people.

However much I might regret the errors that have been committed at Tytherly, I believe, in all sincerity, that they were errors of judgment only.

There is yet another view of the matter which I would like to deal with. It has been stated that Socialists, in establishing a community, would wish to show the world not the advantages of simple co-operation merely, but also the immeasurably superior means for the production and distribution of wealth by the use of all known facts for that purpose—and that unless this were accomplished the superiority of Socialism over every other known system would not be established. The advisability of this aim I at once admit—but then, at the same time, I must deprecate any premature attempt to prove it. I never did approve the Hampshire experiment—I always thought it pre-

nature, and not likely to advance Socialism, but simply to prove the superiority of co-operation over the individual system. Shortly after I joined the Social body I subscribed a trifle to the community fund, not from the most distant idea of ever becoming an inhabitant of a community, for my tastes are not suited for such a life—I prefer the ups and downs of the old world, and the quiet and calm of a community would not be pleasant to me.

Co-operation and community, or some modification of community of goods, I consider to be so natural and so expedient, that it only requires the prejudices which keep men at daggers-drawn with each other to be removed, for them to see their true interests. I think the removal of those prejudices of far more consequence than attempts to establish communities. The Socialists declare that men can only be truly happy when their whole nature is fully developed and amply provided for, and that this can only be accomplished by co-operation and the most superior scientific arrangements, for the benefit of all. Socialism being simply "the greatest good for the greatest number." A co-operative colony of Socialists, wanting the means for developing their peculiar views, would only establish the truth of combination for producing wealth, and this has been already done in a very superior manner by a colony of the most ridiculous fanatics and most ignorant of men on the face of the earth. The great desideratum would still be wanting—the means of proving the superiority of Socialism over all other systems.

For myself, I consider that the Socialists should have continued to disseminate their views, to war with all sorts of ignorance and vice, until the time arrived when they could have commenced an experiment *upon purely Social principles*, without fear of failure. I would have preferred seeing all the other sects in the world establishing co-operative communities—to seeing the Socialists attempt one, except upon the truly philosophical basis which I ever imagined was to be the foundation of Socialists' communities.

I have no doubt but these views will be thought strange—perhaps ridiculous—for I do not remember broaching them to any one who agreed with me. But as I cannot help believing them, I feel no shame in publishing them. W. C.

RELIGION may debase but can never exalt—it may brutalise but cannot ennoble humanity.

THE PLEASURES OF EDITORSHIP.

[Some time ago an article arrived at our office, entitled an "Examination of Dwight's Theology," from one J. P. who informed us how he had taken in our paper. To this we had no objection: but if he had taken us in it would have formed no inducement to the insertion of his paper. His article was examined by Mr. Ryall, and an answer, respectfully and encouragingly couched, was inserted in the *Movement*.

The paper was declined, as insertions go by merit and usefulness and not by favour. The article, as he desired it, we re-posted, an extra editorial duty—and when we were meditating on the gratification our friend would feel at all the trouble we were at on his behalf, we received the following consolatory epistle.—G. J. H.]

HOLYOAKE,—Having seen thy objections for not inserting my letter in the *Movement*, and having likewise seen, as thou sayest, the misplacing of the attributes, but thinking at the same it would have been more to thy credit as a fault-finder, to have substituted a few proper attributes for the improper ones, seeing it would not have occupied much of thy time, but perhaps anticipating no direct interest thou would'st not correct it.

Thou sayest "there is too large a proportion borrowed," there might be, but are thy ideas and reasonings strictly original? and if I commit errors for want of education, there was a time when thou wast under similar difficulties, but instead of accusing me of ignorance, and treating me with contempt, it would have been far more becoming to have pointed out the errors, and guarding me against them for the future; but it is very probable, had I been an esquire I should have had justice done, but being only a labouring man I am treated with everything but justice.

Having taken the *Oracle* from its commencement to its close, &c. with the *Investigator*, and I am now taking 2 numbers of *Movement* weekly, besides all the *Trials* for Blasphemy, and several times supporting the Union, and when asking for one single privilege it is repeatedly refused, but I have not the least doubt had the letter in question been inserted, I should have found sale for dozens, but having been denied the right of its insertion I shall in consequence of not receiving that privilege which others receive, I shall withhold my support, and at the same time button up my breeches-pocket.

From one who never wrote a dozen letters,
J. P.

I may be "set down" as an "ignoramus" for using the word *thou*, those who think proper may do so.

JUST PUBLISHED, *Third Edition*, cloth lettered—Price 1s. 6d.—(For the use of Literary Classes and Mechanics' Institutions),

PRACTICAL GRAMMAR!
OR COMPOSITION DIVESTED OF DIFFICULTIES.
BY G. JACOB HOLYOAKE.

"Mr. Holyoake's grammar is in some passages very smartly written. There is an acuteness of mind shown in this little book, a perspicuity too of intellect which leads us to hope, that time and study will show Mr. Holyoake capable of much better things, though from what we have said we by no means wish it to be induced that this grammar of Mr. Holyoake's is not an exceedingly clever production for so young a man as we take him to be."—*Hunt's London Journal.*

London: J. Watson, 5, Paul's Alley, Paternoster-row.

THE VALUE OF BIOGRAPHY IN THE FORMATION OF INDIVIDUAL CHARACTER.
By G. JACOB HOLYOAKE.

"It is a sincere work; there is no flattering in the manner of its execution; and it is beautifully written. It is a chaste thoughtful style, and expresses what is to be expressed, clearly, distinctly, and with energy. Works of this kind, on a grander scale than the one before us, are needed; and a better set of instructors could not be found for the rising generation."—*The Apprentice.*

London: J. Watson, 5, Paul's Alley, Paternoster-row.

THE VISIT TO HARMONY HALL!
With a New and Curious Vindicatory Chapter, containing the Suppressed Discussions at Branch A 1.
By G. J. H.
London: Hetherington, 40, Holywell Street, Strand.

BRANCH A 1 DISCUSSION.—The debate on the necessity of rescinding the resolution passed at a thinly attended meeting of the members of the above Branch on Sunday, December 29, in reference to the "Visit," was resumed on Sunday morning last by Mr. Hornblower, who, after noticing the rude and uncourteous remarks which appeared in the *New Moral World* of last week in reply to the resolution of the Leicester Branch, placed the position of the two parties before the meeting—and pointed out the injustice of the resolution objected to. Mr. Plastow, Mr. Rowley, and Mr. Jones spoke to the question, and Mr. Hetherington closed the debate by a very able and successful reply. He called upon the Branch to rescind the resolution on the ground that it was contrary to fact, and that as their precipitation had driven them one step in the wrong direction, it would be more in character with their principles to retrace it, than still to persevere in a course which could only irritate and divide the society. Mr. Whitaker, although not approving of the whole of Mr. H.'s resolution, was still of opinion that the resolution on the books was not substantially true, and therefore moved that the resolution of the 29th be rescinded, and that this be inserted in the *New Moral World.* Mr. Jones seconded Mr. Whitaker's amendment—admitting the verbal inaccuracy of the former resolution. Mr. Hetherington and Mr. Hornblower withdrew their resolution—and that of Mr. Whitaker was then put and carried almost unanimously. Mr. Jones then submitted another resolution expressive of the Branch's regret at much that Mr. Holyoake had done, and that his conduct was highly censurable. An adjournment was proposed, as also an amendment to the effect that all censure should be omitted. The adjournment was lost and the amendment carried. The resolution, minus the censure, was then put and carried. J. H.

A COMMUNIST ASSOCIATION has been recently formed at Paris under new auspices—no less than those of the Swedish Ambassador. It is a Scandinavian Society, being composed of natives of three of the northern countries, namely, Sweden, Denmark, and Norway, known formerly by this general title. This forms a most interesting link to the chain of social progress, embracing an outline which includes in its area the three most enlightened states of Northern Europe. These, in addition to the German, French, and English Communists, afford indications which may reasonably cheer and encourage the devoted few everywhere.

ANNOUNCEMENT is made of a "New Advocate of the Rights of Labour," in the shape of a weekly periodical, to be called *The Tribune.* Its principles and plans are stated in the prospectus to consist of "A full Examination and Discussion of the various plans before the Public for the Removal of National Distress; the proceedings of Trade Societies and Bodies for the purpose of effecting social improvements; the Employment of the People upon the LAND; Emigration, with Expositions of the best Localities to select, and Plans on which to proceed." &c., &c. It is now published—a notice will appear.

TO CORRESPONDENTS.

"*Materialist's*" interesting extract from "Vestiges of Creation" is forwarded to Mr. Chilton, who has specially directed his attention to the natural, as contradistinguished from the unnatural, origin of the animate as well as mineral world. "Materialist" will observe in our pages that W. C. now casts a critical eye on the important philosophical work, the merits of which he could at first only convey to us at second-hand, through the literary columns of the *Examiner.*

ANNOUNCEMENTS.—Our readers generally must understand that notices of intended Lectures, Discussions, and Publications received by us are promptly inserted—any omissions are referible to the neglect of secretaries and publishers.

RECEIVED.—"The Total Abstainers Defended," a small pamphlet, the purport of which is sufficiently indicated by the title.—Forwarded, the letter of "*An Ex-Five Years' Member.*"

LECTURES.

Jan. 26.—Social Institution, Market Place, Leicester, Mr. G. J. Holyoake,—The right Interpretation of the Bible decided.
Jan. 27.————— Rhetoric, or the art of communicating thought, explained.
Jan. 26.—Branch A 1, John Street, Tottenham Court Road,—A Lecture. At 7, P.M.
Jan. 26.—Finsbury Institution, Goswell Road, Mr. Cooper,—On the Religion of the New Moral World. Discussion after.—Will the Principles propounded by Robert Owen extinguish sectarian animosity?
Jan. 26.—National Hall, High Holborn, W. J. Fox,—On the "Form of prayer, with Fasting, to be used yearly on the 30th of January." King Charles' Martyrdom.

SUBSCRIPTIONS
TO THE ANTI-PERSECUTION UNION.
B. T.................................... 0 3 0

PATERSON TESTIMONIAL.
W. J. B., sixth subscription............ 1 0 0
G. J. H., Sec.

Printed and Published by G. J. HOLYOAKE, 40, Holywell-street, Strand.
Wednesday, January 22, 1845.

THE MOVEMENT
And Anti=Persecution Gazette.

"Maximise morals, minimise religion."—BENTHAM.

No. 59.   EDITED BY G. JACOB HOLYOAKE, AND M. Q. RYALL.   Price 1½d

THE INDUSTRIOUS ORDERS,
AND "TRADES UNIONS" IN PARTICULAR.

THE establishment of a new organ of the industrious hand-workers has been suggestive of some reflections which, though they have swelled to inappropriate dimensions for our journal, have been thought to present some features differing sufficiently from the "common run" to excuse the space which is devoted to them.

I shall endeavour in the following remarks—not framed according to popular recipes—to give some hints and helps towards advancing the operatives in the right direction, and to draw a line of distinction between their true and false friends.

The publication alluded to, (the *Tribune*), which was announced last week, is since published. It is of the larger size, as periodicals now go, of course excepting such leviathans as the *Family Herald*—its price Twopence. The topics of the first number are comprised principally in an opening article on the "Iniquity of the Game Laws" —Correspondence between Mr. Duncombe, M.P. and Mr. Drury, Secretary to the Sheffield trades,—a narrative Sketch of Poaching life,—Communications on trades, organisations, and the obtainment of Land by the operative classes—an account of Mr. Etzler's Venezuelan scheme of Emigration, with other matters of similar import.

Its sphere of action is one in which much good may be accomplished. Such an organ is capable of contributing most powerfully to the advancement of the "industrious orders" by teaching and urging upon them the necessity of extensive instead of petty, local organisations, and specially the paramount importance of social meliorations *emanating from themselves*.

How this promises to be accomplished by the periodical in question is not so readily to be determined by perusal of a first number. Much more interesting and numerous "reports of industrial progress" are promised, as well as a wider field of intelligence.

A good Trades Unions' advocate as well as reporter—a cheap unstamped one—would be a most valuable auxiliary of democracy, if conducted in an enlightened spirit. The Trade sections do not require, for their best understood and most permanent interests, an upholder of petty tricks and devices— unfortunately too prevalent—but a firm upright organ of their interests, which would scorn to recommend a meanness or injustice even in self-defence, and for the resistance of oppression; one which shall never lose sight of what should be the great ultimate object of the industrious—to which "the fair day's wage for a fair day's work" is but the stepping-stone—namely, *the absolute enjoyment, without the intervention of middle-men, agents, or masters, of the full results of their labour;*

A firm and truthful Mentor of the operative, while exposing the grinding exactions and inexorable oppressions of the masterclass will not flinch from pointing out, with inflexible determination, the errors and follies besetting the objects of his best counsel and affections. It may be a thankless office, his efforts may be taken ill on the part of those upon whom they are intended, and calculated, to enlighten and amend—motives of envy, thirst of distinction, love of paradox, malice, all sorts of unworthy motives may be imputed—the public instructor, guided by conscious integrity and singleness of purpose, must be content to brave all this —nay more, be prepared to hear himself accused of the paltry desire of increasing the sale of his journal, regardless of other results, while he may know, if he calculated results, that he was rather endangering his popularity. Throughout the gulphs and shoals — perils and difficulties of popular journalism, he must continue bidding defiance to power and authority, scorning to flatter and cajole the humble—sternly just to each, yet withal regarding with the kindliest sympathies the bruised reeds of society, those who through the infamous pressure of a system of inequality, are forced into the position of outlaws and outcasts, socially, politically, and morally.

The Trades' unionists would be taught that there is a deep vein of aristocracy running through *them*, and that there is no more contemptible development of aristocracy than that which peeps under the garb of the fustian whose wearer is inveighing against the privileges and usurpations of rank and fortune. While instructed to work out his own emancipation, he must be taught not to fling away arrogantly or contemptuously the proffered services of educated non-workers, who may be as democratic and true lovers of equality as himself. To command the sympathy and alliance of such men, the skilled artisan—of whom the strength and intelligence of Trades' unions are mainly composed—must know or be taught that those beneath him—according to the commonly-accepted false estimate of social gradation—are similarly entitled to his assistance and co-operation, and that he is equally bound to hold out the hand of fellowship, to his less dextrous, or less fortunate brother and sister worker, to the miserable and destitute toiler at the spade, the hand-loom, the needle, or other helpless slave of the profit-mongering of individuals or the tyranny of the system.

The inculcation of such sentiments, the stimulus to such conduct, is one of the highest aims of a working man's organ and advocate. By this course a bold advance would be made in true democratic progress. No such fond fiction would be realised as " the reconciliation between the middle and working classes," much dreamt of by kind, simple men, better endowed with good intentions than sharp-sightedness. Nothing of this most undesirable as well as impossible result would be coveted. The able as well as honest people's advocate would well know that the classes, as such, were irreconcilable —properly and naturally antagonistical. The union, the alliance he would desire, the fraternisation he would aim to bring about, would be between the right principled, honest and intelligent, whether of the same or of adverse classes, whether of the industrious, or privileged orders, or the numerous grades lying between the two extremes.

Disposed to examine with rigid scrutiny, the pretensions of patricians to the favour of the people, there is yet one such instance of popular regard and confidence on which I am disposed to look with peculiar satisfaction. The political connection of the Chartists, Unionists, and the manual workers in general with the Hon. Thomas Duncombe, M.P. appears to be that above almost any similar one of which we have accurate knowledge, in which genuine sympathies, steadiness, good sense, non-conventional boldness, and well merited confidence, distinguished the one or the other party to the alliance. Here the man of titles and privilege has stepped out of the frigid region of aristocracy and offered the hand of fellowship to his oppressed and degraded brother man, and offered it in right good earnest, his heart pulsating with kindred emotions of sympathy—his thoughts directed with the same steadfastness of purpose for the elevation of trampled humanity.

A communication is sent by one of the representatives of the working classes, the Secretary of The United Trades of Sheffield, to Mr. Duncombe, in which the following queries are put. I extract the correspondence from the *Tribune*.

" As the trades of Sheffield (in common with the working classes of the country) regard you as the *veritable* representative of the working millions, I *feel emboldened on their behalf*, to request your opinion and advice on the following subjects:—First, I have long been of opinion (and every day's experience serves but to strengthen it) that it is essentially necessary that there should be a thorough organisation and consolidation of the various trades of this country, and that to effect so desirable an object, they should meet by delegation at a conference to be holden in London, where the wise and virtuous from the various classes of wealth-producers, might be enabled to devise and perfect a plan for the more effectual protection of the working classes from oppression and persecution, whether emanating from the Legislature *or from capitalists*, with whom they are more immediately and individually connected.

"Secondly. It is with feelings of the greatest pleasure that I have seen it suggested that a demonstration should take place in London, to escort you to the House of Commons on the same day on which her Majesty opens the Parliament. This, I conceive, is well calculated to arouse the working classes to increased exertions in defence of their rights, and will at once call forth the masses to rally round you, their champion, and inspire them with a confidence to battle by your side, in such a manner as no other movement can at present effect. It will congregate delegates from all parts of the country, bearing testimony of the respect entertained, and the confidence reposed in you, and at the same time will teach this moral lesson to those who are enemies to Labour's rights— that *the producers of all wealth are fully alive to any attempt that may be made to prostrate Labour still further at the shrine of Capital*. That demonstration, sir, you must allow to go forward, as it is eminently calculated to produce morally a great amount of good.

"Thirdly, I have seen by the the public prints that you intend originating a motion for the *Repeal* of the " ratepaying clauses in the Reform act." As I believe that the efforts of hon. members to effect any measure of reform may be greatly assisted by the support which they receive out of doors, I wish to know if numerous petitions in favour of that object will not be advisable? In short, as it is necessary to strengthen your hands on various questions that may arise, in which the rights of Labour are concerned, I would wish to know how it can be most effectually accomplished."

Mr. Duncombe thus expresses himself, in reply.

"I am much pleased if any information that I can afford to the working classes should lead them seriously to reflect upon their true position; for you may rest assured that thought in the right direction, and acted on wisely, is all that the Trades and industrious classes require to obtain for them not only political emancipation, but some of those practical remedies which the men of Sheffield have so sagaciously adopted ;—I allude principally to their plan of *restriction*, to which my attention was more immediately directed during the discussions of last session upon the "Factory" and " Masters' and Servants'" Bills. If my former note, in which I announced to you the probability of a similar attack upon Labour being made next session, shall have forewarned the Trades and working classes, by stimulating them to such means as through *union* may make their opposition irresistible, I shall consider myself amply repaid. I think we may draw some conclusions as to the tactics likely to be pursued in Parliament by the representatives of wealth, from certain speeches, letters and publications, that have recently appeared, and which leave little doubt in my mind no time should be lost by the working classes, to prepare for a bold and vigorous stand. I fear you overrate my powers of resistance—I am only strong when I represent the *organised* strength of *your* order ; and from my limited knowledge of the machinery by which Trades' Unions are managed, I cannot venture to give you an opinion that should carry weight with it, upon the subject of an improved organisation and consolidation of our various national trades, but if such an object is required, I know of no course (excluded as the working classes are from the parliamentary franchise) better calculated to give effect to that object than that which you suggest, viz., that *the wise and virtuous from all parts of the empire should meet by delegation at a conference in London*, where, co-operating with the metropolitan trades, they shall endeavour to devise such means as shall not only obtain *protection* to the sons of toil from that oppression and persecution of which they have so long and so justly complained, but shall also tend to disabuse the public mind of those prejudices, which I regret to see are now so industriously encouraged against every combination but that of capital and of power.

" As to the time when this conference should be held, I should recommend about Easter, as by that time all ministerial measures, whether affecting trade, commerce, or labour, either will or ought to be before the country, and it could not then be said that it was either premature to discuss them, or too late to resist them. As to the contemplated demonstration on the opening of Parliament, I know nothing of it beyond rumour, and what I read in the public prints; but if it is solely intended as a compliment to myself, and a mere parading through the streets, upon the same day as the Queen, without any definite object, or possible benefit to the working classes, I beg to say that, as far as I am concerned, I will be no party to it, and no man shall leave his employ, or lose his day's wage, on my account.

" I am rejoiced to find you attach some importance to my intended motion for the repeal of the rate-paying clauses, and I certainly think that petitions, numerously signed, and presented by the members representing the localities from which they emanate, will have a most beneficial effect, for I have yet to learn why borough electors —men whom I have always found, if not superior, at all events, equal in intelligence and education to county electors—should be compelled to pay their taxes by a certain day as a condition of their registration, while the small freeholder, and the servile tenant-at-will of an aristocratic landed proprietor, is exempted from any such condition.

" I beg to conclude by assuring you that my untiring and unflinching advocacy of the rights of the industrious classes shall be continued, until, with their assistance, Labour, which is their property, shall be placed upon a perfect equality with the property of all other classes in the state."

This correspondence speaks for itself, admirably illustrating the points endeavoured to be enforced throughout this paper.

Another point in conclusion. The operatives of the Continent are exerting themselves to obtain some meliorations, politically and socially. Among these movements are particularly worthy of attention, the efforts being made in the French capital, to investigate the causes of the wretched depression of the working classes. A loud and indignant cry has gone forth, and the determination on the part of the more advanced reformers to demand a searching systematic inquiry, originating with the "Réforme" newspaper, has been responded to by conductors of Journals in nearly all departments of France.

Our English Trades and their organs will do well to acquaint themselves with what is going on among their Continental brethren. A mutual intelligence would be productive of advantage to both, each are stimulated, strengthened and informed by a mutual intelligence of their respective struggles, failures and successes.

M. Q. R.

THE MANCHESTER BRANCH
versus
BRANCH A 1.

To the Editors of the Movement.

SIRS,—I beg to hand you for insertion in the *Movement* the following resolution which was passed by the Council of the Manchester Branch—and that too, *not* by the promptings or the "*personal presence*" of the individual whom the *New Moral* (?) *World* says wishes to be "whitewashed," or by the influence exercised by "*his near relatives*," but because we conceived that though he had been "heard in his own defence" in Branch A 1, he had not been heard in the *New Moral World*,* and WE *think* that the verdict given in Branch A 1 was a very partial one, and that the chief actors in that Branch were a "*leetle*" too hasty in causing *their* "personal" friends to give it.

I trust we are *not* in the position of the "jury who have given their verdict, after hearing the speech for the plaintiff *only*." yet, had we confined ourselves to the pages of the *New Moral World* we must have done so on hearing the speech *only* of the defendant, or have been silent on the matter, which we don't choose to be.

The *New Moral World* would make it appear that *only in Leicester*, in your "per-

---

[* Respecting the resolution referred to, which appeared in the *New Moral World* of January 4. 1845, Mr. Holyoake was never heard at all—he being absent when it was drawn up].

sonal presence," could such resolutions emanate; but if your *personal presence* was absolutely necessary in the matter, then you must be an *omni*-presence—for, simultaneously with the Leicester resolution, we passed one, and the Stockport Branch were discussing a similar one at the self same time.

We may be condemned for being so "hasty," but we think we only did our *duty* towards Mr. Holyoake—as we would *promptly* do to the parties on the other side the question, under *similar circumstances*—and without saying more on the subject at present, we present the resolution to our friends, as expressive of what we think and feel on the matter.

GEORGE SMITH.

Resolution of the Manchester Branch.

Resolved—"That it is the deliberate opinion of this Council that the insertion of that most cruel and unjust resolution which appeared in the *New Moral World* of January 4th, 1845, condemnatory of Mr. Holyoake's proceedings relative to his late "Visit to Harmony," seems to us contrary to the principles the *New Moral World* professes to advocate—namely, *justice and equality*; it was cruel we *think*, because the resolution was passed in the absence, and without the knowledge of, the individual accused—and unjust because he was *denied* all RIGHT of reply in the paper which published his condemnation. Such gross partiality on the part of the conductors of the *New Moral World*, ill comports with the doctrines and character of the society the paper represents; and *we*, as the head of the Manchester Branch, firm to the principles of justice, deem it our duty thus to express ourselves, and call for an immediate apology for so precipitately publishing the resolution complained of, in order that it may not be considered *we* lend our countenance to such proceedings, and furthermore, to preserve the character and purpose of our organ unsullied for the future.

"JAMES SMITH, Chairman."

PORTUGAL.—The Bishop of Elvas has introduced in the Chamber of Peers a bill prohibiting the importation of immoral and irreligious books, and also "heterodox preaching or teaching in public." The first part, including an index expurgatorius, will probably be struck out; and the latter, supposed to be directed against the missionary labours of Dr. Kalley in Madeira, affirmed.—*Spectator*.

PUBLIC TEA PARTY
IN LEICESTER ON BEHALF OF THE PATERSON TESTIMONIAL FUND.

On Sunday afternoon, January 19, a numerous company of both sexes crowded the Social Institution, Market Place, Leicester, to partake of tea together, and express their regard concerning the incarceration of Mr. Paterson. The assembly was convened by the Leicester Branch of the Anti-Persecution Union, and numbered all the tried friends of free discussion, of both sexes in the town, including Mr. Holyoake's "near relatives." That veteran publicist, and ancient coadjutor of Carlile, Mr. Riley Perry, presided. After the cloth was withdrawn,

Mr. Perry rose and said—The struggle for truth which is continually going on in reference to persecution of opinion, very strongly resembles the storming a town by a body of soldiers, the great mass of the army can never gain admission till a few have volunteered their services as a *forlorn hope* to rush into the "deadly breach," and risk their lives in order to clear the way for their companions to follow them: just so is it requisite for a *forlorn hope* to be continually pushing a-head, and boldly fronting the first discharge of popular indignation, before the mass of mankind can further advance at all. No individual can be more deserving of the esteem, the sympathy, and the support of all enlightened men, than those who, like Paterson, are thus willing to devote themselves, even though they may be wrong in their views, their self-sacrifice is still highly praiseworthy to themselves, and beneficial to the community at large. There can be no fear of truth being endangered by the most searching inquiry, or even by the most furious attacks, if she be left free and unshackled to fight in her own behalf. The only thing to be afraid of is *the suppression of inquiry*, which has a direct tendency to foster error and abuse. The greatest step which society can ever make towards justice and rationality is the acknowledgment of the most unlimited right to all individuals to hold and *express* whatever opinions seem to them most true. It may be conceived that the age of persecution has gone by, but he would say be not too hasty in such judgment, it is true the faggot, the stake, and the torture have been done away with, they were not only exposed to imprisonment on account of religious opinions, but to a still slower species of domestic torture, that of depriving the holder of unpopular or heterodox opinions of the means of a livelihood.

You take my house when you do take the prop
That doth sustain my house. You take my life
When you do take the means whereby I live.

The object of this meeting was to express our sympathy with Thomas Paterson, and he would call upon the Secretary of the parent Anti-Persecution Union to address them.

Mr. G. J. Holyoake of London congratulated the meeting on the numbers present and the animation displayed, and said that on behalf of the London Union he must beg to express their satisfaction at the interest taken in Leicester in the Union's objects, and at the pleasing circumstance that that meeting was presided over by Mr. Perry who has suffered three years imprisonment for the part he had taken with the late Mr. Carlile in supporting free discussion. He (Mr. H.) knew that Mr. Paterson would highly appreciate the honour conferred upon him by Mr. Perry's presence. Mr. H. then expatiated on the general principle sought by the Union to be established, and the direct interest every man and woman had in carrying it forward to success.

The lecture on that evening was preceded by reading a portion of the opening article in this quarter's *Zoist*, and the profits of the tea party, together with that of a private one previously held, and subscriptions given on the present occasion amounted to £2. 10s. Can no other provincial town go and do likewise?

MR. PATERSON'S LIBERATION.
To the Editors of the Movement.

Sirs,—Your No. 55 contained a call on Mr. Paterson to "appear unto his Scottish Atheistical admirers." Is it fair to ask what kind of admirers are those who have never yet thought of the object of their admiration? We have an old English way of estimating professions by practice. But up to the time of Mr. Anderson's letter appearing, besides one shilling from himself, no one person (save Cosmopolite) has ever sent a single sixpence to the Paterson Testimonial Fund.

Is it true that there are "a whole host of towns favourable to free inquiry" in Scotland, and so few have yet thought of contributing to improve the position of one who has been immured among them 15 months for the advocacy of a principle they affect to be in love with? It is not too late, let us hope to have intelligible evidence in the shape of contributions to the Testimonial Fund, that this regard for Mr. Paterson is not very economical affection—unless I see the Testimonial swelled by Scottish subscribers, I shall have an horror of Scottish "admiration."

I trust regard will be had to Mr. Paterson's health. After so long a confinement any sudden excitement must prove injurious. He must not be drawn into public to his own danger. Besides in health or out of it, he can't "coach it" to places around Perth or elsewhere without cash. Then let the means at once be forthcoming to enable Mr. Paterson to "appear unto his friends" like one from the clouds—not as one from the dead.   A WELL KNOWN SUBSCRIBER.

REPORT FROM MANCHESTER.

22nd January, 1845.

DEAR SIR,—For the *Movement* you were kind enough to forward I am much obliged. In the last which has come to hand, it is said you have received several letters expressing approval of the proposed *Atheon*.—I hope the "value" of them is considerable. It was well to drop a hint that little could be done by you in the matter till something was done by others. The Prospectuses you gave me I have distributed among such parties in this locality as are likely to take an interest in the right wise work of studding our priest-ridden country with comfortable Halls of Reason, from which, as a thing of course, all the gods will be excluded. On Sunday the 12th inst. attention was publicly and pointedly called to your Prospectus by the President of this Branch —you may therefore calculate upon communications from this quarter. As to my affairs, all that need be said about them may be said in a few words. They are by no means yet in the state known among Cockneys as *hickledy pickledy*. I have the whole field to myself. Before leaving London, a person told me that Mrs. Martin had laid more Manchester parsons than they had laid ghosts, and if sceptical then, I do now fully believe it, for not so much as half a parson, or even the ghost of one, has honoured me by his presence. But *nil desperandum*, the Rev. Mr. Stephens is to debate with me to morrow and Friday night in Staley Bridge. That distinguished Christian, and no less distinguished Radical, has engaged to make out that the "five fundamental principles of Socialism" are "five lumps of humbug." Of the debate, if it comes off, you shall have an account, unless I happen to be "killed off" in the course of it. On Sunday afternoon, and the evening of Tuesday next, I have engaged to deliver lectures in Ashton-under-Lyne, the proceeds of which (necessary expenses apart) will go to swell and dignify the Paterson Testimonial. My first lecture *here* was attended by about nine hundred persons—a much larger number, *on dit*, than has been brought within the Hall of Science walls since Mrs. M.'s departure. Notwithstanding the potent attractiveness of Mr. Etzler, who, the same evening in Carpenters' Hall charmed "the folk" by his matter of fact description of a Tropical Paradise, my second lecture drew more than a thousand listeners. Its subject was The Nature and Influence of Superstition. Though many very alarming things were said on that occasion, strange to relate, no alarm was manifested. The third and last Sunday evening lecture was equally well attended. On that occasion Feargus O'Connor, Dr. McDouall, and other leading Chartists addressed their friends in Carpenters' Hall. My week or unholy night lectures are various as regards topic, and promise to be productive in a monetary, if in no other sense. Beyond all question, the Manchester investigators are strongly antitheologic in their tendencies—so much so indeed, that the more irreligiously bold their lecturer, the better they like him. Anything short of plain truth will no longer satisfy them. This result we owe in part to you and in part to Mrs. Martin, of whom they speak with enthusiasm.

Sincerely Yours,   C. S.

BEAUTIES OF LAW & RELIGION.

POLITICAL ESAUS,—*Important to Pietists.* —One of the conditions of the right of voting for members of parliament, in the Borough of Wilton, before the passing of the Reform Act, was that the voter should have done all corporate acts and have taken the Sacrament of the Lord's Supper within one year of the election. The Reform Act preserved this right to those who possessed it at the time of the passing of the Act, so long as they continued to be qualified on the 31st of July in every year.

There are now on the Register of Voters for Wilton, twelve persons who claim in respect of this right, but it is said that while they have religiously observed one of the conditons of the right, namely, doing all corporate acts, the principal of which is attending the corporation dinners, they have neglected the less substantial meal—the Lord's Supper.

Here is a pretty little chance for the Lord's Lambs—a nice new way of annoying those who neglect God for Mammon or pleasure—get them struck off the List of Voters.

The pious *Patriot*—that chuckled over the re-appointment, as Consul at the Antipodes, of incendiary Pritchard—showed great alacrity in pointing out the above disqualification.—There is a bible hero who, they tell us, sold his birthright for a mess of pottage. Now good-natured people would excuse Esau, who was well nigh starved by his family, and had not even a " Poor Law Union" to go to—but as the cockneys would say—these " Wilton woters must be wery wicked willains" to like dinner and disfranchisement better than sacred bread and suffrage.

A TRUE " ORACLE.— Somebody, somewhere in the *Oracle*, said something to the following effect—If any body were to be really and positively a Christian among us, very summary consignment to jail or to bedlam would be his fate.—How fully this is made out, a recent newspaper case—a mixture of the horrible and the ludicrous—miserably attests.—A young Christian woman had not only read her master's commands, but was resolved, devoutly, implicitly, and religiously to obey them. She had marked the unmistakable injunction, " If thy right eye offend thee, pluck it out," and detected in the extraordinary and almost unparelleled act of faithfully obeying the divine command.—This was sufficient offence to her fellow Christians, who, finding the offending member on the floor of her apartment, dragged this only obedient Christian to Hanwell Lunatic Asylum. Thus would not these officious religionists suffer a fellow worshipper to settle the account between herself and her eye. How knew they to what extent the young woman's eye had " offended ?" How could they deny its probably numerous, unchristian, unspiritual though most natural wanderings to forbidden ground? Of what use to them was the text "judge not, lest ye be judged ?" Oh vile hypocrites and spiritual Pecksniffs, unworthy pretenders to the name of Christian, with prisons for opponents and madhouses for followers ? what should we Atheists not additionally suffer if ye were not also bent on devouring one another ?

M. Q. R.

THE AUTHORITY OF SCRIPTURE.—*By the Unknown.*—A friendly but fruitless attempt to reconcile religion and philosophy. The author introduces the two parties as " angry" with each other. Whatever religion may be—and we know that it is not often good tempered — philosophy is never "angry" with any one. It understands matters better. The *Unknown* polishes and apologises for the Bible, and suggests for it a universal explanation, but on the same principle and with the same success he might do the same thing with Gulliver's Travels, and prove that work to be a "revelation of truth to all men."

UTILITY.—Rightly understood the doctrine of utility must be regarded as the most certain criterion by which to distinguish between true Philosophy and pseudo-science. The institutions of the past which do not aid actual society are obsolete and dead, the doctrine regarding the future which is not of present utility is a mere dream.—*Athenæum.*

BALANCE SHEET OF THE ANTI-PERSECUTION UNION.

For the Quarter ending December 29, 1844.

RECEIPTS.					EXPENDITURE.			
To Subscriptions, per *Movement* No. 43..	0	10	0		To Balance due to Treasurer............	0	13	3
Do. do. — 44..	1	0	9		To " Paterson Testimonial "............	*6	11	6
Do. do. — 45..	0	2	0		To Mr. Johnson.......................	4	16	10
Do. do. — 46..	0	19	2		1000 " Last of the Martyrs "............	1	6	0
Do. do. — 47..	7	3	1		Mr. Whiting, per Bristol subscription.....	0	5	0
Do. do. — 48..	0	17	5		To printing official and other notices in 12			
Do. do. — 49..	1	12	2½		Gazettes..............................	1	10	0
Do. do. — 50..	4	10	11½		Expenses of Public Meeting respecting Hull,			
Do. do. — 51..	0	12	5		including Posters, small Bills, reports, &c.	1	2	6
Do. do. — 52..	2	15	4		Advertisement of resolution of Public Meeting in three Hull papers................	1	10	0
Do. do. — 53..	1	16	6		To *Gazettes* circulated, containing reports of			
Do. do. — 54..	1	16	5		Public Meeting, official notices, acknowments of Subscriptions, &c............	0	16	0
					To various newspapers, Acts of Parliament	0	8	0
Audited by us and found correct,					General Correspondence, Post Orders, &c..	1	15	3
JOHN ELLIS, } Auditors.					Assistant Secretary.....................	2	0	0
JOHN SKELTON, }					Balance in hand........................	1	1	11
	£23	16	3			£23	16	3

* This Fund now amounts to £16. 7s. 6d.

A COURSE OF FIVE LECTURES
WILL BE DELIVERED BY
MR. G. JACOB HOLYOAKE,

At the Hall of Science, Commercial Place, City Road, on the following subjects:—

Lecture 1. Sunday evening, February 9, 1845,—On the Reputed Recantation (of Atheism) of Frances Wright, now Madame D'Arusmont.

Lecture 2. Sunday evening, February 16,—On the Late Thomas Campbell's description of an Atheist, in his celebrated "Pleasures of Hope."

Lecture 3. Sunday evening, February 23,—The effects of Solitary Confinement, in answer to Luke Roden's article on the Pentonville Prison, in the "Illuminated Magazine."

Lecture 4. Sunday evening, March 2,—The different modes of advocating Popular Rights, as illustrated by the "Chimes" of Charles Dickens.

Lecture 5. Sunday evening, March 9,—The Origin of Man as set forth in that extraordinary work just published, entitled "Vestiges of the Natural History of Creation."

Each lecture to commence at 7 o'clock. Admission 2d. Discussion permitted.

EDINBURGH.—The lectures of Mrs. Martin have created a sensation in Edinburgh which baffles all description. The blood of the Christians has been, during the last few weeks, several degrees above "fever heat." The writer of the article in the *Witness* made a grand mistake when he stated that Mrs. M. "Thicks man's blood with cold," had you seen the feeling manifested yesterday by the Edinburgh Christians, you would have been inclined to think quite the reverse. M. R.

BRISTOL.—This day, (January 29) and February 12, discourses will be delivered at the Public Hall, Temple Street, Bristol, by G. Powel, W. Channing, G. Revell, and W. Cook, on the four Elements of Society,—Knowledge, Government, Production, and Distribution, to which the people of Bristol are respectfully requested to attend.—On February 5, and the following alternate Wednesdays, selections from the writings of Southwell, Holyoake, Ryall, Paterson, &c. will be read by W. Cook, commencing each evening at 8 o'clock.

[This course is stated to have been adopted on account of misrepresentations of the above writings by some members of the Christian body].

RELIGIOUS ILLUMINATION.—We have been accustomed to talk of benighted Christians loving darkness and obscurity, but they have been illuminating the good people of Newtown in Montgomeryshire with a vengeance. A freethinker died, leaving behind him the works of Paine, Combe, &c., his widow consulted her christian neighbours as to their disposal, who determined on buying and burning them. This is not the first time Tom Paine has enlightened the world through Christian fanaticism —and in this way too—but this is certainly a revival, if it is not a burning shame, for 1845.

BRANCH A 1 DISCUSSION.—We understand that our recent publication of Mr. Trevelyan's letter was the subject of severe animadversion on Sunday morning last. Mr. Jones introduced the subject, and a resolution highly censurable of Mr. Holyoake's conduct was proposed by Mr. P. Wood. The question was adjourned till next Sunday morning on the motion of Mr. Hetherington.

MR. HOLYOAKE will meet his Class at Branch 53 on Sunday, February 2nd.

ALL Communications for Mr. Holyoake to be addressed to 40, Holywell Street, Strand, London.

T. S. DUNCOMBE, M.P.—Very opportunely in connection with our notice of this gentleman and the "Trades," an announcement is made of a *Soiree* to be held at the White Conduit Tavern, on Monday the 3rd of February, "in honour to the people's representative." Some of the most radical M.P.'s are invited. Watson and others have tickets and particulars.

TO CORRESPONDENTS.

M. A. SIDDLE.—His letter will receive attention immediately on Mr. Holyoake's return to town.

W. COOK.—No. 2 of the *Plebeian* has not been received in London.—W. C. draws our attention to the case of the Parson prosecuting his servant girl for *selling his dripping*. Clerical delinquencies are too numerous either for insertion, or even notice in our limited space, as they occur. This is the more especial vocation of the *Dispatch*, and right well it does its work. The various Christian newspapers too assist wonderfully by clawing one another, to make us the less regret our inability, even if we had the inclination, to lend a helping hand. These clerical exposes are more properly and appropriately the work of the anti-christian-*abuse*, or deistical and sectarian prints—an *anti-goddist* organ has nobler functions.—W. C. has our acknowledgments for his assiduity. We desire from him and all our readers every piece of information they can furnish that is fully authenticated. If we cannot use such statements in detail, they may help to frame a statistical table which would be valuable.

R. S.—Capital notions those of "Good Old Times," when a fellow could as coolly write down "2s. 8d. for wood, stake and staple to burn a heretic" as he could his washerwoman's bill. Some more "records" would be acceptable. A recommendation of R. S. is worth consideration by our Atheistical friends. It is that they should mingle more with the *Temperance Societies* to procure the exclusion of Christian dogma from their rules and practices *as societies*.

RECEIVED.—J. S.—The "Grave" is the better piece, but neither have *insertible* merit.—Z. P. The same is true of his acrostic.—Address of confidence on the subject of the "Harmony" papers, from James Daly, Rochdale, and other members of Branch 24.—R. G. Gammage's letter and pamphlet, they shall have due attention.

LECTURES.

Feb. 2.—Branch A 1, John Street, Tottenham Court Road,—A Lecture. At 7, P.M.

Feb. 2.—Social Institution, 5, Charlotte Street, Blackfriars Road, Mr. Ellis, subject,—Devils.

Feb. 2.—Finsbury Institution, Goswell Road, Mr. P. Jones,—On Human Destiny. Discussion after,—Can Man be indefinitely Improved?

Feb. 2.—National Hall, High Holborn, W. J. Fox, On the Study of Fact and Fiction.

SUBSCRIPTIONS
TO THE ANTI-PERSECUTION UNION.

Mr. Coltman, piano-forte tuner, Leicester 0 2 6

PATERSON TESTIMONIAL.

Profits of public tea party in Leicester	1	4	6
To private tea party, do	0	7	0
To subscriptions, do	0	18	6
From five friends in Leith, per Mr. Baker	0	1	6
Turnbull Weston, per Miss Roalfe	0	1	4
Thomas Drummond, do	0	1	1
Laurence Hooper, do	0	1	4
R. S	0	1	0

G. J. H., *Sec.*

Printed and Published by G. J. HOLYOAKE, 40, Holywell-street, Strand.
Wednesday, January 29, 1845.

THE MOVEMENT

And Anti=Persecution Gazette.

"Maximise morals, minimise religion."—BENTHAM.

No. 60.   EDITED BY G. JACOB HOLYOAKE, AND M. Q. RYALL.   Price 1½d

DR. KALLEY TO MR. HOLYOAKE.
LETTER V.
Madeira, 24th Nov., 1844.

DEAR SIR,

1st. In consequence of you having addressed your letter to me "*via* France," it arrived covered with post marks, having been about six weeks on the way, which will account for the delay of my reply.

2nd. In paragraph 1st you maintain that the Atheist's field of observation is the same "as the Theist's, his means of observing the same, his powers the same, his interest in exercising them is the same, and his researches are as extensive." You then ask "how I can, under circumstances of such close affinity, and under the operation of equal evidence, allow rational certainty on the one side, and deny it on the other." I answer that the Christian has *certainty*, because in the phenomena within and around him, he finds ample proof of the being of a God. The Atheist, as stated in paragraph 13 of my 2nd to you, after having examined every corner of earth, and all that it contains, without finding any proof of the being of a God, would still not be warranted in concluding with certainty that there is no God. He could have reasonable certainty only with regard to the field which he had examined. He must admit that in other parts of the universe there may exist proofs that would convince even him ; and, therefore, after all his efforts, he cannot get further than to say, "I suppose that there is no God, but (as in paragraph 7 of your 2nd) that there may be a God I admit." The proper meaning of the term "certainty" I believe to be absolute ; and if you had *certainty* in Atheism, I do not know how you could make the admission quoted above. Still further, I cannot grant that there is such an equality of circumstances as you represent, for even in your last letter, paragraph 8, you say that "the crime is but trivial of *dissuading investigation*, where *nothing can be known.*" You take for granted the very thing in dispute, and in virtue of this previous opinion recommend *not to examine*. Now there must be a vast difference between the researches of the Theist and those of the Atheist, seeing Atheism DISSUADES INVESTIGATION, and Theism asks it. Atheism *recommends ignorance*, declaring it to be "*necessary*," while Christianity says "Prove all things."

3rd. I grant that in matters which do not much concern our interests, we may reasonably rest *in quiet ignorance* satisfied without absolute certainty, as is the case with the subject of witches, sylphs, and fairies ; but the existence or non-existence of a God bears so closely on our happiness here, and throughout the duration of our existence, that I cannot think it reasonable to rest without " CERTAINTY," and I believe that a man may attain as much certainty of the being of a God, as of his own.

4th. You regard my return to the argument of design as a result of my mistaking reiteration for new evidence. I did not make that mistake, but returned to the argument of design in compliance with your suggestion that the question should be discussed as one of probability or improbability, wishing simply to recall to your mind the combination of myriads of parts in the human body, and to propose the question, whether the probability is in favour of, or against the idea that such arrangement was designed to produce the end which it, in fact, does produce.

5th. To me it seems very evident on which side probability lies ; and I suspect that, on this point, you are very much of the same opinion with myself, for from paragraph 19 of your letter I understand that your denial of design in the structure of the human body, does not rest on any improbability, or absurdity in the idea that such combination implies design, but on the supposition that the acknowledgment of design must lead to "the monstrous hypothesis of an infinite series of huge beings, disporting in boundless space, rising in awful gradation one above another." The acknowledgment of a Self-Existent quite relieves you from that difficulty ; for then design, instead of leading to the monstrous hypothesis which you have supposed, only leads to the SELF-

Existent. Now if you have no interest in nor taste for evasion, if the proposition that the combination of millions of parts for the production of one end, does not involve the absurdity which you had supposed, and if you have no other objection to that proposition, I hope you will not persist in denying what is so plain to common sense. In this case, however, there is no way of avoiding the conclusion that the Self-Existent is wise. If Atheism require as an essential part of its foundation a denial of the proposition that the combination of millions of parts for one end implies design, its superstructure must be insecure.

6th. You grant that there are "powers co-eval with eternity," but deny the existence of design in the mechanism within and around us. Is there clearer proof of the power whose existence you confess, than there is of the wisdom whose existence you deny? To me the proofs of wisdom appear at least equal to those of power, and I know no principle of reasoning on which the existence of the one is recognized, and that of the other denied.

7th. You object that "a designer of nature only leads to a designer of Deity," and in support of your assertion, state (paragraph 19) that "the intelligent designer involves a material personality, the personality includes an organisation, this implies the presence of contrivance, which again leads to a contriver," and so on. I do not think it worth while to dispute about the word "person" which you quote from Paley in paragraph 4 of your 4th. Could we agree about its meaning, it might be convenient to use the term, but convenience must give place to perspicuity. Therefore I decline it as undefined. The word "personality," which you employ, seems to me still more objectionable for the same reason, and especially when combined with the term "material." I frankly confess that I do not know what a "material personality" is. If it mean *something consisting entirely of matter*, then your assertion that an "intelligent designer involves a material personality," is merely an assumption of what is disputed. If, however, design imply merely *something consisting entirely of matter*, why do you feel obliged for the sake of consistency to deny design in the formation of our frames, and in the movements of the universe, while you acknowledge the existence of matter? If an intelligent designer does not involve only *something consisting altogether of matter*, what else does it involve? Why not an immaterial substance—that is, a substance possessing properties different from those of mere matter, and by way of distinction called "spirit?" Why may not the Self-Existent be a spirit, possessing life, power, wisdom, goodness, and all the attributes essential for the creation and government of the material universe? If design does not involve a *material* personality, it does not imply organisation or contrivance, and therefore does not lead to a contriver.

8th. You tell me that "a self-existent immateriality is nothing," and in this I quite agree with you. The terms immateriality, invisibility, and others of the same class, denote negative qualities of certain substances—and to my mind a *self*-existent *negative quality* is nothing; but who would think of denying the existence of a *substance* because of its possessing a negative quality, such as invisibility? No one doubts the existence of common air, although invisible, and although a self-existent invisibility is as truly nothing as a self-existent immateriality. Air possesses positive qualities which demonstrate its existence, although invisible, and with the same certainty the existence of God is demonstrated, although Deity be immaterial, by the positive attributes or qualities, power, wisdom, goodness, and others.

9th. You add that it is a solecism to say that immateriality exists. I reply that it is neither more nor less a solecism to speak of the existence of immateriality, than it is to speak of the existence of invisibility—both being negative qualities.

10th. You ask if "powers co-eval with eternity, can be inherent in immateriality." Let me reply by asking whether powers may not be inherent in an invisible substance, though they be not inherent in invisibility? Is it customary to propose such questions as whether one *quality*, namely power, is inherent in another *quality*, namely immateriality? Or would it be more in accordance with the common mode of language to ask if a *quality* resides in a *substance*? Or to put the question in a simple form, what would you think if I were to ask if form is inherent in colour? This would be like your question, can power be inherent in immateriality?

11th. You allege further that the question between us is whether the Self-Existent be immateriality, or matter. If your statement were correct, our question would amount merely to this, "Is the Self-Existent something or nothing?" for I have already granted that a self-existent immateriality is nothing. I understand the question, however, to be not merely whether the Self-Existent be, or be not, a negative *property*—equal to nothing—but whether the self-existent *substance* possess the qualities of matter, or others (such as life, wisdom, and goodness) different from those of matter.

12th. I maintain that on the hypothesis of the Self-Existent being mere matter, it is impossible to explain the phenomena of life, and proofs of design, and that it would be as reasonable to deny the *being* of a Self-Existent, as to deny that the Self-Existent is living, wise, powerful, and good. As, however, these are not qualities of matter, I maintain that the self-existent substance must be something different from mere matter.

13th. You assert that "matter is a self-existent being"—"matter always was "—" the human powers can conceive of no other independent existence "—" powers are matter's properties "—" disassociated from matter powers were never known "—" the age of matter is the measure of eternity "—" the only conceivable powers co-eval with eternity are matter's properties "—and that "*consciousness* tells us it is eternal." You thus take for granted the very thing in dispute—but assertions are not proof—reiteration is not evidence—and how *consciousness* can tell us that matter is eternal, I am unable to imagine.

14th. You assert further that " creation is a contradiction," that it is as impossible as the formation " of a triangle in the form of a circle,' and therefore " an absurdity." And you assign my words in proof of your position, "had there ever been absolutely utter nothing, there must have continued to be absolutely utter nothing for ever." If I had said that once there was "absolutely utter nothing," and afterwards a creation took place—or if I had supposed a creation without an adequate cause—there would have been room for your assertions. It would have been absurd and contradictory to hold such views—but I maintain that there is a Self-Existent being, and that in the arrangement and government of the universe there are proofs that the Self-Existent possesses wisdom and power so vast, that human faculties cannot prescribe limits to them—and therefore it is impossible to make good the assertion that creation is a contradiction or impossibility. To me, creation seems no more contradictory, impossible, or absurd, than that I began to live a certain number of years ago.

(*To be concluded next week.*)

ATHEISM AND DEISM.

[The following is the substance of a Speech delivered by Mr. SOUTHWELL, at the Lambeth Branch, in reply to a Lecture delivered a short time ago by Mr. Jones, at Branch A 1. The Central Board wrote to the President of the Lambeth Branch censuring the delivery of Mr. Southwell's reply. At the morning meeting of Branch 53, on Sunday, Jan. 26, the Correspondence between the Central Board and the President was duly canvassed. The result was a general expression of approval and confidence in the President and approbation of the course that he had pursued. On this account Mr. Southwell's reply will be read with interest—but this is not the only reason of its publication, for steps were taken to secure a report of it at the time of its delivery, and of course before it could be dreamed that it was to be the subject of the Central Board's animadversion.]

THIS certainly is the age of oddities broken loose. They come upon us in all shapes, of all kinds, and in all directions. They present themselves every week of the year, every day of the week, and almost every hour of the day. There are Whig oddities, Tory oddities, Chartist oddities, Complete Suffrage oddities, and a " number numberless " of other oddities. But, perhaps, the oddest of all oddities are Socialist oddities, and certainly the oddest of Socialist oddities is Mr. Lloyd Jones, whose lately delivered lecture about what *he* calls Atheism and Deism, I am here to answer. Under favour, however, before proceeding to make good this rather odd assertion, I will make a few preliminary remarks. I presume you are all aware that a novel theory of society, commonly called Socialism, has been vouchsafed to the " Old Immoral World," but it is quite likely that only a few of you are aware that it is a very profane theory, essentially and unalterably irreligious. My authority for thus designating it is no other than Robert Owen himself, its first and ablest promulger ; who over and over again has exhorted his followers to " make short work with priests " by destroying religion " root and branch." I hold in my hand some printed Lectures of his, " On an entire New State of Society," in the fourth of which, after eloquently descanting on the divisions, jealousies, heart-burnings and cruel injustice caused and perpetuated by religion, he concludes with the delaration that, *in the new and superior state of society Truth will supersede Religion.* A declaration which I take to be conclusive, so far as Robert

Owen's published opinion of religion is concerned. But I may be told that he does not *now* think that Truth will supersede Religion in the New Moral World, and if I were so told, my reply would be to this purpose. What Robert Owen *now* thinks about religion, even " prime minds " would be sadly puzzled to determine, for of late his opinions respecting that most important of questions, have been of every sort by turns, and no sort long. But whatever he now may think or say he thinks, I for one shall never cease to *admire*, to *applaud*, and to *act upon* the principles he taught before age had dimmed his perceptions, and impaired his judgment. In 1819, he understood his own theory, or he never understood it, and then it was he thought all the religions of the world " founded upon falsehood," and that in the New Moral World truth would supersede religion. To these opinions I pointedly and emphatically advert upon the present occasion for the purpose of convincing you that years before Socialism, as Socialism, was heard of, its founder declared it a theory of human nature and of human society, totally incompatible with any kind or form of religion. What then is to be thought of those partially informed people, who would fain cajole others into a belief that genuine Socialists are *very* pious, and that Socialism is of all human theories, the most *rationally* religious. Of all cajoleries this, in my judgment, is the most pitiable, and I consider that to pass over those who wantonly practice it would be nothing short of high treason against the majesty of Truth. The most active, and as already said, oddest of their number is Mr. Jones, who in his marvellous *hurry* to extirpate irreligion from the soil of Socialism, really seems to have taken leave of his senses. The lecture on Atheism and Deism, as you will presently perceive, abounds in all sorts of ERRORS, *anomalies*, *and contradictions*, which the most charitable will allow are calculated to breed suspicion, if not certainty, that the person who delivered it was not *compos mentis*. I have somewhere read of a child who, when a new-born infant was put into its arms, cried out, O papa, dear baby has got a little of everything. Just so of Mr. Jones's *Lecture*; it has a little of everything. But what may be called its chief distinguishing feature is paltry vilification of Atheism and Atheists. It appears, indeed, to have been delivered chiefly if not solely for the purpose of convincing his hearers that religion, if false and foolish, is certainly useful; and that Atheists, though " all argument is on their side," are such pornicious wasters of intellect, such everlasting fault-finders, such grossly imaginative nincompoops, such rash exploders of time-honoured, respectable prejudices, and therefore such grievous hindrances to the steady and permanent establishment of a span new state of society, that to *put them down* is the duty of Rationalists. There is an old and just saying, that to a certain class of persons, if you give but rope enough they will not fail to hang themselves. Mr. Jones is one of that class. He commenced his Lecture by observing that he had " no intention of applauding or condemning but simply of ascertaining how much of truth there is in each of them," (Atheism and Deism) and concluded by declaring that Atheism should be scouted from every meeting." Rare inconsistency, and methinks a notable illustration of that saying just quoted. After pledging himself neither to condemn nor applaud any opinion or anybody, he talked rather learnedly about Paine and Voltaire, Deists who do personify God Almighty, and Deists who do not personify God Almighty, but not being a Deist myself I care for none of these things, and pass on to consider his assertions concerning Atheists and Atheism.

One assertion concerning *Atheists* is, that " a bleak and blank denial is their fault." Now, at the risk of being deemed " nothing if not critical," I say that the question is not whether the denial of a God is " bleak and blank," but whether such denial is or is not *warranted by reason*. If some people affirm what is untrue, surely their neighbours are justified in denying what is untrue, nay that is precisely what they *ought* to do. Nor do I suppose a well-founded denial at all the worse because fanciful would-be-Solomons describe it by such coxcombical terms as " bleak and blank." Of *blank* denials I have had some experience, but never before was introduced to a *bleak* one. *Mais revenons à nos moutons*. Another assertion of Mr. Jones's is that " The Atheist has all the argument on his side, so far as external circumstances are concerned." I am by no means disposed to question it. My opinion long has been that the Atheist *has* all the argument on his side. With regard to the " so far as external circumstances are concerned," though doubtless meant for a saving clause, it will not pass, because circumstances being *necessarily* external, there are no other than external circumstances. I am a circumstance to you—you are circumstances to me. *Existences* and *circumstances* are two words of exactly the same signification. Whatever exists is a circumstance to whatever else exists, so that in philosophical strictness, the sum total of circumstances constitutes the sum total of existences; and as, according to Mr. Jones, the Atheist has all the argument on his side so far as external circumstances are concerned, it follows that in repudiating Atheism, he repudiates those philosophical principles of which he claims to be considered the honest and consistent advocate. If Mr. Jones cannot see this, other people can. As to his *facts*, they are of a kind to grow obsolete and perish. He ventured, for example, to call *fact* the oft exposed *falsehood* that "belief in an incomprehensible Power universally prevails." Really, Mr. Jones should in future endeavour to avoid committing himself by a public display of ignorance so disgraceful, not to mention the works of Locke and others, which abound in evidence that whole nations have been found without belief in aught save nature itself. Moffatt, the Christian's, recently published "Missionary Labours in Africa," is a book which, if Mr. Jones had been fortunate enough to read before delivering his Lecture on Atheism and Deism, without doubt the audience assembled to hear it would have been spared the "fact" in question. But even were it true that all tribes and kinds of men believed that the "atom" is pushed and the aggregate "moved on" by an incomprehensible *anything-you-please*, I do not understand how such universal consent can be reasonably adduced as proof of such *anything-you-please*. At a period not very remote, all people thought that the sun's motion caused those appearances and effects which modern science teaches are caused by the motion of our planet. In ancient times, the sun was universally believed a flaming God, but surely no one will contend that such belief can reasonably be quoted as *evidence*, much less *proof* that the sun is a red-hot Deity. Before the birth of Science, our globe was universally believed to be flat or nearly so, and yet we are all convinced it is round as an average orange. But I waste words in confuting assertions which to every person moderately read in the history of human nature must carry its confutation along with it. Mr. Jones thinks that the "fact" of belief in a Deity universally prevailing "is worthy of respectful examination." But I know, and he should know, the fact is mere fiction, and therefore only persons who have more leisure than brains will pay the least attention to it, or the inference, so unfavourable to Atheism, he desires should be drawn therefrom.

(*To be concluded next week*)

A NEW REFUTATION OF THE ARGUMENT A PRIORI.

To the Editors of the Movement.

Sirs,—At the commencement of the Gillespian controversy I wrote to you saying that I regretted that valuable time should be spent in the refutation of such a production, and I should think so still, were it not that I think Mr. Southwell has failed in exposing the Gillespian fallacy, and thereby added plausibility to the so called "Argument A Priori."

The error Mr. Southwell committed is this, he showed that extension is not *an entity*, therefore *cannot have an existence*. Whereas, he should have merely criticised Gillespie's arguments, and shown that Mr. G. does not *prove* his proposition. This course was the more necessary, as Mr. Gillespie seems unable to discriminate between the meaning of the word extension, and the word extended; with him the expressions *has extension*, and *is extended*, seem to be synonymous. He cannot see the distinction. But Mr. S. seems not to have been aware that Mr. G. not only does not prove the existence of infinity of extension, but he does not *attempt* to prove it.

In the commencement of his book he states that, "there are but two ways of proving (attempting to prove) the being of a god," and devotes about thirty four pages to prove the insufficiency of the first or "a posteriori" mode. It follows then that if the second, or "A Priori" mode be also insufficient, that there is no proof of the existence of such a thing.

Mr. G. thus introduces his grand proposition, on the validity of which it is said rests his whole "Argument."

"An Argumemt A Priori for the Being and Attributes of God.

Book 1. Part 1.

Proposition 1. *Infinity of extension is necessarily existing.*

Sec. 1. "For even when the mind endeavours to remove from it the idea of infinity of extension, it cannot, after all its efforts, avoid leaving still there the idea of such infinity. Let there be ever so much endeavour to displace this idea, that is, conceive infinity of extension non-existent; every one, by a review, or reflex examination of his own thoughts, will find it is utterly beyond his power to do so.

Sec. 2. "Now, since even when we would remove infinity of extension out of our mind, we prove it must exist by necessarily leaving the thought of it behind, or, by substituting (so to speak) infinity of extension for infinity of extension taken away; from this it is manifest, infinity of extension is necessarily existing: for, every thing the existence of which we *cannot but* believe, which we *always* suppose, even though we *would* not, is necessarily existing.

Sec. 3. "To deny that infinity of extension exists, is, therefore, an utter contradiction. Just as much a contradiction as this, 1 is equal to 1, therefore 1 is *not* equal to 1 but to 2 : 2 not being identical with 1. As thus: infinity of extension is ever present to the mind, though we desire to banish it, *therefore* it can be removed from the mind. This is just an *application* of the greatest of all contradictions. A thing can be, and not be, at the same time.

In reading this proposition, and its so called *proof*, one is apt to loose sight of a very material difference that exists between the first and following paragraphs, which is, that in the first paragraph he speaks of the *idea* of infinity of extension, but in the following he speaks of *infinity of extension* itself.

The insufficiency of this argument (?) or rather the policy of calling it an argument at all, will be evident if the thing be written thus: (I shall give Mr. G.'s own words, with my insertions, which will enable the reader at once to perceive the force of the argument).

"Infinity of extension is necessarily existing.

"For even when the mind endeavours to remove from it (that is, from the mind) the *idea* of infinity of extension, it (the mind) cannot, after all its (the mind's) efforts, avoid leaving still there (that is, in the mind) the *idea* of such infinity. Let there be ever so much endeavour to displace this *idea*, that is, conceive (or have an *idea* that) infinity of extension (is) non-existent; every one by a review, or reflex examination of his own thoughts, will find that it (that is, the displacing of this idea) is utterly beyond his power to do so." So far he has only treated of the *idea*—but mark the change in the second paragraph.

Sec. 2. "Now, since even when we would remove 'infinity of extension' out of our minds," &c.

Why we have not got "infinity of extension yet, we have only got the *idea*, and the *idea alone* we must keep. Thus, "Now, since even when we would remove (the idea of) infinity of extension out of our mind, we prove it (the idea of infinity of extension) must exist, by necessarily leaving the thought of it (that is, the *idea* of infinity of extension) behind, or, by substituting (so to speak) (the idea of) infinity of extension for (the idea of) infinity of extension taken away; from this it is manifest (*the idea of*) infinity of extension is necessarily existing. For, every thing, (*idea*) the existence of which we cannot but believe, which we always suppose, even though we would not, is necessarily existing.

Sec. 3. "To deny that (the idea of) infinity of extension exists, is, therefore, an utter contradiction," &c.

It is useless to follow this third paragraph to the end, it must be clear to every one that this mode of arguing cannot prove the existence of any thing. Mr. G. does not even prove the existence of the *idea*. If such were to be taken as *proof*, it would be very easy to prove the existence of an " utter contradiction," or any chimera that the deseased brain of fool or fanatic might conjure into existence. I shall apply this boasted "A Priori Argument" to the proving the existence of something else, a ghost to wit.

AN ARGUMENT A PRIORI
FOR
THE BEING AND ATTRIBUTES OF A GHOST.
Book 1. Part 1.

Proposition 1. *A Ghost is necessarily existing.*

Sec. 1. "For even when the mind endeavours to remove from it the idea of a Ghost, it cannot, after all its efforts, avoid leaving still there, the idea of such Ghost. Let there be ever so much endeavour to displace this idea, that is, conceive a Ghost non-existent; every one, by a review, or reflex examination of his own thoughts, will find it is utterly beyond his power to do so.

Sec. 2. "Now, since even when we would remove a Ghost out of our mind, we prove it must exist, by necessarily leaving the thougt of it behind, or, by substituting (so to speak) a Ghost, for a Ghost taken away, from this it is manifest a Ghost is necessarily existing. For everything the existence of which we *cannot but* believe, which we *always suppose*, even though we *would not*, is necessarily existing.

Sec. 3. "To deny that a Ghost exists, is therefore an *utter contradiction*," &c.

The pith of this so called argument seems to rest in the latter part of the second paragraph, which says, that " *everything we cannot but believe*, is necessarily existing."

Now suppose Mr. G. were to "*believe*" that some kind friend had left him £200., and farther, that Mr. G. "*could not but be-*

lieve" that said £200. were deposited in some bank, does Mr. G. really think, that merely having such a belief would ensure the actual existence of the money, and that bankers would credit him the amount.

Divested of its verbiage, the "Argument" would stand thus.

PROP. Infinity of Extension is necessarily existing.

1. Because we have an idea of such infinity.
2. But everything the existence of which we cannot but believe is necessarily existing.
3. Therefore infinity of extension exists, and to deny it is an utter contradiction.

I have thought it worth while to trouble you with these remarks, since Mr. Southwell has said the "entire work might easily be converted into one of the very best Atheistical books extant.

JOHN ALEXANDER.

A MONTH IN LEICESTER.
BY G. J. H.
I

COBBETT used to call London a great "wen," he should have called it an eternal din, an everlasting whirl—its whizzing was in my ears when I reached Tring. nor was I conscious of the pleasures of silence until I arrived in Leicester, which, in contrast with the metropolis, is a Lethe, "a bath to sail in, to refresh, to sleep, to dream in." Never was slumber more balmy than on the first night of staying there—" it wrapped me round like a cloak," and I lay down blessing, with Sancho Panza, the man who first invented sleep. I ought to have been charged double for my bed that night for I had a double measure of repose out of it.

Before I had been long in Leicester, I was informed that a resolution had been for some time agitated there. The Branch thought they were called upon to vindicate the Rational Society in the eyes of the public from *ex-parte* dealing. For my own part, I was too much in love with repose to care anything either for vindication or attack, of myself or others. It must have been something vastly more important than the subject referred to, which would have a-roused me. What the Branch choosed to do they have themselves set forth in the following official report—

"Report of the Leicester Branch of the Rational Society, for the Quarter ending December 31st, 1844,—The President in the Chair. After the preliminary business had been gone through, the attention of the Meeting was called to the consideration of a requisition, bearing the signatures of several members of the Branch, and after a full discussion thereon, the following resolution was passed, a copy of which the Secretary was directed to forward to the Central Board, and also for insertion in the *New Moral World*. Resolved,—That this Meeting strongly disapproves of the conduct of Mr. G. A. Fleming, in inserting the remarks of Branch A 1, (in the *New Moral World* of December 13, 1844), respecting Mr. Holyoake and his " Visit to Harmony Hall," and not inserting the letter of Mr. Holyoake in reply, which appears in No. 55, Vol. 2 of the *Movement*.

" (Signed) J. GIMSON,
" *President of the Branch.*"

It was upon this resolution that Mr. Fleming, in the *N.M.W.* of Jan. 18, paid the Leicester Branch (one of the most independent we have) the compliment of irsinuating that they had no opinion of their own, and that my "*personal presence*" was necessary to induce them to place the resolution on record. The only part that I took in the matter was to tell the Branch that they wasted their time in discussing the resolution, since if they passed it Mr. Fleming would never insert it. "Oh" said all at once, "Mr. Fleming can't reject the insertion of a resolution of a Branch in our own paper. He put in Branch A 1's report, and he must put in ours." "He won't do it," was my reply. They thought me harsh, and I thought them simpletons. The above resolution, it will be seen, makes no attempt to "whitewash" me, as the *New Moral World* has further said. The resolution does not say I was right, but that I ought to be heard where I had been attacked (in the *N.M.W.*), whether I was right or wrong. Among other things not worth noticing, Mr. Fleming said the resolution of the Branch was passed owing to the "influence of my *near* relatives." An ingenious genealogist is Mr. Fleming. There is not a single person in Leicester who spells his name as mine is spelled. I never had a relative in Leicester, unless one went through with Richard III., and he must have been slain at Bosworth Field, as we never heard of him after, and how he took part in the resolution in question the "Central Board" or the next "Congress" will no doubt tell us. However, I do not think lightly of my *New Moral World*-made-" relatives," and have given notice to the family that if any legacy comes into it I shall expect that they will not dispute my claim for a share, and I hereby promise to Mr. Fleming a decent percentage for his services.

THE EDINBURGH PROSECUTIONS FOR BLASPHEMY.

Recent events prove, that although a few individuals may be perfectly convinced of the injustice and irrational tendency of religious prosecutions, there are a vast number who still think that the treatment of the felon is the best prescription for a doubting brother, and who practically declare that the hypocrite and cringing slave is to be preferred to the sincere, upright, and honest thinker. What infatuation! They absolutely believe that they are promoting the advancement of truth, by preventing the free utterance of thought, and the certain result, interchange of knowledge. We refer more particularly to the cases which have lately occurred in the northern metropolis. Four numbers of the *Edinburgh Phrenological Journal* have appeared since two individuals were sentenced to imprisonment and the usual criminal routine, for promulgating opinions which did not square with the orthodox opinions of the day. This is a question which deeply concerns cerebral physiologists. If their science is capable of placing any question on a clear and satisfactory basis, it is this; and yet the journal published in the city where these iniquitous transactions occurred—the journal, whose editor must daily pass the court where these trials took place, and who is a member of the profession more particularly engaged in perpetrating these gross acts of injustice—contains not one word which could authorise the belief that the proceedings were disapproved of—chronicles not one fact or argument which could lead one to suppose that the principles it has been engaged in enforcing for the past twenty years, have in the slightest degree been infringed. Why is this? Is our science to continue a mere record of interesting physiological facts, and not to be made to impress on our laws a more just and humanising spirit? Are the disciples of Gall still to continue to collect the proofs of natural signs and symbols, and not to insist with energy on the adoption of measures in accordance with man's nature? Is science to succumb at the bid of authority, and a blind conformity to take the place of rational conviction? Is this the morality which is to be shamelessly paraded by our judges, and the "Magazine of Moral Science," published in modern Athens, not to record a single protest?—ZOIST.

CATHOLICISM IN GERMANY.—Breslaw, Jan. 19.—The Roman Catholics of this city, who have resolved to withdraw from the supremacy of Rome, will take the first decisive step. We hear, in a few days there is to be a general meeting, as M. Rouge will state his views respecting measures which are now necessary. It is indeed high time that this indecision and inactivity should have an end.—*Times*.

A SIGN OF THE TIMES.—At Woleford—a village situated in a dark corner of loyal, pious, and ignorant Somerset—a missionary meeting is yearly held, and much care taken to supply those who "take no care for the morrow," and who "take neither purse nor scrip," with *the means* to go over and insure the black man's black soul a place in paradise. Missionary boxes ornament every house where there are any pickings to be met with—and, in the course of a year, some of them, singly, have been the recipient of "odds" and "differences" amounting to pounds. But during the whole year past, only one penny had been deposited in one of the principle ones, up to Jan. 19, the day preceding the missionary meeting—which was scantily attended. This display of indifference shows that the people, even here, are getting awake to the cozening of the black-enlightoners. Z. P.

THE JESUITS IN SWITZERLAND.—The journals say that an extraordinary Federal Diet will be convoked towards the end of February, to determine on some settlement of the difference connected with the Jesuit question, by which Switzerland is kept in such a ferment.

BRANCH A 1.—The resolution censuring the publication of Mr. Trevelyan's letter, noticed in our last, has been withdrawn.

P.L., for *Movement*................ 0 1 0

TO CORRESPONDENTS.

W. C.—The liquidation of Mr. Whiting's claim will shortly receive the earnest attention of the Anti-Persecution Union.

J. G.—We hope an explanation will appear next week of the progress made in Mr. Johnson's case.

H. CLARK, Derby.—Mr. Ellis was waiting to know whether the subscription was for the Anti-Persecution Union or the Tract Society. It was instantly handed in on the sight of H. C.'s note. It will be found in the proper place.

Mr. HODSON, Manea, Cambridgeshire.—Received from him an advertisement for a tutor. We do not insert advertisements, and all our notices are in some way connected with *Movement* objects.

An Ex-Five Years Member is thanked for his great attention. Though no direct use can at present be made of the communication, it will not be lost sight of.

P. Q.—The Quarterly Subscription to the *National Reformer* is 2s. 6d., but must be paid in advance. The charge to insular and other subscribers, who don't pay till the end of the quarter, is 3s.

LECTURES.

Feb. 9.—Social Institution, Market Place, Leicester, Mr. Ryley Perry,—On the Transfiguration of Christ.

Feb. 10.————On Historical Evidence.

Feb. 9.—Hall of Science, City Road, Mr. G. J. Holyoake,—On the Reputed Recantation (of Atheism) of Frances Wright, now Madame D'Arusmont.

Feb. 9.—Investigation Hall, 29, Circus Street, Marylebone, Mr. R. Buchanan,—Review of the Popular Theological notions respecting the Creation of the World, the Fall of Man, and the Universal Deluge.

SUBSCRIPTIONS
TO THE ANTI-PERSECUTION UNION.

H. Clark, Derby, per Mr. Ellis, for tickets received from H. Roache.............. 0 2 6

PATERSON TESTIMONIAL.

Per Mr. J. Cook, Theological Depot Ipswich
John Glide, Jun....................... 0 1 0
Mr. and Mrs. Cook.................... 0 2 6
J. P. G., a friend to free discussion........ 0 1 0
James Jervis.......................... 0 1 0
Miss Bird, James Pearce, F. Dennis, E. Gordon............................ 0 1 0
Dungravel, Bennet, Harrel, Lockwood.... 0 1 4
Mr. H. Hetherington, London............ 0 5 0
J. Record and friend, Bethnal Green...... 0 10 0
J. L. Bendall, City Road................ 0 5 0

G. J. H., Sec.

Printed and Published by G. J. HOLYOAKE,
40, Holywell-street, Strand.
Wednesday, February 5, 1845.

THE MOVEMENT

And Anti-Persecution Gazette.

"Maximise morals, minimise religion."—BENTHAM.

No. 61.   EDITED BY G. JACOB HOLYOAKE, AND M. Q. RYALL.   Price 1½d

DR. KALLEY TO MR. HOLYOAKE.

LETTER V.

(CONCLUDED FROM PAGE 43).

15th. You assert farther, that till matter be annihilated no infinite being can exist. If I had maintained that Deity possesses the properties of matter, without being the material universe, and yet that it is infinite, then your objection would have great weight: but I know of no kind of evidence by which you can prove that an *immaterial* substance cannot exist in the same place with *matter*. The properties of the former, life, goodness, wisdom, justice, and holiness are so different from those of the latter, that I know no reason for supposing that the presence of matter can exclude spirit.

16th. I acknowledge that the Self-Existent is incomprehensible, that his wisdom, power, eternity, and other attributes are too vast for the human mind to form any adequate conception of them; and farther, I grant you that no one less than God himself can fully comprehend what God is. While, however, I make these concessions, I cannot admit the deduction that you draw from them, namely, that therefore we should sit down in quiet ignorance. I do not fully comprehend the mechanism of the body, nor the action of remedies, and I never expect to know them perfectly, but this would not be an excuse for neglecting to study them. What branch of study would remain if all were excluded on which man cannot attain perfect knowledge? I cannot grasp the full idea of eternity, wisdom, power, and other attributes of the Deity, but I do know something of them, and know that unless these reside in the Self-Existent, the phenomena of the universe remain unaccounted for.

17th. The difficulty of accounting for these phenomena, on the hypothesis that the Self-Existent is merely matter, is illustrated in a very interesting manner in your letters. In paragraph 5 of your 4th when it was necessary to point out an agent in the movements of the universe, you told me that you "fall back on *nature*, which has peopled space with glittering worlds"— "from which man derives so much"— "from which we learn wisdom, order, and government"—but in paragraph 10 of your last you withdraw these expressions as trespassing on the poetical precincts of personification, and frankly tell me that whence matter's properties or its harmonious adaptations you know not. Every harmonious arrangement, the formation and the life of each individual of all the species of plants and animals, every property of matter, is to you as profound a mystery as the being of a God is to me. Grant that the Self-Existent is living, wise, and powerful, in one word God, and the phenomena of the universe are accounted for. One knot remains, namely, the existence of Deity—all besides are solved. If it be reasonable to receive the doctrine of gravitation, because so many remarkable phenomena, otherwise isolated, and inexplicable, are solved by it, much more reasonable must it be to receive the doctrine that the Self-Existent is a God; for the number of otherwise isolated and inexplicable phenomena solved by this doctrine is infinitely greater than the number of those solved by the doctrine of gravitation.

18th. In reply to my remark that "if man have wisdom, and nature none, then man is greater than nature," you tell me that "human wisdom, knowledge, and discretion come only by observation, study, and intercourse with men," and that "it does not follow that man is nobler than nature." If man were nobler than nature, you think it would be as if a river were rising higher than the level of its source. Nature, *alias* matter, either does, or does not, learn by observation, study, and intercourse. If it *does not*, and man *does so* learn, then it still appears to me that man is nobler than nature. If nature, *alias* matter, does learn by these, and is as noble as man, then it would seem that we have all been mistaken in thinking a living man superior to a clod. If man be living, and nature inanimate, and man be, notwithstanding, the child of nature, then the stream runs higher than its source. Man is nobler than nature.

19th. This reminds me of the similarity between incredulity and superstition. Incredulity says "powers are matter's properties. The only conceivable powers are matter's attributes. All is matter and matter does all. It gives life, wisdom, health, and enjoyment of every kind. To nature, *alias* matter, man owes all." Superstition takes a portion of matter, cuts or moulds it into the shape of a man or beast, and then as if matter had the power of hearing and acting, superstition kneels down and begs matter to give it life, health, wisdom, and enjoyment. Incredulity looks on with a smile of pity, but has little reason to despise superstition as long as it also ascribes so much to matter. Your employment of the expressions "*huge beings*" "rising in awful gradation," (paragraph 19) might indeed lead one to infer that you believe the amount of power in designing and executing designs, to be proportioned to the material bulk of its possessors, but as I cannot at all concur in this idea, I am of opinion that the Romanist who attributes so much to crosses, images, and relics—portions of matter—is as reasonable as the Atheist who ascribes *all* to the whole of matter.

20th. There are several other things in your letter on which I would like to have made a few remarks, but as I am already at my third sheet I fear it would be trespassing too much on your patience. I beg however to call your attention to the following allegory:—

21st. A man was sent to survey a part of ocean, in which it was said that there existed an arch of rock, and when cruising about near the place, in rather hazy weather, he distinctly saw breakers, and then put about his ship and returned, declaring that it was of no use to seek for the rock as nothing could be known about it. When examined before the admiralty the following conversation took place:—Did you see any rock? No. Any indication of a rock? None. Were there any breakers visible? "To this question I before gave the answer of the thoughtless and superficial yes," but now I answer no. Was there anything remarkable about the water? There was broken water (adaptation, harmonious arrangement, &c.) but no breakers (design). Why do you call it broken water and not breakers? Because I have "thought on the subject and see to what it leads." I am convinced that there is no such rock, and therefore the use of the word breakers must lead to "the monstrous hypothesis that there were huge beings disporting" in that part of ocean and lashing it into foam.

I therefore concluded quite satisfactorily to myself that it is just the "nature" of the water, and as "it is the knowledge of the use rather than the origin of things which is necessary to man," I did not search any farther. But did you search so thoroughly as to determine that there is no rock there? "That there may be a rock I admit," (paragraph 7 of your 3rd) but I " treat the subject of its existence as the good sense of mankind now treats the long agitated question of the Philosophers' stone." Even those who maintain that there is a rock, say that no man can grasp it, therefore, "from this investigation both our incapacity and inconsistency warn us to retreat."

22nd. Would you, at the close of such a conversation, be satisfied that the rock does not exist, or that the person did not wish to find it? Is this an unfair illustration of your argument? It is drawn not from any unkindly feeling towards you, but with the hope that it may help to show you that not to enquire after the Self Existent is more unreasonable than you have supposed.

23rd. I shall now only add that our enquiry is not a cold speculative investigation about a fact in natural history, which, though interesting, does not materially affect us. This is about a friend and a father. The question is whether man be a thing of chance—an unheeded child of brute matter — and the sport of circumstances; or, if we have an all-mighty, all-wise, affectionate father, from whom we may seek counsel in the day of prosperity—to whom we may flee for succour when all earthly friends forsake us, in whom we may trust in death—and through whom we may expect an immortality of bliss when our sojourn on earth shall have closed.

Believe me, very sincerely yours,
ROBERT R. KALLEY.

THE Newburyport Watch Tower says that an unsuccessful attempt was made some days ago to steal one of the bones of the celebrated Whitfield, which are deposited beneath the pulpit of the Federal Street church in that town. One of the bones of the arm was stolen several years ago and carried to England. These rogues must have been pious fellows, for you would never catch an Infidel in such a scrape.

THE very privileges which are favourable to religious liberty while exercised by *lay* superiors, became dangerous to the vassals of estates, in process of time, when they were made over to ecclesiastics.—*Encyclopædia Britannica: Art. Waldenses.*

ATHEISM AND DEISM.

(CONCLUDED).

In another part of his Lecture, Mr. Jones said "there is no more knowledge exhibited by the Atheist than by the Deist, the one does not know what he believes, and the other does not know what he disbelieves." Here we have another fiction in the guise of a fact. An Atheist *does* know what he disbelieves. There is no such thing as knowledge or he knows he disbelieves whatever the Deist *says* he believes about impossibles and unnaturals. But the case may be put still closer and better. Mr. Jones is a "philosophical Deist," yet I, who believe myself the "grossest" of Atheists, disbelieve almost every sentence of that gentleman's Lecture on Atheism and Deism. Nothing will be clearer in the view of all Atheists who take the trouble to examine that Lecture, than its bungling inconsistencies, ridiculous sophisms and serious mistakes. As a specimen of the latter, I take the following: "The Deist appeals to design, the Atheist says there is no design at all, it is all right together." Daniel O'Connell, if an Atheist, would designate this "a mere lie," but loving to be charitable, I call it a serious mistake. The words right and wrong you will readily admit are totally void of *abstract* meaning. Like other words they were invented *by* and relate *to* human beings. No Atheist will tell you that Nature is either "all right together" or all wrong together. While your philosophical Deist sees "all things tend to blissful issues," *he* sees that *some* things tend to issues most horrible. He sees that *not seldom* "right and wrong are accidents"—and that what is right to one, is to another intolerably wrong. He denies design but Mr. Jones seems ignorant that Atheists consider the existence of evil (another word for wrong) a fact not easily to be reconciled with the notion of a Deity sufficiently potent to create everything out of nothing. One charge made against the celebrated Hobbes was that no wit could "reconcile himself to himself." I think the same charge may justly be made against Mr. Jones. With unparalleled *consistency* he followed up his assertions that the Atheist declares all right together, by assuring his audience that one bad effect of Atheism is "it leads to fault-finding." Now, how belief in a nature all right together, can beget the disposition to be eternally finding fault as if it were all wrong together, I am unable to explain. That a disposition to find fault should hurry away and tyrannise over the judgment of persons who believe that fault is nowhere to be found savours of the miraculous. The Roman Catholic Count de Montalambert, towards the close of a letter addressed by him to the Camden Society, assures us that miracles never were more plentiful than at this very time. Perhaps the disposition to find fault so strongly manifested by all-right-together-Atheists, is one of the many modern miracles to which that pious person alludes. I would not have it inferred from this part of my harangue that I think Atheists are *not* fault-finders. They certainly are so, and therefore deserve to be thus designated. To call them optimists is to slander them, but no one can justly deny their proneness to annoy *errorists* by exposing their errors, and *backsliders* by checking their retrograde propensity. They are not, however, alone in this particular. A proneness to discover and hold up to popular contempt other false opinions or improper conduct is far from being a characteristic peculiar to Atheists. The best reformers have been the most determined fault-finders. Reformers *must* find fault. There is Robert Owen—see what havoc he makes with every body and everything opposed to the New View of Society. He is the prince of reformers and the prince of fault-finders. Impressed with a conviction that all wisdom is lodged in his own cranium, every act of his life attests his sincerity. Even "genuine disciples of the system" do not escape his censure; for ever and anon he publicly announces them a set of people so utterly stupid as to have much studied his principles without achieving the most distant idea of them. This methinks is fault-finding with a vengeance, and yet I cannot remember that Mr. Jones ever objected to this part of the "venerable founder's" character. And moreover, it occurs to me that Lloyd Jones has reason to *blush* when finding fault with fault-finders. Not long since he was fault-finder general. When most useful he was least disposed to hold his peace about the follies and wickedness of modern civilisation. Parsons detested him as the Devil is said to detest holy water. He went to the work of demolishing creeds, prejudices, and systems with a reckless self-sufficient audacity which paralysed opposition. His love of controversy amounted to a mania. He was looked upon by Socialists themselves as their trump card in the game of revolution. To make men disgusted with old opinions and old practices was his *business*. He was kept for nothing else. To hunt up, chase, and give battle to opponents of "the system" was the work assigned him. He did it well, especially that prime part which consisted in flogging the anti-social parsons. Fault-finding was his *forte*. He could and can do nothing so satisfactorily as point out defects. He does it with an easy confidence in his own opinions, about on a par with that of the disputatious never wrong French woman, who after a sharp debate exclaimed "*Ma foi, c'est singulier, il n'y a que moi qui a toujours raison.*" I have somewhere read that Mr. Brown, the picturesquist, was in such an ecstacy when one of his works was commended, that he cried out "None but your Browns and your God Almighties can do such things as these." The conceit of this Mr. Brown is fairly matched by the conceit of Mr. Jones, who makes satirical saucy speeches as if he *thought* such things could only be done by your Joneses and your God Almighties. And this is the man who waxes eloquent about the folly, the conceit, and the captious fault-finding spirit of Atheists. He does, however, admit that there is "honesty" in them, and that they "deserve respect for honourably avowing their sentiments," which is a compliment so handsome that I much regret not being able *honestly* to return it. I nevertheless agree with Mr. Jones that "there are things to be beloved and believed, as well as to be disbelieved and denied." But care should be taken lest we "belove and believe" what is hateful and false. Society is corrupt no doubt, but corrupt as it is that which is worthy to be loved seldom fails to beget affection in those who come within the sphere of its influence. Nor need Mr. Jones alarm himself about the progress of disbelief. Excess of *belief* is the curse of *this* generation, and if history lie not, has been the curse of *all* generations. Mr. Jones told his audience that Shelley and Leigh Hunt have "become believers in the loving foundations of human nature, and ceased to be destroying." Mr. Hetherington, who was kind enough to furnish notes of the lecture, assured me that in the course of it these very words were spoken, a fact I mention lest you should *disbelieve* Mr. Jones would utter anything so ridiculously false. The idea of Shelley and Leigh Hunt *becoming* believers in the loving foundations of human nature is preposterous in the extreme I should like to be informed when they were not so, and when they began to be so. If the information *can* be given, Atheists will thank Mr. Jones to give it. The Queen Mab of Shelley abounds in the elements of destruction. A poem so eminently calculated to destroy every vestige of belief in the truth or utility of religion, has not appeared before or since. It struck not only at religion, but the two other members of Robert Owen's "trinity of curses," Marriage and Private Property. And yet, who but Mr. Jones or his double, if such a one can be found, would dream of asserting that when Shelley wrote Queen Mab he lacked belief " in the loving foundations of human nature." With respect to Leigh Hunt it is only necessary to observe in the first place that his general estimate of human nature seems the very same as ever it was, and in the second place that he ran by far the most useful part of his career while editor of the *Examiner*, a paper which under his management was remarkable for its vigor, courage, and ability in the work of *destroying* all sorts of error. If Mr. Jones were not the oddest of all oddities he surely never could have committed himself so far as to cite Shelley and Leigh Hunt as illustrations of his notion that we shall cease to be destroying the moment we cease to be ignorant. But really in the lecture before us there is more outrageous frivolity and solemn nonsense than I ever before remember to have met with in any philosophical outpouring of equal length. Take a specimen of solemn nonsense—" Philosophical Deists cannot explain everything—there are thousands of things unexplainable. They bow with all humility to the inexplicable." Now, it occurs to me that if in lieu of bowing to what they know nothing about, and never can know anything about, Mr. Jones and his philosophical Deists would aid in the work of undeceiving the vulgar, there would speedily be less godliness, but more virtue and happiness in the world. Bowing to what is inexplicable is at best a bowing to no purpose. Besides there is nothing like keeping the head erect when the heart is so. Your bowers and scrapers are seldom good for much. Their humility in a majority of cases is only the pride which apes it. I never see men and women hanging their bodies at a tumble down angle, without suspecting them of much that no persons desire to be suspected of. Mr. Jones excited considerable mirth by a fancy sketch of " young Atheists," whom he described as knowing a *little* of everything and something of all; and so utterly unimaginative that they see nothing in a Claude or a Raphael but certain tangible things in the shape of wood, paint, and canvass. Now, although a great lover of facetiousness, and a little facetious myself sometimes, I am clearly of opinion that he who raises a laugh at the cost of truth and justice is rather disgusting than otherwise. Undoubtedly there are Atheists, young and old, who are more than sufficiently impolitic, and do by their advocacy no service to the cause they have espoused, but they are exceptions—few and *very* far between. Fools find their way everywhere, and of course the sanctuary of Atheism is not free from them. Were it worth the while, one might easily gather a rich harvest of such from among philosophical Deists. It is a vulgar libel to say that *Atheists from principle* are insensible to the glories of nature, or unfit to appreciate its wondrous beauties. The effects of Atheism cannot fairly be judged of by reference to a few who though *soi-disant* Atheists, profess irreligious opinions without understanding them, but by reference to the opinions, abilities, and actions of a majority, or say, the bulk of its defenders. Look at the writings of Gassendi, Spinoza, Diderot, D'Alembert, Hume, Stewart, Helvetius and D'Holbach, and then say, if not ashamed to do so, that *Atheism* is the grave of imagination—of the highest intellectual energy, or of the most exalted virtue. When Shelley wrote Queen Mab (and to the day of his death for aught known to the contrary) he was an avowed Atheist. Where is your philosophical Deist who has given evidence of an imagination less impure and more exalted than his. Mr. Jones, as already observed, admits there is *honesty* in Atheism, he might properly have added and *intellect* which I. Lloyd Jones, am not competent to sound the depths of. Here I will observe, for the observation may be useful, that Mr. Jones, who is, I am told, a great admirer of Wordsworth, seems to have derived from him very many of those flighty notions about " all things tending to blissful issues," " bowing with all humility to the inexplicable," and the like, which so mightily disfigure the Lecture on Atheism and Deism My advice to Mr. Jones is, that he do forthwith abandon the study of sentimental poets, especially Wordsworth. An excellent judge declared him " mad beyond all hope," and certainly if all our poets were of his stamp, I should incline to the opinion of the cynic who said a poet and a bellman were only fit to be yoked together. Seriously, my conviction is that Mr. Jones derived his absurd notions concerning Atheism and Atheists from such source. But those notions, absurd though I deem them, affect me little in comparison with the last sentence of his Lecture—ATHEISM SHOULD BE SCOUTED FROM EVERY MEETING. From the lips of a thorough going High Church Parson it would have appeared decent, nay becoming. *He* thinks that one consequence of allowing tinkers and tailors the right to call the truth of religion in question, has been the shaving of Christianity to the block, and naturally desires that Atheism may be " scouted from every meeting." But that Mr. Jones, the charitable, the decent, the anti-find-fault champion of of Socialism, should publicly recommend a proceeding so utterly at variance with every principle of justice, and so fraught with evil to the interests of truth, is indeed astonishing, and fully establishes his claim to be considered the oddest of all possible oddities.

THE ANNEXATION OF JONES.

[BRANCH A 1, SUNDAY FEB. 2.—At this morning's meeting Mr. Clark introduced the subject by saying he hoped Mr. Wood would withdraw his resolution relative to Mr. Trevelyan's letter. Mr. Hetherington said of course he should let the matter drop if the resolution be withdrawn. Mr. Jones promised to watch over the *Movement*, and should anything again occur he would most certainly bring it before the Branch. Mr. Wood, after a few remarks, withdrew his resolution. A conversation followed and the matter dropped. A. IVORY.]

It may be very proper for the matter to *drop in* the Coffee-room of Branch A 1, but with submission, the Conductors of the *Movement* think it high time to *drop in* for a hearing, provided it be considered no intrusion. Their first promptings were to thank Lloyd Jones for kind intentions, and all that sort of thing, in promising to " watch over them." Though censors they are not regardless of courtesies. Further consideration, however, suggested the propriety, or rather policy, of ascertaining the expenses of the said office—and whether it is to be paid by piece-work or salary, also whether it is to come out of the General funds, the Community funds, the funds of A 1, or *our own*! Now as Lloyd Jones has evinced the most imperturbable indifference to the source whence his income is derived, we do not expect him to stoop to such low detail. We Atheists are terrestrial and matter-of-fact enough to evince solicitude to know out of whose coffers the salary—for we take it for granted such services will not be rendered without—is expected to be forthcoming.

The Annexation of Jones no more than " the Annexation of Texas," can be threatened without some emotion on the part of the parties concerned. Sinbad the Sailor had an " Annexation," the perplexities of which everybody knows. The " old man of the mountain" was so well pleased with his berth, and found it so pleasant a situation to *watch over the movements* of Sinbad, and profit by his elevation, that the latter found it no joke to dislodge him.

A famous Jones, too, the *Boy Jones*, was another " annexation " which her most gracious Majesty found it no easy job to cut off. She sent him to sea to learn better manners.

Shall we not then be excused for any slight perturbation we may evince in the antipating such a new and unprecedented " circumstance " as that of Lloyd Jones " watching over the *Movement*."

LETTER FROM MR. DALY.
(*On Branch A-oneism.*)

Although but a unit in the sum total of humanity, I beg to offer an expression of feeling towards G. J. Holyoake under the present attack of A 1-ism. It may serve to shew that London is rot all the world, and that A 1 is not the *Alpha and Omega*.

When I read the first article in the *Movement*, on the visit to Harmony, I thought that it savoured more of wit than of either good sense or good intentions; but the second and third courses made me relish the feast, and I feel confident in saying that the explanations of how business is now carried on has done more to create and establish confidence in the present Executive than all that the *New Moral World*, backed by the Lloyd Joneses, have done since May, 1844.

When I read the article I felt prompted from inclination to thank the writer, but from what has since transpired, I feel compelled from a sense of duty to do so.

JAMES DALY, Rochdale.

P.S. Some of the members of the Rochdale Branch, hearing that I was about writing on this subject, and thinking that he who gives expression to truth without mystery should not be paid with votes of censure by Rational Philosophers, requested leave to attach their names to this letter. But I wish it to be understood that I have neither canvassed for signatures, nor made this letter public with a view of forming a party—had I done so I could have sent a longer list of names.

CHAS. HOWORTH, *President of Branch 24*
WM. M'MALIM, *late President*
JOHN JENKINSON, *Secretary*
WM. COOPER, ROBERT KERSHAW, JOHN CRANNIS, JOHN GARSIDE, SAMUEL TWEEDALE, JOHN BENT, MALCOLM KINCAID, *Members of Branch 24*.

IMPRISONMENT AND RELEASE OF MRS. MARTIN.

THE particular circumstances relative to the arrest and release of Mrs. Martin have not yet arrived—all that is known at present of the singular doings of the Arbroath authorities may be gathered from the following correspondence:—

" Aberdeen.

" I am sorry to inform you that Mrs. Martin has been apprehended in Arbroath, on a charge of Blasphemy. They have thrown her into a felon's cell. I cannot give particulars yet. JAMES MYLES."

" Arbroath.

" Mrs. Martin arrived here last night for the purpose of holding a discussion with Mr. Robert Lowery, a Chartist preacher of Aberdeen, on the question, ' Is Christianity sufficient for the promotion of human happiness.' I met the lady at the railway terminus, and conducted her to the hotel where she had lodged before. We had scarcely been there ten minutes when a gentleman wished to see Mrs. M. alone. This was no other than the Superintendent of Police, with a warrant for her apprehension. This was about six at night. He said she must go before the magistrate, to which she consented. What is the charge against her I know not, for although I called repeatedly I was not allowed to see her, and as late as nine o'clock in the evening I was informed that she was remanded previous to being committed. I asked if the kindness of friends could be permitted in supplying her with meals or any little comforts, but I was informed that no such thing could be allowed. The whole intention I think was more immediately to stop the discussion, which they did, and the discontent of the people was heard on all sides, as they assembled at the place of meeting.

I remain, yours truly, W. C. STUNOC."

" Dundee, Feb. 6th, 1845.

" You will be surprised to hear that I am at liberty again, after having passed two days and nights in Arbroath Prison. They were at last I believe glad to get rid of me. Their chief wish seemed to be to prevent the Discussion, and when they liberated me, an hour ago, the Superintendent of Police, and the Gaoler took me and watched the train until it started. EMMA MARTIN."

The tidings of Mrs. M.'s apprehension excited in us no very great surprise, but by what authority, law or precedent, she was detained and kept on felon's fare, and then summarily dismissed without a formal hearing of the case, must be inquired into.

ASHTON-UNDER-LYNE.

Mr. Southwell has just concluded two lectures in this town, one on Sunday last on the cruelty and injustice of persecuting men for their opinions. The other on Jan. 28, in answer to the question What is Religion? Mr. Southwell treated his subjects in a manner that satisfied the infidel portion of his audiences. To satisfy the christian we need not expect only as a work of time.

Mr. Southwell's object in coming to Ashton was two fold. First, to lay the foundation of truth and justice, and second, to bring Mr. Paterson's case before the public. As might be expected the Paterson Testimonial was introduced to the attention of the audiences. Voluntary collections were entered into at the close of each lecture to go to the Testimonial Fund. The amount (expenses deducted) was £1. 4d. Let it be remembered this is not from aristocratic purses but from the pockets of working men. The sum is small, but let other towns improve upon the example and Paterson will have a substantial Testimonial.

JOHN HINDLE.

THE UNSOCIAL EFFECTS OF RELIGION.—The want of social enjoyments, so generally observable in the West Indies, is sensibly felt in St. Lucia; less perhaps on account of the circumscribed circle of its society, than of the conflicting elements of which that society is composed. Of course, the divisions of colour, and class, and language, and even political antagonism, have their share in widening the breach; but its principal cause is the rage for devotional practices, which of late years has taken possession of the whole female population, both white and coloured. Thus, in addition to the divisions of caste, we have a division of sex. The males and females are severed, as it were, into two hostile camps; and while the gentlemen assemble in the stores to discuss politics and pickles, the ladies repair to their coteries to dilate on salvation and scandal. In a word, dress and devotion are the order of the day—the all-engrossing topics of female society; and both are so harmoniously blended that the greatest devotee is often the greatest coquette. As, however, with the exception of an occasional ball, the opportunities for exhibiting their love of dress are limited to the ceremonies of the church; so, on those occasions, it is no unusual sight to see hundreds of fashionably attired females in the town of Castries, out of a population of 4,000 souls. Never perhaps was religion so emphatically the handmaid of commerce; never were the interests of the one so strenuously promoted by the votaries of the other.—*Breen.*

REFUSAL TO ADMINISTER AN OATH.—At the Police Court, on Tuesday, a message boy was charged with theft by Roalfe, Baker, and Co., stationers. Miss Roalfe appeared to give evidence. When she entered the witness-box, Sheriff Macdonald inquired whether she believed in a future state. She declined to answer the question, but professed her readiness to take the usual oath. The learned Sheriff however declared that, under these circumstances, her evidence was inadmissible. The next witness called was Mr. Baker, whose evidence was refused on the same grounds. Mr. Peddie was then called, and having professed his belief in a future state, the oath was administered, and he proceeded with his evidence, from which it appeared that the boy had come to Mr. Robinson's shop on Wednesday week, when Peddie was present, with twenty-three shillings, which he said was all the money he had received from Miss Roalfe. On the following Friday, Peddie heard Miss Roalfe talk to the boy when he delcared that he paid the whole of the money (twenty-five shillings) to Mr. Robinson. It subsequently appeared from the statement of the lad that he had lost the two shillings. The case was dismissed. Mr. Baker protested against the decision of the learned Sheriff as illegal. He said he was acting under the advice of counsel; and a reference to Lord Campbell's act would prove that the evidence of a witness who took the oath he considered most binding, could not be refused—that he was willing to take the usual oath, and therefore, his evidence ought to be received.—*Edinburgh Chronicle.*

PRIESTLY MACHINATIONS.—Priestcraft, therefore, adapted its policy to the spirit of the people. It gratified their curiosity of the present and the future by mysteries and oracles, their love of grace and festivity by processions and joyous festivals. It captivated and awed their imaginations by aid of the fine arts, erecting magnificent temples, paintings, and sculpture, specimens of which remain to command the admiration, if not the worship of the world. To those were added the appliances of sacrifices, human and celestial, auguries and oracles, games and mysteries. By thus providing for the tastes of all, the priests attained their object—wealth and unbounded influence.—*Howitt.*

THE TYRANT'S WELCOME.

(FROM THE "BOSTON INVESTIGATOR.")

"So great was the anxiety to obtain a glimpse of the Emperor, that noblemen were seen striving against each other to secure the good offices of policemen, in order that their carriages might be allowed to occupy positions calculated to afford the best chance of seeing his Majesty. * * * The crowd, which at this time was greatly increased, cheered him vociferously, the ladies waving their handkerchiefs from the windows in the vicinity."—London *Tablet*, June 8, 1844.

And ye fete him and cheer him, ye sycophants vile,
   And the praise of the Despot's your theme and your song;
And the feet of the tyrant have trod on your isle,
   Which ye boast that to freemen alone should belong

And ye hail the destroyer with shouts of acclaim—
   O shame! that such hearts in your bosoms could beat—
Are ye dead to all feelings of honor and shame,
   That ye crouch and ye bend at the autocrat's feet?

Forget ye the blood that his red hands have spilled?
   The homes he has ruined, the hearts he has riven?
The snow-plains his victims in thousands have filled?
   That his perfidy's thus blotted out and forgiven?

Forget ye the wail of weak woman, when torn
   By his Calmucks and Cossacks from husband and child?
The *knout* she has felt, and the pangs she has borne,
   'Till the fiends at his foul ingenuity smiled?

And has sympathy perished, ye fair ones, who boast
   That no hearts like yours can for misery bleed?
Are Warsaw's dread scenes to your memory lost,
   Where the suckling to exile and death he decreed?

Can ye think of the husband, the child, and the wife,
   Condemned at his will to the ice and the mine—
Where death were relief in the mid-day of life,
   To the slave he has doomed in slow torture to pine?

O! ye nobles of England, who throng round his car,
   To give *Satanides* your homage and cheers;
Ye are worthy the chains and the lash of the Czar—
   Your base adulation has sickened his ears.

Far nobler in nature, in valor, and all,
   On the Caucasus's hills is the poor mountaineer,
Who spurns that hell-hound's dark bondage and thrall,
   And scatters his legions with fire and with spear.

But enough; and wherever the monster may roam,
   He will treasure this truth as he crosses the waves,
No serfdom more sordid awaits him at home,
   Than the *nobles* who greet him to-day as his slaves.

SUBSCRIPTIONS
TO THE ANTI-PERSECUTION UNION.

W. J. B., for Mrs. Martin's expenses in Scotland 0 10 0

PATERSON TESTIMONIAL.

W. B. B., fifth and sixth subscriptions....	1	0	0
Cosmopolite	1	0	0
J. Haxton, per Mr. Ellis.	0	5	0
Mrs. Cooper	0	2	6
John Tonge	0	2	6
T. Bidwell	0	2	0
Mr. Alexander and few friends	0	6	0

Two volumes of the "Investigator," one unbound, from Mr. Read, and one half-bound from Mr. Allen, to be sold for the benefit of the Paterson Testimonial.

G. J. H., *Sec.*

ALL SECTS, PARTIES, AND CLASSES SHOULD READ

THE MOVEMENT!
Anti-Persecution Gazette,

And Record of Progress;

Which neither courts, flatters, nor slanders. It is the only Weekly Periodical containing

ORIGINAL PHILOSOPHICAL ESSAYS,

Plainly and boldly outspoken on all important departments of

Theology, Politics, Social Economy, and Morals,

Most directly bearing on the universal interests and progress of humanity.

Published every Wednesday, price 1½d.

Lectures, discussions, public proceedings, and progress in general, bearing on the topics of the *Movement*, are announced and recorded.

N.B.—The first Volume may be now had in cloth boards, price eight shillings.

Opinion of the Press.

The first volume of this opponent of priestcraft, and champion of free-discussion, is completed, and will make a very handsome addition to the library of the free-thinker. It will do more; it will add to his stock of intellectual weapons with which to fight the battle for truth and freedom against the fiends of superstition and tyranny. A few copies of the first volume, neatly bound, are, we understand, to be had of the publisher. We may remind those disposed to support the *Movement* that the new volume commenced on the 1st inst., and affords a favourable opportunity for them to commence their patronage.—*Northern Star*, Jan. 18, 1845.

ERRATUM.—In the balance sheet of the *Movement*, page 15, for M. A. Liddle, £1. 2s. 6d., read £1. 5s.

TO CORRESPONDENTS.

ARTHUR TREVELYAN.—His letter shall appear.
Mr. G. BEGG.—We shall call on Mr. Carlile, and then write him.
RECEIVED.—George Anderson.
MR. G. SMITH, Salford, writes us that placards were got out there as soon as the news of Mrs. Martin's arrest reached that town. On Sunday night a collection was made at the Hall, when £7. 9s. were given. They were also about to hold public meetings at Oldham and other places, and he states that Mr. Southwell has actually started to Scotland.

LECTURES.

Feb. 16.—Investigation Hall, 29, Circus Street, Marylebone, Mr. R. Buchanan,—Review of the Popular Theological notions respecting the Creation of the World, the Fall of Man, and the Universal Deluge, demonstrating the absurdity of the Bible Chronology and Six Days' Creation.

Feb. 16.—Social Institution, Market Place, Leicester Mr. Ryley Perry,—Internal Evidence of Christianity.

Feb. 17.———Political and Religious opinions of Zoroaster.

Feb. 16.—Finsbury Institution, Goswell Road, Mr. Cooper,—On the Writings of that eminent social reformer Charles Dickens, Esq. Discussion after,—Are the writings of Dickens in accordance with the philosophy of Robert Owen?

Printed and Published by G. J. HOLYOAKE,
40, Holywell-street, Strand.
Wednesday, February 12, 1845.

THE MOVEMENT
And Anti-Persecution Gazette.

"Maximise morals, minimise religion."—BENTHAM.

No. 62.   EDITED BY G. JACOB HOLYOAKE, AND M. Q. RYALL.   Price 1½d

TO ROBERT R. KALLEY, M.D.

LETTER VI.

DEAR DR.,

1st. To the respective degrees of certainty which belong to Theism and Atheism, and what you advance touching Atheism dissuading inquiry, I do not deem it necessary to return, having no wish to add anything to what I have already written on that subject, and not perceiving that you adduce anything more able than that upon which I have before commented. The question of certainty I fully canvassed, and it can hardly be necessary for me to reiterate that it is only at *a certain point* that the Atheist dissuades investigation — the point where examination has been ample, where he is sickened of fruitless research, baffled by deceptive analogies, replete with instances, gathered by the way, of the contradictory hypotheses before him, and satisfied of the non-necessity of the solution of the problem—it is only at this point that the Atheist advises a return from that labyrinth in which mankind from time immemorial have lost themselves. Since the Atheist can better deduce a code of morals from nature than he can from Theism, *his* "happiness here" is not contingent on his belief in the existence of God, and the happiness of a future life will be best taken into consideration when it is entered upon. As small was the preparation exacted from us prior to our appearance here, we are justified in expecting that less will suffice for our next *début*. We can hardly be more "raw" in the next world than we found ourselves in this, or be more in want of initiation.

2nd. You ask me "Is there clearer proof of the power whose existence I confess, than of the wisdom whose existence I deny." I think so. The powers to which I confess are the properties of matter,* the wisdom whose existence I question is that of something independent of matter.† On which side is the truth it would be vanity in me to presume, but which is the more intelligible I think is obvious.

3rd. The close manner in which you turn upon me for passing by as probable the idea of natural objects indicating design, is gratifying in this respect, that it leaves me with the assurance that such arguments as shall be passed over by so acute a reasoner as yourself must indeed be unanswerable. There are indeed other serious objections to the argument of design than the one I have adduced — but sufficient unto the day is the evil thereof? The difficulties I have pointed out, in the instance I have selected, are indeed cut short by the suggestion you make of the "acknowledgment of the Self-Existent," but such acknowledgment is hardly due from me until I am better enabled to perceive the ratiocination whereby it is arrived at. You seem to think that "millions of parts conducing to one end" show strong probability in favour of the existence of design, but when we see the wild and inconsistent conclusions to which such a belief leads, we are warned of the precipitancy of the judgment we had formed, and instructed to reconsider the subject. It is a privilege, I believe never denied to fallible men, that they should re-examine their first impressions and correct them by new accessions of information.

4th. You will remember that I used the term "personality" in connection with the design argument, I did not invent it. I found it. If the idea of an intelligent designer involves a material personality* it is not my fault. When the human eye for instance, is said by the natural theologian to be the work of intelligence, he leads me at once to a person or personality — that is to a being resembling ourselves, furnished as we are with brain and senses, clever, wiser, and more beautiful, doubtless, but still resembling us in being material, organised, and possessing a derived existence. When you ask me whether the various parts in the human structure, combining to produce one end, is not the work of an intelli-

---

* Par. 14 of my 5th.   † Par. 10 of your 4th.   * Par. 7 of your last.

gent designer,* I understand you to mean a personal intelligence, such a one as I have described. For if anything *not a person* may be supposed to be the author of all this, why may not nature be supposed to be the author? If we may reasonably look for the exercise of wisdom in something else than that to which experience leads us, namely, a person, where is the absurdity of supposing wisdom to reside in nature, or in other words, in concluding that the "phenomena and nice adaptation we see around us" are the production of matter? If personality is admitted to belong to what you term the "intelligent designer," it involves organisation, contrivance, a contriver of itself, and consequently a refutation of the Self-Existent—and if a personality is derived it establishes the reasonableness of the Atheist's conclusion, that matter is equal to everything and is all in all?

5th. If "design implies *something consisting entirely of matter*" you enquire, "why I feel obliged for the sake of consistency to deny design in the formation of our frames and in the movements of the universe."† My denial of design in this case is not made for the "sake of consistency" so much as from the force of evidence. Design seems to me to deny itself when it leads us, as we have seen, to a material maker, who is itself made when we seek the Self-Existent.

6th. "Why may not the Self-Existent be a spirit" you further enquire.‡ For the reason I think that a spirit is not anything. You define a spirit to be "an immaterial substance, possessing properties different from those of mere matter." But an immaterial substance is a substance which is not a substance—a negation of all being. It is a figment of the fancy, and the only "properties" which I can conceive it to possess—if it possesses any "different from those of mere matter," are those of imagination. There is no occasion to contend, as you suppose,‖ that matter can exclude spirit — for spirit being nothing matter in such case has nothing to exclude.

7th. In that instance in which you compare Deity to invisibility I agree with you, and think the simile holds good in more senses than you would allow. But if we knew nothing of air save its invisibility, I apprehend that we should trouble ourselves little about it. Its weight, its density, its elasticity, are accurately ascertained, but where has theology its science of pneumatics? On the contrary, the qualities, power, wisdom, goodness, which are ingeniously called the "shadows of Deity," are now more disputed than ever, and are supposed to be reflected from very different objects. Such as were supposed to be indicated in the origin of man, are now ably questioned.*

8th. I care little whether it is or is not a solecism to say that immateriality exists, since you agree with me that a self-existent immateriality is nothing.† You demur to my statement that the question between us is "whether the Self-Existent be immateriality or matter."‡ But must it not be so? If the Self-Existent be matter, then doubtless we see in the universe itself the cause of all things. But if the Self-Existent be not matter, to whom or what do your arguments point?—to some middle existence of which we are entirely ignorant, or to some immateriality which you agree is nothing? In favour of a self-existent spirit we have no experience, and must reject an assumption so entirely unsupported.

9th. That which is merely invisible may have properties, although we cannot search them out, but that which is *immaterial* has no properties to penetrate. The supposition of a self-existent spirit is, no doubt an unconscious but still, a virtual evasion of a matter god. Seeing thus no alternative between matter and immateriality, it was therefore that I proposed the questions you find so difficult to answer. I asked you whether "power and other properties you call the attributes of Deity, could inhere in immateriality," in the hope that seeing these contradictions so plainly exhibited you would be induced to acknowledge the difficulties with which your hypothesis is beset.

10th. I may find difficulties "in explaining the phenomena of nature on the hypothesis of the Self-Existent being mere matter"‖—but are they lessened in your hands by supposing the Self-Existent to be mere spirit? Is not human ingenuity exerted in vain unless we grow wiser by its exercise?

11th. You "maintain§ that the self-existent substance must be something different from mere matter because it is living, wise, powerful, and good," which you say "*are not* qualities of matter." Is this true?

---

* Par. 22 of your 4th.   † Par 7 of your last.
‡ Par. 7 of your last.   ‖ Par. 15 of your last.

* See "Vestiges of the Natural History of Creation."
† Par. 8 of your last.   ‡ Par. 11 of your last.
‖ Par. 12 of your last.   § Par. 12 of your last.

If not yet known to be qualities of all matter, are they not qualities of *educated* matter? and being so does not their presence imply (not a self-existent spirit but) a being dependent, personal, and material?

12th. Consciousness tells us that matter is eternal in the same way that it tells us that two and two must be four, or that for every effect there must be a cause. For such reasons it seems clear to me that a "possible" or impossible creation could never have been. Creation is an absurdity, unless it is reasonable to say that something could come from nothing. To say that the Self-Existent can create is to ascribe to him not only "vast" but contradictory powers. To say that Dr. Kalley "began to live a certain number of years ago"* is an unexceptionable remark, since it includes the prior existence of Dr. Kalley's progenitors, but to assert that Dr. Kalley was created is to say that he never had father and mother—that he came here because he would come, and that he took the resolution of being before he began to exist. Is there no absurdity in all this?

13th. To grant as you propose that the Self-Existent is God, is not to lift the veil of nature's secrets so much as to place an incubus upon it. If philosophy had adopted this easy process of seeming wise, the world would still be ignorant of half the phenomena which research and experiment have already accounted for. We can learn the operations of nature and the uses of natural objects. Thus far we can go and thus far is all that concerns our happiness, the rest, if anything, concerns only our curiosity. After all, may not the "knot which remains" be a supererogatory difficulty. The essential properties of matter being inseparable from matter, of course are eternal, and except in the complaisance of argument it is perhaps unnecessary to admit that we know not "whence they proceed." Is it not idle to ask *why* matter should be harmoniously arranged, since we know of no reason why it should be otherwise? I see no reason why matter should not act as it does as well as be what it is. The existence of matter is a fact and its properties are facts. They form the universe in which we find ourselves produced, and in searching out the relations we bear to it is our ample and rational employment. Matter and its properties we find before us—they precede ratiocination, and out of their operations doubtless arise all the phenomena which we see around us. A Self-Existent, independent of this source—so far from explaining as gravitation might do many things—seems to me to confuse everything.

14th. I will not argue against your conclusions that "man is nobler than nature," but thank you for the compliment you thus pay to our species. I like dominion.

15th. In the comparison which you institute between incredulity and superstition I think you less happy than ingenious. The two things have little in common between them. Superstition fashions a Deity out of a rude log—incredulity chops it up. Superstition bows down to it — incredulity tosses it on the fire. Superstition deceives —incredulity warms itself by it. Superstition is the slave - incredulity the master of matter. Is commerce to be revived?—incredulity sends out the fire winged car—connects the remote ends of the firm earth together—over old ocean paves with steam ships, a broad highway—and interchanges with distant nations arts and manufactures for golden grain or richest viands, while superstition implores heaven's blessing, and starves for want of trade. When blue, ghastly, clammy cholera stalks through the land incredulity seeks medicine's resources, while superstition mutters a prayer and perishes. If lurid fever distils its hot poison abroad incredulity drains the marsh and laves the body and lives, but superstition trusts to heaven and is numbered with the dead. Incredulity goes down to the sea in ships, sound and firm, to give battle to the tempest, while poor superstition (if true to its faith) ventures in its rickety vessel, cries in the storm's fury to a god of mercy, and miserably goes to the bottom. Nor does it ever grow wiser, but " in prosperity it seeks council of its almighty father," and again in distress idly "flees for succour to the same mistaken source." No wonder that on leaving this world, which it has so libelled both by its creed and its practice, it should " expect an immortality of bliss," thinking I suppose that he who has *wasted* one world upon it has a few others to spare. Incredulity is more vigilant, less encroaching, less presumptuous.

16th. Nor can the most refined superstition (philosophical Deism) be successfully confounded with incredulity (Atheism). In every sense they are antipodes—one exalting and the other debasing the world. If I may borrow the language of the first Pantheist of this country,* superstition perpetually forgets that "in spiritualising God nature

---

* Par. 14 of your last.

* W. J. Fox.

is desecrated. For by this spiritualism the stars are robbed of their glory, the flowers of their beauty, and the ocean of its eternity. One God acting on all things makes the things themselves of less value. The Revelations were gorgeous to the fancy but were only imaginative frost work. Mankind feel there is something more divine in what is more human."

Doctor your allegory is so excellent that I must try my hand at a legend myself.

Once upon a time there was a certain ocean, in which existed (said the theological navigators of that day) only *one* being, an " immaterial independent " rock. (Dr. Kalley's Deity). A man, a plain man, one who called something something and nothing nothing, was induced to investigate the phenomenon. On his return home, after many fruitless voyages, the following dialogue was held between him and the admiralty in those parts :—

Admiralty. Well sir, when you were cruising about did you see an "invisible" rock anywhere?

Sailor. You are joking with me gentlemen. Of course I could not see an invisible thing. He would be sharp sighted I guess who could.

Admiralty. Come, come sir, you must be serious on this subject, "it bears closely upon your happiness here and throughout the duration of your existence." Did you observe jets of water (marks of contrivance and design) such as a grampus (an intelligent designer) would eject, and such as nothing save a grampus (intelligence) ever does produce.

Sailor. I did see certain appearances which greatly excited my admiration, but I can hardly conceive that such jets as you describe could proceed from the rock. We never knew rocks to shoot up jets of water. (We never knew intelligence apart from a person). The jets lead me to suppose that they proceed from a grampus. But now I think of it a grampus isn't "immaterial." Besides we should never find *one* grampus only—there would be sure to be a pair, (contrivance implies a contriver) and no doubt there are a family of them (an infinite series). Gentlemen, I must be wrong—for my observations go to prove that instead of one "immaterial independent" rock, there are a series of " huge beings " disporting about, producing the appearances we ascribe to the rock. I think gentlemen that it will be more reasonable in me to say that though the appearances I witnessed were very interesting I am not quite certain about their proceeding from the rock.

Admiralty. Well, now sir, if they do not proceed from the rock " whence do they proceed ?" How do you account for the phenomena?

Sailor. May not the appearances be owing to the natural operation of the wind on the water (matter and its properties). I see no reason to suppose the ocean (nature) unequal to the task of astonishing us. But if reference to the wind and water (natural causes) is insufficient the rock won't do at all, no one ever knew a rock spouting water, (a spirit designing) and we must fall back on the grampuses.

Admiralty. It appears to us that "you do not wish to find the rock."

Sailor. Gentlemen this is very hard. You allow that this rock is "invisible," and yet you expect me to find it out—that the indications of it (its attributes) are such as " the human mind can form no adequate conception of," and still you tell me that I can attain " certainty" concerning it—that it has none of the qualities of a rock, (its properties being different from those of matter) that none but a rock can certainly know a rock, (" God only can fully comprehend what God is,") * yet you would have me waste my whole life in searching after it. Besides what matters it to me ? Suppose there are jets or spouts, my business is to adapt my bark to sail among them unhurt, for if I neglect this I shall go to the bottom, whether they are thrown up (designed) by ocean, (nature) by grampus, (intelligence) or by rock (God). If indeed I discover ocean (nature) to be the cause of the phenomena which I behold I have some chance of directing myself, as its operations are ever before me to study, (to learn its uses) but as for the others I can never know when I have them or when I hav'nt.

Admiralty. My dear sir, that rock is your " father." You are engaged on a very reasonable investigation. " We hope you will not persist in denying what is so plain to common sense." " We believe that you may attain as much certainty of the existence of that rock as of your own."

Our friend the sailor withdrew, as does

Yours, respectfully,
G. JACOB HOLYOAKE.

BEAUTY.—No man receives the true culture of a man, in whom the sensibility to the beautiful is not cherished, and I know of no condition of life from which it should be excluded.—*Self Culture.*

---

* Par. 16 of your last.

"THE MORMON DELUSION,"

ONE OF THE CURRENT CHRISTIAN CANTS BY WHICH THE OLD TALE OF THE "POT AND THE KETTLE" IS NEWLY ILLLUSTRATED.

R. PAYNE writes that he has been to hear a sermon by a Mormonite preacher, at the Assembly Rooms, Theobald's Road. The clerical gentleman in question was a particular friend of the great Joe Smith—not our worthy Socialist friend, the most active of the promoters of the Hampshire Community experiment—but the Joe Smith of transatlantic repute and the victim to transatlantic christian "persecution unto death."

Some of the extravagancies of the "latter day saints," our correspondent recites as follows:

"The lecture was on the restitution of all things spoken of by the prophets, Joe Smith of course included. He first went to shew what was lost by the sinfulness of man, commencing with Adam. The earth, he states, was very different in the time of Adam to what it is in these days of puffing, steaming, &c., for in the days of Adam the waters were gathered together and formed one great sea, while the earth formed one great continent, but through the wickedness of man this great continent has been divided into continents, islands, &c. He did not say how the inhabitants of the earth were supplied with water, nor can I imagine how it was unless they bored Artesian wells to the other side. But this state of things is not to last, the waters are to be again gathered to one place, the mountains are to be leveled, and the earth is to become a smooth plain. The nature of animals is also changed, for in the days of Adam the tiger and the lion were on the most friendly terms with the lamb, and like some of our *modern Economists*, agreed to abstain from animal food and confine themselves to vegetable diet. This, he asserts, will be the case again, all carnivorous animals are to become granivorous or herbivorous animals, and all noxious animals are to become innoxious and harmless. With regard to man he is to return to his primitive state of innocence and ignorance, there is also to be a general restitution of all the books made mention of in the Bible, the Book of Mormon has been already restored, although not mentioned in the Bible. When this general restitution has taken place we may expect the second coming of Christ."

Are we quite certain that these people are more fitly entitled to the term "wild fanatics" than the regularly constituted clergy? It frequently escapes our notice that it is the *novelty* and not the *degree* of the absurdity that excites our pity and contempt.

Watch the demure old foxes in regular canonicals, " surpliced " or non-surpliced—see the disturbances they kick up about the bit of white or bit of black for clerical livery, and the broils of their silly followers clawing each other in the contest—hear the ranting, raving, and cawing of the ill-omened ravens in plain plumage—witness the agitations and flutterings of the silly flocks when holy incomprehensibilities and goblin mysteries, sacred incoherencies and incongruities, almighty-phantom fictions, called revelations, miraculous interpositions, godly and devilish colloquies, incarnations, rovings and roamings—divine floods, fires, and furious massacres, " by command," are blattered forth. Track them through their "horrible and awful" lists of plagues in every variety, frog-gluts and famine, lice and locusts, blood-rivers and all sorts of portentious *judgments* to amuse and horrify the well-duped geese—and by way of a wind-up, the long tale of a tub tacked on, with a cock-and-bull story of sheep and goats divided on general gaol delivery day—when by sound of trump one lot shall be kept above chaunting and blowing hosannahs and the other lot sent *below* for spitting and frizzling and grilling, boiling, steaming and baking, weeping and wailing and gnashing of teeth—with all other concomitants understood in religious jargon by the concluding and drop-scene term of ETERNAL DAMNATION.

When such monstrosities are current—when we know that the state hires a trained band of artful sophists to play at hide-and-seek with words, and make fictions pass for realities—when we know that the said state makes their submissive booby subjects pay for this balderdash—when we further know —oh achme of deplorable absurdity!—that there are hundreds and thousands and tens of thousands ready and willing to pay for this loathsome cant for themselves and wives and even innocent offspring, and to contribute for its exportation to the utmost countries of the globe—let us no longer marvel at Mormon absurdities but conclude that no preternatural follies and duperies are too real to be swallowed by those whose brains are once benuddled by the GOD-IDEA!

R. P. adds, "It is a very rare thing now-a-days to meet our friends as was formerly our wont. Is the spirit dead within us, or have we done all that can be done to exterminate superstition, ignorance and error? Are the advocates of free discussion dead, or do they consider no more agitation necessary? It was with a great degree of pleasure I attended the public meeting at John Street Institution, concerning the treatment Mrs. Martin received at the hands of the Hull Magistrates; since that time we have had no public demonstration of our principles at the west end of London. Could not some of our friends suggest a plan for meeting more frequently?"

The prospectus for the ATHEON, which has appeared in the *Movement*, and which has already called forth many responses, seems to be that which, if carried out, would meet the wishes of our correspondent.

The attention of Atheists cannot be too strenuously directed to the establishment of such an institution. M. Q. R.

SECOND LETTER FROM ARTHUR TREVELYAN.

Newcastle-upon-Tyne, Feb. 2, 1845.

Jacob Holyoake,
  Worthy Friend,

Phrenology teaches that a well developed conscientiousness, could not be content, unless the accounts were capable of being understood by all persons possessing a capacity of understanding any accounts clearly kept*

The agitation, the account of your Visit has caused, and the different discussions and published opinions that have followed, will no doubt do an immense amount of good to the Social cause.

There is still a hampering after the ways of the old world in many professing Socialists, which must be rooted out, whatever amount of pain it may cause to certain individuals, fame, &c. Indeed everything sinks into insignificance, even life itself, when put in competition with the emancipation of the millions of bees, that are crushed to death by a few thousands of drones and bayonets, aided by priests.

I have the greatest faith in the power of the working classes to carry through successfully the Harmony Experiment, if solely in their own hands, or assisted by those who can feel as working men,—the middle-class feeling of gentility is the lever which has caused all the mismanagement, and unhappy squabbles that have taken place, since Harmony came into the possession of the Rational Society.

The largest number of the greatest men the world has yet possessed, have come from the working classes,—and we have seen that almost all institutions, as Mechanics Institutes, Libraries, &c., got up ostensibly for the benefit of that class, have owing to the interference in the management by the middle and higher classes, been eventually lost to the working man: the same fate awaited Harmony, had they not taken it into their own hands, and then only at the eleventh hour.

In the *Zoist*, for January, what an excellent article is " Intellectual Freedom—its advocates and opponents," and what deservedly severe censure is passed on the editors of the " Edin. Phrenological Journal," at their want of moral courage, in not showing the injustice of the late Scotch persecution for Blasphemy, by publishing articles in that Journal exposing the cruelty of punishing any man or woman for opinions sake.

I remain, faithfully yours,
ARTHUR TREVELYAN.

INFINITY MEASURED,
OR VERY PRECISE PARTICULARS OF GOD ALMIGHTY.

[WE have been favoured by Mr. Ellis with the following extract from the Rabbinical traditions of Eisenmenger, contained in the *Jewish Repository* for Jan. 1813.]

" In Sepher Raziel* R. Ismael said, Metatron, the great prince of testimony told me, I testify this of Jehovah the God of Israel, the living and unchangeable God our Lord and Ruler, that from the seat of his glory and upwards is 1,180,000 miles, and from the seat downwards is also 1,180,000 miles; his height is 2,360,000 miles; from his right arm to his left is 770,000 miles; from his eyeball is 300,000 miles, his skull is 30,000 miles in length and breadth,† the crowns of his head are 660,000. The height of his foot soles is 30,000,000 miles, and from his foot soles to his heels 1,000,500 miles, and from his heel to his shin-bones 190,000,004 miles; from his shin-bone to his thigh 121,004 miles; from his thigh to his neck 240,000,000 miles; his neck is 130,000,800 miles; his beard 11,500 miles; the black in his right and left eyes 11,500 each; his right and left hands 220,002 miles

---

* We are not Phrenologists and are not to be held responsible for these opinions. Mr. Lloyd Jones must go to loggerheads with George Combe about them.

* A Manuscript said to have been written by the Angel Raziel, and by him given to Adam.

† A capital development. We should recommend the Phrenological Society to have a cast taken.—Ed. of *Movement*.

each; from his right to his left shoulder 160,000,000 miles; from his right arm to his left 120,000,000 miles; the same is the space between every finger. R. Ismael told me in the presence of his pupils, I and Rabbi Akiva pledge ourselves that whosoever knows the measure of our Creator is sure to be a child of the next world. The ministering angels are at a distance of 360,000,000 miles from the divine Majesty, as is said above, it stood the Seraphims according to Gematrioth,* equal to 36,000 which shews us that the body of the divine Majesty measures 2,360,000 miles, from his loins and upwards, 1,180,000 miles, and the same distance from his loins downwards. Those miles are not like ours, but each mile is 1,000,000 ells long, and each ell is is 4 spans and a hand long, and God's span reaches from one corner of the world to the other, as it is said, "Who has measused the waters in the hollow of his hand, and meted out heaven with his span." Or the words, "he meted out heaven with his span" teaches us that heaven, and the heaven of heavens, is but one span in length, and the same in breadth and height, and that the earth and the deep is a foot-sole in length, and the same in breadth and height even to the firmament. R. Judah said in Rav's name, the day is twelve hours long; the first three hours God sits and studies the laws, the second three, he sits to judge the world; the third three, he provides for the world; and the fourth three hours he sits and plays with Leviathan. To the same effect the Jerusalem Targum on Parsha Haazinu; Moses the prophet said, when I ascended into heaven I saw the Lord of the world dividing the day into four parts; three hours he studies the law; three he is occupied in judging causes; three in maintaining the world; in the fourth three hours he ordains marriages. In Medrash Rabba, R. Acha said, in the name of R. Chanina, When Moses ascended into heaven, he heard the voice of the blessed God studying in the section relative to the red heifer, and stated the opinion of every Rabbi on the subject; together with the name of its author."

LIBERATION OF MR. PATERSON.

We understand that Mr. Paterson was liberated on Monday, Feb. 10. His term of imprisonment expired on the 9th (Sunday). In the English Gaols, when a prisoner's term

* A cabalistic art which consists in reckoning numerically the letters or characters of which Hebrew words are composed, and also in the comparison of different words, which by the transposition of their letters, form the same number.

expires on a Sunday, he is not liberated on that day, it being literally not *lawful* to do that good on the Sabbath day. But the law provides better things; it orders the liberation to take place on the Saturday. But the pious Scotch have their "pound of flesh," and keep their prisoner until the Monday.

Since writing the preceding we have received some interesting Communications from Mr. P. which shall appear next week. The following is a short extract, written on the day of his liberation.

" Parted with my guardians this morning, and although there used to be something in parting that softened my heart, yet so far from melting at the eyes in bidding ' good morning ' to well-known faces, by heaven, I detected myself laughing as I passed under the outer gateway! *I must be becoming hard-hearted, surely.*"

EXTRACTS FROM A LETTER FROM MRS. MARTIN.

"I was subjected to an hour-and-half's scrutiny, before the Magistrates, when every effort was made to discover every thing connected with my private life. Among the rest, they were extremely anxious to know the name of my husband—my residence in London—whether I had a press and types, whether I had ever passed by other names than those which I had given, namely, my maiden name and my public name. To all these queries, I declined *any* answer. I believe the design was, first, to keep me while the Discussion should have been going on, and second, to find out all about my affairs. They endeavoured to extort a promise from me to visit Arbroath no more,—but knowing that I could not get any room to Lecture in, they were satisfied with escorting me to the railway, and seeing me off; cautioning me against coming there again.

" Southwell has gone through Glasgow to-day, and we passed each other (unknowingly) on the railway between Glasgow and Edinburgh. I understand he is come to hold the Discussion in my stead, but I know they will get no room, so his labour will be lost "

We believe Jacob Holyoake's account of Robert Owen's establishment in Hampshire to have been written under a sense of duty, and to be mainly, if not entirely, correct in its criticisms. The abuse he has met with from some of the Owenites, without the liberty of replying to it in their paper, stamps them with disgrace and inconsistency.—*Communist Chronicle.*

Third Edition.—Price 1s. 6d.

PRACTICAL GRAMMAR.
By G. Jacob Holyoake.

This is a very useful little book. To learners of grammar, especially adult persons, it will prove an acceptable and valuable guide. The chapters intitled "Writing for the Press" and "Composition" are well worthy of perusal by writers generally. The hints contained therein are pithy and practical, and, being conveyed in terse smart sentences, afford some instructive and amusing reading.—*Leicester Chronicle.*

London: J. Watson, 5, Paul's Alley, Paternoster-row.

Published by Watson, 5, Paul's Alley, Paternoster Row. Price 2d.

THE VALUE OF BIOGRAPHY IN THE FORMATION OF INDIVIDUAL CHARACTER.
By G. Jacob Holyoake.

The pamphlet gives an excellent outline of the career of Pemberton—and is written in an exceedingly lucid and forcible style. We have derived great pleasure from its perusal and commend it to the attention of all our readers.—*New Moral World.*
A pleasing subject, pleasingly and profitably discoursed of.—*Northern Star.*

Cosmopolite, for *Movement*................ 1 0 0

Another Vial to be Opened.—The last number of the *Communist Chronicle* contains the following portentous proclamation :—

To the Custodiens of the unopened Scriptures of Johanna Southcott; Greeting—

Whereas, certain of the prophetic writings of Johanna Southcott yet remain unopened and unpublished to the people, I hereby publicly demand, *in the name of the learned of the earth*, that the said Scriptures be opened and published : full cause for which shall be shown, either by writing or in person, at any fit time and place hereafter appointed.
(Signed) Goodwyn Barmby.

A believer in Christianity should, at least, have sufficient philanthropy to wish that his religion were not true. Even if he believes that his future happiness is secured, he should feel no enthusiasm for a religion which proclaims "as glad tidings of great joy" that a few are elected to eternal happiness ; but that the greatest number of his departed relatives, friends, and fellow beings are now writhing in torments that are to have no end! It is true, an unbeliever is deprived of the visionary hope of happiness in a future state; but, to compensate for this, he perceives that the doctrine of endless punishment, inflicted for the sins of frail and erring man, is as absurd as it is execrable. A. T.

Arbroath not yet settled.—W. C. M. says, "What a set of unmanly and shameless brutes these Presbyterian spouters must be to put a defenceless *woman* in a Dungeon for exposing the infamy of their infernal cant; who were afraid to touch Mr. Southwell when he was amongst them last winter." They are at any rate to have another chance given them, as the Manchester Branch have announced by placard that Mr. Charles Southwell is to go to beard them in their dens. On the 18th and 19th he is advertised to lecture on " Civil and Religious Liberty," in John Street Hall, Arbroath.

Education.—To educate a child perfectly requires profounder thought and greater wisdom than to govern a state.—*Channing.*

TO CORRESPONDENTS.

Z. P. sends us a long piece on those words of Hunt, " Damn the people of England—they will never do anything for themselves." We cannot undertake to advise Z. P. beyond this that he ought first to attend to those duties which devolve upon him—afterwards let him make himself acquainted with the theory of versification, to which at present he has little attended.

Received.—God's words versus God's works, by W. C.—Article D of Alphabet of Materialism, by C. S.—The *Leicester Chronicle.*

J. C.—We received the money rightly from Mr. Cleave. The error lay with us. He will see it corrected now.

J. G.—We have never been tropically struck, and consequently have paid little attention to Mr. Etzler's plans of emigration. But respecting all schemes of the kind we have one rule to recommend—let each who goes out take money enough to bring himself back if he does not succeed, or does not like it. Emigration without this precaution may prove self-transportation.

Errata.—For Woleford, page 48, read *Coleford.* In subscriptions to Paterson. Testimonial, same page, for Miss Bird, James Pearee, F. Dennis, E. Gordon, 1s., read 2s.

For Mr. Paterson, from " W. W."........ 0 10 0
For Miss Roalfe, from   do............ 0 5 0
For C. S., from   do............ 0 5 0
For G. J. H., from   do............ 0 5 0

LECTURES.

Feb. 23.—National Hall, 242, High Holborn, W. J. Fox,—On the ceremony of Burial ; and the Superstitions and Abuses connected therewith.

Feb. 23.—Hall of Science, City Road, Mr. G. J. Holyoake,—The Effects of Solitary Confinement, in answer to Luke Roden's article on the Pentonville Prison, in the " Illuminated Magazine."

Feb. 23.—Social Institution, Market Place Leicester, Mr. Ryley Perry,—Internal Evidence of Christianity.

Feb. 24.——— Free Discussion.

Feb. 23.—Branch A 1, John Street, Tottenham Court Road,—A Lecture. At 7, p.m.

Feb. 23.—Finsbury Institution, Goswell Road, Mr. Cooper,—On the Writings of that eminent social reformer Charles Dickens, in continuation. Discussion after,—Adjourned question resumed.

SUBSCRIPTIONS
TO THE ANTI-PERSECUTION UNION.

T. G. Hibburd Mansfield, for members' tickets..................... 0 2 6
H. Cook, Theological Depot, Ipswich...... 0 1 0

PATERSON TESTIMONIAL.

H. Spooner......................... 0 1 0
Society for Investigation of Truth, Victoria Coffee House, Portland Town.......... 0 5 0
Per Mr. Hindle, Ashton-under-Lyne, proceeds of Mr. Southwell's Lectures...... 1 0 4
Miss Inge, per Mrs. C. G. H. Hornblower 0 1 0
G. J. H., Sec.

Printed and Published by G. J. Holyoake, 40, Holywell-street, Strand.
Wednesday, February 19, 1845.

THE MOVEMENT
And Anti-Persecution Gazette.

"Maximise morals, minimise religion."—BENTHAM.

No. 63.   EDITED BY G. JACOB HOLYOAKE, AND M. Q. RYALL.   Price 1½d

MR. PATERSON'S ADDRESS ON HIS LIBERATION FROM PERTH.

SOME eighteen moons have filled their horns since the "higher powers" arrested my humble endeavours to illuminate Christianity's dark mass by pouring on it a stream of Infidel philosophy, that would have gone far to dispel its stagnant humours, or at least have made its darkness more visible.

Good men must regret that I had so little opportunity, in my small way, in showing Edina's citizens that it was simply the constellations of priests and clusters of bigots in authority, that, hanging in mid air, obscured reason's rays, that darkened men's visions, so that they could only see dimly, as through a glass, this vale of misery, and the great tide of ignorance rolling through it, and human beings pursuing bubbles light as air. My intentions were disregarded or misrepresented, my advices scorned, and my person, as you well know, handed over to these very bigots and vultures, to whose care Christ's spiritual and this material world are committed. Compelled to give each inquietude the slip by stealing out of active being, the cormorants thought also to immolate our Atheistic works to appease their Jehovah and their own selfishness; but the faggots have been scattered, and Atheism like the Phœnix, has fanned the flame of liberty with its own wings, so that instead of them consigning our principles to the tomb of oblivion, we may soon chaunt *paeans* over the decay of the Christian idolatry.

I forgot to state that no lark ever carroled the morning's dawn with more glee than I ushered in the morning light that should disrobe me of the felon's marks, and enable me again to behold the sight of fields, trees, houses, people, and other glad marks of other days. Though nature was clad in winter's garb, yet I loved to see her again in winter weeds, and her frozen trees sparkled to my fond vision like young diamonds, while the northern blast was as refreshing to my withered face as ever the south wind was to the lap of earth when it kisses away its winding-sheet of snow. Suppose not, however, that I pined in my narrow cell for all this. No, I verily believe I enjoyed more serenity from a conscientious reflection, aided by the approval of the honest and enlightened, than did any one of those bigots who insulted or unjustly treated me, and who triumphed over the supposed ruins of the principles of free expression—still the sight of old friends whom I once valued, and never forgot, sent the blood to my face, and made me glow with the exultation of a liberated school boy.

I feel this moment as if all the world was a stage and I had never acted any part, or that I had drunk a Lethean draught and had forgot all I ever knew. I know not what has been doing among Atheists, nor what they intend doing, but I will venture to make a few observations though I should be set down as one of those antiquated, for whom I formerly entertained so supreme a contempt.

Of the nature of my imprisonment little need be said. It would be only an oft repeated tale, suffice it that all the rigors of an imprisonment, in the first rate " silent system" establishment, were not abated one iota in my case, but were much added to by the conduct of our Chaplain, whom I declare and can prove was the greatest specimen of a human monster it was ever my lot to encounter. I feel indeed humiliated to refer to such a disgrace to humanity and such an ornament of the kirk, but I will do so only to show that Atheists *must* take some steps to curb religion's power, else there will be no end to such pitiable creatures. Only think of Infidels being sent to a prison in a remote corner of the country, where visitors are never admitted, where the public eye never penetrates, and obliged to submit to the abuse, misrepresentation, and petty annoyances of such a man as this Mr. Allan. As I do not wish to set down aught in malice, although to exaggerate his character is impossible, I give a specimen of his kindness, as I complained, and was prepared to the Board to prove.

MR. PATERSON'S REMONSTRANCE TO THE PRISON BOARD AGAINST THE REV. MR. ALLAN.

General Prison, Perth.
Sep. 28, 1844.

"Gentlemen,—Understanding, through Directors, you desire acquaintance with the grievances of prisoners, I think it proper to acquaint you with one which I hope has not your sanction. Within the last six months your Chaplain has indulged himself on Sundays in the most gross, violent, and unjustifiable abuse of myself, friends, and party, imputing to us thoughts and actions never even dreamed of by the worst specimens of humanity which have come under my notice. To be described as thieves, liars, profligates, debauchers, and hypocrites, by a hard-brained, unsentimental, and vulgar spouter must be disagreeable enough. Indeed the ideas could only find a place in the most impure minds, or be echoed by hearts in sympathy with such conceptions.

"I do not complain, nor did I ever in my life complain, of any arguments used against my opinions, so far from that I court them, would be delighted with them, and in expectation of a treat I provided several sheets, detailing my own views and my objections to his, but he has never found it convenient to notice them. Nor am I objecting to anything said by him on Sundays, which appears like argument, I never yet heard any, for I do not call bellowing and roaring, (with frothy and bubbling remarks of groans, hells, and sulphur,) argument. I am complaining of pure misrepresentation and positive falsehoods, cloaked under the pretence of zeal for religion—a cheap way of gaining celebrity, but evidently springs from the gratification of a revengeful temper.

"A just man needs not, to establish his own purity, to wantonly blacken his neighbour; a system based on truth requires neither the support of falsehood or impertinent declamation. A bad man and system require both.

"Bishop Warburton (a man of talent by the bye) declared he scorned a victory over a tonguetied opponent, such a sentiment is too noble to find a place in Mr. Allan's breast; crowing over a dungeoned opponent is too pleasing to a little mind not to be enjoyed at its opportunity—practical kindness forms no part of his morality—' Do unto others, &c.,' forms no practical part of his or any of his profession's creed. I hope it does yours. Justice, at all events, cannot sanction scurrility in a pulpit and condemn it in a shop. Surely imprisonment is not meant for revenge—not meant to steel the heart by injustice, but to soften it by moderation and humanity.

"Is it not worthy of consideration whether these Sunday harangues on pretended Atheism are not likely to induce prisoners to turn their thoughts favourably to systematic disbelief, who otherwise may have remained in utter ignorance of its very meaning? I think it possible, and could, if desired, give many reasons why I think so—however, nothing would give me greater pain than the accession of such converts.

"If the Board asks why I do not complain to Mr. Allan himself, it is simply because since I told him to answer my papers he seldom visits me. The last visit was in June, and in answer to my remonstrance of his conduct he told me, 'That the blackguard origin of my belief should incessantly be his theme.' He spoke truth that time.

"My principal reason for bringing this matter before the Board is not that my character or that of my friends can be injured by the tirades, as our characters I believe would suffer nothing by a comparison with his own, but simply to obtain redress, or if not, that such deliberate tyranny, duplicity, lying, and slander be exposed, and those patronising such conduct obtain the credit due to it.

"Hoping the Board will put a stop to such proceedings, or cause my removal to another part of the prison during their performance, on the principle that 'Evil communications corrupt good manners.'

"Yours, &c.,
"THOMAS PATERSON.
"Prisoner for Libel.
"To the President of the Prison Board."

We have deluded ourselves with the idea that any formal exposure of persecution was unnecessary—that it would die out of itself. It never will until we show by some decided step that we are not to be trifled with. The conduct of this theological frog is but the echo of every real Christian in the country, power and the same opportunity granted. Persons have told me repeatedly that never could any real religionist grant or consent that Atheists be allowed to propagate their sentiments. Every religious publication circulated in Scotland, either plainly or slyly, avows the same sentiments. Nay, even Deists chime in with the Christians at this time, or else by their faint sneers try to damn us. In a word, when a practical application of the principle of private judgment is tested all religionists are persecutors. Our duty is plain. Step boldly into the arena and proclaim, so that EVERY MAN SHALL HEAR, our principles and rights. Let us henceforth pull from the faces of *soi disant* lovers of liberty, the flimsy veils under which they are masked: strip these self idolators and ludicrous self flatterers of their tattered robes of vanity, affectation, and hypocrisy, and show them to the world as the persecutors of the human race, and the supporters of the grossest delusion, and most degrading tenets the sun ever shone upon.

We have not gone wisely to work. We have ransacked our brains for arguments why men should not persecute. How odious is a persecutor! Persecutors admit all we say, but they still go on persecuting as usual, and they smile at our efforts so long as they are directed at themselves, their only dread is lest we may make an impression on the multitude. Atheists have confined their exertions to a few large towns and have no power, the bigots *have power*, and retain it by *misrepresenting* and *blackguarding us in every corner where* we have *no representatives*. In my travels in this country I have often met persons who, from the descriptions given of us by the cunning, have believed we were the scum and refuse of the earth, and our aims the annihilation of morality and the extermination of the pious—others think there are in reality no such persons as Atheists, but only imaginary creatures like the unicorns and such like beasts talked of in "Revelations." I give a specimen of our characters as drawn by one of Scotland's talented and pious clergymen, the Rev. Mr. Dunn of St. Peter's, Glasgow, in a work teeming with tirades against Infidels, and of a large circulation.

"Every Atheistical objection has been met and refuted a hundred times, yet it (Atheism) retails them as unanswerable, or tricks them out under other colours and calls them new. It has been hunted down from the heights of learning and science and sought refuge in the hovel and workshop. Its emissaries are principally men who can neither read nor write. It *dare not* come into the fair field of fight. It minces the opposition it has not the *courage to proclaim*. Why do Infidels not attack Paley and strip him of the name he has borne unchallenged half a century? Why? They are afraid. They cannot. Why do Infidels refuse to inculcate their principles on their children, dependants or neighbours? Why do they shun and hate the light—why grovel in the filth and mire of vice?" &c., &c. Enough has been quoted to cause Infidels to stare with astonishment that such barefaced falsehoods have been publicly delivered to crowded audiences in Glasgow, lately, and now published far and wide. No wonder men look quietly on our persecutions, no wonder juries are lost to all sense of humanity, when such descriptions of us are uppermost in their minds.

Mr. Dunn and others with "pot valor" call on us to come out. Let us do so in earnest. Never mind if a few of us are drawn within a prison's vortex. It will undeceive the gulled, it will do more, it will keep our principles *continually* before mankind. There has been our fault, we have defended ourselves *only*, shook our chains *merely*, *fell back* and *gained nothing*. Our discretion and virtues have been transient, our exertions intermittent, our zeal has lain fallow while it ought to have been assiduously fostered. The enemy has always recovered by our supineness, and we have had continually to renew the combat with the oppressor. I would propose that we alter tactics. Elect a central committee, chalk out the ground we already possess, and begin to break in more, and when broken in, secured, and death before yielding an inch. Collections should be made to enable the committee to print fifteen or eighteen millions of tracts, containing a challenge to all respectable Christians to discuss the fundamentals of their faith; a part devoted to a pithy condensation of the *principles of free inquiry;* a third and last to advertising all Atheistical works, particularly our weekly organ, enlarged, and capable of *being sent by post*, if required, like the new edition of *Chambers' Journal*. The press work might be done gratuitously, and their distribution might be effected in towns where there are Atheists voluntarily, while one or two *travelling advertisers* might be employed to go to all the country villages and towns, calling meetings and giving addresses on free inquiry, and taking advantage of them to circulate the tracts. Every house in the country might be visited, every public work inundated with our views, and almost every body familiarised with our designation. This principle, pursued for one year, would do more to disarm bigotry, silence *bravadoism*, unmask hypocrisy, create new friends, encourage old ones, decide waverers, enlighten public opinion generally, which would be our future safeguard from all but the harmless priestly weapon of anathemas. The expense would not in reality be more than the cost of defending a victim of persecution, and how much more glorious to our safety, to our own energy and courage, than to the godly forbearance. A lasting impression would be made of our determination, and nothing but this impression can arrest the inroads of the godly.

More than this, it is our duty to endeavour to arrest public attention to the delusion of Godism. Do we believe the truth shall make men free? then why stand by sighing with a sickly sentimentality over wishes and prisoned hopes, until we have tried every means to draw attention, tried to unfurl our pinions and soar away beyond the bigots aim, and have failed?

The mental dawn has broken let us hasten on the day. Let a glorious agitation be set on foot—let us no longer be tossed from wave to wave at the caprice of Godly pilots, but take helm in hand and make *direct* for port. Do not let us hang on the words of a Brougham or a Denman, but *create a public opinion*, and our object will be gained by our own exertions. Liberty of speech is no longer in embryo, the shell is burst, let us shiver it into pieces. Irrigate the country again I say, deluge the land with Infidelity, let volunteers in the summer months distribute tracts. I shall cheerfully accept of any position in the good work. I will do anything but tamper with tigers, for it is not policy—it is cowardice, fraud, or both. No benefit can result from it. It is not a truce we want, but a conclusion of the war, that afterwards our energies may be employed in schemes taken in hand for man's mental, moral, and physical benefit.

GOD'S WORDS *versus* GOD'S WORKS.

I

"Behold, my desire is that the Almighty would answer me."—*Jewish and Christian Mythology.*

"Professions are oftimes deceiving," says an ancient and over-true proverb, which has been, from time immemorial, applied alike to the just and the unjust, the simple minded and the artful of this world's inhabitants, but never, that I am aware, have the "divinities" been looked upon as worthy of association with the animal, "a little lower than the angels," in the truth of the above apothegm. What ever the cause of this omission, I believe I may confidently affirm of all descriptions of gods, that the omission is most undeserved—the immortals being quite as prone to "put on appearances" as the mortals. As the people of Japan prefer black teeth, mount their horses from the right side, and wear white for mourning, all of which are the opposites of the customs of this part of the world—so, in endeavouring to appear other than they are, the gods reverse the earthly rule. With us the practice is to "put the best side outside," with them to cry "stinking fish." Whether this arises from ignorance or impudence I am not prepared to say—it may be a product of both, for it is said that "ignorance and impudence usually go together." The exploits of Jupiter with Leda, and the Holy Ghost with the betrothed of Joseph are far from complimentary to the principal personages concerned, and yet we are told in the case of the Christians' God that the record of the transaction was made immediately under his own superintendence, and that a belief in its truth will secure eternal happiness—and as the poets were considered to be favourites of the gods, doubtless the libidinous Jupiter smiled approvingly upon the "inspired" mortal who first conceived the happy thought of transmitting to posterity the *faux pas* of the Greek "thunderer." Pope says, "to err is *human*—to forgive *divine*." The sentence, by implication and assertion, is an artful and abominable falsehood. To err is alike the fate of gods and men—to forgive is a virtue rarely, very rarely practised by divinities. I shall leave to other nations the looking after the foibles of their peculiar deities, and shall confine my research to those who are affirmed to patronise this small (but happy?) isle—for though I may not increase in worldly wealth, as a consequence of minding my own business, I may escape the misfortune usually attending an attempt to do too much.

If we grant, for argument sake, that the Bible was written under divine superintendence, and was really intended for a guide and instructor to man—and, further, that this earth, our planatary system, the universe in fact, was created by the *same* being who indited that book, we shall be astonished, when we examine the two, at the discrepancies which force themselves upon our notice. An old song declares it to be "a wise child that knows its own father," and it would seem to require an infinitely wiser being than the God of the Christians to know his own child—for the account given by the Holy Ghost of the birth of the world, its features, and some particulars of its history, are so much at variance with the facts discovered by men, on a subsequent examination of the earth itself, that no one could possibly identify the one by a reference to the other. Perhaps I am going too far when I say no one—but having no faith in inspiration, or divine "clairvoyance," I use the expression in reference to the assistance derivable from man's *natural* aids only, which I am confident, and which will be readily admitted by some of the godly, would never lead him to a perception of the *harmony* existing or affirmed between the Bible and modern science. I do not remember even to have read a book, a lecture, or a remark, the tendency of which was entirely opposed to some one or the other of the assertions in the Bible, but that it was averred to be another beautiful and striking evidence of the *truth* of scripture. "The greater the truth, the greater the libel," said the late Lord Ellenborough; and to my mind the greater the number of *facts,* the products of philosophical industry, said to be in agreement with the relations in the Bible, or the Bible to be in agreement with them, why the greater the libel on that "holy" book. Before I proceed to place in juxta-position the so-called words and the so-called works of the Christians' Deity, I will give a few quotations from the opinions of some of our most distinguished philosophers in favour of the view that revelation and science will be always found to agree.

The Rev. Dr. Pye Smith, F.G.S., in a course of lectures delivered at the Congregational Library in 1839, says, "The study of revealed religion, *when rightly pursued,* could not but be in perfect harmony with all true science. *The works and the word of God were streams from the same source,* and, though they flowed in different directions, they necessarily partook of the same qualities of wisdom, truth, and goodness. Geology, in an especial manner, possesses a place in this benificent association, and holds also a most interesting connexion with every other branch of natural science." In another part he remarks.—Above all, it was incumbent upon them to beware of that erroneous opinion that certain geological doctrines were at variance with the testimony of the Holy Scriptures, as this notion must work a very pernicious effect. "There is, indeed (said the learned doctor), *the semblance of such variance,* but I confess my conviction that *it is nothing but a semblance,* and that, like many other difficulties, on all the important subjects which have exercised the intellect of man, it vanishes before a careful and sincere examination. The naked fact, however, the mere appearance, is eagerly laid hold of by irreligious men, and is made *an excuse* for dismissing from their minds any serious regard to the law and the gospel of God; whilst they contend that the Mosaic history *lies under such heavy suspicion* as to have but slender claims upon a philosopher's attention."

A kind friend of mine has lent me a report of the doctor's lecture from the *Patriot.* I shall have occasion to make many extracts, when the reader can weigh the doctor against the doctor—can place in the worthy gentleman's own scales revelation and science, and can determine for himself which kicks the beam. It will be seen more clearly in the sequel whether there be a "semblance" of difference *only* between the book of god and the book of nature; whether there be not plenty of substantial, unmistakable discrepancies, upon which the irreligious man may *calmly* lay hold, from the certainty of their not being able to escape him in the hurry; and whether the Mosaic history *undeservedly* "lies under a heavy suspicion."

I have not by me now Babbage's Ninth Bridgewater Treatise, but I find that Dr. P. Smith thus alludes to him, and what I recollect of the work convinces me that it is correct:—"Here was a mind of the highest order, deeply versed in philosophical knowledge, whose acquirements in the exact sciences, and in their highest branches, were the astonishment and admiration of the world; here was one who had deeply studied the nature and the rules of evidence, and who was not an enemy, but a decided friend, to revealed religion, marching boldly up to the front of the imagined discrepancies, and they saw in his own words the strength of his conviction. He was, indeed, satisfied that geology and revelation were not in reality at variance."

The Messrs. Chambers, in a delightful little tract on the "Romance of Geology," say, "It was at *first* thought by some that these curious revelations of science militated against the account of creation given by Moses in the book of Genesis; but this supposition is now *generally dismissed,* and a very prevalent conviction exists that there is nothing in the one history to interfere with a *becoming reverence* for the other." A most carefully-worded sentence, in which the Messrs. Chambers, while saying a great deal, say nothing for *themselves.*

The present Dean of York, who is either a very sincere man or a very wise one, taking the Bible for his guide, fancied, or said he fancied he perceived some wide differences between the so-called facts of geology and the so-called truths of scripture. Preferring revelation to science, like a consistent clergyman, he brought all things to the test of the Bible, and when he found any difference he laid the blame upon science. In this course his reverence was perfectly justified by very high authority, for in the *Church of England Quarterly Review,* for September, 1842, article "Scriptural Geology," it is stated, "Now there is *one* volume which we rank higher than the book of nature, or the volumes of science, and to the standard of which we would bring the book of nature, assured that where they differ we have not read the book of nature aright." Professor Sedgwick, who is one of the great lights of the present day on the subject of geology, was selected by the Geological Section of the British Association to reply to the Dean, and he successfully demolished all the arguments of his very reverend opponent, describing them as puerile and only suited to the nursery ; described the Dean as ignorant of the alphabet of geology, and that in place of coming there to dictate to philosophers, he should rather have come to learn. But even this learned professor, after his fierce onslaught on this pillar of the church, declared that it was only necessary to read the word of God aright to perceive the perfect harmony subsisting between it and the book of nature. Now, the Dean of York is a man, set apart from other men for the express purpose of expounding the word of God, and Professor Sedgwick is an expounder of the work of nature—and the Dean declares that after a careful consideration of Professor Sedgwick's explanation of the book of nature, he finds that book extirely opposed to the book of God, whilst the professor affirms them to be in beautiful agreement.

Another learned professor, Rhymer Jones, F.R.S., of King's College, London, at the conclusion of six splendid lectures, at Manchester, on Palæontology, or the science of extinct animals, every sentence of which was opposed to the statements in the Bible, said, in conclusion, " *What we were told in holy writ exactly corresponds with this*, [the facts he had been relating]. To quote the words of a late illustrious writer: ' Those do wrong, they do no good, who would endeavour to put a few dubiously interpreted words in contradistinction to the 10,000 tablets of stone, *written as they are by the finger of Almighty God himself*, which are displayed to the eye of the geologist.' "

I am satisfied that had 1 Dr. Buckland's works to refer to 1 should find similar sentiments to the foregoing in them—but, in their absence, I must be content to let him pass.

In the " Vestiges of the Natural History of Creation," decidedly the most heterodox of modern works, not excepting those of the " Infidel school," the direct tendency of which is the establishment of materialism, whatever the author may attempt to the contrary, is the following passage : " It will be objected that the ordinary conceptions of christian nations on this subject *are directly derived from scripture*, or, at least, are in conformity with it. If they were clearly and unequivocally supported by scripture, it may readily be allowed that *there would be a strong objection to the reception of any opposite hypothesis*. But the fact is, however startling the present announcement of it may be, that the first chapter of the Mosaic record is not only not in harmony with the ordinary ideas of mankind respecting cosmical and organic creation, but is opposed to them, *and only in accordance with the views here taken*." Of the value of this assertion we shall be able to judge presently.

Before I conclude this portion of my subject, I will quote the opinion of William Thomas Brand, F.R.S., in his " Outlines of Geology," where, after briefly stating the proper objects of geology, he thus proceeds: " The bare mention of these, the genuine and legitimate objects of geological science, naturally brings to the mind the awful and magnificent account of the creation, conveyed to us in scriptural history ; and geological writers have not unfrequently attempted to combine their speculations with the announcement of holy writ. Mixing up the chronology of Moses and the history of the deluge *with their own short-sighted speculations*, and with observations hastily made and imperfectly reasoned upon, *they have presumed*, on the one hand, to verify and illustrate, and on the other, to question and controvert. But the arrogance of imperfect knowledge is nearly equally prevalent in both." Here we see the good gentleman who wrote the above is not angry because parties attribute the Bible and the universe to the same author—but because they should have " presumed " to attempt to make the two *agree*. Whether his displeasure arose from the failure of such attempts, or from other causes, I know not, but I rather suspect that to be the true explanation, for a little further on is the following :

" Far, therefore, from endeavouring to explain or controvert the arguments which have thus been by some annexed to, and blended with, geology, I shall altogether omit them, referring such as are interested in the *legitmate* part of the discussion, to the *masterly* work of Mr. Granville Penn, entitled ' A Comparative Estimate of the Mineral and Mosaical Geologies,' " which work, I presume, *was* sufficiently successful to merit our author's approval. W. C.

ONE great reason why truth is stranger than fiction is, because there is not half so much of it in the world.—*Chartist Pilot*.

THE CENTRAL BOARD & BRANCH 53.

To the Editors of the Movement.

Sir,—Having seen annexed to the Lecture of Mr. Southwell, published in the *Movement*, some prefatory remarks relative to a difference existing between the Central Board and the Lambeth Branch as to the delivery of the Lecture, permit me to state that the Correspondence alluded to was between myself and the Central Board; and that the difference of opinion was not from the recognition by the Branch of the opinions advanced by Mr. Southwell, but simply that the Branch considered the restriction of the free expression of opinion was involved in the resolution of the Central Board. As however the Board disclaim any desire by their Resolution to to fetter free discussion, it is evident that the difference must have existed from the Resolution, as worded, being capable of a construction which was not intended to be conveyed.

Your insertion of this will oblige,

Sir, yours, respectfully,

Thomas Couldery,
Vice President, Lambeth Branch.

Feb. 17 1845.

[This letter is inserted rather from courtesy than any conviction of its necessity. It seems superfluous, inasmuch as it neither contradicts nor corrects any assertion of ours, and scarcely explains more. The reader on turning to page 43, will find nothing contrary to the fact of the correspondence being between the Central Board and the *Branch's Officer*—nor to the difference of opinion not inferring a recognition of Mr. Southwell's opinions. But this may be added—that the Branch Meeting unanimously, by vote, approved of their officer's letters to the Board, and that *no non-recognition* of Southwell's views were expressed.

Mr. Jones lectured in the same Hall, last Sunday, on "Atheism and Deism."—*Eds. of M.*]

AGITATION IN SCOTLAND.

Mr. Southwell.

Mr. Southwell was sent to Scotland by the Manchester Branch, for the purpose of exposing the Authorities of Arbroath for their treatment of Mrs. Martin. You know that £7 9s. were raised for that purpose, and they are still active in collecting. Mr. S. has orders to stay as long as he can do any good in this affair.

Such an act of heroism on the part of the men of Manchester is admirable, indeed it is something so far removed from the actions of the great mass of mankind, that one cannot easily forget. I hope the Glasgow people will not be less energetic and active, so that while Mr. S. is here they will supply him with a little shot to use against the enemy, and I doubt not but that much good will yet be done, and that the mean and tyrannical conduct of the Arbroath wiseacres, may be fully exposed, and held up to public scorn and indignation.

Mr. Southwell has gone to Arbroath, *incog.*, for the purpose of reconnoitring, and if possible, to obtain a room for two or three days next week. The friends here are determined to be active in the matter, for this act of the Manchester people has reanimated them. W. Baker.

Mrs. Martin.

I am now lying concealed in Arbroath—having been smuggled into a friend's house, where I am (by Mr. Southwell's advice) to stay until Saturday night, when I shall lecture if not previously kidnapped again. The bill announcing my lecture will not be posted until Saturday morning, very early, but they will tear them down as soon as they are put up. I do not yet know how our friends obtained the room for me, as when I left Arbroath before, I did so without resisting the Authorities because my friends had told me that the room could not be got for me again—nor any other in the town.

The Manchester people did well in sending Mr. Southwell and money. I can go on no longer without help (*or* lectures). Of course, if I can lecture it will be all right again, but for this last fortnight, I have been doing nothing but travel and spend money, backwards and forwards only to *plan* meetings but not to *hold* them. I lectured, however, at Glasgow on Sunday last, and at Edinburgh the Sunday before.

E. Martin.

Arbroath, Saturday, Feb. 22nd.

We have conquered! the authorities here are *hors-de-combat*. I lectured last night—not even the ghost of a policeman present; only a struggle in distant streets, and they in plain clothes. They received me well—gave me three cheers, *and three groans for the Authorities*. E. Martin.

No Wonder.—A dog that was locked up in one of the meeting houses of Portland last week, effected his escape by breaking two panes of glass and gnawing through one of the blinds, after having gnawed more or less at every window in the house.—*Boston Investigator.*

BRISTOL.—We are informed by Mr. Cook that three members, W. Barton, S. Cowles, and Richards, have been expelled from the "Young Men's Society" for refusing to answer in the affirmative to the following question: "Do you believe that the Bible is the real will and word of God." Pity so few grains of wheat turn up in the lot of chaff.—The different parties are keeping Bristol up to Edinburgh heat—the town is placarded announcing nearly thirty lectures on different subjects.—The religious world have just concluded its annual meetings for the missionary funds—Mr. Archer of London, who was on the platform when Southwell and our correspondent were buffeted by the christian mob and dragged from the rostrum by brute force by the police, delivered a very able speech at Broadmead Rooms, at one of the twelve meetings, on the right of every man promulgating those opinions he thinks beneficial to society. He reminded the meeting that it was Catholics who imprisoned Dr. Kalley.—Did Mr. Archer ever tell his audience who imprisoned English and Scotch Infidels in Protestant Britain?—The Rev C. Dealtry is contending that Christ is going to pay us a visit in April, for certain.—Dr. West, from the Continent, is delivering a course of lectures in Guine Street, on the beauty and harmony of the Scriptures, in opposition to Infidelity and false theories.—Will friend Chilton take notes of anything that may deserve notice?

PROGRESSIVE MOVEMENTS IN GERMANY.—A paragraph in the *Times* informs us that the King of Prussia has commissioned eminent statesmen to draw up a constitution for the Prussian monarchy. From this equivocal manner of wording, the meaning is very obscure, if it was desired to determine or define the prerogatives of *monarchy*, or to concoct a *constitutional code for the nation*, it would be intelligible—as it is we must await further illumination. It is also stated that great joy is felt on account of the announcement, but whether by the master or servant classes does not appear. The Prussian movements are to be watched with great interest—the "enlightened despotism," which, if we mistake not, has found a great admirer in the editor of the official Socialist organ—the general instructedness and superior condition of the people present peculiarities which we shall scarcely find elsewhere.

At the opening of the States of the Rhenish Province, on the 9th, some observations are quoted from the speech of the royal commissioner, which show how completely he appreciates the "blessings of religion." He seems to speak feelingly—"If I may be allowed by you to make a request it would be to remove far from our debates all the quarrels existing between the two religious confessions. You already know in what a deplorable manner religious discussions have again arisen in our province, and how many invectives and animosities have been excited under the mask of a religion of love and resignation."

Rouge, the Reformer priest, is reported to be making extensive inroads in the old papistry. They quote leading magistrates as converts.

The Synod of the Protestant clergy, of the Grand Duchy of Posen, have passed a resolution that religious toleration should be absolutely without limit, and that if a Christian wished to embrace Judaism that the pastor should not prevent him from doing so if his conversion took place from conscientious motives.—This is a step in advance—it amounts to religious toleration—religious liberty is no more enjoyed in Posen than in Britain.

A RARE OPPORTUNITY.—Mr. Thomas Finlay of Edinburgh, has to dispose of a complete set of Carlile's REPUBLICAN, consisting of fourteen vols., half bound in calf, lettered, and wanting only No. 26 of Vol. 12, and that is partly supplied very neatly with the pen. Price £5.

LECTURES AT THE CITY ROAD.—In consequence of the protracted illness of Mr. Holyoake the course of lectures announced in *Movement* 59 has been abandoned until further notice, Mr. H. not having been able to deliver one of them. This circumstance will account for the non-appearance of some papers promised in the *Movement*, and the discontinuation of others begun. For lectures at the City Road now see the usual list.

CLERICAL INTOLERANCE EXPOSED.—By *Theon*. —This is a letter to one Rev. J. Symington, by Mr. Myles. It administers some well merited rebukes, as well as one can judge from the pamphlet, to that rev. gentleman for his vanity and aspersions of the characters of Hume and Shelley. This kind of practice will be of service to *Theon* if he will keep his papers by him, and after a time carefully prune them.

TO CORRESPONDENTS.

MR. RANSOM, Brighton.—Mr. S. called and the remittance was duly paid.

MR. COLTMAN, Leicester, will attend to his request as soon as able.

W. BRITTAIN.—An enquiry shall be immediately made.

RECEIVED.—The first and second numbers of the "Colchester Christian Magazine," got up with neatness and method. Too late to pronounce if the contents are worth comment. We have sent *Movements* in return.

LECTURES.

Mar. 2.—Hall of Science, City Road, Mr. Petch Jones,—On Phrenology. At 7, P.M.
Mar. 2.—National Hall, 242, High Holborn, W. J. Fox,—On the "Labour Market." At 8, P.M.
Mar. 2.—Finsbury Institution, Goswell Road, Mr. Skelton,—On Social, Moral, and Political Reform. Discussion after,—Will the adoption of the People's' Charter secure liberty and prosperity?

SUBSCRIPTIONS TO THE ANTI-PERSECUTION UNION.

Per Mr. G. Smith, Salford, in consequence of Mrs. Martin's arrest.

Mr. Alexander Campbell	0	1	0
Mr. Williamson	0	2	0
George Smith	0	1	0
William Haslam	0	1	0
Henry Ogden	0	1	0
Mrs. E. Edgley	0	5	0
Joseph Smith	0	2	6
J. Frost	0	1	0
James Greenhalgh	0	1	0
J. R. Cooper	0	2	6
Salmon	0	1	0
J. Robinson	0	1	0
Esplin	0	0	6
Thomas Walsh (quarterly)	0	0	6
Edward Hyde	0	0	6

PATERSON TESTIMONIAL.

Per Mr. G. Smith, Salford.

W. J. Williams	0	2	6
Henry Walker	0	1	0
Henry Wood	0	0	6
J. Haxton, London, second subscription	0	5	0

G. J. H., Sec.

Printed and Published by G. J. HOLYOAKE, 40, Holywell-street, Strand.
Wednesday, February 26, 1845.

THE MOVEMENT

And Anti-Persecution Gazette.

"Maximise morals, minimise religion."—BENTHAM.

No. 64.   EDITED BY G. JACOB HOLYOAKE, AND M. Q. RYALL.   Price 1½d

TO THE SCOTCH PRISON BOARD:

COMPOSED OF JUDGES, ADVOCATES, SHERIFFS, PROCURATORS, POLICEMEN, AND PARSONS.

It is finished. The sacrifice is offered—the utmost farthing is paid. Your brutal infliction is determined. Physical force has for a time triumphed over mental. *Cui Bono?* I will answer. It may be a subject of eulogy for your annual report, and a delightful theme of congratulation to the Messrs. Chambers.

The punishment was brutal, because it was unnecessarily severe: because in a civilized community it should have for its object the reformation of the criminal and the protection of society. Where these objects are not obtained, or not sought, punishment is revenge, revenge and brutality.

Disbelief in a *thing* called God and contempt for Bible, *honestly avowed*, being my opinions, and these opinions crimes, what steps were taken to change them? Small room for tracing marks of design in stone walls or floor; I saw not God's handy work in oakum; nor thought highly of Omnipotence when dressed in *handcuffs* or felons garb; nor of omniscience although a spyhole was in the door which exposed my *minutest actions;* nor of benevolence with a limited allowance of porridge and treacle beer: neither was the Bible's authenticity or genuineness proved, by a copy lying in my cell. Should it be said, or thought, that time to study these objects was expected to work a change, I must remind you of your refusal to grant me even an hour's abridgement of labour for such a purpose, and believed it to be your intention by solitude, labour, want of exercise and air, and proper food, by humiliations and well intended mortifications, to produce idiotcy. I do not say but what there may have been benevolence in all this, you may think *that* was the only cure for disbelief in gods and ghosts. Religion and slavery being natural allies, idiotcy may be a mercy, in a country where it is predominant.

Your chaplain entertained similar views. He tried to drive me frantic by abuse; he was too ignorant to be successful. Boasting of an ignorance he could not conceal, yet what he ought to have known he taught me to despise. A man who never addressed me with civility, who affected to honour me by putting me on a level with the vilest criminal, "because I was the chief of sinners" who although he was ignorant of myself, friends, or principles, (by his own confession) yet could, with a settled deliberate malignity, every Sunday, declare that we were "only a batch of theives, robbers, liars, debauchers, and hypocrites," such were his polished expressions, which could not impress me very favorably either with his god or his religion.

I was prepared for priestly hate in such a gaol, away from the public eye and nothing but their own dispositions to check them; I know by experience how they treat infidels in such places. but for such wholesale mendacity, such deliberate hate, such puerile declamation, and Billingsgate tirades, fairly confounded me. I endeavoured to divert his attention by writing whole sheets of arguments on behalf of my sentiments, and against his, but the only answers he vouchsafed me were, " Prisons were the best arguments for such as I." " A man that is an heretic, reject." " He that spareth the rod," &c. " God used such means to bring about his own ends," &c , &c. He believed himself inspired, and I think he often was. He smelt of drink and snuff repeatedly. He has an inordinate development of the lower propensities, and a hearty hatred, and morbid distaste for sincerity—in short he was a *christian parson,* new fledged 'tis true, only admitted to be one of the glorious brigade since the late " strike " in the Kirk. He is a fair specimen of those who, brutal by nature, have their tendencies fostered by their faith, and countenanced by their god. If religion is everything, and morality nothing, he is very virtuous, and the reverse holds good, of course. Fortunately, he only visited me seven times in fifteen months, else, you know the proverb, " Evil communications," &c. Had the Board really been desirous of curing my *errors,* they would have requested a man of good nature to visit me, who at all events might have won by his sympathy if not by his logic.

I have not been benefitted intellectually or morally. Have the public? No! Atheistic works treating Jehovah and the Bible with thorough undisguised contempt, have received an impetus from bigotry's efforts to suppress them, and Atheism, like a tree shaken by the wind, has fixed its roots deeper in the soil, and its branches are now leafy enough to shade those who choose to repose under them. Persecution has ripened into verdure. It has done more; the *gentler* sex have taken the field against the gods, and bigots will find them harder to deal with than the other sex. They are treating bible and bible laws with little ceremony. Much as people may have detested Atheism, they have sympathised with our sufferings, and sympathy sometimes leads to inquiry. The public *are more than ever exposed to the influence of Atheism.*

There are to be found, in every age, a number of beings, who derive their ideas from the preceding century—the refuse of a past age, who value gods and religions, not for their merits, but because they, like themselves, have outlived their day. They have no glow for improvement, and no sympathies but for antiquities — superannuated owls who hate the light of day. Such is the Lord Justice Clerk. He would have graced the bench famously under that notorious knave and blockhead, James the First, by the grace of God, Defender of the faith, and witch burner, &c., but his lordship's puerile twaddle, and "*musty saws*," are no more fit for this age than an almanack of last century is fit for this. I was truly mortified that he should have selected me to frighten with his cant of "dreadful punishments in future," "adorable redeemer," and other rif-raf, delivered in his contradictory and paradoxical speech. Neither his nor his god's threats can make cowards of us, nor are our resolutions "sicklied o'er with pale thoughts" of holy ghosts or hell fires.

What Atheists *can do, that* they *dare* do. Neither godships nor lordships are a hindrance to us. Fearful though it may be to fall into Jehovah's hands, and dreadful though it be to fall into the god-believers' power, yet persons in the discharge of duty care little for either. From experience, we can triumphantly exclaim, "O bigots, where is thy sting, O christianity, where is thy victory? As speech is morning to the mind, I will give a few reasons why you should halt ere you again give encouragement to persecution.

Persecution patrons and bigots are, without doubt, the down-draughts of civilization. They are inexpressibly depraved who sanction a violation of the right of private judgment. Barbarian ignorant are they who do not know that opinons cannot be arbitrarily adopted, but are fruits of conviction. Brutally selfish are those who do know this fact, yet act as if they knew it not, and exult in the triumph of brute force like the uncultivated Cherokee. Levellers of all the courtesies of life, tramplers on all principles of good breeding are those pernicious wasps who burr about society only to sting. Persecutors demonstrate, all infidels prove, that religion is false, for truth needs no props; it stands by itself. Persecutors are walking specimens of pride, the "Sir Oracles" of the day, who in their self-important airs, pull their deity out of his throne and seat themselves in it with wonderful gravity. "Prove all things," Jehovah is said to have said, these Bruins say we must do nothing of the kind. They would persuade us that a second rebellion had taken place in the land of souls, and Jehovah had this time been floored. They set us the example of treating Jove and his book with contempt, and what is fun and fair play for the goose is good amusement for the gander. Law may decide as it pleases, justice is superior to law.

What benefit can the state reap from interfering violently in matters of opinion? It is not necessary either to its welfare or existence that men should be of one opinion, if it were possible, which it is not. What can't be is not necessary. Different natures and different educations necessarily produce different thoughts, especially about a being that is everything by turns, and nothing long. Why should the state strive against the laws of nature, unless to produce discontent, disturbance, and endanger its own existence? It cannot expect compliance with despotic laws either as regards opinions, food, or dress. There have been such laws, but experience has shown they are indefensible either as just or politic.

Could penal laws cause Atheists to forego the open propagation of their sentiments, on the denunciation of delusion, fraud and chicanery, they would still do both secretly. Would the case be bettered think you by that? No brute power on earth now a days, could do more than suppress for a time; it could not change opinions. Reason alone can do this. The brute power, therefore, in full swing can only produce a crop of hypocrisy. It can do no good. The mind is not being stormed like a castle. An appearance of submission would be more dangerous to the state than open rebellion, for reason not being convinced, the elements of opposition pent up, would burst from their barriers the first opportunity, with a power proportioned to its resistance. To persecute what cannot be long suppressed is being cruel for cruelty's sake, and the world can well spare monsters of such dispositions.

Were it clearly established that certain opinions were erroneous and presumptuous, force would be unnecessary; knowledge would suffice to disperse them. This cannot be done. It follows, force patrons are absurd, erroneous and presumptuous, They stab truth by preventing its elucidation in the only way in which it can be done—by free discussion! The fact that I differ from you, does not necessarily prove *me* wrong. Something else than articulated air is required to demonstrate the entity of chimeras. Departure from opinions protected by the state is most often a virtue. Ghosts were as much protected by kings, priests and judges, as their prototypes, the gods, are now; and there were far greater evidences for their existence than there ever was for Jehovah, Christ or Holy Ghost. If private judgment is a crime, the reformation, like christianity, was a forgery. The vessel of catholicism must have been boarded, like merchant vessels, by pirates, hoisting false colours.

When religion was entwined round the state, like the serpent round a tree; when the cassock and the bayonet were accounted indissoluble—when the church could *exterminate* all dissentients and burn their works, then it might be politic to persecute in its behalf. Not now. I speak as a friend to the faith. The persecuted prepare for the combat. They arm themselves to defend their opinions, right or wrong, if attacked. Truth is at a disadvantage, it has prejudice, passion, as well as argument to surmount, and the godly have no extra arguments to throw away—

For never can true reconcilement grow
Where wounds of deadly hate have pierced so deep.

Persecution turns the current of sympathy towards the persecuted,—turns the edge of the bigot's knife, and compensates the physical ills of imprisonment. Even the *gulled* come to wonder that a religion, patronised by an omnipotent god, should depend on the police principally for its support.

Collission brings forth energetic minds, so if trials await the conscientious, characters are not wanting to endure them. Even worms will turn when trod on. Atheists may be defeated by brute-force antagonists, but like Peter the great, they will one day beat the defeaters. Although we may be trodden down, like rushes in a giant's path, yet christian injustice will be our nutriment, and we will rise from under the intended depression. We are not hot-house plants, that wither under the northern blasts. We do not court persecution, but we will fulfil a duty and defend a right. We will not compromise with tyranny, nor wink at fraud. We shall exercise the right of criticism impartially. All published sentiments are legitimate objects of attack; all public characters are fair subjects of comment, *as public characters*; no matter whether the works are bibles, or the characters gods. We force not, nor desire to force others; neither shall any power *force* us to forego a privilege possessed by others. Our condition in society would not be improved were we to cringe and fawn before brutal Jeferies, priestly Bonners, or ideotic Agnews, power and bigotry. Could we become so weak and wicked, we should well deserve the contempt that assuredly would be our portion; and well deserving of execration should we be for surrendering a right dear to all men. We love and desire peace, but not the peace of the oppressed, nor the calm of desolation. All that is necessary is impartial protection, in other words, *to be let alone*.

It is questionable policy of the law interpreters endangering the peace or morality of the country to support a church and a band of desert-making locusts. Truly has it been said, that in its whole history, *there is not a single good action on record* which can be thrown into its teeth. It has done good by *stealth*, if it ever did any, or by attempting to persuade mankind that it was virtuous, it convinced *itself* it really was so. Leave its defenders, the parsons, to prop it up, and let it not be said that that religion which owed its existence to a happy combination of imposture and chicanery in ancient days, was indebted in modern days to the policeman's arm. Some respect is due to its dotage, nor should judges, by their ill-timed bigotry, expose its aged imbecility, or uncover its icy nakedness. Why should the law interfere when neither the public nor the religion are said to require it? Why pay policemen's salaries to support a church sinking into the grave, and only prolonging an existence painful even to its friends?

Mental liberty is as much an element of advancing knowledge as sanatory regulations are a cause of longevity. Intelligence is opposed to creeds. Creeds eclipse nature by putting an opaque body between man and it, and renders dark and doubtful the paths of morality. What a monument of religion's cursed influence does Britain present. Unaccustomed to war's alarms and ravages she might be expected to rank foremost in religion, liberty, and education; yet travellers tell us, that excepting Spain and Russia, she lags behind the continental nations. Britain, the baby in religion, but giant in science, owes the humiliating confession to the rigid nature of its creed and the influence of its priests. Naturally humane, Britons have often had their worst passions roused by the demoniac ravings of priests. Good men see clearly that while religion's supremacy exists, while dissensions are fostered, and perpetuated, by separate educational institutions, men can never be either kind or just. Even now priests are praying heaven and earth to prevent children of different denominations from meeting together in one common school, lest they should forget their parents' prejudices. Divide and conquer is the well known trick of godlies and godly politicians. Let the laws be impartially administered, and religion's power be by that means lessened, so that we may meet its champions in fair and equal combat, and we are fearless as to the result. "Truth was never worsted in a free and open encounter."

Atheists (and by this name are designated men who will not swear, lie, and give their consciences to the keeping of those who have none themselves, and swallow gods, ghosts, and witches, &c., like pills) oppose religion because they *know* it to be false and productive of incalculable evils. They see it makes men slaves to their own passions as well as their fellow men. They see it makes men miserable, but not happy. It is a useless state appendage which does no good and never prevents harm. Well meaning folks think we over estimate its evil tendency because some good men have professed it. Swift has answered them in these words, "Some good men have learned to play the fiddle, and some good men have not; the goodness is not a consequence of playing the fiddle, but from other causes, while they who can't play the fiddle are not necessarily bad." Just so, the good men in religion's ranks are so natured, so tempered by education and organisation, that no form of religion could make them much worse, and *none at all* would leave them better.

Great men, too, have undoubtedly been Christians, but it requires a face of brass to say they owed their scientific or literary greatness to religion. Investigation implies imperfection and improvement—religion is stationary in principle. It supposes *perfection*, and is therefore an inhuman institution. It is a stagnant pool in a cultivatable field—a upas tree in a fertile soil—the deadly night-shade in a flowery plat. Had intellectual men not given themselves up to the tutelage of nature, had they taken the snaky creed to their bosoms, they would have been bitten by it; enfolded in its shiny embrace they would have been warped, stultified, and deadened like the mass of mankind. Bacon's creed dimned his shrine. It is the black spot on Sir M. Hale's escutcheon. The one defended and the other put to death for the impossible crime of witchcraft. Where got they these accursed notions? From the Bible, that repository of all that is wicked, stupid, and abominable. From the same polluted source come gods, ghosts, pigeons, and virgin mothers! Can the dabblers in such a source be pure? Did men fairly give themselves up to the examples of this Jehovah and his favorites, would this be a world for a honest man or virtuous woman. Even the versatile and peccant priesthood would blush to see such a consumation. It would be a world of Fanny Hills, Bishop Cloghers and Neroes. Christianity's entrance into the world was too dark for any person of humane feelings to wish to see it repeated. It has hitherto been called the dark ages. Literature, science, art, and refinement fell beneath its blasting breath. Slowly is Europe recovering from its deadly gripe. What good man would wish to see its pristine power restored?

(*To be concluded next week.*)

GOD'S WORDS versus GOD'S WORKS.
II

Dr. Pye Smith, in his 3rd lecture, states, "The first object presented for consideration was the immense antiquity ascribed to the earth, and the succession of living creatures upon it. *It was the opinion of many that the dependent universe, in all its extent, was brought into existence by the almighty power of its creator in six days,* as mentioned in the book of Genesis. The same conclusion, also, with regard to the commencement and completion of the creation, was drawn from the language of the 4th commandment, 'In six days,' &c. To this position the discoveries of geological science were directly opposed. * * * The rev. doctor then read a quotation from the Ninth Bridgwater Treatise, by Mr. Babbage, in allusion to the antiquity of the earth; in which it was observed, that the mass of evidence which combines to prove this was irresistible, *and so unshaken by any opposing facts*, that none but those who were alike incapable of observing facts, and of appreciating reasoning, could for a moment conceive the present state of its surface to have been the result of only 6000 years of existence. 'It was admitted (said the author, Babbage) by all competent persons, that the formation even of those strata which were nearest the surface must have occupied vast periods, *probably millions of years, in arriving at their present state.*' It must be borne in mind by those who peruse these articles, that I am arguing upon the *literal* meaning of the language of the Bible, which is the *general* understanding of that book—and, further, that a "revelation" proceeding from an infinitely wise and moral being should be without flaw or spec—that it should be a natural impossibility for a finite being to bring any valid objection against such a book—for, if an objection can be sustained, it invalidates the work as the production of an infinitely wise and truth-loving being, and it must henceforth take its legitimate place amongst the productions of men and not aspire to a seat with the gods. But the attempted "revelation" of the revelations of the Bible, would fail to reconcile the Bible to philosophy, as we shall see presently, and nothing can reconcile the Bible with itself. Dr. Pye Smith declares that it is an "erroneous opinion that certain geological doctrines were at variance with the testimony of the holy scriptures," and yet he at the same time says these same scriptures, at least in two places, gives the reader to understand that the *universe* was created in six *days*, that "it is the opinion of many" that this is true—but that geology has proved that it has taken *millions of years* to form *a portion only of the strata of this earth.* What *should* common-sense say to this? In connexion with this part of the subject, there was a very beautiful fact brought to light during the cutting for the Great Western Railway near Bristol, which I am induced to give, as bearing upon the age of the world, although, perhaps, sufficient has already been adduced. Some remarkable *drift* beds occur in abundance in the second and third tunnels. They consist of irregular unconsolidated accumulations of water-worn fragments of sandstone, of drifted stems and leaves of plants, and further of pebbles of previously-formed sandstone and coal. Their place is in the lower part of the upper coal measures, and the inference from a consideration of their position and character is, that parts of the lower formed the margin of those waters at the bottoms of which the upper accumulations were being deposited. Hence an idea may be gained of the enormous length of time which elapsed during the formation of the coal measures, which, although two or three thousand feet in thickness, form scarcely the twentieth part of the total range of stratified rock.

"And the earth was without form and void." How anything could have been created, or *formed*, as some have translated it, without form, I know not—but that, in the beginning, whenever that might have been, it was void, or uninhabited, I think by no means unreasonable, and required no extraordinary exhibition of "second-sight" to perceive; neither is it necessary for a man to be "inspired" to understand it. Dr. Pye Smith says the original idea of the form of the earth was that of an "extended plain," and that some passages in the Bible "spoke of the extremes as boundary lines of the earth, and of pillars and other supports on which it rested"—just as some eastern nations of the present day suppose that the world is supported upon the back of an elephant, which elephant stands upon a tortoise, which tortoise stands upon—nothing : the self-same unsubstantial foundation upon which revelation rests. Dr. P. S. says, "In the primary record in the beginning of the book of Genesis, nothing was affirmed or implied concerning the figure and situation of the earth." This omission was, however, supposed afterwards by the *very correct* information that the earth was flat, a "four-sided plain," with pillars to sustain it, great, and good, and true, is the revelation of the Holy Ghost!

"And darkness was upon the face of the deep. And the Spirit of God moved upon the face of the waters." How this was effected we have no record—this spirit may have been the first Elfin King or Water Sprite. "And God said, let there be light: and there was light. And God saw the light, that *it was* good," which would seem to imply that he was not confident *before hand* of the success of his experiment, and that, if he had not seen that it was good, that we should have had darkness in its place. "And God divided the light from the darkness"—modern philosophers conceive darkness to be merely a negation or absence of light.

"And God called the light day, and the darkness he called night. And the evening and the morning were the first day." In consequence of several paragraphs—arbitrarily fixed by translators, for the supposed convenience of readers — intervening between the statement of the "beginning" and the "first day," some Christians have asserted that an indefinite period of time *may* be meant, and not simply a solar day of twenty-four hours—but this is not the generally received opinion, and has only been attempted since modern discoveries have proved the vulgar opinion to be untenable. But this *ruse* will not serve them in the case of the second and following days —the supposition, in fact, that Moses, or any other man who wrote 4000 years or more since, was well acquainted with the true history and origin of the earth, which is even now, with all our accumulated knowledge, buried in darkness, is too preposterous for any but the most credulous to believe, or the most impudent to assert.

"And God said, let there be a firmament in the midst of the waters, and let it divide the waters from the waters." What is the meaning of this I am at a loss to " divine." The ancients entertained the opinion that the "firmament," or what is now called the sky, was a crystal vault. If this were true, which it is not, it is difficult to imagine how such an immense body of water could have existed at that time. The supposed "firmament," or sky is some two or three miles distant from the surface of the earth. And if the earth were then an aqueous globe, extending to the supposed boundary, or firmament—what became of the water thus cut off? And as there were waters *above* the firmament as well as *under* the firmament—it would appear that the Christians' heaven only rests on a watery foundation after all. On the subject of the "firmament" mentioned in Genesis, Dr. P. Smith remarks: "The Hebrew word commonly translated 'firmament,' after the Septuagint, implied a *solid substance*, by the beating out or working out of a ductile mass; but many modern interpreters had sought to soften the idea of a solid concave shell over their heads, by rendering it 'expanse.' That was, however, *transferring a modern idea to times and persons who did not possess that idea*. The Hebrews supposed, that at a moderate distance above the flight of birds there was a solid concave hemisphere, in which the stars were fixed as lamps, and containing openings to be used or closed as necessary. *It was understood* as supporting a kind of celestial ocean, called 'the waters above the firmament.' That was considered a reservoir containing waters to be discharged as rain, which in Job was called 'water-courses,' or 'pouring out.' Lightning was considered to be preserved in the same regions, and to consist, if ignited, of matter called 'coals of fire.' Of the nature and cause of thunder the Israelites had no idea, they therefore referred it immediately to the Supreme, and called it ' the voice of God.' "

"And God made the firmament, and divided the waters which were under the firmament from the waters which were above the firmament : and it was so. And God called the firmament heaven. And the evening and the morning were the second day.'' Now, in place of the earth having been originally an aqueous body, as this verse and the preceding one would evidently imply, for land, we shall find, was first formed or made to "appear" afterwards —no previous mention of it being made— everything tends to the conclusion that the earth was, at some time or the other, an igneous mass, and previously to that in a nebulous state—its flatness at the poles is just such a form as a body of incondescent matter would assume, in cooling down when whirling round a centre, at a great velocity – its present internal heat, also, is considered to be evidence of the truth of the same hypothesis.

"And God said, let the waters under the heaven be gathered together unto one place, and let the dry land appear : and it was so," &c. Was it ? The land and water have played strange pranks since those days— they are greatly commingled *now*, and geology proves that they were so millions of years before man existed. But this is a striking proof of the very limited geographical knowledge of God's " chosen people " —they thought that the countries which were known to them were all the dry land in the world, and that all beyond was water.

"And God said, let the earth bring forth grass, the herb yielding seed, and the fruit tree yielding fruit after his kind, whose seed is in itself, upon the earth : and it was so. * * * And the evening and the morning were the third day." Mark, reader, this took place on the *third* day - and now hear what Dr. Pye Smith says : " It was stated that the *sun and all the other* heavenly bodies were created on the *fourth* day after the creation of the earth ; that light was created in a diffused state, and that on the *fourth* day it was condensed and collected into a centre, which centre was the sun of our solar system. But those who adopted this hypothesis had forgotten that the creation of vegetables took place on the *third* day, and that *this necessarily implied the presence and the operations of the sun*; unless indeed, (said the lecturer) we resort to some gratuitous supposition of multiplied miracles of the most astounding magnitude. Those, (he continued) who can rest satisfied with such a supposition are out of the sphere of reason; no difficulty, no improbability, no natural; impossibility appals them; they seem to have the attribute of omnipotence at their command, *to help out any hypothesis*, or answer any exigency.'" The doctor has here placed himself and the divine author in " a fix "—for the Bible expressly declares that vegetables *were* created *before* the sun —and the doctor has no less expressly declared that revealed religion and science were "in perfect harmony." These severe strictures upon some class of intellects must, I should think, have been keenly felt by many of his auditory. How true is it, however, that a miserable minority only of "true believers" agree with the doctor? The doctor objects to the use of a modern idea on the subject of the firmament, but does not hesitate to use modern information respecting the necessary presence of the sun for the production of vegetable and animal forms. The cases were different— one was of far more consequence than the other. W. C.

IMPOLITIC FORBEARANCE.

THE Discussion of Mr. O'Connell's unfair trial is scrupulously avoided as calculated " to excite angry feelings." How amiable is this! What a lovely example. Let it but be followed in all other and less important instances, and Parliament will be a society of Friends, a Quaker's Meeting. If we are smitten on one cheek let us offer the other; for to resist is to excite angry feelings.

What a pity it is that this consideration did not occur to men's minds earlier in our history. Had Hampden been governed by it, he would not have resisted ship money, and at a later period, general warrants would have been suffered to pass unnoticed rather than excite angry feelings.

If this consideration had always prevailed, how different would have been the history of our country, how different the form of our Government, and the character of our people. We should have been without our liberties, it is true but what of that? angry feelings would have existed as little as liberty, and what conflicts, what fierce contentions would have been avoided!

It is set down in every copy book that anger is a bad passion. People are moved to ange by injustice; do not then expose injustice for fear of the consequent irritations.

Swift took this view of things when with reference to an offence he asked why the sufferers were so wilful as to struggle. When wrong is done, let us say nothing about it, lest the public anger should arise. To be sure this may have the effect of making wrongs more frequent but is it not better than one bit of angry feeling in the country. Let injustice have its way. Let the evil example silently obtain the force and sanction of precedent; what matters it, so that angry feelings are not stirred.

What's done can't be undone, it is true, but yet there has hitherto seemed to be a prudence in taking measures to the end that what has been done amiss should not be respected; but all that policy of our forefathers is changed for a nice scruple as to the excitement of anger.

This beautiful rule must of course be extended beyond the particular case of Mr. O'Connell's foul trial. The system of the Liberals must in future be to eschew all discussion, no matter what the occasions, if they have a tendency to excite angry feelings. The greater the provocation of the grievance indeed, the greater the obligation to abstain from exposing it.

The gentle Whigs say with Dr. Watts, " Let dogs delight to bark and bite." The liberal should appear in a guise conformable with their new principles of peace. They should wear broad brimmed hats, and buttonless drab. If Hampden and Pym could rise from the grave to see the guardians of public right, how they would blush at their own strong courses maintaining the securities of liberty at all price compared with the goodness of the meek forbearance that characterises our present champions.—*Examiner*, Feb. 15, 1845.

No one but the religious persecutor—a mischievous and overgrown child—wreaks his vengeance on involuntary inevitable compulsory acts or states of the understanding, which are no more affected by blame than the stone which the foolish child beats for hurting him. Reasonable men may apply to every thing which they wish to move, the agent which is capable of moving it—force to outward substances, arguments to the understanding, and blame (together with all other motives whether moral or personal,) to the will alone. It is as absurd to entertain an abhorrence of intellectual inferiority or error, as it would be to cherish a warm indignation against earthquakes or hurricanes.

SOCIAL disunion, persecution, hatred, revenge, and murder, are the great facts of Christianity.

JEHOVAH'S THRONE,
A DIALOGUE.
(For the "Movement.")

"Before Jehovah's awful throne
Ye nations bow, with sacred joy." *Hymn.*
"The Lord Jehovah reigns;
His throne is built on high." *Watts.*
"The Lord Jehovah reigns;
Let all the nations fear,
Let sinners tremble at his throne,
And saints be humble there." *Ibid.*
"Thy throne is established of old." *Jew Book.*

Where is "Jehovah's awful throne?"
In vain thro' history's page I scan,
For search is vain.
  'Tis fixed alone
Deep in the dreamy mind of man.

What is Jehovah's throne?
  'Tis built
Of selfish hopes and slavish fears,
Cemented, by the hand of guilt,
  With human blood, and human tears.

What is Jehovah?
  God.
    And God?
A mask for priestly lust and pride,
An idle word men write in blood,
  When senselessness is deified

And if 'tis but an empty sound,
  That priests have forged in iron chains,
Where shall their rusted roots be found?
  Deep, deep in idiotic brains.

Cans't tell me when the odious word
  Was first pronounced upon the earth?
When the first tyrant's voice was heard,
  When the first trembling slave had birth.

And is "God" but a hideous mask,
  Hiding what bad men hate to see—
Their own vile, hateful, selves?
    Go, ask
The genius of history.

Behold her, as with trembling hand
  She spreads her scroll's recording page,
And slowly points through every land,
  To crime's career in every age.

But, hark! she speaks—
    "I trace, with pain,
Where crime's destroying foot has trod;
And where his foul foot leaves its stain,
It stamps the fearful name of GOD."

Nay, then, blot out the hateful name;
  Oh, how I loathe its utterance now!
Perish the name of God!—or shame
  Be branded on man's recreant brow.

Go, go, my son, a contest wage
  With vice in virtue's stolen dress:
Stamp God's vile name from out life's page,
  And crush it into nothingness!

Such thoughts, unchilled by cold disguise,
  Flowed from the ardent lips of youth:
Such were the stern, but just, replies
  Made by the guileless tongue of truth.

M. A. L.

CONTRIBUTORS TO THE MOVEMENT.—Those, who, by resolution at their last meeting determined on renewing their contributions to the *Movement*, will be shortly summoned, and the result of the Auditors' examination presented. Notice of the evening will be given in the next number.

Letters detained from Mr. Paterson during his Imprisonment in Perth.

Mr. Holyoake, London, 6, Mr. Ryall 7, Mr. Birch 3, Mr. Liddle 10, Mrs. Bagshaw 3, Mr. Lear 1, Mr. Merryman 1, Mr. Dent 2, Mr. Falstaff 1, Mr. Trevelyan, Wallington, 1, Mr. Ross, London, 1, Mr. Knox, Leicester, 1, Mr. Campbell, do., 2, Mr. Emery, do., 1, Mr. Ironside, Sheffield, 1, Mr. Mellor, Oldham, 1, Mr. Cathels, Perth, 1, Mr. Cook, Bristol, 1.

POPLAR SCIENTIFIC INSTITUTION.—On Tuesday evening, Feb. 18, Mr. Goodwyn Barmby lectured on Association as introductory to Societary Science, which he treated as the "philosophy of History, Poetry, and Religion," followed by a beautiful dissertation in his own peculiar language, upon "Paradisation," a few remarks upon Monboddo's theory of human origin, and a review of the doctrines of the "Fall and Resurection."—He then defined "Individualisation and Universalisation" as the "two Societary Orders," and the "critical and the organic" as the "two societary phases," and showed that human beings were formed for society, and led to the idea of association by the observation of animal habit. Lastly, the "Ten Societary States," as propounded by him in his Outlines of Communism, were separately defined as "Paradisatisn, Patriarchalely, Clanism, Barbarisation, Feudality, Municipality, Civilisation, Monopolism, Associality, and Communisation." The elements of the latter state were pointed out as being "common property and industry," not as applied by associations only but by nations and the whole world.

TO CORRESPONDENTS.

Mr. A. Campbell will oblige Mr. B. Hagen, of Nun Street, Derby, by sending him a copy of Joseph Barker's Tract, which appeared in 58 of the *Movement.* Mr. Hagen will pay all expenses.

RECEIVED.—H. Cook.—Aliqus.—W. G. Williams, Manchester. He will see his subscription acknowledged. His hint respecting "gravitation" arrived too late, or it might have received special attention.

LECTURES.

Mar. 9.—Social Institution, 5, Charlotte Street, Blackfriars Road, Mr. Lloyd Jones,—On Christianity and the Christians.

Mar. 9.—Investigation Hall, 29, Circus Street, Marylebone, Mr. Buchanan,—The Immateriality and Immortality of the Soul; with a review of the doctrines of Spirits, Ghosts, Witchcraft, Casting out Devils, &c., &c.

Mar. 9.—Finsbury Institution, Goswell Road, Mr. Jenneson,—On the writings of Eugene Sue—the Wandering Jew, Mysteries of Paris, &c. Discussion after,—Have works of fiction a beneficial tendency?

Mar. 9.—Branch A 1, John Street, Tottenham Court Road,—A Lecture. At 7, P.M.

For Mrs. Martin, Miss Roalfe, T. Paterson, C. S., and G. J. H., 25s.—from W. J.

ERRATUM.—In list of subscriptions to A. P. U., on page 62, for J. Robinson 1s., read 6d.

PATERSON TESTIMONIAL.

M. A. L. and five friends 0 3 0
T. W., per Mr. Hetherington.............. 0 2 0
          G. J. H., Sec.

Printed and Published by G. J. HOLYOAKE,
40, Holywell-street, Strand.
Wednesday, March 5, 1845.

THE MOVEMENT
And Anti-Persecution Gazette.

"Maximise morals, minimise religion."—BENTHAM.

No. 65.   EDITED BY G. JACOB HOLYOAKE, AND M. Q. RYALL.   Price 1½d

ALPHABET OF MATERIALISM.
D.

DES CARTES may be named as the modern philosopher who more than any other helped to perpetuate faith in creative Deity. On that account priests who are "up to snuff," laud him rather extravagantly. Without doubt, he was an acute thinker; but I know not how better to describe his scheme of metaphisics than by the ugly word mistiphysics, which is equivalent to the sentence, *physics in a mist*. Anything more obscure, or more repugnant to reason, the prolific brain of man may safely be challenged to conceive—one might even run the entire circle of philosophy without meeting its match. It is the quintessence—the *ne plus ultra*-or learned foolery, and proof everlasting that no thinker, however acute, patient, or profound, is competent to the thousand times attempted work of bringing about "a marriage union between religion and philosophy." The work famous "Meditations" is compounded of materials singularly heterogeneous—here a page of well aimed truth—there double the quantity of precious trash. Locke was of opinion that they "who would advance in knowledge and not deceive and swell themselves with a little articulated air, should lay down this as a fundamental rule, not to take words for things, nor suppose that names in books signify real entities in nature, till they can frame clear and distinct ideas of those entities." If Des Cartes had laid down and consistently abided by the "fundamental rule" here recommended, he never could have written the "Meditations," which is a book abounding in words significant of nothing whatever, except the imagination run mad of its author, whose ambition to explain the inexplainable hurried him beyond the boundaries of experience, where he found a "philosophy"

"—— of all our vanities the mobliest,
The merest word that ever fooled the ear,
From out the schoolman's jargon."

The reader of this Alphabet has seen that Berkeley, Collier, and others, considered belief in an external world irreconcilable with belief in the God whose existence is "revealed" by Scripture. Des Cartes, on the other hand, took for granted the existence of matter, a belief in the reality of which he deemed quite compatible with belief in Deity.* In common with most philosophers, observes a modern writer, Des Cartes assumed a duality: he assumed a God and a real world created by God. Substance to him was by no means the primal fact of all existence; on the contrary, he maintained that both extension and thought were substances, in other words, that mind and matter were distinct substances, different in essence and united only by God.

The difference, then, between Des Cartes and such writers as Berkeley or Collier is wide, palpable, and fundamental. He assumed, they denied, the reality of matter. He received, they rejected the account of Creation ascribed to Moses. Near the close of Letter B of this Alphabet, I promised to notice the attempt made by Collier to harmonise popular belief in an actual creation rather more than six thousand years ago, with his own disbelief in the reality of an external world. I take the present opportunity of performing that promise.

Collier published what he called "A Specimen of True Philosophy, in a Discourse on Genesis, the first chapter and the first verse, where I find these paragraphs :

"What I would advance is this : that as the visible iconic world exists in the glass, the glass itself exists in the mind or soul of him that perceives it. And, therefore, as the visible object, which we call glass, is of the same nature, or world, or order, with all the bodies of the universe, we must affirm the same of all, indifferently; which is the same as to say, that the whole visible world exists in mind, or the soul of him that perceives it.

"Now, this is the very point which I think I have demonstrated in the little book, (Clavis Universalis), before referred to, where, besides, I have proved at large, by nine several arguments, that an external

---
* G. H. Lewes.

world, or matter not dependent, for its existence, on mind, is an impossibility and a contradiction.

"Well then, in the (Scripture) text, we are told, that God made heaven and earth, or the whole material world *En Arche*. This may be called the major, or universal proposition of the argument I am upon ; and for as much as it is the word of God, it may well pass with us Christians for an unquestionable axiom. Now, to this I subjoin the proposition by me demonstrated, as the minor, namely, that the visible or material world exists in mind, *i. e.* immediately in the mind of him that seeth or perceiveth it ; wherefore, I conclude the meaning of the text to be the same as if Moses had said, *In mente creavit Deus*, &c., *i. e.* that mind, soul or spirit, is the *Arche*, in which God created the heaven and the earth."

What to make of this "rhapsody of words" I hardly know. People good at riddles may perhaps *guess* their meaning. To me they seem void of all sense, save nonsense. The conclusion, however, drawn by their ingenious author is important, and may be true in what *Newmaniacs* call a "non-natural sense," but sure I am it is false in any other.

Collier was a clergyman of the Church of England, and, therefore, it may fairly be presumed, subscribed himself believer of its thirty-nine Articles—one of which declares God "without body, parts, or passions." Pious Mr. Collibeer, in his treatise entitled "The Knowledge of God," assures us that the Deity must have some form, which he intimates may in all likelihood be the spherical. But few believers of any denomination will agree with him. That the creator of heaven and earth is himself without body, parts or passions, is an article of our church which not one of a million of Christians will *say* they reject. They are unable to conceive a Deity without body, &c., but nevertheless display much indignation if accused of adoring a Deity with them. As to Collier, he was anything but Anthropomorphous in his conceptions. The reader knows that he wrote books to disprove the existence of God, which no believer in a material God could dream of doing. It is evident that if Deity have a body, such body (no matter of what composed) must have parts; but Collier would have us believe that body is unreal though visible—in short, that the only realities are God and Mind; what answers to the words "material world" being neither more nor less than an "idol of our imagination."

A person on whose card was written, Professor Byrne, Member of the Royal College of Engineers, invited me, a few months since to debate the God question. I accepted the invitation and at this moment am heartily glad that I did so, for my opponent, a great *mathematician*, urged several mathematical and very novel arguments. One of the several was that as in mathematics there are quantities less than nothing, it manifestly follows to prove God nothing, or even considerably less than nothing is not to prove he don't exist. Another argument of the learned Professor, was to this purpose : Every mathematician knows that nothing divided by nothing gives anything in mathematics—who then can be illogical enough to deny that nothing divided by nothing gives any-*God* in theology.

Arguments such as these no *wary* theologists will disprove. They smack, it is true, of absurdity, but pray, Mr. Faultfinder, what religious arguments do not? Undoubtedly, to the rationalist there is something abundantly ridiculous in the notion that a brace of nothings may be *hocus-pocussed* into an infinite something, without body, parts or passions; or the no less mathematical notion that to prove God a quantity less than nothing is not to disprove his existence. But for the life of me, I cannot discover in these notions what should excite the ire, or provoke the laughter of theologians. So far, indeed, from laughing at, or scouting the attempt of scientific men to demonstrate that from nothing, or even *less than nothing*, everything could come, they should give them hearty encouragement, for sure as fate, unless such demonstration is possible, Immaterialism is a lie, for it rests upon the mere and monstrous assumption that all entities were created by a nonentity of some inconceivable sort. I say with emphasis, *nonentity*, because though many names have been given to the *assumed* being who is *assumed* to have created our, according to some, real, according to others, (only) visible, world ; they are each and all void of meaning—such names add nothing to our stock of knowledge. Dr. Knowlton, in his "Elements of Modern Materialism," distinguishes them as "thingless." At page 23 of that clever work, it is stated that " IGNORANCE has given rise to many thingless names, and these names have so long constituted a part of our language that it is almost impossible to converse without using them; but so long as we use them we ought to acknowledge that we mean nothing, or else use them to denote something that has perchance got a more appropriate name, and show distinctly what this something is. We had better (continues the Dr.) give one thing two or three names, than to suppose that two or three things exist when only one exists.

The materialist will readily admit the soundness of this reasoning. Not so, the opponents of that philosopher, who are perpetually the dupes of "thingless" names, which they fondly imagine must mean something. Deceived and swollen "with a little articulated air," they neglect to lay down this as a fundamental rule, not to take words for things nor suppose that names in books signify real entities in nature, till they can frame clear and distinct ideas of those entities. Hence, faith in God, and other "thingless" names, which represent nothing but the ignorance of those who use them. Hence the metaphysics of immaterialism which, from foundation to apex, is made up of transparent fooleries and flat contradictions. Whole libraries have been written in its support, and yet, at this moment, there breathes not the man who either knows himself or can explain to others what *immaterial* signifies. Dr. Knowlton says the word is not to be found in the Bible; and thanks to close thinkers, if any body ever meant any thing by it, men have been compelled to admit that whatever is immaterial is unextended. Now, talk about unextended mind or unextended being of any sort, has really no more claim to be considered language than the clucking of hens, grunting of hogs, or b-a-a-ing of sheep. An entity to be an entity must have at least two properties, and whatever has more than one property must be matter, what Des Cartes called *empty space*, Dr. Knowlton (properly, I think) observed, is not matter, for space consists of but one single property, to wit, *extension*. Thus much granted, it incontestably follows, that when Des Cartes asserted the independent substantiality of mind and matter, he did so, *in spite* of facts. But, till chaos come again, all assertions in opposition to facts will be the reverse of reasonable. We have the same *quality* of evidence that brains think, as we have that loadstones attract, and if any one were to assume that the attracting action of the loadstone is an entity distinct from the loadstone, he would be just on the level as regards wisdom, with our philosophical Christians, who declare that the thinking and sensing action of a brain is a substance or entity distinct from brain.

Dr. Knowlton urges with great force that the question, *What is it that thinks?* is not to be determined by conceivables or inconceivables; if it were, it would certainly be determined at once that it is the brain which thinks; for (he adds) it is not only as conceivable that actions of the brain should constitute thinking, as that actions of an immaterial *unextended* thing should constitute thinking; but the *existence* of this immaterial thing is inconceivable, whereas it requires no very great stretch of one's faith to admit that a brain exists. Again, we may lay down the position, (which, if disputed, can never be refuted) that we have just the same kind of evidence that sensing and thinking are functions of the nervous system, as we have that the secretion of bile is the function of the liver, or the secretion of urine, a function of the kidnies. And there would be just as much sense and propriety in my saying the bile is secreted by a bilary agent distinct from the liver, as there is in immaterialists saying that thinking is performed by a soul, mind, or thinking agent distinct from the brain. Nor do immaterialists better the matter by acknowledging, as some of them have, that it is as much a function of the brain to think, as it is of the liver to secrete bile, *provided*, they add, the brain is enabled to perform this function by the super-addition of a "percipient principle." A distinct agent is a distinct agent, call it by what name you please, whether mind, soul percipent principle or something else, I will say the liver is enabled to secrete bile by means of a *bile-secreting principle* superadded, and then ask them how this sounds.* If sound, these arguments are *fatal* to the theory of Collier, whose unintelligible assumption that the visible or material world exists in mind, is irreconcilable with the *fact* that actions called sensing and thinking, are no less certainly performed by brain than is action called secreting performed by kidneys or liver. If sound, these arguments are *fatal* to the theory of Des Cartes, whose unintelligible assumptions that mind and matter are distinct substances is irreconcilable with the *fact*, that mind is a "thingless name, which represents certain functions *performed* by substance, not *substance itself*. Spinoza understood by substance, "that which is in itself, and is conceived *per se*." which is precisely what I understood by it. Spinoza thought "It pertains to the nature of substance to exist." I think the very same thought; and thinking it, *cannot* agree with Des Cartes, that mind is substance, or with Collier, that there is no substance; *cannot agree* with the former that real matter was created by real Deity, or with the latter, that mind, soul, or spirit, is the *Arche, in* which God created the heaven and the earth.   C. S.

---

* Elements of Modern Materialism, pp. 43—72.

TO THE SCOTCH PRISON BOARD.

(CONCLUDED FROM PAGE 76).

Judge Hope, in his striking solecisms delivered with vicious delicacy, at the conclusion of my farcical trial, said he left me to the " mercy of his adorable redeemer." If " speech is morning to the mind," a wintry sun illuminates his dark and murky intellect. We may pray to be spared the tender mercies of Christians and their redeemers. Desolation marks the bigot's progress if in anger; misery, poverty and affliction are the results of his amity. They wish to improve Atheists by robbing them of their properties and destroying their businesses ; they desire us to live long in the land which the lord their god gives us, by destroying our lives in *gaols*; to make us heirs of heaven, by beggaring us now. By what right do christians thus trample upon us. By the violation of all rights, the right of the savage who is strongest and rules the rest. The right of the Israelites who murdered without compunction whom they could, who stood in the way of their ambition! Christians call themselves with unblushing mendacity, benefactors to humanity!!! Let the two millions of human carcasses that stank on Asian plains—America's exterminated forest sons; let the Waldenses, Episcopalians, Presbyterians, Jews, Quakers, Catholics, Deists, Atheists, and Hindoos, persecuted and murdered, boast christian *benefactors*; let the aged, lame, idiotic, virtuous but helpless old creatures, whose natural infirmities desired the soothing care of their more fortunate fellow beings, but who suffered the cruelest of tortures and the most horrible of deaths, by christian judges and parsons for the offence of witchcraft! sing christianity's praises. I am no singer. Christian kindness I have lately experienced, and with the remark I agree, " My soul come not thou into their assembly." Such kindness or protection as butchers give to lambs, christians give to us,

For godliness has such a face and mien,
As to be hated, needs but to be seen.

How happy for humanity were these moonstruck madmen, who torture their fellow men for the love of God, in heaven with their gods. They call themselves followers of a meek and humble God. Dreadful mistake. Religion is idolatry. Those religionists who have not a stone or wooden image have a book and from it they draw one to suit their temperaments; in a word gods are only reflections of the individual. They are self worshippers. What humility there is kneeling at your own reflection either in the mind or looking glass I never could discover. Cease to laugh at coquettes. Self worshippers of course admit no virtue not emanating from themselves. Daniel is lauded for refusing to bow to a calf; Carlile, Southwell, Holyoake, and Finlay are execrated for refusing to slaver over a *Lamb*.

Yet Christians, after confounding right and wrong, talk of "danger to public morals" from men who scorn to lie to please them. Protestants cant and whine about the generous tendancy of their branch of the delusion, but test it by the standard of humanity and reason, and it is simply not *so bad* as Druidism, because it has not so much power,

Religions, like glow-worms, afar off shine bright,
But viewed *too near*, hath neither heat nor light.

How pitiful that Judges, Lawers, &c., should become the clients, purveyors, and caterers to the vitiated appetites of pietists ! Cunning priests shelter themselves from the odium of the PERSECUTOR behind weak-minded or knavish Barristers. Judges, like Hope, *may* be so maudlin in conception as to fancy themselves instruments in Jehovah's hands to carry out his revenge. If they think so, it is because they are by nature bigots, and it is hard to resist nature. Justice and humanity are so contrary to every principle of a christian that we may as well look for both from a starving tiger? He thinks human suffering *is still* acceptable to his god, and if the Bible is correct, he is right. The Blackamoor never becomes white. The most rational supposition for the rabidness of the Scotch authorities, however, will be found in a desire to be accounted zealous and notorious by the saintly rabble, and the bewildered mob. They were mere sycophants of the sanctified cheats. Mere puppets pulled by priestly wires. They may not think this themselves, but the impartial spectators see them only as Jackalls for human cannibals. How much more noble the conduct of Judges Powell, Holt, and North, who stood firm amid the many interests that surrounded them, and did not allow their religion to cloud their sense of right and wrong, or distort common sense by the decisions of priest-ridden juries in witchcraft cases. All honour to such men, who, instead of fostering the bloody appetites of the *faithful*, stemmed the torrent of godly barbarities and saved the accused *in spite of* jury verdicts. Sad to see the Bench imitating the conduct of the notorious and brutal Jefferies, and an advocate rivalling the Covenanting persecutor.

It would be both ignorance and impertinence to say much about juries. They are selected from a portion of the community prominent for fawning, cringing, and sneaking to power or prejudice. Fed on such godly garbage as priests dole out, it dwarfs their intellects, stultifies their moral nature, and unfits them for sound judgment or mental independence. It is not to such versatile cravens that we are indebted for any mental liberty: not to such men as my jury were composed of, men whose reading never disentangled them from sacred jungle, who pore only over Bible metaphors and muddy allegories, do we owe any stand against oppression. They were no doubt conscientious, as far as Christians can be said to have a conscience, and no doubt thought they spoke and did, not so much their own ways, as those of a god. Such creatures deceive themselves more than others, they are self impostures. Other men see through the deceit. Piety has been called a "madman's robe, so tattered, that each puff of *reason* parts it, and shows the wearer's nakedness." And true it is, that on the day of my trial a *policeman* whispered to me that "there was not an intellectual face amongst the jury." He must have been a Lavater. The weakness and wickedness of juries is peculiarly Christian. Religion has made them servile and submissive where they should have been erect and independent.

If Scotch authorities have agreed that there must be a religion of some kind, why not the best and cheapest? Boodhism, of course, traduced like everything else by priests, Mr. Malcolm, an enlightened missionary, sent to India in 1835 to ascertain its spiritual condition, gives the following characters:—"No false religion, ancient or modern, is comparable to this. Its philosophy is not exceeded in folly by ANY other, but its doctrines and practical piety bear a strong resemblance to those of the scriptures. Did the people but act up to its *principles* of love and peace, oppression and injury would be unknown within its borders. Its deeds of merit are in ALL CASES either beneficial to mankind or harmless. It has no mythology of obscene and ferocious deities, no sanguinary or *impure* observances, no self inflicting tortures, no tyrannising priesthood, no confounding of right and wrong. Foreigners of every description are allowed the fullest exercise of their religion. The people are happier, milder tempered, and more innocent than Europeans generally."—*Malcolm's travels in the Burman Empire*. I put it to the Board whether our religion does not confound "right and wrong?" whether our mythology of deities are not "ferocious and obscene?" whether Christianity is not often "injurious to mankind?" whether foreigners or even natives, have not been tyrannised over for the exercise of their religion? A Bedlamite would blush to compare our obscene mythology with Boodhism. Let the unprejudiced read the five books of that rapacious bandit Moses, which is a record of detestable cruelties and abominable conceits, interspersed with filthy and disgusting tales, which abandoned licentiousness would scarce conceive—all, all commanded, partaken of, and rewarded by God—let the reader reflect that this book is not hidden, but exposed to the face of day and of females! nay, have actually crucifixes and portraits of a naked god to doat upon as children do dolls! What wonder that there is such a dreadful want of truth amongst Christians, and of which your late Chaplain was a striking example? Their god is a liar, and they try to imitate their heavenly father.

That such is the true character of Christianity, its book, and its supposed author, we have proved over and over again; and I respectfully ask can anything in modern or ancient religion equal it in degradation? Were it not for the little leaven of philosophy which is creeping into the lump, the witchcraft fires, the exterminating persecutions, and drivelling nonsense would again close in darkness over the European world. Pray turn a favourable ear to Boodhism. *It* you see is moralising, and what should be a recommendation in these hard times is, it has no *paid priesthood*.

I do not recommend Atheism. The change from a besotted faith to drink of the pure stream of Infidelity, in whose calm depth the beautiful and true are mirrored, would be asking a withered old beldam, whose haggard lips have quaffed polution's dregs to the bottom, to drink and view herself in a chrystal fountain. Besides, Atheism lays down no dogmas, commands no belief. This is very bad. It claims the right to speak conscientiously, and criticise fairly according to the evidence. It labours for the moral and intellectual welfare of all. Of course, in acheiving so *very* necessary a work as the moral and intellectual welfare of all, useful institutions would not be endangered. It labours to make known the truth to the mass, hoping it may be productive of good, and intends, should idolatries and solemn reveries fall to the ground, to substitute a principle of moral purity and mental energy. Atheism cares nothing about overturning of religions so mankind gain; nothing about sweeping an apartment for fear of disturbing cobwebs: nor of scouring away dirt for fear of incommoding vermin. Atheists think the sun of REASON may shine more gloriously, although it rose in mist; it has already struck sunlight over the surrounding gloom. Though foul and loathsome superstitions hover round its surface, though the dark and wintry clouds of hate, pride, and revenge try to eclipse it from men's views, it glides in "light, and takes no shadows from them."

In summing up to the jury the Lord Justice Clerk said that the style in which my books and placards were written showed clearly my intentions in selling them to be wicked and felonious. Did his lordship mean that I and others were not to express our ideas in our own language? Surely none but a creature in the last stage of dotaged idiotcy would ever conceive peculiarity of diction an offence. Was it offensive to put down in plain language the ideas we meant to convey, to so express ourselves that we could not be misunderstood? Would we not have been punished had we diluted our meanings with all sorts of obscurities like the Bible and his lordship's speech, that may mean something or nothing? It would be idle to answer these questions, every body of sense knows that style is a word used by religious tyrants apologetically for their detested persecutions. I hesitate not to charge Judge Hope with saying what was not true—he is a slanderer, a coward, and a bigot in charging me with other than just motives for my conduct, and should he venture from that Bench where he distorts the laws, I will prove him to be each of these characters.

If style infatuates, and leads men through wilds and labyrinths of error, so does the Christian boast, that Christianity is part and parcel of the law of the land, do the same. If true, a most clear reason why it deserves to be treated with contempt. It is a lie nevertheless. It should be : *the priests in power and their dogmas for the time being are part of the law's care*. What did the law prove against me? Simply what I admitted, that I sold books *proving* that *lies are lies* under any circumstances. Good men will therefore treat laws with contempt that punish the *just* for the gratification of the *unjust*. Law expounders, who strain the laws to conform to prejudices, should be execrated, and their names emblazoned in the scroll of "*scourges*." Blasphemy laws, church attendance laws, and many others are virtually repealed by disuse, and an enlightened opinion even in the government. The test and corporation acts—Campbell's New Libel Bill all show that enlightened men do not approve of these remains of a power exercised by a barbarous church in the zenith of its power, and crafty enough to see that its dominion would one day cease unless supported by physical force.

The fact that cases of this kind can only be brought before courts by public *prosecutors*, would seem to imply that *they* should check, not pander, to a vitiated and pious taste. "Law is law" is not a more ludicrous definition than it is a true one, for what justice is there in allowing Atheists to be traduced, slandered, and spit upon by all sorts of godlies, from all sorts of pulpits and presses, who call upon us to defend ourselves or be branded as cowards, yet the moment we open our lips, *or shops*, are pounced upon and punished. Civil liberty is defined as the permission of as much action to all as does not interfere with the particular welfare of each. But law, as it at present stands, or interpreted, is as much liberty as religionists please at *our* expense. Laws indeed appear at present instituted by godlies as traps to catch the sincere, and reward the hypocritical profligate. Thus everything is lawful that the law allows, and right and justice become words of no meaning, just like the words "religious morality." O'Connell declared that we may drive a coach and six through *any* act of parliament, and true it is, and of verity, that bigot judges warp them to suit themselves or party. Scottish barristers should remember that Scottish law doctrine *was* that "disuse repealed laws," and they should even for their own *ultimate* benefits imitate the liberality of an Erskine and a Denman, who rather try to enlarge than shrink the liberal tendency of opinion statutes. An enlightened public opinion is forming which will not look favorably upon a body of men unfit to suit the law to altered circumstances and times, and who appear not to know that society cannot be benefitted in the aggregate at the expense of any parts suffering. THOS. PATERSON.

MESSRS. GILLESPIE & SOUTHWELL.

SIRS,—*If* Mr. Gillespie's Argument A Priori is false, it is incumbent on the "Movement" party to *prove* it to be so, and that *too* in plain, intelligible, and *decisive* terms. It appears to me this has not been performed yet, and I am therefore induced to offer the following observations, for the purpose of *inciting* such *farther* investigation on this subject as may, if possible, set it finally at rest.

I believe that the controversy which appeared in your columns, between the above named disputants, is capable of being reduced into a small compass.

The basis of Mr. Gillespie's argument is, " Infinity of extension is necessarily existing," and Mr. Southwell admitted that if this proposition could be proved the remainder of the argument was good.

Mr. Southwell denies that there is such a *thing* as infinity of extension—he farther says, extension is *only* an *attribute* of existence, *not* existence *itself*—*attributes* have no *real* existence: they are *qualities* belonging to *matter*. What has no real existence amounts to nothing; an infinity of nothing will not make something, for they just amount to nothing; and nothing is an odd sort of foundation on which an argument is based. If infinity of extension is a real existence it should be shown how it can co-exist with matter, for even if that substance is finite, still it must destroy the infinity of aught else.

Mr. Gillespie does not notice these observations, but considers he has gained the victory, from his opponent having indirectly admitted the existence of infinity of extension, under the terms of matter has extension—matter has existence—matter is infinite.

Mr. Alexander, in your 60th number, takes a new view of the argument: he considers that Mr. Gillespie has neither proved nor *attempted* to prove the existence of infinity of extension. I do not quite agree with him here, as I think that gentleman *has* attempted to prove his first proposition. Admitting, however, for argument sake, that Mr. Alexander is correct, is it quite clear Mr. Editor that this failure would vitiate the entire argument?

Mr. Alexander says, "The pith of this so called argument seems to rest in the latter part of the second paragraph." The words here alluded to stand as follows in the Argument:—"For everything the existence of which we cannot but believe is necessarily existing."

Long before I read Mr. Alexander's paper I was forcibly struck with these words. It appeared their propounder meant them to convey an "axiomatic truth," and I thought they conveyed a fallacy. As Mr. Alexander has taken a similar view to myself I am now induced to request Mr. Gillespie to favour us with his interpretation of them. If by them he means to assert that "ideas," which rest upon what to us appear to be facts, and which in consequence we not only believe to be true, but which we have good reasons for believing to be true, necessarily involve the existence of the things which they (ideas) represent, then I am compelled to tell him he is mistaken indeed.

There is no necessary connexion between the belief of a thing and its reality. Take the following as an illustration of my meaning:

It is now well known that the planets are retained in their orbits by the attraction of the sun, and that they also attract the sun and each other. The mutual attraction of the planets for each other causes what astronomers call " the planetary perturbations," (irregular figures formed by them in their orbits). Thinking of the disturbing action of each planet on the other, it appeared to the great Newton that the part of no body could be perfectly stable, but on the contrary that every orbit must be constantly moved somewhat from its place by these unsteady influences, and he thought that the accumulating disturbances would soon abate the symmetry of existing arrangements, and probably cause their destruction by irregular shocks. When he saw no end to the damaging effect of the planetary perturbation, "*Sorrowful forebodings*" arose in his mind and he called "*for the special interference of the Almighty to avert the catastrophe*."

Now here is a man of the most profound abilities—a sincere enquirer after truth—pondering over a subject with which he was better acquainted than any other man *then* alive—his mind is harrassed by " sorrowful forebodings" *because* he believes certain things (the precipitation of the planets upon the body of the Sun) to be *true*. But will this *belief* involve the *realization* of these things? Mark the sequel.

The dissipation of Newton's fears was reserved for that age whose terminations we are still touching, and " great was the rejoicing" when the subtile analysis of the illustrious Legrange instructed us that *every* one of the perturbations before referred to must be PERIODICAL, or oscillatory; that is, if the earth is approaching the sun, or her orbit drawing in, a time must come when that approach will cease, and when an opposite action, or retrograding will take place, which also will be stopped in subsequent ages by a superior limit; *and so of all other perturbations.*

In addition to the question I have already asked Mr. Gillespie, I will feel obliged if he will inform us, whether he considers *matter* to have a *real* or an *ideal* existence—I wish it to be distinctly understood that by *real existence* I mean has *matter* length, breadth, thickness, ponderosity, hardness, impenetrability and other qualities mentioned in books of natural philosophy.

I have asked these questions from no idle motive, but for the purpose of fairly examining Mr. Gillespie's argument.

ALIQUIS.

EXTRACT FROM MRS. MARTIN'S PETITION TO THE HOUSE OF COMMONS.—" Your petitioner was apprehended in the town of Arbroath on a charge of blasphemy, taken before certain magistrates, examined in a private room, interrogated respecting her private affairs, no evidence being produced against her, or any attempt made to prove the charge from any of her lectures or writings. That your petitioner was confined two days and two nights in a felon's cell, where she endured much suffering from the intense cold, it being February 4th, 5th, and 6th, and from want of food—she was refused bail, and in all respects treated as a condemned felon: she was refused all correspondence with her friends, separated from her child, a girl of twelve years, in a strange town 400 miles from her home—denied all correspondence with any legal adviser; and the authorities having endeavoured to extort a promise from her that she would never again visit Arbroath, which she refused to give, they set her at liberty, without any evidence or reason given for her apprehension, her punishment, or her release. The authorities refused to state under what law they were proceeding, but your petitioner having several times during the examination demanded to be informed under what law she was to be prosecuted, they at last read to her the following ancient enactment, (which the Unitarians are tolerated in the constant breach of):—' Whosoever hereafter shall deny God, or any of the persons of the blessed Trinity, and obstinately continue therein, shall be processed, and being found guilty, that they shall be punished with death.'"

MR. PATERSON arrived in London on Tuesday morning, March 4. He is looking well, though suffering from a cold. While in Perth he lost 14lbs. in weight.

OLDHAM.—A Public Meeting was held in this town on February 14, on behalf of the Anti-Persecution Union. The meeting was addressed by Mr. Joseph Smith, Mr. Alexander Campbell, and Mr. Ambrose Hunt. The proceeds will be seen in our subscription column. Mr. Southwell was to have attended, but was prevented by his absence in Scotland.

LEICESTER.—Mr. Knox has lately removed from Sanvey Gate to the premises lately occupied by Mrs. Cooper, 11, Church Gate. On the premises is a Reading Room, containing the *Movement, New Moral World, Punch, Northern Star*, &c. A Discussion Class has also commenced. It meets on Monday nights. The subject of debate has been, "The Elevation of Woman, and the best means of raising her from her present position," and we are happy to state that "woman" has taken an active part in it. One of them moved for an adjournment of the debate, and opened it the next Monday evening with an excellent speech.

LAWS VERSUS RELIGION.—The truth is, and it is a melancholy truth, that where human laws do not tie men's hands from wickedness, religion too seldom does; and the most certain security which we have against violence is the security of the laws. Hence it is that the making of laws supposes all men naturally wicked, and the surest mark of virtue is the observation of laws that are virtuous. If, therefore, we would look for virtue in a nation we must look for it in the nature of government, the name and model of their religion being no certain symptom nor cause of their virtue.—*Cato's Letters.*

VOTES OF THE HOUSE OF COMMONS, Feb. 17.—Blasphemy Petition of Alexander Quin Campbell, for alteration of the law relating thereto; to lie on the table.

MRS. MARTIN, an Infidel teacher, has been "mobbed" in the streets of Edinburgh. The papers call her an "abandoned creature," but say nothing of the unchristian conduct of the people who treated her with violence. The early Christians were "mobbed," and their persecutors are justly condemned; as every persecuting Christian should be.—*Glasgow Saturday Post.*

This affair [the Arbroath affair] we think requires farther investigation, as it involves a most vital public principle. Suppose for instance that Mrs. Martin should turn out to be "a Jewess," would the magistrates of Arbroath think themselves justified to act, or would the law authorise them to act as they have done?—*Glasgow Argus.*

THE MOVEMENT AND MR. PATERSON.—Meetings in connection with our publication, and Mr. Paterson's Welcome—the first of which was named last week—must still be postponed. In addition to Mr. Holyoake's illness, Mr. Paterson being on the invalid list, for the present suspends our operations.

J. Cooper, for *Movement*................ 0 5 0

TO CORRESPONDENTS.

C. S.—He is quite wrong in his conclusion. We willingly advertise the John Street Lectures when we can find out the particulars which we always have to seek personally. Several times we have desired the secretary to inform us punctually of lectures delivered. But in every case hitherto we have had to find out the particulars by our own industry. We are not to blame for any neglect.

RECEIVED.—"Birmingham Herald," "Felix Farley's Journal," "Bristol Gazette," "Glasgow Saturday Post," "Glasgow Argus."—J. Newman—his case shall receive attention.

LECTURES.

Mar. 16.—National Hall, 242, High Holborn, W. J. Fox,—On the Poet Tennyson.
Mar. 18.—Charlestown Rooms, Ashton-under-Lyne, Mr. C. Southwell,—The Nature and Influence of Superstition.
Mar. 16.—Finsbury Institution, Goswell Road, A Friend,—On Competition and Free Trade. Discussion after,—Ought the Anti-Corn Law League to be supported by the industrious classes?
Mar. 16.— Investigation Hall, 29, Circus Street, Marylebone, Mr. R. Buchanan,—Heaven and Hell; the New Jerusalem and the Lake of Fire and Brimstone.

SUBSCRIPTIONS
TO THE ANTI-PERSECUTION UNION.
Mr. Hindle, Ashton-under-Lyne......... 0 5 6
Per Mr. Mellor, Oldham.
A friend to free discussion............. 0 2 6
Collected at a public meeting on Feb. 14. 0 14 4
James Mellor, annual subscription...... 0 2 0

PATERSON TESTIMONIAL.
Per J. Mellor, Oldham.
Edward Hume........................ 0 1 0
A young Atheist of Gledwick.......... 0 1 0
James Mellor........................ 0 1 0
Jubal Howard........................ 0 1 0
James Taylor........................ 0 1 0
John Nicholson...................... 0 1 0
A hater of religion.................. 0 2 6
A few friends....................... 0 2 6
James Greaves...................... 0 1 0
G. J. H., *Sec.*

Printed and Published by G. J. HOLYOAKE, 40, Holywell-street, Strand.
Wednesday, March 12, 1845.

THE MOVEMENT
And Anti=Persecution Gazette.

"Maximise morals, minimise religion."—BENTHAM.

No. 66.   EDITED BY G. JACOB HOLYOAKE, AND M. Q. RYALL.   Price 1½d

GOD'S WORDS VERSUS GOD'S WORKS.

III

" AND God said, let there be lights in the firmament of the heaven to divide the day from the night; and let them be for signs, and for seasons, and for days and for years: and let them be for lights in the firmament of the heaven to give light upon the earth: and it was so. And God made two great lights; the greater light to rule the day, and the lesser light to rule the night; he made the stars also. And God set them in the firmament of the heaven to give light upon the earth, And to rule over the day and over the night, and to divide the night from the darkness; and God saw that it was good. And the evening and the morning were the fourth day." There is no mistaking these statements, that the sun, moon, and stars were created *after* the creation of the earth. But there is nothing so certain as that there is not a shadow of reason upon which such a supposition can rest. Modern opinion is entirely opposed to it. Astronomy teaches that many of the *planets* are older than our earth, and that the sun is the parent of all. The Bishop of Norwich, at the opening of the Norwich Athenæum lately, in speaking of geology, said " He remembered when in his own county, (Cheshire) often and often had he mused on those boulders or erratic blocks, remnants of former ages, and how much did he learn from them. They carried him back into ages, cycles and cycles, long gone by; and he, as he read from those rocks, as in botany, there were tongues in trees, sermons in streams, so also might be found sermons in rocks, and good in every thing. It told him of that remote and mighty time when it was said in Genesis ' *in the beginning* ' but when was that beginning ? When the earth was without form and void, *unfitted for life of any sort,* rolling in its orbit *round its central sun.*" The worthy Bishop, in his ardour for science, forgot his duty to the church; for in Genesis it is stated that *vegetable life,* at least, existed *before the sun was formed* and as for the idea that, at the time " the earth was without form and void " it was rolling round its central sun," there had been three hard days' work done upon it before there was any sun formed for it to roll round! A scientific bishop! what an anomaly. Most conclusive and satisfactory as the above must be, I have further authority yet.

The author of the " Vestiges of the Natural History of the Creation," after quoting the opinions of many philosophers which support the hypothesis, says, "Thus, in the sublime chronology to which we are directing our inquiries, we find ourselves called upon to consider the globe which we inhabit as a *child of the sun,* elder than Venus and her younger brother Mercury, but *posterior* in date of birth to Mars, Jupiter, Saturn, and Uranus; next to regard our whole system as probably of recent formation in comparison with many of the stars of our firmament. * * * How much *older* Uranus may be no one can tell, *much less how more aged* may be many of the stars of *our* firmament, or the stars of *other* firmaments than ours." The author does not use the word " firmament " in the sense in which it is used in Genesis, but as comprising our astral or stary system. He speaks, too, of *other firmaments,* upon which subject Genesis is silent. I have something yet more extraordinary to note than even these discrepancies and omissions. After relating the beautiful and astounding discoveries of astronomers, he says, " Nor is this all, Sir William Herschel, so early as 1783, detected a motion in our solar system with respect to the stars, and announced that it was tending towards a star in the constellation Hercules. This has been generally verified by recent and more exact calculations. * * According to this view, a time may come when we shall be much more in the thick of the stars of our astral system than we are now, and have of course more brilliant nocturnal skies: but it may be countless ages before the eyes which are to see this added resplendence shall exist." Those who are alive to see this change *will* have a "*firmament*" not created *for them!* And perhaps an Herschel of that day will discover that our system is proceeding to another point, beyond the one noticed by Sir William." "Push along, keep moving," is the universal rule—men and nations, worlds and systems—all are jogging on.

"And God said, let the waters bring forth abundantly the moving creature that hath life, and fowls that may fly above the earth in the open firmament of heaven. And God created great whales, and every living creature that moveth, which the waters brought forth abundantly, after their kind, and every winged fowl after his kind. * * And the evening and the morning were the fifth day." There is either an awful jumble here, or else an equally awful blunder—for it is stated that the *waters* brought forth fishes *as well as fowls*, and a little further on, "*every living creature that moveth*," and this on the *fifth* day, whereas we find in the next verse, as the commencement of the sixth day's work, "And God said, let the earth bring forth the living creature after his kind, cattle, and creeping thing, and beasts of the earth after his kind: and it was so." The meanest tyro in geology must perceive at a glance the utter impossibility of reconciling the assertion that all marine animals were created in one day, or at one period, though it should have been extended over thousands of years, with modern science. But even if he would let that pass, and say that the writer meant all that were known to the world at the time he wrote, he could never admit that birds were created or came into existence contemporaneously with fishes and other marine animals. He may certainly say that the absence of any remains of birds in the very earliest strata is no proof that birds did not exist at the period of their deposit—their bones may have been destroyed: for Lyel says, because we have not found mammifers in the earlier series of rocks we must not conclude they are not there—for if we could dig down into the bed of some ancient ocean we *might* find them: true, and we might not. To such apologies, however, a ready answer can be given—it is altogether beyond the rules of common sense to imagine that millions of delicate shells, of many hundred different sorts, should have been preserved, and not the bones of birds. And if the smallness of the number of birds which might reasonably be expected to have existed at such time, might militate against the chances of finding them—the manner in which the crust of the earth has been explored, without success, justifies the conclusion that we should ere now have found *some* remains if there were any to be found; and if birds did exist at the time of the early formations, we have a right to expect that remains exist now.

God concluded his week's work by making man *and* woman, but subsequently went over this last item of his labour a second time. What became of the *first* woman "God only knows," for there is no record left of her disappearance—perhaps she was devoured by the wild beasts of those times, and it was thought by the "sacred historian" that the least said about so untoward a circumstance the better. I shall show, by and by, that there is no foundation for the notion, drawn from the Bible, that "death" was a result from Adam's sin—for that death in its most hideous form existed cycles of ages before the earth was suited for man's residence on it. In only one particular of all this history do we find anything approaching the truth, and that is with respect to the order, in relation to the other animals, in which man first appeared upon the earth—that he came after all the rest. I have now gone through the main incidents narrated in the first chapter of Genesis, and have placed modern *knowledge* in opposition to ancient *ideas*—I have compared God's words with God's works—have pitted the authority of priests against the authority of philosophers—revelation against science—the fables of other days against the truths of the present: those who have read can determine their relative value.

In a previous article on the subject of "God's Words *versus* God's Works," *Movement* vol. i. p. 442, I said "If there be a Creator, and man has a revelation from him, then the discoveries of science *ought* to be in harmony with such revelation." In that article I simply argued the general question, whether in a supposed revelation from a deity, of certain of his own acts, those acts should not be found to *agree* with his account of them, before we accorded the merit of a revelation to his statement and that, wanting such agreement, we must look to other sources for our explanation. In the present article I have exhibited the particular questions at issue with the God of the Christians' words and the God of the Christians works and while I have, on the one hand, quoted from the anthorised edition of his words, I have, on the other hand, given extracts illustrative of his works from orthodox believers only. I have "nothing extenuated, nor set down ought in malice" I have measured the deity's corn with his own bushel—if the chaff be great and the grains few, the fault is not mine.

It may be objected by some, that in insisting upon a *literal* interpretation of the book of Genesis, I take the Christians at an unfair advantage, inasmuch as the more enlightened of the Christian world consider that it was never meant as a plain statement of facts, and that it is only an allegory. To this I reply that there are as many high orthodox authorities for the one view as for the other—and that, if there were not, it would not benefit Christianity a jot. Southwell, in the *Investigator*, gave an extract from Bishop Burnet, in which that facetious divine very happily burlesques the notion of a literal interpretation of the account of the "fall of man," declaring it to be an allegory. Upon this Southwell pertinently remarks, if the "*fall* of man," through eating an apple, be an allegory, why—the "*redemption*" of man, through the death of Christ, must be an allegory also; for if there were no literal fall there could be no necessity for a literal redemption—the last being a consequence of the first. Now this is tantamount to a destruction of Christianity altogether, and the Christians are at liberty to choose whichever horn of the dilemma may best suit them. Dr. Pye Smith would seem to favour a literal, or rather a grammatical, interpretation of the scriptures, whilst, as we have seen, he *literally* hems the ground from under his own feet. He "rifles up" a trifle at Dr. Buckland, for hinting that geology would require some little concessions from scripture. Dr. P. Smith says, "It would not be deemed presumptuous in him to express some regret on finding an expression used by one of the most accomplished geologists of our own or any country, Dr. Buckland, believing at the same time that it was introduced *more from oversight* than with deliberate intention. 'If geology (said the professor) should seem to require *some little concession* from the literal interpreter of the scriptures, it may fairly be held to afford ample compensation for this demand by the large additions it has made to the evidence of natural religion, in cases where revelation was not designed to give information.'" Upon this Dr. P. Smith declares that "the testimony of the word of heaven did not lie at their disposal, *they had not the power of conceding anything for it.*" I do not quarrel with this view—I conceive it to be a perfectly rational and consistent one. Men, clearly, can be no more justified in tampering with the *words* of God than they would be in tampering with his *works*. What would be thought of the scientific man who would consent to "burke" some obstinate fact, because it would not agree with scripture?—and what should be thought of the religious believer who would consent to the smallest, the most infinitessimal concession on the part of God's words, in order to *make* them agree with science? Men who would attempt it would be deservedly despised. Supposing we take Dr. Smith's view of the matter, what do we get by it? That "The interpretations of the *word* of God must rest upon their own intrinsic evidences, and be determined by a nice grammatical construction of language." The doctor says that the Jewish idea of a "firmament" was that of a ductile mass beaten out—we have no firmament, therefore the Jewish idea was a fiction, *and not a fact*. Lightning was conceived to be "coals of fire"—which is *not a fact*. Thunder was thought to be "God's voice"—which is *not a fact*. The earth was thought to be a flat plain, which is *not a fact*. The doctor, with all his philosophical acumen, cannot make these blacks appear white —and if he could we have the fact of a different reading, being the general one for the last 4000 years, which entrely invalidates the scriptures as a revelation of God's works.

The difficulties in the doctor's path were as innumerable as they were insuperable. It is expressly stated in the Bible, and a most important point it is in the Christian scheme, "By one man sin entered into the world, *and death by sin.*" "But (says the doctor) when they came to establish facts, *they immediately saw a different state of things.*" To be sure they did, for geologists have found in the dung of the extinct saurians, called coprolites, portions of other saurians, forming, as Dr. Buckland observes, "Records of warfare waged by successive generations of inhabitants of one planet *on one another;* and the general law of nature, which bids all to eat and to be eaten in their turn, is shown to have been co-extensive with animal existence upon one globe." (Penny Mag. 1833, p. 349). A fact in connexion with this subject will not be uninteresting. A respected friend of mine, well acquainted with geology, who was once "a believer," told me the other day that his faith in the scriptures was first shaken by reading the above extract in the *Penny Magazine;* he having previously imagined that the world had not seen death until *after* Adam's fall. That orthodox work, the *Penny Magazine,* may lay claim to making one Infidel, at least.

Dr. Smith says "It was assumed as included in the narrative of Moses," that all animated creatures, excepting fishes, were created in pairs upon *one* spot of the earth, and that of very limited extent—but that this was a *natural* impossibility, as many animals could not have existed even for a short time in such a climate, and the Australian region contained animals "completely distinct from those of any other portion of land on the face of the globe." This is certainly very destructive of the notion that all created things were gathered together in the Ark, when the whole world was drowned—which is also a very important point in the Christian theory.

Although Dr. Smith seems so confident that a strict grammatical examination of the language of scripture would enable us to remove the difficulties in the way of an harmonious agreement between science and scripture, Professor Babbage thinks "that we could not so depend upon our ability to construe the ancient holy writings *as to be sure that we had correctly interpreted them!*" And Professor Powell thinks "that the Mosaic account was not to be taken as a literal history, *but as the language of poetry.*" By which is meant, I presume, that the divine poet, like his profane brethren, has taken great liberties with truth.

I have extended this article, unavoidably, to so great a length, that I think I cannot do better than conclude—though I have not given a tithe of the evidence that might be adduced of the discrepancies existing between science and revelation—as a general rule there is no agreement.

"Actions speak louder than words," says the proverb, and we have found it so. God's works speak louder than his words, and all civilised nations are now ringing with their echo. "If the academy has taught pantheism (said the noble Frenchman, Michelet) it was because she believed it to be true—and if she believes it she will continue to teach it in spite of all the priests of all the world." The book of nature has many leaves, and so has the book of the priests—the book of nature is full of truths—but the book of the priests is full of lies. *Nil desperandum.* "Truth is great, and must prevail."

W. C.

THE ATHEIST DISTINGUISHED FROM THE SCOFFER.

Do theologians wilfully mistake the position of an atheist with regard to his belief or non-belief in a god, or are they absolutely blind to the real state of the case? It is a question that needs from them an adequate answer. Do you, when you speak of us in abusive and comdemnatory language, understand the rights of the subject upon which you are talking? Theologians write and talk as if atheists belied their nature ; as if the term atheist was applied to us falsely ; as if, in fact, atheist meant a believer in a god, who chooses to insult that supposed being. They assume, that an atheist, by denying the existence, or even reasoning against the existence of a god, does it only from a carping spirit ; that he believes all the time he is writing or speaking, but that he chooses to act hypocritically before the face of society in that precise point, and in that path which brings neither reputation nor wealth. They either purposely or ignorantly mistake the thoughtless reviler for the reflecting atheist. Even Burns could not or would not notice this distinction. He says—

"An atheist laughs—a poor exchange
For Deity offended."

But the atheist is by position unable to make the "exchange." It is here evidently assumed that you might have your joke at heaven provided heaven took no notice of it ; but the atheist considers heaven a dream, or something only to be realised in this life, therefore he may consistently have his joke at what he deems the fruit of the unhealthy imaginations of mistaken men. What I want explained is this : does any sane priest or layman believe it possible for an *atheist* to be a *scoffer*? If they do not, then are their denunciations of the atheist hypocritical, and merely employed to help a sinking cause ; if they do, then they are miserably blind ; for the distinction is so clear between one who scoffs at what he believes to be of immense importance to man, out of a diabolical or thoughtless spirit, and one who places in a ridiculous light, or in a position that discloses their falsity, the opinions and creeds of men with an earnest and devout mind. By the theologian taking advantage of the existence of these two characters, and wilfully or blindly confounding them, most disingenuously true atheism and atheists are placed in a despicable light, invested by parsonical rhetoric with a repulsive exterior, and held up as hypocritical villians. Every sound mind hates hypocrisy, every earnest man who heartily believes in the reality, the importance of life—that it is a thing that ought not, and must not, to live truly—be played with, but religiously, that is devotedly, heroically treated, as well by those destined to perish in their generation, and the grand minds who will live while man lives—every one of these hates, cordially and with uncompromising fervour, the trifler, the scoffer —the man who degrades and makes contemptible by his actions, our ideas of life. Let not us, oh, ye possessors of estate and name, and who pervert while ye possess that estate, from its legitimate objects—let not us, staunch, consistent, but willing-to-reason atheists, be ranked with those whose estimates of life and its possibilities, is mean and contemptible—who treat it as a "jest," and not as something holy and sacred. We have no fear of being classed with those who declare man is "born in sin," and subject to unredeemable depravity; some other parties, reputable, sanctified, must answer for those degrading doctrines. Give us that idea of life which, loftier than the stars, tells its possessor that nothing he can imagine, grand and magnanimous, is impossible to the soul —give us that hope, quenching despair, and strengthening as an elixir, the aspiring -- give us that hope that ets a valuation upon mind, not body—upon worth not wealth—upon that which a man can nobly do, not upon that which a man has—upon that which he *creates*, not upon that which he *inherits*—give us that pure and sacred faith, that asks for, and as willingly grants, the right of an unmolested, conscientious belief in *any* opinions, generating a true respect for our fellows, animating them and us, with a reliance on, and reverence for, conscience; and above all, give us that creed, come it from heaven or hell, which would conquer the world, not with a "sword," but with love and knowledge. Hope on, my brethren—hope in nature, hope in truth—trust in unconquerable mind—truthfully and earnestly enquire—cultivate the intellect, refine the tastes, elevate the feelings, and the days of happiness will yet come to cheer us all.

ATHEOS.

WHITEHAVEN.

MESSRS. EDITORS, — Being in a tradesman's shop the other day, a conversation was going on with the shopkeeper and his friend, relative to a case for trial at the late Carlisle Assizes, of a woman of intemperate habits, at Lamonby, who, having conceived a violent hatred towards one of her children (a girl about six or seven years of age) for telling tales to the father, had actually held the child over the fire and burned it to death. The principal evidence against the mother was another of her children, a girl also, about eight or nine years of age, I believe. This child the judge remanded *to be educated* ere its evidence could be received. It was so grossly ignorant that it had *no idea*, either innately or otherwise, of either heaven or hell, god or devil—and was *frightened* of nothing but its mother. So the child, the party stated, was remanded—that is, it was sent back to be *educated*, to be taught to be *frightened* at something else besides its mother, and to *know* something about heaven, hell, god, and the devil. Here, Messrs. Editors, one cannot help expressing some wonder as to how much the learned judge himself *knows* about these matters; and if the child can be *taught* anything more than merely to *believe* in the *words*. And when it has learnt to be frightened at the devil, we suppose, will it have learnt to revere truth, or to tell a lie, or speak the truth merely *through fear*, as the motive may be? Strange sort of education this—still more strange the child should have no idea of a god! Really, the circumstance is a melancholy one—the more so as regards the judge, perhaps, than the child.

Yours, Gentlemen, W. W.

MRS. MARTIN ON THE VISIT TO HARMONY.

DEAR SIR,—I have for some time been looking on, somewhat surprised, it is true, but certainly not apprehensive, respecting the ultimate results of your "Visit" and the critiques bestowed upon it. I *had* hope that those who have arrayed themselves as your enemies, if not governed by principle (which they have sufficiently proved they do not understand) would yet see the *impolicy* of their foolish attempt at despotism. Be assured, sir, you have more who sympathise with you than have yet expressed it. I for one am not fond of attaching myself to a party, but if you and your friends are to become the ordinary objects of insane attacks from those who ought to have too much to do to spend time in breaking up the camp instead of attacking enemies who are so numerous without it—I cannot remain a silent witness—if you required defence I would gladly exert myself in so just a cause —but that is unnecessary. I have only therefore to say that as they seem not to be able just now to find business to their mind sufficiently plentiful, out of pity for their idleness I suggest the following, it may furnish them with a little of their favourite occupation : —

I entirely sympathise with Mr G. J. Holyoake under his recent treatment by Branch A 1 and the *New Moral World*, and consider that the attempt made to fetter free discussion, and hide the truth from those so deeply interested in learning it, is conduct unworthy any executive, or branch of a society calling itself rational.

EMMA MARTIN.

Glasgow, March, 1845.

"THERE ARE FAULTS ON BOTH SIDES."

This very phrase, which *seems* to hold in the narrowest compass the moral of all life, and to convey the verdict agreed upon by *truth* in relation to all the vain and aggravated contentions of mankind,—this phrase is made a catch-word, a slang saying, a jest becoming in the very meanest mouths, and fitted for the vilest objects.

There is no form of words which has worked more mischief in the social world, as far as words alone can work it, than this phrase. It is caught up from lip to lip—repeated until sense is lost in mere sound; and the general truth becomes a particular falsehood in thousands of instances. Its real meaning is struck out, and a hollow lie is substituted. Where we should find the white sweet kernel, the maggot fattens. "Faults on both sides" is the language, not of the philosopher or the moralist—but of the self elected juror, concealed and cowardly slanderer, the heartless and abandoned leveller, who would confound vice and virtue, and merge all distinctions, not merely of guilt, but of guilt and innocence, in a loose easy, general, comfortable verdict —a safe one universally,—" faults on both sides."

You are not far from the truth there, is the cry of the sage babblers of society as often as the verdict is delivered—not very, in one sense, but awfully near a lie, dark and silent as assassination, perhaps, in another sense. A reputation is possibly sacrificed in the very utterance of the words—a life's life may be destroyed – a great cause, sacred as virtue, is given up at once—the broadest, simplest points of difference all confused and merged uninquiringly—and honour and shame reduced to the same measure, colour and substance; all by the easy, current verdict, applicable to the most difficult and the most contradictory cases—"there are faults on both sides."

The Father of Evil never invented a more dexterous weapon for his agents to work with. The envenomed point is so concealed, while it looks so open and fair. Candour so shines in it, that enquiry is subdued at once. Remonstrance is silenced by a text so impartial. Once utter this decree and there is no more to be said. "There are faults on both sides" generally settles all to everybody's satisfaction.

The lovers of peace are satisfied, for it cuts short dispute. The sympathisers with virtue submit, for it spares her the dangerous intoxication of a triumph. The allies of the vicious are comforted, for their client is lifted up in repute to the virtuous level. The slanderers exult, because it gives them a cue for reviling both parties. The timed, selfish people are reconciled, for they are relieved from the risk of taking part one way or other. The indolent are saved the trouble of investigating. The hypocrites admit that there may possibly be a fault or more on one side than the other, but protest vehemently against the practice of balancing hairs and re-opening cases that are finally settled. The verdict is given; there is no new trial to be had when once human nature has heard the decree pronounced—"There are faults on both sides."—*Laman Blanchard.*

THE CASE OF MR. NEWMAN.

Our attention has been again drawn to the case of this gentleman. In No. 57 we abridged from the *Inquirer* a statement of his position. Being fully in possession of the mastership of a liberal school—a kind of Free School, in the parish of Long Sutton, Lincolnshire—he was ejected by the vicar's influence on account of holding Unitarian principles. Mr. Newman did not teach them, or in any way diffuse them in his school, he simply held them, and on this account was obnoxious to the church. Further, he was required to change his school procedure from one—so far liberal as to admit children of dissenting denominations—into church sectarianism. This he refused to do, or be a party to it, for which he deserves well of the parishoners, and of all interested in education and the destruction of that insolent interference on the part of churchmen who would subject to their iron domination. We believe the parish never before possessed a vicar till lately, when the present dashing blade arrived, who, if report speak truly, is competent both to take care of hounds as well as cure souls. Most of the parish worthies, never having seen so great a man before, are all obsequiousness— hence a powerful phalanx are influenced to an heterodox and comparatively defenceless individual, but we trust that the public will give attention to a case so deserving of support. Mr Newman has commenced legal proceedings for the recovery of his situation, and needs considerable assistance to support his suit, as his opponents spare nothing that will throw obstacles in his way. Besides this, is the loss of his situation, and he has a large family to maintain. The attention of the Anti-Persecution Union was solicited by a valued friend, on Mr. Newman's behalf, but such a case—Mr. Newman not being imprisoned on account of his opinions — does not come within the Union's sphere. Nevertheless we shall be happy as journalists to aid Mr. Newman, and any subscriptions sent to our office for him shall be acknowledged in the *Movement* and forwarded to him. It ought to be added that many interesting facts connected with this transaction to which we cannot allude even, will be found in the *Inquirer* of the week before last.

PRINCIPLES OF MORALITY.

Hobbes taught that the " laws which the civil magistrates enjoins are the ultimate standards of morality.'

Cadworth that the " origin of our notions of right and wrong is to be found in a particular faculty of the mind which distinguishes truth from falsehood.'

Mandeville that the "moral virtues are mere sacrifices of self interest, made for the sake of public approbation." He calls virtue the " political offspring which flattery begot upon pride."

Dr. Clarke that " virtue consists in acting according to the fitnesses of things."

Hume that " utility is the constituent or measure of virtue."

Dr. Hutcheson that " it originates in the dictates of a moral sense."

Paley that it is " doing good to mankind in obedience to the will of God, and for the sake of everlasting happiness."

Adam Smith that " sympathy is the source of moral approbation."

Reid, Stewart, Brown maintain the " existence of a moral faculty."

Mackintosh says " conscience is made up or compounded of associations."—*Combe's Moral Philosophy.*

General and Local Religion.—Religion is the same everywhere, if men would but believe it ; but the superstitious of the vulgar are always cruel to themselves in proportion to the rigour of their climate. Nature, such as they see it, is their only notion of Providence ; and in a wretched atmosphere, they set down Providence as a very hard taskmaster. They never seek to enliven what is dismal, but to make every thing else agree with it. This is why men worship in Scotland with groans, and in Italy with the most delightful music. This is why, although London weather is bad enough, you cannot wrap us up in perfect Scotch melancholy, unless you could shroud us in perpetual Scotch mists. And as your Glasgow is to our London, so is London to Paris. It is a perfect rule-of-three sum, as to cheerfulness in weather and religion.

Anti-Persecution Union.—A Special Meeting of the Committee, held at Mr. Holyoake's, on Friday ; important matter was brought forward respecting the legal proceedings in Mr. Johnson's Case, which are going on very satisfactorily. The claim of Mr. Whiting, of Bristol, was also considered, and it was resolved that the earnest attention of friends of the Union be called to these cases, that the Committee be at once put in possession of the means of bringing these cases to a successful issue.

Profligacy of the English Government.—The expenses of the English Government are paving the way for future revolutions. The world never yet saw so extravagant a Government as the Government of England. Not only is economy not practised, but it is despised, and the idea of it connected with disaffection, Jacobinism, and Joseph Hume. Every rock on the ocean where a cormorant can perch, is occupied by troops, has a governor, deputy governor, store-keeper, deputy store-keeper, and will soon have an arch-deacon and a bishop. Military colleges with thirty-four professors, educating seventeen ensigns per annum, being half an ensign for each professor, with every species of nonsense, athletic, sartorial, and plumigerous. A just and necessary war costs this country about £100 per minute ; whip-cord £15 000 ; red tape £7000 ; lace for drummers and fifers £19,000 a year. A pension to one man who has had his head broken at the pole ; to another who has shattered his leg at the equator : secret service money to Thibet ; an annuity to Lady Henry Somebody and her seven daughters, the husband having been shot at some place where he never ought to have had any soldiers at all ; and the elder brother returning four members to parliament. Such a scene of extravagance, corruption, and expense as this, must paralyse the industry and mar the fortunes of the most industrious and spirited people that ever existed. — *Sydney Smith.*

Camp Meeting.- " My young friend," said a minister to a boy at camp meeting, " do you ever think of a future state ?"

" No, I never meddle with state affairs, though brother John is a politicianer ?"

" Do you never think about dying ?"

" No; but I guess our Sally did when she got the measles, for she turned all sorts o' colours."

" Whose boy are you ?"

" When any body axes dat, I tell 'em I don't know."—*Boston Investigator.*

PRESENTATION OF MRS. MARTIN'S PETITION.

The petition from which we extracted last week was presented on Friday night by Mr. Duncombe. The following is the hon. member's intimation concerning it:—

March 15, 1845.

Dear Sir,—I presented yesterday Mrs. Martin's petition which you sent in for that purpose. In haste, Yours, truly,

T. S. Duncombe.

H. Hetherington, Esq.

MARYLEBONE.

A meeting took place on Thursday evening last at the Investigation Hall, in order to establish an Atheistical Society in this district. A chairman having been appointed—

1st. "It was resolved that the Society be known as the Marylebone Atheistical Society.

2nd. "That a Committee of three be appointed to draw up rules, and that the same be submitted for adoption on this night fortnight.

3rd. "That the foregoing resolutions be sent to the *Movement* for insertion, to bring those in the district acquainted with the formation of the above society." John Truman, Sec. *pro tem.*

N.B.—All persons in the neighbourhood friendly to the Atheistical principles are most respectfully invited.

CHAPEL TACTICS.

Mr. Anderson sends the following illustration of the coercion necessary to be had recourse to to fill the churches and conventicles of Scotland:—

Sabbath Desecration.—A public meeting was held on this subject in the Free East Church, Aberdeen, on Monday week: Dr. Henderson in the chair. Various resolutions were adopted relative to the sanctity of the Sabbath, the duty of observing it, and of masters forcing those in their employment to attend divine service.—*Edinburgh Weekly Register.*

This is the way Christians get their audiences, and then boast of the religious feeling of the working classes of Scotland.

Mr. Anderson adds, as a kind of "counterblast," as King James would write, to the above, that Sir Andrew Agnew, of maw-worm notoriety, lately attempted to stop the Sunday trains, at a late meeting of the Edinburgh and Glasgow Railway Co.

For Sir Andrew's motion............ 52
Against it......................... 2060

Thus cant stood at a discount of 2008.

The Meeting of Mr. Paterson's Friends.—Mr. Cooper, at the last meeting of the Anti-Persecution Union, has been appointed a member of the Sub-Committee for conducting this meeting in lieu of Mr. Holyoake, who is unable to attend to it. Next week the Sub-Committee will be able to announce all particulars, and name the places where tickets can be purchased.

Progress in Wales.—Extract from a letter in the *Carnarvon and Denbigh Herald*, of March 1, signed "A Churchman." "All denominations of dissenters in Wales are degenerating and dwindling fast into infidelity."

The Catholic Bishop, Geiger, in Switzerland, has published a work in defence of celibacy, among the many arguments is also the following:—"Should marriage be content with only *one* wife; and it is, therefore, as well not to give them any at all."

TO CORRESPONDENTS.

G. Anderson.—The address we believe is Miss Roalfe, Galashiels.

R. Cranston.—We shall comply with his request very willingly.

I. Ironside.—His communication respecting the "detention of Mr. Paterson's letters" shall receive immediate attention.

Aliquis.—We have written for the opinions of a party conversant with the subjects about which he questions, in order to form the sounder judgment. This causes a slight delay in giving answer.

Received.—W. C. and enclosures. The case of Mr. Crouch, Chartist lecturer, who has been persecuted in Kidderminster for having stood foremost as the friend of labour and liberal opinions, and not only has he been refused employment by capitalists, but has had the mortification to find that the very men for whose interests he had laboured were ignorant or base enough to aid his enemies. Unfortunately we might enumerate a thousand cases of similar kind, and can only select one now and then, as we do this, as an example of persecution, of which we trust society will soon grow ashamed.

LECTURES.

Mar. 23.—Charlestown Meeting Room, Ashton-under-Lyne, Mr. Southwell,—On Christian precept and Christian practice.

Mar. 23.—National Hall, 242, High Holborn, W. J. Fox,—Commentary on Passing Events. At 8, p.m.

Mar. 23.—Investigation Hall, 29, Circus Street, Marylebone,—Mr. Buchanan,—General Character of Superstition; its immoral and debasing influence on the human mind, the power it exercises in promoting political despotism and social misery.

Erratum.—In the article on Messrs. Gillespie and Southwell, in No. 65, page 87, 2nd column, 11th line from top, for "part" read *path*.

SUBSCRIPTIONS TO THE ANTI-PERSECUTION UNION.

A few working men at Whitehaven, in consequence of Mrs. Martin's arrest......... 0 4 3
Subscriptions of the Leicester branch of the Anti-Persecution Union, for the quarter ending December 31................. 0 10 6

PATERSON TESTIMONIAL.

Thomas Brittain and family...............	0	1	6
Mr. Kendle..............................	0	1	0
Mr. Stockwell...........................	0	1	0
Mr. Moore...............................	0	0	6
From friends of liberty in Dundee — per James Graham—*not* the letter opener.			
John McIntosh...........................	0	1	0
William Nicol...........................	0	1	0
John Kinnear............................	0	1	0
James Myles.............................	0	1	0
Duncan Mill.............................	0	1	0
David McLaren...........................	0	1	0
James Graham............................	0	1	0
A. A. and T. T..........................	0	1	0
H. F. and A. L..........................	0	1	0
W. Ferguson, C. Colville................	0	1	0
G. Mitchell, J. Thomson.................	0	1	0
W. Pirrie, T. Henderson.................	0	1	0
T. Fife, W. Tait, J. Clark..............	0	1	6
Four friends............................	0	1	1

G. J. H., Sec.

Printed and Published by G. J. Holyoake, 40, Holywell-street, Strand.
Wednesday, March 19, 1845.

THE MOVEMENT
And Anti=Persecution Gazette.

"Maximise morals, minimise religion."—BENTHAM.

No. 67.   EDITED BY G. JACOB HOLYOAKE, AND M. Q. RYALL.   Price 1½d

PANTHEISM.

[Having been requested by "Aliquis" to explain what is Pantheism and what is the religion of Emerson, we answer the first question by presenting chapters 5, 6, and 7 of an unpublished Essay on Pantheism, by a young lady who has devoted considerable attention to the subject, and who is capable of communicating her sentiments in elegant language].

THE first thing which strikes us in examining into nature is the perplexing multiplicity of varying facts which offer themselves for our inspection. But the deeper we go, the more clearly we are able to trace the action of *principles*, the more we see how facts are grouped under laws, and different spheres of thought and feeling revolve in eternal harmony ; the more we see that the same laws rule matter and mind, nature and man — gravitation and attraction are as true of one as of the other. The farther we go into nature the more we find that its laws become simpler, and ever simpler, till at last they are all resolvable into LIFE, the eternal miracle which baffles all analysis.* There it is, this life—burning in the stars, growing in vegetation, moving in animals, and in us—thinking, feeling, and uttering. Ever developing, ever widening—it increases each moment in beauty and in power, and spreads a blessing over all in whom it dwells. Is it not self conscious ? Has not that which gives birth to all a parent's love for all ? Can that which causes love and joy to all be itself unconscious of love and joy ? Ah, surely no! Surely the mysterious power in which we at all exist, however fathomless to us, speaks through our hearts in a language which we cannot mistake. Look up to the summer sky of melting blue, thou who doubtest the existence of a loving parent. Does it not bend softly over us as if to clasp the world in a tender embrace? Gaze on the thoughtful beauty in the delicate petals of a flower. Were those lovely contrasts of colour, satisfying so perfectly the desire for the beautiful, the result of unconscious law ? Thine own mind, with all its intricate and deep thought—could this come from that which had *no thought ?* Thine own heart, with all its wild beating hopes and fathomless feelings—could this come from aught but that which felt, even more deeply than thou ?—that "divinity which shapes our ends, rough-hew them how we will"—whose workings are seen in the *progress of humanity independently of the will of humanity*—and who, as the spring leads on the unconscious flowers, leads us on, and ever on, to a destiny unknown. Oh, there are times when all the turmoil of the world seems hushed, and a deep stillness comes over the soul, which, while gazing on the loveliness of nature, or the exalted triumphs of humanity, "can quite forget earth"—then suddenly comes a flash of inspiration over the mind, and it seems as if the mystic veil were lifted from the Isis-Universe—we feel that we understand the life that throbs through nature's veins, and that our life is a part of it—we feel that that which burns in the stars, rustles in the wind, and rolls in the ocean, is the same as that which thinks and feels in us. *Our life is in all*, and we firmly resolve ever to cherish its lightest beatings, ever to be a true member of the great whole. Then we feel, O, how deeply ! that it matters not whether men call this Life, this Soul of the World, Bramah or Jehovah, God or Nature. It is THE HIGHEST, and it is *there*, livingly present in our heart of hearts. Shall we not render it eternal homage ?

But, it may be said, the existence of evil in the world obliges us to deduct either from the omnipotence or the benevolence of the soul of the world—for if he delighted in giving joy he would not give birth to pain. This proposition is founded on the theory that unmixed pleasure is desirable for man. But, I think, a careful study of the subject will show this not to be the case. Pain or difficulty is necessary for the full development of our being. It is only through re-

---

* In all animal and vegetable forms, the physiologist concedes that no chemistry, no mechanics can account for the facts, that a mysterious principle of life must be assumed, which not only inhabits the organ, but makes the organ.—*Emerson's Lecture, "The Method of Nature."*

peated efforts that we obtain the command over our bodily powers—and the same process is necessary for the acquisition of intellectual strength and moral excellence. Through strength and progress alone are the hidden powers of the soul brought to light and nourished into ever increasing beauty. "And this is not the consequence of an arbitrary 'decree of God,' but of the very nature of things."* No "omnipotence" could have ordered it otherwise, except one which could make things be and not be at the same time, a childish conception, which (though not unlike that of the god of supernaturalism) is unworthy of a rational being. Neither, as it seems to me, need "benevolence" wish it otherwise. A world without pain would have been a world without virtue, heroism, or progression; one in which there would have been nothing to do, and consequently one in which it would not have been worth while to exist. Ever from the deepest grief springs the brightest light, and no circlet ever gave forth such radiant lustre as the Crown of Thorns. Yes, there are moments when we feel that the world may do its worst if it will, but that a love and strength burns within us which can conquer the world —can " brave and bear all things for the right and true," and turn earth's tear-cloud to heaven's rainbow. Who that has felt this has felt his truest highest life thus grow and ripen, but will say—Blest be suffering, for in it also dwells the power of the Highest. And though it may be impossible for us to trace all its beneficial effects throughout the world, we can at least grasp the principle and hold it fast. Arise, lovers of humanity! Happiness never yet dropped from the clouds! Up, and let your courage and patience achieve redemption for yourselves and your fellows – and when a happier world than this shall arise from your efforts, O, give thanks to the beautiful soul of the world which brings light out of darkness, and makes *both* work together for nature's deepest beauty and man's highest happiness.

PANTHEISM DEVELOPED.

Not alone in our devotion,
In all being, life, and motion,
We the present Godhead see. *W. J. Fox.*

Faust was right in the main when he said,
Feeling is all names are but sound and smoke,
O'er clouding heaven's glow!

Still names are necessary when we come to *speak* of feelings or thoughts. The belief

---
* Emerson.

which I have just expressed that there is a loving spirit in the fair universe, whom we should ever adore without us, and cherish within us—is usually called *Pantheism* (from *Pan*, all, and *Theos*, God.—God in all). Is this a new faith? Perhaps *in words* it has only been held by a limited number of individuals, but, *in fact*, it has been the faith of all who have thought, felt, or acted deeply and nobly. In so far as they have stood on reality, in so far have they worshipped Divinity *in* nature, and not out of it— in so far they have been Pantheists, worshippers of Him who dwells in all. Were not the old heathens Pantheists, when they knelt to the sun, and adored the stars? It was the marvellous mystic beauty which burned there so brightly that rivetted their eyes, and captivated their hearts. Were not the Christians Pantheists, when after listening to the tales of Christ's majesty and meekness, his heroism and devotedness, they sank down on the knees of the heart, and called him *God ?* Were not the reformers Pantheists, when, scorning the Church's ban, they dared to seek salvation for themselves, and thus rendered glorious homage to the sacred supremacy of the human mind ? Are not infidels Pantheists, when they cast away revelations and gods which rest on false foundations, and fall at the feet of nature? True, there are errors of omission and commission in each and all ; but there where they set their hearts in earnest —where in faith they truly *worship*—there is the Highest visible to them—the one eternal and identical, under whatever form he may appear. And not only in theological speculations—in all the beautiful and true, there is the god of nature, lighting the soul to the perception of beauty, and encouraging it in the march of progression. He is with a young Raphael, when dreams of unearthly loveliness haunt his spirit, and *will* find their way to the canvass; he is with a Columbus, who dares trust his own heart against all the wise and revered of Europe, and will struggle and conquer Atlantic waves till his eyes rest in blessedness on the shores of the New World. He is with a Beethoven, when waves of melody rush over his soul, and the discords of external life are forgotten in the rapturous harmonies that resound in the inner sanctuary. He is with a Clarkson, when the agony of sympathy drives him to action, and one strong pure will redeems a race from bondage. He is with the mother in her holy bliss, and with the child in its innocent delight—with the young girl in her devotedness, or the youth in his developing intellect. And grief is not without his consoling presence. He is with the bereaved in all the desolation of loneliness, and with the deserted in all the agony of blasted happiness—telling the one of eternal reunion and the other of duties that will bring relief. He is with the sufferer, stretched on the bed of sickness, and with the prisoned patriot in his lonely cell—whispering to the one of patience, which takes the sting from agony, and to the other of heroism, that endures all for the right; and murmuring, while tears rush to the sufferers' eyes,

O love! thou makest all things even,
In earth or heaven;
Finding thy way thro' prison-bars
Up to the stars.

Thus, to all earth's differing children does the Highest speak—if not in one language then in another—in joy or grief—in midnight or in sunshine—at all times and in all places—if we will but listen. Thus do all the different voices of nature and humanity join in one glorious harmony of thanksgiving, which, as it arises from all space, and has continued through all time, shall sound on and on for ever, widening and deepening through all eternity.

PRACTICAL PANTHEISM.

A life of resolute good,
Unalterable will, quenchless desire
Of universal happiness, the heart
That beats with it in unison, the brain
Whose ever wakeful wisdom toils to change
Reason's rich stores for its eternal weal.
Shelley's "Queen Mab."

FULLY to realize the fact that there is god in all creation would require omnipresence and omniscience; but to grasp the *principle*, and strive ever towards its realization, this is to be a Pantheist. From this it follows that the true Pantheist will be devoted to the study of reality. His worship will not consist in poring over dusty parchments to know what he ought to think, or in the repetition of old forms till every feeling has evaporated from them—but in the loving study of the grand principles of science, the high musings of philosophy, the wild soarings of poetry, or the beautiful lessons of psychology. Religion will no longer be a thing of the past, to be recalled with difficulty by the aid of tradition or books, but on ever present principle of life, animating all without and within. No longer will the wings of science be clipped that she may not pass the bounds of tradition's garden—but she shall soar to the stars, unfettered, while humanity, with beating heart and sparkling eyes, follows her wondrous flight and listens to her glorious song. No longer shall high philosophy be driven from the dwellings of men with a curse, or "pledged in the cup of hemlock;" but beaming eyes and grateful hearts shall follow her wherever she may go, and "happy lips shall bless *her* name" who unlocked the door of their own minds and showed them what a paradise lay within. And not only in the study of the speculative sciences but in that of social and political science—in all that by teaching men "to dwell together in unity," tends towards the healthy and happy development of their whole being—in all this will the true Pantheist delight. Wherever liberty lifts her banner to kiss the free breezes of heaven, and deliver nations from bondage—wherever patriots conquer or bleed—wherever the principles of true freedom and enlightened government have to be defended by word, deed, or suffering—there will the heart of the true Pantheist be found—there will he promptly contribute his offering of sympathy or of action to the common cause of humanity. And in individual life, too—in all that adorns the fire-side and brightens the lights of the home circle—there will his hand be found—increasing happiness, soothing discomfort, and turning life's little discords, as well as its great ones, into sweet music, by the harmonising and brightening influences that dwell within him. All that is narrow, harsh, or exclusive in thought, word, or deed, he will strive to overcome—in himself even more than elsewhere. Simple and truthful, earnest and joyous—his way cannot be very dark—for though clouds may lower over him, he has a sun within, whose glorious light can turn midnight to noon, and make life's dreariest

Autumn time
Change to summer's happiest prime

Nor will he feel himself cut off from sympathy with his fellow beings because he has discarded those beliefs which they still consider sacred; for he will feel that each heart has its own idolatries, more or less one-sided—and that under different names all adore pretty much the same things. And while he must lament that others should mix so much dross with their adorations, as they now do, his attempt to purify them will be kept in wholesome check by the recollection that perfect objective truth is unattainable to mortals, and that the difference between the ignorant and the wise is, after all, only one of *degree*, and not of *kind*—and that on such a subject as this it peculiarly becomes us to be humble, and ever ready to receive new light, from whatever source it may come. He will feel true brotherhood with all, of whatever creed, who with pure and earnest souls, worked out what they believed to be right and good—and he will see that in so far as they were true, was the Soul of the world with them, blessing their work. And if those who do not understand him, cry out against him, and abuse him for want of religion, then he will practically demonstrate the contrary by simple truthfulness, and brave, sweet patience, that, conquering its own suffering, grieves most that others should be so hard of heart and blind of sight as to strike the innocent, and yet forgets even this grief in the trust that new light will spring out of the darkness, and that all the harsh and heart-breaking discords of time are but the preparation of those heavenly harmonies which shall embrace all hearts in their lovely dominion.

S. D. C.

[The writer of the preceding paper has taken the idea of Pantheism from general acceptation and worked it out individually. Comparatively it is little disparagement to say that however pleasing the ideas presented, and ingenious the illustrations, there is about the paper in question a certain indescribable vagueness which probably belongs to the subject, as every author, of whatever talent, exhibits it more or less. Good judges are of opinion that Shelley has described Pantheism in his "Queen Mab," at the conclusion of the 6th and beginning of the 7th cantos, but it would be hard for one not initiated in the mysteries of Pantheism to point out the particular passages. W. J. B. once engaged Dr. L— to enlighten the world on this *ism*. The doctor called it the "science of all goddedness," and "the doctrine of the unity and universality of the existing existence." His article can be found in No. 88 of the *Oracle of Reason*—it has been a conundrum from the day of its appearance. According to Böhme, quoted by Mr. Southwell in *Movement* 53, "heaven and earth, the stars and elements, and all that is above all heavens constitute the whole god." To which Mr. S. rejoins—such a "whole god" is exactly an Atheist's *whole matter*, and Pantheism amounts to Atheism. So far it does, but this is not all, there is that which comes after in connection with Pantheism which makes all the difference and all the mystery. The Atheist establishes the existence of matter to the exclusion of the idea of God, and there rests, and leaves morality and reason free course in the world, untramelled by the dogmas of goddism. But the Pantheist has no sooner admitted the whole of matter to be the whole existence than he commences the work of bewilderment, and calls it god. He invests nature with consciousness, worships it, and deduces somehow or other the expectation of immortality. Indeed Pantheism is religion without a bible. It worships God without having a god—or in other words, worships it under the name of nature. This is the source of its mysteries and vagueness. "Pantheism," treated to my satisfaction, would separate itself entirely from Atheism, and develop its own peculiar nature—or if this cannot be done I should like to see it clearly laid down how far Atheism and Pantheism originate and travel together—the point distinctly marked where they separate—where Atheism stop, and the road delineated which Pantheism takes after parting from its companion.—G. J. H.]

BAILEY'S ARGUMENT AGAINST MIRACLES.

THE most concise and conclusive argument against miracles is the comparatively little-known one by Samuel Bailey, in his ingenious essay on the "Fundamental Principles of all Evidence and Expectation." If indeed some consider the basis of Bailey's argument to be the same as Hume's all will allow, at all conversant with his Essay, that it is founded on a strikingly original view supported with ingenuity, and explained with that lucidity by which he is distinguished above all metaphysical writers.

Previously to placing his reasonings before the reader, I wish to advert to a novel performance on the other side of the question, lately announced with no little pomposity.

The *Newry Telegraph* recently said, " we refer our readers to a most interesting letter, on the Scripture Evidence of Miracles from the pen of J. R. Young the learned Professor of Mathematics in the Royal Belfast Institution. We earnestly recommend its attentive perusal to Christians of every class, but, more espicially, to those whose every day occupations lead them much into communication with those who question the truth of those early evidences of the Christian religion. The subject is one of very great moment, and we cannot but feel gratified that we have it in our power to present to our readers so valuable a tribute to the truth of our holy religion as Mr. Y's communication. The learned professor's reputation, high as it stood before, will be much increased by its publication."

Again we are told, that "Hume's argument against the probability of Miracles has regularly "bothered" the first philosophers of the age. We have read various answers to it, and not one of them is conclusive; but Professor Young, of the Belfast College, has, in our paper of this day, given a mathematical demonstration of the problem which appears to set the difficulty at rest."

Thus various portions of the Irish press have landed this new born effort in support of a dogma, which, if I mistake not, Mr. Bailey has, "set at rest for ever."

But first let us hear J. R. Young. The Professor of the Royal Belfast Institution argues that, "The position which Hume labours to establish is in substance this, viz. :—That no amount of human testimony, in favour of the performance of a miracle, can ever render its occurrence so highly *probable*, as the uniform experience of mankind, a violation of " the laws of nature," renders it *improbable*. And the object of preceding writers has always been to show in contravention of this doctrine, that a comparatively limited number of witnesses of ordinary veracity, and without collusion, bearing concurrent testimony to the event, are sufficient to render the probability in favour of its occurence, far greater than the *a priori* probability against it, as inferred from the uniform experience of all mankind. It is the principal object of this communication, by presenting the matter in a light somewhat different from that in which it has hitherto been viewed, to show that the above mentioned condition, as to the veracity of the witnesses, may be altogether dispensed with; and that if these witnesses, without collusion, come voluntary forward to affirm the occurrence of a miracle, and all testify to the *same* miracle, the simple fact of this concurrence in their testimony—if they be at all numerous—will give a probability to the truth of their statement which is altogether irresistible, *however abandoned the character of the witnesses may be.*

The Professor continues " Let us then concede that the witnesses were altogether unworthy of the slightest confidence - that one comes forward, bent upon deception, and affirms that he is eye-witness to the performance of a miracle—the raising of a dead man to live, for instance : and let ten other persons, with the same disposition to deceive, but without collusion, testify to the same thing. Now, let us assume that these ten persons were limited within the very narrow range of only ten fabrications suitable to their purposes of fraud, the probability that they would all fix upon the particular miracle mentioned is the tenth power of 1-10; that is, it is one to one hundred millions. If instead of *ten* other persons, there were *twelve*, the probability would be one to one million millions; that is, the *odds* against the occurrence of this supposed uniformity of testimony is within a unit of a *million millions* to *one*. Now supposing, according to Mr. Babbage and Laplace, that the origin of the human race was about 6,000 years ago, and that 30 years is the average duration of a generation, 200 generations must have passed away ; and allowing that the average population of the earth has been a thousand millions, we find that there have lived and died, since the creation, about two hundred thousand millions of individuals. The experience of all these, in favour of the non-occurrence of a miracle, is therefore *two hundred thousand millions to one.* We have seen above, that if only thirteen individuals bear indipendent testimony to the fact—even supposing that they have only ten other events to choose from—the probability that that fact is *not* a fabrication is a *million millions to one* —a probability far surpassing the former; and it will be observed that this result is wholly independent of the character of the witnesses either as to honesty or intellect."

The world is to be favoured with the mathematical details, whence these conclusions are deduced in an Essay on Probabilities, already it is said in the press. But in the absence of the learned Professor's work, it cannot fail to strike the reader as a monstrous conclusion; that the uniform experience of the *two hundred thousand millions* of individuals, assumed to have lived upon the earth; of the uniform operation of natures laws, is to go for nothing, and to be utterley set aside by the testimony of *thirteen* "abandoned and lying men." Now let us hear Mr. Bailey, and we shall be able to judge what degree of credence can be due to any pretended mathematical or other demonstration of the probability of miracles, when as Mr. Bailey shews no man can believe in such events, without utterly contradicting every principle upon which he believes anything.

The fundamental principle from which Mr. Bailey starts in his reasoning, is the " uniformity of causation." " Man," he remarks, " is placed on the narrow isthmus of the present time, between the two oceans of the past and the future, and the uniformity of causation is the principle by which he sends his glances over both."

There is so much philosophical value in this grand principle of all evidence and expectation, that to introduce it briefly will be to enrich our pages with one of the choicest speculations of modern times, and gratify those of our readers not familiar with it.

"Amongst the primary truths which are necessarily assumed, or taken for granted, one of the most important is the uniformity of causation. In all our anticipations of events, in all cases of applying to the future our experience of the past, we unavoidably assume the fundamental principle that every cause will continue to produce the effect by which we have hitherto found it attended. A very short explanation will be sufficient to make this perfectly clear.

"When I throw a piece of paper into the fire, it is obvious that I do it under the expectation that the paper will be consumed. But *why* do I form this expectation? Because I have found by experience that fire has the property of consuming paper. This is a reason which would be perfectly satisfactory to every mind in actual life: the metaphysician, however, although perfectly satisfied with the validity of the answer, still asks why, because you have found in your past experience that fire has consumed paper, do you conclude that it will now exhibit the same destructive qualities? By what logical process do you infer that the same cause [has produced, or] will continue to produce the same effect? Show me the steps of your reasoning.

"All the reply that can be given to this demand is what philosophers have already given. It is, that I *assume* or expect that fire will destroy paper as it has hitherto done, without any process of reasoning, any deduction from any other principle, I naturally and irresistibly take it for granted. You yourself continually act on a similar assumption; for in putting your questions to me or any other person, you take for granted, you assume without thinking of it, that your words will reach the ears of him for whom they were intended, and excite ideas in his mind, as you have found them to do in time past. In placing your foot on the ground, in taking up your pen, or in eating your breakfast, you still expect that the objects around you, the subjects of your operations, will retain their usual properties —that the earth will not open a gulph beneath your feet, that the pen will not melt in your grasp, and the food which has hitherto nourished you will not turn to poison on your stomach. In a word, from the same causes you and every other human being necessarily anticipate the same effects. This uniformity is the essential principle of all expectation."

Having thus briefly explained, in Mr. Bailey's words, his views of the uniformity of causation, we can now understand his application of it to testimony. His language follows.

"Suppose, for instance, any person to affirm that he had exposed a cubic inch of ice to a temperature of 200 degrees of Fahrenheit, and that at the expiration of an hour it had retained its solidity. Here is a sequence of events asserted which is entirely at variance with the admitted course of nature, and the slightest reflection is sufficient to show that to believe the assertion would involve a logical absurdity. *The intrinsic discrepancy of the facts could never be overcome by any plausible proof of the truth of the testimony.*

"For let us put the strongest case imaginable: let us suppose that the circumstance of the ice remaining unmelted, rests on the concurrent testimony of a great number of people [not persons of abandoned characters, as Professor Young supposes but] people of science and perspicacity, who had no motive for falsehood, who had discernment to perceive and honesty to tell the real truth, and whose interests would essentially suffer from any departure from veracity. Under such circumstances, false testimony, it may be alleged, is impossible.

Now, mark the principle on which this representation proceeds. Let us concede the positions, that what is attested by a great number of witnesses must inevitably be true, that people of reputation and intelligence, without any apparent motive for falsehood are invariably accurate in their testimony,—and that they are, above all, incapable of violating truth, when a want of veracity would be ruinous to their interests. Granting all this, I ask the objector, how he knows that these things are so; that men of this character, and in these circumstances speak truth? He will reply, that he has invariably found them so to act in this manner; but why, because you have found them to act thus in a few or even in many cases, within your own experience, or in the experience of ages, do you conclude that they have acted so in all cases and in the case before us? The only answer is, that it is impossible not to take for granted, that in precisely similar circumstances similar results will ensue, or that like causes have always like effects.

"*Thus, on the ground of the uniformity of causation, he would be maintaining the competency of testimony to prove a fact which implies a deviation from that uniformity.*

"These considerations appear to establish the important rule that *no testimony* can prove any deviation from the known sequences of cause and effect, or that at any time similar effects have not had similar causes, or—*vice versa.*

"In the strongest conceivable case, the argument of an advocate for the power of testimony to prove such deviations would be this : 'It is impossible that human testimony should not be true in these circumstances, because its falsity would be contrary to the principles of human nature; that is, it would imply a deviation from that sequence of motives and voluntary actions which has invariably observed.'

"But—Mr. Bailey replies on precisely the same ground he ought to maintain that the circumstances attested could not take place, because they are contrary to the laws of the material world, unless it can be shown that the certainty or uniformity of causation in voluntary actions is greater than in physical events.

"The rule now laid down, is in fact that by which mankind are universally, though perhaps not consciously nor uniformly, guided. Let us take another case as an illustration. If a number of men were to swear that they had seen the mercury of a barometer remain at the height of 30 inches when placed in the exhausted receiver of an air-pump, their testimony would be instantly rejected. The universal conclusion would be that such an event was impossible. To justify the rejection of the evidence it would not be necessary to account for the origin of so extraordinary a statement, or to trace the concatenation of motives in the minds of those who asserted its truth. The motives of the witnesses might be quite inconceivable, there might be no apparent advantage to any of them in hazarding a falsehood; on the contrary their rank in life, their reputation, their habits of integrity, the disgraceful consequences of detection, might appear irresistible disuasives from a course of deceit. But although these circumstances might concur to render their veracity probable, no man of science would listen to their evidence. People might be perplexed to account for their conduct, but all would agree as to the *credit* due to their statements.

It may be asked, why reject the testimony rather than admit the fact, when the former equally implies a deviation from the uniform sequence of causes and effects; if the circumstances of the witnesses are such as always give use to true testimony, then to consider their evidence as false is to admit that the same causes do not always produce the same effects.

"The answer to this objection is not difficult -should any man affirm himself to have been an eye-witness of any event, contrary to the usual succession of causes and effects, such as those above adduced, I might consistently reply to him in the following terms; I have no ground whatever for believing what you say. You assert that an event has taken place quite at variance with the observed course of nature, I may account for what I hear by supposing that your senses have deceived you, or that your tongue utters words which you do not intend, or that my ears have acquired the property of changing the sounds transmitted to them; or any other mutation which it is possible to conceive. Without this principle should be abandoned to the utmost licence of conjecture and scepticism, nor could I possibly have any reason for supposing one of these events to have taken place rather than another, because every reason that could be assigned would necessarily imply the principle which I had discarded."

There is no occasion to multiply quotations farther. Obviously, Mr. Bailey utterly demolishes all that Professor Young *can possibly* rear up in favour of testimony. Mr. Bailey in his Essay makes no allusion to the miracles of Christ, but the application of his reasonings to the apostles and thier statements is so plain as to require no illustration.   G. J. H.

ON GOVERNMENT.

National prosperity is really, in all cases, the result of the principles of human nature operating in each individual in his private career, and the mistake of ascribing it to any other source has evidently arisen from the power of governments to *mar* what they cannot *make*. In the province of doing evil they are indeed almost omnipotent. There is no limit but the insurgent spirit of outraged humanity to their power of preventing happiness and inflicting misery ; and this power has been amply exercised, both by despotic selfishness, and mischievous, because ignorant, benevolence. By almost all the governments which have yet existed, this tremendous capacity for inflicting evil has been largely exhibited. It is no exaggeration to say, that the prevention of attainable enjoyments, and the creation of positive wretchedness, have been their common, systematic course; and when in any country a departure from this course has taken place, when there has been a cessation of activity in creating evil, a withdrawal of the interference of authority with the sources of individual happiness, an abstinence from mischievous meddling,—the good effects which have resulted, the industry, the enterprise, the wealth, the civilization, the spirit of inquiry, the intelligence, the morality, which have almost immediately sprung up, have been placed to the credit of the supreme power of the state; when in fact the whole merit of government consisted, not in the active production of these good fruits, but in the wisdom of giving the principles of human nature fairer play and further room for development. "Mr. Grenville (says Burke) thought better of the wisdom and power of human legislation than in truth it deserves. He conceived, and many conceived along with him, that the flourishing trade of this country was greatly owing to law and institution, and not quite so much to liberty; for but too many are apt to believe regulation to be commerce, and taxes to be revenue.*"

The delusion respecting the wisdom and power of human legislation is not yet dissipated: there are still too many from whom the truth is hid, that the great fountains of the prosperity and happiness of nations must ever be the principles of human nature, spontaneously guiding the actions of individuals to their own and the general good; and that the most which the supreme authority can beneficially do, is to remove obstructions and to regulate the conflicting play of these principles, when they do not adequately supply their own checks.

Although, on a superficial glance, the representation which has been here given may appear to lessen the importance of government, yet in reality it does not: it tends only to prevent our looking for that importance in the wrong place. An institution must be of immense consequence (even supposing it to be capable of creating a particle of positive good), so long as it has the power both of *preventing* great evils and *inflicting* great evils. The poetical author of the "Traveller" in the celebrated passage on this subject, which every reader's recollection will immediately present to him—

In every government though terrors reign,
Though tyrant kings or tyrant laws restrain,
How small of all that human hearts endure
That part which laws or kings can cause or cure!

was wrong in under-rating the influence of government on private happiness, because he took only a half view;—because he overlooked the difference in intensity between its power of doing good, and its capability of inflicting injury. Kings may be able to cure few ills, except what they themselves have occasioned, and not always those; but it is not true that they are able to cause but few. Their power of affecting human hearts with misery transcends even the imagination of a poet.—*Rationale of Political Representation.*

---

*Speech on American Taxation.

Under the Superintendence of the Anti-Persecution Union.

PATERSON WELCOME!

A SOIREE
OF THE FRIENDS OF
MR. THOMAS PATERSON
Will be held at the Hall of Science, City Road, seven doors from Featherstone-street, on Sunday, April 6, 1845, for the purpose of presenting him with the amount publicly subscribed as a testimony of respect and approval for his eminent services in the cause of free expression of opinion; and sympathy on account of his fifteen months' Imprisonment in Perth Gaol.

MR. H. HETHERINGTON IN THE CHAIR.

Sentiments will be spoken to by English and foreign advocates of Religious Liberty; interspersed with Songs, &c.

Tea on table at half-past four for five.

TICKETS, ONE SHILLING EACH,
Including Refreshments, may be had of Mr. Holyoake, 11, Woburn Buildings, Tavistock Square; Mr. Hetherington, 40, Holywell-street, Strand; Mr. Watson, 5, Paul's Alley, Paternoster Row; Mr. Stewart, 23, John-street, Tottenham Court Road; at the Social Institution, 5, Charlotte-street, Blackfriars Road; at the Social Institution, High-street, Whitechapel; at the Social Institution, Goswell Road; at the Hall of Science, City Road; and of the members of the Committee.

In consequence of the proverbial disappointment of persons at Tea Parties the Stewards have issued only 300 Tickets, that being the number of persons that can be accommodated with convenience and comfort. On no account will a second set be admitted to table.

The Friends of the Union will be admitted at seven o'clock—Admission 3d.

J. B. LEAR, WM. COOPER, Stewards.

DETENTION OF MR. PATERSON'S LETTERS.—Mr. Isaac Ironside, of Sheffield, suggests that a petition from the authors of the letters detained from Mr. Paterson, during his recent imprisonment, should be placed in the care of T. S. Duncombe for presentation. He thinks it should be brief, firm, not humiliating—yet respectful, and should set forth: The offence, conviction and imprisonment: the petitioners deeming the punishment a disgrace to the age, corresponded with Paterson, to lighten the rigours of his confinement, and was surprised to learn that the same had been detained. Enumerate the letters detained, and urge the appointment of a committee to inquire into the matter.

TO CORRESPONDENTS.

J. GRAHAM.—Mr. Paterson was born at a village near New Lanark.

W. C. MEIKLE sends a "Purgative for Puseyism," consisting of extracts from a satirical poem, resembling that famous one by the *Yahoo.* Its insertion is declined, as our readers are already familiar with the poem just mentioned, it would present no new features.

W. B.—The Judge willingly granted a writ of certiorari, and the case against the Hull magistrates will be tried next term. This is the reason why the Union are so anxious about funds.

LECTURES.

Mar. 30.—National Hall, 242, High Holborn, W. J. Fox,—'The Political Influence of the Church Establishment. At 8, P.M.

Printed and Published by G. J. HOLYOAKE, 40, Holywell-street, Strand.
Wednesday, March 25, 1845.

THE MOVEMENT
And Anti-Persecution Gazette.

"Maximise morals, minimise religion."—BENTHAM.

No. 68.   EDITED BY G. JACOB HOLYOAKE, AND M. Q. RYALL.   Price 2d.

THE LAST OF THE MOVEMENTS.
FAREWELL ADDRESS OF MR. HOLYOAKE.

The pecuniary state of the *Movement* being the chief cause of its cessation, and that department having always been in my hands, it devolves on me to explain it. In doing this I shall adhere to my usual custom and state the case with frankness—it being of no consequence to me what is thought, provided one is not thought to deceive. The monetary facts which follow can be verified by reference to my cash books which any person interested may examine.

This year commenced, as those who have seen the Balance Sheet in No. 56, are aware, with a debt of £7 17s. 4d. due to me as treasurer of the *Movement*. Since the commencement of the second volume, of which fourteen numbers are now issued, the weekly sale has failed to return the weekly outlay, exclusive of the expense of management. This deficiency was unwittingly augmented by an expenditure for neat window cards and bills, to increase the publicity of the paper—and by printing, for some weeks, 250 extra for distribution to the press, which we knew would be useful if not productive, and if they did not increase our means would diffuse our principles. Twenty-four Volumes have been bound, and some of them presented to editors and public societies. In other ways well calculated measures were taken to increase the circulation, but as up to this period they have not had time to take effect, the measures taken prove money lost.

To meet these expenses, the only returns beyond the deficient ones from the publisher, have been the half-yearly subscriptions of R. R. and M. C. R , £1. from Cosmopolite, the 2s. 6d. per week, for printing, from the Union, and a few other minor subscriptions. The result is that on balancing my accounts, I find that I have £25. 4s. to pay and nothing to receive, save what the stock may fetch at the trunkmaker's. Consequently, as such a liability greatly exceeds my present means of meeting it, the *Movement* must cease.

It will be asked what was I doing to allow it to come to this. I had little or no suspicion of it till lately. The first month of the year I was in Leicester and since my return, now nine weeks, I have been too ill to attend to anything—without power to scrutinize accounts, and most of the time without hope of life.

In giving up the *Movement* I have come to a hard resolution. Probably no sense of personal danger would have wrung it from me. But to be pursued by debt and death at the same time is an exigency for which I was never prepared—to cease to live can be but a transient event, but to leave claims unsatisfied may be an enduring disgrace.

The present aspect of the *Movement's* affairs, will, no doubt, do with us as similar ones have done before, incite to new exertions which will be undertaken with better educated energies. Some persons will think it is due to subscribers that an effort be made to continue the *Movement* at least till half the volume is completed. To this I should not be averse did I not regard it as a higher duty to devote my spare time and spare means to the liquidation of the liabilities already incurred. It cannot be that subscribers to the *Movement* would consent to be obliged at the expense of creditors.

The *Movement* would have ceased some weeks ago had I been aware of the precise state of its affairs, as I have an unconquerable aversion to debt. I believe that no success achieved by a popular cause, ever compensated for the disgrace resulting—if debts were contracted for its support. If this conviction had not grown up with me, it would be created by the baleful spirit of reaction which I have witnessed Chartist, Socialist, and Atheistical teachers spread around them, by neglect or indifference of pecuniary obligations. Moralists are not wrong in regarding honour in small transactions as the true disipline which insures probity in greater ones. But few have the courage to believe that the only sure basis of confidence lies in the "continuity of little duties well fulfilled"—and are content to seek the admiration of mankind without a foundation laid in their esteem.

Those who are of opinion that a paper ought not to exist unless it pays all its expenses, will conclude that discretion has been wanting in continuing the *Movement*, but upon the propriety of this, before commencing, a sage, judicious and eminent adviser of the people, was consulted. His answer was, " Money is wisely expended in enlightening mankind. Most incipient causes require assistance, and most causes must be well supported before they can lay hold on public attention and become self-supporting."

It is not greatly discouraging that the sale of the *Movement* has been too limited to meet its own expenses. We are assured by the *Printing Machine*, that the *Spectator*, of classical fame, never exceeded 3000; and that the *Rambler*, edited by the Author of Rasselas, never had a circulation of 1500; and without the elegance of Addison, or the power of Johnson, and with sentiments to advocate immeasurably more unpopular now than theirs then, the wonder is that our atheistical organ has so far succeeded so well.

The straitened condition of *Movement* matters here confessed, is no indication of the decline of Atheism, as it has resulted in accident rather than in real apathy. Was my health sufficiently well established, or M. Q. R. less engaged with business, as to enable us to make personal applications, such assistance could be procured as would render the difficulties which now prove fatal, of transient duration. Perhaps the friends of the *Movement* ought to have been vigilant and *secured* its success, and not have needed the formality of special visits - but if otherwise, it is a mortifying reflection that a publication which (including the existence of its predecessor, the *Oracle*) has defied, during three years and half, the efforts of the Attorney-General, and those of the combined bigots of England and Scotland, to suppress it, should at last be put down by the temporary neglect of its friends. A circumstance from which we learn how impotent is power when unjustly exercised and resolutely opposed, and how fatal is supineness in those who struggle for right against might.

What I have said is not to be taken as the language of reproach, nor is the preceding reflection to be understood as of general application. I take the leave of my *Movement* acquaintances, which circumstances force upon me, with the recollection of a thousand kindnesses I never experienced before. When released from Gloucester Gaol, I owed my unbroken health to the generosity of those who participated in my sentiments—and a second time I owe my life to my atheistical friends. Possessing no means but those my weekly exertions procured me, when my health fell off, my resources fell off, and I was in as much danger of perishing from inanition as from disease. From this end I was saved, and my family supported by the unsolicited, and delicate munificence of W. J. B., Aliquis, Mr. Watts, and several other valued friends. It is quite contrary to the wishes of these friends that I thus allude to this circumstance, but I do it in answer to such persons as the Rev. J. Cooper, Chaplain of Gloucester Gaol, and other christians who have taken special trouble to assure me that my atheistical friends would only be the friends of prosperity—and I do it further because on the kindness in question I had no claim. If I choosed to play the part of a reformer, it was my own choice, and its dangers or difficulties concerned nobody but myself. When from these, therefore, I am generously relieved, I am anxious to make a requital, but being precluded from that it is some satisfaction to express one's gratitude.

During the short time we may be without an organ efforts will be made to disparage our exertions, but our past history as spread over the pages of the *Oracle* and *Movement* is no fiction, and our efforts no failure. I speak of Southwell, M. Q. R., W. J. B., Chilton, Paterson, Mr. and Mrs. Adams, M. Roalfe, and Finlay—of all who have contributed literarily or pecuniarily to these papers, or suffered for their publication. The currency given to Atheism, and the support rendered to the Anti-Persecution Union, are subjects for a thousand congratulations. We have given irreligion a new character, and redeemed infidelity from the everlasting taunt of the priest—that it is " wily and cowardly, and shrinks from acknowledging itself." In periodicals and lectures, in courts of law, in conventional England and sanctimonious Scotland the voice of undisguised Atheism has been heard. We have held no terms with hypocrisy. We may often have been wrong but we have always been plain. We have neither mined nor sapped prejudices, and it is our glory to have lived without charity and without deceit.

Once the waters of Socialism ran through the land in refreshing and fertilizing streams, but at last settled into a respectable and stagnant pool, giving forth only the unhealthy effluvia of conventionality, jesuitry, and religion. To stir and sweeten this water, and to open the sluices again which carried its streams by the poor man's cottage, has been with us an earnest work. At the basis of rationalism lies solid truth, which fully displayed is capable of refining morality and extirpating religion. To demonstrating this we addressed ourselves, and not in vain. The general sentiment has been elevated, and we have impressed a large majority of communists with the sentiments of Samuel Bailey, that "There is a growing disposition in the world, amongst the intelligent part of it at least, to prize truth, to look with disdain on all artifice, disingenuity, and disguise—to regard the business of life no longer as an affair which demands unremitted intrigue and perpetual deceit—to consider the great interests of humanity as not requiring to be supported by ignorance and superstition—to believe that suppression and concealment can be of no service, except for the few at the expense of the many, and that every important question should be freely and boldly examined."

The most important consideration connected with the cessation of the *Movement* is the welfare of the Anti-Persecution Union, which is now left without an organ. To remedy this evil the Committee of the Union have adopted a suggestion made by W. J. B., and determined to issue a MONTHLY CIRCULAR, to be edited by myself—to be of four pages the size of the *Movement*—to be published at a penny—the entire cost of 500, including all expenses, not to exceed £2. The difference, if the sale fails to cover the expenses, to be defrayed by the Union. The *Circular* will relate purely to Anti-Persecution Union matters, will acknowledge all subscriptions, register the presentation of petitions, place before the public the cases of all victims of blasphemy laws, and it is trusted will never cease to exist till every law in England and Scotland is repealed which affects the free expression of theological opinions. By this means the Union will seek to preserve its individuality more effectively than hitherto, and to correspond as usual with its members, its friends, and the public. The action now pending against the Hull Magistrates and other important cases demand immediate support. The office of the *Circular* will be at the office of the Union, 5, Paul's Alley, Paternoster Row, London, to which place all communications and subscriptions are to be addressed, to G. J. Holyoake, Secretary. The first number of the *Circular* will be issued on the 1st of May.

The *Atheon*, of which prospectuses were some time since issued, will not be further proceeded with until my return to town, from which I am about to be absent. Consequently the subscriptions offered will not be applied for, and the donations sent will be returned.

I have accepted an engagement as Lecturer to the Glasgow Branch for twelve months to which I proceed at the end of next May. As Mr. Jeffery is returning to England, being engaged by the Manchester branch, and Mrs. Martin is expected to leave to propagandize in our provinces, unless there are new importations, I shall have Scotland to myself. Besides the pleasure I anticipate in visiting my Scotch friends whom I have never seen, I am anxious to do something towards settling certain accounts, which the Procurator Fiscal and Authorities of Perth and Arbroath have contracted with the friends of anti-religious liberty.

It only remains to add that all subscribers to the *Movement*, who have paid in advance, will have returned to them the proportion of their remittances due. For the liability of the *Movement* which I have explained, M. Q. R. holds himself, with me, jointly answerable, but as he has already pressing upon him heavy responsibilities arising out of the *Oracle* and Holywell Street prosecutions he ought not to be charged with new ones. Some friends have expressed an intention of considering the liability of the *Movement* as a species of atheistical debt, therefore any subscriptions received in liquidation of it (they can be addressed to me at 5 Pauls Alley Paternoster Row) will be acknowledged in the *Monthly Circular*, the *National Reformer*, or the *New Moral World*.

G. JACOB HOLYOAKE.

As an addendum to the preceding, in which I concur, I have to request that all our friends will, at their earliest convenience, send their names and addresses to our office, openly or confidentially as they please. It will afford great facilities if it becomes desirable for us to be put in communication with them again.

M. QUESTELL RYALL.

PERSONALITIES.

PERSONAL reproach is more or less offensive to all sorts of public men, but to none so eminently obnoxious as that section of them who pass for philosophical liberals. No less affrighted are *they* at the merest shadow of censure than was conscience-stricken Macbeth when confronted by the ghost of Banquo—he exclaims, "Take any form but that and my firm nerves shall never tremble." Soloman believed open rebuke better than secret love; whereas philosophical liberals seem decidedly of opinion that of the two even hate, if kept snug, is a less evil than rebuke, if openly administered. They dislike excessively to be found fault with, but to being extolled they have no objection. Far from disliking praise their apetite for it is positively insatiable. They lick up flattery, however gross and filthy, with as keen a relish as hungry dogs proverbially do dirty pudding. Some of them hurried away no doubt by their active "love of approbation," play the well known game of *fishing for compliments*, with a self complacent stupidity which reminds one of the modern fable, according to which that renowned ass immortalised by Esop, met him and said— When you again write a history of me, let me speak something witty and wise—You speak something witty and wise, cried Esop in amazement—why if I were to do so people would think you the moralist and I the ass. In justice, however, to this ass, I am bound to declare our philosophically liberal fishers for compliments rather less witty and wise than he, inasmuch as to vanity quite a match for his, they exhibit inconsistency most pitiable. What inconsistency can be grosser than that of men who though "opposed on principle" to the language of praise and blame, which they call "the language of insanity," when such language is applied to themselves quarrel only with the "blame" portion of it. Esop's ass is not fairly chargeable with folly so preposterous as this, but philosophical liberals are; for the praise which *in theory* they repudiate, *in practice* they embrace. No reformers among my pretty large troop of acquaintances sit more "attentive to their own applause," none more uneasily to hear their own condemnation. Openly rebuked for selling a cause or betraying a principle, they are to the full as wrathful, if not quite so rash, as that Duke of Argyle, who declared in the House of Lords, on occasion of some of Pope's "personalities,"—If any man dared to use his name in an invective he would run him through the body—

Be to their faults *entirely* blind,
Be to their virtues very kind,

praise their "talent"—extol their "disinterestedness"—shed tears of sympathy at bare remembrance of the many "sacrifices" they have offered up on the altar of public good, and you may reckon, not only upon their "sincere and heartfelt thanks," but return most gratifying of "such kind though unmerited praise" the very first convenient opportunity. No dealer in personalities *of this kind* need fear being snubbed by philosophical liberals, or accused by their admirers of any desire "to excite angry feelings." An orator may be stupid as the ass just referred to—the stream of his eloquence may be troubled as the waters of a huge cataract. No matter if he do manage to sputter on behalf of some popular partisans the language of servile adulation, ladies with white kerchiefs will call him "a duck of a man," and thundering plaudits from the other sex will leave no room to doubt the profundity of *their* satisfaction.

Quite different is the treatment usually experienced by those who detesting flattery, scorn to flatter; who see no reason for exposing or combating heresies of *aggregate opinion*, which is not equally a reason for laying bare heresies of *individual action*; and who so far as practicable act up to the intelligible and most useful truth, *that though all things are not persons, all persons are things, and should be dealt with accordingly*.

Political delinquents in general, and philosophical liberals in particular, have no fancy for such action. Its actor may be the perfection of gentility and pink of politeness; he may possess purity of intention, combined with great abilities; nay, all the talents in union with "all the virtues under heaven," and yet if he expose the faults of these men, if he dispraise as well as praise them, they will neither love nor forgive him, but heap upon his "mischief-making" head the most unpleasant imputations. Praise and you please, but to please, and at the same time dispraise them is impossible. Punch can be allowed for the rare power of being offensively personal without giving personal offence, a faculty described by Persius in one of his predecessors:

When Horace every foible touched with art,
His smiling friend received him to his heart;
Pleased with the tickling probe, nor felt it smart,
The testy people too could patient stand
While wip'd their follies by his skilful hand.

I am nevertheless "fast wedded" to the opinion that if a greater than Horace were to try the experiment of "wiping out" the "follies" of philosophical liberals with his "skilful hand," he would find them far from "pleased" or willing to "patient stand" under his inflictions. And if as some think, it is a sure sign of the failure of people's faculties when they grow angry at any invective or raillery levelled at their defects, without doubt, the faculties of philosophical liberals are far on the road to a "galloping consumption"—for they, as already intimated, show *very* ill humour when personally *castigated*. Let the castigation be ever so gentle, or ever so well merited, it seldom fails to put them in a "towering passion." Their exquisite sensibility, under circumstances so distressing, reminds one of the naval surgeon, mentioned by Byron, who being under the disagreeable necessity of wearing a wig could by no means relish the frequent jests of his brother officers, allusive to so delicate an appendage, and when in the course of a merry conversation one of them said—Suppose now doctor I should take off your *hat*.—Sir, replied he, I shall talk no longer with you—you grow *scurrilous*.

But though thus ridiculously fearful of unflattering personalities — though when self reputation is in danger, like the poor doctor when his *wig* was in danger, they are alarmed, and say to the tormentor—Sir, I shall talk no longer with you—you grow *scurrilous*. These philosophical liberals are not at all backward in the work of dealing out open rebuke to others. Few are better skilled in this department of human action. To "damn with faint praise" they have the "knack" almost in perfection. They sneer down character in a *style* that Gibbon might have envied. If afraid to assault an opponent *openly* they set about it *covertly*. Lamb like sometimes, they are furious as wolves at others, probably in imitation of Jesus Christ, who, on one page of the gospel is described as preaching up no personality—nonsense—while on the other he is exhibited to us railing at Pharisees and every mothers' son who opposed him with all the virulent bitterness of an exasperated modern fishfag.

What I greatly fear is that these philosophical liberals will succeed in bringing the virtues into contempt by their vicious advocacy of them. Their everlasting talk, for instance, about charitableness, has a direct tendency to lower men's estimate of it. Not long since the editor of this periodical announced himself "sick of charity." So am I most heartily of that spurious charity, under cover of which apostles of mischief perpetrate with impunity their shocking crimes. No philanthropist can desire to see his fellow beings less charitably honest and honestly charitable than they are, but to the enlightened lover of his kind the cant of charity is odious, and charity itself, however pure and disinterested, *at best a secondary, at worst a beggarly virtue*. Did justice preside over human affairs there would be no need of charitable works, and as to charitable speeches they never should be made at the expense of truth. To charity when hand in hand with justice there can be no reasonable objection—on the contrary, we cannot too much admire and applaud it. Only fanatics, who, like Hortensius, crawl about "In hopes of gaining heaven by making earth a hell" can suppose one world would be the worse if its "unfeathered bipeds" were more free, generous, and loving than we usually find them. But, let us not in our ignorant haste to make people charitable, become the dupes and victims of cunning "humanity mongers," so well described by Punch as philosophers who would dress up charity as school boys dress up the effigy of Guy Fawkes—not a white robed angel, but a SOCIAL MONSTER.

In the pleasant operatic piece called the Quaker, a proverb making person complains with great reason, that *charity seldom leaveth the house while ill nature is always roaming abroad*. But I dare hazard the assertion that to no class of reformers is ill nature less agreable than to those who are "sick of charity," as preached and practised by our philosophical liberals.

To the declaimer against *inconvenient* personalities, on the ground of their uncharitableness, it never seems manifest that the principle of justice is immeasureably higher and more important than the principle of charity, that though justice always includes charity, charity does not always include justice, and therefore that a course of conduct very charitable, as regards individuals, may be most unjust as regards the public. When, in the tragedy of Pizarro, Elvira enters the tent of that horrid tyrant and finds that Rolla had neglected to assassinate him, she closes a speech full of keen reproach, by saying, "Oh Rolla soon wilt thou learn that mercy to that man is direct cruelty to all thy race." Let philosophical liberals say what they please, she was right, and the Peruvian was wrong. NO MISTAKE CAN BE GREATER THAN THAT OF SPARING UNITS AT THE EXPENSE OF THOUSANDS.

The poor "unit" convicted of emptying a till or picking a pocket is not spared. On no, any one may call him *thief* without being charged with lack of charity. To call such a vulgar criminal by his proper name is justifiable no doubt; but I want an answer to this question:—If it is right to call a thief a thief, can it be wrong to call a scoundrel a scoundrel? There are many sorts of scoundrelism, and certainly not the least abominable sort is political scoundrelism. Yet its exposure is considered an act of malignancy no charitable person would commit. Thieves are abused right and left without any loss of reputation to the abuser, but let a sentence be breathed in condemnation of some profligate politician, and sure as fate his "brother chips" (especially if he happen to be a philosophical liberal) will begin jabbering lustily in deprecation of "personalities." They are like Sir Robert

Peel, in at least one respect, inasmuch as they object to be held "personally responsible" either for opinions expressed or practice pursued. Now, I cannot get rid of the opinion that public men who shrink from a responsibility at once so tangible and so salutary, are more *sensitive* than *honest.* Were a thief detected in the act of picking a pocket to turn round upon his captors and protest against being held personally responsible, what a laugh would be raised at the poor fellow's expense, and yet our politicians when detected in the act of *something far worse than picking pockets* are not ashamed to take that course. Such conduct is very disgusting, but I confess to having been often greatly amused while observing their feverish anxiety to escape from all personal responsibility. And too long have they been allowed to do so. *It is full time that truth be told as well of* MEN AS MEASURES, *and politicians be made to understand that if it is just to praise their* VIRTUES *it is equally so to censure their* VICES. CHARLES SOUTHWELL.

MR. GILLESPIE'S ARGUMENT A PRIORI.
II.

MR. EDITOR,—I do not intend to enter into a metaphysical disquisition on the merits of this argument, but I will endeavour to bring it to the test of plain common sense, and try it by a standard intelligible to persons of ordinary acquirements.

As a preliminary step I will make some observations on the nature of belief and the duty of inquirers after truth.

[Aliquis had here inserted an interesting proem on these subjects, the object of which was to prove that belief is in all cases involuntary; that if inquirers only act fairly and honestly in their investigations; if they bestow on religion, or any other important subject adequate and impartial attention—then—whether the result be belief, doubt, or disbelief they will be equally innocent. The omission of this part deprives Aliquis's examination of much of its force, but its omission, if his argument is to appear this week, is unavoidable.—G. J. H.]

I believe it is universally acknowledged by all intelligent men, that he who *affirms* a proposition is bound to prove its truth; it is also agreed that if one man affirms a proposition which another man denies, the denier is not to be called upon to make good his denial; it is sufficient for him to say "I deny;" the duty of the affirmer is to prove it; if he cannot do this he should have held his peace, and not have affirmed. It is only wise and proper that arguments should be conducted under such regulations, otherwise the most monstrous and absurd ideas might be passed off for truths.

I will not assert that Mr. Gillespie is ignorant of these rules, but he certainly disregards them—as an instance—"Proposition 3 § 2. And if any one should deny that it (infinity of extension) is a substance it so subsisting; to prove beyond contradiction the utter absurdity of such denial, we have but defy him to show *why* infinity of extension is not a substance *so far forth as it can subsist by itself, or without a substratum.*" Will Mr. Gillespie permit me to observe that it was his duty and his *alone* to prove infinity of extension a *substance* ?

The first proposition, or as I may say the basis of the Argument, commences in these words—

"Infinity of Extension is necessarily existing.

§ 1. Even when the mind endeavours to remove from it the idea of infinity of extension, it cannot after all its efforts avoid leaving there the idea of such infinity. Let there be ever so much endeavour to displace this idea, that is to conceive infinity of extension non-existent; every one by a reflex examination of his own thoughts will find it utterly beyond his power to do so." The remainder of the proposition I need not notice at present, as I most decidedly object to the words "Infinity of Extension is necessarily existing," and cannot allow the argument to proceed until either they or *their* proofs are altered.

As it is not every person who is capable of clearly comprehending the above, I will endeavour to shew *how* it may be brought home to the mind. Suppose a man turns his eyes upwards in a clear frosty night, he will perceive many stars shining in the sky (space*). Let this idea cross his mind, "has the universe then any limits," and whilst pursuing the train of thoughts engendered thereby he might go through a mental process something like this: he would *imagine* himself able to travel with the rapidity of light, and at the same time be capable of penetrating with equal rapidity all material substances — he would journey on for a thousand years and where would he then be? He must either have more sky before him or have arrived at the end of the sky; if he had more sky before him then he might journey onwards; if he had arrived at the end of the sky then the

---

* I am *not* satisfied that Mr. Gillespie's ideas about "space" are correct; astronomers have reasons to believe the celestial regions are filled with an ethereal medium: nor am I convinced the material universe is finite in extent; *if* it is finite Mr. Gillespie, in my opinion, does not prove it to be so.

sky must be bounded by something, and *this* something must be either boundless or bounded by *some other* something, or bounded by sky—if it is boundless then the case is ended, as it is plain he might journey on for ever without impediment; if it is bounded by some other something then he could also pass through that something; if it is bounded by sky then he could proceed onwards. If these journeyings be extended over millions and millions of years, the result will be still the same.

Reflections like these do not prove "*extension*" to be an existence, but they convince the mind that either matter must be infinitely extended or matter and space together must be infinitely extended.

Words are not always the representatives of *even* ideas, much less things, and although no mischief might arise if a chemist, an astronomer, or a geometrician took a fancy to substitute the name of one thing for that of another thing, yet it would be unwise to allow a metaphysician such a latitude.

The following form of the first proposition appears unobjectionable, and such as the human mind can believe to be true:

Prop. 1. Matter is infinitely extended, or matter and space together are infinitely extended.

Sec. 1. Even when the mind endeavours to remove from it the idea of matter being limited in extent, or matter and space together being limited in extent, it cannot after all its efforts avoid leaving there the idea that matter is boundless, or matter and space together are boundless. Let there be ever so much endeavour to displace this idea, that is to conceive matter limited in extent, or matter and space together limited in extent; any one by a reflex examination of his own thoughts will find it utterly beyond his power to do so.

Sec. 2. Now, since even when we would endeavour to remove the notion out of our minds that matter is limited in extent, or that matter and space together are limited in extent we cannot but leave the notion behind; from this it is manifest we are warranted in believing that matter is infinitely extended, or that matter and space together are infinitely extended; for, *every thing which we have " a sufficient reason " to believe in, we must believe to be true*.

Sec. 3. To deny therefore that either matter is infinitely extended, or that matter and space together are infinitely extended, is contrary to the constitution of the human mind.

Sec. 4. Matter then is infinitely extended, or matter and space together are infinitely extended.

If this form is retained, material alterations will require to be made in the argument. To make such alterations is not my business.

It is possible Mr. Gillespie may be disinclined to agree to the proposition in the above form; if so, may I beg he will give the following due consideration.

Natural philosophers consider "*extension*" to be a property belonging to matter; now if they are right, and if Mr. Gillespie is right in calling it an existence, then I am equally right in pronouncing *all* the other properties belonging to matter to be existences also; that is, hardness is an existence—impenetrability an existence—weight an existence, &c., &c. I am afraid natural philosophers will not think much of this information concerning matter.

Mr. Gillespie thinks matter to be finite; even if so, it is extended—it occupies some portion of space—it is moreover a *real* existence—if infinity of extension be a *real* existence, then we have *one* infinite *real* existence, containing in itself *another* finite real existence—"*infinity*" is "*the whole*," and if from "*the whole*" you take away a part, it ceases to be "*infinity;*" now infinity of extension contains matter, therefore it ceases to be "*infinity*," except it *perfectly* penetrates matter; natural philosophers say matter is *impenetrable*, how then can one *real infinite* existence penetrate another *real* existence which is *impenetrable*.

Matter is a *real* existence and it is extended: let extension also be a *real* existence—then matter must be a *compound* existence, made up of itself and *part* of the existence of extension—now take from this compound existence one of its component parts, and we ought (mentally at least) to have the other part remaining—let the part taken away be extension, and where is matter? Vanished.

That extension is *not* matter a simple experiment will prove. Take a glass tube, 40 inches long and 2 inches in diameter—perfectly close this tube at one end and leave the other end open—fill it quite full of mercury, then place it perpendicularly, with its open end downwards, and without spilling any of the mercury, in a basin half full of this metal—the mercury will immediately sink several inches in the tube, and by so doing form what philosophers call a vacuum;[*] now this term means simply in plain language emptiness—an empty space full of nothing —just as a bottle of wine would be called

---

[*] I am taking it for granted that "*space*" is a vacuum, but as before remarked astronomers think differently.

empty after the wine had been poured out, or an empty bottle, or a bottle full of nothing. Suppose an ignorant person said to a good natured philosopher " what is that empty space in the glass tube (vacuum) filled with ?" the philosopher would reply, " that empty space in the glass tube above the mercury is a vacuum, and it is filled with ' *nothing* '—it is quite empty."

I beg to inform the reader that I have a particular object in view in the above explanation of a vacuum, and I request he will bear the explanation in mind, as I shall have occasion to refer to it presently.

If the tube above referred to be greatly lengthened, water, oil and several other fluids will form vacua, although we cannot exhibit the experiment upon other forms of matter, yet the mind can realize them with regard to sugar, beef, bread, clay, gold, silver, and in fact *all* material substances, no matter howsoever dissimilar their properties or qualities may be.

If the foregoing observations and experiments are carefully examined, they will be found to *prove*, 1st, that altho' there can be *no* matter without extension, still there may be extension *without* a particle of matter—matter has properties but we know no instance whatever, of properties distinct from, or disconnected with, matter *—2nd, if extension is a real existence, and possesses properties, these properties must be different from the properties of matter; for if we remove matter, we must remove its properties too; but I have removed matter and left extension behind—therefore extension can have no property belonging to matter.

Mr. Gillespie is convinced extension is an infinite existence, and matter a finite one—be it so; now let the vacuum in the glass tube, instead of being only a minute part of extension be " *the whole*" of it; that is, let it be increased infinitely, and let the mercury be the representative of all the matter in the universe—these the mind can certainly comprehend as clearly as it can comprehend the proof of Mr. Gillespie's first proposition;—now cause the mercury (matter) to vanish,

---

* The intelligent reader may possibly think I ought to make here an exception in favour of the property called extension; if however he reflects that natural philosophers consider extension one of the properties belonging to matter, and that Mr. Gillespie considers it an infinite existence, then my reason will be apparent. If the stars really float in *vacuo*, as Mr. G. is convinced they do, then space would be a much more appropriate word to use than extension—extension is intimately connected with matter; space has no relation whatever to it.

and what have we got? Why we have got an empty space—a vacuum *full of nothing*—the " necessary existence of infinity of extension. '

Mr. Gillespie is convinced extension is an existence; be it so—he is also convinced, " the Being of Infinity of Extension is necessarily of simplicity and unity," be it so also—*as is the part so is the whole*; that is if a sample of a simple body be taken, the entire body will prove to be of the same quality: just as if a tumbler was dipped into a full cask of spring water, and some water taken up, the remainder of the cask would be of the same quality as that contained in the tumbler—if we could, therefore, obtain a sample of extension, we could tell perfectly what was the *quality* of extension—but if the reader refers back to the experiment of the glass tube, he will find I have obtained a sample of extension, standing over the mercury; he will also find it I have examined it and found it to be *perfectly* of the same quality, as that which mankind understand by the term of NOTHING. "The necessary existence of infinity of extension," then, and " *nothing*" have precisely the same meaning.

Mr. Gillespie and I now perfectly understand each other: from this time forth, when he makes use of the words, extension, infinity of extension, or the necessary existence of infinity of extension, I will understand him to mean " *nothing*," and when I make use of the word " *nothing* " he will please to understand that I am alluding to extension, &c. I intend to use the word " nothing" throughout our controversy—it is shorter than infinity of extension, and it is a term in common use, to which plain people have attached a meaning. If Mr. Gillespie would consent to drop the above learned names, and use the term " nothing," it would probably save both of us a great deal of trouble. If Mr. Gillespie's argument is *really* invulnerable, no injury could occur through adopting the same name as I do—as an instance if a mathematician chose to call a right angled triangle a square, and a square a circle, he could, and still demonstrate a sound proposition, provided that his hearers understood that a right angled triangle meant a square and a square a circle. Now he, the public, and I clearly understand that " *nothing*' means extension, and extension means " *nothing* " I shall therefore assume until I hear from him to the contrary, that he agrees to use the word " nothing" instead of extension.

If Mr. Gillespie will not consent to alter the first proposition in the manner suggested by me at paragraph 10, I shall be compelled to require from him a rigid demonstration that " nothing " is an existence—when he has performed this, then, the phrase " Nothing is necessarily existing " may properly be proposed for consideration.

I beg Mr. Gillespie will not take it offensively, when I express my inflexible determination not to allow him to employ either assertion, hypothesis, dogma, or assumption without adequate proof.

It would be very desirable to use, in this controversy as few learned words as possible—to employ no words to which definite meanings are not attached—and not to use the same terms, or words, to designate ideas or things having no relation whatever to each other.

If a mathematician called a square a circle, and a circle a square, and also endowed the square with the properties of the circle, and the circle, with the properties of the square, and then proceeded to demonstrate a problem, in which squares and circles were elements, it is easy to perceive what would be the result.

Men have definite meanings for the words " thing," " substance," " existence," " being :" they convey ideas of things relating to matter only—a house is a thing a substance—man exists—he is a being—I have already shown that " nothing " is not matter ; that if it has properties they must be different from those belonging to matter — then why should " nothing" be termed a " substance "—a " being "—an " existence." Such transmutation of words is sufficient to throw every thing into confusion.

ALIQUIS.

It is perhaps as well to observe that philosophers have discovered that the vacuum above spoken contains a very attenuated vapour; this, however does not alter the *principle* of the illustration, for the mind can readily conceive that it is possible mercury might not have the property of volatising in vacuo at ordinary. In fact, the quantity is so minute as to have escaped the notice of the discoverer of this mode of producing a vacuum.

RATIONALITY IN MEDICINE.

[Some time ago, friend W. B. B. introduced to my notice, " Life, Health, and Disease," by Edward Johnson, Surgeon, a work original, perspicuous, and valuable. The " Fallacies of the Faculty " has the same qualities, and takes a more extensive range, and has so enchanted A. T. that he is anxious to express his obligations to the author, and draw the attention of our friends to his novel and useful performance. —G. J. H.]

Wallington-Cambo, near Morpeth.
March 20, 1845.

Samuel Dickson, M. D , 28, Bolton-street, Piccadilly, London.

Worthy Friend, — Having lately read your invaluable work the " Fallacies of the Faculty,"—I cannot forbear, although non-medical,—and hence, by some individuals, may be styled presumptuous,—from expressing to its author, the pleasing excitement generated by its perusal, in the superior and anterior portions of my brain,—you, Priessnitz, Gall, Read, and Elliotson are in my opinion the five greatest benefactors of the human race in modern times, whose stars have yet illumed the regions of reason and benevolence.

At various times, I have attended courses of medical-lectures in the Edinburgh School, and was a pupil of McIntosh's, and an upholder of his method of treating intermittent fever, until such practice was shaken by Priessnitz's method of the " Cold-water-cure," and now wholly abandoned since studying your lectures. I have gained much medical knowledge from books, but very little from actual practice, as like some of your medical correspondents, I was much dissatisfied with the results, that I saw in the practice of others, who followed the cruel, uncertain, and irrational, old routine mode, thus I feared to venture, and since reading your lectures, only feel too thankful, that such fear restrained me,—that is, the action of my benevolence.

For several years past my brain has been much taken up with the various theories brought forward for removing disease, poverty, misery, and vice, from the face of this beautiful world, now unfortunatly governed by the dishonest and cruel. A man unless an idiot to all sense of conscientiousness, could not be a member of the British letter opening government.

I blame myself much for not having purchased your book earlier,—Hydriatria and Mesmerism I soon studied, but had little idea that the " Fallacies of the Faculty " which I saw so often advertised in the newspapers, contained such rational, benevolent and original views, of the nature of disease, and its cure.

Your theory of the " Unity of Disease," is most convincingly proved, not only by the arguments brought forward in the course of your lectures, but by actual observation on our suffering fellow-creatures,—and I agree with you. that ague in some of its forms, is invariably the accompaniment of all supposed diseases,—remove the intermittent, and then it will be soon enough to treat the symptoms of the other complaint, whatever that may be, provided the symptoms remain after their probable cause, ague, is removed, —and that powerful remedy an emetic, will generally, when given early, render any further medical aid needless,—but yours, let us call it the *Rational Medical Practice*, will not suit the pockets of the unconscientious and acquisitive practitioner,—and unfortunately for the public, they, like the priests and lawyers preponderate over the honest in their profession—it interferes with established interests, and thus some pockets are in danger, which accounts for the abuse heaped on you by your medical brethren. Such has been the fate of all the benefactors of the human race, but more particularly when their philanthropy interfered with priestcraft, law, or medicine. However, you have gained the day, and ere long blood-letting will be read of as a barbarism that once existed (unfortunately too long) in medical practice.

Bleeding and blistering is the practice of the country surgeons in these parts, but our small subscription library having got (at my recommendation) a copy of your book (and I lend other copies) so that ere the end of the present year arrives I expect to have been the means, through the "Fallacies of the Faculty," of stopping much of the slaughter-house practice now followed.

From this time forth all blood-letting practitioners must be looked upon as either ignorant, extra-insane, or dishonest men, and when death follows such practice, if ignorant, they are guilty of the crime of manslaughter, and if dishonest, murder must be laid to their charge.

I agree with all your views, and among them that of the great indelicacy of men attending females in their accouchement, except in cases of extreme danger. Regarding this McIntosh held the same opinion.

I only wish it was in the power of every person, either to obtain a copy of, or to read your lectures of humanity, if such was the case, I guess at the end of six months, many a lancet might become rusty, and leeches might be purchased at a discount.

I beg your acceptance of the accompanying pamphlets, and wishing you the enjoyment of a life of usefulness, health, and happiness,

I remain,
Faithfully yours,
ARTHUR TREVELYAN.

WHAT IS THE RELIGION OF EMERSON?

We cannot answer this question put by *Aliquis* better than by quoting the opinion with which we have been favored by S. D. C., the young lady to whom we were last week indebted for ingenious views of Pantheism—

"With respect to Emerson's religion, he seems to me one of the last men in the world who could be characterized as having a religion, he seems to be so complete a whole, that religion, politics, literature, action—all blend into *one* in him, as colours merge into white light—and it is impossible to select one of these without injury to the rest.

"But if you mean, what do I think Emerson believes about God and Christ, it seems to me that with respect to the first, he is a perfect Pantheist. He believes in one soul animating all nature and humanity, and says "if a man is at heart just, then, in so far is he God." He believes most fully in the immortality of this universal soul, but does not seem quite sure about the continued existence of individuals *as* individuals after death (perhaps his own words may change about it). With respect to Christ, he thinks him a glorious specimen of humanity, calls him "the only soul in history who has appreciated the true worth of a man," but does not think him anything more than man (but as he thinks man an epitome of Divinity, *that* is something great). I think Emerson's Divinity Lecture and the Over Soul, describe more of his direct opinions and ideas about religion than any other of his writings.

S. D. C."

FIRST REFLECTIONS.
BY A NEW BEGINNER.

IF there be a God, and *he*, although invisible, can influence us, that is, cause us to go rightly or wrongly, where is the necessity for religious teachers—do they doubt the integrity or the sagacity of dety?

According to their maxims the deity is pleased to see us go rightly, and if he knows anything at all about it he is more likely to know what is pleasing to himself than we are. Is it not reasonable to ask why we do not leave ourselves to his will, that is, do as he causes us to do, and not as priests tell us?

Why should we think they have such love for our souls when they mock at the miseries the body is subjected to? If they do not mock right out, they take care to say what a virtue poverty is, and that the poor will be rewarded hereafter—and take care not to do anything to reward virtue here, nor to assist in the removal of distress. All they do is to try to satisfy people that the poor are the better Christians for their endurance. E. W. H.

FRANCES WRIGHT'S LAST WORK—LETTERS ON RELIGION AND CIVILIZATION.—*J. Myles Dundee.*—It was my intention to have reviewed this interesting work long ago, but great anxiety to notice it in a manner commensurate with its merit and importance has prevented me reviewing it at all. The virtual recantation of Atheism, and brief views of religion which the work contains, seemed as the once embryo opinions of Fox, Emerson, and Theodore Parke, and led me to the consideration of the religious philosophy of this school, and I intended answering the above letters by others. But recent illness has prevented me following out this idea, and want of space this week leaves me only briefly to say that the above letters are deserving of universal perusal.
G. J. H.

THE DEVIL.—J. H. sends a copy of the work which is published by Sherwood & Co., Paternoster Row, at 1s., and simply entitled THE DEVIL. The book itself consists of 12 lectures, delivered to a metropolitan congregation, and excited so much interest that 1000 copies were subscribed for. The book is a learned and elaborate dissertation on the Devil. The author comes to the conclusion that, "if there be a God there cannot be a Devil." I intended entering upon the merits of the performance, but for obvious reasons the intention must be abandoned. The author advertised in the *Patriot*, and a curious recantation took place on the part of the editor. On some future occasion I must refer to this again. G. J. H.

MRS. MARTIN IN GORBALS.—Mrs. Martin and Mr. and Mrs. Jeffery have been taken to the police office of this place and fined—Mrs. Martin £3 and Mr. Jeffery £2, in consequence of Mrs. Martin having issued a placard, stating her intention of visiting the Rev. Mr. Anderson's church in that parish and criticising his sermon, which drew, say the Glasgow papers, 3000 people together, to the great alarm of the pious kirk people and that of the Rev. Mr. Anderson, who could not reach his own pulpit (we are afraid he did not try). We suppose these fines are for pew rents, and that Mrs. Martin and Mr. Jeffery have paid theirs in advance.

THE REV. MR. ALLAN.—Mr. Paterson sends an interesting account, which it is impossible to find room for, of the public delinquencies of the Rev. Mr. Allan, his late Chaplain, also of the Rev. Mr. Tullock, who kindly told him it would be for his own good if he (Mr. P.) was shot. This Rev. Mr. Tullock has since absconded from his parish to America, with £2000 of parish money, and according to a Glasgow paper has been drowned on his passage.

MR. NEWMAN.—Any of our friends wishing to communicate with Mr. Newman, whose case we recently noticed, can do so by letter, sent to the care of Mr. Hetherington, 40, Holywell Street, Strand.

PREPARING FOR PUBLICATION.
THE MATERIALISM AND INFIDELITY OF SHAKSPERE,
As far as those sentiments may be inferred from his Dramatic Writings, and the opinions of some of his Critics.
BY W. J. B., ESQ.

Under the Superintendence of the Anti-Persecution Union.
PATERSON WELCOME!
A SOIREE
OF THE FRIENDS OF
MR. THOMAS PATERSON
Will be held at the Hall of Science, City Road, seven doors from Featherstone-street, on Sunday, April 6, 1845, for the purpose of presenting him with the amount publicly subscribed as a testimony of respect and approval for his eminent services in the cause of free expression of opinion; and sympathy on account of his fifteen months' Imprisonment in Perth Gaol.
MR. H. HETHERINGTON IN THE CHAIR.
Sentiments will be spoken to by English and foreign advocates of Religious Liberty; interspersed with Songs, &c.
Tea on table at half-past four for five.
TICKETS, ONE SHILLING EACH,
Including Refreshments, may be had of Mr. Holyoake, 11, Woburn Buildings, Tavistock Square; Mr. Hetherington, 40, Holywell-street, Strand; Mr. Watson, 5, Paul's Alley, Paternoster Row; Mr. Stewart, 23, John-street, Tottenham Court Road; at the Social Institution, 5, Charlotte-street, Blackfriars Road; at the Social Institution, High-street, Whitechapel; at the Social Institution, Goswell Road; at the Hall of Science, City Road; and of the members of the Committee.
In consequence of the proverbial disappointment of persons at Tea Parties the Stewards have issued only 300 Tickets, that being the number of persons that can be accommodated with convenience and comfort. On no account will a second set be admitted to table.
The Friends of the Union will be admitted at seven o'clock—Admission 3d.
J. B. LEAR, WM. COOPER, Stewards.
N. B.—The Committee of the Anti-Persecution Union are requested to meet at the Hall at half-past four, A.M. G. J. H., Sec.

A COURSE OF THREE LECTURES
will be delivered by
MR. G. JACOB HOLYOAKE,
At the Hall of Science, Commercial Place, City Road, on the following subjects;

Sunday evening, April 13,—On the Reputed Recantation (of Atheism) of Frances Wright, now Madame D'Arusmont.

Sunday evening, April 20,—On the Late Thomas Campbell's description of an Atheist, in his celebrated " Pleasures of Hope."

Sunday evening, April 27,—The effects of Solitary Confinement, in answer to Luke Roden's article on the Pentonville Prison, in the "Illuminated Magazine."

Each Lecture to commence at seven o'clock precisely.—Admission twopence.—Discussion permitted.

New and Extraordinary Work.
Early in May next will be published, No. 1, price twopence,

The Adventures of Lord William Carisdale in Icaria.

Translated from the French of M. Cabet, Procurator-General and Member of the Chamber of Deputies, at the especial request of the author,

By Dr. P. M. McDOUALL.

"As to the organisation of society—the vital question of the age—that subject has been treated by M. Cabet with remarkable ability—His excellent works have stamped his character at once moral, pacific, and fraternal."—*Eugene Sue.*

London: Hetherington, 40, Holywell Street, Strand; Watson, Paul's Alley, Paternoster Row: and sold by all booksellers in town and country.

TO CORRESPONDENTS.

C. S.—It is impossible to crowd his report of his debate with the Rev. J. R. Stephens in this number.

W. B. B.—Having inserted the letter of Mr. Duncombe respecting the presentation of Mrs. Martin's petition, it is unnecessary to insert the "Vote of the House of Commons." But it is necessary, as W.B.B. desires us, to remind our readers of the duty of petitioning generally.

J. L. BENDALL.—We are sorry that his letter arrived too late for Mr. Cooper's lecture on Dickens to be noticed.

GEORGE ANDERSON writes a surprising letter of complaint, to the effect that "A well known Subscriber," who in No. 59 comments on his (G. A.'s) letter in No. 57, respecting Mr. Paterson visiting the towns of the North. G. A complains that "A well known Subscriber" reproaches him with having only subscribed 1s. to the Testimonial. The fact is that the "W. K. S." mentioned G. Anderson and Cosmopolite as pleasing exceptions, and had not the remotest idea of reproaching either one or the other.

H. B.—The last Congress was no farce, but many of the preceding ones were, and unless the Branches bestir themselves and make judicious selections of delegates this will be one—and all that follow.

J. B.—We believe Mr. Finlay has not yet parted with his "Republicans." Is there no liberal library that would enrich itself by purchasing them?

J. MYLES.—He neglected to forward us a copy of the "Three Impostors," and it not having been at hand has prevented a review of it appearing.

S. LOCKWOOD.—The Library is still issuing, and is likely to continue. The other particulars are not known to us.

RECEIVED.—Reply to the interrogatories of Aliquis by W. Gillespie. Second number of *Colchester Christian Magazine.*

Now READY.—The MOVEMENT, a Revolutionary Journal—Republican in Politics, Materialist in Philosophy, Communitarian in Social Science, and Utilitarian in Morals.

Vol. 1 in boards, lettered, 8s.
The whole of the numbers of Vol. 2 in a stiff wrapper.
Price 1s. 6d.

TO BE HAD complete, in eight numbers of the *Movement—The Discussion on the Comparative Merits of Christianity and Atheism,* between Dr. Robert R. Kalley, imprisoned on account of his religious tenets by the Portuguese authorities of Maderia, and G. Jacob Holyoake, Secretary to the Anti-Persecution Union, London.
In a stiff wrapper.—Price 1s.

Baron Humboldt is about to publish a book, to be entitled "Cosmos," to contain a summary of all his views on the earth's formation, and its various phenomena. It will be the learned author's legacy to the world.

ERRATA.—[Through the printer not beginning my second article on "God's words *versus* God's works" from where he left off on the first, and from the copy being subsequently lost, I must trouble you to insert the following, being, as nearly as I can recollect, the substance of what I had written in my original M.S., and without which the article No. II. is incomplete].

Having now given some specimens of the opinions of scientific men, in favour of the view that God's words and God's works will always be found to agree, if rightly interpreted, I will, without further comment, proceed to contrast the Word of God with the modern discoveries of the Works of God, taking especial care, in the second particular, to make my extracts from the writings of reputed orthodox believers.

"In the beginning God created the heaven and the earth." About this said beginning, and when it began to be, there is a great variety of opinions. The Christian world date back about six thousand years; but the discoveries of geology give reasons for supposing that it may have been as many or more *millions* of years. (And then follows the opinion of Dr. Pye Smith, etc., art. II. page 76 of *Movement*).

In the same article, p. 77, 27 lines from bottom of 2nd col., for "supposed" read *supplied.* P. 78, col. 2, for "incondescent" read incandescent, 22 lines from top.

In article III., No. 66, p. 91, 29 lines from top of 1st col., for "beins" read *hews*; and next line, for "rifles" read *rifes.* 2nd col., 19 lines from bottom, for "one" read *our*; and 4 lines above, for "one" read *our.* W, C.

In No. 67, p. 97, 2nd col., 19 lines from top, for "soil" read *soul*; do. do., 30 lines from top, for "Our" read *One.* P. 98, 1st col., 5 lines from top, for "strength" read *struggle*; do., 2nd col., 35 lines from top, for "faith" read *fact.* S. D. C.

SUBSCRIPTIONS
TO THE ANTI-PERSECUTION UNION.

W. B. B. 0 10 0

PATERSON TESTIMONIAL.

To Vol. of "Investigator" 0 6 0
J. L. Bendall............................ 0 1 0
Mrs. P. 0 1 0
G. J. H., *Sec.*

Printed and Published by G. J. HOLYOAKE,
40, Holywell-street, Strand.
Wednesday, April 2, 1845.

[PUBLISHED ON THE FIRST OF EVERY MONTH.]

THE CIRCULAR

Of the Anti=Persecution Union.

Whoever is not persuaded by reason will not be convinced by authority.—FEYJOO.

No. 1.   EDITED BY G. JACOB HOLYOAKE.   Price 1d.

INTRODUCTION.

GREAT care will be bestowed in writing the Circular. Every paragraph will be patiently condensed that much may be communicated in the small space at disposal. Pains will be taken that little shall be deficient in completeness whatever may be wanting in length. Friends will tolerate the Circular being limited to four pages, as it arises from the desire of the Committee of the Union to limit the expense. It is with them a standing principle, that little shall be spent officially—that the bulk of the funds entrusted to them may be employed in the *direct* protection of persons indicted, or legally molested, for the expression of religious or anti-religious sentiments.

As three Circulars may be posted with a penny stamp, it is hoped that friends will give them an active circulation. Five hundred copies only are printed—but a thousand should be sold to cover the entire expense. If subscribers will endeavour to increase the demand to a thousand, they will (besides extending the publicity of our efforts) save the Union a pound per month—that being the deficiency the Committee will have to meet if 500 only are sold.

Formerly it was deemed objectionable that the organ of the Union expressed ultra opinions on religion—but as *now* the Circular relates purely to the principles of the Union, it claims, and ought to receive, *general* support. It may, without fear of annoying, be put into the hands of liberal persons of any party in politics, or of any sect in religion.

The Circular will be frank, earnest and uncompromising—single in purpose, and, as the Union has ever been, impartial in act. Tenets it will leave to take care of themselves. The Circular declares for Free Trade in religion, and if the public are true to their own interests, it will never cease its exertions, while the state allows to any sects a monopoly of the law to enforce conformity to *their* standard of free expression.

THE EDITOR.

THE ACTION AGAINST THE HULL MAGISTRATES.

I

THE prosecution of Mr. Johnson arose, it will be remembered, out of lectures delivered in Hull by Mrs. Martin, in September last. Mr. Johnson, for the act of having received the admission money at the door on that occasion, was fined £20 and costs—his house was taken possession of by the police, and his goods, to several times the above amount, sold by public auction in payment. To effect this, recourse was had to an infamous and obsolete statute, the 39th of Geo. III., known as the gagging act. As soon as these proceedings were reported to the Anti-Persecution Union the committee called a public meeting in London, where, upon it being shown that the conviction of Mr. Johnson was entirely illegal—a recent act (the 2nd Victoria, c. 12), having ordered that *no conviction on the 39th of Geo. III. shall be valid unless procured by the Attorney General,* it was agreed, that as this prosecution was undertaken at the instigation of a local functionary in Hull, and *not* by the Attorney General, an action for the recovery of the fine would hold good. An action was ordered, and the Union forthwith brought one. Thus much of reiteration is necessary to inform the readers of the Circular (not before acquainted with the case) of the injustice in which it originated, and the grounds on which it is confidently believed that the conviction may be set aside.

It will save confusion by premising that in this matter will appear *two* Johnsons. Mr. Richard Johnson, the person fined, and Mr. B. L. Johnson (no relative) his solicitor in Hull. In addition to Mr. B. L. Johnson, the solicitor, the Union (counsel being necessary) entrusted the case, in London, into the hands of Mr. J. Humphrey Parry, barrister, in whose ability and liberality of sentiment confidence could be placed. Instructions to barristers being (such is legal etiquette) made through a solicitor, Mr. B.

L. Johnson selected Messrs. Hopwood and Son as his London agents, through whom he sends instructions to Mr. Parry, counsel. It is hoped that this recital will not be lost upon our friends, as a case involving (unavoidably indeed) three lawyers, entails serious responsibilities.

As at first it was intended to enter an action against the Magistrates for trespass, as well as appeal to the Queen's Bench to set the verdict aside, *time* became a matter of consequence—formal notices of these steps having to be given within a certain term. *Time* however proving too short for the action of trespass to be laid, it was abandoned, and all attention directed to the case for which there was more time. This explanation is necessary, as an impression has gone forth that because the proceedings were said at first to depend upon time now long since passsd, that the *whole* action was abandoned. This is an error—the case in the Queen's Bench is proceeding, and will be certain (as far as certainty can be predicated of law) to succeed—unless subscribers to the Union fail us.

Long before this time progress would have been reported had not unexpected difficulties appeared in the way. An informal notice, or something of that kind, crept in—which as soon as discovered the counsel ordered every doubtful step to be retraced—deeming delay better than danger. At length every thing has been made secure —a writ of Certiorari has been moved for by Mr. Parry, which was granted by the Judge without hesitation, and the case is expected shortly to come on.

It is necessary that this trial should be brought on to vindicate the right of free discussion, which must not be left at the mercy of fanatic magistrates. Whether this action succeeds or not it must be paid for. The London solicitor has already waited on Mr. Hetherington, who has consented, on behalf of the Union, to give an *unlimited* guarantee for the costs. This step was imperative, that no impediment on our part should be thrown in the way, on which account the trial might be stopped—for should this happen Mr. R. Johnson, who, on giving notice of the action, had to bind himself and a friend under a penalty of £50 to carry the case into court, will forfeit that £50 more in addition to the fine, and the Union will lose all expenses incurred. Our friends will at once see the necessity of sending in subscriptions. The few that have been received hitherto for this case have barely met the contingent expenses of putting the train of law in operation. *Fifty pounds* ought at once to be placed at the Union's disposal on account of this special undertaking. To vindicate the inportant right violated in Mr. Johnson's conviction the Union have incurred serious responsibilities—and should they fail to fulfil them, Mr. Hetherington, their security, will be involved, and Mr. Johnson and his bondsman will be sacrificed by the very men who have ostensibly stepped forward to protect them. The honour and character of the Union are thus at stake— need more be said to our friends? These serious responsibilities have been risked upon the good faith subsisting between the Union, its members, friends, and the public—simply stating this, will be to them, the Committee believe, the only necessary appeal.

G. J. H.

THE PRESENTATION OF THE "TESTIMONIAL" TO Mr. PATERSON.

(*Abridged from the Northern Star.*)

On Sunday, April 6th, a numerous body of friends assembled at the Hall of Science, City-road, to give their meed of approbation to Mr. Thomas Paterson, for his faithfulness under long and bitter suffering in the cause of free expression of opinion. The tea and refreshments, which were of the best quality, were provided under the superintendence of Mr. Bendall, and gave great satisfaction to all parties. After the removal of the cloth, MR. HETHERINGTON, took the chair.

The meeting was very interesting. In the *Northern Star* of April 12th, will be found a report of it. The following is an outline. THE CHAIRMAN after an appropriate speech presented to Mr. Paterson the sum of £30 11s. 6d. (the amount of the "Testimonial" then subscribed) and gave the following sentiment :—"MR. THOMAS PATERSON—The assembled friends of the right of private judgment, and the free expression of opinion, embrace the occasion of presenting to Mr. Paterson the present "testimonial," to convey their warmest respect and approbation to him, who a second time left a quiet retirement to place himself in the thick of danger, and by inflexible defiance, to render the bigot's greatest power abortive, and smooth the path for future friends of freedom."

MR. PATERSON then spoke in acknowledgement.

The CHAIRMAN then proposed the second sentiment, as follows :—" The Anti-Persecution Union, which has for its principles the recognition of the first step towards equality, namely, unrestricted discussion, and for its objects the protection of all whose exercise of this liberty is prohibited or attacked."

To which Mr. Holyoake, Secretary of the Anti-Persecution Union responded.

The CHAIRMAN then introduced to the meeting one who had suffered for the freedom of the publication of opinion, Mr. Julian Harney, to respond to the third sentiment — "The Press. — Honest Journalism, the most potent help to Universal progression.',

MR. HOLYOAKE stated that he had come prepared to enroll members of the Union that they might commence their new *Monthly Circular* in numerous company. (At the conclusion of the meeting more than fifty persons took out tickets of membership.)

THE "MOVEMENT" MEETING AT THE PARTHENIUM.

At a meeting of the friends and subscribers of this paper, held in the Parthenium, St. Martin's Lane, April 15, Mr. Skelton in the chair—the accounts of the second volume (as far as it has proceeded) were presented, and a balance of £25 4s. declared due to the conductors. It was thereupon resolved that "that meeting holds itself in a great measure responsible for the same, agrees to enter into a subscription to repay it, and calls upon subscribers and friends generally to further that object." There and then various sums were entered upon the list, which, with others subsequently tendered, amount to £11 6s. 7d., as will be seen from a column of subscriptions adjoining. On the motion of Mr. Powell, seconded by Mr. Haxton, a committee was formed (of friends of the *Movement* and members of the Anti-Persecution Union) to make arrangements for a Public Tea Party, on the occasion of Mr. Holyoake's departure for Scotland.

Permission has been given by the Union to insert in their *Circular* the list of subscriptions (annexed) referred to in the above report.

SUBSCRIPTIONS RECEIVED IN LIQUIDATION OF THE BALANCE DUE TO THE TREASURER OF THE "MOVEMENT."

At the Parthenium, April 15.

	£	s.	d.
F. Gerhard	0	2	6
David Palmer	0	7	3
J. Haxton	0	5	0
T. Powell	0	5	0
T. Paterson	1	0	0
William Russel	0	2	6
Carried forward	£2	2	3

	£	s.	d.
Brought forward	£2	2	3
"J."	0	10	0
Daniel Ross	0	2	6
J. M. C.	0	5	0
R. R.	0	5	0
Thomas Brittain	0	6	10
H. Plasto	0	5	0
J. Alexander	0	2	6
W. Handby	0	2	6
A. H. Ivory	0	2	6
A Friend	0	1	0
J. G. Hornblower	0	5	0
Edwin Johnson	0	2	6
J. Peat	0	1	0
J. Skelton	0	2	6
W. Goosey	0	2	0
J. Trueman	0	1	0
— Murphy	0	1	0
I. Ironside, Sheffield	1	0	0
E. Walter, Worcester	0	10	0
Cosmopolite, (including £1. 14s. for back stock	5	13	6
W. Taylor	0	1	0
Z. Padfield, Coleford	0	5	0
Barnard Cole, Ipswich	0	1	0
Caroline Bird	0	1	0
John Glide, jun	0	1	0
R. Whiteman (for stock)	0	5	0
William Bendall	0	10	0
George Bird (surgeon)	1	1	0
R. Ridley	0	2	0
Charles White	1	14	0
C. Parke	0	2	0
— Wanfor	0	1	0
F. C. G.	0	5	0
Mr. Palmer	0	2	6
J. T. Dyer	0	1	0
J. W.	0	10	0
— Spooner	0	1	0
— Markhall	0	1	0
— Thornton	0	0	6
	£17	8	7

[Those persons who have intimated their intentions of subscribing to the above will enhance the value of the act by doing so at their earliest convenience, that the list may be closed. Communications to be addressed to G. J. H., 5, Paul's Alley, Paternoster Row, London].

A SOIREE of the Friends of Mr. G. JACOB HOLYOAKE to take leave of him previous to his departure for Glasgow, will be held at the Hall of Science, City Road, on Sunday, May 11, Mr. Julian Harney in the Chair. Tea on table at ½-past Four. Tickets, 1s, to be had at the various Social Institutions, of Watson, Paul's Alley, Hetherington, 40, Holywell Street, and of W Russell, H. Plasto, J. Haxton, and Thos. Powell, Stewards.

THE CIRCULAR

BALANCE SHEET OF THE ANTI-PERSECUTION UNION.

For the Quarter ending March 29, 1845.

RECEIPTS.	£	s.	d.
Balance in hand as per last account	1	1	11
To Subscriptions, per *Movement* No. 55	2	0	6
Do. do. — 56	1	0	0
Do. do. — 57	1	5	0
Do. do. — 58	1	3	0
Do. do. — 59	2	18	9
Do. do. — 60	1	10	10
Do. do. — 61	3	8	0
Do. do. — 62	1	10	10
Do. do. — 63	1	10	0
Do. do. — 64	0	5	6
Do. do. — 65	1	16	4
Do. do. — 66	1	13	4
Do. do. — 68	0	18	0
	22	2	0
Balance due to Treasurer	0	6	4
	£22	8	4

EXPENDITURE.	£	s.	d.
Paid to " Paterson Testimonial "	14	4	0
To Mr. Whiting's account	0	15	0
To Mrs. Martin, as per direction of subscribers, on account of her apprehension in Arbroath	1	15	3
To printing in Gazette during 14 weeks	1	15	0
To general correspondence, post orders, parcels, papers, Gazettes presented, etc.	1	19	1
To Assistant Secretary	2	0	0
	£22	8	4

Audited by us and found correct,

JOHN ELLIS, } Auditors.
JOHN SKELTON,

ANTI-PERSECUTION UNION.

Official Notices.

Office.—The office of the Union and of the *Circular* is 5, Paul's Alley, Paternoster Row, London.

Subscriptions.—All subscriptions and communications for the Union are to be addressed to the office, to Mr. Alfred H. Ivory, Secretary. All post orders to be made payable to him at the Post Office, Tottenham Court Road.

Editor.—All letters, etc., for the Editor, are to be addressed to him at the office of the Union.

New Secretary.—The committe have pleasure in announcing that Mr. Alfred H. Ivory, known to many of their friends as the Secretary of the Rational Tract Society, has accepted the office of secretary, made vacant by Mr. Holyoake's engagement in Scotland.

Mr. Holyoake's address will be the office of the Union until the end of May—afterwards the Social Institution, Glasgow.

TO CORRESPONDENTS.

A SUBSCRIBER TO THE "MOVEMENT," Glasgow, is thanked for the "Record against the Rev. Mr. Allan." Will he secure us a copy of the whole "Trial?" The expense shall be paid.

H. COOK, Bristol.—Deferred.

MRS. MARTIN will oblige by forwarding her address to the editor.

W. C. and other enquirers may bind up the 68 Nos. of the *Movement*, as no continuation is contemplated.

J. G. H.—Aliquis is anxious to conclude his examination of Mr. Gillespie's Argument A Priori, and has proposed to Mr. Gillespie that each shall print his respective article, monthly, at his own expense, and present it to the subscribers of the *Circular*. Mr. G. has objected to this, and up to this time has come to no arrangement.

HOUSE OF COMMONS, MARCH 13th.—Petition of the inhabitants of the town of Arbroath, in Scotland, praying for the repeal of all laws against the free expression of opinion. To lie on the table. Presented by Mr. Hume.

ERRATA in *Movement* No. 68, page 113, 17th line, 2nd col., for " Read" read *Pinel*.

SUBSCRIPTIONS
TO THE ANTI-PERSECUTION UNION.

	£	s.	d.
S. B.	0	2	6
W. Goosey	0	1	0
J. Haxton, per Mr. Paterson	0	0	6
Per Mr. Allen, Collector	0	1	6
Mr. Begg, Hull, to Members' Tickets	0	11	0
Mr. R.	0	2	0
Mr. Miles	0	0	6
Per Mr. Powell, London	0	3	0
Mr. Haxton, for Mrs. Martin	0	2	6
At the City Road Hall of Science, April 6.			
J. Hammon	0	5	0
Per T. Bidwell	0	3	6
J. Simpson, for Hull prosecution	0	1	0
J. F., for do. do.	0	2	6
To Members' Tickets issued at the same time, and minor subscriptions	1	3	6
Messrs. Rough and Griffith	0	1	0
At the same time and subsequent for the " Paterson Testimonial."			
J. Webley	0	1	0
H. Hoy	0	1	0
E. F.	0	5	0
E. A.	0	2	6
J. Hammon	0	5	0
H. Bradley	0	0	6
A friend to the cause of liberty	0	1	0

Alfred Henry Ivory, Sec.

[The following sums, and similar ones which appeared in the *Movement* from "W.J." and "W.W." are occasional remembrances for services rendered, or suffering endured by the parties below in the propagation of their sentiments. "W. W." is the author of "*Yahoo*"—still a hearty and hale old gentleman of 95 years of age. "W. J." is the brother of the author of "*Yahoo*," and approaching the same ancient age. He was present in excellent health at the " Presentation of the Testimonial to Mr. Paterson"]—

M. Q. R., G. J. H., E. H. M., C. S., M. R., T. P. 5s. each, £1 10s., from "W. J."

London : Printed for the Anti-Persecution Union, by John Griffin Hornblower, 77, Myddelton-street, Clerkenwell, and Published by Watson, 5, Paul's Alley, Paternoster Row.

[PUBLISHED ON THE FIRST OF EVERY MONTH.]

THE CIRCULAR

Of the Anti-Persecution Union.

I would rather that the authors of religious libels were answered than prosecuted.—LORD DENMAN.

No. 2. EDITED BY G. JACOB HOLYOAKE. Price 1d.

THE MAYNOOTH QUESTION.

[The editor of the *Circular* has been favoured by Mr. Ivory, of the Rational Tract Society, with a copy of the following unpublished paper, which that body is about to issue as a tract. Amid the hesitancy, narrowness, or error with which the subject of this article is regarded, it is a change to find it reasoned out in a decided tone, and withal having direct reference to those principles of religious liberty advocated by the *Circular*.]

THE question of the endowment of Maynooth, which has for some time agitated the public, involves principles which ought not to be dimly seen—principles touching the foundations of right and wrong—affecting just action and social welfare.

The Maynooth endowment, as a mere matter of policy, is one of those little questions which, in these days of superficial thought and superficial virtue engrosses all attention, and enlists numerous defenders—while the great principle of religious liberty involved in it is neglected as though the triumph of policy was of more importance than the welfare of the people.

Of the thousand and one sects of our country—all (on their own showing) equally true—why should only Protestants be endowed? The continuance of state patronage to the churchman is invidious to every dissenter. Church endowment is but another name for partiality.

What thus originates in injustice, strange to tell, it is proposed to extend. The Catholic clergy are to be the recipients of this increased patronage. A monopoly of state benefits is never well defensible, and least of all defensible when conferred on Catholic priests—a body of men whose sworn objects, from time immemorial are to trample down human reason and subjugate mankind to an iron ecclesiastical sway—whose principles are most inimical to all individual liberty—whose lives are devoted to spiritual dominion, and who can never be conciliated except by corruption. Protestantism does concede the right of private judgment—to those who can get it—but Catholicism says you shall not have it when you do get it.

Some think all would be reasonable were state patronage conferred on all sects alike.

But this principle equitably carried out would lead to the endowment of the anti-religious parties, whose objects are as well defined and (if they are to be believed) quite as moral as those of the orthodox. Thus acting honestly on the principle of the state endowing all parties, would be in effect the state endowing itself—a plan more troublesome and less reasonable than that of the state endowing no sect, but leaving, as it should do, each to public opinion and to truth. Be this accepted as it may, there is no fair or safe course but in the endowment of none or the endowment of all.

The endowment of one or two sects to the exclusion of others ought never to be thought of and never tolerated. England ought not to offer it and Ireland ought not to accept it. Partial endowment is terrible in effect. The state priest ever exhibits vices additional to those natural to his character. The desire of dominion, nearly always fatal to usefulness, seems ever an indigenous element in the religious instructor, and attains a fearful ascendancy in the agent of the state. The life of state priests, let them be inducted from whatever sects they may, has three stages—first, the love of power, then the lust of power, and last the rampancy of power. They begin by attacking reason and end with attacking liberty. This is the answer to those who maintain that were the clergy all provided for by the state, they would, from being comfortable, grow lethargic, and freedom would have a long respite from persecution. Unhappy delusion! That is a precarious peace which depends on the hypothetical supineness of a powerful enemy. But there never is this indifference. Religious patronage can always be turned to new accounts, and religious ambition once awakened is never satiated. The new made state priest can work with more decency than before, and hence it is supposed that he is less industrious—because he is less seen he is less suspected, but he is still the same enemy of reason and liberty—*only with more power.*

Instead of reducing this order of men among us, shall we under the pretence of redressing Ireland's wrongs, propagate them there. Ask the *Nonconformist*, and all Dissenters' organs downwards, "whence originates persecution?" and they will unanimously reply "in a state church—*not* in Christianity but in endowmency." Can it be clearer then that to endow new sects (Catholics or Dissenters) will be to multiply the already too prolific race of persecutors.

The opinion before alluded to, that of a state of clerical comfort will beget comparative supineness, has recently been abundantly confuted by the unanimous voice of alarmed dissent. The grand practical argument against state establishments has ever been that they generate a lazy indifference to proselytism. If this, though said, was *felt* to be true, Dissenters who believe Catholicism to be wrong would rejoice at such a short and easy method as that of endowment for laying asleep the dissemination of error—but the deadly opposition which they have given to the endowment of Maynooth has established their secret and deep conviction of the all powerfulness of state support, and it is to be feared that at no very distant day *policy* will induce them to seek the same fatal power. Friends of freedom, therefore, while there is yet time, repudiate endowments.

The general truth is that the endowment of a few sects is partial, invidious, unjust, dangerous. Considered as a question of merè policy the success of no ministerial stratagem can be held to compensate for the sacrifice of the great principles of impartiality and equality, by which the government of this nation should ever be distinguished. If Ireland has been wronged (which undoubtedly she has) let restitution be made. Give back the chuich property formerly wrested from the Catholics, but give not back to the Catholic church that liberty she formerly wrested from us. Upon this question let it be believed that religion is purest when left as a matter of conscience, not made a matter of interest. Morality is the only public question. Religion, strictly, is a private question, and is best left to private judgment and voluntary support.

It is more easy to reason men into usefulness than to coerce them to obedience.

THE ACTION AGAINST THE HULL MAGISTRATES.
II.

This case, whose historical features were sketched last month, was from the first considered as one which addressed itself to the attention of political and social societies. If such a conviction as that of Mr. Johnson is to be suffered no association is safe—the National Hall and Branch A 1, the Social Institution and the Political Institute are everywhere endangered.

From these bodies the Union will principally look for help, and as far as appearances go they will not look in vain. Soon after the case was made public Mr. Holyoake drew the attention of Branch A 1 to it, when (I think) Mr. Rowley moved a resolution to the effect (if my memory fail me not) that the Branch should assist the Union in its undertaking. It has not yet done so: but it is only necessary that some member again mentions the matter for the resolution to be redeemed.

I believe that the Secretary of the Union is instructed to correspond with the Presidents of the various social and political institutions, and such of our friends as can and will facilitate this object will render a service of great importance.

Dr. Warrenne, of Hull, who takes great interest in this case, has written to intimate his intention of giving a Lecture, "announced to be delivered in aid of the funds of the Anti-Persecution Union," and sending the proceeds to us. This is an example that might be generally followed.

Mrs. Martin has been solicited by the Union to draw the attention of her friends in the North to this case. Mr. Joshua Hopkins writes in reply, "that in consequence of the recent holidays it will be out of her power to do any thing at present, but she expects shortly to arouse the public to a due sense of its importance." Mr. Southwell and several other gentlemen will be written to, to further the same object.

Next month the Secretary hopes to be able to report considerable progress both in subscriptions received and in assistance promised. G. J. H.

THE TEA PARTY AT THE CITY ROAD.

The Tea Party referred to in a short notice in No. 1 of the *Circular* was held at the City Road Hall of Science, on Sunday, May 11. Mr. Bendall purveyor, Mr. Julian Harney chairman. The sentiments given were—

1. The people the chief source of power, and may they soon chiefly wield it, without partiality in politics or bigotry in religion.—2. The Anti-Persecution Union and its secretary, G. Jacob Holyoake: may the prosperity of both be commensurate with their services to the cause of general freedom.—3. The intrepid band who, emancipated from the thraldom of religion, labour in the face of persecution for the enlightenment of mankind: may their sacrifices meet with reward in their own day, and find appreciation through all time.—The speakers were the chairman; Mr. Skelton, and Mr. Marshall; Mr. Hetherington, Mr. Watson, and Mr. Holyoake; Mr. Ryall, Mr. Ridley, and Mr. Powell.

A comprehensive report of the above proceedings may be found in the *Northern Star* of May 17, and some other papers.

THE BRITISH MUSEUM AND THE ORACLE OF REASON.

British Museum,
December 21, 1842.

Sir,—I am to call your attention to the Act to amend the Law of Copyright (5 and 6 Victoria, cap. 45) by which it is directed, under penalties stated therein, that a copy of every book, pamphlet, sheet of letterpress, sheet of music, map, chart or plan, published within the British dominions, shall be delivered at the British Museum.

And I am to acquaint you that it will be my duty to cause the provisions of the Act to be enforced in every case in which a publication shall not be delivered as the Act directs.

I am, Sir, your obedient Servant,
M. Cowtan.
To Mr. Paterson, Bookseller,
Holywell Street, Strand, London.

[The above letter, and two others of a threatening nature, were addressed to Mr. Paterson at a time, when, being within the grasp of the Tothill Field authorities, it was impossible he could attend to them. Shortly after the *Oracle* was out of print and the demand was necessarily passed by. Recently, however, and our friends will be glad to learn it, Mr. Paterson and Mr. Lear jointly presented numerous unbound numbers of that periodical, out of which were made up two complete volumes, to which the conductors of the *Movement* added a set of that work, and the Anti-Persecution Union, in consideration of those books being a record of the Union's existence, agreed to be at the expense of binding the same (in a neat manner) for the Museum. Before Mr. Holyoake left London he lodged them there, assuring Mr. Cowtan that his request was not willingly neglected, as the parties applied to approved the law under which he acted, but that about that time five of them (Mr. Southwell, Mr. Holyoake, Mr. Paterson, and Mr. and Mrs. Adams) were in the hands of the government, and a prosecution from the Museum very little concerned them. Mr. Cowtan said they were very glad now to receive the works].

Tribute to Mr. Holyoake.—Several friends at Branch A 1, (Messrs. Hetherington, Ivory, Trueman, Lupton, Carman, Plasto. Palmer, Dent, Bull, Mayes, and J. M. C.) desirous of offering some tribute of esteem to Mr. Holyoake, have subscribed £2 13s, of which they have desired Mr. Holyoake's acceptance.

SUBSCRIPTIONS TO THE DEFICIENCY DUE TO THE TREASURER OF THE MOVEMENT.

Per first list in *Circular* No 1 ...	17	8	7
E. A. and friends, Colchester ...	0	10	0
A Friend..............................	0	10	0
Mr. Reed.............................	0	2	6
Mr. Stovel	0	2	6
Mr. Clements......................	0	1	0
Mr. James	0	1	0
A friend	0	0	6
William Friend	0	2	6
J. L. Bendall, jun	0	2	6
Henry Hoy..........................	0	2	0
W. B. B...............................	0	2	0
	£19	5	1

Failure of Persecution.—Half a dozen people choose to take up the notion that there is no God, and instead of laughing at them they have been persecuted into importance. Of this absurd exhibition, we had the government of a great nation opposed to a penny journal, the *Oracle*, and *dead beat* by it.—(Dr. P. Y.'s, Hunt *after the Devil, or a Few Hundred Bible Contradictions*, in 3 vols., written during the existence of the *Oracle*.)

Motto. These will be renewed at the head of the *Circular*, monthly. Our friends in the possession of terse and judicious sentiments will oblige by forwarding them for selection.

PRIVATE NOTICES.

On Mr. Holyoake's departure from London, the few Books in his possession, belonging to others, and which he had not been able to deliver, were left (directed to the owners) in the care of Mr. Hetherington, at 57, Judd Street, Brunswick Square, where they can be had on application.

The members of Mr. Holyoake's Improvement Class, at the Lambeth Branch, will confer a favour upon him by sending their addresses as he has a small offering to make them to compensate, in some measure for the neglect of them, which his illness caused.

PERSECUTION
By Dr. Bowring, M.P.

[It is no mean indication of the spread of liberal opinion that the following lines by Dr. Bowring have appeared in many of the English and Scotch newspapers. When another prosecution for blasphemy is undertaken, may the Doctor's eloquent denunciation of the prosecutors be remembered. People who share not in the Doctor's faith, could not urge his arguments, powerful as they are considered in relation to the class of believers they address. We prefer those universal reasons against persecutions which are founded on a sense of justice on religious and intellectual equality. But as the *Circular* is intended to find its way among the religious as well as the liberal, it is proper that the religious should be reminded of the light in which persecution is regarded by so eminent a Christian as Dr. Bowring.]

Let those who *doubt* the heavenly source
Of revelation's page divine,
Use as their weapons fraud and force —
No such unhallow'd arms are mine.
I only wield its holy word —
Reason its shield, and truth its sword.

I doubt not : —My religion stands
A beacon on the eternal rock,—
Let malice* throw her fiery brands ;
Its sacred fane has stood the shook
Of ages—and shall tower sublime
Above the waves and wind of time.

Infinite wisdom form'd the plan ;
Infinite power supports the pile :
Infinite goodness pour's on man
Its radiant light—its cheering smile.
Need they *thine* aid ?—poor worm!—*thine* aid !
O mad presumption—vain parade !

Thou wilt not trust th' Almighty One
With his own thunders—thou wouldst throw
The bolts of heaven !—O senseless son
Of dust and darkness !—Spider ! go,
And with thy cobweb bind the tide,
And the swift, dazzling comet guide.

Yes ! force has conquering reasons given,
And chains and tortures argues well,—
And thou hast proved thy faith from heaven,
By weapons thou hast brought from hell.
Yes ; thou hast made thy title good,
For thou hast signed the deed with blood

Daring imposter ; sure that God
Whose advocate thou feign'st to be,
Will smite thee with that awful rod
Which thou would seize—and pour on thee
The vial of that wrath, which thou
Wouldst empty on thy brother's brow.

[* Why does the Doctor select his weakest enemy ? His faith is most in danger from "fiery brands" thrown from other camps, than those "*malice*" commands.]

TO CORRESPONDENTS.

J.C., Margate,— The Union cannot incur greater risks in respect of the *Circular*. If our friends have patience we shall be better able to supply them with a more efficient organ than we have yet had.

H. Cook of 29, Montague Hill, Bristol, desires it to be announced that he takes orders at his residence for all the works that further the objets of the *Movement*, from the Spirit of Bonner down to the Materialism and Infidelity of Shakespeare," moreover he pledges himself to distribute faithfully any numbers of the *Circular, Movement* or *Oracle*, that may be sent to him carriage free.

A WORD IN SEASON.

Let not our friends, both women and men, neglect this Session of Parliament to trouble their respective representatives with Petitions against the Blasphemy Laws. Each person should send a paper to the following effect.

To the Commons of Great Britain and Ireland in Parliament assembled.

The Petition of [here insert the name, residence, profession, and parish of the petitioner.]

Respectfully sheweth

That your Petitioner is of opinion that prosecutions for Blasphemy (of which to the disgrace of this nation many instances have lately occurred) are an unwise exercise of the powers of the law. As public utility cannot, in this age, be promoted by visiting with legal penalties the concientious convictions of any man. Your petitioner therefore prays your house at once to repeal all laws in any way restricting the publication, by tongue or pen, of theological opinions.

Signed [by the Petitioner].

The Movement Numbers.—Cosmopolite having purchased a quantity of No. 68, and the back stock of Nos. 31 and 58 of the *Movement*, will supply, gratuitously, those Nos. to any person wanting them. Application to be made through the Editor of the *Circular*.

Apiori Errata.— If, in the last notice to Correspondents, on page 4, of *Circular* No. 1, for "Mr. G. has objected to this, and up to this time has come to no arrangement" it is read *Mr. G. has objected to this, and up to this time no arrangement has been decided on.* It will save us the necessity of publishing a very heavy letter from Mr. Gillespie upon the subject.

SUBSCRIPTIONS
TO THE ANTI-PERSECUTION UNION.

A. Park	0	1	6
T. Bownian	0	1	6
N. Brown	0	1	6
E. Stricland	0	1	6
Collector No. 6 (A. Park)	0	7	1
A. Liddle	0	2	0
J. M	0	0	6
Murphy	0	1	0
E. Medley	0	1	0
Collector No. 40 (per Mr. Powell)	0	4	7
T. Messeder, Eliza Shillman	0	1	0
E. Baker, R. Bruce	0	1	0
T. Watts	0	2	6
A friend, for G. J. H., who intended to subscribe it on the occasion of his imprisonment	0	10	6
W. Bull, for "Paterson Testamonial"	0	2	6
J. Chubb, do	0	2	6
Balance from Tea Party to Mr. Paterson	2	1	3
Mr. Coltman, piano-forte tuner, Leicester	0	4	6
J. Glide, jun	0	.1	0
G. Goodwin	0	1	0
For Mr. Johnson's Case, by a few friends at the National Hall,			
Mr. Dell	0	1	0
Mr. Mitchell, Bennett	0	1	6
Mr. Collett	0	1	0
Mr. Makenzie	0	2	6
Mr. Moore	0	1	0

Alfred Henry Ivory, Sec.

Sunday, June 1, 1845.

London : -Printed for the Anti-Persecution Union, by John Griffin Hornblower, 77, Myddelton-street, Clerkenwell, and Published by Watson, 5, Paul's Alley, Paternoster Row.

[PUBLISHED ON THE FIRST OF EVERY MONTH.]

THE CIRCULAR

Of the Anti=Persecution Union.

You may as well cure the colic by brushing a man's clothes, or fill a man's belly with a syllogism, as prosecute for blashemy.—JEREMY TAYLOR.

No. 3.   EDITED BY G. JACOB HOLYOAKE.   Price 1d.

THE ZOIST.

It is not extravagant but just praise to say that this publication, of all others, is the greatest benefactor of society. Not more in the soundness and benevolence of its chief scientific articles than in the example it sets. From the first number to the last it has been uncompromising, and heroic in its language. Its writers, men of great ability, and in a position to command the ear of respectability, have, at serious risks to themselves, uttered such language in that ear as never before vibrated there—language which men of loud pretensions, of humble station, and with comparatively nothing to risk, have shrunk from uttering, and have laboured to persuade themselves it was not prudent to do it. In the pages of the *Zoist* science, for the first time, has spoken out with the dignity of science. Its conductors have resuscitated the dying courage of the liberal world by their example, and have laid both men and letters under obligation to them.

In a recent number appeared an able article in vindication of free expression of opinion, accompanied with severe but justly deserved censures on the *Edinburgh Phenological Journal*, which had allowed the prosecutions for blashphemy there to proceed under its eyes, and with the actual cognizance of the editor, without publishing "one word which could authorise the belief that such proceedings were disproved of by that very journal, which, during twenty years, had advocated principles which these prosecutions directly infringed." This article concluded by a bitter reproach, applicable to some other papers as well as the *Edinburgh Phrenological Journal*, which we intend to subjoin, because its force is not yet spent, and for the following reason.

J. M. C., a friend with whose initials our readers are familiar, pointed out to us that both the *New Moral World* and *Movement* had printed selections from this article in the *Zoist* but both had omitted the paragraph in question, and he desired to know why—giving it as his opinion that the *Movement* could have no motive for passing it by, and that it would be highly useful in the *New Moral World*. We can not be expected to answer for the *New Moral World*. As that paper gave nearly the whole of the article, the particular part omitted might be cut out by the printer, who sometimes for his own convenience, or want of time, omits a paragraph which would otherwise appear. The *Movement* made its extract from the *New Moral World* before it had seen the original article, which sufficiently explains its neglect of so rich a portion. However, for J. M. C.'s and our satisfaction we now append the missing paragraph, and are glad of the curious circumstance related for drawing especial notice to it. The *Zoist's* words are—

"Shame on the men who claim humanity for their theme, and who, when that humanity is crushed, quietly allow the injustice to be perpetuated without advancing to the rescue. Shame on the men who claim the title of philosophers, and are yet wanting the courage to meet the frown of power or the prejudice of the million. Shame, everlasting shame, on the men who know better, yet tremble to avow it—who privately raise their fronts and declaim on the humanizing and civilizing tendency of their principles, but who publicly permit these principles to be invaded, without uttering a sound which can support the dignity of reason or the right of freedom."

DANGER OF UN-REPEALED OBSOLETE STATUTES.

SPEECH OF MR. MILNER GIBSON IN THE HOUSE OF COMMONS 1844.

He was aware of the evil of resuscitating old and worn-out statutes which had fallen into desuetude; but he was of opinion that the country should be made acquainted with those statutes which were and those which were not considered obsolete. (Hear.) If they referred to the report of the Inspectors of Prisons they would find that *the country magistrates were in the habit of resuscitating old statutes*, and by virtue of them fining the people and sending them to gaol. But the house did not think it worth their while to repeal those statutes. In the report of the northern and eastern districts referring to Lancashire, the inspector said, "Amongst other complaints made to me by the prisoners, J. C. came forward and said he was tried for not attending church, and was sentenced to pay a fine of 1s. and 14s. costs. He had been in prison 10 years and had no means of paying the fine. Upon referring to this man's commitment I find he was summarily convicted before two magistrates, because upon the Lord's-day, called Sunday, he did neglect to attend a church, or other place of religious worship, having no reasonable excuse to be absent; and he was ordered to pay a fine of 1s., and 14s. costs, or in default to be kept in prison till he did pay." (Hear. Hear.) It appeared that others were charged with the same offence, and discharged upon paying the fine and costs. (Hear.) No application was made to that house to save those poor persons from the operation of an obsolete law; and when the matter was mentioned by an hon. member in that house he was told that it was an ancient statute, and that the Government were quite ignorant that any proceedings were being taken under it. (Hear.) Eleven persons, in 1839, underwent different periods of confinement for non-attendance at church. One was imprisoned for sixty-three days, another for sixty-one days, another for sixteen days, another for twelve days, another for seventeen days, another for two days, another for sixteen days, another for twenty-six days, another for three days, another for twenty-seven days, another for three days; and *it must be observed when those people were relieved that it was only upon the payment of the fine and costs; not because they had been long imprisoned or hardly dealt by, but because they had paid what was required of them.*

[Our friend W. J. B., who is peculiarly qualified to admonish us upon this subject, sends the above to be pressed upon the attention of the friends of the UNION. The Hull case (at present) is in point, which has arisen *since* he first forwarded it. At the time it arrived Mr. Gibson's speech was deemed hardly to have an application to blasphemy statutes, but experience quickly informed us that they whose liberty is suffered to hang on the chances of Magistrates being supine or liberal, hold it by a precarious thread—At best by mere sufferance. No rest should be allowed the Legislature until liberty of expression is secured by the *repeal* of all statutes affecting it.

WARNING TO BELIEVERS.

The *Tribune*, an American paper, quoted in the *New Moral World* for June 21, has a few scoffing remarks upon the causes which lead to infidelity. Its words are, "Here and there a youth has a severe parent or master, who is a vehement christian—gets badly flogged for going to play instead of to church on Sunday—has religion crammed down his throat in some harsh fashion, or witnesses some gross exposure of hypocrisy or sanctified villainy—and resolves to be an infidel." If to this category (for this modest editor does not for a moment suppose that any persons ever discovered logical defects in the evidences of christianity, and by a course of reasoning were led to its rejection) be added, and the editor, if he wrote in this country, would add, cases of persecution, which being witnessed, might become causes of infidelity, his summary will be complete, and represent the united causes usually assigned by christians for the origin of infidelity. Let them be so—and call them unsound, trifling, impertinent causes, call them what you will—yet, remember, believers, you allow they *are* causes of infidelity, and we give you this piece of intelligence, that these so-made infidels do *not stop here*—they have very active advisers, who, on finding them thus disgusted, also find them disposed to *investigate* into what before they took on authority, and they lead them on, step by step, into thinking, reasoning infidels. They may reason wrongly—that is not here questioned—but they *do reason*, somehow, and at last, sit down more steadfast in their infidelity than *mere disgust* could make them. Beware, then, of "cramming" religion down people's throats—beware of "harshness" and "hypocrisy," and especially beware of *persecution*, which, more than all other causes, generates disgust, leads to doubt, to inquiry, and infidel conviction.

ADVICE FROM LORD KAMES.—In the *Art of Thinking*, by Lord Kames, persecutors are advised that "Slight persecution makes converts; severe persecution, on the contrary, hardens the heart against all convictions." Severity, it appears, defeats its end, but doing the persecutor slightly proselytises. We would add an appendix to this advice in case it should be acted upon, namely—that the persecution to succeed must be *very slight* indeed.

POSTPONEMENT OF THE HULL TRIAL.

36, Savile Street, Hull,
June 13th, 1845.

Mr. Holyoake,

Dear Sir,—Last Sunday morning the Attorney received a communication from his agents, stating that the case was called upon and opened by Mr. Parry, on Saturday, the 6th, but postponed on account of the absence of Mr. Martin, the magistrates' counsel, (supposed to be engaged in the House of Commons, on railway business) and that it was likely to lay over until Michaelmas Term, which does not commence until November.

Thus the case stands at present, another evidence of the *certainty* of the *uncertainty* of the law. Many friends here seem inclined to suppose that it has been purposely delayed, in order that it may, from some possible, if not probable chance, be allowed to pass over entirely. However, it remains for the result to prove.

Hoping your health is re-established, and your exertions likely to prove of service to the cause of truth,

I remain, yours sincerely, R. JOHNSON.

[We can assure Mr. Johnson that it is not the intention of the Committee of the Union to let this important case slip out of the hands of *justice*, and the Committee trust that the friends of the Union are of the same determination. The Committtee believe that these delays of law will not find them less anxious, but better prepared, when the day of issue comes.]

NEW CHARACTER OF THE BLASPHEMY LAWS.

"WE will not be deterred by any fear of misrepresentation from expressing our hearty approbation of the mild and wise manner in which the government have acted with respect to blasphemous publications. We praise them for not having thought it necessary to encircle a religion pure, merciful, and philosophical, with the defences of a false and bloody superstition. The real security of Christianity is to be found in its benevolent morality, in its exquisite adaptation to the human heart, in the facility with which its scheme accommodates itself to the capacity of the human intellect, in the consolation which it bears to the house of mourning, in the light with which it brightens the mystery of the grave. To such a system it can bring no addition of dignity or of strength, that it is *part and parcel of the common law.*" This passage we believe is found in the *Quarterly Review*. Certainly, it came from one of those publications, from one that speaks with authority. It is not necessary to question the estimate in which Christianity is held by these writers, that may pass, but if it be truly stated, not only is Christianity *not* served by its alliance with the "common law," but is disgraced by its dependence upon it, and can never be freed from this dishonour so long as the blasphemy statutes exist. Let it be distinctly understood that these laws are publicly stigmatized by those who cannot be suspected of underating Christianity, to be "*the defences of a false and bloody superstition.*" When, again, people are found calling upon these laws to aid their faith, let it be remembered the kind of aid they seek—let those who listen to such applications be made aware of the kind of aid they render, and let the public know the kind of character Christianity is then unequivocally assuming.

We cannot pretend to determine when it was that our government proceeded in the "mild manner" affirmed, with respect to blasphemous publications. We know of no recent instances in which such praise has been merited. It would at all times be much more to their credit to proceed in no manner in such business. They will not be "wise" until they leave such matters alone.

LORD BROUGHAM'S OPINION ON BLASPHEMY.—"It is evident that, strictly speaking, blasphemy can only be committed by a person who believes in the existence and in the attributes of the Deity whom he impugns, either by ridicule or by reasoning. An Atheist is wholly incapable of the crime. When he heaps epithets of abuse on the Creator, or turns His attributes into ridicule, he is assailing or scoffing at an empty name—at a being whom he believes to have no existence. In like manner if a Deist, one who disbelieves in our Saviour being either the son of God or sent by God as his prophet upon earth, shall argue against his miracles, or ridicule his mission or his person, he commits no blasphemy; for he firmly believes that Christ was a man like himself, and that he derived no authority from the Deity. Both the Atheist and the Deist are free from all guilt of blasphemy, that is, of all guilt towards the Deity or towards Christ."—*Lives of Men of Letters.*

To FRIENDS.—The Subscription to the Anti-Persecution Union, by Members is but one half penny per week—This is paid by persons taking a *quarterly* ticket price 6d., which constitutes membership. If one or two active friends in each town, would apply to the Secretary for 100 tickets, and get them taken at this juncture, it would place the Union in a condition to proceed with ease with the Hull case. Surely some hundreds of people could be found in town and country to give 6d., each to obtain the reversal of the unjust judgment against Mr. Johnson. We know a few persons who are determined to try the experiment. Let each reader of the *Circular* go to each of his acquaintances and say " will you give *one* sixpence, namely, take one quarterly ticket of the Union, to prosecute the Hull magistrates"—who would refuse? Without further application or delay the money would be to hand.

DEATH OF MRS. MARTHA HOWARD.—Mr. James Mellor of Oldham writes to inform us of the death of this excellent friend of liberty. In *Movement* 33, under head of "Notes from the North" is a short notice of a visit to "Old Martha" as her familiar friends were wont to term her. She was then hearty, hale, and full of lively humour, and continued so until the 7th of April, when she was seized with a palsy, that terminated her life in a few days. She was eighty-two years of age. Her interment took place, on the 20th. of April, in the presence of a large number of friends. Her death was a gratifying comment on the usefulness of her life and the strength of her principles.

CLERICAL DUELLING.—The hon. member for Bath has just brought before the House a letter of intimidation, in the shape of a challenge to fight a duel from the member for Sligo. The member for Bath regarded a proposed duel as a species of bullying him out of his right to speak his own sentiments, and refused to be thus coerced by desperadoes carrying pistols. The House applauded his sentiments, and Sir Robert Peel joined in deprecating the conduct of which Mr. Roebuck complained. But while the House of Commons thus discountenances bullying by gentlemen, does it not feel itself equally called upon to discountenance bullying, under similar circumstances, by clergymen? When a man speaks his sentiments against religion, as Mr. Roebuck did against repeal, clergymen send an indietment for blasphemy—which is far more cowardly than a challenge to fight a duel, for the duellist opposes himself to equal danger with his antagonist, but the clergyman strikes in such a manner as to prevent a return of the blow. If the House finds it necessary to dispense with fashionable duelling, they have far stronger reasons to discourage clerical duelling. We hope this question will soon receive the attention of hon. members.

DISCUSSION WITH DR. KALLEY.—To be had in a stiff wrapper, complete, (in eight Nos. of the *Movement*) the Discussion between Dr. Kalley, imprisoned for Blasphemy by the Portuguese Authorities of Madeira, and G. Jacob Holyoake, Secretary to the London Anti-Persecution Union.—Price 1s.

THE EDITOR OF THE LONDON JOURNAL.—This gentleman, we are informed, was lately written to by a Bristol Correspondent—one almost persuaded to be an anti-persecutionist—to enquire "what were the principles and objects of the Anti-Persecution Union, and whether that body merited the support of the Bristol people." The editor answered his correspondent, "Bristollian," that "he had no opinion of the society, and would advise Bristollian to have nothing to do with it." If the Editor of the *London Journal*, by "having no opinion of us," means that he knows nothing of us, he was hardly in a condition to "advise" with any body respecting us. But if by having no opinion he intended it to be understood that he had no high one of us, we tell him he will oblige us by being a little more explicit, and stating what he has found amiss in the Union's proceedings. Mr. Ivory will no doubt furnish this gentleman with a set of the addresses of the Union, and any information he may request.

SUBSCRIPTIONS TO THE FINAL DEFICIENCY OF THE MOVEMENT.

Per *Circular* No 2	19	5	1
Per Mr. John Synes, Coventry.			
E. Roe	0	1	0
J. Morris	0	1	0
J. Farn	0	1	0
T. Cleary	0	1	0
T. A. Marrs	0	1	0
J. Lynes	0	1	3
J. Aston	0	1	0
W. Lynes, W. May	0	1	0
H. Keene, E. Jeffcoat	0	0	9
	19	14	1

ANTI-PERSECUTION UNION.
Official Notices.

Office.—The office of the Union and of the *Circular* is 5, Paul's Alley, Paternoster Row, London.

Subscriptions.—All subscriptions and communications for the Union are to be addressed to the office, to Mr. Alfred H. Ivory, Secretary. All post orders to be made payable to him at the Post Office, Tottenham Court Road.

Editor.—All letters, etc., for the Editor, are to be addressed to him at the office of the Union.

Quarterly Tickets of membership can be had on applying to the Secretary, or writing to the office, enclosing six penny postage stamps, and the initials or name, and address of the applicant.

TO CORRESPONDENTS.

TO FRIENDS IN BRISTOL.—Persons desirous of subscribing to the Union for Johnson's case, of Hull, may do so at Mr. Nickoll's Coffee Rooms, 14, Rosemary Street, and at Mr. Cook's, 29, Montague Hill, Bristol.

RECEIVED.— The "Record" against the Rev. Mr. Allan, late of Perth Gaol.

SUBSCRIPTIONS TO THE ANTI-PERSECUTION UNION.

T. W. (Collector 16)	1	6	6
Liddale	0	2	6
S. B. (for Johnson's case)	0	2	6

Alfred Henry Ivory, Sec.

Tuesday, July 1, 1845.

London : - Printed for the Anti-Persecution Union, by John Griffin Hornblower, 77, Myddelton-street, Clerkenwell, and Published by Watson, 5, Paul's Alley, Paternoster Row.

[PUBLISHED ON THE FIRST OF EVERY MONTH.]

THE CIRCULAR

Of the Anti=Persecution Union.

Conscience is not controllable by human laws nor amenable to human tribunals.—*Chief Justice Mansfield.*

No. 4.   EDITED BY G. JACOB HOLYOAKE.   Price 1d.

BELIEF.*

BY ALIQUIS.

[Judges now only profess to punish the publication of opinion, from respect to the feelings of the public which are said to be outraged by it. It is conceived that a great portion of those persons whose feelings are, in these cases assumed to be wounded, would be tolerably content that opinion should be expressed were they convinced that it could be entertained without criminality. To the consideration of these parties, this paper is submitted, which comprises a masterly summary of the most powerful arguments ever advanced on the nature of belief and the duty of enquiry.—Ed. of *C.*]

THE mistakes which have prevailed on this subject have given rise to more misery—tyranny—rancorous hate—and deliberate cruelty than any other error incidental to humanity. Religious history teems with accounts of the wars of contending sects, and of the merciless punishment inflicted upon such as dared to dissent from established creeds.

The object of this paper, is to shew that *belief* is *involuntary*; that no man can believe as he pleases, or as others please—but only according to the evidence offered to his *understanding*, and consequently that punishment inflicted for *opinions* is contrary to JUSTICE.

A mathematical axiom, cannot be doubted by any man who comprehends the terms in which it is expressed, however ardent may be his desire to disbelieve it. He might be compelled to assert the falsity of the proposition, but all the powers in the world could not make him believe what he thus asserted. In the same way no hopes of gain, no allurements of pleasure, no fear of punishment could make a man really disbelieve a matter of fact which happened under his own observation. The same is also true of innumerable facts which come under the cognizance of our senses; no man in his right mind could by any effort of his will believe a horse to be a dog, or a turnip an orange.

In cases like the above, and others of an analogous nature, it will be acknowledged by all that the *will* can have no power over the convictions. If it exercises any controul at all, it must be looked for in those subjects which admit of diversity of opinions; and yet even here it will be found, on examination, that belief is involuntary. Every one may bring the question to the test of experiment by appealing to his own reflections, and trying whether in any conceivable case he can at pleasure change his opinions. He will soon become sensible of the inefficacy of the attempt. Take for instance any controverted fact in history; let a man make himself perfectly acquainted with the statements and authorities on both sides, and at the end of his investigation he will either believe, doubt, or disbelieve the fact in question. Suppose he disbelieves it. Now blame him, praise him, intimidate him by threats, or allure him by promises, and after all your efforts, do you think you will *really* convert his disbelief into belief. The understanding being passive as to the impressions made upon it, if you wish to change those impressions, you must change the cause which produces them. You can alter perceptions *only* by altering the thing perceived. Every man's reflections will tell him that the *will* can no more modify the effect of an argument on the understanding, than it can change the taste of sugar to the palate, or the fragrance of the rose to the smell. Whatever be the state of a man's understanding in relation to any possible proposition, it is a state of affection devoid equally of desert or culpability. The nature of opinion cannot make it criminal, for in relation to the *same subject*, one person may believe, another doubt, and a third disbelieve, and all with equal innocence.

From these remarks, the reader must not suppose that I consider it of no consequence

---

* I wish the reader to consider this paper as a mere compilation. Those persons conversant with the writings of Mr. Bailey will perceive how very largely I have extracted from the works of that able reasoner.

what opinions a man entertains. Quite the reverse. TRUE opinions are necessarily conducive to the welfare of mankind, and slight reflection is required to shew, that they are deeply concerned not only in clearly understanding the properties of the material world and of their own physical constitution, but in an accurate acquaintance with the consequences of human actions, the results of social regulations, and their *real* position in the universe: and yet it frequently happens in actual life that from ignorance misapprehensions, prejudice, or fearfulness, the acquisition of TRUE opinions, if not positively repudiated, is really evaded.

Without INQUIRY it is impossible for us to KNOW whether our opinions are true or false, and various are the pretences employed for declining investigation: frequently they are masked under vague and metaphorical phrases: " inquiry implies the weighing of evidence and might lead to doubt and perplexity "—" to search into a subject might shake the settled convictions of the understanding "—to examine opposite arguments and contradictory opinions might contaminate the mind with false views.

Every one who alleges pretexts like these for declining *inquiry*, must obviously begin by assuming that his own opinions are unerringly in the right. Nothing could justify a man for declining the investigation of a subject involving important opinions, but the possession of an understanding *free* from liability of error. Not gifted with infallibility, in what way except by diligent inquiry can he obtain any assurance that he is not pursuing a course of injurious action. If he holds any opinion he must have acquired it either by examination, or by instillation, rote, or some process which he cannot recollect. On the supposition that he has acquired it by proper examination, the duty on which I am now insisting has been discharged and the matter is now at an end, but if he has acquired in any *other* manner, the mere plea that his mind might become unsettled, can be no argument against the duty of investigation. For any thing he can allege to the contrary his present opinions are wrong—and in that case the disturbance of his blind convictions instead of being an evil, is an essential step towards arriving at the truth.

It may possibly be assigned as a further reason for his declining inquiry, that he may come to some fallacy which he cannot surmount, although convinced of its character. If he is convinced of its character, he must either have grounds for that conviction or not. If he has grounds let him examine them, draw them out, try if they are valid, and then the fallacy will stand exposed. If he has no grounds for suspecting a fallacy, what an irrational conclusion he confesses himself to have arrived at! But perhaps he will reply—he may be unable to solve the difficulty; his mind may become perplexed, and the issue may prove after all that it would have been much better had he remained in his former strong, though unenlightened conviction. Why better? If he is in perplexity let him read, think, consult the learned and the wise, and in the end he will probably reach a definite opinion on one side or the other. But if he should still remain in doubt, where is the harm, or rather why is it not to be considered a good. The subject is evidently one which admits strong probabilities on opposite sides. Doubt is therefore the proper sentiment for the occasion—it is the result of the best exercise of the faculties—and either positively to believe, or positively to disbelieve, would imply an erroneous appreciation of evidence.

In the minds of some people a strong prejudice appears to exist against that state of the understanding which is termed doubt. A little reflection however will convince any one that on certain subjects "*doubt*" is as appropriate a state of the reasoning faculties as belief or disbelief on others. There are doctrines, propositions, facts, supported and opposed by every degree of evidence, and amongst them by that degree of evidence of which the proper effect is to lean the understanding in an equipoise between two conclusions. In these cases "*doubt*" is the appropriate result, which there can be no reason to shrink from or lament.

But it may be further urged, that inquiry might contaminate the understanding with false views—and therefore it is wise and laudable to abstain from it.

I can comprehend what is meant by contaminating a man's habits or disposition, or even imagination. If a man reads impure books or works of extravagant fiction and false taste, his imagination will be coloured by the ideas presented, and the conceptions which subsequently rise up in his brain will partake of the impurity and extravagance thus made familar to it. But there is no analogy on this point between the understanding and the imagination. There is contamination, there is evil, in preposterous and obscene images crowding before the intellectual vision, notwithstanding a full and distinct perception of their character—but there is no contamination, no evil, in a thousand false arguments coming before the understanding, if their quality is clearly discerned. The only possible evil in this case is mistaking false for true—but the man who shrinks from investigation lest he should mistake false for true, can have no reason for supposing himself free from that delusion in his actual opinions.

Besides the foregoing objections to INQUIRY, there are some other prejudices of a similar character, which form serious impediments to the attainment of truth.

One of these is a fear that we may search too far, and become chargeable with presumption in prying into things we ought not to know—another prejudice is, that we may contract guilt should we arrive at erroneous conclusions, or conclusions at variance with such as are established—and another, that it is a sort of praiseworthy humility to acquiesce in received opinions on the authority of others, and to refrain from thinking for ourselves.

A brief space will not be ill bestowed in setting these prejudices in their true light.

As to the first a few words will suffice to prove that nothing can be more irrational and absurd. I have already shown that *true* opinions are conducive to the welfare of mankind, and the prosecution of *inquiry* is therefore a process from which we have everything to hope and nothing to fear, and to which there are no limits but such as the nature of our own faculties prescribe.

The second of the prejudices before enumerated—that we may contract guilt, if in the course of our researches we miss the right conclusion, and had therefore better let inquiry alone—is still more prevalent and influential in preventing those investigations which it is our duty to make. As our opinions on any subject are not *voluntary* acts, but *involuntary* effects, in whatever conclusions our researches terminate they can involve us in no culpability. All that we have to take care of is to bestow on every subject an adequate and impartial attention. Having done this we have discharged our duty, and it would be irrational and unmanly to entertain any apprehension for the result.

In fact this is the grossest inconsistency in the prejudice now under consideration. If we may contract guilt by searching after truth, we may equally do so by remaining in our present state. The reason alleged in the prejudice itself, and the only reason which can be assigned with any plausibility, why we may commit an offence by embarking in any inquiry is, that we may; by so doing miss the right conclusion, or in other words, fall into error—for no one would seriously contend that we incur any moral culpability by an investigation which conducts us to the truth. But it is obvious that we may equally miss the right conclusion by remaining in our actual opinions. It is then incumbent on us to ascertain whether we are committing an offence by remaining in them—in other words, it is necessary to *examine* whether those opinions are true. Thus the reasons assigned for *not* inquiring, lead to the conclusion that it is *necessary* to inquire.

The third prejudice—that acquiescence in received opinions, or forbearing to think for ourselves, shews a degree of humility highly proper and commendable—if closely examined will be found usually to evince nothing but a great degree of indolent presumption, or intellectual cowardice. There is often, in truth, as great a measure of presumption in this species of acquiescence as in the boldest hypothesis which human invention can start. That received and established opinions are true is one of those sweeping conclusions, which would require very strong reasons, and often elaborate research to justify. On what grounds are they considered to be true by one who declines investigation? Because (on the most favourable supposition) they have been handed down to us by our predecessors, and have been held with unhesitating faith by a multitude of illustrious men. But what comprehensive reasons are these?

What investigation would it require to shew they were valid! As the whole history of mankind teems with instances of the transmission of the grossest errors from one generation to another, and of their having been countenanced by the concurrence of the most eminent of our race—how without examination can we shew that *this* particular instance is an exception from the general lot?

It is then no humility to refrain from inquiry—on the contrary, the proper feeling is, to be determined to do all in our power to make ourselves acquainted with every subject in which it is necessary for us to pronounce, or profess, or act upon an opinion.

From the necessity of using our own judgment, or, in other words, of forming a conclusion for ourselves, we cannot be absolved. We must form our opinions either of the doctrine itself, or of the comparative degrees of confidence, to which those men who have studied the subject are entitled—and it is evident that in the case of disputed doctrines, the latter may be as difficult, and demand as much investigation, as much knowledge and acuteness of judgment, as to come to a decision on the original question.

Let no one, then, deceive himself by supposing that he is exercising the virtue of humility, or modesty, or diffidence, when he is in fact resting in a conclusion, which to reach legitimately requires so much knowledge and ability. Nor let any one suppose that such a plea will exonerate him from the imperative duty of entering upon a rigorous examination of all the evidence within his reach. Far from being a virtue, this kind of acquiescence is in most cases a positive vice, tending to stop all advancement in knowledge, and all improvement in practice.

From the preceding review it is evident that the inquirer may enter on his task with full confidence that he is embarking in no criminal, or forbidden, or presumptuous enterprise, but is, on the contrary, engaging in the discharge of a duty. Let him be as circumspect as he pleases in collecting his facts and deducing his conclusions, cautious in the process, but *fearless* in the result. Let him be fully aware of his liability to error, of the thousand sources of illusions, of the limited powers of the individual, of the paramount importance of truth—but let him dismiss *all apprehensions* of the issue of an investigation conducted with due application of mind and rectitude of purpose.

The duty of every one is not only to enter upon investigation, but to pursue his inquiries as far as his capacity and opportunities permit, till he has come to satisfactory conclusions, or feels thoroughly convinced he has all the light which investigation will supply. The same considerations which render it a duty to commence inquiry, render it a duty to persevere till this satisfactory end has been achieved.

PAYMENT OF THE "TESTIMONIAL."—It has been thought necessary to formally certify, for the satisfaction of the subscribers, that the whole of the Testimonial to Mr. Paterson, including the profits of the Tea Party at the City Road, in all £33 13s. 9d., have been duly paid over to him.

THE HULL SUBSCRIPTION.—The suggestions in the last *Circular* respecting this subscription have been acted upon in Glasgow. Mr. H. procured forty Members' Tickets from the Secretary of the Union, and friends were found immediately to take them. Sixty more tickets have been written for, to make the 100 for Glasgow, which will yield £2 10s. London will no doubt be equal to *four* Glasgows. As soon as the experiment has been tried, other towns will be appealed to.

Errata.—In the par. Editor of London Journal, page 12, for "Bristol people" read *British* people.

BALANCE SHEET OF THE ANTI-PERSECUTION UNION.

For the Quarter ending June 29, 1845.

RECEIPTS.	£ s. d.	EXPENDITURE.	£ s. d.
Per *Circular* No. 1	3 17 0	Balance due to Treasurer last quarter	0 6 4
Do. — 2	4 16 5	Paid to "Paterson Testimonial"	3 2 3
Do. — 3	1 11 6	To printing, ect. 500 *Circulars* each—Nos. 1, 2	4 0 0
Per Mr. Watson, on account of Nos. 1, 2, *Circular*	1 11 3	To G. J. H., as per instruction of "A Friend," *Circular* 2	0 10 6
Audited by us and found correct,		Advertising and distributing *Circulars*	0 8 0
JOHN ELLIS, } Auditors.		Paid to Mr. Whiting on account	1 6 6
JOHN SKELTON, }		Postage, Newspapers, booking, etc.	1 8 9
		Balance in hand	0 13 10
	£11 16 2		£11 16 2

THE DISCUSSION BETWEEN ALIQUIS AND GILLESPIE.—This discussion, "concerning the being of a God," which commenced in the *Movement*, is now being continued in a separate publication, of a convenient form, and got up in a neat manner. No. 1 contains Mr. Gillespie's "First Paper" and Aliquis's "First and Second Papers." Some practical result may be expected from two such accomplished writers. The merits of their respective arguments it is obviously no province of the *Circular* to determine—but our readers have a strong interest in this Controversy, from the fact that Mr. Gillespie is the representative of a Society which professes to extirpate Infidelity by better means than persecution. Both these disputants practically exemplify an honourable confidence in human reason. They put their respective views to the trial of truth. We are treated here to the rare exhibition of Theism venturing to combat without the aid of the policeman. However the argument may end, the example will be of great moral value.

ANTI-PERSECUTION UNION.
Official Notices.

Office.—The office of the Union is 5, Paul's Alley, Paternoster Row, London. Treasurer, Mr. Watson. Secretary, Mr. J. B. Lear, to whom post office orders must be made payable at the Post Office Tottenham Court Road.

DISCONTINUATION OF THE CIRCULAR.—The Committee have come to the resolution of discontinuing the *Circular* after this number. They find the expenses too heavy for their present funds. They think that "short addresses, printed by thousands and freely distributed, would more effectually serve their purposes at less expense. The confidence of the public and satisfaction of subscribers will be still maintained by a slight increase of duties to the Secretary, by letter-writing." This is the account forwarded to me by the Secretary. The information is complete, specifying the reasons of the change and the nature of future proceedings. It precludes the necessity of any addition by me, excepting this: that friends of the Union will please to take notice that the "official notices" in this number still remain in force.—G.J.H.

Members and friends of the Union, desirous of becoming collectors, or otherwise aiding its objects, are requested to forward their names and addresses to the Secretary, at the office, who will be happy to point out the way for so doing, and furnish them with the requisite documents for forming branch-unions in the different towns.

Cards of membership for this quarter are ready, and may be had on application to the Secretary, at the office of the Union.

Petitions to Parliament for the total repeal of the blasphemy laws lie at the following places for signature: 5, Paul's Alley, Paternoster Row ; Hetherington, 40, Holywell Street, Strand. Also at the following institutions :— John Street, Tottenham Court Road ; Goswell Road ; Whitechapel ; Hall of Science, City Road ; and Investigation Hall, Circus Street. Persons desirous of sending separate petitions from themselves alone, may obtain the requisite form on application to the Secretary, at the office of the Union.

Subscriptions to the [25*l*. 4*s*.] *Deficiency of the Movement.*

	£ s. d.
Per last *Circular*, No. 3	19 14 1
Thos. Williams	0 0 6
James Mellor, Oldham	0 5 0
H. Cook, Bristol	0 0 6
From the Tea Party on Mr. H.'s departure from London, per Mr. Thos. Powell	0 15 7
	£20 15 8

TO CORRESPONDENTS.

W. BROOM sends a tract on the "Character and Tendency of Religion"—No. 1 issued by the Infidel Tract Society. These parties are Radical Anti-Persecutionists, who seem to hold that persecution is only to be extirpated by extirpating religion. This has the merit of looking like a *certain* process, if a possible one—and they would contend that the possibility is only a question of time. This society can be heard of at 12, King's Row, Walworth, London, where all communications must be addressed. Their tracts can be had at 2d. per dozen.

H. COOK, Bristol, is thanked for his extracts and mottoes. We use one this week. The Nos. required shall be sent. We are gratified to find that he has taken eighteen *Circulars* during the past month for gratuitous distribution. The example is good. H. C. acknowledges the receipt of a parcel of liberal papers from R. D., Walworth, London. We shall be happy to see the "Prosecution of Blasphemers Vindicated, by the Rev. W. B. Whitehead, A.M., Vicar of Tiverton, Somerset."

SUBSCRIPTIONS
TO THE ANTI-PERSECUTION UNION.

	£ s. d.
W. H. Holyoak, Leicester	0 2 0
T. Emery, do.	0 1 0
Leicester quarterly subscriptions	0 8 3
Mr. Hindle, Newcastle-upon-Tyne	0 12 6
Collector 45 (per Mr. Powell)	0 2 1
Mr. Overton	0 1 0
Mr. J. Hall	0 1 0
Mr. Port Philip	0 1 0
Messrs. Cooke and Glide, for cards of membership	0 1 0
For Union, from different individuals	0 2 6

J. B. LEAR, Sec.

Friday, August 1, 1845.

London : Printed for the Anti-Persecution Union, by John Griffin Hornblower, 77, Myddelton-street, Clerkenwell, and Published by Watson, 5, Paul's Alley, Paternoster Row.